The Oxford Handbook of Infidelity

OXFORD LIBRARY OF PSYCHOLOGY

The Oxford Handbook of Infidelity

Edited by
Tara DeLecce
Todd K. Shackelford

OXFORD
UNIVERSITY PRESS

Oxford University Press is a department of the University of Oxford. It furthers the University's objective of excellence in research, scholarship, and education by publishing worldwide. Oxford is a registered trade mark of Oxford University Press in the UK and certain other countries.

Published in the United States of America by Oxford University Press
198 Madison Avenue, New York, NY 10016, United States of America.

© Oxford University Press 2022

All rights reserved. No part of this publication may be reproduced, stored in a retrieval system, or transmitted, in any form or by any means, without the prior permission in writing of Oxford University Press, or as expressly permitted by law, by license, or under terms agreed with the appropriate reproduction rights organization. Inquiries concerning reproduction outside the scope of the above should be sent to the Rights Department, Oxford University Press, at the address above.

You must not circulate this work in any other form
and you must impose this same condition on any acquirer.

CIP data is on file at the Library of Congress

ISBN 978–0–19–750289–1

DOI: 10.1093/oxfordhb/9780197502891.001.0001

9 8 7 6 5 4 3 2 1

Printed by Integrated Books International, United States of America

This handbook is dedicated to the late Winkie Wartooth, who was among the greatest of feline friends.

SHORT CONTENTS

About the Editors   ix

Contributors   xi

Contents   xiii

Chapters   1–614

Index   615

ABOUT THE EDITORS

Tara DeLecce

Tara DeLecce received her PhD in social, developmental, and cognitive psychology in 2017 from Wayne State University. She is currently a postdoctoral researcher and special lecturer in the Department of Psychology at Oakland University. Dr. DeLecce has published over 20 journal articles, book chapters, and encyclopedia entries. Her research addresses infidelity in humans and how infidelity affects romantic relationships. Dr. DeLecce is a reviewer for several journals, including *Frontiers in Psychology* and *Personality and Individual Differences*.

Todd K. Shackelford

Todd K. Shackelford is Distinguished Professor and Chair of the Department of Psychology at Oakland University in Rochester, Michigan, where he is Co-Director of the Evolutionary Psychology Lab. He received his PhD in evolutionary psychology in 1997 from the University of Texas at Austin. Much of Dr. Shackelford's research addresses sexual conflict between men and women, with a special focus on men's physical, emotional, and sexual violence against their intimate partners.

CONTRIBUTORS

Lidia Dengelegi Abrams
    Resolve Community Counseling Center

Mike Abrams
    New York University

Steven Arnocky
    Nipissing University

Mohammad Hassan Asayesh
    University of Tehran

Brien K. Ashdown
    American University of Sharjah

Emma E. Altgelt
    Florida State University

Charlene F. Belu
    University of New Brunswick

Brian M. Bird
    Simon Fraser University

Lindsay Bochon
    Simon Fraser University

Jonathan M. Bowman
    University of San Diego

Tiffany L. Brown
    California State University, Long Beach

Rebecca L. Burch
    State University of New York, Oswego

Abraham Pieter Buunk
    University of Groningen
    Universidad Católica del Uruguay
    Interdisciplinary Demographic Institute (NIDI)

Kelly Campbell
    California State University, San Bernardino

Benjamin L. Compton
    University of Washington

Jaclyn Cravens Pickens
    Texas Tech University

Adam Davis
    University of Ottawa

Tara DeLecce
    Oakland University

Amanda Denes
    University of Connecticut

Megan R. Dillow
    West Virginia University

Jacqueline M. Di Santo
    State University of New York, New Paltz

Maryanne L. Fisher
    Saint Mary's University
    Kinsey Institute, Indiana University

Carey J. Fitzgerald
    Oregon Institute of Technology

Glenn Geher
    State University of New York, New Paltz

Elaheh Golpasha
    University of Tehran

Limor Y. Gottlieb
    Brunel University

Jana Hackathorn
    Murray State University

Jessica Hehman
    University of Redlands

Yu-Hsun Hsu
    National Cheng Kung University

Mercedes Hughes
    Oakland University

Susan M. Hughes
> Albright College

Daniel J. Kruger
> University of Michigan

Justin J. Lehmiller
> The Kinsey Institute, Indiana University

Ashley Locke
> Nipissing University

Jenna M. Lunge
> Oakland University

Larissa McKelvie
> Nipissing University

Brandyn-Dior McKinley
> Smith College School for Social Work

James K. McNulty
> Florida State University

Andrea L. Meltzer
> Florida State University

Virginia E. Mitchell
> Oakland University

Crystal Moreno
> Oregon Institute of Technology

Alex Orille
> Oakland University

Lucia F. O'Sullivan
> University of New Brunswick

Farid Pazhoohi
> University of British Columbia

Julie A. Planke
> State University of New York, New Paltz

Gemma Sáez
> University of Extremadura

Catherine Salmon
> University of Redlands

David A. Sbarra
> University of Arizona

David P. Schmitt
> Brunel University

Dylan Selterman
> University of Maryland

Caroline E. Shanholtz
> University of Arizona

Adam V. Thomas
> Texas Tech University

Jody Thompson
> Newberry College

Tracy Vaillancourt
> University of Ottawa

Inmaculada Valor-Segura
> University of Granada

T. Joel Wade
> Bucknell University

Dana A. Weiser
> Texas Tech University

Lisa L. M. Welling
> Oakland University

CONTENTS

Part 1 • Predicting Infidelity

1. Are Certain People More Prone Toward Infidelity?: Own and Partner Personality and Individual Difference Predictors of Infidelity 3
   Emma E. Altgelt, James K. McNulty, and Andrea L. Meltzer
2. Predicting Infidelity in the Context of Race and Ethnicity 28
   Kelly Campbell, Tiffany L. Brown, and Brandyn-Dior McKinley
3. Hormonal Predictors of Infidelity: A Life History Perspective on Testosterone and Other Hormonal Mechanisms 61
   Lindsay Bochon and Brian M. Bird
4. Operational Sex Ratio and Infidelity 86
   Daniel J. Kruger
5. It's Not You, It's Us: Relationship-Based Factors That Predict Infidelity 101
   Jana Hackathorn and Brien K. Ashdown
6. Social Versus Sexual Monogamy 121
   Catherine Salmon and Jessica Hehman
7. Cultural Differences and Similarities in Correlates of Infidelity 140
   Inmaculada Valor-Segura, Gemma Sáez, and Abraham Pieter Buunk
8. Predicting Online Infidelity 153
   Carey J. Fitzgerald, Crystal Moreno, and Jody Thompson
9. Predicting Infidelity in Nonheterosexual Relationships 172
   Jonathan M. Bowman and Benjamin L. Compton

Part 2 • The Nature of Infidelity

10. Emotional and Sexual Infidelity: Evolutionary Origins and Large-Scale Implications 195
    Julie A. Planke, Jacqueline M. Di Santo, and Glenn Geher
11. Thank You, Next!: Sexual Novelty Motivations for Infidelity 211
    Limor Y. Gottlieb and David P. Schmitt

12. The Mate Switching Hypothesis for Infidelity   236
    Mike Abrams and Lidia Dengelegi Abrams
13. Deception and Secrecy in Infidelity   260
    Susan M. Hughes
14. Infidelity Across the Ovulatory Cycle   288
    Virginia E. Mitchell, Jenna M. Lunge, Alex Orille, Mercedes Hughes, and Lisa L. M. Welling
15. Long-Term Infidelities   315
    Dana A. Weiser, Jaclyn Cravens Pickens, and Adam V. Thomas
16. Cultural Differences and Similarities in the Nature of Infidelity   349
    Farid Pazhoohi
17. The Nature of Infidelity in Nonheterosexual Relationships   373
    Justin J. Lehmiller and Dylan Selterman

Part 3 • Consequences of Infidelity

18. Relationship Dissolution Following Infidelity   399
    Caroline E. Shanholtz and David A. Sbarra
19. Forgiveness for a Partner's Infidelity   415
    Megan R. Dillow and Amanda Denes
20. Formation of a Primary Relationship with an Infidelity Partner   453
    Charlene F. Belu and Lucia F. O'Sullivan
21. Renewed Love Between Partners Following Infidelity   471
    T. Joel Wade, Rebecca L. Burch, and Maryanne L. Fisher
22. Relationship Quality Between Partners Following Infidelity in the Absence of Renewed Love   493
    Mohammad Hassan Asayesh and Elaheh Golpasha
23. Violence and Homicide Following Partner Infidelity   516
    Steven Arnocky, Adam Davis, Ashley Locke, Larissa McKelvie, and Tracy Vaillancourt
24. Male Sexual Coercion in Response to Mate Infidelity   555
    Lidia Dengelegi Abrams and Mike Abrams
25. Consequences of Infidelity in Nonhuman Animals   576
    Yu-Hsun Hsu
26. Future Directions for Theory and Research on the Predictors, Nature, and Consequences of Infidelity   601
    Tara DeLecce

Index   615

PART 1

Predicting Infidelity

CHAPTER 1

Are Certain People More Prone Toward Infidelity?: Own and Partner Personality and Individual Difference Predictors of Infidelity

Emma E. Altgelt, James K. McNulty, *and* Andrea L. Meltzer

Abstract

Individual differences in personality and other traits may be associated with the likelihood that people or their partners will engage in infidelity. This chapter reviews research examining these possibilities. It begins by reviewing research examining associations between infidelity and (a) the Big Five, (b) Dark Triad, (c) attachment insecurity (i.e., attachment anxiety and attachment avoidance), and (d) sociosexual orientation. For each individual difference, it considers the extent to which each trait is associated with individuals' own as well as their partners' likelihood of engaging in infidelity. This chapter then outlines the importance of using strong methodologies to examine the association between personality and infidelity, including the importance of examining the role of both partners' personalities and using strong measures of infidelity. This chapter concludes by highlighting important avenues for future research in this domain.

Key Words: infidelity, personality, Big 5, Dark Triad, attachment, sociosexuality

Infidelity can harm romantic relationships. Following incidences of infidelity, both partners frequently report lower relationship satisfaction, and relationships are at greater risk of dissolution (Previti & Amato, 2004). In fact, infidelity is the most common predictor of relationship dissolution across more than 150 societies (Betzig, 1989; see Fincham & May, 2017). These consequences make it important to understand who is more or less likely to engage in infidelity—that is, it is important to understand the extent to which personality traits and individual differences are associated with individuals' likelihood of infidelity. Given the interdependent nature of romantic relationships (Kelley & Thibaut, 1978), both couple members' personality and individual differences can influence each couple member's relationship behaviors, including infidelity. Thus, we begin this chapter by reviewing literature examining the associations between own and partner personality traits (as well as other individual differences, including attachment insecurity and sociosexuality) and infidelity. We then offer methodological recommendations and suggest future directions for personality and infidelity research.

Big Five Personality Traits and Infidelity

According to several theoretical and empirical traditions, the five-factor model of personality, which consists of conscientiousness, agreeableness, extraversion, neuroticism, and openness to experience (i.e., the Big Five), captures all, or at least most, aspects of personality (McCrae & Costa, 1997). Numerous studies suggest that the Big Five are associated with infidelity (e.g., Altgelt et al., 2018; Barta & Kiene, 2005; Buss & Shackelford, 1997; Orzeck & Lung, 2005; Schmitt, 2004a; Schmitt, 2004b; Schmitt & Buss, 2001; Schmitt & Shackelford, 2008; Shackelford et al., 2008; Whisman et al., 2007). Nevertheless, considerable variability exists in the (a) extent to which traits are predictive of infidelity, (b) reliability of the associations that have been established, and (c) methodologies used to establish them. Table 1.1 provides a summary of these findings. In an effort to clarify such variability, we address each of the Big Five personality traits in turn, beginning with conscientiousness.

Conscientiousness

Conscientiousness is characterized by self-discipline and reliability (Costa & McCrae, 1992). Numerous studies have linked low conscientiousness (or impulsivity) to a greater likelihood of engaging in infidelity. For example, several studies involving large samples from over 45 countries indicate that individuals low in conscientiousness describe themselves as less faithful (Schmitt, 2004b; Schmitt & Shackelford, 2008). Likewise, other studies indicate that people lower in conscientiousness report a greater likelihood of engaging in infidelity in the future (Buss & Shackelford, 1997) and are more likely to report having engaged in infidelity in a past or current relationship (Barta & Kiene, 2005; Orzeck & Lung, 2005; Schmitt, 2004a; Schmitt & Buss, 2001; Schmitt & Shackelford, 2008). Nevertheless, conscientiousness was not significantly predictive of infidelity in two independent integrative data analyses, each of which pooled the data from two different longitudinal studies of newly married couples (Altgelt et al., 2018; Russell et al., 2013) to simultaneously examine all Big Five personality traits (one additionally controlled for own and partner narcissism as well as partner Big Five personality traits, whereas the other additionally controlled for own and partner attachment insecurity); neither of these analyses revealed a significant association between conscientiousness and infidelity over the first three to four and one-half years of marriage. Likewise, several other studies reported nonsignificant associations between conscientiousness and either describing oneself as unfaithful (Bourdage et al., 2007; Smith et al., 2007) or reporting a past infidelity (Gibson et al., 2016).

Several studies have also linked having a *partner* who is low in conscientiousness to a greater likelihood of engaging in infidelity. In one study, for example, wives (but not

Table 1.1 Big Five Findings

		Own										Partner									
		Consc		Agree		Extra		Neuro		Open		Consc		Agree		Extra		Neuro		Open	
	N	M	W	M	W	M	W	M	W	M	W	M	W	M	W	M	W	M	W	M	W
Algelt et al., 2018	454	ns	ns	ns	ns	ns	+	ns	ns	ns	ns	ns	ns	ns	ns	+	+	+	+	-	ns
Barra & Kiene, 2005	432	-	-	-	-	+	ns	ns	+	ns	ns										
Bourdage et al., 2007	230	ns	ns	-	-	ns	ns	ns	ns	ns	ns										
Buss & Shackelford, 1997	214	-	-	ns	-	+	+	ns	ns	+	ns	ns	ns	ns	ns	ns	ns	ns	ns	ns	ns
Gibson et al., 2016	295	ns	ns	ns	ns	+	+	ns	ns	ns	ns										
Mahambrey, 2020	1,577*	-	-	ns	ns	ns	ns	ns	ns	ns	ns	-	-	+	+	ns	ns	ns	ns	ns	ns
Orzeck & Lung, 2005	104	-	-	ns	ns	+	+	ns	+	+	+										
Russell et al., 2013	414	ns	ns	ns	ns	ns	ns	ns	ns	-	-										
Schmitt, 2004a	16,954	-	-	-	-	ns	ns	ns	ns	ns	ns										
Schmitt, 2004b	16,362	-	-	-	-	+	+	+	+	-	ns										
Schmitt & Buss, 2001	236	-	-	-	-	+	ns	+	+	ns	ns										
Schmitt & Shackelford, 2008	13,243	-	-	-	-	+	+	ns	+	+	+										
Shackelford et al., 2008	214	-	-	ns	ns						ns										
Smith et al., 2007	118	ns	-	ns	ns	+	+	ns	ns	ns	ns			-	-						
Whisman et al., 2007	2,291	ns	ns	ns	ns	ns	ns	+	+	ns	ns										

Note. N = sample size; Consc = Conscientiousness; Agree = Agreeableness; Extra = Extraversion; Neuro = Neuroticism; Open = Openness; M = Men; W = Women; ns = not significant. Mahambrey's (2020) partner findings are based on a subsample of 898 married participants.

husbands) married to partners lower in conscientiousness reported a higher probability of flirting with people other than their partners (Buss & Shackelford, 1997). Nevertheless, when using structural equation modeling to examine the extent to which marital satisfaction mediates the association between partner conscientiousness and infidelity, Shackelford et al. (2008) found no sex differences in this association; both men and women who had spouses lower (versus higher) in conscientiousness were less satisfied with their marriages, which was associated with a higher likelihood of engaging in future infidelities. Moreover, an additional study using a large sample and controlling for multiple confounding variables (e.g., demographics, the other Big Five personality traits, religiosity) found that individuals lower in conscientiousness reported more instances of their partners engaging in infidelity across their lifetime and within their current marriages (Mahambrey, 2020). Nevertheless, the Altgelt et al. (2018) integrative data analysis found no significant associations between partner conscientiousness and the likelihood of engaging in infidelity over the first three years of marriage.

Considering this body of research as a whole, there appears to be fairly consistent evidence that individuals reporting lower levels of conscientiousness and individuals with partners reporting lower levels of consciousness are more likely to engage in infidelity. Although some studies yielded nonsignificant associations, it is important to keep in mind that null associations involving the prediction of infidelity may reflect low power due to underreporting of infidelity. Indeed, three of the studies documenting significant negative associations between conscientiousness and infidelity involved large, multinational datasets, which presumably had ample power (Schmitt, 2004a, 2004b; Schmitt & Shackelford, 2008). Further, the two integrative data analyses demonstrating non-significant associations examined infidelity over the first three to four and one-half years of marriage (Altgelt et al., 2018; Russell et al., 2013), a time when infidelity may be particularly rare. Given the large number of studies revealing a negative association between conscientious and infidelity, we conclude overall that lower (versus higher) conscientiousness is associated with a greater probability of infidelity. Indeed, a recent meta-analysis of some of these studies drew the same conclusion (Allen & Walter, 2018). Given that several studies also demonstrate an association between partner conscientiousness and infidelity, whereas only one study failed to document such an association, we also cautiously conclude that lower partner conscientiousness is associated with a greater probability of infidelity.

Agreeableness

Agreeableness is characterized by a strong adherence to interpersonal norms (e.g., Olver & Mooradian, 2003), and numerous studies have also linked low agreeableness to a higher likelihood of infidelity. Specifically, individuals lower in agreeableness are more likely to (a) describe themselves with infidelity-related words (e.g., promiscuous, adulterous, unfaithful) in Canada (Bourdage et al., 2007) and across more than 45 countries (Schmitt, 2004b; Schmitt & Shackelford, 2008) and (b) report having engaged in past infidelity (Barta & Kiene, 2005; Schmitt, 2004a; Schmitt & Buss, 2001; Schmitt & Shackelford, 2008). Further, wives (but not husbands) lower in agreeableness report being more likely to engage in infidelity in the future (Buss & Shackelford, 1997). Nevertheless, other studies have failed to document that less agreeable people are more likely to describe themselves with infidelity-related words (Smith et al., 2007) or report having been unfaithful in a prior relationship (Gibson et al., 2016; Orzeck & Lung, 2005). Further, the two integrative data analyses described in the previous section (Altgelt et al., 2018; Russell et al., 2013), each of which simultaneously examined all Big Five variables and other traits, failed to detect a significant association between agreeableness and infidelity over the first three to four and one-half years of marriage.

Findings regarding the association between *partner* agreeableness and infidelity are notably inconsistent. Shackelford et al. (2008) found both men and women whose partners reported lower (versus higher) levels of agreeableness were less satisfied with their marriage and thus reported being more likely to engage in a future infidelity. In stark contrast to these studies, however, a study of almost 900 older married individuals that controlled for multiple confounding variables (e.g., demographics, the other Big Five personality traits, religiosity) demonstrated that people *higher* in agreeableness reported more instances of their partner engaging in infidelity (Mahambrey, 2020). The authors speculated that "perhaps individuals with agreeable spouses become accustomed to their highly understanding and accommodating partners, so much so that they assume even infidelity—if discovered—will be pardoned" (p. 294). Consistent with such speculation, other work suggests people do take advantage of partners who appear particularly accommodating (McNulty & Russell, 2016). Nevertheless, an analysis that included nearly 700 participants failed to document a similar association, and two other studies failed to document any significant association between partner agreeableness and infidelity. In one of these studies, for example, husbands and wives with more agreeable partners did not rate themselves as more or less likely to engage in a future infidelity (Buss & Shackelford, 1997). Likewise, the Altgelt et al. (2018) integrative data analysis of two longitudinal studies of married couples revealed no evidence that partner agreeableness was associated with infidelity over the first three years of marriage (controlling for all Big Five variables and narcissism).

What should we make of these findings? Regarding the association between own agreeableness and infidelity, several studies observed a significant association whereas several other studies, including the two integrative data analyses of new marriage, failed to observe such an association. That said, as we noted previously, it is important to keep in mind that null associations involving the prediction of infidelity, particularly as documented in the first few years of marriage, may reflect low power due to underreporting of infidelity. In light of the large number of studies—many that involve large samples (Schmitt, 2004a, 2004b; Schmitt & Shackelford, 2008)—revealing a negative association between agreeableness and infidelity, we cautiously conclude that individuals lower (versus higher) in agreeableness are more likely to engage in infidelity. Indeed, a recent meta-analysis of some of these studies underscored this conclusion (Allen & Walter, 2018). Nevertheless, future research would enhance confidence in this conclusion. With respect to partner agreeableness, the evidence is mixed; one study revealed a negative association between partner agreeableness and infidelity, one study revealed a positive association, and two studies failed to detect any significant association. Given these conflicting results, we argue more research is needed before firm conclusions regarding the association between partner agreeableness and infidelity can be drawn.

Extraversion

Extraversion is characterized by assertiveness, gregariousness, and sociability (Costa & McCrae, 1992), and several studies have demonstrated a positive association between extraversion and infidelity. Indeed, individuals higher (versus lower) in extraversion are more likely to describe themselves with infidelity-related words (Schmitt, 2004b; Schmitt & Shackelford, 2008; Smith et al., 2007) and report having engaged in an infidelity in the past (Gibson et al., 2016; Orzeck & Lung, 2005; Schmitt & Shackelford, 2008). Likewise, Altgelt and colleagues' (2018) integrative data analysis of two longitudinal studies revealed that extraversion was positively associated with infidelity among wives (but not husbands), controlling for the other Big Five traits and narcissism. Nevertheless, other studies have failed to document such an association (Barta & Kiene, 2005; Buss & Shackelford, 2008; Schmitt & Buss, 2001), including Russell et al.'s (2013) integrative data analysis of newlywed couples. Of the three studies of which we are aware that examined the association between *partner* extraversion and infidelity, two revealed no significant associations (Buss & Shackelford, 1997; Mahambrey, 2020), and one revealed a positive association (Altgelt et al., 2018).

In light of the fact that there is more evidence that individuals' own extraversion is associated with their infidelity than evidence that it is not, as well as the fact that a significant association emerged among wives even in one of the conservative integrative data analyses of new couples (Altgelt et al., 2018), our cautious conclusion is that own extraversion is associated with a greater likelihood of infidelity. In contrast, there appears to be little evidence that partner extraversion is associated with the likelihood of infidelity.

Neuroticism

Neuroticism is characterized by dispositional tendencies toward negative affect (Watson & Clark, 1984), and several studies have linked higher levels of neuroticism to an increased likelihood of infidelity. Specifically, several studies indicate that people higher (versus lower) in neuroticism are more likely to report having engaged in infidelity in past relationships (Barta & Kiene, 2005; Schmitt & Buss, 2001; Whisman et al., 2007). Moreover, several additional studies similarly document positive associations between neuroticism and infidelity among women. For example, women (but not men) higher in neuroticism are more likely to (a) describe themselves as less faithful (Schmitt, 2004b; Schmitt & Shackelford, 2008) and (b) report having engaged in a prior infidelity (Schmitt & Shackelford, 2008). Nevertheless, several other studies have failed to document such associations. Specifically, these other studies have suggested that people higher (versus lower) in neuroticism do not reliably (a) describe themselves as less faithful (Bourdage et al. 2007; Smith et al., 2007), (b) forecast future infidelity (Buss & Shackelford, 1997), or (c) report having been unfaithful in prior relationships (Gibson et al. 2016; Orzeck & Lung, 2005). Further, the two integrative data analyses that controlled for various other traits to predict infidelity over the first few years of marriage also failed to document significant associations between neuroticism and the probability of infidelity (Altgelt et al., 2018; Russell et al. 2013).

Results regarding associations between *partner* neuroticism and infidelity are also inconsistent. Altgelt et al.'s (2018) integrative data analysis revealed that, among both men and women, partner neuroticism was associated with a higher probability of infidelity over the first three years of marriage. That said, in one study in which men and women predicted whether they would engage in future infidelity, partner neuroticism was unassociated with infidelity (Buss & Shackelford, 1997). Moreover, a recent analysis of older couples revealed a nonsignificant association between self-reported neuroticism and partner infidelity (Mahambrey, 2020).

Considering all these findings together, we conclude there is weak evidence suggesting that neuroticism is associated with infidelity among men. Among women, however, there is mixed support; specifically, about as much evidence reveals a positive association as there is failing to reveal any association. That said, we are aware of no studies that have documented a negative association, and several of the studies suggesting positive associations between neuroticism and infidelity among women involved large samples (e.g., Schmitt, 2004b; Schmitt & Shackelford, 2008). Accordingly, we tentatively conclude there is likely a small, difficult-to-detect positive association between neuroticism and infidelity among women only. With respect to partner neuroticism, the conservative integrative data analysis of new marriages (Altgelt et al., 2018) detected a positive association among both men and women, whereas two studies failed to detect an associations, including one study involving older couples (Buss & Shackelford, 1997; Mahambrey, 2020). Thus, based on the conflicting available evidence, we hesitate to draw firm conclusions regarding partner neuroticism and infidelity.

Openness

Openness is characterized by curiosity and imaginativeness (Costa & McCrae, 1992), and the research examining the association between openness and infidelity has revealed particularly inconsistent findings. Some studies have documented positive associations between openness and infidelity that vary across men and women. For example, Orzeck and Lung (2005) demonstrated that individuals who reported engaging in infidelity (ranging from kissing to sexual intercourse) in prior relationships were higher in openness than individuals who reported never having engaged in prior infidelities. Nevertheless, another study of married couples found that openness was positively correlated with the likelihood of future infidelity only among men (Buss & Shackelford, 1997), and, when sampling individuals across 46 nations, Schmitt and Shackelford (2008) similarly found a positive correlation between openness and infidelity only among men. Still, other studies have documented *negative* associations between openness and infidelity. For example, Russell et al.'s (2013) integrative data analysis revealed that individuals lower in openness were more likely to report having engaged in an infidelity, controlling for frequency of sex, marital satisfaction, the other Big Five personality traits, own attachment insecurity, and partner attachment insecurity. Likewise, Schmitt (2004b) used a large sample of 16,362 participants from 52 nations to demonstrate that men who were lower in openness were more likely to describe themselves with infidelity-related words. Further still, other studies have failed to document *any* associations between openness and infidelity (Altgelt et al., 2018; Barta & Kiene, 2005; Bourdage et al., 2007; Gibson et al., 2016; Schmitt & Buss, 2001; Smith et al., 2007). For example, Altgelt et al.'s (2018) integrative data analyses revealed that openness was not significantly associated with infidelity over the first three years of marriage.

Research on the association between *partners'* openness and infidelity has also yielded mixed findings. Whereas Altgelt et al. (2018) suggested that men (but not women) whose partners were lower in openness were more likely to engage in infidelity (controlling for the other Big Five traits and narcissism), neither Buss and Shackelford (1997) nor Mahambrey (2020) reported significant associations between partner openness and infidelity.

Looking at the body of research as a whole, evidence regarding the link between both own and partner openness and infidelity is particularly mixed. There are inconsistencies across studies when it comes to sex differences in this association, the direction of the association, and whether the association is significant. We argue future research is necessary before one can draw any firm conclusions on the association between openness and infidelity.

Conclusion

Overall, research examining the associations between own and partner Big Five traits and infidelity is mixed, with some associations emerging somewhat consistently and others being quite inconsistent. The most common and consistent findings are that individuals reporting lower levels of conscientiousness and individuals reporting lower agreeableness demonstrate an increased propensity for infidelity. There is also relatively strong evidence that people higher in extraversion and women higher in neuroticism are more likely to engage in infidelity. Findings regarding the role of own openness in infidelity are mixed. Fewer studies have examined the role of partner qualities in infidelity, but there is fairly consistent evidence that people with partners who are lower in conscientiousness are more likely to engage in infidelity. There is also fairly consistent evidence that partner extraversion is unrelated to infidelity. Nevertheless, the role of partner agreeableness, partner neuroticism, and partner openness remain unclear.

Given some of the inconsistencies, particularly with respect to the nonsignificant associations among all the Big Five traits (for both the self and partner), as well as the opposing associations that emerged for openness and partner agreeableness, we speculate that there are various hidden moderators of the associations between infidelity and these personality traits that contribute to the inconsistencies. For example, it may be that higher levels of openness are associated with an increased probability of infidelity among individuals with certain qualities or facing certain circumstances, whereas lower levels of openness are associated with an increased probability of infidelity among individuals with other qualities or facing other circumstances. Indeed, aspects of the person, partner, or environment have been shown to determine the strength and direction of the association among numerous relationship processes (McNulty, 2016). Future research may benefit from addressing these possibilities.

Dark Triad and Infidelity

The Dark Triad consists of three related personality traits—narcissism, psychopathy, and Machiavellianism—that, collectively, reflect a tendency toward superiority, manipulativeness, and low empathy (Paulhus & Williams, 2002), and, as a recent meta-analysis argues, may simply reflect low agreeableness (Muris et al., 2017). Numerous studies have linked each Dark Triad trait to infidelity (Adams et al., 2014; Alavi et al., 2018; Atkins et al., 2005; Brewer & Abell, 2015; Brewer et al., 2015; Campbell et al., 2002; Hunyady et al., 2008; Jones & Weiser, 2014; McNulty & Widman, 2014; McNulty & Widman, 2018; Buss & Shackelford, 1997), though, as will be seen, some of these associations have emerged somewhat inconsistently. Table 1.2 provides a summary of these associations. In more detail, we address each of the three Dark Triad traits, beginning with narcissism.

Narcissism

Narcissism is characterized by feelings of superiority and low empathy (Campbell et al., 2002; Raskin & Terry, 1988), and research has demonstrated, somewhat inconsistently (for a review, see McNulty & Widman, 2018), that narcissism is positively associated with infidelity. Indeed, research has demonstrated that people high (versus low) in narcissism report (a) more permissive attitudes toward engaging in infidelity (Hunyady et al., 2008), (b) greater interest in infidelity, even when their infidelity may be detected (Adams et al., 2014), and (c) greater likelihood of engaging in concurrent (Atkins et al., 2005; Brewer et al., 2015; Campbell et al., 2002; Jones & Weiser, 2014) and future infidelity (Brewer et al., 2015; Buss & Shackelford, 1997; also see Buunk & Van Direl, 1989). Nevertheless, other research has failed to demonstrate an association. For example, one study used a

Table 1.2 Dark Triad Findings

		Own						Partner					
		Narc		Psych		Mach		Narc		Psych		Mach	
	N	M	W	M	W	M	W	M	W	M	W	M	W
Adams et al., 2014	210	+	+	+	+	ns	ns						
Alavi et al., 2018	140	ns	ns	+	+	+	+						
Altgelt et al., 2018	454	ns	ns						ns				
Atkins et al., 2005	268	+	+										
Brewer & Abell, 2015	282					+	+						
Brewer et al., 2015	102*		+		+		ns						
Buss & Shackelford, 1997	214	+	+	+	+			ns	+	ns	+		
Campbell et al., 2002	100	+	+										
Hunyady et al., 2008	316	+	+					+	ns				
Jones & Weiser, 2014	884	+	+	+	+	+	+						
McNulty & Widman, 2014	246*	ns	ns					ns	ns				

Note. N = sample size; Narc = Narcissism; Psych = Psychopathy; Mach = Machiavellianism; M = Men; W = Women; ns = not significant. Brewer et al.'s (2015) study consisted of women only. McNulty and Widman (2014) additionally assessed sexual narcissism—a facet of global narcissism.

non-Western sample to demonstrate that narcissism is not significantly associated with infidelity (Alavi et al., 2018). Likewise, two independent integrative data analyses (Altgelt et al., 2018; McNulty & Widman, 2014) of newly married couples revealed a similar null association between narcissism and infidelity (controlling for the Big Five traits).

Research regarding the association between *partner* narcissism and infidelity is also somewhat inconsistent. Although several studies report a positive association between partner narcissism and infidelity, some find an association among men (but not women) whereas others find an association among women (but not men). For example, two studies (Altgelt et al., 2018; Hunyada et al., 2008) reported that women (but not men) higher in narcissism were more likely to report being victims of infidelity. Yet, both studies contrast with Buss and Shackelford's (1997) finding that partner narcissism was positively correlated with women's (but not men's) reported likelihood of engaging in future infidelity. It is certainly possible that women whose partners are higher in narcissism report a greater intention to engage in infidelity, but it is men with partners who are higher in narcissism that are more likely to *actually* engage in infidelity. Future research may benefit from examining this possibility. Nevertheless, still other research reports no association between partner narcissism and infidelity (McNulty & Widman, 2014).

Some of the inconsistencies in the observed associations between own and partner narcissism and infidelity (as well as between other personality traits and infidelity) could stem from a mismatch between the level of measurement of the predictor (i.e., global narcissism) and the level of measurement of the outcome (i.e., infidelity—a sexual behavior). Personality may be more predictive of behavior when considered contextually. Consistent with this possibility, McNulty and Widman (2014) used a sample of newlywed couples to demonstrate that people's own *sexual* narcissism (i.e., narcissism that is specific to the sexual domain and consists of sexual entitlement, exploitation, low empathy, and inflated sense of sexual skill; see McNulty & Widman, 2013), but not own *global* narcissism, was associated with their infidelity. Moreover, in this study, individuals whose partners reported inflated sexual skills and sexual entitlement as well as dampened sexual empathy were more likely to retrospectively report infidelity.

Considering this body of research as a whole, these findings seem to suggest that, when assessed at the same contextual level, individuals higher (versus lower) in sexual narcissism and individuals whose partners are higher (versus lower) in sexual narcissism are more likely to engage in infidelity (McNulty & Widman, 2014). Nevertheless, when assessed more broadly, there are greater reported inconsistencies between own narcissism and infidelity (Alavi et al., 2018; Altgelt et al., 2018; Atkins et al., 2005; Brewer et al., 2015; Campbell et al., 2002; Jones & Weiser, 2014; McNulty & Widman, 2014) as well as partner narcissism and infidelity (Altgelt et al., 2018; Buss & Shackelford, 1997; Hunyady et al., 2008; McNulty & Widman, 2014). Of course, the findings regarding narcissism that is specific to the sexual domain emerge in only one study and thus we argue that additional research is needed to better understand the associations between own and partner sexual narcissism and infidelity.

Psychopathy

Psychopathy is characterized by callousness and low empathy (Jonason et al., 2013; McHoskey et al., 1998), and research has consistently linked psychopathy to infidelity. Indeed, several studies reveal that people high (versus low) in psychopathy are more interested in engaging in future infidelity (Alavi et al., 2018; Brewer et al., 2015; Buss & Shackelford, 1997), even when their infidelity may be detected (Adams et al., 2014), and are more likely to report having engaged in infidelity in past relationships (Brewer et al., 2015; Jones & Weiser, 2014).

Although there are consistent findings regarding the association between own psychopathy and infidelity, we are only aware of one study that has examined the role of *partner* psychopathy in infidelity. In that study, Buss and Shackelford (1997) found that women (but not men) were more likely to engage in future infidelity when their partners were higher in psychopathy. Moreover, research examining the role of partner psychopathy in other relationship outcomes has revealed it is relatively harmful. Indeed, people with partners higher (versus lower) in psychopathy are less committed to their relationships (Smith et al., 2014) and less satisfied with those relationships (Weiss et al., 2018). Likewise, heterosexual women (but not men) with partners higher (versus lower) in psychopathy report elevated personal distress and more frequent aggression aimed at their partners (Savard et al., 2011), even when controlling for own psychopathy (Webster et al., 2016). Given the one significant finding and these other harmful relationship outcomes, we speculate that partner psychopathy may play a role in infidelity—particularly among women. Nevertheless, additional future research should continue to explore the association between psychopathy and infidelity.

Machiavellianism

Machiavellianism, which is characterized by the manipulation and exploitation of others (Christie & Geis, 1970; Vecchio & Sussman, 1991), is relatively consistently positively associated with infidelity. Indeed, people high (versus low) in Machiavellianism are more likely to report (a) intentions to engage in future infidelity (Alavi et al., 2018; Brewer & Abell, 2015) and (b) infidelity in prior relationships (Brewer et al., 2015; Jones & Weiser, 2014). Nevertheless, one study using a somewhat small sample of people recruited online ($N = 210$) revealed a null association between Machiavellianism and willingness to engage in infidelity (Adams et al., 2014).

We are not aware of any research directly examining the role of *partner* Machiavellianism in infidelity, though Machiavellianism has been somewhat inconsistently linked to other relationship outcomes. For example, some research has demonstrated that Machiavellianism is positively associated with partner-focused, negative relationship behaviors (e.g., controlling behaviors, emotional abuse, mate guarding; Brewer & Abell, 2017) whereas other research has revealed null associations between partner Machiavellianism and aggression, controlling for own Machiavellianism (Webster et al. 2016). Given such mixed findings, we are hesitant to speculate about the role of partner Machiavellianism in infidelity.

Similar to psychopathy and infidelity, we cautiously conclude that individuals higher (versus lower) in Machiavellianism are more likely to engage in infidelity. Although one study (Adams et al., 2014) revealed a null association, we hesitate to place too much emphasis on that study given its small sample size. Nevertheless, future research could benefit from further exploring this association or even considering potential moderators that could explain these inconsistent findings. Also similar to psychopathy and infidelity, additional research assessing the role of partner Machiavellianism in infidelity is needed.

Conclusion

Considering this broad literature as a whole, there is fairly convincing evidence that individuals higher in any of the Dark Triad traits are more likely to engage in infidelity (Adams et al., 2014; Alavi et al., 2018; Atkins et al., 2005; Brewer & Abell, 2015; Brewer et al., 2015; Campbell et al., 2002; Jones & Weiser, 2014). A few inconsistencies do emerge, however, some of which may be due, in part, to a mismatch between the level of measurement of personality when predicting a sexual behavior (see McNulty & Widman, 2014). For this reason, we recommend that future research examine domain-specific personality traits—a point to which we return later in this chapter.

Research on the link between partner Dark Triad traits and infidelity is less conclusive. The few studies that have examined the association between partner narcissism and infidelity are inconsistent, with some studies finding a positive association in men but not women (Hunyady et al., 2008; Altgelt et al., 2018), at least one study finding a positive association in women but not men (Buss & Shackelford, 1997), and at least one additional study finding no association (McNulty & Widman, 2014). Further, we are aware of only one study that has directly examined the association between partner psychopathy and infidelity, and no research that has directly examined the association between partner Machiavellianism and infidelity. Thus, future research employing the strongest methodologies is needed to better understand the true nature of the associations between own and partner Dark Triad traits and infidelity.

Attachment Insecurity and Infidelity

According to attachment theory (Mikulincer & Shaver, 2003; Mikulincer et al., 2003), people possess working mental attachment models that influence their subsequent behaviors. Attachment theory characterizes these working models as two continuous dimensions: attachment anxiety and attachment avoidance (see Brennan et al., 1998; Fraley & Waller, 1998). Research suggests both dimensions of attachment insecurity are associated with infidelity (e.g., Allen & Baucom, 2004; Bogaert & Sadava, 2002; DeWall et al.,

Table 1.3 Attachment Insecurity Findings

		Own				Partner			
		Anxiety		Avoidance		Anxiety		Avoidance	
	N	M	W	M	W	M	W	M	W
Allen & Baucom, 2004	755	ns	+	+	+				
Bogaert & Sadava, 2002	792	ns	+	ns	ns				
DeWall et al., 2011	2,382*	ns	ns	+	+				
Drigotas et al., 1999	74	+	+	-	-				
Fish et al., 2012	353	+	+	-	-				
McNulty et al., 2018	466	-	-	-	-				
Parker & Campbell, 2017	1024	+	+	ns	ns				
Russell et al., 2013	414	+	+	ns	ns	+	+	-	-

Note. N = sample size; Anxiety = Attachment Anxiety; Avoidance = Attachment Avoidance; M = Men; W = Women; ns = not significant. DeWall et al. (2011) conducted eight studies examining attachment and infidelity.

2011; Fish et al., 2012; Parker & Campbell, 2017; Russell et al., 2013). Table 1.3 provides a summary of these associations.

Attachment Anxiety

People higher in attachment anxiety consistently crave, but at the same time doubt, acceptance and care from current and potential partners (Mikulincer & Shaver, 2003). Accordingly, such individuals tend to engage in a variety of cognitive and behavioral strategies aimed at garnering love and affection. We thus might expect a positive association between attachment anxiety and infidelity. Nevertheless, the association appears somewhat inconsistently—both with regard to the existence of the association and with regard to the extent that it emerges equally across men and women. We are aware of at least three studies demonstrating that both men and women higher (versus lower) in attachment anxiety are more likely to report having previously engaged in both emotional and physical infidelity (Drigotas et al., 1999; Fish et al., 2012; Parker & Campbell, 2017). Likewise, an integrative data analysis of two longitudinal studies of newlywed couples found that husbands and wives higher (versus lower) in attachment anxiety were more likely to report having engaged in infidelity in their marriage, and this association held when controlling for own attachment avoidance, partner attachment anxiety, partner attachment avoidance, sexual frequency, marital satisfaction, and the Big Five personality traits (Russell et al., 2013). Two other studies (Allen & Baucom, 2004; Bogaert & Sadava, 2002), however, observed a positive association among only women. More specifically, Bogaert and Sadava (2002) found that attachment anxiety was positively correlated with women's (but not men's) retrospective reports of infidelity (although this association was not robust to the inclusion of covariates including other sexual behaviors, age, physical attractiveness, income). Likewise, Allen and Baucom (2004) found an interaction between gender and attachment security when predicting undergraduates' number of past extradyadic partners such that anxiously attached women (using categories rather than retaining the scores' continuous nature) reported more extradyadic partners than securely attached women. In contrast to all of these findings, however, eight independent studies (from the same group of researchers; DeWall et al., 2011) of individuals in mostly dating relationships demonstrated that, controlling for attachment avoidance, attachment anxiety was not significantly associated with attitudes toward infidelity, interest in available alternatives—either at an explicit or implicit level, retrospective reports of infidelity, or reports of infidelity over time. It is worth noting that, in contrast to the studies we have reviewed thus far, one additional study controlled for attachment anxiety in an analysis of more proximal cognitive processes that predict infidelity (i.e., attention toward and evaluation of attractive alternatives) and revealed a weak almost significant *negative* association between attachment anxiety and infidelity (McNulty et al., 2018). Nevertheless, we hesitate to make too much out of this finding given the authors controlled for these and several other proximal and distal variables (e.g., marital satisfaction, sexual satisfaction, commitment, availability of alternatives), leaving it unclear what was the nature of the variance in attachment anxiety that remained.

Given individuals higher (versus lower) in attachment anxiety experience more frequent relationship conflict and interact more negatively with their partners (Collins, 1996; Simpson et al., 1996; for a review, see Li & Chan, 2012), we might expect *partners'* attachment anxiety to be similarly positively associated with infidelity. Nevertheless, we are aware of only one study that has examined this association. Consistent with expectations, Russell et al.'s (2013) integrative data analysis demonstrated that, controlling for own attachment anxiety and both couple members' attachment avoidance, people with partners higher (versus lower) in attachment anxiety were more likely to engage in infidelity. Of course, it should be noted that this integrative data analysis was based on newlywed couples, a time when infidelity is rare and thus we are hesitant to draw strong conclusions from this single analysis.

This research as a whole suggests that future research is needed to more rigorously examine the associations between own and partner attachment anxiety and infidelity. Although several studies reveal a positive association between own attachment anxiety and infidelity (Fish et al., 2012; Parker & Campbell, 2017; Russell et al., 2013), two studies suggest this may be particularly (or only) true among women. Nevertheless, we are hesitant to draw this latter conclusion due to various features of these studies; one of the studies found this association no longer emerged when controlling for other variables (Bogaert & Sadava, 2002) and another categorized individuals into one of three attachment styles (rather than measuring attachment anxiety as a continuous variable; Allen & Baucom, 2004). Despite these study features, it is worth acknowledging that these sex-differentiated findings are consistent with other work demonstrating that attachment anxiety impacts sexual outcomes more strongly for women than for men (Cooper et al., 1998; Cooper et al., 2006). Of course, in contrast to these findings highlighting a positive association between own attachment anxiety and infidelity, an impressive eight studies reveal a null association. With regard to partner attachment anxiety and infidelity, we are aware of only one study that has examined this association, and it revealed a positive association.

Attachment Avoidance

In contrast to attachment anxiety, people higher in attachment avoidance see others as relatively unreliable and thus engage in cognitive and behavioral strategies aimed at gaining distance from partners (Mikulincer & Shaver, 2003). It is thus perhaps not surprising that the association between attachment avoidance and infidelity is rather complicated. On the one hand, three studies found a negative association between people's own attachment avoidance and their reports of both emotional and physical infidelity (Drigotas et al., 1999; Fish et al., 2012; McNulty et al., 2018), suggesting people higher in attachment avoidance are less likely to engage in infidelity. On the other hand, several studies have found a positive association between own attachment avoidance and infidelity (Allen & Baucom, 2004; DeWall et al., 2011). For example, in the eight studies of individuals in mostly dating relationships that revealed a null association between attachment anxiety and infidelity, DeWall and colleagues (2011) reported that individuals higher (versus lower) in attachment avoidance had more positive attitudes toward infidelity, showed greater attentional bias toward attractive alternative partners, and reported more infidelity retrospectively and over time. Moreover, they showed this positive association was explained, at least in part, by those individuals' lower commitment. Further still, Russell and colleagues (2013) examined the association in two samples of married couples, controlling for both couple members' attachment anxiety and partner attachment avoidance, and revealed no significant association between own attachment avoidance and reports of infidelity.

To our knowledge, similar to the association between partner attachment anxiety and infidelity, only Russell and colleagues (2013) have examined the association between *partner* attachment avoidance and infidelity. Interestingly, their two longitudinal studies of newlywed couples revealed that individuals with spouses higher (versus lower) in attachment avoidance were *less* likely to report engaging in infidelity. Given the dearth of research in this area, however, we are hesitant to draw firm conclusions from these data.

Taken together, this body of research suggests that, similar to own and partner attachment anxiety, additional research is needed to understand the true nature of the associations between own and partner attachment avoidance and infidelity. DeWall and colleagues (2011) showed a positive association between own attachment avoidance and infidelity across eight studies with mostly dating (though some married) participants using a wide variety of operationalizations of infidelity. However, Russell and colleagues (2013) failed to find an association between own attachment avoidance and infidelity when controlling for partner attachment insecurity. Moreover, given only one study has examined the association between partner attachment avoidance and infidelity, additional research should attempt to replicate the negative association observed in that study (Russell et al., 2013).

Conclusion

Looking at this body of research collectively, we are fairly confident in concluding that more research is needed. Regarding own attachment anxiety and infidelity, some research has revealed positive associations (Fish et al., 2012; Parker & Campbell, 2017; Russell et al., 2013) that may be stronger among women (Allen & Baucom, 2004; Bogaert & Sadava, 2002) whereas other research has revealed null associations (DeWall et al., 2011). Regarding own attachment avoidance and infidelity, some research has revealed negative associations (Drigotas et al., 1999; Fish et al., 2012; McNulty et al., 2018), other research has demonstrated positive associations (DeWall et al., 2011), and yet other research has demonstrated null associations (Russell et al., 2013). Regarding partner attachment insecurity and infidelity, there is some evidence that individuals with partners higher (versus lower) in attachment anxiety are more likely to engage in infidelity and that individuals with partners higher (versus lower) in attachment avoidance are less likely to engage in infidelity (Russell et al., 2013), and no studies that yet challenge this finding. Given the inconsistent findings regarding own attachment insecurity and infidelity as well as the dearth of research regarding partner attachment insecurity and infidelity, we caution against drawing strong conclusions until further research has been conducted.

Sociosexuality and Infidelity

Another notable individual difference that has been relatively consistently linked to infidelity (e.g., Barta & Kiene, 2005; Mattingly et al., 2011; Penke & Asendorpf, 2008; Rodrigues et al., 2017; Seal et al., 1994; Weiser et al., 2018) is the extent to which individuals are motivated to engage in casual, uncommitted sex, or their sociosexual orientations (Simpson & Gangestad, 1991). Table 1.4 provides a summary of the associations between sociosexuality and infidelity. Indeed, previous research has shown that individuals with more unrestricted (versus restricted) sociosexual orientations are more likely to (a) retrospectively report having engaged in past infidelity (Barta & Kiene, 2005; Penke & Asendorpf, 2008; Rodrigues et al., 2017) and (b) engage in future infidelity (Mattingly et al., 2011; Seal et al., 1994; Weiser et al., 2018). One study even found that more

Table 1.4 Sociosexuality Findings

	N	Own		Partner	
		M	W	M	W
Barta & Kiene, 2005	432	+	+		
Mattingly et al., 2011	228	+	+		
McNulty et al., 2018	466	+	+		
Penke & Asendorpf, 2008	2,778*	+	+	-	-
Rodrigues et al., 2017	570*	+	+		
Seal et al., 1994	164*	+	+		
Weiser et al., 2018	550	+	+		

Note. N = sample size; M = Men; W = Women. Rodrigues et al. (2017) and Seal et al. (1994) conducted two studies. Penke and Asendorpf (2008) examined the association between own sociosexuality and infidelity in their first study (N = 2,208) and the association between partner sociosexuality and infidelity in a subsample of their second study (n = 70).

unrestricted (versus restricted) individuals in existing relationships were more likely to enter to win a date with an alternative partner (Seal et al., 1994). Moreover, McNulty and colleagues (2018) found that newly married individuals who reported more short-term partners prior to marriage (a characteristic of a more unrestricted sociosexual orientation) attended more to attractive alternative partners (also see French et al., 2019), and this increased attention was associated with an increased likelihood of engaging in infidelity. In contrast to these numerous studies demonstrating main effects of sociosexuality, two additional studies suggested that it depends on peoples' commitment (Rodrigues et al., 2017; Seal et al., 1994); unrestricted sociosexuality appears unassociated with infidelity among more committed individuals, but positively associated with infidelity among less committed individuals.

In light of recent research demonstrating that newly married individuals whose *spouses* are more unrestricted (versus restricted) experience steeper declines in satisfaction over time (French et al., 2019), we might expect those people to be more likely to engage in infidelity as they become less satisfied with their relationships. To our knowledge, however, only one study has indirectly examined the association between partner sociosexuality and infidelity, and it reveals a counterintuitive finding. Specifically, Penke and Asendorpf (2008) found that individuals whose partners were more unrestricted (versus restricted) flirted *less* when interacting with alternative partners. Flirtation is only one (fairly mild) form of infidelity and thus this finding should be interpreted cautiously.

Collectively, we take this body of research to suggest that less restricted individuals are more likely to engage in infidelity, and this association seems to be driven, at least in part, by individuals' decreased commitment and increased attention to alternatives. The link between partner sociosexuality and infidelity seems less clear, and the one study exploring this association revealed a counterintuitive finding involving a relatively mild form of infidelity. Future research would thus benefit from replicating this counterintuitive association and extending it to other operationalizations of infidelity.

What Does Good Personality and Infidelity Research Look Like?

As may be clear based on our review thus far, research examining the association between personality and infidelity varies widely in methods used, some of which may explain the inconsistencies that emerged. Moving forward, the literature could benefit from adopting practices to conduct the best test of the associations between personality and infidelity. First, research may benefit from strong operationalizations of infidelity. Infidelity is notoriously difficult to measure (see Fincham & May, 2017). As such, it has been operationalized differently across prior studies. For example, infidelity has been operationalized as perceptions of individuals' likelihood that one's self or partner will engage in a host of behaviors in the future (e.g., Buss & Shackelford, 1997; Shackelford et al., 2008), some of which are clearly infidelity (e.g., serious affair) and others of which may not be (e.g., flirting). Likewise, infidelity has been operationalized as descriptions of oneself in terms of various infidelity-related words (e.g., faithful; see DeWall et al., 2011; Fish et al., 2012; Parker & Campbell, 2017; Schmitt, 2004b). Finally, infidelity has been operationalized as reports that people and/or their partners have engaged in an infidelity in their current (e.g., Altgelt et al., 2018; McNulty et al., 2018; McNulty & Widman, 2014; Russell et al., 2013) or any past relationships (Gibson et al., 2007; Mahambrey, 2020; Orzeck & Lung, 2005). These different measures may capture different, though related, processes which may be differently related to various individual differences. For example, some people may report that they are likely to engage in infidelity in the future, but never actually do so. Thus, the associations between personality and infidelity may look different depending on the operationalization of infidelity employed. We recommend that research aimed at examining the associations between personality traits and infidelity clearly operationalize infidelity as reports of ongoing and past instances of that behavior. We also recommend defining and distinguishing across different forms of infidelity (ranging from extrapair sex to flirting to emotional infidelity).

Second, conclusions may be most credible when research examines the influence of both partners' personality traits simultaneously. Given that both partners play a role in shaping relationships (Kelley & Thibaut, 1978), and given assortative mating—particularly in terms of personality and individual differences (Buss, 1984), isolating the effects of each couple member's personality requires assessing both partners' personality and simultaneously accounting for each (see McNulty, 2013). Moreover, given the interdependent nature of romantic relationships, one partner's behavior is difficult, if not impossible, to understand without considering aspects of the other partner. Indeed, Zayas and colleagues (2002) draw on a broad tradition of research examining the role of situational factors in the link between personality and behavior to note that partner personality is a powerful situational factor that predicts behavior; that is, people's behaviors depend not only on their own personality but also on their partner's personality. For example, having a romantic partner who is neurotic and disagreeable creates a negative situation within the relationship for the individual. Thus, this partner's personality traits could influence whether that individual looks for alternative partners outside of the relationship and, ultimately, engages in infidelity. Yet, research examining the associations between partner personality and infidelity is limited in comparison to research examining the associations between own personality and infidelity.

Third, research would benefit from pooling across several large samples. Indeed, in many samples, incidences of infidelity are relatively low (particularly among samples of newly married couples; e.g., Altgelt et al., 2018; Russell et al., 2013), which is fairly consistent with surveys demonstrating that 23% of US men and 15% of US women report engaging in an infidelity at least once in their lifetimes (Atkins & Kessel, 2008). Moreover, infidelity is a sensitive and socially taboo behavior; thus, measuring it is complicated by a myriad of issues (e.g., secrecy, shame, social desirability; Blow & Hartnett, 2005; Krumpal, 2013; see Fincham & May, 2017). These issues likely inhibit individuals' willingness to report infidelity, further reducing reported incidences. Accordingly, research would benefit from taking steps to increase people's willingness to report infidelity. For example, having individuals complete measures of infidelity separate from their partner, making it clear to individuals that their responses are completely confidential, and perhaps even using bogus pipeline procedures (see Alexander & Fisher, 2003) may help to increase the validity of infidelity measures.

Finally, research would benefit from examining diverse samples. When adopting these new methodological considerations, future research should continue to seek out samples that vary in race, ethnicity, nationality, age, socioeconomic status, sexual orientation, etc. For example, despite some of the methodological strengths of Altgelt and colleagues' (2018) study (e.g., large, dyadic, longitudinal, both couple member's reported infidelity independently), their sample was relatively homogeneous in that most participants were young, married, and from the southern United States, limiting the generalizability of their findings to other samples. Indeed, as Fincham and May (2017) suggest, infidelity research should be interpreted with caution prior to replication using representative samples. Several studies employing cross-cultural methods involving over 45 nations (e.g., Schmitt, 2004a, 2004b; Schmitt & Shackelford, 2008) offer nice examples of the utility of obtaining diverse samples.

Future Directions

In addition to offering these methodological recommendations for future research, we proffer several interesting new avenues for future research examining the association between personality and infidelity. First, such research should more frequently consider the important role of context. Personality and infidelity research largely uses global assessments of personality traits; however, in the context of romantic relationships, facets of personality traits specific to that context may be better predictors of outcomes like infidelity. Indeed, as noted earlier, McNulty and Widman (2014) found that global narcissism did not predict sexual infidelity whereas sexual narcissism did. Creating and utilizing relationship-specific measures of personality traits could help clarify other inconsistent findings and reveal new information about the role of personality in predicting infidelity. For example, openness is relatively inconsistently associated with infidelity in the current body of research. It is possible that individuals' global levels of openness are not good predictors of infidelity behaviors, but individuals' levels of openness to sexual behaviors and experiences specifically are good predictors of infidelity. Future research may benefit from exploring this possibility.

Second, future research should continue to explore the mechanisms driving the associations between personality traits and infidelity. For example, it is possible that automatic processes and attitudes drive, at least in part, the association between personality traits and infidelity. Indeed, prior research revealed the number of short-term sexual partners individuals had before marriage (a characteristic of an unrestricted sociosexual orientation) predicted the extent to which they attended to attractive alternatives (also see French et al., 2019), which subsequently predicted their likelihood of engaging in infidelity (McNulty et al., 2018). Likewise, previous research has demonstrated individuals' automatic attitudes toward their partners predict important relationship outcomes like relationship satisfaction and dissolution such that more negative automatic partner attitudes are associated with lower satisfaction (currently and over time; McNulty et al., 2013; Scinta & Gable, 2007) and an increased likelihood of dissolution (Lee et al., 2010). It is thus possible that individuals' personality traits influence their automatic partner attitudes, and these attitudes are associated with their likelihood of engaging in infidelity. As just one example, it is possible that the emotional distress related to the partner and the relationship that is associated with attachment anxiety results in more negative automatic partner attitudes, which may predict subsequent infidelity. Moreover, couples' sexual behaviors could drive the association between their own and their partner's personality traits and infidelity. For example, more (versus less) agreeable individuals engage in sex with their partners more often (Meltzer & McNulty, 2016), and the increased sexual frequency their partner experiences could reduce their partner's likelihood of engaging in infidelity.

General Conclusion

Given the impact infidelity can have on romantic relationship satisfaction and stability (Betzig, 1989; Previti & Amato, 2004), it is necessary to understand the personality and individual differences that are associated with individuals' likelihood of engaging in infidelity. A large body of research has examined the associations between own and partner personality traits and infidelity. Although informative, methodological inconsistencies plaguing this body of research prevent us from making strong conclusions about the nature of the associations between own and partner personality traits and infidelity.

Future research using (a) strong methodologies, (b) examining facet-specific personality traits, and (c) uncovering new avenues will advance our understanding of the role personality and individual differences play in infidelity.

References

Adams, H. M., Luevano, V. X., & Jonason, P. K. (2014). Risky business: Willingness to be caught in an extra-pair relationship, relationship experience, and the Dark Triad. *Personality and Individual Differences, 66,* 204–207.

Alavi, M., Mei, T. K., & Mehrinezhad, S. A. (2018). The Dark Triad of personality and infidelity intentions: The moderating role of relationship experience. *Personality and Individual Differences, 128,* 49–54.

Alexander, M. G., & Fisher, T. D. (2003). Truth and consequences: Using the bogus pipeline to examine sex differences in self-reported sexuality. *Journal of Sex Research, 40,* 27–35.

Allen, E. S., & Baucom, D. H. (2004). Adult attachment and patterns of extradyadic involvement. *Family Process, 43,* 467–488.

Allen, M. S., & Walter, E. E. (2018). Linking Big Five personality traits to sexuality and sexual health: A meta-analytic review. *Psychological Bulletin, 144,* 1081–1110.

Atkins, D. C., & Kessel, D. E. (2008). Religiousness and infidelity: Attendance, but not faith and prayer, predict marital fidelity. *Journal of Marriage and Family, 70,* 407–418.

Atkins, D. C., Yi, J., Baucom, D. H., & Christensen, A. (2005). Infidelity in couples seeking marital therapy. *Journal of Family Psychology, 19,* 470–473.

Altgelt, E. E., Reyes, M. A., French, J. E., Meltzer, A. L., & McNulty, J. K. (2018). Who is sexually faithful? Own and partner personality traits as predictors of infidelity. *Journal of Social and Personal Relationships, 35,* 600–614.

Barta, W. D., & Kiene, S. M. (2005). Motivations for infidelity in heterosexual dating couples: The roles of gender, personality differences, and sociosexual orientation. *Journal of Social and Personal Relationships, 22,* 339–360.

Betzig, L. (1989). Causes of conjugal dissolution: A cross-cultural study. *Current Anthropology, 30,* 654–676.

Blow, A. J., & Hartnett, K. (2005). Infidelity in committed relationships I: A methodological review. *Journal of Marital and Family Therapy, 31,* 183–216.

Bogaert, A. F., & Sadava, S. (2002). Adult attachment and sexual behavior. *Personal Relationships, 9,* 191–204.

Bourdage, J. S., Lee, K., Ashton, M. C., & Perry, A. (2007). Big Five and HEXACO model personality correlates of sexuality. *Personality and Individual Differences, 43,* 1506–1516.

Brennan, K. A., Clark, C. L., & Shaver, P. R. (1998). Self-report measurement of adult attachment: An integrative overview. In J. A. Simpson & W. S. Rholes (Eds.), *Attachment theory and close relationships* (pp. 46–76). Guilford Press.

Brewer, G., & Abell, L. (2015). Machiavellianism and sexual behavior: Motivations, deception and infidelity. *Personality and Individual Differences, 74,* 186–191.

Brewer, G., & Abell, L. (2017). Machiavellianism, relationship satisfaction, and romantic relationship quality. *Europe's Journal of Psychology, 13,* 491–502.

Brewer, G., Hunt, D., James, G., & Abell, L. (2015). Dark Triad traits, infidelity and romantic revenge. *Personality and Individual Differences, 83,* 122–127.

Buss, D. M. (1984). Marital assortment for personality dispositions: Assessment with three different data sources. *Behavior Genetics, 14,* 111–123.

Buss, D. M., & Shackelford, T. K. (1997). Susceptibility to infidelity in the first year of marriage. *Journal of Research in Personality, 31,* 193–221.

Buunk, B. P., & Van Driel, B. (1989). *Variant lifestyles and relationships.* Sage.

Campbell, W. K., Foster, C. A., & Finkel, E. J. (2002). Does self-love lead to love for others? A story of narcissistic game playing. *Journal of Personality and Social Psychology, 83,* 340–354.

Christie, R., & Geis, F. L. (1970). *Studies in Machiavellianism.* Academic Press.

Collins, N. L. (1996). Working models of attachment: Implications for explanation, emotion, and behavior. *Journal of Personality and Social Psychology, 71,* 810–832.

Cooper, M. L., Pioli, M., Levitt, A., Talley, A. E., Micheas, L., & Collins, N. L. (2006). Attachment styles, sex motives, and sexual behavior. In M. Mikulincer & G. S. Goodman (Eds.), *Dynamics of romantic love: Attachment, caregiving, and sex* (pp. 243–274). Guilford Press.

Cooper, M. L., Shaver, P. R., & Collins, N. L. (1998). Attachment styles, emotion regulation, and adjustment in adolescence. *Journal of Personality and Social Psychology, 74*, 1380–1397.

Costa, P. T., & McCrae, R. R. (1992). *NEO PI-R: Professional manual*. Psychological Assessment Resources.

DeWall, C. N., Lambert, N. M., Slotter, E. B., Pond, R. S., Jr, Deckman, T., Finkel, E. J., . . . Fincham, F. D. (2011). So far away from one's partner, yet so close to romantic alternatives: Avoidant attachment, interest in alternatives, and infidelity. *Journal of Personality and Social Psychology, 101*, 1302–1316.

Drigotas, S., Safstrom, C., & Gentilia, T. (1999). An investment model prediction of dating infidelity. *Journal of Personality and Social Psychology, 77*, 509–524.

Fincham, F. D., & May, R. W. (2017). Infidelity in romantic relationships. *Current Opinion in Psychology, 13*, 70–74.

Fish, J. N., Pavkov, T. W., Wetchler, J. L., & Bercik, J. (2012). Characteristics of those who participate in infidelity: The role of adult attachment and differentiation in extradyadic experiences. *American Journal of Family Therapy, 40*, 214–229.

Fraley, R. C., & Waller, N. G. (1998). Adult attachment patterns: A test of the typological model. In J. A. Simpson & W. S. Rholes (Eds.), *Attachment theory and close relationships* (pp. 77–114). Guilford Press.

French, J. E., Altgelt, E. E., & Meltzer, A. L. (2019). The implications of sociosexuality for marital satisfaction and dissolution. *Psychological Science, 30*, 1460–1472.

Gibson, K. A., Thompson, A. E., & O'Sullivan, L. F. (2016). Love thy neighbour: Personality traits, relationship quality, and attraction to others as predictors of infidelity among young adults. *Canadian Journal of Human Sexuality, 25*, 186–198.

Hunyady, O., Josephs, L., & Jost, J. T. (2008). Priming the primal scene: Betrayal trauma, narcissism, and attitudes toward sexual infidelity. *Self and Identity, 7*, 278–294.

Jonason, P. K., Lyons, M., Bethell, E. J., & Ross, R. (2013). Different routes to limited empathy in the sexes: Examining the links between the Dark Triad and empathy. *Personality and Individual Differences, 54*, 572–576.

Jones, D. N., & Weiser, D. A. (2014). Differential infidelity patterns among the Dark Triad. *Personality and Individual Differences, 57*, 20–24.

Kelley, H. H., & Thibaut, J. W. (1978). *Interpersonal relations: A theory of interdependence*. Wiley.

Krumpal, I. (2013). Determinants of social desirability bias in sensitive surveys: A literature review. *Quality & Quantity, 47*, 2025–2047.

Lee, S., Rogge, R. D., & Reis, H. T. (2010). Assessing the seeds of relationship decay: Using implicit evaluations to detect the early stages of disillusionment. *Psychological Science, 21*, 857–864.

Li, T., & Chan, D. K. S. (2012). How anxious and avoidant attachment affect romantic relationship quality differently: A meta-analytic review. *European Journal of Social Psychology, 42*, 406–419.

Mahambrey, M. (2020). Self-reported Big Five personality traits of individuals who have experienced partner infidelity. *Personal Relationships, 27*, 272–304.

Mattingly, B. A., Clark, E. M., Weidler, D. J., Bullock, M., Hackathorn, J., & Blankmeyer, K. (2011). Sociosexual orientation, commitment, and infidelity: A mediation analysis. *Journal of Social Psychology, 151*, 222–226.

McCrae, R. R., & Costa, P. T. (1997). Personality trait structure as a human universal. *American Psychologist, 52*, 509–516.

McHoskey, J. W., Worzel, W., & Szyarto, C. (1998). Machiavellianism and psychopathy. *Journal of Personality and Social Psychology, 74*, 192–210.

McNulty, J. K. (2013). Personality and relationships. In J. A. Simpson & L. Campbell (Eds.), *The Oxford handbook of close relationships* (pp. 535–552). Oxford University Press.

McNulty, J. K. (2016). Highlighting the contextual nature of interpersonal relationships. In J. M. Olson & M. P. Zanna (Eds.), *Advances in experimental social psychology* (Vol. 54, pp. 247–315). Academic Press.

McNulty, J. K., Meltzer, A. L., Makhanova, A., & Maner, J. K. (2018). Attentional and evaluative biases help people maintain relationships by avoiding infidelity. *Journal of Personality and Social Psychology, 115*, 76–95.

McNulty, J. K., Olson, M. A., Meltzer, A. L., & Shaffer, M. J. (2013). Though they may be unaware, newlyweds implicitly know whether their marriage will be satisfying. *Science, 342*, 1119–1120.

McNulty, J. K., & Russell, V. M. (2016). Forgive and forget, or forgive and regret? Whether forgiveness leads to less or more offending depends on offender agreeableness. *Personality and Social Psychology Bulletin, 42*, 616–631.

McNulty, J. K., & Widman, L. (2013). The implications of sexual narcissism for sexual and marital satisfaction. *Archives of Sexual Behavior, 42*, 1021–1032.

McNulty, J. K., & Widman, L. (2014). Sexual narcissism and infidelity in early marriage. *Archives of Sexual Behavior, 43*, 1315–1325.

McNulty, J. K., & Widman, L. (2018). Narcissistic qualities and infidelity. In A. D. Hermann, A. B. Brunell, & J. D. Foster (Eds.), *Handbook of trait narcissism* (pp. 327–333). Springer.

Meltzer, A. L., & McNulty, J. K. (2016). Who is having more and better sex? The Big Five as predictors of sex in marriage. *Journal of Research in Personality, 63*, 62–66.

Mikulincer, M., & Shaver, P. R. (2003). The attachment behavioral system in adulthood: Activation, psychodynamics, and interpersonal processes. *Advances in Experimental Social Psychology, 35*, 56–152.

Mikulincer, M., Shaver, P. R., & Pereg, D. (2003). Attachment theory and affect regulation: The dynamics, development, and cognitive consequences of attachment-related strategies. *Motivation and Emotion, 27*, 77–102.

Muris, P., Merckelbach, H., Otgaar, H., & Meijer, E. (2017). The malevolent side of human nature: A meta-analysis and critical review of the literature on the dark triad (narcissism, Machiavellianism, and psychopathy). *Perspectives on Psychological Science, 12*, 183–204.

Olver, J. M., & Mooradian, T. A. (2003). Personality traits and personal values: A conceptual and empirical integration. *Personality and Individual Differences, 35*, 109–125.

Orzeck, T., & Lung, E. (2005). Big-Five personality differences of cheaters and non-cheaters. *Current Psychology, 24*, 274–286.

Parker, M. L., & Campbell, K. (2017). Infidelity and attachment: The moderating role of race/ethnicity. *Contemporary Family Therapy, 39*(3), 172–183.

Paulhus, D. L., & Williams, K. M. (2002). The Dark Triad of personality: Narcissism, Machiavellianism, and psychopathy. *Journal of Research in Personality, 36*, 556–563.

Penke, L., & Asendorpf, J. B. (2008). Beyond global sociosexual orientations: A more differentiated look at sociosexuality and its effects on courtship and romantic relationships. *Journal of Personality and Social Psychology, 95*, 1113–1135.

Previti, D., & Amato, P. R. (2004). Is infidelity a cause or a consequence of poor marital quality? *Journal of Social and Personal Relationships, 21*, 217–230.

Raskin, R., & Terry, H. (1988). A principal-components analysis of the Narcissistic Personality Inventory and further evidence of its construct validity. *Journal of Personality and Social Psychology, 54*, 890–902.

Rodrigues, D., Lopes, D., & Smith, C. V. (2017). Caught in a "bad romance"? Reconsidering the negative association between sociosexuality and relationship functioning. *Journal of Sex Research, 54*, 1118–1127.

Russell, V. M., Baker, L. R., & McNulty, J. K. (2013). Attachment insecurity and infidelity in marriage: Do studies of dating relationships really inform us about marriage? *Journal of Family Psychology, 27*, 242–251.

Savard, C., Sabourin, S., & Lussier, Y. (2011). Correlates of psychopathic personality traits in community couples. *Personality and Mental Health, 5*, 186–199.

Schmitt, D. P. (2004a). Patterns and universals of mate poaching across 53 nations: The effects of sex, culture, and personality on romantically attracting another person's partner. *Journal of Personality and Social Psychology, 86*, 560–584.

Schmitt, D. P. (2004b). The Big Five related to risky sexual behaviour across 10 world regions: Differential personality associations of sexual promiscuity and relationship infidelity. *European Journal of Personality, 18*, 301–319.

Schmitt, D. P., & Buss, D. M. (2001). Human mate poaching: Tactics and temptations for infiltrating existing mateships. *Journal of Personality and Social Psychology, 80*, 894–917.

Schmitt, D. P., & Shackelford, T. K. (2008). Big Five traits related to short-term mating: From personality to promiscuity across 46 nations. *Evolutionary Psychology, 6*, 246–282.

Scinta, A. & Gable, S. L. (2007). Automatic and self-reported attitudes in romantic relationships. *Personality and Social Psychology Bulletin, 33*, 1008–1022.

Seal, D., Agostinelli, G., & Hannett, C. (1994). Extradyadic romantic involvement: Moderating effects of sociosexuality and gender. *Sex Roles, 31*, 1–22.

Shackelford, T. K., Besser, A., & Goetz, A. T. (2008). Personality, marital satisfaction, and probability of marital infidelity. *Individual Differences Research, 6*, 13–25.

Simpson, J. A., & Gangestad, S. W. (1991). Individual differences in sociosexuality: Evidence for convergent and discriminant validity. *Journal of Personality and Social Psychology, 60*, 870–883.

Simpson, J. A., Rholes, W. S., & Phillips, D. (1996). Conflict in close relationships: An attachment perspective. *Journal of Personality and Social Psychology, 71*, 899–914.

Smith, C. V., Hadden, B. W., Webster, G. D., Jonason, P. K., Gesselman, A. N., & Crysel, L. C. (2014). Mutually attracted or repulsed? Actor–partner interdependence models of Dark Triad traits and relationship outcomes. *Personality and Individual Differences, 67*, 35–41.

Smith, C. V., Nezlek, J. B., Webster, G. D., & Paddock, E. L. (2007). Relationships between daily sexual interactions and domain-specific and general models of personality traits. *Journal of Social and Personal Relationships, 24*, 497–515.

Vecchio, R. P., & Sussman, M. (1991). Choice of influence tactics: Individual and organizational determinants. *Journal of Organizational Behavior, 12*, 73–80.

Watson, D., & Clark, L. A. (1984). Negative affectivity: The disposition to experience aversive emotional states. *Psychological Bulletin, 96*, 465–490.

Webster, G. D., Gesselman, A. N., Crysel, L. C., Brunell, A. B., Jonason, P. K., Hadden, B. W., & Smith, C. V. (2016). An actor-partner interdependence model of the Dark Triad and aggression in couples: Relationship duration moderates the link between psychopathy and argumentativeness. *Personality and Individual Differences, 101*, 196–207.

Weiser, D. A., Niehuis, S., Flora, J., Punyanunt-Carter, N. M., Arias, V. S., & Baird, R. H. (2018). Swiping right: Sociosexuality, intentions to engage in infidelity, and infidelity experiences on Tinder. *Personality and Individual Differences, 133*, 29–33.

Weiss, B., Lavner, J. A., & Miller, J. D. (2018). Self-and partner-reported psychopathic traits' relations with couples' communication, marital satisfaction trajectories, and divorce in a longitudinal sample. *Personality Disorders: Theory, Research, and Treatment, 9*, 239–249.

Whisman, M. A., Gordon, K. C., & Chatav, Y. (2007). Predicting sexual infidelity in a population-based sample of married individuals. *Journal of Family Psychology, 21*, 320–324.

Zayas, V., Shoda, Y., & Ayduk, O. N. (2002). Personality in context: An interpersonal systems perspective. *Journal of Personality, 70*, 851–900.

CHAPTER 2

Predicting Infidelity in the Context of Race and Ethnicity

Kelly Campbell, Tiffany L. Brown, *and* Brandyn-Dior McKinley

Abstract

This chapter describes the intrapersonal, relational, and environmental predictors of infidelity across the major racial/ethnic groups in the United States including African, Asian, European, Latin, and Native Americans. It also reviews cross-cultural research on the topic of race/ethnicity and infidelity. It begins by defining key terms and identifying the predictors of infidelity that apply across racial/ethnic groups. In addition, historical, societal, and cultural factors that influence individuals' intimate relationship beliefs and practices are highlighted throughout to help contextualize the underlying motivations for infidelity. Several theoretical frameworks including social exchange and interdependence, symbolic interaction, intersectionality, and bioecological are used to advance the discussion. It concludes by identifying the limitations of extant work and providing directions for researchers and practitioners.

Key Words: infidelity, power, ethnic minority, culture, race, ethnicity, cross-cultural, interpersonal relationship theories

The purpose of this chapter is to highlight predictors of extradyadic involvements (EDIs) as they relate to race and ethnicity. We begin by defining relevant terms, particularly because concepts such as race and ethnicity are often used interchangeably, and we want to highlight their distinctiveness. Throughout the chapter, we hope to underscore that race and ethnicity rarely serve as direct predictors of outcomes such as infidelity; instead, factors that correlate with race and ethnicity such as socioeconomic status (SES), acculturation, religiosity, and historical antecedents explain findings. This chapter reviews these contextual factors in describing the intrapersonal, relational, and environmental predictors of infidelity for the major racial/ethnic groups in the United States. We first identify predictors that apply across ethnic groups, noting that those studies used predominantly European American samples, and then shift to spotlight the racial/ethnic groups that have been underrepresented in the literature. The available cross-cultural research is also presented. We review theories that can be used to understand infidelity in the context of race/ethnicity and include examples from our empirical review to demonstrate those connections. We conclude with an identification of empirical gaps and provide suggestions for scholars and practitioners who plan to continue this line of work. It is worth noting at the outset that research examining EDI in the context of race/ethnicity is limited in scope and focuses nearly exclusively on heterosexual samples. As highlighted in the future directions section, more work is needed to examine both EDI in the context of race/ethnicity as well as among those with nonheterosexual orientations.

Race

Historically in the United States, attempts were made to biologically classify people into different racial groups so that privileges such as citizenship status and land ownership could be restricted to "White" groups (Bosworth & Flavin, 2007). Although it is now illegal to deny privileges based on race, it is still common to racially classify individuals. The biological classification of people is difficult however, given that humans belong to the same species and are biologically mixed. Phenotypic traits such as skin tone, facial features, and hair type are therefore commonly used as a means of racial identification (Marger, 2015). The federal US Census, which is relied on to provide an official taxonomy, falls short of identifying meaningful racial groupings. The "White" category, to provide just one example, includes "individuals who identify with one or more nationalities or ethnic groups originating in Europe, the Middle East, or North Africa. Examples of these groups include, but are not limited to, German, Irish, English, Italian, Lebanese, Egyptian, Polish, French, Iranian, Slavic, Cajun, and Chaldean" (U.S. Census, 2020). This definition confounds race with ethnicity and also groups together people with distinct phenotypic traits. Given the difficulties of biologically classifying people, this chapter uses ancestral region as a way to organize the material.

Ethnicity

The definition of ethnicity is more useful and less problematic than that of race. While racial conceptualizations rely on biology, ethnicity focuses on socialized features tied to region of origin (Marger, 2015). Ethnic attributes include among other things, language, traditions, rituals, manner of dress, and cuisine. Religion is often but not always associated with ethnicity. For instance, a majority of Latin Americans are Catholic but people from this ethnic group can espouse any spiritual or religious orientation (or none). Another example is Judaism, which is a religion but arguably also an ethnicity because Jewish people engage or practice their own language (Hebrew), traditions, rituals, etc. Ethnicity is relevant to infidelity because it shapes how a group perceives EDI, which then influences the likelihood of its occurrence and outcomes associated with it (e.g., is infidelity forgivable or a deal-breaker?). In most countries, including the United States, EDI is widely considered unacceptable, and women are judged more harshly than men for it (Frayzer, 1985).

Power

People with power have more wealth, status, knowledge, and control over information than those with less power (Marger, 2015). The terms "dominant" and "minority" refer to whether a person's group has power at the macrostructural level. Dominant statuses in the United States, and many parts of the world, include European American/White, men, middle and upper class, heterosexual, Christian, and able-bodied or without a disability. When referring to race, a term used to denote power is "white privilege" (McIntosh, 2003). In the United States, racial/ethnic groups are socially stratified with European Americans at the top, Asian and Middle Eastern Americans in the middle, and African, Latin, and Native Americans in the lower tier. The placement of groups is based on their degree of power and likelihood of experiencing discrimination. Although groups in the middle have higher SES on average than European Americans, they are more likely than White people to experience racial discrimination. Groups in the third tier have significantly lower SES on average than those in upper tiers and like those in the middle, are at risk for experiencing racial discrimination (Marger, 2015).

The concept of power can be defined at the micro, relational level as well. A partner has power if they control a valued resource within the relationship such as money or sex; the greater their partner's desire for that resource, the greater the person's power (Lennon, Stewart, & Ledermann, 2013). The least dependent or least committed person in a relationship also has more power. Dependence and commitment are influenced by the extent to which a person can secure valued resources from alternative partners. The more high-quality alternatives a person has for obtaining resources, the greater their power and the less dependent they are on their partner. Also, the partner who cares least about the relationship continuing (i.e., the one with more options) has the power to exploit the other's resources.

Macro and micro systems of power are interdependent with the macro structure influencing power at the dyadic level (Coontz, 1997). People's identities typically contain a mix of dominant and minority statuses, which interact with their partner's identities. The mismatch of statuses between partners creates the potential for tension and conflict. In relationships, the person with the most power may assume the other shares similar freedoms, but in reality, only the powerful partner can act freely whereas the other operates under constraints. When a person with power does not acknowledge their power or pretends not to have it, the other partner cannot implement change; they require recognition of the imbalance by the power-holder to achieve desired outcomes. In nearly every culture, men have more power than women at the macro level, which provides men greater freedom to exploit women in relationships. Overall, women are more dependent than men in their relationships and are therefore at greater risk for having a partner who engages in EDI. In interracial or interethnic partnerships, the partner with the greatest power at the macro level (e.g., European American) will similarly have more power at the dyadic level with respect to race/ethnicity, leading to potential conflict and/or exploitation within the relationship.

Infidelity

Given that relationship expectations vary widely across people and cultures, the concept of infidelity is best defined by the involved partners (Parker, Berger, & Campbell, 2010; Parker & Campbell, 2017). Scholars and lay people agree that sexual intercourse should be included in definitions, but disagreement exists regarding other behaviors such as masturbation, porn-viewing, and/or sharing an emotional connection with a relationship rival (Allen et al., 2005). Due to the difficulties in operationalizing this construct, some researchers use umbrella terms such as "infidelity" or "affair" rather than asking participants about specific behaviors. This approach is advantageous because people vary in how they define EDI and can apply their own definitions, but disadvantageous in terms of comparing across studies. A defining feature of infidelity is that it involves a violation of implicit and explicit relationship norms (Blow & Hartnett, 2005). In open relationships where EDI is permitted, partners may perceive infidelity only when activities breach the couple's agreed on terms (e.g., prior permission, disclosure; Campbell, 2014; Mint, 2004). The array of behaviors constituting infidelity is one reason why incidence rates vary widely by study.

Commonalities Across Racial/Ethnic Groups

We shift now to the EDI predictors that apply across racial/ethnic groups. It is important to note that a majority of this research has been conducted with European Americans, making it difficult to generalize to other groups; however, a few studies have included diverse samples and afford cross-cultural comparisons (Toplu-Demirtas & Fincham, 2018). In nearly every culture, infidelity acceptance rates are low. Widmer and colleagues (1998) examined infidelity attitudes across nearly 35,000 people in 24 nations and found strong disapproval. One identified exception to their findings are the Danes, who are more tolerant of EDI compared to other cultural groups, likely due to their more liberal orientation toward relationships and life (Solstad & Music, 1999). In terms of actual rates, it is more difficult to draw conclusions across cultures because empirical studies comparing countries are limited. Where available, these statistics are presented in the cross-cultural section. For the United States, data from the General Social Survey indicate that among those who have ever been married, 22% of African Americans, 16% of European Americans, and 13% of Latin Americans have engaged in EDI (Wang, 2018). The section on African Americans provides contextual information to help interpret their higher rates, but it is worth noting here that some studies do not support this finding (Atkins & Kessel, 2008; Choi et al., 1994; Kuroki, 2013). Nationally representative data for the rates of Asian and Native Americans are not currently available, but some research suggests that EDI among Native Americans may be the highest of all groups. In this section, we summarize research on the EDI predictors across racial/ethnic groups, recognizing that the findings predominantly apply to European Americans. We begin by highlighting the historical and societal factors that influence individuals' intimate relationship beliefs and practices.

Around the world, countries have been exposed to White Anglo-Saxon Protestant (WASP) norms through colonization (Marger, 2015). Beginning in the 15th century, Northwestern European settlers traveled to foreign territories and imposed their values and ways of life on the native people they encountered. European norms differed from indigenous cultures in the emphasis on Christianity, patriarchy, individualism, and capitalism (Kincheloe, 1999). These norms have shaped societies across the world. Even in heterogenous societies such as the United States, which contain people from different world regions, dominant WASP norms have informed what is considered "normal" and "acceptable" (Kincheloe, 1999; Marger, 2015). For relationships, these norms have historically included monogamy, heterosexuality, sex solely within the context of marriage, and women's subservience (Burdette, Ellison, Sherkat, & Gore, 2007). Although norms have relaxed over time, WASP values continue to influence relationships (Buunk & Bakker, 1995). The prevailing expectation of monogamy, which appears difficult to uphold considering EDI rates, causes individuals to feel devastated when infidelity occurs (Campbell et al., 2012; Coontz, 2005).

A variety of intrapersonal factors predict EDI across racial/ethnic groups. In nearly every culture studied, men are more likely than women to engage in EDI (Mark et al., 2011); however, a major reason for this gender difference may relate to power differentials between the sexes. When comparisons are made between men and women with similarly high levels of power and status, infidelity rates are comparable (Lammers et al., 2011). In terms of personality, those who are high on neuroticism, and low on both conscientiousness and agreeableness are more likely than others to commit infidelity (Altgelt et al., 2018; Schmitt, 2004; Fernandez & Castro, 2003). People who come from families characterized by abuse, divorce, and/or remarriage are also at risk (Fish et al., 2012; Weiser et al., 2017; Whisman & Snyder, 2007), as are those with insecure attachment orientations and high levels of psychological distress (Hall & Fincham, 2009; Parker & Campbell, 2017; Schmitt & Jonason, 2015). Individuals who engage in premarital sex, cohabit prior to marriage, and participate in first intercourse at a young age are inclined toward EDI (Amato & Rogers, 1997; Whisman & Snyder, 2007). Infidelity is more common among those who desire sexual variety and believe sex without commitment is acceptable (i.e., have an unrestricted sociosexual orientation; Schmitt & Jonason, 2015; Simpson & Gangestad, 1991). In terms of protective factors, people who consistently pray for their spouse and view marriage as sacred, as well as those who espouse a conservative political orientation have lower rates of EDI compared to those without such religious attributes and with more liberal orientations (Atkins et al., 2001; Choi et al., 1994; Cochran et al., 2004; Reich & Kalantar, 2018).

Numerous interpersonal correlates of EDI have also been identified across groups. Individuals in distressed relationships including those with low satisfaction, low sexual satisfaction, high conflict, and/or low partner support are at risk (Atwood & Seifer, 1997; Mark et al., 2011). At times, partners report engaging in EDI because they believe their partner has already done so (Buunk, 1980; Mark et al., 2011). Partner dissimilarity in values, personality, education, and income is associated with EDI (Forste & Tanfer, 1996; Schmitt, 2004; Shackelford et al., 2008). Partners who are high in autonomy, lack interdependence, and perceive more attractive alternatives to their current relationship are at risk (Nowak et al., 2014; Treas & Geisen, 2000). In terms of equity, those who feel overbenefited (i.e., receiving more outcomes than they deserve) as well as underbenefited (i.e., receiving fewer outcomes than they deserve) report more EDI than those in equitable relationships. Equity is linked to power, in that people who are less dependent on their partner for rewards (satisfying outcomes) have more power in a relationship and are more inclined toward EDI (Prins, Buunk, & VanYperen, 1993). In a systematic review of EDI predictors, Mark and colleagues (2011) concluded that incompatible interpersonal characteristics are more predictive of EDI than intrapersonal factors alone. Meanwhile, others point out that relationship factors such as satisfaction are inconsistently measured across studies, making comparisons difficult (Blow & Hartnett, 2005).

Certain environmental factors predispose partners toward infidelity. Some researchers find that increasing one's social status or making career advances predicts EDI (Atwood & Seifer, 1997; Glass & Wright, 1992). These life changes are typically associated with higher income and increased opportunities for travel, which lead to time away from a partner and more access to rivals. People who work in jobs that require touching, personal discussions, and one-on-one time with others are at risk (Treas & Giesen, 2000). Exposure to alternative partners is a major risk factor. Employed people have greater access to alternative partners compared with those who stay at home, and, in the past, men had significantly more access to alternatives than women; but today, with a majority of women in the workforce, infidelity rates among women have been rising (Glass, 2003; South et al., 2001). In terms of geographic region, people who live in urban areas, as opposed to less populated regions, are also more likely to engage in EDI (Mark et al., 2011; Treas & Giesen, 2000). The reason is twofold: Infidelity is more common in metropolitan areas and therefore less stigmatized, and cities have larger numbers of people, which provides greater anonymity and an abundance of alternative partners with whom to commit infidelity. Finally, individuals in communities with an imbalanced sex ratio (i.e., an overabundance of one sex) are more likely to experience infidelity (South et al., 2001). Similar results have been found in gender-imbalanced workplaces, particularly for White men who are outnumbered by women (Munsch & Yorks, 2018).

African Americans

Perspectives and practices of infidelity within the African American community are complex and shaped by a number of sociocultural influences. Factors including the experiences of racism, discrimination, and economic stress have been identified as contributing to relationship instability and EDI (Penn et al., 1997). The legacies of slavery have also been influential in the development of relationship patterns. For example, during US slavery, marriage and committed partnerships were forbidden and slave families were often separated by the selling of African American males to serve as "breeders" on other plantations (Penn et al., 1997). At the same time, African American female slaves were treated as sex objects and often raped by their White slave masters. Long-lasting relationships, commitment to spouses, and the raising of children within a parental unit were not available for enslaved Africans. These practices are believed to have affected generations of African Americans in their views of monogamy, marriage, and commitment (Penn et al., 1997).

Historically, the scholarship on infidelity has portrayed African Americans as more likely to engage in EDI and infidelity is cited as a major reason for marital instability and dissolution (Utley, 2011). Several studies have found that Black men have the highest incidence of infidelity when compared to other race and gender groups (Adamopoulou, 2013; Amato & Rogers, 1997), with some estimating that African American men are twice as likely as White men to have relationships outside their primary partnership (Pinderhughes, 2002). These statistical trends have been attributed to a number of factors, with the most common being the gender ratio imbalance. Largely due to higher mortality and incarceration rates, as well as disproportionate rates of substance abuse and poor healthcare related to racism (Penn et al., 1997), there are more available female partners than there are men within the Black community (Utley, 2011). Consequently, there are fewer African American men with whom to partner, allowing them to have more leverage in heterosexual relationships. Also, because African American men are more likely than African American women to partner outside of their race, their potential pool of partners further expands, while the dating pool shrinks for African American women (Raley et al., 2015). According to Guttentag and Secord (1983) the gender ratio imbalance leads to lower levels of commitment and more short-lived relationships, thereby increasing the likelihood of infidelity (Penn et al., 1997).

As a "cultural adaptation" to the gender ratio imbalance, some African American women engage in a practice termed "man sharing" (Cook, 2007; Gibbs & Campbell, 1999), which involves having a relationship with a man who is already partnered. Cook (2007) proposes that man-sharing allows for single African American women to be in a partnership and become mothers, even if they are unable to marry. Man-sharing aligns with the notion of "something is better than nothing" and can be viewed as an adaptive practice at the macro level because it allows for more women to partner and have children, resulting in stable growth of the African American population (Cook, 2007). However, these arrangements are not usually the preferred type of relationship for Black women and they are often left wanting more stability, consistency, and intimacy (Utley, 2011). Taken together, these factors result in some Black women accepting or overlooking infidelity as a way to maintain their relationship under conditions of scarce resources (i.e., lack of available men). Unfortunately, this normalization can compromise the self-esteem of Black women and negatively impact their mental and physical well-being (Eyre et al., 2012; Utley, 2011).

Among African Americans, it is well documented that spirituality is a key cultural strength (Boyd-Franklin, 1989). Choi et al. (1994) found that higher levels of religious participation served to reduce the likelihood of EDI among African and Latin Americans, but not European Americans. Possibly, findings reported by some researchers regarding the positive effects of religiosity on EDI may be attributable to ethnic minority, rather than White participants in the samples (Atkins et al., 2001; Cochran et al., 2004; Reich & Kalantar, 2018). When ethnic differences are not tested, it is difficult to know.

There is also a body of research regarding infidelity in response to the disproportionate rates of HIV/STIs among Black young adults relative to other racial/ethnic groups. Eyre et al. (2012) examined models of infidelity in an effort to develop HIV/STI prevention and intervention models that were consistent with the cultural constructs of intimate relationships within the African American community. Using focus group data from a sample of 143 African American young adults, the researchers found that 37% of women and 57% of men had sexual relations outside of their committed relationships over the prior month. A main reason for EDI was to engage in more exciting or adventurous sexual activities than were available through the primary relationship. Although both men and women reported these sentiments, a double standard existed regarding the acceptability of EDI with more leniency toward men. Other research conducted by Carey et al. (2010) has supported these assertions through interviews with African American men. The men described the normalization of having more than one sex partner at a time. EDI provided a means for fulfilling sexual needs and offering sexual variety. They also believed it was in men's biological nature to have multiple sex partners (Carey et al., 2010). Some indicated that it would not be acceptable for their female partner to engage in infidelity, although not all the men supported a double standard, with some reporting that infidelity was wrong for both sexes. The men identified various methods for shielding their primary partner from concurrent sexual relationships, which included using condoms and being discrete about outside partners (Carey et al., 2010).

In a mixed-method study of urban African and Puerto Rican American emerging adults, researchers found similarities across gender and ethnicity regarding sexual beliefs, attitudes, and behaviors, and pointed to the important role of environmental factors in shaping beliefs and attitudes about infidelity (Macauda et al., 2011). One of the most salient themes emerging from these data included an acceptance and in some cases expectation of infidelity in romantic partnerships, which corroborated Carey et al.'s (2010) qualitative work described above. Definitions of infidelity were nuanced and depended on the role of the relationship in a person's life. Individuals in urban communities of color are often struggling to survive emotionally and physically due to the lack of resources and choices in their neighborhoods. Therefore, having intimate relationships with multiple partners and at varying emotional levels, provides a network that helps support daily living (Macauda et al., 2011). Participants use infidelity as a way to protect from emotional pain, as in cases where the primary relationship is characterized by challenges, alternate partners can be used as a safety net for emotional need fulfillment (Macauda et al., 2011).

Asian Americans

Asian Americans represent one of the fastest-growing and ethnically diverse populations in the United States. The term "Asian American" is used to refer to "all individuals who identify with one or more nationalities or ethnic groups originating in the Far East, Southeast Asia, or the Indian subcontinent," including Cambodian, Chinese, Indian, Japanese, Korean, Pakistani, Filipino, Thai, and Vietnamese (U.S. Census, 2020). Each of these groups espouses their own language, religious beliefs, immigration histories, and customs (Kim & Hong, 2004). Significant differences also exist in educational achievement, income, poverty rates, English proficiency, and naturalization rates (Budiman et al., 2019). Even so, the economic success and social positioning of Asian Americans (i.e., based on median household income, education, rates of intermarriage, and family stability) relative to other racial/ethnic groups in the United States has contributed to their designation as "model minorities" (Wu, 2014). As Wu explains, the "model minority" stereotype defines Asian Americans as a "racial group distinct from the white majority, but lauded as well assimilated, upwardly mobile, politically nonthreatening, and *definitively not-black*" (p. 2).

There is a paucity of literature on Asian Americans and EDI. The few studies that examine EDI within this population focus on how Asian cultural values influence Asian Americans' perceptions and responses to marital infidelity. Little is known about the predictors of EDI within this community. However, scholarship on Asian American sexuality provides some insight into what factors may increase (or decrease) individual susceptibility to EDI. Scholars have identified cultural values that are salient across Asian ethnic groups including collectivism (Yuan & Weiser, 2019). In contrast to the European American norm of individualism, many Asian cultures emphasize family unity and cohesiveness, prioritizing the interests of the family over those of the individual (Cochran et al., 1991; Yoshioka et al., 2001). Thus, individuals are expected to avoid behaviors that may dishonor the family (Yuan & Weiser, 2019).

Yuan and Weiser (2019) conducted a study with 158 European Americans and 167 Asian Americans, examining how differences in cultural values and beliefs—namely individualism versus collectivism—contributed to relationship decision-making after a spouse's infidelity. The results showed that Asian Americans were less likely to consider relationship satisfaction in making decisions about divorce. Divorce attitudes were a significant predictor of how Asian Americans, and not European Americans, responded to marital infidelity. Because Asian cultural values stress group harmony, divorce is stigmatized, as it not only disrupts the family unit but also brings shame to the family. In this context, Asian Americans were more likely to protect their reputation as a couple and the reputation of their extended family by remaining in the marital relationship. The one exception was that Asian Americans were more likely to divorce if their partner engaged in *both* emotional and sexual infidelity.

In addition to the emphasis on family cohesion, Asian cultural values endorse conformity to norms and respect for authority. As a result of these cultural forces, Asian families tend to be hierarchical and patriarchal. According to Penn et al. (1997), traditional Asian cultural values dictate that the husband is the head of household, breadwinner, and sole decision maker. He is also responsible for enforcing the roles and rules within the family (Penn et al., 1997). The authors posit that the patriarchal gender norms common in many Asian cultures are likely to influence perceptions of infidelity among Asian Americans. Indeed, Yuan and Weiser (2019) found that Asian American men were more likely than women to divorce a partner upon learning of their infidelity. Asian cultural values consider expressions of sexuality outside of marriage to be highly inappropriate (Okazaki, 2002). At the same time, the endorsement of traditional gender roles influences the meanings ascribed to extramarital sex. Whereas a husband's infidelity might be blamed on his wife or the other woman, a wife's infidelity is often considered more shameful (Penn et al., 1997). For example, Yoshioka et al. (2001) found that in a sample of Chinese, Korean, Vietnamese, and Cambodian adults living in the United States, over one-quarter of participants agreed that violence was justified in the case of a wife's sexual infidelity. This reflects the high status afforded Asian American men both inside and outside the family.

Another line of research has explored the effects of acculturation on Asian American sexuality. Many Asian cultures view procreative sex as the most appropriate expression of sexuality. Accordingly, Asian American adolescents and young adults tend to espouse more sexually conservative attitudes and show more conservative rates of sexual behaviors (fewer sexual experiences, fewer sexual partners, and later ages of sexual debut) when compared to other racial/ethnic groups in the United States (Meston & Ahrold, 2010, p. 181). However, more recent data indicate that acculturative effects on sexual attitudes and behaviors may vary based on gender.

A survey of 1,415 college students asked about their attitudes toward homosexuality, gender role traditionality, casual sex, and extramarital sex (Ahrold & Meston, 2010). Attitudes toward extramarital sex were used to determine how different ethnic and cultural groups view the structure and function of marriage as well as the acceptability of sexuality outside of marriage. As predicted, Asian American students reported more conservative sexual attitudes than did Latin or European American students. The researchers found that identification with mainstream culture (i.e., WASP values) was associated with more liberal sexual attitudes but predicted more conservative attitudes toward extramarital sex among Asian and Latin American men. The authors posit that the cultures of origin for

Asian and Latin men may be more liberal regarding extramarital sex. Therefore, increased exposure to WASP values that stress monogamy may lead to greater sexual conservatism.

In another study of college students, acculturated Asian American women (those who adopted mainstream culture) were more likely to engage in casual sex (Meston & Ahrold, 2010). Asian American men reported lower rates of sexual experience and fewer sexual partners than Asian American women, Latin or European Americans. This finding is consistent with previous research, which found that Asian American women have more sexual experience (i.e., kissing and petting, oral sex, and intercourse) than their male counterparts (Cochran et al., 1991). A partial explanation for this difference is the influence of sexual stereotypes that portray Asian women as passive and exotic sexual objects and Asian men as asexual, emasculated nerds and outsiders (Mukkamala & Suyemoto, 2018; Wong et al., 2012). Possibly, the eroticization of Asian women exposes them to more sexual opportunities relative to men.

Research on HIV prevalence within Asian/Pacific Islander (API) communities reveals interethnic differences in Asian women's experiences with EDI. In a study of low-income, first-generation Cambodian, Vietnamese, and Laotian women, participants identified their husband's sexual risk behaviors, including partners' extramarital encounters with sex workers, as increasing their own risk of infection (Jemmott et al., 1999). Several Cambodian participants expressed "fear that their partners would infect them with HIV upon returning home from trips to Cambodia" stating that "such trips are a common occurrence among men in their community" (p. 106). In contrast, participants in the Vietnamese/Laotian group believed that their partners were too afraid to pursue sex with other women, and thus were faithful. However, both groups expressed that men's visits to Cambodia, Vietnam, and Thailand provided opportunity for men to engage in unprotected sex, and thereby increase their partner's exposure to HIV.

Latin Americans

Although the Latin American population is composed of individuals with cultural roots in a number of countries, most EDI research has been conducted with Mexican Americans, who make up a majority of the Latin American population residing in the United States. Furthermore, several of the empirical studies on Latin Americans consider how EDI is experienced and interpreted in relation to gendered Latin(x) cultural scripts that privilege men and oppress women. It has been documented that within Latin(x) culture, men are perceived as the provider, protector, and head of household (Penn et al., 1997). Conversely, Latinas are expected to be the homemakers and nurturers for the family (Penn et al., 1997). As Toro-Morn (2008) notes, there continue to be stereotypes within popular culture and the scholarship of Latina women as "submissive" and accepting of their partner's infidelities (Lopez, 2017). An enduring gender script for Latinas is "marianismo," which "encourages women to be sexually naive, subservient to their male partners, and willing to put the needs of their male partners and families above their own" (Lopez, 2015, p. 216). Meanwhile the dominant gender script for Latino men is "machismo," which Gonzalez-Lopez (2010) characterizes as strong, dominant, and sexually virile. Even in cases where younger generations may reject strict adherence to gendered scripts, there is still reported pressure from parents and elders to comply (Lopez, 2015).

A qualitative study conducted with 305 Latin(x) adolescents, indicated that girls had high levels of concern around not being able to trust their partners, their partners' cheating behaviors, and in some cases partner violence (Williams et al., 2014). Another qualitative study conducted with Mexican American and White adolescents, indicated that in comparison to the other ethnic groups, Mexican American adolescents felt more negatively about cheating than White adolescents (Williams & Hickle, 2011). Mexican American girls voiced the strongest concerns about partner infidelity compared to other adolescents in the study. Williams and Hickle (2011) concluded that the heavy emphasis on commitment and fidelity displayed by Mexican American girls might be reflective of cultural values that prioritize marriage and parenthood.

The literature also addresses connections between infidelity and dating violence within the Mexican American community (Williams et al., 2014). Some of these experiences are steeped in the same cultural values discussed above, wherein men experience more sexual freedom, while women are expected to be sexually chaste and faithful. Williams and colleagues (2014) describe a qualitative study wherein Latina girls described their partners as using violence to keep them from "misbehaving" or to control their potential cheating behaviors. High levels of emotional distress have also been reported among Mexican American women who are suspected of infidelity and fear retaliatory violence from partners (Roberts & Flaskerud, 2008). Some scholars argue that violence may be a response to the value placed on commitment within the Mexican American culture, and perhaps individuals perceive they have more to lose in cases of infidelity (Williams et al., 2014).

Some researchers have investigated levels of adherence to cultural gender role beliefs by examining the role of acculturation. Williams et al. (2014) found that Mexican male adolescents with a strong Mexican identity conceptualized infidelity broadly, called on friends to monitor the cheating behaviors of female partners, and perceived female cheating behaviors as problematic. On the other hand, Mexican American male adolescents who identified with both Mexican and American cultures reported that their cheating resulted from peer pressure and the desirable status gained from having multiple partners (Williams et al., 2014). Other researchers have similarly documented that ethnic minority boys perceive the "player" label to be desirable and associated with a high status among peers (Lopez, 2017). Even Latina adolescents acknowledge that the boys in their neighborhoods are pressured into having sexual relations with multiple girls (Lopez, 2017). It is important to note that despite a recognition of these dynamics, Latina girls felt "resentful," "used," and "objectified" (Lopez, 2017). Nevertheless, the girls accepted the notion that most boys are "players," except for those who are religious or are not as attractive, and also stated that for girls, being in a relationship is associated with a higher social status (Lopez, 2017). Lopez (2017) explained that being in a relationship allows Mexican American Latina girls to be viewed as a "good girl" and live within the parameters of cultural expectations associated with "marianismo." It was also evident from the narratives of Latina adolescents that learning of a partner's infidelity is stressful and hurtful, and results in high levels of partner monitoring (e.g., monitoring social media accounts and text messages) in order to prevent future emotional distress (Lopez, 2017). Furthermore, a hypervigilance was employed on the part of girls to identify red flags that might indicate a partner has cheated or is going to cheat (Lopez, 2017).

Native Americans

There is very little scholarship on Native Americans and infidelity. However, some insight can be gained from Dalla et al.'s (2010) research with Navajo women. The Navajos are a matrilineal society, which has traditionally held women in high social regard and provided them with their own economic resources through owning livestock. However, the economic well-being of women was significantly compromised due to US policies initiated in the 1930s. The Navajo reservation has experienced high levels of poverty, substance abuse, and low levels of educational achievement, which have had implications for intimate relationships and family life (Dalla et al., 2010). The prevalence of infidelity on the Navajo reservation could be tied to the economic context of the reservation where jobs are scarce and many men have to find work away from home, resulting in partner separation for long periods of time (Dalla et al., 2010). Also, within the context of the Navajo reservation, men were given a great deal of liberty with infidelity, even though these behaviors were found to have negative implications for the psychological well-being of women (Dalla et al., 2010). Specifically, women were likely to tolerate cheating in an effort to keep their families together, as many of the women had grown up without their father present (Dalla et al., 2010).

According to DHHS (1991), Navajo teenagers had childbearing rates that were triple that of the larger US population. In Dalla et al.'s (2010) investigation of Navajo teenage mothers' intimate relationships during the transition to parenthood, infidelity was commonly reported. Most of the women in the sample indicated multiple cases of infidelity within the same relationship as well as across relationships with different partners. Although not as prevalent as male infidelity, some women admitted to having extramarital relationships, mainly in response to their partners' EDI. A direct comparison of infidelity rates across samples of adolescent mothers is not possible, but these scholars contended that the rates of infidelity were high for this group of women with 71% indicating that their male partner had been unfaithful during their relationship.

Other historical accounts of Native tribes from the 18th century, such as the Creeks, Chickasaws, Choctaws, and Cherokees, paint a different picture of gender sexuality and fidelity. For example, documentation of Native tribes in the southern United States depicted unmarried women as having full autonomy of their sexual lives, including choice and number of sexual partners, all while supporting the idea that sex was a natural step in the maturation from being an adolescent to becoming a woman (Donohoe, 2012). Once married, fidelity was expected of women, however, given the status and power of women in these communities, the enforcement of these expectations by men was limited (Donohoe, 2012). In other reports, it was not uncommon for Cherokee and Chocktaw women to change husbands frequently. As pointed out by Donohoe (2012), "sex was viewed as a service for the benefit of women and clan rather than men" (p. 116). Examining the gender dynamics within Native American culture is central to understanding their perspectives on infidelity and sexuality. Within Native American culture, scholars argue that it is more constructive to consider marriage and infidelity as they relate to the community rather than the individual partners. Historically within Native American communities, marriage was loosely structured and did not have the same significance as it did for European Americans. Marriage was more about establishing connections between families and once that was done, what happened within or outside the marriage was less important.

It is essential to recognize the diverse sexual customs and perspectives on infidelity across and within Native American tribes in the southeastern United States during earlier centuries (Donohoe, 2012). For example, even within the same clan, depending on the status, there could have been different expectations regarding sexuality and adultery. Both men and women were subject to punishments due to adultery based on the circumstances of the affair and the ranking of the individual within the clan as was reported within the Choctaws (Romans, 1775), whereas others—like the Cherokees—had no formal laws about adultery (Donohoe, 2012). There were also customs that included spouses asking for permission to seek additional lovers, leading to social acceptance and public approval of extramarital affairs. Several aspects of marital life were ambiguous and lacked consistent expectations such that some women lived with husbands, while others did not, some women traveled with spouses, others stayed home, and some were in polygamous marriages. It was at the end of the 18th century when the influence of Euro-Christian beliefs began to shift the perspectives of gender, sexuality, and the role of women within the family to that of subservience and sexual chastity.

Cross-Cultural Research

Limited cross-cultural research examines the social conditions through which race and ethnicity predict EDI. A majority of existing work is grounded in evolutionary psychology and examines universal patterns such as men feeling more jealous about sexual infidelity and women feeling more jealous about emotional infidelity (Buss, 2018). In this section, we focus less on biological universals, and instead highlight cultural distinctions related to EDI. The studies are grouped by continents, starting with Africa.

A major concern regarding EDI in Africa relates to the transmission of HIV. Most commonly, it is men, rather than women, who are having unprotected sex with extramarital partners and put their spouse at risk for HIV. Stephenson (2010) used Demographic and Health Survey data from the African countries of Chad, Ghana, Malawi, Nigeria, Tanzania, Uganda, Zambia, and Zimbabwe to examine the influence of gender equity on EDI among married men. For a majority of countries, gender equity within the community was associated with lower rates of EDI as well as lower rates of unprotected extramarital sex. Men who resided in communities with conservative values, including those that endorsed violence against women had higher rates of both EDI and unprotected extramarital sex.

HIV transmission in the context of EDI has been investigated among the Igbo tribe in Nigeria. Smith (2010) describes a common pattern whereby married men engage in EDI with younger, unmarried women. The older married man is termed a "sugar daddy" and the arrangement helps ease economic concerns for the young women. Once married, women become highly valued for their familial roles and are perceived in less sexual terms. The institution of marriage and the process of building a family are considered paramount, and yet men engage in extramarital relations and put their wives at risk for contracting HIV. Oyediran and colleagues (2010) similarly describe HIV risks associated with unprotected extramarital sex in Nigeria. Using nationally representative data from married and cohabiting men, they reported that 16% engaged in extradyadic sex over the previous year and with an average of 1.82 partners. The researchers noted that the power imbalance between men and women puts wives at risk and recommended reform to encourage married couples to use condoms. Ogwokhademhe and Ishola (2013) identified the most common reasons for extramarital affairs in Lagos, Nigeria, which included: sexual dissatisfaction, socioeconomic stressors, occupational stressors, age-related factors (e.g., spousal mismatch in age), and infertility issues.

Parker and colleagues (2014) examined infidelity in South Africa, where HIV rates are among the highest in the world at 20%–25% of the population, and ethnic minorities are disproportionately affected. The researchers interviewed 10 couples, who reported that EDI is considered unacceptable and yet is a common occurrence. One reason for its prevalence is that a significant portion of the non-White population are migrant laborers, traveling through the country for work and engaging in EDI while away from home for long periods. Their partners who are similarly lonely while men are away, are also at risk for engaging in EDI. This migrant labor system, which keeps families apart for most of the year was popularized under the racial segregationist system of Apartheid. Although Apartheid ended in the mid-1990s, the migrant labor system remains intact and adversely impacts communities of color. Partners are reluctant to discuss safe-sex practices because it implies lack of trust and is associated with relational tension and conflict. Therefore, they leave the topic unaddressed, are unlikely to use contraception because they are in a committed relationship, and are at risk for transmitting HIV to each other (Parker et al., 2014).

We found two studies examining EDI in Africa that were specific to women. Kwena and colleagues (2014) examined predictors for fishermen's wives in Kenya. Infidelity rates for these women over the previous six months was 6.2%. The most common reasons for engaging in EDI included domestic violence in the marital relationship and sexual dissatisfaction with the spouse. In terms of protective factors, women over the age of 24 and those who were sexually satisfied in their relationships exhibited lower rates of EDI. One of the rarer perspectives on EDI comes from the Himba tribe in Namibia. Women in this tribe are more likely than men to commit infidelity, and EDI is largely considered acceptable. Emotional and sexual infidelity rarely elicit jealousy (Scelza et al., 2020), and approximately 20% of babies result from extramarital relations (Scelza, 2011). For this ethnic group, extramarital childbearing is more common in arranged marriages than in those based on love or in which partners selected their own spouse.

Similar to the research conducted in Africa, HIV is a major concern for women who experience EDI in Asia. As in many African countries and other parts of the world, the power imbalance between men and women leads men to engage in EDI at much higher rates than women. Thapa, Yang, and Chan (2020) examined extramarital sex in Cambodia and noted that the practice is culturally acceptable for men and that their involvements put wives at significant risk of HIV contraction. The researchers interviewed high-school students about their relationship expectations and found even among youth, Cambodian girls expected their future husbands to engage in EDI and attributed the prospective infidelity to their own behaviors or perceived shortcomings, which included their participation in the workforce. Knodel and colleagues (1997) reported a similar pattern in their Thai sample. Participants described men as having a stronger sex drive than women and less control over their sexual desires. For women, infidelity was perceived as completely unacceptable whereas for men, attitudes were more lenient, provided their family responsibilities were not neglected.

Two studies examined how Asian men's separation from their families for work reasons led to a practice of taking second wives or long-term secondary partners in other regions. Lang and Smart (2002) reported on this practice among Hong Kong men who establish extramarital relationships in mainland China, and Shen (2005) described the practice among Taiwanese businessmen. These relationships parallel the "sugar daddy" arrangement described among the Nigerian Igbo in that the affairs are often with younger, unmarried women who are benefiting economically from the relationship. Shen further stated that the Chinese mistresses are perceived in particularly negative terms, whereas less stigma is associated with the men who are perpetrating the affairs.

Liu-Farrer (2010) examined the EDI motivations of Chinese immigrants in Japan. Of note, she included women who perpetrate EDI in her sample, which is a group that has been largely omitted in prior work. The qualitative study found economic, sexual, and emotional motivations for the EDI perpetrated by Chinese men and women. The men participants were married to Chinese women, whereas the women were married to Japanese citizens. The motivations for infidelity included common predictors such as unsatisfying marital relationships, but the reasons unique to this population were loneliness resulting from the migration process that required separation from a spouse, coping with feelings of alienation or missing one's culture of origin, feeling disconnected from a spouse because of the utilitarian and/or economic basis of marriage, cultural distancing between spouses due to their interethnic relationship, and rebelling against traditional gender roles and norms.

Madathil and Sandhu (2008) examined infidelity in the context of Asian Indian marriages. They noted that in India, marriage is considered a fundamentally important institution, which unifies not only the partners but their families as well. Given that the decision about whom to marry is not made solely by the partners, EDI may occur when spouses are unhappy in their relationship and seeking love and fulfillment. The caste system prescribes that women marry into a higher socioeconomic status, resulting in a power imbalance not only from cultural norms of patriarchy but also because men have greater resources. Infidelity is considered more culturally acceptable for men; women who engage in EDI risk losing their family, home, and support network.

Jahan and colleagues (2017) examined reasons for EDI among married individuals in Bangladesh where approximately 90% of the population is Muslim. Rather than collecting data from participants, they reviewed newspaper articles, books, Internet materials, and journal articles published between 1980 and 2016. The main reasons they identified for EDI were: sexual dissatisfaction, marital factors (e.g., early marriage, arranged marriage, marrying for the "wrong" reasons), the transition to parenthood, financial stressors, need for excitement, spousal dissimilarity, self-esteem issues (e.g., feeling unloved), and the availability of alternatives particularly through online/social media platforms.

Shifting to Europe and the Middle East, Apostolou and Panayiotou (2019) examined reasons Greek participants identified for *not* engaging in EDI. Using qualitative methodology, they identified 47 reasons, which were categorized according to the costs of EDI versus the relational benefits that protect against EDI. Men exhibited a greater predisposition to EDI, as did those who were high on the personality trait of openness. Conscientiousness served to protect against EDI, as did relationship satisfaction and feelings of guilt among women. Reich and Kalantar (2018) also investigated factors that prevent EDI but in Tehran, Iran. They found that among married participants, praying for one's spouse and viewing marriage as sacred (i.e., perceiving the manifestation of God within the relationship) correlated with lower EDI.

Toplu-Demirtas and Fincham (2018) investigated EDI among dating participants in Turkey, which is a democratic, Muslim country. In this culture, family honor and female purity are paramount and when threatened, women risk execution (Cetin, 2015). In their study, dating infidelity rates were approximately 15% for both men and women, which is relatively low and likely due to prohibitions on premarital sex, which would discourage EDI in a dating context. Despite their comparable EDI rates, the genders differed in attitudes toward infidelity, with men indicating a greater willingness to engage in it. The pro-infidelity attitudes for both genders were considerably lower than in Western samples, however.

Male honor culture, which refers to a man's reputation regarding masculinity and ability to protect his family and home, is prevalent in many parts of the world including the Mediterranean, Middle East, Latin America, and southern United States. In a series of lab studies, Vandello and Cohen (2003) investigated the influence of male honor with Brazilian and US participants. Compared to those in the United States, they found that Brazilian people perceived men as less masculine, of poor character, and responsible for a wife who engages in EDI. Compared to participants in the northern United States, those from honor cultures (i.e., Brazil, southern United States) were less critical of men who used violence in response to a wife's EDI, believing that it partly restored his honor. Those from the northern United States were more judgmental about the violence, believing that men who used it loved their wives less and were less trustworthy than those who did not. Participants from honor cultures also assessed women more favorably when they stayed with their husbands after discovering EDI compared to those from the northern United States, who regarded women more favorably when they left their husbands.

Rivera-Aragon and colleagues (2011) examined EDI and jealousy among Mexican couples. Although their study largely addressed responses to rather than predictors of infidelity, they reported the well-established gender difference of men desiring EDI more than women due to their greater interest in sexual variety. Pulerwitz et al. (2001) examined EDI in Mexico City and found that approximately half of participants who engaged in extramarital sex did not use protection, which put their primary partners at risk for STIs. This latter finding coincides with concerns reported by women around the world who experience health risks due to men's EDI.

Theories

Various theories can be used to further our understanding of EDI in the context of race/ethnicity. Here, we describe four, which we identified as among the most relevant. We begin with social exchange and interdependence, which are among the most widely used theories for studying couple relationships. Next, we consider the influence of socialization and social interactions on thoughts and behaviors with a discussion of the symbolic interaction framework. Intersectionality theory is more specific to the study of race/ethnicity and therefore provides an avenue for new lines of inquiry in the study of EDI with racially and ethnically diverse populations. As the most commonly implemented framework in EDI research, we end with the bioecological model as it offers an integrative framework in which to consider the influence of multiple environments on an individual's development (Bronfenbrenner, 1979, 2005).

Social Exchange and Interdependence

Social exchange theory assumes that humans seek to maximize rewards and minimize costs in their intimate relationships (Nye, 1979). Satisfying relationships are ones in which the rewards exceed the costs and exceed personal expectations for desired outcomes.

Individuals who have been involved in few rewarding relationships, and who are unaware of others in such relationships, will have low expectations for their partner and be easily satisfied, whereas those whose relationship outcomes fall below expectations (or who have high expectations that go unfulfilled), will feel unsatisfied and be at risk for infidelity and/or dissolution. Partners who fulfill each other's needs and are responsible for the rewarding outcomes experienced by the other are considered interdependent (Thibaut & Kelley, 1959). When few attractive alternatives are available, one will be more dependent on and committed to their relationship. People in costly relationships and with abundant alternatives are less dependent on the relationship, and prone to infidelity or dissolution.

Rusbult and colleagues (1998) developed the investment model of commitment, which is based on social exchange principles. According to the model, commitment is high for people who are satisfied, perceive of few good relationship alternatives, and have high relationship investments. The investment model has been used across thousands of participants in different countries to predict commitment and explain how commitment influences the likelihood of relationship outcomes such as infidelity (Le & Agnew, 2003). However, it is worth noting that at least for studies conducted in the United States, there is a possibility that the investment model is a better predictor of relationship commitment for European Americans than ethnic minority participants (Yuan & Weiser, 2019).

Social exchange and the investment model can be used to contextualize the research reviewed in this chapter. Across groups, low interdependence predisposes individuals to EDI (Treas & Geisen, 2000). Other major predictors of infidelity across racial/ethnic groups included unfulfilling, dissatisfying relationships (Atwood & Seifer, 1997; Prins et al., 1993), and the abundance of relationship alternatives (Nowak et al., 2014). In the case of African American men who are reported to have among the highest rates of EDI, several instances exist wherein levels of investment are low due to contextual factors such as racism, legacies of slavery, and poverty, while the presence of alternative partners is high (Adamopoulou, 2013; Amato & Rogers, 1997; Penn et al., 1997). With the gender ratio imbalance in the African American community, Black men may invest less in their relationships knowing they have access to a high number of alternatives, which can compromise levels of commitment in a primary relationship and elevate the likelihood of EDI (Secord, 1983; Penn et al., 1997). Factors that may protect against infidelity for this population include high satisfaction with the primary relationship as well as adherence to religious practices such as praying for a spouse and viewing marriage as sacred (Atkins et al., 2001; Choi et al., 1994; Cochran et al., 2004; Mark et al., 2011; Reich & Kalantar, 2018).

A common pattern evidenced in the cross-cultural research involved an exchange of financial resources for sex, which predisposed men toward EDI. Smith (2010) described a "sugar daddy" arrangement in Nigeria wherein married men partnered with younger, less economically stable women for extramarital affairs. In Asia, scholars described a similar pattern of married men who traveled for work and partnered with women who benefited economically (Lang & Smart, 2002; Shen, 2005). Although the exchange of money for sex is common, other types of exchanges were evident in the research reviewed. Several scholars noted that EDI was common among spouses involved in arranged or utilitarian-based marriages. When spouses do not attain emotional fulfilment from their spouse, EDI is used as a way to cope with loneliness, augment satisfaction, and in some cases, birth a child (Jahan et al., 2017; Liu-Farrer, 2010; Scelza et al., 2020).

Symbolic Interaction

Symbolic interaction theory is centrally focused on shared meanings created through social interactions (LaRossa & Reitzes, 1993). It is through socialization that individuals learn how the world and relationships work (Berger & Kellner, 1984; Berger & Luckman, 1966; LaRossa & Reitzes, 1993). People's actions are guided and constrained by social norms. As noted in other sections, the norms guiding behaviors in the United States and many parts of the world are guided by WASP values of monogamy, patriarchy, individualism, and capitalism (Buunk & Bakker, 1995). These norms were not common to Indigenous populations prior to European conquest. As Donohoe (2012) noted, among some Native American tribes, multiple sexual partners, spouse swapping, and polygamy were not necessarily considered taboo. The monogamy expectation has caused most of the world's societies to view infidelity as immoral, unacceptable, and deviant (Campbell, 2014; Widmer et al., 1998). Despite its widespread disapproval, EDI is arguably a common occurrence over the duration of a partnership. Campbell and Wright (2010) comment on how changes can be implemented at the individual, relational, and macro levels to reconcile the incongruence that exists between EDI beliefs and practices:

> At the intrapersonal level, individuals could question whether they are inclined toward monogamy and make a decision to marry only if they expect to remain faithful. Given that socially acceptable alternatives to marriage exist, individuals who are not suited for monogamy have other options. Individuals who choose to marry should communicate their needs to their spouse and work hard at their relationship to maintain satisfaction and protect against infidelity. At the interpersonal level, spouses should commit to working as hard as possible at their marriage to ensure that the needs of both partners are being met. When partners are unable to work things out, they have the option of divorce, which can be enacted prior to engaging in extramarital relations. At the cultural level, Americans could expand their definition of marriage to include non-monogamous relationships. They could also be more tolerant and forgiving of infidelity when it does occur. If cultural values were more relaxed about infidelity, perhaps individuals would experience fewer adverse effects from its occurrence. (pp. 336–337)

The monogamy expectation can be considered in conjunction with patriarchy, which is also characteristic of most societies, and causes EDI to be perceived as more acceptable for men than women. This theme was exemplified across several groups in this chapter including Asian and Latin Americans (Lopez, 2017; Penn et al., 1997; Toro-Morn, 2008) and nearly every group reviewed in the cross-cultural section, especially those espousing male honor culture. In these groups, some condone violence against women as a way to ensure women's faithfulness (Black & Weisz, 2005; Lopez et al., 2012; Roberts & Flaskerud, 2008; Williams et al., 2014). Patriarchy provides men with greater power and freedom than women and is one reason why men engage in infidelity at higher rates than women across the world. The gendered power imbalance and cultural scripts that prioritize men and contribute to high rates of EDI put women at risk for HIV and other sexually transmitted infections both in the United States and abroad (Choi et al., 1994; Eyre et al., 2012; Oyediran et al., 2010; Parke et al., 2014; Pulerwitz et al., 2001; Smith, 2010; Stephenson, 2010; Thapa et al., 2020). Our review found few cultures in which EDI was more common among women; the notable exceptions were some Native American tribes and the Himba tribe in Namibia (Donohoe, 2012; Scelza et al., 2020). The value of individualism similarly relates to infidelity because it causes people to prioritize personal fulfillment over relational, family, or collective goals. A person may therefore feel entitled to fulfill their needs through EDI, particularly when relationship satisfaction is low, even if it damages the primary relationship (Attridge & Berscheid, 1994). This premise is supported by research in this chapter demonstrating that sexual and relationship satisfaction is a leading cause for infidelity across cultures.

Historically, the norms of patriarchy and capitalism have encouraged infidelity by prioritizing men's paid work over the domestic sphere with the latter traditionally being assigned to women (Coontz, 2005). It is only when women can financially support themselves that they have the power to leave an unhappy relationship. Similarly, women who are not financially independent are at great risk if they engage in EDI because relationship dissolution threatens their livelihood. These dilemmas were exemplified in several cultures including Asian Indian marriages, wherein women who participate in EDI risk losing their family, home, and friends (Madathil & Sandhu, 2008), and Thapa and colleagues' (2020) interviews with Cambodian girls who indicated that husbands' EDI would be justified if wives were to work outside the home. Capitalism has caused individuals to prioritize work even if their employment impedes healthy family functioning. We noted a number of instances wherein employment perpetuated EDI because of exposure to alternatives (Treas & Giesen, 2000) or separation from a primary partner for extended work-related travel (Dalla et al., 2010; Lang & Smart, 2002; Parker et al., 2014; Shen, 2005). These extended work-travel arrangements tend to disproportionately affect people of color (Dalla et al., 2010; Parker et al., & 2014).

Intersectionality

The intersectionality framework describes how social identities (e.g., gender, race, socioeconomic status, sexual orientation, education, religion) intersect to create a unique social location for each person (Crenshaw, 1991). Historically, intersectionality emerged out of the lived experience of Black women who sought to articulate how race, gender, class, and sexuality shaped women's experiences of oppression. In the process, Crenshaw (1993) delineated three mechanisms by which multiple social statuses (i.e., intersecting identities) operate simultaneously to create differences in experiences and outcomes among Black women (Cole, 2009). From this view, women of color may (a) experience racism and sexism in ways that are similar to men of color or White women, (b) experience the combined effects of racist and sexist practices, or (c) experience a specific form of oppression unique to their particular social location (intersectional experience) (Mukkamala & Suyemoto, 2018). The latter represents a "locational" analytic approach in that researchers investigate the experiences of those individuals and groups whose social location is defined by multiple disadvantaged statuses (i.e., Black women).

As a conceptual framework, intersectionality also provides opportunities to examine the intersectional effects of holding both disadvantaged and privileged statuses. However, social identities are not simply individual attributes; they are sociopolitical categories that "position individuals and groups in asymmetrical relation to one another" (Cole, 2009, p. 173). This "relational" approach to intersectional analyses reveals how multiple social identities are codified in institutional practices that create unique patterns of social inequality and stigma (Ferree, 2010). In other words, the combination of dominant and/or minority identities situate individuals within the larger social context and result in varying degrees of oppression and privilege. These identities relate to infidelity because those with dominant identities have more power at the macro and micro levels and interact in complex ways with their partner's social location. Consider that in most of the cultures reviewed, men have more power than women and their rates of EDI are also significantly higher.

Although scholars often have distinguished between "locational" and "relational" intersectionality approaches, both are useful in understanding EDI in the context of race/ethnicity. The "locational" approach can be used to explain sexual practices among Asian Americans. Previous research has found that Asian American men have fewer sexual experiences and partners than Asian American women (Cochran et al., 1991; Meston & Ahrold, 2010). One potential reason for this finding is that Asian men have been stereotyped as weak and unmasculine whereas Asian women have been cast as exotic and submissive (Mukkamala & Suyemoto, 2018; Wong et al., 2012). In this case, there is a unique intersectional experience of race and gender (gendered racism) that is specific to Asian Americans wherein the differential stereotypes of Asian American men and women provide each group with differential sexual opportunities. Younger generations of Asian Americans are increasingly likely to espouse permissive views about casual sex, yet the environments in which they live and socialize (i.e., conservative immigrant communities or majority-white environments that stigmatize Asian male sexuality) may limit access to casual sexual encounters, thereby reducing the likelihood of EDI.

A "relational" intersectionality approach reminds us that race is fundamentally a relational concept. In other words, racial groups are defined in relation to each other wherein some groups have more power, resources, and advantages than others. We can see the effects of social inequality in the strategies (i.e., cultural practices) that different racial/ethnic groups deploy to manage their intimate and family lives. A cross-cultural example can be found in South Africa, where the vestiges of Apartheid are evident in the migration labor system, which remains racially stratified. Because non-White South Africans are more likely to be migrant laborers spending long periods away from home, rates of EDI are significantly higher among this population, with devastating health consequences (i.e., HIV prevalence) for communities of color (Parker et al., 2014).

Bioecological

As Haseli and colleagues (2019) point out, EDI is a complex phenomenon that is influenced by interactions between individual characteristics and social contexts. The application of the bioecological model highlights the ways that person characteristics (values, beliefs, previous experiences, temperament, motivation), context (culture, social class, immediate environment) and historical time mutually influence the processes that shape an individual's development (Rosa & Tudge, 2013). For example, examining individual characteristics provides us with a lens from which to account for the intersections of race and gender and how these factors impact processes related to EDI across multiple systems of the ecological model. Moreover, ecological perspectives provide a framework from which to better understand the protective factors and risk factors associated with EDI. Factors related to EDI can be found within the multiple systems of the ecological model (e.g., microsystem, mesosystem, exosystem, macrosystem, and chronosystem) as well as in the interactions between these systems. Not only do these frameworks account for the factors that might contribute to infidelity but also ecological models can support with assessing the consequences of EDI for individuals and family units, as well as inform the ways in which EDI is dealt with in clinical settings.

One of the most compelling aspects of these frameworks is the recognition that "cultural values, beliefs, and practices are not static, but change over time" (Tudge et al., 2017, p. 51) in response to broader shifts in demands in the immediate environment. In this way, the changes that accompany a particular historical moment might support or discourage risk factors related to infidelity. This can be seen when examining how the legacies of slavery, Jim Crow segregation, and mass incarceration have impacted the partnering behaviors of contemporary African American couples. The concept of time within the ecological model also helps us to recognize the importance of when EDI occurs in the developmental timeline for an individual and/or a couple. For example, experiences of infidelity might have different consequences for a person based on whether it happens early in their romantic career versus later. Similarly, the timing of EDI whether it is early or later in the relationship may also have varying consequences. Furthermore, the concept of adaptation within the ecological model allows us to investigate the ways that EDI may function as an adaptation to particular environmental demands. This is most clearly illustrated within the African American community as women negotiate intimate relationships with African American men under conditions of a skewed gender ratio. As pointed out previously, some African American women may ignore or even condone EDI not because it is a desired outcome but because it is a way to have partnership under conditions of partner scarcity.

Some microsystems (e.g., neighborhood) and exosystems (e.g., place of employment) provide more or fewer opportunities for EDI and as discussed throughout this chapter, this can differ across ethnic groups. This can be seen in the EDI risks associated with employment that requires physical contact (i.e., touching) (Treas & Giesen, 2000) and/or when workplaces have a gender ratio imbalance (Munsch & Yorks, 2018). Another example can be found when looking at research by Macauda et al. (2011) that highlights how living in underresourced neighborhoods of color might support higher risks of EDI. More specifically, their work found that ethnic minority women and men in these neighborhood contexts reported having multiple partners as a means to meet their needs, as one person might not have adequate resources to fully provide all that is required to sustain a monogamous relationship (Macauda et al., 2011).

Lastly, bioecological frameworks are especially useful for unpacking the role of gender in EDI. The research has consistently documented that men are more likely to engage in infidelity than women. Many of the factors that explain these gender differences come from culturally grounded gender scripts, demonstrating an interaction between person characteristics and macrolevel cultural factors. This interaction can be seen across all of the ethnic groups reviewed for the chapter, and provided explanations for how individuals perceive, experience, and cope with EDI. For example, among Mexican Americans, the gendered notions of "marianismo" and "machismo" make EDI more acceptable for men and also allow for men to use their power and privilege to prevent women from engaging in EDI.

Implications, Limitations, and Future Directions

A number of recommendations for clinical practice derive from the work reviewed. In a meta-analysis, Mark and colleagues (2011) identified partner incompatibility as a critical EDI risk factor. Correspondingly, researchers have identified partner similarity as a predictor of long-term satisfaction and stability (Watson et al., 2014). Based on this information, Haseli and colleagues (2019) suggest examining partners' compatibility including sociodemographic similarity in both premarital and marital counseling as a way to prevent and treat infidelity. With respect to sociodemographic and cultural factors, therapists need to understand their clients' values and beliefs regarding EDI in order to provide optimal treatment. Latin and Native American wives, for example, may expect their husbands to engage in infidelity at some point in the marriage, and the value placed on family motivates partners to stay together through this occurrence (Dalla et al., 2010; Parker & Campbell, 2017; Parra-Cardona & Busby, 2006; Williams & Hickle, 2011). By contrast,

European Americans are less inclined to expect infidelity and more likely to perceive EDI as cause for relationship dissolution (McLellan-Lemal et al., 2013).

In their review article, Blow and Hartnett (2005) noted that a majority of infidelity research has focused on European American, middle-class samples and that more research is needed across cultural groups, including international work. Twelve years later, Parker and Campbell (2017) reinforced this view, stating that most EDI research "has included predominantly European American samples, which serves to perpetuate a Western bias. This bias involves using Euro-based norms, such as monogamy, individualism, hierarchical decision-making, and patriarchy as the standard" (p. 174). We wish to underscore that research with diverse participants is still needed. Very few studies examine EDI in the context of race/ethnicity, and only two of the international studies reviewed included representative samples (Oyediran et al., 2010; Stephenson, 2010). Given that Western values are spreading to cultures across the world, it is imperative that research be conducted soon, before WASP norms dilute rich cultural traditions. There is a need for more cross-cultural research with adolescent and emerging adult populations as well, to examine conceptualizations of and reactions to infidelity, as it has been documented that relationship patterns established early in one's developmental trajectory have an influence on later romantic relationship experiences (Savin-Williams, 2018).

In addition to expanding research to include more cultural groups, research is needed to examine EDI in nonheterosexual relationships and across different relationship types, such as polyamorous and open relationships. We did not come across any publications that addressed race/ethnicity and EDI within nonheterosexual and/or alternative relationship types. From the available research, it appears that infidelity views and practices are misaligned in that most people disapprove of infidelity, yet a significant number of people engage in it (Campbell & Wright, 2010). The Western norm of monogamy therefore does not work well, and it would be worth identifying different models that could help individuals and relationships thrive.

With respect to our suggestions for the individual groups reviewed, several researchers note that African American men have higher rates of infidelity relative to other racial/gender groups, yet limited information exists on what distinguishes African American men who engage in infidelity from those who do not. Some of this can be attributed to the sex-ratio imbalance, sociocultural contexts that support multiple partners, and cultural adaptations to the relationship landscape present in the Black community. Certainly, more research is needed to elucidate the unique consequences of infidelity for Black families, in particular Black women, as they may be in relationship arrangements (e.g., man sharing) that do not offer enough security and stability for their families. Researchers have also identified cases where African American women feel the need to overlook cheating behaviors in order to maintain their relationship. Utley (2011) addresses this in her work, however, additional research is needed to examine the psychological and physical ramifications of these relationships. Although the literature has focused on the STI/HIV risks associated with infidelity in the Black community, examining the role of infidelity stress and how it relates to other health outcomes is warranted. This is true not only for the person who experiences EDI but also for those who commit infidelity. Carey and colleagues (2010) note that several of the African American men in their study reported feeling guilt and shame for having sexual partners outside of the primary relationship. These kinds of emotions can have a negative impact on a person's well-being and should be explored empirically. Examining the association between African American cultural values (e.g., religiosity, collectivism, racial/ethnic pride, etc.) and EDI also requires additional attention.

More research is needed on the EDI experiences of Asian Americans. Some research has found that employment in middle- and high-income occupations leads to infidelity as people spend more time away from their partners and have greater access to alternative partners (South et al., 2001; Treas & Giesen, 2000). Data show that Asian Americans as a whole have higher incomes and are better educated than other groups. Do these variables operate as risk or protective factors in relation to EDI? Asian Americans also continue to be treated as a homogeneous group. However, patterns of immigration influence the socioeconomic status of different Asian ethnic groups. Although recent Asian immigrants are nearly twice as likely as those who came three decades ago to have a college degree and work in high-paying fields (Pew Research Center, 2013, para. 31), vast economic disparities exist between Asian immigrants who came to the United States on visas designated for high-skilled workers and those who arrived through refugee resettlement programs. These differences have possible implications for the acculturation process (i.e., levels of social integration or access to mainstream culture), and by extension, the ways Asian ethnic groups may perceive or respond to EDI. Finally, more research is needed regarding the effects of gender-specific ethnic stereotypes of Asian Americans and their access to alternative partners, as well as the ways gendered and racial power may function within the interracial relationships of Asian American women and White men.

For Latin Americans, future research should continue to examine the relationship between acculturation and appraisals of cheating behaviors. As scholars suggest, more acculturated Latin Americans are less likely to adhere to traditional roles, which could shift their perceptions of infidelity (Lopez, 2015; Williams et al., 2014). Penn et al. (1997) propose that the more acculturated a Latin(x) couple is, the more likely they are to perceive infidelity as disruptive to the marital relationship. This connection is supported by Lopez's (2015) research with Mexican American girls in which 2 of the 24 participants reported that they remained in relationships after experiencing infidelity due to their strong affiliation with traditional Mexican beliefs. These participants were born in Mexico and stated that it was acceptable for men to cheat because of the higher status afforded to them in Mexican culture (Lopez, 2015). Results from the work of Williams et al. (2014) mirror these findings and support the importance of considering acculturation in Latin(x) relationships. Similar to research on infidelity within the African American community, more research should be conducted on the overall well-being of Latina women who subscribe to traditional beliefs that condone behaviors of infidelity among men and can leave women feeling disempowered (Williams et al., 2014).

Only a handful of EDI studies have focused on Native Americans, making this a glaring research gap. Scholars have highlighted great ethnic diversity within the Native American group, with Donohoe (2012) noting that even among members of the same tribe, dissimilarity regarding relationship norms and practices exists. It is important that EDI researchers explore this diversity. Prior to conquest, Native American societies were governed by values that largely opposed European American norms (Takaki, 2008). The limited available research presented in this chapter demonstrated that nonmonogamy, matrilineal societies, and collectivism were attributes of Native American culture. Given that so few matrilineal societies have been identified, it would be worth comparing their norms to patriarchal cultures in order to elucidate the impact of biological sex, gender, and power on EDI to provide one potentially fruitful avenue for exploration with this group.

In conclusion, the research on EDI in the context of race and ethnicity is no longer in its infancy, and yet much work remains to be done. The bulk of research has consisted of predominantly European American samples and additional work is needed to examine racial/ethnic minority groups in the United States as well as cultural groups abroad. Researchers and practitioners must be cognizant of the extent to which minority and dominant norms are guiding the values and behaviors of their participants and patients or clients. They must consistently challenge personal biases to ensure that Western prejudices are not influencing their work. Without regular reflection, non-White voices and experiences risk remaining on the periphery or being overlooked completely. Much can be gained from a better understanding of non-White perspectives and practices, particularly because based on the literature, the European American norm of monogamy appears both challenging and, in some cases, maladaptive.

References

Adamopoulou, E. (2013). New facts on infidelity. *Economics Letters*, *121*(3), 458–462. https://doi.org/10.1016/j.econlet.2013.09.025

Ahrold, T. K., & Meston, C. M. (2010). Ethnic differences in sexual attitudes of U.S. college students: Gender, acculturation, and religiosity factors. *Archives of Sexual Behavior*, *39*(1), 190–202. https://doi.org/10.1007/s10508-008-9406-1

Allen, E. S., Atkins, D. C., Baucom, D. H., Snyder, D. K., Gordon, K. C., & Glass, S. P. (2005). Intrapersonal, interpersonal, and contextual factors in engaging in and responding to extramarital involvement. *Clinical Psychology: Science and Practice*, *12*, 101–130. https://doi.org/10.1093/clipsy/bpi014

Altgelt, E. E., Reyes, M. A., French, J. E., Meltzer, A. L., & McNulty, J. K. (2018). Who is sexually faithful? Own and partner personality traits as predictors of infidelity. *Journal of Social and Personal Relationships*, *35*(4), 600–614. https://doi.org/libproxy.lib.csusb.edu/10.1177/0265407517743085

Amato, P. R., & Rogers, S. J. (1997). A longitudinal study of marital problems and subsequent divorce. *Journal of Marriage and the Family*, *59*, 612–624. https://doi.org/10.2307/353949

Apostolou, M., & Panayiotou, R. (2019). The reasons that prevent people from cheating on their partners: An evolutionary account of the propensity not to cheat. *Personality & Individual Differences*, *146*, 34–40. https://doi.org.libproxy.lib.csusb.edu/10.1016/j.paid.2019.03.041

Atkins, D. C., Baucom, D. H., & Jacobson, N. S. (2001). Understanding infidelity: Correlates in a national random sample. *Journal of Family Psychology, 15,* 735–749. https://doi.org.10.1037//0893-3200.15.4.735

Atkins, D. C., & Kessel, D. E. (2008). Religiousness and infidelity: Attendance, but not faith and prayer, predict marital fidelity. *Journal of Marriage & Family, 70*(2), 407–418. https://doi.org.libproxy.lib.csusb.edu/10.1111/j.1741-3737.2008.00490.x

Attridge, M., & Berscheid, E. (1994). Entitlement in romantic relationships in the United States: A social-exchange perspective. In M. J. Lerner & G. Mikula (Eds.), *Entitlement and the affectional bond: Justice in close relationships* (pp. 117–147). Plenum.

Atwood, J. D., & Seifer, M. (1997). Extramarital affairs and constructed meanings: A social constructionist therapeutic approach. *American Journal of Family Therapy, 25,* 55–75. https://doi.org/10.1080/01926189708251055

Berger, P., & Kellner, H. (1984). Marriage and the construction of reality. In G. Handel (Ed.), *The psychosocial interior of the family* (3rd ed., pp. 1–23). Aldine.

Berger & Luckman (1966). *The social construction of reality.* Doubleday.

Black, B. M., & Weisz, A. N. (2005). Dating violence: A qualitative analysis of Mexican American youths' views. *Journal of Ethnic & Cultural Diversity in Social Work: Innovation in Theory, Research & Practice, 13*(3), 69–90. https://doi.org/10.1300/J051v13n03_04

Blow, A., & Hartnett, K. (2005). Infidelity in committed relationships II: A substantive review. *Journal of Marital and Family Therapy, 31*(2), 217–233. https://doi.org/0.1111/j.1752–0606.2005.tb01556.x

Bosworth, M., & Flavin, J. (2007). *Race, gender, and punishment: From colonialism to the War on Terror.* Rutgers University Press.

Boyd-Franklin. (1989). Five key factors in the treatment of Black families. *Journal of Psychotherapy & the Family, 6*(1-2), 53–69. https://doi.org/10.1300/J287v06n01_04

Bronfenbrenner, U. (1979). *The ecology of human development, experiments by nature and design.* Harvard University Press.

Bronfenbrenner, U. (Ed.). (2005). *Making human beings human, bioecological perspectives on human development.* Sage Publications.

Budiman, A., Cilluffo, A., & Ruiz, N. G. (2019, May 22). *Key facts about Asian origin groups in the U.S.* https://www.pewresearch.org/fact-tank/2019/05/22/key-facts-about-asian-origin-groups-in-the-u-s/

Burdette, A. M., Ellison, C. G., Sherkat, D. E., & Gore, K. A. (2007). Are there religious variations in marital infidelity? *Journal of Family Issues, 28*(12), 1553–1581. https://doi.org.libproxy.lib.csusb.edu/10.1177/0192513X07304269

Buss, D. M. (2018). Sexual and emotional infidelity: Evolved gender differences in jealousy prove robust and replicable. *Perspectives on Psychological Science, 13*(2), 155–160. https://doi.org.libproxy.lib.csusb.edu/10.1177/1745691617698225

Buunk, B. P. (1980). Extramarital sex in the Netherlands. *Alternative Lifestyles, 3,* 11–39. https://doi.org/10.1007/BF01083027

Buunk, B. P., & Bakker, A. B. (1995). Extradyadic sex: The role of descriptive and injunctive norms. *Journal of Sex Research, 32*(4), 313–318. https://doi.org.libproxy.lib.csusb.edu/10.1080/00224499509551804

Campbell, K. (2014). Swinging: Socially deviant or genetically advantageous? In Copes, H., & Forsyth, C. J. (Eds.), *Encyclopedia of social deviance* (pp. 717-719). SAGE. https://dx.doi.org/10.4135/9781483340470.n287

Campbell, K., & Wright, D. W. (2010). Marriage today: Exploring the incongruence between Americans' beliefs and practices. *Journal of Comparative Family Studies, 41*(3), 329–345. https://www.jstor.org/stable/41604361

Campbell, K., Wright, D. W., & Flores, C. (2012). Newlywed women's marital expectations: Lifelong monogamy? *Journal of Divorce and Remarriage, 53*(2), 108–125. https://doi.org/10.1080/10502556.2012.651966

Carey, M. P., Senn, T. E., Seward, D. X., & Vanable, P. A. (2010). Urban African-American men speak out on sexual partner concurrency: Findings from a qualitative study. *AIDS and Behavior, 14*(1), 38–47. https://doi.org/10.1007/s10461-008-9406-0

Cetin, I. (2015). Defining recent femicide in modern Turkey: Revolt killing. *Journal of International Women's Studies, 16,* 346–360. https://doi.org/10.1007/s10461-008-9406-0

Choi, K. H., Catania, J. A., & Dolcini, M. M. (1994). Extramarital sex and HIV risk behavior among US adults: Results from the National AIDS Behavioral Survey. *American Journal of Public Health, 84,* 2003–2007. https://doi.org/10.2105/ajph.84.12.2003

Cochran, J. K., Chamlin, M. B., Beeghley, L., & Fenwick, M. (2004). Religion, religiosity, and nonmarital sex conduct: An application of reference group therapy. *Sociological Inquiry*, *74*, 102–127.

Cochran, S. D., Mays, V. M., & Leung, L. (1991). Sexual practices of heterosexual Asian-American young adults: Implications for risk of HIV infection. *Archives of Sexual Behavior*, *20*, 381–391. https://doi.org/10.1007/BF01542618

Cole, E. R. (2009). Intersectionality and research in psychology. *American Psychologist*, *64*(3), 170–180. https://doi.org/10.1037/a0014564

Cook, C. T. (2007). Polygyny: Did the Africans get it right? *Journal of Black Studies*, *38*(2), 232–250. https://doi.org/10.1177/0021934705285695

Coontz, S. (1997). *The way we really are: Coming to terms with America's changing families*. Basic Books.

Coontz, S. (2005). The new fragility of marriage, for better or for worse. *Chronicle Review*, *51*, B7.

Crenshaw, K. (1991). Mapping the margins: Intersectionality, identity politics, and violence against women of color. *Stanford Law Review*, *43*(6), 1241–1299. https://doi.org/10.2307/1229039

Crenshaw, K. (1993). Demarginalizing the intersection of race and sex: A Black feminist critique of antidiscrimination doctrine, feminist theory and antiracist politics. In D. K. Weisbert (Ed.), *Feminist legal theory: Foundations* (pp. 383–395). Temple University Press.

Dalla, R. L., Marchetti, A. M., Sechrest, E. A., & Whie, J. L. (2010). "All the men here have the Peter Pan Syndrome—they don't want to grow up": Navajo adolescent mothers' intimate partner relationships— A 15-year perspective. *Violence Against Women*, *16*(7), 743–763. https://doi.org/10.1177/1077801210374866

Donohoe, F. (2012). To beget a tame breed of people: Sex, marriage, adultery, and Indigenous North American women. *Early American Studies: An Interdisciplinary Journal*, *10*(1), 101–131. https://www.jstor.org/stable/23546683

Eyre, S. L., Flythe, M., Hoffman, V., & Fraser, A. E. (2012). Concepts of infidelity among African American emerging adults. *Journal of Adolescent Research*, *27*(2), 231–255. https://doi.org/10.1177/0743558411417865

Fernandez, M., & Castro, R. Y. (2003). The Big Five and sexual attitudes in Spanish students. *Social Behavior and Personality*, *31*, 357–362. https://doi.org/10.2224/sbp.2003.31.4.357

Ferree, M. M. (2010). Filing the glass: Gender perspectives on families. *Journal of Marriage and Family*, *72*(3), 420–439.https://doi.org/10.1111/j.1741-3737.2010.00711.x

Fish, J., Pavkov, T., Wetchler, J., & Bercik, J. (2012). Characteristics of those who participate in infidelity: The role of adult attachment and differentiation in extradyadic experiences. *American Journal of Family Therapy*, *40*(3), 214–229. https://doi.org/libproxy.lib.csusb.edu/10.1080/01926187.2011.601192

Forste, R., & Tanfer, K. (1996). Sexual exclusivity among dating, cohabiting, and married women. *Journal of Marriage and the Family*, *58*, 33–47. https://www.jstor.org/stable/353375

Frayzer, S. G. (1985). *Varieties of sexual experience: An anthropological perspective on human sexuality*. HRAF Press.

Gibbs, T., & Campbell, J. (1999). Practicing polygyny in Black America: Challenging definition, legal and social considerations for the African American community. *Western Journal of Black Studies*, *23*(3), 144–153.

Glass, S. P. (2003). *Not "just friends": Protect your relationship from infidelity and heal the trauma of betrayal*. Free Press.

Glass, S. P., & Wright, T. L. (1992). Justifications for extramarital relationships: The association between attitudes, behaviors, and gender. *Journal of Sex Research*, *29*, 361–387. https://doi.org/10.1080/00224499209551654

Gonzalez-Lopez, G. (2010). Heterosexuality exposed: Some feminist sociological reflections on heterosexual sex and romance in U.S. Latina/o communities. In M. Asencio (Ed.), Latina/o sexualities: Probing powers, passions, practices, and policies (pp. 103–116). New Brunswick, NJ: Rutgers University Press.

Hall, J. H., & Fincham, F. D. (2009). Psychological distress: Precursor or consequence of dating infidelity? *Personality and Social Psychology Bulletin*, *35*(2), 143–159. https://doi.org/libproxy.lib.csusb.edu/10.1177/0146167208327189

Haseli, A., Shariati, M., Nazari, A. M., Keramat, A., & Emamian, M. H. (2019). Infidelity and its associated factors: A systematic review. *Journal of Sexual Medicine*, *16*(8), 1155–1169. https://doi.org/libproxy.lib.csusb.edu/10.1016/j.jsxm.2019.04.011

Jahan, Y., Chowdhury, A. S., Rahman, S. M. A., Chowdhury, S., Khair, Z., Ehsanul Huq, T. M., & Rahman, M. M. (2017). Factors involving extramarital affairs among married adults in Bangladesh. *International*

Journal of Community Medicine and Public Health, 4(5), 1379–1386. https://doi.org/10.18203/2394-6040.ijcmph20171506

Jemmott, L. S., Maula, E. C., & Bush, E. (1999). Hearing our voices: Assessing HIV prevention needs among Asian and Pacific Islander women. *Journal of Transcultural Nursing, 10*(2), 102–111. https://doi.org/10.1177/104365969901000203

Kim, B. S. K., & Hong, S. (2004). A psychometric revision of the Asian Values Scale using the Rasch model. *Measurement and Evaluation in Counseling and Development, 37*(1), 15–27. https://doi.org/10.1080/07481756.2004.11909747

Kincheloe, J. L. (1999). The struggle to define and reinvent whiteness: A pedagogical analysis. *College Literature, 26*(3), 162–194.

Knodel, J., Low, B., Saengtienchai, C., & Lucas, R. (1997). An evolutionary perspective on Thai sexual attitudes and behavior. *Journal of Sex Research, 34*, 292–303. https://doi.org/10.1080/00224499709551895

Kuroki, M. (2013). Opposite-sex coworkers and marital fidelity. *Economics Letters, 118*(1), 71–73. https://doi.org/0.1016/j.econlet.2012.09.023

Kwena, Z., Mwanzo, I., Shisanya, C., Camlin, C., Turan, J., Achiro, L., & Bukusi, E. (2014). Predictors of extra-marital partnerships among women married to fishermen along Lake Victoria in Kisumu County, Kenya. *PLoS ONE, 9*(4), 1–9. https://doi.org/libproxy.lib.csusb.edu/10.1371/journal.pone.0095298

Lammers, J., Stoker, J. I., Jordan, J., Pollmann, M., & Stapel, D. A. (2011). Power increases infidelity among men and women. *Psychological Science, 22*(9), 1191–1197. https://doi.org/10.1177/0956797611416252

Lang, G., & Smart, J. (2002). Migration and the "second wife" in South China: Toward cross-border polygyny. *International Migration Review, 36*(2), 546–569. https://www.jstor.org/stable/4149464

LaRossa, R., & Reitzes, D. C. (1993). Symbolic interactionism and family studies. In P. G. Boss, W. J. Doherty, R. LaRossa, W. R. Schumm, & S. K. Steinmetz (Eds.), *Sourcebook of family theories and methods: A contextual approach* (pp. 135–163). Plenum Press.

Le, B., & Agnew, C. R. (2003). Commitment and its theorized determinants: A meta-analysis of the investment model. *Personal Relationships, 10*, 37–57. https://doi.org/10.1111/1475-6811.00035

Lennon, C. A., Stewart, A. L., & Ledermann, T. (2013). The role of power in intimate relationships. *Journal of Social and Personal Relationships, 30*, 95–114. https://doi.org/10.1177/0265407512452990

Liu-Farrer, G. (2010). The absent spouses: Gender, sex, race and the extramarital sexuality among Chinese migrants in Japan. *Sexualities, 13*(1), 97–121. https://doi.org/libproxy.lib.csusb.edu/10.1177/1363460709352727

Lopez, V. (2015). Breaking up is hard to do: Mexican American girls' reactions to boyfriends' infidelity. *Journal of Human Behavior in the Social Environment, 25*(3), 214–227. https://doi.org/10.1080/10911359.2014.1003731

Lopez, V. (2017). Love is a battlefield. *Youth & Society, 49*(1), 23–45. https://doi.org/10.1177/0044118X14521223

Macauda, M. M., Erickson, P. I., Singer, M. C., & Santelices, C. C. (2011). A cultural model of infidelity among African American and Puerto Rican young adults. *Anthropology & Medicine, 18*(3), 351–364. https://doi.org/10.1080/13648470.2011.615908

Madathil, J., & Sandhu, D. S. (2008). Infidelity in Asian Indian marriages: Implications for counseling and psychotherapy. *Family Journal, 16*(4), 338–343. https://doi.org/libproxy.lib.csusb.edu/10.1177/1066480708323086

Marger, M. N. (2015). *Race and ethnic relations: American and global perspectives*. Cengage/Wadsworth.

Mark, K., Janssen, E., & Milhausen, R. (2011). Infidelity in heterosexual couples: Demographic, interpersonal, and personality-related predictors of extradyadic sex. *Archives of Sexual Behavior, 40*(5), 971–982. https://doi.org/libproxy.lib.csusb.edu/10.1007/s10508-011-9771-z

Meston, C. M., & Ahrold, T. (2010). Ethnic, gender, and acculturation influences on sexual behaviors. *Archives of Sexual Behavior, 39*(1), 179–189. https://doi.org/10.1007/s10508-008-9415-0

McLellan-Lemal, E., Toledo, L., O'Daniels, C., Villar-Loubet, O., Simpson, C., Adimora, A., & Marks, G. (2013). A man's gonna do what a man wants to do: African American and Hispanic women's perceptions about heterosexual relationships: A qualitative study. *Women's Health, 13*(27), 1–14. https://doi.org/10.1186/1472-6874-13-27.

McIntosh, P. (2003). White privilege: Unpacking the invisible knapsack. In S. Plous (Ed.), *Understanding prejudice and discrimination* (pp. 191–196). McGraw-Hill.

Mint, P. (2004). The power dynamics of cheating: Effects on polyamory and bisexuality. *Journal of Bisexuality, 4*(3/4), 55–76. https://doi.org/libproxy.lib.csusb.edu/10.1300/J159v04n03_04

Mukkamala, S., & Suyemoto, K. L. (2018). Racialized sexism/sexualized racism: A multimethod study of intersectional experiences of discrimination for Asian American women. *Asian American Journal of Psychology*, *9*(1), 32–46. https://doi.org/10.1037/aap0000104

Munsch, C. L., & Yorks, J. (2018). When opportunity knocks, who answers? Infidelity, gender, race, and occupational sex composition. *Personal Relationships*, *25*(4), 581–595. https://doi.org/libproxy.lib.csusb.edu/10.1111/pere.12261

Nowak, N. T., Weisfeld, G. E., Imamoğlu, O., Weisfeld, C. C., Butovskaya, M., & Shen, J. (2014). Attractiveness and spousal infidelity as predictors of sexual fulfillment without the marriage partner in couples from five cultures. *Human Ethology Bulletin*, *29*, 18–38.

Nye, F. I. (1979). Choice, exchange, and the family. In W. R. Burr, R. Hill, F. I. Nye, & I. Reiss (Eds.), *Contemporary theories about the family* (Vol. 2, pp. 1–41). Free Press.

Ogwokhademhe, M., & Ishola, C. A. (2013). Factors responsible for extramarital affairs as perceived by married adults in Lagos, Nigeria. *Problems of Psychology in the 21st Century*, *6*, 37–46.

Okazaki, S. (2002). Influences of culture on Asian Americans' sexuality. *Journal of Sex Research*, *39*(1), 34–41. https://doi.org/10.1080/00224490209552117

Oyediran, K., Isiugo-Abanihe, U. C., Feyisetan, B. J., & Ishola, G. P. (2010). Prevalence of and factors associated with extramarital sex among Nigerian men. *American Journal of Men's Health*, *4*(2):124–134. https://doi.org/10.1177/1557988308330772

Parker, L., Pettifor, A., Maman, S., Sibeko, J., & MacPhail, C. (2014). Concerns about partner infidelity are a barrier to adoption of HIV-prevention strategies among young South African couples. *Culture, Health & Sexuality*, *16*(7), 792–805. https://doi.org/libproxy.lib.csusb.edu/10.1080/13691058.2014.905707

Parker, M. L., Berger, A. T., & Campbell, K. (2010). Deconstructing infidelity: A narrative approach for couples in therapy. *Journal of Couple and Relationship Therapy*, *9*, 66–82. https://doi.org/10.1080/15332690903246119

Parker, M. L., & Campbell, K. (2017). Infidelity and attachment: The moderating role of race/ethnicity. *Contemporary Family Therapy*, *39*(3), 172–183. https://doi.org/10.1007/s10591-017-9415-0

Parra-Cardona, J., & Busby, D. (2006). Exploring relationship functioning in premarital Caucasian and Latino/a couples: Recognizing and valuing cultural differences. *Journal of Comparative Family Studies*, *37*(3), 345–359. https://doi.org/10.3138/jcfs.37.3.345

Penn, C. D., Hernandez, S. L., & Bermúdez, J. M. (1997). Using a cross-cultural perspective to understand infidelity in couples therapy. *American Journal of Family Therapy*, *25*(2), 169–185. https://doi.org/10.1080/01926189708251064

Pew Research Center. (2013, April 4). *The rise of Asian Americans*. https://www.pewsocialtrends.org/2012/06/19/the-rise-of-asian-americans/

Pinderhughes. (2002). African American marriage in the 20th century. *Family Process*, *41*(2), 269–282. https://doi.org/10.1111/j.1545-5300.2002.41206.x

Prins, K. S., Buunk, B. P., & Van Yperen, N. W. (1993). Equity, normative disapproval, and extramarital relatioships. *Journal of Social and Personal Relationships*, *10*, 39–53. https://doi.org/10.1177/0265407593101003

Pulerwitz, J., Izazola-Licea, J. A., & Gortmaker, S. L. (2001). Extrarelational sex among Mexican men and their partners' risk of HIV and other sexually transmitted diseases. *American Journal of Public Health*, *91*, 1650–1652. https://doi.org/10.2105/ajph.91.10.1650

Raley, R. K., Sweeney, M. M., & Wondra, D. (2015). The growing racial and ethnic divide in U.S. marriage patterns. *Future of Children*, *25*(2), 89–109. https://doi.org/10.1353/foc.2015.0014

Reich, N., & Kalantar, S. M. (2018). The role of praying for the spouse and sanctification of marriage in reducing infidelity. *Mental Health, Religion & Culture*, *21*(1), 65–76. https://doi.org/libproxy.lib.csusb.edu/10.1080/13674676.2018.1447555

Rivera-Aragon, S., Diaz-Loving, R., Velasco-Matus, P. W., & Montero-Santamaria, N. (2011). Jealousy and infidelity among Mexican couples. In F. Deutsch, M. Boehnke, U. Kühnen, & K. Boehnke (Eds.), *Rendering borders obsolete: Cross-cultural and cultural psychology as an interdisciplinary, multi-method endeavor: Proceedings from the 19th International Congress of the International Association for Cross-Cultural Psychology*. https://scholarworks.gvsu.edu/iaccp_papers/81/

Roberts, S. T., & Flaskerud, J. H. (2008). Traditional Mexican immigrant women and distress over infidelity. *Issues in Mental Health Nursing*, *29*, 913–916. https://doi.org/10.1080/01612840802182953

Rosa, E. M., & Tudge, J. (2013). Urie Bronfenbrenner's theory of human development: Its evolution from ecology to bioecology. *Journal of Family Theory & Review*, 5(4), 243–258. https://doi.org/10.1111/jftr.12022

Rusbult, C. E., Martz, J., & Agnew, C. R. (1998). The Investment Model Scale: Measuring commitment level, satisfaction level, quality of alternatives, and investment size. *Personal Relationships*, 5(4), 357–391. https://doi.org/10.1111/j.1475-6811.1998.tb00177.x

Savin-Williams, R. (2018). Developmental trajectories and milestones of sexual-minority youth. In *The Cambridge Handbook of Sexual Development* (pp. 156–179). Cambridge University Press. doi:10.1017/9781108116121.009

Scelza, B. (2011). Female choice and extra-pair paternity in a traditional human population. *Biology Letters*, 7, 889–891. https://doi.org/10.1098/rsbl.2011.0478

Scelza, B.A., Prall, S. P., Blumenfield, T., et al. (2020). Patterns of paternal investment predict cross-cultural variation in jealous response. *Nature Human Behavior*, 4, 20–26. https://doi.org/10.1038/s41562-019-0654-y

Schmitt, D. P. (2004). The Big Five related to risky sexual behaviour across 10 world regions: Differential personality associations of sexual promiscuity and relationship infidelity. *European Journal of Personality*, 18, 301–319. https://doi.org/10.1002/per.520

Schmitt, D. P., & Jonason, P. K. (2015). Attachment and sexual permissiveness: Exploring differential associations across sexes, cultures, and facets of short-term mating. *Journal of Cross-Cultural Psychology*, 46(1), 119–133. https://doi.org/libproxy.lib.csusb.edu/10.1177/0022022114551052

Secord. (1983). Imbalanced sex ratios: The social consequences. *Personality & Social Psychology Bulletin*, 9(4), 525–543. https://doi.org/10.1177/0146167283094002

Shackelford, T. K., Besser, A., & Goetz, A. T. (2008). Personality, martial satisfaction, and probability of marital infidelity. *Individual Differences Research*, 6(1), 13–25.

Shen, H. H. (2005). "The first Taiwanese wives" and "the Chinese mistresses": The international division of labour in familial and intimate relations across the Taiwan Strait. *Global Networks*, 5(4), 419–437. https://doi.org/libproxy.lib.csusb.edu/10.1111/j.1471-0374.2005.00127.x

Smith D. J. (2010). Promiscuous girls, good wives, and cheating husbands: Gender inequality, transitions to marriage, and infidelity in Southeastern Nigeria. *Anthropological Quarterly*, 83(1). https://doi.org/10.1353/anq.0.0118

Solstad, K., & Mucic, D. (1999). Extramarital sexual relationships of middle-aged Danish men: Attitudes and behavior. *Maturitas*, 32, 51–59. https://doi.org/10.1016/s0378-5122(99)00012-2

South, S. J., Trent, K., & Shen, Y. (2001). Changing partners: Toward a macrostructural opportunity theory of marital dissolution. *Journal of Marriage and Family*, 63, 743–754. https://www.jstor.org/stable/3654646

Stephenson, R. (2010). Community-level gender equity and extramarital sexual risk-taking among married men in eight African countries. *International Perspectives on Sexual & Reproductive Health*, 36(4), 178–188. https://doi.org/libproxy.lib.csusb.edu/10.1363/3617810

Takaki, R. (2008). *A different mirror: A history of multicultural America*. Back Bay Books.

Thibaut, J. W., & Kelley, H. H. (1959). *The social psychology of groups*. Wiley.

Thapa, R., Yang, Y., & Chan, S. (2020). Young rural women's perceptions of sexual infidelity among men in Cambodia. *Culture, Health & Sexuality*, 22(4), 474–487. https://doi.org/libproxy.lib.csusb.edu/10.1080/13691058.2019.1608469

Toplu-Demirtaş, E., & Fincham, F. D. (2018). Dating infidelity in Turkish couples: The role of attitudes and intentions. *Journal of Sex Research*, 55(2), 252–262. https://doi.org/libproxy.lib.csusb.edu/10.1080/00224499.2017.1365110

Toro-Morn. (2008). Beyond gender dichotomies: Toward a new century of gendered scholarship in the Latina/o experience. In *Latinas/os in the United States: Changing the Face of América* (pp. 277–293). Springer US. https://doi.org/10.1007/978-0-387-71943-6_18

Treas, J., & Giesen, D. (2000). Sexual infidelity among married and cohabiting Americans. *Journal of Marriage and Family*, 62, 48–60. https://doi.org/10.1111/j.1741-3737.2000.00048.x

Tudge, J. R. H., Merçon-Vargas, E. A., Liang, Y., & Payir, A. (2017). The importance of Urie Bronfenbrenner's bioecological theory for early childhood education. In L. E. Cohen & S. Waite-Stupiansky (Eds.), *Theories of early childhood education: Developmental, behaviorist, and critical* (pp. 45–57). Routledge.

U.S. Census (2020, May 23). *2020 Census questions: Race*. United States Census Bureau. https://2020census.gov/en/about-questions/2020-census-questions-race.html

Utley, E. (2011). When better becomes worse: Black wives describe their experiences with infidelity. *Black Women, Gender Families*, 5(1), 66–89. https://www.jstor.org/stable/10.5406/blacwomegendfami.5.1.0066

Vandello, J. A., & Cohen, D. (2003). Male honor and female fidelity: Implicit cultural scripts that perpetuate domestic violence. *Journal of Personality and Social Psychology*, *84*(5), 997–1010. https://doi.org/libproxy.lib.csusb.edu/10.1037/0022-3514.84.5.997

Wang, W. (2018, January 10). *Who cheats more? The demographics of infidelity in America*. Institute for Family Studies. https://ifstudies.org/blog/who-cheats-more-the-demographics-of-cheating-in-america

Watson, D., Beer, A., & McDade-Montez, E. (2014). The role of active assortment in spousal similarity. *Journal of Personality*, *82*, 116–129. https://doi.org/10.1111/jopy.12039

Weiser, D. A., Weigel, D. J., Lalasz, C. B., & Evans, W. P. (2017). Family background and propensity to engage in infidelity. *Journal of Family Issues*, *38*(15), 2083–2101. https://doi.org/libproxy.lib.csusb.edu/10.1177/0192513X15581660

Whisman, M. A., & Snyder, D. K. (2007). Sexual infidelity in a national survey of American women: Differences in prevalence and correlates as a function of method of assessment. *Journal of Family Psychology*, *21*(2), 147–154. https://doi.org/libproxy.lib.csusb.edu/10.1037/0893-3200.21.2.147

Widmer, E. D., Treas, J., & Newcomb, R. (1998). Attitudes toward nonmarital sex in 24 countries. *Journal of Sex Research*, *35*, 349–358. https://doi.org/10.1080/00224499809551953

Williams, L. R., Rueda, H. A., & Nagoshi, J. (2014). Trust, cheating, and dating violence in Mexican American adolescent romantic relationships. *Journal of the Society for Social Work and Research*, *5*(3), 339–360. https://doi.org/10.1086/677174

Williams, L. R., & Hickle, K. E. (2011). "He cheated on me, I cheated on him back": Mexican American and White adolescents' perceptions of cheating in romantic relationships. *Journal of Adolescence*, *34*(5), 1005–1016. https://doi.org/0.1016/j.adolescence.2010.11.007

Wong, Y. J., Owen, J., Tran, K. K., Collins, D. L., & Higgins, C. E. (2012). Asian American male college students' perceptions of people's stereotypes about Asian American men. *Psychology of Men & Masculinity*, *13*(1), 75–88. https://doi.org/10.1037/a0022800

Wu, E. D. (2014). *The color of success: Asian Americans and the origins of the model minority*. Princeton University Press.

Yoshioka, M. R., DiNoia, J., & Ullah, K. (2001). Attitudes toward marital violence: An examination of four Asian communities. *Violence Against Women*, *7*(8), 900–926. https://doi.org/10.1177/10778010122182820

Yuan, S., & Weiser, D. A. (2019). Relationship dissolution following marital infidelity: Comparing European Americans and Asian Americans. *Marriage & Family Review*, *55*(7), 631–650. https://doi.org/libproxy.lib.csusb.edu/10.1080/01494929.2019.1589614

CHAPTER 3

Hormonal Predictors of Infidelity: A Life History Perspective on Testosterone and Other Hormonal Mechanisms

Lindsay Bochon *and* Brian M. Bird

Abstract

Life-history theory provides a framework for understanding the resource trade-offs that are inherent in the struggle to maximize reproductive fitness. Hormones, and testosterone in particular, play important roles in mediating some of the morphological, behavioral, and physiological traits that are implicated in these trade-offs—one of the most widely studied of which is mating versus parenting. In this chapter, we use a life history perspective to review literature examining hormones and infidelity or related proxies (e.g., interest in extrapair sex), and how these links may be understood as a function of the mating vs. parenting trade-off. This chapter focuses the review primarily on testosterone, but also reviews other hormones and hormone systems that have been implicated in infidelity or relevant behavioral and psychological proxies. Further, it touches on contextual considerations for understanding the link between hormones and infidelity and mating, such as the type of mating system (e.g., monogamy vs. polygamy) and the menstrual cycle. The chapter concludes with a discussion of some of the limitations of current, and potential avenues for future, research on hormones and infidelity.

Key Words: infidelity, life history theory, hormone, testosterone, mating vs. parenting, monogamy, polygamy, estradiol

Infidelity describes the violation of the common cross-cultural norm (de Roda et al., 1999; Haavio-Mannila & Kontula, 2003) of sexual and emotional fidelity within the context of an exclusive, monogamous relationship. Despite widespread disapproval (Treas & Giesen, 2000) and serious relational consequences (Amato & Previti, 2003; Scott et al., 2013) associated with the violation of this norm, sexual behavior outside of the primary relationship appears to be remarkably common (Wiederman, 1997). Some reports estimate a lifetime prevalence of 49% and 29% for heterosexual men and women, respectively, with a similar sex difference in homosexual men (34%) versus women (4%) (Haversath & Kröger, 2014). While there are clear sex differences in the prevalence of infidelity, with men reporting higher levels than women (Martins et al., 2016), there is some evidence to suggest these differences are lessening over time (Allen et al., 2005; Wysocki & Childers, 2011; reviewed in Fincham & May, 2017).

From an evolutionary perspective, infidelity may be understood through a framework in which fitness is maximized by balancing energy expenditure toward different aspects of reproductive behavior. In this context, males and females undergo different selection pressures leading to varying reproductive strategies which are differentially moderated by sex steroids (Del Giudice et al., 2015). For example, extradyadic sexual desire has been linked to various levels of progesterone and estradiol in women (Grebe et al., 2016; Roney & Simmons, 2016) and infidelity has been linked to increased concentrations of testosterone in men (Klimas et al., 2019). In this chapter, we provide an overview of such hormonal modulation and reactivity to sexual behavior within the overarching framework of life history theory, and outline how unfaithful behavior, as well as relevant behavioral and psychological proxies (e.g., relationship commitment, interest in extrapair sex) in men and women can be understood within this context. We focus our review primarily on the steroid hormone testosterone among men, given the historical focus on this population, but we also provide an overview of similar research involving women, in addition to other steroid hormones (e.g., estradiol), and contextual considerations for female hormonal influence, such as the menstrual cycle.

Life History Theory

Life history theory is an evolutionary biological framework for understanding the allocation of limited resources toward major life functions—such as bodily maintenance, growth, and reproduction—to optimize fitness (Ellis et al., 2009; Del Giudice et al., 2015). The substantial energetic investment associated with these processes confines expenditure to any single function at one time. Following sexual maturation, adult reproductive function involves a basic trade-off between mating and parenting effort, in which resources are respectively devoted to increasing reproductive opportunities or raising existing offspring. This necessary trade-off is theoretically relevant to understanding infidelity, given that men who allocate more resources to mating effort increase their chances of successful reproduction. Heavy investment in mating effort may be beneficial for males of good genetic quality (Maynard-Smith, 1989); however, exclusive pursuit of this strategy is also costly, including increased risk of pathogen contraction and physical harm from aggressive intrasexual competition (Kokko & Jennions, 2008). Investment in parenting effort can alternatively increase male reproductive fitness by producing stable mating relationships and supporting offspring through provisioning or direct paternal care. Smaller obligate investments in offspring allow males more flexibility in achieving an optimal balance between these two opposing functions (Trivers, 1972). However, heightened levels of male intrasexual competition produces variation in mate quality that, along with the unusual degree to which human males invest in their mates and offspring (relative to some other species), engenders significant intrasexual competition among females as well (Campbell, 2013). Therefore, there is variation both within and between sexes in the extent to which somatic energy allocation is diverted toward mating and parenting effort, the balance of which is mediated by varying levels of the sex steroid testosterone in both males and females (Motta-Mena & Puts, 2017; Muehlenbein & Bribiescas, 2005). Our understanding of the relationship between testosterone (and other hormones) and infidelity can be more easily clarified and conceptualized by understanding testosterone's functions in mediating the mating versus parenting trade-off (Shirazi et al., 2019), reviewed below.

Testosterone and Trade-Offs in Reproductive Effort
MALES

In adult males, elevated testosterone enhances anabolic and androgenic effects—associated with somatic growth and sexual differentiation—that reflect distribution of resources toward mating effort. Testosterone, for example, modulates morphological characteristics such as muscle mass and strength (Bhasin et al., 1996), 2D:4D digit ratio (Manning et al., 2000), indicators of facial masculinity (Lefevre et al., 2013; Penton-Voak & Chen, 2004; Roney et al., 2006; Verdonck et al., 1999; Welker et al., 2016; but see Bird et al., 2016; Hodges-Simeon et al., 2016; Peters et al., 2008) and vocal pitch (Dabbs & Mallinger, 1999; Evans et al., 2008; Puts et al., 2012), that are positively associated with female ratings of attractiveness (Penton-Voak & Chen, 2004; but see Swaddle & Reierson, 2002), particularly in short-term mating contexts (Roney et al., 2006; Valentine et al., 2014).

Testosterone also fluctuates in response to fitness relevant cues indicating the presence of potential mating opportunities (Roney, 2015; Zilioli & Bird, 2017). For example, testosterone increases following interactions with potential mating partners (Flinn et al. 2012; Roney et al., 2007; van der Meij et al., 2008), after participating in sporting events with a larger ratio of opposite-sex to same-sex spectators (Miller et al., 2012), following exposure to olfactory cues of female ovulation (Cerda-Molina, 2013; Miller & Maner, 2010; but see Roney & Simmons, 2012), and in response to sexually explicit fantasies (Goldey et al., 2014). In this way, testosterone serves as an internal signal that coordinates behavioral, motivational, and physiological shifts toward mate attraction and acquisition (Bird & Zilioli, 2017). In line with this, testosterone influences a range of downstream behaviors that are indirectly associated with reproductive success, including competitive and aggressive interactions with intrasexual rivals (Archer, 2006; Carré & Olmstead, 2015; Fales et al., 2014; Geniole et al. 2017; Geniole et al., 2020; Geniole & Carré, 2018; Zilioli & Bird, 2017), increased risk-taking (Ronay & von Hippel, 2010), and affiliative behavior (van der Meij et al., 2012) in the presence of an attractive woman (reviewed in Gray et al., 2020). Testosterone also promotes responses directly related to reproduction, such as increased sexual arousal (Hellhammer et al., 1985; Ponzi et al., 2016; Stoléru et al., 1993; but see van Anders, 2013 and Zilioli et al., 2016), sexual motivation (Isidori et al., 2005; Wallen, 2001), and sexual activity (Dabbs & Mohammed, 1992; Peters et al., 2008) and is associated with greater number of lifetime sexual partners (Peters et al., 2008; Pollet et al., 2011).

Investment in reproductive effort, however, is metabolically costly and must be balanced against testosterone's potential negative impact on immunocompetence (Foo et al., 2017; Muehlenbein & Bribiescas, 2005). In line with this, reactivity to mating opportunities has been shown to be conditional on the likelihood of mate pursuit (Flinn et al., 2012), suggesting that elevated testosterone should be adaptive only under conditions in which competition for mates is functional. Therefore, to the extent that it reflects a reduction in mate acquisition behavior, participation in committed, monogamous relationships should be associated with functional reductions in testosterone. Indeed, men in long-term committed relationships have been found to have lower testosterone (Burnham et al., 2003; Caldwell-Hooper et al., 2011; van Anders & Watson, 2006; see Grebe et al., 2019, for meta-analysis), and experience significant declines over time compared to men who remain single (Gettler et al., 2011). Furthermore, age-related declines in testosterone were found to be accelerated in men transitioning from unmarried to married over a 10-year period, a decline that was attenuated in those who became divorced over the same period (Holmboe et al., 2017). Reductions in testosterone, then, appear to facilitate nurturing behaviors that are associated with enhanced relationship quality. This is illustrated by results showing that testosterone is negatively related to marital commitment and satisfaction (Caldwell-Hooper et al., 2011; Edelstein et al., 2014), partner ratings of marital quality (Edelstein et al., 2014), and declines in sexual activity that are thought to enhance the marital relationship before the arrival of offspring (Gettler et al., 2013; but see Sakaguchi et al., 2007). Furthermore, studies show that fathers typically have lower testosterone concentrations compared to nonfathers (Alvergne et al., 2009; Gettler et al., 2011; Gettler et al., 2012; Gray, Yang, et al., 2006; Muller et al., 2009), suggesting that decreased testosterone concentrations also play a functional role in dampening pursuit of reproductive opportunities (e.g., extrapair partnerships) in favor of increased attention to offspring care. In support of this, fathers engaging in more direct caregiving, including holding, cleaning, feeding (Alvergne et al., 2009; Muller et al., 2009), and co-sleeping with infants (Gettler et al., 2012; Lawson et al., 2017), have lower testosterone than less involved fathers.

FEMALES

Constraints on overall lifetime reproductive success and the extensive energy expenditure associated with offspring care may predispose women towards heavily investing in parenting effort. Provisioning from males, however, is often constrained by the fact that resources cannot easily be shared among multiple females. Thus, female intrasexual competition for access to high-quality mates is common (Puts, 2010, 2016), albeit to a lesser extent than seen in males (Campbell, 2013). However, while heightened salivary testosterone is associated with intrasexual competitiveness (Edwards et al., 2006; Hahn et al., 2016; Oliveira et al., 2009), it does not appear to play a significant role in female aggressive behavior (Geniole et al., 2020). Competition among females, then, is more likely to take the form of mate attraction than direct intrasexual confrontation. Grammer et al. (2004), for example, found positive associations between testosterone and revealing clothing choice among women attending an Austrian discotheque. Furthermore, the fitness benefits associated with mate attraction are likely most beneficial during the high fertility phase of the menstrual cycle. This is in line with some evidence suggesting that behaviors designed to enhance attractiveness, such as wearing revealing clothing (Durante et al., 2008; Fisher, 2004; Haselton et al., 2007), peak around ovulation.

In human females, however, ovulation is concealed, and sexual activity evenly distributed across the menstrual cycle (Motta-Mena & Puts, 2017). Female sexual behavior, then, is at least partially independent from ovulation. Given that potential mates could be met at any time during the menstrual cycle, rapid hormonal responses may allow for the activation of mate acquisition behaviors outside of the fertile window (Roney, 2015). Testosterone in females thus appears to serve a similar function as in males, in that it facilitates courtship behaviors directed at attracting men of high mate-value. López, Hay, and Conklin, (2009), for example, report that naturally cycling women experience significant increases in testosterone in response to a video clip of an attractive man courting a young woman. These rapid fluctuations serve as an internal signal of mating opportunities that produces downstream physiological and behavioral changes to facilitate successful mate attraction in a manner that is independent of cycle phase. Additionally, testosterone increases prior to and in response to sex (Dabbs & Mohammed, 1992; van Anders, Hamilton, Schmidt, & Watson, 2007), is associated with satisfying sexual activity (Braunstein et al., 2005; Buster et al., 2005; van Anders & Dunn, 2009), sexual desire (Raisanen et al. 2018; van Anders, 2012), attractiveness ratings of masculine men's faces (arguably because they are high-quality mates for short-term relationships; Welling et al., 2007), and masturbation frequency (van Anders, 2012), suggesting that it plays a role in moderating at least some aspects of female sexual behavior, thus potentially holding relevance for infidelity.

The contribution of testosterone in mediating other aspects of female reproductive effort, however, is less apparent. Some research, for example, suggests that monogamously partnered women have lower testosterone than single women (Edelstein et al., 2011; van Anders & Goldey, 2010; van Anders & Watson, 2006, 2007), although others have failed to find this association (Caldwell-Hooper et al., 2011). Furthermore, mothers have been found to have significantly lower testosterone than nonmothers (Barrett et al., 2013; Kuzawa et al., 2010). The association between testosterone and motherhood, however, appears to be moderated by the age of the child, with lower testosterone in mothers of younger children than mothers of older children. To the extent that testosterone is associated with sexual activity in women, reductions in testosterone are functional in shifting energetic investment away from mating and toward provisioning of the current offspring. This may be particularly important for young offspring as the metabolic demands immediately postpartum are the most energetically intensive (Valeggia & Ellison, 2009). Mothers with higher postpartum testosterone show reduced positive affect and affectionate behavior toward their offspring (Fleming et al., 1997), suggesting that reductions in testosterone are necessary for the functional display of nurturing behavior. These results suggest that, similar to males, testosterone is an important mechanism in females for shifting metabolic and behavioral priorities between mating and parenting effort.

Diversity in Human Mating and Parenting Systems

Most research on reproductive behavior in humans, including desire and participation in extrapair sex, has been conducted on North American populations in which monogamous romantic relationships and some degree of direct paternal care are the norm. However, this represents only a narrow portion of the considerable crosscultural variation in global mating and parenting strategies, suggesting that inclusion of more diverse populations is important to contextualize associations with testosterone. Polyamory, for example, represents a variation on reproductive behavior characterized by consensual engagement in multiple loving and committed relationships (van Anders, Hamilton, & Watson, 2007). Polyamorous individuals, while still engaged in long-term, romantic relationships, differ from monogamous individuals in that they maintain the possibility of entering multiple relationships. In line with this, testosterone is found to be higher in polyamorous men and women than those in monoamorous relationships (van Anders, Hamilton, & Watson, 2007), suggesting that mating effort remains elevated. Furthermore, in a sample of Kenyan Swahili men, polygynously married men were found to have higher testosterone concentrations than monogamously married men (Gray, 2003). Of course, the emotional and sexual fidelity that is typically expected in monogamous relationships is different among polyamorous and polygynous populations, but the evidence presented here nevertheless supports an association between higher testosterone and increased effort or interest in mating, thus having relevance for our understanding of testosterone's relationship to extrapair interest in monogamous populations.

Later research has been mixed, with some replicating previous effects among polygynous populations (Alvergne et al., 2009; Lawson et al., 2017) and others finding no differences (Gray et al., 2007; Muller et al., 2009). Other non-Western samples, however, reveal a moderating role of paternal investment in polygynous populations. The Hadza foragers and Datoga pastoralists, for example, are groups living in close proximity in northern Tanzania and exhibiting divergent levels of paternal investment (Muller et al., 2009). Hadza fathers, who display high levels of involvement with their offspring, have lower testosterone concentrations than nonfathers. However, in the Datoga, for whom paternal involvement is significantly lower, fathers have testosterone concentrations comparable to nonfathers (Muller et al., 2009). These results suggest that testosterone concentrations within the context of polygynous mating strategies reflects continued investment in mating effort aimed at obtaining more wives. The degree to which testosterone remains elevated in these populations, however, may depend on cross-cultural variation in direct paternal investment in offspring.

Hormonal Modulation of Extradyadic Sexual Behavior

Life history theory provides an overarching framework for understanding testosterone dynamics in the modulation of energetic investment between mating and parenting effort. Conceptually, the idea that testosterone promotes mating at the expense of nurturing behavior across various contexts, including polygynous and polyamorous populations in which the pursuit of multiple mating partners is contextually appropriate, provides a theoretical basis from which relationships with infidelity can be hypothesized. Specifically, given that infidelity is associated with pursuing novel partners outside of the existing romantic relationship, we might expect that those with high testosterone would participate in more infidelity. Evidence for the role that testosterone (and other hormones) plays in mediating infidelity and its related proxies (e.g., relationship commitment, sexual dimorphism in morphological characteristics) is reviewed below.

Testosterone

INFIDELITY

A small number of studies have directly examined the link between testosterone and infidelity (i.e., extra-marital, -pair, -dyadic sex). With some exceptions (e.g., Maestripieri et al., 2014), results suggest that testosterone is positively and significantly related to infidelity. For example, in one of the earliest studies, Booth and Dabbs (1993) found that among a large sample of army veterans, married men with high testosterone levels were more likely to report extramarital sex than their lower-testosterone counterparts. Similarly, Fisher and colleagues (2009) found that among a large sample of men with sexual dysfunction, those with higher androgenization—as indexed by higher testosterone levels and testis volume—reported more extramarital affairs than their low-androgenization counterparts. Recent work from a sample of middle-aged men is also consistent with this in finding that among healthy men, testosterone levels were positively predictive of the frequency of unfaithful behavior reported (Klimas et al., 2019). Although these studies are few in number, they provide evidence to suggest that testosterone, at least among men, may play an important role in infidelity.

Given that few studies have directly examined the relationship between testosterone or other hormones and infidelity specifically, another way to understand these relationships is to use closely related proxies to infidelity. The relationship between testosterone and several of these proxies is reviewed below.

RELATIONSHIP COMMITMENT

Relationship commitment may serve as one proxy for infidelity, given that individuals with lower relationship commitment have been found to report more permissive attitudes toward, as well as participate in more instances of, previous and future infidelity (Drigotas et al., 1999; Rodrigues et al., 2017). Consistent with this idea, recent work has found that among a community sample of young men and women, high concentrations of salivary testosterone for men (but not women) were predictive of lower relationship commitment (Caldwell-Hooper et al., 2011); this builds on other work showing that testosterone levels are higher among men and women who are involved in multiple emotional and/or sexual relationships versus those with a single partner (Alvergne et al., 2009; van Anders, Hamilton, & Watson, 2007). Similarly, in a dyadic association study with heterosexual couples, testosterone concentrations among both men and women were not only negatively associated with self-reported relationship commitment and satisfaction, but also predictive of their partner's commitment and satisfaction (Edelstein et al., 2014). Other work suggests that higher testosterone may predict psychological processes that are conceptually related to commitment, and which hold relevance for short-term and/or extrapair affairs. For example, in a study of college students, young men in romantic relationships had lower testosterone, but this relationship was moderated by their extrapair sexual interest; specifically, paired men with sustained high levels of testosterone also showed higher interest in sexual encounters outside of the relationship (McIntyre et al., 2006).

RELATIONSHIP ORIENTATION

Relationship status (e.g., married, dating) is likely less meaningful for testosterone concentrations than the emotions and behaviors underlying these relationships. For example, when compared to men in stable, long-term relationships, those recently entered into a relationship (Farrelly et al., 2015), those engaged in casual relationships (van Anders & Goldey, 2010), and those going through relationship dissolution (Dibble et al., 2017; Mazur & Michalek, 1998) were found to have heightened testosterone concentrations. Testosterone is thus more likely to be attuned to relationship orientation and the degree of investment than the relationship label, per se (van Anders, 2013). Several authors (e.g., Grebe et al., 2019; McIntyre et al., 2006) additionally report that men in committed relationships, who nevertheless maintain elevated testosterone concentrations, exhibit behavior indicative of extrapair sexual interest (e.g., self-reported willingness to have an affair, history of extrapair sexual activity). These results suggest that for men, testosterone is associated with continued investment in mating effort, regardless of current relationship status—which is in line with findings that higher testosterone is associated with greater likelihood of divorce and higher rates of sexual infidelity in men (Booth & Dabbs, 1993; Klimas et al., 2019; Mazur & Michalek 1998).

SOCIOSEXUAL ORIENTATION

Perhaps one of the most widely studied constructs of relevance to infidelity is sociosexual orientation. Sociosexual orientation reflects a continuum ranging from restricted to unrestricted beliefs and behaviors regarding sex (Simpson & Gangestad, 1991). Individuals with a restricted sociosexual orientation prefer to engage in sexual intercourse within the context of a close and committed relationship. In contrast, unrestricted individuals can engage in sexual intercourse in the absence of commitment and have lower commitment when engaged in a romantic relationship (Jones, 1998). Given that low commitment is often cited as a predictor of sexual infidelity (Drigotas et al., 1999), it is perhaps unsurprising that unrestricted sociosexual orientation is associated with a greater willingness to engage in unfaithful behavior (Barta & Kiene, 2005; Mattingly et al., 2011; Ostovich & Sabini, 2004; Seal et al., 1994), particularly when relationship quality is low (Rodrigues & Lopes, 2017). Additionally, those reporting a prior history of sexual infidelity are more likely to be sociosexually unrestricted and to perceive ambiguous and deceptive behavior (such as talking on the internet; lying to romantic partners) as not representative of infidelity (Rodrigues et al., 2017).

The fact that unrestricted sociosexuality is associated with motivational states related to the pursuit of new mating partners implies relatively greater investments in mating effort, which may be related to a tendency to engage in sex outside a committed relationship (Roney & Gettler, 2015). Furthermore, given the relationship between testosterone and mating effort reviewed above, the extent to which sociosexuality predicts unfaithful behavior may be associated with relatively higher testosterone concentrations. This may be particularly relevant for men, who are typically more unrestricted in their sociosexual orientation than women (Rodrigues & Lopes, 2017) and more likely to engage in extradyadic sexual behavior (Fisher et al., 2012). In line with this, partnered men with greater unrestricted sociosexuality retain testosterone concentrations similar to that of single men (McIntyre et al., 2006). Furthermore, masculinized morphological characteristics known to vary with prenatal and pubertal androgen exposure, have been associated with greater unrestricted sociosexuality (Arnocky et al., 2018; Polo et al., 2019) and intended infidelity among men (Arnocky et al., 2018). However, within sex variability in sociosexual orientation has been shown to be greater than between sex variability (Simpson et al., 2004), and sociosexuality appears to be a reliable predictor of sexual infidelity in both sexes (Shaw et al., 2013). This is in line with research showing that indicators of pubertal androgen exposure (Clark, 2004) and adult testosterone concentrations positively predict sociosexuality in women as well (Shirazi et al., 2019; but see Charles & Alexander, 2011; Farrelly et al., 2015; van Anders, Hamilton, & Watson, 2007).

Despite associations with testosterone found in some studies, inconsistent results (van Anders, Hamilton, & Watson, 2007) suggest that the use of a global measure may not fully capture the multifaceted nature of sociosexuality. In light of this, Penke and Asendorpf

(2008) advocate for distinguishing between sociosexual desire, attitudes, and behavior to give a more nuanced picture not captured when aggregating these distinct components. Using this method, partnered men reporting greater sociosexual desire, defined as interest in uncommitted sexual activity, had testosterone concentrations comparable to single men (Edelstein et al., 2011). However, partnered women reporting greater sociosexual behavior, defined as actual engagement in uncommitted sexual activity, had comparable testosterone to single women. Sex differences in sociosexual desire may constrain men's ability to engage in uncommitted sexual activity because relatively fewer women are inclined to do so. However, due to the availability of willing men, women interested in uncommitted sex are relatively less constrained in their sociosexual behavior (Edelstein et al., 2011). Thus, the motivation to engage in uncommitted sex may differentially map onto testosterone concentrations in men and women, with testosterone more closely tied to sociosexual desire in men and sociosexual behavior in women.

Seeking and engaging in extrapair mating opportunities comes with costs associated with long-term maintenance of elevated testosterone, including increased risk of injuries from aggressive and competitive interactions (Archer, 2006; Carré & Olmstead, 2015; Fales et al., 2014; Geniole et al., 2017; Geniole et al., 2020; Geniole & Carré, 2018) and reduced immune function (Foo et al., 2017; Muehlenbien & Bribiescas, 2005). Therefore, testosterone should mediate sociosexual behavior only in so far as it facilitates opportunities for actual sexual intercourse, after which it should reduce to mitigate the costs of maintaining high concentrations. Puts et al. (2015) report that testosterone positively predicts sociosexual psychology, an aggregate of sociosexual attitudes and desires, in a sample of male undergraduate students. After controlling for sociosexual psychology, however, testosterone negatively predicts sociosexual behavior, measured as the number of sexual partners in the previous year. Thus, while testosterone promotes sociosexual behavior by increasing desire for uncommitted sex, successful engagement in these mating opportunities results in decreased testosterone production. Puts et al. (2015) hypothesize that copulatory success produces negative feedback on testosterone such that concentrations are reduced following satisfaction of sexual desires.

Links between sociosexual psychology and testosterone may be particularly strong in partnered men, for whom the risks associated with uncommitted sex are particularly high (Puts et al., 2015). Therefore, partnered men with a greater desire for sexual intercourse outside of the primary relationship should have elevated testosterone concentrations. However, to the extent that sexual desire is fulfilled by extrapair sex, testosterone may be reduced following engagement in unfaithful behavior, perhaps to offset its potential physiological and relational costs. Contrarily, there is evidence to suggest plasticity in sociosexual orientation such that men become relatively more restricted as mating opportunities become scarce (Arnocky et al., 2016) and as they transition from single into marriage and fatherhood (Gettler et al., 2019). Thus, men's sociosexuality appears malleable to contextual conditions that alter the functionality of investing in mating effort, bringing into question the causal direction of links between testosterone and sociosexuality, and testosterone and infidelity.

SEXUAL DIMORPHISM IN THE FACE, BODY, AND VOICE

Masculine and feminine facial characteristics, and preferences for such traits, have also been studied in the context of infidelity. For example, some evidence suggests that women with more characteristically feminine faces are accurately rated as showing greater interest in short-term relationships and extrapair sex, particularly near ovulation (e.g., Boothroyd et al., 2011; reviewed in Gangestad & Thornhill, 2008). Masculine men, however, are perceived to have more interest in, and to actually participate in more, short-term partnerships than more feminine men (e.g., Kruger, 2006; Rhodes et al., 2005). Research by Welling and colleagues suggests that preferences for these sexually dimorphic facial characteristics—including women's attractiveness ratings of masculine men's faces (Welling et al., 2007) and men's attractiveness ratings of feminine women's faces (Welling et al., 2008)—are associated with elevated endogenous testosterone concentrations (but see Marcinkowska et al., 2019). Similarly, work on exogenous testosterone administration finds that men show the highest attractiveness ratings for feminine faces in short-term mating contexts versus long-term contexts (Bird et al., 2016). Collectively, this research suggests that elevated testosterone may predict preferences or increased interest in those who are more likely receptive of short-term mates, thus potentially increasing the chance of extrapair copulation. This possibility has not been directly tested and will require future work to determine if elevated testosterone, either endogenously or from exogenous administration, precedes interest in facial sexual dimorphism, and whether this preference in turn leads to infidelity.

Further clues about the relationship between testosterone and infidelity can be found by examining the link between human characteristics that are influenced by, correlate with, or show between-subject differences in, testosterone. At the most basic level, men—who, even at the low end, have roughly four to five times higher testosterone than women (Clark et al., 2019)—have been repeatedly found to show greater desire, willingness, and likelihood of infidelity than women, although this gap may be narrowing among young adults (reviewed in Fincham & May, 2017). Moreover, men with high shoulder-to-hip ratios (a relatively masculine, testosterone-dependent trait) self-report more sex partners and extrapair partners (Hughes & Gallup, 2003). Research has also found that human vocal frequencies are lower among men with higher testosterone levels (Evans et al., 2008), which is notable given that men with lower vocal frequencies are preferred as short-term (versus long-term) mates, and are accurately judged by female raters to have been more unfaithful in the past relative to those with higher vocal frequencies (Hughes & Harrison, 2017; O'Connor et al., 2011; O'Connor et al., 2014). Further, in non-Western hunter-gatherer populations, breastfeeding women show a preference for partner voices that are higher (Apicella & Feinberg, 2009), potentially because those partners have lower testosterone and are thus more likely to provide necessary resources for child rearing (and by extension, are less likely to stray). Taken together, sexually dimorphic cues that are dependent on developmental levels of, and can reflect differences in, circulating hormones, may map onto variation in mate preferences because they provide clues to behavioral proclivities, such as an individual's likelihood of engaging in extrapair relations.

Beyond Testosterone
ESTRADIOL AND PROGESTERONE

Although testosterone has implications for both men's and women's mating, the study of women's interest in extrapair mating has historically been more focused on other hormones, such as estradiol and progesterone. One of the dominant theoretical approaches to understanding women's mating psychology is the dual mating strategy hypothesis (e.g., Gangestad & Simpson, 2000), which argues that women's preferences for casual sex and/or extrapair mating with high-mate-value men increases in the ovulatory phase of the menstrual cycle—which is characterized by high estradiol (the primary estrogen during reproductive years) and low progesterone. This view suggests that during high fertility, women may be more inclined to prefer individuals with characteristics indicative of high genetic quality, particularly if their existing partner is low on these traits. Here, like many studies with men, researchers have often used proxies for extrapair sex, such as interest in faces that are more masculine, with the argument that masculine (versus feminine) men are more likely to participate in short-term relationships (Rhodes et al., 2005), and that masculine faces may be indicative of desirable characteristics that could then be passed onto offspring (e.g., health; Thornhill & Gangestad, 2006). While some highly influential research is consistent with this hypothesis in finding, for example, that women show increased preferences for masculine male faces during high fertility versus other points in the menstrual cycle, particularly when rating for short-term relationships (e.g., Penton-Voak et al., 1999; see Gildersleeve et al., 2014, for meta-analysis), experts have recently raised some methodological concerns about past work, citing low power, limitations in determining menstrual cycle phase from self-report data, and reliance on cross-sectional designs (Jones et al., 2019).

Of course, proxies such as preferences for facial masculinity are not equivalent to interest or actual participation in infidelity. Similar to men, studies with women examining hormones other than testosterone are limited, but evidence indicates that hormones such as estradiol may indeed hold predictive value for women's infidelity. For example, Durante and Li (2009) found that women's salivary estradiol was positively related to self- and other-perceived attractiveness, as well as greater likelihood of flirting, kissing, and having a serious affair with someone other than the primary partner. Similarly, Pillsworth et al. (2004) reported that naturally cycling women were more likely to flirt with individuals outside the primary relationship during high fertility days, particularly for those who were not in new relationships, and Bellis and Baker (1990) found that rates of reported extrapair copulations were the highest during the late follicular phase (but see Motta-Mena & Puts, 2017, for some methodological limitations of this work).

As with men who have high shoulder-to-hip ratios, women with low waist-to-hip ratios—a trait that correlates with high levels of estradiol relative to progesterone, fecundity, and men's ratings of women's attractiveness (reviewed in Dixson, 2016)—report more sexual partners and more extrapair partners than their high waist-to-hip ratio counterparts (Hughes & Gallup, 2003). More recently, a study examined the extent to which oral contraceptive (OC) use was associated with extrapair behavior, given that OCs work by interfering with the hypothalamic-pituitary-ovarian feedback loop, thus preventing a drop in progesterone (and affecting estrogen, depending on the form of OC). While the authors did not find any main effects of OC use on extrapair partnerships, they did find that among those women who had engaged in extrapair sexual behavior, women taking OC (versus not) had fewer one-night stands and fewer partners (Klapilová et al., 2014), thus providing indirect evidence that disruption of the natural variation in ovarian hormones can reduce interest in extrapair sex. Others have not replicated these findings, however, suggesting that these relationships are not clear (e.g., Marcinkowska et al., 2019).

Naturally, the extent to which ovarian hormones map onto variation in infidelity can be studied in the context of the ovulatory cycle, where hormones fluctuate in a relatively predictable way. Although a review of infidelity and related indices across the ovulatory cycle is beyond the scope of the present chapter, it is worth noting that ovulatory shifts in mating psychology represent a rich area of research for understanding hormone-infidelity links. Some studies provide evidence of a positive association for estradiol and a negative association for progesterone on within-cycle shifts in women's sexual desire (e.g., Roney & Simmons, 2013; but see Grebe et al., 2016; see also Roney & Simmons, 2016), while others find that among naturally cycling women, increases in estradiol predict sociosexual desires (i.e., interest in short-term mating) but not general sexual desire, especially in the context of simultaneous progesterone decreases (Shirazi et al., 2019). A recent diary study with a total sample of over 1,000 women and 26,000 diary entries similarly found strong evidence that naturally cycling women experienced ovulatory increases in extrapair desire and behavior (e.g., flirting; Arslan et al., 2021). The theoretical explanations for such effects remain under debate, however, and thus future work in this area will be important.

OTHER STEROIDS AND PEPTIDES

Additional research on human sexual behavior suggests that infidelity, and related proxies, are influenced by hormonal mechanisms—such as steroid (e.g., cortisol) and peptide (e.g., oxytocin and vasopressin) systems—other than those already discussed. Wilson et al. (2015), for example, report that cortisol reactivity to a socioevaluative stressor mediates the relationship between extraversion and short-term mating orientation—a component of unrestricted sociosexuality. Extraversion has previously been linked with greater mating success (Randler et al., 2012), extrapair mating (Nettle, 2005), and relatively unrestricted sociosexual orientation (Simpson & Gangestad, 1991; Wright & Reise, 1997), suggesting that reduced cortisol reactivity in the face of psychosocial stress may be a mechanism by which extraverted individuals are able to engage in uncommitted sexual relationships. Higher cortisol reactivity, on the other hand, may interfere with sociosexual behavior in introverted individuals (Wilson et al., 2015) and those with higher autistic-like traits (Ponzi et al., 2016)—personality dimensions that have previously been linked with sexual restraint (Schmitt, 2004; Schmitt & Shackelford, 2008) and restricted sociosexuality (Del Giudice et al., 2010).

Moreover, a substantial body of research on the sexual behavior of several closely related species of voles implicates peptide hormones such as vasopressin, oxytocin, and their associated receptor genes—the arginine vasopressin receptor 1A gene (AVPR1A) and the oxytocin receptor gene (OXTR)—in the regulation of monogamous and nonmonogamous behavior (see Insel, 2010, for a review). Research in humans suggests that affiliative behavior is similarly affected by genetic variation in these hormonal systems. For example, Walum and colleagues report that marital quality and affection towards romantic partners is associated with variation in AVPR1A (Walum et al., 2008) and OXTR (Walum et al., 2012). Variation in single nucleotide polymorphisms (SNPs) in the AVPR1A gene has also been found to be associated with extrapair mating in women (Zietsch et al., 2015; but see Cherkas et al., 2004).

Limitations in Our Understanding of Hormone-Infidelity Links

A number of limitations exist in our understanding of hormonal modulation or prediction of infidelity. First, there exist a limited number of studies that have directly examined the link between hormones and infidelity, rather than related proxies like extrapair or sociosexual desire. While several studies indicate that hormones, such as testosterone in men (Klimas et al., 2019) and estradiol in women (Durante & Li, 2009) may be directly associated with unfaithful and flirtatious behavior, more research that incorporates infidelity specifically will improve our understanding of these relationships. Furthermore, existing research on hormone-infidelity relationships has focused almost exclusively on sexual infidelity, perhaps because sexual infidelity has the most direct consequences for reproductive fitness. Nevertheless, the definition of what constitutes extradyadic behavior is not always clearly stipulated (Luo et al., 2010), and other forms of nonsexual involvement with extrapair partners may be important predictors of subsequent infidelity. Early work by Kinsey et al. (1948) distinguishes between sexual and emotional infidelity, with men more likely to pursue sexual opportunities and women more likely to engage in emotionally unfaithful behavior outside of the primary relationship (Glass & Wright, 1977). Restricting analyses to exclusively sexual behavior likely conceals sex-specific patterns of behavior (Luo et al., 2010; McAnulty & Brineman, 2007) that may be important for hormone-infidelity relationships, and thus future work might consider incorporation of both emotional and sexual infidelity. Further, the consideration of sexual and gender minorities may help improve our understanding of hormone-infidelity relationships, given past work showing differences in, for example, sociosexuality and personality among heterosexual versus nonheterosexual (e.g., gay, lesbian, bisexual) individuals (Schmitt, 2007).

Beyond the limited research, however, there remain additional considerations for our understanding of these relationships. As indicated in several theoretical models (Zilioli & Bird, 2017; Geniole & Carré, 2018; Roney & Gettler, 2015), testosterone is similar to other hormones in that it not only has the potential to drive behavior, but also to respond flexibly to environmental cues of challenge and/or mating opportunities. Although these bidirectional relationships are often studied within the context of acute fluctuations and behaviors that follow in close succession, there is evidence that feedback from hormones may influence behavior at greater intervals. This is illustrated by Zilioli and Watson (2014), who found that testosterone increase as a result of winning a competition predicted performance on a subsequent competition the following day. Longitudinal studies have been helpful in clarifying how basal testosterone shifts over time in committed relationships (Gettler et al., 2011; Holmboe et al., 2017; Grebe et al., 2019), surrounding relationship status transitions (Dibble et al., 2017; Mazur & Michalek, 1998), and in association with changes in sexual activity in long-term relationships (Gettler, 2013). Further, as noted by Puts et al. (2015), there is evidence that while testosterone can drive sociosexual desires, circulating testosterone can also flexibly change once such desires are fulfilled. These results illustrate the bidirectional nature of testosterone–behavior relationships and will likely be important for our understanding of how infidelity could potentially influence hormones, eventually feeding back to further influence behavior. Exogenous administration studies have been used to examine how steroid and peptide hormones are involved in various psychological and behavioral processes (reviewed in Bos et al., 2012; Zilioli & Bird, 2017), and may be additionally helpful for understanding the degree to which hormones play a causal role in infidelity.

It will also be important to examine how relevant demographic variables known to vary with testosterone affect infidelity. For example, men with children, who are in committed relationships, may be older on average than those who are single and childless. Further, testosterone typically declines across the lifespan in males, although the extent of this decline is a matter of contention (Kelsey et al., 2014; Handelsman et al., 2015). In a sample of Kenyan Ariaal pastoralists, for example, polygynously married men had equivalent testosterone levels compared to their monogamously married counterparts (Gray et al., 2007). Importantly, marriage among the Ariaal is based on an age-grade system in which men do not transition from single to married until around age 30 (Gray et al., 2007). Polygynously married men, however, are older than men in monogamous marriages, suggesting that age and the continued acquisition of wealth and sociopolitical power is more important for marital status than testosterone-mediated behavior. To the extent that age predicts fatherhood and participation in committed relationships, then, associations between testosterone and extradyadic sexual activity may be relatively reduced as a consequence of these age-related declines. As a result, the elevated testosterone concentrations associated with continued investment in mating effort and higher rates of infidelity may be more consistently found in younger rather than older, married men.

However, there is variability across populations in the extent to which testosterone declines with age (Ellison et al., 2002), illustrating the importance of including more diverse samples. For example, a recent meta-analysis on the role of testosterone in mediating life-history strategies reports that 73% of reviewed effects for paired vs. unpaired men and 88% for behavior within romantic relationships were drawn from Western populations (Grebe et al., 2019). This is representative of a pervasive limitation in the social sciences in which empirical findings are drawn disproportionally from WEIRD (Western, Educated, Industrialized, Rich, and Democratic) populations (Henrich et al., 2010). To this end, much of the research reporting positive relationships between testosterone and mating effort are drawn from a restricted range of populations in which monogamous relationships and direct parental care are the norm. Ellison and Gray (2009) report significant between-population geographical differences in testosterone concentrations, with higher testosterone typically found in males living in modern, Western cultures when compared to small-scale, preindustrial societies (Bribiescas, 1995; Ellison et al., 1989; Ellison & Panter-Brick, 1996). Testosterone also appears to fluctuate across social strata, such that males of higher socioeconomic status, living in urban settings, have higher concentrations than those living in more rural, socioeconomically disadvantaged areas (Gray, Kruger, et al., 2006). These results suggest that testosterone varies along with factors associated with urbanization. The diet, energetic stresses, and disease burden associated with living in rural, preindustrial communities sustained by subsistence food production is, thus, associated with lower average testosterone levels (Gray, Kruger, et al., 2006). More research is required to determine whether rates of infidelity in less urbanized areas are associated with cross-cultural differences in average testosterone concentrations.

Conclusion

Infidelity is a broadly disapproved of (Treas & Giesen, 2000), but widespread (Haversath & Kröger, 2014; Wiederman, 1997), violation of the common expectation of fidelity within romantic relationships. Understanding the underlying mechanisms leading to infidelity is important due to the associated serious relational consequences (Amato & Previti, 2003; Scott et al., 2013), including relationship dissolution and divorce (Harris, 2002). This review sheds light on some of the hormonal mechanisms underlying infidelity by conceptualizing human sexual behavior under the framework of life history theory. Specifically, lower testosterone in fathers (Alvergne et al., 2009; Gettler et al., 2011; Gettler et al., 2012; Gray, Yang, et al., 2006; Muller et al., 2009) and men in committed relationships (Burnham et al., 2003; Caldwell-Hooper et al., 2011; van Anders & Watson, 2006; see Grebe et al., 2019, for meta-analysis) illustrates the mediation of energetic trade-offs between mating and parenting associated with testosterone. On the other hand, relationships characterized by low commitment, satisfaction, and interest in extradyadic sex are associated with elevated testosterone and are suggestive of the predictive potential of testosterone for infidelity.

Evidence consistent with a positive relationship between testosterone and infidelity has been found among men when examining actual infidelity (Booth & Dabbs, 1993; Fisher et al., 2009; Klimas et al., 2019) and related proxies such as sociosexual desire (Edelstein et al., 2011). Findings are less consistent in women, with some research suggesting a similar relationship with testosterone (e.g., Edelstein et al., 2011; Shirazi et al., 2019) and others showing no relationship (e.g., Caldwell-Hooper et al., 2011; van Anders & Goldey, 2010). Other research, however, suggests that hormones such as estradiol and progesterone may be more relevant for understanding infidelity in women. Women with high estradiol relative to progesterone, for example, are more likely to engage in flirting and extrapair sexual behavior (Durante & Li, 2009), display higher levels of relevant proxies such as lower waist-to-hip ratios (reviewed in Dixson, 2016), as well as within-cycle fluctuations in sexual desire (e.g., Roney & Simmons, 2013; but see Grebe et al., 2016; see also Roney & Simmons, 2016) and interest in short-term mating (Shirazi et al., 2019).

Future research will help add to the existing body of work by clarifying direct relationships between hormones and infidelity and including more nuanced definitions that acknowledge potential differences between sexual and emotional infidelity. Furthermore, the inclusion of longitudinal designs and exogenous administration studies will help to disentangle potential bidirectional relationships between testosterone and infidelity, and help determine the extent to which unfaithful behavior can feedback to influence testosterone concentrations. Finally, extending research to include more diverse samples (e.g., older individuals, non-WEIRD populations) and other steroid (e.g., cortisol) and peptide (e.g., oxytocin and vasopressin) hormones will likely be helpful in clarifying relationships with infidelity as well.

References

Allen, E. S., Atkins, D., Baucom, D., Snyder, D., Gordon, K., & Glass, S. (2005). Intrapersonal, interpersonal, and contextual factors in engaging in and responding to extramarital involvement. *Clinical Psychology: Science and Practice, 12*, 101–130.

Alvergne, A., Faurie, C., & Raymond, M. (2009). Variation in testosterone levels and male reproductive effort: Insight from a polygynous human population. *Hormones and Behavior, 56*, 491–497.

Amato, P. R., & Previti, D. (2003). People's reasons for divorcing gender, social class, the life course, and adjustment. *Journal of Family Issues, 24*(5), 602–626.

Apicella, C. L., & Feinberg, D. R. (2009). Voice pitch alters mate-choice-relevant perception in hunter-gatherers. *Proceedings of the Royal Society B: Biological Sciences, 276*(1659), 1077–1082.

Archer, J. (2006). Testosterone and human aggression: An evaluation of the challenge hypothesis. *Neuroscience and Biobehavioral Reviews, 30*, 319–345.

Arnocky, S., Carré, J. M., Bird, B. M., Moreau, B. J. P., Vaillancourt, T., Ortiz, T., . . . Marley, N. (2018). The facial width-to-height ratio predicts sex drive, sociosexuality, and intended infidelity. *Archives of Sexual Behavior, 47*, 1375–1385.

Arnocky, S., Woodruff, N., & Schmitt, D. P. (2016). Men's sociosexuality is sensitive to changes in mate availability. *Personal Relationships, 23*, 172–181.

Arslan, R. C., Schilling, K. M., Gerlach, T. M., & Penke, L. (2021). Using 26,000 diary entries to show ovulatory changes in sexual desire and behavior. *Journal of Personality and Social Psychology*, *121*(2), 410–431.

Barrett, E. S., Tran, V., Thurston, S., Jasienska, G., Furberg, A., Ellison, P. T., . . . Thune, I. (2013). Marriage and motherhood are associated with lower testosterone concentrations in women. *Hormones and Behavior*, *63*(1), 72–79.

Barta, W. D., & Kiene, S. M. (2005). Motivations for infidelity in heterosexual dating couples: The roles of gender, personality, differences, and sociosexual orientation. *Journal of Social and Personal Relationships*, *22*(3), 339–360.

Bellis, M. A., & Baker, R. R. (1990). Do females promote sperm competition? Data for humans. *Animal Behaviour*, *40*(5), 997–999.

Bhasin, S., Storer, T. W., Berman, N., Callegari, C., Clevenger, B., Philips, J., . . . Casaburi, R. (1996). The effects of supraphysiological doses of testosterone on muscles size and strength in normal men. *The New England Journal of Medicine*, *335*(1), 1–7.

Bird, B. M., Jofré, V. S. C., Geniole, S. N., Welker, K. M., Zilioli, S., Maestripieri, D., . . . Carré, J. M. (2016). Does the facial width-to-height ratio map onto variability in men's testosterone concentrations? *Evolution and Human Behavior*, *37*, 392–398.

Bird, B. M., Welling, L. L., Ortiz, T. L., Moreau, B. J., Hansen, S., Emond, M., . . . Carré, J. M. (2016). Effects of exogenous testosterone and mating context on men's preferences for female facial femininity. *Hormones and Behavior*, *85*, 76–85.

Bird, B. M., & Zilioli, S. (2017). Testosterone. In T. K. Shackelford & V. A. Weekes-Shackelford (Eds.), *Encyclopedia of evolutionary psychological science*. Springer.

Booth, A., & Dabbs, M., Jr. (1993). Testosterone and men's marriages. *Social Forces*, *72*(2), 463–477.

Boothroyd, L. G., Cross, C. P., Gray, A. W., Coombes, C., & Gregson-Curtis, K. (2011). Perceiving the facial correlates of sociosexuality: Further evidence. *Personality and Individual Differences*, *50*(3), 422–425.

Bos, P. A., Panksepp, J., Bluthé, R., & van Honk, J. (2012). Acute effects of steroid hormones and neuropeptides on human social-emotional behavior: A review of single administration studies. *Frontiers in Neuroendocrinology*, *33*(1), 17–35.

Braunstein, G. D., Sundwall, D. A., Katz, M., Shifren, J. L., Buster, J. E., Simon, J. A., . . . Watts, N. B. (2005). Safety and efficacy of a testosterone patch for the treatment of hypoactive sexual desire disorder in surgically menopausal women. *Archives of Internal Medicine*, *165*(14), 1582–1589.

Bribiescas, R. G. (1995). Testosterone levels among Aché hunter-gatherer men. *Human Nature*, *7*(2), 163–188.

Burnham, T. C., Chapman, J. F., Gray, P. B., McIntyre, M. H., Lipson, S. F., & Ellison, P. T. (2003). Men in committed, romantic relationships have lower testosterone. *Hormones and Behavior*, *44*, 119–122.

Buster, J. E., Kingsberg, S. A., Aguirre, O., Brown, C., Breaux, J. G., Buch, A., . . . Casson, P. R. (2005). Testosterone patch for low sexual desire in surgically menopausal women: A randomized trial. *Obstetrics & Gynecology*, *105*(5, Part 1), 944–952.

Caldwell-Hooper, A. E., Gangestad, S. W., Thompson, M. E., & Bryan, A. D. (2011). Testosterone and romance: The association of testosterone with relationship commitment and satisfaction in heterosexual men and women. *American Journal of Human Biology*, *23*, 553–555.

Campbell, A. (2013). The evolutionary psychology of women's aggression. *Philosophical Transactions: Biological Sciences*, *368*(1631), 1–11.

Carré, J. M., & Olmstead, N. A. (2015). Social neuroendocrinology of human aggression: Examining the role of competition-induced testosterone dynamics. *Neuroscience*, *286*, 171–186.

Cerda-Molina, A. L., Hernández-Lopez, L., de la O, C. E., Chavira-Ramírez, R., & Mondragón-Ceballos, R. (2013). Changes in men's salivary testosterone and cortisol levels, and in sexual desire after smelling female axillary and vulvar scents. *Frontiers in Endocrinology*, *4*(159), 1–9.

Charles, N. E., & Alexander, G. M. (2011). The association between 2D:4D ratios and sociosexuality: A failure to replicate. *Archives of Sexual Behavior*, *40*, 587–595.

Cherkas, L. F., Oelsner, E. C., Mak, Y. T., Valdes, A., & Spector, T. D. (2004). Genetic influences on female infidelity and number of sexual partners in humans: A linkage and association study of the role of the vasopressin receptor gene (AVPR1A). *Twin Research*, *7*, 649–658.

Clark, A. P. (2004). Self-perceived attractiveness and masculinization predict women's sociosexuality. *Evolution and Human Behaviour*, *25*, 113–124.

Clark, R. V., Wald, J. A., Swerdloff, R. S., Wang, C., Wu, F. C., Bowers, L. D., . . . Matsumoto, A. M. (2019). Large divergence in testosterone concentrations between men and women: Frame of reference for elite athletes in sex-specific competition in sports, a narrative review. *Clinical Endocrinology*, *90*(1), 15–22.

Dabbs, J. M, & Mallinger, A. (1999). High testosterone levels predict low voice pitch among men. *Personality and Individual Differences*, *27*, 801–804.

Dabbs, J. M., & Mohammed, S. (1992). Male and female salivary testosterone concentrations before and after sexual activity. *Physiology & Behavior*, *52*, 195–197.

Del Giudice, M., Angeleri, R., Brizio, A., & Elena, M. R. (2010). The evolution of autistic-like and schizotypal traits: A sexual selection hypothesis. *Frontiers in Psychology*, *1*(41), 1–18.

Del Giudice, M., Gangestad, S. W., & Kaplan, H. S. (2015). Life history theory and evolutionary psychology. In D. M. Buss (Ed.), *The handbook of evolutionary psychology*. Wiley.

de Roda, A. B. L., Martınez-Iñigo, D., de Paul, P., & Yela, C. (1999). Romantic beliefs and myths in Spain. *Spanish Journal of Psychology*, *2*, 64–73.

Dibble, E. R., Goldey, K. L., & van Anders, S. M. (2017). Pair bonding and testosterone in men: Longitudinal evidence for trait and dynamic associations. *Adaptive Human Behavior and Physiology*, *3*, 71–90.

Dixson, B. J. W (2016). Waist-to-hip ratio. In T. K. Shackelford & V. A. Weekes-Shackelford (eds.), *Encyclopedia of evolutionary psychological science*. Springer.

Drigotas, S. M., Safstrom, C. A., & Gentilia, T. (1999). An investment model of dating infidelity. *Journal of Personality and Social Psychology*, *77*(3), 509–524.

Durante, K. M., & Li, N. P. (2009). Oestradiol level and opportunistic mating in women. *Biology Letters*, *5*(2), 179–182.

Durante, K. M., Li, N. P., & Haselton, M. G. (2008). Changes in women's choice of dress across the ovulatory cycle: Naturalistic and laboratory task-based evidence. *Personality and Social Psychology Bulletin*, *34*(11), 1451–1460.

Edelstein, R. S., Chopik, W. J., & Kean, E. L. (2011). Sociosexuality moderates the association between testosterone and relationship status in men and women. *Hormones and Behavior*, *60*, 248–255.

Edelstein, R. S., van Anders, S. M., Chopik, W. J., Goldey, K. L., & Wardecker, B. M. (2014). Dyadic associations between testosterone and relationship quality in couples. *Hormones and Behavior*, *65*, 401–407.

Edwards, D. A., Wetzel, K., & Wyner, D. R. (2006). Intercollegiate soccer: Saliva cortisol and testosterone are elevated during competition, and testosterone is related to status and social connectedness with teammates. *Physiology & Behavior*, *87*, 135–143.

Ellis, B. J., Figueredo, A. J., Brumbach, B. H., & Schlomer, G. L. (2009). Fundamental dimensions of environmental risk: The impact of harsh versus unpredictable environments on the evolution and development of life history strategies. *Human Nature*, *20*, 204–268.

Ellison, P. T., Bribiescas, R. G., Bentley, G. R., Campbell, B. C., Lipson, S. F., Panter-Brick, C., & Hill, K. (2002). Population variation in age-related decline in male salivary testosterone. *Human Reproduction*, *17*(12), 3251–3253.

Ellison, P. T., & Gray, P. B. (Eds.). (2009). *Endocrinology of social relationships*. Harvard University Press.

Ellison, P. T., Lipson, S. F., & Meredith, M. D. (1989). Salivary testosterone levels in males from the Ituri forest of Zaïre. *American Journal of Human Biology*, *1*, 21–24.

Ellison, P. T., & Panter-Brick, C. (1996). Salivary testosterone levels among Tamang and Kamimales of central Nepal. *Human Biology*, *68*(6), 955–965.

Evans, S., Neave, N., Wakelin, D., & Hamilton, C. (2008). The relationship between testosterone and vocal frequencies in human males. *Physiology and Behavior*, *93*, 783–788.

Fales, M. R., Gildersleeve, K. A., & Haselton, M. G. (2014). Exposure to perceived male rivals raises men's testosterone on fertile relative to nonfertile days of their partner's ovulatory cycle. *Hormones and Behavior*, *65*, 454–460.

Farrelly, D., Owens, R., Elliott, H. R., Walden, H. R., & Wetherell, M. A. (2015). The effects of being in a "new relationship" on levels of testosterone in men. *Evolutionary Psychology*, *13*(1), 250–261.

Fincham, F. D., & May, R. W. (2017). Infidelity in romantic relationships. *Current Opinion in Psychology*, *13*, 70–74.

Fisher, M. L. (2004). Female intrasexual competition decreases female facial attractiveness. *Proceedings of the Royal Society B: Biological Sciences*, *271*, 283–285.

Fisher, A. D., Corona, G., Bandini, E., Mannucci, E., Lotti, F., Boddi, V., . . . Maggi, M. (2009). Psychobiological correlates of extramarital affairs and differences between stable and occasional infidelity among men with sexual dysfunctions. *Journal of Sexual Medicine, 6*(3), 866–875.

Fisher, T. D., Moore, Z. T., & Pittenger, M. (2012). Sex on the brain? An examination of frequency of sexual cognitions as a function of gender, erotophilia, and social desirability. *Journal of Sex Research, 49*(1), 69–77.

Fleming, A. S., Steiner, M., & Corter, C. (1997). Cortisol, hedonics, and maternal responsiveness. *Hormones and Behavior, 32*, 85–98.

Flinn, M. V., Ponzi, D., & Muehlenbein, M. P. (2012). Hormonal mechanisms for regulation of aggression in human coalitions. *Human Nature, 23*, 68–88.

Foo, Y. Z., Nakagawa, S., Rhodes, G., & Simmons, L. W. (2017). The effects of sex hormones on immune functions: A meta-analysis. *Biological Reviews, 92*(1), 551–571.

Gangestad, S. W., & Simpson, J. A. (2000). The evolution of human mating: Trade-offs and strategic pluralism. *Behavioral and Brain Sciences, 23*(4), 573–587.

Gangestad, S. W., & Thornhill, R. (2008). Human oestrus. *Proceedings of the Royal Society B: Biological Sciences, 275*(1638), 991–1000.

Geniole, S. N., Bird, B. M., McVittie, J. S., Purcell, R. B., Archer, J., & Carré, J. M. (2020). Is testosterone linked to human aggression? A meta-analytic examination between baseline, dynamic, and manipulated testosterone in human aggression. *Hormones and Behavior, 123*, 104644.

Geniole, S. N., Bird, B. M., Ruddick, E. L., & Carré, J. M. (2017). Effects of competition outcome on testosterone concentrations in humans: An updated meta-analysis. *Hormones and Behavior, 92*, 37–50.

Geniole, S. N., & Carré, J. M. (2018). Human social neuroendocrinology: Review of the rapid effects of testosterone. *Hormones and Behavior, 104*, 192–205.

Gettler, L. T., Kuo, P. X., Rosenbaum, S., Avila, J. L., McDade, T. W., & Kuzawa, C. W. (2019). Sociosexuality, testosterone, and life history status: Prospective associations and longitudinal changes among men in Cebu, Philippines. *Evolution and Human Behavior, 40*, 249–258.

Gettler, L. T., McDade, T. W., Agustin, S. S., Feranil, A. B., & Kuzawa, C. W. (2013). Do testosterone declines during the transition to marriage and fatherhood relate to men's sexual behavior? Evidence from the Philippines. *Hormones and Behavior, 64*, 755–763.

Gettler, L. T., McDade, T. W., Feranil, A. B., & Kuzawa, C. W. (2011). Longitudinal evidence that fatherhood decreases testosterone in human males. *PNAS, 108*(39), 16194–16199.

Gettler, L. T., McKenna, J. J., McDade, T. W., Agustin, S. S., & Kuzawa, C. W. (2012). Does cosleeping contribute to lower testosterone levels in fathers? Evidence from the Philippines. *PLoS One, 7*(9), e41559.

Gildersleeve, K., Haselton, M. G., & Fales, M. R. (2014). Do women's mate preferences change across the ovulatory cycle? A meta-analytic review. *Psychological Bulletin, 140*(5), 1205.

Glass, S., & Wright, T. (1977). The relationship of extramarital sex, length of marriage, and sex differences on marital satisfaction and romanticism: Athanasiou's data reanalyzed. *Journal of Marriage and the Family, 39*, 691–704.

Goldey, K. L., Avery, L. R., & van Anders, S. M. (2014). Sexual fantasies and gender/sex: A multimethod approach with quantitative content analysis and hormonal responses. *The Journal of Sex Research, 51*(8), 917–931.

Grammer, K., Renninger, L., & Fischer, B. (2004). Disco clothing, female sexual motivation, and relationship status: Is she dressed to impress? *The Journal of Sex Research, 41* (1): 66–74.

Gray, P. B. (2003). Marriage, parenting, and testosterone variation among Kenyan Swahili men. *American Journal of Physical Anthropology, 122*, 279–286.

Gray, P. B., Ellison, P. T., & Campbell, B. C. (2007). Testosterone and marriage among the Ariaal men of northern Kenya. *Current Anthropology, 48*(5), 750–755.

Gray, P. B., Kruger, A., Huisman, H. W., Wissing, M. P., & Vorster, H. H. (2006). Predictors of South African male testosterone levels: The THUSA study. *American Journal of Human Biology, 18*, 123–132.

Gray, P. B., Straftis, A. A., Bird, B. M., McHale, T. S., & Zilioli, S. (2020). Human reproductive behavior, life history, and the challenge hypothesis: A 30-year review, retrospective and future directions. *Hormones and Behavior, 123*, 104530.

Gray, P. B., Yang, C. F., & Pope, H. G., Jr. (2006). Fathers have lower salivary testosterone levels than unmarried men and married non-fathers in Beijing, China. *Proceedings of the Royal Society B: Biological Sciences, 273*, 333–339.

Grebe, N. M., Sarafin, R. E., Strenth, C. R., & Zilioli, S. (2019). Pair-bonding, fatherhood, and the role of testosterone: A meta-analytic review. *Neuroscience and Biobehavioral Reviews, 98*, 221–233.

Grebe, N. M., Thompson, M. E., & Gangestad, S. W. (2016). Hormonal predictors of women's extra-pair vs. in-pair sexual attraction in natural cycles: Implications for extended sexuality. *Hormones and Behavior, 78*, 211–219.

Haavio-Mannila, E., & Kontula, O. (2003). Single and double sexual standards in Finland, Estonia, and St. Petersburg. *Journal of Sex Research, 40*, 36–49.

Hahn, A. C., Fisher, C. I., Cobey, K. D., DeBruine, L. M., & Jones, B. C. (2016). A longitudinal analysis of women's salivary testosterone and intrasexual competitiveness. *Psychoneuroendocrinology, 64*, 117–122.

Handelsman, D. J., Yeap, B. B., Flicker, L., Martin, S., Wittert, G. A., & Ly, L. P. (2015). Age-specific population centiles for androgen status in men. *European Journal of Endocrinology, 173*(6), 809–817.

Harris, C. R. (2002). Sexual and romantic jealousy in heterosexual and homosexual adults. *Psychological Science, 13*, 7–12.

Haselton, M. G., Mortezaie, M., Pillsworth, E. G., Bleske-Rechek, A., & Frederick, D. A. (2007). Ovulatory shifts in human female ornamentation: Near ovulation, women dress to impress. *Hormones and Behavior, 51*(1):40–45.

Haversath, J., & Kröger, C. (2014). Extradyadic sex and its predictors in homo- and heterosexuals. *Psychotherapie, Psychosomatik, Medizinische Psychologie, 64*(12), 458–464.

Hellhammer, D. H., Hubert, W., & Schürmeyer, T. (1985). Changes in saliva testosterone after psychological stimulation in men. *Psychoneuroendocrinology, 10*(1), 77–81.

Henrich, J., Heine, S. J., & Norenzayan, A. (2010). The weirdest people in the world? *Behavioral and Brain Sciences, 33*, 61–135.

Hodges-Simeon, C. R., Sobraske, K. N. H., Samore, T., Gurven, M., & Gaulin, S. J. C. (2016). Facial width-to-height (fWHR) is not associated with adolescent testosterone levels. *PLoS One, 11*(4). e0153083.

Holmboe, S. A., Priskorn, L., Jørgensen, N., Skakkebaek, N. E., Linneberg, A., Juul, A., . . . Andersson, A. (2017). Influence of marital status on testosterone levels—A ten year follow-up of 1113 men. *Psychoneuroendocrinology, 80*, 155–161.

Hughes, S. M., & Gallup, G. G., Jr. (2003). Sex differences in morphological predictors of sexual behavior: Shoulder to hip and waist to hip ratios. *Evolution and Human Behavior, 24*(3), 173–178.

Hughes, S. M., & Harrison, M. A. (2017). Your cheatin' voice will tell on you: Detection of past infidelity from voice. *Evolutionary Psychology, 15*(2), 1474704917711513.

Insel, T. R. (2010). The challenge of translation in social neuroscience: A review of oxytocin, vasopressin, and affiliative behavior. *Neuron, 65*(6), 768–779.

Isidori, A. M., Giannetta, E., Gianfrilli, D. Greco, E. A., Bonifacio, V. Aversa, A., . . . Lenzi, A. (2005). Effects of testosterone on sexual function in men: Results of a meta-analysis. *Clinical Endocrinology, 63*(4), 381–394.

Jones, M. (1998). Sociosexuality and motivations for romantic involvement. *Journal of Research in Personality, 32*, 173–182.

Jones, B. C., Hahn, A. C., & DeBruine, L. M. (2019). Ovulation, sex hormones, and women's mating psychology. *Trends in Cognitive Sciences, 23*(1), 51–62.

Kelsey, T. W., Li, L. Q., Mitchell, R. T., Whelan, A., Anderson, R. A., & Wallace, W. H. B. (2014). A validated age-related normative model for male total testosterone shows increasing variance but no decline after age 40 years. *PLoS One, 9*(10): e109346.

Kinsey, A., Pomeroy, W., & Martin, C. (1948). *Sexual behavior in the human male*. W.B. Saunders.

Klapilová, K., Cobey, K. D., Wells, T., Roberts, S. C., Weiss, P., & Havlíček, J. (2014). Current hormonal contraceptive use predicts female extra-pair and dyadic sexual behavior: Evidence based on Czech National Survey data. *Evolutionary Psychology, 12*(1), 147470491401200103.

Klimas, C., Ehlert, U., Lacker, T. J., Waldvogel, P., & Walther, A. (2019). Higher testosterone levels are associated with unfaithful behavior in men. *Biological Psychology, 146*, 107730.

Kokko, H., & Jennions, M. D. (2008). Parental investment, sexual selection and sex ratios. *Journal of Evolutionary Biology, 21*, 919–948.

Kruger, D. J. (2006). Male facial masculinity influences attributions of personality and reproductive strategy. *Personal Relationships, 13*(4), 451–463.

Kuzawa, C., Gettler, L. T., Huang, Y., & McDade, T. W. (2010). Mothers have lower testosterone than non-mothers: Evidence from the Philippines. *Hormones and Behavior, 57*(4–5), 441–447.

Lawson, D. W., Nuñez-de la Mora, A., Cooper, G. D., Prentice, A. M., Moore, S. E., & Sear, R. (2017). Marital status and sleeping arrangements predict salivary testosterone levels in rural Gambian men. *Adaptive Human Behavior and Physiology, 3*, 221–240.

Lefevre, C. E., Lewis, G. J., Perrett, D. I., & Penke, L. (2013). Telling facial metrics: Facial width is associated with testosterone levels in men. *Evolution and Human Behavior, 34*(4), 273–279.

López, H. H., Hay, A. C., & Conklin, P. H. (2009). Attractive men induce testosterone and cortisol release in women. *Hormones and Behavior, 56*, 84–92.

Luo, S., Cartun, M., & Snider, A. (2010). Assessing extradyadic behavior: A review, a new measure, and two new models. *Personality and Individual Differences, 49*, 155–163.

Maestripieri, D., Klimczuk, A., Traficonte, D., & Wilson, M. C. (2014). Ethnicity-related variation in sexual promiscuity, relationship status, and testosterone levels in men. *Evolutionary Behavioral Sciences, 8*(2), 96.

Manning, J. T., Barley, L., Walton, J., Lewis-Jones, D. I., Trivers, R. L., Singh, D., . . . Szwed, A.(2000). The 2nd:4th digit ratio, sexual dimorphism, population differences, and reproductive success: Evidence for sexually antagonistic genes? *Evolution and Human Behavior, 21*(3), 163–183.

Marcinkowska, U. M., Hahn, A. C., Little, A. C., DeBruine, L. M., & Jones, B. C. (2019). No evidence that women using oral contraceptives have weaker preferences for masculine characteristics in men's faces. *PloS One, 14*(1). e0210162.

Marcinkowska, U. M., Helle, S., Jones, B. C., & Jasienska, G. (2019). Does testosterone predict women's preference for facial masculinity? *PloS One, 14*(2). e0210636.

Martins, A., Pereira, M., Andrade, R., Dattilio, F. M., Narciso, I., & Canavarro, M. C. (2016). Infidelity in dating relationships: Gender-specific correlates of face-to-face and online extradyadic involvement. *Archives of Sexual Behavior, 45*, 193–205.

Mattingly, B. A., Clark, E. M., Weidler, D. J., Bullock, M., Hackathorn, J., & Blankmeyer, K. (2011). Sociosexual orientation, commitment, and infidelity: A mediation analysis. *Journal of Social Psychology, 151*(3), 222–226.

Maynard-Smith, J. M., 1989. *Evolutionary genetics*. Oxford University Press.

Mazur, A., & Michalek, J. (1998). Marriage, divorce, and male testosterone. *Social Forces, 77*(1), 315–330.

McAnulty, R., & Brineman, J. (2007). Infidelity in dating relationships. *Annual Review of Sex Research, 18*, 94–114.

McIntyre, M., Gangestad, S. W., Gray, P. B., Chapman, J. F., Burnham, T. C., O'Rourke, M. T., . . . Thornhill, R. (2006). Romantic involvement often reduces men's testosterone levels—but not always: The moderating role of extrapair sexual interest. *Journal of Personality and Social Psychology, 91*(4), 642–651.

Miller, S. L., & Maner, J. K. (2010). Scent of a woman: Men's testosterone responses to olfactory ovulation cues. *Psychological Science, 21*(2), 276–283.

Miller, S. L., Maner, J. K., & McNulty, J. K. (2012). Adaptive attunement to the sex of individuals at a competition: The ratio of opposite- to same-sex individuals correlates with changes in competitors' testosterone levels. *Evolution and Human Behavior, 33*, 57–63.

Motta-Mena, N. V., & Puts, D. A. (2017). Endocrinology of human female sexuality, mating, and reproductive behavior. *Hormones and Behavior, 91*, 19–35.

Muehlenbein, M. P., & Bribiescas, R. G. (2005). Testosterone-mediated immune functions and male life histories. *American Journal of Human Biology, 17*, 527–558.

Muller, M. N., Marlowe, F. W., Bugumba, R., & Ellison, P. T. (2009). Testosterone and paternal care in East African foragers and pastoralists. *Proceedings of the Royal Society B: Biological Sciences, 276*, 347–354.

Nettle, D. (2005). An evolutionary approach to the extraversion continuum. *Evolution and Human Behavior, 26*(4), 363–373.

O'Connor, J. J., Pisanski, K., Tigue, C. C., Fraccaro, P. J., & Feinberg, D. R. (2014). Perceptions of infidelity risk predict women's preferences for low male voice pitch in short-term over long-term relationship contexts. *Personality and Individual Differences, 56*, 73–77.

O'Connor, J. J., Re, D. E., & Feinberg, D. R. (2011). Voice pitch influences perceptions of sexual infidelity. *Evolutionary Psychology, 9*(1), 147470491100900109.

Oliveira, T., Gouveia, M. J., & Oliveira, R. F. (2009). Testosterone responsiveness to winning and losing experiences in female soccer players. *Psychoneuroendocrinology, 34*, 1056–1064.

Ostovich, J. M., & Sabini, J. (2004). How are sociosexuality, sex drive, and lifetime number of sexual partners related? *Personality and Social Psychology Bulletin, 30*(10), 1255–1266.

Penke, L., & Asendorpf, J. (2008). Beyond global sociosexual orientations: A more differentiated look at sociosexuality and its effects on courtship and romantic relationships. *Journal of Personality and Social Psychology*, *95*, 1113–1135.

Penton-Voak, I. S., & Chen, J. Y. (2004). High salivary testosterone is linked to masculine male facial appearance in humans. *Evolution and Human Behavior*, *25*, 229–241.

Penton-Voak, I. S., Perrett, D. I., Castles, D. L., Kobayashi, T., Burt, D. M., Murray, L. K., & Minamisawa, R. (1999). Menstrual cycle alters face preference. *Nature*, *399*(6738), 741–742.

Peters, M., Simmons, L. W., & Rhodes, G. (2008). Testosterone is associated with mating success but not attractiveness or masculinity in human males. *Animal Behaviour*, *76*, 297–303.

Pillsworth, E. G., Haselton, M. G., & Buss, D. M. (2004). Ovulatory shifts in female sexual desire. *Journal of Sex Research*, *41*(1), 55–65.

Pollet, T. V., van der Meij, L., Cobey, K. D., & Buunk, A. P. (2011). Testosterone levels and their associations with lifetime number of opposite sex partners and remarriage in a large sample of American elderly men and women. *Hormones and Behavior*, *60*(1), 72–77.

Polo, P., Muñoz-Reyes, J. A., Pita, M., Shackelford, T. K., & Fink, B. (2019). Testosterone-dependent facial and body traits predict men's sociosexual attitudes and behaviors. *American Journal of Human Biology*, *31*(3), 1–10.

Ponzi, D., Henry, A., Kubicki, K., Nickels, N., Wilson, M. C., & Maestripieri, D. (2016). Autistic-like traits, sociosexuality, and hormonal responses to socially stressful and sexually arousing stimuli in male college students. *Adaptive Human Behavior and Physiology*, *2*, 150–165.

Puts, D. A. (2010). Beauty and the beast: Mechanisms of sexual selection in humans. *Evolution and Human Behavior*, *31*(3), 157–175.

Puts, D. A. (2016). Human sexual selection. *Current Opinion in Psychology*, *7*, 28–32.

Puts, D. A., Apicella, C. L., & Cárdenas, R. A. (2012). Masculine voices signal men's threat potential in forager and industrial societies. *Proceedings of the Royal Society B: Biological Sciences*, *279*, 601–609.

Puts, D. A., Pope, L. E., Hill, A. K., Cárdenas, R. A., Welling, L. L. M., Wheatley, J. R., . . . Breedlove, S. M. (2015). Fulfilling desire: Evidence for negative feedback between men's testosterone, sociosexual psychology, and sexual partner number. *Hormones and Behavior*, *70*, 14–21.

Raisanen, J. C., Chadwick, S. B., Michalek, N., & van Anders, S. M. (2018). Average associations between sexual desire, testosterone, and stress in women and men over time. *Archives of Sexual Behavior*, *47*, 1613–1631.

Randler, C., Ebenhöh, N., Fischer, A., Höchel, S., Schroff, C., Stoll, J. C., . . . Piffer, D. (2012). Eveningness is related to men's mating success. *Personality and Individual Differences*, *53*(3), 263–267.

Rhodes, G., Simmons, L. W., & Peters, M. (2005). Attractiveness and sexual behavior: Does attractiveness enhance mating success? *Evolution and Human Behavior*, *26*(2), 186–201.

Rodrigues, D., & Lopes, D. (2017). Sociosexuality, commitment, and sexual desire for an attractive person. *Archives of Sexual Behavior*, *46*, 775–788.

Rodrigues, D., Lopes, D., & Pereira, M. (2017). Sociosexuality, commitment, sexual infidelity, and perceptions of infidelity: Data from the Second Love web site. *Journal of Sex Research*, *54*(2), 241–253.

Ronay, R., & von Hippel, W. (2010). The presence of an attractive women elevates testosterone and physical risk taking in young men. *Social Psychological and Personality Science*, *1*(1), 57–64.

Roney, J. R. (2015). Evolutionary psychology and endocrinology. In D. M. Buss (Ed.), *The handbook of evolutionary psychology* (pp. 1067–1083). Wiley.

Roney, J. R., & Gettler, L. T. (2015). The role of testosterone in human romantic relationships. *Current Opinion in Psychology*, *1*, 81–86.

Roney, J. R., Hanson, K. N., Durante, K. M., & Maestripieri, D. (2006). Reading men's faces: Women's mate attractiveness judgments track men's testosterone and interest in infants. *Proceedings of the Royal Society B: Biological Sciences*, *273*, 2169–2175.

Roney, J. R., Lukaszewski, A. W., & Simmons, Z. L. (2007). Rapid endocrine responses of young men to social interactions with young women. *Hormones and Behavior*, *52*, 326–333.

Roney, J. R., & Simmons, Z. L. (2012). Men smelling women: Null effects of exposure to ovulatory sweat on men's testosterone. *Evolutionary Psychology*, *10*(4), 703–713.

Roney, J. R., & Simmons, Z. L. (2013). Hormonal predictors of sexual motivation in natural menstrual cycles. *Hormones and Behavior*, *63*(4), 636–645.

Roney, J. R., & Simmons, Z. L. (2016). Within-cycle fluctuations in progesterone negatively predict changes in both in-pair and extra-pair desire among partnered women. *Hormones and Behavior*, *81*, 45–52.

Sakaguchi, K., Oki, M., Honma, S., Uehara, H., & Hasegawa, T. (2007). The lower salivary testosterone levels among unmarried and married sexually active men. *Journal of Ethology, 25*, 223–229.

Schmitt, D. P. (2004). The Big Five related to risky sexual behaviour across 10 world regions: Differential personality associations of sexual promiscuity and relationship infidelity. *European Journal of Personality, 18*, 301–319.

Schmitt, D. P. (2007). Sexual strategies across sexual orientations: How personality traits and culture relate to sociosexuality among gays, lesbians, bisexuals, and heterosexuals. *Journal of Psychology & Human Sexuality, 18*(2–3), 183–214.

Schmitt, D. P., & Shackelford, T. K. (2008). Big Five traits related to short-term mating: From personality to promiscuity across 46 nations. *Evolutionary Psychology, 6*, 246–282.

Scott, S. B., Rhoades, G. K., Stanley, S. M., Allen, E. S., & Markman, H. J. (2013). Reasons for divorce and recollections of premarital intervention: Implications for improving relationship education. *Couple & Family Psychology, 2*(2), 131–145.

Seal, D. W., Agostinelli, G., & Hannett, G. A. (1994). Extradyadic romantic involvement: Moderating effects of sociosexuality and gender. *Sex Roles, 3*(1/2), 1–22.

Shaw, A. M. M., Rhoades, G. K., Allen, E. S., Stanley, S. M., & Markman, H. J. (2013). Predictors of extradyadic sexual involvement in unmarried opposite-sex relationships. *Journal of Sex Research, 50*(6), 598–610.

Shirazi, T. N., Self, H., Dawood, K., Rosenfield, K. A., Penke, L., Carré, J. M., . . . Puts, D. A. (2019). Hormonal predictors of women's sexual motivation. *Evolution and Human Behavior, 40*, 336–344.

Simpson, J. A., & Gangestad, S. W. (1991). Individual differences in sociosexuality: Evidence for convergent and discriminant validity. *Personality Processes and Individual Differences, 60*(6), 870–883.

Simpson, J., Wilson, C., & Winterheld, H. (2004). Sociosexuality and romantic relationships. In J. H. Harvey, A. Wenzel, & S. Sprecher (Eds.), *The handbook of sexuality in close relationships* (pp. 87–112). Erlbaum.

Stoléru, S. G., Ennaji, A., Cournot, A., & Spira, A. (1993). LH pulsatile secretion and testosterone blood levels are influenced by sexual arousal in human males. *Psychoneuroendocrinology, 18*(3), 205–218.

Swaddle, J. P., & Reierson, G. W. (2002). Testosterone increases perceived dominance but not attractiveness in human males. *Proceedings of the Royal Society B: Biological Sciences, 269*, 2285–2289.

Thornhill, R., & Gangestad, S. W. (2006). Facial sexual dimorphism, developmental stability, and susceptibility to disease in men and women. *Evolution and Human Behavior, 27*(2), 131–144.

Treas, J., & Giesen, D. (2000). Sexual infidelity among married and cohabitating Americans. *Journal of Marriage and the Family, 62*, 48–60.

Trivers, R. L. (1972). Parental investment and sexual selection. In B. Campbell (Ed.), *Sexual selection and the descent of man: 1871–1971* (pp. 136–179). Aldine.

Valeggia, C., & Ellison, P. T. (2009). Interactions between metabolic and reproductive functions in the resumption of postpartum fecundity. *American Journal of Human Biology, 21*(4), 559–566.

Valentine, K. A., Li, N. P., Penke, L., & Perrett, D. I. (2014). Judging a man by the width of his face: The role of facial ratios and dominance in mate choice at speed dating events. *Psychological Science, 25*(3), 806–811.

van Anders, S. M. (2012). Testosterone and sexual desire in healthy women and men. *Archives of Sexual Behavior, 41*, 1471–1484.

van Anders, S. M. (2013). Beyond masculinity: Testosterone, gender/sex, and human social behavior in a comparative context. *Frontiers in Neuroendocrinology, 34*, 198–210.

van Anders, S. M., & Dunn, E. J. (2009). Are gonadal steroids linked with orgasm perceptions and sexual assertiveness in women and men? *Hormones and Behavior, 56*, 206–213.

van Anders, S. M., & Goldey, K. L. (2010). Testosterone and partnering are linked via relationship status for women and "relationship orientation" for men. *Hormones and Behavior, 58*, 820–826.

van Anders, S. M., Hamilton, L. D., Schmidt, N., & Watson, N. V. (2007). Associations between testosterone secretion and sexual activity in women. *Hormones and Behavior, 51*(4), 477–482.

van Anders, S. M., Hamilton, L. D., & Watson, N. V. (2007). Multiple partners are associated with higher testosterone in North American men and women. *Hormones and Behavior, 51*, 454–459.

van Anders, S. M., & Watson, N. V. (2006). Relationship status and testosterone in North American heterosexual and non-heterosexual men and women: Cross-sectional and longitudinal data. *Psychoneuroendocrinology, 31*, 715–723.

van Anders, S. M., & Watson, N. V. (2007). Testosterone levels in women and men who are single, in long-distance relationships, or same-city relationships. *Hormones and Behavior, 51*, 286–291.

van der Meij, L., Almela, M., Buunk, A. P., Fawcett, T. W., & Salvador, A. (2012). Men with elevated testosterone levels show more affiliative behaviors during interactions with women. *Proceedings of the Royal Society B: Biological Sciences, 279*, 202–208.

van der Meij, L., Buunk, A. P., van den Sande, J., & Salvador, A. (2008). The presence of a woman increases testosterone in aggressive dominant men. *Hormones and Behavior, 54*(5), 640–644.

Verdonck, A., Gaethofs, M., Carels, C., & de Zegher, F. (1999). Effect of low-dose testosterone treatment on craniofacial growth in boys with delayed puberty. *European Journal of Orthodontics, 21*, 137–143.

Wallen, K. (2001). Sex and context: Hormones and primate sexual motivation. *Hormones and Behavior, 40*(2), 339–357.

Walum, H., Lichtenstein, P., Neiderhiser, J. M., Reiss, D., Ganiban, J. M., & Spotts, E. L., . . . Westberg, L. (2012). Variation in the oxytocin receptor gene is associated with pair-bonding and social behavior. *Biological Psychiatry, 71*, 419–426.

Walum, H., Westberg, L., Henningsson, S., Neiderhiser, J. M., Reiss, D., Igl, W., . . . Lichtenstein, P. (2008). Genetic variation in the vasopressin receptor 1a gene (AVPR1A) associates with pairbonding behavior in humans. *Proceedings of the National Academy of Sciences, 105*, 4153–14156.

Welker, K. M., Bird, B. M., & Arnocky, S. (2016). Commentary: Facial width-to-height ratio (fWHR) is not associated with adolescent testosterone levels. *Frontiers in Psychology, 7*(1745). 1–3.

Welling, L. L. M., Jones, B. C., DeBruine, L. M., Conway, C. A., Smith, M. J. L., Little, A. C., . . . Al-Dujaili, E. A. S. (2007). Raised salivary testosterone in women is associated with increased attraction to masculine faces. *Hormones and Behavior, 52*, 156–161.

Welling, L. L., Jones, B. C., DeBruine, L. M., Smith, F. G., Feinberg, D. R., Little, A. C., & Al-Dujaili, E. A. (2008). Men report stronger attraction to femininity in women's faces when their testosterone levels are high. *Hormones and Behavior, 54*(5), 703–708.

Wiederman, M. W. (1997). Extramarital sex: Prevalence and correlates in a national survey. *Journal of Sex Research, 34*(2), 167–174.

Wilson, M. C., Zilioli, S., Ponzi, D., Henry, A., Kubicki, K., Nickels, N., . . . Maestripieri, D. (2015). Cortisol reactivity to psychosocial stress mediates the relationship between extraversion and sociosexuality. *Personality and Individual Differences, 86*, 427–431.

Wright, T. M., & Reise, S. P. (1997). Personality and unrestricted sexual behavior: Correlations of sociosexuality in Caucasian and Asian college students. *Journal of Research in Personality, 31*(2), 166–192.

Wysocki, D. K., & Childers, C. D. (2011). "Let my fingers do the talking": Sexting and infidelity in cyberspace. *Sexuality and Culture, 15*, 217–239.

Zietsch, B. P., Westberg, L., Santtila, P., & Jern, P. (2015). Genetic analysis of human extrapair mating: Heritability, between-sex correlation, and receptor genes for vasopressin and oxytocin. *Evolution and Human Behavior, 36*(2), 130–136.

Zilioli, S., & Bird, B. M. (2017). Functional significance of men's testosterone reactivity to social stimuli. *Frontiers in Neuroendocrinology, 47*, 1–18.

Zilioli, S., Ponzi, D., Henry, A., Kubicki, K., Nickels, N., Wilson, M. C., . . . Maestripieri, D. (2016). Interest in babies negatively predicts testosterone responses to sexual visual stimuli among heterosexual young men. *Psychological Science, 27*(1), 114–118.

Zilioli, S., & Watson, N. V. (2014). Testosterone across successive competitions: Evidence for a "winner effect" in humans? *Psychoneuroendocrinology, 47*, 1–9.

CHAPTER 4

Operational Sex Ratio and Infidelity

Daniel J. Kruger

> **Abstract**
> The operational sex ratio is a powerful influence on behavior in humans and other species. Although stable on an evolutionary time scale, specific populations may have an imbalanced sex ratio. Following the economic patterns of supply and demand, the rare sex is more valuable in the reproductive market and has lower mating competition and greater selectivity for partners. Because men and women have somewhat divergent reproductive strategies, imbalances in the sex ratio have differential effects. Men leverage their market scarcity for greater sexual access while avoiding long-term relationship commitments. Lower sex ratios, where men are less numerous, are associated with more promiscuous mating strategies, higher rates of infidelity, and low relationship stability. Women can leverage their market scarcity in high sex ratio populations to secure commitment from partners, marry at earlier ages, and obtain greater resource investment; however, women's ability to pursue infidelity or multiple relationships is typically constrained by cultural practices regulating female sexuality. High sex ratios are associated with greater emphasis on traditional sex roles and norms that both protect and constrain women. Harsh penalties, including death, are possible consequences of women violating cultural norms in such societies. In part due to rates of infidelity, biased sex ratios create important implications for social conditions and public health.
>
> **Key Words:** operational sex ratio, demography, infidelity, mating strategies, intrasexual competition

Introduction to the Sex Ratio

Darwin (1871) recognized the importance of the ratio of females and males in a population and deduced that a species' sex ratio was usually nearly balanced over evolutionary time scales. On average, males and females in a population will have equivalent reproductive success because each offspring has one genetic mother and one genetic father. If there are more of one sex in a population than the other, the scarcer sex will have higher average reproductive success and selection will favor the production of the scarcer sex. Thus, a stable equilibrium is generated on an evolutionary time scale. Darwin's (1871) textual description of influential factors related to the sex ratio would be formalized decades later in mathematical models by Düsing (1884) and Fisher (1930).

The numerical balance of males and females occurs on an evolutionary time scale; at any given point in time, however, some human populations will exhibit imbalanced sex ratios (Darwin, 1871). Because of the larger necessary investment required for females, females have much lower potential reproductive output than males. Thus, females are more discriminating in selecting mates and males expend comparatively more effort in acquiring and retaining mates in most animal and all mammalian species (Trivers, 1972). Following the economic patterns of supply and demand, the rare sex is more valuable in the mating market (Fisher, 1958). Because men and women have somewhat divergent reproductive strategies, imbalances in the sex ratio have differential effects consistent with the strategies of each sex. Females are the limiting factor in reproduction in most animal and all mammalian species because they provide most of the physiological resources required for reproduction. Thus, females are more discriminating in selecting mates and males expend comparatively more effort in acquiring and retaining mates (Trivers, 1972).

Definitions of the Sex Ratio

Emlen and Oring (1977) originally defined the operational sex ratio (OSR) as the ratio of sexually active males to sexually receptive females in a population, multiplied by 100. Thus, an OSR of 100 is a sex ratio with balanced proportions of males and females. An OSR below 100 is considered a low sex ratio representing a female-biased population (e.g., more available females than males). An OSR above 100 is considered a high sex ratio representing a male-biased population (e.g., more available males than females). It may be more difficult to determine the actual number of sexually active males and sexually receptive females in human populations than in other species. Researchers have operationally defined the human OSR in terms of raw population counts (e.g., Barber, 2000) and as the ratio of unmarried adult men to unmarried adult women (e.g., Kruger et al., 2010). Because the reproductive strategies of men and women are somewhat divergent, imbalances in the OSR exhibit directional effects consistent with the strategies of each sex. Some researchers use the adult sex ratio (ASR), the proportion of adult males in the population (Liker et al., 2014).

Consequences of Biased Sex Ratios Across Species

Understanding behavioral patterns across species helps inform our understanding of our own species (Tinbergen, 1963). We share evolutionary heritage with our very distant relatives and are part of the natural world despite our complex cultures and advanced technological capacities. The sex ratio influences reproductive and related behaviors across species from insects to mammals, including katydids, pipefish, frogs, squirrels, macaques, chimpanzees, and humans (Berglund, 1994; Elmberg, 1990; Emlen & Oring, 1977; Gwynne, 1990; Kvanermo & Ahnesjö, 1996; Michener & McLean, 1996; Mitani et al., 1996; Symington, 1987; Takahashi, 2001; Valero et al., 2006). There is a general pattern whereby imbalances in the sex ratio result in greater leverage in reproductive dynamics for the rare sex. There is greater competition among males for female partners when the sex ratio is more male-biased and greater competition among females for male partners when the sex ratio is more female-biased (e.g., Gwynne, 1991; Mills & Reynolds, 2003).

Even insects demonstrate the influence of sex ratio. Both female and male katydids (bush crickets) are more selective in choosing mating partners when their own sex is scarce (Gwynne & Simmons, 1990). Female coreid bugs glue their eggs to the backs of other coreid bugs because this decreases their vulnerability to predation. In this monogamous insect species, the females are usually not very selective of the individuals hosting their eggs; however, when researchers induced a male-biased sex ratio, females were more likely to glue their eggs to the backs of the males who fertilized the eggs (Kaitala & Miettinen, 1997). For the males, carrying the eggs represents a form of paternal investment and may also interfere with male attempts to pursue additional mates.

The two-spotted goby is a small, socially monogamous fish living in the eastern Atlantic Ocean. Males become territorial and create nests under stones in the sand on the seafloor during the summer mating season. When males successfully attract females and fertilize their eggs, they will guard the eggs until they hatch. Over the course of the mating season, the sex ratio gradually transitions from female-biased to male-biased. At the beginning of the short breeding season, there is intense male competition and intensive male courtship of females. This gradually transitions to intense female–female competition and intensive female courtship of males (Forsgren et al., 2004).

Male Panorpa scorpionflies have two contrasting mating strategies; they can attract female mating partners by offering a dead insect as a nutritional gift or they can coerce females into copulation by holding their wings without providing a gift. Each strategy has costs and benefits for males. Nutritional gifts are a form of paternal investment that increases the likelihood of the production of viable offspring, but prey insects are limited and hunting them exposes males to predation risks. More male-biased sex ratios intensify male competition and make prey insects more difficult to acquire. Males are more likely to use a forced copulation strategy in these male-biased environments (Thornhill, 1980).

Across nonhuman primates, males compete more intensely for fewer females as sex ratios become increasingly male-biased. Both male body size and sexual size dimorphism (the size of males compared to females) increase, consistent with greater levels of conflict between males (Mitani et al., 1996). Spider monkeys usually have a very female-biased population (Chapman et al., 1989; Symington, 1987; Valero et al., 2006); however, the OSR for one wild spider monkey population in the Yucatan increased from 58.8 in 2000 to 100.0 in 2002 as an increasing number of females became pregnant. Males who were used to having higher selective power due to their scarcity experienced increasing competition with other males, resulting in the first documented fatal intragroup coalitional aggression in spider monkeys (Valero et al., 2006).

Infidelity and the Sex Ratio in Other Species

Snapping shrimp are socially monogamous and territorial; mated pairs establish a common habitat and defend it together. After researchers created a very female-biased sex ratio, males were more likely to abandon their mates and leave their commonly established territories (Mathews, 2002). Female-biased sex ratios also destabilize monogamous bonds in other aquatic animals, such as the rainbow cichlid (Keenleyside, 1983) and Kentish plover (Székely et al., 1999).

Across avian species, divorce rates (separation from previous-year partners in species with long-term pair bonds) are higher in birds with female-biased sex ratios, but infidelity rates are higher in birds with male-biased sex ratios (Liker et al., 2014). Pair-bonded males may initiate divorce in response to their partner's infidelity (Moody et al., 2005) or may switch mates when unmated females are readily available in female-biased populations (Poirier et al., 2003). Unmated females are more efficient in poaching paired males than unmated males are in poaching paired females. Deserting males will leave their territory and establish a new territory; however, females can be evicted from their territories by harassment from other females (Taborsky & Taborsky, 1999). Imbalanced sex ratios are also associated with short-term pair bonding; when females outnumber males, males are more frequently polygamous. When males outnumber females, females are more frequently polygamous (Liker et al., 2014). The sex ratio has a weaker effect on infidelity in polygynous bird species than in monogamous species because females are less constrained to mate with their preferred mate in polygamous mating systems (Liker et al., 2014).

High-ranking males have the most opportunities to mate with highly fecund females in primate societies, although lower-ranking males have increased mating opportunities when the sex ratio is female-biased. Dominant macaque males can control females and ward off competitors when the sex ratio is balanced or female-biased, but when there are more females than males it becomes more difficult for the dominant males to monitor all the fecund females (Berard et al., 1993). When females are more numerous, it is easier for them to evade the watch of the dominant male and mate surreptitiously with other males, weakening the relationship between a male's social rank and his reproductive success (Berard et al., 1993). There is a similar dynamic for troop membership, which enhances a male macaque's reproductive success when the OSR is equal or male-biased, as male troop coalitions are better able to protect their females from nontroop males (Takahashi, 2001). However, female biased OSRs make it easier for nontroop males to infiltrate troops and mate with females because troop males cannot simultaneously guard all fecund females (Takahashi, 2001).

In species in which the sex roles are reversed after gametic production (i.e., females invest more in larger gametes, but males invest more in offspring afterward), males make a greater overall parental contribution compared to females and females display greater intrasexual competition for partners than do males and have brighter coloration (Berglund & Rosenqvist, 2003). Males in the Syngnathidae family of pipefish, seahorses, and seadragons have brood pouches that receive the eggs of female mates and fertilize them internally. Males carry their offspring for several weeks until they hatch and swim away. Because of the required parental investment, male pipefish predominantly engage in monogamous behavior, even though the local sex ratio is female-biased for most of the mating season. Female pipefish without mates often attempt to poach male partners from mated females, but mated females are vigilant to mate-poaching attempts and will disrupt them (Matsumoto & Yanagisawa, 2001). Males are sometimes receptive to extrapair copulations when they are not disrupted by their partners.

Patterns Associated With Biased Human Sex Ratios

The economics of supply and demand affect what individuals can demand from prospective mates, and human preferences for potential romantic or sexual partners in part reflect the differential roles and contributions made by men and women in successful reproduction. There is considerable overlap in men's and women's criteria for potential partners, but there is also divergence following reproductively relevant attributes. Both sexes prefer partners who exhibit characteristics such as kindness, understanding, and intelligence (Buss, 1989; Kenrick & Simpson, 1997).

Women and men actively seek the resources related to reproductive value that the opposite sex provides in reproductive relationships (Kruger, 2008). Women provide nearly all the physiological investment in offspring and the majority of the nonphysiological parental investment; however, men's parental investment is much larger than that of other male primates (Buss & Schmitt, 1993; Geary & Flinn, 2001). Paternal investment may enhance the child's reproductive success (Geary, 2005). Investment from fathers promotes positive child outcomes (Lamb, 2004) and protects against negative outcomes such as delinquency (Harris, 2002) in modern populations. Children in foraging populations who grow up without a father present suffer higher mortality rates, indicating the importance of paternal investment throughout our evolutionary history (Hill & Hurtado, 1996). Men seek as partners women that display cues of fecundity, the physiological potential for bearing offspring, whereas women prefer men that display the ability and willingness to commit to a long-term relationship and provide substantial paternal investment (Buss, 1989). Men with higher social status and greater resource control have higher reproductive success across a wide variety of societies (Hopcroft, 2006). Men across many cultures have historically preferred chastity in a potential spouse, as this assures men that their paternal investment will be directed to their own offspring (Barber, 2000).

In populations with male-biased sex ratios, males compete more intensely for fewer females, and females have greater power in choosing partners. These factors raise the quality of valued male attributes necessary for securing female partners. In male-biased populations, men offer more resources to potential relationship partners, invest more time in wooing, are more emotionally invested in interactions with relationship partners, and make greater effort to advertise their potential for long-term resource investment

(Guttentag & Secord, 1983). Men compete more so in signals of both paternal investment and relationship commitment (Pedersen, 1991). Women have higher expectations for husbands to be of relatively higher social status, to be kind, loving, and generous, and to share the responsibilities of parenting (Guttentag & Secord, 1983). Men who are relatively lower in socioeconomic status have an especially difficult time securing a spouse when there is a surplus of men relative to women (Pollet & Nettle, 2007).

Because women can secure male commitment earlier in relationships, they tend to marry at younger ages (Kruger et al., 2010). Some men also marry at younger ages as they have greater incentives to secure a prospective partner before another man does. The variance in male marital age increases as the population becomes increasingly male-biased, because men need to acquire greater social status and resources to be considered eligible for marriage, which can take considerable time and effort (Kruger et al., 2010). Women in high sex ratio societies can enhance their value in the marriage market by making sexual access a scarce commodity (Guttentag & Secord, 1983). Both women and men claim to be less willing to engage in uncommitted sexual relationships when women are scarce (Kandrik et al., 2015).

In female-biased populations, women compete more intensely for male partners and men have lower requirements for securing relationships with women. Women compete most intensely in the attributes related to female mate value that men seek in partners, such as fecundity and sexual availability (Cunningham, 1986; Tesser & Martin, 1996). These attributes are emphasized in fashion trends for revealing clothing, such as shorter skirt lengths, which advertise sexuality and fecundity (Barber, 1999; Time Out New York, 2007). Women are more self-conscious about physical appearances for both themselves and other women. Women will both wear revealing clothing and derogate other women for wearing the same revealing fashions that they display themselves (Guttentag & Secord, 1983; Time Out New York, 2007). Men have lower incentives to provide relationship commitment and paternal investment when women are more numerous than men (Pederson, 1991). Female-biased sex ratios are associated with lower paternal investment, more out-of-wedlock births and single mother households, and higher divorce rates (Guttentag & Secord, 1983; Trent & South, 1989). Promiscuous mating strategies are more prevalent in women in nations with female biased sex ratios (Schmitt, 2005).

Polygyny, polyandry, and the Sex Ratio

The higher the degree of polygyny in a population, the degree to which high status men are able to attract and/or retain multiple female partners, the higher the effective sex ratio will be. For every woman who is polygynously mated, there is one less woman available to other men. A polygynous population with a numerical balance of reproductive aged men and women may have an effectively male-biased sex ratio (Hendrix, 1996). The degree of polygyny will constrain the effects of female numerical surplus, as well as exacerbate male competition in balanced or male-biased populations. The proportion of polygynously married men is higher when the sex ratio is more female-biased (Pollet & Nettle, 2009). Higher degrees of polygyny are associated with greater male mating competition (Kruger, 2010). Polyandry, in which one woman is married to multiple men, is more prevalent in male-biased populations, especially those which are more egalitarian in gender roles and norms (Starkweather & Hames, 2012).

Historical Patterns in Cultures With Biased Human Sex Ratios

The frequent invasions of Germanic tribes during and after the collapse of the Western Roman Empire corresponded with a reduction in the European population and the abandonment of cities (Herlihy, 1973). Most people engaged in subsistence agriculture in rural areas, and the need for agricultural labor generated a strong preference for sons (Coleman, 1976). Preferential treatment of sons resulted in a high sex ratio, which increased along with the size of the household (Herlihy, 1973). Due to the shortage of adult women, women who survived to reproductive age were highly valued (Herlihy, 1973). These male-biased populations saw the emergence of "Courtly love," whereby men emphasize devotion to their partners, tenderness, and avoidance of hedonistic pleasure. Many men were unable to marry, and some of these men established unconsummated relationships devoted to the approval of a woman who was already married (Guttentag & Secord, 1983).

In the late Middle Ages, the Western European sex ratio became female-biased because of the loss of men to the Crusades, monasteries, and differential mortality from plagues of infectious diseases (Herlihy, 1976). The redevelopment of urban areas freed women from the physical labor of agriculture and extended their longevity, facilitating an expansion of the population. Over time, marriage payments gradually shifted from contributions to the woman's family (bride prices) to contributions to the man's family (dowries; Guttentag & Secord, 1983). Many women were unable to marry because of the relative scarcity of men as well as the reluctance of these men to marry. In this environment with relatively lower female selective power, sexually libertarian male bachelors proliferated (Herlihy, 1974). Beguine communities, resembling quasi-secular communes of women, produced feminist literature that was radical for the time, although the general female population was largely illiterate and uneducated and thus these writings generated little support (Bolton, 1976).

Colonial New England began with a high sex ratio from predominantly male migration, though it declined quickly and became female-biased from the 18th century onward. The meaning of the term "spinster" shifted from female yarn spinner to unmarried woman because there were so many unmarried women engaged in yarn production for outside income (Cott, 1977). Industrialization in the 19th century greatly reduced the need for manual labor and improved living conditions sufficiently for women to return to their homes (Bloch, 1978). Men of the Colonial era married respectable women and supported their households and family members. However, many of these men also had ongoing affairs with one or more women who were not considered respectable (Guttentag & Secord, 1983).

Near the end of the 19th century, "free love" groups argued against the institution of marriage on the grounds that marital constraints stifled "real" love. These groups were often led by men, and though they never became very large, they shared beliefs with Suffragettes and other social reformers that women should have access to birth control (Gordon, 1976). Many feminist movements emerged in New England at this time, arguing that motherhood should be voluntary and that women should have greater independence (Gordon, 1976). These movements were remarkably similar in beliefs to the self-organized female religious groups of the late Middle Ages, who questioned traditional marriage and raised and educated girls abandoned by their parents (Herlihy, 1973).

The sex ratio in the United States was male-biased before World War II, due to higher immigration rates for men than for women. The US sex ratio became less male biased from 1910 to the early 1940s, when the country reached gender parity, then became increasingly female-biased through 1970. Sex ratio dynamics are reflected in American cultural patterns (Guttentag & Secord, 1983). From the 1930s to the 1950s, male protagonists were motivated to make lifelong commitments to and considerable investments in their partners. Screwball comedies featured women that socially dominated the central male character. In contrast, the male characters of the 1960s and 1970s expressed "love 'em and leave 'em" attitudes and focused on short-term relationships. These fictional portrayals coincided with increasing divorce rates and other parallels in the sociopolitical climate that lasted until the 1980s (Pedersen, 1991).

In addition to temporal trends, there is geographical variation in the sex ratio. Large cities in the Northeastern United States tend to have low (female-biased) sex ratios because of the migration of women from more rural areas to larger cities for white-collar employment opportunities (Gwin, 2007). The abundance of single women creates intersexual dynamics typical in female-biased populations. Women have considerable trouble finding a stable and reliable partner. Single men are scarce and the men who are available are often not interested in long-term relationships (Time Out New York, 2007). Women express a preference for a settle-down partner, but often end up settling for less; they find it difficult to stay with one person, partially because the men they are dating are not interested in marriage. Relationships are often "fast and casual," even when the women are middle-aged, and women find themselves becoming accepting of this fact. Women are puzzled why many of their friends, who are intelligent, have good careers, and interesting personalities, are still unmarried (Time Out New York, 2007). In contrast, men have disproportionally moved to cities and surrounding areas in the Western United States for technology-oriented careers and agricultural labor, resulting in male-biased sex ratios (Gwin, 2007).

Infidelity and Biased Human Sex Ratios

Female-biased sex ratios are associated with greater likelihoods of male infidelity (Warner et al., 2011). Higher sex ratios are associated with lower divorce rates across nations (Trent & South, 1989), though highly biased sex ratios with a surplus of either men or women are associated with higher divorce rates than more balanced sex ratios (South & Lloyd, 1995). In highly female-biased environments, women report ending up single with children often because their child's father cheated on them (Time Out New York, 2007). Many men are seen as emotionally unavailable or unsuitable for a partnership because they are interested in being simultaneously polygynous, cheating on their partner, or are just looking for short-term sexual relationships. Men may exhibit serial infidelity, where they cheat on their partner, form a new relationship with the woman in the affair, and then cheat on her as well. Women note the availability of potentially promiscuous women who provide easy sexual access and reduce incentives for male commitment (Time Out New York, 2007). Those living in areas with strongly female-biased populations may be less likely to use online infidelity matchmaking services (e.g., Ashley Madison) because of the lesser difficulty in finding infidelity partners (Chohaney & Panozzo, 2018).

Adult women outnumber men in England and Wales; however, there is also geographical variation in the sex ratio. In areas where the sex ratio is more balanced, there are lower rates of infidelity and lower numbers of serial sex partners (Kang & Pongou, 2019). Areas with more balanced sex ratios also have lower rates of sexually transmitted infections (Kang & Pongou, 2019). Variation in the sex ratio appears to be more strongly related to variation in sexual behavior for men than for women, but more strongly related to sexually transmitted infections in women than in men (Kang & Pongou, 2019).

African Americans have higher rates of infidelity than White Americans, a pattern which has been attributed to highly female-biased sex ratios within African American communities (Choi et al., 1994; Hutchinson, 1999; Wiederman, 1997). The sex-ratio imbalance is partially a result of higher mortality and incarceration rates for Black men, as well as a long history of often violent discrimination (Utley, 2011). One of the consequences is a higher rate of sexually transmitted infections, in part because women may not be aware that their partners are having sex with other women (Choi, Catania, & Dolcini, 1994).

Workplace environments may be another venue for sex ratio dynamics. Sexual integration in the workplace lowers the costs of mate search, including for extramarital partners (Kuroki, 2013; McKinnish, 2007). Men who work in environments with greater proportions of women are more likely to have committed infidelity; however, there is no relationship between the sex ratio and the likelihood of women's infidelity (Kuroki, 2013). However, both men and women are more likely to be divorced when there is a greater proportion of members of the other sex in their workplace, demonstrating a broader pattern of mate-switching (Aberg, 2003; McKinnish, 2007).

Cultural Practices Constraining Female Infidelity

Men will use their social power to reduce women's potential advantages associated with numerical scarcity, especially in populations where legal structures facilitate greater male social power. High sex ratios predict greater emphasis on traditional sex roles and norms that both protect and constrain women, though women who can choose their own marriage partners will have more power and control (Guttentag & Secord, 1983). Women will be loved, respected, admired, and cherished, but only within a narrowly defined traditional role that limits their ability to take advantage of their market scarcity (Guttentag & Secord, 1983). Men may also increase enforcement of social norms that favor stability in relationships, devaluing promiscuity in women to reduce the perceived alternatives for their female partners. Valuation of sexual morality will be especially directed toward women, who will be treated as a valuable resource, with intensified guarding of their virginity and reproductive output (Guttentag & Secord, 1983). Some cultural practices are extreme and include sequestering high-caste women in India in their homes and surgical infibulations to physically prevent women from having sex in the Sudan and other parts of Africa (Daly & Wilson, 1978).

The British colonies which became the central Atlantic states of the early United States had high sex ratios due to the importation of White male indentured servants. Georgia avoided recruiting single women because the colonial administrators feared that these women might take husbands away from military garrisons, increasing the threat of invasion by the Spanish colonists to the south (Spruill, 1938). The southern colonies began with extremely male-biased sex ratios, and though the extreme disparities attenuated quickly, the sex ratio then declined more gradually until there was just a slight male bias immediately before the Civil War. The male-biased sex ratio was reflected in local cultures and legislation. For example, the governor of Virginia prohibited women from committing themselves to more than one man at a time and taking unfair advantage of their scarcity (Calhoun, 1945). The Southern Belle was an archetypal cultural character in the antebellum (pre-Civil War) American South. Although she had high social status, the Southern Belle was expected to love, honor, and obey her husband and raise his children. These women were highly admired, but they were less able to leverage their numerical advantages because of social restrictions and cultural expectations. Although thought to be intuitive and adept at understanding people, women were also thought to be physically weak and dependent on men for protection (Scott, 1970). Protection of women included monitoring and guarding their behavior, preventing their infidelity or other unacceptable behavior. These restrictions were not applied to high-status men, as plantation owners would often have sex with female slaves and even produce offspring with them (Scott, 1970).

The construction of transcontinental railroads in the late 19th-century United States initiated another period of male-biased immigration. Male Chinese laborers were recruited to build railroads in the American West, though few Chinese women immigrated, resulting in local populations where there were as many as 200 men for every woman (Lyman, 1974). The male Chinese immigrants brought sometimes secret fraternal associations and other social structures based on village affiliation or kinship that suppressed female social power. Many Chinese women either worked as prostitutes in brothels or were married to wealthy Chinese American men who sheltered and protected them to the point of virtual imprisonment (Lyman, 1974). In modern China, the implementation of the 1979 single-child law led to a surplus of men through higher rates of sex-specific abortions and higher rates of female infant mortality (Ding & Hesketh, 2006; Zhu & Hesketh, 2009). The sex ratio varied geographically and was especially high in rural areas. The more male-biased an area, the less extensive women's education was in comparison to men, the less likely women were to be employed, the less likely women who were employed were to be in professional positions, and the lower their wages and income (Edlund et al., 2013). Women in higher sex ratio areas were more likely to be sexually active, to have had premarital sexual intercourse, to have been forced to have sex, and to test positive for a sexually transmitted infection (Trent & South, 2012).

Polygyny and concubinage in Iran predates the rise of Islam (Jackson, 1928), which limits polygynous marriages to four wives, but allows for men's sexual relations with indentured servants or slaves (Qur'an, Sura 4 [An-Nisa], Ayah 3). Iranian folklore depicts polygyny as the ideal of luxurious living, as economic success was necessary for men to acquire multiple wives (Miller & Windle, 1960). Iran also has a male-biased sex ratio, and polygyny further increases the effective sex ratio of available reproductive partners. Islamic honor culture includes strong norms of protecting and guarding female kin (Tabatabai, 1973), reducing the risks of sexual coercion or infidelity. However, the cultural importance of honor may lead to fatal violence in reaction to violations of these norms. In Pakistan, those who are older, live in rural areas, and belong to extended family systems have higher acceptance of honor-based killings (Huda & Kamal, 2020). Chesler (2010) reports that in 70% of cases of honor killings, victims were killed by members of their families of origin and not their romantic partner or husband and that 60% of perpetrators provided the motive that victims were "too Western," defined as being seen as too independent, not subservient enough, refusing to wear varieties of Islamic clothing (including forms of the veil), wanting an advanced education and a career, having non-Muslim friends or boyfriends, refusing to marry a first cousin, wanting to choose one's own husband, choosing a socially "inferior" or non-Muslim husband; or leaving an abusive husband (Chesler, 2010). Another study in Pakistan suggests that the family fear of "what will other people say" regarding their female relative violating cultural expectations motivates acts of honor violence for the sake of maintaining respect in the eyes of the society (Nazar, 2020).

In West African preliterate societies with high sex ratios, women were unable to use their market scarcity to their advantage but were instead treated as chattel. Male power was related to physical strength and prowess as a warrior, and husbands were allowed to beat or kill their wives for infidelity (Ardener et al., 1960). Then British colonizers suppressed the traditional social structures of the Bakweri in Cameroon, West Africa, creating a British-style justice system and effective state government. This destroyed the old order of male power, despite the very high sex ratio due to the constant migration of men from other areas for plantation labor (Ardener et al., 1960). Under the British protectorate,

Bakweri society was characterized by unstable marriages where women divorced men for insufficient support. Men made substantial bride wealth payments in order to secure a marriage. Women could generate substantial incomes in exchange for casual sex. Some women sought new male partners with the wealth to buy out their previous bride wealth, and some women paid off the bride wealth themselves to leave their husbands (Ardener et al., 1960).

Conclusion

The sex ratio is an important aspect of the social environment in shaping relationship dynamics and rates of infidelity. Populations with biased sex ratios exhibit patterns following from the differential reproductive strategies of each sex. Male scarcity enhances mating opportunities for men and decreases incentives for long-term commitment and fidelity. Men can leverage their market scarcity for greater sexual access, even when retaining long-term relationships. Female scarcity enhances women's ability to secure commitment from their partners and to demand higher levels of resource investment. However, male social power often constrains women's ability to leverage their market scarcity for serial or simultaneous polyandry, whether in recognized relationships or infidelity to their primary partners. As documented above, there are important social and public health implications of infidelity and biased human sex ratios, including for rates of violence and sexually transmitted infections. Overall, these patterns are best understood in an evolutionary framework that affords rich explanations of psychological, behavioral, and cultural patterns.

References

Aberg, Y. (2003). *Social interactions: Studies of contextual effects and endogenous processes* [PhD Dissertation, Department of Sociology, Stockholm University].
Ardener, E., Ardener, S., & Warmington, W.A. (1960). *Plantation and village in the Cameroons: Some economic and social studies*. London: Oxford University Press.
Barber, N. (2000). On the relationship between country sex ratios and teen pregnancy rates: A replication. *Cross-Cultural Research*, 34, 26–37.
Barber, N. (1999). Women's dress fashions as a function of reproductive strategy. *Sex Roles*, 40, 459–471.
Berard, J. D., Nürnberg, P., Epplen, J. T., & Schmidtke, J. (1993). Male rank, reproductive behavior, and reproductive success in free-ranging rhesus macaques. *Primates*, 4, 481–489.
Berglund, A. (1994). The operational sex ratio influences choosiness in a pipefish. *Behavioral Ecology*, 5, 254–258.
Berglund, A., & Rosenqvist, G. (2003). Sex role reversal in pipefish. *Advances in the Study of Behavior*, 32, 131–167.
Bloch, R. H. (1978). Untangling the roots of modern sex roles: A survey of four centuries of change. *Signs: Journal of Women in Culture and Society*, 4, 237–252.
Bolton, B. M. (1976). *Muliers sanctae*. In S. M. Stuard (Ed.), *Women in medieval society* (pp. 141–158). University of Pennsylvania Press.
Buss, D. M. (1989). Sex difference in human mate preferences: Evolutionary hypotheses tested in 37 cultures. *Behavioral and Brain Sciences*, 12, 1–49.
Buss, D. M., & Schmitt, D. P. (1993). Sexual strategies theory: An evolutionary perspective on human mating. *Psychological Review*, 100, 204–232.

Calhoun, A. W. (1945). *A social history of the American family from Colonial times to the present* (Vol. 1). Barnes & Noble.

Chapman, C. A., Fedigan, L. M., Fedigan, L., & Chapman, L. J. (1989). Post-weaning resource competition and sex ratios in spider monkeys. *Oikos, 54*, 315–319.

Chesler, P. (2010). Worldwide trends in honor killings. *Middle East Quarterly, 17*, 3–11.

Chohaney, M. L., & Panozzo, K. A. (2018). Infidelity and the Internet: The geography of Ashley Madison usership in the United States. *Geographical Review, 108*, 69–91.

Choi, K.-H., Catania, J. A., & Dolcini, M. M. (1994). Extramarital sex and HIV risk behavior among U.S. adults: Results from the National AIDS Behavioral Survey. *American Journal of Public Health, 84*, 2003–2007.

Coleman, E. (1976). Infanticide in the early Middle Ages. In S. M. Stuard (Ed.), *Women in medieval society* (pp. 47–70). University of Pennsylvania Press.

Cott, N. F. (1977). *The bonds of womanhood: "Woman's sphere" in New England, 1780–1835*. Yale University Press.

Cunningham, M. (1986). Measuring the physical in physical attractiveness: Quasi-experiments on the sociobiology of female facial beauty. *Journal of Personality and Social Psychology, 50*, 925–935.

Daly, M., & Wilson, M. (1978). *Sex, evolution, and behavior: Adaptations for reproduction*. Duxbury Press.

Darwin, C. (1871). *The descent of man, and selection in relation to sex*. John Murray.

Ding, Q. J., & Hesketh, T. (2006). Family size, fertility preferences, and sex ratio in China in the era of the one child family policy: Results from national family planning and reproductive health survey. *British Medical Journal, 333*, 371–373.

Düsing, C. (1884). On the regulation of the sex-ratio. *Theoretical Population Biology, 58*, 255–257.

Edlund, L., Li, H., Yi, J., & Zhang, J. (2013). Sex ratios and crime: Evidence from China. *Review of Economics and Statistics, 95*, 1520–1534.

Elmberg, J. (1990). Long-term survival, length of breeding season, and operational sex ratio in a boreal population of common frogs, *Rana temporaria L. Canadian Journal of Zoology, 68*, 121–127.

Emlen, S., & Oring, L. (1977). Ecology, sexual selection, and the evolution of mating systems. *Science, 197*, 215–223.

Fisher, R. A. (1930). *The genetical theory of natural selection*. Oxford University Press.

Fisher, R. A. (1958). *The genetical theory of natural selection* (2nd ed). Dover.

Forsgren, E., Amundsen, T., Borg, A. A., & Bjelvenmark, J. (2004). Unusually dynamic sex roles in a fish. *Nature, 429*, 551–554.

Geary, D. C. (2005). Evolution of paternal investment. In D. Buss (Ed.), *The handbook of evolutionary psychology* (pp. 483–505). Wiley.

Geary, D. C., & Flinn, M. V. (2001). Evolution of human parental behavior and the human family. *Parenting: Science and Practice, 1*, 5–61.

Gordon, L. (1976). *Woman's body, woman's right: A social history of birth control in America*. Viking Press.

Guttentag, M., & Secord, P. F. (1983). *Too many women? The sex ratio question*. Sage.

Gwin, P. (2007). Geography: Singles. *National Geographic, 211*, 22.

Gwynne, D. T. (1990). Testing parental investment and the control of sexual selection in katydids: The operational sex ratio. *American Naturalist, 136*, 474–484.

Gwynne, D. T. (1991). Sexual competition among females: What causes courtship-role reversal? *Trends in Ecology & Evolution, 6*, 118–121.

Gwynne, D. T., & Simmons, L. W. (1990). Experimental reversal of courtship roles in an insect. *Nature, 346*, 172–174.

Harris, S. M. (2002). Father absence in the African American community: Toward a new paradigm. *Race, Gender & Class, 9*, 111–133.

Hendrix, L. (1996). *Illegitimacy and social structures: Cross-cultural perspectives on nonmarital birth*. Westport, CT: Greenwood.

Herlihy, D. (1973). Alienation in medieval culture and society. In F. Johnson (Ed.), *Alienation: Concept, term and meanings* (pp. 125-140). Seminar Press.

Hill, K., & Hurtado, A. M. (1996). *Ache life history: The ecology and demography of a foraging people*. Aldine de Gruyter.

Hopcroft, R. L. (2006). Sex, status, and reproductive success in the contemporary United States. *Evolution and Human Behavior, 27*, 104–120.

Huda, S., & Kamal, A. (2022). Assessing demographics-based differences in attitude toward honor killings. *Journal of Interpersonal Violence, 37,* NP3224-NP3241.

Hutchinson, J. F. (1999). The hip-hop generation: African male–female relationships in a nightclub setting. *Journal of Black Studies, 30,* 62–84.

Jackson, A. V. (1928). *Zoroastrian studies.* Columbia University Press.

Kaitala, A., & Miettinen, M. (1997). Female egg dumping and the effect of sex ratio on male egg carrying in a coreid bug. *Behavioral Ecology, 8,* 429–432.

Kandrik, M., Jones, B. C., & DeBruine, L. M. (2015). Scarcity of female mates predicts regional variation in men's and women's sociosexual orientation across US states. *Evolution and Human Behavior, 36,* 206–210.

Keenleyside, M. H. (1983). Mate desertion in relation to adult sex ratio in the biparental cichlid fish *Herotilapia multispinosa. Animal Behaviour, 31,* 683–688.

Kenrick, D. T., & Simpson, J. A. (1997). Why social psychology and evolutionary psychology need one another. In J. Simpson & D. Kenrick (Eds.), *Evolutionary social psychology* (pp. 1–20). Erlbaum.

Kang, Y., & Pongou, R. (2019, April 18). Sex ratios, sexual infidelity, and sexual diseases: Evidence from the United Kingdom. *SSRN Electronic Journal, 1*–44.

Kruger, D. J. (2008). Young adults attempt exchanges in reproductively relevant currencies. *Evolutionary Psychology, 6,* 204–212.

Kruger, D. J., Fitzgerald, C. J., & Peterson, T. (2010). Female scarcity reduces women's marital ages and increases variance in men's marital ages. *Evolutionary Psychology, 8,* 420–431.

Kuroki, M. (2013). Opposite-sex coworkers and marital infidelity. *Economics Letters, 118,* 71–73.

Kvarnemo, C., & Ahnesjö, I. (1996). The dynamics of operational sex ratios and competition for mates. *Trends of Ecology & Evolution, 11,* 404–408.

Lamb, M. E. (2004). *The role of the father in child development* (4th ed.). Wiley.

Liker, A., Freckleton, R. P., & Székely, T. (2014). Divorce and infidelity are associated with skewed adult sex ratios in birds. *Current Biology, 24,* 880–884.

Lyman, S. (1974). *Chinese Americans.* New York: Random House.

Mathews, L. M. (2002). Tests of the mate-guarding hypothesis for social monogamy: Does population density, sex ratio, or female synchrony affect behavior of male snapping shrimp (*Alpheus angulatus*)? *Behavioral Ecology and Sociobiology, 51,* 426–432.

Matsumoto, K., & Yanagisawa, Y. (2001). Monogamy and sex role reversal in the pipefish *Corythoichthys haematopterus. Animal Behaviour, 61,* 163–170.

McKinnish, T. G. (2007). Sexually-integrated workplaces and divorce: Another form of on-the-job search. *Journal of Human Resources, 42,* 331–335.

Michener, G. R., & McLean, I. G. (1996). Reproductive behavior and operational sex ratio in Richardson's ground squirrels. *Animal Behavior, 52,* 743–758.

Miller, M.K., & Windle, C. (1960) Polygyny and Social Status in Iran. *Journal of Social Psychology, 51,* 307–311.

Mills, S. C., & Reynolds, J. D. (2003). Operational sex ratio and alternative reproductive behaviours in the European bitterling, *Rhodeus sericeus. Behavioral Ecology and Sociobiology, 54,* 98–104.

Mitani, J. C., Gros-Louis, J., & Richards, A. F. (1996). Sexual dimorphism, the operational sex ratio, and the intensity of male competition in polygynous primates. *American Naturalist, 147,* 966–980.

Moody, A. T., Wilhelm, S. I., Cameron-MacMillan, M. L., Walsh, C. J., & Storey, A. E. (2005). Divorce in common murres (*Uria aalge*): Relationship to parental quality *Behavioral Ecology and Sociobiology, 57,* 224–230.

Nazar, M. (2020). *The analysis of honor killings in Pakistan and how it is related to the notion of "what will other people say?* Undergraduate Honors Theses 5. Vestal, NY: SUNY Binghamton.

Pedersen, F. A. (1991). Secular trends in human sex ratios: Their influence on individual and family behavior. *Human Nature, 2,* 271–291.

Poirier, N. E., Whittingham, L. A., & Dunn, P. O. (2003). Effects of paternity and mate availability on mate switching in house wrens. *Condor, 105,* 816–821.

Pollet, T. V., & Nettle, D. (2007). Driving a hard bargain: Sex ratio and male marriage success in a historical US population. *Biology Letters, 4,* 31–33.

Pollet, T. V., & Nettle, D. (2009). Market forces affect patterns of polygyny in Uganda. *Proceedings of the National Academy of Sciences, 106,* 2114–2117.

Schmitt, D. P. (2005). Sociosexuality from Argentina to Zimbabwe: A 48-nation study of sex, culture, and strategies of human mating. *Behavioral and Brain Sciences, 28,* 247–311.

Scott, A. F. (1970). *The southern lady: From pedestal to politics, 1830–1930*. University of Chicago Press.

Scott, S., & Lloyd, K. (1995). Spousal alternatives and marital dissolution. *American Sociological Review, 60*, 21–35.

Spruill, J. C. (1938). *Women's life and work in the southern colonies*. University of North Carolina Press.

Starkweather, K. E., & Hames, R. (2012). A survey of non-classical polyandry. *Human Nature, 23*, 149–172.

Symington, M. M. (1987). Sex ratio and maternal rank in wild spider monkeys: When daughters disperse. *Behavioral Ecology and Sociobiology, 20*, 421–425.

Székely, T., Cuthill, I. C., & Kis, J. (1999). Brood desertion in Kentish plover: Sex differences in remating opportunities. *Behavioral Ecology, 10*, 185–190.

Tabatabai, M. H. (1996). *Al-mizan fi tafsir al-Qur'an*. Islamic Publications Society of Seminary Teachers of Qom.

Taborsky, B., & Taborsky, M. (1999). The mating system and stability of pairs in kiwi *Apteryx spp. Journal of Avian Biology, 30*, 143–151.

Takahashi, H. (2001). Influence of fluctuation in the operational sex ratio to mating of troop and non-troop male Japanese macaques for four years on Kinkazan Island, Japan. *Primates, 42*, 183–191.

Tesser, A., & Martin L. (1996). The psychology of evaluation. In E. Higgins & A. Kruglanski. *Social psychology: Handbook of basic principles* (pp. 400–432). Guilford Press.

Thornhill, R. (1980). Rape in *Panorpa* scorpionflies and a general rape hypothesis. *Animal Behavior, 28*, 52–59.

Time Out New York. (2007, June 28). Single women: Single minded. *Time Out New York, 613*, 28–34.

Tinbergen, N. (1963). On aims and methods in ethology. *Zeitschrift für Tierpsychologie, 20*, 410–433.

Trent, K., & South, S. J. (1989). Structural determinants of the divorce rate: A cross-societal analysis. *Journal of Marriage and Family, 51*, 391–404.

Trent, K., & South, S. J. (2012). Mate availability and women's sexual experiences in China. *Journal of Marriage and Family, 74*, 201–214.

Trivers, R. (1972). Parental investment and sexual selection. In B. Campbell (Ed.), *Sexual selection and the descent of man* (pp. 136–179). Aldine-Atherton.

Utley, E. A. (2011). When better becomes worse: Black wives describe their experiences with infidelity. *Black Women, Gender & Families, 5*, 66–89.

Valero, A., Schaffner, C. M., Vick, L. G., Aureli, F., & Ramos-Fernandez, G. (2006). Intragroup lethal aggression in wild spider monkeys. *American Journal of Primatology, 68*, 732–737.

Warner, T. D., Manning, W. D., Giordano, P. C., & Longmore, M. A. (2011). Relationship formation and stability in emerging adulthood: Do sex ratios matter? *Social Forces, 90*, 269–295.

Wiederman, M. W. (1997). Extramarital sex: Prevalence and correlates in a national survey. *Journal of Sex Research, 34*, 167–74.

Zhu, W. X., & Hesketh, T. (2009). China's excess males, sex selective abortion, and one child policy: Analysis of data from 2005 national intercensus survey. *British Medical Journal, 338*, b1211.

CHAPTER 5

It's Not You, It's Us: Relationship-Based Factors That Predict Infidelity

Jana Hackathorn *and* Brien K. Ashdown

Abstract

Infidelity is often defined as perceived as a violation of relationship exclusivity rules, and many view infidelities as immoral. Thus, one can imagine the importance of understanding why up to a fifth of research samples report cheating in their current relationships. There is considerable literature regarding what factors predict infidelity. Although individual characteristics associated with infidelity do exist, relationship-based variables tend to be the most consistent and robust factors. This chapter will discuss various theories and research findings that suggested different relationship-based factors and frameworks with which to consider and predict why some people engage in infidelity. This chapter reviews some major ideas and research through the lens of the investment model of commitment (i.e., satisfaction, investment, quality of alternatives, commitment), as well as other relationship-based variables (e.g., opportunities and boredom, relationship type and length) that have received empirical support. Finally, the chapter ends with a nod to future directions in this area, and a notion of what researchers should expect from the literature in the future.

Key Words: infidelity, investment model, commitment, satisfaction, alternatives

Whether using the term "adultery," "unfaithful," "extramarital," "extradyadic," "infidelity," or simply "cheating," what is typically being referred to is a betrayal of the expectancy of sexual and romantic monogamy in a relationship (Moller & Vossler, 2014). As the vast majority of romantic relationships have such expectations, especially in America (DeMaris, 2009; Scheinkman, 2005; Wiederman & Allgeier, 1996), it is not surprising that most relationships, whether formalized by marriage or not, have unwritten and sometimes never-verbalized agreements regarding loyalty, fidelity, and betrayal (Sevi et al., 2020). In a recent sample of almost 500 people, over 90% reported expecting romantic and sexual exclusivity from a partner, and over 95% reported that their partners expected romantic and sexual exclusivity from them. Moreover, most of the participants (84%) reported having an exclusivity agreement, either explicit, as a mutual understanding, or merely implied (Gibson et al., 2016). Infidelity is often perceived as a violation of such exclusivity ground rules, and many view infidelities as immoral (Fincham & May, 2017; Sevi et al., 2020; Thompson, 1984). Hence, one can imagine the importance of understanding why up to a fifth of research samples report cheating in their current relationships, regardless of its cultural unacceptability (e.g., Mark et al., 2011).

The ability to predict who might cheat in their relationships could be valuable information for therapists, counselors, and anyone in a romantic relationship. In a fantasy world, it would be ideal if researchers could identify a particular trait in a person who cheats on their partner(s). Perhaps a test could be developed that could be sold at a local pharmacy to help identify those who will betray. Even more tantalizing is the idea that individuals could simply look at another person and determine, perhaps even on a first date, that the person is a "cheater." They could walk around with a giant label that says "Adulterer" on their chest, like Hester Prynne, for all the world to see (Hawthorne, 1850). It might make life easier and save a lot of time and emotional distress. However, as everyone knows, it is not that simple.

In the real world, the motivation to remain monogamous, and conversely one's motivation toward infidelity, are influenced by various sources. Arguably, individuals might be motivated to be monogamous to meet cultural expectations (Haseli et al., 2019; Solstad & Mucic, 1999). Or, perhaps they are motivated to avoid punishment, as a recent study that asked participants to explain why they remained monogamous revealed that most people do it to avoid negative sanctions, such as guilt, shame, family disapproval, or divorce (Emmers-Sommer et al., 2010). People's attitudes about fidelity may also reflect gender roles and norms (Glass & Wright, 1985; Haseli et al., 2019), the type of relationship (e.g., sexual orientation, dating, or marriage (Parsons et al., 2012;), the type of cheating behaviors (e.g., explicit or ambiguous; Mattingly et al., 2010), the source of the cheating behaviors (e.g., online; Hackathorn & Harvey, 2011), whether an individual has a past experience with infidelity (Donovan & Emmers-Sommers, 2012; Knopp et al., 2017) or if they have been "burned" before (Sharpe et al., 2013).

People tend to be inaccurate when predicting their own likelihood of cheating. For instance, when Buss and Shackleford (1997) asked participants to estimate the probability that they would engage in various extramarital behaviors during the first year of their marriage, about 35% reported expecting that both they and their partner would probably flirt with another person, approximately 15% predicted that both they and their partner might passionately kiss another person, and approximately 2% expected they or their partner would go on a romantic date, have a one-night stand, or a brief affair (Buss & Shackleford, 1997). Seeing as rates of reported infidelity tend to be around 20%, people apparently underestimate the likelihood that they or their partner will engage in cheating behaviors.

Research has examined hundreds of factors that predict infidelity, including individual differences and relationship/circumstantial factors. While demographic (e.g., sex, age) and individual difference factors (e.g., personality) are empirically associated with infidelity, the most consistent and robust predictors are found within the relationship (Fincham & May, 2017; Gibson et al., 2016; Haseli et al., 2019; Silva et al., 2017; Tsapelas et al.,

2010; Vowels et al., 2020). This is especially true when one considers that any relationship encompasses the intricate behaviors that a couple engages in, including the macrosystems (e.g., religion) microsystems (e.g., infidelity experience), exosystems (e.g., home instability), and mesosystems (e.g., satisfaction) that are interacting to influence the relationship and the individuals within that relationship (Haseli et al., 2019). In fact, relationship factors such as satisfaction, need fulfillment, boredom, emotional support, and communication account for up to one-fourth of the variance in infidelity (Atkins et al., 2001; Tsapelas et al., 2010).

Various theories and research findings have suggested different relationship-based factors and frameworks with which to consider and predict why some people engage in infidelity. In this chapter, we review some of the main theories (e.g., the investment model of commitment) as well as relevant variables from previous research (e.g., boredom, communication, conflict) that have empirical support as relational factors involved in infidelity. Before discussing these theories and frameworks, however, we want to state an important caveat: none of these variables or theories—individually or in combination with one another—guarantees a person will engage in infidelity; nor, for that matter, are any of these frameworks or variables required to be present for someone to be unfaithful in their relationship. The decision to engage in infidelity is always a decision made by the person involved, and the following theories and variables are aspects that might play a role in that person's decision-making.

Investment Model of Commitment

Commitment (i.e., the intention to stay in one's current romantic relationship) is probably the most powerful and relevant factor in predicting whether an individual will cheat in a relationship, and allows for systematic prediction of infidelity behavior (Drigotas et al., 1999; Le & Agnew, 2003). Interdependence theory (Rusbult & Buunk, 1993) and, more specifically, the investment model of commitment (Rusbult, 1980; Rusbult et al., 1998) posits that relationship commitment is based on the combination of three factors: high satisfaction, high investment, and low quality of potential alternatives. Moreover, the investment model is central to explaining relationship functioning, and comprises both attachment and motivation to continue the relationship via those three factors (Drigotas et al., 1999; Fincham & May, 2017; Le & Agnew, 2003).

Commitment refers to a long-term, subjective state that includes an emotional attachment to one's partner and/or the relationship, and a desire to maintain the relationship (Lambert et al., 2014; Rubsult & Buunk, 1993). One's commitment reflects the amount of investment, involvement, satisfaction, constraints, or barriers to terminating the relationship, and intention to stay in the relationship (Emmers-Sommers et al., 2010; Roloff et al., 2001). Importantly, a sense of commitment motivates and influences a range of relationship behaviors. Desiring to continue a relationship promotes prorelationship maintenance behaviors (e.g., compromise; Meyer et al., 2011) and discourages relationship-damaging behaviors, such as infidelity (Maddox Shaw et al., 2013; Rusbult & Buunk, 1993). An individual's decision to damage a relationship, particularly through acts of infidelity, is often mediated by feelings of commitment to the relationship, and speaks to the strength of the investment model (Drigotas et al., 1999; Rusbult & Buunk, 1993). Simply put, if one plans to continue the relationship, the likelihood of engaging in infidelity decreases significantly (Maddox Shaw et al., 2013).

As relationships increase in commitment, people become more invested both tangibly (e.g., resources, income) and intangibly (e.g., time, energy, emotions), and satisfaction increases as a result. Conversely, the quality of potential alternatives diminishes as commitment increases, including new potential partners and other outside options (e.g., moving to a different location without one's partner). In one study, 220 participants currently in a relationship were asked to report reasons for being unfaithful to their partner (if they had been). A lack of commitment, lack of investment, and perceiving better alternatives were all mentioned, and a lack of satisfaction with the relationship was the most commonly reported reason (Emmers-Sommer et al., 2010).

Satisfaction

One's relationship satisfaction is based on comparisons that are shaped by previous experiences as well as upward and downward social comparisons (Rubult & Buunk, 1993). According to the deficit model of infidelity (Thompson, 1984; Tsapelas et al., 2010), when a relationship exceeds an individual's generalized expectations, or if they benefit from social comparisons, they feel satisfied. When the appraisal of the relationship falls short, they feel dissatisfied. For example, if Brien looks at his close friends' romantic relationship and perceives their relationship to be of a higher quality than his own, he may become dissatisfied with his current relationship.

However, satisfaction can be more nuanced and complicated. According to equity theory, one's feelings of satisfaction do not just depend on the absolute value of what one is getting from the relationship but also on an input-to-output ratio relative to the partner's input-to-output ratio (Rusbult & Buunk, 1993). When these ratios differ, individuals are dissatisfied. For example, if Brien feels he is putting much more into his romantic relationship than he is getting out of his relationship, he may be unsatisfied. Furthermore, if he feels that his input/output discrepancy is greater than his partner's input/output discrepancy, Brien will feel unsatisfied in the relationship.

Inequity predicts higher engagement in infidelity, and this appears to be exacerbated for women, and has been shown to be independent of dissatisfaction (Prins et al., 1993). Infidelity is more likely among those who are in poorer-quality relationships (Mattingly et al., 2010), arguably because individuals turn to people outside of their relationship to meet their needs for intimacy (which they would prefer to have met by their partner), and thus become more satisfied with their lives but not with their relationships. In the infidelity literature, there has been much research on satisfaction as a predictor, and satisfaction is arguably the most robust predictor of the relationship-related predictors. However, the source of the satisfaction impacts how well it predicts infidelity. Researchers have focused on two main sources of satisfaction in regard to infidelity: relationship satisfaction and sexual satisfaction.

RELATIONSHIP SATISFACTION

A recent study of individuals who were actively engaging in infidelity via a facilitating website (i.e., AshleyMadison.com) indicated that above and beyond any personal factors, low satisfaction with the primary partner was the largest contributor to their decision to be unfaithful (Hackathorn & Ashdown, 2021). This finding was true for motivations that were based on relationship satisfaction (e.g., I have fallen out of love with my primary partner), as well as for feeling neglected (e.g., I feel neglected by my partner) and less satisfied sexually (e.g., I want more frequent sex than I am getting with my current partner).

Satisfaction within various domains (e.g., sexual satisfaction, neglect, etc.) in one's primary relationship predicts a person's attitudes toward infidelity, and less satisfaction increases the likelihood to engage in an affair, as individuals who are happy tend not to stray from the things that make them happy (Emmers-Sommer et al., 2010; Garg & Ruhela, 2015; Hackathorn & Ashdown, 2021; Larson et al., 2014; Maddox Shaw et al., 2013; Mark et al., 2011; Martins et al., 2016; Silva et al., 2017; Treas & Giesen, 2000; Vowels et al., 2020; Whisman et al., 2007). For example, in another large study in which respondents were asked to report reasons for engaging in infidelity, the most frequent reason was lack of satisfaction with their current relationship (Emmers-Sommer et al., 2010). Interestingly, in a recent study, relationship satisfaction was the main predictor in a machine-learning algorithm that predicted infidelity by both men and women (Vowels et al., 2020).

No single variable can explain all the variance in models predicting infidelity; yet, satisfaction interacts with other variables to play an instrumental role in predicting infidelity. Satisfaction is not only correlated with the number of extradyadic partners people admit to having (Wiggins & Lederer, 1984), but also predicts the degree of involvement of the infidelity (e.g., one-night stand versus an ongoing relationship; Glass & Wright, 1985; Tsapelas et al., 2010), and the type of affair (e.g., sexual versus emotional; McDaniel et al., 2017). In fact, relationship satisfaction is a significant predictor of online-only infidelity related behavior, even after controlling for demographic variables (e.g., gender, age) and other relationship factors, such as marital status or relationship length (Martins et al., 2016; McDaniel et al., 2017; Whisman et al., 2007).

GENDER AND SATISFACTION

In various studies, the pattern of relationship satisfaction predicting infidelity is stronger for women than men (Allen et al., 2008; Blow & Hartnett, 2005; Glass & Wright, 1985; Mark et al., 2011; Prins et al., 1993; Wiggins & Lederer, 1984), and relationship variables, such as satisfaction, are particularly important to women's sexual functioning and overall satisfaction (Basson, 2005; Dennerstein et al., 2005; Prins et al., 1993). For example, among people who engage in extramarital infidelity, women report being less satisfied in their marriage than are men (Blow & Hartnett, 2005; Glass & Wright, 1985). In one study, women's level of unhappiness in their current relationship predicted a 200% increase in engaging in infidelity, and levels of incompatibility in sexual values predicted an almost 300% increase in engaging in infidelity, even after controlling for demographics (e.g., age) and relationship type (e.g., marital status; Mark et al., 2011).

These gender differences suggest that, for women, relationship factors may be more relevant in predicting infidelity than demographic (e.g., marital status) or social variables, such as religiosity (Atkins et al., 2001; Mark et al., 2011). It is important to note these variables likely interact. For example, the difference in the likelihood of engaging in infidelity for people low in marital satisfaction was four times greater for those also low in religiosity than for those higher in religiosity (Fincham & May, 2017; Whisman et al., 2007), suggesting that religiosity may act as an "infidelity buffer" and hinders commitment-damaging behaviors. Future empirical research should continue to explore how demographic variables (e.g., gender identity, marital satisfaction) interact with social and cultural variables, such as religiosity or gender role expectations.

In another survey of people's likelihood of engaging in infidelity (Buss & Shackelford, 1997), males' marital satisfaction was negatively correlated with their expectations of how likely they were to engage in kissing, dating, and having serious affairs with women other than their committed partner. Men who were unhappy in their relationship reported higher probabilities of flirting with and having a brief affair with extradyadic women. Similarly, women who were unhappy in their marriage anticipated a higher likelihood that they would flirt, date, kiss, and have brief and serious affairs with other men, and also that their husbands were more likely to kiss, and have one-night stands and brief affairs with other women (Buss & Shackelford, 1997). These findings suggest that unhappy individuals expect to cheat, and expect their spouses to cheat as well (Tsapelas et al., 2010; Buss & Shackelford, 1997).

It is unclear why relationship satisfaction interacts with sex and gender as it does. It is also unclear what other factors might interact with or predict relationship dissatisfaction and infidelity in the way it appears that sex and gender does. Potential explanations for the relationship that have been discussed in the literature include boredom (Garg & Ruhela, 2015), a lack of communication and emotional intimacy (Gonzalez-Rivera et al., 2020), involvement in poor-quality relationships (Demaris, 2009; Gibson et al., 2016), ignoring dissatisfaction early in the relationship until the shortcomings negatively impact the relationship (Huston & Houts, 1998), or simply too much conflict (Atkins et al., 2005).

SATISFACTION AND COMMUNICATION

Communication is important for the success of a relationship, and ineffective communication can have serious consequences, including less relationship satisfaction and greater likelihood for infidelity (Buss & Shackelford, 1997; Maddox Shaw et al., 2013).

For instance, women who report that love and affection were not expressed much in their marriage anticipated a higher likelihood for themselves of engaging in a brief affair during the first year of marriage, and their husbands had similar expectations for their wives' behavior in this situation (Buss & Shackelford, 1997).

One possibility for why relationship satisfaction has such a strong influence on infidelity is because of the way that dissatisfaction and a lack of communication (which we discuss in the next section) have far-reaching consequences in a relationship. For instance, couples in therapy dealing with issues of infidelity had higher levels of dishonesty and more arguments about trust (Atkins et al., 2005). Husbands who complained about their partner's moodiness and withholding of sex reported a greater likelihood of flirting and kissing other women, while women with moody husbands anticipated kissing and having brief affairs with other men. Additionally, women who complained that their husbands sexualized others (e.g., commenting about the attractiveness of other women) estimated higher likelihood of themselves engaging in flirting, kissing, and having a one-night stand with other men (Buss & Shackelford, 1997). Women who complained that their husbands are jealous or possessive reported a higher likelihood of brief affairs, in line with the predictions that the husbands made about their wife's behavior—perhaps suggesting a self-fulfilling prophecy (Buss & Shackelford, 1997).

The influence of relationship satisfaction on infidelity underscores the importance of communication for predicting infidelity. Relationship satisfaction and communication within the relationship are strongly connected (Yoo et al., 2014). This link between relationship satisfaction and communication is revealed in research that explored how technology has impacted communication among partners; for example, smartphone use increases communication (Lapierre & Custer, 2021), but too much online intrusion into a partner's life decreases satisfaction (Norton et al., 2018). The communication does not have to involve major issues or deep conversations—the men in couples who doubled their "pillow talk" during a three-week experimental period had greater relationship satisfaction than the control group after a laboratory-induced conflict (though there was no increase in satisfaction for women, nor was there lower stress for either; Denes et al., 2020). Communication is related to relationship satisfaction across cultures, even if the mode of communication is culturally specific (Williamson et al., 2012). The direct effect of communication on infidelity, as well as the effect of communication on relationship satisfaction (which then predicts infidelity) warrants deeper examination.

In a study of 72 (White, educated) couples that used a diathesis-stress model (i.e., understanding unhealthy or problematic behavior as a result of the interaction between genetic predispositions and the stress caused by environmental factors; Ingram & Luxton, 2005) to understand infidelity, the most robust and consistent effects were found among relationship variables (stress), particularly communication effects (Allen et al., 2008). The findings showed that couples who engage in infidelity have more problematic communication even before marriage, such as lower levels of positive communication and higher levels of negative communication. Positive communication includes positive affect, problem solving, and support, whereas negative communication includes negative affect, denial, dominance, withdrawal, and conflict (Allen et al., 2008). A specific type of negative communication is emotional invalidation, which refers to communication behaviors including insults, negative comments, sarcasm, and "mind-reading," coupled with negative affect. High levels of this particular type of negative communication premaritally were highly predictive of engaging in infidelity after getting married.

Men who cheated, as compared to those who did not, reported less positive communication from their female partner, higher levels of their partner's emotional invalidation, and higher levels of their own negative communication and invalidation (Allen et al., 2008). In fact, women's invalidation continues to predict men's infidelity even after controlling for men's invalidation. Women who cheated, as compared to those who did not, reported higher levels of positive communication, lower levels of men's positive communication, higher levels of both women's and men's negative communication, and higher levels of both men's and women's invalidation (Allen et al., 2008). This suggests that it is not necessarily one partner ruining the relationship, but instead that couples (or, at least, heterosexual couples) who have lower levels of positive communicative interactions are at higher risk for future infidelity. That is, rather than one partner driving the other into the arms of another, the communication problems in the relationship may lead an individual to be more receptive or open to the idea of an extramarital relationship.

Moreover, it appears that worrying about the relationship and whether both partners are satisfied increases the likelihood of infidelity. In a longitudinal study with participants in relationships where infidelity had not yet occurred, higher levels of divorce proneness (e.g., thinking the marriage is in trouble, thinking about divorce, talking about divorce) predicted greater likelihood that at least one spouse would eventually engage in infidelity. Moreover, the relationship between satisfaction and infidelity was not unidirectional. Extramarital infidelity increased the odds of divorce, as well as indirectly increasing the odds of divorce via decreasing marital happiness and increasing divorce proneness and discussions. In fact, the odds of divorce were more than twice as high among individuals who reported infidelity than those who did not (Previti & Amato, 2004).

Finally, infidelity is often a secretive, concealed behavior and thus not usually communicated to the partner (Weiser et al., 2014). Moreover, once engagement in infidelity is discovered or suspected, a majority of individuals deny involvement, especially if the infidelity was short-lived (Moller & Vossler, 2014), and the communication tactics and strategies to do so are usually negative in nature, such as destructive strategies that actively work against the partner or relationship (e.g., revenge; Donovan & Emmers-Sommers, 2012). That is, while communication issues may have existed before the cheating, once infidelity has occurred, the partnership is more likely to suffer from communication problems. This pre-existing and continuing lack of positive and healthy communication can present particular problems for couples (and their counselors) as they work through the consequences of infidelity.

SEXUAL SATISFACTION

A person's perception that their needs are not being met is correlated with higher susceptibility to infidelity, and this includes sexual needs (Lewandowski & Ackerman, 2006). A lack of satisfaction with or a greater desire for certain sexual activities is one of the top 10 predictors of infidelity (Vowels et al., 2020). Both men and women who are unhappy with the sexual components of their married relationships are more likely to anticipate that they could become sexually involved with extramarital individuals, especially in the context of one-night stands (Buss & Shackelford, 1997). Many studies have examined the impact of sexual satisfaction on infidelity, and the conclusion appears to be that low sexual satisfaction predicts higher engagement in infidelity, particularly for men (Allen et al., 2008; Atkins et al., Buss & Shackleford, 1997; Liu, 2000; Mark et al., 2011; Vowels et al., 2020). Men who have cheated, as compared to those who have not cheated, report lower sexual satisfaction (Allen et al., 2008; Mark et al., 2011); however, a study of couples in therapy discussing issues related to infidelity showed that sexual dissatisfaction interacted with gender, in that men who had affairs were more sexually dissatisfied than women who had affairs (Atkins et al., 2005).

Moreover, the relationship between sexual satisfaction and infidelity exists not only for the sexual satisfaction component of frequency of sexual activity but also for incompatibility in sexual attitudes, sexual values, and sexual importance. Liu (2000), using National Health and Social Life Survey data, concluded that declining frequency of sexual activity in a heterosexual marriage led to a higher incidence of infidelity, especially for men. Additionally, men were prone to seek sexual partners outside of their marriage when they perceived their wife to be withholding sex (Buss & Shackelford, 1997).

For both men and women, perceived incompatibility related to the couple's sexual attitudes and sexual values was associated with infidelity. Mark and colleagues (2011) found that approximately two-thirds of men and 51% of women who engaged in infidelity reported lower sexual compatibility with their committed partner compared to those who did not engage in infidelity. In that same study, 70% of men who engaged in infidelity reported low compatibility with their partners in terms of the importance of sex for their lives and relationships (Mark et al., 2011). It should be noted that there is potential overlap between attitudes and behaviors in this case. For example, if one does not believe that sex is important, then avoidant behavior may result. As such, there is still much research needed to distinguish between sex-related attitudes and behaviors, and how they relate to satisfaction and ultimately infidelity.

As explained by the investment model of commitment (Rusbult, 1980; Rusbult et al., 1998), people's satisfaction with their relationships—including communication and sexual satisfaction—plays a major role in predicting infidelity. At the same time, no one variable (such as satisfaction) can account for all of the variance in infidelity. Another important variable in the investment model of commitment, as well as a predictor of infidelity, is the amount of resources people perceive they have invested into their current relationship.

Investment

Investments into one's romantic relationship includes anything that binds an individual to their partner or the partnership, and something that would be devalued or lost if the relationship were to end (Coy et al., 2019; Goodfriend & Agnew, 2008; Rusbult, 1980). Those investments could include intangible resources such as time, energy, self-disclosure, sacrifice, or compromises, and could also include tangible resources such as mutual friends, finances, or possessions (Goodfriend & Agnew, 2008). Commitment to one's relationship is increased not only by investment of resources into the relationship (Rubsult & Buunk, 1993), but also by the partner's investment, even after controlling for the individual's level of satisfaction and their perceived alternatives to the relationship (Coy et al., 2019).

The specific investment of sacrifice has been studied as a correlate of commitment in a few studies. For example, in situations when one partner does not agree with the other partner, sacrificing one's own needs or preferences so that the partner is benefited demonstrates a dedication to the partner's happiness and the relationship (Etcheverry & Le, 2005; Le & Agnew, 2003). One's willingness to sacrifice is positively related to commitment, in that individuals who are willing to sacrifice are more committed to the relationship, and shows that the individual is partner- and couple-focused rather than consumed with their own desired outcomes. Across studies, individuals who sacrifice or forego their own needs to resolve a conflict with their partner experience enhanced mood and increased satisfaction in their relationship, especially when they underestimate their costs and overestimate their benefits, suggesting that sacrifices protect one's well-being and perceptions of the relationship (Visserman et al., 2021).

One potential explanation for the positive outcomes resulting from investment is via cognitive dissonance theory and effort justification. Cognitive dissonance theory (Festinger, 1957; Harmon-Jones & Mills, 2019) posits that individuals strive to remain consistent in their thoughts, attitudes, and behaviors. Once those elements become misaligned, individuals experience an aversive emotion (i.e., dissonance arousal) that they are motivated to reduce by engaging in behaviors such as changing the misaligned element or engaging in rationalization and justification. Although initial research on cognitive dissonance focused on nonrelationship projects or tasks (Festinger & Aronson, 1960), the same behavioral process can be seen in various aspects of relationships. Specifically, when an individual considers abandoning a relationship in which they have highly invested, dissonance is the potential (and common) result (Nicholson & Lutz, 2017). Thus, individuals may increase their perceptions of satisfaction with the relationship in an attempt to justify the amount of effort (i.e., investment) that they have put into the relationship (Aronson & Mills, 1959).

In contrast to satisfaction and alternatives, which have a theoretical focus on what happens when an individual chooses to stay in a relationship, the investment portion of the investment model focuses on what happens (or may happen) when one leaves the relationship (Coy et al., 2019). As one's investments in a relationship increase, the costs of betraying or damaging the relationship increase as well. Individuals who are not invested in their current romantic partners are more likely to engage in infidelity than those who are invested (Drigotas et al., 1999; Mattingly et al., 2010). And, in cyclical fashion, infidelity is then related to subsequent declines in investments (Drigotas et al., 1999).

SELF-EXPANSION OPPORTUNITIES

Investments can be in the past or planned for the future. Another intangible source of investment in a relationship could be related to one's identity (Rusbult & Buunk, 1993). The self-expansion model (SEM; Aron & Aron, 1996; Aron et al., 1998) posits that people are motivated to enhance their perceptions of self via close relationships, new resources, perspectives, skills, abilities, and insights that increase self-efficacy and enhance their senses of self. That is, as individuals increase their emotional investments in their relationships, they begin thinking of themselves as part of a unit rather than as an individual. That is, Jana may begin to see herself as a member of the Todd-and-Jana unit, but also that the Todd-and-Jana unit makes up an important feature of who Jana is and how she perceives herself. The inclusion of the other in the self (i.e., viewing one's relationship partner as part of one's self), blurs the distinction between the two partners (Aron et al., 1991). To damage that relationship would then also inflict damage on Jana's own identity and sense of self.

Tying one's identity to another person is an intangible investment, but also provides a buffer against infidelity via new opportunities for self-expansion within the relationship. Sharing novel activities and experiences is one way to gain self-expansion and avoid boredom in a relationship, and is positively correlated with relationship quality (Reissman et al., 1993). If the process of self-expansion declines or stops, partners become less satisfied. That is, if an individual believes that their current relationship has the potential to provide self-expansion opportunities, then the need to terminate the relationship or seek alternatives is reduced. Conversely, if there is little opportunity in the current relationship, then the need for self-expansion might be found through alternative relationships (Lewandowski & Ackerman, 2006).

In fact, the perceived potential for self-expansion in one's possible future relationships predicts susceptibility to infidelity, even after controlling for gender, relationship length, and need fulfillment (e.g., intimacy, companionship, and sexual, security, and emotional involvement; Lewandowski & Ackerman, 2006). This is because extradyadic others, or extradyadic relationships, can provide self-expansion opportunities that the primary relationship may be failing to offer (Lewandowski & Ackerman, 2006). This is particularly true if alternate partners and relationships are perceived to be of higher quality than the current partner or relationship.

Quality of Alternatives

People who are in relationships where exclusivity is desired are not immune to the existence of tempting others. More so, individuals feel more committed to their relationships when they believe they have poor quality alternatives (Rusbult & Buunk, 1993). That is, the perceived attractiveness of one's other possible options (that is, if they were not in their current relationship) directly influences one's level of commitment. These alternatives could include nonromantic friendships, hobbies, moving to a new geographical location, and, as specifically related to infidelity, other tempting partners, relationships, or sexual opportunities. The quality of one's alternatives refers to the "siren's call" that may pull one away from their current relationship.

An increasing number of desirable alternatives predicts participants' reported propensities for engaging in infidelity if they believe they could get away with it. Moreover, higher quality of alternatives is among the strongest predictors of cheating (Emmers-Sommer et al., 2010). Specifically, relationship quality is negatively related to intense attraction to others and to infidelity (Gibson et al., 2016). The more alternatives someone thinks they have and the higher quality they think those alternatives are, the more likely they are to engage in infidelity. This is particularly true if they perceive the quality of those potential alternative partners to be greater than that of their current partner.

One way to manipulate (albeit often unconsciously) one's perceptions of the quality of alternatives is to derogate and devalue those alternatives (DeWall, Lambert, et al., 2011). Studies have shown that individuals who are happy and committed in their relationships restrict the time they spend on alternatives (e.g., time-consuming hobbies), wear symbols to ward off potential alternatives (e.g., wedding rings), actively avoid the temptation or even gazing at the tempter, and emphasize negative aspects of potential alternatives (DeWall, Maner, et al., 2011; Etcheverry et al., 2013; Meyer et al., 2011; Rodrigues et al., 2017). These studies speak to the power of commitment to shape one's behaviors, where the urge to engage in infidelity or even attend to attractive alternatives is reduced by the rewards of the current relationship (DeWall, Lambert, et al., 2011). In a classic infidelity study, Johnson and Rusbult (1989) found that the tendency to derogate the alternative was correlated with increases in the attractiveness of a potential alternative. That is, the more attractive the potential alternative was, the tendency to derogate occurred more often and to a greater degree. Presumably, the tendency to derogate alternatives in the first place is a relationship maintenance strategy that helps to buffer the relationship against infidelity.

The derogation of alternatives must be voluntary as opposed to enforced by a partner or situational demands. That is, if one partner restricts, or attempts to restrict, the ability of the partner to attend to alternatives, the effects are negative for the relationship (DeWall, Lambert, et al., 2011). This is likely because forcing individuals to reduce their attention toward attractive alternatives simultaneously increases their positive attitudes toward the alternative, increases their long-term memory of the alternative, increases their positive attitudes toward infidelity, and decreases their relationship satisfaction and commitment. That is, the restrictive partner unknowingly creates a forbidden fruit (DeWall, Lambert, et al., 2011; Ogolsky et al., 2017). Thus, the relationship maintenance behavior must come from the motivation of the tempted, not the threatened, or it might produce a type of relational reactance.

Other Potential Relationship Factors That Predict Infidelity

The investment model of commitment is a validated and replicated theory that explains various processes that engage relationship factors (Le & Agnew, 2003). The theory is useful in predicting relationship commitment and the outcomes associated with it. However, the quality of the interdependence among partners in a relationship (e.g., satisfaction, communication, investment) are not the only relationship-based factors that predict infidelity. Myriad other variables connected to the relationship, such as the details and demographics of the relationship (e.g., marriage versus cohabitation), also account for variance in predicting infidelity.

RELATIONSHIP TYPE

Married women are less likely to engage in infidelity than women who are cohabitating or dating, suggesting that there might be a commitment mechanism in marriage that serves as a protective factor against infidelity, although this may also be due to the level of commitment or investment in the relationship rather than speaking directly to the institution of marriage (Blow & Hartnett, 2005; Emmers-Sommer et al., 2010). Respondents who were married at a young age (i.e., 16 years or younger) were four times more likely to report infidelity than those who were married in their early 20s. Finally, the likelihood of infidelity decreases steadily as the age at which participants were married increases (Atkins et al., 2001).

RELATIONSHIP LENGTH

The length of a relationship has an interesting and sometimes curvilinear relationship with infidelity. Many studies have shown that relationship length negatively predicts infidelity behavior, in that infidelity was more likely to occur in shorter relationships (e.g., DeMaris, 2009)—possibly because relationships might end after an instance of infidelity, keeping those relationships short. This correlation often interacts with gender. For women, infidelity is more likely to occur in longer primary relationships than in shorter relationships, regardless of the commitment level of the relationship (e.g., dating, cohabitating, married; Blow & Hartnett, 2005). However, for married women, the rates of infidelity increase until about the seventh year and then begin to decline (Liu, 2000). For married men, this relationship is the opposite, in that relationship time is negatively related to likelihood of engaging in infidelity, until the 18th year, at which point the likelihood begins to increase again (Liu, 2000; Blow & Hartnett, 2005). For dating relationships, men show a positive relationship between the length of time in the relationship and the likelihood of committing infidelity (Blow & Hartnett, 2005).

It is possible that the duration of the relationship is correlated with commitment, but other studies show that, again, it could be the number of quality investments that couples have made that is the better predictor. For example, couples in therapy who reported infidelity showed greater marital instability, spent more time apart from one another, enjoyed time together less, and engaged in more steps toward separation and divorce (Atkins et al., 2005). Moreover, couples who live apart are more likely to engage in nonmonogamous behaviors (Blow & Hartnett, 2005), perhaps because living apart provides greater opportunities and more potential alternative partners for infidelity.

OPPORTUNITIES FOR INFIDELITY

As it pertains to cyber-infidelity, there is a clear sense that the Internet makes cheating behavior more possible, particularly infidelity that might not have been possible otherwise, because the Internet creates opportunities for coincidental online contact (Martins et al., 2016; Vossler & Moller, 2020). That is, individuals can intentionally seek partners through social media (e.g., Facebook) or infidelity-facilitating websites (e.g., AshleyMadison.com), but they may also find potential partners through means that are not directly related to relationship building, such as gaming (e.g., World of Warcraft). The Internet presents an array of ways to meet potential partners.

However, opportunity also increases by simply leaving the house. For example, Atkins and colleagues (2001) found that participants reported less infidelity when neither partner was employed as opposed to other employment categories (e.g., both are employed, one works). Respondents who were working outside the home but whose spouse was not working outside the home were the most likely to engage in infidelity (Atkins et al., 2001; Brooks & Monaco, 2013). Arguably, this is because the work environment adds opportunity, provides potential alternative partners, and individuals spend approximately 40 hours or more with these individuals weekly (Blow & Hartnett, 2005; Treas & Giesen, 2000).

Another argument may be that this likelihood of infidelity is because of similarity in assortative mating (Brooks & Monaco, 2013). That is, if one spouse works and the other one does not, there is a lack of similarity, producing what could be referred to as a bad pairing and motivating the working individual to find someone who is more similar to themselves. Regardless of the reason, one study (Wiggins & Lederer, 1984) showed how prolific this pattern is, as half of the participants who had engaged in infidelity reported being involved with one of their coworkers.

Moreover, respondents earning $75,000 or more annually were 1.5 times more likely to engage in infidelity than respondents earning less than $30,000 annually (Atkins et al., 2001). This may not be due to the money itself, but to other factors related to income such as stress, entitlement, and opportunity (Atkins et al., 2001; Blow & Hartnett, 2005). Lower relative income (i.e., economic dependency on one's current partner) is associated with higher odds of engaging in infidelity, even after controlling for race, age, education, hours worked, religious attendance, and the presence or age of children (Munsch, 2015). Of course, this relationship was mediated by relationship satisfaction or amount of conflict. For women, those who are economically dependent on their partner are more likely to engage in infidelity than either women who provide all the income in a household (i.e., the breadwinners) or women who are in an economically equal relationship (Munsch, 2015).

Future Directions

There is a considerable literature regarding what factors predict infidelity. Although demographic and individual characteristics are inconsistently associated with infidelity, relationship variables are the most consistent and robust across multiple studies (Haseli et al., 2019; Vowels et al., 2020). However, this research on relationship factors accounts for, on average, only one-fourth of the variance in infidelity behavior (e.g., Atkins et al., 2001; Blow & Hartnett, 2005; Tsapelas et al., 2010), leaving a large amount of variance unexplained. Simply put, infidelity does sometimes occur in happy relationships (Perel, 2017), and we still do not fully know why.

Perhaps some of the variance can be explained not by *what* we are studying, but *how* we are studying it. No one would argue that a beautifully modeled longitudinal study examining the interconnectedness of couples would not be groundbreaking in discovering that missing link (or links) of why people cheat. Following a large sample of individuals as they interact, influence, and potentially betray one another over a long period of time may be imperative for understanding how this behavior occurs. The analysis would be complicated, the study would be expensive, and the time required could be career-ending, but the mechanisms that underlie the transition from monogamous to betrayed (or betrayer) might be uncovered for all the world to see. For the time being, though, psychology must continue to examine potential factors, and how those factors interact with other known factors, mostly with cross-sectional and correlational designs. The good news is that the more studies that find consistent links, the more we can trust the results.

Future studies may want to start asking broader questions about infidelity. For example, rather than asking *why* individuals seek out extradyadic others, we might ask what individuals get out of an extradyadic relationship or affair. That is, most of the research has focused on predicting infidelity based on individuals' motives, disappointments, or other such factors. But few studies have asked why an individual continues the affair (or affairs). We know that individuals who cheat are likely to repeat the behavior (Knopp et al., 2017), but do we know what they gain from it? If the source of their discontent lies in the relationship, do they keep finding themselves in poor quality relationships? Or, is there something they get from the extradyadic relationship that is fulfilling a need?

For example, Hackathorn and Ashdown (2021) found that individuals may be motivated to cheat through sex-based motives (e.g., higher desired frequency), but may not be finding the satisfaction they crave for those motives in the extradyadic relationships they form. Instead, participants reported being emotionally satisfied with their extradyadic relationships, even if a sex-based motive drove them to cheat in the first place. This might suggest that their sex-based needs are now being met with the extradyadic partner, and they are able to progress toward fulfilling other needs, such as emotional intimacy. Or, it might suggest that there is a disconnect between what people think they need or want and what they actually need or want. Future research should examine what individuals get out of extradyadic relationships.

Lastly, in knowing the consistent and robust predictors of engaging in infidelity, such as a lack of relationship satisfaction, what can we do about it? Perhaps addressing relationship-based issues early on might provide a buffer against infidelity, whether through one's own behavior or the partner's, or through the partners' interactions with one another. Perhaps in an ideal future, experimental studies in which couples voluntarily attend infidelity or conflict prevention therapy will begin to shed light on which factors to pay attention to—including aspects of the relationship—in order to reduce the siren's call. If we can identify which of those factors can be isolated, manipulated, or reduced, perhaps we can help improve relationships. We need to keep adding evidence to the notion that it is not that the cheater is a bad person, or a type of person whom we can easily profile or spot in a crowd. It is the interacting dyadic nature of the relationship that may be the root cause. That is, it's not you, and it's not me . . . it's us.

References

Allen, E. S., Rhoades, G. K., Stanley, S. M., Markman, H. J., Williams, T., Melton, J., & Clements, M. L. (2008). Premarital precursors of marital infidelity. *Family Process, 47*(2), 243–259. https://doi.org/10.1111/j.1545-5300.2008.00251.x

Aron, E. N., & Aron, A. (1996). Love and expansion of the self: The state of the model. *Personal Relationships, 3*(1), 45–58.

Aron, A., Aron, E. N., Tudor, M., & Nelson, G. (1991). Close relationships as including other in the self. *Journal of Personality and Social Psychology, 60*(2), 241.

Aron, A., Norman, C. C., & Aron, E. N. (1998). The self-expansion model and motivation. *Representative Research in Social Psychology 22, 1-13.*

Aronson, E., & Mills, J. (1959). The effect of severity of initiation on liking for a group. *Journal of Abnormal and Social Psychology, 59*(2), 177–181.

Atkins, D. C., Baucom, D. H., & Jacobson, N. S. (2001). Understanding infidelity: Correlates in a national random sample. *Journal of Family Psychology, 15*(4), 735–749. https://psycnet.apa.org/doi/10.1037/0893-3200.15.4.735

Atkins, D. C., Yi, J., Baucom, D. H., & Christensen, A. (2005). Infidelity in couples seeking marital therapy. *Journal of Family Psychology*, *19*(3), 470–473. https://doi.org/10.1037/0893-3200.19.3.470

Basson, R. (2005). Women's sexual dysfunction: Revised and expanded definitions. *Canadian Medical Association Journal*, *172*(10), 1327–1333.

Blow, A. J., & Hartnett, K. (2005). Infidelity in committed relationships II: A substantive review. *Journal of Marital and Family Therapy*, *31*(2), 217–233. https://doi.org/10.1111/j.1752-0606.2005.tb01556.x

Brooks, T. J., & Monaco, K. (2013). Your cheatin' heart: Joint production, joint consumption and the likelihood of extramarital sex. *Applied Economics Letters*, *20*(3), 272–275. https://doi.org/10.1080/13504851.2012.690845

Buss, D. M., & Shackelford, T. K. (1997). Susceptibility to infidelity in the first year of marriage. *Journal of Research in Personality*, *31*(2), 193–221. https://doi.org/10.1006/jrpe.1997.2175

Coy, A. E., Davis, J. L., Green, J. D., & Etcheverry, P. E. (2019). A dyadic model of investments: Partner effects on commitment. *Journal of Social and Personal Relationships*, *36*(11–12), 3471–3491. https://doi.org/10.1177/0265407518822783

DeMaris, A. (2009). Distal and proximal influences on the risk of extramarital sex: A prospective study of longer duration marriages. *Journal of Sex Research*, *46*(6), 597–607. https://doi.org/10.1080/00224490902915993

Denes, A., Crowly, J. P., Winkler, K. L., Dhillon, A., Ponivas, A. L. P., & Bennet, M. (2020). Exploring the effects of pillow talk on relationship satisfaction and physiological stress responses to couples' difficult conversations. *Communications Monographs*, *87*(3), 267–290. https://doi.org/10.1080/03637751.2020.1726424

Dennerstein, L., Lehert, P., & Burger, H. (2005). The relative effects of hormones and relationship factors on sexual function of women through the natural menopausal transition. *Fertility and Sterility*, *84*(1), 174–180.

DeWall, C. N., Lambert, N. M., Slotter, E. B., Pond, R. S., Deckman, T., Finkel, E. J., Luchies, L. B., & Fincham, F. D. (2011). So far away from one's partner, yet so close to romantic alternatives: Avoidant attachment, interest in alternatives, and infidelity. *Journal of Personality and Social Psychology*, *101*(6), 1302–1316. https://doi.org/10.1037/a0025497

DeWall, C. N., Maner, J. K., Deckman, T., & Rouby, D. A. (2011). Forbidden fruit: Inattention to attractive alternatives provokes implicit relationship reactance. *Journal of Personality and Social Psychology*, *100*(4), 621–629. https://doi.org/10.1037/a0021749

Donovan, S., & Emmers-Sommer, T. M. (2012). Attachment style and gender as predictors of communicative responses to infidelity. *Marriage & Family Review*, *48*(2), 125–149. https://doi.org/10.1080/01494929.2011.626670

Drigotas, S. M., Safstrom, C. A., & Gentilia, T. (1999). An investment model prediction of dating infidelity. *Journal of Personality and Social Psychology*, *3*, 509–524.

Emmers-Sommer, T. M., Warber, K., & Halford, J. (2010). Reasons for (non)engagement in infidelity. *Marriage & Family Review*, *46*(6–7), 420–444. https://doi.org/10.1080/01494929.2010.528707

Etcheverry, P. E., & Le, B. (2005). Thinking about commitment: Accessibility of commitment and prediction of relationship persistence, accommodation, and willingness to sacrifice. *Personal Relationships*, *12*(1), 103–123. https://doi.org/10.1111/j.1350-4126.2005.00104.x

Etcheverry, P. E., Le, B., Wu, T.-F., & Wei, M. (2013). Attachment and the investment model: Predictors of relationship commitment, maintenance, and persistence. *Personal Relationships*, *20*(3), 546–567. https://doi.org/10.1111/j.1475-6811.2012.01423.x

Festinger, L. (1957). *A theory of cognitive dissonance*. Row, Peterson.

Festinger, L., & Aronson, E. (1960). The arousal and reduction of dissonance in social contexts. *Group Dynamics*, *2*, 214–231.

Fincham, F. D., & May, R. W. (2017). Infidelity in romantic relationships. *Current Opinion in Psychology*, *13*, 70–74. https://doi.org/10.1016/j.copsyc.2016.03.008

Garg, A., & Ruhela, S. (2015). Investigation of attitude of college youth towards infidelity. *International Journal of Education and Psychological Research*, *4*(1), 72–75.

Gibson, K. A. V., Thompson, A. E., & O'Sullivan, L. F. (2016). Love thy neighbour: Personality traits, relationship quality, and attraction to others as predictors of infidelity among young adults. *Canadian Journal of Human Sexuality*, *25*(3), 186–198. https://doi.org/10.3138/cjhs.253-A2

Glass, S. P., & Wright, T. L. (1985). Sex differences in type of extramarital involvement and marital dissatisfaction. *Sex Roles, 12*(9/10), 1101–1120.

González-Rivera, J. A., Aquino-Serrano, F., & Pérez-Torres, E. M. (2020). Relationship satisfaction and infidelity-related behaviors on social networks: A preliminary online study of Hispanic women. *European Journal of Investigation in Health, Psychology and Education, 10*(1), 297–309.

Goodfriend, W., & Agnew, C. R. (2008). Sunken costs and desired plans: Examining different types of investments in close relationships. *Personality and Social Psychology Bulletin, 34*(12), 1639–1652. https://doi.org/10.1177/0146167208323743

Hackathorn, J., & Ashdown, B. K. (2021). The webs we weave: Predicting infidelity motivations and extradyadic relationship satisfaction. *Journal of Sex Research, 58*(2), 170–182.

Hackathorn, J., & Harvey, R. (2011). Sexual double standards: Bias in perceptions of cyber-infidelity. *Sexuality & Culture, 15*, 100–113.

Hackathorn, J., Mattingly, B. A., Clark, E. M., & Mattingly, M. J. B. (2011). Practicing what you preach: Infidelity attitudes as a predictor of fidelity. *Current Psychology, 30*(4), 299–311. https://doi.org/10.1007/s12144-011-9119-9

Harmon-Jones, E., & Mills, J. (2019). An introduction to cognitive dissonance theory and an overview of current perspectives on the theory. In E. Harmon-Jones (Ed.), *Cognitive dissonance: Reexamining a pivotal theory in psychology* (2nd ed., pp. 3–24). American Psychological Association. https://doi.org/10.1037/0000135-001

Haseli, A., Shariati, M., Nazari, A. M., Keramat, A., & Emamian, M. H. (2019). Infidelity and its associated factors: A systematic review. *Journal of Sexual Medicine, 16*(8), 1155–1169.

Hawthorne, N. (1850). *The scarlet letter*. Tickner, Reed, & Fields.

Huston, T. L., & Houts, R. M. (1998). The psychological infrastructure of courtship and marriage: The role of personality and compatibility in romantic relationships. In T. N. Bradbury (Ed.), *The developmental course of marital dysfunction* (1st ed., pp. 114–151). Cambridge University Press. https://doi.org/10.1017/CBO9780511527814.006

Ingram, R. E., & Luxton, D. D. (2005). Vulnerability-stress models. In B. L. Hankin & J. R. Z. Abela (Eds.), *Development of psychopathology: A vulnerability-stress perspective* (pp. 32–46). Sage Publications.

Johnson, D. J., & Rusbult, C. E. (1989). Resisting temptation: Devaluation of alternative partners as a means of maintaining commitment in close relationships. *Journal of Personality and Social Psychology, 57*(6), 967.

Knopp, K., Scott, S., Ritchie, L., Rhoades, G. K., Markman, H. J., & Stanley, S. M. (2017). Once a cheater, always a cheater? Serial infidelity across subsequent relationships. *Archives of Sexual Behavior, 46*(8), 2301–2311. https://doi.org/10.1007/s10508-017-1018-1

Lambert, N. M., Mulder, S., & Fincham, F. (2014). Thin slices of infidelity: Determining whether observers can pick out cheaters from a video clip interaction and what tips them off. *Personal Relationships, 21*(4), 612–619. https://doi.org/10.1111/pere.12052

Lapierre, M. A., & Custer, B. E. (2021). Testing relationships between smartphone engagement, romantic partner communication, and relationship satisfaction. *Mobile Media & Communication, 9*(2), 155–176. https://doi.org/10.1177%2F2050157920935163

Larson, J. M. (2014). *Relationship satisfaction, attitudes toward infidelity, Facebook, and infidelity*. Trevecca Nazarene University.

Le, B., & Agnew, C. R. (2003). Commitment and its theorized determinants: A meta-analysis of the investment model. *Personal Relationships, 10*(1), 37–57. https://doi.org/10.1111/1475-6811.00035

Lewandowski, G. W., & Ackerman, R. A. (2006). Something's missing: Need fulfillment and self-expansion as predictors of susceptibility to infidelity. *Journal of Social Psychology, 146*(4), 389–403. https://doi.org/10.3200/SOCP.146.4.389-403

Liu, C. (2000). A theory of marital sexual life. *Journal of Marriage and the Family, 62*(12), 363–374.

Maddox Shaw, A. M., Rhoades, G. K., Allen, E. S., Stanley, S. M., & Markman, H. J. (2013). Predictors of extradyadic sexual involvement in unmarried opposite-sex relationships. *Journal of Sex Research, 50*(6), 598–610. https://doi.org/10.1080/00224499.2012.666816

Mark, K. P., Janssen, E., & Milhausen, R. R. (2011). Infidelity in heterosexual couples: Demographic, interpersonal, and personality-related predictors of extradyadic sex. *Archives of Sexual Behavior, 40*(5), 971–982. https://doi.org/10.1007/s10508-011-9771-z

Martins, A., Pereira, M., Andrade, R., Dattilio, F. M., Narciso, I., & Canavarro, M. C. (2016). Infidelity in dating relationships: Gender-specific correlates of face-to-face and online extradyadic involvement. *Archives of Sexual Behavior*, *45*(1), 193–205. https://doi.org/10.1007/s10508-015-0576-3

Mattingly, B. A., Wilson, K., Clark, E. M., Bequette, A. W., & Weidler, D. J. (2010). Foggy faithfulness: Relationship quality, religiosity, and the perceptions of dating infidelity scale in an adult sample. *Journal of Family Issues*, *31*(11), 1465–1480.

McDaniel, B. T., Drouin, M., & Cravens, J. D. (2017). Do you have anything to hide? Infidelity-related behaviors on social media sites and marital satisfaction. *Computers in Human Behavior*, *66*, 88–95. https://doi.org/10.1016/j.chb.2016.09.031

Meyer, M. L., Berkman, E. T., Karremans, J. C., & Lieberman, M. D. (2011). Incidental regulation of attraction: The neural basis of the derogation of attractive alternatives in romantic relationships. *Cognition & Emotion*, *25*(3), 490–505. https://doi.org/10.1080/02699931.2010.527494

Moller, N. P. & Vossler, A. (2014). Defining infidelity in research and couple counseling: A qualitative study. *Journal of Sex & Marital Therapy*, *41*(5), 487–497. https://doi.org/10.1080/0092623X.2014.931314

Munsch, C. L. (2015). Her support, his support: Money, masculinity, and marital infidelity. *American Sociological Review*, *80*(3), 469–495. https://doi.org/10.1177/0003122415579989

Nicholson, S. B., & Lutz, D. J. (2017). The importance of cognitive dissonance in understanding and treating victims of intimate partner violence. *Journal of Aggression, Maltreatment & Trauma*, *26*(5), 475–492. https://doi.org/10.1080/10926771.2017.1314989

Norton, A. M., Baptist, J., & Hogan, B. (2018). Computer-mediated communication in intimate relationships: Associations of boundary crossing, intrusion, relationship satisfaction, and partner responsiveness. *Journal of Marital and Family Therapy*, *44*(1), 165–182. https://doi.org/10.1111/jmft.12246

Ogolsky, B. G., Monk, J. K., Rice, T. M., Theisen, J. C., & Maniotes, C. R. (2017). Relationship maintenance: A review of research on romantic relationships. *Journal of Family Theory & Review*, *9*(3), 275–306. https://doi.org/10.1111/jftr.12205

Parsons, J. T., Starks, T. J., Gamarel, K. E., & Grov, C. (2012). Non-monogamy and sexual relationship quality among same-sex male couples. *Journal of Family Psychology*, *26*(5), 669–677. https://doi.org/10.1037/a0029561

Perel, E. (2017). *The state of affairs: Rethinking infidelity—A book for anyone who has ever loved*. Hachette UK.

Previti, D., & Amato, P. R. (2004). Is infidelity a cause or a consequence of poor marital quality? *Journal of Social and Personal Relationships*, *21*(2), 217–230. https://doi.org/10.1177/0265407504041384

Prins, K. S., Buunk, B. P., & VanYperen, N. W. (1993). Equity, normative disapproval and extramarital relationships. *Journal of Social and Personal Relationships*, *10*(1), 39–53. https://doi.org/10.1177/0265407593101003

Reissman, C., Aron, A., & Bergen, M. R. (1993). Shared activities and marital satisfaction: Causal direction and self-expansion versus boredom. *Journal of Social and Personal Relationships*, *10*(2), 243–254.

Rodrigues, D., Lopes, D., & Kumashiro, M. (2017). The "I" in us, or the eye on us? Regulatory focus, commitment and derogation of an attractive alternative person. *PLoS One*, *12*(3), e0174350. https://doi.org/10.1371/journal.pone.0174350

Roloff, M. E., Soule, K. P., & Carey, C. M. (2001). Reasons for remaining in a relationship and responses to relational transgressions. *Journal of Social and Personal Relationships*, *18*(3), 362–385. https://doi.org/10.1177%2F0265407501183004

Rusbult, C. E. (1980). Commitment and satisfaction in romantic associations: A test of the investment model. *Journal of Experimental Social Psychology*, *16*(2), 172–186.

Rusbult, C. E., & Buunk, B. P. (1993). Commitment processes in close relationships: An interdependence analysis. *Journal of Social and Personal Relationships*, *10*(2), 175–204.

Rusbult, C. E., Martz, J. M., & Agnew, C. R. (1998). The investment model scale: Measuring commitment level, satisfaction level, quality of alternatives, and investment size. *Personal Relationships*, *5*(4), 357–387.

Scheinkman, M. (2005). Beyond the trauma of betrayal: Reconsidering affairs in couples therapy. *Family Process*, *44*(2), 227–244.

Sevi, B., Urganci, B., & Sakman, E. (2020). Who cheats? An examination of light and dark personality traits as predictors of infidelity. *Personality and Individual Differences*, *164*, 110126. https://doi.org/10.1016/j.paid.2020.110126

Sharpe, D. I., Walters, A. S., & Goren, M. J. (2013). Effect of cheating experience on attitudes toward infidelity. *Sexuality & Culture*, *17*(4), 643–658. https://doi.org/10.1007/s12119-013-9169-2

Silva, A., Saraiva, M., Albuquerque, P. B., & Arantes, J. (2017). Relationship quality influences attitudes toward and perceptions of infidelity. *Personal Relationships*, *24*(4), 718–728. https://doi.org/10.1111/pere.12205

Solstad, K., & Mucic, D. (1999). Extramarital sexual relationships of middle-aged Danish men: Attitudes and behavior. *Maturitas*, *32*(1), 51–59. https://doi.org/10.1016/S0378-5122(99)00012-2

Thompson, A. P. (1984). Emotional and sexual components of extramarital relations. *Journal of Marriage and the Family*, *46*(1), 35. https://doi.org/10.2307/351861

Treas, J., & Giesen, D. (2000). Sexual infidelity among married and cohabiting Americans. *Journal of Marriage and Family*, *62*(1), 48–60. https://doi.org/10.1111/j.1741-3737.2000.00048.x

Tsapelas, I., Fisher, H. E., & Aron, A. (2010). *Infidelity: When, where, and why?* In WR Cupach and BH Spitzberg (eds), The Dark Side of Close Relationships II, NY.

Visserman, M. L., Righetti, F., Muise, A., Impett, E. A., Joel, S., & Van Lange, P. A. M. (2021). Taking stock of reality: Biased perceptions of the costs of romantic partners' sacrifices. *Social Psychological and Personality Science*, *12*(1), 54–62. https://doi.org/10.1177/1948550619896671

Vossler, A., & Moller, N. P. (2020). Internet affairs: Partners' perceptions and experiences of internet infidelity. *Journal of Sex & Marital Therapy*, *46*(1), 67–77.

Vowels, L. M., Vowels, M. J., & Mark, K. P. (2020). Is infidelity predictable? Using interpretable machine learning to identify the most important predictors of infidelity Journal of Sex Research, 59(2), 224-237. https://doi.org/10.31234/osf.io/4crxu

Weiser, D. A., Lalasz, C. B., Weigel, D. J., & Evans, W. P. (2014). A prototype analysis of infidelity. *Personal Relationships*, *21*(4), 655–675. https://doi.org/10.1111/pere.12056

Whisman, M. A., Gordon, K. C., & Chatav, Y. (2007). Predicting sexual infidelity in a population-based sample of married individuals. *Journal of Family Psychology*, *21*(2), 320–324. https://doi.org/10.1037/0893-3200.21.2.320

Wiederman, M. W., & Allgeier, E. R. (1996). Expectations and attributions regarding extramarital sex among young married individuals. *Journal of Psychology & Human Sexuality*, *8*(3), 21–35. https://doi.org/10.1300/J056v08n03_02

Wiggins, J. D., & Lederer, D. A. (1984). Differential antecedents of infidelity in marriage. *American Mental Health Counselors Association Journal*, *6*(4), 152–161.

Williamson, H. C., Ju, X., Bradbury, T. N., Karney, B. R., Fang, X., & Liu, X. (2012). Communication behavior and relationship satisfaction among American and Chinese newlywed couples. *Journal of Family Psychology*, *26*(3), 308–315. https://psycnet.apa.org/doi/10.1037/a0027752

Yoo, H., Bartle-Haring, S., Day, R. D., & Gangamma, R. (2014). Couple communication, emotional and sexual intimacy, and relationship satisfaction. *Journal of Sex & Marital Therapy*, *40*(4), 275–293. https://doi.org/10.1080/0092623X.2012.751072

CHAPTER 6

Social Versus Sexual Monogamy

Catherine Salmon *and* Jessica Hehman

> **Abstract**
> Monogamy is sometimes understood as a type of relationship in which an individual has only one partner during their lifetime. Thus, serial monogamy refers to the practice of having only one partner during a specific period of time. Based on current divorce rates in modern Western populations, humans are often referred to as serially monogamous. However, there is also a distinction to be made between social and sexual monogamy. Social monogamy reflects a socially recognized relationship in which two individuals live together, have sexual relations, and cooperate in the acquisition and sharing of resources, and often the care of offspring. Sexual monogamy consists of two individuals who are sexually exclusive, having no sexual partners outside of the pair. While many pairings can be both socially and sexually monogamous, sexual monogamy is not always found in socially monogamous relationships. This chapter reviews research that examines the factors influencing social and sexual monogamy and the role infidelity can play in social monogamy in humans and nonhuman animals.
>
> **Key Words:** monogamy, infidelity, serial monogamy, social monogamy, sexual monogamy, relationship

Introduction

Much research across a wide range of species has focused on monogamy, despite its rarity in the animal world, perhaps due to its commonality among human populations today (Birkhead & Moller, 1996; Klug, 2018; Low, 2003; Lukas & Clutton-Brock, 2013; Marlowe, 2000; Reichard, 2003). A substantial proportion of published work has focused on evaluating models of how monogamy evolved or what conditions could have led to such a mating system including the role of biparental care in offspring survival, male protection of offspring from predation or infanticide, resource distribution, male ability to mate guard, and female territoriality (Clutton-Brock, 1991; Gowaty, 1996a; Lukas & Clutton-Brock, 2013; Reichard, 2003; Ribble, 2003). The distribution of monogamy across species ranges from 90% in birds, to 9% in mammals, though it is worth noting that 29% of nonhuman primates (Lukas & Clutton-Brock, 2013), and 17% of human societies have some form of monogamy (Low, 2003). Polygyny is much more common than monogamy, presumably because the fitness benefits under such a system are greater than the costs, at least for some individuals. Male reproductive success is largely influenced by sexual access to multiple females, and this has been used to explain male sexual strategies in a wide variety of species (Jones & Ratterman, 2009; Symons, 1979; Trivers, 1972). However, females can also benefit from mating with multiple males, which has been associated with greater female reproductive success in birds (Reding, 2015) and infanticide avoidance (Hrdy, 1979). With these sorts of multiple mating benefits, why, or in what sorts of circumstances, does monogamy occur?

Before going any further, it is important to distinguish what we mean by the term "monogamy." There are two main forms of monogamy that will be distinguished in this chapter. Social monogamy occurs when a male and female pair bond and live together for a period of time (one breeding season to over many years). Social monogamy does not necessarily imply sexual monogamy (Gowaty, 1996a; Klug, 2018). Sexual monogamy entails sexual exclusivity between the mated pair for a specified period of time. Genetic monogamy can also occur even in the absence of sexual monogamy if no extrapair paternity occurs. In many cases, whether social or sexual, monogamy is often serial. The time frame can be variable from a breeding season to the death of one member of the pair, at which point, re-pairing may occur (Reichard, 2003). Re-pairing often occurs in a number of mammalian species as well as in birds and humans. Some of the early research on social monogamy, particularly in birds, assumed social was sexual monogamy but later work documented infidelity leading to sperm competition and extrapair paternity that has been further examined via genetic analysis (Bellis et al., 2005; Birkhead & Moller, 1996; Kleven et al., 2019; Rice et al., 2018; Shackelford et al., 2002). These extrapair copulations (EPCs) are engaged in by both male and female members of some socially monogamous pairs. The idea that the relationship between social and sexual monogamy is highly variable has been demonstrated in a number of species, some of which will be discussed in greater detail later in this chapter. For example, there are birds that are socially and sexually monogamous such as the long-eared owl (Marks et al., 1999) and ones that are socially monogamous but with high rates of EPCs, including many songbirds such as warblers, cardinals, and thrushes (Brouwer & Griffith, 2019). Rodents also vary from the socially monogamous prairie vole (*Microtus ochrogaster*) where the majority of males engage in sexual monogamy but some do engage in extrapair mating (Ophir et al., 2008), to the socially and sexually monogamous California mouse (*Peromyscus californicus*) (Ribble, 2003) and Malagasy giant jumping rat (*Hypogeonys antimena*) (Sommers, 2003). And, of course, there are human societies that practice social monogamy with varying degrees of sexual monogamy (Bauch & McElreath, 2016; Bellis et al., 2005; Gallup et al, 2003; Low, 2003).

Theoretical Perspectives on Monogamy

What factors influence the development and maintenance of social and/or sexual monogamy? Biparental care is often associated with monogamy, and it has often been suggested that a need for significant investment from both parents has been a driving factor in the development of monogamy. From this perspective, successful rearing of offspring requires the investment of both parents, such as in birds, where provisioning and incubation by both members of the mated pair can be essential (Clutton-Brock, 1991; Hall, 1999; Schneider & Lamprecht, 1990), though significant paternal care occurs in a number of mammals as well, the majority of which are socially monogamous (Fernandez-Duque et al., 2009; Gubernick & Teferi, 2000; Malcolm, 1985; Stockley & Hobson, 2016). However, others have pointed out that some monogamous species do not have much paternal care and that biparental care may be a product of monogamy rather than a causal factor in its evolution (Brotherton & Komers, 2003; Gowaty, 1996a; Iwasa & Harada, 1998; Lukas & Clutton-Brock, 2013).

Another factor, often implicated in monogamy for humans and birds, is the role of mate guarding (Kokko & Morrell, 2005). In humans, mate guarding can lead to monogamy as it allows males a greater degree of paternity certainty (Schacht & Bell, 2016). Of course, in humans, mate guarding does not have to be done only by the male partner (Lowe, 2003; Marlowe, 2000). His social allies and kin as well as cultural practices like menstrual hut sequestration and female circumcision (Strassman, 2003) can influence the likelihood of females engaging in extrapair sexual activities and drastically reduce any extrapair paternity. In birds, mate guarding males stay in close proximity to their females and are able to dissuade other males from encroaching and prevent females from seeking out extrapair opportunities. They may stay with their partners almost continuously until eggs are in the nest. Of course, such males face a trade-off in that they cannot simultaneously mate guard and seek extrapair opportunities for themselves, but they may be able to take advantage once the eggs are being incubated if the females do not have synchronous fertility (Fishman et al., 2003).

Lukas and Clutton-Brock (2013) suggest that monogamy in many of its mammalian versions resulted from low female population density and the resulting inability of males to defend multiple females from other males due to either large female home ranges or aggression between females. Others have also reported a correlation between social monogamy, female home range, and biparental care but have suggested that infanticide is a key factor, perhaps the key factor for primates (Opie et al., 2013). Here the argument is that social monogamy could develop when the risks of infanticide are high and the presence of a resident male partner can provide protection against infanticidal males (Opie et al., 2013; Palombit, 1999; van Schaik & Kappeler, 1997).

Sexual, or genetic monogamy, is more unusual than social monogamy, as many socially monogamous species have low to high levels of extrapair copulations (Carballo et al., 2019; Reichard, 2003) including some human populations (Bellis et al., 2005; Low, 2003). However, sexual monogamy should also be examined with regard to the costs and benefits experienced by males and females in such a mating system. The question of what added benefits males and female experience and what ecological conditions foster sexual monogamy, including life history factors (Gavrilets, 2012; Lambert, Sabol, & Solomon, 2018; Marlowe, 2000; Quinn et al., 1999) will be examined.

In the rest of this chapter, we will review the literature on social and sexual monogamy focusing on how different pressures in birds, mammals, and nonhuman primates and humans have influenced the forms of monogamy (social and sexual) that are observed. Understanding how male and female reproductive success benefits under these different forms of monogamy is essential to a comprehensive theory of mating systems and their development and maintenance.

Birds

There was a time when the avian literature suggested that the majority of birds were socially and sexually monogamous (Lack, 1968). However, the introduction of modern molecular genetic analysis to the examination of nestling parentage has highlighted a variety of alternative reproductive strategies including extrapair paternity (EPC) and intraspecific brood parasitism (IBP). In this section, we will examine mating systems in a variety of bird species and discuss the factors that influence the reproductive strategies displayed including social, sexual, and genetic monogamy. A number of studies suggest that obligatory paternal care and low annual mortality are important factors associated with the shift from social to sexual monogamy in birds.

Social Monogamy

A majority of birds engage in social monogamy where there is a social association but females engage in various levels of extrapair sexual activity. Passerine species are ones in which male parental food provisioning is not required for successful rearing of offspring and, in a number of passerines, females seek out extrapair copulations (Birkhead & Moller, 1992; Gowaty, 1996a). Females presumably engage in these EPCs because they are beneficial in terms of female fitness, perhaps in a variety of ways including genetic quality benefits (Hasselquist et al., 1996) and security against the infertility of her partner (Whitekiller et al., 2000). Male benefits for engaging in EPCs in terms of additional reproductive success are clear, with females being a limiting factor on their success, but then that raises the question of why males might stay in close proximity to their social mate rather than leaving. A number of reasons have been suggested, including limited mating options due to female–female aggression (or large female territories). However, if it is females seeking out extrapair opportunities, males may stay on a primary territory because other females know where they are and so advertise their availability for EPCs (Gowaty, 1996a). In such systems, females control EPCs by seeking out males (Graves et al., 1995). Females also can control EPCs by refusing unwanted copulations by males (Mills, 1994). Much of the sexual conflict that arises over EPCs in socially monogamous birds is influenced by whether extrapair paternity is driven largely by the extrapair male (male benefits) or the within-pair female (female benefits). In addition, rates of extrapair paternity in birds are highly influenced by adult mortality in that future cooperation in a breeding pair requires surviving to the next breeding season which decreases with increasing mortality rates. Longer lived species (like the parrots discussed later in this section) have more years together for the benefits of fidelity to accumulate and tend to have lower extrapair paternity (Chaine et al., 2015). Many of these factors influencing level of EPCs, or infidelity, in birds, including adult mortality and male parental care, will be revisited in the section on monogamy in humans.

Female hooded warblers appear to avoid interference in EPC attempts by their social mate by engaging in extraterritorial forays (Neudorf et al., 1997). Hooded warblers are socially monogamous but have relatively high levels of EPCs, with between a quarter and a half of nests reported to contain extrapair young. Neudorf et al.'s (1997) results suggest that females leave their territories more frequently when fertile and that 22% of the extrapair mating females had extrapair young. While females may be engaging in EPCs with males of higher genetic quality than their social mates, evidence for this was not found in these warblers.

As socially monogamous species vary widely in the frequency of extrapair paternity (Griffith et al., 2002), substantial interest has focused on the factors that influence this. Modeling studies suggest that male attractiveness and male trade-offs in terms of time spent mate guarding versus time spent obtaining EPCs are factors influencing extrapair paternity (Kokko & Morrell, 2005). The ability of males to mate guard has also been implicated in the development and/or maintenance of systems of sexual monogamy, as we will see in the next section. Other modeling studies have examined how, in altricial birds, where the successful rearing of chicks requires significant investment from males and females, female competition can lead to social monogamy despite the frequency of genetic promiscuity (Iwasa & Harada, 1998), as both female mate preferences and male decisions about parental care are related.

Interestingly, studies of both brain size and sperm morphology in birds have highlighted the different pressures males and females face in social versus sexual monogamy. West's (2014) study of brain size in birds indicates that there is a strong positive relationship such that brain size is related to social but not genetic monogamy. Large brain size appears to be related to the challenges of pursuing extrapair copulations while maintaining a socially monogamous relationship. Extrapair copulations also create a situation where the sperm of different males can be in competition to fertilize the same egg and this competition has been suggested to have played a role in the evolution of sperm morphology (Calhim et al., 2007; Lifjeld et al., 2010). Socially monogamous macaws, for example, show little indication of significant sperm competition in terms of their sperm quality/morphology, while the polygynandrous Eclectus parrot has much higher sperm density, indicative of the greater degree of sperm competition in their mating system (Bublat et al., 2017). Carbello and colleagues (2019) examined sperm morphology in parrots with results suggesting that the greatest levels of sperm competition were found in two species where females mate promiscuously and males provide food to the females they copulate with. The sperm competition level indicators within social monogamous species were also influenced by breeding density, likely due to opportunities for extrapair copulations resulting in greater sperm competition.

Sexual and/or Genetic Monogamy

Given some of the reproductive success benefits of social monogamy with extrapair mating, why do some species engage in sexual or genetic monogamy and under what circumstances does this occur? Cooperatively breeding birds, at first glance, might not seem like the most obvious place to find genetic monogamy. However, evidence suggests a lack of extrapair fertilizations or egg dumping in the Florida scrub jay (Quinn et al., 1999). In the population studied, the behavioral fathers and mothers were the genetic parents, evidence of genetic monogamy. The authors suggest that large territory size may limit opportunities for cuckoldry and the intense competition for limited breeding space may be responsible for low variance in quality between the male breeders. This would reduce the opportunities and benefits of engaging in extrapair copulation in this species for females.

Other examples of genetic or strict monogamy, as it is sometimes referred to, are found in a variety of species, mostly ones with long-term pair bonds and high levels of paternal care, which are often associated with high paternity confidence. While colonial living is often assumed to increase the frequency of EPCs due to opportunity, the jackdaw is a semicolonial passerine with long-term pair bonds and high levels of paternal care. In this species male provisioning is associated with fledging success (Henderson & Hart, 1993) though they also have frequent nestling loss due to brood reduction. Research conducted in the United Kingdom has reported no evidence of extrapair fertilizations (EPFs) or intraspecific brood parasitism (IBP) and this was the case despite the frequent absence of males during their female's fertile window (Henderson et al., 2000). The authors suggest an essential role for paternal care in genetic monogamy as females are unable to raise broods unassisted and high paternity confidence facilitates substantial paternal investment in offspring. Interestingly, extrapair copulations have been documented in wild jackdaws in the absence of actual extrapair fertilizations (Gill et al., 2019). Other colonial and semicolonial birds with high paternal care and long-term pair bonds include the black vulture (Decker et al., 1993), and the European bee-eaters (Jones et al., 1991). Interestingly, kin interference in EPC opportunities has also been raised as having a function in maintaining sexual monogamy in black vultures (Decker et al., 1993), something that will be discussed with regard to the maintenance of sexual monogamy in humans later in this chapter. The semicolonial flammulated owl is also considered to be socially monogamous, and there is evidence that they are genetically monogamous with very active parental care on the part of social fathers (Arsenault et al., 2002). Social and genetic monogamy have also been documented in long-lived high-parental-care species of parrots, including the burrowing parrot (Masello et al., 2002) and the crimson rosella (Eastwood et al., 2018).

In addition to obligatory paternal care, low annual mortality has also been suggested to play a role in variation in rates of extrapair paternity across avian species. The fact that low annual mortality (long life span) and paternal care are often correlated makes it difficult to detangle their relative importance. If paternal care is essential, genetic monogamy should be more commonly seen (Arnold & Owens, 2002), whether a species has low annual mortality or not. A study of two long-lived passerines, New Zealand saddlebacks and robins, revealed genetic monogamy (with one extrapair paternity exception in robins). The degree to which paternal care is required for fledging success in these species is not known. These results indicate that low annual mortality rates likely do play a role in in genetic monogamy (Taylor et al., 2008).

Mammals

In contrast to birds, social monogamy is more often associated with genetic monogamy in mammals with a relatively low reported incidence of extrapair mating in socially monogamous mammals (Lukas & Clutton-Brock, 2013; van Schaik, 2000). However, the majority of mammals are not monogamous, with some studies suggesting rates of less than 3% (Kleiman, 1977). Numerous studies examining the evolution of monogamy in mammals generally, have suggested the following two factors to have played possible roles: paternal care, sometimes associated with protection from male infanticide or male provisioning (Gubernick & Teferi, 2000; Malcolm, 1985), and male mate guarding (in that social monogamy evolved where females were solitary with distinct territories and males are unable to mate guard more than one female at a time). However, some genetic and socially monogamous species, like the dik-dik engage in no obvious paternal care (Brotherton, et al., 1997) leading some to suggest that social monogamy came first and then paternal care evolved under some conditions. Lukas and Clutton-Brock (2013) suggest that social monogamy evolved in mammals under conditions in which males were unable to successfully mate guard more than one female at a time, rendering monogamy a more efficient breeding strategy for males under those ecological conditions. In this section we will examine monogamy in prairie voles, which have been well studied, as well as in primates, which, as a group, have been characterized as having a greater proportion of monogamous species (Diaz-Munoz & Blaes, 2016; Munshi-South, 2007).

Social Monogamy

One of the most frequently highlighted examples of nonhuman mammalian monogamy is the prairie vole, in which adults typically form long-term male–female pairs with high levels of paternal care (Ophir et al., 2008). While some studies have suggested exclusive mating based on embryo fingerprinting (Getz & Carter, 1996), others have reported some females to have litters of mixed paternity (Solomon et al, 2004) raising the possibility of extrapair mating (though it was not known in this study whether the females were members of mating pairs). It may be that individual differences in the pairing status of adult animals (so-called wandering males) may have a role in influencing litter paternity (Getz & McGuire, 1993). Ophir and colleagues' (2008) examination of breeding success in a captive population of prairie voles indicated that there were more extrapair fertilizations than would be expected under genetic monogamy, indicating that they were socially but not genetically monogamous. However, a majority of litters were sired exclusively by the paired males, which brings us back to questions about ecological factors, or individual differences, shaping extrapair mating. Some studies have examined proximal links such as that between oxytocin receptor density and male mating tactics, finding that within prairie voles, monogamous males had greater oxytocin receptor density in the forebrain than nonmonogamous males (Ophir et al., 2012). The connection between oxytocin receptor distribution (and vasopressin) and pair bonding/parental care are implicated in vole mating systems (Insel & Shapiro, 1992) and have received interest as possible models for human monogamy. In addition, a number of studies have documented the role of female home ranges in constraining male mating strategies, such as in the round-eared sengi or elephant-shrew (Schubert et al., 2009).

While the majority of mammals are not socially monogamous (more commonly multiple males mate with multiple females during a breeding season), social monogamy is more common in primates than in other orders of mammal (Opie et al., 2013) with some researchers suggesting it is the result of male infanticide creating pressure for both parents to be available to defend dependent young with other forms of paternal care and more discrete female ranges developing as a consequence (Opie et al., 2013; Opie et al., 2014). Others have argued that nongregarious females would also be required as a precondition for social monogamy to evolve (Lukas & Clutton-Brock, 2013; Reichard, 2017). Male mate guarding of nongregarious females would likely make it difficult for males to guard more than one at once. Others have reported that male infanticide is not consistently associated with social monogamy and that again, female territoriality and spacing may be a relevant factor (Fernandez-Duque, 2016; Lukas & Clutton-Brock, 2014). Interestingly, the wild owl monkeys studied by Fernandez-Duque (2016) are often argued to be both socially and genetically monogamous (Fuentes, 1999; Huck et al., 2014), and while ranges may play a role in their monogamy, no one factor seems to provide sufficient explanation. This suggests that a number of factors may be necessary or that different pathways to social and sexual monogamy exist.

The frequency of extrapair mating in socially monogamous primates is highly variable. In the socially monogamous nocturnal fat-tailed dwarf lemur, rates of extrapair paternity of up to 44% have been reported (Fietz et al., 2000) while a study of white handed gibbons reported an extrapair copulation rate of 12% (Reichard, 1995). Rates over 20% have also been reported in Lariang tarsiers (Driller et al., 2009). Extrapair copulations have been documented in a number of socially monogamous primates from gibbons (Kenyon et al., 2011; Oka and Takenaka, 2001; Palombit, 1994) to marmosets (Digby, 1999), dwarf lemurs (Fietz et al., 2000), and fork-marked lemurs (Schülke et al., 2004). An examination of the impact of the social structure and of the type of pair bonding on interspecific variations in extrapair paternity rates by Cohas and Allaine (2009) suggests that solitary and family-living species present higher extrapair paternity rates than pair-living species. Living with sexual competitors results in higher levels of male–male competition and more opportunities for female choice. In general, extrapair mating can be influenced by a number of factors including ecological circumstances (including male ability to mate guard), availability and quality of potential male mates as well as current mate, and female reproductive status.

Sexual and/or Genetic Monogamy

Sexual monogamy in mammals can mean mating with one partner during one, multiple, or a lifetime of mating seasons or cycles. While sexual monogamy and genetic monogamy may coincide, they do not always, as a female may mate with several males but only one may have paternity over her offspring. It's unclear if lifetime genetic monogamy occurs due to limited long-term research on lifetime reproductive success, however, genetic monogamy has been documented in at least one pair-living primate, Azara's owl monkeys (Huck et al., 2014). Azara's owl monkeys have only one reproductive male and female in a group and the male contributes substantially to the care of their infant. Data from a wild-living Argentinian population indicates genetic monogamy despite the presence of extrapair males, providing an explanation for the intense level of paternal care.

Lambert et al. (2018) conducted a meta-analysis of 41 socially monogamous species where there was also information on genetic parentage. They concluded that living as a socially monogamous pair rather than in a group was the best predictor of genetic monogamy (and was often also associated with high levels of paternal care). A male-biased sex ratio and low population density were predictive of lower levels of genetic monogamy, again suggesting that multiple factors are likely involved in the development of genetic monogamy in mammals. Higher levels of paternal care were associated with lower levels of EPCs.

Humans

The diversity of human mating systems has led to interestingly different conclusions, suggesting that humans are either generally monogamous, polygynous, promiscuous, or adapted for both polygyny and polyandry (Wilson et al., 2017). Indeed, the wide variability of human mating strategies has led some researchers to propose humans are the model species in which to investigate ecological factors that drive different mating systems (Wilson et al., 2017). In a review of 186 societies, 82% were found to be polygynous, 17% monogamous, and 1% polyandrous (Marlowe, 2000). As others have pointed out, however, these general categorizations do not acknowledge the tremendous amount of variability within each society (Wilson et al., 2017). For example, within the polygynous societies, only between 5% and 12% of married men had more than one wife (Marlowe,

2000). Therefore, even in societies where marriage to more than woman is permitted, most marriages are monogamous. However, consistent with the nonhuman literature described earlier, socially monogamous relationships are not necessarily sexually monogamous. Within monogamous societies, recent investigations of extrapair paternity rates indicate between 1% and 2% of offspring are from extrapair copulations, though it should be noted that there is considerable variability in those rates between different human societies (Anderson, 2006; Larmuseau et al., 2016; Simmons et al., 2004). Regardless of the tremendous amount of variation in human mating systems (both between as well as within different human groups), the most frequent human mating system is serial social monogamy (Chapais, 2013). Though monogamy is much more common in societies with more evolved political systems (Sanderson, 2001), anthropologists have documented long-term pair bonds in all known human societies (Muller & Pilbeam, 2017). Monogamy in humans is thought to have evolved from an increase in male provisioning and paternal care (Gavrilets, 2012), mate guarding (Marlowe, 2000), and the transition of human societies from collecting food as mobile foragers to producing food as sedentary groups (Betzig, 2012). In this section, we will examine the different factors that may have led to social and sexual monogamy within humans, the potential benefits for males and females under such a mating system, how sexual monogamy is maintained, and factors that influence infidelity.

Social Monogamy

Many ethnographers agree that social monogamy is more common in harsh ecological environments in which care from both parents is vital for reproductive success (Low, 2003). Investigation of large cross-cultural databases has found that monogamous societies have significantly lower plant production than those that are polygynous (Low, 2003). While there was no evidence that mating systems varied as a function of temperature or rainfall extremes, the consistency and predictability of seasonal changes (including rainfall) was associated with monogamous mating systems. Furthermore, in regions with very high pathogen loads, monogamy was not present (Low, 2003). Bauch and McElreath (2015) suggest that as humans began living in larger social groups, socially imposed monogamy evolved from a pressure to avoid sexually transmitted infections (STIs) that threaten fertility and quality of offspring. Others have suggested that social monogamy increased with the increasing population size due to problems imposing and enforcing unequal reproductive rewards in a larger population (Low, 2003). As population size increases, the availability of mates also increases, leading to increased competition for mates. Some researchers have proposed social monogamy evolved from the greater mate competition and increased need for mate guarding (i.e., to protect one's mate from other potential mates and to ensure paternity certainty for males) (Gowaty, 1996b).

Using mathematical modeling, Gavrilets (2012) proposed evidence that pair bonds coevolved from an increase in male provisioning (including paternal investment) and an increase in female faithfulness. According to the model, pair bonds arose as low-ranking males increased their levels of investment to compete with higher-ranking males for mates. Therefore, it was females' desire for investment from their mate and males' desire to invest in a mate that is faithful that led to a shift from promiscuity to monogamous pair bonding (Gavrilets, 2012). This transition to enduring pair bonds has allowed for energy and resources devoted to competition between males over mates to instead be used for greater paternal investment (Chapais, 2008), creating stronger alliances and coalitions (Gavrilets et al., 2008), and ultimately leading to greater cooperation essential for living with other families in a multilevel society (Boomsma, 2009; Chapais, 2008).

Demographers have highlighted several reproductive advantages in modern societies associated with the transition to social monogamy, including reduced mortality, reduced fertility, and fewer children with greater investment (Low, 2003). The result of social and genetic monogamy with greater investment in offspring benefits both males and females in modern societies (Low, 2003). However, as women attain greater education and resource accrual on their own in modern societies, women have begun to delay reproduction (Low, 2003; Low et al., 2002, 2003) and the reproductive advantage of wealthy men has been decreasing (Kaplan & Lancaster, 2003; Perusse, 1993, 1994). This suggests that the benefits associated with the demographic transition to monogamy may not apply to postindustrial societies (Low, 2003).

While a great deal of theoretical attention has historically focused on male motivations for short-term mating (mostly concentrating of increased reproductive success), more recent work has also focused on female motivation for short-term mating, and particularly on extrapair mating (Grebe et al., 2016; Greiling & Buss, 2000; Gangestad & Thornhill, 2008; Pillsworth & Haselton, 2006; Scelza, 2013). While many people disapprove of extramarital sexual activity (Negash et al., 2014), estimates of lifetime prevalence of marital infidelity ranges from 20% to 50% (Allen & Atkins, 2012; Greiling & Buss, 2000; Parker-Pope, 2008). Several hypothesized benefits to women of extrapair mating have been suggested including: immediate resource acquisition, genetic benefits, mate switching, mate skill acquisition, and mate manipulation (Greiling & Buss, 2000). While studies have found support for several of these hypotheses, for example, mate switching and resource acquisition (Buss et al., 2017; Buss & Schmitt, 2019; Dillon et al., 2018; Greiling & Buss, 2000), little evidence has been collected to speak to the question of the genetic benefits of extrapair mating, as ideally this would compare the genetic quality of in-pair and extrapair offspring which would be challenging to do.

It is important to note that while the previously mentioned cross cultural study of nonpaternity (Anderson, 2006) reported quite low rates of extrapair paternity, the majority of the samples were from industrialized countries. There has been relatively little data on nonpaternity rates in small-scale societies. However female infidelity is reported as common in over 50% of societies in the Standard Cross-Cultural Sample (Broude, 1980; Broude & Green, 1976; Marlowe, 2000). Ethnographic reports of female infidelity in small-scale societies have been reported in a number of studies conducted among the !Kung (Howell, 2000), Ache (Hill & Hurtado, 1996), Yanomamo (Chagnon, 1968), and Tsimane (Stieglitz et al., 2012). Among the Himba, a seminomadic pastoral population in the northwest of Namibia, 17% of recorded marital births were attributed by women to extrapair paternity, a rate much higher than in most small-scale societies. However, the Himba women who were in "love matches" of their choice rather than arranged ones that were not, had no reported extrapair children (Scelza, 2011). This difference in extrapair paternity across Himba marriages highlights the female choice aspect of infidelity.

Sexual Monogamy

The relationship between social and sexual monogamy is highly variable across human societies. Specifically, social monogamy with varying degrees of sexual monogamy is common both between as well as within societies (Bauch & McElreath, 2016; Bellis et al., 2005; Gallup et al., 2003; Low, 2003). Few studies have investigated nonpaternity rates (i.e., likelihood that the male is not the genetic father of a child) in humans, and many of the studies that do report nonpaternity rates appear to be flawed either due to small sample sizes or lack of empirical data to support their claims (Anderson et al., 2006). In a recent meta-analysis of 67 studies investigating nonpaternity in humans, Anderson (2006) categorized the samples from those studies into three groups: those with high paternity certainty (e.g., based on genetic testing), those with low paternity certainty (e.g., men seeking genetic testing based on their doubts the offspring is theirs), and those whose paternity certainty was unknown. Median nonpaternity rates varied across the three groups ranging from 1.9% nonpaternity in the high paternity certainty group, to 16.7% for the unknown paternity certainty group, and 29.8% for the low paternity group. While these numbers do not apply to a general population as the samples were not randomly selected, the rates of nonpaternity do demonstrate varying degrees of sexual (or genetic) monogamy in socially monogamous relationships.

Sexual monogamy is enforced via many cultural practices across human societies. An example of a society with such cultural practices are the Dogon, an agricultural society that resides in the rocky hills, mountains, and plateaus of Mali (West Africa) (Strassman, 2003). The Dogon live in patrilineage clans descended from a common male ancestor. Due to (1) the scarcity of arable land which is essential to survival and reproduction of the clans and (2) the patrilineal control over resources, cuckoldry is seen as particularly offensive as it threatens the inheritance of resources by true descendants of the clan (Strassman, 2003). As such, mate guarding in this society is extreme. All little girls in the village undergo clitoridectomy (Strassman, 2003). Timing of female menstruation is tracked, with Dogon women required to indicate to the entire male lineage their menstrual timing at a menstrual hut (Strassman, 2003). Husbands and other kin continually monitor females' reproductive status, including which wives are fertile, which are experiencing their menstrual cycle, which are pregnant, and which are experiencing lactational amenorrhea (Strassman, 2003). Mate guarding in this society extends to kin and other social allies from extended family within the clan to ensure that potentially fertile wives are not engaging in extrapair copulations. Taboos surrounding menstruation, threats of loss of social status for the mothers, and exclusion of any male offspring of questionable paternity also serve to deter female engagement in EPCs (Strassman, 2003). Presumably, the threat of losing paternal investment, which would be essential for the survival (and ultimately) reproductive success of potential offspring in this scarce resource environment, serves as deterrence against females engaging in EPCs.

Given the (oftentimes) extreme lengths used in human societies to enforce sexual monogamy, what factors influence infidelity? A twin study investigating infidelity and number of sexual partners in over 1,600 female twin pairs from the United Kingdom found that approximately 40% of the variability in engaging in EPCs and number of sexual partners is explained by genetic variation (Cherkas et al., 2004). Furthermore, although shared environment did significantly explain individual differences in attitudes toward infidelity and casual sex, there was no evidence that shared environmental factors explained any variance in the actual sexual behavior of the twins (i.e., engaging in EPCs or number of sexual partners). These findings suggest that female infidelity under certain circumstances did provide a fitness advantage for females' reproductive success in our evolutionary past (Cherkas et al., 2004). Females in established socially monogamous relationships may have benefited by engaging in EPCs if those extrapair matings were with genetically superior males (i.e., relative to their long-term partner). Interestingly, infidelity in females does not seem to be regulated by vasopressin as has been observed in other mammalian species described earlier (Cherkas et al., 2004).

Limitations and Future Directions

One main limitation in the monogamy literature is the lack of studies and empirical evidence for nonpaternity rates in humans. As mentioned earlier, the few studies of nonpaternity in humans are often flawed due to small sample sizes, lack of generalizability, and absence of empirical data to support their claims (Anderson et al., 2006). In addition, the measurement of nonpaternity is often indirect using measures of paternity confidence in men (e.g., Anderson et al., 2006) and/or self-report of extrapair offspring (e.g., Scelza, 2011). Genetic testing, as has been conducted with nonhuman species, is necessary to validate the self-report claims and to obtain a direct measure of in-pair versus extrapair offspring. Obviously this is a challenging research objective, though perhaps one that could at least be partially addressed through medical research that involves genetic testing. Even in the nonhuman animal literature, more genetic paternity testing is needed as observations of copulations can be somewhat unreliable and copulations are, in themselves, evidence of extrapair mating and not necessarily extrapair paternity.

Another limitation in the monogamy literature is that there is little evidence regarding the genetic benefits of extrapair mating. It is interesting that the presumption that a benefit of engaging in EPCs for females would be the potential to mate with a male of superior genetic quality to their partner has not been systematically (nor directly) tested. This may be due to the difficulty of conducting such a study in humans, which would require a comparison of the genetic quality of in-pair and extrapair offspring. Such research could be conducted with nonhuman animals, though more easily in captive than wild populations, which would also raise the question of the ecological validity of results depending on the captive conditions.

The heritability of female infidelity and number of sex partners in humans (Cherkas et al., 2004) also warrants more investigation of genetic and hormonal regulators of that behavior. Although Cherkas and colleagues (2004) did not find evidence that vasopressin was involved in female infidelity, other genes and hormones should be investigated. Candidates for this exploratory physiological evidence would include examination of genes (and receptors) for estrogen (i.e., the primary female sex hormone) as well as oxytocin and dopamine, which have been linked with sexual behavior, social bonding, and reward pathways in the hypothalamus (Cherkas et al., 2004).

Conclusions

Factors associated with the different types of monogamy in nonhuman species are basically the same factors associated with monogamy in humans. An exception to this includes findings regarding the regulatory role of vasopressin in the monogamous behavior of some nonhuman mammals (Insel & Shapiro, 1992) that does not appear to extend to humans (Cherkas et al., 2004). Other factors related to whether a species is socially and/or sexually monogamous, however, appear to apply to both human and nonhuman species. These factors include population size, availability of potential mates (including the genetic quality of other potential mates), reproductive status of females, mortality rates, the need for paternal investment in the raising of offspring, and mate guarding.

References

Allen, E. S., & Atkins, D. C. (2012). The association of divorce and extramarital sex in a representative U.S. sample. *Journal of Family Issues, 33,* 1477–1493.

Anderson, K. G. (2006). How well does paternity confidence match actual paternity? *Current Anthropology, 47,* 513–520.

Anderson, K. G., Kaplan, H., & Lancaster, J. B. (2006). Demographic correlates of paternity confidence and pregnancy outcomes among Albuquerque men. *American Journal of Physical Anthropology, 131,* 560–571.

Arnold, K. E., & Owens, I. P. (2002). Extra-pair paternity and egg dumping in birds: Life history, parental care and the risk of retaliation. *Proceedings of the Royal Society of London. Series B: Biological Sciences, 269*(1497), 1263–1269.

Arsenault, D. P., Stacey, P. B., & Hoelzer, G. A. (2002). No extra-pair fertilization in flammulated owls despite aggregated nesting. *Condor, 104,* 197–202.

Bauch, C. T., & McElreath, R. (2016). Disease dynamics and costly punishment can foster socially imposed monogamy. *Nature Communications, 7,* 11219.

Bellis, M. A., Hughes, K., Hughes, S., & Ashton, J. R. (2005). Measuring paternal discrepancy and its public health consequences. *Journal of Epidemiology & Community Health, 59,* 749–754.

Betzig, L. (2012). Means, variances, and ranges in reproductive success: Comparative evidence. *Evolution and Human Behavior, 33*(4), 309–317.

Birkhead, T. R., & Moller, A. P. (1992). *Sperm competition in birds: Evolutionary causes and consequences.* Academic Press.

Birkhead, T. R., & Moller, A. P. (1996). Monogamy and sperm competition in birds. In J. M. Black (Ed.), *Partnerships in birds: The study of monogamy* (pp. 323–343). Oxford University Press.

Boomsma, J. J. (2009). Lifetime monogamy and the evolution of eusociality. *Philosophical Transactions of the Royal Society B: Biological Sciences, 364*(1533), 3191–3207.

Brotherton, P. N., Pemberton, J. M., Komers, P. E., & Malarky, G. (1997). Genetic and behavioural evidence of monogamy in a mammal, Kirk's dik–dik (; Madoqua kirkii). *Proceedings of the Royal Society of London B: Biological Sciences, 264*(1382), 675–681.

Broude, G. J. (1980). Extramarital sex norms in cross-cultural perspective. *Cross-Cultural Research, 15*, 181–218.

Broude, G. J., & Green, S. J. (1976). Cross-cultural codes on twenty sexual attitudes and preferences. *Ethology, 15*, 409–429.

Brouwer, L., & Griffith, S. C. (2019). Extra-pair paternity in birds. *Molecular Ecology, 28*, 4864–882.

Bublat, A., Fischer, D., Bruslund, S., Schneider, H., Meinecke-Tillmann, S., Wehrend, A., & Lierz, M. (2017). Seasonal and genera-specific variations in semen availability and semen characteristics in large parrots. *Theriogenology, 91*, 82–89.

Buss, D. M., Goetz, C., Duntley, J. D., Asao, K., & Conroy-Beam, D. (2017). The mate switching hypothesis. *Personality and Individual Differences, 104*, 143–149.

Buss, D. M., & Schmitt, D. P. (2019). Mate preferences and their behavioral manifestations. *Annual Review of Psychology, 70*, 77–110.

Calhim, S., Immler, S., & Birkhead, T. R. (2007). Postcopulatory sexual selection is associated with reduced variation in sperm morphology. *PLoS One, 2*(5), e413.

Carballo, L., Battistotti, A., Teltscher, K., Lierz, M., Bublat, A., Valcu, M., & Kempenaers, B. (2019). Sperm morphology and evidence for sperm competition among parrots. *Journal of Evolutionary Biology, 32*, 856–867. https://doi.org/10.1111/jeb.13487

Chagnon, N. A. (1968). *Yanomamo: The fierce people.* Holt, Rinehart & Winston.

Chaine, A. S., Montgomerie, R., & Lyon, B. E. (2015). Sexual conflict arising from extrapair matings in birds. *Cold Spring Harbor Perspectives in Biology, 7*(3), a017590.

Chapais, B. (2008). *Primeval kinship: How pair-bonding gave birth to human society.* Harvard University Press.

Chapais, B. (2013). Monogamy, strongly bonded groups, and the evolution of human social structure. *Evolutionary Anthropology, 22*, 52–65.

Cherkas, L. F., Oelsner, E. C., Mak, Y. T., Valdes, A., & Spector, T. D. (2004). Genetic influences on female infidelity and number of sexual partners in humans: A linkage and association study of the role of the vasopressin receptor gene (AVPR1A). *Twin Research, 7*(6), 649–658.

Clutton-Brock, T. H. (1991). *The evolution of parental care.* Princeton University Press.

Cohas, A., & Allainé, D. (2009). Social structure influences extra-pair paternity in socially monogamous mammals. *Biology letters, 5*(3), 313–316.

Decker, M. D., Parker, P. G., Minchella, D. J., & Rabenold, K. N. (1993). Monogamy in black vultures: Genetic evidence from DNA fingerprinting. *Behavioral Ecology, 4*, 29–35.

Díaz-Muñoz, S. L., & Bales, K. L. (2016). "Monogamy" in primates: Variability, trends, and synthesis: Introduction to special issue on primate monogamy. *American Journal of Primatology, 78*, 283–287.

Digby, L. J. (1999). Sexual behavior and extragroup copulations in a wild population of common marmosets (*Callithrix jacchus*). *Folia Primatologica, 70*, 136–145.

Dillon, L. M., Nowak, N. T., & Weisfeld, G. E. (2018). Sex and Infidelity. In C. C. Weisfeld, G. E. Weisfeld, & L. M. Dillon (Eds.), *The psychology of marriage: An evolutionary and cross-cultural view* (pp. 251–264). Lexington Books.

Driller, C., Perwitasari-Farajallah, D., Zischler, H., & Merker, S. (2009). The social system of Lariang tarsiers (*Tarsius lariang*) as revealed by genetic analyses. *International Journal of Primatology, 30*, 267–281.

Eastwood, J. R., Berg, M. L., Ribot, R. F., Stokes, H. S., Martens, J. M., Buchanan, K. L., . . . Bennett, A. T. (2018). Pair fidelity in long-lived parrots: Genetic and behavioural evidence from the crimson rosella (*Platycercus elegans*). *Emu-Austral Ornithology, 118*, 369–374.

Fernandez-Duque, E. (2016). Social monogamy in wild owl monkeys (*Aotus azarae*) of Argentina: The potential influences of resource distribution and ranging patterns. *American Journal of Primatology, 78*, 355–371.

Fernandez-Duque, E., Valeggia, C. R., & Mendoza, S. P. (2009). The biology of paternal care in human and nonhuman primates. *Annual Review of Anthropology, 38*, 115–130.

Fietz, J., Zischler, H., Schwiegk, C., Tomiuk, J., Dausmann, K. H., & Ganzhorn, J. U. (2000). High rates of extra-pair young in the pair-living fat-tailed dwarf lemur, *Cheirogaleus medius. Behavioral Ecology and Sociobiology, 49*, 8–17.

Fishman, M. A., Stone, L., & Lotem, A. (2003). Fertility assurance through extrapair fertilizations and male paternity defense. *Journal of Theoretical Biology, 221*, 103–114.

Fuentes, A. (1999. Re-evaluating primate monogamy. *American Anthropologist, 100*, 890–907.

Gallup, G. G., Jr., Burch, R. L., Zappieri, M., Parvez, R., & Stockwell, M. (2003). The human penis as a semen displacement device. *Evolution and Human Behavior, 24*, 277–289.

Gangestad, S. W., & Thornhill, R. (2008). Human oestrus. *Proceedings of the Royal Society B, 275*, 991–1000.

Gavrilets, S. (2012). Human origins and the transition from promiscuity to pair-bonding. *Proceedings of the National Academy of Sciences, 109*, 9923–9928.

Gavrilets, S. Duenez-Guzman, E. A., & Vose, M. D. (2008). Dynamics of alliance formation and the egalitarian revolution. *PLoS One, 3*, e3293.

Getz, L. L., & Carter, C. S. (1996). Prairie-vole partnerships. *American Scientist, 84*, 56–63.

Getz, L. L., & McGuire, B. (1993). A comparison of living singly and in male-female pairs in the prairie vole, *Microtus ochrogaster. Ethology, 94*, 265–278.

Gill, L. F., van Schaik, J., von Bayern, A. M., & Gahr, M. L. (2019). Genetic monogamy despite frequent extrapair copulations in "strictly monogamous" wild jackdaws. *Behavioral Ecology*, 31, 247–260.

Gowaty, P. A. (1996a). Multiple mating by females selects for males that stay: Another hypothesis for social monogamy in passerine birds. *Animal Behaviour, 51*, 482–484.

Gowaty, P. A. (1996b). Battles of the sexes and origins of monogamy. In J. Black (Ed.), *Partnerships in birds: The study of monogamy* (pp. 21–52). Oxford University Press.

Graves, J., Ortega-Ruano, J., & Slater, P. J. B. (1993). Extra-pair copulations and paternity in shags: Do females choose better mates? *Proceedings of the Royal Society London B, 253*, 3–7.

Grebe, N. M., Thompson, M. E., & Gangestad, S. W. (2016). Hormonal predictors of women's extra-pair vs. in-pair sexual attraction in natural cycles: Implications for extended sexuality. *Hormones and Behavior, 78*, 211–219.

Greiling, H., & Buss, D. B. (2000). Women's sexual strategies: The hidden dimension of extra-pair mating. *Personality and Individual Differences, 28*, 929–963.

Griffith, S. C., Owens, I. P., & Thuman, K. A. (2002). Extra pair paternity in birds: a review of interspecific variation and adaptive function. *Molecular ecology, 11*(11), 2195–2212.

Gubernick, D. J., & Teferi, T. (2000). Adaptive significance of male parental care in a monogamous mammal. *Proceedings of the Royal Society of London. Series B: Biological Sciences, 267*, 147–150.

Hall, M. L. (1999). The importance of pair duration and biparental care to reproductive success in the monogamous Australian magpie-lark. *Australian Journal of Zoology, 47*, 439–454.

Hasselquist, D., Bensch, S., & von Schantz, T. (1996). Correlation between male song repertoire, extra-pair paternity, and offspring survival in the great reed warbler. *Nature, 381*, 229–232.

Henderson, I. G., & Hart, P. J. (1993). Provisioning, parental investment and reproductive success in Jackdaws *Corvus monedula. Ornis Scandinavica, 24*, 142–148.

Henderson, I. G., Hart, P. J. B., & Burke, T. (2000). Strict monogamy in a semi-colonial passerine: The jackdaw *Corvus monedula. Journal of Avian Biology, 31*, 177–182.

Hill, K., & Hurtado, A. M. (1996). *Ache life history: The ecology and demography of a foraging people*. Aldine de Gruyter.

Howell, N. (2000). *Demography of the Dobe!Kung*. Aldine de Gruyter.

Hrdy, S. B. (1979). Infanticide among animals: A review, classification, and examination of the implications for the reproductive strategies of females. *Ethology and Sociobiology, 1*, 13–40.

Huck, M., Fernandez-Duque, E., Babb, P., & Schurr, T. (2014). Correlates of genetic monogamy in socially monogamous mammals: Insights from Azara's owl monkeys. *Proceedings of the Royal Society B: Biological Sciences, 281*, 20140195.

Insel, T. R., & Shapiro, L. E. (1992). Oxytocin receptor distribution reflects social organization in monogamous and polygamous voles. *Proceedings of the National Academy of Sciences, 89*, 5981–5985.

Iwasa, Y., & Harada, Y. (1998). Female mate preference to maximize paternal care. II. Female competition leads to monogamy. *American Naturalist*, *151*, 367–382.

Jones, A. G., & Ratterman, N. L. (2009). Mate choice and sexual selection: What have we learned since Darwin? *Proceedings of the National Academy of Sciences*, *106*(Supplement 1), 10001–10008.

Jones, C. S., Lessells, C. M., & Krebs, J. R. (1991). Helpers-at-the-nest in European bee-eaters (*Merops apiaster*): A genetic analysis. In T. Burke, G. Dolf, A. J. Jeffreys, & R. Wolff (Eds.), *DNA fingerprinting: Approaches and applications* (pp. 169–192). Birkhäuser Basel.

Kaplan, H. S., & Lancaster, J. B. (2003). An evolutionary and ecological analysis of human fertility, mating patterns, and parental investment. *Offspring: Human Fertility Behavior in Biodemographic Perspective*, 1, 170–223.

Kenyon, M., Roos, C., Binh, V. T., & Chivers, D. (2011). Extrapair paternity in golden-cheeked gibbons (Nomascus gabriellae) in the secondary lowland forest of Cat Tien National Park, Vietnam. *Folia Primatologica*, *82*(3), 154–164.

Kleiman, D. G. (1977). Monogamy in mammals. *Quarterly Review of Biology*, *52*, 39–69.

Kleven, O., Fiske, A. N., Håvik, M., Kroglund, R. T., Østnes, J. E., & Schmoll, T. (2019). Extra-pair paternity and sperm length variation in the socially monogamous fieldfare *Turdus pilaris*. *Journal of Ornithology*, *4*, 1043–1051.

Klug, H. (2018). Why monogamy? A review of potential ultimate drivers. *Frontiers in Ecology and Evolution*, *6*, 30. https://doi.org/10.3389/fevo.2018.00030.

Kokko, H., & Morrell, L. J. (2005). Mate guarding, male attractiveness, and paternity under social monogamy. *Behavioral Ecology*, *16*, 724–731.

Lack, D. (1968). *Ecological adaptations for breeding in birds*. Methuen.

Lambert, C. T., Solomon, N. G., & Sabol, A. C. (2018). Genetic monogamy in socially monogamous mammals is primarily predicted by multiple life history factors. *Frontiers in Ecology and Evolution*, *6*, 139. https://doi.org/10.3389/fevo.2018.00139.

Larmuseau, M. H., Matthijs, K., & Wenseleers, T. (2016). Cuckolded fathers rare in human populations. *Trends in Ecology & Evolution*, *31*(5), 327–329.

Lifjeld, J. T., Laskemoen, T., Kleven, O., Albrecht, T., & Robertson, R. J. (2010). Sperm length variation as a predictor of extrapair paternity in passerine birds. *PLoS One*, *5*(10), e13456.

Low, B. S. (2003). Ecological and social complexities in human monogamy. In U. H. Reichard & C. Boesch (Eds.), *Monogamy: Mating strategies and partnerships in birds, humans, and other mammals* (pp. 161–176). Cambridge University Press.

Low, B. S., Simon, C. P., & Anderson, K. G. (2002). An evolutionary perspective on demographic transitions: Modeling multiple currencies. *American Journal of Human Biology*, *14*, 149–167.

Low, B. S., Simon, C. P., & Anderson, K. G. (2003). The biodemography of modern women: Tradeoffs when resources become limited. In J. L. Rodgers & H. P. Kohler (Eds.), *The biodemography of human reproduction and fertility* (pp. 105–134). Springer.

Lukas, D., & Clutton-Brock, T. H. (2013). The evolution of social monogamy in mammals. *Science*, *341*, 526–530.

Lukas, D., & Clutton-Brock, T. H. (2014). Evolution of social monogamy in primates is not consistently associated with male infanticide. *Proceedings of the National Academy of Sciences USA*, *111*, E1674.

Malcolm, J. R. (1985). Paternal care in canids. *American Zoologist*, *25*, 853–859.

Marks, J. S., Dickinson, J. L., & Haydock, J. (1999). Genetic monogamy in long-eared owls. *Condor*, *101*, 854–859.

Marlowe, F. (2000). Paternal investment and the human mating system. *Behavioural Processes*, *51*, 45–61.

Masello, J. F., Sramkova, A., Quillfeldt, P., Epplen, J. T., & Lubjuhn, T. (2002). Genetic monogamy in burrowing parrots *Cyanoliseus patagonus*? *Journal of Avian Biology*, *33*, 99–103.

Mills, J. A. (1994). Extra-pair copulations in the red-billed gull: Females with high-quality attentive males resist. *Behaviour*, *128*, 41–64.

Muller, M. N, & Pilbeam, D. R. (2017). Evolution of the human mating system. In M. Muller, R. Wrangham, & D. Pilbeam (Eds.), *Chimpanzees and human evolution* (pp. 383–426). Harvard University Press.

Munshi-South, J. (2007). Extra-pair paternity and the evolution of testis size in a behaviorally monogamous tropical mammal, the large tree shrew (*Tupaia tana*). *Behavioral Ecology and Sociobiology*, *62*, 201–212.

Negash, S., Cui, M., Fincham, F. D., & Pasley, K. (2014). Extradyadic involvement and relationship dissolution in heterosexual women university students. *Archives of Sexual Behavior*, *43*, 531539.

Neudorf, D. L., Stutchbury, B. J. M., & Piper, W. H. (1997). Covert extraterritorial behavior of female hooded warblers. *Behavioral Ecology, 8*, 595–600.

Oka, T., & Takenaka, O. (2001). Wild gibbons' parentage tested by non-invasive DNA sampling and PCR-amplified polymorphic microsatellites. *Primates, 42*, 67–73.

Ophir, A. G., Gessel, A., Zheng, D. J., & Phelps, S. M. (2012). Oxytocin receptor density is associated with male mating tactics and social monogamy. *Hormones and Behavior, 61*, 445–453.

Ophir, A. G., Phelps, S. M., Sorin, A. B., & Wolff, J. O. (2008). Social but not genetic monogamy is associated with greater breeding success in prairie voles. *Animal Behaviour, 75*, 1143–1154.

Opie, C., Atkinson, Q. D., Dunbar, R. I., & Shultz, S. (2013). Male infanticide leads to social monogamy in primates. *Proceedings of the National Academy of Science USA, 110*, 13328–13332.

Opie, C., Atkinson, Q. D., Dunbar, R. I., & Shultz, S. (2014). Reply to Lukas and Clutton-Brock: Infanticide still drives primate monogamy. *Proceedings of the National Academy of Sciences, 111*, E1675–E1675.

Palombit, R. A. (1994). Extra-pair copulations in a monogamous ape. *Animal Behaviour, 47*, 721–723.

Palombit, R. A. (1999). Infanticide and the evolution of pair bonds in nonhuman primates. *Evolutionary Anthropology: Issues, News, and Reviews: Issues, News, and Reviews, 7(4)*, 117–129.

Parker-Pope, T. (2008, October 28). "Love, sex, and the changing landscape of infidelity." *New York Times*.

Perusse, D. (1993). Cultural and reproductive success in industrial societies: Testing the relationship at proximate and ultimate levels. *Behavior and Brain Sciences, 16*, 267–322.

Perusse, D. (1994). Mate choice in modern societies: Testing evolutionary hypotheses with behavioral data. *Human Nature, 5*, 255–278.

Pillsworth, E. G., & Haselton, M. G. (2006). Male sexual attractiveness predicts differential ovulatory shifts in female extra-pair attraction and male mate retention. *Evolution and Human Behavior, 27*, 247–258.

Quinn, J. S., Woolfenden, G. E., Fitzpatrick, J. W., & White, B. N. (1999). Multi-locus DNA fingerprinting supports genetic monogamy in Florida scrub-jays. *Behavioral Ecology and Sociobiology, 45*, 1–10.

Reding, L. (2015). Increased hatching success as a direct benefit of polyandry in birds. *Evolution, 69*, 264–270.

Reichard, U. (1995). Extra-pair copulations in a monogamous gibbon (*Hylobates lar*). *Ethology, 100*, 99–112.

Reichard, U. H. (2003). Monogamy: Past and present. In U. H. Reichard & C. Boesch (Eds.), *Monogamy: Mating strategies and partnerships in birds, humans, and other mammals* (pp. 3–25). Cambridge University Press.

Ribble, D. O. (2003). The evolution of social and reproductive monogamy in *Peromyscus*: Evidence from *Peromyscus californicus* (the California mouse). In U. H. Reichard & C. Boesch (Eds.), *Monogamy: Mating strategies and partnerships in birds, humans, and other mammals* (pp. 81–108). Cambridge University Press.

Rice, M. A., Restrepo, L. F., & Ophir, A. G. (2018). When to cheat: Modeling dynamics of paternity and promiscuity in socially monogamous prairie voles (*Microtus ochrogaster*). *Frontiers in Ecology and Evolution, 6*, 141.

Sanderson, S. K. (2001). Explaining monogamy and polygyny in human societies: Comment on Kanazawa and Still. *Social Forces, 80(1)*, 329–335.

Scelza, B. A. (2011). Female choice and extra-pair paternity in a traditional human population. *Biology Letters, 7(6)*, 889–891.

Scelza, B. A. (2013). Choosy but not chaste: Multiple mating in human females. *Evolutionary Anthropology, 22*, 259–269.

Schacht, R., & Bell, A. V. (2016). The evolution of monogamy in response to partner scarcity. *Scientific Reports, 6(1)*, 1–9. https://doi.org/10.1038/srep32472

Schneider, J., & Lamprecht, J. (1990). The importance of biparental care in a precocial, monogamous bird, the bar-headed goose (*Anser indicus*). *Behavioral Ecology and Sociobiology, 27*, 415–419.

Schubert, M., Pillay, N., Ribble, D. O., & Schradin, C. (2009). The round-eared sengi and the evolution of social monogamy: Factors that constrain males to live with a single female. *Ethology, 115*, 972–985.

Schülke, O., Kappeler, P. M., & Zischler, H. (2004). Small testes size despite high extra-pair paternity in the pair-living nocturnal primate *Phaner furcifer*. *Behavioral Ecology and Sociobiology, 55*, 292–301.

Shackelford, T. K., LeBlanc, G. J., Weekes-Shackelford, V. A., Bleske-Rechek, A. L., Euler, H. A., & Hoier, S. (2002). Psychological adaptation to human sperm competition. *Evolution and Human Behavior, 23*, 123–138.

Simmons, L. W., Firman, R. C., Rhodes, G., & Peters, M. (2004). Human sperm competition: Testis size, sperm production and rates of extrapair copulations. *Animal Behaviour, 68(2)*, 297–302.

Solomon, N. G., Keane, B., Knoch, L. R., & Hogan, P. J. (2004). Multiple paternity in socially monogamous prairie voles (*Microtus ochrogaster*). *Canadian Journal of Zoology, 82*, 1667–1671.

Sommer, S. (2003). Social and reproductive monogamy in rodents: The case of the Malagasy giant jumping rat (*Hypogeonys antimena*). In U. H. Reichard & C. Boesch (Eds.), *Monogamy: Mating strategies and partnerships in birds, humans, and other mammals* (pp. 109–124). Cambridge University Press.

Stieglitz, J., Gurven, M., Kaplan, H., & Winking, J. (2012). Infidelity, jealousy, and wife abuse among Tsimane forager–farmers: Testing evolutionary hypotheses of marital conflict. *Evolution and Human Behavior, 33*, 438–448.

Strassmann, B. L. (2003). Social monogamy in a human society: Marriage and reproductive success among the Dogon. In U. H. Reichard & C. Boesch (Eds.), *Monogamy: Mating strategies and partnerships in birds, humans, and other mammals* (pp. 177–189). Cambridge University Press.

Stockley, P., & Hobson, L. (2016). Paternal care and litter size coevolution in mammals. *Proceedings of the Royal Society B: Biological Sciences, 283*, 20160140.

Symons, D. (1979). *The evolution of human sexuality*. Oxford University Press.

Taylor, S. S., Boessenkool, S., & Jamieson, I. G. (2008). Genetic monogamy in two long-lived New Zealand passerines. *Journal of Avian Biology, 39*, 579–583.

Trivers, R. L. (1972). Parental investment and sexual selection. In B. Campbell (Ed.), *Sexual selection and the descent of man: 1871–1971* (pp. 136–179). Aldine.

van Schaik, C. P. (2000). Social counterstrategies against infanticide by males in primates and other mammals. In P. Kappeler (Ed.), *Primate males: Causes and consequences of variation in group composition* (pp. 34–54). Cambridge University Press.

van Schaik, C. P., & Kappeler, P. M. (1997). Infanticide risk and the evolution of male–female association in primates. *Proceedings of the Royal Society of London. Series B: Biological Sciences, 264*, 1687–1694.

West, R. J. D. (2014). The evolution of large brain size in birds is related to social, not genetic, monogamy. *Biological Journal of the Linnean Society, 111*, 668–678.

Whitekiller, R. R., Westneat, D. F., Schwagmeyer, P. L., Mock, D. W. (2000). Badge size and extra-pair fertilizations in the house sparrow. *Condor, 102*, 342–348.

Wilson, M. L., Miller, C. M., & Crouse, K. N. (2017). Humans as a model species for sexual selection research. *Proceedings of the Royal Society B: Biological Sciences, 284*(1886), 20171320.

CHAPTER 7
Cultural Differences and Similarities in Correlates of Infidelity

Inmaculada Valor-Segura, Gemma Sáez, *and* Abraham Pieter Buunk

Abstract

Infidelity is negatively judged all over the world, but there are substantial cultural differences in this respect. Moreover some variables seem globally consistently associated with the occurrence of infidelity. The current chapter examines cross-cultural differences about what infidelity means and the social and psychological correlates associated with infidelity, including intrapersonal, relational, and ideological factors. Of the intrapersonal factors that predict infidelity, it explores especially the roles of gender, religiosity, education, income, mental health, and personality. Moreover, of the interpersonal factors related to infidelity, it focuses on factors like commitment, satisfaction, and dependency. Finally, it analyzes some ideological factors, such as religiosity and attitudes toward extramarital sex that are associated with engaging in infidelity.

Key Words: infidelity correlate, cultural difference, intrapersonal factor, relational factor, attitude, extradyadic sex

Introduction

Monogamy or fidelity has been observed as a relational expectation worldwide (Watkins & Boon, 2016). Hence, violation of this expectation is perceived as a relational problem (Sharpe et al., 2013) and usually causes resentment and relationship breakdown (Prieto-Ursúa et al., 2012; Sharpe et al., 2013). It has been estimated that, in therapeutic practice, infidelity is the most damaging event (after physical violence) for relationship health (Olmstead et al., 2009; Prieto-Ursúa et al., 2012). Although the literature includes multiple definitions for infidelity, there is no consensus regarding its meaning (e.g., Thompson & O'Sullivan, 2016a; Thompson et al., 2017). However, a common definition is that infidelity is a violation of the commitment to relational exclusivity—implicit or manifest—which may include short-term or longer-lasting sexual or emotional involvement with a third person without the prior consent of the regular partner (Dillow et al., 2011; Fife et al., 2013; Prieto-Ursúa et al., 2012). The conception of infidelity may differ considerably even within the same culture. Whereas in monogamous relationships it is not tolerated to seek out emotional or sexual interactions with any person other than one's partner (Jonason & Balzarini, 2016), in polyamorous relationships it is acceptable to have multiple emotionally or sexually close relationships, with the consent of everyone involved (Buunk, 1980a; Barker & Langdridge, 2010; Martell & Prince, 2005; Moller & Vossler, 2015).

Notwithstanding the typical disapproval of infidelity cross-culturally, there are considerable cross-cultural differences in how infidelity is perceived and understood. For example, infidelity is not typically accepted or approved in Western countries such as Spain, Great Britain, or the United States, and is seriously disapproved of in many Islamic countries, with often serious consequences for the adulterer. On the other hand, in many African countries infidelity is sometimes tolerated, while in Eastern countries such as Thailand, people are more tolerant because sex has traditionally been marketed, thus increasing the approval or consent of extradyadic sex (Mackay, 2001). Furthermore, Mackey and Immerman's review (2001) of 216 cultures showed that extramarital sex by husbands is less unacceptable than the same behavior by wives. Even today in many cultures, a wife's infidelity is viewed as an act for which the betrayed husband may exact revenge on the guilty parties (Buunk et al., 2018).

Types of Extradyadic Behaviors

Although the conceptualization of infidelity may vary with the culture or the type of relationship, it is important to distinguish different extradyadic behaviors that may be considered infidelity. One of the most widely used classifications was provided by Thompson and O'Sullivan (2016b), who established four groups of infidelity behaviors:

1. *Actual sexual behaviors.* These include sexual behaviors with someone outside the primary relationship (Whitty & Quigley, 2008). Some of the behaviors included in this category are vaginal or anal penetration, oral sex, and erotic touching.
2. *Technology-facilitated involvement.* Technological changes have added new variations to the dynamics of extradyadic sexual involvement. This involves when someone has a romantic or sexual relationship with another person through the use of the Internet or cellular phones and it is perceived by the partner as an intolerable transgression of their relationship (Hertlein & Piercy, 2008). This category includes behaviors such as sending sexually explicit or affectionate text messages or emails to another person or browsing online dating websites for single people.
3. *Actual emotional and affectionate behaviors.* These behaviors constitute emotional infidelity, referred to as the "development of an emotional bond" with a third person (Mattingly et al., 2010, p. 1466). This category includes

behaviors such as sharing secrets with, or providing emotional support to, a person outside the couple.
4. *Solitary behaviors.* Solitary behaviors may be judged as infidelity depending on the expectations of the relationship (Bergner & Bridges, 2002). Some examples of this category might include masturbation and viewing pornographic magazines and videos.

Of the behaviors in the classification above, recent research has found that behaviors of a sexual nature are considered the most typical of infidelity, and are viewed as less ambiguous than the other behaviors (e.g., Rodrigues et al., 2016; Thompson et al., 2017). In contrast, technology-facilitated, emotional, and solitary behaviors are perceived as more ambiguous and judged as infidelity depending on the situation and the interpretation of the offended partner (e.g., Thompson & O'Sullivan, 2016a, 2017).

Demographic Factors

Previous research has distinguished between incomes, education, occupational status, age and gender as the most relevant demographic factor predicting involvement in extradyadic relationships.

Incomes, Education, and Occupational Status

Research has examined the extent to which involvement in extradyadic relationships depends on income, education, and occupational status. Research in Western cultures has shown that extradyadic involvement is associated with income and employment status. Specifically, in a sample representative of the population of the United States (Atkins et al., 2001), participants earning more than $30,000 per year were more likely to engage in extramarital sex because they could afford the costs associated with having an affair. However, according to the authors, "It might be a marker of something else that contributes to infidelity. For example, individuals with higher incomes might be considered to have higher status, to travel more, or to interact professionally with more appealing individuals" (Atkins et al., 2001, p. 744). Moreover, discrepancy between men's and women's occupational status (e.g., people who work and whose spouses do not) increases the likelihood of extramarital relationships, which might be explained by the differential relational power between men and women (Atkins et al., 2001). A study by Smith (2012) in the United States, Germany, and the United Kingdom showed that the lower people's educational level, the more likely they were to be involved in an extramarital relationship, holding occupational status constant. The same study showed that the higher men's work status, the more likely they were to be involved in an extramarital relationship, which corroborates Atkins's (2001) findings. Specifically, Smith asserts that there are robust results across the three national samples indicating that people with higher socioeconomic status are involved to a greater extent in extramarital relationships, whereas a college education hinders involvement in extradyadic affairs, perhaps because educated people are more concerned about the costs (e.g., economic impact of separation) related to the extradyadic relationships.

Studies in non-Western samples show mixed results. In India, Schensul et al. (2006) investigated a sample of married couples from Mumbai and found that men's educational level was negatively related to involvement in extradyadic relationships. In Africa, Kimuna, and Djamba (2005) showed that occupational status was not associated with extramarital sexual behaviors among Zambian men, after controlling for other demographic variables. We have to be cautious when integrating and comparing these results because some of the studies included both men and women (e.g., Atkins et al., 2001; Smith, 2012), whereas other studies were based on only men's responses (e.g., Kimuna & Djamba, 2005). Few of these studies controlled for extraneous variables (e.g., Kimuna & Djamba, 2005), and different studies used different measures for assessing the dependent and independent variables. Moreover, the correlational nature of the studies prevents us from asserting that education, socioeconomic status, or incomes leads to extradyadic involvement; we only can conclude that, globally, income and occupational status have a positive association with involvement in extradyadic sexual relationships whereas educational level has a negative association with involvement in such relationships.

Gender

Gender is the most studied variable in predicting extradyadic sexual involvement, but there is evidence that the possible moderating effect of age should be considered. In Western culture, American men older than 40 years are more likely to be involved in extradyadic relationships than American women in the same age group, but this is not true for American participants younger than 40 years (Wiederman, 1997), as younger women and men reported being similarly involved in extradyadic sexual relationships (Atkins et al., 2001; Negasha et al., 2016). In contrast, McAlister et al. (2005), studying an Australian undergraduate sample, found that men are more inclined to engage in extradyadic sex than women, controlling by participant's age. Even though several studies confirmed that the gender differences are becoming smaller than in the past (e.g., Atkins et al., 2001; Negasha et al., 2016), there may be gender differences in the motivation for being involved in extradyadic relationships. Sex is the most important feature for American men motivating involvement in extradyadic relationships, whereas for women dissatisfaction with a regular partner is the most important motive for being involved in extradyadic relationships (Barta & Kiene, 2005).

In Asian cultures, there also are gender differences in extradyadic sexual attitudes and behaviors. Indonesian men have more positive attitudes toward infidelity compared to Indonesian women (Isma &Turnip, 2019), and 4.5% of Chinese women reported infidelity in the last 12 months, whereas this was true for 11% of Chinese men (Zhang et al., 2012). Finally, mixed results have been found in other cultures. In a study in a predominantly Muslim culture, the sample did not yield gender differences in reported infidelity (Toplu-Demirtaş & Fincham, 2018). In the Caribbean culture of Puerto Rico, men reported higher rates of infidelity than women.

Age

In a recent systematic review, Haseli et al. (2019) showed that age is one of the weakest predictors of involvement in extradyadic relationships, given the mixed results in the literature. In Western cultures, the findings about the effect of age on involvement in extradyadic relationships are mixed. Earlier studies found a curvilinear relationship between age and extramarital sex in a sample from the United States, with men aged 55–65 years and women aged 40–45 years at the time of survey reporting the highest levels of involvement in extramarital sex (Atkins et al., 2001). In contrast, more recent studies have found that the likelihood of infidelity decreases with age among North American married women (Whisman & Snyder, 2007). However, an important consideration is that we cannot be certain that these effects are age effects rather than generation effects.

In non-Western cultures, there is no clear evidence that age has an effect on extradyadic affairs. Whereas in Asia, Zhang and colleagues (2020) found a negative association between age and engagement in extramarital sex among Chinese men and women, studies with African samples found a positive association between age and extradyadic relationships among Tanzanian men (Mbago & Sichona, 2014). Additionally, a study from India has shown that the partner's age as well as the discrepancy between the wife's and husband's age predict men's extradyadic sexual relationships (Schensul et al., 2006).

Personality and Intrapersonal Factors

Big Five

Focusing on the five-factor model of personality or Big Five (neuroticism, agreeableness, conscientiousness, extraversion, and openness to experience; McCrae & Costa, 1997), several studies in different world regions have shown the predictive role of each factor in fostering extradyadic involvement.

Neuroticism, characterized by low emotional regulation and emotional instability, has been related to higher involvement in extradyadic relationships in different cultures. Most studies have found that among men and women from the United States, neuroticism predicts involvement in extradyadic relationships (Barta & Kiene, 2005; Whisman & Coop Gordon, 2007). For example, Schmitt (2004) found in a North American sample that, among women, but not among men, there was a relationship between being unfaithful and scoring high in neuroticism. Gibson and collaborators (2016) explains this finding on the basis of the "lower likelihood of neurotic people attracting extradyadic partners, given the negative personality profile of neurotic individual" (p. 193). However, some studies do not find neuroticism as a predictor of involvement in extradyadic relationships (Gibson et al., 2016; Schmitt, 2004).

Also, in a number of non-Western cultures, neuroticism has been found to be a predictor of extradyadic relationship involvement. For example, neuroticism predicted positive attitudes toward infidelity among married young adult men and women living in Indonesia (Isma & Turnip, 2019). However, Schmitt (2004) found different results in 10 world regions regarding the relationship between extradyadic relationships and neuroticism, being negatively related in women from South America, positively related in men from Africa, and positively related in both genders in South and Southeast Asia.

Extraversion, which is characterized by high sociability and assertiveness, does not seem to have a clear effect on involvement in extradyadic relationships (Altgelt, 2018). In Western cultures, some studies failed to find extraversion as a predictor of extradyadic relationships in a sample from the United States (e.g., Barta & Kiene, 2005), whereas other studies in North American samples have found extraversion to be a weak predictor of involvement in extradyadic relationships (Gibson et al., 2016; Schmitt, 2004). In the same vein, in the global study in 10 different world regions, Schmitt (2004) found that extraversion was a weak or nonsignificant predictor of extradyadic involvement. It might be concluded that across countries extraversion does not consistently predict extradyadic involvement.

There is no consistent evidence for an effect of *openness to experience*, which characterizes people that expose themselves to challenging and new experiences and sensations, on extradyadic relationship involvement. On the one hand, openness has been found to be unrelated to the occurrence of infidelity among North Americans (Gibson et al., 2016) and to attitudes toward infidelity among Indonesians (Isma & Turnip, 2019). On the other hand, the global study by Schmitt (2004) showed that the effect of openness depended on the cultural context: Openness to experience was negatively related to extradyadic involvement for men from North America, eastern Europe, and South and Southeast Asia, whereas there was a positive relationship between openness to experience and extradyadic relationships for women from eastern and southern Europe (Schmitt, 2004).

Conscientiousness has been found to be a universal and consistent predictor of low involvement in extradyadic relationships. For example, conscientiousness predicted negative attitudes toward infidelity in Indonesian men and women (Isma & Turnip, 2019). In the same vein, there is evidence that in North American culture, low conscientiousness predicts participants' self-reported infidelity during the first year of marriage (e.g., Buss & Shackelford, 1997). That conscientiousness seems to be a universal predictor of a low involvement in, and negative attitudes toward, extradyadic relationships for both men and women (Schmitt, 2004) may be explained by the finding that conscientiousness is negatively related to impulsive sensation-seeking. Indeed, dysfunctional impulsivity is related to extradyadic relationship inclination in Australian male and female undergraduates (McAlister et al., 2005), and sensation seeking is related to infidelity among Puerto Rican men and women (Galarza et al., 2009).

Like conscientiousness, *agreeableness*, which is characterized by trustworthiness, historically has been considered to negatively predict extradyadic involvement. Findings in North

American culture are mixed. For example, whereas Bart and Kiene (2005) found that low agreeableness predicted extradyadic involvement, Gibson et al. (2016) using a North American sample did not find that low agreeableness predicts involvement in extradyadic relationships. Studies in non-American samples show a universal trend in which agreeableness is negatively associated with involvement in extradyadic relationships (Schmitt, 2004).

In addition to the McCrae and Costa's (1997) five factor model of personality, there are other personality traits and psychological factors that have been found to be predictors of extradyadic relationships in Western culture. Specifically, in North American samples, *self-esteem* was found to be negatively related to infidelity (Whisman et al., 2007), *psychopathy* was found to be related to a positive attitude toward infidelity (Sevia et al., 2020), and *psychological distress* has been found to positively predict infidelity (Hall & Fincham, 2009). Focusing on sexual motivations for extradyadic sex, Barta and Kiene (2005) found that those American women and men who scored higher in *sociosexual orientation* (SO) endorsed higher sexual motivations for extradyadic sex. Moreover, among Dutch women, *exchange orientation*, defined as a disposition to reciprocity, has been found to be related to the desire to engage in extradyadic relationships (Prins et al., 1993). Summarizing, culture has an important role moderating the effect that personality variables have on extradyadic sexual behavior (Schmitt, 2004).

History of Alcohol Use

In American samples, mixed results have been found on the effect of alcohol use on engagement in extradyadic sex. Maddox et al. (2013), using a sample of American undergraduate women and men, found a positive relationship between problematic alcohol use and involvement in extradyadic sex. Moreover, Graham et al. (2016), in a representative sample of the United States, found that alcohol problems predicted future extradyadic sexual involvement. However, Graham et al. (2016), in a study of American undergraduates from a southeastern university, failed to find a link between alcohol consumption and engagement in extradyadic relationships.

Among people from Africa, Kongnyuy and Wiysonge (2007) found in a sample of Cameroonian married or cohabiting men, that alcohol consumption predicted involvement in extramarital sexual relationships. Furthermore, in Uganda such a relationship is higher for circumcised men compared to uncircumcised men (Bailey et al., 1999). In Asia, the scant research that has explored the relationship between alcohol consumption and extradyadic relationships showed that, among Indian married men, alcohol consumption predicts extradyadic sexual involvement (Schensul et al., 2006).

Relational Factors

Commitment, Satisfaction, and Dependency

Research has shown that a number of relational factors are related to the occurrence of infidelity. Specifically, poor dyadic adjustment, dissatisfaction, low emotional dependence, and low commitment with the primary relationship have been found to be important determinants of actual infidelity, or of the willingness to be involved in an extradyadic relationship (Buunk & Bakker, 1997; Martins et al., 2016; Treas & Giesen, 2000). Martins et al. (2016) found, in a Portuguese dating relationships sample, that lower relationship satisfaction and lower commitment were associated with extradyadic involvement. In a Dutch sample, Buunk (1980b) found that the more people felt emotionally dependent on their spouse, the less often they had been involved in extradyadic sexual and erotic relationships and the less likely they expected to be involved in these relationships.

Nevertheless, gender differences emerge in the relational features associated with the occurrence of extradyadic affairs. Among men, infidelity has been related to feelings of sexual deprivation in the primary relationship; meanwhile, among women, infidelity has been related to emotional displeasure with the primary relationship (e.g., Atkins et al., 2001; Cheng & Smyth, 2015). For example, Omarzu et al. (2012) found that infidelity among men was more motivated by the desire for additional sexual encounters, curiosity, and sensation seeking, and among women more by the desire for additional emotional involvement or validation from others. Moreover, Zhang et al. (2012) showed that Chinese men who commit infidelity did so in response to sexual dissatisfaction with their primary partner, while women's infidelity was more responsive to a loss of love.

History of Sexual and Romantic Interactions

In Western cultures, research has shown that an individual's history of sexual and romantic relationships is associated with the number of reported extradyadic relationships. Specifically, the prevalence of extramarital sex is higher among North Americans married at younger ages (Atkins et al., 2001) and among female Americans who had cohabited with their partner prior to marriage or were remarried (Whisman & Snyder, 2007). In addition, results from samples of North American women and Australian undergraduate men and women samples showed that a greater number of previous sexual partners was positively related to the probability of sexual infidelity (McAlister et al., 2005; Whisman & Snyder, 2007).

In non-Western cultures, the results depend on the region. In Asia, the results of a study of 5,502 married women showed that, among men, a longer relationship and having sex before marriage was related to extradyadic sexual relationships (Ahlburga et al., 1997). However, it is important to point out that the conclusions come from women's reports of their husbands' behaviors. Data from Africa have shown similar factors associated with involvement in extradyadic sexual relationships. Specifically, Mbago and Sichona (2010) found that sex before marriage was associated with higher likelihood of engagement in extramarital relationships among Tanzanian married men. Mitsunaga et al. (2005) found among Nigerian married men that an earlier age of sexual debut predicted engagement in extradyadic sexual relationships. In addition, among African men, there are mixed results regarding the effect that peri- and postpartum sexual abstinence has on extradyadic involvement: Among married men from Ivory Coast, postpartum abstinence was related to extradyadic sex (Ali & Cleland, 2001), but this was not found for Nigerian men (Mitsunaga et al., 2005).

Ideological Factors
Religiosity

In Western cultures, religiosity (Whisman & Gordon, 2007), and biblical beliefs and church attendance (Atkins et al., 2001; Burdette et al., 2007) are associated with less self-reported extramarital sexual involvement. However, religiosity has not been found to predict involvement in extradyadic relationships among American undergraduates in dating relationships. These mixed results might be explained because of the importance of marital union fidelity among religious people (Negasha et al., 2016), which might explain the finding that, among religious people, marital dissatisfaction may less often lead to extradyadic involvement than among nonreligious people (Whisman & Gordon, 2007).

Moreover, in Latin American cultures, similar results have been found. Specifically, attendance at religious services is negatively related to involvement in extramarital sex among Puerto Rican men and women (González et al., 2009). Furthermore, among Brazilians, evangelical religious affiliation is negatively related to having extramarital partners (Hill et al., 2004). In addition, in Africa there are some differences in infidelity depending on religious affiliation (e.g., Muslim, Catholic, or Protestant). Specifically, among Nigerian men, Mitsunaga et al. (2005) found that Muslim men are less likely to engage in extradyadic sex compared to Catholic and Protestant men. The authors explained that these results are because of "stronger religious taboos against sex outside marriage for Muslims" (Mitsunaga et al., 2005, p. 486). Moreover, if husband and wife have different religious affiliations, this predicts extramarital sex among West African participants (Ali & Cleland, 2001).

Attitudes Toward Extramarital Sex

Research has shown a positive association between attitudes toward infidelity and actual infidelity (Brase et al., 2014; Martins et al., 2016; Toplu-Demirtaş & Fincham, 2018; Wiederman, 1997; Whisman & Snyder, 2007). Several studies have shown that unfaithful individuals with more liberal sexual attitudes have a higher predisposition toward sexual excitation, which is associated with an increased frequency of extramarital sexual involvement (Haseli et al., 2019; Mark et al., 2011). Toplu-Demirtaş and Fincham (2018) investigated in a Muslim culture the associations between attitudes toward infidelity and reported infidelity. In a sample of male and female college students, attitudes toward infidelity were related to the intention to engage in extradyadic involvement. Moreover, men compared to women and cheaters compared to noncheaters expressed more positive attitudes and stronger intentions to pursue infidelity. In a US sample, Wiederman (1997) found that men and women who had engaged in extramarital sex were less likely to disapprove of infidelity than were their peers without extramarital sexual experience. The same was found in a Dutch sample by Buunk (1980b). In both studies, men and women who denied ever engaging in extramarital involvement did not differ in their attitudes toward extramarital sex. However, the direction of the relationship between attitudes and involvement in extramarital sex is not clear. Are more accepting attitudes toward extramarital sex responsible for an increased likelihood of engaging in extramarital sex? Or, does engaging in extramarital sex result in more positive attitudes as a rationalization of one's behavior? It seems likely that both processes occur.

Conclusions

Although infidelity is negatively judged all over the world, there are considerable cultural differences in this respect, and in general, infidelity by women is evaluated more negatively than infidelity by men. Infidelity is not an unambiguous concept, but it is most commonly considered to be sexual involvement outside the primary relationship. There have not been many cross-cultural studies on the determinants of this type of behavior. In general, the demographic determinants appear similar across cultures. First, there is evidence that, globally, involvement in extradyadic sexual relationships is found more among people with a higher income and a higher occupational status, but less among people with more education. Second, globally, men are more inclined to engage in extradyadic sex, although there is some evidence that among younger people this sex difference is decreasing, or even disappearing. Third, of all demographic variables, religiosity is one of the most consistent predictors of a lack of extradyadic sexual involvement.

The effects of personality characteristics on extradyadic sexual involvement are weak. Extraversion and openness to experience are not consistently associated with extradyadic sexual involvement, but a lack of conscientiousness is. There is also evidence that individuals high in neuroticism engage more in extradyadic sex, and that in non-Western cultures this is also true for individuals low in agreeableness. In contrast to the role of personality, there are clear relational correlates of actual or intended extradyadic sexual involvement, including low commitment, low sexual satisfaction for men, low relational satisfaction for women, and a more active premarital sexual history.

To conclude, some variables, including socioeconomic status, religiosity, gender, and relational satisfaction, seem globally consistently associated with the occurrence of infidelity. Nevertheless, there is little consistent evidence for cross-cultural differences in the factors associated with infidelity. And as far as such differences have been established these have mostly only been found in a single study. Therefore, there is a need for more cross-cultural research on the factors associated with engaging in extradyadic sex.

References

Ahlburg, D. A., Jensen, E. R., & Perez, A. E. (1997). Determinants of extramarital sex in the Philippines. *Health Transition Review, 7*, 467–479. http://www.jstor.org/stable/40652317

Ali, M. M., & Cleland, J. G. (2001). The link between postnatal abstinence and extramarital sex in Cote d'Ivoire. *Studies in Family Planning, 32*(3), 214–219. https://doi.org/10.1111/j.1728-4465.2001.00214.x

Altgelt, E. E., Reyes, M. A., French, J. E., Meltzer, A. L., & McNulty, J. K. (2018). Who is sexually faithful? Own and partner personality traits as predictors of infidelity. *Journal of Social and Personal Relationships, 35*(4), 600–614. https://doi.org/10.1177/0265407517743085

Atkins, D. C., Baucom, D. H., & Jacobson, N. S. (2001). Understanding infidelity: Correlates in a national random sample. *Journal of Family Psychology, 15*(4), 735. https://doi.org/10.1037/0893-3200.15.4.735

Bailey, R. C., Neema, S., & Othieno, R. (1999). Sexual behaviors and other HIV risk factors in circumcised and uncircumcised men in Uganda. *Journal of Acquired Immune Deficiency Syndromes, 22*(3), 294–301. http://doi.org/10.1097/00126334-199911010-00012

Barker, M., & Langdridge, D. (2010). Whatever happened to non-monogamies? Critical reflections on recent research and theory. *Sexualities, 13*, 748–772. https://doi.org/10.1177/1363460710384645

Barta, W. D., & Kiene, S. M. (2005). Motivations for infidelity in heterosexual dating couples: The roles of gender, personality differences, and sociosexual orientation. *Journal of Social and Personal Relationships, 22*(3), 339–360. https://doi.org/10.1177/0265407505052440

Bergner, R. M., & Bridges, A. J. (2002). The significance of heavy pornography involvement for romantic partners: Research and clinical implications. *Journal of Sex and Marital Therapy, 28*, 193–206. https://doi.org/10.1080/009262302760328235

Brase, G. L., Adair, L., & Monk, K. (2014). Explaining sex differences in reactions to relationship infidelities: Comparisons of the roles of sex, gender, beliefs, attachment, and sociosexual orientation. *Evolutionary Psychology, 12*, 73–96. https://doi.org/10.1177/147470491401200106

Burdette, A. M., Ellison, C. G., Sherkat, D. E., & Gore, K. A. (2007). Are there religious variations in marital infidelity? *Journal of Family Issues, 28*(12), 1553–1581. https://doi.org/10.1177/0192513X07304269

Buss, D. M., & Shackelford, T. K. (1997). Susceptibility to infidelity in the first year of marriage. *Journal of Research in Personality, 31*(2), 193–221.

Buunk, A. P. (1980a). Sexually open marriages: Ground rules for countering potential threats to marriage. *Alternative Lifestyles, 3*, 312–328.

Buunk, A. P. (1980b). Extramarital sex in the Netherlands: Motivations in social and marital context. *Alternative Lifestyles, 3*, 11–39.

Buunk, A. P., & Bakker, A. B. (1997). Commitment to the relationship, extradyadic sex, and AIDS-preventive behavior. *Journal of Applied Social Psychology, 27*, 1241–1257.

Buunk, A., Dijkstra, P., & Massar, K. (2018). The universal threat and temptation of extradyadic affairs. In A. Vangelisti & D. Perlman (Eds.), *The Cambridge handbook of personal relationships* (pp. 353–364). Cambridge Handbooks in Psychology. Cambridge University Press. https://doi.org/10.1017/9781316417867.028

Cheng, Z., & Smyth, R. (2015). Sex and happiness. *Journal of Economic Behavior & Organization, 112*, 26–32. https://psycnet.apa.org/doi/10.1016/j.jebo.2014.12.030

Dillow, M. R., Malachowski, C. C., Brann, M., & Weber, K. (2011). An experimental examination of the effects of communicative infidelity motives on communication and relational outcomes in romantic relationships. *Western Journal of Communication, 75*, 473–499. https://doi.org/10.1080/10570314.2011.588986

Fife, S. T., Weeks, G. R., & Stellberg-Filbert, J. (2013). Facilitating forgiveness in the treatment of infidelity: An interpersonal model. *Journal of Family Therapy, 35*, 343–367. doi: 10.1111/j.1467-6427.2011.00561.x

Galarza, J. G., Martínez-Taboas, A., & Ortiz, D. M. (2009). Factores psicológicos asociados a la infidelidad sexual y/o emocional y su relación a la búsqueda de sensaciones en parejas puertorriqueñas. *Revista Puertorriqueña de Psicología, 20*, 59–81.

Gibson, K. A., Thompson, A. E., & O'Sullivan, L. F. (2016). Love thy neighbour: Personality traits, relationship quality, and attraction to others as predictors of infidelity among young adults. *Canadian Journal of Human Sexuality, 25*(3), 186–198. https://doi.org/10.3138/cjhs.253-A2

Graham, S. M., Negash, S., Lambert, N. M., & Fincham, F. D. (2016). Problem drinking and extradyadic sex in young adult romantic relationships. *Journal of Social and Clinical Psychology, 35*(2), 152–170. https://doi.org/10.1521/jscp.2016.35.2.152

Hall, J. H., & Fincham, F. D. (2009). Psychological distress: Precursor or consequence of dating infidelity? *Personality and Social Psychology Bulletin*, *35*(2), 143–159. https://doi.org/10.1177/0146167208327189

Haseli, A., Shariati, M., Nazari, A. M., Keramat, A., & Emamian, M. H. (2019). Infidelity and its associated factors: A systematic review. *Journal of Sexual Medicine*, *16*(8), 1155–1169. https://doi.org/10.1016/j.jsxm.2019.04.011

Hertlein, K. M., & Blumer, M. L. (2014). *The couple and family technology frame-work: Intimate relationships in a digital age*. Brunner-Routledge.

Hill, Z. E., Cleland, J., & Ali, M. M. (2004). Religious affiliation and extramarital sex among men in Brazil. *International Family Planning Perspectives*, *30*(1), 20–26. http://www.jstor.org/stable/3181012

Isma, M. N. P., & Turnip, S. S. (2019). Personality traits and marital satisfaction in predicting couples' attitudes toward infidelity. *Journal of Relationships Research*, 10, e13, 1–5 https://doi.org/10.1017/jrr.2019.10.

Jonason, P. K., & Balzarini, R. N. (2016). Unweaving the rainbow of human sexuality: A review of one-night stands, serious romantic relationships, and the relationship space in between. In K. Aumer (Ed.), *The psychology of love and hate in intimate relationships* (pp. 13–28). Springer International.

Kimuna, S. R., & Djamba, Y. K. (2005). Wealth and extramarital sex among men in Zambia. *International Family Planning Perspectives*, *31*(2), 83–89. https://www.jstor.org/stable/3649483

Kongnyuy, E. J., & Wiysonge, C. S. (2007). Alcohol use and extramarital sex among men in Cameroon. *BMC International Health and Human Rights*, *7*(1), 6. https://doi.org/10.1186/1472-698X-7-6

Mackay, J. (2001). Global sex: Sexuality and sexual practices around the world. *Sexual and Relationship Therapy*, *16*, 71–82. https://doi.org/10.1080/14681990020021575

Mackey, W. C., & Immerman, R. S. (2001). Restriction of sexual activity as a partial function of disease avoidance: A cultural response to sexually transmitted diseases. *Cross-Cultural Research*, *35*, 400–423.

Maddox Shaw, A. M., Rhoades, G. K., Allen, E. S., Stanley, S. M., & Markman, H. J. (2013). Predictors of extradyadic sexual involvement in unmarried opposite-sex relationships. *Journal of Sex Research*, *50*(6), 598–610. https://doi.org/10.1080/00224499.2012.666816

Mark, K. P., Janssen, E., & Milhausen, R. R. (2011). Infidelity in heterosexual couples: Demographic, interpersonal, and personality-related predictors of extradyadic sex. *Archives of Sexual Behavior*, *40*, 971–982.

Martell, C. R., & Prince, S. E. (2005). Treating infidelity in same-sex couples. *Journal of Clinical Psychology*, *61*, 1429–1438. https://doi.org/10.1002/jclp.20192

Martins, A., Pereira, M., Andrade, R., Dattilio, F. M., Narciso, I., & Canavarro, M. C. (2016). Infidelity in dating relationships: Gender-specific correlates to face-to-face and online extradyadic involvement. *Archives of Sexual Behavior*, *45*, 193–205.

Mattingly, B., Wilson, K., Clark, E., Bequette, A., & Weidler, D. (2010). Foggy faithfulness: Relationship quality, religiosity, and the perceptions of dating infidelity scale in an adult sample. *Journal of Family Issues*, *31*, 1465–1480. https://doi.org/10.1177/0192513X10362348

Mbago, M. C., & Sichona, F. J. (2010). Determinants of extramarital sex by men in Tanzania: A case study of Mbeya region. *SAHARA-J: Journal of Social Aspects of HIV/AIDS*, *7*(4), 33–38. https://doi.org/10.1080/17290376.2010.9724975

McAlister, A., Pachana, N., & Jackson, C. J. (2005). Predictors of young dating adults' inclination to engage in extradyadic sexual activities: A multi-perspective study. *British Journal of Psychology*, *96*(3), 331–350. https://doi.org/10.1348/000712605X47936

McCrae, R. R., & Costa, P. T., Jr. (1997). Personality trait structure as a human universal. *American Psychologist*, *52*(5), 509. https://doi.org/10.1037/0003-066X.52.5.509

Mitsunaga, T. M., Powell, A. M., Heard, N. J., & Larsen, U. M. (2005). Extramarital sex among Nigerian men: Polygyny and other risk factors. *JAIDS: Journal of Acquired Immune Deficiency Syndromes*, *39*(4), 478–488. httpd://doi.org/10.1097/01.qai.0000152396.60014.69

Moller, N. P., & Vossler, A. (2015). Defining infidelity in research and couple counseling: A qualitative study. *Journal of Sex and Marital Therapy*, *41*, 487–497. https://doi.org/10.1080/0092623X.2014.931314

Negash, S., Veldorale-Brogan, A., Kimber, S. B., & Fincham, F. D. (2019). Predictors of extradyadic sex among young adults in heterosexual dating relationships: A multivariate approach. *Sexual and Relationship Therapy*, *34*(2), 153–172. https://doi.org/10.1080/14681994.2016.1219334

Olmstead, S. B., Blick, R. W., & Mills, L. I., III. (2009). Helping couples work toward the forgiveness of marital infidelity: Therapists' perspectives. *American Journal of Family Therapy*, *37*(1), 48–66.

Omarzu, J., Miller, A. N., Schultz, C., & Timmerman, A. (2012). Motivations and emotional consequences related to engaging in extramarital relationships. *International Journal of Sexual Health*, *24*(2), 154–162. https://psycnet.apa.org/doi/10.1080/19317611.2012.662207.

Prieto-Ursúa, M., Carrasco, M. J., Cagigal de Gregorio, V., Gismero, E., Martínez, M. P., & Muñoz, I. (2012). El perdón como herramienta clínica en terapia individual y de pareja. *Clínica Contemporánea, 3*, 121–134. https://doi.org/10.5093/cc2012a8

Prins, K. S., Buunk, A. P., & Van Yperen, N. W. (1993). Equity, normative disapproval and extramarital relationships. *Journal of Social and Personal Relationships, 10*, 39–53.

Rodrigues, D., Lopes, D., & Pereira, M. (2016). Sociosexuality, commitment, sexual infidelity, and perceptions of infidelity: Data from the second love web site. *Journal of Sex Research, 54*, 241–253. https://doi.org/10.1080/00224499.2016.1145182

Schensul, S. L., Mekki-Berrada, A., Nastasi, B. K., Singh, R., Burleson, J. A., & Bojko, M. (2006). Men's extramarital sex, marital relationships and sexual risk in urban poor communities in India. *Journal of Urban Health, 83*(4), 614–624. https://doi.org/10.1080/14681994.2016.1219334

Schmitt, D. P. (2004). The Big Five related to risky sexual behaviour across 10 world regions: Differential personality associations of sexual promiscuity and relationship infidelity. *European Journal of personality, 18*(4), 301–319.

Sevi, B., Urganci, B., & Sakman, E. (2020). Who cheats? An examination of light and dark personality traits as predictors of infidelity. *Personality and Individual Differences, 164*, 110126. https://doi.org/10.1016/j.paid.2020.110126

Sharpe, D., Walters, A., & Goren, M. (2013). Effect of cheating experience on attitudes toward infidelity. *Sexuality & Culture, 17*, 643–658. https://doi.org/10.1007/s12119-013- 9169-2

Smith, I. (2012). Reinterpreting the economics of extramarital affairs. *Review of Economics of the Household, 10*(3), 319–343. https://doi.org/10.1007/s11150-012-9146-9

Thompson, A. E., & O'Sullivan, L. F. (2016a). I can but you can't: Inconsistencies in judgments of and experiences with infidelity. *Journal of Relationship Research, 7*, 1–13. https://doi.org/10.1017/jrr.2016.1

Thompson, A. E., & O'Sullivan, L. F. (2016b). Drawing the line: The development of a comprehensive assessment of infidelity judgments. *Journal of Sex Research, 53*, 910–926. https://doi.org/10.1080/00224499.2015.1062840

Thompson, A. E., & O'Sullivan, L. F. (2017). Understanding variations in judgments of infidelity: An application of attribution theory. *Basic and Applied Social Psychology, 39*, 262–276. https://doi.org/10.1080/01973533.2017.1350578

Thompson, A. E., Zimmerman, C. N., Kulibert, D., & Moore, E. A. (2017). Sex differences and the effect of rival characteristics on adults' judgments of hypothetical infidelity. *Evolutionary Psychological Science, 3*, 97–108. https://doi.org/10.1007/s40806-016-0076-2

Toplu-Demirtaş, E., & Fincham, F. D. (2018). Dating infidelity in Turkish couples: The role of attitudes and intentions. *Journal of Sex Research, 55*(2), 252–262. https://doi.org/10.1080/00224499.2017.1365110

Treas, J., & Giesen, D. (2000). Sexual infidelity among married and cohabiting Americans. *Journal of Marriage and the Family, 62*, 287–300. https://doi.org/10.1111/j.1741-3737.2000.00048.x

Watkins, S. J., & Boon, S. D. (2016). Expectations regarding partner infidelity in dating relationships. *Journal of Social and Personal Relationships, 33*, 237–256. https://doi.org/10.1177/0265407515574463

Whisman, M. A., Gordon, K. C., & Chatav, Y. (2007). Predicting sexual infidelity in a population-based sample of married individuals. *Journal of Family Psychology, 21*(2), 320. https://doi.org/10.1037/0893-3200.21.2.320

Whisman, M. A., & Snyder, D. K. (2007). Sexual infidelity in a national survey of American women: Differences in prevalence and correlates as a function of method of assessment. *Journal of Family Psychology, 21*(2), 147–154. https://doi.org/10.1037/0893-3200.21.2.147

Whitty, M. T., & Quigley, L. (2008). Emotional and sexual infidelity offline and in cyberspace. *Journal of Marital and Family Therapy, 34*, 461–468. https://doi.org/10.1111/j.1752-0606.2008.00088.x

Wiederman, M. W. (1997). Extramarital sex: Prevalence and correlates in a national survey. *Journal of Sex Research, 34*(2), 167–174. https://doi.org/10.1080/00224499709551881

Zhang, N., Parish, W. L., Huang, Y., & Pan, S. (2012). Sexual infidelity in China: Prevalence and gender-specific correlates. *Archives of Sexual Behavior, 41*(4), 861–873. https://doi.org/10.1007/s10508-012-9930-x

Zhang, Y., Wang, X., & Pan, S. (2020). Prevalence and patterns of extramarital sex among Chinese men and women: 2000–2015. *Journal of Sex Research, 41*–50. https://doi.org/10.1080/00224499.2020.1797617

CHAPTER 8

Predicting Online Infidelity

Carey J. Fitzgerald, Crystal Moreno, *and* Jody Thompson

Abstract
Infidelity, as well as emotional and behavioral responses to infidelity, have been extensively studied in the evolutionary and social psychological literature. However, changing Internet usage by the general population continues to afford new directions to this body of research. With the advent of such websites and applications as Ashley Madison, Seeking Arrangement, and Tinder, the Internet has provided a new environment for humans to engage in both sexual and emotional infidelity on an unprecedented level. This chapter defines sexual infidelity and emotional infidelity within the context of the Internet, then reviews the literature regarding online infidelity (specifically, usage of Ashley Madison and Tinder) with a focus on the situational, dispositional, and cultural factors that influence these behaviors. Variables such as gender, age, income, attachment style, relationship satisfaction, and personality traits—including the five factor model (i.e., the "Big Five") and the dark triad model—are examined. Same sex infidelity, nonbinary infidelity, and suggestions for future research on this topic are also discussed.

Key Words: emotional infidelity, evolutionary psychology, fidelity, fidelity management, sexual infidelity

Introduction

Engaging in monogamous long-term mating provides many benefits to both women and men. Both sexes can transmit copies of their genes, and both sexes can work together to care for their offspring, and thereby increasing the survival of their offspring. However, long-term mating also has costs. For example, while the female is pregnant, the male cannot reproduce with her until she gives birth and physically recovers. This creates a (minimum) 40-week period during which the male cannot transmit his genes with that same female. In humans' ancestral past, it may have been reproductively beneficial for males to engage in extrapair copulation to enhance their reproductive output (Trivers, 1996). This may account for the fact that 33%–75% of men have engaged in infidelity at some point in their lives (Buss, 1994). Similarly, a mated female may seek a new mate who has greater access to resources than her current mate, which would in turn enhance the probability of her—and her future offspring's—survival (Trivers, 1996). Both males and females may also seek a new mate who is genetically superior (i.e., more "fit") than their current mate, as the new mate's "better" genes may produce healthier offspring, thus enhancing the probability of offspring survival (Trivers, 1996).

There can be severe costs associated with infidelity. If a woman engages in infidelity, this could effectively eliminate her long-term partner's only opportunity for reproduction (either by cuckolding her long-term mate, or by leaving her long-term mate for a new mate)—which would be an evolutionary death sentence for her current long-term mate. In addition, if a man engages in infidelity, he may leave his current long-term mate and take his resources with him—which could be a literal death sentence for her and any offspring she may have. In fact, even in modern times, human offspring mortality rates increase after the death of a parent (Rostila & Saarela, 2011).

Given these potentially deadly costs, humans may have evolved mechanisms to prevent their romantic partners from engaging in infidelity. In a seminal study, Buss and colleagues (1992) hypothesized that jealousy in romantic relationships evolved as a means of preventing a partner from engaging in infidelity. Specifically, Buss and colleagues argued that sex differences in jealousy may arise as a product of the type of partner infidelity that would have been most costly to men and women in humans' ancestral past. This led to the differentiation between sexual infidelity—the act of engaging in sexual intercourse with someone who is not one's long-term mate—and emotional infidelity—developing a deep emotional bond with someone who is not one's long-term mate. Across three experiments, the researchers asked participants to indicate whether they were more upset at the thought of their romantic partner having sex with another person or at the thought of their partner falling in love with another person. Their results indicated a robust sex difference—men were more upset at the thought of their partner's sexual infidelity, while women were more upset at the thought of their partner's emotional infidelity. These results have been corroborated in many studies (Buss, 2018; Hughes et al., 2004; Kruger et al., 2015; Takahashi et al., 2006), and they reflect a deeper truth regarding perceptions of infidelity. Men are more sensitive to their partner's potential sexual infidelity because it could lead to cuckoldry. On the other hand, women are more sensitive to their partner's potential emotional infidelity because it could lead to their mate leaving for a new mate.

While these mechanisms influencing mating, infidelity, and jealousy have evolved over thousands of generations, they remain the same today. Humans' environment, however, has changed dramatically in many ways in just the past few thousand years. Most humans no longer live in small hunter-gatherer groups. As technology continues to develop, humans embrace new ways of meeting and interacting across the globe. The Internet is now commonplace in most humans' environments, and it is frequently used to meet new people. In fact, 93% of individuals in the United States regularly use the Internet today (Pew Research Center, 2021), and approximately 91% of single adults in the United States today have used online dating sites to meet new people offline (Statistic Brain Research Institute, 2017)—which has increased from 40% in 2013 (Smith & Duggan,

2013). Moreover, some data suggest that people are now using the Internet and dating applications as regular "preinteraction" processes to facilitate communication with potential new friends and/or mates before meeting them in person (LeFebvre, 2018). This novel environment for human interaction and mating still brings with it the same costs and benefits that humans ancestrally faced when mating. In this chapter, we focus on the situational, dispositional, and cultural predictors of online sexual and emotional infidelity, as well as how men and women use the Internet for mating purposes, how men and women engage in infidelity via the Internet, whether similar trends are seen across cultures, and how scientists can predict the likelihood of infidelity in this technological age.

Online Sexual Infidelity

Sexual infidelity is often defined as engaging in some form of sexual behavior with an individual who is not one's current long-term romantic partner. While these behaviors can range from "sending erotic messages to someone" to "sexual intercourse" (Kruger et al., 2010), most men and women both rate the following definition of sexual infidelity as accurate: "Sexual infidelity is when you are in a relationship or a marriage, and engage in sexual activity with another individual that is not your girlfriend/boyfriend, husband or wife. Having an affair or cheating in a sexual manner" (Guitar et al., 2017, pp. 439–440). While this definition of sexual infidelity may seem straightforward, the advent of online dating has provided many caveats.

What is perceived as conventional (in-person) infidelity might not be perceived as infidelity in an online context. Whitty's (2003) results indicated three primary categories of online (heterosexual) infidelity: Cybersex, emotional intimacy (sharing sensitive emotional information with someone of the opposite sex), and pornography use (however, pornography use was viewed as less of a betrayal than cybersex or sharing intimate information). Online sexual infidelity is usually defined in terms of cybersex—when two or more people engage in sexual talk for the purposes of sexual gratification (Daneback et al., 2005). Thus, online sexual infidelity may be somewhat differently defined than conventional sexual infidelity. Online sexual infidelity involves sexual discussion with another person—with the usual intention of sexual gratification—but with no physical contact with the other person.

While trying to understand what online sexual infidelity is, and how humans react to it, scientists have found conflicting results. Some researchers have shown that perceptions of infidelity via online interaction lead to similar responses in a long-term partner as perceptions of conventional infidelity. For example, when thinking about their partner engaging in online infidelity, the results are consistent with Buss and colleagues' (1992) hypotheses regarding sex differences in jealousy—men are more upset by their partner's sexual infidelity, while women are more upset by their partner's emotional infidelity (Groothoff et al., 2009; Guadagno & Sagarin, 2010; Whitty & Quigly, 2008). It is important to note, though, that some researchers have found that both men and women perceive online sexual infidelity as more upsetting than online emotional infidelity (Docan-Morgan & Docan, 2007; Whitty, 2003). Conversely, other researchers' data indicate that men and women may be more upset by online emotional infidelity than online sexual infidelity (Henline et al., 2007). Clearly, more research into perceptions of online infidelity is needed.

A study of members of the website Ashley Madison (www.AshleyMadison.com)—a website designed for individuals to seek extramarital affairs—found multiple factors to be predictors of individuals' sexual motivations for seeking an extramarital partner. Having an unrestricted sociosexual orientation, low relationship satisfaction, and identifying as Christian were all predictors of individuals' sexual motivations (Hackathorn & Ashdown, 2021). Similarly, usage of cellular phone-based dating applications, such as Tinder, has been found to be positively correlated with risky behaviors—including drug and alcohol use, unprotected sex, and number of sexual partners in one's lifetime (Sawyer et al., 2018). Consistent with previous research on conventional sexual infidelity, men were more likely than women to report sexual motivations for engaging in online infidelity (Hackathorn & Ashdown, 2021).

While the factors that influence an individual to engage in an affair vary from person to person, and are dependent on circumstances that range from relationship dynamics to attachment insecurity (Russell et al., 2013), the influence of easy online access, and the dominance of social media platforms, present unique challenges for research. The now infamous Ashley Madison data breach brought the growing prevalence of online infidelity into the national spotlight—exposing personally identifying information of those engaging in extradyadic activities from varying social and economic strata (Cross et al., 2019). Touting itself as a site catering to the "married dating," Ashley Madison has approximately 60 million members, with a "join rate" of 14,500 new accounts per day (Dodgson, 2019). However, only about 15% of Ashley Madison users are female, with the remaining "female" accounts being bots that the Ashley Madison organization uses to entice heterosexual males into creating new accounts on the site (Newitz, 2016). With approximately 85% of Ashley Madison users being male, these percentages corroborate previous evolutionary psychological research indicating that more men engage in sexual infidelity than women (Buss, 1994).

In an anonymous interview conducted with a man who continued to use the Ashley Madison site with full knowledge of the data breach, and the site's stated purpose as a venue in which to engage in infidelity, the individual gave the reasons why he continued to access the site as a resource. The married male user, who had been using the site for approximately 18 months, stated that he joined because he was "intrigued to see what it was all about. . . . It feels really nice flirting and getting to know a lady," he said. "I love the temptation, and I get feelings that are missing in my marriage." This is consistent with research that found infidelity on social media is positively correlated with attachment avoidance, ambivalence, and anxiety, and negatively correlated with relationship satisfaction (McDaniel et al., 2017, p. 1).

While use of Ashley Madison is explicitly for the purpose of engaging in extradyadic activities, the impact of Tinder, Grindr, and other websites that connect individuals for romantic purposes based on geographic location or proximity to a poster cannot be discounted when forming an understanding of online sexual infidelity. Tinder, for example, is an application used in 196 countries by over 10 million users with reports stating that 25%–42% of users are in committed relationships (Dredge, 2015; Timmermans et al., 2018). Consistent with previous research on traditional infidelity (Buss, 1994), approximately 65% of Tinder users are male (Dredge, 2015).

Recent research into the personality traits of Tinder users found differences in personality traits and various sexual behaviors of single users (i.e., not in a committed romantic relationship) and nonsingle users (i.e., in a committed romantic relationship but seeking a new sexual partner). Specifically, nonsingle Tinder users—when compared to single Tinder users and general nonusers of Tinder in a committed romantic relationship—reported lower levels of agreeableness and conscientiousness, and higher levels of neuroticism, psychopathy, and Machiavellianism (Timmermans et al., 2018). Similarly, nonsingle Tinder users reported more sexual partners and relationships than single Tinder users. These results suggest that nonsingle Tinder users are less considerate, less honest, and more manipulative than single Tinder users and nonusers in committed relationships.

While these sites are ostensibly dating sites for single individuals, the intent of use is determined by the user, and as such they have become synonymous in the public consciousness as a platform for creating connections for the purpose of engaging in sexual activity. This creates both ease of access and temptation based on what users perceive as low risk of exposure (for indulging in extradyadic relations) to a current partner. However, "low risk" may be a misperception by users, as many of these sites often link directly to social media accounts, such as Facebook, and use information on that platform to facilitate the ease of creating a dating profile. In comparison to Ashley Madison, whose users eschewed revealing any personally identifying information, applications like Tinder use personally identifying information such as employment, education, and personal interests revealed on various platforms—potentially leading to less than clearly marked lines of demarcation in boundaries when it comes to extradyadic activities. Researchers assessing the intent of people who use Tinder for purposes of infidelity stated that:

> participants reported that they themselves had used Tinder to engage in infidelity, although more than half reported having seen somebody on Tinder who they knew was in an exclusive relationship (63.9%). Additionally, 73.1% of participants reported that one of their male friends had used Tinder while in a relationship and 56.1% of participants reported that one of their female friends had used Tinder while in a relationship. Participants indicated that they believed people used Tinder to cheat on romantic partners at least some of the time.
> (Weiser et al., 2018, p. 32)

The most commonly reported activity was having used the site to message someone in a flirtatious or potentially extradyadic capacity, while the lowest reported activity was engaging in sexual relations with another offline (Weiser et al., 2018).

Online Emotional Infidelity

While the term "sexual infidelity" refers to instances in which an individual engages in extrapair sexual behavior, definitions of *emotional infidelity* are more nuanced (Guitar et al., 2017). One consistent theme of emotional infidelity focuses on the development of a deep emotional bond between a mated individual and someone with whom this individual is not in a monogamous relationship. To elicit emotional jealousy, Buss and colleagues (1992) asked participants to imagine "your partner forming a deep emotional attachment" (p. 252) with another person, and to imagine "your partner falling in love" (p. 252) with another person. However, this definition of emotional infidelity—as well as Buss and colleagues' (1992) methods—has been criticized for being oversimplified (DeSteno & Salovey, 1996).

Researchers employing qualitative methods have found that definitions and examples of emotional infidelity vary by participants' sex. For instance, women are more likely to define emotional infidelity as an emotional connection (i.e., feelings of "love") one develops with an individual who is not one's partner, while men are more likely to define emotional infidelity as emotional distance (i.e., neglect) that develops between pair-bonded individuals as a result of a partner becoming emotionally closer to a new person (Guitar et al., 2017). Other behaviors that have been defined as emotional infidelity include sharing secrets, hugging, cuddling, holding hands, and communicating too often (Guitar et al., 2017; Kruger et al., 2010).

Perceptions of emotional infidelity are influenced by more than one's biological sex. The nuanced nature of definitions regarding infidelity identifies a range of behaviors that may be considered "cheating." One's attachment style (Bowlby, 1969) can influence whether one perceives certain ambiguous behaviors—such as holding hands, spending time together, and sleeping in the same hotel room—as emotional infidelity. Specifically, individuals with insecure-ambivalent/anxious attachment styles are more likely to perceive these ambiguous behaviors as "cheating" on a romantic partner. Conversely, individuals with insecure-avoidant attachment styles are less likely to perceive these behaviors as instances of emotional infidelity (Kruger et al., 2013).

While there is consensus regarding the fact that online emotional and sexual infidelity presents unique challenges, both sexual and emotional infidelity can also be interpreted along more traditionally defined views of extrapartner intimate relations. The varying levels of emotional reaction and response are dependent on multiple factors, with research denoting the degree of response based on both sex and type of infidelity. When emotional infidelity occurs online, the violation of the intimate relationship "contract" can result in the cessation of a relationship, often with antipathy and enmity in both partners.

Online emotional infidelity involves intimate self-disclosure—such as disclosing love for someone or experiencing feelings for someone—via the Internet with someone other than one's romantic partner (Docan-Morgan & Docan, 2007). Online infidelity is often viewed as more emotional, and less sexual, than conventional infidelity (Parker & Wampler, 2003). This is exacerbated by the fact that people self-disclose more quickly online than in person (Walther, 1996). Some research suggests that both men and women feel greater jealousy in response to online emotional infidelity than online sexual infidelity (Henline et al., 2007). This may be due, in part, to the fact that online sexual infidelity may not involve sexual intercourse. For example, cybersex is considered online sexual infidelity (Adam, 2019; Whitty, 2003) even though physical sexual intercourse has not occurred.

The emotional component of online infidelity may account for many of the predictors of jealousy identified by previous research. Loneliness and decreased marital quality are both predictors of online infidelity (Isanejad & Bagheri, 2018). Yet, other situational factors that sometimes lead to conventional infidelity—such as low sexual satisfaction with one's romantic partner—do not predict online infidelity (Aviram & Amichai-Hamburger, 2005). These results indicate that online infidelity may involve a greater emotional component than sexual component, and factors associated with negative emotionality may be better predictors of online infidelity than sexual factors. It is possible that most people engage in online infidelity to satisfy a missing emotional component in their current romantic relationship. It might also serve as an alternative to one's "real-world" relationship—an alternative in which individuals can explore new relationship roles and new sexual experiences (Aviram & Amichai-Hamburger, 2005).

Researchers have also found certain personality traits—many of which correlate with low relationship quality and satisfaction—predict the likelihood of engaging in online infidelity. For instance, high levels of neuroticism and narcissism (specifically, manipulation and exhibitionism) are positively correlated with prevalence of online infidelity (Aviram & Amichai-Hamburger, 2005; Ferron et al., 2016). Similarly, low self-disclosure in one's romantic relationship predicts online infidelity (Aviram & Amichai-Hamburger, 2005). The correlations between these personality traits and online infidelity are indicative of a deeper emotional component rather than a sexual one. This would also account for why insecure-avoidant attachment styles also predict online infidelity (Ferron et al., 2016)—individuals who are more emotionally distant from their romantic partners are more likely to engage in online infidelity.

Due to the strong emotional component associated with online infidelity, therapists who treat couples recovering from online infidelity employ a series of steps related to developing a deeper emotional connection within the relationship (Hertlein & Piercy, 2012). These steps involve self-disclosure with one's romantic partner—defining the infidelity, acknowledging the negative effects the infidelity has had on the relationship, discussing positive experiences in the relationship, setting psychological boundaries, and developing trust.

Websites such as Ashley Madison and Seeking Arrangement (www.seeking.com), however, have dramatically impacted the ability for individuals to seek extradyadic relationships (Pardiwalla, 2016). While individuals may assume that these are sexual relationships, this is not always the case. For example, Pardiwalla (2016) describes a phenomenon called *sugaring*. Sugaring occurs when older and wealthier males—known as *sugar daddies*—use their status and wealth to seek attention from younger females—known as *sugar babies*. The wealthier individuals pay a monthly fee for companionship and even intimacy. For example, a *sugar daddy* may give their *sugar baby* upward of several thousands of dollars per month to talk to them, spend time with them, and enjoy something called the *girlfriend experience*. The *girlfriend experience* is described as a longer encounter that involves role playing as a boyfriend/girlfriend (Read, 2016). The role play may involve acting as if the individuals have a detailed history, and these experiences often do not culminate in sexual intercourse. These dates are more about an emotional connection with another individual rather than sexual gratification.

Sugaring has been gaining popularity among female college students as a means to pay tuition. Soon after Seeking Arrangement launched in 2006, about two million college students had joined (Pardiwalla, 2016). Seeking Arrangement has a portion of their website titled Sugar Baby University (Tapper, 2019). The potential benefits of enrolling in Sugar Baby University is that students can obtain money to pay tuition by going on dates with older individuals. These websites do seem to show a connection between frequency of dates and those who have greater wealth. There is even a term for older men who want to be a *sugar daddy*, but do not have the wealth to attract and pamper a *sugar baby*. These less than wealthy older men are known as *Splenda daddies* (SugarDaddy.World, 2021). These men are called *Splenda daddies* because they act like "sugar," but do not contain the "extras" of real "sugar."

While *sugaring* typically describes interactions between an older wealthier male and younger female, this is not always the case. A *sugar mamma* is a wealthy woman who has a *sugar baby* (Chou, 2018). Instances of younger males being attracted to and pursuing older females have been well documented in the psychological literature. In fact, evolutionary psychological research indicates that young males—particularly adolescents—are more attracted to females who are several years older (as opposed to females of similar age) (Kenrick et al., 1996). This preference for older females seems to be linked to female fertility and the potential for older females to possess more resources than younger (adolescent) females.

Sugaring is also not limited to heterosexual couples. A *sugar daddy* can have a male *sugar baby*, and *sugar mammas* sometimes have a female *sugar baby*. There can be some sex differences in how *sugar babies* approach these relationships. Chou (2018) interviewed three female *sugar babies* and one male *sugar baby*. Though this is a small and nonrepresentative sample, Chou noted that the female *sugar babies* thought of the relationship much like a job but did intend to marry their *sugar daddies*. The male *sugar baby* did not see their arrangement as much more than a short-term relationship. The male *sugar baby* saw it as a financial arrangement and did not view the arrangement as leading to a long-term relationship. Similarly, Hsieh (2018) interviewed three male *sugar babies* about their experiences. One male *sugar baby* described himself as a serial monogamist who was seeking a long-term relationship; however, the other two *sugar babies* both were interested in short-term dating with the financial benefits.

Because of the Internet, these sites have made it easier for individuals to form a connection with someone they have not previously met, and easier to discreetly seek emotional relationships with someone other than their long-term partner. However, these websites are prone to hacking, often leading to the names of those who have accounts being released to the public (Doffman, 2020). Finding that one's long-term partner has an account for a website that encourages discrete emotional and/or sexual relationships can create distrust and potentially end a relationship.

Social media websites such as Facebook, Instagram, and Twitter provide simple routes for communication between individuals who may never meet otherwise. Being able to search by names and locations has made it easier to find old friends and old romantic partners. These platforms also make it easy to send direct messages in a discrete manner. This has provided ample opportunities for individuals to communicate with someone who they may have had a previous emotional connection with, and thus renew that emotional connection. Rumination on former relationships could lead to new emotional connections and spark an emotional relationship (Marshall et al., 2013). While these new emotional relationships with former romantic partners may never become sexual relationships, this emotional infidelity can damage a current relationship.

Emotional infidelity may also occur in the form of the colloquial *work spouse*—an individual with whom someone works but also shares a deep emotional connection. Popular news sites like the *Huffington Post* and the *Wallstreet Journal* (Feintzeig, 2014; Chun, 2012; Dold, 2012) have discussed this type of relationship; however, it is difficult to define. McBride and Bergen (2015) attempted to define what a *work spouse* is by analyzing five different categories. Those categories were (1) the characteristics of a work spouse, (2) conditions for the work spouse relationship, (3) characteristics of the relationship, (4) the functions of the relationship, and (5) ways to manage the relationship. From their study, the definition developed was "a special, platonic friendship with a work colleague characterized by a close emotional bond, high levels of disclosure and support, and mutual trust, honesty, loyalty, and respect" (McBride & Bergen, 2020, p.16). The authors found that the *work spouse* relationship is typically between opposite-sex colleagues, and often does not stop at the end of the workday. It is important to note, however, that *work spouse* relationships are not exclusive to opposite-sex colleagues.

The *work spouse* phenomenon has increased in recent years (McBride et al., 2020b; Office Pulse, 2017). It may be beneficial for businesses to foster *work spouse* relationships (Feintzeig, 2014). This could, for instance, lead to employees developing more of a familial connection with their place of work, which could lead to less turnover and absenteeism, as well as increased worker satisfaction. As a consequence, businesses studied different facets of the *work spouse* relationship—including privacy rules and communication styles between *work spouses*, to better understand *work spouse* relationships (McBride et al., 2020a, 2020b; Whitman & Mandeville, 2021). However, there has been little research on the impacts of blurred boundaries between work and family (McBride et al., 2020b). While these relationships can be good for the business, this encouraged emotional infidelity can cause problems for personal relationships at home. The *work spouse* relationship can even lead to divorce among married individuals (Cade, 2017). As definitions above suggest, the *work spouse* relationship is not typically a romantic or sexual relationship; however, it does rely on a strong emotional relationship to someone other than one's romantic partner.

Cultural Differences in Perceptions of Infidelity

While differences in the impact and interpretation of infidelity evolves as changing technology provides new routes of access for extradyadic involvement, the need for understanding cultural contexts bears examination. Research on the intersection of race and attachment theory indicate few racial and ethnic differences in the likelihood of committing infidelity, as well as in responses to infidelity (Bassett 2005; Campbell et al. 2012; Choi et al. 1994). This lack of difference is especially true when individuals possess secure attachments (Parker & Campbell, 2017). However, some distinctions between races have been reported (Allen et al. 2005). When racial or ethnic differences are found, it is typically Black men who are reported as having the highest rate of extradyadic involvement (Amato & Rogers 1997; Treas & Giesen, 2000; Wiederman, 1997). It is important to contextualize these findings though. For example, Black participants did not differ from White participants in terms of lifetime incidences of infidelity; rather, Black men reported higher rates over the past year (Wiederman, 1997). This finding can be explained by a variety of factors, including an imbalanced sex ratio within the African American community caused by higher incarceration rates of African American men (when compared to incarceration rates of European American men) (Parker & Campbell, 2017).

Research within Latina/o communities identifies different sociocultural factors as potential influences of individuals' responses to infidelity. For instance, Latina women report an expectation of acceptance of their partner's infidelity (McLellan-Lemal et al. 2013; Parker & Campbell, 2017; Parra-Cardona & Busby, 2006). Researchers infer that this expectation and acceptance stems from the greater value that Latino couples place on the male's role as the provider. On average, Latina women would rather preserve their relationship than engage in the conflict that ensues from confronting their romantic partner's infidelities, which leads to a strong reluctance to communicate their suspicions to their partner (Parra-Cardona & Busby, 2006).

While this study speaks to analyzing aspects of extradyadic involvement among Western microcosms along cultural/racial/ethnic categories, it can be viewed against a larger, global perspective on infidelity. In a study of 40 countries, approximately 78% of individuals stated that infidelity was morally unacceptable, while approximately 7% believed infidelity was morally acceptable, and 10% stated infidelity was not a moral issue (Poushter, 2014). Thus, while only 17% of respondents believed infidelity was either ethical or unrelated to ethics, other research has shown that over 25% of men and women have engaged in infidelity (Brand et al., 2007; Wiederman, 1997)—and some research has indicated upward of 75% of men have engaged in infidelity at some point in their lives (Buss, 1994). This indicates a stark difference between individuals' judgments and their behaviors.

While the studies mentioned above represent a strong concentration of research in Western societies, there are also many studies of extradyadic involvement in Eastern/Asiatic societies. For example, researchers in China examined the influences of *covert fidelity management*—tactics used by one partner to monitor another partner's potential for engaging in extradyadic activity both online and off, and then use this information to prevent their partner from engaging in infidelity (Eyre et al., 1998; Li et al., 2012).

Specifically, individuals in a committed relationship are motivated by feelings of suspicion and jealousy to perform surveillance behaviors. Surveillance leads to three possible results: (1) infidelity is discovered, (2) uncertainty continues, and (3) after partner fidelity is reassured, the suspicious partner repeats the series of actions, beginning with suspicion and jealousy, and eventually leading into covert surveillance of one's partner again. Women are more likely to employ covert fidelity management tactics than men (Li et al., 2012). While Li and colleagues (2012) address the specifics of Chinese culture and the impact of covert fidelity management, they also identify sex differences in the intrinsic motivational factors of employing covert tactics and the correlates with satisfaction in the relationship. For instance, male covert fidelity management was negatively correlated with men's self-esteem, but women's self-esteem was not a predictor of women's covert fidelity management. Similarly, men's relationship satisfaction was negatively correlated with covert fidelity management, but there was no such relationship found between women's relationship satisfaction and their covert fidelity management. Li and colleagues also note that covert fidelity management is a normatively understood and accepted behavior within intimate partner relationships in China.

In the United States, there is legal precedent for those tempted to use technology for the purpose of covert surveillance of a romantic partner. In an article for National Public Radio, the subject of using technology such as keyboard loggers (monitoring software designed to count keystrokes), Global Positioning System (GPS) software, and specialized applications for covert fidelity management was summarized via the statement, "it could violate federal and state laws, and may constitute stalking. . . . If you try to use spyware, you may go from trying to prove your partner is an adulterer, to having to prove you're not a criminal" (Simon, 2018, p.1). The temptation to use spyware technology to monitor one's partner may be caused by one's desire for vindication; however, in the United States, the intersection of law and online infidelity can be a moot point because many states have no-fault divorce.

In contrast to the above examples, in nations where cultural, religious, and/or governmental proscriptions are a challenge to technology usage (or where Internet access is limited), there can be further barriers in defining, as well as creating an inherent response to, infidelity in officially recognized heterosexual marital unions. Also, in theocratically governed nations, there can be highly punitive, legally sanctioned actions brought against individuals who engage in infidelity. For example, in Iran, all laws and regulations are required to be based on Islamic criteria—which is biased in favor of males (Gashtili, 2013). Moreover, Muslim men view infidelity more positively than Muslim women (Toplu-Demertas & Fincham, 2018). This showcases one of the cultural barriers to further exploration and understanding of cultural definitions regarding online infidelity.

While conducting research in theocratic nations such as Iran may be hindered, there have been advances in the research on perceptions of infidelity among Iranian individuals. For instance, Nooripour and colleagues' (2017) study of young Iranians showed that many ambiguous behaviors (e.g., watching pornography with someone other than one's romantic partner, sharing personal details with someone who is not one's romantic partner) engaged in by individuals seeking extradyadic involvement within their culture were considered betrayal by some individuals. This correlates with Western studies indicating that defining infidelity is often subject to the personal ideologies of the participants within the intimate partner union (Ferron et al., 2016; Whitty, 2003).

Same-Sex Infidelity

While variability exists among all intimate partner unions, the use of online social media platforms indicates usage via dating apps is a preferred method of contact among individuals who identify as lesbian, bisexual, gay, trans, queer, asexual, or other. For example, online dating is particularly popular among young gay, lesbian, and bisexual individuals. In fact, Grindr—a dating application for gay men—has over 1,000,000 active users (Weiss & Samenow, 2010). Similarly, approximately 55% of LGB adults have used a dating website or application, and about 20% of those individuals reported being in a committed relationship with someone they met through one of those websites or applications (Anderson et al., 2020).

While not much research has been conducted on online infidelity within same-sex couples, there is data to suggest no significant differences in emotional jealousy (i.e., responses to emotional infidelity) between heterosexual and gay individuals. However, some data suggest that gay individuals may feel less jealousy about sexual infidelity compared to heterosexual individuals (Dijkstra et al., 2013).

It is possible that same-sex couples are in the position of navigating and establishing new relationship norms under the auspice of greater social acceptance. There have been many stereotypes regarding gay individuals and same-sex relationships. For example, gay men are stereotyped as aggressively sexual, and lesbian women are stereotyped as excessively "clingy" in their relationships (Martell & Prince, 2005). These stereotypes may fuel general perceptions of same-sex couples, and lead to a societal double standard regarding what constitutes infidelity in same-sex relationships. To date, we could not locate any published research regarding *online* infidelity within same-sex relationships.

Internet Addiction and Online Infidelity

Internet addiction disorder (IAD) has been incorporated into the latest edition of the *Diagnostic and Statistical Manual of Mental Disorders V* (DSM-5; American Psychiatric Association, 2013) with five diagnostic criteria for recognition of the disorder: (1) Preoccupation with the Internet—consistent thoughts about previous, or next, online sessions; (2) A strong need to use the Internet for increased amounts of time to achieve satisfaction; (3) Efforts to control, decrease, or end Internet use have been unsuccessful; (4) Restless, moody, depressed, or irritable disposition when attempting to decrease Internet use; (5) Consistently remains online for more time than originally intended (Cash, 2012).

Approximately 70% of Facebook users log on every day. Similarly, 59% of Snapchat and Instagram members view their sites daily, and approximately 46% of Twitter members engage in daily use (Villanti et al., 2017). Many individuals are also on multiple platforms, although there is a preferred primary account among users. On average, social media users subscribe to 7.6 social media sites, with the large majority (approximately 85%) using six or more social media sites (Villanti et al., 2017). These numbers correspond to the prevalence of opportunities for extradyadic activities, such as infidelity, to occur. As previous researchers have stated, individuals with a greater number of opportunities to engage in extradyadic activities are at greater risk of infidelity (Barta & Kiene, 2005). While Internet addiction afflicts only 3.3% of Internet users, males are three times more likely to suffer from Internet addiction than females—with one of the primary reasons for Internet addiction being obtaining sex-related material (Adiele & Olatokun, 2014).

Researchers have attempted to define the differences between Internet sex addiction and online infidelity—with emphases on individual activities for Internet sex addiction, and a second party being involved for online infidelity (Cash et al., 2012). While the issues of addiction are not the primary factor of motivation for engaging in extradyadic behavior, they may play a causal role in some instances of online infidelity.

Directions of Future Research

Current research indicates that the definition of sexual infidelity is relatively unchanged among a modern demographic (i.e., though there are sex differences in response to, as well as motivation for, sexual and emotional infidelity, these reactions adhere to many of the same behavioral edicts in online interactions). Nevertheless, clear definitions of "online sexual infidelity" and "online emotional infidelity" are still needed. For instance, many researchers have noted that some individuals perceive viewing of pornography as infidelity, while many other individuals do not (Ferron et al., 2016; Whitty, 2003). Thus, it is important to develop clearer definitions of these phenomena to better understand this topic. However, other researchers have noted that many individuals define online sexual infidelity in a rather similar light as in-person sexual infidelity.

One potential factor responsible for the ambiguity within definitions of online infidelity may be that there has been little research conducted on cohort effects impacting changing trends and interpretations of infidelity among nontraditional relationships—such as a polyamourous "throuple"—a committed relationship between more than two individuals—as well as those within an emotionally monogamous yet sexually open relationship. Another consideration that may bear further examination is generational differences in how infidelity is interpreted, as this varies among individuals across different age groups (CITATION).

The same struggle to define infidelity in heterosexual relationships can also be applied to same-sex relationships, as well as the current movement toward recognition of polyamorous connections. Moreover, online extrapartner infidelity has had a profound impact on how these liaisons are structured. With conversation regarding the fluidity of gender and nonbinary self-identification gaining attention in the national consciousness (Monro, 2019), there is a growing number of individuals who engage in extrapartner infidelity online by creating new personas. While these individuals may live daily lives that adhere to a more traditional construct of a "nuclear" family, their online existence may mark them as presenting a gender of their choosing or—in some instances—no gender. There is currently a dearth of empirical literature on this subject.

Conclusion

The prevailing social norms, family censure, and/or religious edicts that espoused strict doctrines to behaviors—all entailing undesirable consequences for those engaging in infidelity—were prohibitive enough to curtail individual action in the past. However, the swift ingress and access to technology that allowed for seemingly anonymous interactions to fulfill both emotional and sexual desires created an unprecedented opportunity to engage in these behaviors.

Today in the United States, 93% of adults access the Internet. This contrasts with just over 50% of adult users 20 years ago (Pew Research Center, 2021) with the majority of users (72%) ranging between 18–29 years of age. Recent research on websites and applications designed for romantic encounters and infidelity (e.g., Ashley Madison, Tinder, etc.) have found large user bases with a substantial percentage of those users currently in a committed romantic relationship (Cross et al., 2019; Dodgson, 2019; Dredge, 2015; Timmermans et al., 2018; Weiser et al., 2018).

The personality traits and situational factors linked to individuals' likelihood of engaging in online infidelity vary significantly. While males are more likely to engage in online infidelity—and infidelity, in general—researchers have found that certain Big Five and Dark Triad personality traits, such as extraversion, neuroticism, psychopathy, and narcissism, are positively correlated with men's and women's likelihood to engage in online infidelity (Aviram & Amichai-Hamburger, 2005; Ferron et al., 2016). Conversely, the Big Five traits of agreeableness and conscientiousness are negatively correlated with likelihood of engaging in online infidelity (Timmermans et al., 2018). Social and situational factors—such as loneliness, low sexual and marital satisfaction, and insecure attachment styles—have also been linked to online infidelity (Aviram & Amichai-Hamburger, 2005; Isanejad & Bagheri, 2018).

The extensive study of these various correlates have allowed psychologists to uncover a list of potential predictors of online infidelity. However, further psychological research in this area is still needed. As the internet becomes more accessible around the world, and the number of websites and applications focused on romantic arrangements, sexual engagement, and infidelity continues to grow, it is likely that online infidelity will increase in frequency.

References

Adam, A. (2019). Perceptions of infidelity: A comparison of sexual, emotional, cyber-, and parasocial behaviors. *Interpersona: An International Journal on Personal Relationships, 13*(2), 237–252.

Adiele, I., & Olatokun, W. (2014). Prevalence and determinants of Internet addiction among adolescents. *Computers in Human Behavior, 31*, 100–110.

Allen, E. S., & Atkins, D. C. (2005). The multidimensional and developmental nature of infidelity: Practical applications. *Journal of Clinical Psychology, 61*(11), 1371–1382.

Amato, P. R., & Rogers, S. J. (1997). A longitudinal study of marital problems and subsequent divorce. *Journal of Marriage and the Family*, 612–624.

American Psychiatric Association. (2013). *Diagnostic and statistical manual of mental disorders* (5th ed.). https://doi.org/10.1176/appi.books.9780890425596

Anderson M., Vogels E. A., & Turner E. (2020). The virtues and downsides of online dating. Pew Research Center. Available at: https://www.pewresearch.org/internet/2020/02/06/the-virtues-and-downsides-of-online-dating/

Aviram, I., & Amichai-Hamburger, Y. (2005). Online infidelity: Aspects of dyadic satisfaction, self-disclosure, and narcissism. *Journal of Computer-Mediated Communication, 10*(3), 1037.

Barta, W., & Kiene, S. (2005). Motivations for infidelity in heterosexual dating couples: The roles of gender, personality differences, and sociosexual orientation. *Journal of Social and Personal Relationships, 22*, 339–360.

Bassett, J. F. (2005). Sex differences in jealousy in response to a partner's imagined sexual or emotional infidelity with a same or different race other. *North American Journal of Psychology, 7*(1), 71–84.

Brand, R. J., Markey, C. M., Mills, A., & Hodges, S. D. (2007). Sex differences in self-reported infidelity and its correlates. *Sex Roles, 57*(1), 101–109.

Bowlby, J. (1969). *Attachment and loss* (Vol. 1). Basic Books.

Buss, D. M. (1994). *The evolution of desire*. Basic Books.

Buss, D. M. (2018). Sexual and emotional infidelity: Evolved gender differences in jealousy prove robust and replicable. *Perspectives on Psychological Science, 13*(2), 155–160.

Buss, D. M., Larsen, R. J., Westen, D., & Semmelroth, J. (1992). Sex differences in jealousy: Evolution, physiology, and psychology. *Psychological Science, 3*(4), 251–256.

Cade, A. (2017). The "work wife": Platonic or invitation to divorce? *Divorce Marketing Group.* https://divorcedmoms.com/blogs/divorce-warrior/work-wife-platonic-fun-invitation-divorce

Campbell, K., Wright, D. W., & Flores, C. G. (2012). Newlywed women's marital expectations: Lifelong monogamy? *Journal of Divorce & Remarriage, 53*(2), 108–125.

Cash, H., Rae, C. D., Steel, A. H., & Winkler, A. (2012). Internet addiction: A brief summary of research and practice. *Current Psychiatry Reviews, 8*(4), 292–298.

Choi, K. H., Catania, J. A., & Dolcini, M. M. (1994). Extramarital sex and HIV risk behavior among US adults: Results from the National AIDS Behavioral Survey. *American Journal of Public Health, 84*(12), 2003–2007.

Chou, J. (2018). I'm a sugar baby—and my sugar mama Venmos me $3,300 a month. *Business Insider.* https://www.sugardaddy.world/blog/splenda-daddy/#:~:text=A%20Splenda%20daddy%20is%20a,the%20thing%20that%20is%20re

Chun, J. (2012). Signs you've crossed the line with your work spouse. *Huffington Post.* http://www.huffingtonpost.com/2012/09/26/work-spouse_n_1901577.html

Cross, C., Parker, M., & Sansom, D. (2019). Media discourses surrounding "non-ideal" victims: The case of the Ashley Madison data breach. *International Review of Victimology, 25,* 53–69.

Daneback, K., Cooper, A., & Månsson, S. A. (2005). An Internet study of cybersex participants. *Archives of Sexual Behavior, 34*(3), 321–328.

DeSteno, D. A., & Salovey, P. (1996). Evolutionary origins of sex differences in jealousy? Questioning the "fitness" of the model. *Psychological Science, 7*(6), 367–372.

Dijkstra, P., Barelds, D. P., & Groothof, H. A. (2013). Jealousy in response to online and offline infidelity: The role of sex and sexual orientation. *Scandinavian Journal of Psychology, 54*(4), 328–336.

Docan-Morgan, T., & Docan, C. A. (2007). Internet infidelity: Double standards and the differing views of women and men. *Communication Quarterly, 55*(3), 317–342.

Dodgson, L. (2019, April 29). The infidelity dating site Ashley Madison now has 60 million users. Two men told us why they use it. *Business Insider.* https://www.businessinsider.co.za/why-men-use-ashley-madison-online-dating-2019-4

Doffman, Z. (2020, February 1). Ashley Madison hack returns to "haunt" its victims: 32 million users now watch and wait. *Forbes.* https://www.forbes.com/sites/zakdoffman/2020/02/01/ashley-madison-hack-returns-to-haunt-its-victims-32-million-users-now-have-to-watch-and-wait/?sh=657b72c35677

Dold, K. (2012, February 29). Work husband: Married, 9 to 5. *Women's Health.* Retrieved from http://www.womenshealthmag.com/life/work-husband

Dredge, S. (2015, May 7). 42% of people using dating app Tinder already have a partner, claims report. *Guardian.* https://www.theguardian.com/technology/2015/may/07/dating-app-tinder-married-relationship

Eyre, S. L., Auerswald, C., Hoffman, V., & Millstein, S. G. (1998). Fidelity management: African-American adolescents' attempts to control the sexual behavior of their partners. *Journal of Health Psychology, 3*(3), 393–406.

Feintzeig, R. (2014, February 13). *Workplace love: Good for business. Wall Street Journal.* http://blogs.wsj.com/atwork/2014/02/14/workplace-love-good-for-business/

Ferron, A., Lussier, Y., Sabourin, S., & Brassard, A. (2016). The role of Internet pornography use and cyber infidelity in the associations between personality, attachment, and couple and sexual satisfaction. *Social Networking, 6*(1), 1–18.

Gashtili, P. (2013). Is an "Islamic feminism" possible? Gender politics in the contemporary Islamic Republic of Iran. *Philosophical Topics, 41*(2), 121–140.

Groothof, H. A., Dijkstra, P., & Barelds, D. P. (2009). Sex differences in jealousy: The case of Internet infidelity. *Journal of Social and Personal Relationships, 26*(8), 1119–1129.

Guadagno, R. E., & Sagarin, B. J. (2010). Sex differences in jealousy: An evolutionary perspective on online infidelity. *Journal of Applied Social Psychology, 40*(10), 2636–2655.

Guitar, A. E., Geher, G., Kruger, D. J., Garcia, J. R., Fisher, M. L., & Fitzgerald, C. J. (2017). Defining and distinguishing sexual and emotional infidelity. *Current Psychology, 36*(3), 434–446.

Hackathorn, J., & Ashdown, B. K. (2021). The webs we weave: Predicting infidelity motivations and extradyadic relationship satisfaction. *Journal of Sex Research, 58*(2), 170–182.

Henline, B. H., Lamke, L. K., & Howard, M. D. (2007). Exploring perceptions of online infidelity. *Personal Relationships, 14*(1), 113–128.

Hertlein, K. M., & Piercy, F. P. (2012). Essential elements of Internet infidelity treatment. *Journal of Marital and Family Therapy, 38*, 257–270.

Hsieh, C. (2018). Three guys on what it's really like to be a male sugar baby. *Cosmopolitan.* https://www.cosmopolitan.com/sex-love/a15898507/male-sugar-baby/

Hughes, S. M., Harrison, M. A., & Gallup, G. G. (2004). Sex differences in mating strategies: Mate guarding, infidelity and multiple concurrent sex partners. *Sexualities, Evolution & Gender, 6*(1), 3–13.

Isanejad, O., & Bagheri, A. (2018). Marital quality, loneliness, and Internet infidelity. *Cyberpsychology, Behavior, and Social Networking, 21*(9), 542–548.

Kenrick, D. T., Keefe, R. C., Gabrielidis, C., & Cornelius, J. S. (1996). Adolescents' age preferences for dating partners: Support for an evolutionary model of life-history strategies. *Child Development, 67*(4), 1499–1511.

Kruger, D. J., Fisher, M. L., Edelstein, R. S., Chopik, W. J., Fitzgerald, C. J., & Strout, S. L. (2013). Was that cheating? Perceptions vary by sex, attachment anxiety, and behavior. *Evolutionary Psychology, 11*(1), 159–171.

Kruger, D. J., Fisher, M. L., Fitzgerald, C. J., Garcia, J. R., Geher, G., & Guitar, A. E. (2015). Sexual and emotional aspects are distinct components of infidelity and unique predictors of anticipated distress. *Evolutionary Psychological Science, 1*(1), 44–51.

Kruger, D. J., Fitzgerald, C. J., & Peterson, T. (2010). Female scarcity reduces women's marital ages and increases variance in men's marital ages. *Evolutionary Psychology, 8*(3), 420–431.

LeFebvre, L. E. (2018). Swiping me off my feet: Explicating relationship initiation on Tinder. *Journal of Social and Personal Relationships, 35*(9), 1 205–1229.

Li, Y. M., Chan, D. K. S., & Law, V. W. S. (2012). Gender differences in covert fidelity management among dating individuals in China. *Sex Roles, 67*(9–10), 544–558.

Martell, C. R., & Prince, S. E. (2005). Treating infidelity in same-sex couples. *Journal of Clinical Psychology, 61*(11), 1429–1438.

McLellan-Lemal, E., Toledo, L., O'Daniels, C., Villar-Loubet, O., Simpson, C., Adimora, A. A., & Marks, G. (2013). "A man's gonna do what a man wants to do": African American and Hispanic women's perceptions about heterosexual relationships: A qualitative study. *BMC Women's Health, 13*(1), 1–14.

Marshall, T. C., Bejanyan, K., & Ferenczi, N. (2013). Attachment styles and personal growth following romantic breakups: The mediating roles of distress, rumination, and tendency to rebound. *PLoS One, 8*(9), e75161.

McBride, M. C., & Bergen, K. M. (2015). Work spouses: Defining and understanding a "new" relationship. *Communication Studies, 66*(5), 487–508. https://doi.org/10.1080/10510974.2015.1029640

McBride, M. C., Thorson, A. R., & Bergen, K. M. (2020a). Privacy rule decision criteria: An examination of core and catalyst criteria that shape disclosures in the work-spouse relationship. *Management Communication Quarterly, 34*(4), 527–557. https://doi.org/10.1177/0893318920949328

McBride, M. C., Thorson, A. R., & Bergen, K. M. (2020b). An examination of individually performed and (co) managed facework: Unique communication within the work-spouse relationship. *Communication Studies, 71*(4), 489–510. https://doi.org/10.1080/10510974.2020.1749866

McDaniel, B. T., Drouin, M., & Cravens, J. D. (2017). Do you have anything to hide? Infidelity-related behaviors on social media sites and marital satisfaction. *Computers in Human Behavior, 66*, 88–95.

Monro, S. (2019). Non-binary and genderqueer: An overview of the field. *International Journal of Transgenderism, 20*(2–3), 126–131.

Newitz, A. (2016, July 8). Ashley Madison admits using fembots to lure men into spending money. *Ars Technica.* https://arstechnica.com/tech-policy/2016/07/ashley-madison-admits-using-fembots-to-lure-men-into-spending-money/

Nooripour, R., Abdi, M. R., Bakhshani, S., Alikhani, M., Hosseinian, S., & Ebrahim, T. P. (2017). Exploring validity and reliability of Internet infidelity questionnaire among Internet users in Iran. *International Journal of High-Risk Behaviors and Addiction, 6(1),* e34928. doi:10.5812/ijhrba.34928

Office Pulse Editorial Team. (2017). Cubicle comradery and the proliferation of the work spouse. *Office Pulse.* http://officepulse.captivate.com/workspouse_2017

Pardiwalla, A. (2016, April 20). Sugaring: A new kind of irresistible. *Huffington Post.* https://www.huffpost.com/entry/post_10274_b_9683356#:~:text=Exercising%20power%20and%20control%20is,that%20is%20rapidly%20gaining%20momentum.

Parker, M. L., & Campbell, K. (2017). Infidelity and attachment: The moderating role of race/ethnicity. *Contemporary Family Therapy*, *39*(3), 172–183.

Parker, T. S., & Wampler, K. S. (2003). How bad is it? Perceptions of the relationship impact of different types of Internet sexual activities. *Contemporary Family Therapy*, *25*(4), 415–429.

Parra-Cardona, J. R., & Busby, D. M. (2006). Exploring relationship functioning in premarital Caucasian and Latino/a couples: Recognizing and valuing cultural differences. *Journal of Comparative Family Studies*, *37*(3), 345–359.

Pew Research Center (2021, April 2). *Demographics of Internet and home broadband in the United States*. Washington D.C.: Pew Research Center.https://www.pewresearch.org/internet/fact-sheet/internet-broadband/

Poushter, J. (2014, April 15). *What's morally acceptable? It depends on where you live*. Pew Research Center. Washington D.C.: Pew Research Center.https://www.pewresearch.org/fact-tank/2014/04/15/whats-morally-acceptable-it-depends-on-where-in-the-world-you-live/

Read, K. (2016, November 14). Peek under the covers of "The Girlfriend Experience"—Clients and sex workers weigh in. *Pop Sugar*. https://www.popsugar.com/love/What-Girlfriend-Experience-42547412

Rostila, M., & Saarela, J. M. (2011). Time does not heal all wounds: Mortality following the death of a parent. *Journal of Marriage and Family*, *73*(1), 236–249.

Russell, V. M., Baker, L. R., & McNulty, J. K. (2013). Attachment insecurity and infidelity in marriage: Do studies of dating relationships really inform us about marriage? *Journal of Family Psychology*, *27*, 242–251.

Sawyer, A. N., Smith, E. R., & Benotsch, E. G. (2018). Dating application use and sexual risk behavior among young adults. *Sexuality Research and Social Policy*, *15*(2), 183–191.

Simon, M. (2018, January 4). *What to do if spyware comes up in your relationship*. National Public Radio. https://www.npr.org/sections/alltechconsidered/2018/01/04/556185863/what-to-do-if-spyware-comes-up-in-your-relationship

Smith, A., & Duggan, M. (2013). *Online dating and relationships*. Washington, DC: Pew Internet & American Life Project.

Statistic Brain Research Institute. (2017, May 12). *Online dating*. http://www.statisticbrain.com/onlinedating-statistics/

SugarDaddy.World (2021). *What is a Splenda daddy, and what's the difference from a sugar daddy?* https://www.sugardaddy.world/blog/splenda-daddy/#:~:text=A%20Splenda%20daddy%20is%20a,the%20thing%20that%20is%20real

Takahashi, H., Matsuura, M., Yahata, N., Koeda, M., Suhara, T., & Okubo, Y. (2006). Men and women show distinct brain activations during imagery of sexual and emotional infidelity. *NeuroImage*, *32*(3), 1299–1307.

Tapper, M. K. (2019). Enrolling in sugar baby university. *Crimson*. https://www.thecrimson.com/article/2019/5/20/sugar-baby-university/#:~:text=Sugar%20Baby%20University%20is%20part,and%20sometimes%20to%20have%20sex.

Timmermans, E., De Caluwe, E., & Alexopoulos, C. (2018). Why are you cheating on Tinder? Exploring users' motives and (dark) personality traits. *Computers in Human Behavior*, *89*, 129–139.

Toplu-Demirtaş, E., & Fincham, F. D. (2018). Dating infidelity in Turkish couples: The role of attitudes and intentions. *Journal of Sex Research*, *55*(2), 252–262.

Treas, J., & Giesen, D. (2000). Sexual infidelity among married and cohabiting Americans. *Journal of Marriage and Family*, *62*(1), 48–60.

Trivers, R. L. (1996). Parental investment and sexual selection. In L. D. Houck & L. C. Drickamer (Eds.), *Foundations of animal behavior: Classic papers with commentaries* (pp. 795–838). University of Chicago Press.

Villanti, A. C., Johnson, A. L., Ilakkuvan, V., Jacobs, M. A., Graham, A. L., & Rath, J. M. (2017). Social media use and access to digital technology in US young adults in 2016. *Journal of Medical Internet Research*, *19*(6), e196.

Walther, J. B. (1996). Computer-mediated communication: Impersonal, interpersonal, and hyperpersonal interaction. *Communication Research*, *23*, 3–43.

Weiderman, M. W. (1997). Extramarital sex: Prevalence and correlates in a national survey. *The Journal of Sex Research*, *34*, 167–174

Weiser, D. A., Niehuis, S., Flora, J., Punyanunt-Carter, N. M., Arias, V. S., & Baird, R. H. (2018). Swiping right: Sociosexuality, intentions to engage in infidelity, and infidelity experiences on Tinder. *Personality and Individual Differences*, *133*, 29–33.

Weiss, R., & Samenow, C. P. (2010). Smart phones, social networking, sexting and problematic sexual behaviors—A call for research. *Sexual Addiction & Compulsivity, 17*(4), 241–246.

Whitman, M. V., & Mandeville, A. (2021). Blurring the lines: Exploring the work spouse phenomenon. *Journal of Management Inquiry, 30*(3), 1–15.

Whitty, M. T. (2003). Pushing the wrong buttons: Men's and women's attitudes toward online and offline infidelity. *CyberPsychology & Behavior, 6*(6), 569–579.

Whitty, M. T., & Quigley, L. L. (2008). Emotional and sexual infidelity offline and in cyberspace. *Journal of Marital and Family Therapy, 34*(4), 461–468.

CHAPTER 9

Predicting Infidelity in Nonheterosexual Relationships

Jonathan M. Bowman *and* Benjamin L. Compton

> **Abstract**
> Myriad factors impact the likelihood of infidelity in relationships, and the literature on those impacts as found in nonheterosexual relationships is in some ways still an emerging field. At the same time, robust research on the nature of infidelity has been completed over many years, research that finds both similarities and differences between heterosexual and nonheterosexual relationships in the factors that predict infidelity. Factors that are considered in this chapter include individual differences (encompassing the categories of nonheterosexuality that one uses to describe oneself) and personality characteristics, as well as broader social factors based on perceived group membership. These broader social factors include one or both partners' racial and ethnic identity, and one or both partners' cultural backgrounds as well as the impact of those group memberships on other characteristics of the self and the relationship. The chapter also includes a discussion of the impact of perceptions of the third party on predicting infidelity. Finally, the ability to predict infidelity is discussed in terms of the limitations of the current research and offers a call for future research in specific areas of interest for how best to predict infidelity in nonheterosexual relationships.
>
> **Key Words:** nonheterosexual, gay, lesbian, bisexual, asexual, open relationships, polyamorous, queer

Characterizing Nonheterosexual Relationships

As noted in other chapters throughout this handbook, infidelity is among the great social equalizers in that the occurrence of infidelity is common in a variety of relationships even if the impact of that infidelity may vary widely. Infidelity can occur across every sociodemographic indicator, including racial and ethnic identities, socioeconomic statuses, religious background and/or degree of religiosity, age, length of relationship, and the sexual identities of one or more partners. In this chapter, we explore relationships that are broadly defined as nontraditional, with emphasis on those relationships that are not heterosexual. While the literature in such areas is still emerging and our ability to predict infidelity using research has not been developed to the same extent that one might find for heterosexual relationships, there are enough individual research projects that allow for a sense of these predictions to emerge. To begin the discussion of predicting infidelity in nonheterosexual relationships, however, we must first unpack a characterization of what nontraditional relationships look like.

Proudly Flouting "Straight": Lesbian, Gay, Bisexual, and Pansexual

To begin, a brief definition of "nonheterosexual" must include a variety of relationships and individuals within those relationships; at the same time, it would be difficult to be exhaustive in listing all relational combinations given the complexity of human relational pairings (and groupings). Even more disheartening, with APA style reinforcing a gender binary in research reporting (APA, 2020) and the majority of research forcing self-reports of sex/gender following this model, even the most "familiar" terminology of sexuality and sexual identity that follows in this chapter often misrepresents the identities of the diversity of participants in infidelity research, perhaps exacerbated by the focus on cisgender representation and the underrepresentation of research on infidelity practices of transgender individuals. The most commonly researched nonheterosexual relationships include lesbian, gay, bisexual, and pansexual individuals. Lesbians are typically described as female-identified individuals whose primary orientation of sex and affection are toward other female-identified individuals (LGBTQIA Resource Center, 2020). While the term "gay" can be used to describe individuals who identify as primarily oriented toward people of the same gender, gay men are typically described as male-identified individuals whose primary orientation of sex and affection are toward other male-identified individuals. Non-binary individuals who do not primarily identify as male or female can also identify as gay or lesbian because of their identification with manhood or womanhood and their primary attraction to men or women, respectively. Bisexual individuals typically have orientations of sex and affection toward people of the same gender and people of the "opposite" gender, while pansexual individuals might have orientations of sex and affection toward people of all genders and all sexes. While some people use the terms "bisexual" and "pansexual" interchangeably, not all bisexual or pansexual individuals identify with both terms (LGBTQIA Resource Center, 2020).

Proudly Flouting "Monogamy": Polyamory, Polyfidelity, and Open Relationships

In addition to the variety of dyadic relationships characterized by two individuals coming together in monogamous pairings—a cultural exhortation described as mononormativity (Ferrer, 2018)—some relationships are not characterized by being limited to two individuals and/or to monogamous couplings. While the legal definition of such relationships is still emerging (Tweedy, 2010) and the arguments around polyamory as a sexual orientation are being waged (Klesse, 2014), typically polyamory is described as a relationship type in which members maintain intimate and sexual relationships with multiple partners at the same time, often over a long period of time (Haritaworn et al., 2006). These consensual nonmonogamous relationships typically do not consider the presence of multiple partners as infidelity (Levine et al., 2018; Woodruff-Diaz, 2010), although situations or contexts can emerge within these relationships where rules are violated and one or more partner may choose to label the violation as infidelity (Hosking, 2013). Polyamory is differentiated from polyfidelity in that polyfidelous members maintain a closed group of intimate and sexual relationships with multiple partners, where all members are involved with one another in an egalitarian group relationship (Peterson, 2017). In contrast to both polyamory and polyfidelity, each of which are characterized by long-term relationships among participants, "open" relationships are intimate yet sexually nonmonogamous relationships characterized by a primary partnership in which each of the primary partners has agreed that the other can have additional sexual partners (Kim, 2019) for various durations. Interestingly, much infidelity research uses "sex with more than one person" as a measure of infidelity, regardless of the transgressive (or lack thereof) nature of multiple partnerships or agreements within a particular relationship (Whisman et al. 2007). Such paradigms operationally consider polyamory, polyfidelity, and open relationships as infidelity regardless of the level of commitment and mutual agreement found among members of the group.

Proudly Flouting "Labels": Asexual and Other Queer Pairings

In exploring the variety of nonheterosexual relationships, one must turn attention to those individuals who identify as asexual, typically described as individuals who do not experience sexual attraction (Cerankowski & Milks, 2014). At the same time, some researchers have highlighted that asexual individuals may simply experience significantly less sexual desire, arousability, and sexual excitation (Prause & Graham, 2007) for another person (although notably these asexual individuals do not *necessarily* have lower desires leading to lower rates of masturbation than the general population; Prause & Graham, 2007). In talking about individuals who identify as asexual, it is important to distinguish the use of this term from that of individuals who have been labeled (unjustly) by *others* as asexual because of their physical appearance or ability (Kim, 2011), a group of people often disenfranchised by the application of the term (Milligan & Neufeldt, 2001). Individuals who self-identify as asexual often have fulfilling long-term relationships across a variety of heterosexual and queer pairings, with the terms "Boston Marriage" sometimes used to describe long-term asexual lesbian pairings (Rothblum & Brehony, 1993) and "romantic friendships" used to describe similar long-term asexual gay pairings (National Park Service, 2020). At the same time, not all asexual individuals desire such long-term relationships, and those that don't will often identify as "aromantic" to express this lack of desire for partnership (Scherrer, 2010). Another category of queer pairings that questions the privileging of romantic relationships are those individuals that identify with "relationship anarchy" (Barker, 2017) or profess to challenge amatonormativity (i.e., the assumption that people *should* be in a long-term relationship; Brake, 2011), describing queerplatonic relationships (also known as quasiplatonic relationships) in which individuals have deep commitment and love toward one another that go beyond that of stereotypical platonic relationships but do not have the sexual element that often characterizes romantic relationships (Queerplatonic, 2020).

Characterizing Infidelity in Nonheterosexual Relationships

The majority of researchers studying infidelity across the social sciences define infidelity according to the heteronormative, amatonormative "ideal" of the heterosexual marriage (Blow & Hartnett, 2005a). Indeed, infidelity is often reduced to sexual (or erotic) behavior that occurs outside of the marriage between a man and a woman. At the same time, scholars critiquing this state of the scholarship have long identified three conditions that should be identified in describing infidelous behaviors: consensuality, relationship type, and behavior type (Thompson, 1983). It is to the last of these three conditions—behavior types associated with infidelity—that we now turn our attention.

Sexual Monogamy vs. Social Monogamy

Typically, infidelity is characterized by a transgression wherein one partner violates a relational rule (implicit or explicit) with a person outside the relationship unit (Bowman, 2019). However, in order for that relational rule to have developed, there must be some sort of implicit or explicit relationship that has emerged between the two (or more) partners against whom the transgression occurs. While we have already outlined a variety of relationships that may emerge that involve more than a dyadic pair (i.e., polyamory, polyfidelity, or open relationships) it is helpful to distinguish between two components of monogamy that serve as precursors for infidelity to emerge. Sexual monogamy is characterized by two people engaging in sexual activity exclusively with one another, not having sexual partners outside of the dyad. Social monogamy, however, is characterized by two individuals who only partner with one another (Reichard, 2003), but need not *necessarily* include a sexual relationship (e.g., either sexually monogamous partners or asexual committed partners). Multipartner relationships can also have a version of sexual and/or social "monogamy" where encounters are limited exclusively to the "group" of partners who have agreed to be sexually exclusive with other members of the group. One or more partners can exhibit infidelity within a socially monogamous relationship without necessarily having engaged in sexual activity outside of the dyad or group. This leads into a discussion of the distinctions between sexual infidelity and emotional infidelity.

Sexual Infidelity vs. Emotional Infidelity

As discussed, the myriad definitions of infidelity can be both problematic and difficult to manage, due to the multiplicity of ways in which scholars and laypersons "count" a behavior as an act of infidelity (Blow & Hartnett, 2005a; Thompson, 1983) or as a relational transgression (Bowman, 2019). That being said, there are two broad categories of infidelity that are widely agreed on. Notably, these two categories—sexual infidelity and emotional infidelity—are not mutually exclusive; a partner in a relationship can commit an act of sexual infidelity, emotional infidelity, both sexual and emotional infidelity, or no act of infidelity at all. The main distinction emerges wherein sexual infidelity is relationally defined by sexual or erotic physical behaviors that are engaged in with someone outside of the committed relationship, while emotional infidelity is relationally defined by intimacy or an emotional connection to someone outside of the committed relationship. To muddle the waters somewhat, this intimacy or emotional connection typically must be seen by one or both partners as transgressive, something which breaks a relational rule. A partner's emotional connection to or intimacy with a parent, for example, does not fall into a category of infidelity, leading some scholars to define emotional infidelity as the formation of a romantic attachment with someone other than your romantic partner (Bowman, 2019). Researchers have seen differences in perceptions of severity between sexual vs. emotional infidelity based on the gender of the person cheated on, but that difference can be attenuated (or ameliorated) depending on features of the relationship including the nonheterosexuality of the cheater and/or of the extradyadic partner (Compton & Bowman, 2017; Sagarin et al. 2003).

Relationship Type and Infidelity in Nonheterosexual Relationships

Another factor impacting the nature of infidelity in nonheterosexual relationships is the type of relationship that is under threat from the infidelity. To be sure, relational transgressions are likely to cause conflict whether one or both parties see the behavior as transgressive, yet the relationship type may influence the degree of impact that acts of infidelity can cause within a relationship. Additionally, the type of relationship (and the degree to which that relationship is explicitly defined by all parties) may influence the likelihood of extradyadic behaviors as being perceived as infidelity at all.

Casual vs. Committed

One relational distinction that impacts perceptions of infidelity is the degree to which a couple is casual (e.g., nonmonogamous) with one another or committed (i.e., monogamous) to one another. As anyone who reflects on their teen years can attest, relationships are difficult to characterize, and the need to make a relationship description explicit has led to a movement among some young people in recent decades to explicitly and verbally define the relationship (a turning-point relationship event; Bowman, 2019) in order to know where they stand with one another (England et al., 2008). Often, however, people move from being independent casual partners to being a committed couple through the process of implicitly "sliding" into a relationship rather than explicitly "deciding" that they are monogamous (Owen et al., 2013). Partners may not be on the same page about the monogamous nature (or lack thereof) of their relationship, and may disagree about whether an act of infidelity has occurred. Indeed, the distinction between casual and committed can be hard to pinpoint, and the partners may have different understandings of what behaviors are acceptable and unacceptable—nowhere is this more obvious than in the *Friends* episode with Ross and Rachel fighting over the "infidelity" that occurred despite the fact that Ross vehemently believed that "We were on a break!," which quickly became a cultural touchstone for the difficulties of defining acceptable relational behaviors (Knox & Schwind, 2019).

Open vs. Closed vs. the Lifestyle

To complicate matters, relationships may differ on whether partners are allowed or encouraged to have extradyadic sexual partners while still following other relationship rules. While traditional (closed) relationships often are characterized by expressions of monogamy, open relationships may allow one or both parties to engage in sexual or erotic activity with partners outside the relationship despite sharing both commitment and/or emotional intimacy with one another. Relationships that include "swinging" or "the Lifestyle" may not only allow for extradyadic sexual encounters while remaining in a committed relationship, but may also encourage those encounters through shared activities or events that allow for both partners to find extradyadic partners (Ruzansky & Harrison, 2019). In such partnerships, relational rules (and the interdependent identity as a couple) must be mutually explicated and negotiated to allow for emotions and perceptions of infidelity to be carefully managed within the relationship (de Visser & McDonald, 2007).

THE IMPACT OF MARRIAGE EQUALITY

While infidelity occurs in both heterosexual and nonheterosexual relationships, the progressive forward gains that led to marriage equality may have added additional nuance to the impact of acts of infidelity within a committed nonheterosexual relationship. While some studies have addressed differences in attitude toward infidelity across sexual orientations (Leeker & Carlozzi, 2014), there is not enough data regarding the impact of marriage equality on attitudes toward infidelity (Balsam et al., 2017). Indeed, much of the research on such issues focuses on complications associated with legal status rather than on the antecedent relational issues that may cause these commitments to be dissolved (Oppenheimer, 2011). While scholars and practitioners argue that the expanded definition of marriage must impact nonheterosexual relationships, insufficient research into the impact of marriage on infidelity has reached publication. This is an important future area of exploration for scholars of infidelity in nonheterosexual relationships.

Predictions Based on Relationship Type

Past research has focused on the disparate natures of heterosexual and nonheterosexual relationships in terms of the relational norms and regulatory mechanisms that have developed over the decades, highlighting the impact of nonheterosexual behaviors (and gay or lesbian sexual encounters especially) being forced to be hidden (Leeker & Carlozzi, 2014), a state of affairs that continues in many countries where nonheterosexual relationships are frowned upon or illegal (Notaro, 2020). Such research highlights the likelihood of nonheterosexual relationships being more sexually permissive (or at least less sexually restrictive) than their heterosexual counterparts (Bringle, 1995; Armstrong & Reissing, 2014; Heaphy et al., 2004; Hickson et al., 1992; Leeker & Carlozzi, 2014). Indeed, some research has found smaller negative outcomes of infidelity (e.g., jealousy, upset, distress, anger, anxiety, humiliation) in nonheterosexual relationships than those found in heterosexual relationships (Barelds & Dijkstra, 2006; Barelds et al., 2017; Heaphy, Donovan, & Weeks 2004; Leeker & Carlozzi, 2014). Researchers have also found differences in perceptions of infidelity for nonheterosexual relationships from those that would be predicted using models of heterosexual partnerships (Frederick & Fales, 2016). Some nonheterosexual partners may even focus on reconceptualizing infidelity and jealousy to remove the negative, transgressive connotations (Ferrer, 2019).

Rather unsatisfyingly, the impact of relationship type on predictions of infidelity (or even likelihood of infidelity) is so dependent on the norms and rules established in each individual relationship that it is difficult to derive meaningful conclusions from the literature. Nonheterosexual couples are said to "design their relationships differently" without the norms and/or the legal status of heterosexual partnerships (Martell & Prince, 2005). For example, while partners in open relationships and/or swinging relationships likely have many more sexual partners than those in monogamous relationships, those sexual encounters are less likely to be described as transgressive (and ultimately as acts of infidelity) precisely *because* of the open nature of those relationships (Wosick-Correa, 2010). As a result, we may be able to better predict extradyadic sexual activity in those relationships but may be relatively incompetent at correctly predicting perceptions of infidelity from one or more individuals within the relationship.

At the same time, in relationships that are not explicitly monogamous (or committed), partners may differ in their understanding of the level of sexual exclusivity that is expected. One partner may view an extradyadic sexual encounter as an act of infidelity, while the other partner may be comfortable with the behavior and unable (or unwilling) to see the transgressive nature of the act from the perspective of the "offended" partner. While research has highlighted that heterosexual couples find extradyadic nonheterosexual sexual activity to be less negatively perceived (or differently perceived) than if the extradyadic partner were heterosexual (Compton & Bowman, 2017; Denes et al., 2015; Frederick & Fales, 2016), the rules and norms of nonheterosexual relationships may vary more on a case-by-case basis. As a result, predictions of infidelity must be based on the degree to which those norms, rules, and transgressive acts were made explicit and/or the degree to which the relationship was explicitly monogamous.

For explicitly nonmonogamous relationships, infidelity is relationally defined and therefore more difficult to capture than one might expect. At the same time, while it may be hard to define infidelity, partners often "know" it when they experience it. The impacts of infidelity in these nonmonogamous relationships are certainly felt. While men in open gay relationships report less passion, but similar levels of intimacy and commitment to those in a closed couple or closed "throuple" (three persons in a committed, exclusive relationship), people who broke the rules established for the open gay relationship had lower ratings of overall relationship quality (Hosking, 2013). Monogamous gay couples experiencing infidelity were less satisfied and adjusted than were nonmonogamous couples and faithful monogamous couples (LaSala, 2004). In addition, bisexual individuals have lower self-reported positive attitudes toward monogamy as "enhancing" than do straight, gay, and lesbian individuals (Mark et al., 2014), leading to a higher desire for nonmonogamous relationships among those individuals. Interestingly, regardless of sexual orientation, consensually nonmonogamous individuals were less worried that their partner would cheat on them but spent more time thinking about the extradyadic partner (Mogilski et al., 2019). Nonmonogamous gay partnerships (across a variety of styles) report relationship quality similar to monogamous partnerships (Parsons et al., 2012). While it may be difficult to make explicit predictions based on the nonmonogamous nature of a relationship, it is often the impact of the individual perceptions and shared understanding of the "open" relationship rules and norms that will determine the degree to which infidelity occurs, or at least the degree to which it is labeled as such.

Personality and Individual Differences and Infidelity in Nonheterosexual Relationships

Overview and Definitions

While relationship type, partner identity, and a variety of cultural contexts are likely to influence the nature of infidelity across all relationships (inclusive of nonheterosexual relationships), personality characteristics and individual differences are likely to impact the likelihood of one or more partners engaging in acts of infidelity while in a self-identified committed relationship.

One set of personality characteristics studied in research on relational transgressions is known as the Dark Triad, a composite of three separate personality characteristics. These three personality characteristics—narcissism (characterized by perceptions of entitlement and superiority), psychopathy (characterized by impulsive and antisocial behavior), and Machiavellianism (characterized by manipulation and a sort of social charisma or charm) (Barelds et al., 2017)—strongly relate to jealousy toward a romantic partner, but not necessarily predicting the likelihood of infidelity. That is, we may be able to better predict the relational outcomes of infidelity than the likelihood of an actual act of infidelity (Barelds et al., 2017).

Another individual difference that manifests as a prejudicial attitude—notably one that can even be self-prejudicial—is "binegativity," the prejudice expressed toward bisexual people by members of both the heterosexual and nonheterosexual population (Armstrong & Reissing, 2014). This binegativity (also known as biphobia in some research) is characterized by an unfounded belief that the bisexual individual is promiscuous and/or incapable of monogamy (Armstrong & Reissing, 2014).

While we discuss sociodemographic characteristics to some degree later in the chapter, it is important to note that there are a variety of individual differences that might influence one's attitudes toward relationships, relationship norms, acceptable relationship behavior, likelihood of infidelity in relationships, and even the acceptability of one's own identity as a nonheterosexual individual (Joseph & Cranney, 2017; Kosciw et al., 2009; Lassiter & Ceballos, 2018; Vosvick & Stem, 2019).

Predictions Based on Personality and Individual Difference

One of the measures that influences attitudes around infidelity (including the likelihood of jealousy that results from—and even influences the likelihood of—infidelity in committed relationships) is the Dark Triad of narcissism, psychopathy, and Machiavellianism. Bisexual women are more likely to rate higher on Machiavellianism than straight or lesbian women (Lippa, 2020) and on the Dark Triad (Semenyna et al., 2018). Neuroticism and narcissism are positively associated with likelihood of infidelity (Fincham & May, 2017). Neuroticism occurs more frequently within nonheterosexual individuals (Zietsch et al., 2011), with a greater preponderance in bisexual men and women (Lippa, 2020) and in gay men (Allen & Robson, 2020; Lippa, 2020). As a result, one can predict that a nonheterosexual individual who displays the Dark Triad, or neuroticism and narcissism specifically, may be more likely to commit infidelity than someone who does not.

We also discussed the self-prejudicial attitude of binegativity (or biphobia) as related to the idea that bisexual people are unable or unwilling to be monogamous. While a person who self-identifies as unable to be monogamous may be less likely to do so, this has been confirmed in research for only one group of bisexuals. Bisexual women with higher levels of binegativity are more likely to commit infidelity than those with lower levels (Hoang et al., 2011). Further research needs to be conducted in order to know the impact of this individual attitude on bisexual men.

In terms of basic demographic characteristics, we will discuss some of these throughout the rest of the chapter in dedicated areas. Specifically, racial and ethnic identity as well as cultural influences will be discussed in later sections. However, there is at least one consistent finding based on other demographic characteristics. People who identify as men are typically more likely to engage in infidelity than are people who identify as women, a finding which does not aid in the prediction of same-sex relationships about whether one partner is more likely to cheat than the other but does allow us to make some guesses about the likelihood of infidelity between same-sex male-identified partnerships and same-sex female-identified partnerships (Fincham & May, 2017). Also, a variety of demographic characteristics like age, education, and income have been linked to infidelity, but scholars have noted that the pattern of findings is not stable enough to provide clear guidance about trends in these categories.

Race and Ethnicity in Nonheterosexual Relationships

Overview and Definitions

Without even taking into account sexuality, the research on the relationship between race, ethnicity, and infidelity is mixed; while some findings provide evidence for racial and ethnic differences, others do not replicate these differences (Blow & Hartnett, 2005). One problem has been a reliance on Caucasian samples, with a lack of research focusing on or including diverse populations (Sheff & Hammers, 2011). Of the few studies that include race as a predictor, most focus on consensual nonmonogamy rather than nonconsensual nonmonogamy (Parsons et al., 2012; Rubin et al., 2014; Noël, 2016). Now taking into account sexuality *and* the relationship between race and ethnicity on infidelity, there are few published findings on the interaction of these factors (Levine et al. 2018).

Scholars claim that race is inseparable from sexual identity (McQueeney, 2009). Historically, some argued that monogamy and the construct of marriage is embedded in Whiteness, and thus the very idea of monogamy is racialized (Willey, 2006). Two examples of this are the antipromiscuity discourse targeted at non-White women and the "down low" discourse targeted at non-White men. Klesse (2016) argued that the antipromiscuity discourses, which posits that women's sexual agency is restricted and threatened under the guise of being negatively stigmatized, is unfairly attributed to bisexual women of color. This discourse threatens non-White women's sexual autonomy, thus emphasizing more pressure to play into the confines of monogamy. The second example is the "down low" discourse. The phrase "down low" refers to Black men who secretly have extradyadic sex with other men while sustaining heterosexual relationships with women (Phillips, 2005). While research has found that men in heterosexual relationships who engage in extradyadic sexual activities are an occurrence that transcends any racial barrier (Boykin, 2005), the cultural conversation around the "down low" has primarily been aimed at Black men (Han, 2015). Both of these examples showcase that while there might be limited support to the claim of racial differences within infidelity in nonheterosexual relationship, the discourse around race and sexuality is very much present.

Predictions Based on Race and Ethnicity

Despite there being a lack of concrete evidence, there have been a few studies that might help to predict or at least infer relationships between race, ethnicity, and infidelity. While sexual jealousy and sexual infidelity are different phenomena, jealousy can often be a predecessor or reaction to infidelity (Harris & Christenfeld, 1996). Parsons et al. (2012) compared gay men who identified themselves as being in monogamous relationships with gay men who identified themselves as being in nonmonogamous relationships and found that race was unrelated to the amount of sexual jealousy reported by the participants. Additionally, Rubin et al. (2014) examined consensual nonmonogamous relationships and found that both Caucasian and non-Caucasian individuals were equally likely to participate in both monogamous and consensual nonmonogamous relationships.

While both of these examined extradyadic behavior in the realm of agreed consent between at least two partners, Levine et al. (2018) looked specifically at infidelity and found that individuals who identified as bisexual and Black were more likely to report having engaged in nonconsensual nonmonogamy. It should be noted that in this study, both bisexuality and race/ethnicity were treated as individual predictors, and that no indication of a test of interaction was reported. Therefore, based on the findings from Levine et al. (2018), we might conclude that while race/ethnicity and bisexuality *might* influence whether an individual engages in infidelity, more research is needed to better understand whether these two variables together have any sort of significant difference from the average likelihood of infidelity across all relationship types. While it is one thing to examine these factors under the lens of consensual nonmonogamy, it is too difficult to predict how might breaking of a relational agreement might relate to maintaining consent.

Without an abundance of research aiming to better understand and explain the intersectionality of race, ethnicity, and sexuality on infidelity in nonheterosexual relationships, the current body of literature is robbed of potentially provocative and rich findings on the topic which may contribute to our understanding of human sexual behavior.

Cultural Difference and Infidelity in Nonheterosexual Relationships
Overviews and Definitions

Culture can influence the norms and expectations around the perceptions of appropriateness and the subsequent reaction to the discovery that individuals are in violation of seemingly exclusive intimate relationships (Buunk & Hupka, 1987). Depending on the specific culture, even the nature or terminology we use to determine or describe infidelity, such as calling it an "affair," can hold different meanings in different cultures (Heaphy et al., 2004).

Defining culture has been a tricky task for researchers over the last 50 years, given the complexity and vagueness with which it has sometimes been studied (Williams, 1976). Despite many scholars adding nuance to the concept of culture, the ability to operationalize and conceptualize culture has proved somewhat of a struggle (Geertz, 1973; Jepperson & Swidler, 1994). To that end, we accept the idea that culture is the process of the complex interactions of thought, feelings, and actions made up of the knowledge structures that are shared and distributed among networks of persons (Patterson, 2014). It should be noted that much scholarship has been conducted on the influence and relationship between "gay" culture and "straight" culture (Ghaziani, 2014; Heaphy et al., 2004), as well as scholarship on nonnormative relationships such as the culture of polyamory, which in itself challenge the culture of mononormativity (Klesse, 2014; Ritchie & Barker, 2016; Sheff, 2020). Within differing cultures centered around sexuality, one's own personal experience of culture might be predisposed by both implicit and explicit aspects of networked culture, thus leading to variation based on cultural knowledge (Lizardo, 2017). However, in this chapter, we focus on an aspect of culture as a concept primarily related to national affiliation, and thus include the findings from cross-cultural research done on infidelity in non-heterosexual relationships. On a global level, much of the modernized world is relatively similar in the prevailing views on extradyadic sexual behaviors (Widmer et al., 1998). However, while there might be minimal between-country variation, factors like sexuality might influence the within-country perceptions and engagement in infidelity.

Much research has examined the role of sexual jealousy within romantic relationships. Jealousy has been argued to be shaped by socialization that could be the product of one's culture (DeSteno & Salovey, 1996). Sexual jealousy, as well as emotional jealousy, has been linked as either a precursor or response to both sexual and emotional infidelity (Harris & Christenfeld, 1996). Throughout the late 20th century, many scholars argued for an evolution-based explanation pointing toward sex differences in perceptions around sexual jealousy. It wasn't until the 1990s that scholars began to uncover evidence that pushed back against this nature-focused stance, presenting data that suggested variation in sexual jealousy is more influenced not by biological sex differences, but rather by cultural socialization (Harris & Christenfeld, 1996; DeSteno & Salovey, 1996).

Within any culture, learned expectations and norms can be applied to both gender norms and sexuality norms. A given culture may vary in terms of how gender is constructed and treated, as well as how social support is given for those outside the gender binary or outside heteronormative dyads. The discounting hypothesis, which is embedded in the belief of a gender double standard, argues that men are privileged and presented with greater freedom to participate in extradyadic sex compared to women (Sheets & Wolfe, 2001). Depending on the nature of gender equality expressed within a given country, this discounting standard might place less negative valence on men who engage in infidelity. Comparing heterosexual and nonheterosexual men and women, Sheets and Wolfe (2001) found that straight women, lesbians, and gay men were more likely to fear being abandoned (i.e., relationship dissolution) if they engaged in infidelity compared to heterosexual men. This finding suggests that both gay men and lesbian women might be more likely to fear that if they cheat, their partner might decide to terminate the relationship. In addition, Sheets & Wolfe also argued that the amount of social support an individual receives also might vary dependent on the culture in which they reside. For lesbian and gay individuals influenced by their country's acceptance of LGBT rights, each might have a higher fear of social isolationism if a partner were to break off the relationship (Sheets & Wolfe, 2001). If their partner might be one of their primary providers of social support, to risk terminating that relationship might hold more significance than it would to heterosexual individuals.

While both intercultural gender expectations and the social support one might receive from a romantic partner may play a role in an individual's decision-making process to engage in either infidelity behavior or risky behavior that might create jealousy in a partner, it is important to examine the intersectionality of identities (e.g., identifying as not just a man, but a gay man). Worth et al. (2002) interviewed 20 New Zealand men who identified as gay, and found that these men were more tolerant and accepting of sex outside of their immediate relationship, but at the same time finding that the extradyadic behavior still led to feelings of jealousy and pain. These findings were similar to findings by Blumstein and Schwartz (1983), who focused on an American sample of couples and found that gay men were the least likely to be concerned if their partners were nonmonogamous.

Predictions Based on Cultural Differences

Unfortunately, limited research has been conducted that directly compares cross-cultural and international gay and lesbian populations on their perceptions of cheating (Blow & Hartnett, 2005). Such research is highly important for future study, given the inherent diversity between cultures and countries that are highly accepting of nonheterosexual relationships to those that closely police and restrict nonheterosexual relationships. However, we do know that regardless of cultural group identity, infidelity can be incredibly painful for those who break or lose trust within their relationship or experience sexual jealousy (Druckerman, 2008).

Despite the lack of direct research on international differences in infidelity between cultures, we can still use previous literature to predict the role of national affiliation with nonheterosexual views on infidelity. Looking at the literature on jealousy might help us to indicate how individuals might also approach actually participating in extradyadic behavior. Given that sexual jealousy varies among cultures (Buunk & Hupka, 1987), we might also predict that this variation is inhibited in a similar fashion to that of enacted sexual infidelity. With sexual jealousy being a rational response to infidelity (Harris & Chrisenfeld, 1996), one can assume there is some relationship between sexual jealousy and acts of infidelity; Still, whether that relationship is in fact positively or negatively correlated among a variety of nonheterosexual relationships would call for more research to be conducted across that variety of sexual identities.

Another predictor that may lend greater understanding could result from a country's dominant perceptions of gender roles. Using the aforementioned discounting hypothesis (Sheets & Wolfe, 2001), in countries where there is low gender equality, more defined gender roles, and a maximized "double standard," men in that particular country might be more likely to engage in more extradyadic sexual behaviors than women. For a gay couple involving two men, some scholars may argue that there is the potential to have two actors in a relationship who believe it is more culturally acceptable to cheat. That being said, it is worth noting that countries with low gender inequality might also tend to have lower prevailing beliefs in the importance of LGBT rights, thus causing gay men to be less able to openly engage in sexual activity. For lesbian or bi-sexual women, this "double standard" might run the risk of threatening their sexual autonomy for fear of negative stigmatization, ostracization, or potential exposure to violence (Klesse, 2016). On the other hand, in countries where there is high gender equality, less defined gender roles, and a minimized "double standard," we might predict nonheterosexual infidelity somewhat mirroring the rates of heterosexual infidelity within that culture.

Perceptions of the Third Party and Infidelity in Nonheterosexual Relationships

Overviews and Definitions

Within the last 10 years, a handful of studies have examined the role of third-party perceptions on infidelity with cross-sex and same-sex partners. Unfortunately, these studies have mainly looked at self-identified heterosexual individuals in hypothetical situations, rather than diverse sexualities who may or may not be involved in an exclusive relationship. However, the findings might still shed light on individuals in an exclusive nonheterosexual relationship on issues like the manner in which they might terminate a relationship after an extradyadic act of infidelity (Confer & Cloud, 2011), respond to cheating (Confer & Cloud, 2011; Denes et al., 2015) and even conceptualize which specific behaviors an individual would perceive as cheating (Compton & Bowman, 2017).

To explore that further, we must consider the influences on relationship termination that occur after a monogamous partner were to cheat. Confer and Cloud (2011) looked at sex differences in reactions to imagining if a partner were to engage in sexual relations with someone of the same sex and someone of the opposite sex. They found that males were more likely to continue in a relationship with their female partner if the female partner engaged in sexual relations with another female than if it had been with a male. However, the opposite was found for female participants, who reported being less likely to maintain a relationship if their male partner engaged in nonheterosexual infidelity as compared to heterosexual infidelity. It should be noted that sex differences associated with the likelihood of continuing in a relationship were characterized as having a wider range for male participants than for women participants. In other words, men perceived their female partners who cheated with other women as the least threatening to the relationship, as compared to female partners cheating with other men (Confer & Cloud, 2011). In addition, women were more likely to maintain a relationship if their male partners cheated with other men than if their male partners cheated with other women (Confer & Cloud, 2011). One biological explanation for this might be found in sexual strategies theory (Buss & Schmitt, 1993), based on the idea that men have less obligation to invest heavily in offspring, and women who partake in sexual activity with other women might provide opportunity for the men to mate with more than one woman. On the other hand, a cultural explanation for this might include cultural factors around gender, where extradyadic sexual behaviors are perceived as male privilege (Scheinkman, 2005).

While Confer and Cloud (2011) look at how sex might influence a reaction to cross-sexual orientation cheating, Denes et al. (2015) looked at the impact of gender on the response to same-sex infidelity outside of heterosexual relationships. Specifically, they focused on emotional, relational, and communicative responses to cross-sexual orientation infidelity. It was found that participants experienced higher negative emotional responses to their partners' cross-sex infidelity than to their partners' same-sex infidelity. They also found that heterosexual men were more likely to report higher levels of sexual arousal as a result of their female partner's same-sex infidelity, but that heterosexual women's levels of sexual arousal was similar across both same-sex or cross-sex infidelity. In terms of specific communicative responses, heterosexual women were more likely to use denial messages for same-sex infidelity, but were more likely to use possession messages for cross-sex infidelity. That is, if a heterosexual woman's partner were to cheat with another man, the woman might be more likely to deny the behavior occurred; if a heterosexual woman's partner cheated with another woman, the woman would use a possessive response. However, for men, it was found that heterosexual men's responses to jealousy (as a result of cheating) did not change for same-sex or cross-sex infidelity. So if a heterosexual man's partner were to cheat with either another woman or a man, the man would be equally likely to respond with either messages of possession or messages of denial.

The previous studies examined how heterosexual individuals might respond *after* extradyadic sexual relations occur within an exclusive relationship, but what behaviors do individuals specifically perceive as acts of infidelity if it occurs with a same-sex extradyadic individual as compared to a cross-sex extradyadic individual? Compton and Bowman (2017) provided insight into how a behavior might influence whether or not a heterosexual individual perceives an extradyadic act as infidelity, specifically based on heterosexual participants' gay and lesbian disdain and prejudices. The researchers looked at three potential infidelity behaviors: sexual/erotic behaviors (e.g., oral sex; watching porn together), close relational behaviors (e.g., sharing secrets; hugging for more than 10 seconds), and casual social interaction behaviors (e.g., going out to dinner; giving $5 to the other person). They found that perceptions of same-sex infidelity varied depending on what type of behavior it was, with sexual and erotic behaviors being perceived as the most likely to be deemed cheating by a partner. Similar to previous findings (e.g., Confer & Cloud, 2011; Denes et al., 2015), it was discovered that there was a gender difference in what was perceived as infidelity and what was not, with men rating sexual behaviors as less likely to be perceived as infidelity than female participants. Overall, men were found to be more accepting of infidelity if their female partners engaged in sexual or erotic behaviors, whereas neither men nor women differed in their views of close relational or casual social interaction behaviors as potential infidelity.

Predictions Based on Perceptions of the Third Party

Without an abundance of studies looking specifically at either the experience or perceptions of nonheterosexual individuals as related to whether their exclusive partner cheated (or might cheat), scholars can only engage in informed speculation about how these individuals would respond. However, the aforementioned studies shed light on how sex differences and attitudes might predict how individuals in nonheterosexual relationships perceive what "counts" as cheating and what does not, and how they might respond.

Given the consistent findings that men perceive same-sex cheating as less threatening (Confer & Cloud, 2011; Denes et al. 2015; Compton & Bowman, 2017), we can predict that gender does in fact influence individuals' perceptions of cheating. We predict that men involved in a gay relationship would perceive the extradyadic behavior of their partner less negatively when compared to women involved in a lesbian relationship. Based on the response findings from Denes et al. (2015), we predict that for gay couples where extradyadic behaviors occur, the partner who was cheated on would likely use possessive or denial messages regardless of whether their partner engaged in acts of infidelity with a man or a woman. For lesbians, if one partner were to engage in extradyadic behaviors with another woman, then the faithful partner likely might respond using possessive messages, whereas they would be more likely to use messages of denial if the extradyadic behavior occurred with a man.

Clearly there needs to be more research focusing specifically on nonheterosexual individuals and nonheterosexual relationships, disentangling how partners might differ in their perceptions of what is considered cheating for their partner(s). As much as the current literature begins the conversation about how an individual might judge or respond to specific extradyadic behaviors, more research using nonheterosexual participants is essential.

Summarizing Infidelity Predictions in Nonheterosexual Relationships
Review

To conclude, there is much literature that might begin to influence our understanding of how infidelity is engaged in and perceived by one or both partners in nonheterosexual relationships. To be sure, factors that were considered in this chapter included individual differences (encompassing but not limited to the categories of nonheterosexuality that a person uses to describe oneself) and personality characteristics, as well as a variety of broader social factors based on perceived group membership. These larger social factors included (but were not limited to) one or both partners' racial and ethnic identity, and one or both partners' cultural backgrounds as well as the impact of those group memberships on a variety of other characteristics of the self and the relationship. Even the perceptions of a third party were found to possibly have some influence on predicting infidelity in nonheterosexual relationships.

Limitations

At the same time, much of the research on infidelity focuses on heterosexual, dyadic partnerships that have expressions or expectations of monogamy. The literature is beginning to emerge for gay and lesbian marital partnerships, but there is an absolute dearth of information about infidelity within the wide range of nontraditional nonheterosexualities.

Polyamorous, polyfidelous, swinging, and open relationships are often treated by default as relationships with constant infidelity, despite the mutual agreement of partners within those relationships and the preferences of those partners for the behavior to occur for the good of the relationship. Even more concerning, intersectional identities are understudied in terms of infidelity in relationships. While one might find some research exploring the impact of race and gender on infidelity and perceptions of acts of infidelity, there is not a substantive body of literature exploring the impact of race and gender on infidelity among the variety of nonheterosexual relationships that exist. Similar statements can be made for the variety of personality characteristics and individual differences—as well as group and cultural influences—on nonheterosexual relationship pairings or groupings and their perceptions or experiences with infidelity. While the careful scholar can piece together a variety of relationships in order to make informed predictions, we need much more hard evidence to truly claim a social science approach to infidelity in nonheterosexual relationships.

Future Directions

In closing, scholars should be exhorted to do more work across intersectional identities regardless of topic, in order to have a better understanding of the myriad social influences of identity and identity constructions that individuals and groups experience in their solitary and social life. For a topic like infidelity—one that is characterized by the confluence of multiple intersectionalities as couples come together—there is even greater need for the study of those factors that influence acts of infidelity, perceptions of infidelity, and responses to infidelity across the variety of nonheterosexual pairings and groupings. The field of infidelity research has been historically heteronormative, amatonormative, and overly reliant on White research participants while simultaneously reinforcing the gender binary. In order to better understand and to predict behavior with confidence, scholars should actively work to better engage in the recruitment of diverse research samples across the great variety of intersectional identities and sociodemographic characteristics. Such attempts can only further enhance our ability as an interdisciplinary field to better predict infidelity and its outcomes in nonheterosexual relationships.

References

Allen, M. S., & Robson, D. A. (2020). Personality and sexual orientation: New data and meta-analysis. *Journal of Sex Research*, 1–13.

Armstrong, H. L., & Reissing, E. D. (2014). Attitudes toward casual sex, dating, and committed relationships with bisexual partners. *Journal of Bisexuality*, *14*(2), 236–264.

APA (2020, November 12). *Gender*. https://apastyle.apa.org/style-grammar-guidelines/bias-free-language/gender

Balsam, K. F., Rothblum, E. D., & Wickham, R. E. (2017). Longitudinal predictors of relationship dissolution among same-sex and heterosexual couples. *Couple and Family Psychology: Research and Practice*, *6*(4), 247.

Barelds, D. P. H., & Dijkstra, P. (2006). Reactive, anxious and possessive forms of jealousy and their relation to relationship quality among heterosexuals and homosexuals. *Journal of Homosexuality*, *51*(3), 183–98.

Barelds, D. P. H., Dijkstra, P., Groothof, H. A. K., & Pastoor, C. D. (2017). The Dark Triad and three types of jealousy: Its relations among heterosexuals and homosexuals involved in a romantic relationship. *Personality and Individual Differences, 116*, 6–10.

Barker, M. J. (2017). *Gender, sexual, and relationship diversity (GSRD)*. British Association for Counselling and Psychotherapy.

Blow, A. J., & Hartnett, K. (2005). Infidelity in committed relationships I: A methodological review. *Journal of Marital and Family Therapy, 31*(2), 183–216.

Blumstein, P., & Schwartz, P. (1983). *American couples: Money, work, sex*. William Morrow.

Boykin, K. (2005). *Beyond the down low: Sex, lies, and denial in Black America* (1st Carroll & Graf ed.). Carroll & Graf.

Bowman, J. M. (2019). *Interconnections: Foundations and Contexts in Interpersonal Communication*. Cengage Learning.

Brake, E. (2011). *Minimizing marriage: Marriage, morality, and the law*. Oxford University Press.

Bringle, R. G. (1995). Sexual jealousy in the relationships of homosexual and heterosexual men: 1980 and 1992. *Personal Relationships, 2*(4), 313–325.

Buss, D. M., & Schmitt, D. P. (1993). Sexual strategies theory: An evolutionary perspective on human mating. *Psychological Review, 100*, 204–232.

Buunk, B., & Hupka, R. B. (1987). Cross-cultural differences in the elicitation of sexual jealousy. *Journal of Sex Research, 23*(1), 12–22.

Cerankowski, K. J., & Milks, M. (2014). *Asexualities: Feminist and queer perspectives*. Routledge.

Compton, B. L., & Bowman, J. M. (2017). Perceived cross-orientation infidelity: Heterosexual perceptions of same-sex cheating in exclusive relationships. *Journal of Homosexuality, 64*(11), 1469–1483.

Confer, J. C, & Cloud, M. D. (2011). Sex differences in response to imagining a partner's heterosexual or homosexual affair. *Personality and Individual Differences, 50*(2), 129–134.

Denes, A., Lannutti, P. J., & Bevan, J. L. (2015). Same-sex infidelity in heterosexual romantic relationships: Investigating emotional, relational, and communicative responses. *Personal Relationships, 22*(3), 414–430.

de Visser, R., & McDonald, D. (2007). Swings and roundabouts: Management of jealousy in heterosexual "swinging" couples. *British Journal of Social Psychology, 46*(2), 459–476.

DeSteno, D. A., & Salovey, P. (1996). Jealousy and the characteristics of one's rival: A self-evaluation maintenance perspective. *Personality and Social Psychology Bulletin, 22*(9), 920–932.

Druckerman, P. (2008). *Lust in translation: Infidelity from Tokyo to Tennessee*. Penguin.

England, P., Shafer, E. F., & Fogarty, A. C. (2008). Hooking up and forming romantic relationships on today's college campuses. *Gendered Society Reader, 3*, 531–593.

Ferrer, J. N. (2018). Mononormativity, polypride, and the "mono–poly wars." *Sexuality & Culture, 22*, 817–836.

Ferrer, J. N. (2019). From romantic jealousy to sympathetic joy: Monogamy, polyamory, and beyond. *International Journal of Transpersonal Studies, 38*(1), 185–202.

Fincham, F. D., & May, R. W. (2017). Infidelity in romantic relationships. *Current Opinion in Psychology, 13*, 70–74.

Frederick, D. A., & Fales, M. R. (2016). Upset over sexual versus emotional infidelity among gay, lesbian, bisexual, and heterosexual adults. *Archives of sexual behavior, 45*(1), 175–191.

Geertz, C. (1973). *The interpretation of cultures*. Basic Books.

Ghaziani, A. (2014). Measuring urban sexual cultures. *Theory and Society, 43*(3/4), 371–393.

Han, C. (2015). No brokeback for black men: Pathologizing black male (homo)sexuality through down low discourse. *Social Identities, 21*(3), 228–243.

Haritaworn, J., Lin, C. J., & Klesse, C. (2006). Poly/logue: A critical introduction to polyamory. *Sexualities, 9*(5), 515–529.

Harris, C. R, & Christenfeld, N. (1996). Jealousy and rational responses to infidelity across gender and culture. *Psychological Science, 7*(6), 378–379.

Heaphy, B., Donovan, C., & Weeks, J. (2004). A different affair? Openness and nonmonogamy in same sex relationships. In *The state of affairs* (1st ed., pp. 167–186). Routledge.

Hickson, F., Davis, P. M., Hunt, A. J., Weatherburn, P., McManus, T. J., & Coxon, A. (1992). Maintenance of open gay relationships: Some strategies for protection against HIV. *AIDS Care, 4*(4), 409–419.

Hoang, M., Holloway, J., & Mendoza, R. H. (2011). An empirical study into the relationship between bisexual identity congruence, internalized biphobia and infidelity among bisexual women. *Journal of Bisexuality*, *11*(1), 23–38.

Hosking, W. (2013). Agreements about extra-dyadic sex in gay men's relationships: Exploring differences in relationship quality by agreement type and rule-breaking behavior. *Journal of Homosexuality*, *60*(5), 711–733.

Jepperson, R. L, & Swidler, A. (1994). What properties of culture should we measure? *Poetics (Amsterdam)*, *22*(4), 359–371.

Joseph, L. J., & Cranney, S. (2017). Self-esteem among lesbian, gay, bisexual and same-sex-attracted Mormons and ex-Mormons. *Mental Health, Religion & Culture*, *20*(10), 1028–1041.

Kim, E. (2011). Asexuality in disability narratives. *Sexualities*, *14*(4), 479–493.

Kim, J. (2019, December 26). Do open relationships work? *Psychology Today*. https://www.psychologytoday.com/us/blog/the-angry-therapist/201912/do-open-relationships-work

Klesse, C. (2014). Polyamory: Intimate practice, identity or sexual orientation? *Sexualities*, *17*(1–2), 81–99.

Klesse, C. (2016). Bisexual women, non-monogamy and differentialist anti-promiscuity discourses. *Sexualities*, *8*(4), 445–464.

Knox, S., & Schwind, K. H. (2019). *Friends: A reading of the sitcom*. Springer Nature.

Kosciw, J. G., Greytak, E. A., & Diaz, E. M. (2009). Who, what, where, when, and why: Demographic and ecological factors contributing to hostile school climate for lesbian, gay, bisexual, and transgender youth. *Journal of Youth and Adolescence*, *38*(7), 976–988.

LaSala, M. C. (2004). Extradyadic sex and gay male couples: Comparing monogamous and nonmonogamous relationships. *Families in Society*, *85*(3), 405–412.

Lassiter, P. S., & Ceballos, P. L. (2018). Self-acceptance, parental self-efficacy, and impression management in lesbian and gay parents. *Journal of LGBT Issues in Counseling*, *12*(2), 72–86.

Leeker, O., & Carlozzi, A. (2014). Effects of sex, sexual orientation, infidelity expectations, and love on distress related to emotional and sexual infidelity. *Journal of Marital and Family Therapy*, *40*(1), 68–91.

Levine, E. C., Herbenick, D., Martinez, O., Fu, T.-C., & Dodge, B. (2018). Open relationships, nonconsensual nonmonogamy, and monogamy among U.S. adults: Findings from the 2012 National Survey of Sexual Health and Behavior. *Archives of Sexual Behavior*, *47*(5), 1439–1450.

LGBTQIA Resource Center. (2020, November 1). *LGBTQIA Resource Center Glossary*. https://lgbtqia.ucdavis.edu/educated/glossary

Lippa, R. A. (2020). Interest, personality, and sexual traits that distinguish heterosexual, bisexual, and homosexual individuals: Are there two dimensions that underlie variations in sexual orientation? *Archives of sexual behavior*, *49*(2), 607–622.

Lizardo, O. (2017). Improving cultural analysis: Considering personal culture in its declarative and nondeclarative modes. *American Sociological Review*, *82*(1), 88–115.

Mark, K., Rosenkrantz, D., & Kerner, I. (2014). "Bi" ing into monogamy: Attitudes toward monogamy in a sample of bisexual-identified adults. *Psychology of Sexual Orientation and Gender Diversity*, *1*(3), 263.

Martell, C. R., & Prince, S. E. (2005). Treating infidelity in same-sex couples. *Journal of Clinical Psychology*, *61*(11), 1429–1438.

McQueeney, K. (2009). "We are God's children, y'all": Race, gender, and sexuality in lesbian- and gay-affirming congregations. *Social Problems (Berkeley, Calif.)*, *56*(1), 151–173.

Milligan, M. S., & Neufeldt, A. H. (2001). The myth of asexuality: A survey of social and empirical evidence. *Sexuality and Disability*, *19*(2), 91–109.

Mogilski, J. K, Reeve, S. D, Nicolas, S. C A, Donaldson, S. H., Mitchell, V. E, & Welling, L. L. M. (2019). Jealousy, consent, and compersion within monogamous and consensually non-monogamous romantic relationships. *Archives of Sexual Behavior*, *48*(6), 1811–1828.

National Park Service. (2020, November 1). *An era of romantic friendships: Sumner, Longfellow, & Howe*. https://www.nps.gov/articles/an-era-of-romantic-friendships-sumner-longfellow-and-howe.htm

Noël, M. J. (2016). Progressive polyamory: Considering issues of diversity. *Sexualities*, *9*(5), 602–620.

Notaro, S. R. (2020). *Marginality and global LGBT communities*. Palgrave Macmillan.

Oppenheimer, E. (2011). No exit: The problem of same-sex divorce. *North Carolina Law Review*, *90*(1), 73–124.

Owen, J., Rhoades, G. K., & Stanley, S. M. (2013). Sliding versus deciding in relationships: Associations with relationship quality, commitment, and infidelity. *Journal of Couple & Relationship Therapy*, *12*(2), 135–149.

Parsons, J. T., Starks, T. J., Gamarel, K. E., & Grov, C. (2012). Non-monogamy and sexual relationship quality among same-sex male couples. *Journal of Family Psychology*, *26*(5), 669.

Patterson, O. (2014). Making sense of culture. *Annual Review of Sociology*, *40*(1), 1–30.

Peterson, J. R. (2017). *Polyfidelity and the dynamics of group relationships* [Doctoral dissertation, Walden University]. Walden University ScholarWorks.

Phillips, L. (2005). Deconstructing "down low" discourse: The politics of sexuality, gender, race, AIDS, and anxiety. *Journal of African American Studies (New Brunswick, N.J.)*, *9*(2), 3–15.

Prause, N., & Graham, C. A. (2007). Asexuality: Classification and characterization. *Archives of Sexual Behavior*, *36*(3), 341–356.

Queerplatonic. (2020, November 1). Aromantics Wiki. https://aromantic.wikia.org/wiki/Queerplatonic

Reichard, U. H. (2003). Monogamy: Past and present. In *Monogamy: Mating strategies and partnerships in birds, humans and other mammals* (pp. 3–25).

Ritchie, A., & Barker, M. (2016). "There aren't words for what we do or how we feel so we have to make them up": Constructing polyamorous languages in a culture of compulsory monogamy. *Sexualities*, *9*(5), 584–601.

Rothblum, E. D., & Brehony, K. A. (1993). *Boston marriages: Romantic but asexual relationships among contemporary lesbians*. University of Massachusetts Press.

Rubin, J. D., Moors, A. C., Matsick, J. L., Ziegler, A., & Conley, T. D. (2014). On the margins: Considering diversity among consensually non-monogamous relationships. *Journal für Psychologie*, *22*.

Ruzansky, A. S., & Harrison, M. A. (2019). Swinging high or low? Measuring self-esteem in swingers. *Social Science Journal*, *56*(1), 30–37.

Sagarin, B. J., Becker, D. V., Guadagno, R. E., Nicastle, L. D., & Millevoi, A. (2003). Sex differences (and similarities) in jealousy: The moderating influence of infidelity experience and sexual orientation of the infidelity. *Evolution and Human Behavior*, *24*(1), 17–23.

Scheinkman, M. (2005). Beyond the trauma of betrayal: Reconsidering affairs in couples therapy. *Family Process*, *44*, 227–244. doi:10.1111/j.1545-5300.2005.00056.x

Scherrer, K. S. (2010). Asexual relationships: What does asexuality have to do with polyamory? In *Understanding non-monogamies* (pp. 166–171). Routledge.

Semenyna, S. W., Belu, C. F., Vasey, P. L., & Honey, P. L. (2018). Not straight and not straightforward: The relationships between sexual orientation, sociosexuality, and Dark Triad traits in women. *Evolutionary Psychological Science*, *4*, 24–37.

Sheets, V., & Wolfe, M. D. (2001). Sexual jealousy in heterosexuals, lesbians, and gays. *Sex Roles*, *44*(5), 255–276.

Sheff, E. (2020). Polyamory is deviant—but not for the reasons you may think. *Deviant Behavior*, *41*(7), 882–892.

Sheff, E., & Hammers, C. (2011). The privilege of perversities: Race, class and education among polyamorists and kinksters. *Psychology & Sexuality*, *2*(3), 198–223.

Thompson, A. P. (1983). Extramarital sex: A review of the research literature. *Journal of Sex Research*, *19*(1), 1–22.

Tweedy, A. E. (2010). Polyamory as a sexual orientation. *University of Cincinnati Law Review*, *79*(4), 1461–1515.

Vosvick, M., & Stem, W. (2019). Psychological quality of life in a lesbian, gay, bisexual, transgender sample: Correlates of stress, mindful acceptance, and self-esteem. *Psychology of Sexual Orientation and Gender Diversity*, *6*(1), 34.

Whisman, M. A., Gordon, K. C., & Chatav, Y. (2007). Predicting sexual infidelity in a population-based sample of married individuals. *Journal of Family Psychology*, *21*(2), 320.

Widmer, . D, Treas, J., & Newcomb, R. (1998). Attitudes toward nonmarital sex in 24 countries. *Journal of Sex Research*, *35*(4), 349–358.

Willey, A. (2006). "Christian nations," "polygamic races" and women's rights: Toward a genealogy of non/monogamy and whiteness. *Sexualities*, *9*(5), 530–546.

Williams, R. (1976). *Keywords: A vocabulary of culture and society*. Oxford University Press.

Woodruff-Diaz, S. K. (2010). *Polyamory as "ethical nonmonogamy": A viable alternative to infidelity: A project based upon an independent investigation* (Publication no. 1109). [Masters thesis, Smith College]. Smith ScholarWorks.

Worth, H., Reid, A., McMillan K. (2002). Somewhere over the rainbow: Love, trust and monogamy in gay relationships. *Journal of Sociology: The Journal of the Australian Sociological Association*. *38*(3), 237–253.

Wosick-Correa, K. (2010). Agreements, rules and agentic fidelity in polyamorous relationships. *Psychology and Sexuality*, *1*(1), 44–61.

Zietsch, B. P., Verweij, K. J., Bailey, J. M., Wright, M. J., & Martin, N. G. (2011). Sexual orientation and psychiatric vulnerability: A twin study of neuroticism and psychoticism. *Archives of Sexual Behavior*, *40*(1), 133–142.

PART 2

The Nature of Infidelity

CHAPTER 10

Emotional and Sexual Infidelity: Evolutionary Origins and Large-Scale Implications

Julie A. Planke, Jacqueline M. Di Santo, *and* Glenn Geher

Abstract

Infidelity can wreak havoc on the emotional, familial, and social lives of people. Reactions to infidelity may be erratic and pronounced, including anger, depression, violence, and even homicide. Reactions to infidelity motivate a substantial proportion of violent crimes across cultures. Understanding the psychology of infidelity thus has the capacity to shed light on substantial social and emotional issues. Importantly, work on the psychology of infidelity has identified two broad categories of infidelity: *emotional infidelity* and *sexual infidelity*. The current chapter will address research on the foundational psychological features that bear on these two categories of infidelity, using an evolutionarily informed framework as a guide. Sex-differentiated reactions to infidelity will be addressed in this discussion to shed light on the ways that infidelity and reactions to infidelity manifest in sex-specific ways. The integrative framework presented here will elucidate paths for future research as well as potential implications and applications of the research in this field.

Key Words: Infidelity, evolutionary psychology, emotion, mating, sex differences

Pair bonding in relationships is a foundational feature of our social structures. Thus, while monogamy and its variants constitute only a subset of the human mating-system experience (see Barash, 2016), pair bonding within mateships of some variety is a ubiquitous aspect of intimate relationships across the globe (see Hrdy, 2009). Pair bonding facilitates bi-parental care for offspring. Given how altricial (helpless) human offspring are in the early part of life, bi-parental care has the effect of substantially increasing the support and help that offspring receive during early development, increasing their likelihood of survival and eventual reproduction (see Trivers, 1971). Thus, a tendency toward monogamous (or, at least, quasi-monogamous) mating systems in humans seems to map onto the relatively high levels of parental investment needed for raising offspring in our species. From this landscape, we can consider threats to a mateship as critical from an evolutionary perspective as such threats have the capacity to reduce care and support for developing offspring. Infidelity serves as such an evolutionarily relevant threat to human mateships.

This chapter explores various forms of infidelity, with a focus on emotional-based versus sexual-based infidelity, to shed light on the evolutionary psychology of infidelity.

Infidelity in Evolutionary Perspective

Threats to a mateship, indirectly but importantly, exert evolutionarily relevant costs to developing offspring. Such threats are highly from an evolutionary perspective (see Barbaro et al., 2019). Infidelity represents perhaps the costliest threat to a mateship. For this reason, understanding the psychological mechanisms that surround infidelity is critical to understanding our evolved psychology.

From an evolutionary perspective, infidelity is a major threat for various reasons. The classic paper on this topic, by Buss et al. (1992), discusses these threats as adaptive hurdles. Infidelity can dissolve important emotional bonds between partners. Such bonds have the capacity to help members of a couple working in a coordinated fashion in raising children. Once the bonds are compromised as the result of the betrayal of infidelity (see De Jesus et al., in press), the capacity for a couple to effectively co-parent may be compromised. Thus, infidelity can have adverse effects on all aspects of a family, particularly coordinated support for developing offspring.

Further, given the nature of sex-differentiated reproductive strategies, infidelity plays out differently between the sexes (see Buss et al., 1992). Given the fact of internal fertilization (characteristic of mammals) coupled with the altricial nature of human offspring, women must commit considerable investment in offspring. They often play a primary role in raising offspring (including breastfeeding, teaching basic skills, caregiving, etc.; see Buss, 2017) and, as such, securing help in the process is important. And, similarly, being abandoned and thus stuck in a position that includes no help from a partner, can be evolutionarily devastating. This concern (which is likely partly conscious and partly unconscious) about being abandoned underlies female psychology associated with a partner's infidelity.

For males, a different adaptive hurdle that relates to the psychology of infidelity exists. Given the fact of internal fertilization, it is possible that a baby that is related to a mother may not be related genetically to the man who believes himself to be the father. A woman's infidelity may make a man a cuckold, a man who invests in a child that he thinks is his but is sired by another man. This adaptive hurdle is by no means minor. Andersson (2006) found that a nontrivial proportion of people around the world today have fathers different from the men they think are their fathers. From an evolutionary perspective, being a cuckold is nearly the ultimate evolutionary tax and, as such, it makes good sense that natural selection would have favored processes that made men hyper-vigilant about female infidelity.

Infidelity and Significant Social Outcomes

Based on extensive research regarding the social psychology of infidelity, conducted over decades, infidelity has effects on various broader social outcomes. In a landmark set of studies conducted by Wilson, Daly, and their colleagues (see Daly & Wilson, 1988), the role of infidelity in various criminal activities was examined. Of the various findings that emerged from this line of research, one of the most visceral to consider pertains to the relationship between homicide and infidelity. Based on thousands of data points across multiple regions of the world, these researchers documented the fact that approximately 1/3 of the homicides have some connection with infidelity. Such homicides may take the form of a man killing a woman who has cheated on him. Or a man killing the interloper with whom his female partner had an affair. Or the man getting killed by either the partner or the interloper in a struggle that emerged from an infidelity (see Wilson et al., 1982).

Before Daly and Wilson's work that applied an evolutionary lens to crime statistics, the ultimate causes of so many classes of violent crimes, such as homicide, were poorly known. It was their work in this area, using an evolution-based framework, that shed light on so many of the ultimate causes of violent crime. Relevant to the current chapter, the work of Daly and Wilson made it clear that infidelity and violent crime often go hand-in-hand. Thus, understanding the evolutionary psychology of infidelity can shed light on our understanding of violent criminal behaviors.

Another broad social issue related to infidelity is marital dissolution or divorce. Marital separation and divorce inflict many costs on families and on developing children, in particular (see D'Onofrio & Emery, 2019). These issues have broader implications at the level of the society, with effects that bear on such issues as drug use, academic success, and mental health (D'Onofrio & Emery, 2019). For these reasons, we can think of infidelity as, indirectly but importantly, having substantial implications for societal outcomes across a range of issues.

Better understanding the psychology of infidelity has can inform various features of societal functioning. From our vantage point, an evolutionarily informed approach (see Geher, 2014; Geher & Kaufman, 2013) has the effect of providing a powerful and ultimate understanding of the nature of infidelity as it relates to our evolutionary heritage.

Classes of Infidelity

Although previous research shows two main categories of infidelity (Buss et al., 1992), there are multiple forms of infidelity that fall under both emotional and sexual infidelity. In today's social world, one could argue that an affair may be *easier* to have (i.e., with cell phones, social media, and anonymous sites devoted to risky communication) and may look *different* from the stereotypical affair we think of. There are social media and dating sites, such as Ashley Madison, devoted to individuals who are married or in a current relationship. Ultimately, the intent behind an affair is the same—a desire for a sexual or emotional connection outside the current relationship.

Within sexual infidelity, the most obvious form is a physical, sexual relationship with someone other than the regular partner. And this sexual relationship can take many forms; the relationship may be an ongoing affair with the same individual, a one-night stand with one or multiple different individuals, or even hiring a sex-worker for a sexual relationship. Because sex is an important part of a healthy relationship, if there are intimacy issues in the current relationship, an individual may seek out physical intimacy outside the relationship.

What one individual considers as cheating may be different from what the next individual considers as cheating. As previously mentioned, with the Internet and many other electronic resources, infidelity can take many forms. For example, an individual may be using pornographic resources frequently without their partner's knowledge, or the partner may be receiving explicit images and videos from individuals other than their partner. And although these explicit images and pornography may not be the typical physical relationship we view as an affair, there exists a sexual component to the infidelity. And again, whether a partner views certain behavior as infidelity is up to the individual; one may see pornography use as cheating, whereas the other may view their partner's actions as expressing a need for more sexual intimacy in their relationship.

According to the National Marriage Project's 2019 report on iFidelity: Interactive Technology and Relationship Faithfulness (2019), Internet infidelity is more common and accepted among young adult Americans than other generations. For instance, 26% of baby boomers believe that Internet behaviors that blur the lines between faithfulness and infidelity are inappropriate, but only 18% of millennials believe these behaviors to be unacceptable while in a relationship. The project also attempts to identify which specific actions are considered cheating and which are not. For example, it appears that Americans mostly agree that behaviors such as vaginal, anal, or oral sex, sexting, cybersex, secret online or in-person relationships, and sexual talk online are cheating. However, behaviors such as flirting with someone in real life, following an old partner on social media, or watching pornography is not typically considered cheating.

And like sexual infidelity, emotional infidelity may take many forms. An emotional affair may be over the telephone, on the Internet, at the workplace, or even through written letters in the mail. On this point, it is noteworthy that in a recent large-scale study of online infidelity, a large majority of Americans judge online affairs to be as damaging and hurtful as affairs that include an in-person, physical component (National Marriage Project, 2019). Such online-based affairs often include both sexual and emotional elements.

Thus, regardless of how the emotional affair is taking place, emotional infidelity occurs when an individual has strong feelings for someone outside their current relationship. These feelings may be short-term, such as a workplace crush, or they may be long-term and may change the future plans of the unfaithful individual. Some individuals may only consider sexual infidelity as cheating and may not consider emotional infidelity to be a threat to their relationship. However, an emotional affair may also be detrimental to a relationship because it may indicate that the partner committing the emotional affair is no longer invested in their current relationship and is seeking an emotional connection elsewhere (Rusbult, 1980).

Perceptions of infidelity differ globally. Cross-cultural data show that sexual infidelity is understood globally as a betrayal and detrimental to a relationship (Buss et al., 1999; Jankowiak et al., 2002). In addition to infidelity being an emotionally taxing situation, in many places around the world, infidelity is viewed as a crime punishable by law. Historically in the United States, many states viewed infidelity as a punishable offense, and in the US military, infidelity may result in a court-martial. However, laws against infidelity in the United States are rarely enforced today. In other countries around the world, infidelity is a much more serious crime and may even be punishable by death. More recently, in 2018, the Supreme Court of India ruled adultery not a crime, where previously adultery could result in a jail sentence for the man involved in the sexual relationship but not the woman. The previous law criminalizing adultery was challenged by arguing the law was gender-discriminating by only holding the man responsible and punishable by law, while viewing women as objects owned by men. There have been similar critiques of adultery laws around the world as gender discriminatory.

Defining Sexual and Emotional Infidelity

When studying infidelity, researchers often differentiate and operationally define the types of infidelity. However, in the real world, not much is known about how individuals distinguish between types of infidelity, or what these individuals consider infidelity. We can imagine that sexual infidelity might be easy to characterize. Emotional infidelity, on the other hand, may be less clear when it comes to identifying and categorizing. Especially now, in today's world, with the Internet and social media, where the lines between infidelity and remaining faithful to a partner may be blurry. In a study aimed at investigating how people conceptualize and define emotional and sexual infidelity, Guitar et al. (2016) found that individuals were more consistent in defining sexual infidelity than emotional infidelity, suggesting that emotional infidelity is more complex than sexual infidelity. The study also revealed that when asking participants to define sexual and emotional infidelity, individuals focused on specific behaviors and actions, but when asked to differentiate between sexual and emotional infidelity, participants described feelings (Guitar et al., 2016). Further, the study found sex differences in the defining features of definitions for sexual and emotional infidelity, suggesting that women are more likely to conflate definitions of sexual and emotional infidelity, and men are more likely to differentiate between the two. Sex differences in the way that individuals define these types of infidelity could also be related to the differences in the way males and females react and respond to types of infidelity.

Emotional Responses to Infidelity

In addition to severe physical responses to infidelity, or even jealousy due to suspicion of infidelity (i.e., physical abuse and killing of wife; Daly et al., 1982; Wilson & Daly,

1992), there is a wide range of emotional responses to infidelity that differ depending on the type of infidelity committed. Most studies evaluating emotional responses to infidelity focus on assessing jealousy in response to infidelity; however, subsequent research has made attempts to dive deeper into the emotional responses to infidelity. In a study asking participants to nominate emotional responses they believe to follow infidelity, Shackelford et al. (2000) found a main effect for infidelity type; for example, participants nominated nauseated/repulsed as more likely to follow sexual infidelity and undesirable/insecure as more likely to follow emotional infidelity.

As previously mentioned, with the Internet, infidelity can take many forms aside from the traditional physical, sexual affair. Research has made attempts to investigate whether online infidelity elicits the same emotional responses as an offline relationship. Whitty (2003) found that online infidelity is not its own discrete category separate from offline infidelity. Moreover, when Whitty asked participants to rate online acts of infidelity, participants rated online acts almost as severely as sexual intercourse.

Research has also found sex differences in the emotional responses to online and Internet infidelity. Whitty (2005) found that women are more likely to end a relationship over finding out their partner has been involved in an online affair than men and that women perceive an online affair as an emotional betrayal more than do men. It appears that much of the research on sexual and emotional infidelity focuses on sex differences in emotional responses to infidelity—a facet of infidelity that an evolutionary perspective has productively addressed.

The Interface of Sexual and Emotional Infidelity

Studies examining sexual versus emotional infidelity often address sex differences, and in particular, one central question: Are affective reactions to each type of infidelity sex-differentiated? However, we need to first consider a more fundamental question: Is each category of infidelity distinct, or is this a false dichotomy? This second question does not deny the existence of the sexual and emotional aspects of infidelity; rather, it questions whether emotional infidelity can exist in the absence of sexual infidelity and vice versa. The following section discusses and integrates relevant empirical evidence to address both questions.

Opposing an evolutionary perspective and critiquing Buss and colleagues' (1992) original work, DeSteno and Salovey (1996) offered the *double-shot* hypothesis, which argues that men and women do not perceive sexual and emotional infidelity to be independent. Rather, with decades of socialization, humans learn to carry sex-differentiated beliefs about the covariation of the types of infidelity. It is a commonly believed stereotype that women only have sex with individuals whom they are emotionally attached to, and thus men identify sexual infidelity as more distressing because they (subconsciously or consciously) assume both forms of infidelity are present. In contrast, women may stereotype men and believe that their male partner who forms a deep emotional attachment to an interloper is likely also having sex with her (or is going to). Guitar and colleagues (2016) queried participants about their conceptualizations of sexual and emotional infidelity, finding that women were more likely than men to associate sexual activity with emotional infidelity. In essence, according to this *double-shot* perspective, sexual and emotional infidelity are intertwined and difficult to tease apart (DeSteno & Salovey, 1996; DeSento et al., 2002; Harris & Christenfeld, 1996).

As previously discussed, both emotional and sexual infidelity have defining features in terms of their capacity to elicit jealousy, other negative emotions, and behavioral tactics within partnerships (see Buss, 2013; Kruger et al., 2015). On the one hand, evolutionists maintain that the robust and replicable sex-differentiated reactions to sexual and emotional infidelity are the result of evolved mechanisms that solve adaptive problems faced by each sex (Buss et al., 1992; Buss et al., 1996). On the other hand, those coming from a social-cognitive perspective argue these sex differences are a result of socially learned expectations that sexual and emotional infidelity are rarely mutually exclusive (DeSento & Salovey, 1996; Harris & Christenfeld, 1996; Harris, 2003). Considering the latter *double-shot* perspective, the validity and simplicity of the methodology commonly used by Buss and others requires evaluation.

Evolved Sex Differences or Artifact of Measurement

If the choice between sexual versus emotional infidelity presents a false dichotomy for most individuals, a forced-choice format would not capture the extent of participants' phenomenological experience. Instead, participants identify the form of infidelity that they believe is most likely to result in a *double-shot*, or both types of infidelity occurring, as more distressing (DeSento & Salovey, 1996; Harris & Christenfeld, 1996). Moreover, if the documented sex differences regarding reactions to infidelity are a product of evolution, these differences should then generalize across response formats.

DeSento and colleagues (2002) used multiple convergent measures, including the forced-choice items; 7-point Likert-scale measures in which participants indicated the degree to which they would feel angry, jealous, calm, threatened, relieved, and hurt in response to each type of infidelity; agree-disagree measures; and a checklist measure. These convergent methodologies revealed that the sex difference was only present when participants were forced to choose between emotional or sexual infidelity. In the alternative response formats, men and women *both* reported greater distress in response to sexual than to emotional infidelity, even when accounting for within-sex differences. In a follow-up study in which the researchers manipulated participants' cognitive load to enhance automatic (innate) processing, the sex difference in response to the forced-choice questions was diminished. Like men, women reported greater distress and upset to sexual infidelity, compared to emotional infidelity.

Other researchers continued to find analogous patterns, only replicating the sex-differentiated findings of Buss et al. (1992) when presenting the questions to the participants in the same exact way. Buss and colleagues (1999) directly responded to the aforementioned theoretical and methodological critiques, arguing the superiority of the forced-choice response format by suggesting that continuous measures may be subject to ceiling effects. However, ceiling effects have been unfounded in studies using continuous measures. These studies again have found that women report more distress in response to emotional infidelity (versus sexual infidelity) compared to males, and in others, sexual infidelity is more bothersome than emotional infidelity for *both* sexes (DeSteno et al., 2002; Harris, 2003; Leeker & Carlozzi, 2014). Even within a forced-choice context, if participants are provided a third option to indicate that both forms of infidelity were equally upsetting, the majority of men and women select this third option (Lishner et al., 2008). Within-sex analyses in past research suggest that men may react to emotional and sexual infidelity similarly or imagine emotional infidelity as being more upsetting (see Harris, 2002; Leeker & Carlozzi, 2014). The intensity of female reactions specifically to emotional infidelity alone may therefore account for the observed sex differences.

Buss and colleagues (1999) responded to the early criticism of their evolutionary model by conducting four studies designed to clarify the nature of sex differences in reactions to infidelity. The first study altered the previously used forced-choice questions to explicitly convey that sexual and emotional infidelity were mutually exclusive ("Imagining your partner forming a deep emotional (but not sexual) relationship with that person; Imagining your partner enjoying a sexual (but not emotional) relationship with that person." p. 130). The second study instructed participants to imagine that their partner had formed an emotional attachment *and* had sexual intercourse with another person, and asked participants to select which aspect upset them more. The results of both studies replicated the original Buss et al. (1992) findings. The remaining two cross-cultural studies replicated the findings of the second study in Korean and Japanese samples.

More recently, Buss (2018) has directly responded to theoretical and methodological critiques of his work on infidelity. First, Buss maintains that the competing social-cognitive (*double-shot*) theory for sex differences in reaction to infidelity types was falsified by his 1999 publication controlling for conditional probabilities. Second, Buss refers to the cognitive load manipulation (used by DeSteno et al., 2002) as a "theory-irrelevant manipulation" (Buss, 2018, p. 159). And last, Buss states that the sex difference in reactions to types of infidelity are robust and replicable across multiple methods (citing Edlund & Sagarin, 2017), and are therefore not a result of methodological artifact.

Carpenter (2012) directly compared the response formats (forced choice versus continuous) in a meta-analysis, finding that when forced to choose between the two infidelity types, both sexes identified emotional infidelity as causing more upset. When rating their distress separately for emotional and sexual infidelity on a continuous measure though, sexual infidelity was identified as more distressing by both sexes. Carpenter's analysis replicated that of Harris's (2003) meta-analysis reviewing sex differences in sexual jealousy, both works suggesting that sex differences in reactions to infidelity are the result of an artifact of measurement. Yet, the meta-analysis conducted by Edlund and Sagarin (2017) provides a comprehensive review of this research and claims consistent sex differences are present across a variety of measures.

Is it possible that ideological biases of social psychologists cause them to be resistant to the sex differences themselves that are proposed by evolutionary research (see von Hipple & Buss, 2017)? Alternatively, is it possible that evolutionists have been too insular in their methodological approaches and interpretation of findings? To resolve this contention and elucidate the nature of the effects of infidelity, we use an integrative approach in reviewing additional pertinent literature. This review then serves to inform directions for future research and showcases important implications and potential applications of this research.

Integrating Inconsistent Findings
OPERATIONALIZING EMOTIONAL REACTIONS TO INFIDELITY

An additional critique of Buss et al.'s (1992) original work concerns the construct validity of his original questions; specifically, his use of the terms "distress" and "upset" to capture the construct of jealousy. Subsequently, researchers began to identify and measure individual components of emotional reactions to infidelity to determine whether the prevalence of these components was sex-differentiated and/or specific to the type of infidelity. In short, participant-generated emotional reactions to infidelity included 15 components of emotions which account for 60% of the variance in participants' responses (Shackelford et al., 2000). Undesirable/insecure, depressed, happy, shocked, humiliated, tired, forgiving, and sexually aroused are a sample of the emotion components identified by the researchers. Evidently, emotional reactions to infidelity are more complex than "distress" or "upset," and range widely in terms of affect.

Within these 15 components of emotional reactions to infidelity, consistent differences can be found when considering both the infidelity type and the participant's sex (Shackelford et al., 2000). Nine out of 15 of the emotional components were sex-differentiated. For example, men reported higher levels of homicidal/suicidal reactions compared to women, whereas women reported higher levels of feeling undesirable/insecure compared to men. Emotional reactions to infidelity depend more on the infidelity type than the participant sex, however. Twelve out of 15 of the emotional components differed in intensity based on the infidelity type. For example, nauseated/repulsed was associated with sexual infidelity more than emotional, and undesirable/insecure was associated with emotional infidelity more than sexual.

Offering an integrative viewpoint, Green and Sabini (2004, 2006) suggest that the intensity of participants' emotional reactions to infidelity depends on the particular emotional component. While evolution has differentially shaped some of these emotional components in each sex, there are also emotional components involved in reactions to infidelity that are not sex-differentiated. Imagining sexual infidelity elicited more anger and blame, and emotional infidelity elicited more hurt feelings in both male and female undergraduates and nonstudents (Green & Sabini, 2006). However, the evolutionary-predicted sex difference failed to replicate in the nonstudent sample. Though there were no effects for age or socioeconomic status (Sabini & Green, 2004), private university students reported more sex-differentiated emotional reactions compared to the public university sample. Findings from related work suggest the inconsistency in results across samples may be related to cultural differences (Geary et al., 1995; Harris, 2003) and differential past experiences with infidelity (Harris, 2000, 2002).

Additionally, when using a continuous measure to assess the intensity of participants' emotional reactions (e.g., anger, hurt, blame, upset) to imagined infidelity, both male and female participants reported a stronger emotional response to sexual than to emotional infidelity (Green & Sabini, 2006; Sabini & Green, 2004). This last finding aligns with previous studies also using continuous, Likert-type measures (see DeSteno et al., 2002; Harris, 2003; Leeker & Carlozzi, 2014). Further highlighting the importance of methodology, when participants were queried about their emotional reaction to one type of infidelity *without hearing the other type*, sexual infidelity elicited more upset, hurt, and anger in both sexes than emotional infidelity (Sabini & Green, 2004).

The emotion of blame was more strongly associated with sexual infidelity than emotional in all cases. Sexual infidelity may elicit stronger reactions compared to emotional infidelity because of the component of choice involved in engaging in a sex act with an interloper (Vaughn Becker et al., 2004). In comparison, participants may perceive emotional infidelity as less intentional. Relative to women, men are less likely to forgive their partners and are more likely to end the relationship in response to sexual infidelity than emotional infidelity (Shackelford et al., 2002). The converse, evolutionarily predicted results were also found for women, and so it does appear that sex is a significant factor in particular facets within overall reactions to infidelity (at least in forced-choice, hypothetical contexts).

Using a situational control scale and multiple measures of emotion, Nannini and Myers (2000) found that men and women are less likely to feel and accept responsibility for their own role in their partner's actions in events of sexual infidelity compared to emotional infidelity. Moreover, women reported feeling less responsible for their partner's infidelity than men, and also greater emotional distress across all three infidelity conditions (emotional, sexual, and combination). The researchers highlighted this relationship between emotional upset and perceived responsibility: The less control (and thus responsibility) an individual feels surrounding the infidelity, the more likely he or she will react with feelings of upset, such as feeling insecure. Considering participants' cognitive appraisals of infidelity helps us understand specific emotional reactions, sex differences, and why sexual infidelity often elicits more distressing emotions in participants (see DeSteno et al., 2002; Harris, 2003; Green & Sabini, 2006; Kruger et al., 2015; Leeker & Carlozzi, 2014; Nannini & Myers, 2000; Sabini & Green, 2004).

Much insight is gained from examining the individual emotions involved in reactions to imagined infidelity. Reconsidering Buss's original focus of "upset" and "distress," and his subsequent theory (Buss, 2013), we shift our attention to the emotion of jealousy. Following the work of Shackelford and colleagues (2000) and using a hypothetical scenario in which *both* sexual and emotional infidelity occurred and continuous emotional measures, the findings of Becker et al. (2004) suggest that jealousy is specifically and uniquely sex-differentiated. Levels of hurt, anger, and disgust were dependent on the infidelity type, whereas the results for jealousy replicate Buss et al.'s (1992, 1999) original work. Other studies that operationally define the affective reaction to infidelity as jealousy continue to find support for this evolved sex difference (Schützwohl, 2007; Schützwohl & Koch, 2004), especially when decisions are made spontaneously or automatically.

EXAMINING THE ROLE OF ECOLOGICAL VALIDITY

Many of the studies examining reactions to infidelity discussed thus far share a methodological limitation: unknown ecological validity. Consequently, the results discussed ought to be prefaced as "hypothetical" or "imagined" infidelity. Directly comparing actual and hypothetical infidelity, Harris (2002) found that ~70% of participants had previous experience with infidelity, and that no sex differences were found when participants recalled this experience. Reactions to hypothetical infidelity assessed using forced-choice items were more consistent with an evolutionary view, albeit arguably limited in terms of ecological validity.

Studies have shown that the more vivid an imagined/hypothetical infidelity is presented within a laboratory setting, the more psychological distress reported by participants (Kato, 2014). Men, in particular, imagine these scenarios more vividly than women, and are also more sensitive to visual stimuli of potential rival mates (Lanfolfi et al., 2007). Supporting this cognitive difference, fMRI results reveal differential brain activation in men and women while imagining both forms of infidelity (Takashashi et al., 2006). Areas involved in sex and aggression, such as the amygdala and hypothalamus, were activated more in men than in women. These findings complement those of Daly et al. (1982) and Wilson et al. (1992, 1993), providing an understanding of the neuropsychological aspects of sex-differentiated jealousy-related behaviors.

Future Research Directions

Resolving the contention regarding the sex-differentiated nature of reactions to infidelity has both empirical and practical implications. Future research in this area should use an integrative theoretical approach (e.g., Leeker & Carolozzi, 2014), considering both evolutionary and social-cognitive perspectives. The pervasiveness of evolution's influence on human behavior—mating behavior, in particular—is clear (Buss, 2017; Geher, 2014). A comprehensive theory of how we process and function within intimate relationships might better situate previous opposing findings, however. The role of methodological limitations,

participants' cognitive appraisals of infidelity, and an unknown number of unmeasured related factors must be considered. Herein lies suggestions for future investigators to improve on previous research design and explore the subtleties of the proposed sex differences:

- Include multiple question types (forced-choice and continuous) to account for measurement artifact (e.g., DeSteno et al., 2002) and address issues of reliability.
- Strengthen construct validity by being intentional and specific in how reactions to infidelity are operationally defined and presented to the participant (e.g., Shackelford et al., 2000).
- Improve ecological validity by querying participants' experiences with *actual* infidelity using qualitative and quantitative measures to capture the depth and complexity of responses.
- Increase external validity by including cross-cultural comparisons (e.g., Geary et al., 1995) and use random sampling when possible to ensure demographic variables such as age, sexual orientation, relationship history, and racial identity are accurately represented in the sample. Moreover, consider these variables directly to identify potential generational differences and other potential group differences based on sexuality, marital status, etc.
- Continue to explore additional independent variables and individual differences relating to the psychology of infidelity, such as:
  - The quality of participants' current relationships (i.e., level of commitment, intimacy, passion), and the impact of expectations about infidelity (Cramer et al., 2008; Leeker & Carolizzi, 2014).
  - Self-esteem and how it is impacted in each sex during events of various types of infidelity (Goldenberg et al., 2003).
  - Characteristics of the rival or interloper, such as his/her attractiveness, financial status (Wade & Fowler, 2006), and genetic and social relational proximity (Fisher et al., 2009).
  - The presence of offspring between the individual and the adulterer, considering Hamilton's (1964) theory of inclusive fitness.
  - Evolutionarily relevant factors such as participants' mating effort (Jones et al., 2007).
  - Participants' personality and childhood experiences, specifically within the context of the parent–child relationship (Geary et al., 1995).
  - Participants' cognitive appraisals of the infidelity, such as his/her perception of personal responsibility (Nannini & Myers, 2000) and beliefs surrounding infidelity (DeSteno & Salovey, 1996). Doing so may also shed light on

why participants sometimes report feeling positive emotions in reaction to an imagined infidelity (Shackelford et al., 2000).
- The role of the respondents' sexual orientation (Frederick & Fales, 2016; Harris, 2002; Howard & Perilloux, 2017; Leeker & Carlozzi, 2014). However, future work should accurately operationalize sexuality to capture the fluidity inherent in human sexuality (see Diamond, 2015).
- Lastly, an important next step for future work could be to assess the potential function of reactions to infidelity. For example, do the behavioral displays associated with male sexual jealousy serve as a signal of impending spousal violence?

Implications and Applications

Infidelity can be catastrophic when it comes to problems in intimate relationships. An evolutionary perspective has been successful in helping us understand the psychology of infidelity in terms of why it is so devastating as well as why there are so many cognitive, emotional, and behavioral adaptations that underlie this broader part of the human experience (see Buss & Haselton, 2005). The sex-differentiated nature of reactions to infidelity, presented herein, speak importantly to different adaptive hurdles that our male versus female ancestors experienced across human evolutionary history (see Buss, 2017). Although the science surrounding sex-differentiated psychology pertaining to infidelity is a work in progress, much in the way of applicable insights has been garnered over the past few decades on this front.

Bottom Line

Infidelity and reactions to it connect strongly with such adverse societal outcomes as domestic violence, filicide, and homicide (see Daly & Wilson, 1988; Buss, 2005). The fact that a full one-third of homicides in North America can be tied to infidelity speaks volumes about the societal impact of this issue in the broadest sense (see Daly et al., 1982). And on a slightly more micro scale, the ramifications of parental infidelity on mental health outcomes of children can be devastating (see D'Onofrio & Emery, 2019). Better understanding the psychology of infidelity, along with the sex-differentiated patterns associated with it, has the capacity to help us understand modern social problems in a larger sense (see Gallup & Burch, in press).

References

Anderson, K. G. (2006). How well does paternity confidence match actual paternity? Evidence from worldwide nonpaternity rates. *Current Anthropology, 48*, 511–518.

Barash, D. (2016). *Out of Eden*. Oxford University Press.

Barbaro, N., Sela, Y., Atari, M., Shackelford, T. K., & Zeigler-Hill, V. (2019). Romantic attachment and mate retention behavior: The mediating role of perceived risk of partner infidelity. *Journal of Social and Personal Relationships, 36*, 940–956.

Buss, D. M. (2005). *The murderer next door: Why the mind is designed to kill*. Penguin Press.
Buss, D. M. (2013). Sexual jealousy. *Psychological Topics, 22*(2), 155–182.
Buss, D. M. (2017). *The evolution of desire: Strategies of human mating* (Rev. ed.). Basic Books.
Buss, D. M. (2018). Sexual and emotional infidelity: Evolved gender differences in jealousy prove robust and replicable. *Perspectives on Psychological Science, 13*(2), 155–160.
Buss, D. M., & Haselton, M. (2005). The evolution of jealousy. *Trends in Cognitive Sciences, 9*(11), 506–507.
Buss, D. M., Larsen, R. J., & Westen, D. (1996). Sex differences in jealousy: Not gone, not forgotten, and not explained by alternative hypotheses. *Psychological Science, 7*(6), 373–375.
Buss, D. M., Larsen, R. J., Westen, D., &; Semmelroth, J. (1992). Sex differences in jealousy: Evolution, physiology, and psychology. *Psychological Science, 3*, 251–255.
Buss, D. M., Shackelford, T. K., Kirkpatrick, L. A., Choe, J. C., Lim, H. K., Hasegawa, M., . . . Bennett, K. (1999). Jealousy and the nature of beliefs about infidelity: Tests of competing hypotheses about sex differences in the United States, Korea, and Japan. *Personal Relationships, 6*(1), 125–150.
Carpenter, C. J. (2012). Meta-analyses of sex differences in responses to sexual versus emotional infidelity: Men and women are more similar than different. *Psychology of Women Quarterly, 36*(1), 25–37.
Cramer, R. E., Lipinski, R. E., Meteer, J. D., & Houska, J. A. (2008). Sex differences in subjective distress to unfaithfulness: Testing competing evolutionary and violation of infidelity expectations hypotheses. *Journal of Social Psychology, 148*(4), 389–406.
D'Onofrio, B., & Emery, R. (2019). Parental divorce or separation and children's mental health. *World Psychiatry, 18*(1), 100.
Daly, M., & Wilson, M. (1988). *Homicide*. Aldine de Gruyter.
Daly, M., Wilson, M., & Weghorst, S. J. (1982). Male sexual jealousy. *Ethology and Sociobiology, 3*, 11–27.
De'Jesús, A. R., Cristo, M., Ruel, M., Kruchowy, D., Geher, G., Nolan, K., & Zezula, V. (2021). Betrayal, outrage, guilt, and forgiveness: The Four Horsemen of the human social-emotional experience. *EvoS Journal of the Evolutionary Studies Consortium, 9*, 1–13.
DeSteno, D., Bartlett, M. Y., Braverman, J., & Salovey, P. (2002). Sex differences in jealousy: Evolutionary mechanism or artifact of measurement? *Journal of Personality and Social Psychology, 83*(5), 1103–1116.
DeSteno, D. A., & Salovey, P. (1996). Evolutionary origins of sex differences in jealousy? Questioning the "fitness" of the model. *Psychological Science, 7*(6), 367–372.
Diamond, L. M. (2015). Sexual fluidity. In P. Whelehan & A. Bolin (Eds.), *The International Encyclopedia of Human Sexuality*, 1115–1354. John Wiley & Sons.
Edlund, J. E., & Sagarin, B. J. (2017). Sex differences in jealousy: A 25-year retrospective. *Advances in Experimental Social Psychology, 55*, 259–302.
Fisher, M., Cox, A., Tran, U. S., Hoben, A., Geher, G., Arrabaca, A., . . . Voracek, M. (2009). Impact of relational proximity on distress from infidelity. *Evolutionary Psychology, 7*(4), 560–580.
Frederick, D. A., & Fales, M. R. (2016). Upset over sexual versus emotional infidelity among gay, lesbian, bisexual, and heterosexual adults. *Archives of Sexual Behavior, 45*(1), 175–191.
Gallup, G. G. Jr. & Burch, R. L. (in press). Paternal Resemblance and Investment. To appear in Mogilski, J., & Shackelford, T. (eds.). *The Oxford Handbook of Evolutionary Psychology and Romantic Relationships*. Oxford University Press.
Geary, D. C., Rumsey, M., Bow-Thomas, C. C., & Hoard, M. K. (1995). Sexual jealousy as a facultative trait: Evidence from the pattern of sex differences in adults from China and the United States. *Ethology and Sociobiology, 16*(5), 355–383.
Geher, G. (2014). *Evolutionary psychology 101*. Springer.
Geher, G., & Kaufman, S. B. (2013). *Mating intelligence unleashed: The role of the mind in sex, dating, and love*. Oxford University Press.
Goldenberg, J. L., Landau, M. J., Pyszczynski, T., Cox, C. R., Greenberg, J., Solomon, S., & Dunnam, H. (2003). Gender-typical responses to sexual and emotional infidelity as a function of mortality salience induced self-esteem striving. *Personality and Social Psychology Bulletin, 29*(12), 1585–1595.
Green, M. C., & Sabini, J. (2006). Gender, socioeconomic status, age, and jealousy: Emotional responses to infidelity in a national sample. *Emotion, 6*(2), 330.
Guitar, A. E., Geher, G., Kruger, D., Garcia, J. R., Fisher, M., & Fitzgerald, C. J. (2016). Defining and interpreting definitions of emotional and sexual infidelity. *Current Psychology, 36*(3), 434–446.
Hamilton, W. D. 1964. The genetical evolution of social behaviour, Part I. *Journal of Theoretical Biology, 7*, 1–16

Harris, C. R. (2000). Psychophysiological responses to imagined infidelity: The specific innate modular view of jealousy reconsidered. *Journal of Personality and Social Psychology, 78*(6), 1082.

Harris, C. R. (2002). Sexual and romantic jealousy in heterosexual and homosexual adults. *Psychological Science, 13*(1), 7–12.

Harris, C. R. (2003). A review of sex differences in sexual jealousy, including self-report data, psychophysiological responses, interpersonal violence, and morbid jealousy. *Personality and Social Psychology Review, 7*(2), 102–128.

Harris, C. R., & Christenfeld, N. (1996). Gender, jealousy, and reason. *Psychological Science, 7*(6), 364–366.

Howard, R. M., & Perilloux, C. (2017). Is mating psychology most closely tied to biological sex or preferred partner's sex? *Personality and Individual Differences, 115*, 83–89.

Hrdy, S. B. (2009) *Mothers and others: The evolutionary origins of mutual understanding.* Harvard University.

Jankowiak, W., Nell, M., & Buckmaster, A. (2002). Managing infidelity: A cross-cultural perspective. *Ethnology, 41*, 85.

Jones, D. N., Figueredo, A. J., Dickey, E. D., & Jacobs, W. J. (2007). Relations among individual differences in reproductive strategies, sexual attractiveness, affective and punitive intentions, and imagined sexual or emotional infidelity. *Evolutionary Psychology, 5*(2), 387–410.

Kato, T. (2014). A reconsideration of sex differences in response to sexual and emotional infidelity. *Archives of Sexual Behavior, 43*(7), 1281–1288.

Kruger, D. J., Fisher, M. L., Fitzgerald, C. J., Garcia, J. R., Geher, G., & Guitar, A. E. (2015). Sexual and emotional aspects are distinct components of infidelity and unique predictors of anticipated distress. *Evolutionary Psychological Science,* 1(1), 44–51.

Landolfi, J. F., Geher, G., & Andrews, A. (2007). The role of stimulus specificity on infidelity reactions: Seeing is disturbing. *Current Psychology, 26*(1), 46–59.

Leeker, O., & Carlozzi, A. (2014). Effects of sex, sexual orientation, infidelity expectations, and love on distress related to emotional and sexual infidelity. *Journal of Marital and Family Therapy, 40*(1), 68–91.

Lishner, D. A., Nguyen, S., Stocks, E. L., & Zillmer, E. J. (2008). Are sexual and emotional infidelity equally upsetting to men and women? Making sense of forced-choice responses. *Evolutionary Psychology, 6*(4), 667–675.

Nannini, D. K., & Meyers, L. S. (2000). Jealousy in sexual and emotional infidelity: An alternative to the evolutionary explanation. *Journal of Sex Research, 37*(2), 117–122.

National Marriage Project. (2019). State of our unions: iFidelity: Interactive technology and relationship faithfulness. http://nationalmarriageproject.org/wp-content/uploads/2019/07/SOU2019.pdf

Rusbult, C. E. (1980). Commitment and satisfaction in romantic associations: A test of the investment model. *Journal of Experimental Social Psychology, 16*, 172–186.

Sabini, J., & Green, M. C. (2004). Emotional responses to sexual and emotional infidelity: Constants and differences across genders, samples, and methods. *Personality and Social Psychology Bulletin, 30*(11), 1375–1388.

Schützwohl, A. (2007). Decision strategies in continuous ratings of jealousy feelings elicited by sexual and emotional infidelity. *Evolutionary Psychology, 5*(4), 815–828.

Schützwohl, A., & Koch, S. (2004). Sex differences in jealousy: The recall of cues to sexual and emotional infidelity in personally more and less threatening context conditions. *Evolution and Human Behavior, 25*(4), 249–257.

Shackelford, T. K., Buss, D. M., & Bennett, K. (2002). Forgiveness or breakup: Sex differences in responses to a partner's infidelity. *Cognition & Emotion, 16*(2), 299–307.

Shackelford, T. K., LeBlanc, G. J., & Drass, E. (2000). Emotional reactions to infidelity. *Cognition & Emotion, 14*(5), 643–659.

Takahashi, H., Matsuura, M., Yahata, N., Koeda, M., Suhara, T., & Okubo, Y. (2006). Men and women show distinct brain activations during imagery of sexual and emotional infidelity. *NeuroImage, 32*(3), 1299–1307.

Trivers, R. L. (1971). The evolution of reciprocal altruism. *Quarterly Review of Biology, 46*, 35–57.

Vaughn Becker, D., Sagarin, B. J., Guadagno, R. E., Millevoi, A., & Nicastle, L. D. (2004). When the sexes need not differ: Emotional responses to the sexual and emotional aspects of infidelity. *Personal Relationships, 11*(4), 529–538.

von Hipple, W., & Buss, D. M. (2017). Do ideologically driven scientific agendas impede the understanding and acceptance of evolutionary principles in social psychology? In L. Jussim & J. Crawford (Eds.), *Political bias in psychology* (7–25). Cambridge University Press.

Wade, T. J., & Fowler, K. (2006). Sex differences in responses to sexual and emotional infidelity: Considerations of rival attractiveness and financial status. *Journal of Cultural and Evolutionary Psychology, 4*(1), 37–50.

Whitty, M. T. (2003). Pushing the wrong buttons: Men's and women's attitudes toward online and offline infidelity. *CyberPsychology & Behavior, 6*(6), 569–579.

Whitty, M. T. (2005). The "realness" of cyber-cheating: Men and women's representations of unfaithful Internet relationships. *Social Science Computer Review, 23*, 57–67.

Wilson, M. I., & Daly, M. (1992). Who kills whom in spouse killings? On the exceptional sex ratio of spousal homicides in the United States. *Criminology, 30*(2), 189–216.

Wilson, M., & Daly, M. (1993). Spousal homicide risk and estrangement. *Violence and victims, 8*(1), 3–16.

CHAPTER 11

Thank You, Next!: Sexual Novelty Motivations for Infidelity

Limor Y. Gottlieb *and* David P. Schmitt

> **Abstract**
> Pair bonding is a central feature of human mating. We are designed to fall in love and to feel the breaking of a romantic bond is something to be avoided. Even so, people vary in their propensity to remain in lifelong marriages and infidelity is often a source of this relational instability. One of the key motivations for engaging in infidelity is the desire for *sexual novelty*. This chapter outlines the psychological origins of novelty-seeking as a motivation for infidelity. It places this motivation within broader research on infidelity and its links with biological substrates, including personality traits, sociosexuality, executive control, and a wide range of demographic factors. In particular, it reviews evidence that biological sex may play an important role in novelty-seeking and infidelity. According to sexual strategies theory (Buss & Schmitt, 1993), men and women have evolved distinct psychological mechanisms adapted for the pursuit of short-term mating, including infidelity or extrapair mating. From this perspective, men may have evolved a stronger desire for sexual variety, and so are expected to be more likely than women to be unfaithful with multiple partners. Even so, the gender gap in infidelity may be closing, especially in younger adults from the United States, with married women between the ages of 18–29 years more likely to cheat than men. The chapter concludes with a discussion of the importance of age and nuances of culture in explaining sex differences in novelty-seeking motivations for infidelity.
>
> **Key Words:** infidelity, novelty-seeking, relationship, personality, marriage

In humans, the institution of marriage, pair bonding between two people, occurs in all known societies (Buss, 1985; Epstein & Guttman, 1984; Henrich et al., 2012). Yet, some individuals take actions breaching the sexual exclusivity of their pair-bond commitments—they engage in infidelity. Infidelity is defined as a person's emotional or physical intimacy with individuals outside their relationship. In the United States, infidelity is frequent, with a prevalence ranging from 20% to 40% among married couples (Atkins et al., 2001; Lauman et al., 1994), and 70% among dating couples (Allen & Baucom, 2006; Schmitt & Buss, 2001).

High rates of infidelity are not confined to American couples (Druckerman, 2007). In China, infidelity rates have risen over the period 2000–2015 from 12.9% to 33.4% for men, and from 4.7% to 11.4% for women (Zhang et al., 2021). In a large examination of 160 human cultures worldwide, infidelity was the most often cited reason for divorce (Betzig, 1989). In a study of 53 nations from around the world, mate poaching—attracting a partner who is already in a committed relationship—was found to be common, with 56.9% of men and 34.9% of women admitting they had tried to attract someone already in a relationship for a short-term affair (Schmitt, 2004a). Not only is infidelity a leading cause of divorce or separation, but also it can lead to the spread of sexually transmitted infections (STIs), harsh social as well as professional implications, intersexual and intrasexual violence, and even homicide (e.g., Daly & Wilson, 1988). As a consequence, the topic of infidelity has been the focus of intensive scholarly investigation. In particular, many studies have addressed novelty-seeking as a motivation for infidelity. A key question is how novelty-seeking fits with the adaptive landscape of human sexuality.

Marital Satisfaction

A prominent psychological factor associated with infidelity is satisfaction in one's primary, committed relationship. The extent to which individuals are satisfied with and committed to their intimate relationship plays a role in infidelity. For instance, individuals who are unhappy in their marriages expect to engage in infidelity in the future, and they expect their spouses to do the same (Buss & Shackelford, 1997). Relationship dissatisfaction also correlates with the number of extradyadic partners (Wiggins & Lederer, 1984) and with the degree of emotional and sexual involvement with an extramarital partner (e.g., Allen & Baucom, 2001; Glass & Wright, 1985). According to Rusbult's investment model (Rusbult, 1980; Rusbult et al., 1994), the degree of investment in a primary partnership and the perceived quality of alternatives may also predict commitment to a relationship, including self-perceived ability to do without the relationship and the benefits that might be lost if the relationship ends, including material possessions, friends, and social connections. Moreover, boredom in a marriage can lead to an increased risk of infidelity (Allen & Atkins, 2005), as can poor communication and a lack of emotional support (Allen et al., 2008). This is in line with the "deficit model" of infidelity (Thompson, 1983), which holds that extradyadic relationships may result from personal needs in the primary relationship not being met, the frequency and quality of sexual activity with the primary partner, as well as the degree of love and the duration of the primary relationship. From this deficit perspective, it could be that people seek a new *experience* rather than a new romantic partner. In that sense, affairs may reflect personal exploration, self-discovery, a search for a new identity, and an interest in personal growth and transformation.

According to the self-expansion model, by including the other in the self (Aron & Aron, 1996; Aron et al., 1998), people may seek to enhance the self through extradyadic relationships or fulfill needs that are unmet in their primary relationship (Buunk & Dijkstra, 2004). Therefore, some individuals may be motivated to seek novelty in extradyadic relationships as a means of self-expansion. Indeed, the potential for self-expansion and the extent to which the other is included in the self was found to be associated with susceptibility to infidelity among dating college students (Lewandowski & Ackerman, 2006). This self-expansion starts as new partners begin to share and participate in novel experiences which counteract the boredom experienced in their primary relationship (Aron et al., 2000; Tsapelas et al., 2009). Indeed, among dating, cohabiting, and married couples, the longer the primary relationship continues, the more likely it is that sexual infidelity will occur (e.g., Forste & Tanfer, 1996; Hansen, 1987). Specifically, for married women, the likelihood of extramarital involvement peaks in the 7th year of marriage, then declines; but for married men, the likelihood of extramarital involvement decreases over time until the 18th year of matrimony, after which the likelihood of extramarital involvement increases (Liu, 2000). Similarly, in a sample of couples in therapy for infidelity, sexual infidelity first occurred after an average of seven years of marriage (Wiggins & Lederer, 1984), whereas Lawson and Samson (1988) showed that among younger cohorts the length of marriage prior to initial sexual infidelity was decreasing. This may suggest that the need for novelty-seeking in extrapair relations increases over time in an effort to combat boredom in the primary relationship.

Certain developmental stages in a marriage, including pregnancy and the months following the birth of a child, may be times of greater infidelity risk among males (Allen & Baucom, 2001; Brown, 1991; Whisman et al., 2007). Additionally, sexual satisfaction in a relationship could play a role in individuals' decisions to commit infidelity (Liu, 2000). Using data from the National Health and Social Life Survey, Liu (2000) found that the decline of sexual activity frequency in a marriage could lead to infidelity, especially for men. However, given that over two-thirds of adulterous men indicated that they would not have predicted their own infidelity, relationship satisfaction may not be necessarily linked to infidelity. Provided that individuals cheat regardless of marital satisfaction and given the sex differences in the context of length of the primary relationship and infidelity, novelty-seeking may be a motivation for infidelity. Evolutionary psychology provides a rationale for these sex differences in infidelity and novelty-seeking.

Sex Differences

When the United States President Calvin Coolidge (United States, 1923–1929) and the First Lady were visiting a government farm in the state of Kentucky, Mrs. Coolidge asked the guide why there was only one cockerel and yet so many hens. The guide replied the cockerel could copulate many times a day, to which she replied, "Tell that to Mr. Coolidge." When President Coolidge found out, he was equally stunned and asked the guide whether it was the same hen every time, to which the tour guide replied, "Oh, no, Mr. President, a different one every time." The president then replied, "Tell that to Mrs. Coolidge" (Kelley et al., 1999; Wilson, Kuehn, & Beach, 1963).

The term "Coolidge effect" originated from this anecdote and refers to the tendency for men to be more aroused by sexual novelty than women. This effect has been observed in many species. For example, in male Norway rats, sexual satiation is reached after about

1.5 hours when housed with a single female, but males can be kept sexually active for almost 8 hours with the introduction of novel females at regular intervals (Fisher, 1962). Another example comes from fish, in which male guppies that were familiarized with a set of females subsequently directed courtship behavior at unfamiliar females (Kelley et al., 1999). In humans, men rate faces as less attractive after being exposed to them twice, suggesting that men may be more attracted to novelty as opposed to familiarity (Little et al., 2013). Little and colleagues (2014) proposed that men's attraction to novelty may reflect an adaptation promoting the acquisition of new sexual partners. To further examine the Coolidge effect in human sexuality, Hughes and colleagues (2020) investigated sex differences in preferences for sexual novelty and found that men preferred variety in short-term mates more than women did. In addition, they showed that men displayed a preference for frequent modifications in their long-term partners' physical appearance, and that women reported changing their physical appearance more frequently than men. This could suggest that women may attempt to appeal to men's preference for novelty in mating. A second study by Hughes et al. (2020) found that men were more likely to choose a new short-term dating partner in a hypothetical dating task, although the sample size was small (i.e., men [n = 40]; women [n = 56]). To further demonstrate the Coolidge effect in human mating, Joseph et al. (2015) showed that men who were exposed to a novel woman had a significant decrease in time to ejaculation and an increase in sperm count compared to when they were exposed to the same woman six times. Therefore, men may invest more in ejaculates and ejaculation may be quicker when mating with new sexual partners. Consequently, such sex differences in preferences for sexual novelty may have evolved as a male-specific mating strategy (e.g., Hughes et al., 2020).

Indeed, the Coolidge effect is thought to reflect the asymmetric investment in reproduction between males and females. Most evolutionary theories of human mating are rooted in Trivers's (1972) parental investment theory, which notes that the relative amount of obligatory parental investment—the time and energy minimally required to raise viable offspring—varies between males and females and is related to sexual selection processes in ways that generate sex differences in mating behavior across species (Buss & Schmitt, 1993; Kenrick et al., 1990). For example, men in comparison to women incur much lower obligatory parental investment in offspring. That is, men are not obligated to invest as much as women to produce viable offspring (Symons, 1979). Women are obligated, for example, to incur the costs of internal fertilization, placentation, and gestation to successfully reproduce. The minimum physiological obligations of men are considerably less—requiring only the contribution of sperm. Consequently, men's mate preferences are less discriminating than women's, especially in the context of short-term mating (Buss & Schmitt, 1993; Kenrick et al., 1990; Regan, 1998; Regan & Berscheid, 1997; Simpson & Gangestad, 1992). According to parental investment theory, men are the lesser investing sex of and should therefore be less discriminative than women in their choice for mates.

Buss and Schmitt (1993) extended Trivers's (1972) theory by proposing men and women have evolved a repertoire of mating strategies (i.e., sexual strategies theory; SST). One strategy within this repertoire is long-term committed mating. Long-term mating is marked by extended courtship, heavy investment, the emotion of love, and the dedication of resources to the mate and their offspring. Another strategy within this repertoire is short-term mating, which includes anything from intermediate-term relationships to prolonged romances, and brief affairs. Although SST views both sexes as having long-term and short-term strategies within their repertoire, men and women are predicted to differ in certain respects. In long-term mating, for example, the sexes are hypothesized to differ in their expressed mate preferences. For instance, men are predicted to place a greater premium on signals of fertility and reproductive value, such as a woman's youth and physical appearance, whereas women are predicted to place a greater premium on a man's status, maturity, and ability and willingness to devote resources to herself and their children (Buss & Schmitt, 1993; Ellis, 1992). In each case, the differing qualities that men and women preferentially desire solve adaptive problems that men and women have faced over human evolutionary history.

According to SST, both sexes are also hypothesized to pursue short-term mating in delimited contexts, but for different reproductive reasons that reflect sex-specific adaptive problems. For example, when men pursue short-term mates, they are motivated by a desire for sexual variety. Such a desire leads short-term seeking men (not all men) to pursue numerous mates and to consent relatively quickly to sex (Buss & Schmitt, 1993; Symons, 1979). From an evolutionary perspective, considering that short-term seeking men can produce as many as 100 offspring by indiscriminately mating with 100 women in a given year, whereas monogamous men will sire only one child with their partner during that same time period, this represents a strong selective pressure for short-term mating to prefer sexual variety (Barash & Lipton, 2001; Buss & Schmitt, 1993; Symons, 1979). In humanity's ancestral past, there were many adaptive benefits men could reap from securing multiple sexual partners and, in many societies, children of nonmarital unions survive to maturity even without the assistance of the father, due to support provided by kin, charities, or the state (Geary, 2000; Hrdy, 1999). There are also emotional advantages that men gain as a result of short-term mating such as increasing their social status among other men (Greiling & Buss, 2000), and experiencing boosts of self-esteem (Schmitt & Jonason, 2019; Spencer et al., 2002). In contrast, the asymmetry in obligatory parental investment means that women have little to gain in reproductive output by engaging in indiscriminate short-term mating (Bjorklund & Shackelford, 1999; Hinde, 1984). Indeed, sex differences in the desire for sexual variety are cross-culturally universal (Schmitt et al., 2001; Schmitt et al., 2003). Although there could be costs to an unfaithful man such as divorce, diversion of resources from his children, and punishment (e.g., retaliatory infidelity), the societal penalties for unfaithful men in most cultures are relatively minor, especially if the sex partners are not married (Daly & Wilson, 1983).

Provided that the potential reproductive benefits from mating with numerous partners are much higher for men than for women, adaptive desires for sexual variety motivate some men to seek novelty and therefore to actively pursue short-term mates (Bateman, 1948; Buss & Schmitt, 1993; Symons, 1979). From an evolutionary perspective, when pursuing a short-term mating strategy, men likely possess psychological adaptations to secure a many sexual partners (Buss & Schmitt, 1993), and, therefore, motivate novelty-seeking. However, given that not all men are unfaithful, and provided that some women are, another important question is what the individual differences are that distinguish those who seek sexual novelty from those who do not, and whether these novelty-driving individual differences are similar within men and women.

Sociosexual Orientation

Sociosexual orientation (SO) refers to the willingness to engage in sexual activities outside a committed pair bond (Simpson & Gangestad, 1991). Individuals with an unrestricted SO were found to be more likely to engage in sexual activity early on in their relationships and can date and have sex with more than one partner at a time (Simpson & Gangestad, 1991). Such individuals are also more likely to invest less and be less committed to their relationship partners (Simpson & Gangestad, 1991). Morover, Ostovich and Sabini (2004) showed that SO was positively related to sex drive. However, whereas sex drive alone did not seem to be associated with lifetime number of partners, SO was associated with having numerous sexual partners. It may therefore be that sex drive may only affect a person's sexual behavior if the individual has an unrestricted SO. Individuals with an unrestricted SO further display sexually assertive behaviors such as flirting more frequently and engaging in socially dominant behaviors such as maintaining close physical proximity and eye contact during social engagements (Simpson et al., 1996). Seal and Agostinelli (1994) also found that unrestricted individuals are highly responsive to situational sexual cues. Moreover, individuals who have an unrestricted SO are more comfortable having sex outside of a committed relationship and report higher levels of and engagement in extradyadic sex than those with a more restricted SO (Barta & Kiene, 2005; Seal et al.1994; Simpson & Gangestad, 1991). It may therefore be that individuals with an unrestricted SO are more motivated to seek sexual novelty than those with a restricted SO.

Individuals who report greater intentions of committing infidelity (conceptualized as one's perceived likelihood of cheating if the opportunity occurred) are also more likely to have committed infidelity in the past (Buunk, 2011; Weiser, 2012). This means that those with greater intentions to commit infidelity also view it more favorably. Indeed, Martins and colleagues (2016) showed that greater acceptability of infidelity is related to greater likelihood of committing infidelity. Consistent with the parental investment and sexual strategies theories, men are far more likely to exhibit an unrestricted SO than women (Gangestad & Simpson, 1990) and are also more likely to report a primarily sexual motive for committing infidelity than women (Glass & Wright, 1985; Thompson, 1984). Using data from 53 nations, Lippa (2009) found consistent cross-cultural sex differences in sex drive, sociosexuality, and height. Specifically, women are consistently more variable in sex drive than men. Moreover, whereas across nations gender equality and economic development predicted sex differences in SO, no sex differences were found in sex drive or height. This could suggest that such sex differences may be due to biological factors. Indeed, Schmitt's (2005) cross-cultural study of 48 nations showed that in reproductively demanding environments sex differences in SO were large in comparison to nations with more political and economic gender equality.

Infidelity Gender Gap?

Although sex differences in infidelity have been found in most past research (Choi et al., 1994; Laumann et al.1994; Feldman & Cauffman, 1999), male and female rates of infidelity are becoming more similar, particularly in younger cohorts in developed countries (Atkins et al., 2001; Oliver & Hyde, 1993).[1] For instance, Wiederman (1997) found no sex differences in extramarital sex among men and women under age 40 years, while Seal and colleagues (1994) showed that although men are more likely to report a desire for extradyadic partners, when it comes to actual extrapair sex there is no gender difference. The decreasing sex difference in infidelity may be due to social changes, including rising female economic and reproductive independence (Fisher, 1999), or the use of more sensitive measurements of infidelity based on broader definitions of philandering. Overall, however, according to data from the General Social Survey (GSS, 2010–2016), men are more likely to report infidelity (i.e., having sex with someone other than spouse) while married (20%) in comparison to women (13%). Yet it could be that this gender gap varies by age. For example, women between the ages of 18 and 29 years were more likely to cheat (11%) than men (10%), but this gender gap reverses soon after between the ages of 30–34 years and grows wider in older age groups.

From an evolutionary perspective, there are many ways women may reproductively benefit from novelty-seeking in short-term mating, including benefits specific to selective infidelity (Greiling & Buss, 2000). For instance, married women's short-term strategy may be designed for women to obtain men of higher genetic quality than their husbands, especially finding men who possess heritable traits related to high status or physical attractiveness that their husbands do not possess (Banfield & McCabe, 2001; Gangestad & Thornhill, 1997; Greiling & Buss, 2000). According to the "sexy son" hypothesis (Weatherhead, & Robertson, 1979), and strategic pluralism theory (Gangestad, & Simpson, 2000), women may increase their likelihood of bearing attractive sons by mating with attractive men, therefore increasing the chances that such sons will attract more women. Indeed, due

---

[1] Note: the word "gender" in the context of "gender gap" refers to differences between self-identitified men and women.

to the trade-offs women face in choosing mates, they may pursue a dual-mating strategy (Gangestad & Simpson, 2000; Pillsworth & Haselton, 2006), whereby investment is secured through one partner and good genes through other partners. This is in line with the good-genes hypothesis of female extrapair mating (Buss & Schmitt, 1993; Gangestad & Simpson, 2000; Gangestad et al., 2007). Therefore, sexual novelty may play a role in women's short-term mating, specifically for adding genetic diversity to their offspring, providing a hedge against pathogens and diseases. For instance, when women were asked to sniff the t-shirts of anonymous men and to select those they considered sexiest, they chose the t-shirts of men with different genes in a specific part of the immune system, the major histocompatibility complex (Wedekind et al., 1995). Indeed, women who were married to men with similar genes in this part of the immune system were more adulterous and have more extradyadic affairs when they shared these same genes with their husbands (Garver-Apgar et al., 2006).

Fisher (1992) suggested that beyond increasing genetic variety in offspring, unfaithful women may also gain economic resources from their extramarital partners, as well as additional support with parenting duties in case they are abandoned by their primary partner. This would be in line with Buss's (2000) "back-up" mate theory, whereby women may use extradyadic partners as a means of finding a more desirable mate (i.e., trading up) or finding someone who could supply protection or resources when the primary partner is not around. It could therefore be that under certain ecological conditions (i.e., harsh or unpredictable environments), women may be more likely to seek sexual novelty from extradyadic partners who are willing and able to provide better or back-up financial support for their offspring. Indeed, Olderbak and Figueredo (2010) found that in adverse conditions people are more likely to pursue a "fast life strategy" (Giudice et al. 2015), which is characterized by high novelty seeking (Figueredo et al., 2006), short-term temporal orientations (Kruger et al., 2008; Ponzi et al., 2015), early puberty (Webster et al., 2014), insecure attachment (Belsky et al., 1991; Chisholm, 1993), and having larger numbers of sexual partners (Dishion et al., 2012; Luoto et al., 2019). However, Barbaro and colleagues (2017) proposed an alternative hypothesis whereby these correlational relationships may be confounded by shared genes.

Attachment Model

According to attachment theory (Bowlby, 1988), internal representations or working models of close attachment relationships begin in childhood and are incorporated into an individual's developing personality structure (Bowlby, 1973). These working models guide the formation and maintenance of romantic pair-bonds by motivating and regulating behavioral and cognitive responses to specific social circumstances (Hazan & Shaver, 1987). The lack of an internalized secure base and positive feedback could affect the extent to which individuals perceive themselves worthy of love and attention from others and the extent to which they perceive others to be supportive of them. For instance, as a relationship develops, there is a shift away from the initial phases of sexual attraction, fueled by reactivity to novelty and reward, toward the appreciation of familiarity. This is a change from a reward system triggered by external cues to a system responsive to internal cues. Indeed, individuals with a secure attachment have more stable relationships and less extradyadic relationships (Schmitt & Jonason, 2015). However, those who have experienced inconsistent and unpredictable feedback in their early childhood, or, according to some research, early romantic relationships in adolescence (Allen et al., 2018), may not develop feelings of security and familiarity in their romantic relationships confounded with shared genes (Barbaro et al., 2017). Such individuals are likely to develop an insecure attachment style (i.e., anxious or avoidant), and according to life history theory, are also more likely to adopt a faster life history strategy (Belsky, 1997). Individuals high in attachment anxiety feel that their needs for intimacy are not being met in their current relationships (for review, see Shaver & Mikulincer, 2007) and use sex to meet their unmet needs (Birnbaum et al., 2006). Accordingly, they may be more likely than individuals low in attachment anxiety to seek novelty in sexual partners to fulfill their need for intimacy and reassurance from others. Individuals high in attachment avoidance are chronically less committed to their relationships (DeWall et al., 2011) and have more permissive sexual attitudes (Brennan & Shaver, 1995; Gentzler & Kerns, 2004; Hazan & Zeifman, 1994). This in turn can make them more likely to pursue novelty in extrapair mateships to fulfill their need for independence and autonomy in their primary relationship. Indeed, both styles of insecure attachment are associated with infidelity (Bogaert & Sadava, 2002; Drigotas et al., 1999; Smith, 1994). Additionally, there may be sex differences in attachment style and infidelity. For example, Allen and Beacom (2004) found that men with a more avoidant attachment style had the largest number of extradyadic partners, whereas women who have had affairs had a more anxious attachment style. Moreover, women high in attachment anxiety were more likely to seek sexual novelty through infidelity than men (Bogaert & Sadava, 2002).

The question is in what ways does novelty-seeking motivate the links between attachment anxiety and avoidance and infidelity. Schmitt and Jonason (2015) suggested that the sex-specific links between dismissing attachment and permissive sexuality are likely not cross-cultural universals, often failing to show up in African and Asian cultures. This could have implications for novelty-seeking being a factor in WEIRD (i.e., Western Educated, Industrialized, Rich, and Democratic) samples and their infidelity, but not in all cultures. It may be, for instance, that aspects of non-WEIRD cultures might overwhelm novelty-seeking mechanisms that lead to infidelity in WEIRD cultures. Moreover, the associations slightly differed across sexes and across short-term mating indicators, such that infidelity differed from sociosexuality (e.g., Schmitt & Shackelford, 2008).

Provided that humans have evolved to maintain attachment to protective individuals, early insecure attachment and psychosocial stress could heighten sensitivity to cues about risks in the environment and therefore may motivate a switch toward reproductive strategies that favor higher mating effort and early reproduction (Del Giudice, 2009). As such, novelty-seeking in the form of infidelity may be an adaptive trait or strategy in a risky or unpredictable environment (Del Giudice, 2009).

Big Five

Researchers have also explored the relationship between infidelity and the "Big Five" personality traits—openness to new experience, conscientiousness, extraversion, agreeableness, and neuroticism—and related traits. Individuals who engage in infidelity are more open to new experiences and extroverted than their partners (Orzeck & Lung, 2005; Wiederman & Hurd, 1999; Yeniceri & Kokdemir, 2006), as well as more susceptible to boredom (Hendrick & Hendrick, 1987). Sexual infidelity has also been associated with low agreeableness (Costa & McCrae, 1992; Graziano & Eisenberg, 1997), low conscientiousness, and higher neuroticism, or lacking positive psychological adjustment (Whisman, 2007). In fact, individuals whose spouses have a low degree of agreeableness or conscientiousness were more likely to engage in infidelity (Shackelford et al., 2008). Further, individuals in relationships with a similar degree of agreeableness, conscientiousness, neuroticism, and openness to new experiences to their partner were more likely to be faithful (Drigotas et al., 1999; Orzeck & Lung 2005). Based on the available data, both low agreeableness and conscientiousness are most strongly related to infidelity (compared to the other "Big Five" traits) and these associations are found across cultures. For instance, a study of 10 world regions, including North America, South America, western Europe, eastern Europe, southern Europe, the Middle East, Africa, Oceania, South Asia and East Asia, individuals with a low degree of agreeableness or conscientiousness were found to be more unfaithful (Schmitt, 2004b). This is in line with previous findings showing that novelty-seeking was linked to the Big Five traits of high extraversion and openness to experience as well as low agreeableness and conscientiousness (Gocłowska et al., 2019; Hoyle et al., 2000; Wills et al., 1994). This could suggest that individuals with these specific trait-combinations of the Big Five may be particularly likely to seek sexual novelty and to pursue extradyadic relationships to fulfill their need for new experiences.

Dark Triad

The Dark Triad, a cluster of personality traits including psychopathy, narcissism, and Machiavellianism (Paulhus & Williams, 2002), represents a self-serving style of social interaction whereby individuals may manipulate and exploit social groups or individuals for resources (Jonason & Webster, 2012). The Dark Triad is further characterized by low rates of conscientiousness, higher rates of risk-taking impulsivity, and an aggressive nature and need for sexual variety (Jonason et al., 2009; Jonason et al., 2010; Jonason et al., 2010; Mealey, 1995; Paulhus & Williams, 2002; Vazire & Funder, 2006). Moreover, individuals who possess these traits tend to have a less restricted mating style and more sexual partners (Jonason et al., 2009). Consequently, those who are involved in romantic relationships, may be especially susceptible to leave their pair bonds for new mates (Foster et al., 2006). In addition, these individuals may be more likely to develop a strategy of mate poaching to satisfy their competitive, aggressive, and novelty-seeking nature (Schmitt & Buss, 2001).

Indeed, all the Dark Triad traits have been linked with low commitment in relationships and with sexual promiscuity (Aly & Chamorro-Premuzic, 2010; Brewer & Abell, 2015). Moreover, higher scores on these traits are associated with poaching others from existing relationships, being poached by others to form new relationships, and greater involvement in infidelity (Browne, 2015; Buss & Shackelford, 1997; Hurlbert et al., 1994). Specifically, in a longitudinal study of 123 married couples, McNulty and Widman (2014) demonstrated that sexual narcissism was positively related to infidelity. In addition, Brewer and colleagues (2015) found that among heterosexual women (n = 102, age = 18-42 years), higher scores of narcissism were associated with greater infidelity as well as intentions to be unfaithful in the future. Conversely, Jones and Weiser (2014) did not find this association in narcissistic women, but only in narcissistic men. Individuals who score high on this trait tend to also have early sexual activity and more sex partners (Visser et al., 2010). Indeed, in their study of 884 participants (age = 18–74 years) Jones and Weiser (2014) reported that psychopathy is a robust predictor of infidelity in romantic relationships. This was further supported by Brewer and colleagues (2015) who showed that among 102 heterosexual women (age = 18–42 years), psychopathy was positively associated with intentions of being unfaithful. But also, Machiavellianism has been associated with infidelity. A large-scale study that included Caucasians, East and South Asians, and participants of other ethnicities (age range 18–74 years) showed that Machiavellianism was positively related to infidelity (Jones & Weiser, 2014). It could therefore be argued that the novelty-seeking, risk-taking, aggressive, and impulsive nature of such opportunistic individuals may facilitate access to more novel sexual or romantic partners. Indeed, when measured as the number of partners and the variability associated with a disinhibited sexual style, the Dark Triad traits demonstrate increased reproductive success (Jonason et al., 2009).

Especially, the robust link between psychopathy and novelty-seeking and infidelity (in both men and women) could indicate that psychopathy may serve as a reproductive strategy (Mealey, 1995). Therefore, psychopathy as a strategy may be aligned with a fast life history strategy (Jonason, Koenig, & Trost, 2010). It is further possible that the antisocial, impulsive, and manipulative nature of psychopathic individuals may predispose them to seek sexual novelty. However, Jones and Weiser (2014) found that whereas psychopathy was the primary predictor of infidelity in men, both psychopathy and Machiavellianism predicted infidelity in women. One explanation as to why Machiavellianism predicted infidelity among women, but not men, is that women are likely to suffer greater consequences following infidelity. For example, a woman's infidelity is more likely to result in dissolution of the relationship (Brand et al., 2007).

Consequently, adopting a Machiavellian strategy could facilitate committing infidelity in a more risk-averse way that would maximize a woman's benefits. Indeed, Jones and Weiser (2014) found that Machiavellian individuals did not ruin their relationship as a result of infidelity as compared with psychopathic individuals. Their findings could be explained in several ways. For one, Machiavellian individuals are generally not impulsive, tend to delay gratification, and are better at hiding their behaviors such as through planning alibis to make their infidelity difficult to detected (Jones & Paulhus, 2011b). For instance, when a woman seeks sexual novelty to cultivate the genes of a more attractive and dominant man, she would need to make sure that her primary partner is unaware of the infidelity. In such a scenario, she would benefit from the calculated Machiavellian strategy. It may therefore be that novelty-seeking may be especially linked to Machiavellian women. Future studies could focus on exploring this gender difference further, including evolved mechanisms that specifically link parts of the Dark Triad to sexual novelty-seeking and infidelity across different cultures and ecologies.

Combined, these findings provide strong support for the origins of individual differences in the context of sexual strategies (Buss, 2009; Penke et al., 2007) and could explain why some individuals may be particularly likely to seek sexual novelty. Alternatively, certain genetic variants may predispose individuals for such antisocial traits which appear to be especially favorable for mating success (Jonason et al., 2009).

Is it All in Our Genes?

Data from genetics suggests that there may be biological mechanisms that could influence the persistence of sexual novelty seeking and frequency of infidelity worldwide. For example, the relationship between dopamine and sexual desire and behavior in humans was initially proposed when patients with Parkinson's disease noticed having an increase in sex drive as a result of L-DOPA (Bowers et al., 1971). Indeed, due to the dopaminergic reward pathway's influence on pleasure, physiological arousal, and intrinsic reward (Peterson, 2005), polymorphisms along dopamine receptor genes have been previously associated with various behavioral phenotypes such as sensation-seeking (Congdon et al., 2008; Ding et al., 2002). For instance, individuals who carry the dopamine receptor gene (DRD4) have increased sexual desire and arousal (Ben Zion et al., 2006), and score higher on impulsivity (Eisenberg et al., 2007), novelty-seeking (Ebstein et al., 1996), and risk-taking (Carpenter et al., 2011; Dreber et al., 2011). Specifically, individuals with at least one allele containing seven or more repeats (7R+) on the DRD4 have reduced binding affinities and receptor densities for dopamine neurotransmission in the reward pathway (Schoots & Van Tol, 2003). Consequently, those carrying these long alleles are susceptible to sensation-seeking behaviors, which include novelty-seeking, and may lead to differential reproduction and survival (see Harpending & Cochran, 2002; Wang, 2004). Moreover, Garcia and colleagues (2010) found that men and women with longer dopamine genes are more promiscuous (e.g., have more one-night stands and casual sex) and are more likely to be unfaithful. It could be that instead of having more dopamine, those promiscuous thrill-seekers may have particular types of dopamine receptors that could require more dopamine to have the same effect as that experienced by a non-thrill-seeking person. In other words, an individual with these long alleles may feel the need for more sensation-seeking behaviors to boost their dopamine levels and experience a thrill.

Moreover, variation in certain genes (polymorphism) could lead to individual differences in mating systems. For instance, monogamous male voles were shown to express higher oxytocin receptor density in the nucleus accumbens than nonmonogamous male voles (Ophir et al., 2012). Such differences have also been found in humans. For instance, Zietsch and colleagues (2015) tried to determine whether some people are more inclined toward infidelity by looking at the link between promiscuity and specific variants of vasopressin and oxytocin receptor genes. The study investigated Finnish twins and their siblings (n = 7378) who had been in a relationship for at least one year and found that 9.8% of men and 6.4% of women reported that they had two or more sexual partners in the previous year. The study further demonstrated that while oxytocin genes were not linked with sexual behavior in either gender, there was a significant relationship between five different variants of the vasopressin gene and infidelity but only in women. Specifically, 40% of the variation in promiscuous behavior could be attributed to genes in women. To investigate the role of oxytocin in sexual behavior, Scheele and colleagues (2013) conducted two experiments with heterosexual men in a long-term relationship. Participants received either a dose of oxytocin intranasally or a placebo and were shown photographs of their female partners and photographs of other (unfamiliar) women. fMRI scans of the participants' brains revealed that indeed, intranasal oxytocin treatment led these men to perceive their partner's face as more attractive than that of an unfamiliar woman. These findings indicate that it may not be familiarity which activates the reward system, but rather oxytocin that leads to pair-bonded men's enhanced perception of their partner's attractiveness and reward value compared with other women. Similarly, men in monogamous relationships who received oxytocin intranasally kept a greater distance when approaching or being approached by an unfamiliar attractive woman compared to those who received a placebo (Scheele et al., 2012). Conversely, in single men, oxytocin had no effect. Therefore, although oxytocin was previously shown to increase trust toward others, it seems that for men in committed relationships, oxytocin may reinforce monogamy. Indeed, from an evolutionary perspective, oxytocin should strengthen pair bonds and motivate the provision of partners and offspring.

However, when interpreting such findings, it is important to note their limitations. For example, given that most data were collected from self-report measures, it may be that instead of being more promiscuous, individuals with the DRD4 or 7R+ were more likely to report that they had more one-night stands and were more unfaithful compared to others. Moreover, a single gene cannot be associated with a specific behavioral trait. Therefore, it cannot be concluded that a set of genes can hardwire individuals to be unfaithful. It is, however, likely that different groups of genes could be responsible for multiple traits, which could influence individuals' decisions to be unfaithful and potentially drive people to commit infidelity. The question then becomes whether humans, unlike animals, can have complete rational control over their behaviors and actions.

Self-Control

Self-control refers to the capacity for resisting impulses or desires and refraining from acting on them to attain long-term goals (Baumeister et al., 2007). It is related to better adjustment, better relationships, and emotional responses as well as secure attachment (Tangney et al., 2004). In addition, self-control has been linked to the Big Five traits, such as low neuroticism and high agreeableness, extraversion, and openness (Andrei et al., 2014; De Vries & Van Gelder, 2013; Green et al., 2016).

In recent years, research on self-control and self-regulatory processes has contributed to the understanding of relationship dynamics (e.g., Finkel & Campbell, 2001; Finkel & Rusbult, 2008). However, it has also sparked the debate of whether men tend to be more unfaithful than women due to having less self-control. In order to explore this sex difference, Tidwell and Eastwick (2013) conducted two experiments. In the first study, participants (n male = 70, n female = 148) were asked to recall an instance when they were attracted to a member of the opposite sex who was unavailable ("off limits"). Participants were further asked to rate the strength of their attraction and sexual desire as well as their attempt to intentionally control that desire. The study demonstrated that although men were more likely to report acting on their attraction than were women, they did not differ in the extent to which they exerted self-control. Instead, men experienced stronger impulses to pursue attractive alternatives relative to women and consequently were more likely to act on those impulses. This suggests that rather than having less self-control than women, men's stronger sexual impulses could override their ability for self-control, which then leads to greater sexual novelty-seeking.

To further investigate the strength of sexual impulse relative to the strength of impulse control, Tidwell and Eastwick (2013) conducted a second study for which they recruited 600 participants (n male = 326, n female = 274) to take part in in a "Partner Selection Game." Both men and women viewed images of opposite-sex individuals that were tagged either "good for you" or "bad for you" and had to accept or reject potential partners based on these computer-generated tags. Whereas in some trials, participants were instructed to either accept or reject the potential candidates, in other trials, they were instructed to go against their impulse by accepting undesirable candidates or rejecting desirable candidates. The study demonstrated that men displayed greater self-control than women, however they also experienced a much stronger impulse (measured by longer response times) to accept the desirable partners and this impulse partially explained men's poor performance on the task in comparison to women. From an evolutionary perspective, there are two explanations. For one, it could be that men performed worse because they tend to pay more attention to women's physical attractiveness. As such, although men were shown to have self-control over their attention, it may be that they are more likely to be impulsively drawn to women who are attractive. Another explanation is that sexual impulses are older than self-control, which may have evolved later with the emergence of transmitted culture (see Finkel et al., 2009) in order to suppress people's sexual urges that could lead to breaking cultural norms and being ostracized by society (Baumeister et al., 2005; Baumeister et al., 2009). Therefore, while men may have stronger sexual impulses than women, they may have developed the ability to exert self-control to prevent having sex with someone who is "off limits" (e.g., a married woman) which could have severe societal consequences. Indeed, Pronk and colleagues (2011) similarly found that individuals in a romantic pair bond who had greater trait self-regulation, flirted less with attractive opposite-sex research confederates.

In addition, Durante and Arsena (2015) demonstrated that fertility status predicted an increase in women's desire for variety, but only for those whose commitment to their marriage had been manipulated by having female participants remove their wedding rings. The manipulation of bondedness may have therefore reduced the desire for sexual novelty in women who kept on their wedding rings. This prorelationship transformation, moving from conflict to confluence (conflict-confluence model, Durante et al., 2016) depends not only on individuals' capacity for self-regulation but moreover on the context and status of the relationship. For instance, when relationship partners have strong conflicts of interest, they should be motivated to act on their own self-interests, whereas when there are strong confluences of interest between partners, they should be motivated to act in line with what would be best for the relationship (Burnette et al., 2014; Finkel & Campbell, 2001; Finkel, De Wall, et al., 2009).

Although the ability to self-regulate evolved sexual impulses should not have been sex differentiated, it is possible that there are differences between men and women in terms of the strength of such impulses and desires (Eastwick, 2009). In comparison to women, men may therefore be more susceptible to seek sexual novelty due to experiencing stronger sexual impulses, however this sex difference seems to disappear once self-control is exerted.

Conclusion

Pair bonding has been suggested to be a critical factor in the evolutionary development of the social brain (Henrich & Muthukrishna, 2021), and although humans have adaptations that motivate them to form intimate pair-bonds (Fisher, 2016; Fisher et al., 2005), novelty-seeking may have provided biological payoffs for both ancestral men and women (Buss & Schmitt, 1993). However, not everyone has a built-in Coolidge effect; therefore, one question is why novelty-seeking is an expressed trait only in certain individuals. Depending partly on their genetic makeup, personality, attachment style, and current relationship qualities, some people may be more prone to seek sexual novelty and pursue extrapair relationships that put them at risk of losing their committed relationship, their reputation, and in some cases careers (e.g., President Bill Clinton, United States 1993–2001). However, there are many important reasons why people benefit from remaining in committed long-term pair bonds, such as well-being, stress relief, and better physical and mental health (Collins & Feeney, 2000; Tay et al., 2013; Myers, 2000). Hence, humans may have evolved mechanisms that lead them to be motivated to remain in romantic pair bonds and aspire to be monogamous, at least long enough to raise viable offspring.

Even so, many couples who remain in a long-term committed relationship will face boredom, which is a predictor of low relationship quality (e.g., Tsapelas et al., 2009) and will therefore need to come up with ways to generate novelty (Aron et al., 2000; Riggle et al., 2016). Although some experimental research showed that it may be possible to manipulate physical intimacy in long-term relationships by increasing partners' oxytocin levels and thereby encouraging more loving pair bonds, such studies do not imply that the answer for high novelty-seekers is to carry oxytocin spray in their pocket. Alternatively, sexual novelty in relationships can be generated by introducing new erotic stimuli or trying new sexual acts and may help restore sexual arousal and relationship satisfaction (e.g., Dawson & Chivers, 2014). For instance, a recent study conducted during the COVID-19 pandemic demonstrated that people who made new additions such as trying new sexual positions and sharing sexual fantasies were more likely to report that their sex life improved (Lehmiller et al., 2020). Similarly, participating in new activities together has been shown to reduce relationship boredom and increase relationship satisfaction (Aron et al., 2000; Carson et al., 2007; Graham, 2008). Indeed, relationship and sexual satisfaction have been consistently shown to be increased by engaging in new and arousing behaviors (Aron et al., 200; Morton & Gorzalka, 2015). It may therefore be that sexual novelty in long-term committed relationships can serve as a buffer for relationship quality as well as sexual satisfaction (e.g., Aron et al., 2000; Rosa et al., 2019; Watson et al., 2016).

Finally, having noted the various factors that could help identify individuals who may be more at risk of experiencing sexual boredom and may therefore be more likely to commit infidelity, it is important to gain an understanding of the underlying motivations both psychosocially and neurobiologically that play a role in individuals' sexual behaviors to self-regulate unconscious urges. Making sense of the evolved mechanisms that can facilitate infidelity can help individuals better understand their own as well as their partners' behaviors. Yet, while evolutionary psychology and biology can shine a light on *why* certain individuals seek sexual novelty, the issue of infidelity needs to be examined from multiple additional perspectives, including legal, political, and religious perspectives (Schmitt & Fuller, 2015). Moreover, given that there may be distinct neurobiological pathways that could be associated with infidelity as well as relationship stability, these behaviors could be perpendicular to each other rather than being complete opposites. Paying attention to the evolved psychological motivations underlying affairs may aid counselors and clinical psychologists in designing more effective, personalized treatments to help patients recover from the psychological distress and trauma infidelity can cause (Gilbert, 2019; Josephs, 2018).

References

Ali, F., & Chamorro-Premuzic, T. (2010). The dark side of love and life satisfaction: Associations with intimate relationships, psychopathy and Machiavellianism. *Personality and Individual Differences*, *48*(2), 228–233.

Allen, E. S., & Atkins, D. C. (2005). The multidimensional and developmental nature of infidelity: Practical applications. *Journal of Clinical Psychology*, *61*(11), 1371–1382.

Allen, E. S., & Baucom, D. H. (2004). Adult attachment and patterns of extradyadic involvement. *Family Process*, *43*(4), 467–488.

Allen, E. S., & Baucom, D. H. (2006). Dating, marital, and hypothetical extradyadic involvements: How do they compare? *Journal of Sex Research*, *43*(4), 307–317.

Allen, E. S., Baucom, D. H., Burnett, C. K., Epstein, N., & Rankin-Esquer, L. A. (2001). Decision-making power, autonomy, and communication in remarried spouses compared with first-married spouses. *Family Relations*, *50*(4), 326–334.

Allen, J. P., Grande, L., Tan, J., & Loeb, E. (2018). Parent and peer predictors of change in attachment security from adolescence to adulthood. *Child Development*, *89*(4), 1120–1132. https://doi.org/10.1111/cdev.12840

Allen, E. S., Rhoades, G. K., Stanley, S. M., Markman, H. J., Williams, T., Melton, J., & Clements, M. L. (2008). Premarital precursors of marital infidelity. *Family Process*, *47*(2), 243–259.

Andrei, F., Mancini, G., Trombini, E., Baldaro, B., & Russo, P. M. (2014). Testing the incremental validity of trait emotional intelligence: Evidence from an Italian sample of adolescents. *Personality and Individual Differences*, *64*, 24–29.

Aron, A., Aron, E. N., & Norman, C. (2004). Self-expansion model of motivation and cognition in close relationships and beyond. In M.B. Brewer & Hewstone (eds.), Self and social identity (pp99-123). Blackwell Publishing.

Aron, A., Norman, C. C., & Aron, E. N. (1998). The self-expansion model and motivation. *Representative Research in Social Psychology*, *22*, 1–13.

Aron, A., Norman, C. C., Aron, E. N., McKenna, C., & Heyman, R. E. (2000). Couples' shared participation in novel and arousing activities and experienced relationship quality. *Journal of Personality and Social Psychology*, *78*(2), 273.

Atkins, D. C., Baucom, D. H., & Jacobson, N. S. (2001). Understanding infidelity: Correlates in a national random sample. *Journal of Family Psychology: JFP: Journal of the Division of Family Psychology of the American Psychological Association (Division 43)*, *15*(4), 735–749. https://doi.org/10.1037//0893-3200.15.4.735

Banfield, S., & McCabe, M. P. (2001). Extra relationship involvement among women: Are they different from men? *Archives of Sexual Behavior*, *30*(2), 119–142.

Barash, D. P., & Lipton, J. E. (2001). *The myth of monogamy*. W.H. Freeman.

Barbaro, N., Boutwell, B., Barnes, J. C., & Shackelford, T. (2017). Genetic confounding of the relationship between father absence and age at menarche. *Evolution and Human Behavior*, *38*, 357–365. https://doi.org/10.1016/j.evolhumbehav.2016.11.007.

Barta, W. D., & Kiene, S. M. (2005). Motivations for infidelity in heterosexual dating couples: The roles of gender, personality differences, and sociosexual orientation. *Journal of Social and Personal Relationships*, *22*(3), 339–360.

Bateman, A. J. (1948). Intra-sexual selection in Drosophila. *Heredity*, *2*(3), 349–368.

Baumeister, R. F., & Alquist, J. L. (2009). Is there a downside to good self-control? *Self and Identity*, *8*(2–3), 115–130.

Baumeister, R. F., DeWall, C. N., Ciarocco, N. J., & Twenge, J. M. (2005). Social exclusion impairs self-regulation. *Journal of personality and social psychology*, *88*(4), 589.

Baumeister, R. F., Vohs, K. D., & Tice, D. M. (2007). The strength model of self-control. *Current Directions in Psychological Science*, *16*(6), 351–355.

Belsky, J. (1997). Theory testing, effect-size evaluation, and differential susceptibility to rearing influence: The case of mothering and attachment. *Child Development*, *68*(4), 598–600.

Belsky, J., Steinberg, L., & Draper, P. (1991). Childhood experience, interpersonal development, and reproductive strategy: An evolutionary theory of socialization. *Child Development, 62*(4), 647–670.

Betzig, L. (1989). Causes of conjugal dissolution: A cross-cultural study. *Current Anthropology, 30*(5), 654–676. https://doi.org/10.1086/203798

Birnbaum, G. E., Reis, H. T., Mikulincer, M., Gillath, O., & Orpaz, A. (2006). When sex is more than just sex: Attachment orientations, sexual experience, and relationship quality. *Journal of Personality and Social Psychology, 91*(5), 929.

Bjorklund, D. F., & Shackelford, T. K. (1999). Differences in parental investment contribute to important differences between men and women. *Current Directions in Psychological Science, 8*(3), 86–89.

Bogaert, A. F., & Sadava, S. (2002). Adult attachment and sexual behavior. *Personal Relationships, 9*(2), 191–204.

Bowlby, J. (1973). *Attachment and loss. Volume 2: Separation, anxiety and anger.* London: The Hogarth Press and the Institute of Psychoanalysis.

Bowlby, J. (1988). Developmental psychiatry comes of age. *The American Journal of Psychiatry, 145*(1), 1-10.

Bowers, M. B., Jr., Van Woert, M., & Davis, L. (1971). Sexual behavior during L-dopa treatment for Parkinsonism. *American Journal of Psychiatry, 127*(12), 1691–1693.

Brand, R. J., Markey, C. M., Mills, A., & Hodges, S. D. (2007). Sex differences in self-reported infidelity and its correlates. *Sex Roles, 57*(1), 101–109.

Brennan, K. A., & Shaver, P. R. (1995). Dimensions of adult attachment, affect regulation, and romantic relationship functioning. *Personality and Social Psychology Bulletin, 21*(3), 267–283.

Brewer, G., & Abell, L. (2015). Machiavellianism and sexual behavior: Motivations, deception and infidelity. *Personality and Individual Differences, 74*, 186–191.

Brown, E.M. (1991). Patterns of infidelity and their treatment. New York: Brunner/Mazel.

Browne, A. (2015). Online infidelity: Gender, narcissism and extraversion as predictors of behaviour and jealousy responses.

Burnette, J. L., Davisson, E. K., Finkel, E. J., Van Tongeren, D. R., Hui, C. M., & Hoyle, R. H. (2014). Self-control and forgiveness: A meta-analytic review. *Social Psychological and Personality Science, 5*(4), 443–450.

Buss, D.M (1985). Human mate selection: Opposites are sometimes said to attract, but in fact we are likely to marry someone who is similar to us in almost every variable. *American Scientist, 73*(1), 47–51.

Buss, D. M. (2000). Desires in human mating. *Annals of the New York Academy of Sciences, 907*(1), 39–49.

Buss, D. M. (2009). How can evolutionary psychology successfully explain personality and individual differences? *Perspectives on Psychological Science, 4*(4), 359–366.

Buss, D. M., & Schmitt, D. P. (1993). Sexual strategies theory: An evolutionary perspective on human mating. *Psychological Review, 100*(2), 204.

Buss, D. M., & Shackelford, T. K. (1997). Susceptibility to infidelity in the first year of marriage. *Journal of Research in Personality, 31*(2), 193–221.

Buunk, B. (2011). Extramarital behavioral intentions scale. In T. D. Fisher, C. M. Davis, W. L. Yarber, & S. L. Davis (Eds.), *Handbook of sexuality related measures* (3rd ed., pp. 250–251). Routledge.

Buunk, B. P., & Dijkstra, P. (2004). Gender differences in rival characteristics that evoke jealousy in response to emotional versus sexual infidelity. *Personal Relationships, 11*(4), 395–408.

Carpenter, J. P., Garcia, J. R., & Lum, J. K. (2011). Dopamine receptor genes predict risk preferences, time preferences, and related economic choices. *Journal of Risk and Uncertainty, 42*(3), 233–261.

Carson, J. W., Carson, K. M., Gil, K. M., & Baucom, D.H. (2007).Self-expansion as a mediator of relationship improvements in a mindfulness intervention. *Journal of marital and family therapy. 33*(4): 517–28. https://doi.org/10.1111/j.1752-0606.2007.00035.x. PMID: 17935533

Chisholm, J. (1993). Death, hope, and sex: Life-history theory and the context of reproductive strategies. *Current Anthropology, 34(1), 1-24.* 10.1086/204131.

Choi, K. H., Catania, J. A., & Dolcini, M. M. (1994). Extramarital sex and HIV risk behavior among US adults: Results from the National AIDS Behavioral Survey. *American Journal of Public Health, 84*(12), 2003–2007.

Collins, N. L., & Feeney, B. C. (2000). A safe haven: An attachment theory perspective on support seeking and caregiving in intimate relationships. *Journal of Personality and Social Psychology, 78*(6), 1053.

Congdon, E., Lesch, K. P., & Canli, T. (2008). Analysis of DRD4 and DAT polymorphisms and behavioral inhibition in healthy adults: Implications for impulsivity. *American Journal of Medical Genetics Part B: Neuropsychiatric Genetics, 147*(1), 27–32.

Costa, P. T., & McCrae, R. R. (1992). Normal personality assessment in clinical practice: The NEO Personality Inventory. *Psychological Assessment*, *4*(1), 5.

Daly, J. A., & Wilson, D. A. (1983). Writing apprehension, self-esteem, and personality. *Research in the Teaching of English*, *17*(4), 327–341.

Daly, M., & Wilson, M. (1988). *Homicide*. Transaction.

Dawson, S. J., & Chivers, M. L. (2014). Gender differences and similarities in sexual desire. *Current Sexual Health Reports*, *6*(4), 211–219.

Del Giudice, M. (2009). Sex, attachment, and the development of reproductive strategies. *Behavioral and Brain Sciences*, *32*(1), 1.

De Vries, R. E., & Van Gelder, J. L. (2013). Tales of two self-control scales: Relations with Five-Factor and HEXACO traits. *Personality and Individual Differences*, *54*(6), 756–760.

DeWall, C. N., Lambert, N. M., Slotter, E. B., Pond, R. S., Jr., Deckman, T., Finkel, E. J., . . . Fincham, F. D. (2011). So far away from one's partner, yet so close to romantic alternatives: Avoidant attachment, interest in alternatives, and infidelity. *Journal of Personality and Social Psychology*, *101*(6), 1302.

Ding, Y. C., Chi, H. C., Grady, D. L., Morishima, A., Kidd, J. R., Kidd, K. K., . . . Moyzis, R. K. (2002). Evidence of positive selection acting at the human dopamine receptor D4 gene locus. *Proceedings of the National Academy of Sciences*, *99*(1), 309–314.

Dishion, T. J., Ha, T., & Véronneau, M. H. (2012). An ecological analysis of the effects of deviant peer clustering on sexual promiscuity, problem behavior, and childbearing from early adolescence to adulthood: An enhancement of the life history framework. *Developmental Psychology*, *48*(3), 703.

Dreber, A., Rand, D. G., Wernerfelt, N., Garcia, J. R., Vilar, M. G., Lum, J. K., & Zeckhauser, R. (2011). Dopamine and risk choices in different domains: Findings among serious tournament bridge players. *Journal of Risk and Uncertainty*, *43*(1), 19–38.

Drigotas, S. M., Safstrom, C. A., & Gentilia, T. (1999). An investment model prediction of dating infidelity. *Journal of Personality and Social Psychology*, *77*(3), 509.

Druckerman, P. (2007). *Lust in Translation: The Rules of Infidelity from Tokyo to Tennessee*. Penguin Press.

Durante, K. M., & Arsena, A. R. (2015). Playing the field: The effect of fertility on women's desire for variety. *Journal of Consumer Research*, *41*(6), 1372–1391.

Durante, K. M., Eastwick, P. W., Finkel, E. J., Gangestad, S. W., & Simpson, J. A. (2016). Pair-bonded relationships and romantic alternatives: Toward an integration of evolutionary and relationship science perspectives. In J.M. Olson & M.P. Zanna (Eds), *Advances in experimental social psychology*, 2016 (pp. 1–74). Academic Press. (Advances in Experimental Social Psychology; Vol. 53). Academic Press Inc. http://doi.org/10/1016/bs.aesp.2015.09.001

Eastwick, P. W. (2009). Beyond the pleistocene: Using phylogeny and constraint to inform the evolutionary psychology of human mating. *Psychological Bulletin*, *135*(5), 794.

Ebstein, R. P., Novick, O., Umansky, R., Priel, B., Osher, Y., Blaine, D., . . . Belmaker, R. H. (1996). Dopamine D4 receptor (D4DR) exon III polymorphism associated with the human personality trait of novelty seeking. *Nature Genetics*, *12*(1), 78–80.

Eisenberg, D. T., Campbell, B., MacKillop, J., Lum, J. K., & Wilson, D. S. (2007). Season of birth and dopamine receptor gene associations with impulsivity, sensation seeking and reproductive behaviors. *PLoS One*, *2*(11), e1216.

Ellis, B. J. (1992). The evolution of sexual attraction: Evaluative mechanisms in women. *The Adapted Mind: Evolutionary Psychology and the Generation of Culture* (pp. 267–288). Oxford University Press.

Epstein, E., & Gutman, R. (1984) Mate selection in man: Evidence, theory, and outcome. *Social Biology*, *31*(3-4), 243–278.

Feldman, S. S., & Cauffman, E. (1999). Your cheatin' heart: Attitudes, behaviors, and correlates of sexual betrayal in late adolescents. *Journal of Research on Adolescence*, *9*(3), 227–252.

Figueredo, A. J., Vásquez, G., Brumbach, B. H., Schneider, S. M., Sefcek, J. A., Tal, I. R., . . . Jacobs, W. J. (2006). Consilience and life history theory: From genes to brain to reproductive strategy. *Developmental Review*, *26*(2), 243–275.

Finkel, E. J., & Campbell, W. K. (2001). Self-control and accommodation in close relationships: An interdependence analysis. *Journal of Personality and Social Psychology*, *81*(2), 263.

Finkel, E. J., DeWall, C. N., Slotter, E. B., Oaten, M., & Foshee, V. A. (2009). Self-regulatory failure and intimate partner violence perpetration. *Journal of Personality and Social Psychology*, *97*(3), 483.

Finkel, E. J., & Rusbult, C. E. (2008). Prorelationship motivation: An interdependence theory analysis of situations with conflicting interests. In J. Y. Shah & W. L. Gardner (Eds.), *Handbook of motivation science* (pp. 547–560). Guilford Press.

Fisher, A. E. (1962). Effects of stimulus variation on sexual satiation in male rat. *Journal of Comparative and Physiological Psychology, 55*, 614–620.

Fisher, H. E (1992). *Anatomy of love: The natural history of monogamy, adultery, and divorce*. Norton.

Fisher, H. E. (1999). *The first sex: The natural talents of women and how they are changing the world.* New York: Random House.

Fisher, H. (2016). *Anatomy of love: A natural history of mating, marriage, and why we stray (completely revised and updated with a new introduction)*. Norton.

Fisher, H., Aron, A., & Brown, L. L. (2005). Romantic love: An fMRI study of a neural mechanism for mate choice. *Journal of Comparative Neurology, 493*(1), 58–62.

Forste, R., & Tanfer, K. (1996). Sexual exclusivity among dating, cohabiting, and married women. *Journal of Marriage and the Family, 58*(1) 33–47.

Foster, J. D., Shrira, I., & Campbell, W. K. (2006). Theoretical models of narcissism, sexuality, and relationship commitment. *Journal of Social and Personal Relationships, 23*(3), 367–386.

Gangestad, S. W., Garver-Apgar, C. E., & Simpson, J. A. (2007). Changes in women's mate preferences across the ovulatory cycle. *Journal of Personality and Social Psychology, 92*, 151–163.

Gangestad, S. W., & Simpson, J. A. (2000). The evolution of mating: Trade-offs and strategic pluralism. *Behavioral and Brain Sciences, 23*, 675–687.

Gangestad, S. W., & Thornhill, R. (1997). The evolutionary psychology of extrapair sex: The role of fluctuating asymmetry. *Evolution and Human Behavior, 18*(2), 69–88.

Garcia, J. R., MacKillop, J., Aller, E. L., Merriwether, A. M., Wilson, D. S., & Lum, J. K. (2010). Associations between dopamine D4 receptor gene variation with both infidelity and sexual promiscuity. *PLoS One, 5*(11), e14162.

Garver-Apgar, C. E., Gangestad, S. W., Thornhill, R., Miller, R. D., & Olp, J. J. (2006). Major histocompatibility complex alleles, sexual responsivity, and unfaithfulness in romantic couples. *Psychological Science, 17*(10), 830–835.

Geary, D. C. (2000). Evolution and proximate expression of human paternal investment. *Psychological Bulletin, 126*(1), 55.

General Social Survey. (2010–2016). Smith, T.W., Marsden, P., Hout, M., & Kim, J. (2012). General social surveys. National Opinion Research Center. https://gss.norc.org/Lists/gssNewsArticles/DispForm.aspx?ID=101&ContentTypeId=0x010097F51E04B6E29A4DA5088910B198C118001E89468CD12E6047A9101BE0A48227BC

Gentzler, A. L., & Kerns, K. A. (2004). Associations between insecure attachment and sexual experiences. *Personal Relationships, 11*(2), 249–265.

Gilbert, P. (2019). Psychotherapy for the 21st century: An integrative, evolutionary, contextual, biopsychosocial approach. *Psychology and Psychotherapy: Theory, Research and Practice, 92*(2), 164–189.

Giudice, M. D., Gangestad, S. W., & Kaplan, H. S. (2015). Life history theory and evolutionary psychology. In D.M. Buss (Ed.), The handbook of evolutionary psychology – Vol 1: Foundations (2nd ed.) (pp.88–114). Wiley.

Glass, S. P., & Wright, T. L. (1985). Sex differences in type of extramarital involvement and marital dissatisfaction. *Sex Roles: A Journal of Research, 12*(9–10), 1101–1120. https://doi.org/10.1007/BF00288108

Gocłowska, M. A., Ritter, S. M., Elliot, A. J., &Baas, M. (2019). Novelty seeking is linked to openness and extraversion, and can lead to greater creative performance. *Journal of personality 87*(2), 252–266.

Graham, J. M. (2008). Self-expansion and flow in couples' momentary experiences: An experience sampling study. *Journal of Personality and Social Psychology, 95*(3), 679–694. https://doi.org/10.1037/0022-3514.95.3.679.

Graziano, W. G., & Eisenberg, N. (1997). Agreeableness: A dimension of personality. In *Handbook of personality psychology* (pp. 795–824). Academic Press.

Green, J. A., O'Connor, D. B., Gartland, N., & Roberts, B. W. (2016). The Chernyshenko Conscientiousness Scales: A new facet measure of conscientiousness. *Assessment, 23*(3), 374–385. https://doi.org/10.1177/1073191115580639

Greiling, H., & Buss, D. M. (2000). Women's sexual strategies: The hidden dimension of extra-pair mating. *Personality and individual Differences, 28*(5), 929–963.

Hansen, G. L. (1987). Extra-dyadic relations during courtship. *Journal of Sex Research, 23*, 382–390.

Harpending, H., & Cochran, G. (2002). In our genes. *Proceedings of the National Academy of Sciences, 99*(1), 10–12.

Hazan, C., & Shaver, P. (1987). Romantic love conceptualized as an attachment process. *Journal of Personality and Social Psychology, 52*(3), 511.

Hazan, C., & Zeifman, D. (1994). *Sex and the psychological tether*. In K. Bartholomew & D. Perlman (Eds.), Attachment processes in adulthood (pp. 151–178). Jessica Kingsley Publishers.

Hendrick, S. S., & Hendrick, C. (1987). Love and sexual attitudes, self-disclosure and sensation seeking. *Journal of Social and Personal Relationships, 4*(3), 281–297.

Henrich, J., Boyd, R., & Richerson, P. J. (2012). The puzzle of monogamous marriage. *Philosophical Transactions of the Royal Society B: Biological Sciences, 367*(1589), 657–669.

Henrich, J., & Muthukrishna, M. (2021). The origins and psychology of human cooperation. *Annual Review of Psychology, 72*, 207–240.

Hinde, R. A. (1984). Why do the sexes behave differently in close relationships? *Journal of Social and Personal Relationships, 1*(4), 471–501.

Hoyle, R. H., Fejfar, M. C., & Miller, J. D. (2000). Personality and sexual risk taking: A quantitative review. *Journal of Personality, 68*(6), 1203–1231.

Hrdy, S. B. (1999). Mother nature: A history of mothers, infants, and natural selection. *New York*: Pantheon books.

Hughes, S. M., Aung, T., Harrison, M. A., LaFayette, J. N., & Gallup, G. G. (2020). Experimental evidence for sex differences in sexual variety preferences: Support for the Coolidge effect in humans. *Archives of Sexual Behavior, 50*(2), 495–509.

Hurlbert, D. F., Apt, C., Gasar, S., Wilson, N. E., & Murphy, Y. (1994). Sexual narcissism: A validation study. *Journal of Sex & Marital Therapy, 20*(1), 24–34.

Jonason, P. K., Koenig, B. L., & Tost, J. (2010). Living a fast life. *Human Nature, 21*(4), 428–442.

Jonason, P. K., Li, N. P., & Teicher, E. A. (2010). Who is James Bond? The Dark Triad as an agentic social style. *Individual Differences Research, 8*(2), 111.

Jonason, P. K., Li, N. P., Webster, G. D., & Schmitt, D. P. (2009). The Dark Triad: Facilitating a short-term mating strategy in men. *European Journal of Personality, 23*(1), 5–18.

Jonason, P. K., & Webster, G. D. (2012). A protean approach to social influence: Dark Triad personalities and social influence tactics. *Personality and Individual Differences, 52*(4), 521–526.

Jones, D. N., & Paulhus, D. L. (2011). The role of impulsivity in the Dark Triad of personality. *Personality and Individual Differences, 51*(5), 679–682. https://doi.org/10.1016/j.paid.2011.04.011

Jones, D. N., & Weiser, D. A. (2014). Differential infidelity patterns among the Dark Triad. *Personality and Individual Differences, 57*, 20–24.

Joseph, P. N., Sharma, R. K., Agarwal, A., & Sirot, L. K. (2015). Men ejaculate larger volumes of semen, more motile sperm, and more quickly when exposed to images of novel women. *Evolutionary Psychological Science, 1*(4), 195–200.

Josephs, L. (2018). *The dynamics of infidelity: Applying relationship science to psychotherapy practice*. American Psychological Association. https://doi.org/10.1037/0000053-000.

Kelley, J. L., Graves, J. A., & Magurran, A. E. (1999). Familiarity breeds contempt in guppies. *Nature, 401*, 661–662.

Kenrick, D. T., Sadalla, E. K., Groth, G., & Trost, M. R. (1990). Evolution, traits, and the stages of human courtship: Qualifying the parental investment model. *Journal of Personality, 58*(1), 97–116.

Kruger, D. J., Reischl, T., & Zimmerman, M. A. (2008). Time perspective as a mechanism for functional developmental adaptation. *Journal of Social, Evolutionary, and Cultural Psychology, 2*(1), 1.

Laumann, E., Gagnon, J., Michael, R., & Michaels, S. (1994). *The social organization of sexuality*. University of Chicago.

Lawson, A., & Samson, C. (1988). Age, gender, and adultery. *British Journal of Sociology, 39*, 409–440.

Lehmiller, J. J., Garcia, J. R., Gesselman, A. N., & Mark, K. P. (2020). Less sex, but more sexual diversity: Changes in sexual behavior during the COVID-19 coronavirus pandemic. *Leisure Sciences, 43*(1-2), 295–304.

Lewandowski, G. W., & Ackerman, R. A. (2006). Something's missing: Need fulfillment and self-expansion as predictors of susceptibility to infidelity. *Journal of Social Psychology, 146*(4), 389–403.

Lippa, R. A. (2009). Sex differences in sex drive, sociosexuality, and height across 53 nations: Testing evolutionary and social structural theories. *Archives of Sexual Behavior, 38*(5), 631–651.

Little, A., DeBruine, L., & Jones, B. (2013). Sex differences in attraction to familiar and unfamiliar opposite-sex faces: Men prefer novelty and women prefer familiarity. *Archives of Sexual Behavior, 43*(5), 973–981. https://doi.org/10.1007/s10508-013-0120-2.

Liu, C. (2000). A theory of marital sexual life. *Journal of Marriage and the Family, 62,* 363–374.

Luoto, S., Krams, I., & Rantala, M. J. (2019). A life history approach to the female sexual orientation spectrum: Evolution, development, causal mechanisms, and health. *Archives of Sexual Behavior, 48*(5), 1273–1308.

Martins, A., Pereira, M., Andrade, R., Dattilio, F.M., Narciso, I., & Canavarro, M.C. (2016). Infidelity in dating relationships: Gender-specific correlates of face-to-face and online extradyadic involvement. *Archives of Sexual Behavior, 45*(1), 193–205.

McNulty, J. K., & Widman, L. (2014). Sexual narcissism and infidelity in early marriage. *Archives of Sexual Behavior, 43*(7), 1315–1325. https://doi.org/10.1007/s10508-014-0282-6.

Mealey, L. (1995). The sociobiology of sociopathy: An integrated evolutionary model. *Behavioral and Brain Sciences, 18*(3), 523–541.

Morton, H., & Gorzalka, B. B. (2015). Role of partner novelty in sexual functioning: A review. *Journal of Sex & Marital Therapy, 41*(6), 593–609.

Myers, D. G. (2000). The funds, friends, and faith of happy people. *American Psychologist, 55*(1), 56.

Neubeck, G., & Schletzer, V. M. (1962). A study of extra-marital relationships. *Marriage and Family Living, 24*(3), 279–281.

Olderbak, S. G., & Figueredo, A. J. (2010). Life history strategy as a longitudinal predictor of relationship satisfaction and dissolution. *Personality and Individual Differences, 49*(3), 234–239.

Oliver, M. B., & Hyde, J. S. (1993). Gender differences in sexuality: A meta-analysis. *Psychological Bulletin, 114*(1), 29.

Ophir, A. G., Gessel, A., Zheng, D. J., & Phelps, S. M. (2012). Oxytocin receptor density is associated with male mating tactics and social monogamy. *Hormones and Behavior, 61*(3), 445–453.

Ostovich, J. M., & Sabini, J. (2004). How are sociosexuality, sex drive, and lifetime number of sexual partners related? *Personality and Social Psychology Bulletin, 30*(10), 1255–1266.

Paulhus, D. L., & Williams, K. M. (2002). The Dark Triad of personality: Narcissism, Machiavellianism, and psychopathy. *Journal of Research in Personality, 36*(6), 556–563.

Penke, L., Denissen, J. J., & Miller, G. F. (2007). The evolutionary genetics of personality. *European Journal of Personality: Published for the European Association of Personality Psychology, 21*(5), 549–587.

Peterson, R. L. (2005). The neuroscience of investing: fMRI of the reward system. *Brain Research Bulletin, 67*(5), 391–397.

Pillsworth, E. G., & Haselton, M. G. (2006). Male sexual attractiveness predicts differential ovulatory shifts in female extra-pair attraction and male mate retention. *Evolution and Human Behavior, 27*(4), 247–258.

Ponzi, D., Henry, A., Kubicki, K., Nickels, N., Wilson, M. C., & Maestripieri, D. (2015). The slow and fast life histories of early birds and night owls: Their future-or present-orientation accounts for their sexually monogamous or promiscuous tendencies. *Evolution and Human Behavior, 36*(2), 117–122.

Pronk, T. M., Karremans, J. C., & Wigboldus, D. H. (2011). How can you resist? Executive control helps romantically involved individuals to stay faithful. *Journal of Personality and Social Psychology, 100*(5), 827.

Pronk, T. M., & Karremans, J. C. (2014). Does executive control relate to sacrificial behavior during conflicts of interests?. *Personal Relationships, 21*(1), 168–175.

Regan, P. C. (1998). What if you can't get what you want? Willingness to compromise ideal mate selection standards as a function of sex, mate value, and relationship context. *Personality and Social Psychology Bulletin, 24*(12), 1294–1303.

Regan, P. C., & Berscheid, E. (1997). Gender differences in characteristics desired in a potential sexual and marriage partner. *Journal of Psychology & Human Sexuality, 9*(1), 25–37.

Riggle, E. D., Rothblum, E. D., Rostosky, S. S., Clark, J. B., & Balsam, K. F. (2016). "The secret of our success": Long-term same-sex couples' perceptions of their relationship longevity. *Journal of GLBT Family Studies, 12*(4), 319–334.

Rosa, M. N., Matthews, S. A., Giuliano, T. A., Thomas, K. H., Swift, B. A., & Mills, M. M. (2019). Encouraging erotic variety: Identifying correlates of, and strategies for promoting, sexual novelty in romantic relationships. *Personality and Individual Differences, 146,* 158–169.

Rusbult, C. E. (1980). Commitment and satisfaction in romantic associations: A test of the investment model. *Journal of Experimental Social Psychology*, *16*(2), 172–186.

Rusbult, C. E., Drigotas, S. M., & Verette, J. (1994). The investment model: An interdependence analysis of commitment processes and relationship maintenance phenomena. In D.J. Canary & L. Stafford (Eds.), Communication and relational maintenance (pp. 115–139). Academic Press.

Scheele, D., Striepens, N., Güntürkün, O., Deutschländer, S., Maier, W., Kendrick, K. M., & Hurlemann, R. (2012). Oxytocin modulates social distance between males and females. *Journal of Neuroscience*, *32*(46), 16074–16079.

Scheele, D., Wille, A., Kendrick, K. M., Stoffel-Wagner, B., Becker, B., Güntürkün, O., . . . Hurlemann, R. (2013). Oxytocin enhances brain reward system responses in men viewing the face of their female partner. *Proceedings of the National Academy of Sciences*, *110*(50), 20308–20313.

Schmitt, D. P. (2004a). Patterns and universals of mate poaching across 53 nations: The effects of sex, culture, and personality on romantically attracting another person's partner. *Journal of Personality and Social Psychology*, *86*(4), 560–584.

Schmitt, D. P. (2004b). The Big Five related to risky sexual behaviour across 10 world regions: Differential personality associations of sexual promiscuity and relationship infidelity. *European Journal of Personality*, *18*(4), 301–319.

Schmitt, D. P. (2005). Sociosexuality from Argentina to Zimbabwe: A 48-nation study of sex, culture, and strategies of human mating. *Behavioral and Brain Sciences*, *28*, 247–275.

Schmitt, D. P., Alcalay, L., Allik, J., Ault, L., Austers, I., Bennett, K. L., et al. (2003). Universal sex differences in the desire for sexual variety: Tests from 52 nations, 6 continents, and 13 islands. *Journal of Personality and Social Psychology*, *85*, 85–104.

Schmitt, D. P., & Buss, D. M. (2001). Human mate poaching: Tactics and temptations for infiltrating existing mateships. *Journal of Personality and Social Psychology*, *80*(6), 894.

Schmitt, D. P., & Fuller, R. C. (2015). On the varieties of sexual experience: Cross-cultural links between religiosity and human mating strategies. *Psychology of Religion and Spirituality*, *7*(4), 314.

Schmitt, D. P., & Jonason, P. K. (2015). Attachment and sexual permissiveness: Exploring differential associations across sexes, cultures, and facets of short-term mating. *Journal of Cross-Cultural Psychology*, *46*(1), 119–133.

Schmitt, D. P., & Jonason, P. K. (2019). Self-esteem as an adaptive sociometer of mating success: Evaluating evidence of sex-specific psychological design across 10 world regions. *Personality and Individual Differences*, *143*, 13–20.

Schmitt, D. P., & Shackelford, T. K. (2008). Big Five traits related to short-term mating: From personality to promiscuity across 46 nations. *Evolutionary Psychology*, *6*, 246–282.

Schmitt, D.P., Shackelford, T.K., Duntley, J., Tooke, W., & Buss, D.M. (2001). The desire for sexual variety as a key to understanding basic human mating strategies. *Personal Relationships*, *8*(4), 425–455.

Schoots, O., & Van Tol, H. H. M. (2003). The human dopamine D4 receptor repeat sequences modulate expression. *Pharmacogenomics Journal*, *3*(6), 343–348.

Seal, D. W., Agostinelli, G., & Hannett, C. A. (1994). Extradyadic romantic involvement: Moderating effects of sociosexuality and gender. *Sex Roles*, *31*, 1–22.

Shackelford, T. K., Besser, A., & Goetz, A. T. (2008). Personality, marital satisfaction, and probability of marital infidelity. *Individual Differences Research*, *6*(1), 13–25.

Shaver, P. R., & Mikulincer, M. (2007). Adult attachment strategies and the regulation of emotion. *Handbook of emotion regulation*, *446*, 465.

Simpson, J. A., & Gangestad, S. W. (1991). Individual differences in sociosexuality: Evidence for convergent and discriminant validity. *Journal of Personality and Social Psychology*, *60*(6), 870.

Simpson, J. A., & Gangestad, S. W. (1992). Sociosexuality and romantic partner choice. *Journal of Personality*, *60*(1), 31–51.

Simpson, J. A., Gangestad, S. W., & Nations, C. (1996). Sociosexuality and relationship initiation: An ethological perspective of nonverbal behavior. In G. J. O. Fletcher & J. Fitness (Eds.), *Knowledge structures in close relationships: A social psychological approach* (pp. 121–146). Lawrence Erlbaum Associates, Inc.

Smith, M. R. (1994). *The moral problem*.

Spencer, J. M., Zimet, G. D., Aalsma, M. C., & Orr, D. P. (2002). Self-esteem as a predictor of initiation of coitus in early adolescents. *Pediatrics*, *109*(4), 581–584.

Symons, D. (1979). *The evolution of human sexuality*. Oxford University Press.

Tangney, J. P., Baumeister, R. F., & Boone, A. L. (2004). High self-control predicts good adjustment, less pathology, better grades, and interpersonal success. *Journal of Personality, 72*(2), 271–324.

Tay, L., Tan, K., Diener, E., & Gonzalez, E. (2013). Social relations, health behaviors, and health outcomes: A survey and synthesis. *Applied Psychology: Health and Well-Being, 5*(1), 28–78. https://doi.org/10.1111/aphw.12000

Thompson, A. P. (1983). Extramarital sex: A review of the research literature. *Journal of Sex Research, 46*, 35–42.

Thompson, A. P. (1984). Emotional and sexual components of extramarital relations. *Journal of Marriage and the Family, 46*(1) 35–42.

Tidwell, N. D., & Eastwick, P. W. (2013). Sex differences in succumbing to sexual temptations: A function of impulse or control? *Personality and Social Psychology Bulletin, 39*(12), 1620–1633.

Trivers, R. (1972). Parental investment and sexual selection. In Campbell, B. (Ed.), Sexual Selection and the Descent of Man (pp.136–179). New York: Aldine de Gruyter.

Tsapelas, I., Aron, A., & Orbuch, T. (2009). Marital boredom now predicts less satisfaction 9 years later. *Psychological Science, 20*(5), 543–545.

Vazire, S., & Funder, D. C. (2006). Impulsivity and the self-defeating behavior of narcissists. *Personality and Social Psychology Review, 10*(2), 154–165.

Visser, B. A., Pozzebon, J. A., Bogaert, A. F., & Ashton, M. C. (2010). Psychopathy, sexual behavior, and esteem: It's different for girls. *Personality and Individual Differences, 48*(7), 833–838.

Wang, E., Ding, Y. C., Flodman, P., Kidd, J. R., Kidd, K. K., Grady, D. L., . . . Moyzis, R. K. (2004). The genetic architecture of selection at the human dopamine receptor D4 (DRD4) gene locus. *American Journal of Human Genetics, 74*(4), 931–944.

Watson, E. D., Séguin, L. J., Milhausen, R. R., & Murray, S. H. (2016). The impact of a couple's vibrator on men's perceptions of their own and their partner's sexual pleasure and satisfaction. *Men and Masculinities, 19*(4), 370–383.

Weatherhead, P. J., & Robertson, R. J. (1979). Offspring quality and the polygyny threshold: "The sexy son hypothesis." *American Naturalist, 113*(2), 201–208.

Webster, G. D., Graber, J. A., Gesselman, A. N., Crosier, B. S., & Schember, T. O. (2014). A life history theory of father absence and menarche: A meta-analysis. *Evolutionary Psychology, 12*(2), 147470491401200202.

Wedekind, C., Seebeck, T., Bettens, F., & Paepke, A. J. (1995). MHC-dependent mate preferences in humans. *Proceedings of the Royal Society of London. Series B: Biological Sciences, 260*(1359), 245–249.

Weiser, D. A. (2012). *Family background and propensity to engage in infidelity: Exploring an intergenerational transmission of infidelity* [Unpublished dissertation, University of Nevada].

Whisman, M. A. (2007). Marital distress and DSM-IV psychiatric disorders in a population-based national survey. *Journal of Abnormal Psychology, 116*(3), 638.

Whisman, M. A., Gordon, C. C., & Chatav, Y. (2007). Predicting sexual infidelity in a population-based sample of married individuals. *Journal of Family Psychology, 21*, 320–324.

Wiederman, M. W. (1997). Extramarital sex: Prevalence and correlates in a national survey. *Journal of Sex Research, 34*(2), 167–174.

Wiederman, M. W., & Hurd, C. (1999). Extradyadic involvement during dating. *Journal of Social and Personal Relationships, 16*(2), 265–274.

Wiggins, J. D., & Lederer, D. A. (1984). Differential antecedents of infidelity in marriage. *American Mental Health Counselors Association Journal, 6*(4), 152-161.

Wills, T. A., Vaccaro, D., & McNamara, G. (1994). Novelty seeking, risk taking, and related constructs as predictors of adolescent substance use: An application of Cloninger's theory. *Journal of Substance Abuse, 6*(1), 1–20.

Wilson, J. R., Kuehn, R. E., & Beach, F. A. (1963). Modification in the sexual behavior of male rats produced by changing the stimulus female. *Journal of Comparative and Physiological Psychology, 56*(3), 636–644. https://doi.org/10.1037/h0042469

Yeniceri, Z., & Kökdemir, D. (2006). University students' perceptions of, and explanations for, infidelity: The development of the Infidelity Questionnaire (INFQ). *Social Behavior & Personality: An International Journal, 34*(6), 639–650.

Zhang, Y., Wang, X., & Pan, S. (2021). Prevalence and patterns of extramarital sex among Chinese men and women: 2000–2015. *Journal of Sex Research, 58*(1), 41–50.

Zietsch, B. P., Westberg, L., Santtila, P., & Jern, P. (2015). Genetic analysis of human extrapair mating: Heritability, between-sex correlation, and receptor genes for vasopressin and oxytocin. *Evolution and Human Behavior, 36*(2), 130–136.

Zion, I. B., Tessler, R., Cohen, L., Lerer, E., Raz, Y., Bachner-Melman, R., . . . Ebstein, R. P. (2006). Polymorphisms in the dopamine D4 receptor gene (DRD4) contribute to individual differences in human sexual behavior: Desire, arousal and sexual function. *Molecular Psychiatry, 11*(8), 782–786.

CHAPTER 12

The Mate Switching Hypothesis for Infidelity

Mike Abrams *and* Lidia Dengelegi Abrams

Abstract

Infidelity toward obtaining a new partner is commonly abetted by the tendency, especially during the peak reproductive years, to continually assess other potential companions' mate value, suitability, and availability. The strategy of maintaining a relationship while seeking other partners can be adaptive for several reasons: (1) Whether in service of finding a new partner or not, infidelity offers the male more potential childbearing partners and provides the female a means to obtain genes from a partner with a superior phenotype, (2) extradyadic sex potentially creates a bond with a new partner and can add to one's perceived security in a relationship while paradoxically easing leaving it, and (3) infidelity can act to mitigate the financial or emotional risks of leaving a partner who has become less desirable. Mate switching infidelity is abetted by many intrinsic factors such as males' tendency to reflexively attend to those with salient sexual features and females' propensity to remain vigilant for new partners who offer superior genes, status, and resources. This chapter details these and several other cultural and evolutionary forces that underlie the mate switching hypothesis of infidelity. It also presents case studies to illuminate the psychological and clinical implications of this practice.

Key Words: mate switching, infidelity, CBT, evolutionary psychology, counseling

When people form romantic bonds there is usually a strong correlation between the intensity of their passion and their expectations for the duration of the relationship. People in love hope and expect to be with their paramour for life. If romantic love were both deep and reliable, most relationships would fulfill this expectation. Unfortunately, the factors that bring people together are often volatile and have short half-lives. The fact that approximately half of all marriages end in divorce (Abrams, 2016) supports this. This results from the volatility of the bonds that sustain relationships, most notably romantic love that tends to diminish in just a few years. Since monogamous relationships are accompanied by partners increasingly performing reassessments of the value of their mate along with vigilance for new mates, most couplings will be precarious.

As Buss has pointed out (Buss et al., 2017), people continue to assess their marketability and to evaluate new potential mates even when in a stable relationship. The self-assessment for marketability to a new mate increases with weak attachment, low relationship satisfaction, a decline in sexual passion (Negash et al., 2019; Guilbault et al., 2020), distrust in a partner's fidelity, and one's having a large number of prior lovers (Maddox, 2013).

The forces that drive people to seek new mates are in a continual battle with a socially endorsed ideal of lifelong bonds. This social imperative contrasts with our tendency for transient monogamy and multiple sexual partners, which we share with other primates. Despite the best efforts of many well-intentioned individuals, innate inclinations often overwhelm the imperatives imposed by marriage or partners' strong intentions of fidelity. We humans simply are not evolved to remain with one partner exclusively and indefinitely. When we nevertheless do so, it is often with frustration and resentment. Intimate bonds during our ancestral past did not adhere to the Western standard of stable monogamy. Indeed, monogamy is rare. In their book *The Myth of Monogamy*, Barash and Lipton (2001) convincingly argue for an innate human tendency for polygamy. They point out that virtually no animals are monogamous, including birds, the genus most often cited as emblematic of monogamy and lifetime mating. Extrapair copulations (EPCs), or what human couples would denote as cheating, are common in birds. Birds like the passerine (*Passeriformes*) and the cockatiel (*Nymphicus hollandicus*), which are known to have stable bonds, also have a significant number of offspring fathered by males outside the pair bond (Fossøy et al., 2006; Spoon et al., 2007). There is also the disillusioning case for the paradigmatic lifetime mating of the prairie vole. These rodents do indeed stay together for life, but the female very often finds the time to mate with other males (Ledford, 2008).

The idyllic goal of marriage for life is more a function of social mores, imposed chiefly in Western countries and in modern times, than a biological reality. Indeed, Helen Fisher and her colleagues observed that 84% of human societies had permitted some form of polygyny (Tsapelas et al., 2011). And when social values permit polygyny, monogamous marriage for life becomes somewhat rare. The tendency to seek extrarelationship lovers is documented in every culture throughout history (Abrams, 2016). In the staid 1950s, C. S. Ford and the psychologist Frank A. Beach (1951) studied 185 human societies and found that 39% approved of extramarital sexual relationships. The bonds of matrimony and other committed relationships are viewed with wariness by the evolutionary psychologist Gordon Gallup, who has estimated that 10%–30% of children are sired by men who are not their legal fathers (cited in Abrams, 2016).

Just as humans have evolved mechanisms to identify people who exploit reciprocal obligations, it seems that we also have them to detect potentially unfaithful mates. This existence of a fidelity cheater detection mechanism is supported by the 15-fold higher nonpaternity rates among men suspicious of their paternity than males with high paternity confidence. Gallup has also pointed out (cited in Abrams, 2016) that the high rate of extrapair pregnancy is a proxy measure of the high rate of female infidelity. Suppose one assumes that most women who engage in extrapair copulations (EPCs) actively attempt to prevent pregnancy. In that case, the 10%–30% rate of nonpaternity implies a much higher rate of EPCs among women.

The ability to detect infidelity may result from an adaptation that underlies jealousy and mate-guarding behaviors (e.g., Buss, 2002). From an evolutionary psychological perspective, an individual who can read an unfaithful partner's affective and behavioral cues would have increased fitness and thereby pass along more offspring. A woman who can identify a man prone to infidelity can minimize the risk of losing resources. Such a man would divert resources away from her and her progeny. In turn, a man who can detect the cues that signal potential or ongoing infidelity by a female partner can minimize the high costs of cuckoldry. Ancestral times were characterized by lethal violence, disease, and deprivation, which yielded a life expectancy not much longer than 30 years (Kaplan et al., 2000). A man in such an epoch spending even a year or two providing sustenance and care to the progeny of another male paid a devastating price in genetic fitness. Men who were vigilant for competing males, put significant effort into mate guarding, and responded with violent rage when their monogamy was threatened, were more successfully in avoiding cuckoldry. The violent rage that was adaptive eons ago continues to be expressed by evolved mechanisms in modern men, often with very adverse consequences. These evolved mechanisms still compel male behaviors that may be destructive to male reproductive potential in modern times. The profound trauma that ensues when discovering that the person to whom one is emotionally or sexually committed has been unfaithful has its origins in the evolved psychological mechanism that protects a man from the genetically destructive act of providing time and resources to the progeny of a competitor. An early human who took a laissez-faire approach to his mate's behavior would have an increased chance of investing in other males' offspring and a diminished likelihood of leaving his own offspring and genes to survive in posterity. As a result, "jealous" genes are more prevalent in modern men.

Besides sexual infidelity, there is also romantic infidelity. The latter is more common in women, who might develop a deep romantic bond with another man (or on occasion with a woman) without ever having sex. Although husbands and lovers find this disturbing, it does not approach the emotional firestorm that ensues when the infidelity is sexual and might expose them to the risk of raising another man's child. David Buss's contention that it is a male adaptation that produces violent jealousy in the face of sexual infidelity is supported by the negative relationship between the length of the second finger to the fourth finger ratio and increased anger with sexual jealousy (Fussell et al., 2011). The second digit to fourth digit ratio correlates with prenatal testosterone levels such that men or women with ring fingers longer than their index fingers were exposed to higher testosterone levels. Those with a more masculinized brain will likely experience more significant distress in response to a partner's sexual infidelity (Buss, 2006). A masculinized brain is not limited to men; it can be found in women whose mothers had congenital adrenal hyperplasia (CAH) or who were exposed to higher levels of androgens in utero (e.g., Fleming et al.

2017). And women born to mothers with CAH tend to display more traditional male behaviors like aggression and jealousy (Abrams, 2016).

Infidelity as the Norm—Prevalence and Incidence

Infidelity is common and even allowing for people's aversion to acknowledging it in surveys (Whisman & Snyder, 2007), it still is disclosed at high rates. In a recent survey study of sexual preferences, I queried 549 participants about whether they had ever cheated in a relationship. The results showed that 28.7% of men and 24.3% of women acknowledged having done so. This infidelity estimate is concordant with data compiled from the General Social Survey conducted six times over 16 years (Schmitt, 2014), which reported that between 22% and 25% of men admitted infidelity. With women, this percentage was somewhat lower, ranging between 10% and 18% in these earlier surveys.

Animals who mate for life, such as birds, offer unique insight into short- and long-term mating benefits. Both birds of a mated pair increase their fitness because they can provide superior protection and nutrition for their hatchlings when working together. However, both sexes also benefit from extrapair copulations, although for different reasons. EPCs are beneficial for the male as he can procreate with more females, which increases the chance of his genes being transmitted to future generations. Females benefit from EPCs by acquiring genes from a male more genetically fit than her mate. Female birds have evolved the ability to discern the correlates of good genes in males. Male birds evolved cues to their genetic endowments like the extravagant plumage of the peacock (Loyau et al., 2005), or the maintenance of coveted territory by the bowerbird (Pruett-Jones & Pruett-Jones, 1994), or displays of fighting ability by the cowbird (O'Loghlen & Rothstein, 2012). Physically attractive attributes can be as important to humans as they are to other animals. Humans prefer symmetrical faces absent of lesions or other indicators of immune deficiency. They prefer a body structure that reveals sex-typical hormone levels. This is exemplified by a male preference for women with more gluteofemoral fat—especially when that fat results in hips about a third wider than the waist. For women's preferences, broad shoulders, lower body fat, and greater height are desirable. In addition to the importance of physical attributes, humans' choice of mates is more complex, with state of mind and intent being a factor, and many nonphysical features being considered. The markers of attractiveness vary in importance based on an individual's circumstances and intent. For example, a masculinized face and body are more important criteria for a one-night stand for a woman (Kenrick et al., 1993). In contrast, this masculinized appearance becomes less significant when the woman's goal is commencing a steady relationship or marriage.

Sexual competition has endowed female birds, humans, and most sexually reproducing species to seek males with attributes indicating high-quality genes. We have evolved to perceive and respond to indicators of genetic fitness as beauty. A paradox arises from this evolutionary principle—the lek paradox. That is, why haven't all men and women (or birds, in leks) been selected to all be beautiful, thereby eliminating a significant portion of the motive for infidelity and mate switching? It seems (Petrie et al., 2009) that traits associated with beauty—especially in males, are linked to other characteristics like an efficient immune system or rapid tissue repair. High variability in these related traits allows for mutations that can be adaptive in the face of new environmental challenges. Without this variability, we would all be beautiful but would ultimately lose in the battle against parasites and other infectious organisms.

It may be an unkind paradox that our inclination for mate switching infidelity, which is a source of so much emotional suffering, is a vital survival attribute. It is common among species like birds that mate for life as well as promiscuous species like chimpanzees and bonobos. These two close genetic relatives of humans are both nonmonogamous and highly sexually competitive. When a female chimpanzee is in estrus, she will typically have a series of brief matings with multiple partners. The closest chimpanzees come to monogamy is in the form of a tryst lasting a few days in which a mating pair will bond for a few days in what is called a consort relationship (Fisher, 1992; McGinnis, 1979). More commonly, chimpanzees will participate in frenzies of multiple male–female pairings. During these encounters, there is rarely intermale aggression so long as the dominant male's access to females is not impeded. Rather than battling for access to females, chimpanzee and bonobo sperm compete. The sperm competition among chimpanzee males is abetted by producing roughly 223 times more sperm than gorillas living in small groups consisting of one male and multiple females (Fujii-Hanamoto et al., 2011). Male gorillas, who have small genitals relative to body size, do not need high sperm counts to compete with other males; they compete with their great size and strength. And they only need to do so intermittently, as they do not live in troops with competing males. Nevertheless, all male apes use some mechanism to compete with other males to maximize their genetic fitness.

In humans, alertness to potential alternate partners increases as the passion in a long-term relationship declines. Intimately bonded people increasingly become aware of the flaws and blemishes of their partners that they did not discern in the earlier phases of the relationship. Each will become exasperated by aspects of their lover's personality that they once found unremarkable or even charming and engaging. One reason is that emotional states guide the ancient brain circuits that alter perception. Sexual arousal can undermine many limbic survival defenses in favor of facilitating genetic survival. Even fundamental visceral responses like disgust are attenuated when one is sexually attracted to another person (Stevenson et al., 2011). For example, think about your typical reaction to noticing a bolus of saliva on the rim of a cup offered by a casual friend—you would quickly reject it with a grimace. Now think of the times you were sexually aroused and eagerly imbibed the saliva of your paramour—in the act often called French kissing. Many people, when sexually excited, will orally stimulate portions of their lover's body immediately proximate to the wellsprings of body wastes. The perceptual changes affected by sexual arousal diminish moral revulsion as much as visceral disgust. Passion will make the antisocial miscreant seem empathic and loving when someone is strongly attracted to them.

Since a central function of the brain is the continuous creation of a working model of the world, the unfaithful partner will construct explanations to justify their behavior to themselves (Seth, 2013; Böhm & Pfister, 2015). These explanations usually include an adverse evaluation of their current relationship that absolves them from guilt about pursuing new mates. They can also include revisionist premises that one's partner was never appropriate, that the exiting partner never felt loved, or the relationship was always unfulfilling. However, clinical experience strongly indicates that these perceptions and assessments are post hoc in response to a recent decline in attraction to a current mate along with the perceived availability of a more desirable partner. The combination of these factors leads to one of several exit schemes to conveniently leave the relationship. The selected one is often contingent on the exiting partner's risk aversion, level of dissatisfaction, and emotional dependency on the relationship (Conroy-Beam et al., 2015; Gangestad & Simpson, 2000; Schmitt & Buss, 2001). It seems that marital dissatisfaction is a greater impetus for the affairs of women than of men. This effect was supported by a classic study (Glass, 1985) that found that 56% of men, but only 34% of women involved in affairs reported that their marriages were happy.

The decision to have an affair is based on several factors, foremost of which are conflict in the relationship, or changes in a partner's appearance or status that makes them less desirable. If one or both of these are combined with the availability of a desirable alternative, the risk precipitously increases. And these factors come about quite often as the degradation of romantic bonds is nearly inevitable. Even in the most passionate connections, it tends to degrade, as it is an adaptation that evolution seems to have given a short life (Fisher, 1994). Of course, it can evolve into a companionate love that may create an even stronger bond than that engendered by romance (Epstein et al., 2013). However, the high rate of divorce or relationship dissolution suggests that this progression is less common than one would hope for.

The social barriers to fidelity give way to the adaptations that drive people to extradyadic relationships more in some than in others. Infidelity as an adaption is supported by the connection between highly heritable personality traits (e.g., Abrams, 2020) and cheating. For example, low conscientiousness and high openness to experience predict infidelity in women, and low agreeableness predicts infidelity in men (Botwin et al., 1997). Moreover, high agreeableness correlates with greater relationship satisfaction along with more guilt after infidelity (and presumably less mate switching) (Apostolou & Panayiotou, 2019). Of the many possible personality correlates of infidelity, the most intuitive is narcissism. In a longitudinal study of married couples, narcissism was related to infidelity, even after controlling for marital and sexual satisfaction (McNulty & Widman, 2014). The fact that many personality traits are linked to infidelity is particularly relevant, as personality is an evolved and fitness-enhancing aspect of the psyche (Ellis & Abrams, 2008). If all personality measures are heritable and many significantly correlated with infidelity, it follows that infidelity is also likely to be heritable and adaptive. And this is precisely what a study of 7,378 twin pairs revealed. Specifically, extrarelationship sex among these twins was demonstrated to have a heritability of 62% in men and 40% in women (Zietsch et al., 2015). The higher heritability of infidelity in men is concordant with the larger fitness benefits infidelity provides to men relative to women. The evolutionary basis of this finding is evident as men who engage in sex with more partners increase their fitness far more than women who do so. Since women do not increase their reproductive output with more male partners, they benefit less directly by infidelity. The authors of this study (Zietsch et al., 2015) also found that the vasopressin receptor gene and oxytocin receptor gene variants were linked to extrapair mating. Thus, qualities like personality and genetic profiles are related to infidelity.

Men who remained faithful to one woman would be less fecund than men who impregnated many partners (Buss, 2006). On the other hand, those who remained within a partnership long enough to ensure their young's survival would probably have had increased fitness than those who sired children and then left. In essence, romantic love is an adaptation that encourages males to stay long enough to wean a child. This conclusion is supported by the work of Helen Fisher (Fisher et al., 2005), who has conducted fMRI studies revealing that romantic love has precise neurological signatures. People who experience romantic love have distinct activation in the motivational and reward centers of the basal ganglia. As a result, love leads to a near-obsessive attentional focus on the paramour and would have guided our distant ancestors to commit to one partner at least long enough to rear a couple of children. However, as compelling as romantic love can be, it does not stop all partners from straying.

The proximate goal of producing children in a heterosexual relationship is a factor that enhances the strength of that bond and consequently reduces the vigilance for or pursuit of other partners. Although Westerners may view sex as primarily for pleasure rather than for procreation, most motivating adaptations were selected because they resulted in more offspring throughout our evolutionary history.

Romantic love added to fitness in the EEA by increasing the duration of reproductive bonds, but it plays much less of a role in procreation in current societies. In an era with long life spans and permanent marriages, love's relative brevity tends to lead to disappointment. Romantic love almost inevitably fades within a few years, leading to diminished commitment and broken vows. The transience of love does not invariably lead to infidelity, but it does lead to increased demands on the part of one or both partners. If a male has high status or attractive features such as an androgenized face, absence of facial lesions—suggesting immune competence, and a masculine scent offering a desirable genetic profile (Jacob et al. 2002), the decline in romantic love is more likely to be survived. Similarly, if the woman has many of the markers of reproductive health that we associate with beauty, such as a .7 waist-to-hip ratio, symmetrical body fat, and a neotenous face, in that case, the relationship is more likely to successfully transition into a new stable bond. However, if the diminution of love awakens a partner to deficiencies in their mate, a typical response is to reevaluate the relationship. And if this reassessment process leads to the tacit or overt conclusion that one could do better, or be happier with someone new, the process of mate switching often begins.

Infidelity as an Exit Strategy

Infidelity is an ineluctable aspect of sexuality and is ensconced in the human behavioral repertoire. Despite the just-world perspective, sexual infidelity is an anomalous deviation from the norm; it is an essential, even adaptive aspect of sexual reproduction. Some of the evolved motivations for infidelity—attempts to increase one's fecundity and produce offspring with better genes—were described above. However, it seems that infidelity, in humans and animals, has a strategic, if unkind, function as a means to exit a committed relationship. It is difficult for most people to leave a person with whom they have shared a substantial portion of their lives, have procreated with, have loved. People develop affinities and attachment to people or even places by mere exposure (e.g., Zajonc, 1980). The stronger the attachment to a person, the greater the distress in leaving them. This can be the case even if the person is unloved—even if hated (e.g., Dutton & Painter, 1993).

Leaving a significant other, even if the original bonds have morphed from love to aversion, commonly leads to intense feelings of loss, anxiety, or depression. These aversive reactions to separation seem to be innate. They have a substantial heritability, and those with the most severe reactions to partner loss have measurable differences in their amygdala (Abrams, 2020; Redlich et al., 2014). Particularly intense adverse reactions to the loss of a partner often result when the loss is believed to be the result of infidelity (Shackelford at al., 2004, p. 284). Relationships that end after infidelity are often preceded by periods of suspicious conflict and accusations. Suspicions may be potentiated by long-term partners who learned to "read" behavioral clues of their partner's potential infidelity (Shackelford & Buss, 1997a). If the suspicion this engenders has been long denied it can lead to a vengeful rage when the infidelity is confirmed (e.g., Buss, 2006). The fear of discovery by a suspicious partner frequently leads to deceptions such as professing commitment to that current partner. In many cases, such lies are difficult to detect, as humans seem to have evolved the ability to believe our own fabrications to make them less detectable (Trivers, 2011).

The desire, or even openness, for new partners, includes both the conscious and implicit evaluation of the comparative value of one's existing partner. Men are more reflexive in their assessment of new paramours. The male inclination to react to attractive females is instantiated by the "wandering eye" that is so vexing to many women in relationships. Women, in comparison, are more subtle in their assessment of their current partners for relative attractiveness, emotional security, and economic viability (Buss et al., 2017). If this assessment leads to the feeling that a mate is not worthy of their attention, it is often a cue to start the process of leaving the relationship and attempting to mate with a higher quality partner. Even if the affairs are meant to be exploratory, they present a greater risk to the relationship if conducted by women, as women are more inclined to fall in love with extradyadic partners. Approximately 80% of women fall in love with their extramarital paramours, while only about a third of men do (Buss et al., 2017). Successfully engaging in EPC must include accurately assessing one's mate value relative to the perceived value of a partner in a liaison (Buss et al., 2017; Conroy-Beam et al., 2015). Otherwise, those seeking EPCs would make numerous unsuccessful attempts to attract partners. Adding one's value to the equation helps make judgments about whether the potential new partners on the market are attainable. Studies of women's approaches to finding new mates show that these include displaying non-verbal behaviors to gauge the interest of potential new partners (e.g., Moore, 1985). Thus, flirting is often ascribed to irrational jealousy (e.g., Buss & Abrams, 2017).

Those men who are the beneficiaries of a novel woman's interest will meet three criteria to minimize the risk of switching mates (Conroy-Beam et al., 2015). The first criterion requires that the prospective new mate exhibit interest in the form of expressed attraction and desire. The greater the expressed interest, the more likely a woman will be willing to take the risk of leaving a committed partner. Also, her positive reaction to his looks, terms of endearment, etc., will indicate that she is not fully committed to her current relationship. Having assessed the potential new mate as having a viable interest in her, she will then evaluate a second criterion, rating the value of the new suitor relative to her current paramour. This rating typically includes evaluating attributes like social or financial status, health, and attractiveness. The third selection criterion for women assessing potential new mates is eligibility: a man who is, or least appears to be, free of encumbrances such as children, a solid bond to another woman, or other social obligations that would impede his availability.

Women who are particularly vigilant for new mates, especially those with a higher willingness to engage in extramarital couplings, are those who have come to perceive their current mate as unattractive (Pillsworth & Haselton, 2006). If a woman accurately judges herself to be of a higher value than her current partner, mate switching is deemed to be potentially beneficial. However, this judgment is not a consequence of a sudden epiphany, in either men or women. In most cases, it is the product of a gradual change in perspective that may or may not result from objective changes in mate value. Such an attitudinal change can occur when one partner becomes less attractive relative to their mate due to differential aging. Or, one mate achieves social, educational, or professional status that radically elevates them close to their partner. As the self-assessed value in the ascendant partner increases, they will frequently experience an increasing dissonance between their self-assessed value and their commitment to the relationship (e.g., Schmitt & Buss, 2001). This dissonance arises as a slow and insidious process that leads the disaffected partner to attribute their dissatisfaction to their partner's shortcomings (Abrams, 2012). This process not only makes infidelity more likely, but it also allows the unfaithful partner to feel justified in being unfaithful. Having decided that their diminished attraction to their partner results from the partner's own failures, they are unlikely to feel remorse about their infidelity. The infidelity will lead to increased devaluation of their partner, who will increasingly be viewed as inferior to the new lover. The progressive devaluation of one's partner leads to a closer bond to the new lover, which increases the chance of infidelity being a gateway to mate switching.

Just as some people rate themselves as more desirable or marketable than their partner, others labor through life feeling that they are unworthy of their partner. This perspective becomes problematic if it becomes evident to their partner. If one conveys that one feels unworthy of the partner, it is not improbable they will inadvertently convince a partner that this is the case. Paradoxically, the solicitations and amenities the self-effacing partner offers to secure the esteem of their lover may have the undesired effect of having the solicited partner reevaluate the equity of the relationship. Such a reevaluation can destabilize a relationship and increase vulnerability to mate poaching and subsequent infidelity (Schmitt, & Buss, 2001; Arnocky et al., 2013). Thus, the efforts of the self-effacing paramour to secure their lover might paradoxically lead to their becoming amenable to accepting the advances of a suitor.

Sexual infidelity in relationships in which a partner perceives their mate to have less value may be explained by the "good genes hypothesis." In this case, women have evolved a dual mating strategy—obtaining parental and other investment from one man while surreptitiously seeking and mating with those they find more sexually attractive. A woman being drawn to a man who is more sexually attractive represents her nonconscious quest for "better" genes. Indeed, the willingness of many women to risk the consequences of an affair denotes the compelling attraction to someone with a superior genome. The quest for better genes is more motivation for women than for men, who, unlike women, will often have affairs even when satisfied with their current relationship. Studies (Shackelford & Buss 1997b) have shown that most men who cheat report that they are happy with their long-term partners. Their motives are the quest for novelty and opportunity to propagate their genes (consciously or unconsciously).

The tendency for partners in relationships to reevaluate their own and their partner's worth likely underlies the high divorce and dissatisfaction rate in marriages (Abrams, 2016). In addition, the high frequency of divorce and the instability of courting relationships leads to both mate guarding and efforts to evade a partner's mate guarding. This leads to implicit competition in relationships that increase the chances of seeking more desirable mates. Additionally, mates who are vigilant for potential new partners will be more likely to convey availability to those who practice mate poaching (Schmitt & Buss, 2001). This practice usually involves detecting unstable or conflictual relationships and exploiting their vulnerability by courting one with overt or implicit promises of offering more relationship equity than their current relationship can provide. The offers of the mate poacher will be compelling to the individual who is desirous of a higher-value mate and perceives their current relationship to be unsatisfactory.

Understanding mate switching, mate poaching, the substrates of infidelity, and related complexities of love and sex is essential for researchers and clinicians examining couples with sexual and physical intimacy problems. Too often, sexual problems are viewed as primarily cultural or learned. In fact, most aspects of love and bonding indicate that they are biological processes. Of course, their specific expressions are culturally defined, but their essential functions are evolved to optimize procreation. Even romantic love, an idealized aspect of human mating, is a genetic and biological phenomenon that evolved to create a bond enduring enough to mate and rear a child (Fisher, 2005). Research has demonstrated that the passionate emotions of romantic love may be more than a result of programmed activation of brain reward centers (Aron et al., 2005). Despite its cross-cultural idealization, romantic love is explained by innate neuropsychological systems. The evolutionary and biological nature of romantic love is exemplified by the tendency to fall in love with people who have sufficiently similar major histocompatibility complexes (Garver-Apgar, 2006). The fact that genetic compatibility, such as having similar major histocompatibility complex genes underlies attraction and romance strongly supports the biological nature of love. And just as love is innate, so too are many of the impulses that disrupt it. This does not mean that we are destined to fall in love with people with the right genes just long enough to procreate, but it does mean that people require conscious effort to sustain relationships.

Case Studies

To this point, this chapter has reviewed many of the theories about infidelity as a route to mate-switching. Clinical experience provides little doubt that it does occur often. Below are two typical cases of the many couples with whom I have worked who have experienced infidelity. The cases are accurate descriptions of clients. They have been altered to protect the individuals' confidentiality without detracting from the essential elements of biographies that are archetypal of people who have lived through this phenomenon.

Case One: A Man Seeking Younger Mates

The following is based on a client typical of many male clients with whom I have worked. Although disguised for confidentiality, it captures the motivation, attitudes, and actions of a man who used infidelity to find a new mate.

Tyler worked hard at looking fit and youthful in his early 50s. He was above average in height and had an athletic build that was not typical of men his age. The fact that he had acquired substantial savings and a high-status position made his evident efforts into optimizing his appearance even more notable. Tyler was the mayor of a wealthy suburban city in a northeastern state and a practicing attorney in the same town. This was legal and acceptable in his state, and Tyler's law practice benefited from clients who eagerly sought out a respected political figure as their lawyer. He decided to seek guidance from a psychologist sufficiently far from him to minimize any chances of being seen by his constituents or clients. He said he needed an objective opinion on his next steps in a significant life change. It was not his upcoming congressional race or his practice moving into a larger office that troubled him. Instead, it was finding a means to exit his marriage that would cause the least pain for his wife and three adolescent and young teen children. Tyler confided that younger women had always found him attractive and have continually tempted him. He admitted that he had succumbed to temptation at least three times. His sexual affairs lasted from a few months to two years. These entanglements were with women substantially younger than himself. His lovers were women who had been employees of either the city he governed or the law firm he managed. He noted that he had mutually agreeable separations from the first two. However, one of the two did clarify that she would feel uncomfortable continuing with his firm and would need help getting a fresh start elsewhere. Tyler had helped her get this start with $50,000 and a recommendation that led to a more remunerative job in a nearby state. He emphasized that these payments were purely out of love and generosity.

The third affair was the one that was the most problematic. Tyler poignantly described his great love for this young woman who was more than two decades younger than him. He enthusiastically described her as precociously prudent and intelligent. She was his confidant, his best friend, and she inspired more passion than he had felt for any woman. The passion he felt for Anna had led him to realize that he had never truly loved his wife, Kelly. He complained that he married her to satisfy his parents, who repeatedly assured him that he loved her and that she was "perfect for him." Now 24 years later, he claimed that the love he professed to her, and even his marriage proposal, were no more than his echoing his parents' assertions and yielding to their tacit demands. When asked if he thought his wife loved him, he stated that she probably did, "in her own way." But it wasn't "real love," just a love of "convenience." When asked if she ever said anything specific to validate his perception, he said she didn't, but she didn't have to as her life was centered around the home and her children. To avoid potential image problems, Tyler had arranged for his paramour Anna to get a new position in another locale. He made it clear that it was the first step in a plan to extricate himself from his unfulfilling marriage. He planned to wait at least a year after Anna no longer worked for him before moving in with her and asking for a divorce.

In subsequent meetings, Tyler could not detail any aspect of his marriage that jibed with his characterizations of an unhappy union originating out of pressure. They had traveled and celebrated together, planned their children, and had been affectionate for most of their relationship. Any estrangement on the part of his wife seemed to be a response to Tyler's growing emotional distance. Sex had become virtually nonexistent between Tyler and Kelly. He attributed it to her unwillingness to work at making herself more attractive for him. Despite his claims that it was Kelly's indifference to her appearance that led to their sexual estrangement, his declining interest seemed to be more correlated with her age and role as a mother, as well as his extramarital relationships with much younger women.

Rather than encourage Kelly to work on her appearance and emotional expressiveness, Tyler distanced himself from her with his love affairs and general indifference. Kelly probably suspected Tyler had lost his passion, but she did not even imagine that he was having an affair with an implicit goal of finding a new partner. She found out after Easter dinner with Tyler and their children at her parents' house. He accurately guessed that she would hide her hurt and humiliation when he told her he wanted a divorce. This saved him the distress of seeing her suffer from his rejection and betrayal. Kelly doubtlessly suffered the worst day of her life, but she maintained a heroically stoic demeanor to save her parents and children from distress. Tyler said he was proud of her. Within a few weeks and some family counseling sessions to help his children adjust to the separation, Tyler moved into a luxury condominium a few miles away. Anna moved in shortly after that. But Anna and Tyler's plan was not carried out to Anna's satisfaction. She was assured that after a "cooling off" period, they would get married and have a family of their own. Yet, for many months after moving in with Anna, Tyler not only evaded any discussions of marriage but seemed to have a waning interest in the relationship. The relationship deteriorated in a series of arguments and complaints. As Anna increased her demands for marriage and children, Tyler responded with complaints about Anna's personality. These were typically red herring diversions from the main issue that he had broken his commitment to Anna and did not seem to have any intentions to marry or have children with her. Tyler even told Anna he was doubtful of her trustworthiness as she had an affair with a married man— himself.

At Anna's insistence, Tyler agreed to couples counseling. He chose this author, probably believing that a psychologist he had previously seen would be biased in his favor. During the first session, Tyler proclaimed his love and commitment to Anna but said he could no longer bear Anna's complaints and nagging. Anna was distraught throughout the session, and Tyler used her frustrated grief as evidence of her irrationality and his victimization. This would be the theme for the subsequent few sessions. Despite the best efforts of the counselor, the plan that Tyler had set for the counseling could not be derailed. After three sessions, Anna refused to continue, stating that it was pointless and frustrating. Tyler made it clear to Anna that he felt she had given up trying, which made him confident that he had the moral standing to begin seeing other women. Although he made a minimal effort to hide his connections, Anna would find messages on his social media and dating sites, making it clear that he was active in other romantic pursuits. She had sought help from the counselor whom she had seen for couples counseling. The counselor made it clear that Tyler was following a pattern that was unlikely to change. Despite the counselor's warnings, she persisted in her efforts to make Tyler love her again. To her numerous sexual overtures and acts of affection, Tyler responded with indifference or even hostility. He would seemingly wait for Anna to make any mistake or omission to point out her deficiencies. This pattern continued for approximately two months until Anna had no choice but to leave.

In a relatively brief period, Tyler was unfaithful at least twice and switched two mates. His professed love for Anna facilitated Tyler's ability to leave his wife and children. However, once convinced of his ready access to younger women, Anna had lost her appeal. Like many men who have affairs with an implicit or explicit goal of finding a new partner, Tyler was not satisfied with the partner that eased his exit from the relationship.

Case Two:—An Unfaithful Woman in Quest of a More Fit Partner

Karen was a teacher specializing in children with special needs. She was 32 and, being aware of the duration of her fertility, had a growing sense of urgency about finding a life partner. She wanted to have children and was becoming increasingly proactive about finding an appropriate husband. Karen knew that her archetypal lover—the tall, blonde, Norse god type— was not likely to come anytime soon. So, she established that she would be open to a nice man who was reasonably handsome and financially secure. Shortly after she decided on this compromise, a new vice-principle was hired. He was not tall and blonde; he was of average height and appeared Mediterranean in origin. However, he was well educated, articulate, and, as Karen would later discover, relatively well off. Val was both frugal and the only heir to his parent's estate. These attributes were sufficient for Karen to forgive him for not possessing the physical qualities of her dream man. She reasoned that his superior intellect, educational, and professional accomplishments made him a much more viable breeding stock than the Vikings that she found sexually compelling. Karen made her final decision that he would make the best partner for a husband and father of her children. Afterward, Karen began doing everything that dignity and decorum would permit to let Val know that she was interested in him. Her efforts paid off when Val approached her in the teacher's cafeteria, told her that he had two tickets to a concert, and she was welcome to the extra one. It was an awkward way to ask her out, but she gracefully accepted the ticket and the offer to accompany him to the concert. This event marked the beginning of a brief courtship that culminated with Karen and Val moving in together, renting a house in an upscale neighborhood a short drive from their school. A year later, Karen was pregnant, and they were married three months into the pregnancy. Karen wanted children, and if she was going to marry a man other than her Norse god, she wanted to be sure that he was equipped to fulfill this critical goal before marrying him.

Things were going well after the birth of their son and seemed to be getting better when a former classmate of Val offered him an executive position in a well-funded start-up that provided educational programs to school systems. This seemed to be an excellent opportunity as the company was highly rated and quickly expanding. It had innovated AI systems to augment learning for every student level. Val would have to quit his tenured teaching job, but this seemed a small cost for a job that more than doubled his salary. He gave notice, and within a month, he managed sales for the tech start-up. Karen was happy to be expecting their second child, and their relationship was flawless. Things even improved from good to better with Val's new salary that allowed for household amenities and weekend getaways. Then six months into his new job, Val was informed that the company was being audited by one of the venture capital firms that funded the company. He initially was unconcerned, thinking it was a formality. However, the sudden increase in meetings and the persistent concern exhibited by senior staff told Val something ominous was happening. He was right. The CEO and the CFO were fired, and the rest of the senior staff were told that there would be more changes and cuts. As best as Val could determine, his company's product was not as original as he was told. Besides, sales had not been growing as reported. In short, the company was on its way to dissolution, and Val was on his way to unemployment.

Had Val left for another school administrator position, he might have been able to find a new job relatively quickly. However, as a senior staff member of a company that was still under investigation, he found his job market quite limited. He ended taking a position as a permanent substitute teacher in a low-SES school district. The pay was a small fraction of what he had been getting, and his status and self-esteem plummeted. His self-rebuke worsened when Karen took a second job at a test preparation company. She had to work two jobs to offset his salary reduction, making him feel worthless—a feeling that was evident to almost anyone who observed him. In his despair, Val made the common mistake of seeking reassurance from a spouse going through an emotional crisis of her own. Karen's priorities were her child and child to be, and their life quality now seemed at risk. Her anxieties were leading her to question the trajectory of their marriage. Val's new self-effacing demeanor and his apologetic efforts to do more at home had the paradoxical effect of diminishing his status in Karen's eyes. She now pitied him, and pity is not attractive. As this tension in their marriage increased, their sexual encounters radically decreased in frequency.

At this point in their relationship, Karen went on maternity leave after the birth of their daughter. What would have been a celebratory time was one of distress as Karen lost the income from her second job, and now they also had the increased expenses of a second child. These additional financial pressures increased Karen's resentment toward Val. He could little more than apologize and promise a better future. Over the coming months, their debt kept growing, and their relationship continued deteriorating. Fortunately, Karen and Val found some salvation in Val's college friend Bert. For many years he had been a casual friend of Val. But during this dark period, he began to stop by more often, offering moral support and sometimes bringing small gifts. Bert's upbeat demeanor was a happy offset to Val's open anguish. He then did more than offer cheer; he offered the couple a substantial loan that would not need to be repaid until Val got a good job. Karen was effusive and quickly accepted with a hug while Val responded coldly; he would later complain that he was not adequately consulted about the loan. Over several months, Bert would make two more loans which would substantially improve Val and Karen's financial situation. This generosity further endeared him to Karen while increasing Val's envy. Bert was never reticent about the details of his successes and his financial security. He would frame this information in the form of assurances to Val and Karen that his loans had no adverse impact on his financial situation.

With his debt to Bert, Val could not express his discomfort about Bert's frequent visits—very often when Karen was home alone. It took several of these visits before Val asserted his frustration; his damaged self-esteem and debt to Bert had kept him silent. He angrily told Karen that he didn't want Bert coming to their home when he wasn't home. She responded by calling him jealous and childish. The more he insisted, the lower her blows would fall. She called him a failure and a loser. She had won. Val had given up and stopped asking her to stop. And he wouldn't ask Bert as he felt too ashamed of his jealousy of a friend who had been helping him.

Bert's visits abruptly stopped after a couple of months. Paradoxically, this did not provide a great deal of relief to Val, as Bert's disappearance was accompanied by a resurgence of Karen's interest in Val. She was suddenly affectionate and sexual again. These changes only piqued Val's suspiciousness and jealousy, as the confluence of these two life changes seemed too coincidental. Val increased his questioning of Karen, telling her that he knew what had been going on—a gambit that worked. Karen confessed that Bert had been poaching on their relationship. He had become a reassuring confidant who offered Karen guidance and suggestions on improving her life. These suggestions increasingly included a future with him. On reflection, Karen realized that Bert never promised to marry her if she left Val—but it was strongly implied. She acknowledged her frustration with Val's professional failures had made Bert seem more exciting and attractive.

Bert and Karen had an affair that lasted six months but ended when Karen moved to divorce Val. She was shocked and disappointed when Bert encouraged her to take her time. Karen began to press Bert about their future, and he soon made it clear that much as he was fond of her, he would not take on the responsibility of marriage—especially to a woman with two children. She was enraged and broke off the relationship, something that Bert seemed amenable to. Bert was a mate poacher, and Karen had an affair with him with at least a nonconscious goal of obtaining a more fit partner. When this failed, she sought to reconcile with Val. She suggested that they attend the couple's counseling. Val said that he had only agreed for the sake of their children.

At last contact, Val was still angry and suspicious of Karen, but they collaborated in parenting and reestablishing their finances. Val did get a new tenured teaching position, and he did pay Bert everything that was owed. They are no longer friends.

Assessing Couples Experiencing Infidelity

People have extrarelationship sex for many reasons, but the modal reason is quite apparent: The desire and pleasure of sex are often more compelling than the deterrents of guilt or remorse. Unfortunately for many marriages and other unions, the emotions that can discourage cheating usually fade to insignificance in the face of the nonconscious evolutionary modules that can make infidelity feel right or justified. This phenomenon is best understood in light of other sexual activities that are condemned by many cultures. People who have gay, lesbian, bisexual, or even paraphilic sexualities tend to feel the sex is healthy and appropriate, even in societies that condemn nonnormative sexualities (Abrams, 2016). The ability to accept and identify with one's sexual behavior despite social rebuke directly results from sexuality being an innate and largely immutable aspect of one's identity. Comparably, the innate modules that lead to mate switching are very likely innate adaptations that will overcome society proscriptions and personal commitments. This includes the near universal vigilance for new and more desirable partners, the tendency for romantic love to weaken, and the inclination to use extrarelationship sex to find a new partner.

Thus, a clinical assessment of a sexually estranged couple requires that a counselor have a working knowledge of evolutionary psychology and conceptualize a couple's conflicts in terms of evolved psychological mechanisms. The assessment needs to include apprising both partners of the evolutionary motives that underlie the desire for extradyadic sex. The assessment also must include elicitation of the unfaithful partner's overt explanations for their actions. It also must involve evaluating the level of hurt and betrayal being experienced by the betrayed partner. The application of evolutionary psychology to the counseling process must include educating clients about the evolution of the nonconscious motives and drives that lead to changing desires and emotions. Clients need to be given a working knowledge of the evolutionary foundations of love and mating to help them accurately understand the trajectory that their relationship has taken. An evolutionarily informed clinician working with estranged couples needs to evaluate both the factors that led to one of the partners seeking sexual or emotional satisfaction from another and the potential for both to reestablish a stable bond. The partners need to be educated on the true nature of nonconscious motivational forces that underlie so many of the actions and feelings that underlie love, sex, and bonding. The knowledge that one's partner has been motivated by an ancient and evolved propensity to seek new partners will not engender immediate forgiveness. But it will help both partners understand the significance of the evolved love and sex proclivities that help motivate the infidelity. It will enable the couple to accept that a restoration of the relationship will require a substantial change to each of their views of intimacy and require a new look at each other.

The assessment needs to determine whether both partners are genuinely open to developing a new understanding of their relationship. Both partners will be re-engaging in a relationship in which one will be aggrieved for some time, and the other will be a risk for future infidelity. If it is clear that both are fully committed to overcoming such significant obstacles, the assessment can continue to help both partners understand the trajectory of their troubled relationship. This should include identifying what external factors led one partner to seek a new mate. Some of the antecedents of the infidelity as a means to a new partner include:

- Diminished attraction on the part of one or both partners.
- Persistent anger at actions or attitudes of a partner.
- A reduction in status, perceived appearance, or life functioning of one of the partners.
- Personality disorders or clinical conditions on either side that became apparent as romantic feelings began to fade.

When a change has taken place in a partner's feelings, the counselor must assist each partner in understanding and accepting it. Such changes can include loss of sexual attraction, the development of hostile feelings, or affections for a third party. When such a change leads to infidelity, the counselor must insist that the transgressed partner explores the beliefs and values that underlie their anger or vindictiveness. Specifically, they need to make explicit their tacit demands and other irrational beliefs. The offended partner needs to be assisted to see that vengeance and rage are not compatible with either leaving or restoring the relationship. This help must be in the form of a dialogue where the thoughts, beliefs, and attitudes that underlie the angry intentions are elicited. Similarly, the irrational demands and values that led the unfaithful partner to stray also must be detailed and examined.

Counseling Couples Facing Infidelity

The goal of finding a new mate through having an affair sometimes is not reached, and the unfaithful partner stays with the original mate. They end up back with an aggrieved spouse or paramour. Some couples will seek help in restoring their relationship after infidelity. As with all couples' therapy, treatment for a couple with an unfaithful partner should begin with an individual session with each partner to assess each partner's feelings and view of the situation and their goals for the therapy sessions. One or both members of the dyad will often use couples' therapy as an exit strategy. Even if there is no sincere desire to remain together, it is painful to leave a relationship for reasons that include guilt, inertia, social responsibility, or feelings of obligation. The counselor is placed in a no-win situation in which the partner who secretly desires a way out is not trying to reconcile but only wants to claim that he or she has tried everything to make the relationship work. Worse, the counselor's interventions can be blamed for pulling the relationship asunder. A requisite of doing couple counseling is being thick-skinned, but the job does not include billing for wasted time. Thus, the counselor must determine whether both partners are committed to continuing the relationship. This may not be immediately obvious. As the research previously presented shows, a great deal of sexual motivation is innate, evolutionarily old, and not always consciously accessible to the individual.

When and if a change has taken place and becomes evident in counseling, the counselor must assist each partner in understanding and accepting this. Changes in a relationship can include loss of sexual passion, the development of anger or resentment, or introducing a third party. When a change such as a reduction in allure leads to infidelity, the counselor must insist that the offended partner understand his or her hurt, anger, and vengefulness in terms of his or her demands and other irrational beliefs. The offended partner must be helped to see that retribution and rage are not compatible with restoring the relationship. This is accomplished by enabling the partners to discover and challenge their irrational beliefs and tacit demands collaboratively.

Similarly, any beliefs or demands that led the unfaithful partner to stray must be identified. The unfaithful partner must be helped to accept that they were guided by irrational, demanding, or rigid thinking that encouraged them to violate their values. They then have to commit to replacing their beliefs with ones that will promote commitment and stability. Ultimately, both partners must be helped to see that creating a new relationship without the ruminations about the past is the best path to resolution. If both can view the infidelity as bad but not terrible or unredeemable, it can eventually become no more relevant than the sexual encounters before the relationship.

Clinical Approaches to Infidelity

Cognitive-behavioral therapy (CBT) has become the de facto gold standard of psychotherapy modalities (David et al., 2018). The sine qua non of this approach is identifying and changing beliefs, personal philosophies, and attitudes that lead to dysfunctional emotions or behaviors. Since the foundation of many cognitive processes is evolutionarily endowed modules of mind, clinicians need to take a new look at the motivation of the many behaviors and emotions that underlie relationship conflicts like infidelity. While a long-term, monogamous relationship is a goal for many, it has only recently become the ideal, and not in all societies. According to the research, we often vastly overestimate the importance of romantic love and mutual attraction and desire that last forever, as they diminish over time, and only a small number of relationships "survive" these changes. While none of this justifies adultery, it offers another outlook on it and can help both therapist and client understand the infidelity (Abrams, 2016).

Once the counselor understands the motivations of the infidelity and whether the unfaithful partner is earnest about his or her commitment to reestablishing the relationship, the counselor should enlighten the client about significant factors that underlie much of human behavior. Clients need to be informed that a preponderance of human behavior—especially those relating to love and sex—is guided by heritable and evolved mechanisms. This explanation should emphasize that heritability does not inevitably determine human thinking and acting. Still, it will increase the probability of many problematic behaviors such as infidelity and the activities that precede it. With this information, the client can more effectively understand the undesirable actions of their mate and their impulses.

In a relationship in which a partner is progressing from an affair to leaving a relationship, both parties must explore the beliefs and emotions that led them or their partner to seek someone else. The counselor should be aware that a sincere desire to be faithful does not erase the inclinations in the person or deficits in a relationship that led to the infidelity. Once clients are briefed on the evolutionary nature of love and sex, they can be educated on how their innate inclinations usually take the form of distorted perceptions and irrational beliefs about their own or their partner's behavior. Below are some of the common distorted or irrational beliefs that both cause and exacerbate the distress associated with infidelity—especially infidelity as a path to a new partner.

Distorted Cognitions Associated With Infidelity

Common beliefs of the betrayed partner include:
- "I have been completely humiliated and must shame him/her to restore my self-respect."
- "My mate is completely worthless, and I must punish them."
- "I can never trust any partner again."
- "I must punish the cheater by fighting for custody or refusing to end the relationship."
- "It is absolutely unbearable that people will know that my partner cheated."
- "I am a worthless lover, and no one will ever want me."
- "The infidelity permanently tainted me, and I cannot be with this person."
- "They deceived me, and so everything they ever said to me must have been a lie."

Common beliefs on the part of the unfaithful partner include:
- "I have an absolute right to pursue my gratification elsewhere if my spouse/partner doesn't meet my needs."
- "It is completely his/her fault that they have become unattractive to me. They forced me to find someone else."
- "My lover completely understands me and loves me far more than they did, so I am justified."
- "They are no longer the person I fell in love with, so I had no choice but to find someone like they used to be."
- "My partner absolutely should understand that I had to do this."

Even though these irrational and demanding beliefs are likely to arise due to innate inclinations, they can be modified by CBT. After each irrational belief is identified through therapeutic discussion, they can be illuminated and modified using one of the many disputation techniques. Each member of the couple has to be helped to see that their alienation from their partner is partially a result of their change in the perception of the other. This is especially important for the unfaithful partner who blames their partner's shortcomings for their unfaithfulness and the aggrieved partner who blames the infidelity for all their negative feelings. An essential initial step is to encourage each partner to specify specific changes they have identified in their partner that are currently troubling them. They then have to explore the specific transformations required of both of them to have a satisfactory new relationship.

The clinician should remain vigilant for signs that that one or both partners have made therapeutic efforts futile. A significant percentage of those suffering infidelity will never forgive the offense (Shackelford et al., 2002), and a substantial number of the unfaithful will be recidivists. If it seems that infidelity represents an unforgivable transgression or that the straying partner is still intent on finding a new mate, then the couple needs to be counseled accordingly. It is crucial to convey realistic expectations. For example, the unfaithful partner needs to be warned that staying in the relationship may be associated with prolonged hostility and resentment even with counseling. And the aggrieved partner needs to be warned that the desire for some to switch mates is often a need that resurfaces. However, if both partners want to stay together, they are helped by accepting the rational idea that infidelity is painful but not disastrous (Abrams, 2016).

The ultimate goal of CBT for infidelity or mate switching is to help people identify and regulate the evolutionarily endowed impulses that lead them to behaviors that may feel adaptive but no longer are. Many of our evolved psychological mechanisms are at odds with the demands and standards of modern life (Abrams, 2020). Like our sexual desires, we have many innate appetites that motivate self-defeating behaviors that can lead to obesity, substance abuse, or the morbid use of salt or sugar. The cravings can lead to destructive lifestyles that were once highly adaptive. The cravings for fats, sugar, and salt were appropriate motivations when these necessary nutrients were in chronic short supply. Now, in Western societies, they are chronically overabundant, and these cravings shorten our lives. However, we can override these nonconscious mechanisms with ongoing conscious efforts.

The research into mating and love suggests that enduring relationships may require the same conscious efforts to override the impulses that lead to mate reappraisal, infidelity, and so on. The fact that arranged marriages often endure longer than marriages based on romantic love (Abrams, 2016) is a hopeful sign. People in these marriages are paired based on their shared backgrounds and similar familial and economic support levels. Their bond tends to increase when they have worked together to overcome adversity, face life challenges, and share successes. Such marriages are structured such that innate tendencies are suppressed. However, the fact is that we do have these tendencies, and they will put relationships at risk unless they are recognized and managed. This can be accomplished by a

CBT clinician who has practical knowledge of evolutionary psychology. This clinician can help couples in conflict understand the origins of their irrational and self-defeating beliefs or demands that are causing or exacerbating their contentions. Very often, it only takes a shift in perspective, an attenuation of extreme emotions, and some time to reconstruct perspectives to salvage a relationship.

References

Abrams, M. (2012). Helping couples deal with intimacy and sexuality. In A. Vernon (Ed.), *Cognitive and rational-emotive behavior therapy with couples*. (pp. 97–115). Springer.

Abrams, M. (2016). *Sexuality and its disorders: Development, cases, and treatment*. Sage.

Abrams, M. (2020). *The new CBT: Clinical evolutionary psychology*. Cognella Academic.

Apostolou, M., & Panayiotou, R. (2019). The reasons that prevent people from cheating on their partners: An evolutionary account of the propensity not to cheat. *Personality and Individual Differences, 146*, 34–40.

Arnocky, S., Sunderani, S., & Vaillancourt, T. (2013). Mate-poaching and mating success in humans. *Journal of Evolutionary Psychology, 11*(2), 65–83.

Aron, A., Fisher, H., Mashek, D. J., Strong, G., Li, H., & Brown, L. L. (2005). Reward, motivation, and emotion systems associated with early-stage intense romantic love. *Journal of Neurophysiology, 94*(1), 327–337.

Böhm, G., & Pfister, H. R. (2015). How people explain their own and others' behavior: A theory of lay causal explanations. *Frontiers in Psychology, 6*, 139.

Botwin, M. D., Buss, D. M., & Shackelford, T. K. (1997). Personality and mate preferences: Five factors in mate selection and marital satisfaction. *Journal of Personality, 65*(1), 107–136.

Buss, D. M. (2002). Human mate guarding. *Neuroendocrinology Letters, 23*, 23–29.

Buss, D. M., & Abrams, M. (2017). Jealousy, infidelity, and the difficulty of diagnosing pathology: A CBT approach to coping with sexual betrayal and the green-eyed monster. *Journal of Rational-Emotive & Cognitive-Behavior Therapy, 35*(2), 150–172.

Buss, D. M., Goetz, C., Duntley, J. D., Asao, K., & Conroy-Beam, D. (2017). The mate switching hypothesis. *Personality and Individual Differences, 104*, 143–149.

Buss, D. M. (2006). Strategies of human mating. *Psihologijske Teme, 15*(2), 239–260.

Conroy-Beam, D., Goetz, C. D., & Buss, D. (2015). Why do humans form long-term mateships? An evolutionary game-theoretic model. *Advances in Experimental Social Psychology, 51*, 1–39.

David, D., Cristea, I., & Hofmann, S. G. (2018). Why cognitive behavioral therapy is the current gold standard of psychotherapy. *Frontiers in Psychiatry, 9*, 4.

Dutton, D. G., & Painter, S. (1993). Emotional attachments in abusive relationships: A test of traumatic bonding theory. *Violence and Victims, 8*(2), 105–120.

Ellis, A., & Abrams, M. (2008). *Theories of personality: A critical perspective*. Sage.

Epstein, R., Pandit, M., & Thakar, M. (2013). How love emerges in arranged marriages: Two cross-cultural studies. *Journal of Comparative Family Studies, 44*(3), 341–360.

Fisher, H. E. (1992). *Anatomy of love: The natural history of monogamy, adultery, and divorce*. Simon & Schuster.

Fisher, H. (1994). The nature of romantic love. *Journal of NIH Research, 6*, 59–59.

Fisher, H. (2005). *Why we love: The nature and chemistry of romantic love*. Macmillan.

Fisher, H., Aron, A., & Brown, L. L. (2005). Romantic love: An fMRI study of a neural mechanism for mate choice. *Journal of Comparative Neurology, 493*(1), 58–62.

Fleming, L., Knafl, K., Knafl, G., & Van Riper, M. (2017). Parental management of adrenal crisis in children with congenital adrenal hyperplasia. *Journal for Specialists in Pediatric Nursing: JSPN, 22*(4), 10.1111.

Ford, C. S., & Beach, F. A. (1951). *Patterns of sexual behavior*. Harper and Paul B. Hoeber.

Fossøy, F., Johnsen, A., & Lifjeld, J. T. (2006). Evidence of obligate female promiscuity in a socially monogamous passerine. *Behavioral Ecology and Sociobiology, 60*(2), 255–259.

Fujii-Hanamoto, H., Matsubayashi, K., Nakano, M., Kusunoki, H., & Enomoto, T. (2011). A comparative study on testicular microstructure and relative sperm production in gorillas, chimpanzees, and orangutans. *American Journal of Primatology, 73*(6), 570–577.

Fussell, N. J., Rowe, A. C., & Park, J. H. (2011). Masculinised brain and romantic jealousy: Examining the association between digit ratio (2D:4D) and between-and within-sex differences. *Personality and Individual Differences*, *51*(2), 107–111.

Gangestad, S. W., & Simpson, J. A. (2000). The evolution of human mating: Trade-offs and strategic pluralism. *Behavioral and Brain Sciences*, *23*(4), 573–587.

Garver-Apgar, C. E., Gangestad, S. W., Thornhill, R., Miller, R. D., & Olp, J. J. (2006). Major histocompatibility complex alleles, sexual responsivity, and unfaithfulness in romantic couples. *Psychological Science*, *17*(10), 830–835.

Glass, S. P., & Wright, T. L. (1985). Sex differences in type of extramarital involvement and marital dissatisfaction. *Sex Roles*, *12*, 1101–1120.

Guilbault, V., Bouizegarene, N., Philippe, F. L., & Vallerand, R. J. (2020). Understanding extradyadic sex and its underlying motives through a dualistic model of sexual passion. *Journal of Social and Personal Relationships*, *37*(1), 281–301.

Kaplan, H., Hill, K., Lancaster, J., & Hurtado, A. M. (2000). A theory of human life history evolution: Diet, intelligence and longevity. *Evolutionary Anthropology*, *9*(4), 156–185.

Kenrick, D. T., Groth, G. E., Trost, M. R., & Sadalla, E. K. (1993). Integrating evolutionary and social exchange perspectives on relationships: Effects of gender, self-appraisal, and involvement level on mate selection criteria. *Journal of Personality and Social Psychology*, *64*(6), 951.

Ledford, H. (2008). "Monogamous" vole in love-rat shock. *Nature*, *451*(7179), 617.

Loyau, A., Jalme, M. S., & Sorci, G. (2005). Intra-and intersexual selection for multiple traits in the peacock (*Pavo cristatus*). *Ethology*, *111*(9), 810–820.

Maddox Shaw, A. M., Rhoades, G. K., Allen, E. S., Stanley, S. M., & Markman, H. J. (2013). Predictors of extradyadic sexual involvement in unmarried opposite-sex relationships. *Journal of Sex Research*, *50*(6), 598–610.

McGinnis, L. M. (1979). Maternal separation vs removal from group companions in rhesus monkeys. *Journal of Child Psychology and Psychiatry*, *20*(1), 15–27.

McNulty, J. K., & Widman, L. (2014). Sexual narcissism and infidelity in early marriage. *Archives of Sexual Behavior*, *43*(7), 1315–1325

Moore, M. (1985). Nonverbal courtship patterns in women: Context and consequences. *Ethology and Sociobiology*, *6*, 237–247.

Negash, S., Veldorale-Brogan, A., Kimber, S. B., & Fincham, F. D. (2019). Predictors of extradyadic sex among young adults in heterosexual dating relationships: A multivariate approach. *Sexual and Relationship Therapy*, *34*(2), 153–172.

O'Loghlen, A. L., & Rothstein, S. I. (2012). When less is best: Female brown-headed cowbirds prefer less intense male displays. *PLoS One*, *7*(5), e36130.

Petrie, M., Cotgreave, P., & Pike, T. W. (2009). Variation in the peacock's train shows a genetic component. *Genetica*, *135*, 7–11.

Pillsworth, E. G., & Haselton, M. G. (2006). Male sexual attractiveness predicts differential ovulatory shifts in female extrapair attraction and male mate retention. *Evolution and Human Behavior*, *27*, 247–258.

Pruett-Jones, S., & Pruett-Jones, M. (1994). Sexual competition and courtship disruptions: Why do male bowerbirds destroy each other's bowers? *Animal Behaviour*, *47*(3), 607–620.

Redlich, R., Grotegerd, D., Opel, N., Kaufmann, C., Zwitserlood, P., Kugel, H., Heindel, W., Donges, U. S., Suslow, T., Arolt, V., & Dannlowski, U. (2015). Are you gonna leave me? Separation anxiety is associated with increased amygdala responsiveness and volume. *Social Cognitive and Affective Neuroscience*, *10*(2), 278–284.

Schmitt, D. P. (2014). Evaluating evidence of mate preference adaptations: How do we really know what *Homo sapiens sapiens* really want? In V. A. Weekes-Shackelford & T. Schackelford (Eds.), *Evolutionary perspectives on human sexual psychology and behavior* (pp. 3–39). Springer.

Schmitt, D. P., & Buss, D. M. (2001). Human mate-poaching: Tactics and temptations for infiltrating existing mateships. *Journal of Personality and Social Psychology*, *80*(6), 894.

Seth, A. (2013). Interoceptive inference, emotion, and the embodied self. *Trends in Cognitive Sciences*, *17*, 565–573.

Shackelford, T. K., & Buss, D. M. (1997a). Cues to infidelity. *Personality and Social Psychology Bulletin*, *23*(10), 1034–1045.

Shackelford, T. K., & Buss, D. (1997b). Marital satisfaction in evolutionary psychology perspective. In R. J. Sternberg & M. Hojat (Eds.), *Satisfaction in close relationships* (pp. 7–25). Guilford Press.

Shackelford, T. K., Buss, D. M., & Bennett, K. (2002). Forgiveness or breakup: Sex differences in responses to a partner's infidelity. *Cognition & Emotion, 16*(2), 299–307.

Shackelford, T. K., Voracek, M., Schmitt, D. P., Buss, D. M., Weekes-Shackelford, V. A., & Michalski, R. L. (2004). Romantic jealousy in early adulthood and in later life. *Human Nature, 15*(3), 283–300.

Spoon, T. R., Millam, J. R., & Owings, D. H. (2007). Behavioural compatibility, extrapair copulation and mate switching in a socially monogamous parrot. *Animal Behaviour, 73*(5), 815–824.

Stevenson, R. J., Case, T. I., & Oaten, M. J. (2011). Effect of self-reported sexual arousal on responses to sex-related and non-sex-related disgust cues. *Archives of Sexual Behavior, 40*(1), 79–85.

Trivers, R. (2011). *The folly of fools: The logic of deceit and self-deception in human life*. Basic Books.

Tsapelas, I., Fisher, H. E., & Aron, A. (2011). Infidelity: When, where, why. In W. R. Cupach & B. H. Spitzberg (Eds.), *The dark side of close relationships* (Vol. 2, pp. 175–195). Routledge/Taylor & Francis Group.

Whisman, M. A., & Snyder, D. K. (2007). Sexual infidelity in a national survey of American women: Differences in prevalence and correlates as a function of method of assessment. *Journal of Family Psychology, 21*(2), 147–154

Zajonc, R. B. (1980). Feeling and thinking: Preferences need no inferences. *American Psychologist, 35*(2), 151–175.

CHAPTER 13

Deception and Secrecy in Infidelity

Susan M. Hughes

Abstract

Infidelity is rooted in secrecy and deceit. The deception can include both falsification (i.e., active lying) and concealment (i.e., omission of information) of extrapair liaisons. Infidelity deception can also take the form of engagement in secret online indiscretions. Those who are more likely to engage in infidelity deception possess certain qualities related to high sociosexuality and Machiavellianism, and also have a history of serial infidelity. Given the secretive nature of infidelity, there are strategies that individuals use to uncover secrets. These cheater detection strategies may involve active information seeking (e.g., snooping on partner) or the use of implicit cues such as assessing subtle behavioral changes or examining the facial and vocal patterns of a cheater. Deception can also be directed toward the extrapair partner to attain or maintain the extradyadic relationship. Further, there is deception involved with a potential consequence of infidelity—cuckoldry; misattributed paternity is definitive proof of infidelity that has been kept hidden. Even after a sexual infidelity has been exposed, the responses presented to one's partner may not always be laden with truth and transparency with regard to the unfaithful acts and the feelings toward the extrapair partner. The motivation to maintain an in-pair partnership and the amount of knowledge already gathered by an in-pair partner about the transgressions can facilitate different incentives for exposing the disloyalty and/or offering concessions. This chapter presents an overview of the literature that examines the secret and deceptive aspects of infidelity.

Key Words: deception, secrecy, infidelity, detection, concealment, cuckoldry

Deception and Secrecy Define Infidelity

Infidelity can be defined as participation in a range of behaviors with an extrapair partner that could include flirting, holding hands, cuddling, kissing, oral sex, penetrative vaginal and/or anal sex, and even emotional involvement with another whether online or in person (Hughes & Harrison, 2017; Kruger et al, 2013). A commonality across all categorizations of infidelity is that it involves secret activity. That is, infidelity is rooted in secrecy and deceit. It is common for most dictionaries to define "affair" by incorporating the terms "secret" or "illicit" to explain the sexual relationship (Andrews et al., 2008). Most synonyms for infidelity (e.g., cheating, affair, unfaithfulness, extradyadic involvement, stepping out, straying) are indicative of the secretive nature of the romantic activity with an extrapair partner that occurs outside of another relationship, usually in the context of an exclusive, committed relationship such as a marriage (Fincham & May, 2017).

Extramarital affairs, in particular, typically involve having to lie to one's spouse about the extrapair involvement. An exception is the "open-marriage" arrangement, in which extradyadic activities are either openly discussed with candor or are tolerated with acknowledgment and permission (Gass & Nichols, 1988). However, some argue that when both parties have mutual consent to establish a nonmonogamous arrangement in a relationship, this cannot be classified as infidelity since there is no attempt at deceiving the other person of any outside sexual and/or emotional activities (see Rokach & Philibert-Lignières, 2015). Thus, the betrayal of both intimate and sexual exclusivity through deception seems to be critical to defining infidelity. Whether it be in marriage or other long-term romantic commitments, monogamy is the socially accepted norm in serious intimate relationships, and a betrayal of such is typically accomplished through lies and deception that some consider the defining features of adultery (Drigotas & Barta, 2001; Rokach & Philibert-Lignières, 2015).

Infidelity is often delineated to represent two types: sexual infidelity and emotional infidelity (see chapter 10). Guitar et al. (2017) asked participants to provide definitions of each type of infidelity using open-answer questions. When defining emotional infidelity, one of the most reported themes was deceiving one's partner about feelings toward an extrapair partner. When defining sexual infidelity, deception by one's partner of the extrapair sexual activity was listed by many in the sample. Although participants seemed to link deception more with emotional than sexual infidelity, it appears to be a critical aspect for both types of infidelity.

Others have attempted to classify specific behaviors and attitudes associated with infidelity into categories where deception is an integral part of classification. Wilson et al. (2011) developed the Perceptions of Dating and Infidelity Scale and in their analysis identified three categories of distinct behaviors related to infidelity: (1) ambiguous, (2) deceptive, and (3) explicit behaviors. Ambiguous behaviors were categorized as those acts where one's motivations to cheat may be unclear, but in and of itself were benign behaviors such as communicating on the Internet or hugging another person. Deceptive behaviors were those mainly kept hidden such as lying and actively deceiving one's partner or withholding information from one's partner. Explicit behaviors were ones where it was clear that a person breaks the agreement of monogamy by engaging in sexual acts with someone outside of the primary relationship. Deceptive behaviors such as flirting, fantasizing, and lying, or withholding information from a partner was rated as being a moderate indication of cheating but was not considered as severe or indicative of cheating as were explicit behaviors. Further, explicit behaviors appeared to be more directly related to sexual infidelity, whereas a combination of the ambiguous and deceptive behaviors was related to emotional infidelity. Roscoe et al. (1988) also found that people considered keeping secrets from a partner as a defining feature of unfaithfulness. It was ranked fourth on a list of behaviors identifying infidelity and was preceded only by the categories of: their partner was dating/spending time with another, had sexual intercourse with another, or had a sexual interaction with another.

There appears to be a sex difference when it comes to the importance placed on partner deception as a defining sign of infidelity. Compared to men, women perceive deceptive behaviors such as lying or withholding information from one's partner as being more indicative of cheating (Wilson et al., 2011). This was even the case when examining what older adolescents considered was cheating while dating; more teen women than men indicated that keeping secrets from a partner constituted unfaithfulness (Roscoe et al., 1988). Whereas men saw engaging in sexual interactions as being more indicative of cheating, women viewed keeping secrets from a partner as more indicative of cheating.

The Nature of Infidelity Deceit

Infidelity is an aspect of human behavior that cannot be easily observed (Adamopoulou, 2013), thus making it ideal for concealment. Estimates of infidelity are difficult to determine due to its secretive nature. Wiederman and Hurd (1999) found that 75% of men and 68% of women admitted to engaging in at least one form of extradyadic dating and/or sexual behavior (e.g., kissing, fondling, intercourse) while involved in a committed, romantic relationship. Several surveys administered to college students showed that most students reported regularly lying to sex partners about having cheated on the partner (see Williams, 2001). Because secrecy and deception are concomitant with partner infidelity, it makes sense that the rates for both infidelity and sexual deception are equivalently high.

Deception can be conceptualized as any intentional behavior that creates an impression that the deceiver knows to be untrue (Rokach & Philibert-Lignières, 2015) and can entail a variety of misleading acts such as lying or breaking promises and confidences (Feeney, 2004). Those attempting to evade infidelity detection can lie either by falsification or through concealment (Gass & Nichols, 1988). Falsification involves presenting false information as truth. Concealment involves withholding information without communicating untruth or by diverting attention away from vital facts to avoid discussing a particular topic. It is thought that concealment of affairs is easier and happens earlier in the course of an extradyadic relationship whereas outright falsification and fabricating stories occurs later and is a riskier part of the deceit (Gass & Nichols, 1988). Sometimes a person will combine the two and tell "half-truths" so as to be misleading (Drigotas & Barta, 2001; Rokach & Philibert-Lignières, 2015).

At times, cheaters deal with their partners who either learn about or suspect their infidelity by "gaslighting," a term used to describe when a person manipulates information and distorts reality in such a way that the victim questions their own sanity (Gass & Nichols, 1988). Cheaters may lie, falsify the facts, and distort reality to convince their mates that they are crazy and that what their mate perceives is not happening. As a result, victims may feel as if they are losing their mind because they know that certain events occurred but cannot prove that they did. The reactions to gaslighting by the infidelity victim can conjure a variety of responses; victims can feel an overwhelming sense of numbness, fear, despair, confusion, anger, guilt, and depression and will wish for the restoration of the past (Gass & Nichols, 1988). As a result of gaslighting behaviors, some victims may experience denial and be dismissive of the frequency or meaning of their partner's affairs, and think it will stop if the victim changes some behavior.

Deception Involved With Online Cheating

The opportunity to engage in and hide infidelity has increased with the introduction of the Internet and "cyber-cheating." Some Internet sites exist for the express purpose of facilitating offline sexual infidelity. For instance, AshleyMadison.com is a website where married individuals can connect with others looking for extramarital relationships and possible sexual liaisons. The service is advertised as a discrete or secret means of engaging in affairs while allowing people to remain in their primary relationships (Hackathorn et al., 2017). The site became popular in media reports when there was breach of terms and information about the users was released, thus violating the understanding that registering for the site would be kept confidential and private.

AshleyMadison is not the only site that exists for the purposes of seeking infidelity online. Individuals who are motivated to engage in infidelity can also pay to register for a variety of other sites such as Second Love, which also facilitates infidelity. A study examining a sample of those who had registered for Second Love documented that most users of the site had done so without their partner being aware (Rodrigues, 2017). They reported deliberately withholding information and lying to their partner about having registered for the site and they perceived their deceptive behaviors as moderately indicative of infidelity, possibly acknowledging their behavior as a form of betrayal.

Beyond using the Internet for the intention of an actual meeting with a possible extra-pair partner, the anonymity of electronic transactions allows users to engage in erotic chats and have other communication without the fear of being caught by their partner (Young et al., 2000). Cooper et al. (1999) conducted a study during the early stages of Internet use and found that 70% of 9,177 users who indicated using the Internet for sexual pursuits at least once kept the fact they went online for such reasons a secret. They found that more men (72%) than women (62%) reported keeping their time involvement online a secret. Thus, since the advent of making sexual content and interaction available online, indulging in such is an activity one elects not to disclose to a partner, especially if it involves behaviors that could be classified as being unfaithful. Although most individuals in Cooper and colleagues' study felt compelled to keep their online activity a secret, the majority (92%) reported that their online sexual pursuits were not problematic. They did not feel they spent excessive time on it and reported it had little interference in their daily lives.

A more recent study reported lower rates of digital cheating behaviors. McDaniel et al. (2017) found that only a small percentage of their sample of 338 married/cohabitating individuals reported engaging in private, online indiscretions facilitated by social media platforms. Fewer than 10% had reported that they had engaged in behaviors online that they would hide from their partner; participated in chats they would keep hidden from their partner; become defensive or angry if their partner saw their online behavior; or thought their partners would get upset if they read their online written interactions. However, for both sexes, higher engagement of infidelity-related behaviors on social media was related to lower relationship satisfaction and higher relationship ambivalence.

Some researchers question reported statistics about rates of Internet infidelity because it is conducted so secretly, particularly emotional infidelity (see Octaviana & Abraham, 2018). They claim that accurate and reliable statistical data on such matters is difficult to find and document. Newer technologies have presented additional challenges to examining rates of infidelity because it is so much easier to hide and deny such as the use of smartphone apps that can easily erase any visible traces (Schneider et al., 2012).

Young et al. (2000) discussed how users may go to great lengths to hide the truth about their online indiscretions from their partners. They may move their computers to more secluded areas in the house away from visibility, move to a locked room, change or add passwords, wait until late hours of the night to use the Internet, or show a greater need for privacy during computer usage. If disturbed or interrupted when online, they may react defensively or with anger. In addition, some may hide credit card bills, telephone bills, or lie about the reason for extensive Internet use.

Given the modern era of online and mobile technology, defining what it means to cheat has become more difficult. As pointed out by Octaviana and Abraham (2018), Internet infidelity does not have a consensus definition, but one component central to most definitions is that the online contact is kept secret from a partner/spouse. Indeed, social media infidelity-related behaviors are often categorized similarly to offline infidelity. The types of behaviors seen with online indiscretions include hiding information, being secretive, forming secret emotional connections with others instead of one's partner, and getting defensive about their behaviors if confronted about it (McDaniel et al., 2017). Sometimes the online relationship will progress into secret phone calls, letters, and offline meetings, whereas other times they will remain relatively anonymous and be confined to cyberspace (Young et al, 2000). Some prefer the latter situation because it allows users to secretly engage in erotic exchanges with reduced fear that they will be caught by their partner. It also offers the user more control over the nature of the online indiscretion, as Internet use can occur in privacy, can be anonymous, and can be untraceable.

While explicit acts such as cyber-sex and erotic chatting have been more readily perceived as acts of online infidelity (see Hackathorn et al., 2017), some view their partner's consumption of pornography as a form of online cheating, a sort of "virtual sexual infidelity." Wives report experiences with their husbands' pornography use and concomitant deception as an attachment threat in the adult pair-bond relationship (Zitzman & Butler, 2009). As with other online infidelity, the deception and lying used to hide and protect pornography use can have a negative impact on relationship trust. It can be perceived by partners as the first step to the possibility of engaging in a real-life infidelity. Thus, many view pornography use as a heightened sexual fidelity risk, especially if it is something one's partner feels compelled to keep a secret.

Loss in partner trust can occur when the cybersex user either lies about or underreports the degree of their Internet-related sexual activity (Schneider et al., 2012). Schneider et al. (2012) found that only 22% of their sample of cybersex abusers had voluntarily disclosed their activities prior to their partner's discovery. There was also a large percentage of the sample who reported uncertainty with regard to the extent of their partner's online sexual activities. The majority of participants did not believe that their partner had disclosed the full extent of their online behaviors, and this frequently led to attempts of investigating their partner's online activity further. They found that the cybersex user's repeated deception and dismissal of the partner's concerns appeared to be a significant contributor to the spouse's trauma reactivity. Betrayed partners of cybersex abusers consistently report that it is not the online cheating itself or any specific sexual act that caused them the deepest pain, but rather the lying, denial, and inability to maintain relationship trust with their partner (Schneider et al., 2012). Further, the emotional connections and even sexual fantasies about an online extradyadic partner can be perceived as acts of deceitful infidelity (Hackathorn et al., 2017).

Traits Related to Infidelity Deception

Chapter 1 provides an overview of the various personality traits and other individual differences that predict infidelity. Here, I discuss the traits that specifically predict deception involved with infidelity.

Sociosexuality

Sociosexuality reflects a person's beliefs and attitudes toward sex whereby those with higher sociosexuality do not have a need to be in a committed relationship in order to have sex (Mattingly et al., 2011). Not surprisingly, higher sociosexuality, or the propensity toward more uncommitted relations, is associated with a greater willingness to engage in infidelity (see Mattingly et al., 2011). More specifically, those with higher sociosexuality have a greater willingness to engage in deceptive infidelity, which involves acts of deliberately lying to or withholding information from one's partner about the infidelity (Mattingly et al., 2011). Because those with unrestricted sexualities invest less in relationships, they may feel they have less to lose if the relationship terminates because of their deceit. Indeed, the relationship between sociosexual orientation and willingness to engage in deceptive behaviors was reduced slightly when considering one's commitment to their relationship.

Other studies have also demonstrated a link between high sociosexuality and the use of deception related to infidelity. Wilson et al. (2011) asked participants to rate the level of cheating they associated with different types of behavior if one were to engage in such behavior with someone other than his or her romantic partner. They found that those with an unrestricted sociosexual orientation and who had the tendency to act on a sexual attraction to an opposite-sex friend were less likely to rate both explicit acts (e.g., having sex with another) and deceptive acts (i.e., flirting with others, fantasizing about others, lying, or withholding information from partner) as indicative of cheating. The less likely participants were to psychologically avoid temptation and distance themselves from sexual situations with someone other than their partner, the less they perceived the use of deceptive behaviors were indicative of cheating. Likewise, when examining a sample of individuals who registered for an online site meant to promote infidelity, more permissive perceptions of deceptive infidelity were associated with unrestricted sociosexual desire and with lower commitment levels (Rodrigues et al., 2017). Perhaps those with higher sociosexuality perceive deceptive behaviors as not indicative of infidelity, simply because they, themselves, engage in them. That is, individuals who find these behaviors as not indicative of cheating may be more likely to engage in those behaviors because they do not perceive their own actions as unacceptable in the context of a romantic relationship.

Dark Triad

Other personal traits linked to deceptive infidelity are those constituting the Dark Triad. Specifically, Machiavellianism, a personality trait defined as being cunning, distrustful, and exploitative, is a significant predictor of intention to engage in infidelity and to use several forms of sexual deception (Brewer & Abell, 2015). Those high in the trait are more likely to engage in blatant lying to pursue sexual activity with a current or prospective partner. They were also more likely to sexually deceive for self-serving intents and were more likely to avoid subsequent confrontations with their partner. Those high in Machiavellian traits often control the type and depth of information they reveal to others, which may facilitate their ability to deceive and hinder the detection of blatant lies by their deceived relationship partners. Indeed, individuals with high levels of Machiavellianism tell more plausible lies and, in turn, demonstrate confidence in their ability to deceive and endorse lying for self-gain (Giammarco et al., 2013). Because Machiavellian individuals demonstrate confidence in their ability to deceive their partners, they seem to be more encouraged or enabled to engage in blatant lies rather than partake in the less risky deception of omission (Brewer & Abell, 2015). Nonetheless, Machiavellianism is also associated with detection risk aversion in the context of infidelity (Adams et al., 2014), so they may be careful with their deceptive tactics. In addition to their confidence in their ability to avoid detection, they may lack empathy and concern for their partner's feelings which further enables using deception with ease.

The other traits of the Dark Triad, psychopathy and narcissism, are also associated with having greater extrapair, low-commitment relationship experiences (Adams et al., 2014). Individuals high on both psychopathy and narcissism were found to accept a greater risk to engage in a variety of low-commitment extrapair relationships such as one-nightstands, booty-call relationships, and extrapair friends-with-benefits relationships. Those high in the Dark Triad may employ more deceptive sexual practices in their relationships and have increased levels of infidelity probability because of their callous nature.

Prior Infidelity

Prior infidelity is a risk factor for infidelity in subsequent relationships (Adamopoulou, 2013). Those who reported engaging in extradyadic sexual involvement in the first relationship were three times more likely to report engaging in it for their next relationship compared to those who were faithful during their first relationship (Knopp et al., 2017). Adamopoulou (2013) also found that those who cheated in a past relationship were more likely to cheat on their current partner. The author concluded that if someone cheats many times, they may develop and refine strategies that best keep their secrets hidden from their partners. Thus, learning to acquire different successful tactics of concealment may be accomplished with repeated cheating behaviors.

Infidelity Detection Mechanisms

Given the secretive nature of infidelity, there are several tactics that individuals use to uncover those secrets. Just as there is an active nature to the strategies individuals employ to conceal their engagement in relationship-threatening behaviors, there appears to be an active nature to the strategies used to unearth those secrets (Dowd, 2012). Indeed, a partner's deceptive acts should require special attention because they may be indicative of infidelity (Sobraske et al., 2013). Suspicious partners are motivated to engage in a variety of seemingly paranoid acts such as consistently monitoring their partners, snooping through their partner's belongings, isolating their partner, or attempting to cut off their partner's social contacts in order to mitigate violations of relationship fidelity (Buss & Abrams 2017).

Buss and Abrams (2017) describe the relationship between a cheater and their deceived partner as a coevolutionary arms race where the cheater has evolved abilities to deceive the partner, and the jealous partner has evolved mechanisms to detect the deception. Thus, because infidelity is driven by secrecy, feelings of jealousy are often accompanied by sophisticated defenses against the infidelity. As one sex became more sensitive to subtle cues of infidelity, the other became more adept at skillfully concealing those cues (Buss & Abrams, 2017) and evolved effective strategies for disguising extrapair involvement (Brand et al., 2007). As such, many infidelity victims are not knowledgeable of their partner's transgression, which allows the transgressors the ability to sustain their primary relationship (Weiser & Weigel, 2015). Dowd (2012) found that most participants (78%)

in the study never disclosed their infidelity to their partner, so it remained unknown. If infidelity was uncovered, many of the victims reported not having seen any signs or indications of infidelity, and only a few (5.4%) were able to catch their partner in some kind of lie. Thus, it appears that extradyadic involvement can be largely concealed quite successfully.

The potential of getting caught has to impact the decision of whether someone would consider engaging in an extrapair relationship. As follows, the consideration as to when and where the cheating occurs appears to be based on the likelihood of getting caught and being able to keep the act a secret. For example, Adamopoulou (2013) examined infidelity among married, cohabiting, and dating couples at each month during the years 1996–2001 and found that infidelity in all types of relationships displayed a seasonal peak during summertime. What may explain the seasonal pattern of infidelity peaking in the summer months is that it is a period associated with increased travel, which could facilitate sex with a partner in a geographical location distant from the in-pair relationship. When one selects an extrapair partner in a place different from the same area in which they reside, it could decrease the chances of detection and the prospects of constant accountability.

Infidelity Detection Through Information Seeking

Deception detection can entail a variety of active information-seeking strategies. These active strategies can range from seeking out third-party confessions, finding physical evidence, and even espionage (Dowd, 2012). Espionage can be categorized as snooping through a partner's belongings, phone, email, social media accounts, reading a partner's diary or personal letters, and listening in on their phone calls. Some even go so far as using cell phone tracking GPS, text-mail rerouting, hacking email accounts, going through phone records, or using a keystroke capture program to record emails and passwords (Dowd, 2012). These varied acts demonstrate how a suspicious partner is very motivated to increase their attention to their partner's behavior, whereabouts, and associates (Sobraske et al., 2013).

Dowd (2012) found that espionage was the most popular information-seeking strategy (41%), followed by accidental discovery (20.9%), then by speaking with mutual friends and direct disclosure (13% each), receiving the unsolicited truth (12.4%), interrogation (7.8%), and observation of behavior (7.0%). People often use a combination of various methods when trying to confirm deceit of their partner and rarely relied on the use of a single strategy. On average, participants used two strategies in order to detect their partner's infidelity, and reported relying primarily on physical evidence and third-party disclosure.

Direct interrogation of a suspected mate is another active information-seeking strategy used to unveil unfaithfulness. Confession solicitation tactics involve asking one's partner more of a battery of questions (e.g., "I badgered him with questions") rather than a single question of guilt (Dowd, 2012). When deception detection occurs through direct probing, those deceived become even more suspicious when their partners sound defensive, dominate the conversation, or show hesitation to questioning (Burgoon et al., 1996). In turn, the interrogator probing can force the liar to adapt and make their deceptive message sound more believable. Thus, it makes sense that one of the least common infidelity detection strategies reported by participants in Dowd's study was using some form of interrogation (7.8%), because it may not necessarily result in a revelation of truth.

Another infidelity detection strategy that men may use is performing oral sex on their suspected partner. Pham and Shackelford (2013) documented that men who perceived having a higher partner infidelity risk had a greater interest in and spent more time performing oral sex on their partner. Thornhill (2006) hypothesized that oral sex performed by a man on his regular partner may allow him to taste and smell rival semen near or within her vagina, providing cues to her recent sexual history and a possible infidelity. Further, oral sex induced orgasm could serve as a mate retention strategy if there is indeed a threat that their partner has strayed. Although women's propensity for performing oral sex on their partner was unrelated to infidelity risk (Pham et al., 2013), women who perceived higher risk of partner infidelity seemed to use fake orgasms as a deceptive tactic for mate retention; women who reported greater likelihood of pretending orgasm perceived a higher risk that their partner would cheat and were more likely to engage in other mate-retention behaviors (Kaighobadi et al., 2012).

Infidelity Detection by Implicit Behavioral Cues

Because infidelity is not usually an overt act and is kept hidden, there are also several implicit behavioral cues that are used to uncover infidelity of one's partner. Observation of a suspected partner's behavior could include watching their partner interact with friends and coworkers or monitoring their behavior on the phone (Dowd, 2012). Nonetheless, infidelity is an aspect of human behavior that cannot be easily observed (Adamopoulou, 2013), which may explain why observation of behavior (7%) was low on the list of active information-seeking strategies used (Dowd, 2012).

Shackelford and Buss (1997) identified a lengthy list of specific behavioral cues that can lead people to suspect a partner's infidelity whether they were real or alleged. Among that list, they found that partners can be sensitive to subtle cues of infidelity such as unexplained absences, strange scents, changes in sexual interactions, or observations of their partner engaging in changes that are outside of their normal routines (Shackelford & Buss, 1997). Some noticed their partners were becoming more territorial or protective of their belongings than before (Dowd, 2012). Cheating partners may have a reluctance to discuss a particular individual with their partner (Shackelford & Buss, 1997) or try to conceal information by diverting attention away from vital facts in order to avoid discussing what they consider are touchy subjects (Gass & Nichols, 1988).

Dowd (2012) reported that withdrawal was the most commonly reported sign (39.5%) of a partner's infidelity. Different types of withdrawal patterns included less frequency in phone contact, less physical contact, a diminishing sex life, a general loss of interest in their partner, being less communicative, emotional detachment, and breaking patterns of usual behavior (Dowd, 2012; Shackelford & Buss, 1997). Partners who stray frequently displayed a passive rejection, were apathetic, and were reluctant to spend time with one's partner (Shackelford & Buss, 1997).

Some suspicious partners noticed that their partners had also become antagonistic, confrontational (10.1%) (Dowd, 2012), overly critical, or argumentative (Shackelford & Buss, 1997), and would try to pick fights or degrade their partners, causing the victims to feel they were responsible for their partner's unhappiness (Dowd, 2012). Alternatively, some unfaithful partners showed exaggerated affection or a sudden increase in sexual interest toward their in-pair partner (Shackelford & Buss, 1997), which could be considered a display of a reaction formation defense mechanism.

Other Implicit Cues for Identifying Cheaters

Beyond the tactics used to uncover infidelity of one's own partner, there is evidence that certain implicit cues are used to detect another's proclivity and/or history of infidelity.

Behaviors

People are able to identify infidelity in others' romantic relationships simply from viewing brief observations of their behavior. For instance, Lambert et al. (2014) found that participants who watched a short video clip of a couple interacting could accurately detect which targets had cheated on their romantic partners. They found that this detection was mediated by ascriptions of commitment and trustworthiness of the persons they were observing. It is quite astonishing that the presence of infidelity may be among the characteristics that observers can intuitively surmise after only brief exposure of watching an unknown person's behavior.

Faces

Women were also able to accurately judge unfamiliar men's past unfaithfulness simply from viewing facial photographs (Rhodes et al., 2013). Facial masculinity seemed to mediate women's accuracy, with women rating more masculine-looking men as more likely to be unfaithful and as having a sexual history of being unfaithful. Women were correct in their estimates because masculinity ratings correlated significantly with men's infidelity. This evidence suggests that in addition to using brief behavioral cues to identify cheaters, minimal facial cues can also be used to judge unfaithfulness.

Voices

Another cue that is used to detect a person's proclivity to cheat is the sound of their voice. There is evidence that it is possible to accurately detect a cheater based solely on hearing a brief voice sample. Hughes and Harrison (2017) found that participants rated the voices of unseen persons who had a history of cheating as more likely to cheat than those who reported never having cheated, thus demonstrating that perceptions of a speaker's history of infidelity could be determined through voice alone.

So what is driving this assessment? The study had controlled for aspects that may clue a listener to the speaker's mate value such as voice attractiveness, age, voice pitch, and other acoustic measures to assure that greater attractiveness was not driving this effect. Although Hughes and Harrison (2017) were unable to pinpoint all the features about a voice that allow our perceptual system to make this assessment, voice pitch seemed to play some role in infidelity detection, though it did not represent the entire picture. It appears that listeners can unconsciously tune into voice pitch to ascribe infidelity risk to speakers. O'Connor et al. (2011) also found that listeners would make cheating ascriptions based on voice pitch alone when they had manipulated the pitch of men's and women's voices. Similarly, Hughes and Harrison (2017) found that for both sexes, voices manipulated to have a lower pitch were thought to be more likely to have cheated than those with higher pitches. Likewise, others have shown when it comes to trusting in mating-related contexts such as with infidelity or mate stealing, higher pitched voices of both sexes are perceived as being more trustworthy (O'Connor & Barclay, 2017).

There were a few reasons offered as to why a lower pitch voice was met with such suspicion when it comes to infidelity and trust. Because a lower pitch voice is linked to higher levels of testosterone (Abitbol et al., 1999; Evans et al., 2008), which contributes to a higher sex drive (Abitbol et al., 1999; Davis, 2000; Halpern et al., 1998), people may come to associate lower pitch voices with those who are motivated to seek a variety of sexual encounters such as affairs. Further, both men and women speak with deeper voices when communicating with someone they find attractive (Hughes et al., 2010) and both sexes lower their pitch when asked to intentionally display a "sexy voice" (Hughes et al., 2014; Tuomi, & Fisher, 1979). Therefore, it is possible that raters related lower pitched voices with those who were intentionally trying to sound sexy and attempting to seek casual sexual encounters and affairs.

The findings that infidelity detection can be made by either watching short video clips, seeing pictures of faces, or hearing brief voice samples demonstrate the validity of the "thin slice theory," which posits that one can make accurate assessments of another based on merely brief observations (Ambady & Rosenthal, 1992). These data suggest that cognitive strategies have evolved to facilitate wise mate choices to detect individuals who may have a proclivity to practice mating strategies that involve secretive extradyadic relations.

Factors Influencing Infidelity Detection
Previous Infidelity Experience

When asked to detect cues of infidelity during an experimental task, people who cheated on their romantic partner versus those who did not were better at detecting lies and dishonesty (Ein-Dor et al., 2017). It is possible that people who cheat on their romantic partner have developed optimized techniques to keep their affairs hidden. So when the need to detect unfaithfulness arises, they may draw on their own experience with dishonesty to detect other cheaters with greater accuracy than would faithful people. On the other hand, people who have been cheated on by their partner were no more accurate in detecting infidelity than those whose partner had not cheated on them (Ein-Dor et al., 2017). Thus, those who have previous experience being victims of infidelity do not seem to be at an advantage when it comes to detection of future infidelity.

Other researchers found that people who either engaged in infidelity themselves, knew about a partner's infidelity, or suspected a partner of infidelity had a higher risk of having those same infidelity experiences again in their next romantic relationships (Knopp et al., 2017). Those who suspected their first-relationship partners of infidelity were four times more likely to report suspicion of their partner's affair again in their next relationships. Further, those who had knowledge that their partners in the first relationships had engaged in extradyadic sexual interaction were twice as likely to report the same behavior from their next relationship partners. Hence prior experience with infidelity clearly seems to impact suspicion and detection of one's partner's activity.

Gender Differences

Men and women employ different infidelity-detection strategies and display different levels of sensitivity and accuracy in detecting potential threats to their relationship. Women were more attentive than men to indications of a specific rival threat and tried to ensure that other women were not attempting to poach their partner (Sobraske et al., 2013). Women also employ more indirect strategies for fidelity management such as covertly monitoring their partner's faithfulness or imposing "secret tests" of commitment (Ein-Dor et al., 2015). Men, on the other hand, engage in more mate-guarding behaviors to ensure that their partner is not responsive to the advances of other men. The one area in which there is no apparent sex difference when it comes to suspicions of infidelity is the attention that is paid to deception used by one's partner (Sobraske et al., 2013).

Relative to women, men are typically more likely to be suspicious of infidelity (Brand et al., 2007). Further, men are more likely than women to judge that their partners would commit sexual infidelity in the future (Goetz & Causey, 2009). Men may experience more motivation to be suspicious of their partner so as to reduce the risk of being cuckolded, and thus have evolved an infidelity detection system designed to overestimate the likelihood of their partner's infidelity. In other words, it may be adaptive for men to determine whether their partner has been unfaithful so that they do not invest resources in the relationship and in providing for offspring that may not be their own (Brand et al., 2007).

Men are not only more suspicious of their partner's infidelity but also more likely to find out and learn about their partner's infidelity both by discovering it on their own and hearing about it from their partners (Brand et al., 2007). When examining a sample of young couples, it was found that men made more accurate inferences about their partner's cheating behaviors, and this occurred even after accounting for sex differences of women underreporting their extrapair acts (Andrews et al., 2008). Further, for participants who had partners reporting their infidelity, men were less likely than women to harbor unresolved suspicions about their partners because those men were more motivated to seek out confirming information, which was subsequently validated. However, the idea that men are better detectors of infidelity is up to some debate. A few studies showed that men made more mistakes in detecting infidelity than women during experimental detection tasks (Ein-Dor et al., 2015; Ein-Dor et al., 2017). Further research on sex differences in infidelity detection is warranted in order to better understand this phenomenon.

Insecure Attachment Styles

People higher on attachment insecurity are better at catching cheaters than people who experience interpersonal security. Ein-Dor et al. (2017) found those who have insecure attachment style (anxious and avoidant) demonstrated their adept ability by making fewer mistakes in detecting infidelity during an experimental task. People with a history of dishonesty may have heightened attention and vigilance that allows for better infidelity detection. This ability to detect infidelity cannot be ascribed as simply an exaggerated suspicion or general mistrust in people because there was no tendency for insecure individuals to indiscriminately judge people as cheaters overall. Further, those high in attachment anxiety or avoidance were more likely to cheat on their romantic partners, so it is possible that their own experiences allowed them to be better at detecting infidelity than more secure individuals. The authors of this study concluded that these findings demonstrate how attachment insecurity may seem maladaptive at the personal level, but can confer advantages at the interpersonal level; those with insecure attachment are seemingly better at portending their partner's thoughts and feelings in situations that pose a threat to their romantic relationship.

Projection Affects Detection

People who are attracted to alternative partners themselves may be more suspicious and show more anger toward their own partner because they assume that their partner is also interested in alternative partners (Neal & Lemay, 2019). This projection can overpower the use of valid cues in discerning their partners' attraction to others. Thus, perception of a partners' extradyadic attraction depends more on the perceiver's own attraction to others.

Also, by exaggerating their partner's perceived interests in others, they can try to alleviate their own guilt and/or justify their own extradyadic attraction.

Is Suspicion Normal?

It may be difficult to distinguish between normal and pathological jealousy that leads to infidelity detection tactics. Indeed, many evolutionary psychologists view acts of cheater detection and partner monitoring not as signs of pathology, but rather adapted, normal reactions to effectively detect subtle signals of concealment and deception of the philanderer (Buss & Abrams, 2017). Behaviors that are intended to hide or deceive are often good indicators that a betrayal has occurred (Fife et al., 2008). Because infidelity involves secrecy, deception, and often withdrawal from the primary partner, these behaviors are frequently met with suspicion by the in-pair partner (Dowd, 2012).

When therapists are confronted with clientele that show signs of suspicion and jealousy of their partner, they would need to ascertain whether their client was being overly protective of their partner, or whether their client was sensitive to behaviors that underlie diminishing commitment from their partner (Buss & Abrams, 2017). Some may be overly mistrustful or suspicious of their partner despite any real changes to the relationship or actual deceptions by their partner. In such a case, therapy should focus to illuminate the source of the distortions or exaggerations of the jealous partner. However, in other cases, the client's suspicions may be substantiated. Again, it is believed that humans have evolved adept means to detect cheating or deception in others. In these cases, therapists may need to shift their focus on jealousy as the primary issue and to view the jealousy as a symptom of other problems in the relationship which need to be addressed first.

Deceit Toward Infidelity Partner and Others

When it comes to infidelity, deceit is not only directed toward the in-pair partner, but also can be directed toward the infidelity partner. Most infidelity partners reported that they were initially unaware that they were the "other man/woman" and were involved in a situation of infidelity (Weiser & Weigel, 2015), thus suggesting that they were lied to before entering the relationship. One of the strategies used to first attain an extrapair mate can involve keeping their in-pair relationship a secret, although this appears to be more the case for men than women who are seeking extradyadic partners. It has been shown that men who sought extrapair partners were more likely than women to conceal that they were already in a committed relationship (Hughes & Harrison, 2019). Along with evidence that shows men will often lie and feign commitment and investment simply to attract a mate (Tooke & Camire, 1991), men apparently will also lie about their in-pair relationship in order to attain an extrapair mate. It may not be in a man's best interest to reveal his current relationship status to a potential affair partner because he could not offer her the time and commitment she desires in the relationship. He would also be limited in providing her with resources. Especially if the extradyadic relationship resulted in a pregnancy, the woman would have to sustain the enormous costs of bearing offspring without his support. Single women involved with married men report suffering from the negative consequences of the strategies the man uses to try to conceal the relationship from his wife (Richardson, 1988). These tactics involve time constraints, expectations of temporariness, and extreme privacy. It has been shown that this increases a woman's dependence on the relationship and reduces her power within it.

On the other hand, it was found that women seeking an extrapair mating were more likely to reveal they had a committed partner (Hughes & Harrison, 2019). A situation of a woman taking interest in an already committed man would present an ideal mating opportunity for the man. He could take advantage of having uncommitted sex. If their sexual interaction resulted in a pregnancy, there is a possibility that her in-pair partner would be the cuckold who would provide the resources and parental effort for his child, thus perpetuating his genetic legacy with little effort on his part. So it may be advantageous for a woman to disclose to a potential extrapair partner that she is in a current, committed relationship.

People already in a relationship use several other deceptive tactics when trying to attract or entice someone new while disguising it from their current partner. Schmitt and Shackelford (2003) examined the specific behaviors or acts that people who are already in a relationship do to let others know that they are willing to have another relationship. They termed these tactics as mate-poaching enticements. In order to be successful, mate poaching attraction needs to be secretive and disguised. Each sex seems to employ different tactics to disguise the fact that they are attempting to attract someone else while still in a relationship. Men who want to deceive both their in-pair partner and the community at large about their potential poaching enticements will display greater acts of commitment to their current partner. Men try to disguise their poaching attempts by overly satisfying their current partner's resource and commitment needs. They will discuss their future as a family with their current partner, pay closer attention to their current partner, and engage in deep emotional talks with them. Men will often express their satisfaction with their current relationship in hopes that their in-pair partner would be diverted away from the fact that they are seeking outside relations. To reduce the risk of having a poaching relationship become known, men are also careful in regard to what they reveal to others. Men will often try to camouflage their mate poaching to others by limiting discussion about the other relationship or by isolating that relationship from others (Schmitt & Shackelford, 2003).

For women, the most effective way to deceive their current partner and others of their extrapair pursuits was to maintain everyday routine and activities (Schmitt & Shackelford, 2003). In other words, women's mate poaching enticements were more inconspicuous if their daily life did not become noticeably altered. Women also tried to disguise their extradyadic pursuits by satisfying their current partner's need for sexual access. Women had more sex with their in-pair partner as well as became more romantic with their current partner. Thus, men and women use different deceptive tactics to achieve the goal of hiding the fact that they are trying to attract another partner while maintaining their current relationship.

Children of Unfaithful Parents

Parents may also lie to their children about infidelity to help save face. If a parent decides to share their affair with their child, and subsequently insists the child not share this information with anyone else, then the burden of secrecy and lying now transfers to the child. It has been shown that children of parents who have engaged in infidelity often have to keep their parents' infidelity a secret, and these attempts to maintain the privacy of their parents' infidelity are often fraught with stress and anxiety (Thorson, 2015). Adult children can be greatly affected by their parent's infidelity and experience quite a bit of turbulence having to keep that knowledge a secret.

Deceit by the Infidelity Partner

The infidelity partner is also involved in the deception surrounding infidelity. The "other man/woman" can be aware of their lover's in-pair partner (Dowd, 2012), and therefore willing to keep their extradyadic relationship a secret. In some cases, there is open discussion of the in-pair partner and the other man/woman understands his or her role in the extradyadic involvement. In other cases, even though the extrapair pair is aware of the primary relationship, they elect not to fully acknowledge it and the extradyadic couple does not discuss the partner, thereby fostering a climate of ignorance (Dowd, 2012). In either scenario, the infidelity partner is mindful that the secret must remain intact for the extradyadic relationship to persist. So why engage in such a relationship and keep this secret? It may be a case of mate availability. Many single women willing to engage in infidelity with married men indicated it was the closest thing they could find to a conventional relationship in comparison to other available men whom they perceived as unappealing or unacceptable relationship partners (Richardson, 1985).

Weiser and Weigel (2015) found that most of their participants did not initially know they were engaging in infidelity as the extrapair partner, but later found out. However, only slightly less than half ended the relationship upon learning of the infidelity, and many stayed with the infidelity transgressor for at least some time after learning the true nature of the relationship. Further, men were less likely than women to end an extradyadic relationship upon learning they were engaging in infidelity (Weiser & Weigel, 2015).

Who is the "other man/woman"? Those who knowingly and willingly become an infidelity partner and are amenable to conceal the transgression possess certain traits. Individuals who scored high on all Dark Triad personality traits (e.g., neuroticism), extraversion, unrestricted sociosexuality, and insecure attachment and low on agreeableness were more likely to knowingly enter infidelity relationships (Weiser & Weigel, 2015). Further, individuals with these clusters of traits also indicated a greater willingness to keep these infidelity relationships concealed and not inform the infidelity victim of the transgression. They were unlikely to even consider telling the infidelity victim. In contrast, individuals who are securely attached were less likely to knowingly become infidelity partners, and were more likely to have considered telling or did tell of the infidelity.

Infidelity partners who are aware they are engaging in a relationship transgression and willing to keep the infidelity hidden appear to possess a personality profile that is self-focused. They show little regard for the infidelity victim. In particular, those low in agreeableness are less considerate and caring of others, so it may be easier for them to be complicit in being an infidelity partner (Weiser & Weigel, 2015). Individuals high in anxious attachment may be willing to risk engaging in a secretive infidelity relationship as the other man/woman simply because it is a way in which they can receive a self-esteem boost and feel greater intimacy that they so desire.

The Deception of Cuckoldry

There is great deception involved with a potential consequence of infidelity— cuckoldry. Misattributed paternity is definitive proof of infidelity that has been kept hidden (Draper, 2007). Men face a considerable risk of cuckolding if their partners are unfaithful and would have to invest valuable resources in children who are not their own (Brand et al, 2007). In other words, it would be adaptive for men to detect if their partner has been unfaithful so that they do not invest resources in a relationship and provide for unrelated offspring (Brand et al., 2007). Because men can become fathers as a result of deception and infidelity, it may explain why men are more likely than women to be suspicious of infidelity, even when it is not occurring (Brand et al., 2007), and why men are more likely detect it when it is occurring (Andrews et al., 2008). It also helps explain men's strong reactions to a partner's infidelity which can often result in fatal consequences for women who are suspected of infidelity (Daly & Wilson, 1988).

Misattributed paternity is sometimes referred to as paternity fraud, which suggests that the mother (and even the extrapair partner) knew about the true paternity and deliberately deceived the cuckold for either financial gain or for other provisioning (Draper, 2007). Men who become fathers through deception not only bear the costs of child rearing, but also the cost of meeting a child's other needs (i.e., time, emotional investment, protection, etc.). If the discovery that a man has been wronged through deception of misattributed paternity happens many years into fatherhood, his decision and ability to leave or be compensated for his lost autonomy can become complicated. There are many aspects involved in leaving at that point. The purported father would have likely developed a deep emotional attachment, care, and love for a child that would be difficult to break. It probably would be in the best interest for the child to remain in a stable family and not be separated from the man who has been actively fathering them. It is also not in the child's best interest to encourage the view that fathering is primarily about providing financial child support or that their "real" father is simply a sperm donor (Draper, 2007).

Men find sexual infidelity more upsetting than women, particularly in the long-term situations than in short-term contexts (Haselton et al., 2005). If sexual infidelity signals a compromised paternity and the potential for adaptively misdirected long-term investment, then it makes sense this would be of greater concern for men in long-term relationships than short-term ones. Haselton et al. also found that men felt more upset than women in response to deception about a long-term partner's flirtation with others, whereas within short-term relationships, men's and women's ratings did not significantly differ. Further, not only did more men than women report feeling emotionally upset in response to deception about a partner's sexual infidelity, but they were also more upset about deception surrounding their partner's sexual fantasies about others, as sexual fantasies may be a predictor of sexual infidelity. Men's reactions to infidelity that could result in cuckoldry is considered an evolved defense to guard against investment in children that are not genetically their own.

Another study examined responses to a hypothetical situation where participants were asked to imagine that they found their significant other cheating on them and had to decide which sex of the infidelity partner they would find most disturbing (Hughes et al., 2004). Men found it more distressful if the sex of the interloper was another man than woman presumably because another male could potentially impregnate his partner and it could result in cuckoldry. If the interloper was a woman, this would pose no threat to a man's paternity. Women, on the other hand, who do not have to contend with the possibility of being cuckolded, were equally distressed if the extrapair person was either the same- or opposite-sex because both situations could lead to abandonment and the potential diversion of resources and attention.

Choice to Conceal or Reveal

There are several factors involved in the decision to either reveal or conceal one's own infidelity to their in-pair partner. As Kruger et al. (2015) found, people are more likely to expose infidelity when they have a strong reason to do so. Dowd (2012) found that the number one reason offered for discussing the infidelity secret was when some sort of crisis occurred that necessitated the disclosure. Cheaters were also substantially more truthful and willing to speak about their transgressions as their partner's knowledge of it increased (Mongeau & Schulz, 1997). Further, the desire to continue with the primary relationship may also factor into the decision for disclosure. Individuals with high motivation to maintain their current relationship offer more mitigating accounts of their affairs in order to achieve their goal of maintaining the relationship (Mongeau & Schulz, 1997). Likewise, individuals who reported having greater satisfaction with their relationship were more likely to reveal their infidelity secret to their partner than those in less satisfying relationships (Dowd, 2012). The betrayer may think that revealing infidelity portrays their willingness to now be open and honest and provides redemption of their good character.

In addition to an attempt to reconcile, disclosing infidelity can offer the cheater other benefits too. The cheater could unload the heavy burden of keeping this secret (Slepian et al., 2012). By telling the secret of infidelity to a partner, the cheater could also transfer the responsibility for determining whether the relationship should continue onto their in-pair partner. Revealing not only then shifts the determination of the relationship onto the one betrayed, but it also can give the cheater a sense of restoring morality (Miller, 2013).

Despite reasons to disclose infidelity, it seems that in most cases, acts of infidelity are not revealed. Slepian et al. (2012) surveyed participants regarding disclosure of their infidelity and found that the majority sampled (80%) did not tell their partners about their infidelities and it remained a secret. Many (42.5%) indicated that they told no one of their indiscretions, 37.5% told a friend, and only 20% told their partner. Dowd (2012) found similar rates of nondisclosure (78%) in another sample. Thus, most acts of infidelities seem to be untold and are kept quiet from others. Likewise, victims of infidelity reported similar rates of their partner's disclosure. Dowd (2012) showed that only 12.4% of the participants sampled noted that their partner had directly told them of their infidelity without solicitation or provocation by the victim in attempt to confirm the victim's own suspicions. It makes sense to keep infidelity a secret because if a cheater feels like they have gotten away with their infidelity, they have less need to blame themselves, feel guilty, or find themselves responsible for their actions (Mongeau & Schulz, 1997).

Further, the longer the extradyadic relationship, the less likely a cheating partner was to disclose their infidelity (Dowd, 2012). During the time of the extradyadic involvement, the cheater may increase their satisfaction with the extrapair partner, which then prompts them to further conceal the infidelity in order to continue those relations. Cheaters also often report keeping their secret from their partner out of a need to protect their partner from getting hurt or out of their own feelings of guilt while still indulging in the extrapair liaisons (Dowd, 2012). Some concealers may feel as if they have done nothing wrong and leaving something out may be less hurtful for their partner to hear.

Experience with prior infidelity may also impact decisions to reveal or conceal future infidelity. Williams et al. (2002) found that those who had previously cheated on a primary partner rated their recalled lies as more serious and as less acceptable than did those who had never cheated. The authors suggest that this finding raises a question: Would those who have sexually dishonest histories of lying/cheating on previous partners and recognize the seriousness of their lies be more or less likely to lie again? It is possible they would be less likely to lie again because of moral considerations. But it is also possible they would be more likely to lie again because they realize they have more to lose by telling the truth. In either instance, those with more self-protective motivations may perceive their own dishonesty more negatively.

There is also a sex difference when it comes to infidelity disclosure. Women are more likely to tell their partners when they were unfaithful than are men, and men reported that they often learn of their partner's unfaithfulness by hearing it directly from their partners (Brand et al., 2007). Women were also marginally more likely than men to break up with their partner after they had cheated and subsequently more likely to then start a new relationship with the affair partner. Thus, women may be more likely to reveal their infidelity partly due to their interest in terminating their current relationship and trade-up from their current partner to a more resourceful partner. If women are more likely to use infidelity to mate-swap, keeping the infidelity a secret would not be of paramount importance and women would be more prone to tell on themselves (Brand et al., 2007).

In addition to deciding on whether to keep the infidelity a secret from one's partner, cheaters also have to consider to whom else they should reveal their secret. Cheaters have an adaptive interest in not letting the larger community know about their indiscretions because in the past, such revelations were often met with violence and outrage from others (Schmitt & Shackelford, 2003). Particularly for women, the consequences could be dangerous and/or fatal if they are suspected of infidelity (Daly & Wilson, 1988). As such, people tend not to flaunt their affairs before their partner, their children, or society at large (Gass & Nichols, 1988). If an infidelity secret is revealed to others, then there is a greater risk that the victim may discover the information from others' disclosure. Indeed, suspicious partners primarily rely on third-party testimony as means of discovering infidelity (Dowd, 2012). Kruger et al. (2015) found that several factors influenced the likelihood of exposing sexual infidelity of another person. For instance, people might expose infidelity when they have a close connection to the victim (i.e., the person is a close friend or kin), when they want to date the victim themselves, or if they feel the relationship is likely to end regardless. Participants were also more willing to expose infidelity of others either when there seemed to be a strong emotional bond or when the affair seemed purely sexual (Kruger et al., 2015).

Many people often report keeping at least a few secrets from relational partners (Caughlin et al., 2009). However, a secret about infidelity is far less trivial than telling white lies, and keeping such serious secrets is evidently burdensome. As a matter of fact, secrets about infidelity can be experienced as physical burdens, and literally can weigh a person down. For instance, one experimental study showed that the more cheaters thought about their infidelities, the greater effort and energy they estimated would be required to engage in certain physical tasks, such that the weight of their secret took a physical toll on their well-being (Slepian, 2012). Thus, if cheaters become preoccupied with, constantly ruminate about, or try to repress their secret of infidelity, it can be physically impactful and prompt them to reveal their secret. Further, Wilson et al. (2011) found that the more a person categorized deceptive acts such as flirting, fantasizing, lying, and withholding information as indicative of cheating, the more guilt they would feel if they engaged in those behaviors. These factors could all come into play when making the decision of revealing infidelity.

Aftermath of Infidelity Deception

In the aftermath of discovering infidelity, it appears that issues surrounding the betrayal stem mainly from the secrecy and deception used to conceal the extradyadic relations (Lusterman, 2001). Some even report that it is not the affair itself but rather how their unfaithful partner lied and deceived them that was most hurtful, and the victim was unable to get past that use of deceit (Gass & Nichols, 1988). Even for couples seeking reconciliation via therapy, it appears that one of the primary issues that emerges during therapy in the aftermath of infidelity is dealing with the hurt feelings from the deception (Feeney, 2004). Therapists are advised to convey in a nonjudgmental manner that infidelity and the associated deception are never acceptable in any committed relationship and therapists should especially consider the level of deception used and the type of infidelity (whether emotional, sexual, Internet, etc.) when providing therapy to couples grappling with infidelity (Fife et al., 2008).

Serious distress can result when marriages are challenged by tensions caused by lies and deceit from infidelity (Rokach & Philibert-Lignières, 2015). Deception and lying can spoil a good and loving relationship and can result in intense loneliness (Rokach & Philibert-Lignières, 2015). Individuals victimized from infidelity may also develop depressive symptoms, feelings of shame and anger, and their own concept of romance and intimacy can be shattered (see Rokach & Philibert-Lignières, 2015). Some can experience a posttraumatic reaction after discovering their partner's affair (Lusterman, 2001), and these reactions often develop specifically from the deception involved with infidelity. It is also common for deceived partners to experience self-blame and feel that they are responsible for the betrayal and consequently feel inadequate or unattractive (see Rokach & Philibert-Lignières, 2015).

The general negative reaction caused by discovered deceptions does not appear to be gender specific (see Gordon & Miller, 2000). However, it seems that the nature of the distress experienced in response to infidelity is influenced by an individual's perceived mate value. Those who perceived themselves to be high in mate value reported greater levels of indignation in response to infidelity, whereas those who perceived themselves to be lower in mate value reported greater levels of insecurity (Phillips, 2010). This may be one explanation for why certain individuals are able to forgive their partners and choose to work toward reconciliation whereas others seek to immediately terminate the relationship following infidelity.

Infidelity victims can often feel humiliated or stupid for not detecting the infidelity or the lies told by their partner (see Rokach & Philibert-Lignières, 2015). Victims may question why they were such a fool or so blind not to recognize what was transpiring. Dowd (2012) noted that participants often had hindsight after discovering their partner's infidelity. That is, many signs of their partner's infidelity were noticed only after the fact. Some claimed that when looking back, they were angry that they should have picked up on some of the lies and deception but had not. Some of their partner's behaviors that were relatively innocuous at the time were later ascribed a suspicious context in hindsight. Dowd suggested that perhaps subsequent suspicion was needed for the victims to make sense of the relationship termination. Realizing a partner's previous suspicious behavior appeared to be more easily recognized after the event.

Further, victims can be confronted with even more deception when their partner recounts stories about the infidelity. The responses presented to one's partner accounting their previous actions may not be laden with truth and transparency. Lies can continue to be told in the aftermath of infidelity to prevent a relationship partner from knowing about the true nature of the extradyadic relationship or the devotion and time spent with the extrapair interest. Cheaters' deceptions are often downplayed, attributed to the situation, or otherwise rationalized (Gordon & Miller, 2000). Lie-tellers' accounts focus on minimizing the importance of their indiscretions, whereas lie-receivers' accounts seemed to focus on the damage done to the relationship (Gordon & Miller, 2000).

Smith (1991) discussed a case study of a couple who sought therapeutic consultation after infidelity. The wife was willing to forgive her husband for cheating and decided to remain in the marriage but was particularly unsettled by the lying that had occurred. She stated that she did not find her husband's cover-up stories credible and thought they consisted of a string of coincidences and omissions, even when retelling the details during the therapy sessions. In turn, the husband was angered that his wife had not believed him despite his previous devotion to her. Thus, infidelity and deception can elicit a considerable amount of anger from both parties (Feeney, 2004). Because uncovering the deception of infidelity can cause such a great deal of anger (Gordon & Miller, 2000), some couples even resort to violence and perceive that reaction to be an ordinary, predictable, and justifiable response to a partner's unfaithful behavior (Guerrero & Andersen, 1998).

Many lie tellers claimed that the reason they told the lie was to prevent their current partner from experiencing unnecessary worry, distress, or hurt feelings (Gordon & Miller, 2000). However, cheaters should realize that learning that an affair is continuing after a partner's repeated denials sometimes allows the victim to end his/her ambiguous situation and start to fully accept the loss (Gass & Nichols, 1988).

The motivation to maintain an in-pair relationship can also influence the type of accounts produced and attributions of the infidelity disclosure. Mongeau and Schulz (1997) examined college student responses to their own hypothetical sexual infidelity and found that those highly motivated to maintain their current relationship provided more mitigating accounts and excuses for their infidelity. They presented kinder responses to their partners and were more willing to offer concessions/apologies, admit responsibility, and feel guilt or blame for their actions. Thus, a person with high motivation to maintain a relationship was more likely to produce an account that was nonthreatening to their partner to achieve the goal of repairing the relationship by being as conciliatory as possible. On the other hand, a person with low motivation of maintaining the in-pair relationship was less worried about their partner's reaction to their account of their infidelity or to the future of their relationship. As follows, because those with a low motivation to continue their in-pair relationship do not feel a strong desire to protect their partner's feelings, they often provided more aggravating accounts of their infidelity. For instance, they offered more refusals of their behavior by asserting that it never happened, they felt no need to provide any explanations, or felt it was unnecessary to give an exact account of their transgression to their partners. They also presented more justifications for their behavior such that they took responsibility for their actions yet denied it was wrong, unwarranted, or serious (Mongeau & Schulz, 1997).

Further, Mongeau and Schulz (1997) showed that accounts were much more prevalent and honest as the partner's knowledge of the transgression increased. In other words, participants' descriptions of the transgression were substantially more truthful if they were aware that their partner had previous knowledge of it. Only when philanderers were certain that their partner knew the particulars of their transgressions did they mention the intimate details of the infidelity. Otherwise, cheaters wanted to be apologetic but did not want to give away too much information.

Those who have been deceived by their unfaithful partner ultimately have to decide whether to remain in the relationship. Divorce rates are significantly higher for secret infidelity couples than for revealed infidelity and non-infidelity couples (Marín et al., 2014). The negative outcomes of the secret infidelity couples suggest that disclosing the affair is an important step toward repairing a relationship and is something that is worth working through in therapy. However, it must be noted that 40% of infidelity couples who disclosed the affair and processed it during therapy still get divorced (see chapter 18 for a more detailed review of relationship dissolution following infidelity). The feelings of being violated and exploited due to the deceit may be so strong that it overrides desires to make the relationship last (Gass & Nichols, 1988). Further, because infidelity is often accompanied by deception, more than one type of relationship violation is at play, and the two combined can elicit even higher levels of anger and can reinforce the revelation that the relationship is no longer viable (Feeney, 2004).

Women's relationships were more likely to end after their own infidelity than were men's relationships, perhaps because women were more likely to begin a new relationship with the extrapair partner afterward (Brand et al, 2007). Thus, women may be using an extradyadic relationship as part of the transition of mate swapping (see chapter 20 for more on the formation of primary relationship with infidelity partner).

A partner who has committed infidelity has violated the trust in the relationship and has been deceptive about it, and betrayed partners do not want to be deceived or hurt further (Fife et al., 2008). After infidelity is brought to light and a couple decides to work on their relationship, it is recommended that unfaithful partners should adhere to a specific communication plan in which partners keep in touch regularly and inform each other of their schedules in order to help build accountability and trust. Failure to do so after an infidelity disclosure can perpetuate the mistrust and pain. Lie receivers reported that if their partner was more upfront about their engagements with a potential threat, then suspicions and arguments could have been avoided (Gordon & Miller, 2000).

As Gass and Nichols (1988) pointed out, there will be scars left from infidelity and the concomitant deception used to hide it, but issues can fade if the partner who breached the contract of the relationship plays their part in the healing process (see chapter 19 for discussion on forgiveness for a partner's infidelity). This will involve being more transparent and taking the responsibility to avoid giving any impressions that an extrapair relationship is still taking place outside of the primary relationship. Because a cheater has elected to use deception to deliberately misinform or mislead their partner, only the cheater can remedy the resultant damage and repair a relationship of trust.

References

Abitbol, J., Abitbol, P., & Abitbol, B. (1999). Sex hormones and the female voice. *Journal of Voice, 13,* 424–446. https://doi.org/10.1016/s0892-1997(99)80048-4

Adamopoulou, E. (2013). New facts on infidelity. *Economics Letters, 121*(3), 458–462. https://doi.org/10.1016/j.econlet.2013.09.025

Adams, H. M., Luevano, V. X., & Jonason, P. K. (2014). Risky business: Willingness to be caught in an extra-pair relationship, relationship experience, and the Dark Triad. *Personality and Individual Differences, 66,* 204–207. https://doi.org/10.1016/j.paid.2014.01.008

Ambady, N., & Rosenthal, R. (1992). Thin slices of expressive behavior as predictors of interpersonal consequences: A meta-analysis. *Psychological Bulletin, 111,* 256–274. https://doi.org/10.1037/0033-2909.111.2.256

Andrews, P. W., Gangestad, S. W., Miller, G. F., Haselton, M. G., Thornhill, R., & Neale, M. C. (2008). Sex differences in detecting sexual infidelity: Results of a maximum likelihood method for analyzing the sensitivity of sex differences to underreporting. *Human Nature, 19*(4), 347–373. https://doi.org/10.1007/s12110-008-9051-3

Brand, R. J., Markey, C. M., Mills, A., & Hodges, S. D. (2007). Sex differences in self-reported infidelity and its correlates. *Sex Roles: A Journal of Research, 57*(1–2), 101–109. https://doi.org/10.1007/s11199-007-9221-5

Brewer, G., & Abell, L. (2015). Machiavellianism and sexual behavior: Motivations, deception and infidelity. *Personality and Individual Differences, 74,* 186–191. https://doi.org/10.1016/j.paid.2014.10.028

Burgoon, J. K., Buller, D. B., Ebesu, A. S., White, C. H., & Rockwell, P. A. (1996). Testing interpersonal deception theory: Effects of suspicion on communication behaviors and perceptions. *Communication Theory, 6,* 243–267. https://doi.org/10.1111/j.1468-2885.1996.tb00128.x

Buss, D. M., & Abrams, M. (2017). Jealousy, infidelity, and the difficulty of diagnosing pathology: A CBT approach to coping with sexual betrayal and the green-eyed monster. *Journal of Rational-Emotive & Cognitive-Behavior Therapy, 35*(2), 150–172. https://doi.org/10.1007/s10942-016-0248-9

Caughlin, J. P., Scott, A. M., Miller, L. E., & Hefner, V. (2009). Putative secrets: When information is supposedly a secret. *Journal of Personal and Social Relationships, 26,* 713–743. https://doi.org/10.1177/0265407509347928

Cooper, A., Scherer, C. R., Boies, S. C., & Gordon, B. L. (1999). Sexuality on the Internet: From sexual exploration to pathological expression. *Professional Psychology: Research and Practice, 30*(2), 154–164. https://doi.org/10.1037/0735-7028.30.2.154

Daly, M., & Wilson, M. (1988). *Homicide.* Transaction.

Davis, S. (2000). Testosterone and sexual desire in women. *Journal of Sex Education and Therapy, 25,* 25–32. https://doi.org/10.1080/01614576.2000.11074325

Dowd, M. M. (2012). *The secrets of infidelity.* Dissertation Abstracts International Section A: Humanities and Social Sciences. ProQuest Information & Learning. Retrieved from http://search.ebscohost.com/login.aspx?direct=true&db=psyh&AN=2013-99150-256&site=ehost-live

Draper, H. (2007). Paternity fraud and compensation for misattributed paternity. *Journal of Medical Ethics: Journal of the Institute of Medical Ethics, 33*(8), 475–480. https://doi.org/10.1136/jme.2005.013268

Drigotas, S. M., & Barta, W. (2001). The cheating heart: Scientific explorations of infidelity. *Current Directions in Psychological Science, 10*(5), 177–180. https://doi.org/10.1111/1467-8721.00143

Ein-Dor, T., Perry-Paldi, A., Hirschberger, G., Birnbaum, G. E., & Deutsch, D. (2015). Coping with mate poaching: Gender differences in detection of infidelity-related threats. *Evolution and Human Behavior, 36*(1), 17–24. https://doi.org/10.1016/j.evolhumbehav.2014.08.002

Ein-Dor, T., Perry-Paldi, A., Zohar-Cohen, K., Efrati, Y., & Hirschberger, G. (2017). It takes an insecure liar to catch a liar: The link between attachment insecurity, deception, and detection of deception. *Personality and Individual Differences, 113*, 81–87. http://doi.org/10.1016/j.paid.2017.03.015

Evans, S., Neave, N., Wakelin, D., & Hamilton, C. (2008). The relationship between testosterone and vocal frequencies in human males. *Physiology and Behavior, 93*(4–5), 783–788. https://doi.org/10.1016/j.physbeh.2007.11.033

Feeney, J. A. (2004). Hurt feelings in couple relationships: Towards integrative models of the negative effects of hurtful events. *Journal of Social and Personal Relationships, 21*(4), 487–508. https://doi.org/10.1177/0265407504044844

Fife, S. T., Weeks, G. R., & Gambescia, N. (2008). Treating infidelity: An integrative approach. *Family Journal, 16*(4), 316–323. https://doi.org/10.1177/1066480708323205

Fincham, F. D., & May, R. W. (2017). Infidelity in romantic relationships. *Current Opinion in Psychology, 13*, 70–74. https://doi.org/10.1016/j.copsyc.2016.03.008

Gass, G. Z., & Nichols, W. C. (1988). Gaslighting: A marital syndrome. *Contemporary Family Therapy: An International Journal, 10*(1), 3–16. https://doi.org/10.1007/BF00922429

Giammarco, E. A., Atkinson, B., Baughman, H., Veselka, L., & Vernon, P. A. (2013). The relation between antisocial personality and the perceived ability to deceive. *Personality and Individual Differences, 54*, 246–250. https://doi.org/10.1016/j.paid.2012.09.004

Goetz, A. T., & Causey, K. (2009). Sex differences in perceptions of infidelity: Men often assume the worst. *Evolutionary Psychology, 7*(2), 253–263. https://doi.org/10.1177/147470490900700208

Gordon, A. K., & Miller, A. G. (2000). Perspective differences in the construal of lies: Is deception in the eye of the beholder? *Personality and Social Psychology Bulletin, 26*(1), 46–55. https://doi.org/10.1177/0146167200261005

Guerrero, L. K., & Andersen, P. A. (1998). The dark side of jealousy and envy: Desire, delusion, desperation, and destructive communication. In B. H. Spitzberg & W. R. Cupach (Eds.), *The dark side of close relationships* (pp. 33–70). Erlbaum.

Guitar, A. E., Geher, G., Kruger, D. J., Garcia, J. R., Fisher, M. L., & Fitzgerald, C. J. (2017). Defining and distinguishing sexual and emotional infidelity. *Current Psychology: A Journal for Diverse Perspectives on Diverse Psychological Issues, 36*(3), 434–446. https://doi.org/10.1007/s12144-016-9432-4

Hackathorn, J., Daniels, J., Ashdown, B. K., & Rife, S. (2017). From fear and guilt: Negative perceptions of Ashley Madison users. *Psychology and Sexuality, 8*(1–2), 41–54. https://doi.org/10.1080/19419899.2017.1316767

Halpern, C. T., Udry, J. R., & Suchindran, C. (1998). Monthly measures of salivary testosterone predict sexual activity in adolescent males. *Archives of Sexual Behavior, 27*(5), 445–465. https://doi.org/10.1023/a:1018700529128

Haselton, M. G., Buss, D. M., Oubaid, V., & Angleitner, A. (2005). Sex, lies, and strategic interference: The psychology of deception between the sexes. *Personality and Social Psychology Bulletin, 31*(1), 3–23. https://doi.org/10.1177/0146167204271303

Hughes, S. M., Farley S. D., & Rhodes, B. C. (2010). Vocal and physiological changes in response to the physical attractiveness of conversational partners. *Journal of Nonverbal Behavior, 34*, 155–167. https://doi.org/10.1007/s10919-010-0087-9

Hughes, S. M., & Harrison, M. A. (2017). Your cheatin' voice will tell on you: Detection of past infidelity from voice. *Evolutionary Psychology, 15*(2), 1–12. https://doi.org/10.1177/1474704917711513

Hughes, S. M., & Harrison, M. A. (2019). Women reveal, men conceal: Current relationship disclosure when seeking an extra-pair partner. *Evolutionary Behavioral Sciences, 13*(3), 272–277. http://doi.org/10.1037/ebs0000133

Hughes, S. M., Harrison, M. A. & Gallup, G. G., Jr. (2004). Sex differences in mating strategies: Mate guarding, infidelity, and multiple concurrent sex partners. *Sexualities, Evolution, and Gender, 6*, 3–13. https://doi.org/10.1080/14616660410001733588

Hughes, S. M., Mogilski, J., & Harrison, M. A. (2014). The perception and parameters of intentional voice manipulation. *Journal of Nonverbal Behavior, 38*, 107–127. https://doi.org/10.1007/s10919-013-0163-z

Kaighobadi, F., Shackelford, T. K., & Weekes-Shackelford, V. A. (2012). Do women pretend orgasm to retain a mate? *Archives of Sexual Behavior, 41*(5), 1121–1125. https://doi.org/10.1007/s10508-011-9874-6

Knopp, K., Scott, S., Ritchie, L., Rhoades, G. K., Markman, H. J., & Stanley, S. M. (2017). Once a cheater, always a cheater? Serial infidelity across subsequent relationships. *Archives of Sexual Behavior, 46*(8), 2301–2311. https://doi.org/10.1007/s10508-017-1018-1

Kruger, D. J., Fisher, M. L., Edelstein, R. S., Chopik, W. J., Fitzgerald, C. J., & Strout, S. L. (2013). Was that cheating? Perceptions vary by sex, attachment anxiety, and behavior. *Evolutionary Psychology, 11*(1), 159–171. https://doi.org/10.1177/147470491301100115

Kruger, D. J., Fisher, M. L., & Fitzgerald, C. J. (2015). Factors influencing the intended likelihood of exposing sexual infidelity. *Archives of Sexual Behavior, 44*(6), 1697–1704. https://doi.org/10.1007/s10508-014-0469-x

Lambert, N. M., Mulder, S., & Fincham, F. (2014). Thin slices of infidelity: Determining whether observers can pick out cheaters from a video clip interaction and what tips them off. *Personal Relationships, 21*(4), 612–619. https://doi.org/10.1111/pere.12052

Lusterman, D.-D. (2001). Treating betrayal issues after the discovery of marital infidelity. *NYS Psychologist, 13*(1), 13–16.

Marín, R. A., Christensen, A., & Atkins, D. C. (2014). Infidelity and behavioral couple therapy: Relationship outcomes over 5 years following therapy. *Couple and Family Psychology: Research and Practice, 3*(1), 1–12. https://doi.org/10.1037/cfp0000012

Mattingly, B. A., Clark, E. M., Weidler, D. J., Bullock, M., Hackathorn, J., & Blankmeyer, K. (2011). Sociosexual orientation, commitment, and infidelity: A mediation analysis. *Journal of Social Psychology, 151*(3), 222–226. https://doi.org/10.1080/00224540903536162

McDaniel, B. T., Drouin, M., & Cravens, J. D. (2017). Do you have anything to hide? Infidelity-related behaviors on social media sites and marital satisfaction. *Computers in Human Behavior, 66*, 88–95. https://doi.org/10.1016/j.chb.2016.09.031

Miller, B. (2013). On the analysis of cheating. *Journal of Analytical Psychology, 58*(4), 530–546. https://doi.org/10.1111/1468-5922.12031

Mongeau, P. A., & Schulz, B. E. (1997). What he doesn't know won't hurt him (or me): Verbal responses and attributions following sexual infidelity. *Communication Reports, 10*, 143–152. https://doi.org/10.1080/08934219709367670

Neal, A. M., & Lemay, E. P. (2019). The wandering eye perceives more threats: Projection of attraction to alternative partners predicts anger and negative behavior in romantic relationships. *Journal of Social and Personal Relationships, 36*(2), 450-468. https://doi.org/10.1177/0265407517734398

O'Connor, J. J. M., & Barclay, P. (2017). The influence of voice pitch on perceptions of trustworthiness across social contexts. *Evolution and Human Behavior, 38*(4), 506–512. https://doi.org/10.1016/j.evolhumbehav.2017.03.001

O'Connor, J. J. M., Re, D. E., & Feinberg, D. R. (2011). Voice pitch influences perceptions of sexual infidelity. *Evolutionary Psychology, 9*(1), 64–78. https://doi.org/10.1177/147470491100900109

Octaviana, B. N., & Abraham, J. (2018). Tolerance for emotional Internet infidelity and its correlate with relationship flourishing. *International Journal of Electrical and Computer Engineering, 8*(5), 3158–3168. https://doi.org/10.11591/ijece.v8i5.pp3158-3168

Pham, M. N., & Shackelford, T. K. (2013). Oral sex as infidelity-detection. *Personality and Individual Differences, 54*(6), 792–795. https://doi.org/10.1016/j.paid.2012.11.034

Pham, M. N., Shackelford, T. K., & Sela, Y. (2013). Women's oral sex behaviors and risk of partner infidelity. *Personality and Individual Differences, 55*(4), 446–449. https://doi.org/10.1016/j.paid.2013.04.008

Phillips, A. (2010). Indignation or insecurity: The influence of mate value on distress in response to infidelity. *Evolutionary Psychology, 8*(4), 736–750. https://doi.org/10.1177/147470491000800413

Rhodes, G., Morley, G., & Simmons, L. W. (2013). Women can judge sexual faithlessness from unfamiliar men's faces. *Biology Letters, 9*. https://doi.org/10.1098/rsbl.2012.0908

Richardson, L. (1985). *The new other woman: Contemporary single women in affairs with married men.* Simon and Schuster.

Richardson, L. (1988). Secrecy and status: The social construction of forbidden relationships. *American Sociological Review, 53*, 209–219. http://doi.org/10.2307/2095688

Rodrigues, D., Lopes, D., & Pereira, M. (2017). Sociosexuality, commitment, sexual infidelity, and perceptions of infidelity: Data from the Second Love Web site. *Journal of Sex Research, 54*(2), 241–253. https://doi.org/10.1080/00224499.2016.1145182

Rokach, A., & Philibert-Lignières, G. (2015). Intimacy, loneliness, and infidelity. *Open Psychology Journal, 8*, 71–77.

Roscoe, B., Cavanaugh, L. E. & Kennedy, D. R. (1988). Dating infidelity: Behaviors, reasons and consequences. *Adolescence, 23*(89), 35–43.

Schmitt, D. P., & Shackelford, T. K. (2003). Nifty ways to leave you lover: The tactics people use to entice and disguise the process of human mate poaching. *Personality and Social Psychology Bulletin, 29*(8), 1018–1035. https://doi.org/10.1177/0146167203253471

Schneider, J. P., Weiss, R., & Samenow, C. (2012). Is it really cheating? Understanding the emotional reactions and clinical treatment of spouses and partners affected by cybersex infidelity. *Sexual Addiction and Compulsivity, 19*(1–2) 123–139. https://doi.org/10.1080/10720162.2012.658344

Shackelford, T. K., & Buss, D. M. (1997). Cues to infidelity. *Personality and Social Psychology Bulletin, 23*(10), 1034–1045. https://doi.org/10.1177/01461672972310004

Slepian, M. L., Masicampo, E. J., Toosi, N. R., & Ambady, N. (2012). The physical burdens of secrecy. *Journal of Experimental Psychology: General, 141*(4), 619–624. https://doi.org/10.1037/a0027598

Smith, T. E. (1991). Lie to me no more: Believable stories and marital affairs. *Family Process, 30*(2), 215–225. https://doi.org/10.1111/j.1545-5300.1991.00215.x

Sobraske, K. H., Boster, J. S., & Gaulin, S. J. (2013). Mapping the conceptual space of jealousy. *Ethos, 41*(3), 249–270. https://doi.org/10.1111/etho.12021

Thornhill, R. (2006). Human sperm competition and women's dual sexuality. In T. K. Shackelford & N. Pound (Eds.), *Sperm competition in humans: Classic and contemporary readings* (pp. v–xix). Springer.

Thorson, A. R. (2015). Investigating adult children's experiences with privacy turbulence following the discovery of parental infidelity. *Journal of Family Communication, 15*(1), 41–57. https://doi.org/10.1080/15267431.2014.980824

Tooke, W., & Camire, L. (1991). Patterns of deception in intersexual and intrasexual mating strategies. *Ethology and Sociobiology, 12*, 345–364. https://doi.org/10.1016/0162-3095(91)90030-T

Tuomi, S. K., & Fisher, J. E. (1979). Characteristics of a simulated sexy voice. *Folia Phoniatrica, 31*, 242–249. https://doi.org/10.1159/000264171

Weiser, D. A., & Weigel, D. J. (2015). Investigating experiences of the infidelity partner: Who is the "other man/woman"? *Personality and Individual Differences, 85*, 176–181. https://doi.org/10.1016/j.paid.2015.05.014

Wiederman, M. W., & Hurd, C. (1999). Extradyadic involvement during dating. *Journal of Social and Personal Relationships, 16*, 265–274. https://doi.org/10.1177/0265407599162008

Williams, S. S. (2001). Sexual lying among college students in close and casual relationships. *Journal of Applied Social Psychology, 31*, (11), 2322–2338. https://doi.org/10.1111/j.1559-1816.2001.tb00178.x

Williams, S. S., & Payne, G. H. (2002). Perceptions of own sexual lies influenced by characteristics of liar, sex partner, and lie itself. *Journal of Sex and Marital Therapy, 28*(3), 257–267. https://doi.org/10.1080/009262302760328299

Wilson, K., Mattingly, B. A., Clark, E. M., Weidler, D. J., & Bequette, A. W. (2011). The gray area: Exploring attitudes toward infidelity and the development of the Perceptions of Dating Infidelity Scale. *Journal of Social Psychology, 151*(1), 63–86. https://doi.org/10.1080/00224540903366750

Young, K. S., Griffin-Shelley, E., Cooper, A., O'Mara, J., & Buchanan, J. (2000). Online infidelity: A new dimension in couple relationships with Implications for evaluation and treatment. *Sexual Addiction and Compulsivity, 7*(1/2), 59–74. https://doi.org/10.1080/10720160008400207

Zitzman, S. T., & Butler, M. H. (2009). Wives' experience of husbands' pornography use and concomitant deception as an attachment threat in the adult pair-bond relationship. *Sexual Addiction and Compulsivity, 16*(3), 210–240. https://doi.org/10.1080/10720160903202679

CHAPTER 14

Infidelity Across the Ovulatory Cycle

Virginia E. Mitchell, Jenna M. Lunge, Alex Orille, Mercedes Hughes, *and* Lisa L. M. Welling

Abstract

The circumstances under which infidelity occurs are numerous and several characteristics predict prior and future infidelity (e.g., religiosity, number of lifetime sexual partners, sociosexuality). Evolutionary perspectives inform why steroid hormones that vary across the ovulatory cycle have been associated with both women's interest in extrapair partners and shifting expressions of men's anti-infidelity behavior across their partner's ovulatory cycle. This chapter provides an overview of the ovulatory cycle to establish the physiological basis of the hormonal changes that occur across it. It then provides requisite background on evolutionary theories of human mating, which provide a framework to predict *when* women should express the most interest in extrapair partnerships, how current partner qualities are associated with desire for extrapair mating opportunities, and the types of qualities women may be seeking in extrapair partners. Evidence that supports and contradicts these accounts of ovulatory phase-dependent changes in extrapair partnerships, as well as research on male anti-infidelity strategies, is then considered. Finally, the chapter reviews evidence that hormonal contraceptives may alter partner preference patterns established in naturally cycling women and their opposite-sex partners. It concludes by identifying current gaps in hormone-linked shifts in women's infidelity desires and behavior, and makes recommendations for future research.

Key Words: ovulatory cycle, menstrual cycle, steroid hormones, progesterone, estrogen, Dual Mating Hypothesis, Strategic Pluralism Theory

Introduction

There is a myriad of factors associated with the likelihood that women will commit or have committed infidelity, such as, for example, their current relationship quality, their sociosexual orientation (i.e., attitudes toward casual sex; Mark et al., 2011; Rodrigues et al., 2017), their romantic attachment style (e.g., DeWall et al., 2011), personality characteristics (e.g., dark personality traits such as Machiavellianism; Brewer & Abell, 2015), childhood experiences of trauma (e.g., Yumbul et al., 2010), and their individual mate value (e.g., Starratt et al., 2017). Evolutionary theory provides a powerful lens for describing another factor that influences *when* women may be most interested in pursuing extrapair partnerships and *what types* of characteristics they seek in extrapair partners: hormonal status.

Women's interest in extrapair partnerships (e.g., Gangestad & Thornhill, 2002) and in-pair investment (e.g., Grebe et al., 2016; Grøntvedt et al., 2017) is linked to their fertility status and levels of circulating hormones associated with the ovulatory cycle. In this chapter, a brief overview of the ovulatory cycle and associated hormonal changes will first be provided, followed by a primer on evolutionary theories of female mate preferences that provide a framework for explaining why women's hormonal status should be associated with their mate preferences and extrapair interest. Next, we discuss the association between steroid hormones and changes in women's mate preferences, sexual desire, and sexual attractivity and proceptivity, along with an explanation of research demonstrating that both men and women have psychological anti-infidelity mechanisms attuned to hormonal changes across the ovulatory cycle. Finally, we outline the ways in which hormonal contraceptives, which interrupt hormonal fluctuations across the ovulatory cycle, influence women's interest in extrapair partners versus their current romantic and sexual partners.

Overview of the Ovulatory Cycle

The ovulatory cycle (also referred to as the menstrual cycle) consists of the follicular phase, beginning with the first day of menstrual bleeding and ending with the release of the mature follicle at ovulation, and the luteal phase, beginning at ovulation and ending just prior to the next menstrual onset. The hypothalamic-pituitary-ovarian (HPO) axis promotes development of ovarian follicles through the release of neuropeptides, gonadotropins, and sex steroid hormones, in turn regulating the female ovulatory cycle. Specifically, the hypothalamus secretes the neuropeptide gonadotropin-releasing hormone (GnRH) in a pulsatile fashion (Belchetz et al., 1978; Clarke & Cummins, 1982), resulting in subsequent pulsatile secretions of gonadotropins from the anterior pituitary (Levine, 1997). These gonadotropins, follicle-stimulating hormone (FSH) and luteinizing hormone (LH), travel through the bloodstream to the ovaries to stimulate development of the ovarian follicles. As a dominant follicle develops, it secretes the steroid hormones testosterone and estrogen (Hillier et al., 1981). Estrogen negatively feeds back to the hypothalamus and anterior pituitary to inhibit the release of GnRH (Caraty et al., 1989) and the gonadotropins (reviewed in Shupnik, 1996), respectively, which results in one dominant follicle developing (Zeleznik, 1981). High levels of estrogen from the developing dominant follicle cause a shift to positive feedback and the anterior pituitary produces a midcycle surge of gonadotropins (Liu & Yen, 1983). This surge finalizes the development of the dominant follicle and increases the production of sex steroid hormones. This point in the late-follicular phase is characterized by the highest circulating levels of estrogen and testosterone during the ovulatory cycle. Ovulation, the release of the ovum from the ovarian follicle, occurs approximately 37 hours following the midcycle gonadotropin surge (Testart & Frydman, 1982).

During the luteal phase immediately after ovulation, the site of the ruptured follicle forms into the corpus luteum, a temporary structure that secretes primarily progesterone and some estrogen to prepare the body for possible implantation and pregnancy (Wuttke et al., 1998). Together, progesterone and estrogen inhibit the production of gonadotropins via negative feedback on the hypothalamus and anterior pituitary (Nippoldt et al., 1989). Progesterone reaches its highest levels in the midluteal phase (i.e., the low fertility phase) of the ovulatory cycle, which is characterized by a low estrogen-to-progesterone ratio (i.e., lower levels of estrogen relative to progesterone). If conception has not occurred, the corpus luteum regresses and production of progesterone and estrogen decline, triggering the next menstrual onset. Declining levels of sex steroid hormones in the late-luteal phase also ends the negative feedback acting on the hypothalamus and anterior pituitary, causing GnRH, FSH, and LH levels to increase pulsatile secretions in preparation for the development of new ovarian follicles in the next ovulatory cycle (McCartney et al., 2002).

Conception can only result from insemination during a finite "fertile window" surrounding ovulation. Live sperm have been found in the female reproductive tract five days after intercourse (Gould et al., 1984) and can cause conception from intercourse up to six days before ovulation, whereas conception does not occur from intercourse 24 hours or longer after ovulation (Wilcox et al., 1995). Thus, researchers typically identify the fertile window as including the 5–6 days before ovulation and 12–24 hours after ovulation (e.g., Baird et al., 1995; Schwartz et al., 1980; Wilcox et al., 1998). The hormonal profile of the fertile window includes high levels of estrogen and testosterone, and low levels of progesterone. Conception cannot occur outside of this fertile window, and conception probability is highest 1–2 days before ovulation (i.e., in the late-follicular phase; Schwartz et al., 1980).

In addition to their biological functions, hormonal fluctuations across the ovulatory cycle may influence women's mating-related behaviors, such as their preferences for specific traits in a romantic or sexual partner. Women report an increase in attraction to and preference for more masculine faces (e.g., DeBruine et al., 2019; Little & Jones, 2012; Little et al., 2002; Marcinkowska et al., 2018; Penton-Voak & Perrett, 2000; Welling et al., 2007; although see Jones, Hahn, Fisher, Wang, Kandrik, Han, et al., 2018), voices (e.g., Feinberg et al., 2006; Pisanski, et al., 2014; Puts, 2006; although see Jünger et al., 2018), and bodies (e.g., Gangestad et al., 2019; Little, Jones, et al., 2007), and report stronger attraction to behavioral displays of male dominance (e.g., Havlíček et al., 2005; Lukaszewski & Roney, 2009; Thornhill et al., 2013; Gangestad et al., 2004), near ovulation compared to other times in their menstrual cycles (reviewed by Gildersleeve et al., 2014; Welling & Burriss, 2019; Welling & Puts, 2014). Although there is currently some debate over the hormonal mechanisms that underlie these shifts in preferences (reviewed by Welling & Burriss, 2019; Welling & Puts, 2014), there is evidence that testosterone (e.g., Bobst et al., 2014; Welling et al., 2007; although see Marcinkowska et al., 2019) and estradiol (e.g., Dixson et al., 2018; Roney & Simmons, 2016; Roney et al., 2011) are positively associated with women's preferences for facial masculinity, whereas progesterone is negatively associated with facial masculinity preferences (e.g., DeBruine et al., 2019; Marcinkowska et al., 2018). Estradiol levels are also positively associated with women's preferences for masculine male voices (e.g., Feinberg et al., 2006; Pisanski et al., 2014) and their preferences for behavioral displays of dominance (e.g., Lukaszewski & Roney, 2009, although these authors used estimated rather than measured hormonal assessments). These findings have been interpreted as possibly reflecting an adaptive shift toward preferences for cues to genetic immunocompetence when pregnancy is most likely to occur (reviewed in, e.g., Little, 2014). In other words, when women are most fertile, they may shift their attention and preferences toward traits in potential mates that would confer an advantage to their resulting offspring.

Evolutionary Theories of Women's Mate Preferences

An element of many evolutionary theories of female mate preference focuses on putative male traits that may be indicators of high genetic quality. Arguably, women should be attracted to cues of genetic immunocompetence because procreating with men who possess these traits could confer direct benefits to shared offspring (i.e., her offspring will have stronger genes for survival). The Handicap Hypothesis (Zahavi, 1975) and the Immunocompetence Handicap Hypothesis (Folstad & Karter, 1992) argue that traits maintained by testosterone (i.e., masculine traits) are good candidates for indicators of genetic quality because the same hormones that mediate the expression of sex-typical traits (mainly testosterone in men) are also immunosuppressants (see, e.g., Muehlenbein & Bribiescas, 2005). So, the argument is that only those with strong immune systems develop exaggerated sex-typical (i.e., masculine in males, feminine in females) traits. Put another way, maintaining traits that are dependent on testosterone, such as facial (e.g., Skrinda et al., 2014; Pound et al., 2009; Penton-Voak & Chen, 2004) and vocal masculinity (Cartei et al., 2014), may be an indicator that one has a particularly strong immune system because only individuals with strong immune systems would be capable of sustaining the burden of high levels of circulating testosterone. Certainly, men's facial masculinity is related to their circulating testosterone level (Penton-Voak & Chen, 2004; Pound et al., 2009; Roney et al., 2006), and it predicts reports of men's health (Thornhill & Gangestad, 2006; Rhodes et al., 2003; Rantala et al., 2013; Phalane et al., 2017; but see Boothroyd et al., 2013) and mating success (Rhodes et al., 2005). Recently, Foo et al. (2020) found an association between several measures of immunity during adolescence (the period during which sexually dimorphic traits develop) and sex-typical traits in adulthood, providing compelling evidence that sexual dimorphism in faces signals immune health during critical developmental periods. An increased preference for these traits when conception is most likely could lead to secondary benefits, whereby women who reproduce with immunocompetent men will be more likely to produce immunocompetent offspring (i.e., the genes for strong immune systems will be passed on to shared offspring) who will be more likely to survive until adulthood. That these traits are preferred by women more for short-term rather than long-term relationships (e.g., Little, Cohen, et al., 2007; but see Stower et al., 2020) and when women are most likely to conceive (e.g., DeBruine et al., 2019) may indicate that these traits are particularly desirable for sexual extrapair partners.

Understanding when women are most interested in extrapair partnerships, the qualities they look for in an extrapair partner, and how steroid hormones influence these preferences, can be informed by other evolutionary theories of female mate choice. These frameworks are important for understanding which women are predicted to be most interested in extrapair partnerships and why preferences for certain traits in extrapair partners may be sensitive to hormonal fluctuations across the ovulatory cycle (e.g., Welling et al., 2007). Trivers (1972) summarized the selective pressures on ancestral men and women in his Parental Investment Theory. According to Parental Investment Theory, sex differences in selective pressures have led to differences in mating strategies. The number of offspring that males can produce is limited mainly by their access to fertile partners and mating opportunities, whereas females are limited by the number of viable gametes an individual can produce. For females, gamete production is costlier, and the cost of a poor mating decision is more damaging to lifetime fitness because of the limited number of lifetime reproductive opportunities. Once a female conceives, she is unable to conceive again for a considerable amount of time (i.e., gestation and early lactation), whereas the male can theoretically continue to mate with numerous other females in order to continue reproducing. Due to this asymmetry in opportunity costs for males and females, men and women have faced different selective pressures that adjust both male-typical mating strategies (e.g., greater tendency toward short-term mating orientation, more permissive sexual attitudes; Buss & Schmitt, 1993) and female-typical mating strategies (e.g., greater tendency toward long-term mating orientation, more stringent mate preferences and less permissive sexual attitudes; Buss & Schmitt, 1993). Trivers's foundational work on Parental Investment Theory is the basis of two other overarching theories of human mate preferences: Sexual Strategies Theory (Buss & Schmitt, 1993) and Strategic Pluralism (Gangestad & Simpson, 2000).

Sexual Strategies Theory (Buss & Schmitt, 1993) and Strategic Pluralism Theory (Gangestad & Simpson, 2000) are founded on the notion that finding a suitable mate was an adaptive challenge for both ancestral men and women, and that this challenge shaped sex-specific mating behavior and psychology. Both theories recognize that investment in offspring is critical for both male and female fitness. Sexual Strategies Theory tends to emphasize that ancestral men's fitness would have been increased more, relative to ancestral women, by pursuing a short-term mating strategy (i.e., seeking more sexual partners and mating opportunities). Strategic Pluralism Theory, however, focuses on the breadth of mating strategies within the sexes and provides a framework to contextualize the variation in "sex-typical" mating strategies. Put another way, Sexual Strategies Theory focuses on women's "average" mating strategy, whereas Strategic Pluralism Theory evaluates both women's short-term and long-term preferences and argues that natural and sexual selection may have shaped these preferences very distinctly. Strategic Pluralism Theory is particularly suitable for characterizing and investigating hypotheses about female infidelity because it accounts for possible trade-offs between important partner characteristics; men with indicators of high immune quality (such as qualities that are linked to testosterone production; e.g., Foo et al., 2020; Muehlenbein & Bribiescas, 2005) are more likely to invest in mating effort relative to parenting effort compared to men with indicators of lower immune quality (e.g., Alvergne et al., 2009; Muller et al., 2009). Masculine men are also more likely to commit infidelity, are more likely to get a divorce, and have more lifetime partners than do relatively feminine men (e.g., Pollet et al., 2011). There is also evidence that these same individuals are poorer fathers; Fleming et al. (2002) found that men with higher testosterone levels were less emotionally responsive to the sound of infant cries, indicating that testosterone levels may impede parenting quality to a degree (see also Kuo et al., 2012, 2016). Thus, women may face a conundrum when it comes to mate choice: It may be difficult to find men displaying markers of immunocompetence who are willing to invest in relationship maintenance and offspring care.

The putative trade-off between investment potential and genetic quality is also the focus of the Dual Mating Hypothesis (Pillsworth & Haselton, 2006a), which centers on women's short-term and long-term mating preferences. According to this hypothesis, women have evolved a dual mating strategy wherein individuals seek suitable long-term partners who are cooperative and willing to invest in potential offspring, while concurrently seeking short-term partners with indicators of good genes around ovulation when conception is most likely. In other words, because signals of high investment potential and high genetic quality are less likely to be found in a single individual, women may attempt to strike a balance by opportunistically seeking extrapair partnerships with men of high genetic quality under certain circumstances while maintaining a long-term relationship with an investing partner. The Dual Mating Hypothesis argues that shifts in women's preferences for partner characteristics (e.g., masculinity) across the cycle are examples of "good genes" hypotheses of mate preferences. In other words, these preferences for genetically fit men at peak fertility increase the likelihood that women will reproduce with men who can confer genes that are associated with high immune function, developmental stability, and attractiveness to their shared offspring. If an individual's long-term partner does not display indicators of high genetic quality, that may increase the likelihood that infidelity will occur.

Whereas the Dual Mating Hypothesis focuses on the target of women's high fertility sexual interests, Extended Sexuality Theory (Grebe et al., 2013) focuses on the function of nonconceptive sex that occurs during the low-fertility luteal phase. Extended Sexuality Theory posits that nonconceptive sex, particularly for pair-bonded women, may be important for supporting the long-term social bonds necessary for successful pregnancies and long-term parenting (Thornhill & Gangestad, 2008; Grebe et al., 2013). During nonconceptive phases of the menstrual cycle, Extended Sexuality Theory argues evolutionary pressures have shaped women's mate preferences and behaviors in ways that favor investment in current pair bonds. During this phase of the cycle, ancestral women may have gained direct benefits from their current partner, such as protection from potential sexual coercion and direct provisioning of resources and food. Consequently, behavioral strategies that shifted ancestral women's focus to their primary partner during periods of low fertility may have been adaptive.

The theories of female mate choice discussed above provide a useful perspective through which to contextualize the qualities that women may seek in extrapair partners insofar as these preferences are linked to fluctuations in hormones across the menstrual cycle, although, as already noted, there are certainly other factors that contribute to the likelihood that sexual infidelity will occur (e.g., religiosity, number of lifetime sexual partners, sociosexuality; Whisman & Snyder, 2007). For many mammals, peak fertility is readily apparent through sexual swellings (Nunn, 1999), changes in body odors (Clarke et al., 2009), and receptive behaviors (Baum et al., 1977). During this fertile period, female sexual activity occurs exclusively (i.e., estrus) or increases (Dixson, 2015; Thornhill & Gangestad, 2015). Conversely, in human females, the fertile window is not easily discernable from nonfertile periods (Nunn, 1999), and sexual behaviors are not limited to times during which conception may occur (Grebe et al., 2013; Martin, 2007). Certainly, women have sex outside of their fertile window and across their entire ovulatory cycle (Dixson & Altmann, 2000). That women lack overt signals of fertility via easily discernable physiological or behavioral changes that may cue potential mates to their ovulatory status has led researchers to categorize their ovulation as "concealed."

In support of a dual mating strategy, concealed ovulation and extended sexuality across the ovulatory cycle may have evolved in part to allow women to secure good genes from extrapair males (should their partner not possess the desired traits) while still gaining the benefits of a pair-bonded partner (Pillsworth & Haselton, 2006a; Thornhill & Gangestad, 2015). Specifically, concealed ovulation and extended sexuality may have prevented ancestral males from monopolizing ancestral female's mating opportunities during high fertility. Due to concealment of high-fertility points during the ovulatory cycle, ancestral men would have had to mate guard women for longer spans of time or across their entire cycle to successfully monopolize mating opportunities that were likely to result in offspring, which would leave little time for other survival-related tasks (e.g., gathering food). Ovulatory concealment increases the cost of highly effective mate guarding strategies for males and may have influenced ancestral men to invest in regular female partner across the ovulatory cycle rather than selectively pursuing multiple mating opportunities with fertile, short-term mating partners. Because male mate-guarding is dispersed across the entire ovulatory cycle rather than specifically focused on women's high-fertility windows, this may have enabled ancestral women to seek extrapair partnerships when maximally fertile. In addition to increasing the opportunities that women may have had for pursuing extrapair partners, concealed ovulation and extended sexuality may have also functioned to reduce paternity certainty. When individuals are unable to consciously pinpoint peak fertility, there is less certainty surrounding the paternity of cuckolded males. Strategies that reduce paternity certainty reduce the likelihood that cuckolded males will commit infanticide (Hrdy, 1979), even when their partners have mated with other males, because they are less certain that the offspring they are killing *are not* genetically related to them (i.e., infanticide when paternity is uncertain could result in accidentally killing one's own offspring). When combined with other research aimed at understanding fluctuations in women's sexual desire, the target of their sexual desire, and sexually desirable traits across the ovulatory cycle, findings broadly suggest that women have evolved strategies to increase sire choice.

Women's Sexual Desire for Extrapair Partners

Understanding patterns of sexual infidelity requires identifying changes in sexual desire. Research aimed at understanding women's sexual desire across the menstrual cycle has yielded some conflicting results (for review see Brown et al., 2011; Schreinger-Engel, 1980), but most studies have reported a peak in sexual desire near ovulation (e.g., Adams et al., 1978; Arslan et al., 2018; Bullivant et al., 2004; Dennerstein et al., 1994; Jones, Hahn, Fisher, Wang, Kandrik, & DeBruine, 2018; Matteo & Rissman, 1984; Pillsworth et al., 2004; Roney & Simmons, 2013; Stanislaw & Rice, 1988; Udry & Morris, 1968; Van Goozen et al., 1997; but see Bancroft, 1987; Meuwissen & Over, 1992). Female-initiated sexual behavior is also consistently shown to increase in the fertile phase of the ovulatory cycle (e.g., Bullivant et al., 2004; Burleson et al., 2002; Guillermo et al., 2010; Prasad et al., 2014), including among lesbian women (Burleson et al., 2002). However, desire does not necessarily translate into action; some research finds that women's overall intercourse frequency across the ovulatory cycle is less consistent (Baker & Bellis, 1995; Clayton et al., 1999; Matteo & Rissman, 1984; Udry & Morris, 1968; Wilcox et al., 2004). It is likely that this increase in sexual desire is driven by estradiol and/or testosterone (reviewed by Motta-Mena & Puts, 2017), both of which peak near ovulation (e.g. Abraham, 1974; Korenman & Sherman, 1973).

Women's increased sexual desire during the fertile phase of the ovulatory cycle is accompanied by changes in behavior that are indicative of an increased mating mindset. For instance, women use more cosmetics, report an increased interest in dressing provocatively (Röder et al.2009), and are perceived by men to be dressed more provocatively (Schwarz & Hassebrauck, 2008) near ovulation compared to other times. Women also perceive themselves to be more attractive and desirable during the fertile days of their cycle (Haselton & Gangestad, 2006; Röder et al., 2009), and men seem to agree; men rate women in their fertile windows as having more attractive faces (Puts et al., 2013; Roberts et al., 2004), increased body symmetry (Manning et al., 1996), more attractive voices (Pipitone & Gallup, 2008), more attractive body scents (Gildersleeve et al., 2012;

Havlíček et al., 2006), and more attractive gaits (Provost et al., 2008) compared to women outside their fertile windows.

This research demonstrates that women's sexual desire increases around the fertile window and that women may also perform behaviors that increase their sexual appeal, thus increasing the likelihood they will secure mates during this time. The specific target of women's sexual interest (i.e., in-pair versus extrapair) has also been linked to hormonal changes across the ovulatory cycle and current-partner qualities in a manner consistent with both the Dual Sexuality Hypothesis and the Extended Sexuality Theory. Arslan et al. (2018) found that women expressed more interest in extrapair partners (e.g., increased attraction to, fantasizing about, flirting with) as well as an increase in direct behaviors that may lead to extrapair partnerships (e.g., going out to meet with other men) when near ovulation compared to other times of the ovulatory cycle. Bellis and Baker (1990) found that partnered women do report increased rates of extrapair copulations in the late-follicular phase compared to other phases, whereas copulations with their primary partner remained constant across the cycle. However, extrapair interest is not universal or indiscriminate; women's interest in extrapair partnerships appears to be partially dependent on aspects of their current romantic relationship (e.g., women's own mate quality, mate availability, male partners' mate quality; Gangestad et al., 2002; Gangestad et al., 2005). Women who rate their partners as being lower in sexual attractiveness report more sexual interest in extrapair partners during high fertility compared to low fertility points in their ovulatory cycle (Gangestad et al., 2002; Gangestad et al., 2005; Haselton & Gangestad, 2006; Pillsworth & Haselton, 2006b). Moreover, women with more sexually desirable partners report feeling closer to their partners and experiencing more relationship satisfaction around ovulation than women who have less sexually desirable partners. Conversely, women with less sexually desirable partners report being less critical of and feeling closer to their partner during low-fertility versus high-fertility points in their menstrual cycle (Larson et al., 2013). It is likely that steroid hormones that fluctuate across the menstrual cycle play a role in driving these shifts in partner interest, with elevated estrogen levels associated with extrapair interest and progesterone positively associated with in-pair sexual interest (Arslan et al., 2018; Grebe et al., 2016; Righetti et al., 2020). This shift in prioritization of partner characteristics when conception probability is highest may function to increase the likelihood that women with partners who have poorer signals of genetic quality are motivated to secure extrapair mating opportunities with individuals possessing cues to high genetic quality. Thus, this preference shift may increase fitness benefits to potential offspring via seeking higher quality extrapair partners when it is optimal to do so.

Outside of peak fertility, research supporting Extended Sexuality Theory has found that women initiate sex with their partner more often during the luteal phase, relative to the late-follicular phase, when they perceive their partner's investment in their relationship to be lesser than their own (Grebe et al., 2013). Women's commitment to their current relationship has also been positively associated with progesterone levels, with higher levels of commitment reported during the luteal phase of the menstrual cycle when progesterone levels are highest and lower levels reported during the follicular phase, when progesterone levels are relatively low (Jones, Little, et al., 2005). Whereas estradiol may play an important role in shifting women's interest in extrapair partners during the late-follicular phase, progesterone levels may underlie the shift in focus to in-pair bonds and sexual activity during the luteal phase of the menstrual cycle (Grebe et al., 2016). Overall, the Dual Mating Hypothesis and Extended Sexuality Theory provide a theoretical foundation linking women's desire to seek extrapair partners to specific hormonal states and conception probability, as well as some insight into the types of characteristics that women may seek in extrapair partners.

These patterns highlight the types of partner traits that moderate women's interest in extrapair partners; both women's mate quality and their male partner's mate quality moderate how sensitive women's interest in extrapair males is across their ovulatory cycle (e.g., Haselton & Gangestad, 2006; Larson et al., 2013; Larson et al., 2012). Furthermore, women who are currently in relationships display stronger preference shifts across their ovulatory cycle relative to women who are single (e.g., DeBruine et al., 2019; Gangestad et al., 2019; Havlíček et al., 2005; Marcinkowska et al., 2018; Pillsworth Larson et al.,, 2004). This research suggests that hormonally attuned changes in preferences may be calibrated for increasing the likelihood that women in relationships seek extrapair partners around high conception risk specifically for the potential direct benefits these partners may provide to potential offspring. According to the Dual Mating Hypothesis, this shift is more relevant for pair-bonded women, particularly if their partners do not display these qualities, but not as important for single women because their future reproductive opportunities are not yet linked to a particular individual.

Overall, changes in partnered women's sexual desire for extrapair partners around midcycle paired with changes in their behavior (e.g., dressing more provocatively, increased grooming behaviors, being more flirtatious) and perceptible differences in their physical appearance (e.g., their faces and voices being more attractive at midcycle), may set the stage for partnered women to find and secure valuable extrapair partnerships when conception probability is highest. In other words, hormonallyassociated changes in the target of women's sexual desire and their appearance and behavior may increase the likelihood that sexual infidelity occurs specifically around high fertility points of the ovulatory cycle. The increases in desire (e.g., Bullivant et al., 2004; Dennerstein et al., 1994; Pillsworth et al., 2004; Roney & Simmons, 2013; Stainslaw & Rice, 1988; Van Goozen et al., 1997), female-initiated sexual behavior (e.g., Arslan et al., 2018; Bellis & Baker, 1990; Bullivant et al., 2004; Burleson et al., 2002; Guillermo et al., 2010; Prasad et al., 2014), and increased attractivity (e.g. Gildersleeve et al., 2012; Havlíček et al., 2006; Manning et al., 1996; Pipitone & Gallup, 2008; Provost et al., 2008; Puts et al., 2013; Roberts et al., 2004) all peaking near ovulation could be a driving influence for increased infidelity across the ovulatory cycle.

Male Adaptations to Prevent Infidelity Linked to the Ovulatory Cycle

Adaptations or strategies for female reproductive success often come at a cost for females in the form of evolved male counterstrategies. These counterstrategies are often challenged by further evolution of female counterstrategies, thus allowing for a cycle of sexually antagonistic coevolution between males and females, otherwise known as sexual conflict (for a review, see Stumpf et al., 2011). For example, women's increased interest in extrapair partners during the fertile phase of the ovulatory cycle may be an adaptive mechanism for *women*, as it would potentially secure "good genes" while retaining a long-term in-pair partner for resources during the luteal phase (Gangestad & Simpson, 2000; Gangestad et al., 2002), but this strategy would increase the likelihood that their in-pair partner would provide paternal care for offspring to which he is not genetically related (i.e., the rival's offspring). Therefore, it would be advantageous for men to evolve counterstrategies to reduce or prevent infidelity so that their paternal care and resources would not be spent on another man's offspring. These strategies, such as jealousy, mate guarding, and mate retention behaviors, have been investigated in humans (e.g., Arnocky et al., 2014; Buss, 2002; Buss & Shackelford, 1997; Daly et al., 1982; Shackelford et al., 2005), and the expression of these traits in men and women has been linked to hormonal fluctuations across the ovulatory cycle.

Researchers have hypothesized that jealousy is designed to reduce infidelity (e.g., Buss et al., 1993; Buss & Haselton, 2005; Daly et al., 1982), and indeed male sexual jealousy seems to have components to it that are present cross-culturally (Daly et al., 1982). In humans, jealousy is usually presented as mate guarding or mate retention behaviors (Buss & Shackelford, 1997; Shackelford et al., 2005). According to Buss (2002), mate guarding refers to strategies designed to (a) retain a mate, (b) prevent potential rivals' access to a mate, and (c) prevent a mate from leaving the partnership. Researchers measure mate guarding by assessing the frequency of mate retention tactics (Buss, 1988; Leivers et al., 2014; Shackelford et al., 2006) or by measuring a participant's willingness to aggress against a same-sex rival (Arnocky et al., 2014). Mate retention tactics can be divided into two subcategories: cost-inflicting strategies and benefit-provisioning strategies (Miner et al., 2009). Cost-inflicting strategies are performed to reduce infidelity at the cost of the woman's interests or freedom, such as derogating her in front of others or monopolizing her time (e.g., McKibbin et al., 2007). Benefit-provisioning strategies function to reduce infidelity by making the current partnership seem more desirable. For example, men might buy their partner an expensive gift, compliment her on her looks, or improve his own looks (Buss et al., 2008). Interestingly, jealousy, mate-guarding, and willingness to aggress toward a rival male increase in conditions of mate scarcity (as opposed to mate abundance; Arnocky et al., 2014). Of course, these behaviors are still present in conditions of mate abundance, albeit to a lesser extent (Arnocky et al., 2014), which suggests that specific contexts may allow for the evolved psychological mechanisms for preventing infidelity to be expressed to different extents. That is, male jealousy and mate guarding may be much higher in contexts where female infidelity is much more likely or costlier (i.e., when extrapair conception is more likely and/or risk of relationship defection is high).

Given that research has shown that jealousy and mate retention behaviors are sensitive to the risk of partner infidelity, it could then be predicted that the male mechanisms for preventing infidelity would be most active during their partner's fertile phase of the ovulatory cycle. For example, chimpanzees almost exclusively guard parous high-fertility females, rather than nulliparous low fertility females. In humans, however, this prediction is difficult to investigate because women possess relatively concealed ovulation (for review, see Burley, 1979; Strassman, 1981). Because of concealed ovulation, it is theoretically more difficult for men to attune their jealousy and mate-guarding behaviors to their partner's ovulatory cycle. Indeed, concealed ovulation may have evolved precisely for the purpose of reducing men's ability to prevent infidelity and extrapair mating (Benshoof & Thornhill, 1979). However, men may perceive subtle changes in women's physiology and behavior during ovulation. Men report finding women more attractive when they are more likely to conceive (i.e., near ovulation), leading to the hypothesis that men have evolved to detect subtle physiological and psychological cues to fertility (Bobst & Lobmaier, 2012; Puts et al., 2013; Roberts et al., 2004; Thornhill & Gangestad, 2008). Consistent with this hypothesis, men express higher levels of jealousy and mate guarding when their partner's conception risk is higher (Gangestad et al., 2002; Haselton & Gangestad, 2006; Pillsworth & Haselton, 2006b). For example, Gangestad et al. (2002) found not only that women report an increase in extrapair, nonprimary partners around midcycle but also that women report that their male partners perform more mate-retention behaviors at midcycle compared to during the luteal phase. Moreover, Righetti et al. (2020) found that although females find their partners less attractive when estradiol is high, men seem to detect these changes in their partners, as they perceived their female partner's relationship satisfaction and attraction to themselves to be lower. These results suggest that the increase in mate guarding surrounding ovulation is caused by the male partner perceiving a threat to the relationship.

Women also experience jealousy and exhibit behaviors designed to reduce partner infidelity that also appear to be sensitive to hormonal status and fluctuations across the ovulatory cycle (Cobey et al., 2012; Geary et al., 2001), although there are sex differences in male and female jealousy. On average, women are more upset at the prospect of a partner's emotional infidelity compared to men, whereas men are more upset at the prospect of a partner's sexual infidelity compared to women, although both sexes are upset by both types of infidelity (Buss et al., 1992; Shackelford et al., 2004). These sex differences could lead to differences in how jealousy is expressed; for example, De Miguel and Buss (2011) found that men used more resource displays (e.g., bought their partner an expensive gift) to retain their mates, and women used more appearance-enhancing behaviors (e.g., making sure they look nice for their partner).

In terms of hormonal correlates of women's expression of jealousy, women are more jealous during the fertile part of the ovulatory cycle (Cobey et al., 2012) and jealousy increases with estradiol (Geary et al., 2001). However, this cyclic shift in women's jealousy is somewhat counterintuitive in light of other findings regarding increased extrapair interest (e.g., Gangestad & Thornhill, 2002). Similar to jealousy, high estradiol in women is associated with increased sexual attraction and interest in extrapair partners, whereas high progesterone is associated with increased sexual attraction and interest in one's current partner (Grebe et al., 2016). If female extrapair interest increases during high fertility, why, then, would male partner infidelity be much more of a concern? Cobey et al. (2012) put forth the explanation that an increase in jealousy during the fertile phase could be a byproduct of the male partner's increase in jealousy. That is, Cobey et al. (2012) proposed that men increase jealousy during their partner's fertile window to counteract the potential risk of cuckoldry, and this in turn provokes reactionary jealous behaviors in women (although others have argued that it is men responding to women's jealous behaviors; see Welling et al., 2012). If women benefit from having their current partners provide resources throughout the ovulatory cycle, then it would be detrimental to have that partner commit infidelity and allocate those resources elsewhere, even if the woman is also interested in extrapair partners. In fact, as estradiol decreases and progesterone increases (i.e., the luteal phase), women's loyalty and faithfulness become more positively associated with frequency of intercourse (Grøntvedt et al., 2017), and an increase in copulations facilitates pair bonds and reduces infidelity (Thornhill & Gangestad, 2008).

Overall, past research has shown that both men and women have evolved mechanisms to reduce their partner's infidelity by way of jealousy and mate guarding. Additionally, men and women have evolved mechanisms that detect infidelity threat and increase jealousy and mate guarding behavior. Still, infidelity detection and prevention across the ovulatory cycle requires more research to fully understand it. Using methods that incorporate comparisons between naturally cycling women and women who use hormonal contraceptives can allow for a more precise grasp of how ovarian hormones interact with infidelity-prevention behaviors over the ovulatory cycle.

Hormonal Contraceptives and Jealousy

Hormonal contraceptives (HCs) work by artificially altering steroid reproductive hormone levels in order to prevent pregnancy. HCs supply a synthetic progestin, often in combination with ethinyl estradiol, to halt the functioning of the HPO-axis. Combined HCs (i.e., oral contraceptive pills with a progestin and ethinyl estradiol) halt the development of the ovarian follicles through negative feedback at the hypothalamus and pituitary, thus inhibiting the release of GnRH and gonadotropins, and by extension reducing endogenous estrogen and progesterone (Odell & Molitch, 1974). Progestin-only contraceptives (e.g., mini-pill, vaginal ring, hormonal intrauterine devices) primarily work by altering the cervical and uterine environment to prevent implantation (Kessurü-Koos,

1971; Moghissi & Marks, 1971), though many users may also experience partially or completely suppressed ovulation like those using combined HCs (Kim-Björklund et al., 1991; Rivera et al., 1999). HC users do not experience cyclical fluctuations in their estrogen and progesterone levels, but instead have relatively stable and reduced levels of estrogen and artificially inflated levels of progesterone in amounts that approximate endogenous progesterone levels during the midluteal phase (Grøntvedt et al., 2017; Odell & Molitch, 1974). In other words, the hormone levels of HC users resemble those of naturally cycling women at low fertility, when progesterone levels are high and estrogen is low.

Because sex hormones and ovulatory cycle phase are associated with various aspects of mating psychology, HC users may display preferences and behaviors that differ from their naturally cycling counterparts (for a review, see Alvergne & Lummaa, 2010; Mitchell & Welling, 2020; Welling, 2013). Certainly, HC users report mate preferences similar to those of naturally cycling women at low fertility (e.g., Klapilová et al., 2014; Jones, Perrett, et al., 2005); naturally cycling women have stronger preferences for masculine male faces at high fertility (e.g., Johnston et al., 2001; but see Jones, Hahn, Fisher, Wang, Kandrik, Han, et al., 2018), but stronger preferences for feminine male faces (an indicator of paternal investment; e.g., Perrett et al., 1998) at low fertility (e.g., Puts, 2006). HC users, however, display reduced preferences for male masculinity (Feinberg et al., 2008; Gori et al., 2014; Little et al., 2002; Little, Jones, & Burriss, 2007; but see Jones, Hahn, Fisher, Wang, Kandrik, Han, et al., 2018) and choose less facially masculine partners compared to women who are naturally cycling (Little et al., 2013). Also, contrary to naturally cycling women, HC users do not show adaptive variations in masculinity preferences based on relationship context (i.e., short- versus long-term relationship; Smith et al., 2009), their own attractiveness (Vukovic et al., 2008), nor across their ovulatory cycle (Penton-Voak & Perrett, 2000; Penton-Voak et al., 1999). Furthermore, unlike naturally cycling women, HC users do not show adaptive midcycle increases in physiological measures of sexual interest (e.g., pupillary dilation; Laeng & Falkenberg, 2007), sexual desire (Adams et al. 1978; Arslan et al., 2018; Elaut et al., 2016; Guéguen, 2009; Wallwiener et al., 2010), attentional bias to flirtatious messages (Rosen & López, 2009), sexual receptivity (Gueguen, 2009), or their own attractiveness (for a review, see Alvergne & Lummaa, 2010; Mitchell & Welling, 2020; Welling, 2013). Compared to naturally cycling women at high fertility, HC users are not rated as having more attractive body odors (Kuukasjärvi et al., 2004) or voices (Ostrander et al., 2018), and exotic dancers using HCs do not see a midcycle increase in their tips like their naturally cycling counterparts (Miller et al., 2007). It therefore appears that altering women's hormonal profile to artificially mimic the low fertility midluteal phase disrupts several mechanisms of women's mating psychology, including dynamic mate preferences, sexual behaviors, and attractiveness.

Women who begin taking HCs after entering a romantic relationship also experience changes in their own mate preferences. Little and colleagues (2013) measured partnered women's preferences for facial masculinity before and after the initiation of an HC regimen and found that the initiation of HCs reduced their preferences for masculinity in male faces. Because attraction to one's partner is a significant predictor of relationship satisfaction (Mark & Herbenick, 2014; Roberts et al., 2012), it is possible that a change in mate preferences (e.g., masculinity) due to a change in HC use could have negative impacts on relationship quality. Indeed, several studies (e.g., French & Meltzer, 2020; Roberts et al., 2012; Roberts et al., 2014; Russell et al., 2014) have found that women's relationship satisfaction is disrupted among those whose current HC use (i.e., either using or not using HCs) is incongruent with their HC status when they began their relationship.

The Congruency Hypothesis argues that relationship satisfaction is predicted by the congruency between current HC use and HC use at the formation of a relationship, rather than current HC use alone (Roberts et al., 2014). Women who used an HC when their relationship begins but later discontinue their HC, as well as women who formed a relationship while naturally cycling but later begin using an HC, report significantly lower satisfaction in their sexual, but not nonsexual, experiences with their romantic partner (French & Meltzer, 2020; Roberts et al., 2012; Roberts et al., 2014). Roberts and colleagues (2012) found that women who used HCs at the onset of a romantic relationship, but later stopped using them, reported lower sexual satisfaction and attraction to their partners, and were more likely to initiate a separation in those relationships that dissolved, compared to women not using HCs at the beginning of their relationship. Interestingly, the women who used HCs at the onset of their romantic relationship were more satisfied with their partner's financial support and, overall, were less likely to have broken up with their partner (Roberts et al., 2012; but see Birnbaum et al., 2017), further suggesting that HC users may prioritize indicators of long-term relationship investment over sexual attraction.

The relationship between HC incongruency and nonsexual marital satisfaction appears to be influenced by the attractiveness of a woman's romantic partner, such that women with relatively attractive partners experience greater marital satisfaction after terminating HC use, whereas women with relatively unattractive partners experience reduced marital satisfaction. On the other hand, women who began their relationship while naturally cycling did not experience changes in their marital satisfaction (Russell et al., 2014). HC congruency, therefore, appears to be a significant predictor in maintaining partnered women's sexual satisfaction and, specifically for women who are partnered with less attractive men, in maintaining their marital satisfaction. It is important to note, however, that more recent large-sample research has not supported the Congruency Hypothesis (Jern et al., 2018; Jones, Hahn, Fisher, Wang, Kandrik, Han, et al., 2018), so future research is needed to further investigate inconsistencies between studies.

Given the aforementioned hormone-mediated fluctuations in extrapair interest (Gangestad et al., 2002; Haselton & Gangestad, 2006), it is reasonable to expect that HCs might similarly have an influence on women's extrapair mating motivation. Klapilová and colleagues (2014) investigated the frequency of partnered women's sexual behaviors and, although there was no difference between HC users and naturally cycling women in the number of extrapair partners, HC users engaged in more in-pair sexual interactions. Furthermore, among those who did engage in extrapair mating, HC users had fewer partners and fewer one-night stands compared to naturally cycling women. Yet, the specific composition of the HC may be more important for predicting the effects of HC use on women's psychology rather than considering all HC users as a single homogeneous group (see Mitchell & Welling, 2020, for a review). High levels of synthetic estrogen, but not progesterone, contained in HCs is positively associated with reported jealousy (Cobey et al., 2011) and their frequency of partner-directed mate retention behaviors (Welling et al., 2012). More recently, Grøntvedt et al. (2017) found that the women who reported being least committed to their relationships reported high frequencies of intercourse only when using HCs with a higher synthetic estrogen to progesterone ratio (i.e., they were using a contraceptive type that contained a relatively stronger dose of estrogen, although all contraceptives contain higher dosages of progestin compared to estrogen), whereas women most committed to their partner reported high frequencies of intercourse when using HCs with a low estrogen to progesterone ratio (i.e., they were using a contraceptive with little to no estradiol). To best understand the influences of synthetic hormones on women's mating psychology, it is therefore important to include HC composition in future investigations (see also Mitchell & Welling, 2020).

Although some research suggests that HCs dampen or eliminate cyclical variations in women's mating psychology, the influence of HCs on relationship dynamics is currently relatively understudied, particularly with regard to extrapair mating motivations and infidelity risk. Despite HC users not experiencing cyclic hormone fluctuations in the way that naturally cycling women do, evidence suggests the synthetic hormones in their contraceptives are still influencing mating psychology. Future research should continue to investigate these relationships and also focus on the specific influences of synthetic hormone type, dosage, and administrative route.

Conclusion

Women's mating motivations are, in part, influenced by their current hormonal state, although to what degree is still debated (e.g., Gangestad et al., 2019; Stern et al., 2019; Jones, Hahn, Fisher, Wang, Kandrik, Han, et al., 2018). As such, hormonal fluctuations across the ovulatory cycle also influence when women may be most likely to seek extrapair partners as well as the types of qualities they may seek in these individuals. The Dual Mating Hypothesis (Pillsworth & Haselton, 2006a) provides a cogent theoretical framework in which to situate empirical findings that women, particularly those with male partners that have relatively poorer indicators of genetic quality (e.g., lower facial and vocal masculinity), are more likely to experience desire for extrapair partners at times of high fertility (e.g., Gangestad et al., 2005; Larson et al., 2013; Pillsworth & Haselton, 2006b). Fluctuating steroid hormones across the ovulatory cycle appear to mediate changes in preferences and interest in an extrapair versus in-pair partner. In-pair sexual interest has been positively associated with progesterone levels, whereas extrapair interest has been positively associated with estrogen and negatively with progesterone (e.g., Arslan et al., 2018; Grebe et al., 2016; Righetti et al., 2020). Both men and women have evolved anti-infidelity counteradaptations that are also attuned to the ovulatory cycle. Male jealousy and mate-guarding behavior peak around the late follicular phase, possibly as a counteradaptation to the period when female extrapair interest would be highest and potentially costliest. Although steroid hormones have been associated with female jealousy (e.g., Cobey et al., 2012; Geary et al., 2001), the exact adaptive function of the link between steroid hormones, cycle phase, and female jealousy is still unclear. Hormonal contraceptives, which interrupt patterns of naturally cycling hormones, alter both the pattern shifts in preferences for opposite-sex characteristics as well as shift the target of women's preferences more toward the Extended sexuality profile (i.e., increase preference for cues to investment; e.g., Little et al., 2013).

Although research documenting hormonal predictors of women's mate preferences has blossomed in the last 20 years, much more research is necessary to understand how women's fertility status and hormonal profile is associated with their interest in extrapair partnerships. One of the largest gaps in the present literature linking infidelity to the ovulatory cycle is that most research assesses women's self-reported interest or desire in engaging in interactions with extrapair partners, rather than measuring instances of actual behaviors. There are some notable exceptions to this, such as Arslan et al. (2018), which documented women's mating interests by collecting diary entries recorded over a span of time. Approaches like this may be more sensitive to capturing instances of extrapair behavior (e.g., flirtation, going out to see an opposite-sex individual without a partner's knowledge, having sexual interactions with an extrapair partner) outside survey measures developed to assess interest in infidelity or infidelity risk. These approaches are also critical for accurately capturing the time at which extrapair interactions are most likely to occur based on an individual's ovulatory cycle. Future research should also define infidelity and extrapair interest and extrapair behaviors more clearly; there are a broad range of extrapair behaviors outside of extrapair copulation that might be considered "cheating" in monogamous relationships, such as nonsexual behaviors that may still be important for understanding how extrapair interest is linked to the ovulatory cycle. Although these behaviors may not result in an immediate opportunity to attain high-quality genetic material from a partner, they may contribute to other important relationship processes, such as mate-switching (Buss et al., 2017).

Future research also needs to address hormonal associations in nonheterosexual mate preferences as well as how extrapair interest and experiences differ between heterosexual and nonheterosexual relationships. For instance, how does the experience of what is known as "lesbian bed death," or the cessation of sexual activity in long-term relationships between two women despite the presence of consistent emotional intimacy (van

Rosmalen-Nooijens et al., 2008), influence the likelihood that individuals in these relationships will commit infidelity? Are naturally cycling women experiencing this in their relationship more likely to commit infidelity around periods of high fertility versus low fertility? Similarly, future research should focus on hormonal influences on extrapair desire in women who are in consensually nonmonogamous relationships (i.e., they have an explicit agreement with their current partner(s) that having sexual and/or romantic relationships outside of the dyad is permissible; Barker & Langdridge, 2010). The concepts of sexual and romantic infidelity, as well as jealousy, within the consensually nonmonogamous community is understudied (see Mogilski et al., 2019). There are numerous consensually nonmonogamous relationship structures or orientations that define (and may condemn) extrapair activity uniquely. Some multipartner relationship structures are "closed," meaning that the members of the relationship have agreed that multipartner mating is permissible within the relationship (e.g., within a group of three individuals), but not outside of it. It is possible that open or closed access to extrapair partnerships may alter the association between ovulatory cycle phase and extrapair interest described in monogamous women. In some cases, studying infidelity and extrapair partnerships may necessitate a reconsideration of how mononormative research has framed these processes.

Shifts in female jealousy over the ovulatory cycle clearly require additional research. However, using methods that incorporate comparisons between naturally cycling women and women who use hormonal contraceptives can allow for a more precise understanding of how ovarian hormones interact with infidelity-prevention behaviors. Certainly, future research must also evaluate hormonal mechanisms that influence extrapair interest in samples that include nonheterosexual, nonmonogamous women in order to fully evaluate the extent to which shifting ovulatory hormones influence processes related to infidelity. Regardless, both emotional and sexual infidelity inflict costs on monogamous, heterosexual pair bonds, but the extent to which hormones influence these processes in sexual minority groups remains unknown. The continued exploration into the causes and effects of behaviors that decrease infidelity, or behaviors that facilitate successful extrapair mating, will surely contribute to the overall knowledge on the evolution of human relationships and mating patterns.

References

Abraham, G. E. (1974). Ovarian and adrenal contribution to peripheral androgens during the menstrual cycle. *Journal of Clinical Endocrinology & Metabolism, 39*, 340–346.

Adams, D. B., Gold, A. R., & Burt, A. D. (1978). Rise in female-initiated sexual activity at ovulation and its suppression by oral contraceptives. *New England Journal of Medicine, 299*, 1145–1150.

Alvergne, A., Faurie, C., & Raymond, M. (2009). Variation in testosterone levels and male reproductive effort: Insight from a polygynous human population. *Hormones and Behavior, 56*, 491–497.

Alvergne, A., & Lummaa, V. (2010). Does the contraceptive pill alter mate choice in humans? *Trends in Ecology & Evolution, 25*, 171–179.

Arnocky, S., Ribout, A., Mirza, R. S., & Knack, J. M. (2014). Perceived mate availability influences intrasexual competition, jealousy and mate-guarding behavior. *Evolutionary Psychology, 12*, 45–64.

Arslan, R. C., Schilling, K. M., Gerlach, T. M., & Penke, L. (2018). Using 26,000 diary entries to show ovulatory changes in sexual desire and behavior. *Journal of Personality and Social Psychology, 121*(2), 410–431.

Baird, D. D., McConnaughey, R., Weinberg, C. R., Musey, P. I., Collins, D. C., Kesner, J. S., Knecht, E. A., & Wilcox, A. J. (1995). Application of a method for estimating day of olvulation using urinary estrogen and progesterone metabolites. *Epidemiology, 6*, 547–550.

Baker, R., & Bellis, M. A. (1995). *Human sperm competition: Copulation, masturbation and infidelity*. Chapman & Hill.

Bancroft, J. (1987). Hormones, sexuality and fertility in women. *Journal of Zoology, 213*, 445–454.

Barker, .M, & Langdridge, D. (2010). *Understanding non-monogamies*. Routledge.

Baum, M. J., Everitt, B. J., Herbert, J., & Keverne, E. B. (1977). Hormonal basis of proceptivity and receptivity in female primates. *Archives of Sexual Behavior, 6*, 173–192.

Belchetz, P. E., Plant, T. M., Nakai, Y., Keogh, E. J., & Knobil, E. (1978). Hypophysial responses to continuous and intermittent delivery of hypothalamic gonadotropin-releasing hormone. *Science, 202*, 631–633.

Bellis, M. A., & Baker, R. R. (1990). Do females promote sperm competition? Data for humans. *Animal Behaviour, 40*, 997–999.

Benshoof, L., & Thornhill, R. (1979). The evolution of monogamy and concealed ovulation in humans. *Journal of Social and Biological Structures, 2*, 95–106.

Birnbaum, S., Birnbaum, G. E., & Ein-Dor, T. (2017). Can contraceptive pill affect future offspring's health? The implications of using hormonal birth control for human evolution. *Evolutionary Psychological Science, 3*, 89–96.

Bobst, C., & Lobmaier, J. S. (2012). Men's preference for the ovulating female is triggered by subtle face shape differences. *Hormones and Behavior, 62*, 413–417.

Bobst, C., Sauter, S., Foppa, A., & Lobmaier, J. S. (2014). Early follicular testosterone level predicts preference for masculinity in male faces—but not for women taking hormonal contraception. *Psychoneuroendocrinology, 41*, 142–150.

Boothroyd, L. G., Scott, I., Gray, A. W., Coombes, C. I., & Pound, N. (2013). Male facial masculinity as a cue to health outcomes. *Evolutionary Psychology, 11*, 1044–1058.

Brewer, G., & Abell, L. (2015). Machiavellianism and sexual behavior: Motivations, deception and infidelity. *Personality and Individual Differences, 74*, 186–191.

Brown, S. G., Calibuso, M. J., & Roedl, A. L. (2011). Women's sexuality, well-being, and the menstrual cycle: Methodological issues and their interrelationships. *Archives of Sexual Behavior, 40*, 755–765.

Bullivant, S. B., Sellergren, S. A., Stern, K., Spencer, N. A., Jacob, S., Mennella, J. A., & McClintock, M. K. (2004). Women's sexual experience during the menstrual cycle: Identification of the sexual phase by noninvasive measurement of luteinizing hormone. *Journal of Sex Research, 41*, 82–93.

Burleson, M. H., Trevathan, W. R., & Gregory, W. L. (2002). Sexual behavior in lesbian and heterosexual women: Relations with menstrual cycle phase and partner availability. *Psychoneuroendocrinology, 27*, 489–503.

Burley, N. (1979). The evolution of concealed ovulation. *American Naturalist, 114*, 835–858.

Buss, D. M. (1988). The evolution of human intrasexual competition: Tactics of mate attraction. *Journal of Personality and Social Psychology, 54*, 616–628.

Buss, D. M. (2002). Human mate guarding. *Neuroendocrinology Letters, 23*, 23–29.

Buss, D. M., Goetz, C., Duntley, J. D., Asao, K., & Conroy-Beam, D. (2017). The mate switching hypothesis. *Personality and Individual Differences, 104*, 143–149.

Buss, D., & Haselton, M. (2005). The evolution of jealousy. *Trends in Cognitive Sciences, 9*, 506–507.

Buss, D. M., Larsen, R. J., Westen, D., & Semmelroth, J. (1992). Sex differences in jealousy: Evolution, physiology, and psychology. *Psychological Science, 3*, 251–256.

Buss, D. M., & Schmitt, D. P. (1993). Sexual strategies theory: An evolutionary perspective on human mating. *Psychological Review, 100*, 204–232.

Buss, D. M., & Shackelford, T. K. (1997). Susceptibility to infidelity in the first year of marriage. *Journal of Research in Personality, 31*, 193–221.

Buss, D. M., Shackelford, T. K., & McKibbin, W. F. (2008). The Mate Retention Inventory-Short Form (MRI-SF). *Personality and Individual Differences, 44*, 322–334.

Caraty, A., Locatelli, A., & Martin, G. B. (1989). Biphasic response in the secretion of gonadotrophin-releasing hormone in ovariectomized ewes injected with oestradiol. *Journal of Endocrinology, 123*, 375–382.

Cartei, V., Bond, R., & Reby, D. (2014). What makes a voice masculine: Physiological and acoustical correlates of women's ratings of men's vocal masculinity. *Hormones and Behavior, 66,* 569–576.

Clarke, I. J., & Cummins, J. T. (1982). The temporal relationship between gonadotropin releasing hormone (GnRH) and luteinizing hormone (LH) secretion in ovariectomized ewes. *Endocrinology, 111,* 1737–1739.

Clarke, P. M. R., Barrett, L., & Henzi, S. P. (2009). What role do olfactory cues play in chacma baboon mating? *American Journal of Primatology, 71,* 493–502.

Clayton, A. H., Clavet, G. J., McGarvey, E. L., Warnock, J. K., & Weiss, K. (1999). Assessment of sexual functioning during the menstrual cycle. *Journal of Sex & Marital Therapy, 25,* 281–291.

Cobey, K., Buunk, A., Roberts, S., Klipping, C., Appels, N., Zimmerman, Y., . . . Pollet, T. (2012). Reported jealousy differs as a function of menstrual cycle stage and contraceptive pill use: A within-subjects investigation. *Evolution and Human Behavior, 33,* 395–401.

Cobey, K., Pollet, T., Roberts, S., & Buunk, A. (2011). Hormonal birth control use and relationship jealousy: Evidence for estrogen dosage effects. *Personality and Individual Differences, 50,* 315–317.

Daly, M., Wilson, M., & Weghorst, S. J. (1982). Male sexual jealousy. *Ethology and Sociobiology, 3,* 11–27.

DeBruine, L. M., Hahn, A. C., & Jones, B. C. (2019). Does the interaction between partnership status and average progesterone level predict women's preferences for facial masculinity? *Hormones and Behavior, 107,* 80–82.

de Miguel, A., & Buss, D. (2011). Mate retention tactics in Spain: Personality, sex differences, and relationship status. *Journal of Personality, 79,* 563–586.

Dennerstein, L., Gotts, G., Brown, J. B., Morse, C. A., Farley, T. M., & Pinol, A. (1994). The relationship between the menstrual cycle and female sexual interest in women with PMS complaints and volunteers. *Psychoneuroendocrinology, 19,* 293–304.

DeWall, C. N., Lambert, N. M., Slotter, E. B., Pond, R. S., Jr., Deckman, T., Finkel, E. J., . . . Fincham, F. D. (2011). So far away from one's partner, yet so close to romantic alternatives: Avoidant attachment, interest in alternatives, and infidelity. *Journal of Personality and Social Psychology, 101,* 1302.

Dixson, A. (2015). Primate sexuality. In A. Bolin & P. Whelehan (Eds.), *The international encyclopedia of human sexuality* (pp. 861–1042). Wiley.

Dixson, A., & Altmann, J. (2000). Primate sexuality: Comparative studies of the prosimians, monkeys, apes, and human beings. *Nature, 403,* 481–481.

Dixson, B. J., Blake, K. R., Denson, T. F., Gooda-Vossos, A., O'Dean, S. M., Sulikowski, D., . . . Brooks, R. C. (2018). The role of mating context and fecundability in women's preferences for men's facial masculinity and beardedness. *Psychoneuroendocrinology, 93,* 90–102.

Elaut, E., Buysse, A., De Sutter, P., Gerris, J., De Cuypere, G., & T'Sjoen, G. (2016). Cycle related changes in mood, sexual desire, and sexual activity in oral contraception-using and nonhormonal-contraception-using couples. *Journal of Sex Research, 53,* 125–136.

Feinberg, D. R., DeBruine, L. M., Jones, B. C., & Little, A. C. (2008). Correlated preferences for men's facial and vocal masculinity. *Evolution and Human Behavior, 29,* 233–241.

Feinberg, D. R., Jones, B. C., Smith, M. L., Moore, F. R., DeBruine, L. M., Cornwell, R. E., . . . Perrett, D. I. (2006). Menstrual cycle, trait estrogen level, and masculinity preferences in the human voice. *Hormones and Behavior, 49,* 215–222.

Fleming, A. S., Corter, C., Stallings, J., & Steiner, M. (2002). Testosterone and prolactin are associated with emotional responses to infant cries in new fathers. *Hormones and Behavior, 42,* 399–413.

Folstad, I., & Karter, A. J. (1992). Parasites, bright males, and the immunocompetence handicap. *American Naturalist, 139,* 603–622.

Foo, Y. Z., Simmons, L., Perrett, D. I., Holt, P. G., Eastwood, P. R., & Rhodes, G. (2020). Immune function during early adolescence positively predicts adult facial sexual dimorphism in both men and women. *Evolution and Human Behavior, 41,* 199–209.

French, J. E., & Meltzer, A. L. (2020). The implications of changing hormonal contraceptive use after relationship formation. *Evolution and Human Behavior, 41,* 274–283.

Gangestad, S. W., Dinh, T., Grebe, N. M., Del Giudice, M., & Thompson, M. E. (2019). Psychological cycle shifts redux: Revisiting a preregistered study examining preferences for muscularity. *Evolution and Human Behavior, 40,* 501–516.

Gangestad, S. W., & Simpson, J. A. (2000). The evolution of human mating: Trade-offs and strategic pluralism. *Behavioral and Brain Sciences, 23,* 573–587.

Gangestad, S. W., Simpson, J. A., Cousins, A. J., Garver-Apgar, C. E., & Christensen, P. N. (2004). Women's preferences for male behavioral displays change across the menstrual cycle. *Psychological Science, 15*, 203–207.

Gangestad, S. W., Thornhill, R., & Garver, C. E. (2002). Changes in women's sexual interests and their partner's mate-retention tactics across the menstrual cycle: Evidence for shifting conflicts of interest. *Proceedings of the Royal Society of London. Series B: Biological Sciences, 269*, 975–982.

Gangestad, S. W., Thornhill, R., & Garver-Apgar, C. E. (2005). Women's sexual interests across the ovulatory cycle depend on primary partner developmental instability. *Proceedings of the Royal Society B: Biological Sciences, 272*, 2023–2027.

Geary, D., DeSoto, M., Hoard, M., Sheldon, M., & Cooper, M. (2001). Estrogens and relationship jealousy. *Human Nature, 12*, 299–320.

Gildersleeve, K., Haselton, M. G., & Fales, M. R. (2014). Do women's mate preferences change across the ovulatory cycle? A meta-analytic review. *Psychological Bulletin, 140*, 1205.

Gildersleeve, K. A., Haselton, M. G., Larson, C. M., & Pillsworth, E. G. (2012). Body odor attractiveness as a cue of impending ovulation in women: Evidence from a study using hormone-confirmed ovulation. *Hormones and Behavior, 61*, 157–166.

Gori, A., Giannini, M., Craparo, G., Caretti, V., Nannini, I., Madathil, R., & Schuldberg, D. (2014). Assessment of the relationship between the use of birth control pill and the characteristics of mate selection. *Journal of Sexual Medicine, 11*, 2181–2187.

Gould, J. E., Overstreet, J. W., & Hanson, F. W. (1984). Assessment of human sperm function after recovery from the female reproductive tract. *Biology of Reproduction, 31*, 888–894.

Grebe, N. M., Gangestad, S. W., Garver-Apgar, C. E., & Thornhill, R. (2013). Women's luteal-phase sexual proceptivity and the functions of extended sexuality. *Psychological Science, 24*, 2106–2110.

Grebe, N. M., Thompson, M. E., & Gangestad, S. W. (2016). Hormonal predictors of women's extra-pair vs. in-pair sexual attraction in natural cycles: Implications for extended sexuality. *Hormones and Behavior, 78*, 211–219.

Grøntvedt, T., Grebe, N., Kennair, L., & Gangestad, S. (2017). Estrogenic and progestogenic effects of hormonal contraceptives in relation to sexual behavior: Insights into extended sexuality. *Evolution and Human Behavior, 38*(3), 283–292.

Gueguen, N. (2009). The receptivity of women to courtship solicitation across the menstrual cycle: A field experiment. *Biological Psychology, 80*, 321–324.

Guillermo, C. J., Manlove, H. A., Gray, P. B., Zava, D. T., & Marrs, C. R. (2010). Female social and sexual interest across the menstrual cycle: The roles of pain, sleep and hormones. *BMC Women's Health, 10*, 19.

Haselton, M. G., & Gangestad, S. W. (2006). Conditional expression of women's desires and men's mate guarding across the ovulatory cycle. *Hormones and Behavior, 49*, 509–518.

Havlíček, J., Dvořáková, R., Bartoš, L., & Flegr, J. (2006). Non-advertized does not mean concealed: Body odour changes across the human menstrual cycle. *Ethology, 112*, 81–90.

Havlíček, J., Roberts, S. C., & Flegr, J. (2005). Women's preference for dominant male odour: Effects of menstrual cycle and relationship status. *Biology Letters, 1*(3), 256–259.

Hillier, S. G., Reichert, L. E., Van Hall, E. V. (1981). Control of preovulatory follicular estrogen biosynthesis in the human ovary. *Journal of Clinical Endocrinology & Metabolism, 52*, 847–856.

Hrdy, S. B. (1979). Infanticide among animals: A review, classification, and examination of the implications for the reproductive strategies of females. *Ethology and Sociobiology, 1*, 13–40.

Jern, P., Kärnä, A., Hujanen, J., Erlin, T., Gunst, A., Rautaheimo, H., Öhman, E., Roberts, S. C., & Zietsch, B. P. (2018). A high-powered replication study finds no effect of starting or stopping hormonal contraceptive use on relationship quality. *Evolution and Human Behavior, 39*, 373–379.

Johnston, V. S., Hagel, R., Franklin, M., Fink, B., & Grammer, K. (2001). Male facial attractiveness: Evidence for hormone-mediated adaptive design. *Evolution and Human Behavior, 22*, 251–267.

Jones, B. C., Hahn, A. C., Fisher, C. I., Wang, H., Kandrik, M., & DeBruine, L. M. (2018). General sexual desire, but not desire for uncommitted sexual relationships, tracks changes in women's hormonal status. *Psychoneuroendocrinology, 88*, 153–157.

Jones, B. C., Hahn, A. C., Fisher, C. I., Wang, H., Kandrik, M., Han, C., Fasolt, V., Morrison, D., Lee, A. J., Holzleitner, I. J., O'Shea, K. J., Roberts, S. C., Little, A. C., & DeBruine, L. M. (2018). No compelling evidence that preferences for facial masculinity track changes in women's hormonal status. *Psychological Science, 29*, 996–1005.

Jones, B. C., Little, A. C., Boothroyd, L., DeBruine, L. M., Feinberg, D. R., Smith, M. L., . . . Perrett, D. I. (2005). Commitment to relationships and preferences for femininity and apparent health in faces are strongest on days of the menstrual cycle when progesterone level is high. *Hormones and Behavior, 48*, 283–290.

Jones, B. C., Perrett, D. I., Little, A. C., Boothroyd, L., Cornwell, R. E., Feinberg, D. R.,Tiddeman, B. P., Whiten, S., Pitman, R. M., Hillier, S. G., Burt, D. M., Stirrat, M. R., Law Smith, M. J., & Moore, F. R. (2005). Menstrual cycle, pregnancy and oral contraceptive use alter attraction to apparent health in faces. *Proceedings of the Royal Society B: Biological Sciences, 272*, 347–354.

Jünger, J., Motta-Mena, N. V., Cardenas, R., Bailey, D., Rosenfield, K. A., Schild, C., . . . Puts, D. A. (2018). Do women's preferences for masculine voices shift across the ovulatory cycle? *Hormones and Behavior, 106*, 122–134.

Kesserü-Koos, E. (1971). Influence of various hormonal contraceptives on sperm migration in vivo. *Fertility and Sterility, 22*, 584–603.

Kim-Björklund, T., Landgren, B. M., & Johannisson, E. (1991). Morphometric studies of the endometrium, the fallopian tube and the corpus luteum during contraception with the 300 μg norethisterone (NET) minipill. *Contraception, 43*, 459–474.

Klapilová, K., Cobey, K. D., Wells, T., Roberts, S. C., Weiss, P., & Havlíček, J. (2014). Current hormonal contraceptive use predicts female extra-pair and dyadic sexual behavior: Evidence based on Czech National Survey data. *Evolutionary Psychology, 12*, 36–52.

Korenman, S. G., & Sherman, B. M. (1973). Further studies of gonadotropin and estradiol secretion during the preovulatory phase of the human menstrual cycle. *Journal of Clinical Endocrinology & Metabolism, 36*, 1205–1209.

Kuo, P. X., Carp, J., Light, K. C., & Grewen, K. M. (2012). Neural responses to infants linked with behavioral interactions and testosterone in fathers. *Biological Psychology, 91*, 302–306.

Kuo, P. X., Saini, E. K., Thomason, E., Schultheiss, O. C., Gonzalez, R., & Volling, B. L. (2016). Individual variation in fathers' testosterone reactivity to infant distress predicts parenting behaviors with their 1-year-old infants. *Developmental Psychobiology, 58*, 303–314.

Kuukasjärvi, S., Eriksson, C. J. P., Koskela, E., Mappes, T., Nissinen, K., & Rantala, M. J. (2004). Attractiveness of women's body odors over the menstrual cycle: The role of oral contraceptives and receiver sex. *Behavioral Ecology, 15*, 579–584.

Laeng, B., & Falkenberg, L. (2007). Women's pupillary responses to sexually significant others during the hormonal cycle. *Hormones and Behavior, 52*, 520–530.

Larson, C. M., Haselton, M. G., Gildersleeve, K. A., & Pillsworth, E. G. (2013). Changes in women's feelings about their romantic relationships across the ovulatory cycle. *Hormones and Behavior, 63*, 128–135.

Larson, C. M., Pillsworth, E. G., & Haselton, M. G. (2012). Ovulatory shifts in women's attractions to primary partners and other men: Further evidence of the importance of primary partner sexual attractiveness. *PLoS One, 7*, e44456.

Leivers, S., Rhodes, G., & Simmons, L. (2014). Sperm competition in humans: Mate guarding behavior negatively correlates with ejaculate quality. *PLoS One, 9*, e108099.

Levine, J. E. (1997). New concepts of the neuroendocrine regulation of gonadotropin surges in rats. *Biology of Reproduction, 56*, 293–302.

Little, A. C. (2014). Facial attractiveness. *Wiley Interdisciplinary Reviews: Cognitive Science, 5*, 621–634.

Little, A. C., Burris, R. P., Petrie, M., Jones, B. C., & Roberts, S. C. (2013). Oral contraceptive use in women changes preferences for male facial masculinity and is associated with partner facial masculinity. *Psychoneuroimmunology, 38*, 1777–1785.

Little, A. C., Cohen, D. L., Jones, B. C., & Belsky, J. (2007). Human preferences for facial masculinity change with relationship type and environmental harshness. *Behavioral Ecology and Sociobiology, 61*, 967–973.

Little, A. C., & Jones, B. C. (2012). Variation in facial masculinity and symmetry preferences across the menstrual cycle is moderated by relationship context. *Psychoneuroendocrinology, 37*, 999–1008.

Little, A. C., Jones, B. C., & Burriss, R. P. (2007). Preferences for masculinity in male bodies change across the menstrual cycle. *Hormones and Behavior, 51*, 633–639.

Little, A. C., Jones, B. C., Penton-Voak, I. S., Burt, D. M., & Perrett, D. I. (2002). Partnership status and the temporal context of relationships influence human female preferences for sexual dimorphism in male face shape. *Proceedings of the Royal Society of London. Series B: Biological Sciences, 269*, 1095–1100.

Liu, J. H., & Yen, S. S. (1983). Induction of midcycle gonadotropin surge by ovarian steroids in women: A critical evaluation. *Journal of Clinical Endocrinology & Metabolism, 57*, 797–802.

Lukaszewski, A. W., & Roney, J. R. (2009). Estimated hormones predict women's mate preferences for dominant personality traits. *Personality and Individual Differences, 47*, 191–196.

Manning, J. T., Scutt, D., Whitehouse, G. H., Leinster, S. J., & Walton, J. M. (1996). Asymmetry and the menstrual cycle in women. *Ethology and Sociobiology, 17*, 129–143.

Marcinkowska, U. M., Helle, S., Jones, B. C., & Jasienska, G. (2019). Does testosterone predict women's preference for facial masculinity? *PloS One, 14*, e0210636.

Marcinkowska, U. M., Kaminski, G., Little, A. C., & Jasienska, G. (2018). Average ovarian hormone levels, rather than daily values and their fluctuations, are related to facial preferences among women. *Hormones and Behavior, 102*, 114–119.

Mark, K. P., & Herbenick, D. (2014). The influence of attraction to partner on heterosexual women's sexual and relationship satisfaction in long-term relationships. *Archives of Sexual Behavior, 43*, 563–570.

Mark, K. P., Janssen, E., & Milhausen, R. R. (2011). Infidelity in heterosexual couples: Demographic, interpersonal, and personality-related predictors of extradyadic sex. *Archives of Sexual Behavior, 40*, 971–982.

Martin, R. D. (2007). The evolution of human reproduction: A primatological perspective. *American Journal of Physical Anthropology, 134*, 59–84.

Matteo, S., & Rissman, E. F. (1984). Increased sexual activity during the midcycle portion of the human menstrual cycle. *Hormones and Behavior, 18*, 249–255.

McCartney, C. R., Gingrich, M. B., Hu, Y., Evans, W. S., & Marshall, J. C. (2002). Hypothalamic regulation of cyclic ovulation: Evidence that the increase in gonadotropin-releasing hormone pulse frequency during the follicular phase reflects the gradual loss of the restraining effects of progesterone. *Journal of Clinical Endocrinology & Metabolism, 87*, 2194–2200.

McKibbin, W., Goetz, A., Shackelford, T., Schipper, L., Starratt, V., & Stewart-Williams, S. (2007). Why do men insult their intimate partners? *Personality and Individual Differences, 43*, 231–241.

Meuwissen, I., & Over, R. (1992). Sexual arousal across phases of the human menstrual cycle. *Archives of Sexual Behavior, 21*, 101–119.

Miller, G., Tybur, J. M., & Jordan, B. D. (2007). Ovulatory cycle effects on tip earnings by lap dancers: Economic evidence for human estrus? *Evolution and Human Behavior, 28*, 375–381.

Miner, E., Starratt, V., & Shackelford, T. (2009). It's not all about her: Men's mate value and mate retention. *Personality and Individual Differences, 47*, 214–218.

Mitchell, V. E., & Welling, L. L. M. (2020). Not all progestins are created equally: Considering unique progestins individually in psychobehavioral research. *Adaptive Human Behavior and Physiology, 6*, 381–412.

Moghissi, K. S., & Marks, C. (1971). Effects of microdose norgestrel on endogenous gonadotropic and steroid hormones, cervical mucus properties, vaginal cytology, and endometrium. *Fertility and Sterility, 22*, 424–434.

Mogilski, J. K., Reeve, S. D., Nicolas, S. C. A., Donaldson, S. H., Mitchell, V. E., & Welling, L. L. M. (2019). Jealousy, consent, and compersion within monogamous and consensually non-monogamous romantic relationships. *Archives of Sexual Behavior, 48*, 1811–1828.

Motta-Mena, N. V., & Puts, D. A. (2017). Endocrinology of human female sexuality, mating, and reproductive behavior. *Hormones and Behavior, 91*, 19–35.

Muehlenbein, M. P., & Bribiescas, R. G. (2005). Testosterone-mediated immune functions and male life histories. *American Journal of Human Biology: The Official Journal of the Human Biology Association, 17*, 527–558.

Muller, M. N., Marlowe, F. W., Bugumba, R., & Ellison, P. T. (2009). Testosterone and paternal care in East African foragers and pastoralists. *Proceedings of the Royal Society B: Biological Sciences, 276*, 347–354.

Nippoldt, T. B., Reame, N. E., Kelch, R. P., & Marshall, J. C. (1989). The roles of estradiol and progesterone in decreasing luteinizing hormone pulse frequency in the luteal phase of the menstrual cycle. *Journal of Clinical Endocrinology & Metabolism, 69*, 67–76.

Nunn, C. L. (1999). The evolution of exaggerated sexual swellings in primates and the graded-signal hypothesis. *Animal Behavior, 58*, 229–246.

Odell, W. D., & Molitch, M. E. (1974). The pharmacology of contraceptive agents. *Annual Review of Pharmacology, 14*, 413–434.

Ostrander, G. M., Pipitone, R. N., Shoup-Knox, M. L. (2018). Interactions between observer and stimuli fertility status: Endocrine and perceptual responses to intrasexual vocal fertility cues. *Hormones and Behavior, 98*, 191–197.

Penton-Voak, I. S., & Chen, J. Y. (2004). High salivary testosterone is linked to masculine male facial appearance in humans. *Evolution and Human Behavior, 25*, 229–241.

Penton-Voak, I. S., & Perrett, D. I. (2000). Female preference for male faces changes cyclically: Further evidence. *Evolution and Human Behavior, 21*, 39–48.

Penton-Voak, I. S., Perrett, D. I., Castles, D. L., Kobayashi, T., Burt, D. M., Murray, L. K., & Minamisawa, R. (1999). Menstrual cycle alters face preference. *Nature, 399*, 741–742.

Perrett, D. I., Lee, K. J., Penton-Voak, I., Rowland, D., Yoshikawa, S., Burt, D. M., Henzi, S. P., Castles, D. L., & Akamatsu, S. (1998). Effects of sexual dimorphism on facial attractiveness. *Nature, 394*, 884–887.

Phalane, K. G., Tribe, C., Steel, H. C., Cholo, M. C., & Coetzee, V. (2017). Facial appearance reveals immunity in African men. *Scientific Reports, 7*, 1–9.

Pillsworth, E. G., & Haselton, M. G. (2006a). Women's sexual strategies: The evolution of long-term bonds and extrapair sex. *Annual Review of Sex Research, 17*, 59–100.

Pillsworth, E. G., & Haselton, M. G. (2006b). Male sexual attractiveness predicts differential ovulatory shifts in female extra-pair attraction and male mate retention. *Evolution and Human Behavior, 27*, 247–258.

Pillsworth, E. G., Haselton, M. G., & Buss, D. M. (2004). Ovulatory shifts in female sexual desire. *Journal of Sex Research, 41*, 55–65.

Pipitone, R. N., & Gallup, G. G., Jr. (2008). Women's voice attractiveness varies across the menstrual cycle. *Evolution and Human Behavior, 29*, 268–274.

Pisanski, K., Hahn, A. C., Fisher, C. I., DeBruine, L. M., Feinberg, D. R., & Jones, B. C. (2014). Changes in salivary estradiol predict changes in women's preferences for vocal masculinity. *Hormones and Behavior, 66*, 493–497.

Pollet, T. V., van der Meij, L., Cobey, K. D., & Buunk, A. P. (2011). Testosterone levels and their associations with lifetime number of opposite sex partners and remarriage in a large sample of American elderly men and women. *Hormones and Behavior, 60*, 72–77.

Pound, N., Penton-Voak, I. S., & Surridge, A. K. (2009). Testosterone responses to competition in men are related to facial masculinity. *Proceedings of the Royal Society B: Biological Sciences, 276*, 153–159.

Prasad, A., Mumford, S. L., Louis, G. M. B., Ahrens, K. A., Sjaarda, L. A., Schliep, K. C., . . . Schisterman, E. F. (2014). Sexual activity, endogenous reproductive hormones and ovulation in premenopausal women. *Hormones and Behavior, 66*, 330–338.

Provost, M. P., Quinsey, V. L., & Troje, N. F. (2008). Differences in gait across the menstrual cycle and their attractiveness to men. *Archives of Sexual Behavior, 37*, 598–604.

Puts, D. A. (2006). Cyclic variation in women's preferences for masculine traits. *Human Nature, 17*, 114–127.

Puts, D. A., Bailey, D. H., Cárdenas, R. A., Burriss, R. P., Welling, L. L., Wheatley, J. R., & Dawood, K. (2013). Women's attractiveness changes with estradiol and progesterone across the ovulatory cycle. *Hormones and Behavior, 63*, 13–19.

Rantala, M. J., Coetzee, V., Moore, F. R., Skrinda, I., Kecko, S., Krama, T., . . . Krams, I. (2013). Adiposity, compared with masculinity, serves as a more valid cue to immunocompetence in human mate choice. *Proceedings of the Royal Society B: Biological Sciences, 280*, 20122495.

Rhodes, G., Chan, J., Zebrowitz, L. A., & Simmons, L. W. (2003). Does sexual dimorphism in human faces signal health? *Proceedings of the Royal Society of London. Series B: Biological Sciences, 270*, S93–S95.

Rhodes, G., Simmons, L. W., & Peters, M. (2005). Attractiveness and sexual behavior: Does attractiveness enhance mating success? *Evolution and Human Behavior, 26*, 186–201.

Righetti, F., Tybur, J., Van Lange, P., Echelmeyer, L., van Esveld, S., Kroese, J., . . . Gangestad, S. (2020). How reproductive hormonal changes affect relationship dynamics for women and men: A 15-day diary study. *Biological Psychology, 149*, 107784.

Rivera, R., Yacobson, I., & Grimes, D. (1999). The mechanism of action of hormonal contraceptives and intrauterine contraceptive devices. *American Journal of Obstetrics and Gynecology, 181*, 1263–1269.

Roberts, S. C., Havlíček, J., Flegr, J., Hruskova, M., Little, A. C., Jones, B. C., Perrett, D. I., & Petrie, M. (2004). Female facial attractiveness increases during the fertile phase of the menstrual cycle. *Proceedings of the Royal Society of London. Series B: Biological Sciences, 271*, 270–272.

Roberts, S. C., Klapilová, K., Little, A. C., Burriss, R. P., Jones, B. C., DeBruine, L. M., Petrie, M., & Havlíček, J. (2012). Relationship satisfaction and outcome in women who meet their partner while using oral contraception. *Proceedings of The Royal Society B: Biological Sciences, 279*, 1430–1436.

Roberts, S. C., Little, A. C., Burriss, R. P., Cobey, K. D., Klapilová, K., Havlíček, J., . . . Petrie, M. (2014). Partner choice, relationship satisfaction, and oral contraception: The congruency hypothesis. *Psychological Science, 25*, 1497–1503.

Röder, S., Brewer, G., & Fink, B. (2009). Menstrual cycle shifts in women's self-perception and motivation: A daily report method. *Personality and Individual Differences, 47*, 616–619.

Rodrigues, D., Lopes, D., & Pereira, M. (2017). Sociosexuality, commitment, sexual infidelity, and perceptions of infidelity: data from the second love web site. *Journal of Sex Research, 54*, 241–253.

Roney, J. R., Hanson, K. N., Durante, K. M., & Maestripieri, D. (2006). Reading men's faces: Women's mate attractiveness judgments track men's testosterone and interest in infants. *Proceedings of the Royal Society B: Biological Sciences, 273*, 2169–2175.

Roney, J. R., & Simmons, Z. L. (2013). Hormonal predictors of sexual motivation in natural menstrual cycles. *Hormones and Behavior, 63*, 636–645.

Roney, J. R., & Simmons, Z. L. (2016). Within-cycle fluctuations in progesterone negatively predict changes in both in-pair and extra-pair desire among partnered women. *Hormones and Behavior, 81*, 45–52.

Roney, J. R., Simmons, Z. L., & Gray, P. B. (2011). Changes in estradiol predict within-women shifts in attraction to facial cues of men's testosterone. *Psychoneuroendocrinology, 36*, 742–749.

Rosen, M. L., & López, H. H. (2009). Menstrual cycle shifts in attentional bias for courtship language. *Evolution and Human Behavior, 30*, 131–140.

Russell, V. M., McNulty, J. K., Baker, L. R., & Meltzer, A. L. (2014). The association between discontinuing hormonal contraceptives and wives' marital satisfaction depends on husbands' facial attractiveness. *Proceedings of the National Academy of Sciences, 111*, 17081–17086.

Schreiner-Engel, P. (1980). *Female sexual arousability: Its relation to gonadal hormones and the menstrual cycle* (Order No. 8017527). Available from ProQuest Dissertations & Theses Global.

Schwarz, S., & Hassebrauck, M. (2008). Self-perceived and observed variations in women's attractiveness throughout the menstrual cycle—A diary study. *Evolution and Human Behavior, 29*, 282–288.

Schwartz, D., MacDonald, P. D. M., & Heuchel, V. (1980). Fecundability, coital frequency and the viability of ova. *Population Studies, 34*, 397–400.

Shackelford, T. K., Goetz, A. T., & Buss, D. M. (2005). Mate retention in marriage: Further evidence of the reliability of the Mate Retention Inventory. *Personality and Individual Differences, 39*, 415–425.

Shackelford, T., Goetz, A., Guta, F., & Schmitt, D. (2006). Mate guarding and frequent in-pair copulation in humans. *Human Nature, 17*, 239–252.

Shackelford, T., Voracek, M., Schmitt, D., Buss, D., Weekes-Shackelford, V., & Michalski, R. (2004). Romantic jealousy in early adulthood and in later life. *Human Nature, 15*, 283–300.

Shupnik, M. A. (1996). Gonadal hormone feedback on pituitary gonadotropin genes. *Trends in Endocrinology & Metabolism, 7*(8), 272–276.

Skrinda, I., Krama, T., Kecko, S., Moore, F. R., Kaasik, A., Meija, L., . . . Krams, I. (2014). Body height, immunity, facial and vocal attractiveness in young men. *Naturwissenschaften, 101*, 1017–1025.

Smith, F. G., Jones, B. C., Little, A. C., DeBruine, L. M., Welling, L. L. M., Vukovic, J., & Conway, C. A. (2009). Hormonal contraceptive use and perceptions of trust modulate the effect of relationship context on women's preferences for sexual dimorphism in male face shape. *Journal of Evolutionary Psychology, 7*, 195–210.

Stanislaw, H., & Rice, F. J. (1988). Correlation between sexual desire and menstrual cycle characteristics. *Archives of Sexual Behavior, 17*, 499–508.

Starratt, V. G., Weekes-Shackelford, V., & Shackelford, T. K. (2017). Mate value both positively and negatively predicts intentions to commit an infidelity. *Personality and Individual Differences, 104*, 18–22.

Stern, J., Arslan, R. C., Gerlach, T. M., & Penke, L. (2019). No robust evidence for cycle shifts in preferences for men's bodies in a multiverse analysis: A response to Gangestad, Dinh, Grebe, Del Giudice, and Emery Thompson (2019). *Evolution and Human Behavior, 40*, 517–525.

Stower, R. E., Lee, A. J., McIntosh, T. L., Sidari, M. J., Sherlock, J. M., & Dixson, B. J. (2020). Mating strategies and the masculinity paradox: How relationship context, relationship status, and sociosexuality shape women's preferences for facial masculinity and beardedness. *Archives of Sexual Behavior, 49*, 809–820.

Strassmann, B. I. (1981). Sexual selection, paternal care, and concealed ovulation in humans. *Ethology and Sociobiology, 2*, 31–40.

Stumpf, R. M., Martinez-Mota, R., Milich, K. M., Righini, N., & Shattuck, M. R. (2011). Sexual conflict in primates. *Evolutionary Anthropology: Issues, News, and Reviews, 20*, 62–75.

Testart, J., & Frydman, R. (1982). Minimum time lapse between luteinizing hormone surge or human chorionic gonadotropin administration and follicular rupture. *Fertility and Sterility, 37*, 50–53.

Thornhill, R., Chapman, J. F., & Gangestad, S. W. (2013). Women's preferences for men's scents associated with testosterone and cortisol levels: Patterns across the ovulatory cycle. *Evolution and Human Behavior, 34*, 216–221.

Thornhill, R., & Gangestad, S. W. (2006). Facial sexual dimorphism, developmental stability, and susceptibility to disease in men and women. *Evolution and Human Behavior, 27*, 131–144.

Thornhill, R., & Gangestad, S. W. (2008). *The evolutionary biology of human female sexuality*. Oxford University Press.

Thornhill, R., & Gangestad, S. W. (2015). The functional design and phylogeny of women's sexuality. In Shackelford, T., & Hansen, R. (eds) *The evolution of sexuality* (pp. 149–184). Springer.

Trivers, R. (1972). Parental investment and sexual selection. In B. Campbell's *Sexual selection and the descent of man*, 136–179. *Aldine de Gruyter*.

Udry, J. R., & Morris, N. M. (1968). Distribution of coitus in the menstrual cycle. *Nature, 220*, 593–596.

Van Goozen, S. H., Wiegant, V. M., Endert, E., Helmond, F. A., & Van de Poll, N. E. (1997). Psychoendocrinological assessment of the menstrual cycle: The relationship between hormones, sexuality, and mood. *Archives of Sexual Behavior, 26*, 359–382.

van Rosmalen-Nooijens, K. A. W. L., Vergeer, C. M., & Lagro-Janssen, A. L. M. (2008). Bed death and other lesbian sexual problems unraveled: A qualitative study of the sexual health of lesbian women involved in a relationship. *Women & Health, 48*, 339–362.

Vukovic, J., Feinberg, D. R., Jones, B. C., DeBruine, L. M., Welling, L. L. M., Little, A. C., & Smith, F. G. (2008). Self-rated attractiveness predicts individual differences in women's preferences for masculine men's voices. *Personality and Individual Differences, 45*, 451–456.

Wallwiener, C. W., Wallwiener, L. M., Seeger, H., Mück, A. O., Bitzer, J., & Wallwiener, C. W. (2010). Prevalence of sexual dysfunction and impact of contraception in female German medical students. *Journal of Sexual Medicine, 7*, 2139–2148.

Welling, L. L. M. (2013). Psychobehavioral effects of hormonal contraceptive use. *Evolutionary Psychology, 11*, 718–742.

Welling, L. L. M., & Burriss, R. P. (2019). Investigating the ovulatory cycle: An overview of research and methods. In L. L. M. Welling & T. K. Shackelford (Eds.), *The Oxford handbook of evolutionary psychology and behavioral endocrinology* (pp. 109–124). Oxford University Press.

Welling, L. L. M., Jones, B. C., DeBruine, L. M., Conway, C. A., Smith, M. L., Little, A. C., . . . Al-Dujaili, E. A. (2007). Raised salivary testosterone in women is associated with increased attraction to masculine faces. *Hormones and Behavior, 52*, 156–161.

Welling, L. L. M., & Puts, D. A. (2014). Female adaptations to ovulation. In V. A. Weekes-Shackelford & T. K. Shackelford (Eds.), *Evolutionary perspectives on human sexual psychology and behavior* (pp. 243–260). Springer .

Welling, L. L. M., Puts, D. A., Roberts, S. C., Little, A. C., Burriss, R. P. (2012). Hormonal contraceptive use and mate retention behavior in women and their male partners. *Hormones and Behavior, 61*, 114–120.

Whisman, M. A., & Snyder, D. K. (2007). Sexual infidelity in a national survey of American women: Differences in prevalence and correlates as a function of method of assessment. *Journal of Family Psychology, 21*, 147.

Wilcox, A. J., Day Baird, D., Dunson, D. B., McConnaughey, D. R., Kesner, J. S., & Weinberg, C. R. (2004). On the frequency of intercourse around ovulation: Evidence for biological influences. *Human Reproduction, 19*, 1539–1543.

Wilcox, A. J., Weinberg, C. R., & Baird, D. D. (1995). Timing of sexual intercourse in relation to ovulation—Effects on the probability of conception, survival of the pregnancy, and sex of the baby. *New England Journal of Medicine, 333*, 1517–1521.

Wilcox, A. J., Weinberg, C. R., & Baird, D. D. (1998). Post-ovulatory ageing of the human oocyte and embryo failure. *Human Reproduction, 13*(2), 394–397.

Wuttke, W., Theiling, K., Hinney, B., & Pitzel, L. (1998). Regulation of steroid production and its function within the corpus luteum. *Steroids, 63*, 299–305.

Yumbul, C., Cavusoglu, S., & Geyimci, B. (2010). The effect of childhood trauma on adult attachment styles, infidelity tendency, romantic jealousy and self-esteem. *Procedia—Social and Behavioral Sciences, 5,* 1741–1745.

Zahavi, A. (1975). Mate selection—a selection for a handicap. *Journal of Theoretical Biology, 53,* 205–214.

Zeleznik, A. J. (1981). Premature elevation of systemic estradiol reduces serum levels of follicle-stimulating hormone and lengthens the follicular phase of the menstrual cycle in rhesus monkeys. *Endocrinology, 109,* 352–355.

CHAPTER 15

Long-Term Infidelities

Dana A. Weiser, Jaclyn Cravens Pickens, *and* Adam V. Thomas

Abstract
This chapter provides a comprehensive exploration of the development and nature of long-term infidelities (i.e., infidelity characterized by emotional attachment and that persists over time). We will discuss the frequency of such long-term infidelities and explore individual, relational, and contextual factors associated with committing long-term infidelities. Specific focus will be given to the nature of long-term infidelities that form and transpire online. Emotional responses to long-term infidelities and relationship outcomes following discovery of long-term infidelities will be explored. We will also examine how long-term infidelities have the potential to impact a broader family system, beyond the infidelity transgressor and victim. Finally, we offer suggestions for future research about long-term infidelities.

Key Words: long-term infidelity, infidelity, extramarital affair, extradyadic relationship, online infidelity, internet infidelity, predictors, prevalence, outcomes

The broadest definition of infidelity is any type of secret emotional, sexual, or romantic behavior that violates the exclusivity norms of a committed, romantic partnership (Glass, 2002). Other researchers have used narrower definitions by focusing on the presence of specific behaviors, such as spending time with another person, flirting, sending/receiving affectionate messages, watching pornography, oral sex, and coitus (Blow & Hartnett, 2005; Thompson & O'Sullivan, 2016). Kruger et al. (2013) asked 456 ethnically diverse undergraduate students (67% women, 33% men) to rate 27 different behaviors that can exist in casual, romantic, and sexual relationships. Participants were asked to indicate the extent to which they believed a person in a long-term relationship enacting each behavior would be cheating. Sexual and erotic interactions were rated as highly indicative of cheating and penile-vaginal intercourse, oral sex, taking a shower together, kissing on the lips, emailing naked pictures, texting erotic messages, watching a pornographic movie together, sleeping in the same bed, and holding hands were the behaviors most consistently rated as infidelity (Kruger et al., 2013). Weiser et al. (2014) conducted a four-study prototype analysis to assess laypeople's definitions of infidelity and found that undergraduate students conceptualized infidelity as a multifaceted construct characterized by betrayal, secretiveness, and immorality with negative emotions for the noninvolved partner and consequences to the relationship. Instead of focusing on the presence of specific behaviors as indicators of infidelity, Weiser et al. (2014) found that participants focused more on the concealment of these behaviors and the emotional turmoil resulting from transgressions. These findings suggest that infidelity remains a subjective experience and there are numerous challenges for researchers to craft a singular definition of infidelity.

Despite these varied definitions of infidelity, researchers have long acknowledged that there are multiple types of infidelity and have typically characterized infidelity as falling into one of three categories: sexual only, emotional only, and combined sexual/emotional (Blow & Hartnett, 2005). The focus of this chapter is long-term infidelity, which is infidelity characterized by an emotional/romantic attachment to the infidelity partner (i.e., the third party) and that persists over time. The challenge in writing this chapter is that few researchers or clinicians have used the terminology "long-term infidelity" and little empirical attention has been paid to defining and studying long-term infidelities. Therefore, for the current chapter we had to make decisions about how to define and conceptualize long-term infidelity. We state these challenges and decisions upfront to highlight that there is a great deal of information to be gained about long-term infidelities and this is an area ripe for exploration. In the following sections, we share the extant knowledge of long-term infidelities and conclude with numerous recommendations about how researchers can further study this construct. Foremost, though, we had to create a working definition for long-term infidelities.

First, we decided that an emotional and/or romantic intimacy should be a defining feature of long-term infidelity, as this emotional closeness likely explains why an infidelity would continue. This means that the involved partner (i.e., the transgressor) and the infidelity partner have some type of emotional bond, including but not necessarily defined by feelings of love and romance. There is less consensus about what constitutes emotional infidelity, compared to sexual infidelity, and women and men seem to differ slightly in their definitions of emotional infidelity. In a study using 73 undergraduate students (34% women, 66% men), Guitar et al. (2017) had participants rate how strongly they agreed or disagreed with 68 different infidelity definitions (36 emotional, 32 sexual) generated by a separate sample of undergraduate students. Women and men were in high agreement that "emotional infidelity is 'being in love' or more dedicated emotionally to someone other than the partner, or family, someone with romantic potential" and "emotional infidelity is when a person in a relationship creates an emotional distance by spending an excessive amount of time with, or thinks about, another person outside of the relationship, to the point that the other partner becomes ignored or rejected emotionally" (Guitar et al., 2017, p. 440). In contrast, women were more likely than men to agree with the statements "emotional infidelity is pretending you feel a certain way for your current partner when you really don't feel that way most of the time and most likely feel that way for another person" and "emotional infidelity is becoming attached to another with the intention of having a sexual relationship" (Guitar et al., 2017, p.440). In a small qualitative study of

White British adults, participants also conceptualized emotional infidelity as romantic feelings or falling in love with another person, and that these feelings impinge on the primary relationship (Moller & Vossler, 2015). In a different qualitative study of mainly heterosexual White women in their 30s and 40s, researchers found participants defined emotional infidelity as having feelings toward another, putting time into and confiding in another person, acting on an attraction, and keeping information from their partner (Morrissey et al., 2019). These findings suggest that people view emotional infidelity as a romantic bond that draws the involved partner away emotionally, physically, and potentially sexually from the primary relationship.

Second, we decided that sexual infidelity would *not* be a defining feature of long-term infidelity. While many extradyadic pairs will undertake sexual activities, whether in-person or in cyberspace, it is likely that there are emotionally bonded extradyadic couples who have not engaged in such physical activities. Even without sexual activities, emotional infidelity has the capacity to diminish the involved partner's connection and commitment to the noninvolved partner by drawing focus and energy away from the primary relationship (Emerson-Potter & Emerson-Potter, 2008). Furthermore, Guitar et al. (2017) found that 88% of women and 79% of men thought emotional infidelity could occur without sexual infidelity. Thus, long-term infidelity may be of the emotional-only type or a combined sexual/emotional type.

Third and finally, long-term infidelity is infidelity that is maintained and continued over time, in contrast to one-night stands or extradyadic partnerships that quickly dissipate. This time feature requires future empirical research, as we can find no research that quantifies a specific time period in which infidelity transitions from short-term to long-term. Researchers commonly discuss short-term mating vs. long-term mating but have similarly left the time component of these concepts broad and nebulous. For example, Buss and Schmitt (1993) note that short-term sexual relationships "can last for a few months, a few days, a few hours, or even a few minutes" (p. 204). However, an extradyadic partnership that lasts even a few months may seem long-term to the noninvolved relationship partners. The conceptualization of long-term infidelity likely depends on relationship length, relationship type, and age of relationship partners. Whether an infidelity is long-term or short-term is likely viewed differently for partners who have been together for 40 years compared to partners who have been together for 4 months. In sum, our definition of long-term infidelity should be viewed as a work in progress, although we believe we have reached a tenable working definition for the current chapter.

Prevalence of Long-Term Infidelities

It is a notable limitation of the infidelity literature writ large that few scholars have explicitly asked about long-term infidelity. Indeed, most infidelity researchers have not asked participants about the length of infidelity or specifically probed the emotional/romantic intimacies of the extradyadic involvement. Most infidelity researchers, particularly researchers utilizing nationally representative samples, have operationalized infidelity solely in terms of whether an extradyadic *sexual* relationship occurred or not (e.g., Atkins et al., 2001; Labrecque & Whisman, 2017). Other researchers have assessed infidelity by asking whether an extradyadic involvement of a sexual and/or romantic nature occurred (e.g., Glass & Wright, 1992). The phrasing of the question as "and/or" prohibits an examination of infidelity that is characterized by an emotional intimacy compared to infidelity that is solely of a sexual nature. Because of how infidelity has been measured throughout the research literature, only a few studies shed light on the prevalence and nature of long-term infidelity. Indeed, only two studies located by our research team appear to have asked participants about the length of their extradyadic involvements.

Omarzu, Miller, Schultz, and Timmerman (2012) recruited 77 participants (55 women, 22 men) from a website for adults who engage in marital infidelity. All participants had participated in at least one extradyadic partnership, and number of partnerships ranged from 1 to 22, with an average of 3.94 extradyadic involvements. Participants were asked what type of extradyadic involvement they had the most experience with, and 53.24% of participants reported ongoing extradyadic relationships, whereas 19.48% reported sporadic encounters and only 6.49% reported one-night stands (Omarzu et al., 2012). The researchers asked participants to report length of their ongoing extradyadic relationships. 52.1% of participants reported that their extradyadic relationships lasted more than one year, with 15.8% of participants indicating their infidelity lasted more than five years. Another third of participants reported their extradyadic involvements lasted less than a year, and 18.5% reported the involvements lasted less than 6 months. Notably, all the extradyadic involvements motivated by love lasted for over a year (Omarzu et al., 2012). Findings from this specialized sample suggest that long-term infidelities are common, and that emotional intimacy appears to be linked with longevity of infidelity.

Allen (2001) in her dissertation work assessed the emotional nature and length of her participants' extradyadic partnerships. In her sample of 251 predominantly White married individuals (132 women, 118 men), 46% reported at least one extradyadic involvement. Among these individuals, 17% of participants reported no emotional involvement, 63% reported moderate emotional involvement, and 26% reported deep emotional involvement. The duration of these infidelities lasted from an hour to 15 years, the modal duration was 6 months, and 55% of participants reported that the extradyadic partnership lasted 6 months or longer.

Other researchers have examined the emotional intimacies of extradyadic partnerships more specifically. Glass and Wright (1985) collected data from 301 White middle-class individuals (153 women, 148 men) who were recruited either while waiting at the airport or during lunchtime at a busy downtown area. Participants received a paper-and-pencil questionnaire along with a pre-addressed, stamped envelope to mail the questionnaire back to the researchers upon completion in a private location. Participants were asked about their sexual involvement and emotional involvement with a person other than their spouse. Participants were also asked to describe the nature of the extradyadic involvement and were able to indicate whether involvement was: (a) entirely sexual, (b) mainly sexual, (c) more sexual than emotional, (d) more emotional than sexual, (e) mainly emotional, and (f) entirely emotional. Men were more likely to describe their infidelity as more sexual compared to women. However, men and women did not differ in their reporting of emotional extradyadic involvement with 51% of men and 49% of women reporting some emotional connection to the infidelity partner (Glass & Wright, 1985). Moreover, Glass and Wright (1985) found a positive correlation between incidence of sexual and emotional involvements, although this correlation was stronger for women than men. Indeed, 44% of men reported slight or no emotional involvement with an extradyadic sexual partner, whereas only 11% of women reported slight or no emotional involvement. These findings, however, do suggest that most women and men do have at least some emotional connection to their infidelity partner.

Thompson (1984) recruited 378 Australian participants (223 women, 155 men) through a randomly selected telephone sample as well as students attending a university. All participants completed a paper-and-pencil questionnaire and returned their finished survey in a preaddressed, stamped envelope to the researchers. Participants were first asked whether they had been intimately involved with a person other than their partner while cohabiting or married. Participants were then asked to indicate yes/no as to whether this involvement was: (a) emotional (in love) only, (b) sexual (intercourse) only, (c) emotionally and sexually involved. 43.7% of participants indicated an extradyadic involvement and most participants responded affirmatively to all three involvement-type options (Thompson, 1984). Men were more likely to report sexual only involvements compared to women (Thompson, 1984). Participants rated extradyadic involvements that were both emotional and sexual as more wrong and detractive to the primary relationship compared to the other involvement types, and reported that they would be least likely to pursue an extradyadic involvement that was emotional and sexual (Thompson, 1984). Thus, although participants seemed to view these extradyadic involvements as most problematic, participants who had engaged in infidelity were most likely to report an infidelity characterized by both emotional and sexual components.

Allan (2004) used data from the Mass-Observation Archive (M-OA) initiative at the University of Sussex. For the initiative, a panel of volunteers write on a regular basis about their everyday lives and each year the M-OA sends out three directives for participants. Allan (2004) analyzed the content provided by 246 participants (185 women; 61 men) for the directive on "having an affair." Allan (2004) found that 40% of women and about one-third of men who had engaged in infidelity reported feeling deep emotional connections to their infidelity partners and that love was the main justification given for more long-term infidelities, although they did not provide a definition of long-term infidelities. Allan (2004) found that men were more likely to report short-term sexual infidelities whereas women were more like to report participating in infidelity characterized by an emotional attachment. Banfield and McCabe (2001) examined data from 112 women recruited through newspaper advertisements and found that only 1.8% of their participants had engaged in extradyadic sexual activities without any emotional involvement. In a study using nine waves of data from the General Social Survey, Labrecque and Whisman (2017), found that participants of all genders were most likely to report having extramarital sex with a close personal friend, a neighbor, a coworker, or a long-term acquaintance, and were less likely to engage in infidelity with casual acquaintances or hookups. In other words, participants were more likely to engage in infidelity in which some emotional connection may be inferred rather than a purely sexual encounter. As a whole, these findings suggest that long-term infidelity is a common occurrence although researchers should be more precise in asking participants about the nature of their infidelity and querying the length of extradyadic involvement to get a more exact statistic about the prevalence of long-term infidelity.

Predictors of and Motivations for Long-Term Infidelities

Scholars have gained a better understanding of predictors of and motivations for infidelity over the past few decades through empirical research and clinical studies. However, factors predicting long-term infidelity have not garnered much attention given that few researchers have explicitly studied long-term infidelities. This section will review the little research there is on predictors of long-term infidelities and why infidelity may persist in the long-term, with particular attention to individual, relational, and contextual factors. Because of the lack of focus on long-term infidelity, much of the literature addressed in this section uses language inferred to examine long-term infidelity, such as maintenance of infidelity, obsessive or needy infidelity, and extradyadic love relationships. As Allen and Atkins (2005) acknowledge, there is "virtually no research" which has examined how extradyadic involvements are maintained and persist over time (p. 1376). From their clinical experience, Allen and Atkins (2005) argue that extradyadic relationships continue because of an increased attachment to the infidelity partner, fear of ending the extradyadic involvement, and increased rationalization on the part of the involved partner. Additionally, the involved partners may have their behaviors reinforced by experiencing the pleasure and fun of the infidelity, and lessening guilt about the infidelity (Allen & Atkins, 2005). However, these maintaining factors of extradyadic involvements have yet to be studied empirically.

Individual Factors

Individual factors are those intrapersonal, intrinsic components of the individual who engages in infidelity (Allen et al., 2005). Gender is one of the most common individual qualities examined by researchers to understand willingness and reasons to engage in extradyadic relationships. It should be noted that the majority of existing infidelity literature exploring gender as a predictor uses a binary and dated approach to studying gender, leaving out gender nonconforming individuals and transgender individuals. Researchers commonly find that men engage in infidelity at higher rates compared to women (Allen et al., 2005; Fincham & May, 2017; Labrecque & Whisman, 2017). More recent studies in the U.S have found this gender gap may be closing and women are engaging in extradyadic activities at higher rates, possibly due to changing societal gender roles and greater participation of women in the workplace (Allen et al., 2005; Atkins et al., 2001; Fincham & May, 2017).

Researchers suggest that men and women differ in the types of infidelity in which they engage. The research consistently finds that men are more likely to engage in sexual only infidelity and to separate feelings of love from sexual activity when engaging in infidelity (Allen et al., 2005; Fincham & May, 2017; Glass & Wright, 1985; Thompson, 1984). Labrecque and Whisman (2017), found that men were more likely than women to have extramarital sex with a casual date or hookup, or pay for extramarital sex. Research also finds women tend to have greater emotional involvements with their extradyadic partners and are more likely to report their infidelity as "a long-term love relationship" (Allen et al., 2005; Tsapelas et al., 1998).

These gender differences in short-term sexual extradyadic relationships and long-term emotionally intimate extradyadic partnerships can possibly be explained by the motivations for engaging in infidelity. Men tend to report more sexual justifications whereas women report more intimacy justifications for engaging in infidelity (Allan, 2004; Allen et al., 2005; Buunk & Dijkstra, 2004; Vangelisti & Gerstenberger, 2004). Women report becoming involved in extradyadic activities because of dissatisfaction within their primary relationship and a desire to find a new long-term relationship partner (Buunk & Dijkstra, 2004; Allan, 2004; Martins et al., 2016). Buunk and Dijkstra (2004) go so far as to say, "it will be unlikely for a happily married woman, but not for a happily married man, to enter an affair" (p. 105).

Glass and Wright (1992) used data from 303 participants (155 women, 148 men) recruited at an airport or a busy downtown location during lunchtime to develop a typology of infidelity motivations, and asked participants to complete the survey in a private location and return the survey to researchers in preaddressed, stamped envelope. Participants were asked to rate 17 different justifications for infidelity and found that four motivation categories emerged: (a) sexual, (b) emotional intimacy, (c) extrinsic, and (d) love (Glass & Wright, 1992). Among participants, 30% of women and 20% of men were consistently disapproving of all justifications for infidelity. Glass and Wright (1992) found that men were more likely to endorse sexual justifications for having infidelity whereas women endorsed love as a reason for infidelity to a greater degree. Women and men did not differ in their endorsement of emotional intimacy for engaging in infidelity (Glass & Wright, 1992).

Omarzu et al. (2012) extended the work of Glass and Wright's (1992) model of infidelity motivations and found eight categories of motivations for extradyadic involvement.

Among the identified motivations, two were physical (lack of sexual satisfaction, desire for additional sexual encounters), two were emotional (lack of emotional satisfaction, desire for additional emotional connection or validation), two were about love (falling out of love with primary partner, falling in love with another person), one was revenge (getting back at partner), and one was curiosity/sensation seeking. The researchers found men were more likely to report seeking additional sexual encounters and curiosity/sensation seeking as motivations for infidelity. In contrast, women were more likely to report seeking additional emotional connection or validation as reasons for infidelity. Interestingly, there were no gender differences for either sexual dissatisfaction or emotional dissatisfaction as a motivator (Omarzu et al., 2012).

Barta and Kiene (2005) also examined motivations for engaging in infidelity and found four factors: (a) sexual frequency and variety, (b) dissatisfaction with one's partner, (c) neglect of and lack of attentiveness from one's partner, and (d) anger and desire to punish partner. These motivation dimensions are similar to those identified by both Omarzu et al. (2012) as well as Glass and Wright (1992). Moreover, women were more likely to endorse the dissatisfaction motivation and men were more likely to endorse the sexual motivation (Barta & Kiene, 2005). In their qualitative study of mainly heterosexual White women, Morrissey et al. (2019) conducted semistructured interviews and asked participants a variety of questions including "I'm wondering what physical/sexual infidelity means to you?," "Tell me what emotional infidelity means to you," and "What makes emotional infidelity different than sexual/physical infidelity, if at all?" Morrisey et al. (2019) found that participants organically volunteered factors that explain why emotional infidelity occurs when asked to define emotional infidelity. Specifically, all participants endorsed that emotional infidelity would occur because emotional needs were met by the infidelity partner, and that emotional infidelity could permit a person to feel validated, valued, and supported. Participants also viewed sharing interests with the infidelity partner as a factor that could lead to emotional infidelity (Morrissey et al., 2019). Collectively these findings suggest that one reason why women may be more likely to engage in emotionally involved and long-term infidelities is because they are seeking love, support, and attention that they are not getting from the primary relationship (Jeanfreau et al., 2014). While men appear to share these motives, their desire for sexual variety and frequency, as well as greater sexual freedom affored by society, also seem to play a role which likely explains why they are more likely to engage in short-term sexual infidelities.

Attachment style and personality traits are also individual factors commonly examined as predictors of infidelity. Russell et al. (2013), collected data from two separate samples of heterosexual newlywed couples (72 couples in Study 1, 135 couples in Study 2). Participants were regularly surveyed across 3.5 years (Study 1) and the first 4.5 years of marriage (Study 2). During each of the six waves of the study, participants completed an attachment measure, were asked if they "had a romantic affair/infidelity" in the past 6 months, and if they found out their partner "had been unfaithful." Partner's attachment anxiety was positively associated with individuals engaging in infidelity and contrary to expectations, partner's attachment avoidance was negatively associated with infidelity. These findings replicate previous research that indicates an individual's attachment style can impact motivations cited for emotional, likely long-term extradyadic involvement. Fearful and preoccupied attachment styles resulted in a higher likelihood of engaging in an obsessive or needy infidelity relationship, and infidelity that is motivated by intimacy related issues (Allen & Baucom, 2004; Blow & Hartnett, 2005). Fearful attachment has also been found to be associated with greater ambivalence regarding extradyadic involvement, possibly leading to individuals maintaining their extradyadic relationships for longer periods of time (Allen & Baucom, 2004).

There is a plethora of literature linking personality traits to infidelity, with neuroticism, extraversion, and narcissism being the main traits predicting infidelity (Allen et al., 2005; Altgelt et al., 2018). Unfortunately, the current literature exploring personality traits as predictors to infidelity do not specify length of the extradyadic relationships or emotional involvement. Other individual variables often linked with infidelity, such as religiosity, sociosexual orientation, and attitudes toward infidelity, have not been examined with regard to long-term infidelity (Blow & Harnett, 2005; Fincham & May, 2017). Most Americans believe infidelity is immoral and unacceptable (Watkins & Boon, 2016; Blow & Hartnett, 2005), given these personal values those who do engage in infidelity may experience cognitive dissonance (Allen et al., 2005). This dissonance can likely have one of two infidelity maintenance outcomes. The first being longer maintenance of the extradyadic relationship. The individual may find ways to adopt beliefs that encourage the continuation of extradyadic behaviors, such as "the marriage was over anyway" (Allen et al., 2005). They may also perceive the extradyadic partner more favorably than their primary partner. These approaches can help to explain how psychological factors may sustain an infidelity. Conversely, with dissonance the individual changes their behavior by ending the extradyadic involvement, to better match their values and beliefs. This research suggests attitudes toward infidelity may play a key role in understanding how infidelity continues.

Relational Factors

Several studies using a multivariate approach to examining predictors of infidelity have found that relational factors have a greater contribution to the likelihood of engaging in infidelity compared to individual factors (Finchman & May, 2017; Gibson et al., 2016). Relationship dissatisfaction has repeatedly been found to be a powerful predictor of extradyadic involvement (Blow & Hartnett, 2005; Fincham & May, 2017). Relationship dissatisfaction is closely associated with emotional infidelity and even more so with combined sexual and emotional infidelity (Blow & Hartnett, 2005), and likely long-term infidelities. These findings coincide with the previously reviewed research that relationship dissatisfaction is an important individual motivator for engaging in an extradyadic relationship.

Relationship history and relationship status also may be associated with propensity to engage in long-term infidelity. Some studies have found greater incidence of infidelity among individuals who have previously engaged in infidelity (Knopp et al., 2017; Martins et al., 2016). This pattern of serial infidelity may occur because of lack of commitment to the relationship or more favorable views of infidelity. It is clear that relationship history is associated with infidelity, and perhaps these patterns play a role in maintaining long-term infidelity. Furthermore, marriage may act as a deterrent, with married couples engaging in infidelity less often than cohabiting couples or dating couples, making marriage a protective factor due to the increase in commitment (Blow & Hartnett, 2005). Although researchers consistently find that satisfaction, commitment, and relationship status are associated with infidelity, further research is required to understand how relational factors are associated with long-term infidelities.

Contextual Factors

Predictors of infidelity can also take the form of contextual factors, which involve variables outside of the primary relationship. These external factors most often studied are sources of opportunity to engage in infidelity and cultural context. Opportunity is conceptualized as the availability of willing extradyadic partners and the means to attract those partners as well as facilitate the infidelity (Allen et al., 2005). Ideas such as working outside of the home, cultural norms surrounding infidelity and sexuality, and geographic location can all be indicators of greater opportunity (Blow & Hartnett, 2005). Studies differ in their operationalization of opportunity, with some measuring the concept by employment status and income, others measure based on geographic location such as urban versus rural settings (Blow & Hartnett, 2005).

OPPORTUNITIES TO ENGAGE IN INFIDELITY

Perhaps the most compelling of these contextual factors is work status. Several studies have investigated the link between work and infidelity, finding greater opportunity by means of expanded access to available alternative partners, funds and time outside of the home to facilitate the affair, and means to attract available alternatives (Allen et al., 2005). Approximately 46%–62% of individuals who have engaged in infidelity met their extradyadic partner through work (Allen et al., 2005). Labrecque and Whisman (2017) found work was a common location to meet extradyadic partners. Interestingly, the highest rates of infidelity were found among couples in which one partner worked outside the home and the other remained at home (Allen et al., 2005). The relationship between work status and infidelity can be explained through income, as finances can help attract available alternatives and facilitate opportunities for infidelity (Allen et al., 2005; Atkins et al., 2001; Blow & Hartnett, 2005). Work environment also impacts likelihood of engaging in infidelity, with jobs with closer contact and greater chances of being alone with others leading to increased likelihood of infidelity (Allen et al., 2005). Supporting this correlation, other studies have found individuals who engage in infidelity with coworkers report greater relationship satisfaction in their primary relationship compared to those who engage with non-coworkers (Blow & Hartnett, 2005).

Gender composition of the work environment is an additional factor associated with engaging in infidelity (Munsch & Yorks, 2017). Using data from the NLSY97, a nationally representative sample, Munsch and Yorks (2017) tested the association between gender makeup of the workplace and infidelity. They found that women tokens (i.e., women working in a male dominated workplace) were no more or less likely to engage in infidelity. However, White men tokens (i.e., men working in a female dominated workplace) were statistically more likely to engage in infidelity; whereas, non-White men tokens were statistically less likely to engage in infidelity. This work suggests that opportunity may be more impactful for specific demographic groups, particularly White, heterosexual men. Future research on infidelity as it relates to work and income should further query participants about length of their extradyadic involvement.

CULTURAL INFLUENCES

The cultural significance and taboo nature of infidelity may contribute to its longevity among some individuals (Allen et al., 2005). Across cultures, sexual double standards continue to exist in which men's infidelity is more sanctioned compared to women's, and women's extradyadic activities are stigmatized to a greater degree (Buunk & Dijkstra, 2004). Betzig (1989) studied extradyadic involvements in 88 different societies to assess relationship dissolution following infidelity. Results showed that relationship dissolution occurs following infidelity by either partner in 25 societies, only on the woman's part in 54 societies, and in only on the husband's part in 2 societies. Additionally, in many cultures, society has continually reinforced the notion that men are allowed to be sexually permissive, whereas women are expected to associate sex with love (Martins et al., 2016). These patterns suggest far greater societal permissiveness for men's infidelity, particularly short-term sexual infidelity. These societal sanctions may motivate women to risk stigmatization only when drawn emotionally into another relationship. The internalization of these beliefs may be why women report increased feelings of guilt and their male partners blame them at a higher rate than women blame men for their extradyadic activities (Buunk & Dijkstra, 2004). Women also invest more in emotional extradyadic relationships, possibly prolonging the infidelity due to the societal taboo revolving around women's sexuality (Allen et al., 2005; Tsapelas, 1998; Martin et al., 2016).

Online Long-Term Infidelities

The past three decades have witnessed an increasing integration of technology and digital media into the lives of those living in Westernized society. While little doubt remains today that certain technology-based behaviors constitute infidelity, researchers initially sought to understand to what extent individuals experienced online behaviors to be a breach of their romantic relationship, and how these behaviors compared to traditional offline infidelity (Cravens et al., 2013; Henline & Lamke, 2003; Henline et al., 2007; Parker & Wampler, 2003; Whitty, 2003, 2005; Whitty & Quigley, 2008). A detailed examination of online infidelity is an essential component to understanding long-term infidelities, as numerous extradyadic involvements are initiated and sustained through technology.

One of the first studies conducted, revealed that participants viewed online infidelity to consist not only of sexual but emotional components as well (Henline & Lamke, 2003). Whitty (2003) recruited a large sample ($n = 1,117$) of men and women ranging in age from early to late adulthood, asking participants to rate the level of infidelity from "not considered infidelity" to "extreme infidelity" for 15 predetermined behaviors (11 sexual, 4 emotional). These behaviors were identified from previous literature on offline infidelity, and included behaviors such as cybersex, hot chatting, emotional disclosure, and pornography use. Findings indicated that individuals do believe that some online behaviors are indicative of cheating, and that certain behaviors, specifically cybersex, are considered a greater relational betrayal than others, such as viewing pornography. Using factor analysis, the study also resulted in the creation of three groups of online infidelity: sexual infidelity, emotional infidelity, and pornography use.

Several researchers conducted studies that asked participants to respond to scenarios of online infidelity, using story completion methods to examine perceptions to different online scenarios. Parker and Wampler (2003) recruited 242 undergraduate college students to respond to eight different scenarios of online infidelity, in which the gender of the character in the committed relationship rotated and different types of online behaviors were presented. The scenarios were designed to explore emotional involvement, sexual involvement, and distraction from the primary relationship. The infidelity behaviors included scenarios of having cybersex, having cybersex various times, adult chatrooms behaviors (joining, visiting without interaction, interacting), visiting adult websites, having telephone sex, and one offline behavior of having sex in a hotel room. The gender of the partner had no impact on participants' responses, and all of the online behaviors were considered cheating and harmful to the primary relationship. Further, this study revealed that online behaviors may not be perceived as being as damaging as on offline affair, but that these behaviors are still problematic to primary relationships. Similar to Parker and Wampler's study, Whitty (2005) had third-year college students enrolled in a psychology course in Australia ($n = 234$) respond to a story completion task, where the cue sentence was the same for all participants, but the gender of the partner engaging in the online behavior was randomized across participants. Results of the study indicated that online behaviors are perceived as real forms of infidelity, and the impact to romantic relationships can be just as impactful as offline infidelity. Commonly reported consequences of the online behavior included a loss of trust within the relationship, emotional hurt experienced by the noninvolved partner, and the couple ending the relationship.

Henline et al. (2007) were the first researchers to explore individuals' beliefs about what constitutes online infidelity. Participants were recruited from a college campus in the southeastern region of the United States ($n = 123$). To participate, participants had to be in a committed relationship; however, the researchers did not report a minimum relationship length to define what they meant by committed. Participants primarily reporting being in a dating relationship (79.6%), 12.2% were engaged, and 8.1% were married. The researchers asked what online behaviors they would consider cheating and the impact of online infidelity, comparing these results to previous research on offline infidelity (Buss et al., 1999; Roscoe et al., 1988). Their findings indicated that respondents identified a greater range of both sexually and emotionally based online behaviors when compared to offline behaviors that would be labeled as infidelity. The four highest-rated online infidelity behaviors were online sex, emotional involvement with an online contact, online dating, and other online sexual interactions. No gender differences were found in evaluations, which differs from previous research on offline infidelity (Buss et al., 1999; Kitzinger & Powell, 1995), and that greater distress occurred following an emotionally based online behavior.

Combined, these researchers demonstrate that certain online behaviors constitute infidelity, that these behaviors can be just as damaging as offline infidelity, that online infidelity can consist of an emotional and/or sexual component, and that individuals are more likely to perceive online behaviors to have a stronger emotional than sexual component due to the nature of technology-based behaviors. These findings suggest that long-term infidelity is likely to occur online, as well as offline, given the centrality of emotional infidelity in defining online infidelity.

Experiences of Online Infidelity

Within the last decade, researchers have attempted to recruit individuals who have experienced online infidelity, to better understand this phenomenon from those who have lived it. These studies have focused on the noninvolved partner, or those on the receiving end of the online affair; however, Mileham (2007) studied chat room users who engage in cyberaffairs. Using an ethnographic qualitative interview, Mileham asked participants about their online behaviors and whether they believed the behaviors were affairs. The majority of participants in the study stated that their behaviors were not cheating, with the primary justification being that no physical contact had occurred. Mileham theorized that the Internet afforded individuals a way to engage in relationships with parties outside of their relationship, due to a sense of a disembodied self in cyberspace. Despite the participating partners in Mileham's study rationalizing their online behaviors as not being harmful, research on the nonparticipating partners of online infidelity report contradictory feelings. This contradiction and ability to justify online infidelity may be associated with more sustained, long-term infidelities.

In one of the first studies to examine the experiences of the noninvolved partner, Schneider (2000) interviewed 94 individuals, 91 of which identified as women, who had experienced cybersex in their committed romantic relationship. Results of the qualitative study found that two-thirds of the participants had lost interest in sex with their spouse due to the cyberaffair, and that 22% of the respondents separated or divorced. Building off of the previous study, Schneider et al. (2012) surveyed 35 individuals whose partners had been engaging in cybersex, finding that the noninvolved partners described a loss of trust for the partner, feeling betrayed and traumatized, and that the participants sought mental health services to cope with the experience. While qualitative researchers focus on reaching saturation rather than a specific sample size, both of Schneider's studies were critiqued for having a small sample size, and the results only being generalizable to women.

Addressing previous concerns about sample size, Cavaglion and Rashty (2010) conducted a narrative analysis of 1,130 messages from female members of online Italian self-help groups for men "addicted" to cybersex and pornography and their female partners. Results of the study showed that the female partners felt a sense of loss, distress, and ambivalence toward their partner. Finally, specific to social media, Cravens et al. (2013) used grounded theory methodology to analyze 90 stories from individuals whose partners had engaged in Facebook infidelity behaviors. Results of the study indicate that after Facebook infidelity has occurred, the noninvolved partner may experience a host of negative emotions and struggle with their decision on whether to remain in or end the relationship.

As more researchers were attempting to understand the influence of online infidelity on individuals and their romantic relationship, researchers had yet to explore the extent to which those in committed relationship were engaging in online infidelity behaviors. Media sources have stated that one-third of US divorces cite Facebook (Lumpkin, 2012), but only a limited number of studies have examined problematic online infidelity-reflated behaviors. Recently, McDaniel et al. (2017) used family data to explore whether individuals in committed relationships are engaging in online infidelity relationships using social media sites. The researchers recruited 338 individuals, mostly White, college-educated, and married, to indicate whether they had engaged in seven social media-based infidelity behaviors while in their current committed relationship. Only a small percentage of participants reported engaging in the online behaviors, and these individuals reported lower relationship satisfaction, higher relationship ambivalence, and greater attachment avoidance in both female- and male-identifying participants. McDaniel's study was unique in its focus on whether those in committed relationships were engaging in social media-based infidelity behaviors. Additionally, attachment anxiety and gender interacted with relationship satisfaction in predicting online infidelity-related behaviors when controlling for other variables.

Why Online Cheating

A review of the research focused on online infidelity leaves us with a clear lack of empirical understanding of long-term online infidelities. In the absence of empirical support for extradyadic relationships of this nature, understanding the nature of the Internet and how it makes relationships vulnerable to infidelity may help to better conceptualize long-term online infidelity. With the recognition that individuals are using technology as a means to engage in and maintain extradyadic involvements, questions have arisen concerning the motivational factors or specific vulnerabilities that are introduced into romantic relationships. Initially proposed models included the "Triple A" engine (Cooper, 2002), ACEs (Young, 1999), and the proposal of a fourth *A*, approximation (Ross & Kauthm, 2003). Both the Triple A and the ACEs model describe how aspects of the Internet may make individuals vulnerable to breaching relational boundaries. The ACEs model discusses how the Internet allows for anonymity, convenience, and escape, while the Triple A engine describes access, affordability, and anonymity. Based on existing theories of Internet vulnerabilities, Hertlein and Stevenson (2010) developed a theory of the ecological vulnerabilities of the Internet, which included the four "As" identified by Cooper (2002) and Ross and Kauthm (2003), and three additional "As": acceptability, accommodation, and ambiguity.

Each vulnerability highlights the ways in which specific aspects of the Internet and technology-based behaviors can influence an individual's decision to engage in and maintain online infidelity behaviors. Both the ACEs model and Triple A engine identify the importance of anonymity, as a vulnerability factor. The nature of the Internet allows individuals to interact anonymously with other online users, creating an environment in which an individual does not have to share their identity with others. Anonymity is associated with lower inhibitions and can lead individuals to engage in behaviors that they would not otherwise do if they were not protected by a hidden identity (Crocket, 2017; Hertlein, 2012). Therefore, a perceived sense of protection may increase an individual's likelihood of engaging in an affair due to a belief that they are less likely to be caught since their behaviors are not directly linked to their identity. The next two A's, access and affordability, highlight the ease at which individuals access others through the convenience of technology and digital media from anywhere at any time, as well as the affordability that has allowed most individuals to have access to the Internet both at home and on a mobile device. The Internet has effectively broken down barriers that in past decades may have limited a person from maintaining a long-term relationship with someone else, by allowing them to contact and interact with another party despite geographical distances or obligations with a primary committed partner. Ross and Kauthman's (2003) A, approximation, describes how advances in technology have allowed computer-mediated interactions to approximate in-person interactions. This approximation allows individuals to develop meaningful, intimate relationships through technology and perhaps sustain emotionally intimate long-term extradyadic involvements.

Hertlein and Stevenson's final three A's build on the existing ecological factors. Accommodation describes the ways in which the Internet can allow an individual to access and engage in behaviors that may not be available in their offline environment. With the Internet's ability to cater to a diverse range of interests and proclivities, an individual interested in a certain sexual fantasy or who shares a common intellectual interest that is not enjoyed by their primary offline partner can go online and find someone to share these parts of themselves with another like-minded individual. The accommodation of a shared interest, whether emotional or sexual, may lead to the development of a meaningful extradyadic relationship, one that can be easily maintained long-term online. The final two As, acceptability and ambiguity, are related constructs. Acceptability highlights how our technologically saturated society has high acceptance over the use of technology and digital media, making the use of the Internet throughout one's day accepted and supported. The Internet has also brought with it ambiguity over what behaviors cross a boundary and are considered inappropriate. Considering the findings of Mileham's (2007) study, individuals who engage in online affairs rationalized their behaviors as not being inappropriate because no in-person interactions had occurred. Therefore, the acceptance individuals may feel over their use of the Internet, paired with ambiguity over when certain behaviors breach fidelity in one's primary relationship may reinforce an individual's long-term commitment to an extradyadic partner. The ecological theories provide one conceptualization of how technology and the Internet can make an individual and their relationship vulnerable to an online extradyadic involvement.

Technology has transformed the ways in which individuals are able to connect and communicate with another, including text messaging, sending emails, sharing experiences on social media, and video chatting. Computer-mediated communication (CMC), any form of technology-based communication, has offered a new way for individuals to connect with one another regardless of one's physical location (Kennedy et al., 2008; Spears & Lea, 1994). Walther (1996) proposed the hyperpersonal model, suggesting that CMC offers different affordances than offline, face-to-face interactions. Similar to the ecological models that have been proposed, Walther identifies anonymity, asynchronicity, selective self-presentation, and a lack of nonverbal cues as unique aspects of CMC. Empirical support exists for the influence of online-based anonymity promoting self-disclosure (Bargh & McKenna, 2004; Joinson, 2001), and that selective self-presentation and impression management influence what information is shared to potential romantic online partners (Gibbs et al., 2006; Hancock & Toma, 2009). The Internet offers users an added protection to disclose personal information to others online, with the potential anonymity or lack of facial cues related to many formats of computer-mediated communication. This leads to individuals not only disclosing more personal information through CMC than in-person, but also omitting less desirable aspects of their identity (Hancock & Toma, 2009; Toma et al., 2008). Finally, with the growing popularity of online dating, Gibbs et al. (2006) found that self-disclosure with online dating was positively associated with reports of feelings of attachment, caring, and intimacy, providing further evidence that online interactions can facilitate romantic connections. This polished self-presentation as well as ability to gain emotional intimacy rapidly, makes the Internet a potentially ripe arena for long-term infidelities to form and persevere.

These theories and the research conducted on computer-mediated communication highlight the reasons that online interactions can lead to the development of an online extradyadic involvement. Media attention has been given to individuals using the Internet to meet extradyadic romantic partners and/or reconnect online with past romantic partners (Brockway, 2016; Bulger, 2021). While a minimal number of studies have been conducted focusing on individuals who engage in online affairs (Mileham, 2007), researchers have not explored reconnecting with past romantic partners online while in a committed relationship. The publications on this form of online infidelity have been limited mostly to popular media and magazines. A quick Internet search of "reconnecting online with an ex-partner" produces a plethora of articles published on the topic, and although these publications often quote clinicians who specialize in working with couples and infidelity, they are not empirically driven articles. These articles discuss the risks that individuals in relationship take when they search for past romantic partners due to curiosity, boredom, or problems within their primary relationship and describe how online interactions can be innocently initiated but quickly escalate to crossing boundaries (Brockway, 2016; Bulger, 2021). Social media makes it increasingly easy to reconnect with previous romantic partners, due to shared connections within your online social network and the nature of the Internet. Locating an ex-partner online may result in a belief that this person's edited online presentation indicates an attractive alternative to their offline relationship, and the ambiguity of online interactions may motivate someone to "catch-up" with their ex-partner. These factors combined with the ease of access to computer-mediated communication may increase an individual's vulnerability for engaging in an online affair.

Several studies have been conducted that have examined the concept of "back burner" relationships, desired prospective romantic/sexual partners that an individual communicates with to establish a potential future relationship with (Dibble & Drouin, 2014; Dibble et al., 2015; Drouin et al., 2015). Further, these relationship interactions can range from platonic communication to flirting or romantic/sexual interactions (Dibble & Drouin, 2014). Recently, researchers have explored how social media sites are used to initiate and maintain back burner relationships, despite individuals being in committed, offline relationships (Dibble & Drouin, 2014; Dibble et al., 2015; Drouin et al., 2015). Dibble and Drouin (2014) recruited 374 undergraduates from the United States and asked them whether they had back burners, the number of back burners, and the nature of their interaction with these individuals. Participants averaged 5.5 back burner partners that they maintained communication with, the interactions were maintained mostly through text messaging or Facebook, and the communication was platonic more than romantic or sexual. No differences existed between single participants and participants in a committed relationship and for those in a relationship, level of commitment and investment did not impact back burner relationships.

Research on back burner relationships indicate that technology and the Internet may be making it increasingly easy for individuals to secretively maintain back burner relationships and raises questions about whether these behaviors are becoming normalized. Researchers in these studies do not distinguish between back burner relationships of a romantic or sexual nature and infidelity behaviors. Thus, these studies further complicate the issue of an operationalized definition of online infidelity, fail to ask participants about the nature of the back burner partners (i.e., offline or online only interactions, history of the relationship), and whether the participant and their committed romantic partner would consider the interactions to be infidelity.

Due to the ambiguity of online behaviors, research indicates that couples living in today's technology-saturated society should revisit the rules and boundaries for technology use within their romantic committed relationships. Helsper and Whitty (2010) were interested in whether married couples shared similarities in their online netiquette—the rules and assumptions about appropriate online behaviors. They recruited couples (n = 992) and asked them to rate how they would react to 10 online activities if their partner were to engage in the behavior. Results of the study found that couples had the strongest agreement with one another on infidelity behaviors, specifically falling in love with someone else online and engaging in cybersex, and the most disagreement about other problematic online behaviors such as online gaming, gambling, and shopping. Norton and Baptist (2014) found that couples in long-term marriages often have rules for social media and that these rules can be categorized into boundaries about openness and fidelity, finding that as trust within the marriage increased, the use of both types of boundaries for the Internet also increased. Pickens and Whiting (2019) explored how couples communicate about and monitor rules and boundaries related to use of technology in their committed relationships. Using constructivist grounded theory, 25 couples in committed relationships were interviewed, resulting in a process model of couples' communication about technology use. Results indicate that some couples develop explicit rules about technology use, but many couples rely on implicit rules or have not communicated about technology-related issues.

Researchers have concluded that there are barriers to resolving this issue due to the vastly different opinions within and across romantic relationships (Pickens & Whiting, 2019; Whitty & Quigley, 2008), which are influenced by gender identity, age, personal and moral values, and one's experiences with infidelity (Vossler, 2016). Hertlein and Piercy (2006, p. 367) attempted to develop an operational definition that addresses the ambiguity within other studies, by stating that online infidelity remains stable by one element across definitions— secrecy. Despite this proposed operational definition, research conducted since their publication in 2006 have not used this definition, perpetuating the problem of variation in how researchers are operationalizing online infidelity. Similar to limitations to the research on traditional offline infidelity, researchers studying online infidelity have failed to give appropriate attention to the nature of the online infidelity and while research suggests the Internet may facilitate long-term infidelity such concrete conclusions are beyond the scope of the literature currently. Therefore, future research is required to understand how factors related to the extradyadic relationship, including length of relationship, type of relationship, who the third party(ies) are, and frequency of contact, influence the primary relationship and subsequent outcomes.

Outcomes of Long-Term Infidelities

Whether an individual has engaged in offline or online infidelity, researchers have consistently identified a host of negative outcomes at both an interpersonal and intrapersonal level. Prior to an in-depth discussion of research on the outcomes of infidelity, it should be stressed that researchers have failed to assess for and consider the nature of the extradyadic relationship and it is unknown the extent to which these studies represent short- or long-term infidelities. While limited to an untested, but empirically based hypothesis at this time, there is the potential that extradyadic relationships that are long-term in nature may intensify or exacerbate the findings discussed in this section of the chapter (Thompson, 1984), but research is needed to test this hypothesis. Several critical reviews of the publications on infidelity (Blow & Hartnett, 2005; Hertlein & Piercy, 2006; Vossler, 2016) have identified a range of covered topics, including emotional responses, psychological well-being, family disruption, interpersonal conflict, reconciliation and forgiveness, and relationship dissolution. An additional area concerns physical health, specifically sexual health (Bull & McFarlane, 2000; McFarlane et al., 2000). Ultimately, the toll of infidelity, paired with the prevalence of infidelity makes it one of the primary precipitating factors for couples seeking therapy (Fife et al., 2008; Glass & Wright, 1997; Moller & Vossler, 2014), and mental health professionals regard it as the second most difficult clinical issue to treat following physical abuse (Whisman et al., 1997). Indeed, individuals rank extramarital sex as being the relational concern with the most significant impact on likelihood to divorce (Amato & Rogers, 1997).

To date, researchers have conducted a number of studies specific to the emotional impact of infidelity. While not all of the studies recruited participants who had experienced an affair (Apostolou et al., 2019; Becker et al., 2004; Buss et al., 1992; Shackelford et al., 2000), researchers have designed studies specifically seeking individuals who have experienced an affair (Bergener et al., 2003; Charny & Parnass, 1995; Cravens et al., 2013; King, 1999; Olson et al., 2002; Schneider, 2000; Schneider et al., 1998; Zitzman & Butler, 2005). Researchers have found that noninvolved partners report experiencing a wide range of emotions in response to infidelity, including betrayal, loss of trust, loss of identity, hurt, rejection, abandonment, devastation, loneliness, shame, shock, isolation, humiliation, jealousy, and anger (Cano & O'Leary, 2000; Charny & Parnass, 1995; Schneider et al., 1998). When comparing the emotional impact of online to offline infidelity, researchers have found analogous impacts on the noninvolved partner (Bergner et al., 2003; Cravens et al., 2013; King, 1999; Schnneider, 2000; Zitzman & Butler, 2005) and that these behaviors were a direct threat to their primary relationship (Bergner et al., 2003). To further understand emotional reactions to infidelity, Sabini and Green (2004) tested the evolutionary hypothesis across a diverse sample of student and nonstudent participants, finding that participants were more hurt and upset by emotional infidelity and reported more anger and blame for sexual infidelity. Researchers studying how couples manage the impact of infidelity disclosure have referred to the wide range of emotional reactions to infidelity and fluctuations in mood as the "emotional roller coaster" (Olson et al., 2002). The range of emotional experiences, paired with the violation of the foundation of their relationship and uncertainty about the partner and the relationship increases the risk of noninvolved partners developing psychological disorders (Baucom et al., 2004; Cano & O'Leary, 2000; Gordon & Baucom, 1998).

An area of growing interest by researchers is whether noninvolved partner's experiences of and reactions to infidelity are similar to posttraumatic stress disorder (PTSD). Gordon and Baucom (1999) refer to infidelity as an "interpersonal trauma" as a way to describe the impact affairs have on the noninvolved partner (p. 382). Researchers have found that a number of their participants met diagnostic criteria for PTSD, reporting that they experience frequent intrusive thoughts, flashbacks to the discovery, and hypervigilance related to their partner's actions (Lasser et al., 2017; Ozgun, 2010; Ross et al., 2018; Stefens & Rennie, 2006). In their study, Lasser et al. (2017) report that nearly their entire sample of female participants rated the infidelity as at least "very traumatic," with over 60% of the sample meeting the *Diagnostic and Statistical Manual for Mental Disorders* (DSM-5; American Psychiatric Association, 2013) criteria for PTSD. While these are concerning findings, Lasser and colleagues also assessed for experiences of posttraumatic growth (Tedeschi & Calhoun, 1996, 2004), finding that 80% of the participants also had some degree of posttraumatic growth through the healing process of the affair. In addition to PTSD, researchers have found that infidelity can increase the noninvolved partners' risk for having a major depressive episode, even when controlling for levels of marital discord, stressful life events, and personal and family history of depression (Cano & O'Leary, 2000).

In the limited number of studies that have assessed the involved partner's emotional experience, researchers have found increased psychological distress (Beach et al., 1985; Hall & Fincham, 2009; Spanier & Margolis, 1983), including heightened levels of anxiety, depressive symptoms, and guilt and lower levels of general well-being (Atwater, 1979; Hall & Fincham, 2009; Hunt, 1974; Lawson, 1988). The majority of these studies are cross-sectional in nature and focus on treatment seeking populations. Hall and Fincham (2009) conducted two studies seeking to determine whether nontreatment seeking populations have higher levels of psychological distress (study 1) and whether longitudinal data would support existing research on infidelity increasing psychological distress in perpetrators of infidelity (study 2). Study 1 confirmed past findings; whereas, study 2 indicated that psychological distress predicts having an affair, but the affair did not increase psychological distress.

Although a focus has been on the impact of infidelity on the noninvolved partner, researchers have also explored the influence of the affair on couple and family relationships. Examination of the impact of infidelity on couple outcomes has included physical health, family environment, and relationship dissolution. The emotional toll of the infidelity can lead couples to experience a loss of sense of security, stability, and control (Humphrey, 1987; Rosenau, 1998), and interpersonal conflict and violence (Amato & Hohmann-Marriott, 2007; Cano & O'Leary, 2000; Kaighobadi et al., 2009; Kaighobadi et al., 2008; Levine, 2005; Scheinkman, 2005; Snyder, 2005). Physical health may also be at risk following an affair, due to the potential that involved partners may engage in unprotected sex with the extradyadic partner as well as their primary partner (Choi et al., 1994), putting both partners at risk for sexually transmitted infections (Bull & McFarlane, 2000; McFarlane et al., 2000). Infidelity has been found to be associated with relationship dissolution (Marin et al., 2014; Negash et al., 2013) and family disruption (Lusterman, 2005; Nemeth et al., 2012).

Divorce

When couples experience a breach to the boundaries of their committed relationship, both partners are tasked with reevaluating the relationship and determining whether to remain in or leave the relationship (Berger & Bridges, 2002; Manning, 2006). Contradictory findings have come from researchers exploring the influence of infidelity on decisions to divorce. Some researchers have found that infidelity is the most commonly cited cause of marital dissolution (Amato & Rodgers, 1997; Kitson et al., 1985; Spanier & Margolis, 1983), whereas others have identified additional factors that may play a more prominent role in decisions.

Initially, researchers examining traditional offline infidelity found that participants attributed the decision to divorce to the infidelity (Amato & Rodgers, 1997; Marin et al., 2014; Previti & Amato, 2004; Shackelford & Buss, 1997;). In an attempt to address the research limitations of retrospective reports from participants, Amato and Rodgers (1997) explored factors that predict divorce using a nationally representative sample of married couples in the United States that followed couples from 1980 to 1992 finding that reports of infidelity was one of the most significant predictors of divorce. A 17-year longitudinal study revealed that infidelity is both a cause and consequence of relationship deterioration (Previti & Amato, 2004). Marin et al. (2014) compared therapeutic outcomes, with a 5-year follow-up for two groups of couples, those who had experienced infidelity, and noninfidelity couples. By 5 years post therapy, 53% of the infidelity couples had divorced compared to 23% of the noninfidelity couples, revealing that couples who had experienced infidelity were more at risk of divorce than other distressed couples entering therapy. Researchers have also explored the impact of infidelity in dating relationships, finding similar results to those on marital relationships and divorce, that the experience of infidelity influenced decisions to end the relationship (Hall & Fincham, 2006a, 2006b; Harris, 2002; Negash et al., 2013).

While numerous researchers have identified a direct link between experiencing infidelity and the decision to divorce, other researchers have explored factors that explain why not all couples who experience infidelity end their relationship. Factors that have been examined include overall relationship satisfaction, the motivations for the affair, level of conflict due to the infidelity, attitudes held about affairs (Bunnk, 1987), and how committed the involved partner was within their infidelity relationship (Charny & Parnass, 1995). Other researchers have indicated that while many couples initially threaten separation and divorce following the disclosure of an affair, less than one-fourth of those couples go on to end their marriage (Schneider et al., 1990). Researchers have also tested how infidelity influences who is likely to file for divorce, finding that the involved partner is more likely to file for divorce due to the affair or to have an affair due to their decision to file for divorce more so than the noninvolved partner (England et al., 2014). The impact that divorce can have on those who decide to file for divorce is influenced by who initiates the divorce. Researchers found that if the involved partner initiates the divorce, the noninvolved partner experiences worse depression than if the noninvolved partner initiates the divorce (Sweeney & Horwitz, 2001).

Positive Outcomes, Reconciliation, and Forgiveness

While the vast majority of existing research has focused on negative consequences associated with infidelity, researchers have attempted to understand the potential positive outcomes. Early research conducted in this area indicated that only a small percentage of couples who experience infidelity will improve their relationship following the affair (Charny & Parnass 1995; Hansen, 1987); however, other researchers found that regardless of the quality of the relationship couples who experience infidelity do not all end their relationship (Buunk, 1987; Charny & Parnass, 1995). In a more comprehensive study, Olson and colleagues (2002) conducted a qualitative interview finding that couples experienced a number of unintended positive outcomes following an affair, including a closer marital relationship, increased assertiveness, placing a higher value on family, taking better care of oneself, and realizing the importance of good marital communication. Finally, researchers explored the influence of couples therapy on addressing infidelity, concluding that those who dealt openly with the affair changed at a quicker rate than other distressed couples in therapy (Atkins et al., 2005).

In conclusion, researchers studying the impact of infidelity on dating and marital relationships have identified a range of outcomes. These studies have sought to recruit participants who have experienced infidelity, although some studies relied on hypothetical scenarios (Sabini & Green, 2004). Some researchers have successfully used longitudinal designs and nationally representative data to explore the impact of infidelity on divorce (Amato & Rogers, 1997; England et al., 2014; Previti & Amato, 2004; Shackelford & Buss, 1997), although more longitudinal research is needed. Unfortunately, researchers who have examined the influence of infidelity on individuals and committed relationships have failed to assess for the nature of the extradyadic relationship. This is a major limitation, as the nature of the extradyadic relationship is likely to influence how partners react to an extradyadic involvement and relationship dissolution.

Family, Friends, and Long-Term Infidelities

One of the unique features of long-term infidelities is that there is a higher likelihood that the noninvolved partner will become aware of the extradyadic relationship compared to short-term sexual infidelities. Subsequently, individuals within the couple's family system and social network will also learn of and be impacted by the extradyadic relationship (Allan & Harrison, 2010; Vangelisti & Gerstenberger, 2004). Because long-term infidelities are also viewed more negatively and more damaging to the primary relationship, family members and friends may also be called on for support and advice to a greater extent. A growing body of literature particularly illuminates how children become aware of and are impacted by a parent's infidelity.

Children and Parental Infidelity

The impact of an affair is not confined to the romantic relationship. Researchers have found that between 11%–21% of participants in their studies have children (Spence, 2012; Weigel et al., 2003), and the affair can have deleterious implications for the entire family system. Parents who are struggling to cope with the ramifications of an affair risk exposing their children to increased levels of conflict (Blodgett Salafia et al., 2013). Further, parental infidelity can lead children to experience a range of negative emotions including guilt, fear, anxiety, depression, worry, shock, and grief-like symptoms (Dean, 2011). Exposure to these environments can negatively affect a child's healthy emotional development (Ablow et al., 2009; Blodgett Salafia et al., 2013; Lusterman, 2005).

As Duncombe and Marsden (2004) report, the minority of parents consider how their infidelity may impact their children, although research suggests that a high percentage of children become aware of their parents' extradyadic involvements (Reibstein & Richards, 1993). Adolescents are more likely to be aware of the sexual nature of infidelity whereas younger children merely understand the hurt feelings and resultant parental conflict. With long-term infidelity, the involved partner may have spent time and energy away from their family, which can negatively impact children of all ages (Duncombe & Marsden, 2004). Further within-family disruptions can occur as siblings may place responsibility differently with parents and be more or less willing to accept an infidelity partner into their lives (Duncombe & Marsden, 2004). Moreover, the experience of parental infidelity sends messages about trust and what to expect from relationship partners. Children may lose respect and trust for the involved parent (Duncombe & Marsden, 2004) and parental infidelity may also send the message to children that future relationship partners should not be trusted either (Sori, 2007). Researchers have consistently found that the experience of a parental infidelity is associated with relational ethics, particularly reduced trust in parents as well as partners (Kawar et al., 2018; Schmidt, Green, & Prouty, 2016; Schmidt, Green, Sibley, et al., 2016).

Thorson (2017, 2015, 2014) has conducted a series of qualitative studies examining how communication about infidelity is experienced by adult children with knowledge of a parental extradyadic involvement. Through descriptions of the parental extradyadic involvement and how participants negotiated family turmoil, it is apparent that most individuals in these studies are discussing long-term infidelities. For example, the adult children discuss how they became aware of the extradyadic involvement, explicit communications with parents, and in some cases, the need to navigate a relationship with the infidelity partner. Thorson (2014) conducted qualitative interviews with 38 individuals who had at least one parent who engaged in infidelity and found participants recalled messages from family members that both discouraged and encouraged feelings of being caught between their parents. Parents discouraged children from feeling caught by limiting their exposure to conflict about infidelity, discussing how both parents have shortcomings, and emphasizing that family transitions and changes can be positive. In contrast, some parents asked their children to provide or discover details about the infidelity or directly put their children in the middle by making them an intermediary. Other family members also engendered discomfort by sharing their negative opinions of the parents with regard to infidelity (Thorson, 2014). Thorson (2015) examined how participants managed family privacy and the taboo nature of infidelity, and found that participants faced a number of dilemmas regarding discovery and sharing of a parent's infidelity. Some participants were explicitly asked to keep information from noninvolved parents, others accidentally discovered an infidelity, and still other participants reported that their parents did a poor job of concealing the extradyadic activity. A handful of participants also reported distress about being lied to by the involved parent or being accused of lying when revealing the infidelity to the noninvolved parent (Thorson, 2015). These findings suggest that some parents do a better job of protecting their children from the fallout of long-term infidelities than others.

Thorson (2017) reported on how participants managed and responded to knowledge of a parental infidelity. Participants indicated that they withheld terms of endearment and affection, refused to use parent's family title (i.e., dad), and would refuse communications with the involved parent. Some participants also indicated that they would knowingly share and use knowledge of the parental infidelity as a way of hurting or embarrassing the involved parent. Still others reported that new family boundaries were enacted with rules created about how and when to discuss infidelity, as well as rules about whether participants would interact with their parent's infidelity partner (Thorson, 2017). Finally, some participants reported distress about being forced to resolve their feelings about a parental infidelity prematurely and failing to recognize that children were also aggrieved about the infidelity. These findings showcase that children respond to their parents' infidelities in varied ways and that acknowledging how children may also be aggrieved by long-term infidelities is essential to their coping.

There is a growing literature which suggests that an additional way children are impacted by parents' infidelity is that they are more likely to engage in infidelity themselves as they grow up and enter their own relationships (Platt et al., 2008; Weiser et al., 2017). Weiser and Weigel (2017) conducted three separate studies to assess intergenerational patterns of infidelity. Study 1 (n = 267) and Study 2 (n = 269) consisted of an undergraduate student sample and Study 3 (n = 718) consisted of a combined undergraduate student and MTurk sample. Across all three studies, Weiser and Weigel (2017) found that adults with knowledge of parental infidelity were about two times more likely to have engaged in some type of infidelity compared to individuals whose parents did not engage in infidelity. In Study 3, the researchers also found that parents who had engaged in infidelity were more likely to communicate that infidelity is acceptable relationship behavior.

Other Family Members and Friends

Research is beginning to emerge to understand how other family members may respond to infidelity. Currently, most of the work has been theoretical in nature and testing tenets of evolutionary theory to examine how parents and siblings respond to knowledge of a family member's emotional or sexual infidelity (Bohner et al., 2010; Michalski et al., 2007; Shackelford et al., 2004). Given the impact of long-term infidelity on an entire family system, future work to understand how extended family members learn of and respond to long-term infidelities is a needed step.

During long-term infidelity, friends may be confided in and turned to as a source of support and advice. Friends must make decisions about whether they will support an involved partner's extradyadic involvement, try to end the extradyadic involvement, or perhaps take a step back from the friendship (Vangelisti & Gerstenberger, 2004). Friends may have greater loyalties or responsibilities to the involved partner, the noninvolved partner, or both partners equally that will ultimately color how they proceed. Harrison (2004) analyzed open-ended responses about how women supported their female friends during an infidelity, either as a noninvolved or involved partner. Participants reported a sense of duty to support their friends who experienced a partner's infidelity and offered substantial emotional support. The participants did note that providing such intense emotional and instrumental support could be trying and laborious but recognized the importance of this support when the person's involved partner was no longer a source of trust and support (Harrison, 2004). Friends of involved partners seemed to have more ambivalent loyalties and expressed disagreement with their partner's engagement in extradyadic activities. Some individuals reported resentment if they were drawn into deception while covering up for their friend's infidelity (Harrison, 2004). Others worried that a similar fate may befall their own marriages and distanced themselves from the friendship. Such concerns may be valid as there is research which suggests that when one thinks individuals approve of infidelity, they are more likely to engage in infidelity and as such infidelity in one's social network may beget further infidelities (Vangelisti & Gerstenberger, 2004).

Future Directions and Limitations

It is clear that prevalence of long-term infidelities has been overlooked by researchers. Specifically, the majority of existing literature on infidelity does not specify length of extradyadic involvement and therefore long-term infidelity has been empirically ignored. The literature lacks specificity on type of infidelity, including emotional vs. sexual, short-term vs. long-term, serial vs. one involvement. We have done our best to propose a working definition of long-term infidelity, speculate on the prevalence of online and offline long-term infidelity, present predictors, and discuss outcomes of long-term infidelity. We conclude by stating there are countless directions that the research literature can take, and a better understanding of long-term infidelities will have implications for researchers and clinicians. We identify six major limitations currently in the infidelity literature and offer suggestions as to how scholars can better study long-term infidelities moving forward.

First and foremost, researchers must conduct research to better operationalize the definition of long-term infidelity. While we believe we have crafted a workable definition, more research is needed to refine and assess what long-term infidelity means to laypeople, clinicians, and scholars. While we feel confident that emotional intimacy is a defining feature of long-term infidelity, we are less certain about how time of extradyadic involvement, relationship length for the primary relationship, and relationship type for the primary relationship may operate in defining long-term infidelity. Moreover, it is possible that long-term infidelity can refer to an extradyadic involvement over time or perhaps serial infidelity with multiple partners over the course of a certain period. Numerous scholars have spent tremendous energy defining infidelity, emotional infidelity, and online infidelity (Hertlein & Piercy, 2006). The next step is to understand the defining features of short-term vs. long-term infidelity.

Second, there are major limitations within the infidelity literature in how researchers have measured infidelity. It is recommended that researchers are more specific in how they measure infidelity or ask participants to indicate how they are defining infidelity. It is imperative that research move beyond ambiguous assessment of "Have you ever engaged in an affair?" and query the specific nature of the infidelity. Lack of information about the nature and length of infidelity inherently limits our understandings of infidelity. We recommend infidelity researchers ask about the type of extradyadic involvement, the length of the relationship, number of partners, how it started/how it was maintained, was it sexual/emotional/online/all of the above, attitudes toward infidelity, length of time since the infidelity occurred, who was the partner(s) (e.g., previous history, known to the couple, same-gender or different-gender partner). Researchers may also directly ask participants about why they had an affair, how it began, why it continued, and why it ended. Researchers who ask questions broadly about "sexual and/or emotional" or merely sexual infidelity are limiting conclusions about the infidelity literature.

Third, there are numerous limitations about the methodologies used by researchers. As a whole, researchers have relied on retrospective, cross-sectional studies. More longitudinal research will help to understand how long-term infidelities develop, are maintained, and may impact the primary relationship. Several researchers have also relied on the use of treatment-seeking samples to test their hypotheses (Marin et al., 2014), which limits the generalizability of the findings. Longitudinal research may also help researchers catch participants prior to extradyadic experiences and gain not only a more complete picture of the length and nature of the extradyadic involvement, but also a less biased sample. Infidelity research has also relied on individual participants and dyadic data collection (or even triadic data collection) could help to illuminate the differing perspectives of all those involved with infidelity.

Fourth, another limitation in the existing research is that researchers have relied on convenience samples of college-aged students in the U.S. who not only tend to be a homogeneous sample of predominantly White heterosexual individuals but also are not always in committed relationships, and may or may not have any experience with the phenomenon in question. In the case of online infidelity, research that does exist, has been limited to the study of those who have been impacted by their partners engaging in online infidelity (Cavaglion & Rashty, 2010; Cravens et al., 2013; King, 1999; Schneider, 2000; Schneider et al., 2012), or the characteristics of those who have sought out extramarital affairs using online chatrooms (Dew et al., 2006; Mileham, 2007). To date, only one study has been published that has explored married/cohabitating adults' use of social media to engage in online infidelity behaviors (McDaniel et al., 2017). Thus, the existing research may not generalize to diverse populations, and researchers may find that older couples, who reflect digital immigrants instead of digital natives, have vastly different norms related to online behaviors.

Fifth, as with many fields of study, LGBTQ+ and racial/ethnic minoritized populations have been widely understudied. Few researchers have gone beyond examining how basic racial/ethnic demographics are associated with infidelity and studied how individuals with diverse racial/ethnic identities experience infidelity (see Parker & Campbell, 2017; Utley, 2011 for examples). Harris (2011) examined the infidelity experiences of gay and heterosexual individuals although far greater research is needed. Researchers must pay attention to these marginalized groups, as a lack of empirical research limits the ability for clinicians and therapists to serve a diverse group of clients.

Sixth, we also argue for an increase in understanding of the specific mechanisms through which gender acts as a predictor of infidelity. The research suggests that gender plays a role in long-term infidelity experiences through differing motivations for infidelity. Rather than simply comparing women and men, and reinforcing a false gender binary, research should further examine how social forces and biological factors may interact to predict motivations, attitudes, and infidelity experiences across genders. Although recent studies have found intriguing results regarding the role of hormones, particularly testosterone, and likelihood of engaging in infidelity, none have specifically examined these associations with long-term infidelity (Barta & Keine, 2005; Booth & Dabbs, 1993; Edelstein et al., 2011; Edelstein et al., 2014; van Anders & Goldey, 2010). Sexual double standards and social factors undoubtedly are also associated with engaging in long-term infidelity. Future research on gender and long-term infidelity should elucidate why individuals may be more or less likely to be motivated by intimacy, love, and sexual passion.

In conclusion, we believe this is an area for exciting new research. Long-term infidelities occur, and may be one of the most common infidelity experiences. These extradyadic involvements may develop or be maintained in person or online, or in some combination. Importantly, it is likely that long-term infidelities are the most hurtful to all parties involved, and may disrupt family systems and social networks. This is a topic that warrants far more empirical attention and we are hopeful that infidelity researchers will adopt some of our recommendations.

References

Ablow, J. C., Measelle, J. R., Cowan, P. A., & Cowan, C. P. (2009). Linking marital conflict and children's adjustment: The role of young children's perceptions. *Journal of Family Psychology*, *23*, 485–499. https://doi.org/10.1037/a0015894

Allan, G. (2004). Being unfaithful: His and her affairs. In J. Duncombe, K. Harrison, G. Allan, & D. Marsden (Eds.), *The state of affairs: Explorations in infidelity and commitment* (pp. 121–140). Lawrence Erlbaum.

Allan, G., & Harrison, K. (2009). Affairs and infidelity. In A. L. Vangelisti (Ed.), *Feeling hurt in close relationships* (pp. 191–208). Cambridge University Press.

Allen, E. S. (2001). *Attachment styles and their relation to patterns of extradyadic and extramarital involvement* [Unpublished dissertation, University of North Carolina, Chapel Hill].

Allen, E. S., & Atkins, D. C. (2005). The multidimensional and developmental nature of infidelity: Practical applications. *Journal of Clinical Psychology*, *61*(11), 1371–1382. https://doi.org/10.1002/jclp.20187

Allen, E. S., Atkins, D. C., Baucom, D. H., Snyder, D. K., Gordon, K. C., Glass, S. P. (2005). Intrapersonal, interpersonal, and contextual factors in engaging in and responding to extramarital involvement. *Clinical Psychology: Science & Practice*, *12*, 101–130. https://doi.org/10.1093/clipsy/bpi014

Allen, E., & Baucom, D. (2004). Adult attachment and patterns of extradyadic involvement. *Family Process*, *43*(4), 467–488. https://doi.org/10.1111/j.1545-5300.2004.00035.x

Altgelt, E., Reyes, M., French, J., Meltzer, A., McNulty, J., Impett, E., & Muise, A. (2018). Who is sexually faithful? Own and partner personality traits as predictors of infidelity. *Journal of Social and Personal Relationships*, *35*(4), 600–614.

Amato, P. R., & Hohmann-Marriott, B. (2007). A comparison of high- and low-distress marriages that end in divorce. *Journal of Marriage and Family*, *69*, 621–638. https://doi.org/10.1111/j.17413737.2007.00396.x

Amato, P. R., & Rogers, S. J. (1997). A longitudinal study of marital problems and subsequent divorce. *Journal of Marriage and the Family*, *59*, 612–624. https://doi.org/10.2307/353949

Apostolou, M., Aristidou, A., & Eraclide, C. (1029). Reactions to and forgiveness of infidelity: Exploring severity, length of relationship, sex, and previous experience effects. *Adaptive Human Behavior and Physiology*, *5*(4) 317–330. https://doi.org/10.1007/s40750-019-00119-y

Atkins, D., Jacobson, N., & Baucom, D. (2001). Understanding Infidelity: Correlates in a National Random Sample. *Journal of Family Psychology*, *15*(4), 735–749. https://doi.org/10.1037/0893-3200.15.4.735

Atwater, L. (1979). Getting involved: Women's transition to first extramarital sex. *Alternative Lifestyles, 2*, 33–68. https://doi.org/10.1007/BF01083662

Aviram, I., & Amichai-Hamburger, Y. (2006). Online infidelity: Aspects of dyadic satisfaction, self-disclosure, and narcissism. *Journal of Computer-Mediated Communication, 10*(3). https://doi.org/10.1111/j.1083-6101.2005.tb00249.x

Banfield, S., & McCabe, M. P. (2001). Extra relationship involvement among women: Are they different from men? *Archives of Sexual Behavior, 30*(2), 119–142. https://doi.org/10.1023/A:1002773100507

Bargh, J. A., & McKenna, K. Y. (2004). The Internet and social life. *Annual Review of Psychology, 55*(1), 573–590. https://doi.org/10.1146/annurev.psych.55.090902.141922

Barta, W., & Kiene, S. (2005). Motivations for infidelity in heterosexual dating couples: The roles of gender, personality differences, and sociosexual orientation. *Journal of Social and Personal Relationships, 22*(3), 339–360. https://doi.org/10.1177/0265407505052440

Beach, S. R., Jouriles, E. N., & O'Leary, K. (1985). Extramarital sex: Impact on depression and commitment in couples seeking marital therapy. *Journal of Sex & Marital Therapy, 11*(2), 99–108. https://doi.org/10.1080/00926238508406075

Becker, D. V., Sagrin, B. J., Guadagno, R. E., Millevoi, A., & Nicastle, L. D. (2004). When the sexes need not differ: Emotional responses to the sexual and emotional aspects of infidelity. *Personal Relationships, 11*, 529–538. https://doi.org/10.1111/j.1475-6811.2004.00096.x

Betzig, L. (1989). Causes of conjugal dissolution: A cross-cultural study. *Current Anthropology, 30*(5), 654–676. https://doi.org/10.1086/203798

Blodgett Salafia, E. H., Schaefer, M. K., & Haugen, E. C. (2013). Connections between marital conflict and adolescent girls' disordered eating: Parent–adolescent relationship quality as a mediator. *Journal of Child and Family Studies, 22*, 1–11. https://doi.org/10.1007/s10826-0139771-9

Blow, A. J., & Hartnett, K. (2005). Infidelity in committed relationships ii: A substantive review. *Journal of Marital and Family Therapy, 31*(2), 217–233. https://doi.org/10.1111/j.17520606.2005.tb01556.x

Bohner, G., Echterhoff, G., Glaß, C., Patrzek, J., & Lampridis, E. (2010). Distress in response to infidelities committed by the partners of close others: Siblings versus friends. *Social Psychology, 41*(4), 223–229. https://doi.org/10.1027/1864-9335/a000030.

Booth, A., & Dabbs, J. M., Jr. (1993). Testosterone and men's marriage. *Social Forces, 72*, 463–477. https://doi.org/10.1093/sf/72.2.463

Brockway, L. S. (September 30, 2016). 13 Things you need to know before searching for an ex on social media. Retrieved on December 17, 2019. https://www.womansday.com/relationships/dating-marriage/advice/a56511/things-youneed-to-know-before-searching-for-an-ex-on-social-media/

Bulger, A. (2021). Social media infidelity is a very modern problem. Retrieved on May 12, 2021 from: https://www.fatherly.com/love-money/digital-infidelity-ruin-marriage/

Bull, S., & McFarlane, M. (2000). Soliciting sex on the Internet: What are the risks for sexually transmitted diseases and HIV? *Sexually Transmitted Diseases, 27*(9), 545–550. https://doi.org/10.1097/00007435-200010000-00008

Buss, D. M., Larsen, R. J., Westen, D., & Semmelroth, J. (1992). Sex differences in jealousy: Evolution, physiology, and psychology. *Psychological Science, 3*, 251–255. https://doi.org/10.1111/j.1467-9280.1992.tb00038.x

Buss, D. M., & Schmitt, D. P. (1993). Sexual strategies theory: An evolutionary perspective on human mating. *Psychological Review, 100*(2), 204–232.

Buss, D. M., Shackelford, T. K., Kirkpatrick, L. A., Choe, J. C., Lim, H. K., Hasegawa, M., et al. (1999). Jealousy and the nature of beliefs about infidelity: Tests of competing hypotheses about sex differences in the United States, Korea, and Japan. *Personal Relationships, 6*, 125–150. https://doi.org/10.1111/j.1475-6811.1999.tb00215.x

Buunk, B. P. (1995). Sex, self-esteem, dependency, and extradyadic sexual experience as related to jealousy responses. *Journal of Social and Personal Relationships, 12*, 147–153. https://doi.org/10.1177/0265407595121011

Buunk, B. P., & Dijkstra, P. (2004). Men, women, and infidelity: Sex differences in extradyadic sex and jealousy. In J. Duncombe, K. Harrison, G. Allan, & D. Marsden (Eds.), *The state of affairs: Explorations in infidelity and commitment* (pp. 103–120). Erlbaum.

Cano, A., & O'Leary, K. D. (2000). Infidelity and separations precipitate major depressive episodes and symptoms of nonspecific depression and anxiety. *Journal of Consulting and Clinical Psychology, 68*, 774–781. https://doi.org/10.1037/0022-006X.68.5. 774

Choi, K. H., Catania, J. A., & Dolcini, M. M. (1994). Extramarital sex and HIV risk behavior among US adults: results from the National AIDS behavioral survey. *American Journal of Public Health*, *84*(12), 2003–2007. https://doi.org/10.2105/AJPH.84.12.2003

Cooper, A. (Ed.). (2002). *Sex and the Internet: A guidebook for clinicians*. Brunner Routledge.

Cravens, J. D., Leckie, K., & Whiting, J. B. (2013). Facebook and infidelity: When poking becomes problematic. *Contemporary Family Therapy*, *35*(1), 74–90. https://doi.org/10.1007/s10591012-9231-5

Cravens, J. D., & Whiting, J. B. (2014). Clinical implications of Internet infidelity: Where Facebook fits in. *American Journal of Family Therapy*, *42*(2), 325–339. https://doi.org/10.1080/01926187.2013.874211

Cravens, J. D., & Whiting, J. B. (2016). Fooling around on Facebook: The perceptions of infidelity on social networking sites. *Journal of Couple & Relationship Therapy*, *15*(3), 231–231. https://doi.org/10.1080/15332691.2014.1003670

Crocket, M. J. (2017). Moral outrage in the digital age. *Nature Human Behavior*, *1*, 769–771. https://doi.org/10.1038/s41562-017-0213-3

Dean, C. J. (2011). Psychoeducation: A first step to understanding infidelity-related systemic trauma and grieving. *Family Journal*, *19*, 15–21. https://doi.org/10.1177/1066480710387487

Dibble, J. L., & Drouin, M. (2014). Using modern technology to keep in touch with backburners: An investment model analysis. *Computers in Human Behavior*, *34*, 96–100. https://doi.org/10.1016/j.chb.2014.01.042

Dibble, J. L., Drouin, M., Aune, K. S., & Boller, R. R. (2015). Simmering on the back burner: Communication with and disclosure of relationship alternatives. *Communication Quarterly*, *63*, 329–344. https://doi.org/10.1080/01463373.2015.1039719

Dibble, J. L., Punyanunt-Carter, N. M., & Drouin, M. (2018) Maintaining relationship alternatives electronically: Positive relationship maintenance in back burner relationships, *Communication Research Reports*, *35*(3), 200–209. https://doi.org/10.1080/08824096.2018.1425985

Drouin, M., Miller, D. A., & Dibble, J. L. (2014). Ignore your partners' current Facebook friends; beware the ones they add! *Computers in Human Behavior*, *35*, 483–488. https://doi.org/10.1016/j.chb.2014.02.032

Drouin, M., Miller, D. A., & Dibble, J. L. (2015). Facebook or memory: Which is the real threat to your relationship? *Cyberpsychology, Behavior, and Social Networking*, *18*(10), 561566. http://dx.doi.org/10.1089/cyber.2015.0259.

Duncombe, J., & Marsden, D. (2004). Affairs and children. In J. Duncombe, K. Harrison, G. Allan, & D. Marsden (Eds.), *The state of affairs: Explorations in infidelity and commitment* (pp. 187–202). Erlbaum.

Edelstein, R., Chopik, W., & Kean, E. (2011). Sociosexuality moderates the association between testosterone and relationship status in men and women. *Hormones and Behavior*, *60*(3), 248–255. https://doi.org/10.1016/j.yhbeh.2011.05.007

Edelstein, R., Van Anders, S., Chopik, W., Goldey, K., & Wardecker, B. (2014). Dyadic associations between testosterone and relationship quality in couples. *Hormones and Behavior*, *65*(4), 401–407. https://doi.org/10.1016/j.yhbeh.2014.03.003

England, P., Allison, P. D., & Sayer, L. C. (2014). When one spouse has an affair, who is more likely to leave? *Demographic Research*, *30*(18), 535–546. https://doi.org/10.4054/DemRes.2014.30.18

Fincham, F. D., & May, R. W. (2017). Infidelity in romantic relationships. *Current Opinion in Psychology*, *13*, 70–74. https://doi.org/10.1016/j.copsyc.2016.03.008

Gibbs, J. L., Ellison, N. B., & Heino, R. D. (2006). Self-presentation in online personals: The role of anticipated future interaction, self-disclosure, and perceived success in Internet dating. *Communication Research*, *33*(2), 152–177. https://doi.org/10.1177/0093650205285368

Gibson, K. A. V., Thompson, A. E., & O'Sullivan, L. F. (2016). Love thy neighbour: Personality traits, relationship quality, and attraction to others as predictors of infidelity among young adults. *Canadian Journal of Human Sexuality*, *25*(3), 186–198. https://doi.org/10.3138/cjhs.253-A2

Glass, S. P. (2002). Couple therapy after the trauma of infidelity. In A. S. Gurman & N.S. Jacobson (Eds.), *Clinical handbook of couple therapy* (3rd ed., pp. 488–507). Guilford Press.

Glass, S. P., & Wright, T. L. (1985). Sex differences in type of extramarital involvement and marital dissatisfaction. *Sex Roles*, *12*(9–10), 1101–1120. https://doi.org/10.1007/BF00288108

Glass, S. P., & Wright, T. L. (1992). Justifications for extramarital relationships: The association between attitudes, behaviors, and gender. *Journal of Sex Research*, *29*(3), 361–387. https://doi.org/10.1080/00224499209551654

Gordon, K. C., & Baucom, D. H. (1998). Understanding betrayals in marriage: A synthesized model of forgiveness. *Family Process*, *37*, 425–250. https://doi.org/10.1111/j.15455300.1998.00425.x

Gordon, K. C., & Baucom, D. H. (1999). A forgiveness-based intervention for addressing extramarital affairs. *Clinical Psychology: Science and Practice, 6*, 382–399. https://doi.org/10.1093/clipsy/6.4.382

Guitar, A. E., Geher, G., Kruger, D. J., Garcia, J. R., Fisher, M. L., & Fitzgerald, C. J. (2017). Defining and distinguishing sexual and emotional infidelity. *Current Psychology, 36*(3), 434–446. https://doi.org/10.1007/s12144-016-9432-4

Hall, J. H., & Fincham, F. D. (2006a). Relationship dissolution following infidelity: The roles of attributions and forgiveness. *Journal of Social and Clinical Psychology, 25*(5), 508–522. https://doi.org/10.1521/jscp.2006.25.5.508

Hall, J. H., & Fincham, F. D. (2006b). Psychological distress: Precursor or consequence of dating infidelity? *Personality and Social Psychology Bulletin, 35*(2), 143–159. https://doi.org/10.1177/0146167208327189

Hancock, J. T., & Toma, C. L. (2009). Putting your best face forward: The accuracy of online dating profile photographs. *Journal of Communication, 59*(2), 367–386. https://doi.org/10.1111/j.1460-2466.2009.01420.x

Harris, C. R. (2002). Sexual and romantic jealousy in heterosexual and homosexual adults. *Psychological Science, 13*, 7–12. https://doi.org/10.1111/1467-9280.00402

Harrison, K. (2004). The role of female friends in the management of affairs. In J. Duncombe, K. Harrison, G. Allan, & D. Marsden (Eds.), *The state of affairs: Explorations in infidelity and commitment* (pp. 203–222). Erlbaum.

Helsper, E. J., & Whitty, M. T. (2010). Netiquette within married couples: Agreement about acceptable online behavior and surveillance between partners. *Computers in Human Behavior, 26*, 916–926. https://doi.org/10.1016/j.chb.2010.02.006

Henline, B. H., Lamke, L. K., & Howard, M. D. (2007). Exploring perceptions of online infidelity. *Personal Relationships, 14*, 113–128. https://doi.org/10.1111/j.1475-6811.2006.00144.x

Hertlein, K. M. (2012). Digital dwelling: Technology in couple and family relationships. *Family Relations, 61*, 374–387. https://doi.org/10.1111/j.1741-3729.2012.00702.x

Hertlein, K. M., & Piercy, F. P. (2006). Internet infidelity: A critical review of the literature. *Family Journal: Counseling and Therapy for Couples and Families, 14*, 366–371. https://doi.org/10.1177/1066480706290508

Hertlein, K. M., & Stevenson, A. (2010). The seven "As" contributing to Internet-related intimacy problems. *Cyberpsychology & Behavior, 7*, 207–230.

Hunt, N. (1974). *Sexual behavior in the 1970s*. Dell.

Jeanfreau, M. M., Jurich, A. P., & Mong, M. D. (2014). Risk factors associated with women's marital infidelity. *Contemporary Family Therapy, 36*(3), 327–332. https://doi.org/10.1007/s10591-014-9309-3

Jiang, L., Bazarova, N. N., & Hancock, J. T. (2011). The disclosure–intimacy link in computer mediated communication: An attributional extension of the hyperpersonal model. *Human Communication Research, 37*(1), 58–77. https://doi.org/10.1111/j.1468-2958.2010.01393.x

Joinson, A. N. (2001). Self-disclosure in computer-mediated communication: The role of self awareness and visual anonymity. *European Journal of Social Psychology, 31*(2), 177–192. https://doi.org/10.1002/ejsp.36

Kaighobadi, F., Shackleford, T. K., Popp, D., Moyer, R. M., Bates, V. M., & Liddle, J. R. (2009). Perceived risk of female infidelity moderates the relationship between men's personality and partner-directed violence. *Journal of Research in Personality, 43*, 10331039. https://doi.org/10.1016/j.jrp.2009.09.001

Kaighobadi, F., Starratt, V. G., Shackleford, T. K., & Popp, D. (2008). Male mate retention mediates the relationship between female sexual infidelity and female-directed violence. *Personality and Individual Differences, 44*, 1422–1431. https://doi.org/10.1016/j.paid.2007.12.010

Katz-Wise, S. L., Williams, D. N., Keo-Meier, C. L., Budge, S. L., Pardo, S., & Sharp, C. (2017). Longitudinal associations of sexual fluidity and health in transgender men and cisgender women and men. *Psychology of Sexual Orientation and Gender Diversity, 4*(4), 460–471. https://doi.org/10.1037/sgd0000246

Kawar, C., Coppola, J., & Gangamma, R. (2019). A contextual perspective on associations between reported parental infidelity and relational ethics of the adult children. *Journal of Marital and Family Therapy, 45*(2), 354–363. https://doi.org/10.1111/jmft.12331

Kitson, G. C., Babri, K. B., & Roach, M. J. (1985). Who divorces and why: A review. *Journal of Family Issues, 6*, 255–293. https://doi.org/10.1177/019251385006003002

Kitzinger, C., & Powell, D. (1995). Engendering infidelity: Essentialist and social constructionist readings of a story completion task. *Feminism and Psychology, 5*, 345–372. https://doi.org/10.1177/0959353595053004

Knopp, K., Scott, S., Ritchie, L., Rhoades, G. K., Markman, H. J., & Stanley, S. M. (2017). Once a cheater, always a cheater? Serial infidelity across subsequent relationships. *Archives of Sexual Behavior, 46*(8), 2301–2311. https://doi.org/10.1007/s10508-017-1018-1

Kruger, D. J., Fisher, M. L., Edelstein, R. S., Chopik, W. J., Fitzgerald, C. J., & Strout, S. L. (2013). Was that cheating? Perceptions vary by sex, attachment anxiety, and behavior. *Evolutionary Psychology*, *11*(1), 159–171. https://doi.org/10.1177/147470491301100115

Labrecque, L., & Whisman, M. (2017). Attitudes toward and prevalence of extramarital sex and descriptions of extramarital partners in the 21st century. *Journal of Family Psychology*, *31*(7), 952–957. https://doi.org/10.1037/fam0000280

Lawson, A. (1988). *Adultery*. Basic Books

Levine, S. (2005). A clinical perspective on infidelity. *Sexual & Relationship Therapy*, *20*, 143–153. https://doi.org/10.1080/14681990500113203.

Lusterman, D. (2005). Helping children and adults cope with parental infidelity. *Journal of Clinical Psychology*, *61*, 1439–1451. https://doi.org/10.1002/jclp.20193

Marin, R. A., Christensen, A., & Atkins, D. C. (2014). Infidelity and behavioral couple therapy: Relationship outcomes over five years following therapy. *Couple and Family Psychology: Research and Practice*, *3*, 1–12. https://doi.org/10.1037/cfp0000012.

Martins, A., Pereira, M., Andrade, R., Dattilio, F., Narciso, M., & Canavarro, I. (2016). Infidelity in dating relationships: Gender-specific correlates of face-to-face and online extradyadic involvement. *Archives of Sexual Behavior*, *45*(1), 193–205. https://doi.org/10.1007/s10508-015-0576-3

McDaniel, B. T., Druin, M., & Cravens, J. D. (2017). Do you have anything to hide? Infidelity related behaviors on social networking sites and marital satisfaction. *Computers in Human Behavior*, *66*, 88–95. https://doi.org/10.1016/j.chb.2016.09.031

McFarlane, M., Bull, S. S., & Rietmeijer, C. A. (2000). The Internet as a newly emerging risk environment for sexually transmitted diseases. *JAMA*, *284*(4), 443–446. https://doi.org/10.1001/jama.284.4.443

Michalski, R. L., Shackelford, T. K., & Salmon, C. A. (2007). Upset in response to a sibling's partner's infidelities. *Human Nature*, *18*(1), 74–84. https://doi.org/10.1007/BF02820847

Mileham, B. (2007). Online infidelity in Internet chat rooms: An ethnographic exploration. *Computers in Human Behavior*, *23*, 11–31. https://doi.org/10.1016/j.chb.2004.03.033

Moller, N. P., & Vossler, A. (2015). Defining infidelity in research and couple counseling: A qualitative study. *Journal of Sex & Marital Therapy*, *41*(5), 487–497. https://doi.org/10.1080/0092623X.2014.931314

Morrissey, L., Wettersten, K. B., & Brionez, J. (2019). Qualitatively derived definitions of emotional infidelity among professional women in cross-gender relationships. *Psychology of Women Quarterly*, *43*(1), 73–87. https://doi.org/10.1177/0361684318806681

Munsch, C. L., & Yorks, J. (2018). When opportunity knocks, who answers? Infidelity, gender, race, and occupational sex composition. *Personal Relationships*, *25*, 581–595. https://doi.org/10.1111/pere.12261

Negash, S., Cui, M., Fincham, F. D., & Pasley, K. (2013). Extradydadic involvement and relationship dissolution in heterosexual women university students. *Archives of Sexual Behavior*, *43*, 531–539. https://doi.org/10.1007/s10508-013-0213-y

Nemeth, J. M., Bonomi, A. E., Lee, M. A., & Ludwin, J. M. (2012). Sexual infidelity as trigger for intimate partner violence. *Journal of Women's Health*, *21*, 942–949. https://doi.org/10.1089/jwh.2011.3328.

Norona, J. C., Khaddouma, A., Welsh, D. P., & Samawi, H. (2015). Adolescents' understandings of infidelity. *Personal Relationships*, *22*(3), 431–448. https://doi.org/10.1111/pere.12088

Norton, A. M., & Baptist, J. (2014). Couple boundaries for social networking in middle adulthood: Associations of trust and satisfaction. *Cyberpsychology*, *8*(4), article 2. https://doi.org/10.5817/CP201 4-4-2.

Olson, M. M., Russell, C. S., Higgins-Kessler, M., & Miller, R. B. (2002). Emotional processes following disclosure of an extramarital affair. *Journal of Marital and Family Therapy*, *28*(4), 423–434. https://doi.org/10/1111/j.1752-0606.2002.tb00367.x

Omarzu, J., Miller, A. N., Schultz, C., & Timmerman, A. (2012). Motivations and emotional consequences related to engaging in extramarital relationships. *International Journal of Sexual Health*, *24*(2), 154–162. https://doi.org/10.1080/19317611.2012.662207

Parker, M. L., & Campbell, K. (2017). Infidelity and attachment: The moderating role of race/ethnicity. *Contemporary Family Therapy*, *39*(3), 172–183. https://doi.org/10.1007/s10591-017-9415-0

Parker, T. S., & Wampler, K. S. (2003). How bad is it? Perceptions of the relationship impact of different types of Internet sexual activities. *Contemporary Family Therapy*, *25*(4), 415–429. https://doi.org/10.1023/A:1027360703099

Pickens, J. C., & Whiting, J. B. (2019). Tech talk: Analyzing the negotiations and rules around technology use in intimate relationships. *Contemporary Family Therapy*. https://doi.org/10.1007/s10591-019-09522-9

Platt, R. A., Nalbone, D. P., Casanova, G. M., & Wetchler, J. L. (2008). Parental conflict and infidelity as predictors of adult children's attachment style and infidelity. *American Journal of Family Therapy*, *36*(2), 149–161. https://doi.org/10.1080/01926180701236258

Potter-Emerson, R. T., & Potter-Emerson, P. S. (2008). *The emotional affair: How to recognize emotional infidelity and what to do about it*. New Harbinger Publications.

Previti, D., & Amato, P. R. (2004). Is infidelity a cause or a consequence of poor marital quality? *Journal of Social and Personal Relationship*, *21*(2), 217–230. https://doi.org/10.1177/0265407504041384

Reibstein, J., & Richards, M. (1993). *Sexual arrangement: Marriage and the temptation of infidelity*. Charles Scribner's Sons.

Russell, V. M., Baker, L. R., & McNulty, J. K. (2013). Attachment insecurity and infidelity in marriage: Do studies of dating relationships really inform us about marriage? *Journal of Family Psychology*, *27*(2), 242–251. https://doi.org/10.1037/a0032118

Scheinkman, M. (2005). Beyond the trauma of betrayal: Reconsidering affairs in couples therapy. *Family Process*, *44*, 227–244. https://doi.org/10.1111/j.1545-5300.2005.00056.x

Schmidt, A. E., Green, M. S., & Prouty, A. M. (2016). Effects of parental infidelity and interparental conflict on relational ethics between adult children and parents: A contextual perspective. *Journal of Family Therapy*, *38*(3), 386–408. https://doi.org/10.1111/1467-6427.12091

Schmidt, A. E., Green, M. S., Sibley, D. S., & Prouty, A. M. (2016). Effects of parental infidelity on adult children's relational ethics with their partners: A contextual perspective. *Journal of Couple & Relationship Therapy*, *15*(3), 193–212. https://doi.org/10.1080/15332691.2014.998848

Schneider, J. P. (2000). A qualitative study of cybersex participants: Gender differences, recovery issues, and implications for therapists. *Sexual Addiction & Compulsivity*, *7*, 249–278. https://doi.org/10.1080/10720160008403700

Shackelford, T. K., & Buss, D. M. (1997). Anticipation of marital dissolution as a consequence of spousal infidelity. *Journal of Social and Personal Relationships*, *14*, 793–808. https://doi.org/10.1177/0265407597146005.

Shackelford, T. K., Michalski, R. L., & Schmitt, D. P. (2004). Upset in response to a child's partner's infidelities. *European Journal of Social Psychology*, *34*(4), 489–497. https://doi.org/10.1002/ejsp.215

Snyder, D. K. (2005). Treatment of clients coping with infidelity: An introduction. *Journal of Clinical Psychology*, *61*, 1367–1370. https://doi.org/10.1002/jclp.20186.

Sori, C. F. (2007). An affair to remember: Infidelity and its impact on children. In P. R. Peluso (Ed.), *Infidelity: A practitioner's guide to working with couples in crisis* (pp. 247–276). Routledge.

Spanier, G. B., & Margolis, R. L. (1983). Marital separation and extramarital sexual behavior. *Journal of Sex Research*, *19*(1), 23–48. https://doi.org/10.1080/00224498309551167

Spence, A. M. (2012). *Adult children's accounts of parental infidelity and divorce: Associations with own infidelity, risky behaviors, and attachment*.[Unpublished doctoral dissertation, University of Colorado].

Thompson, A. P. (1984). Emotional and sexual components of extramarital relations. *Journal of Marriage and the Family*, *46*(1) 35–42. https://doi.org/10.2307/351861

Thompson, A. E., & O'Sullivan, L. F. (2016). Drawing the line: The development of a comprehensive assessment of infidelity judgments. *Journal of Sex Research*, *53*(8), 910–926. https://doi.org/10.1080/00224499.2015.1062840

Thorson, A. R. (2014). Feeling caught: Adult children's experiences with parental infidelity. *Qualitative Research Reports in Communication*, *15*(1), 75–83. https://doi.org/10.1080/17459435.2014.955595

Thorson, A. R. (2015). Investigating adult children's experiences with privacy turbulence following the discovery of parental infidelity. *Journal of Family Communication*, *15*(1), 41–57. https://doi.org/10.1080/15267431.2014.980824

Thorson, A. R. (2017). Communication and parental infidelity: A qualitative analysis of how adult children cope in a topic-avoidant environment. *Journal of Divorce & Remarriage*, *58*(3), 175–193. https://doi.org/10.1080/10502556.2017.1300019

Toma, C. L., Hancock, J. T., & Ellison, N. (2008). Separating fact from fiction: An examination of deceptive self-presentation in online dating profiles. *Personality and Social Psychology Bulletin*, *34*(8), 1023–1036. https://doi.org/10.1177/0146167208318067

Tsapelas, I., Fisher, H. E., & Aron, A. (1998). Infidelity: When, where, why. In W. R. Cupach & B. H. Spitzberg (Eds.), *The dark side of close relationships II* (pp.175–195). Routledge.

Utley, E. A. (2011). When better becomes worse: Black wives describe their experiences with infidelity. *Black Women, Gender & Families, 5*(1), 66–89. https://doi.org/10.5406/blacwomegendfami.5.1.0066

Van Anders, S., & Goldey, K. (2010). Testosterone and partnering are linked via relationship status for women and "relationship orientation" for men. *Hormones and Behavior, 58*(5), 820–826. https://doi.org/10.1016/j.yhbeh.2010.08.005

Vangelisti, A., & Gerstenberger, M. (2004). Communication and marital infidelity. In J. Duncombe, K. Harrison, G. Allan, & D. Marsden (Eds.), *The state of affairs: Explorations in infidelity and commitment* (pp. 59–78). Erlbaum.

Watkins, S., & Boon, S. (2016). Expectations regarding partner fidelity in dating relationships. *Journal of Social and Personal Relationships, 33*(2), 237–256. https://doi.org/10.1177/0265407515574463

Weigel, D. J., Bennett, K. K., & Ballard-Reisch, D. S. (2003). Family influences on commitment: Examining the family of origin correlates of relationship commitment attitudes. *Personal Relationships, 10*, 453–474. https://doi.org/10.1046/j.1475-6811.2003.00060.x

Weiser, D. A., Lalasz, C. B., Weigel, D. J., & Evans, W. P. (2014). A prototype analysis of infidelity. *Personal Relationships, 21*(4), 655–675. https://doi.org/10.1111/pere.12056

Weiser, D. A., & Weigel, D. J. (2017). Exploring intergenerational patterns of infidelity. *Personal Relationships, 24*(4), 933–952. https://doi.org/10.1111/pere.12222

Weiser, D. A., Weigel, D. J., Lalasz, C. B., & Evans, W. P. (2017). Family background and propensity to engage in infidelity. *Journal of Family Issues, 38*(15), 2083–2101. https://doi.org/10.1177/0192513X15581660

Whisman, M. A., Dixon, A. E., & Johnson, B. (1997). Therapists' perspectives of couple problems and treatment issues in couple therapy. *Journal of Psychology, 11*, 361–366. https://doi.org/10.1037/0893-3200.11.3.361

Whitty, M. T. (2003). Pushing the wrong buttons: Men's and women's attitudes towards online and offline infidelity. *CyberPsychology & Behavior, 6*, 569–579. https://doi.org/10.1089/109493103322725342

Whitty, M. T. (2005). The "realness" of cyber-cheating: Men and women's representations of unfaithful Internet relationships. *Social Science Computer Review, 23*, 57–67. https://doi.org/10.1177/0894439304271536

Whitty, M. T., & Quigley, L. (2008). Emotional and sexual infidelity offline and in cyberspace. *Journal of Marital and Family Therapy, 34*, 461–468. https://doi.org/10.1111/j.17520606.2008.00088.x

Wilson, K., Mattingly, B. A., Clark, E. M., Weidler, D. J., & Bequette, A. W. (2011). The gray area: Exploring attitudes toward infidelity and the development of the Perceptions of Dating Infidelity Scale. *Journal of Social Psychology, 151*(1), 63–86. https://doi.org/10.1080/00224540903366750

CHAPTER 16

Cultural Differences and Similarities in the Nature of Infidelity

Farid Pazhoohi

Abstract

This chapter highlights the variations and diversity of human mating systems and cultural differences and similarities in the nature of and attitudes toward infidelity. Altogether, this chapter reviews and shows what is constituted as infidelity in one culture might not necessarily be considered as infidelity in another culture. While there has been some cross-cultural research to evaluate differences and similarities across societies and populations in infidelity, the literature still lacks proper research on what is considered as infidelity in different cultures, societies, and traditions. The current issues of research such as lack of diversity, (i.e., sample limitation to heterosexual, middle-to-upper-class, white, undergraduate students, from Western and industrialized societies, majority from the United States) are noted. Moreover, this chapter argues that the intense interest among behavioral researchers in identifying a universal sex difference in distress over sexual and emotional aspects of infidelity has resulted in neglect of exploring the nature of infidelity and the cultural variations in the attitudes toward infidelity. Finally, by signifying a limited research that employed a behavioral ecological approach, this chapter calls for cross-cultural research based on a behavioral ecological approach on cultural differences and similarities in the nature of infidelity.

Key Words: infidelity, culture, cross-cultural research, nature of infidelity, human behavioral ecology, cultural differences

On the Nature and Definition of Infidelity

Researchers typically assume infidelity is occurring in the population they study, and then begin to test for its variations, including personality correlates of infidelity and individual differences in infidelity. However, what is considered infidelity might vary across cultures and even among individuals within a culture. Historically, infidelity is defined as a breach of the social contract of sexual exclusivity between two individuals in a committed relationship, or it is defined as sexual intercourse with someone besides one's partner and without that partner's permission (Hertlein et al., 2005). However, infidelity might include behaviors other than sexual intercourse with someone other than one's partner. For some individuals, infidelity might include cybersex (i.e., online sexual engagement with another person), watching pornography, or variations of intimate physical behaviors such as touching, holding hands, kissing, and cuddling of someone other than the partner, or varying degrees of emotional intimacy (Hertlein et al., 2005).

Blow and Hartnett (2005) highlight the lack of consistency in the definition and conceptualization of infidelity by pointing to the activities that might be considered infidelity, such as having an affair, extramarital relationship, cheating, oral sex, friendships, etc. The problem of definition looms larger when one thinks about the fact that even those in the same relationship might differently define infidelity and have different opinions about what constitutes infidelity (Blow & Hartnett, 2005; Hertlein et al., 2005; Moller & Vossler, 2015). Additionally, individuals in different forms of relationships (e.g., dating, in a relationship, engaged, marriage, cohabiting, polyamory, etc.) might have different views as to what constitutes infidelity (Blow & Hartnett, 2005). Some individuals might consider only sexual behaviors as infidelity, such as engaging in sexual intercourse with someone other than the partner, engaging in sexual play with, receiving oral sex from, or giving oral sex to, someone else, romantic kissing and nonromantic kissing (e.g., on cheek); others may consider sexual fantasies about someone else or nonsexual/romantic fantasies about someone else to be infidelity. Some individuals might consider casual flirting with someone, having lunch or dinner with someone other than the partner, recurrent lunch at work with a colleague, sharing emotional details with an opposite-sex colleague (in the case of heterosexual orientation), or even dancing at a party with someone other than the partner to be infidelity. Infidelity might even include behaviors such as sexual or romantic online conversations (see below) or engagement with sex robots (Rothstein et al., 2021). On the other extreme, married prostitutes, sex workers, or married porn stars might not be regarded necessarily as behaving unfaithfully to their regular, long-term partners.

The nature of infidelity has been explored in several research. For example, in a study, the majority of a sample of college students in the United States reported dating and spending time with someone other than the partner, sexual intercourse with someone other than the partner, and sexual interactions including flirting, kissing, and petting someone other than the partner as infidelity, while few reported keeping secrets from the partner or emotional involvement with another person to be infidelity (Roscoe et al., 1988). While the majority of US college students (with men significantly more than women) report they have sexual fantasies about someone other than their primary partners (Yarab et al., 1998), they considered sexual fantasy to be a form of infidelity (Yarab & Allgeier, 1998). Both men and women considered a partner's sexual fantasies about other people to be infidelity whereas they did not think their own sexual fantasies about other people counted as infidelity (Yarab & Allgeier, 1998).

Luo et al. (2010) reviewed the literature from 1982 to 2009 on the definition of infidelity and pointed to the lack of clarity and comprehensiveness about the conceptualization and definition of infidelity. They tested the factor structure underlying a wide range of various extrapair relationships including physical and emotional aspects as well as online and offline infidelities. The researchers included 23 items assessing face-to-face interactions and 13 items assessing online interactions, and developed a new measure of infidelity (Luo et al., 2010). Their results using a sample of university students from the United States showed that receiving and giving genital and nongenital stimulation, romantically dating, kissing, spending time with romantic interests, masturbation in another's presence, and oral and vaginal sex were instances of face-to-face infidelity, and sharing intimate pictures, phone sex, and visiting dating websites were instances of online infidelity (Luo et al., 2010). Kruger and colleagues (2013) recruited more than 450 psychology students from two universities in the United States. Participants were asked to indicate to what extent they perceived 27 items including sexual behaviors (e.g., intercourse, oral sex), erotic behaviors (e.g., sexting, watching a pornographic movie together), behaviors implying relationship status (e.g., holding hands, kissing on the lips), emotional bonding (e.g., forming a deep emotional bond, sharing secrets), financial support (e.g., supporting the other person financially, giving them $500), and extensive socialization (e.g., frequently talking on the phone) as infidelity. Their results showed that US university students ranked sexual behaviors as most exemplary of infidelity, followed by erotic behaviors, then behaviors reflecting emotional bonding, and then behaviors related to financial support (Kruger et al., 2013). Using undergraduate students from the United States, Wilson and colleagues (2011) showed that some of these behaviors (e.g., hugging, talking on phone or Internet, dancing, etc.) are ambiguous to the participants in terms of whether they reflect infidelity (Mattingly et al., 2010; Wilson et al., 2011). Asking Canadian university students, Randall and Byers (2003) reported that both men and women have a similar definition about which activities are considered infidelity, and although some of these behaviors may not reflect "having sex" with someone, they are nevertheless considered infidelity. For example, around 90% of participants did not think that if someone other than their partner touches their genitals resulting in orgasm to reflect "having sex," but 99% reported that they considered such behavior to reflect a partner's infidelity.

While these studies shed light on which behaviors are considered infidelity by individuals in the United States and Canada, they do not address perceptions and attitudes of individuals from other cultures. In other words, the picture of what constitutes infidelity may be more complex when we consider the ambiguity in definition from a cross-cultural perspective.

Cross-Cultural Research on Infidelity

Half a century ago, Christensen conducted cross-cultural research on attitudes toward marital infidelity, asking men and women about their approval of extramarital coitus (Christensen, 1973). Specifically, university students from Denmark, Sweden, Belgium, Taiwan and five demographic groups in the United States (i.e., black Americans, Midwesterners, Mormon-oriented university students, Mennonite-oriented university students, and Catholic-oriented university students) were asked to indicate their approval for men's and women's extramarital behaviors under different circumstances (i.e., never, if fallen in love with an unmarried person, if fallen in love with a married person, or need for sexual release with prostitutes during long spousal absence). Women compared to men had more conservative opinions about extramarital sex across all cultures, and Taiwanese and religious-oriented college students were less permissive of extramarital sex compared to people in Scandinavian countries. When comparing the frequency of openness toward extramarital sex across Chinese, Russian, and Turkish men and women, similar sex differences emerged, with men more than women reporting sexual fulfillment outside of the marital bond as a more acceptable reason for their own infidelity (Nowak et al., 2014). In another study, Maykovich (1976) recruited suburban, middle-aged, middle-class women from the United States and Japan and asked them about their attitudes and behaviors regarding extramarital sexual relations. While it was hypothesized that women from Japan—with a male dominant social structure in which sexual activities and norms are more restrictive for women—would report fewer incidents of extramarital relationships, the percentage of American women (32%) and Japanese women (27%) that had had experienced extrapair sexual relation was not statistically significantly different. However, Japanese women were more conservative than American women; 31% approved extramarital sex compared to 56% of American women. It is argued that women from male-dominated societies such as Japan in the 1970s do not approve extramarital infidelity; however, once they are exposed to such an opportunity they are as likely as American women to be unfaithful (Maykovich, 1976).

Scott (1998) shows that American and British men's and women's attitudes toward extramarital relationships did not change during the three decades from the mid-1960s to the mid-1990s. In a more recent study, Labrecque and Whisman (2017) used the nine most recent waves of the General Social Survey, which has secured data since 1972 on American attitudes and behaviors, and showed that from 2000 to 2016, the percentage of American adults who report that extramarital sex is always wrong has declined from 79.4% to 75.8%, while no significant change was observed in the percentage respondents who reported they had extramarital sex. This suggests that Americans' negative attitude toward extramarital sex has decreased in the last two decades (Labrecque & Whisman, 2017), and points to the attitude change in a single culture, potentially as a result of Internet access (Rosenfeld & Thomas, 2012; Vossler, 2016) and perhaps socioeconomic changes. A similar trend has been observed in China (Farrer & Zhongxin, 2003; Zhang et al., 2012; Zhang et al., 2021), a less individualistic society with more respect for social hierarchy compared to the United States (Higgins et al., 2002). Using data from a nationally representative sample drawn from a repeated cross-sectional survey in China, Zheng and colleagues (2021) assessed extrapair sexual behavior by asking whether individuals engaged in sexual activity with someone other than their current partner during their marital relationship. Across four waves of data secured from 2000 to 2015, they showed that there has been a considerable increase in the proportion of individuals that report extramarital sex. Specifically, the occurrence rate has increased from 12.9% to 33.4% for men and from 4.7% to 11.4% for women during this period (Zhang et al., 2021). The researchers argue that access to the Internet and to social media may be causes of this increase in frequency of infidelity and extramarital sexual behaviors, regardless of social structures across different cultures.

Cultural Similarities and Differences in Attitudes Toward Infidelity

Attitudes toward infidelity as well as the behaviors that are considered to constitute infidelity are somewhat variable across cultures. Weinberg et al. (1995) investigated the attitudes of Swedish and American university students to sexual infidelity and found no significant difference between women from these two countries, though contrary to expectations Swedish men were more disapproving of sexual infidelity than were American men. In a survey conducted by Pew Research Center in 2013, participants from 39 countries were asked to indicate whether having an extramarital affair is morally unacceptable (Pew Research Center, 2014). Results showed that France, Germany, Italy, Spain, and South Africa—with 47%, 60%, 64%, 64%, and 65% of the respondents reporting affairs are morally unacceptable, respectively—were the most sexually permissive countries, while Palestine (94%), Turkey (94%), Indonesia (93%), Jordan (93%) and Egypt (93%) were ranked the least permissive. Vera Cruz and colleagues (2010) compared sexual permissiveness between African adults from Mozambique and European Adults living in France. They recruited around 300 individuals living in Maputo, Mozambique, and similar numbers of participants from Toulouse, France, and documented that French participants had more permissive attitudes than Mozambicans. The cultural difference in sexual permissiveness was significant regardless of religiosity (Vera Cruz et al., 2010). Vera Cruz et al. (2010) showed that sexual permissiveness ratings from Mozambicans were close to the scores of Americans reported previously by Hendrick and Hendrick (1987). Accordingly, French adults were more permissive compared to American adults (Le Gall et al., 2002). In another study, Vera Cruz (2018) recruited 225 Mozambican women from the general population with diverse socioeconomic and ethnic backgrounds, asking them to indicate their willingness to forgive a husband's sexual infidelity in different hypothetical scenarios varying in the degree of emotional involvement of the husband with the other woman, husband's regret, and husband's commitment to the marriage. While results showed that women's willingness to forgive was dependent on both the intensity of involvement as well as regretful attitude of the offending husband, the researchers argued that Mozambican women are more forgiving than their Western counterparts, accounting in part for why there is a lower rate of divorce as a result of extramarital sexual relationships among Mozambicans than Western peoples. In other words, it appears Mozambican women have a more relaxed attitude compared to those from Western countries to a husband's extramarital sex.

Immigrant Garifuna women from Honduras living in New York City also have a relaxed attitude toward men's infidelity and most of them believe men are unable to be monogamous (Grieb & Nielsen-Bobbit, 2013). Such attitudes are attributed to the cultural norms, in which Garifuna men in Central America might maintain multiple households in different villages. Macauda and colleagues (2011) also report a more relaxed attitude toward infidelity among African American and Puerto Rican youth (between 18 to 25 years of age) living in the inner city of Hartford, Connecticut, in which most people are to some degree emotionally and physically involved with someone other than their partners while in a committed relationship. Data were collected using mixed methods (e.g., interviews, surveys, coitus diaries, etc.) during a 5-year study on the sexual and emotional life history of participants and showed that it is culturally normal and common to have concurrent partners, and individuals even in a committed relationship expect their partners to have another sexual and/or emotional relationship (Macauda et al., 2011). As for the nature of infidelity, most of the participants did not regard autoeroticism (i.e., looking at pornography, masturbation, or going to a strip club) to be infidelity, and considered behaviors such as hugging someone, kissing on the cheek, giving money, gift giving, and confiding in someone else, etc., as not necessarily infidelity, but interactions that are suggestive of infidelity or what might develop into infidelity (Macauda et al., 2011).

If given the opportunity, both men and women from Peponi, a rural Swahili Muslim fishing village in coastal Tanzania, expect their partners to have extramarital sex (Keefe, 2019). In this culture, men more frequently than women report jealousy about a spouse's infidelity, and for women, their husbands' infidelity and extramarital affairs are preferred than being in a polygynous marriage in which their husband takes a second wife (Keefe, 2019). While women from Western and industrialized cultures are distressed over their partner's emotional infidelity such as flirtations with other women, among Hmub in eastern Guizhou, extramarital flirtation is practiced and accepted (Chien, 2009). The extramarital flirtations among Hmub are an approved and institutionalized practice and are mostly performed in forms of singing love songs by both men and women to express their emotions (Chien, 2009).

Emotional vs. Sexual Aspects of Infidelity: A Cross-Cultural Perspective

Around three decades ago, Thompson (1984; see also Symons, 1979) suggested that there are two distinct components of sexual infidelity and emotional infidelity. A sample of Australian men and women were asked about their actual extrapair relationship as "Have you ever been intimately involved with a person other than your partner while cohabiting or being married?" They reported their actual involvement by answering either "yes" or "no" to three alternative choices of (a) emotionally (in love) only, (b) sexually (intercourse) only, (c) emotionally (in love) and sexually (intercourse). Results showed that 43.7% of respondents were in some sort of extrapair relationship, with men reporting more sexual only involvements compared to women. Moreover, Thompson asked men and women about their attitudes by directing participants to "indicate the degree to which you think it is right or wrong for partners to be involved outside of a committed (married or *de facto*) relationship," on a 7-point scale ranging from "definitely all right" to "definitely wrong." Those participants who were not previously involved in extrapair relationships reported all three categories of infidelity (i.e., emotional, sexual, or both) as more wrong than those who previously were involved with infidelity. In terms of sex difference, men had significantly more positive attitude toward sexual infidelity compared to women, while women were more positive about emotional infidelity. Following Thompson's (1984) suggestion of two components of infidelity, researchers began to consider this approach in their research; however, it gained momentum among researchers after Buss and colleagues' (1992) paper in which they employed an evolutionary perspective and used a forced-choice paradigm to document that women were more distressed over a partner's emotional infidelity with someone else compared to men, while men were more upset compared to women when imagining a partner's sexual infidelity. After the proposal of these two aspects of sexual and emotional jealousy and infidelity (Thompson, 1984), the researchers investigated these sex differences in different countries, overshadowing any potential cross-cultural similarities and differences in the nature of infidelity (i.e., cultural difference in which behaviors are regarded as infidelity and their variations in intensity). In the first cross-cultural attempts to test the evolutionary proposed sex differences in infidelity by Buss et al. (1992), Buunk and colleagues (1996) recruited participants from the United States, Germany, and the Netherlands, asking men and women whether imagining a partner's sexual infidelity or emotional infidelity is more distressing. While German and Dutch cultures are regarded as having more permissive attitudes toward sexuality and extramarital sex compared to the United States, the results confirmed a similar pattern of sex difference. A plethora of cross-cultural studies have since been conducted, most with college students in industrialized and Western cultures, testing and confirming the sex difference in sexual jealousy and emotional jealousy and attitude toward extrapair relationships. Results from Spanish-speaking university students from Chile and Spain replicated the finding that men are more distressed by sexual infidelity than by emotional infidelity of their partners, while women report the reverse (Fernandez et al., 2006, 2007). In a similar fashion, Korean and Japanese university female students indicated more distress than did male students to emotional infidelity, while male students more than female students chose sexual infidelity as more distressing (Buss et al., 1999). The sex difference in response to hypothetical sexual and emotional infidelity scenarios in the context of a committed relationship was replicated for African American university students (Abraham et al., 2001). While the same pattern emerged among both Chinese and American university students, Chinese students reported less distress overall than their American counterparts (Geary et al., 1995). Likewise, English and Romanian university student men were more upset than women by a partner's hypothetical sexual infidelity, and women were more distressed by a partner's hypothetical emotional infidelity (Brase et al., 2004). Similar to the cultural differences found when comparing American and Chinese men and women (Geary et al., 1995), the effect for English participants was larger than for Romanians (Brase et al., 2004). Studies using Austrian (Ward & Voracek, M. (2004), German (Schützwohl & Koch, 2004), Norwegian (Bendixen et al., 2015), and Swedish (Wiederman & Kendall, 1999) university students also replicated the sex difference in regard to hypothetical partner infidelity.

While these cross-cultural studies have merit in showing that men's and women's degree of jealous responses to hypothetical infidelity scenarios are to some extent similar across different populations, it fails to elucidate the causes in the variations and intensities found across different cultures. The strive to find a global pattern for sex difference in response to hypothetical infidelity among university students falls short further when researchers tend to ignore human ecological behavioral diversities in an effort to identify human universals. These limitations are evident from meta-analyses in which such behavioral variations are not addressed (Carpenter, 2012; Harris, 2003a; Sagarin et al., 2012). Using different inclusion criteria—in which all fail to consider cultural differences in their study inclusions—the different meta-analyses appear to refute each others' conclusions (Edlund & Sagarin, 2017).

Human understanding of infidelity and attitudes toward infidelity are diverse and might not necessarily follow the patterns mostly found in industrialized and Western populations. In fact, the frequency of extramarital partnerships is variable across societies and it may range from moderate to ubiquitous in prevalence and permissiveness (Broude & Greene, 1976). Research should move beyond the attitude in which cultural differences are considered minor or absent, and in which investigations are conducted mostly on university students. The overemphasis on the sex difference in response to the aspects of sexual and emotional infidelity has resulted in negligence of other questions, such as of the nature of infidelity or what behaviors are regarded as infidelity across different cultures, and to what extent and why these attitudes and perceptions vary. Cross-cultural research based on a behavioral ecological approach (see Scelza et al. 2020a study below for an example using behavioral ecology approach; see Sng et al., 2018, for a discussion) on sex differences in emotional and sexual aspects of infidelity is timely and encouraged.

Behavioral Ecological Approach on Cross-Cultural Infidelity

Scelza et al. (2020a) used a behavioral ecological approach to test the variations in the perception of infidelity and jealousy cross-culturally. The researchers recruited more than 1,000 participants from 11 diverse cultures (i.e., Hadza, Himba, India, Japan, Karo Batak, Mayangna, Mosuo, Shuar, Tsimane, US, and Yasawa), and report a large association between the level of paternal investment and jealous response to infidelity. In other words, the researchers identified level of paternal investment as an important factor in explaining the variance in jealousy across cultures. Where men invest more in their children, people view and respond to infidelity more severely. Interestingly, the researchers showed that both men and women viewed male more than female sexual and emotional infidelities more harshly in cultures in which direct paternal investment and provisioning is higher. Moreover, the frequency and permissiveness of social norms toward extramarital sex in a population were associated with higher female-biased sex ratios and lower paternal investment. Scelza et al. (2020a) also report mixed results about the sex difference in intensity of response to sexual and emotional infidelities, challenging the standard interpretations of jealous response in the evolutionary literature identified in industrialized populations. In particular, they indicate that women from Yasawa, and men and women from Tsimane, report sexual infidelity to be more upsetting than emotional infidelity. Such difference between the populations is interpreted as examples where sexual rather than emotional infidelity is associated with resource diversion. For example, Tsimane and Himba women report that men's sex with another woman compared to love for another woman is more important in resource diversion (Scelza et al., 2020a).

There are cross-cultural variations in the prevalence of affective touch (Sorokowska et al., 2021). Less conservative individuals, and individuals residing in areas with lower history of parasitic and contagious diseases, and individuals from less religious and conservative countries, report more frequent affective touch (i.e., embrace, hug, kiss, and stroke) toward their partners. Similarly, individuals more frequently report affective touch in less conservative and warmer countries toward a male friend, and in warmer countries toward a female friend and strangers (Sorokowska et al., 2021). Such cross-cultural diversity in affective touch can indicate individuals from different regions potentially have different opinions about what is considered as a friendly interaction versus a sign of romantic interaction or infidelity. For example, around 57% of women from Belgium reported kissing a male friend during a previous week compared to 1.5% prevalence in Malaysia (Sorokowska et al., 2021). Such drastic differences in interpersonal behaviors across different countries suggest diverse judgements and different jealousy responses cross-culturally, e.g., kissing a male friend by a woman in Malaysia might more readily be interpreted as an act of infidelity compared to a parallel behavior in Belgium.

Other research reported cross-cultural variation in romantic jealousy across the nations of Hungary, Ireland, Mexico, The Netherlands, the Soviet Union, the United States, and Yugoslavia (Hupka et al., 1985), which might be caused by variation in what is considered infidelity. Hypothesizing that there are cross-cultural variations in the interpretation of a partner's sexual interest in another person, Buunk and Hupka (1987) investigated cross-cultural differences in evoked sexual jealousy using a variety of behaviors. Specifically, they asked over 2,000 university students from Hungary, Ireland, The Netherlands, the Soviet Union, the United States, and Yugoslavia, about the degree of jealousy in response to observing their lover in six behaviors of flirting, kissing, dancing, hugging, sexual relationship and sexual fantasizing with another person. While flirting and sexual relationship evoked the most negative reaction, the intensity of jealousy reactions and the type of behavior that is perceived as a threat were different across countries. For example,

Yugoslavians reported the most jealousy reaction to a partner's flirting while they scored the least negative reaction to kissing compared to other countries; on the other hand, among Hungarians, kissing evoked a strong negative reaction and flirting was more acceptable, when compared to responses provided by participants from the other nations (Buunk & Hupka, 1987). Hupka and Ryan (1990) examined the cross-cultural severity of aggression in sexual jealousy situations and used information on pair bonding, property, progeny, and sexual gratification from the Human Relations Area Files (HRAF) in 92 preindustrial societies. They showed that there is cross-cultural variation in men's severity of aggression resulting from sexual jealousy and their reactions increased where pair bonding and ownership of property are more important and the possibility of sexual gratification is limited (sexual activity and gratification is restricted to matrimony). Such associations were not found for women, potentially due to women's higher probability of nonaggressive or less aggressive coping with men's infidelity (Hupka & Ryan, 1990).

While parental investment theory predicts that, from an evolutionary perspective, women gain less from additional mating and should behave less promiscuously compared to men (Trivers, 1972), behavioral ecology indicates that women might gain from multiple mating, and therefore variation in women's sexual behaviors as well as cross-cultural variation in normative attitudes toward women's extrapair relationships are expected (Scelza, 2013). There have been previous attempts to explain the diversity of human mating systems. A few potential predictors of cultural variation in human mating system are mentioned below; however, for a full discussion on the factors influencing variation in human mating, see other chapters in this volume.

In an analysis of the Standard Cross-Cultural Sample, Marlowe (2000, 2003) suggests that among foragers, where men provide a greater contribution to subsistence due to environmental conditions, societies are more monogamous. Another factor might be the cost of paternal investment in harsh and demanding environments. Pazhoohi (2017), analyzing aggregated cross-cultural data, showed that child mortality rate predicts the frequency of polygyny, arguing that in harsher environments paternal care is more important for child survival; therefore, to secure paternal investment, men's preference for multiple partners is recognized, normative, and institutionalized through legalizing polygyny in these regions. Hrdy (2000) argues that among matrilocal societies women have greater reproductive autonomy, hence the power relation between men and women is in favor of women and therefore polyandrous mating systems are more beneficial. By rejecting the universality of monogamy and arguing that similar to polygyny, polyandrous behaviors (or women's strategies in which they are linked to several men) are more common than expected in humans, Hrdy (2000, p. 85) comments, "We would expect mothers to hedge their bets by trading off certainty of paternity for the advantages to be obtained from several fathers." While cross-cultural research mostly with data from urbanized areas points to men's greater desire for sexual variety compared to women, there is cultural variation in this sex difference (Schmitt, 2003). Similarly, men's and women's attitudes toward having multiple partners seem to be diverse and subject to environmental differences such as sex ratio and pathogen prevalence (Schaller & Murray, 2008; Schmitt, 2005).

Quinlan and Quinlan (2007) investigated the relationship between parenting (i.e., father involvement in early childhood) and variation in attitudes toward infidelity across cultures. They used data from Murdock and White's (1969) Standard Cross Cultural Sample and predicted that higher levels of parental care are associated with less acceptability of extramarital sex across cultures. Specifically, Quinlan and Quinlan (2007) included four parenting variables (i.e., father sleeping location, father involvement in early childhood, parents' response to infant crying, and age at weaning) in a multivariate analysis as predictors of attitudes toward extramarital sex, ranging from 1 (extramarital sex equally condemned for both men and women) to 4 (both men and women equally allowed to engage in extramarital sex). Their results showed that father's sleeping proximity to the infant and parental responsiveness to infant crying were negatively associated with extramarital sex acceptance across cultures, suggesting that in unpredictable and hazardous environments parents are less responsive or unresponsive to their child, which influences cultural patterns related to conjugal stability (Quinlan & Quinlan 2007).

Jankowiak et al. (2002) examined the similarities and differences in men's and women's perception of and responses to a partner's infidelity by using ethnographic literature. They used different sources in which both men and women's responses were recorded, including those cultures from Murdock and White (1969) as well as other ethnographic sources and using data from contemporary ethnographers. Defining infidelity as sexual intercourse without a spouse's permission, Jankowiak et al. evaluated the responses of men and women across 66 cultures and reported that in all the societies, both women and men were equally vigilant about their spouse' extramarital sexual liaisons, though they differed in the tactics employed in response to spousal infidelity. Men more than women rely on physical violence, while women prefer to emotionally distance themselves from the relationship. Another strategy that men and women employ to confront infidelity is appeal to higher authorities, which increases in frequency and effectiveness as the stratification in society becomes more pronounced. Moreover, employing gossip and appeal to curb and control a spouse's infidelity is a tactic that is more prevalent in patrilineal-descent based societies compared to matrilineal ones (Jankowiak et al., 2002).

Extrapair relationships are common among married and unmarried Himba men and women, and are normatively permitted for both men and women (Scelza, 2014). Such informal extramarital unions can span from short-term encounters or long-term concurrent partnership alongside their primary partner (Scelza & Prall, 2018). For example, Scelza, and Prall (2018) report that 84% of married men and 63% of married women have had at least one informal partner concurrent to their marriage, and they are open in discussing such extra-pair relationships with their kin or even with their spouses (Scelza, 2011; Scelza & Prall, 2018). Such normative attitudes in permissiveness and social acceptance of partnership concurrency is suggested to be associated with low paternal investment of Himba men (Scelza, 2014). Extrapair paternity rate (children sired by a man other than the primary partner) is 48% in the Himba population, and Himba men and women are accurate in detecting the extrapair paternity (reporting whether the children are fathered by husband or another man), with men being accurate more than 70% of the time (Scelza et al., 2020b). Such high extrapair paternity as well as men's high paternity confidence indicates that men choose to provide care for nonbiological children and are permissive of the extrapair relationships of their spouses (Scelza et al., 2020b). In a recent paper, Scelza et al. (2021) report the evidence on Himba men's and women's attitudes about female extrapair sexual relationships. When Himba men were asked whether it was OK for a married woman to have a regular sexual relationship with a boyfriend, about one-fourth of them replied positively, and more than 20% reported there are no repercussions for women's nonmarital partnership. Interestingly, almost all interviewed Himba men indicated that they were aware that such nonmarital partnerships are happening frequently. Scelza et al. (2021) show that such a normative concurrent partnership system would provide wealth and food security benefits to women which positively affects the fitness of both the wife and her husband; "Men can accrue the kinds of standard gains to fitness that are predicted through sexual selection theory, and any paternity loss that occurs in their marriage is buffered by support from other men" (Scelza et al., 2021, p. 18).

Is An Extramarital Partnership Necessarily Infidelity?

Wife sharing and wife lending is reported in about 40% of societies in the Standard Cross-Cultural Sample, and in 12.5% of these societies, extramarital relationships for women is reported to be universal (Broude & Greene, 1976). Polyandry is even more common when a broadened definition of polyandrous relationship (linking a woman with several men) be taken into account, such as a woman's extrapair sex (for reviews see Hrdy, 2000, and Starkweather & Hames, 2012). In other words, while formal polyandrous marriages seem to be rare across cultures, informal polyandry (practiced through women's extramarital affairs) is not (Hrdy, 2000).

Four decades ago, Broude (1980, p. 181) reviewed the ethnographic literature at that point in time and wrote that she was "struck by the incongruity in attitudes regarding sexual behavior for males and females that regularly characterizes society after society, especially in the area of extramarital sex." While she argued that there is a double standard in attitudes toward men's infidelity and women's infidelity in most of the societies, such that not only were men less condemned for infidelity compared to women, but also they were less severely penalized for infidelity than women; but women's extramarital sex is not rare. Broude reviews a diverse range of attitudes toward extrapair relationships across cultures, for example pointing to permissive relationships of Lesu and Lepcha people in south Asia. Among both the Lesu and the Lepcha, spouses are expected to engage in extrapair relationships. The Lesu expect wives, especially when younger, to have extramarital relationships and considered those who did not as abnormal. The Lepcha were not concerned about their wife's infidelity as long as they do not have sex with other men in their presence. Among the Maasai of Kenya, men are not concerned about their wives' intercourse with other men, "provided that they do not do so actually at a time when their husbands want them themselves" (Leakey, 1930, p. 202). Maasai girls are betrothed to their husbands in their early infancy or even prior to their birth, and as women their sexual life begins immediately after menstruation. Their earliest sexual intercourses are not necessarily with their husbands, and "all children born to a woman who is married are considered to be the children of her husband, no matter who their actual father may be. Owing to this system it may happen that by the time a man leaves the warrior stage and passes into the Elders' stage, and goes to live with his wife, he may find that she already has one or more children" (Leakey, 1930, p. 201). Among the Gaddang of the Philippines, spousal exchange is a legitimate form of cohabitation, which is likely to enhance the reproductive success of the parties involved or may establish kinship-like relationships among nonkin resulting in creating new economic and social opportunities (Wallace et al., 1969). Similarly, among certain groups of Inuit in Northern Alaska, wife exchange and wife trading from socially distant families may be practiced as a strategy for building social ties and thereby contributing to the maintenance of the larger society (Hennigh, 1970). Another example is wife sharing among the Qulla (also Qolla) of southern Peru and Bolivia, in which two couples form a cooperative association with emotional and sexual bonds (Bolton, 1973). Such approved, normative, and institutionalized forms of extramarital sex are reported in other cultures, e.g., among Nage and Keo of the southern Indonesia (Forth, 2004), Mosuo of southwest China (Mattison et al., 2014), lowland South America (Walker et al., 2010), or Himba pastoralists of northwest Namibia (Scelza et al., 2021). These instances point to the cross-cultural diversity of attitudes toward infidelity when compared with other traditional societies in which men and women are heavily stigmatized and punished for small breaches from their marital unions. For example, Yolngu people (referred to as the Murngin in Broude's [1980] review), the indigenous inhabitants of the northern territories in Australia demand fidelity of both men and women and unfaithful husbands and wives are sanctioned socially and personally by the spouse. Similarly, K'iche' (spelled as Quiche in Broude's [1980] review) are Mayan people living in the midwestern highlands of Guatemala, and condemn and penalize both husband and wife for infidelity. Another region which has had a severe attitude toward extrapair relationships is in West Asia or the region also known as the Middle East. Such marital practices and attitudes toward infidelity, which may have been cultural adaptations to the environmental pressures in that region, were exported to the other parts of the globe through religious doctrines (Pazhoohi et al., 2017). These sexual norms originating from the Middle East, in which both men and women are punished severely for infidelity were propagated through Christianity and Islam to the African, European, and American continents and replaced norms of those regions' native inhabitants (Burdette et al., 2007; Pazhoohi & Kingstone, 2020).

Are Polyamory and Polygyny Infidelity?

Anecdotal evidence supports the existence of negotiated nonmonogamous sexual relationships among married couples in Western societies (Jamieson, 2014). Similarly, there is negotiated sexual nonmonogamy among "swinging" couples in these societies (De Visser & McDonald, 2007). In addition to existence of nonmonogamous relationships among heterosexual partners, some homosexual couples also report negotiated nonmonogamous sexual relationships (LaSala, 2004). Weeks and colleagues (2001, p. 122) assert that "among gay male couples particularly, fidelity is frequently seen in terms of emotional commitment and not sexual behavior" (cited in Jamieson, 2014). In addition to the complexity of evaluating the nature of polyamorous relationships, and whether such relationships are regarded as infidelity, one might also ask whether polygynous relationships, in which cowives live with one man, should be considered as the approval of sexual and emotional infidelity by each of the wives in this sort of mating and marriage arrangement. It is known that there are various degrees of conflict and rivalry among cowives across cultures, as much as the cooperation among them varies culturally (Jankowiak, 2008; Jankowiak et al., 2005), yet whether such practices are considered as emotional and/or sexual infidelity by the cowives, and the cultural variations in such attitudes, remain to be determined.

Pornography and Online Infidelity: Cross-Cultural Perspective

In an exploratory study to identify individuals' opinions on what constitutes an act of infidelity, Whitty (2003) recruited participants mostly from the Western cultures of Australia, New Zealand, and the United States and showed that regular cybersex (i.e., obtaining sexual gratification by interacting with another person online) and regular "hot chat" were scored and perceived almost equal to sexual intercourse as infidelity. This study not only showed that online infidelity is considered similar to offline infidelity, but also that individuals consider pornography including viewing pornographic videos and magazines and going to strip clubs, as acts of infidelity to their partners. While attributed as infidelity, consumption of online sexual content and involvement in online sex is rated less of an affair than physical sex (Parker & Wampler, 2003). Such findings (e.g., Bridges et al., 2003; Schneider, 2002; Whitty, 2003) are in contrast to more recent studies that report married or cohabiting couples do not consider watching pornography and consumption to be infidelity (Poulsen et al., 2013). Using university students from the United States and Spain, Negy et al. (2018) asked whether viewing sexually explicit material (e.g., pornography) indicates committing infidelity. While the majority of participants from both countries (73% of US participants and 77% of Spanish participants) did not consider viewing sexually explicit content as infidelity, their results showed that compared to Spanish participants, those from the United States were more likely to consider viewing pornography as infidelity (Negy et al., 2018). The researchers attributed this difference to the higher conservativeness and religiosity of US adults compared to Europeans and Spanish adults, in particular.

The definition of online infidelity and what constitutes infidelity is a challenge, and not all individuals consider a partner's pornography consumption and watching necessarily as infidelity. For example, similar to the findings of Whitty (2003), when university students from the United States were asked to answer on a 7-point scale ranging from 1 (totally disagree) to 7 (totally agree) the degree to which they believed phone sex, viewing pornography, and cybersex in a committed relationship constituted infidelity, most of them did not think watching pornography is infidelity (Guadagno & Sagarin, 2010). However, cybersex and phone sex were considered infidelity, though women perceived such activities to be infidelity more than did men (Guadagno & Sagarin, 2010). Olmstead et al. (2013) conducted qualitative research and asked a large number of heterosexual men and women college students from the United States to answer what they think about viewing sexually explicit materials (i.e., porn videos, pictures, websites) while married or in a relationship, and if there are circumstances where viewing these materials alone is okay. The results of the content analysis showed that a majority of men (70.8%) and around half of the women (45.5%) reported that watching pornography, either alone, together, or both were acceptable in a relationship context.

Through interviewing participants, Mileham (2007) provides an analysis on whether online interactions and, in particular, online sexual interactions in chat rooms are considered infidelity. Those who engage in online interactions of a sexual nature mention it can provide individuals with degrees of anonymity and safety especially among married individuals, while online sexual interactions especially in chat rooms are considered innocuous and harmless to marital vows and effortless to avoid (Mileham, 2007). The main argument for people engaging in online infidelity was that disembodiment and the lack of physical contact makes it a weaker form of infidelity or not infidelity altogether. Whitty (2005) recruited Australian university students and asked them whether forming a relationship on the Internet with someone other than one's offline partner is infidelity. Their results showed that some of the participants did not consider forming virtual relationships as a real threat or an actual betrayal, but regarded such relationships as friendship. It appeared for some of the participants that as long as the relationship was not intended to develop into a face-to-face relationship, such relationships are regarded as interactions with objects. Henline et al. (2007) asked university students from the United States to nominate behaviors that are considered online infidelity by answering the open-ended question: "What online behaviors or activities would you consider to be 'unfaithful' to a dating partner if the couple is in an exclusive dating relationship?" Participants most frequently nominated the four behaviors of online sex, emotional involvement with an online contact, online dating (including making plans to meet and actually meeting), and other online sexual interactions as online infidelity. The researchers argued that these behaviors are similar to those behaviors considered as in traditional (offline) infidelity, i.e., sexual intercourse, dating or spending time together, and sexual interactions (Roscoe et al., 1988). In line with the disembodiment argument (Mileham, 2007), the majority of the participants (60% to 82%) considered emotional online infidelity as more distressing than online sexual infidelity (Henline et al., 2007). In a similar attempt to define what constitutes online infidelity, Docan-Morgan and Docan (2007) showed that American students consider a partner's goal-directed online acts such as disclosing love and making plans to meet someone as clearer indicators of infidelity and less acceptable compared to superficial and informal acts, e.g., chatting about sports, talking about current events, and joking.

Among Chinese subjects the relationship-related variables that contribute to offline infidelity (e.g., lower relationship satisfaction, insecure adult attachment, and negative communication patterns) also predicted online sexual activities and infidelity; moreover, dyadic satisfaction among Chinese individuals was negatively associated with online sexual activities and infidelity (Li & Zheng, 2017). Similar associations between marital quality and Internet infidelity is found among Iranian subjects (Isanejad & Bagheri, 2018). While both Iranian men and women consider online sexual activities of their partner as infidelity, women reported more negative attitudes in regards to their partners' online activities. Moreover, Iranian women compared to men considered a broader range of online behaviors, including friendly and emotional activities, as a partner's infidelity (Abdi et al., 2012). Such sex differences in the severity of online infidelity were also reported among men and women college students from the United States (Docan-Morgan & Docan, 2007).

In a study with a sample of Taiwanese college students, participants considered engaging in online sexual relationships as reflecting a high degree of infidelity, compared to building and maintaining online friendships, which was considered low on infidelity. Also, Taiwanese women compared to men had lower thresholds for attributing infidelity to online interactions and relationships, especially those involving sex such as engaging in online sexual relationships and hot chats (Wang & Hsiung, 2008). In a study using a sample from urban areas of Delhi and neighboring states in northern India, married and in-relationship individuals were asked to report the possible reasons behind their engagement in as well as avoidance of online infidelity (Jain & Sahni, 2017). Around one-third (34%) of the sample admitted that they have engaged in online infidelity, with men more than women and those in a nonmarital relationship more than married ones. For those in a nonmarital relationship, peer pressure and desire to explore were the main reasons for pursuing online infidelity, while for married subjects, emotional support, loneliness, boredom, and frustration were reported as the reasons (Jain & Sahni, 2017). Considering India as a collectivistic society compared to the Western countries, where divorce is frowned on and not acceptable, and adults live in a sexually conservative and repressive society (Medora et al., 2002), the frequency of online infidelity is notable.

Across cultures as diverse as India, China, Iran, and the United States, though potentially with higher or lower intensity depending on the region, individuals have to some extent similar understandings about which online sexual behaviors and interactions are considered infidelity. Vossler and Moller (2020) asked English participants to rate online activities that constituted infidelity, and found high agreements among participants in the activities that are categorized as cybersex (e.g., sexual engagement with another person online), which had both a sexual component and the potential to develop into an offline relationship. Online activities that involved emotional interactions with someone other than the partner, and also those activities that were deceptive in nature (e.g., hiding online that someone is already in a relationship) are also regarded as infidelity; though these latter ones (i.e., online emotional interactions and deceptive behaviors) were rated as less reflective of infidelity compared to cybersex (Vossler & Moller, 2020). It is noteworthy that when Vossler and Moller (2020) asked participants using an open-ended question of "You have indicated that you have experienced Internet infidelity yourself. Can you please describe your experience with as much detail as possible?" to describe their experience of online infidelity, the analysis of the qualitative data indicated that online infidelity is multifaceted and ambiguous in definition. Online infidelity might not only include online sexual and emotional behaviors, but also could be considered in a more broad and fluid sense, be defined by secrecy, deceit and betrayal (Vossler & Moller, 2020). In a similar fashion, Chinese men and women were asked to indicate whether each of several online sexual activity items of seeking sexual partners (i.e., seeking sexual partners online), cybersex (i.e., having real-time sexual fantasies via text, voice, or video chat with members of the opposite sex), flirting with the opposite sex online, and maintaining an online relationship with members of the opposite sex are indicative of infidelity (Liu & Zheng, 2019). Among Chinese individuals, those with more permissive perceptions of infidelity did not consider certain behaviors as infidelity, while individuals with stricter perceptions regarded the same behaviors as infidelity (Liu & Zheng, 2019).

Among Swedes, viewing sexually explicit materials and pornographic contents along with seeking sexual partners online, cybersex, and online flirting are considered online infidelity (Cooper et al., 2003). However, it appears among Chinese individuals there is a distinction between viewing online sexually explicit materials and the online activities of seeking sexual partners, engaging in cybersex and flirting (Li & Zheng, 2018). Chinese men compared to women do not regard viewing online sexually explicit materials as infidelities, pointing to men's more open attitude toward and higher likelihood of engaging in online sexual activities than women (Li & Zheng, 2018). Results from China indicating that individuals do not consider viewing online sexually explicit materials and pornography as online infidelity are in contrast to what has been reported from Western societies, where viewing pornography and other online sexual contents are considered as online infidelity (Whitty, 2003).

Jain and Sen (2018) argue that the definition of the online infidelity is limited and not clear. They highlight limitations that researchers should address when studying online infidelity. First, the current research is limited by a reliance on the convenience sampling method, which primarily secures data from university students, potentially affecting the generalizability of the results. Moreover, they argue that there should be a clearer distinction between those who imagine online infidelity and those who have actually experienced online infidelity, with future research privileging the latter. Such studies in which hypothetical scenarios are presented to participants do not necessarily measure attitudes or perceptions of online infidelity or what might occur in a real life situation, but instead they may measure reactions to those hypothetical situations (Jain & Sen, 2018). In line with this argument, previous research has shown that attitudes toward infidelity in hypothetical or imaginative situations differ to some degree from actual experience (Harris, 2003b, but see Zengel et al., 2013 for a contrary argument; Pazhoohi et al., 2019). Finally, Jain and Sen (2018) argue that there is a need for conducting studies exploring the impact and consequences of online infidelities, across different social and cultural contexts.

In a study using Hofstede's (1991) cultural dimensions model, Ramanujam et al. (2018) explored the cultural differences in online infidelity. Specifically, they used Hofstede's cultural scores and linked them with leaked data from an extramarital dating website, AshleyMadison.com. They contrasted a few countries, i.e., the United States and Canada (the countries with the highest number of accounts per capita on the website), China and India (with the lowest number of accounts), the United Kingdom and Finland, with an average number of accounts. They argued that Hofstede's low individualistic and indulgence scores of China and India compared to other countries contributed to lower number of accounts created on the extramarital dating website. Also, they argued that Asian countries including China and India are higher on Hofstede's uncertainty avoidance index and thereby favor security in their institutions, including marriage. In contrast, the United States and Canada score higher on Hofstede's individualism and lower on uncertainty avoidance indices, thereby have had higher number of accounts on the website (Ramanujam et al., 2018). While such cross-cultural approaches in explaining differences in online infidelity are encouraging, unless proper behavioral ecological research is conducted, we cannot identify the ultimate reasons explaining these differences (see Scelza et al. 2020a study for an example using behavioral ecology). In other words, unless we cannot identify what forces and factors are causing human variation, similarities and differences in adoption of conservative versus liberal attitudes toward infidelity, arguments about the existence of cultural differences based on another predefined cultural value, such as Hofstede's cultural distances, amount to circular arguments, leading nowhere (Barber, 2020). Altogether, research on online infidelity still lacks a proper cross-cultural investigation into which online behaviors and to what extent or intensity are regarded as infidelity. Accordingly, a behavioral ecological approach to investigate the nature of online infidelity and its variations across cultures is timely and encouraged.

Conclusion and Future Remarks

While there has been some cross-cultural research to evaluate differences and similarities across societies and populations in infidelity, the literature still lacks proper research on what is considered as infidelity in different cultures, societies, and traditions. In reviewing the studies on infidelity, Blow and Hartnett (2005) raised the issue of diversity and noted that almost all the studied samples were limited to heterosexual, middle-to-upper-class, White individuals. The majority of these studies also report the attitudes of Western and industrialized societies, mostly from the United States. More than 15 years later, the problem of cultural diversity in samples remains. The problem of overusing the convenient university sample adds more to this issue, when considering that this population is still in their early stages of experimenting with relationships and might have different understandings, opinions, and attitudes toward infidelity compared to an older age group with more experience in relationships. Moreover, while there have been instances of cross-cultural comparison in regard to attitudes toward infidelity, it seems that researchers use convenient cultures for data collection (e.g., where they have a colleague that can translate surveys and collect data) or they mostly use archival ethnographic data (e.g., Murdock and White's (1969) Standard Cross Cultural Sample).

This chapter aimed to highlight the variations and diversity of human mating systems and potential cultural differences in the nature of and attitudes toward infidelity. However, as is reviewed, what constitutes as infidelity in one culture might not necessarily be considered as infidelity in another culture. Furthermore, the interest in identifying a universal sex difference in distress over sexual and emotional aspects of infidelity—which has also been somewhat limited in its cultural scope—has resulted in neglect of exploring the nature of infidelity and the cultural variations in the attitudes toward infidelity among behavioral researchers. Therefore, this chapter calls for cross-cultural research based on a behavioral ecological approach on sex differences in emotional and sexual aspects of infidelity, as well as cultural differences in the nature of infidelity, both in offline and online contexts and their variations.

References

Abdi, M., Nazari, A., Mohseni, M., & Zabihzadeh, A. (2012). Internet infidelity: Exploration of attitudes towards partners Internet behaviors. *Zahedan Journal of Research in Medical Sciences, 14*, 72–75.

Abraham, W. T., Cramer, R. E., Fernandez, A. M., & Mahler, E. (2001). Infidelity, race, and gender: An evolutionary perspective on asymmetries in subjective distress to violations-of-trust. *Current Psychology, 20*(4), 337–348.

Barber, N. (2020). *Evolution in the here and now: How adaptation and social learning explain humanity*. Prometheus Books.

Bendixen, M., Kennair, L. E. O., & Buss, D. M. (2015). Jealousy: Evidence of strong sex differences using both forced choice and continuous measure paradigms. *Personality and Individual Differences, 86*, 212–216.

Blow, A. J., & Hartnett, K. (2005). Infidelity in committed relationships I: A methodological review. *Journal of Marital and Family Therapy, 31*(2), 183–216.

Bolton, R. (1973). Tawanku: Intercouple bonds in a Qolla village (Peru). *Anthropos, 68*(H. 1/2), 145–155.

Brase, G. L., Caprar, D. V., & Voracek, M. (2004). Sex differences in responses to relationship threats in England and Romania. *Journal of Social and Personal Relationships, 21*(6), 763–778.

Bridges, A. J., Bergner, R. M., & Hesson-McInnis, M. (2003). Romantic partners use of pornography: Its significance for women. *Journal of Sex & Marital Therapy, 29*(1), 1–14.

Broude, G. J. (1980). Extramarital sex norms in cross-cultural perspective. *Behavior Science Research, 15*(3), 181–218.

Broude, G. J., & Greene, S. J. (1976). Cross-cultural codes on twenty sexual attitudes and practices. *Ethnology*, *15*(4), 409–429.

Burdette, A. M., Ellison, C. G., Sherkat, D. E., & Gore, K. A. (2007). Are there religious variations in marital infidelity? *Journal of Family Issues*, *28*(12), 1553–1581.

Buss, D. M., Larsen, R. J., Westen, D., & Semmelroth, J. (1992). Sex differences in jealousy: Evolution, physiology, and psychology. *Psychological Science*, *3*(4), 251–256.

Buss, D. M., Shackelford, T. K., Kirkpatrick, L. A., Choe, J. C., Lim, H. K., Hasegawa, M., . . . Bennett, K. (1999). Jealousy and the nature of beliefs about infidelity: Tests of competing hypotheses about sex differences in the United States, Korea, and Japan. *Personal Relationships*, *6*(1), 125–150.

Buunk, B. P., Angleitner, A., Oubaid, V., & Buss, D. M. (1996). Sex differences in jealousy in evolutionary and cultural perspective: Tests from the Netherlands, Germany, and the United States. *Psychological Science*, *7*(6), 359–363.

Buunk, B., & Hupka, R. B. (1987). Cross-cultural differences in the elicitation of sexual jealousy. *Journal of Sex Research*, *23*(1), 12–22.

Carpenter, C. J. (2012). Meta-analyses of sex differences in responses to sexual versus emotional infidelity: Men and women are more similar than different. *Psychology of Women Quarterly*, *36*(1), 25–37.

Chien, M. L. (2009). Extramarital court and flirt of Guizhou Miao. *European Journal of East Asian Studies*, *8*(1), 135–159.

Christensen, H. T. (1973). Attitudes toward marital infidelity: A nine-culture sampling of university student opinion. *Journal of Comparative Family Studies*, *4*(2), 197–214.

Cooper, A. L., Månsson, S. A., Daneback, K., Tikkanen, R., & Ross, M. (2003). Predicting the future of Internet sex: Online sexual activities in Sweden. *Sexual and Relationship Therapy*, *18*(3), 277–291.

De Visser, R., & McDonald, D. (2007). Swings and roundabouts: Management of jealousy in heterosexual "swinging" couples. *British Journal of Social Psychology*, *46*(2), 459–476.

Docan-Morgan, T., & Docan, C. A. (2007). Internet infidelity: Double standards and the differing views of women and men. *Communication Quarterly*, *55*(3), 317–342.

Edlund, J. E., & Sagarin, B. J. (2017). Sex differences in jealousy: A 25-year retrospective. In James M. Olson. *Advances in experimental social psychology* (Vol. 55, pp. 259–302). Academic Press.

Farrer, J., & Zhongxin, S. (2003). Extramarital love in Shanghai. *China Journal*, *50*, 1–36.

Fernandez, A. M., Sierra, J. C., Zubeidat, I., & Vera-Villarroel, P. (2006). Sex differences in response to sexual and emotional infidelity among Spanish and Chilean students. *Journal of Cross-Cultural Psychology*, *37*(4), 359–365.

Fernandez, A. M., Vera-Villarroel, P., Sierra, J. C., & Zubeidat, I. (2007). Distress in response to emotional and sexual infidelity: Evidence of evolved gender differences in Spanish students. *Journal of Psychology*, *141*(1), 17–24.

Forth, G. (2004). Public affairs; Institutionalized nonmarital sex in an eastern Indonesian society. *Bijdragen tot de taal-, land-en volkenkunde/Journal of the Humanities and Social Sciences of Southeast Asia*, *160*(2–3), 315–338.

Geary, D. C., Rumsey, M., Bow-Thomas, C. C., & Hoard, M. K. (1995). Sexual jealousy as a facultative trait: Evidence from the pattern of sex differences in adults from China and the United States. *Ethology and Sociobiology*, *16*(5), 355–383.

Grieb, S. M. D., & Nielsen-Bobbit, J. (2013). Monogamy and secondary sexual partnerships among Afro-Amerindian immigrant women in New York City: A qualitative study. *Journal of Immigrant and Minority Health*, *15*(2), 365–371.

Guadagno, R. E., & Sagarin, B. J. (2010). Sex differences in jealousy: An evolutionary perspective on online infidelity. *Journal of Applied Social Psychology*, *40*(10), 2636–2655.

Harris, C. R. (2003a). A review of sex differences in sexual jealousy, including self-report data, psychophysiological responses, interpersonal violence, and morbid jealousy. *Personality and Social Psychology Review*, *7*(2), 102–128.

Harris, C. R. (2003b). Factors associated with jealousy over real and imagined infidelity: An examination of the social-cognitive and evolutionary psychology perspectives. *Psychology of Women Quarterly*, *27*(4), 319–329.

Hertlein, K. M., Wetchler, J. L., & Piercy, F. P. (2005). Infidelity: an overview. *Journal of Couple & Relationship Therapy*, *4*(2–3), 5–16.

Hendrick, S., & Hendrick, C. (1987). Multidimensionality of sexual attitudes. *Journal of Sex Research*, *23*(4), 502–526.

Henline, B. H., Lamke, L. K., & Howard, M. D. (2007). Exploring perceptions of online infidelity. *Personal relationships*, *14*(1), 113–128.

Hennigh, L. (1970). Functions and limitations of Alaskan Eskimo wife trading. *Arctic*, *23*(1), 24–34.

Higgins, L. T., Zheng, M., Liu, Y., & Sun, C. H. (2002). Attitudes to marriage and sexual behaviors: A survey of gender and culture differences in China and United Kingdom. *Sex Roles*, *46*(3), 75–89.

Hofstede, G. (1991). *Cultures and organizations*. McGraw-Hill.

Hrdy, S. B. (2000). The optimal number of fathers: Evolution, demography, and history in the shaping of female mate preferences. *Annals of the New York Academy of Sciences*, *907*(1), 75–96.

Hupka, R. B., Buunk, B., Falus, G., Fulgosi, A., Ortega, E., Swain, R., & Tarabrina, N. V. (1985). Romantic jealousy and romantic envy: A seven-nation study. *Journal of Cross-Cultural Psychology*, *16*(4), 423–446.

Hupka, R. B., & Ryan, J. M. (1990). The cultural contribution to jealousy: Cross-cultural aggression in sexual jealousy situations. *Behavior Science Research*, *24*(1–4), 51–71.

Isanejad, O., & Bagheri, A. (2018). Marital quality, loneliness, and Internet infidelity. *Cyberpsychology, Behavior, and Social Networking*, *21*(9), 542–548.

Jain, G., & Sahni, S. P. (2017). Understanding attribution bias and reasons behind Internet infidelity in India. In Emilio C. Viano. *Cybercrime, organized crime, and societal responses* (pp. 47–65). Springer.

Jain, G., & Sen, S. (2018). Adultery in the age of technology: Complexities and methodological challenges in studying Internet infidelity. *Internet Infidelity*. In: Sahni, S., Jain, G. (eds) Internet Infidelity (pp. 31–43). Springer, Singapore.

Jamieson, L. (2014). Intimacy, negotiated nonmonogamy, and the limits of the couple 1. In Jean Duncombe, Kaeren Harrison, Graham Allan, Dennis Marsden (eds). *The state of affairs* (pp. 35–57). Routledge.

Jankowiak, W., Nell, M. D., & Buckmaster, A. (2002). Managing infidelity: A cross-cultural perspective. *Ethnology*, *41*(1), 85.

Jankowiak, W., Sudakov, M., & Wilreker, B. C. (2005). Co-wife conflict and co-operation. *Ethnology*, *44*(1), 81–98.

Jankowiak, W. (2008). Co-wives, husband, and the Mormon polygynous family. *Ethnology*, *47*(2/3), 163–180.

Keefe, S. (2019). "Looking outside the marriage": Polygyny, infidelity, and divorce in coastal Tanzania. *Gendered Perspectives on International Development: Working Papers*, (314), 0_1–20.

Kruger, D. J., Fisher, M. L., Edelstein, R. S., Chopik, W. J., Fitzgerald, C. J., & Strout, S. L. (2013). Was that cheating? Perceptions vary by sex, attachment anxiety, and behavior. *Evolutionary Psychology*, *11*(1), 147470491301100115.

Labrecque, L. T., & Whisman, M. A. (2017). Attitudes toward and prevalence of extramarital sex and descriptions of extramarital partners in the 21st century. *Journal of Family Psychology*, *31*(7), 952.

LaSala, M. C. (2004). Extradyadic sex and gay male couples: Comparing monogamous and nonmonogamous relationships. *Families in Society*, *85*(3), 405–412.

Leakey, L. S. B. (1930). Some notes on the Masai of Kenya Colony. *Journal of the Royal Anthropological Institute of Great Britain and Ireland*, *60*, 185–209.

Le Gall, A., Mullet, E., & Shafighi, S. R. (2002). Age, religious beliefs, and sexual attitudes. *Journal of Sex Research*, *39*(3), 207–216.

Li, D., & Zheng, L. (2017). Relationship quality predicts online sexual activities among Chinese heterosexual men and women in committed relationships. *Computers in Human Behavior*, *70*, 244–250.

Li, D., & Zheng, L. (2018). Influence of the perceived infidelity of online sexual activities (OSAs) on OSA experiences among Chinese heterosexual individuals in committed relationships. *Journal of Sex & Marital Therapy*, *44*(8), 746–758.

Liu, Y., & Zheng, L. (2019). Influences of sociosexuality and commitment on online sexual activities: The mediating effect of perceptions of infidelity. *Journal of Sex & Marital Therapy*, *45*(5), 395–405.

Luo, S., Cartun, M. A., & Snider, A. G. (2010). Assessing extradyadic behavior: A review, a new measure, and two new models. *Personality and Individual differences*, *49*(3), 155–163.

Macauda, M. M., Erickson, P. I., Singer, M. C., & Santelices, C. C. (2011). A cultural model of infidelity among African American and Puerto Rican young adults. *Anthropology & Medicine*, *18*(3), 351–364.

Marlowe, F. (2000). Paternal investment and the human mating system. *Behavioural Processes*, *51*(1–3), 45–61.

Marlowe, F. W. (2003). The mating system of foragers in the standard cross-cultural sample. *Cross-Cultural Research*, *37*(3), 282–306.

Mattingly, B. A., Wilson, K., Clark, E. M., Bequette, A. W., & Weidler, D. J. (2010). Foggy faithfulness: Relationship quality, religiosity, and the Perceptions of Dating Infidelity Scale in an adult sample. *Journal of Family Issues*, *31*(11), 1465–1480.

Mattison, S. M., Scelza, B., & Blumenfield, T. (2014). Paternal investment and the positive effects of fathers among the matrilineal Mosuo of southwest China. *American Anthropologist, 116*(3), 591–610.

Maykovich, M. K. (1976). Attitudes versus behavior in extramarital sexual relations. *Journal of Marriage and the Family,* 38, 4.

Medora, N. P., Larson, J. H., Hortacsu, N., & Dave, P. (2002). Perceived attitudes towards romanticism: A cross-cultural study of American, Asian-Indian, and Turkish young adults. *Journal of Comparative Family Studies, 33*(2), 155–178.

Mileham, B. L. A. (2007). Online infidelity in Internet chat rooms: An ethnographic exploration. *Computers in Human Behavior, 23*(1), 11–31.

Moller, N. P., & Vossler, A. (2015). Defining infidelity in research and couple counseling: A qualitative study. *Journal of Sex & Marital Therapy, 41*(5), 487–497.

Murdock, G. P., & White, D. R. (1969). Standard cross-cultural sample. *Ethnology, 8*(4), 329–369.

Negy, C., Plaza, D., Reig-Ferrer, A., & Fernandez-Pascual, M. D. (2018). Is viewing sexually explicit material cheating on your partner? A comparison between the United States and Spain. *Archives of sexual behavior, 47*(3), 737–745.

Nowak, N. T., Weisfeld, G. E., Imamoğlu, O., Weisfeld, C. C., Butovskaya, M., & Shen, J. (2014). Attractiveness and spousal infidelity as predictors of sexual fulfilment without the marriage partner in couples from five cultures. *Human Ethology Bulletin, 29*(1), 18–38.

Olmstead, S. B., Negash, S., Pasley, K., & Fincham, F. D. (2013). Emerging adults' expectations for pornography use in the context of future committed romantic relationships: A qualitative study. *Archives of Sexual Behavior, 42*(4), 625–635.

Parker, T. S., & Wampler, K. S. (2003). How bad is it? Perceptions of the relationship impact of different types of Internet sexual activities. *Contemporary Family Therapy, 25*(4), 415–429.

Pazhoohi, F. (2017). Polygyny as a strategy for controlling male sexuality to secure child survival. *Human Ethology Bulletin, 32*(2), 24–35.

Pazhoohi, F., & Kingstone, A. (2020). Sex difference on the importance of veiling: A cross-cultural investigation. *Cross-Cultural Research, 54*(5), 486–501.

Pazhoohi, F., Lang, M., Xygalatas, D., & Grammer, K. (2017). Religious veiling as a mate-guarding strategy: Effects of environmental pressures on cultural practices. *Evolutionary Psychological Science, 3*(2), 118–124.

Pazhoohi, F., Silva, C., Pereira, L., Oliveira, M., Santana, P., Rodrigues, R., & Arantes, J. (2019). Is imagination of the infidelity more painful than actual infidelity? *Current Psychology, 38*(2), 572–578.

Pew Research Center. (2014, January 14). *Extramarital affairs topline.* https://www.pewresearch.org/global/2014/01/14/extramarital-affairs-topline/

Poulsen, F. O., Busby, D. M., & Galovan, A. M. (2013). Pornography use: Who uses it and how it is associated with couple outcomes. *Journal of Sex Research, 50*(1), 72–83.

Quinlan, R. J., & Quinlan, M. B. (2007). Parenting and cultures of risk: A comparative analysis of infidelity, aggression, and witchcraft. *American Anthropologist, 109*(1), 164–179.

Ramanujam, P., Goyal, Y., & Sridhar, S. (2018). Cultural institutions in new technology: Evidence from Internet infidelity. In Sahni, S., Jain, G. (eds) *Internet infidelity* (pp. 45–67). Springer.

Randall, H. E., & Byers, E. S. (2003). What is sex? Students' definitions of having sex, sexual partner, and unfaithful sexual behaviour. *Canadian Journal of Human Sexuality, 12*(2), 87.

Roscoe, B., Cavanaugh, L. E., & Kennedy, D. R. (1988). Dating infidelity: Behaviors, reasons and consequences. *Adolescence, 23*(89), 35.

Rosenfeld, M. J., & Thomas, R. J. (2012). Searching for a mate: The rise of the Internet as a social intermediary. *American Sociological Review, 77*(4), 523–547.

Rothstein, N. J., Connolly, D. H., de Visser, E. J., & Phillips, E. (2021, March). Perceptions of infidelity with sex robots. In *Proceedings of the 2021 ACM/IEEE International Conference on Human–Robot Interaction* (pp. 129–139) March 8–11, 2021, Boulder, CO, USA. ACM, New York, NY, USA, 11 pages. https://doi.org/10.1145/3434073.3444653.

Sagarin, B. J., Martin, A. L., Coutinho, S. A., Edlund, J. E., Patel, L., Skowronski, J. J., & Zengel, B. (2012). Sex differences in jealousy: A meta-analytic examination. *Evolution and Human Behavior, 33*(6), 595–614.

Scelza, B. A. (2011). Female choice and extra-pair paternity in a traditional human population. *Biology Letters, 7*(6), 889–891.

Scelza, B. A. (2013). Choosy but not chaste: Multiple mating in human females. *Evolutionary Anthropology: Issues, News, and Reviews, 22*(5), 259–269.

Scelza, B. A. (2014). Jealousy in a small-scale, natural fertility population: The roles of paternity, investment and love in jealous response. *Evolution and Human Behavior*, *35*(2), 103–108.

Scelza, B. A., & Prall, S. P. (2018). Partner preferences in the context of concurrency: What Himba want in formal and informal partners. *Evolution and Human Behavior*, *39*(2), 212–219.

Scelza, B. A., Prall, S. P., Blumenfield, T., Crittenden, A. N., Gurven, M., Kline, M., . . . McElreath, R. (2020a). Patterns of paternal investment predict cross-cultural variation in jealous response. *Nature Human Behaviour*, *4*(1), 20–26.

Scelza, B., Prall, S., & Starkweather, K. (2021) The role of spousal separation on norms related to gender and sexuality among Himba pastoralists. *Social Sciences*, *10*, 174. https://doi.org/10.3390/socsci10050174

Scelza, B. A., Prall, S. P., Swinford, N., Gopalan, S., Atkinson, E. G., McElreath, R., . . . Henn, B. M. (2020b). High rate of extrapair paternity in a human population demonstrates diversity in human reproductive strategies. *Science Advances*, *6*(8), eaay6195.

Schaller, M., & Murray, D. R. (2008). Pathogens, personality, and culture: Disease prevalence predicts worldwide variability in sociosexuality, extraversion, and openness to experience. *Journal of Personality and Social Psychology*, *95*(1), 212.

Schmitt, D. P. (2003). Universal sex differences in the desire for sexual variety: Tests from 52 nations, 6 continents, and 13 islands. *Journal of Personality and Social Psychology*, *85*(1), 85.

Schmitt, D. P. (2005). Sociosexuality from Argentina to Zimbabwe: A 48-nation study of sex, culture, and strategies of human mating. *Behavioral and Brain Sciences*, *28*(2), 247.

Schneider, J. P. (2002). Effects of cybersex problems on the spouse and family. In A. Cooper (Ed.), *Sex and the Internet: A guidebook for clinicians* (pp. 169–186). Brunner/Routledge.

Schützwohl, A., & Koch, S. (2004). Sex differences in jealousy: The recall of cues to sexual and emotional infidelity in personally more and less threatening context conditions. *Evolution and Human Behavior*, *25*(4), 249–257.

Scott, J. (1998). Changing attitudes to sexual morality: A cross-national comparison. *Sociology*, *32*(4), 815–845.

Sng, O., Neuberg, S. L., Varnum, M. E., & Kenrick, D. T. (2018). The behavioral ecology of cultural psychological variation. *Psychological Review*, *125*(5), 714.

Sorokowska, A., Saluja, S., Sorokowski, P., Frąckowiak, T., Karwowski, M., Aavik, T., . . . Croy, I. (2021). Affective interpersonal touch in close relationships: A cross-cultural perspective. *Personality and Social Psychology Bulletin*, *47*(12), 1705–1721..

Starkweather, K. E., & Hames, R. (2012). A survey of non-classical polyandry. *Human Nature*, *23*(2), 149–172.

Symons, D. (1979). *The evolution of human sexuality*. Oxford University Press.

Thompson, A. P. (1984). Emotional and sexual components of extramarital relations. *Journal of Marriage and the Family*, *46*(1), 35–42.

Trivers, R. (1972). Parental investment and sexual selection. In Bernard G. Campbell. *Sexual Selection and the Descent of Man* (pp. 136–179), Aldine de Gruyter.

Vera Cruz, G. (2018). Would Mozambican women really "tolerate" their husbands' extramarital sexual relationships as socially recommended? *Sexuality & Culture*, *22*(4), 1263–1278.

Vera Cruz, G., Vinsonneau, G., Le Gall, A., Rivière, S., & Mullet, E. (2010). Sexual permissiveness: A Mozambique–France comparison. *Journal of Applied Social Psychology*, *40*(10), 2488–2499.

Vossler, A. (2016). Internet infidelity 10 years on: A critical review of the literature. *Family Journal*, *24*(4), 359–366.

Vossler, A., & Moller, N. P. (2020). Internet affairs: Partners' perceptions and experiences of Internet infidelity. *Journal of Sex & Marital Therapy*, *46*(1), 67–77.

Walker, R. S., Flinn, M. V., & Hill, K. R. (2010). Evolutionary history of partible paternity in lowland South America. *Proceedings of the National Academy of Sciences*, *107*(45), 19195–19200.

Wallace, B. J. (1969). Pagan Gaddang spouse exchange. *Ethnology*, *8*(2), 183–188.

Wang, C. C., & Hsiung, W. (2008). Attitudes towards online infidelity among Taiwanese college students. *International Journal of Cyber Society and Education*, *1*(1), 61–78.

Ward, J., & Voracek, M. (2004). Evolutionary and social cognitive explanations of sex differences in romantic jealousy. *Australian Journal of Psychology*, *56*(3), 165–171.

Weinberg, M. S., Lottes, I. L., & Shaver, F. M. (1995). Swedish or American heterosexual college youth: Who is more permissive? *Archives of Sexual Behavior*, *24*(4), 409–437.

Whitty, M. T. (2003). Pushing the wrong buttons: Men's and women's attitudes toward online and offline infidelity. *CyberPsychology & Behavior*, *6*(6), 569–579.

Whitty, M. T. (2005). The realness of cybercheating: Men's and women's representations of unfaithful Internet relationships. *Social Science Computer Review, 23*(1), 57–67.

Wiederman, M. W., & Kendall, E. (1999). Evolution, sex, and jealousy: Investigation with a sample from Sweden. *Evolution and Human Behavior, 20*(2), 121–128.

Wilson, K., Mattingly, B. A., Clark, E. M., Weidler, D. J., & Bequette, A. W. (2011). The gray area: Exploring attitudes toward infidelity and the development of the Perceptions of Dating Infidelity Scale. *Journal of Social Psychology, 151*(1), 63–86.

Weeks, J., Heaphy, B. and Donovan, C. (2001). Same sex intimacies: families of choice and other life experiments. Routledge, London.

Yarab, P. E., & Allgeier, E. R. (1998). Don't even think about it: The role of sexual fantasies as perceived unfaithfulness in heterosexual dating relationships. *Journal of Sex Education and Therapy, 23*(3), 246–254.

Yarab, P. E., Sensibaugh, C. C., & Allgeier, E. R. (1998). More than just sex: Gender differences in the incidence of self-defined unfaithful behavior in heterosexual dating relationships. *Journal of Psychology & Human Sexuality, 10*(2), 45–57.

Zengel, B., Edlund, J. E., & Sagarin, B. J. (2013). Sex differences in jealousy in response to infidelity: Evaluation of demographic moderators in a national random sample. *Personality and Individual Differences, 54*(1), 47–51.

Zhang, N., Parish, W. L., Huang, Y., & Pan, S. (2012). Sexual infidelity in China: Prevalence and gender-specific correlates. *Archives of Sexual Behavior, 41*(4), 861–873.

Zhang, Y., Wang, X., & Pan, S. (2021). Prevalence and patterns of extramarital sex among Chinese men and women: 2000–2015. *Journal of Sex Research, 58*(1), 41–50.

CHAPTER
17

The Nature of Infidelity in Nonheterosexual Relationships

Justin J. Lehmiller *and* Dylan Selterman

Abstract

This chapter describes research on nonmonogamous practices in nonheterosexual relationships. Specifically, it explores (1) the prevalence of both consensual nonmonogamy (e.g., open relationships, polyamory) and nonconsensual nonmonogamy (i.e., infidelity) in this population, (2) factors that may explain why both types of nonmonogamy appear to be more prevalent among sexual minorities, (3) predictors of attitudes toward and experiences with infidelity (including personality traits and attachment style), and (4) reactions to infidelity among sexual minorities compared to heterosexual persons. We also describe several important directions for future research in this area, including suggestions for improving measurement, given that much previous research on sexual minorities has conflated all forms of nonmonogamy, regardless of whether it was consensual or nonconsensual. This review establishes an ambitious agenda for continued work in this area, while also challenging popular ideas and assumptions about various nonmonogamous practices.

Key Words: infidelity, consensual nonmonogamy, sexual orientation, personality, attachment style, same-sex relationship, LGBTQ, jealousy, compersion

> If one person is completely done with sex and the other person is not done with sex, what do you advise people to do in that circumstance? Divorce? Traumatize their children? I look at that and I say "You know, do what you need to do to stay married and stay sane. And maybe that involves cheating, but as the lesser of two evils. Divorce is an evil, cheating is an evil, there are circumstances in which cheating is the lesser evil."
>
> —*Dan Savage*

In the United States, Americans' views on sexual morality have evolved substantially over time and, according to public opinion polls, they are more liberal than ever (Brenan,

2021). However, while attitudes toward same-sex relationships, casual sex, divorce, and birth control have become more favorable, not all sexual attitudes have shifted to majority approval. One area where relatively little movement has occurred and disapproval remains widespread is nonmonogamy. Nonmonogamy can take both consensual (e.g., open relationships, polyamory, swinging) and nonconsensual forms (i.e., cheating or infidelity), and both are viewed by wide swaths of the population as morally unacceptable. For example, in the 2021 Moral Values Survey conducted by the Gallup Organization, just 10% said that having an affair is morally acceptable, while 20% said the same of having multiple marriages (the only form of consensual nonmonogamy assessed in this survey). Compared to polling from approximately two decades earlier, acceptability of both practices has increased slightly, but the vast majority of adults retain negative attitudes toward them. However, these numbers obscure significant variability across demographic subgroups.

Attitudes toward nonmonogamy—including both its consensual and nonconsensual variants—differ on average across persons of varying genders and sexual orientations. The quote we used to open this chapter comes from the American sex advice columnist Dan Savage, an openly gay man. Savage is infamous for being vocal about the virtues of both open relationships and infidelity, with his comments echoing long-standing differences in the values ascribed to monogamy and nonmonogamy in the gay community relative to heterosexual adults (see Blumstein & Schwartz, 1983). The idea that relationships can survive—and sometimes thrive—when partners do not maintain sexual exclusivity is a difficult concept for many outside of this community to comprehend, despite academic work showing that relationship quality does not differ between monogamists and consensual nonmonogamists (Rubel & Bogaert, 2015) and that infidelity—while mostly having negative effects on relationships—can sometimes end up strengthening a relationship (see Perel, 2017).

So what accounts for sexual orientation differences in attitudes toward infidelity and other forms of nonmonogamy? How common are nonmonogamous experiences in the LGBTQ + community? How are the predictors of infidelity similar or different for heterosexual and nonheterosexual persons? And how do felt experiences of infidelity differ across persons of varying sexual orientations?

In this chapter, we sought to explore these questions. We initially sought to emphasize infidelity in nonheterosexual relationships specifically; however, we also found it necessary to give due consideration to the practice of consensual nonmonogamy because (1) many studies of same-sex relationships have conflated all forms of nonmonogamy, regardless of whether they are consensual, (2) consensual nonmonogamy is sometimes used as an infidelity avoidance strategy, and (3) infidelity can still occur in consensually nonmonogamous relationships, and this type of infidelity can look very different compared to infidelity that occurs within a monogamous arrangement.

We begin by exploring the prevalence of both consensual and nonconsensual nonmonogamy in nonheterosexual relationships, followed by a review of factors that may explain why both practices appear to be more prevalent among sexual minorities. We also explore factors that predict attitudes toward and experiences with infidelity (including personality traits and attachment style), as well as reactions to infidelity among sexual minorities compared to heterosexual persons. Finally, we review important directions for future research in this area.

Prevalence of Infidelity in Nonheterosexual Relationships

Surprisingly little is known about the prevalence of infidelity in nonheterosexual relationships. In our review of the literature, we came across paper after paper declaring this to be an important and much-needed topic of study; however, most studies of infidelity appear to have excluded nonheterosexual participants from investigation for various reasons (e.g., small sample size, beyond study scope) and/or did not employ measurement methods that allowed for investigation of this subject. For example, many national surveys that have included such measures defined "infidelity" specifically as having sexual contact with someone other than one's spouse (e.g., Atkins et al., 2001). National, legal recognition of same-sex marriage is a recent phenomenon (it was not legalized throughout the United States until a 2015 Supreme Court decision); consequently, most studies of marital infidelity are ill-equipped to report on the prevalence of infidelity in same-sex couples because they were conducted at a time when legal marriage was not an option for LGBTQ + persons.

Most academic papers that make reference to same-sex infidelity cite just one study—Blumstein and Schwartz (1983)—which, while representing an important contribution to the literature, has long been regarded as "limited and dated" in terms of its ability to speak to modern-day dating and relationships (McAnulty & Brineman, 2007).

Blumstein and Schwartz (1983) surveyed thousands of couples from across the United States about their intimate lives in the 1970s and 1980s, and their sample included a sizable number of gay men and lesbians, most of whom were from large US cities (e.g., San Francisco, New York). When asked whether they had ever engaged in nonmonogamy (broadly defined) since beginning their relationship, 82% of gay men and 28% of lesbians responded affirmatively. For comparison purposes, 26% of men and 21% of women in mixed-sex marriages reported nonmonogamy. However, in this and many other studies of nonmonogamy, consensual (i.e., sexually open relationships) and nonconsensual practices (i.e., infidelity) were not clearly differentiated, which means that these numbers do not reflect the true prevalence of infidelity. In this particular study, 65% of gay men, 29% of lesbians, and 15% of mixed-sex married couples reported having an agreement that permitted outside sex under certain circumstances. Thus, it would appear that a majority of the couples who reported nonmonogamy in Blumstein and Schwartz's research did so in the context of an open relationship.

A handful of more recent studies have reported on the prevalence of nonmonogamy in same-sex relationships. For example, in a German study of 1,899 adults of diverse genders and sexualities, 4% of lesbian women and 34% of gay men reported having had extradyadic sexual involvements; by contrast, 29% of heterosexual women and 49% of heterosexual men reported the same (Haversath & Kroger, 2014). Again, however, it appears that consensual and nonconsensual nonmonogamy were conflated in this study.

This was also the case in a study of same-sex couples who were and were not in civil unions in Vermont (Solomon et al., 2005). This study found that, among lesbian women in civil unions, 9% reported sex outside of their relationship, compared to 7.3% of those who were not in civil unions. However, 5% of lesbian women in this study reported that they had an agreement with their partner that outside sex is acceptable. Likewise, among gay men in civil unions, 58.3% reported having had sex outside of their relationship, compared to 61.1% of gay men who were not in civil union; however, more than 40% of gay men in this study said they had an agreement with their partner that permitted outside sex under some circumstances. Thus, while rates of extradyadic sexual activity in same-sex relationships might appear to be high (particularly among gay men), it appears that most of this behavior is occurring under consensual arrangements and, thus, does not reflect cheating or infidelity.

Attempts to clearly distinguish consensual from nonconsensual nonmonogamy in same-sex couples are rare, but some research can speak to this. For example, LaSala (2004) interviewed 242 gay men in relationships from the United States and found that most (60.3%) reported being in monogamous relationships, with the remainder reporting some type of open relationship. Of those who had agreed to be monogamous, nearly half (45.2%) reported that one or both partners had sex outside of the relationship at some point. Of that subgroup, a majority (51.5%) reported that infidelity had occurred in the past year.

While LaSala's study examined broken agreements in monogamous couples, it did not appear to assess broken agreements among those who were consensually nonmonogamous. Infidelity can and does sometimes occur in sexually open relationships, although it may look quite different than it does in monogamous relationships. While open relationships permit some degree of sexual contact outside of a primary relationship, there are often rules in place limiting frequency or location of contact (e.g., one-time only, permissible only when traveling), as well as specific sexual activities that may take place. For example, while sexual intercourse with another person may be permitted, kissing or other intimate activities such as spending the night might be off limits. Likewise, condom usage may be essential with outside partners, but not with primary partners. Infidelity in an open relationship is thus defined relative to the rules that a given couple negotiates. In a qualitative study by Hoff and Beougher (2010) involving 39 gay male couples (of whom the majority—64%—reported being in open relationships), 22 couples (56%) reported having experienced a broken agreement (e.g., having sexual or intimate contact that was not permitted under the couple's rule set). Similarly, in a study by Prestage and colleagues (2006) of 822 gay men (of whom 67.6% were in open relationships), 27.7% reported having broken their agreement in some way.

While one might assume that infidelity transgressions among consensually nonmonogamous partners would be more varied and depend on the specific, idiosyncratic agreements within couples compared to those in monogamous relationships, research has shown that a substantial proportion of dating couples (33%) disagree on whether there was an agreed-on monogamous framework for their own relationship, and an even greater number disagree (50%–55%) about whether their monogamous agreement was violated (Warren et al., 2012). A hallmark of most consensually nonmonogamous relationships (especially polyamorous relationships) is clear and straightforward communication. Indeed, monogamy agreements and infidelity norms may be even less clearly defined in "monogamous" contexts because monogamy is often assumed rather than being negotiated or defined.

The findings of LaSala (2004), Hoff and Beougher (2010), and Prestage and colleagues (2006) suggest that infidelity is a common occurrence in gay men's relationships, regardless of whether those relationships are monogamous or consensually nonmonogamous. However, given that these studies are based on small convenience samples, they cannot provide a firm basis for population prevalence, nor can they speak to the experiences of other sexual minorities, including bisexuals.

There is just one nationally representative US survey we are aware of that distinguished consensual from nonconsensual nonmonogamy and that separately reported on rates of infidelity for lesbian, gay, bisexual, and heterosexual participants (Levine et al., 2018). These data, which came from the National Survey of Sexual Health and Behavior, revealed that:

- Overall, about 8% of heterosexual participants, 14% of gay participants, 6% of lesbian participants, 18% of bisexual participants, and 6% of those who reported "other" sexualities indicated nonconsensual nonmonogamy. By contrast, 2% of heterosexual participants, 32% of gay participants, 5% of lesbian participants, 22% of bisexual participants, and 14% of those who reported "other" sexualities described being in open relationships.
- Among male-identified participants only, about 8% of heterosexual men, 14% of gay men, 34% of bisexual men, and 6% of "other" men reported nonconsensual nonmonogamy (i.e., infidelity). By contrast, 3% of heterosexual men, 33% of gay men, 23% of bisexual men, and 24% of "other" men reported open relationships.
- Among female-identified participants only, about 7% of heterosexual women, 6% of lesbian women, 12% of bisexual women, and 6% of "other" women reported nonconsensual nonmonogamy. By contrast, 2% of heterosexual women, 5% of lesbian women, 22% of bisexual women, and 8% of "other" women reported open relationships.

Putting all of this research together, it seems that sexual minorities are more open to consensual nonmonogamy than heterosexuals and, further, that sexual minority men are more open to it than sexual minority women, with the exception of bisexual women (although see Moors et al., 2014, for evidence from a nonrepresentative online community sample finding that sexual minority women and men are equivalently interested in consensual nonmonogamy). With respect to nonconsensual nonmonogamy, the accumulated body of research is quite limited; however, results from nationally representative US data suggest that, among women, heterosexual and lesbian women report similarly low rates of infidelity, with bisexual women being almost twice as likely to report it. Among men, gay men were about twice as likely to report infidelity as heterosexual men, while bisexual men were about four times more likely to do so relative to their heterosexual counterparts.

Given the limited representative datapoints, it would be important to replicate these findings before drawing firm conclusions; however, the available evidence suggests that, on average, gay men and those who identify as bisexual report higher rates of both consensual and nonconsensual nonmonogamy than do heterosexual persons.

Understanding Sexual Orientation Differences in Nonmonogamous Practices

Elevated rates of nonmonogamous practices among gay- and bisexual-identified persons are likely explained by a combination of factors. One contributing variable may simply be differences in the importance ascribed to being monogamous. Blumstein and Schwartz (1983) found that 75% of men and 84% of women in mixed-sex relationships and 71% of lesbian women espoused the importance of being monogamous; by contrast, 36% of gay men said the same. Thus, gay men appear less likely to see monogamy as an essential component of a relationship. Bisexual individuals were not included in Blumstein and Schwartz's study; however, given the high prevalence of nonmonogamy in this community reported in other studies, it seems likely that bisexual persons (across genders) would be likely to ascribe less importance to monogamy than heterosexual persons.

There may be both social psychological and evolutionary explanations behind this. Given a high documented prevalence of nonmonogamy in male same-sex relationships tracing back several decades, it may be that this behavior has come to be seen as a normative component of relationships in this community, thereby reinforcing prevalence of nonmonogamous practices. Put another way, nonmonogamy in male same-sex relationships could potentially be viewed as a descriptive norm—an understanding of what most people in a particular group do, which then guides individual behavior (Cialdini et al., 1990).

Related to this is the fact that there is also less pressure on sexual minorities to uphold the standards and ideals of traditional relationships. Because same-sex relationships already violate traditional notions of what a relationship "should" be, those who enter such relationships may feel less bound to follow other relationship "rules," especially rules based in understandings of morality that disapprove of any orientation other than strict heterosexuality. Likewise, social dictations for monogamy are strongest in the context of marriage, and legal marriage is not something that has been an option for most sexual minorities until very recently. Thus, there have historically been fewer social and cultural constraints on nonmonogamy among sexual minorities.

That said, elevated rates of nonmonogamy (both consensual and nonconsensual) are higher among sexual minority men than they are among sexual minority women (with the exception of bisexual women), which also points to explanations rooted in sex/gender. Research has shown that, relative to women, men express more interest in casual sex (Clark & Hatfield, 1989), report more desire for sexual variety (Schmitt, 2003), and have a more unrestricted sociosexual orientation, or an ability to decouple sex from love (Lippa, 2009). All of these sex differences have been explained through an evolutionary lens based in differences in the parental investment required to produce offspring (Buss & Schmitt, 1993). However, Moors and colleagues (2014) challenged this idea and noted that the existing literature has focused less on sexual minority women's interest in and engagement with open relationships. Their findings from a nonrepresentative community sample indicate that sexual minority women and men are just as interested in consensual nonmonogamy, so it may be the case that in certain subcultures, gender does not play as big of a role as other variables in the pursuit of nonmonogamy.

To the extent that heterosexual women report less interest in casual sex and having multiple partners on average compared to men, this would create a natural limit on heterosexual men's ability to practice nonmonogamy. However, in a context in which men are pursuing other men for sex, they will likely face fewer constraints. Put another way, sexual minority men may simply be more successful than heterosexual men in fulfilling desires for casual sex and sexual variety simply because their desired partners are more aligned with their own sexual psychology. Sex/gender differences in attitudes toward sex may therefore partly explain sexuality differences in nonmonogamy (both consensual and nonconsensual): sexual minority men may simply have more opportunities available, which could explain higher prevalence of nonmonogamous practices.

Of course, other explanations are possible. Below, we explore the extent to which sexual orientation differences in various personality traits (the Big Five, sexual sensation seeking) and attachment style may help us to understand reasons for infidelity and differences in infidelity prevalence among sexual minorities. We also explore the extent to which these same factors may help to explain elevated rates of consensual nonmonogamy in nonheterosexual relationships.

Infidelity in Nonheterosexual Relationships: The Role of Personality

Several theories of personality have relevance for the study of romantic infidelity. The Big Five trait model, for instance, suggests that individuals' tendencies to prefer and engage in romantic infidelity is associated with higher *extraversion* (i.e., more outgoingness and sociability), lower *agreeableness* (i.e., less warmth and cooperation) and lower *conscientiousness* (i.e., less diligence and responsibility). In cross-cultural research spanning dozens of countries on several continents, these three personality traits were consistently linked with infidelity (Schmitt & Shackelford, 2008), although the correlations are small. Small correlations are to be theoretically expected, given that the Big Five model posits general personality traits, which predict different types of behavior across many domains, each to a small degree. Other studies also suggest that Big Five traits are linked with infidelity in part due to preferences for short-term mating and promiscuity (Schmitt, 2004). Put another way, general personality traits including higher extroversion, lower agreeableness, and lower conscientiousness, are associated with a tendency to prefer uncommitted sex and multiple sex partners. Infidelity is one behavioral outcome of such a tendency. However, one thing that is not clear from this body of research is the causal direction: Do specific personality traits create predispositions toward promiscuity and infidelity, or is it the other way around? Researchers generally argue for the former explanation. For example, Schmitt (2004) notes that "extraverts may need to raise their habitually low levels of cortical arousal to a more comfortable level by engaging in risky sex" (p. 303). However, more research is needed to better understand the nature of these associations.

Another limitation of this area of research is that virtually all studies do not account for sexual orientation in their analyses, and heterosexuality is often assumed (especially in studies with an evolutionary framework). This raises the question: Do these associations between the Big Five traits and infidelity generalize to nonheterosexual relationships? To our knowledge, no study has directly examined associations between Big Five traits and infidelity in nonheterosexuals, but some ancillary data may provide useful clues.

Analyses that focus only on the traits themselves find that there is similarity in Big Five trait scores across individuals with heterosexual, homosexual, and bisexual orientations. Some significant group differences emerge in the data, however. For instance, gay men score higher than heterosexual men on average for agreeableness, openness to experience, and neuroticism (Lippa, 2005), and bisexual men score even higher on these traits than both other groups (Ifrah et al., 2018); however, those effect sizes are small (Lippa & Arad, 1997) and they pale in comparison to sexual orientation differences in gender-related traits such as *expressiveness* or *instrumentality* (Lippa, 2005). There is some evidence that gendered traits such as these manifest in reverse-stereotypical ways, with gay men more similar to straight women and lesbian women more similar to straight men (Bailey et al., 2016; Lippa, 2005).

The sexual orientation differences in Big Five traits discussed above do not offer a compelling explanation for why sexual minority men report elevated rates of infidelity compared to heterosexual men. Of the Big Five traits linked to infidelity (i.e., extraversion, agreeableness, and conscientiousness), just one shows a sexual orientation difference—agreeableness—and it is in the direction opposite of what would be expected if it were an explanatory variable here. Gay and bisexual men are higher on agreeableness—a characteristic that should theoretically predict less infidelity—yet they appear *more* likely to engage in infidelity.

An alternative possibility is therefore that sexual orientation differences in Big Five traits are indirectly linked to infidelity, or that other personality traits are more important to attend to in understanding why sexual minorities may have a higher propensity for infidelity. For example, some have theorized that links between certain Big Five traits and infidelity are explained by the fact that those traits are also linked with *sensation seeking*, which is a tendency to prefer novel, high-intensity experiences and stimulation (Zuckerman, 1979, 2007). This is especially true for low conscientiousness and high openness, both of which are correlated with sensation-seeking—and, importantly, gay and bisexual men have elevated levels of openness to experience (Ifrah et al., 2018; Lippa, 2005). While sensation seeking characterizes a tendency toward novel/intense experiences in several different domains (e.g., adventuresome outdoor activities such as skydiving), more specific variants of this trait such as *sexual sensation seeking*, which captures the tendency to seek novel/intense experiences during sexual activity (Kalichman & Rompa, 1995), have been studied thoroughly in the context of nonheterosexual populations, in addition to heterosexuals (Gaither & Sellbom, 2003).

Sexual sensation seeking, measured by items such as, "I have said things that were not exactly true to get a person to have sex with me," is linked with risky sex (e.g., sex without contraception) as well as a tendency to prefer multiple sex partners. The sensation-seeking trait has been found to be higher among bisexual persons (Stief et al., 2014) and is also linked with positive attitudes toward sexual infidelity (Lalasz & Weigel, 2011). If we theoretically connect these lines of research together, we arrive at some tentative ideas about the experience of infidelity in nonheterosexual relationships. It could be the case that elevated levels of certain personality traits among sexual minorities create predispositions to sensation seeking that, in turn, create predispositions to infidelity. Future research would do well to provide a more complete test of this theoretical pathway.

It is worth noting that Big Five traits also predict interest in and engagement with consensual nonmonogamy (CNM) in nonheterosexual populations. Moors et al. (2017) found in a sample of gay, lesbian, and bisexual participants that higher openness and lower conscientiousness predicted more positive attitudes toward and more proclivity to engage in multipartner relationships. It is notable that the associations between Big Five traits and CNM are conceptually similar to the associations between Big Five traits and infidelity. Some research also suggests that people who engage in consensual nonmonogamy are motivated by the excitement of having multiple partners (Moors, Matsick, & Schechinger, 2017), which suggests sensation-seeking motives. This suggests a multifaceted psychological similarity between the experiences of nonconsensual and consensual nonmonogamy in terms of personality traits and motivations, despite the fact that they are also quite different functionally and behaviorally.

This leads us to pose an important question: Why do some individuals or couples gravitate toward infidelity while others gravitate toward CNM, especially when both of these behaviors are predicted by similar underlying traits? Future research can investigate this, but one potential factor could be social norms. Previous research has shown that a large proportion of the variability in personality traits such as the Big Five is attributable to genetic heritability (Bouchard & McGue, 2003; Jang et al., 1996). To the extent that underlying biological processes are responsible for much of the variance between individuals in their personality traits, this points to social psychological mediators in terms of whether these traits end up predicting infidelity versus CNM. As indicated by the National Survey of Sexual Health and Behavior, infidelity is more common than CNM among heterosexual adults, while the reverse is true among sexual minorities (Levine et al., 2018). Given that attitudes toward nonmonogamy are significantly more positive in LGBT populations and there is more stigma against nonmonogamy in heterosexual populations (e.g., Schwartz & Blumstein, 1983), this could potentially lead individuals in heterosexual relationships who are high on traits such as extroversion or low on traits such as conscientiousness to end up cheating on their partners because CNM is not seen as a viable option. By contrast, individuals in nonheterosexual relationships with the same traits may be more likely to gravitate towards consensual nonmonogamy because such relationship arrangements are more widely accepted. Again, this is speculative, but perhaps an idea that future research can address.

Infidelity in Nonheterosexual Relationships: The Role of Attachment Style

Attachment traits or "styles" predict a wide range of variables that pertain to intimate relationships, including those between parents and children, romantic partners, and friends (Mikulincer & Shaver, 2007). Among other things, attachment style is also related to the experience of infidelity. Attachment theory and research indicates that these traits develop in ways that are distinct from generalized personality traits such as Big Five, which are at least partly heritable. Rather than being highly heritable, attachment patterns develop as a function of interactions with attachment figures, including our early caregivers (Ainsworth et al., 1978) and our romantic partners (Fraley, 2019). When our attachment *figures* consistently exude warmth, supportiveness, availability, and emotional skill, people come to trust that the attachment bond is positive and they grow more confident in exploring the world. This is known as secure base exploration. Although most work to date has focused on how children use parents/caregivers to develop healthy exploration, many theorists have connected this line of evidence with concurrent research on adult partners' support-giving and receiving (Feeney, 2004; 2007, Feeney & Collins, 2015; Feeney et al., 2013), as well as human sexuality (Birnbaum, 2015; Birnbaum & Reis, 2018; Selterman, Gesselman, & Moors, 2019).

Before discussing how attachment is connected to infidelity experiences, it is notable that research has demonstrated similarities in attachment relational dynamics across sexual orientations. Insecure traits predict suboptimal relationship functioning such as lower trust, intimacy, and satisfaction in same-sex couples (Mohr et al., 2013), just as they do in heterosexual couples. However, some studies have found gender-atypical patterns of attachment in nonheterosexual individuals. Heterosexual women exhibit higher attachment anxiety and lower avoidance, while the inverse is true for heterosexual men. By contrast, lesbian women report higher avoidance and lower anxiety compared to gay men, while gay men report lower avoidance and higher anxiety (Ridge & Feeney, 1998). Some theorists have suggested that these attachment patterns may emerge, in part, because of nonheterosexual individuals' motivation to resist conventional gender norms (O'Neil, 2008) and is similar to other gender-atypical behaviors in nonheterosexual individuals. This has implications for the experience of infidelity in nonheterosexual relationships, which we discuss below.

According to attachment theory, when partners or caregivers do not serve as an effective secure base, patterns of insecurity develop. This often takes the form of an anxious/preoccupied style, or an avoidant/dismissing style (Mikulincer & Shaver, 2007). Although they are very similar, some research suggests that those high in anxious/preoccupied attachment exhibit *hyperactivating* tendencies (Fraley et al., 2006) which can manifest in failed attempts to increase intimacy through conflict-approach strategies. By contrast, those high in avoidant/dismissing attachment exhibit *deactivating* tendencies (Mikulincer & Shaver, 2003) which can manifest in failed attempts to inhibit intimate feelings and behaviors by reducing contact with attachment figures. Both types of insecurity (anxiety and avoidance) are linked with relational difficulties in terms of intimacy, support, communication, satisfaction, and conflict, among a host of other variables (Mikulincer & Shaver, 2007). The literature on infidelity in relationships suggests that these relationship dysfunctions are significant predictors of infidelity. This is known as the *deficit model of infidelity* (Thompson, 1983; Tsapelas, 2011). One possibility is that these indirect links explain why attachment insecurity is linked with infidelity. That is, insecure traits lead to poor relationship health, which then leads to infidelity. There is some evidence that low commitment and satisfaction mediate the association between attachment avoidance and infidelity (DeWall et al., 2011).

However, not all studies show consistent links between attachment traits and infidelity. In a study of married couples, individuals' attachment avoidance was unrelated to infidelity over a 4-year period, which is inconsistent with other findings from unmarried couples (Russell et al., 2013). In addition, Russell and colleagues (2013) found that higher attachment anxiety in individuals and their partners was linked with a higher likelihood of infidelity while controlling for dyadic variables such as relationship satisfaction. This suggests a second possibility: links between attachment insecurity and infidelity may be orthogonal to relationship deficits. In this view, those who are high in insecurity traits are drawn to infidelity because of their insecurities and their dysfunctional approaches toward intimate relationships, and infidelities would occur even in healthy relationships. Some clinical evidence and anecdotal accounts in a therapy context illuminate the experiences people have during episodes of infidelity as stemming from attachment dysregulation (Butler et al., 2009; Schade & Sandberg, 2012), and some recent empirical work shows that infidelity motivated by personal insecurities is separate from infidelity motivated by dyadic deficits (Selterman, Garcia, & Tsapelas, 2019). Other lines of related evidence show that attachment traits are (sometimes) linked with individual differences in experiences that are tangential to the experience of infidelity, such as feelings of jealousy and reactions to a partner's real/hypothetical infidelity (Levy & Kelly, 2010; Tagler & Gentry, 2011; Treger & Sprecher, 2011).

Yet a third possibility is that the links between attachment and infidelity are moderated by other variables, including other individual differences and demographic factors, which may be relevant in explaining these inconsistencies. Some studies suggest that attachment avoidance predicts infidelity more so in men, whereas attachment anxiety predicts infidelity more so in women (Allen & Baucom, 2004). Fearful attachment has been linked with infidelity among African American/Black participants, but not among European/White or Hispanic participants (Parker & Campbell, 2017).

Adding to this complexity, there is virtually no research specifically examining the experience of engaging in infidelity itself as a function of attachment patterns in nonheterosexuals. This means we must speculate somewhat, based on how well the attachment literature generalizes across individual and relationship contexts. If the gender-inverted patterns for attachment traits/styles that we identified earlier (Ridge & Feeney, 1998) are robust, then gay men may be more likely to experience infidelity stemming from attachment anxiety, which can foment a fear of abandonment. By contrast, lesbian women may be more likely to experience infidelity stemming attachment avoidance, which can motivate emotional distancing. Given some evidence that infidelity is linked with higher attachment anxiety and lower attachment avoidance (see Fish et al., 2012), this may be the psychological mechanism that explains why gay men appear to engage in infidelity more than lesbian women. Still, gender differences in attachment traits are small in magnitude, so even if these associations are robust, they would not likely reveal a taxonomic difference between sexual minority men and women. Future research probing these variables would help us better understand the attachment-relevant experiences that nonheterosexuals have when they engage in infidelity.

As with the generalized personality traits discussed above, attachment variables also predict experiences with consensual nonmonogamy (CNM). In this case, however, attitudes seem to diverge from behavioral experiences with CNM. Within self-identified monogamous, heterosexual individuals, avoidant attachment predicts more positive attitudes toward CNM (e.g., "If my partner wanted to be nonmonogamous, I would be open to that"), while anxious attachment predicted more negative attitudes toward CNM (Moors et al., 2015). However, when comparing respondents who reported being monogamous versus engaging in CNM, the CNM practitioners were significantly *lower* in attachment avoidance relative to their monogamous counterparts, while no differences were observed with respect to attachment anxiety (Moors et al., 2015). Although it may be tempting assume that attachment styles should predict behavioral engagement with CNM in ways that line up with attitudinal reports, there are also theoretical reasons to expect attitudes and behaviors to diverge. Attachment styles are not perfectly stable over time and may change, for example, in response to ending a relationship or starting a new one (e.g., Kirkpatrick & Hazan, 1994). Persons who engage in CNM are likely to have more relationships over the course of their lives than monogamous persons, which creates more opportunities for change. One possible outcome is that perhaps people become less avoidant over time as a function of practicing CNM. It is therefore difficult to draw firm conclusions about whether attachment styles predict engagement in monogamous versus CNM relationships from cross-sectional data due to the possibility of CNM affecting attachment stability, which points to the need for longitudinal research in this area.

Separately, results from dyadic research examining attachment and monogamy in same-sex couples revealed that those couples who identified as nonmonogamous reported relationship health (e.g., satisfaction, trust, commitment) that was just as high as it was for monogamous couples, except when attachment anxiety was high—in that case, relationship health was lower for the nonmonogamous couples (Mohr et al., 2013). Perhaps this is due, in part, to the fact that insecure attachment is linked with sexual minority stress; however, a likelier explanation is that suboptimal relationship behaviors are more prevalent in insecure partners. Insecurity poses potential problems in any relationship, regardless of whether that relationship is monogamous or nonmonogamous. However, to the extent that someone who is anxiously attached enters a CNM relationship specifically as a hedge against their fear of abandonment and this is coupled with suboptimal relationship behaviors across multiple partners, the end result may be difficulty finding the level of trust and commitment they need to soothe that fear.

Subsequent research has found that people's relationship-specific attachment traits correlate across partners in CNM relationships. Put another way, when individuals are more anxious or avoidant with one partner, they also have higher anxiety/avoidance with their concurrent partners (Moors et al., 2019), a finding that has been replicated (Muise et al., 2019). It is also notable that attachment insecurity with one partner was not associated with the relationship quality (e.g., satisfaction) with concurrent partners (Moors et al., 2019). Other findings suggest that as sexual satisfaction increases with one partner, relationship satisfaction increases with concurrent partners (Muise et al., 2019). This remained while controlling for attachment style and sexual orientation, meaning that attachment traits for both heterosexual and nonheterosexual relationships predict relationship outcomes in consensually nonmonogamous relationships in similar ways.

In summary, the pattern of results suggests that secure attachment is linked with more optimal outcomes in nonmonogamous relationships (just as they are in monogamous ones), and these results likely generalize across sexual orientation, although evidence is limited to only a handful of studies. A major strength of this (albeit small) literature is that it has shed light on the dyadic and interrelational effects of attachment variables, something relatively neglected in the literature on infidelity. On the other hand, most of the research in this area is relatively recent, and we lack long-term investigations of attachment and interrelational functioning in consensually nonmonogamous relationships.

Felt Experiences with a Partner's Infidelity: Differences in Heterosexual and Nonheterosexual Relationships

There has been a fruitful academic inquiry into the felt experience of infidelity-related distress. Beginning with a seminal study purporting to show differences between women's and men's distress at the thought of their partners' infidelity (Buss et al., 1992), this has been the subject of much debate and dissention. Some studies have shown a consistent pattern, such that women are more likely than men to respond with more distress at the thought of their partners' emotional infidelity (i.e., falling in love with a different person) compared to a sexual infidelity. By contrast, men are more likely than women to respond with distress at their partners' sexual infidelity compared to an emotional infidelity. These researchers posit that these gender-typed psychological and physiological reactions are the result of sexual strategies designed by evolution to enhance mating success. However, this theoretical reasoning has been challenged, along with methodological critiques and mixed findings, which are beyond the scope of coverage in this chapter (see Carpenter, 2012; Edlund & Sagarin, 2017; Harris, 2003; Sagarin et al.2012 for summaries).

Some findings suggest that when nonheterosexual participants are asked to report on their infidelity-related distress on a forced-choice survey item, the same pattern emerges as it does for heterosexuals (Harris, 2002). That is, gay men are more likely than lesbian women to report sexual infidelity as more distressing. However, for most people, regardless of gender or sexual orientation, emotional infidelity arouses more distress in real and imagined scenarios (Harris, 2002). In addition, while gay and lesbian participants seem somewhat less bothered by various types of infidelities than do heterosexual participants, their responses are more similar than they are different (Dijkstra et al., 2013).

However, other patterns have emerged in different studies. For example, one analysis found that gay men, lesbian women, and heterosexual women all reported emotional infidelity as more distressing, while heterosexual men were the one group to report sexual infidelity as more distressing (Sheets & Wolfe, 2001). Further analyses reveal a gender-inversion pattern, such that gay men (like heterosexual women) were more likely to report emotional infidelity as more distressing, while lesbian women (like heterosexual men) were more likely to report sexual infidelity as more distressing (Dijkstra et al., 2001). This finding also emerged for continuous measures of infidelity distress (de Souza et al.,

2006). Notably, this pattern is consistent with some findings on attachment traits discussed earlier (Ridge & Feeney, 1998). However, some studies have found null gender differences among gay, lesbian, and bisexual individuals, with gender effects only emerging for heterosexuals (Frederick & Fales, 2016). Consistent with this idea, research on bisexual individuals has found that the traditional gender effect only emerges for relationships between men and women, whereas when bisexuals have same-gender relationships, the effect disappears (Scherer et al., 2013).

Numerous other studies have investigated infidelity distress in the context of nonheterosexual affairs. Here, again, the findings are quite mixed. Both men and women express less distress at the thought of their partner having a same-gender affair, relative to a different-gender affair (Denes et al., 2015), and the felt distress after a partner's same-gender affair varies more as a function of other factors such as blameworthiness and intentionality (Denes et al., 2020). Men are especially tolerant toward their partners' same-gender infidelities, and this effect emerges across cultures (Wang & Apostolou, 2019). Men may be more willing to continue a relationship with a female partner if she has an affair with another woman, in contrast to women who are less likely to report wanting to continue the relationship even if their male partner's affair was with another man (Confer & Cloud, 2011). Other studies have similarly found the difference in distress between men and women for emotional and sexual affairs disappears when the affair is with a same-gender partner (Sagarin et al., 2003).

Why would people (especially men) be more accepting of their partners' same-gender affairs? Given that homosexuality is more stigmatized than heterosexuality, a sociocultural framework would lead us to expect that people would likely be *more*, not less upset if their partners had same-gender affairs—and, indeed, the felt distress about a partner's same-gender affair seems to be driven, in part, by negative attitudes toward homosexuality (Brewer, 2014). By contrast, evolutionary theory would suggest that people would be less threatened if their partners' affairs carry a lower risk of reproductive disadvantages. This is bolstered by men and women reporting less distress at the thought of their partners' sexual affairs with same-gender partners, which would not result in offspring (Apostolou, 2018), and the fact that parents'/siblings' reactions also depend on the type of infidelity and gender of the affair partner, rather than the participants' gender (Apostolou, 2016; Hellstrand & Chrysochoou, 2015). In sum, while some scholars have used the findings for nonheterosexual infidelities to challenge theoretical assumptions and generalizability of evolutionary perspectives, the truth is that the existing data may support both the sociocultural and evolutionary perspectives. However, the results from these studies are quite mixed, and a notable limitation from most methodologies is that they involve imagined experiences of infidelity.

We also recognize the long-standing debate about this line of research, with dramatically different conclusions across ideologically different subfields (Edlund & Sagarin, 2017). While different subfields may consider the debate resolved (but in different directions and for different reasons), we encourage more research into the experience of infidelity distress. This fruitful line of inquiry can help illuminate the emotional and cognitive experiences people have about relational issues of importance to them, including the morals and ethics of nonmonogamy, which receives great emphasis in couples and cultures all over the world.

In contrast to romantic jealousy, the idea of *compersion* has gained attention as it occurs particularly within consensually nonmonogamous relationships. Jealousy is regarded as a negative affective state that stems from perceived threat to a relational bond (e.g., the thought of a partner engaging sexually or emotionally with someone else). Compersion can occur within the same context, but is experienced as a positive affective state in which people believe that their partners are happily involved with someone else. What could otherwise be experienced negatively by monogamous couples may be experienced joyfully within a consensually nonmonogamous context, in part because the extradyadic relationship is consensual and mutually agreed-on (Barker & Langdridge, 2010; Ritchie & Barker, 2006). While the experiences of extradyadic engagement are certainly different across monogamous and consensually nonmonogamous contexts, research on compersion could further illuminate the experience of jealousy and infidelity. It may be the case for some couples that jealousy and compersion are not emotional "opposites." Rather, people have the potential to feel jealousy and compersion in their relationships, and whether one or the other occurs depends on factors such as open communication and agreed-on boundaries.

While only a small number of empirical studies to date have examined compersion (Aumer et al., 2014; Mogilski et al., 2019), it appears that even people who are monogamous have the potential to feel compersion while imagining their partners engaging in infidelity, although the type of infidelity and gender play a role. For instance, monogamous men were more likely to report feeling pleasure at the thought of their female partners' emotional infidelity, and the inverse was true for monogamous women, a pattern which mimics the traditional gender effect described above (Mogilski et al., 2019).

Future Directions

In this chapter, we have reviewed the literature on the nature of infidelity (and, to a lesser degree, consensual nonmonogamy) in nonheterosexual relationships. As our review makes clear, there is much work to be done to increase our understanding in this area. In this section, we identify several important directions for future research on this topic.

One of the most important future directions is for researchers to commit to decoupling nonconsensual from consensual nonmonogamy when assessing prevalence of infidelity. Most studies appear to have conflated these things, which has resulted in numerous missed opportunities to establish population prevalence. Survey questions that simply ask whether people have had sex with anyone other than their spouse or primary partner are insufficient and must be more clearly worded to capture the nuances of different relationship behaviors and structures. While researchers often find themselves under pressure to limit number of questions asked on large surveys for the sake of efficiency and/or to enhance completion rates, it is theoretically possible to capture experiences with consensual and nonconsensual nonmonogamy in the span of just one carefully worded question. For example:

> *Monogamy refers to a type of relationship where both people have agreed to engage in intimacy and sexual activities only with each other and no one else. Consensual nonmonogamy refers to a type of relationship where people have agreed that intimacy and sexual activities are permitted with multiple partners. Which statement below best describes your current relationship?*
>
> 1. *We are practicing monogamy and neither of us has broken our agreement or rules.*
> 2. *We are practicing monogamy, but one or both of us have broken our agreement or rules at some point.*
> 3. *We are practicing consensual nonmonogamy and neither of us has broken our agreement or rules.*
> 4. *We are practicing consensual nonmonogamy, but one or both of us have broken our agreement or rules at some point.*

The above question is just one possibility and it could be revised, reworded, or expanded in various ways depending on one's research aims or goals. However, we believe that questions like this are useful because they clearly distinguish monogamous from consensually nonmonogamous relationships, while also capturing experiences with infidelity in each. An alternative approach would be to simplify the question to capture monogamy versus consensual nonmonogamy, while offering a follow-up question to inquire about whether agreements have been broken and by whom. Additional follow-up questions could potentially be added to inquire about the nature of broken agreements, or about the structure of those relationships that are consensually nonmonogamous (e.g., polyamory vs. swinging vs. open relationships). Whether researchers use the exact sample question we provided or not, we hope that they will think more carefully about the way they assess nonmonogamous practices in future research so as to yield more nuance and capture diverse relationship structures in heterosexual and nonheterosexual populations alike.

Another important direction for future research on infidelity is to incorporate more studies of couples (and especially nonheterosexual couples) and to take a longitudinal approach. Many studies to date have allowed individuals and couples to decide for themselves whether infidelity occurred, and research concurrently addresses other variables such as personality traits or dyadic variables that help illuminate the experience of infidelity. However, this picture is obscured by the fact that so many couples disagree about the specific monogamous boundaries in their own relationships, as well as whether or not there was in fact an infidelity at all (Warren et al., 2012). This would likely be a fruitful avenue for future research to uncover what infidelity experiences look like when there is (and is not) agreement within couples about those details. Perhaps there are physical or emotional differences across levels of agreement. We also lack knowledge about the ongoing processes (from a longitudinal perspective) on how couples navigate experiences of infidelity when there is such disagreement, and the ways in which those experiences predict long-term relationship outcomes. We have some evidence about personality traits such as attachment style and sociosexuality, among others, predicting the likelihood of defining ambiguous or "gray area" behaviors as constituting infidelity or moral violations (Selterman & Koleva, 2015; Wilson et al., 2011). These traits may moderate or amplify the ongoing, dyadic infidelity experiences in couples.

The extant research has also presented a set of paradoxical findings with regard to infidelity and consensual nonmonogamy. Functionally and behaviorally, these are quite distinct, especially in terms of increased and detailed communication within consensually nonmonogamous couples, and a different set of moral norms within communities of nonmonogamous people compared to the majority population. However, as we noted earlier, many of the same variables (e.g., Big Five traits) are linked with tendencies toward both infidelity and consensual nonmonogamy. This presents an intriguing puzzle for future research to sort out. Perhaps there exist other individual, dyadic, or cultural variables that clearly differentiate the two. Similarly, future research can disentangle how heterosexual and nonheterosexual couples make decisions about navigating monogamy violations. While some research has investigated how couples overcome infidelity violations in monogamous couples, there is less research on how couples overcome violations in consensually nonmonogamous couples, as well as research that compares and contrasts how couples with these differing monogamy agreements deal with violations. Overall, more studies that compare and contrast different arrangements on the monogamy continuum will help illuminate how people can communicate effectively and solve problems in their relationships. Such work will have important clinical implications in terms of helping therapists assist clients of different sexual orientations who may be coping with infidelity, as well as those who are attempting to navigate consensually nonmonogamous relationships or are seeking to delineate relationship boundaries.

Summary and Conclusions

Infidelity is one of the most statistically robust and strongest predictors of relational distress, poor dyadic health, relationship dissolution/divorce, and even violence. If scientists wish to understand what constitutes healthy (and unhealthy) relationships, we must seek a deeper understanding of the ways in which people navigate and negotiate monogamy. Research on infidelity in sexual minority populations is crucial to this understanding. Nationally representative US surveys find that sexual minorities constitute as much as 7% of the population (Herbenick et al., 2010), yet they are conspicuously absent from much research on cheating and infidelity.

Notably, there are important similarities in terms of the way that infidelity is experienced across persons of varying sexual orientations. Nonheterosexual people, much like their heterosexual counterparts, are driven to infidelity for a variety of reasons, including psychological traits and dyadic variables. Sometimes people cheat because they are unsatisfied with their partners, looking for excitement, or trying to cope with underlying insecurities. At the same time, however, there may be some differences in the specific factors that prompt infidelity most often for persons of different orientations, given that some average differences exist in personality traits, attachment styles, and social norms. Similarities and differences aside, across sexual orientations, infidelity is perhaps best understood as a biopsychosocial phenomenon.

In addition, it is worth noting that the experience of infidelity distress appears to be very similar across persons of differing sexualities. In this light, infidelity in nonheterosexuals appears to be just like infidelity in heterosexuals, even taking into account some limited evidence for gender-inverted tendencies in gay men and lesbian women.

Of course, we must again highlight that attitudes toward infidelity, as well as attitudes toward consensual nonmonogamy, are less negative and more positive (respectively) in sexual minorities compared to heterosexuals. This is, in part, due to subcultures of sexual minority groups adopting different moral codes and standards for gender and sexuality that subvert the norms of the majority population. Because of this, the experience of nonmonogamy (consensual or otherwise) can therefore present itself differently among nonheterosexual persons. One could potentially make the argument that nonheterosexual couples have stronger socioemotional tools with which to handle monogamy violations given these subcultural normative trends.

Research on nonheterosexuals has revealed that monogamy is a nuanced phenomenon, with many elusive and inconsistent aspects. Monogamy (and violations of monogamy) may exist on a continuum. Yet scientists often treat monogamy violations as unequivocally immoral if they are linked with negative relational outcomes at all. As scientists, we must look to our own sociocultural biases in order to improve our analytic methods.

Returning to the quote from Dan Savage at the beginning of the chapter, we suggest that just as people often treat monogamy violations as a corrupting phenomenon to be avoided at all costs, the scientific community may also have unknowingly adopted a similarly moralistic view, as evidenced by the consistent conflation of consensual and nonconsensual nonmonogamy throughout much of the literature. However, the experience of infidelity in nonheterosexual contexts can help revise and correct this type of thinking. In light of this, we suggest reframing the study of infidelity as a stressor—one that may result in negative or positive outcomes for people, depending on a wide range of interpersonal and intrapersonal variables. Health psychologists have long known that stress has the potential to motivate both positive and negative effects, as exemplified in the constructs of *eustress* and *distress*, respectively (e.g., Loving & Wright, 2012). While infidelity may be unpleasant for many, it may not necessarily always be disastrous and distressing—and for some, infidelity may ultimately bear some positive consequences.

References

Ainsworth, M. D. S., Blehar, M. C., Waters, E., & Wall, S. (1978). *Patterns of attachment: A psychological study of the strange situation*. Erlbaum.

Allen, E. S., & Baucom, D. H. (2004). Adult attachment and patterns of extradyadic involvement. *Family Process, 43*(4), 467–488.

Apostolou, M. (2016). The evolution of same-sex attractions: Parental and intimate partners' reactions to deviations from exclusive heterosexual orientation. *Personality and Individual Differences, 101*, 380–389.

Apostolou, M. (2018). The evolution of same-sex attraction in women. *Journal of Individual Differences, 40*(2).

Atkins, D. C., Baucom, D. H., & Jacobson, N. S. (2001). Understanding infidelity: Correlates in a national random sample. *Journal of Family Psychology, 15*(4), 735–749.

Aumer, K., Bellew, W., Ito, B., Hatfield, E., & Heck, R. (2014). The happy green eyed monogamist: Role of jealousy and compersion in monogamous and non-traditional relationships. *Electronic Journal of Human Sexuality, 17*(1), 77–88.

Bailey, J. M., Vasey, P. L., Diamond, L. M., Breedlove, S. M., Vilain, E., & Epprecht, M. (2016). Sexual orientation, controversy, and science. *Psychological Science in the Public Interest, 17*(2), 45–101.

Barker, M., & Langdridge, D. (2010). Whatever happened to non-monogamies? Critical reflections on recent research and theory. *Sexualities, 13*(6), 748–772.

Birnbaum, G. E. (2015). On the convergence of sexual urges and emotional bonds: The interplay of the sexual and attachment systems during relationship development. In J. A. Simpson, W. S. Rholes, J. A. Simpson, & W. S. Rholes (Eds.), *Attachment theory and research: New directions and emerging themes* (pp. 170–194). Guilford Press.

Birnbaum, G. E., & Reis, H. T. (2018). Evolved to be connected: The dynamics of attachment and sex over the course of romantic relationships. *Current Opinion in Psychology, 25*, 11–15.

Blumstein, P., & Schwartz, P. (1983). *American couples*. Morrow.

Bouchard, T. J., Jr., & McGue, M. (2003). Genetic and environmental influences on human psychological differences. *Journal of Neurobiology, 54*(1), 4–45.

Brewer, G. (2014). Heterosexual and homosexual infidelity: The importance of attitudes towards homosexuality. *Personality and Individual Differences, 64*, 98–100.

Buss, D. M., Larsen, R. J., Westen, D., & Semmelroth, J. (1992). Sex differences in jealousy: Evolution, physiology, and psychology. *Psychological Science, 3*(4), 251–256.

Buss, D. M., & Schmitt, D. P. (1993). Sexual strategies theory: An evolutionary perspective on human mating. *Psychological Review, 100*(2), 204–232.

Butler, M. H., Harper, J. M., & Seedall, R. B. (2009). Facilitated disclosure versus clinical accommodation of infidelity secrets: An early pivot point in couple therapy. Part 1: Couple relationship ethics, pragmatics, and attachment. *Journal of Marital and Family Therapy, 35*(1), 125–143.

Carpenter, C. J. (2012). Meta-analyses of sex differences in responses to sexual versus emotional infidelity: Men and women are more similar than different. *Psychology of Women Quarterly, 36*(1), 25–37.

Cialdini, R. B., Reno, R. R., & Kallgren, C. A. (1990). A focus theory of normative conduct: Recycling the concept of norms to reduce littering in public places. *Journal of Personality and Social Psychology, 58*(6), 1015–1026.

Clark, R. D., & Hatfield, E. (1989). Gender differences in receptivity to sexual offers. *Journal of Psychology & Human Sexuality, 2*(1), 39–55.

Confer, J. C., & Cloud, M. D. (2011). Sex differences in response to imagining a partner's heterosexual or homosexual affair. *Personality and Individual Differences, 50*(2), 129–134.

Denes, A., Dillow, M. R., DelGreco, M., Lannutti, P. J., & Bevan, J. L. (2020). Forgive and forget? Examining the influence of blame and intentionality on forgiveness following hypothetical same-sex infidelity in the context of heterosexual romantic relationships. *Journal of Sex Research, 57*(4), 482–497.

Denes, A., Lannutti, P. J., & Bevan, J. L. (2015). Same-sex infidelity in heterosexual romantic relationships: Investigating emotional, relational, and communicative responses. *Personal Relationships, 22*(3), 414–430.

de Souza, A. A. L., Verderane, M. P., Taira, J. T., & Otta, E. (2006). Emotional and sexual jealousy as a function of sex and sexual orientation in a Brazilian sample. *Psychological Reports, 98*(2), 529–535.

DeWall, C. N., Lambert, N. M., Slotter, E. B., Pond, R. S., Jr., Deckman, T., Finkel, E. J., . . . Fincham, F. D. (2011). So far away from one's partner, yet so close to romantic alternatives: Avoidant attachment, interest in alternatives, and infidelity. *Journal of Personality and Social Psychology*, *101*(6), 1302.

Dijkstra, P., Barelds, D. P., & Groothof, H. A. (2013). Jealousy in response to online and offline infidelity: The role of sex and sexual orientation. *Scandinavian Journal of Psychology*, *54*(4), 328–336.

Dijkstra, P., Groothof, H. A., Poel, G. A., Laverman, E. T., Schrier, M., & Buunk, B. P. (2001). Sex differences in the events that elicit jealousy among homosexuals. *Personal Relationships*, *8*(1), 41–54.

Edlund, J. E., & Sagarin, B. J. (2017). Sex differences in jealousy: A 25-year retrospective. In J. Olson (Ed.) *Advances in experimental social psychology* (Vol. 55, pp. 259–302). Academic Press.

Feeney, B. C. (2004). A secure base: Responsive support of goal strivings and exploration in adult intimate relationships. *Journal of Personality and Social Psychology*, *87*(5), 631–648. https://doi.org/10.1037/0022-3514.87.5.631.

Feeney, B. C. (2007). The dependency paradox in close relationships: Accepting dependence promotes independence. *Journal of Personality and Social Psychology*, *92*, 268–285.

Feeney, B. C., & Collins, N. L. (2015). A new look at social support: A theoretical perspective on thriving through relationships. *Personality and Social Psychology Review*, *19*(2), 113–147.

Feeney, B. C., Collins, N. L., Van Vleet, M., & Tomlinson, J. M. (2013). Motivations for providing a secure base: Links with attachment orientation and secure base support behavior. *Attachment & Human Development*, *15*(3), 261–280.

Fish, J. N., Pavkov, T. W., Wetchler, J. L., & Bercik, J. (2012). Characteristics of those who participate in infidelity: The role of adult attachment and differentiation in extradyadic experiences. *American Journal of Family Therapy*, *40*(3), 214–229.

Fraley, R. C. (2019). Attachment in adulthood: Recent developments, emerging debates, and future directions. *Annual Review of Psychology*, *70*, 401–422.

Fraley, C. R., Niedenthal, P. M., Marks, M., Brumbaugh, C., & Vicary, A. (2006). Adult attachment and the perception of emotional expressions: Probing the hyperactivating strategies underlying anxious attachment. *Journal of Personality*, *74*(4), 1163–1190.

Frederick, D. A., & Fales, M. R. (2016). Upset over sexual versus emotional infidelity among gay, lesbian, bisexual, and heterosexual adults. *Archives of Sexual Behavior*, *45*(1), 175–191.

Gaither, G. A., & Sellbom, M. (2003). The sexual sensation seeking scale: Reliability and validity within a heterosexual college student sample. *Journal of Personality Assessment*, *81*(2), 157–167.

Brenan, M. (2021, June 11). Changing one's gender is sharply contentious moral issue. *Gallup*. https://news.gallup.com/poll/351020/changing-one-gender-sharply-contentious-moral-issue.aspx

Harris, C. R. (2002). Sexual and romantic jealousy in heterosexual and homosexual adults. *Psychological Science*, *13*, 7–12.

Harris, C. R. (2003). A review of sex differences in sexual jealousy, including self-report data, psychophysiological responses, interpersonal violence, and morbid jealousy. *Personality and Social Psychology Review*, *7*, 102–128.

Haversath, J., & Kröger, C. (2014). Extradyadic sex and its predictors in homo-and heterosexuals. *Psychotherapie, Psychosomatik, Medizinische Psychologie*, *64*(12), 458–464.

Hellstrand, D., & Chrysochoou, E. (2015). Upset in response to a sibling's partner's infidelity: A study with siblings of gays and lesbians, from an evolutionary perspective. *Evolutionary Psychology*, *13*(3), 1474704915598491.

Herbenick, D., Reece, M., Schick, V., Sanders, S. A., Dodge, B., & Fortenberry, J. D. (2010). Sexual behavior in the United States: Results from a national probability sample of men and women ages 14–94. *Journal of Sexual Medicine*, *7*(Suppl. 5), 255–265. https://doi.org/10.1111/j.1743-6109.2010.02012.x

Hoff, C. C., & Beougher, S. C. (2010). Sexual agreements among gay male couples. *Archives of Sexual Behavior*, *39*(3), 774–787.

Ifrah, K., Shenkman, G., & Shmotkin, D. (2018). How does sexual orientation relate to openness to experience in adulthood. *Personality and Individual Differences*, *131*, 164–173.

Jang, K. L., Livesley, W. J., & Vernon, P. A. (1996). Heritability of the Big Five personality dimensions and their facets: A twin study. *Journal of Personality*, *64*(3), 577–592.

Kalichman, S. C., & Rompa, D. (1995). Sexual sensation seeking and sexual compulsivity scales: Validity, and predicting HIV risk behavior. *Journal of Personality Assessment*, *65*(3), 586–601.

Kirkpatrick, L. A., & Hazan, C. (1994). Attachment styles and close relationships: A four-year prospective study. *Personal Relationships, 1*(2), 123–142.

Lalasz, C. B., & Weigel, D. J. (2011). Understanding the relationship between gender and extradyadic relations: The mediating role of sensation seeking on intentions to engage in sexual infidelity. *Personality and Individual Differences, 50*(7), 1079–1083.

LaSala, M. C. (2004). Extradyadic sex and gay male couples: Comparing monogamous and nonmonogamous relationships. *Families in Society, 85*(3), 405–412.

Levine, E. C., Herbenick, D., Martinez, O., Fu, T. C., & Dodge, B. (2018). Open relationships, nonconsensual nonmonogamy, and monogamy among US adults: Findings from the 2012 National Survey of Sexual Health and Behavior. *Archives of Sexual Behavior, 47*(5), 1439–1450.

Levy, K. N., & Kelly, K. M. (2010). Sex differences in jealousy: A contribution from attachment theory. *Psychological Science, 21*(2), 168–173.

Lippa, R. A. (2005). Sexual orientation and personality. *Annual Review of Sex Research, 16*(1), 119–153.

Lippa, R. A. (2009). Sex differences in sex drive, sociosexuality, and height across 53 nations: Testing evolutionary and social structural theories. *Archives of Sexual Behavior, 38*(5), 631–651.

Lippa, R., & Arad, S. (1997). The structure of sexual orientation and its relation to masculinity, femininity, and gender diagnosticity: Different for men and women. *Sex Roles, 37*(3–4), 187–208.

Loving, T. J., & Wright, B. L. (2012). Eustress in romantic relationships. In L. Campbell, J. G. La Guardia, J. M. Olson, & M. P. Zanna (Eds.), *The Ontario symposium on personality and social psychology: Vol. 12. The science of the couple* (p0. 169–184). Psychology Press.

McAnulty, R. D., & Brineman, J. M. (2007). Infidelity in dating relationships. *Annual Review of Sex Research, 18*(1), 94–114.

Mikulincer, M., & Shaver, P. R. (2003). The attachment behavioral system in adulthood: Activation, psychodynamics, and interpersonal processes. In M. P. Zanna (Ed.), *Advances in Experimental Social Psychology, 35,* 53–152. Elsevier Academic Press.

Mikulincer, M., & Shaver, P. R. (2007). *Attachment in adulthood: Structure, dynamics, and change.* Guilford Press.

Mogilski, J. K., Reeve, S. D., Nicolas, S. C., Donaldson, S. H., Mitchell, V. E., & Welling, L. L. (2019). Jealousy, consent, and compersion within monogamous and consensually non-monogamous romantic relationships. *Archives of Sexual Behavior, 48*(6), 1811–1828.

Mohr, J. J., Selterman, D., & Fassinger, R. E. (2013). Romantic attachment and relationship functioning in same-sex couples. *Journal of Counseling Psychology, 60*(1), 72.

Moors, A. C., Conley, T. D., Edelstein, R. S., & Chopik, W. J. (2015). Attached to monogamy? Avoidance predicts willingness to engage (but not actual engagement) in consensual non-monogamy. *Journal of Social and Personal Relationships, 32*(2), 222–240.

Moors, A. C., Matsick, J. L., & Schechinger, H. A. (2017). Unique and shared relationship benefits of consensually non-monogamous and monogamous relationships. *European Psychologist, 22*(1).

Moors, A. C., Rubin, J. D., Matsick, J. L., Ziegler, A., & Conley, T. D. (2014). It's not just a gay male thing: Sexual minority women and men are equally attracted to consensual non-monogamy. *Journal für Psychologie, 22,* 38–51.

Moors, A. C., Ryan, W., & Chopik, W. J. (2019). Multiple loves: The effects of attachment with multiple concurrent romantic partners on relational functioning. *Personality and Individual Differences, 147,* 102–110.

Moors, A. C., Selterman, D. F., & Conley, T. D. (2017). Personality correlates of desire to engage in consensual non-monogamy among lesbian, gay, and bisexual individuals. *Journal of Bisexuality, 17*(4), 418–434.

Muise, A., Laughton, A. K., Moors, A., & Impett, E. A. (2019). Sexual need fulfillment and satisfaction in consensually nonmonogamous relationships. *Journal of Social and Personal Relationships, 36*(7), 1917–1938.

O'Neil, J. M. (2008). Summarizing 25 years of research on men's gender role conflict using the Gender Role Conflict Scale: New research paradigms and clinical implications. *Counseling Psychologist, 36*(3), 358–445.

Parker, M. L., & Campbell, K. (2017). Infidelity and attachment: The moderating role of race/ethnicity. *Contemporary Family Therapy, 39*(3), 172–183.

Perel, E. (2017). *The state of affairs: Rethinking infidelity; A book for anyone who has ever loved.* Hachette.

Prestage, G., Mao, L., McGuigan, D., Crawford, J., Kippax, S., Kaldor, J., & Grulich, A. E. (2006). HIV risk and communication between regular partners in a cohort of HIV-negative gay men. *AIDS Care, 18*(2), 166–172.

Ridge, S. R., & Feeney, J. A. (1998). Relationship history and relationship attitudes in gay males and lesbians: Attachment style and gender differences. *Australian and New Zealand Journal of Psychiatry, 32*(6), 848–859.

Ritchie, A., & Barker, M. (2006). "There aren't words for what we do or how we feel so we have to make them up": Constructing polyamorous languages in a culture of compulsory monogamy. *Sexualities, 9*(5), 584–601.

Rubel, A. N., & Bogaert, A. F. (2015). Consensual nonmonogamy: Psychological well-being and relationship quality correlates. *Journal of Sex Research, 52*(9), 961–982.

Russell, V. M., Baker, L. R., & McNulty, J. K. (2013). Attachment insecurity and infidelity in marriage: Do studies of dating relationships really inform us about marriage? *Journal of Family Psychology, 27*(2), 242.

Sagarin, B. J., Becker, D. V., Guadagno, R. E., Nicastle, L. D., & Millevoi, A. (2003). Sex differences (and similarities) in jealousy: The moderating influence of infidelity experience and sexual orientation of the infidelity. *Evolution and Human Behavior, 24*(1), 17–23.

Sagarin, B. J., Martin, A. L., Coutinho, S. A., Edlund, J. E., Patel, L., Skowronski, J. J., et al. (2012). Sex differences in jealousy: A meta-analytic examination. *Evolution and Human Behavior, 33*, 595–614.

Schade, L. C., & Sandberg, J. G. (2012). Healing the attachment injury of marital infidelity using emotionally focused couples therapy: A case illustration. *American Journal of Family Therapy, 40*(5), 434–444.

Scherer, C. R., Akers, E. G., & Kolbe, K. L. (2013). Bisexuals and the sex differences in jealousy hypothesis. *Journal of Social and Personal Relationships, 30*(8), 1064–1071.

Schmitt, D. P. (2003). Universal sex differences in the desire for sexual variety: Tests from 52 nations, 6 continents, and 13 islands. *Journal of Personality and Social Psychology, 85*(1), 85–104.

Schmitt, D. P. (2004). The Big Five related to risky sexual behaviour across 10 world regions: Differential personality associations of sexual promiscuity and relationship infidelity. *European Journal of Personality, 18*(4), 301–319.

Schmitt, D. P., & Shackelford, T. K. (2008). Big Five traits related to short-term mating: From personality to promiscuity across 46 nations. *Evolutionary Psychology, 6*(2), 147470490800600204.

Selterman, D., Garcia, J. R., & Tsapelas, I. (2019). Motivations for extradyadic infidelity revisited. *Journal of Sex Research, 56*(3), 273–286.

Selterman, D., Gesselman, A. N., & Moors, A. C. (2019). Sexuality through the lens of secure base dynamics: Individual differences in Sexploration. *Personality and Individual Differences, 147*, 229–236.

Selterman, D., & Koleva, S. (2015). Moral judgment of close relationship behaviors. *Journal of Social and Personal Relationships, 32*(7), 922–945.

Sheets, V. L., & Wolfe, M. D. (2001). Sexual jealousy in heterosexuals, lesbians, and gays. *Sex Roles, 44*(5–6), 255–276.

Solomon, S. E., Rothblum, E. D., & Balsam, K. F. (2005). Money, housework, sex, and conflict: Same-sex couples in civil unions, those not in civil unions, and heterosexual married siblings. *Sex Roles, 52*(9–10), 561–575.

Stief, M. C., Rieger, G., & Savin-Williams, R. C. (2014). Bisexuality is associated with elevated sexual sensation seeking, sexual curiosity, and sexual excitability. *Personality and Individual Differences, 66*, 193–198.

Tagler, M. J., & Gentry, R. H. (2011). Gender, jealousy, and attachment: A (more) thorough examination across measures and samples. *Journal of Research in Personality, 45*(6), 697–701.

Thompson, A. P. (1983). Extramarital sex: A review of the research literature. *Journal of Sex Research, 19*(1), 1–22.

Treger, S., & Sprecher, S. (2011). The influences of sociosexuality and attachment style on reactions to emotional versus sexual infidelity. *Journal of Sex Research, 48*(5), 413–422.

Tsapelas, I., Fisher, H. E., & Aron, A. (2011). Infidelity: When, where, why. In W. R. Cupach & B. H. Spitzberg (Eds.), *The Dark Side of Close Relationships II* (pp. 175–195). Routledge/Taylor & Francis Group.

Wang, Y., & Apostolou, M. (2019). Male tolerance to same-sex infidelity: A cross-cultural investigation. *Evolutionary Psychology, 17*(2), 1474704919843892.

Warren, J. T., Harvey, S. M., & Agnew, C. R. (2012). One love: Explicit monogamy agreements among heterosexual young adult couples at increased risk of sexually transmitted infections. *Journal of Sex Research, 49*(2-3), 282–289.

Zuckerman, M. (1979). Sensation seeking and risk taking. In *Emotions in personality and psychopathology* (pp. 161–197). Springer, Boston, MA.

Zuckerman, M. (2007). *Sensation seeking and risky behavior*. American Psychological Association.

PART 3

Consequences of Infidelity

CHAPTER 18

Relationship Dissolution Following Infidelity

Caroline E. Shanholtz *and* David A. Sbarra

Abstract

Although marital infidelity is often cited as a primary reason for divorce, it does not always signify the end of a relationship. Many researchers and clinicians have questioned whether an extramarital affair is a symptom of a dysfunctional marriage that is headed for divorce or the proximal cause of the separation. More than half of individuals who have extramarital affairs divorce or separate from their spouse. In the current chapter, we answer the question: In what ways can infidelity shape postdivorce emotional reactions and recovery—that is, trajectories of adjustment over time? There are two identified factors that inhibit postdivorce adjustment: attachment-related emotion regulation and emotional suppression. Further, the mechanisms driving postdivorce adjustment, self-concept clarity and narrative coherence, are discussed in the context of how infidelity can be interpreted as a humiliating event and predict poorer postdivorce adjustment. When infidelity occurs and divorce follows, if infidelity is interpreted as a humiliating event, or if it is experienced as a targeted rejection to one's sense of self, these predict poorer divorce adjustment and depression. Suggestions for future research in this area are discussed.

Key Words: marital separation, divorce, infidelity, divorce adjustment, emotion regulation, narrative

Although marital infidelity is often cited as a primary reason for divorce (Amato & Previti, 2003; Kitson et al., 1985), it does not always signify the end of a relationship. Some couples can repair and even improve their relationship following an affair; for other couples, infidelity is either the proximal cause of relationship dissolution or a manifestation of the corrosive relationship processes that set a couple on a trajectory toward this endpoint. In this chapter, we argue that in order to provide the necessary care and services to couples coping with an affair, it is important to understand the broad literature on infidelity and divorce. Are affairs a marker of underlying distress or the causal agents of a relationship's demise? And, how does infidelity impact postdivorce adjustment?

Prevalence and Demographics

Each year, approximately 2%–4% of spouses engage in relationship infidelity (Choi et al., 1994; Whisman et al., 2007), although the prevalence of extramarital affairs over the course of a lifetime ranges from 20% to 25% of all marriages (Wiederman, 1997). Given that the majority of Americans disapprove of infidelity (90% reported that infidelity was "immoral"; Negash et al., 2014), it raises the question of how infidelity impacts both an individual and the couple.

Demographics are such that rates of infidelity are higher among African Americans and Hispanics than Caucasians (Amato & Rogers, 1997; Greeley, 1994; Wiederman, 1997); however, the rates of divorce following infidelity for individuals of these ethnicities are similar to Caucasian couples. Further, those with narcissistic personality traits and those who have a more insecure attachment style are more likely to have an affair (Fincham & May, 2017). Couples who share a religion and are more involved in their religion (attend religious services, engage in prayer focused on partner well-being) are less likely to experience infidelity than couples of different religions (Fincham & May, 2017). Finally, spouses who frequently travel for work and have frequent contact with potential sexual partners are more likely to engage in infidelity than those who do not (Fincham & May, 2017).

Historically, there have been robust findings of gender differences for who perpetrates infidelity (Previti & Amato, 2004; Buss, 1994; Fischer, 1992) in that men had extramarital affairs more often than women. More recent research has indicated that the gender gap is closing and men and women are engaging in infidelity at similar rates (Treas & Giesen, 2000; Whisman et al., 2007). Brand and colleagues (2007) found that women showed a greater likelihood of infidelity if unhappy in their relationship. In terms of ending a marriage after infidelity, some studies have indicated that divorce is more likely if a woman has an affair (Beitzig, 1989) but others have not found gender differences leading to divorce (Spanier & Margolis, 1983).

A Symptom or a Cause?

Many researchers and clinicians have questioned whether an extramarital affair is a symptom of a dysfunctional marriage that is headed for divorce or the proximal cause of the separation, but few studies address this question empirically. Previti and Amato (2004) examined this question in a 17-year longitudinal study. Through collecting data on infidelity, marital happiness, and divorce proneness at three separate time points, this study explored whether infidelity alone increased a couple's likelihood of divorce or if infidelity contributed to marital unhappiness and divorce proneness ultimately leading to divorce. The basic design involved telephone interviews with both husbands and wives from a national sample and measured marital happiness, or how happy an individual was in their marriage, divorce proneness, or the stability of an individual's marriage, and whether an individual had extramarital sex. The results suggested that an extramarital affair played what appeared to be a causal role in a couple's divorce. Affairs were more common in couples with low marital satisfaction, but couples who experienced infidelity—regardless of their marital satisfaction at baseline—evidenced an increase in divorce proneness and a decrease in marital satisfaction post-affair, which was ultimately associated with an increased probability that the relationship would end in divorce.

In many respects, the Previti and Amato (2004) findings are seminal: As a main effect, relationship infidelity appears to increase risk for divorce. There are many cases, of course, where main effects are moderated by important individual differences. Although infidelity may increase the risk for the end of marriage, not all couples who experience extramarital affairs proceed to divorce, and thus it is important to differentiate the cases where infidelity leads to divorce versus cases where couples choose to stay together. Alternatively, Amato and Rogers (1997) found that there were many overlapping factors that predicted both infidelity and divorce, which makes it difficult to determine if infidelity is a causal agent of divorce or simply associated with other factors that lead to divorce.

There are several factors that contribute to the decision to divorce following infidelity. Allen and Atkins (2012) used a large representative community sample in the United States to determine how often couples experience infidelity and, subsequently, divorce. The results indicated that more than half of individuals who have extramarital affairs divorce or separate from their spouse. However, this study only looked at individuals who engaged in infidelity, rather than looking at both the individual committing the infidelity and their partner. Further, this study also only included individuals who had extramarital sex. Among the types of infidelity (emotional, sexual, and emotional/sexual), men are more likely to leave if their partners engage in sexual infidelity and women are more likely to leave after a partner's emotional infidelity (Shackelford et al., 2000). Divorce is the most common among emotional/sexual affairs where the more serious the extramarital relationship, the more imminent the divorce (Shackelford et. al., 2000).

Should I Stay or Should I Go?

What helps couples rebuild their relationship after infidelity? A recent qualitative study explored this question (Abrahamson et al., 2012). Interviews were conducted and analyzed from couples who had experienced infidelity and had remained together for at least 2 years following the discovery of infidelity. A key theme resulting from the narrative coding was that couples found it important to better understand the reason for the affair. Some couples noted that at the time of the affair, there were external stressors such as the death of a family member or work stress. They also indicated that there was opportunity for the affair at the time that they were feeling vulnerable. When determining whether to stay together, motivation was an important factor. Couples who were more motivated to repair their relationship were less likely to divorce after an affair. This motivation may come from the previous investment of time, money, and resources into the relationship, or added life pressures that would make divorce too costly, including becoming a single parent or financial strain.

After the couple decided to stay together, there were several active reconciliation tactics that were used to reunite the couple. First, the couples talked about the process of forgiveness and that once the decision was made to forgive the unfaithful partner, the negative feelings slowly dissipated. Further, the majority of couples in the study engaged in couples counseling and found that having a neutral third party was beneficial in learning new communication skills and processing their feelings. Next, spouses whose partners were unfaithful often found that they had to learn how to manage their memories of discovering the affair to move forward. This often came in the form of learning from others who had dealt with similar infidelity in their own relationship. Finally, couples who stayed together after infidelity found that changing their couple dynamic was critical in changing their relationship for the better. This often meant changing the power dynamic in the relationship and establishing new boundaries. Couples who decided to stay together shared that there was a lot of work put into the relationship following the infidelity (see Abrahamson et al., 2012).

Other research studied whether the method of how an infidelity is revealed or discovered is predictive of divorce. One study found that if the affair is confessed, the likelihood of the couple repairing the relationship increases, but when an unfaithful partner is confronted about the affair, the partners end the relationship approximately 86% of the time (Afifi et al., 2001). If the faithful partner heard about the affair from a third party, divorce occurs 68% of the time, and if the unfaithful partner is caught being unfaithful, 83% of relationships end in divorce (Afifi et al., 2001). Another study revealed that after the affair is known, the faithful partner is more upset by the affair if the primary reason for the affair was relationship dissatisfaction. Conversely, the faithful partner is the least upset if the affair occurred without an obvious reason (e.g., drunken one night stand; Wiederman & Allgeier, 1996).

Other relationship factors that predict divorce from infidelity include if the couple is in the earlier years of marriage (Glass & Wright, 1977) and if the couple was in a high conflict marriage where women are more likely to initiate divorce after infidelity if the husband is unkind (Shackelford & Buss, 1997). Across these relationship factors, divorce is more likely when infidelity is coupled with lower relationship satisfaction (Buunk, 1987).

Infidelity and Divorce Recovery

In this section of the chapter we focus on a relatively nuanced question: In what ways can infidelity shape postdivorce emotional reactions and recovery—that is, trajectories of adjustment over time? We have a reasonable amount of scholarship investigating whether infidelity is a specific and/or a unique predictor of divorce (e.g., Amato & Previti, 2002), and we have a reasonable amount of scholarship investigating specific emotional reactions following infidelity (e.g., Cano & O'Leary, 2000), but despite the prior work cited here, there are few studies of the ways in which infidelity may shape the course of divorce adjustment. Given the relative paucity of work in this area, we borrow from a variety of literatures to outline a model of the key individual differences that may shape the course of adjustment to divorce when an affair is involved.

The end of marriage through divorce is strongly associated with a range of negative outcomes, negative health outcomes and increased risk for early death (Sbarra et al., 2011), financial hardship (Teachman & Paasch, 1994), higher levels of stress (Sbarra et al., 2009), and reduced numbers of friends (Hughes, 1988). Even when accounting for prior mental health problems, divorce exacerbates underlying emotional and mental health problems (Wade & Pevalin, 2004). The majority of research in this area compared divorced to married adults; however, Amato (2000) proposed a model that conceptualizes divorce adjustment as a process that begins well before the decision to end the marriage is made and continues well after the final legal documents are signed. This model posits that postdivorce adjustment is influenced by the magnitude of ongoing stressors, such as prolonged conflict with an ex-spouse or financial strain following divorce. At the same time, these risk processes must be weighed against positive influences—e.g., social support, meaning-making, or having a new romantic partner—that appear to promote recovery. Thus, and most simply, the combination of these stressors and protective factors plays a key role in shaping the course of postdivorce adjustment/recovery.

Building on Amato's divorce-stress-adjustment model (described above), Sbarra and colleagues (2015) argued that although the end of marriage poses an average-level risk for poor outcomes, statistical averages (1) are susceptible to the influence of outliers and (2) mask considerable individual differences. The vast majority of people appear resilient to the end of a marriage (Mancini et al., 2011); that is, the *modal response* to divorce—regardless of its causes(s)—is one that is characterized by relatively little long-term emotional suffering. In these cases, there is typically a period of transition, adaptation, and recovery that runs its course within 12 to 18 months (Bourassa et al., 2017).

For some people, the process of recovery is much more protracted (Borelli et al., 2019). Sbarra and colleagues (2015) suggested that individual differences in attachment-related emotion regulation play key roles in organizing this adjustment process (see Sbarra & Borelli, 2019); in effect, individual differences in attachment anxiety and avoidance—that is, relatively greater attachment *insecurity*, constitute important background risk factors for shaping how people respond to the end of marriage as well as how they recover over time. For example, Lee and colleagues (2011) found that, following a recent marital separation, adults reporting greater attachment anxiety and who evidenced a greater degree of experiential overinvolvement (operationalized via high scores on a composite of first-person, present-oriented experiential language use when describing their marital separation experience) evidenced the greatest blood pressure reactivity when they were asked to think about their separation and divorce experience later in the same laboratory session. Experiential overinvolvement reflects an inability to let go of upsetting thoughts and feelings—it is conceptually similar to rumination and can manifest as jealousy, preoccupation, or other forms of perseverative thought (Kross & Ayduk, 2008; Mikulincer & Shaver, 2019).

Whereas people prone to depression and attachment anxiety may share the underlying tendency toward maladaptive repetitive thought, which can give rise to risk (following separation and divorce) via overinvolvement with one's psychological experiences, evidence also suggests that the tendency toward emotional suppression can heighten risk as well. For example, in one of the longest psychological follow-up studies of divorce adaptation, Bourassa and colleagues (2019) found the greatest risk for poor emotional adjustment four and a half years after a marital separation was observed among people who reported a high degree of attachment avoidance, which is a dimension of attachment-related emotion regulation characterized by *deactivation* or the tendency toward emotional suppression. In a conceptual replication of prior research, Borelli and Sbarra (2013) found that, following a marital separation, people high in attachment avoidance showed greater decreases in self-concept clarity when they also showed a corresponding decrease in an indicator of heart rate variability (HRV) while thinking about their separation and divorce experience. In this report, and consistent with a prior study on the experience of a painful loss in adolescence (Fagundes et al. 2012), the authors interpreted decreases in HRV as reflecting greater preparedness for action. From this perspective, people high in avoidance who experienced no such emotion regulation demands—that is, people high in avoidance who were able to successfully suppress their emotional experiences—showed greater evidence of self-concept clarity following their separation. It is well known that as an emotion-regulation strategy, expressive suppression is highly effortful (Gross & Levenson, 1993), and the conclusion from this series of studies appears to be that emotional avoidance is a reasonable coping strategy in the face of divorce *if* it works. That is, people high in avoidance who are able to successfully engage their preferred emotion-regulatory strategy seem to do well over time, but the opposite is true if that strategy breaks down. This conclusion is consistent with findings from the larger social psychology literature suggesting that the emotional suppression characterizing highly avoidant young adults breaks down under cognitive load (Mikulincer et al., 2002). If you have a tendency toward avoidance, but the emotional pain of an experience is too great, your favored emotion regulatory strategies may be ill-suited to demands of this situation, which is a point we return to below when considering how infidelity might interact with these individual difference strategies.

Emotion-Regulatory Risk Operates Through Self-Concept Disturbances and Narrative Coherence

Before discussing the ways in which infidelity may shape how people cope with the end of marriage, it is important to add one more piece to the general understanding of adjustment to divorce. If these individual differences in (attachment-related) emotion-regulatory strategies—either being overinvolved with or too experientially distanced from the emotions associated with the end of marriage—moderate adjustment to divorce, what are the mediators or mechanisms that may explain why these processes confer risk as they do? Here there is evidence for at least two processes: (1) self-concept clarity/disturbance and (2) narrative coherence (see Sbarra & Borelli, 2019).

In many respects, marital separation and divorce are abhorrent blows to our self-concept. When relationships end, people frequently return to basic questions about their identity, their friends, and even how they should use their time. Said differently, we come to know ourselves through our close relationships (Agnew, 2000). Following nonmarital breakups, improvements in self-concept disturbance are leading indicators of improved psychological well-being; we begin feeling better after a separation as a consequence of an improved sense of self, not the other way around (see Mason et al., 2012). Among adults experiencing a recent marital separation, greater self-concept disturbance is associated with greater separation-related emotional distress three months later (Manvelian et al., 2018). This association appears to be driven by a lack of differentiation between one's self and an ex-partner (Manvelian et al., 2018). In this study, participants, "differentiate themselves from their ex by emphasizing that their former partner is someone who has different qualities, goals, communication styles, hobbies, personalities, or values from themselves" (Manvelian et al., 2018, p. 309). Lower scores on differentiation were associated with higher scores on self-concept disturbance. Whether this effect reflects a potential mechanism of recovery (in that people who show improvements in their self-concept ultimately work to differentiate themselves from their ex-partner) or a simple marker of risk (in that people who have a disturbed self-concept cannot differentiate themselves from their ex-partner), remains to be determined, but this work certainly suggests that a disturbed self-concept is highly associated with poor adjustment to marital separation. Behavioral evidence also exists for this assertion. For example, adults who were judged (when speaking about their separation and divorce experience) to be more highly attached to their ex-partner (1) reported that they were more highly attached to their ex-partner; (2) used more we-talk language to describe their separation experience, which may reflect a greater psychological interdependence with their ex-partner; and (3) this we-talk language mediated the association between self-reported and judged-rated attachment to one's ex-partner, suggesting that this manner of speaking was a behavior cue used to infer the degree of continued attachment with an ex-partner (Borelli et al., 2019).

Related to self-concept clarity is the idea of narrative coherence. One reason emotion regulatory overinvolvement may be associated with poor adjustment to divorce is that this tendency is associated with recalling life events, or recounting personal events repetitively without meaning, rather than reconstruing these experiences into a coherent narrative (Kross & Ayduk, 2011). Reconstruing is an adaptive form of self-reflection that involves focusing on the broader context of one's life experiences to create meaning from difficult experiences. Bourassa and colleagues (2017) found that following a recent separation experience people with a tendency toward overinvolved and maladaptive thoughts developed less coherent narratives about their separation experience, and these less coherent narratives, in turn, statistically explained the association between greater over involvement at the start of the study and greater separation-related emotional distress seven and a half months later. Interestingly, in an exploratory analysis, this study also reported that the negative association between overinvolvement and narrative coherence was attenuated when participants were asked to write about "the story of their marriage and separation experience." Said differently, people with a tendency toward overinvolvement may benefit from a scaffolding that helps create a more coherent narrative about their separation experience (Bourassa et al., 2017). Other work from this study showed that narrative expressive writing *caused* decreases in resting heart rate and increases in resting HRV, and these effects persisted seven and a half months later (Bourassa et al., 2017). In this sense, an intervention task designed to promote narrative coherence in the face of divorce clearly altered and potentially improved resting indices of cardiovascular functioning.

Adding Infidelity to the Mix

Thus far, we have reviewed evidence on two key risk factors associated with poor adjustment to divorce (attachment anxiety and avoidance) and suggest that these individual differences are associated with two forms of maladaptive emotion-regulation (attachment-related overinvolvement and deactivation/suppression). These risk factors are associated with poor outcomes, we argued, because they impair adults' sense of self-concept clarity and disrupt their ability to create a coherent narrative about their separation. When we add infidelity to the mix, it is easy to see ways in which some people may become especially stuck in their distress, either by virtue of overinvolvement with the pain of the infidelity or feeling like the affair has shaken their fundamental sense of self.

Although few studies of infidelity in the context of divorce have studied these types of psychological responses, existing research does suggest that the formation of narrative plays a key role in how adults navigate the end of marriage in the face of an affair. Reissman (1989), for example, conducted detailed, open-ended, structured interviews with 104 separated adults, then reported on three narrative themes to illustrate major differences in how different people react to the same life event. Reissman's analysis centered on three themes that characterized the subjective meaning of the infidelity: (1) as a betrayal centered on the duplicitousness of one's ex-partner, (2) as understandable given the context ("Her alcoholism impaired her decision making."), and (3) as a minor role in an otherwise very turbulent marriage. In discussing the interviews, Reissman highlights her central thesis about infidelity and divorce:

> The three cases analyzed in this paper show the extent of individual differences in the meaning of marital infidelity and, in turn, of divorce. Although on traditional life events scales the three cases might look alike in that they were exposed to the same stressors—divorce and

infidelity—the analysis has suggested that these were not the same "objective" events but, phenomenologically, somewhat different experiences. Importantly, because the meanings of the events and actions were different, the feelings and actions that followed varied as well. . . . Obviously, there are complex causal order issues here. For example, does an account that minimizes the significance of infidelity change its emotional import, or is this construction of the problem itself evidence of a degree of psychological resilience, on the one hand, or denial, on the other? Also, where does personal history fit in? As Brown and Harris have empirically documented, the effect of a major stressor is related to features of a person's biography, as well as to the current circumstances of their life. (p. 749)

The final element of this quote may be especially germane to the present analysis: Background individual differences interact with current circumstances to shape the interpretive lens adults use to narrate their divorce experience in the context of an affair, and this point is consistent with the broad stress literature in documenting that there are some distinct features of life events that are associated with risk for developing depression. For example, severely threatening life events, especially those that involves the experience of humiliation and entrapment (e.g., sexual assault, major financial problems), are especially potent risks for provoking depression in women (Brown et al., 1995; Whisman, 2016). Indeed, targeted rejection, which involves the active and intentional rejection of one specific individual by another, is an interpersonal stress that is highly associated with the onset of major depressive disorder (Slavich et al., 2009). Relative to many other negative or stressful life events, it is easy to envision the ways in which affairs can involve humiliation, entrapment, and, especially targeted rejection. For example, although there is considerable debate around changes in financial status following divorce (see Braver, 1999), many women experience a substantial decline in household income and an increased risk of falling into poverty when their marriage ends (Dewilde & Uunk, 2008). It is not a stretch to call this a form of entrapment; to the extent than an affair ends a relationship and leaves the ex-partner in a more dire financial situation, we would expect a course of emotional adjustment to be more pernicious. Indeed, financial debt is a unique and independent predictor of suicidal ideation (Meltzer et al., 2011), and this effect appears to be mediated by a sense of hopelessness.

Other work has studied infidelity through the lens of a humiliating event. Cano and O'Leary (2000), for example, compared depression rates in women who experienced an extramarital affair to those who did not but had similar levels of marital discord. The results indicated that those who had experienced their partner having an affair—especially one that resulted in the end of marriage—had significantly higher rates of depression than those who did not experience their partner engaging in an extramarital affair (Cano & O'Leary, 2000). Further, Kitson and Holmes (1992) found that individuals who divorce following infidelity are more distressed than those who divorce without the occurrence of an extramarital affair and these individuals are also more attached to their former spouse

(Amato & Previti, 2003). This work is consistent with a study conducted by Whisman (2016) with married/cohabitating couples who had a previous major depressive episode and discovered their partner had an affair. Discovering an affair was associated with a major depressive episode in the past year, even when accounting for demographic variables and marital adjustment (Whisman, 2016). These negative outcomes are typically found for the individual whose spouse had the affair rather than the perpetrator of the infidelity. Sweeney and Horwitz (2001) found that when a partner initiated a divorce, they were less likely to be depressed than those who did not initiate the divorce from a spouse who engaged in infidelity. Alternatively, spouses that committed the infidelity also have negative outcomes including guilt (Spanier & Margolis, 1983) and depression (Beach et al., 1985).

When we combine these findings with the ideas discussed above, a model emerges for understanding divorce adjustment in the context of infidelity. To the extent that people have difficulty regulating their emotional experiences (by virtue of high attachment insecurity or a history of mood or anxiety difficulties), the stress of divorce in the context of an affair may be greatly magnified, and we expect to see these struggles in a more protracted period of grief and recovery, largely because the circumstances around the affair compel toward maladaptive overinvolvement where they repetitively focus on the betrayal and the terribleness of their ex-partner or perhaps even become stuck in a narrative about their own role in the affair. Self-compassion after a separation—the ability to relate to yourself with kindness, to be mindful, and to experience difficult life events in relation to a larger common humanity—is associated with a more adaptive course of recovery after marriage ends (Sbarra et al., 2012). To the extent that a humiliating infidelity provokes self-recrimination ("I should have seen it coming," or, "I'm a doormat—always have been and always will be."), we would expect an adverse course of recovery, one that may be associated with more conflict with an ex-partner (interpersonal conflict) or individual (internal) emotional distress.

Perhaps unsurprisingly, and especially when children are involved, interpersonal conflict often goes hand-in-hand with intrapersonal distress. For example, in one of the only completely dyadic studies of marital dissolution, Sbarra and Emery (2008) reported that fathers evidenced the highest degree of coparenting conflict when mothers reported the greatest degree of acceptance of the separation, and the authors suggested that coparenting custody conflict is a sanctioned means of emotional protest to the end of marriage. In this study, as mothers pulled away, fathers' conflict increased (Sbarra & Emery, 2008). We can envision many ways in which the experience of infidelity overlays increased emotional complications on top of already tense interpersonal dynamics.

Although this basic model in which infidelity can potentiate underlying vulnerabilities toward emotional regulatory dysfunction is useful, it is only part of the story about divorce, and if the field uses psychological science methods for a deeper inquiry into this area we may also find that infidelity is a catalyst toward growth *after* a separation.

We offer this hypothesis following work showing that women who end very low-quality marriages show *gains* in psychological well-being over time and appear to be relatively free of the tumultuous period of adjustment that often surrounds the end of marriage (Bourassa et al., 2015). Here we suggest that it might be useful not to think about divorce as a context for humiliation and entrapment but instead to think of the end of low-quality marriages—especially those that have repeated infidelity as a main feature or theme (Riessman, 1989)—as a signal of freedom, relief, and empowerment, especially for women, rather than suffering, entrapment, and humiliation. This is a hypothesis that will require additional investigations, but it is worthy of study and consistent with an emerging literature on posttraumatic growth (Tedeschi & Calhoun, 2004).

Summary and Conclusions

Infidelity occurs in approximately one-quarter of all married couples but does not always lead to divorce (Wiederman, 1997). It has long been debated whether infidelity is a cause of divorce or a symptom of an already distressed marriage. Relatively recent research points to a causal role for infidelity in predicting divorce (Previti & Amato, 2004). To the extent that an affair plays such a causal role, this raises the question: How does infidelity impact the course of a given person's adjustment once a couple separates? Unfortunately, there is a scarcity of research addressing this specific question, although we can pull from other literature to hypothesize a model for coping with infidelity post-divorce. Amato's divorce-stress-adjustment model (Amato, 2000) posits that coping with divorce occurs over a period of time and is dependent on certain risk factors (e.g., financial strain) and protective factors (e.g., social support) and recognizes that most people return to normalcy relatively quickly post-divorce (Amato, 2000). However, there are two identified factors that inhibit an individual's ability to adjust post-divorce. The first is attachment-related emotion regulation. Individuals with greater attachment insecurity have a more difficult time adjusting to divorce (Sbarra et al., 2015; Lee et al., 2011), and it appears that the secondary emotion regulation of hyperactivation and deactivation play a critical role in adults' adjustment to the end of marriage (Mikulincer & Shaver, 2019). The evidence is fairly clear that when people become overinvolved in their psychological experiences (typical of hyperactivating strategies), this portends a worsened course of adjustment. On the other hand, when people suppress their emotional experiences (typical of deactivating strategies) it appears that this may be associated with positive outcomes *to the extent that these strategies are successful*, and it is well known that suppressive emotion regulation is quite effortful. Further, we highlighted two mechanisms driving divorce adjustment: self-concept clarity and narrative coherence (Sbarra & Borelli, 2019). When infidelity occurs and divorce follows, if infidelity is interpreted as a humiliating event, or if it is experienced as a targeted rejection to one's sense of self, these predict poorer divorce adjustment and depression (Cano & O'Leary, 2000).

To better understand how infidelity impacts postdivorce adjustment, we recommend work on several different fronts. The first is the gender gap. As discussed above, there is disagreement in the literature about whether there is a higher prevalence of men engaging in extramarital affairs than women (Previti & Amato, 2004; Buss, 1994; Fischer, 1992; Hite, 1987), with more recent research finding that men and women engage in infidelity at similar rates (Treas & Giesen, 2000; Whisman et al., 2007). Given that women are more likely to file for divorce and have better postdivorce adjustment outcomes (Diedrick, 1991; Zeiss et al., 1981), will their engagement in infidelity impact their adjustment? For example, if a woman engages in infidelity and her partner files for divorce, will she still have the same gendered adjustment outcomes as indicated by the current available research, or will her course of adjustment be more pernicious because she was ultimately left by her partner? Further, will infidelity be viewed as a humiliating event across genders, or are women uniquely likely to feel humiliated upon learning their partner was/is having an affair? Do men interpret an affair differently and make meaning of an affair that is not humiliating? Men are more likely to leave a marriage if a woman has a sexual affair (Beitzig, 1989; Kinsey et. al., 1953), but if more women are engaging in extramarital sex, will it become more acceptable for couples to remain together? More research is needed on how men and women engage in infidelity and their reactions as individuals and as a couple.

Next, the populations in which infidelity is primarily studied is also limited. Historically, the samples in the bulk of the infidelity literature have been primarily married heterosexual couples. Relatively little is known about infidelity in same-sex couples, couples who are cohabitating and choose not to marry, and the perpetrators of infidelity themselves. More research is needed to determine how infidelity impacts a variety of couples at both the individual and couple level. Most of the dyadic research in the literature uses samples already engaging in couples therapy post infidelity. More longitudinal research is needed tracking the outcomes of both individuals to determine how infidelity impacts the perpetrator, the victim, and the couple. Further, increasing the cultural diversity of samples is also important. There is, again, relatively little data comparing infidelity in people of different ethnicities and how they adjust post-divorce involving infidelity. Using a variety of methodologies such as dyadic, longitudinal, and mixed method studies will provide a deeper insight into couples who divorce post infidelity.

A third limitation in this area is better understanding how technology aids or inhibits postdivorce adjustment. How does seeing an ex-partner with the person they had an affair with on social media impact one's ability to suppress rumination or create a cohesive narrative about the affair? The divorce literature asserts that more frequent contact with an ex-spouse inhibits postdivorce adjustment (O'Hara et al., 2020; Trinder et al., 2008), but there has yet to be research done in the context of infidelity. Technology has made infidelity more accessible both in terms of "catching people in the act" of an affair and the types of infidelity that occur (Brimhall et al., 2017; Hertlein & Stevenson, 2010). It is unclear how technology impacts adjustment both at an individual and couple level, and what it could mean for dealing with the infidelity moving forward. With dating apps, widespread access to pornography, and instant messaging more available than ever, how do couples navigate the potential for infidelity and cope with infidelity once it occurs through a technological medium?

Finally, couples therapists routinely state that infidelity is one of the most challenging issues to treat in couples therapy (Fife et al., 2008). It is critical to develop empirically supported interventions that target the mechanisms through which research tells us that couples can heal from infidelity identified in our proposed model. Further, therapists also must have empirically supported treatments to help individuals who decide to divorce post-infidelity. The mechanisms identified in this chapter serve as references for potential intervention development. For example, helping individuals or couples create cohesive narratives and make meaning of the affair can help them to adjust to their postdivorce sense of self. Existing interventions facilitate forgiveness, improve communication skills, and target the factors that contributed to the perpetration of infidelity (see Fife et al., 2008), but modifying these treatments for individuals or couples facing divorce would be a high priority.

In conclusion, it is important to gather more information on how infidelity impacts postdivorce adjustment. This information will be essential in developing effective interventions for this population both for couples who divorce and those who stay together. Future researchers and clinicians should recognize the unique needs of couples who experience infidelity and how to treat both individuals and the couple if and when their relationship dissolves.

References

Abrahamson, I., Hussain, R., Khan, A., & Schofield, M. J. (2012). What helps couples rebuild their relationship after infidelity? *Journal of Family Issues, 33*(11), 1494–1519.

Afifi, W. A., Falato, W. L., & Weiner, J. L. (2001). Identity concerns following a severe relational transgression: The role of discovery method for the relational outcomes of infidelity. *Journal of Social and Personal Relationships, 18*(2), 291–308.

Agnew, C. R. (2000). Cognitive interdependence and the experience of relationship loss. In J. H. Harvey & E. D. Miller (Eds.), *Loss and trauma: General and close relationship perspectives* (pp. 385–398). New York: Brunner-Routledge.

Allen, E. S., & Atkins, D. C. (2012). *The association of divorce and extramarital sex in a* representative US sample. *Journal of Family Issues, 33*(11), 1477–1493.

Amato, P. R. (2000). The consequences of divorce for adults and children. *Journal of Marriage and Family, 62*(4), 1269–1287.

Amato, P. R., & Previti, D. (2003). People's reasons for divorcing: Gender, social class, the life course, and adjustment. *Journal of Family Issues, 24*(5), 602–626.

Amato, P., & Rogers, S. (1997). A longitudinal study of marital problems and subsequent divorce. *Journal of Marriage and the Family, 59*(3), 612–624.

Beach, S., Jouriles, E., & O'Leary, K. (1985). Extramarital sex: Impact on depression and commitment in couples seeking marital therapy. *Journal of Sex and Marital Therapy, 11*(2), 99–108.

Betzig, L. (1989). Causes of conjugal dissolution: A cross-cultural study. *Current Anthropology, 30*(5), 654–676.

Borelli, J. L., Sbarra, D. A., & Mehl, M. (2019). Convergence of naïve coders and participant report ratings of attachment to a former partner: When we should be me? *Journal of Social and Personal Relationships*, *36*(3), 977–999.

Bourassa, K. J., Hasselmo, K., & Sbarra, D. A. (2019). After the end: Linguistic predictors of psychological distress 4 years after marital separation. *Journal of Social and Personal Relationships*, *36*(6), 1872–1891.

Bourassa, K. J., Manvelian, A., Boals, A., Mehl, M. R., & Sbarra, D. A. (2017). *Tell me a story*: The creation of narrative as a mechanism of psychological recovery following marital separation. *Journal of Social and Clinical Psychology*, *36*(5), 359–379.

Bourassa, K. J., Sbarra, D. A., & Whisman, M. A. (2015). Women in very low quality marriages gain life satisfaction following divorce. *Journal of Family Psychology*, *29*(3), 490–499.

Brand, R., Markey, J., Mills, C., & Hodges, M. (2007). Sex differences in self-reported infidelity and its correlates. *Sex Roles*, *57*(1–2), 101–109.

Braver, S. L. (1999). The gender gap in standard of living after divorce: Vanishingly small. *Family Law Quarterly*, *33*, 111.

Brimhall, A. S., Miller, B. J., Maxwell, K. A., & Alotaiby, A. M. (2017). Does it help or hinder? Technology and its role in healing post affair. *Journal of Couple and Relationship Therapy*, *16*(1), 42–60.

Brown, Harris, T. O., & Hepworth, C. (1995). Loss, humiliation and entrapment among women developing depression: a patient and non-patient comparison. *Psychological Medicine*, *25*(1), 7–21. https://doi.org/10.1017/S003329170002804X

Buss, D. M. (1994). The strategies of human mating. *American Scientist*, *82*(3), 238–238.

Buunk, B. P. (1987). Conditions that promote break ups as a consequence of extradyadic involvements. *Journal of Social and Clinical Psychology 5*, 271–284.

Cano, A., & O'Leary, K. D. (2000). Infidelity and separations precipitate major depressive episodes and symptoms of nonspecific depression and anxiety. *Journal of Consulting and Clinical Psychology*, *68*(5), 774.

Choi, K. H., Catania, J. A., & Dolcini, M. M. (1994). Extramarital sex and HIV risk behavior among US adults: Results from the National AIDS Behavioral Survey. *American Journal of Public Health*, *84*(12), 2003–2007.

Dewilde, C., & Uunk, W. (2008). Remarriage as a way to overcome the financial consequences of divorce—A test of the economic need hypothesis for European women. *European Sociological Review*, *24*(3), 393–407.

Diedrick, P. (1991). Gender differences in divorce adjustment. *Journal of Divorce and Remarriage*, *14*(3–4), 33–46.

Fagundes, C. P., Diamond, L. M., & Allen, K. P. (2012). Adolescent attachment insecurity and parasympathetic functioning predict future loss adjustment. *Personality and Social Psychology Bulletin*, *38*(6), 821–832.

Fife, S. T., Weeks, G. R., & Gambescia, N. (2008). Treating infidelity: An integrative approach. *Family Journal*, *16*(4), 316–323.

Fincham, F., & May, R. (2017). Infidelity in romantic relationships. *Current Opinion in Psychology*, *13*, 70–74.

Fischer, G. J. (1992). Gender differences in college student sexual abuse victims and their offenders. *Annals of Sex Research*, *5*(4), 215–226.

Glass, S. P., & Wright, T. L. (1977). The relationship of extramarital sex, length of marriage, and sex differences on marital satisfaction and romanticism: Athanasiou's data reanalyzed. *Journal of Marriage and the Family*, *39*(4), 691–703.

Greeley, A. (1994). Marital infidelity. *Society*, *31*(4), 9–13.

Gross, J. J., & Levenson, R. W. (1993). Emotional suppression: Physiology, self-report, and expressive behavior. *Journal of Personality and Social Psychology*, *64*, 970–986.

Hertlein, K. M., & Stevenson, A. (2010). The seven "As" contributing to Internet-related intimacy problems: A literature review. *Cyberpsychology*, *4*(1), 1–8.

Hite. (1987). *The Hite report : women and love : a cultural revolution in progress / Shere Hite*. (1st ed.). Knopf.

Hughes. (1988). Divorce and Social Support: A Review. *Journal of Divorce*, *11*(3-4), 123–145. https://doi.org/10.1300/J279v11n03_10

Kitson, G., Babri, K., & Roach, M. (1985). Who divorces and why: A review. *Journal of Family Issues*, *6*(3), 255–293.

Kitson, G. C., & Holmes, W. M. (1992). *Portrait of divorce: Adjustment to marital breakdown*. Guilford Press.

Kross, E., & Ayduk, O. (2008). Facilitating adaptive emotional analysis: Distinguishing distanced-analysis of depressive experiences from immersed-analysis and distraction. *Personality and Social Psychology Bulletin*, *34*(7), 924–938.

Kross, & Ayduk, O. (2011). Making Meaning out of Negative Experiences by Self-Distancing. *Current Directions in Psychological Science, 20*(3), 187–191. https://doi.org/10.1177/0963721411408883

Lee, L. A., Sbarra, D. A., Mason, A. E., & Law, R. W. (2011). Attachment anxiety, verbal immediacy, and blood pressure: Results from a laboratory analog study following marital separation. *Personal Relationships, 18*(2), 285–301.

Mancini, A. D., Bonanno, G. A., & Clark, A. E. (2011). Stepping off the hedonic treadmill. *Journal of Individual Differences, 32*(3), 144–152.

Manvelian, A., Bourassa, K. J., Lawrence, E., Mehl, M. R., & Sbarra, D. A. (2018). With or without you? Loss of self following marital separation. *Journal of Social and Clinical Psychology, 37*(4), 297–324.

Mason, A. E., Law, R. W., Bryan, A. E., Portley, R. M., & Sbarra, D. A. (2012). Facing a breakup: Electromyographic responses moderate self-concept recovery following a romantic separation. *Personal Relationships, 19*(3), 551–568.

Meltzer, H., Bebbington, P., Brugha, T., Jenkins, R., McManus, S., & Dennis, M. (2011). Personal debt and suicidal ideation. *Psychological Medicine, 41*(4), 771–778.

Mikulincer, M., Gillath, O., & Shaver, P. R. (2002). Activation of the attachment system in adulthood: Threat-related primes increase the accessibility of mental representations of attachment figures. *Journal of Personality and Social Psychology, 83*, 881–895.

Mikulincer, M., & Shaver, P. R. (2019). Attachment orientations and emotion regulation. *Current Opinion in Psychology, 25*, 6–10.

Negash, S., Cui, M., Fincham, F., & Pasley, D. (2014). Extradyadic involvement and relationship dissolution in heterosexual women university students. *Archives of Sexual Behavior, 43*(3), 531–539.

O'Hara, K. L., Grinberg, A. M, Tackman, A. M., Mehl, M. R., & Sbarra, D. A. (2020). Contact with an ex-partner is associated with psychological distress after marital separation. *Clinical Psychological Science, 8*(3), 450–463. https://doi.org/10.1177/2167702620916454

Previti, D., & Amato, P. (2004). Is infidelity a cause or a consequence of poor marital quality? *Journal of Social and Personal Relationships, 21*(2), 217–230.

Riessman, C. K. (1989). Life events, meaning and narrative: The case of infidelity and divorce. *Social Science and Medicine, 29*(6), 743–751.

Sbarra, D. A., & Borelli, J. L. (2019). Attachment reorganization following divorce: Normative processes and individual differences. *Current Opinion in Psychology, 25*, 71–75.

Sbarra, D. A., & Emery, R. E. (2008). Deeper into divorce: Using actor-partner analyses to explore systemic differences in coparenting conflict following custody dispute resolution. *Journal of Family Psychology, 22*(1), 144–152.

Sbarra, D. A., Hasselmo, K., & Bourassa, K. J. (2015). Divorce and health beyond individual differences. *Current Directions in Psychological Science, 24*(2), 109–113.

Sbarra, Law, R. W., Lee, L. A., & Mason, A. E. (2009). Marital Dissolution and Blood Pressure Reactivity: Evidence for the Specificity of Emotional Intrusion-Hyperarousal and Task-Rated Emotional Difficulty. *Psychosomatic Medicine, 71*(5), 532–540. https://doi.org/10.1097/PSY.0b013e3181a23eee

Sbarra, Law, R. W., & Portley, R. M. (2011). Divorce and Death: A Meta-Analysis and Research Agenda for Clinical, Social, and Health Psychology. *Perspectives on Psychological Science, 6*(5), 454–474. https://doi.org/10.1177/1745691611414724

Sbarra, D. A., Smith, H. L., & Mehl, M. R. (2012). When leaving your ex, love yourself. *Psychological Science, 23*, 261–269.

Shackelford, T. K., & Buss, D. M. (1997). Anticipation of marital dissolution as a consequence of spousal infidelity. *Journal of Social and Personal Relationships, 14*(6), 793–808.

Shackelford, LeBlanc, G. J., & Drass, E. (2000). Emotional reactions to infidelity. *Cognition and Emotion, 14*(5), 643–659. https://doi.org/10.1080/02699930050117657

Slavich, G. M., Thornton, T., Torres, L. D., Monroe, S. M., & Gotlib, I. H. (2009). Targeted rejection predicts hastened onset of major depression. *Journal of Social and Clinical Psychology, 28*(2), 223–243.

Spanier, G. B., & Margolis, R. L. (1983). Marital separation and extramarital sexual behavior. *Journal of Sex Research, 19*(1), 23–48.

Sweeney, M. M., & Horwitz, A. V. (2001). Infidelity, initiation, and the emotional climate of divorce: Are there implications for mental health? *Journal of Health and Social Behavior, 42*(3), 295–309.

Teachman, & Paasch, K. M. (1994). Financial Impact of Divorce on Children and Their Families. *The Future of Children, 4*(1), 63–83. https://doi.org/10.2307/1602478

Tedeschi, R. G., & Calhoun, L. G. (2004). Posttraumatic growth: Conceptual foundations and empirical evidence. *Psychological Inquiry, 15*(1), 1–18.

Treas, J., & Giesen, D. (2000). Sexual infidelity among married and cohabiting Americans. *Journal of Marriage and Family, 62*(1), 48–60.

Trinder, L., Kellet, J., & Swift, L. (2008). The relationship between contact and child adjustment in high conflict cases after divorce or separation. *Child and Adolescent Mental Health, 13*(4), 181–187.

Wade, & Pevalin, D. J. (2004). Marital Transitions and Mental Health. *Journal of Health and Social Behavior, 45*(2), 155–170. https://doi.org/10.1177/002214650404500203

Whisman, M. (2016). Discovery of a partner affair and major depressive episode in a probability sample of married or cohabiting adults. *Family Process, 55*(4), 713–723.

Whisman, M., Gordon, K., & Chatav, Y. (2007). Predicting sexual infidelity in a population-based sample of married individuals. *Journal of Family Psychology, 21*(2), 320–324.

Wiederman, M. (1997). Extramarital sex: Prevalence and correlates in a national survey. *Journal of Sex Research, 34*(2), 167–174.

Wiederman, M. W., & Allgeier, E. R. (1996). Expectations and attributions regarding extramarital sex among young married individuals. *Journal of Psychology and Human Sexuality, 8*(3), 21–35.

Zeiss, A. M., Zeiss, R., & Johnson, S. (1981). Sex differences in initiation of and adjustment to divorce. *Journal of Divorce, 4*(2), 21–33.

CHAPTER 19

Forgiveness for a Partner's Infidelity

Megan R. Dillow *and* Amanda Denes

Abstract

This chapter offers a brief treatment of infidelity as a major relational transgression and discusses several types of infidelity (i.e., sexual, emotional, communicative, and same-sex infidelity). It overviews numerous aspects of granting forgiveness, beginning with a summary of the various conceptualizations of forgiveness, including motivation-based, therapeutic, and communicative perspectives. The measurement of forgiveness is considered, including assessments of forgiveness at varying levels of specificity. Common correlates and predictors of granting forgiveness are identified, including dispositional, situational, physiological, physical, relationship, and social network considerations. Interventions that encourage forgiveness are presented, such as the decision-based model of forgiveness of marital infidelity and the integrative model of forgiveness. Cross-cultural similarities and differences with regard to the antecedents of forgiveness are acknowledged, although available research is limited primarily to Western cultures at this point. Typical strategies for communicating forgiveness to a transgressor are identified, including direct, indirect, and conditional tactics. The limited research on seeking forgiveness is also reviewed by way of an analysis of offender behavior that is most likely to elicit forgiveness (e.g., sincerely apologizing, displaying remorse, taking responsibility). Finally, the chapter concludes with a discussion of the consequences of forgiveness for both the forgiver and the offender, including physical, physiological, psychological, and relational outcomes. Attention is given to the potential dark side of forgiveness, such as exploitation risk for the forgiver, the possibility of prolonging an unhealthy relationship, and compromised extradyadic relationships with close friends and family members who disagree with the decision to forgive the offender.

Key Words: forgiveness, granting, seeking, antecedents, outcomes, interventions

Although our close relationships with others are perhaps our greatest source of personal fulfillment and emotional well-being, it is also in these relationships that we are most vulnerable to negative consequences that are incurred as a byproduct of such involvement. It is practically a foregone conclusion that we will experience harm of some sort—intentionally or inadvertently inflicted—at the hands of close others, as people are prone to behaving badly even in their closest relationships (Rusbult et al., 1991). Such bad behavior has been studied under several monikers, including relationship transgressions in the communication discipline and aversive interpersonal behaviors (which deny others the positive outcomes or rewards they desire and/or inflict negative outcomes or costs on the other) in the psychological field of study (Kowalski, 1997; Metts, 1994).

Relationship transgression is a term for a variety of wrongdoings that are perpetrated or otherwise occur in the context of relationships. More formally, transgressions are defined as violations of implicit or explicit rules that dictate behaviors that are acceptable within the context of the close relationship (Metts, 1994). Although transgressions can and do occur across different types of relationships (e.g., friendships, family relationships), they have been most often considered and studied in the context of romantic relationships. Transgressions and aversive interpersonal behaviors vary in their severity, and therefore their harmfulness, and severe transgressions have been shown to diminish the quality and constrain the longevity of the relationship. Transgressions and aversive interpersonal behaviors—particularly severe ones—can set the stage for uncomfortable "social confrontation episodes" (Kowalski, 1997, p. 216), which entail an offended person's direct or indirect contention that their partner has violated a guideline or expectation for appropriate relational behavior and the relationship talk that follows such a contention. Such communication includes addressing the offender's reaction to the contention of a rule violation, which can take several forms, including denial, admitting guilt, apologizing, or attempting to justify the behavior (Newell & Stutman, 1988). Paradoxically, positive outcomes may at times result from relationship transgressions or from aversive interpersonal behaviors, even severe ones (Kowalski, 1997; Perlman & Carcedo, 2011).

In the remainder of this chapter, various types of infidelity are introduced before focusing the discussion more narrowly on sexual infidelity primarily in the context of heterosexual relationships, as the bulk of related research centers on this type of relationship. From there, an in-depth discussion of forgiveness comprises the majority of this chapter. Various conceptualizations and measurements of forgiveness are presented from the forgiveness granter's perspective, as most available literature has focused on the forgiveness granter nearly to the exclusion of the forgiveness seeker. Numerous antecedents and correlates of forgiveness are discussed, as are several ways in which forgiveness can be communicated. Models of forgiveness in the therapeutic context are also presented before moving into a necessarily brief treatment of research from the forgiveness seeker's perspective, including motivations for seeking forgiveness and strategies by which to do so. The chapter concludes by overviewing the consequences of forgiveness, both positive and negative in nature.

Infidelity as a Relationship Transgression

Infidelity occurs in various forms, including sexual, emotional, and communicative infidelity. Sexual and emotional infidelity have been the focus of decades of empirical work, and the latter is often studied in juxtaposition with the former (see "Emotional Infidelity versus Sexual Infidelity"). Some scholars combine the two conceptually into a consideration of infidelity more broadly, defined as "a violation of relationship commitment in which sexual or emotional intimacy, or both, is directed away from the primary relationship without the consent of one partner" (Fife et al., 2013, p. 344). The distinction between sexual and emotional infidelity is to some degree a function of the types of exclusivity rules that are broken (i.e., physical or affective, respectively). Prominent scholars of infidelity have adopted a resource-based perspective in conceptualizing these two types (Shackelford & Buss, 1997). When a romantic partner engages in unsanctioned extrarelationship sexual activity, therefore expending their sexual resources on someone other than their partner, an instance of sexual infidelity has occurred. Although extrarelationship sexual intercourse is the exemplar of sexual infidelity, intercourse is not required, as other sexual behaviors may qualify as well (e.g., kissing). When a romantic partner expends their emotional resources on someone other than their relational partner, there is evidence of emotional infidelity. Falling in love with someone outside of the primary romantic relationship is perhaps the clearest example of emotional infidelity, although other behaviors may qualify as well (e.g., providing consistent emotional support to or investing significant time in another). Sexual and emotional infidelity may co-occur (sometimes termed an affair) or may be independent of each other (see "Long-Term Infidelities").

Two other forms of infidelity have gained recent research attention: communicative infidelity and same-sex infidelity. Both may be seen as particular types of sexual infidelity. Communicative infidelity is defined as extradyadic sexual activity that is at least partly intended to send a message to a partner (Tafoya & Spitzberg, 2007). In other words, communicative infidelity is sexual infidelity that is used strategically and/or manipulatively in order to achieve personal or relational goals (e.g., to get revenge against the partner for a previous transgression or to communicate the presence of sociosexual issues such as sexual preoccupation). In this way—and unlike most instances of sexual infidelity—communicative infidelity is meant to be discovered by the partner in order to successfully send the intended message and to obtain the desired result (Dillow et al., 2011).

Researchers have also explored instances of same-sex infidelity in heterosexual relationships. This line of research focuses on the ways in which heterosexual partners respond to a partner's infidelity with someone of the same sex. Much of the research in this domain has employed hypothetical scenarios to determine the expected individual and relational outcomes associated with such behavior and addresses differences in women's and men's responses to same-sex infidelity. For example, Denes et al. (2015) found that women and men both reported more negative emotional responses to different-sex infidelity, but that men were more likely to terminate the relationship in response to different-sex infidelity whereas women were more likely to end the relationship in response to same-sex infidelity. Similarly, women report being more upset than men when imagining a partner cheating with someone of the same sex and report more negative outcomes (e.g., upset, relationship termination) when imagining a male partner's same-sex compared to different-sex infidelity (Confer & Cloud, 2011; Wiederman & LaMar, 1998). Other work further supports the premise that men have a higher tolerance for same-sex infidelity than women, finding that 65% of women would prefer their male partner cheat with another woman rather than a man, whereas men were four times more likely than women to report a preference for the female partner cheating with someone of the same sex (Apostolou, 2019). Yet, other findings paint an inconsistent picture, revealing that same-sex and different-sex infidelity are equally distressing for women (Hughes et al., 2004). Evidence for the lack of sex differences also arises when examining jealous responses to same-sex infidelity, where women and men respond in similar ways (Sagarin et al., 2003; Sagarin et al., 2012).

Merging work on same-sex infidelity and communicative infidelity, Denes et al. (2020a) explored motivations for engaging in same-sex infidelity. First, they identified unique reasons people engage in same-sex infidelity: for sexual experimentation (i.e., they were curious what sex with someone of the same sex would be like), due to attraction (i.e., they did so because they desired someone of the same sex), and because they did not feel that same-sex infidelity "counted" as infidelity and thus should not be categorized as such. The sexual exploration narrative has also arisen in other work on same-sex infidelity as part of an individual recognizing their "true self" (Clarke et al., 2015). Similarly, the "not cheating" motivation may speak to Compton and Bowman's (2017) finding that same-sex sexual behavior between two female friends was less likely to be perceived as cheating by men than women. Together, explorations of communicative infidelity and same-sex infidelity in heterosexual relationships extend research on sexual infidelity, providing nuanced information regarding motivations behind acts of infidelity and ensuing outcomes.

Prevalence of Infidelity

Sexual infidelity has been identified as the prototypical relational transgression, and it is virtually always evaluated as quite severe in nature (Metts, 1994; Metts & Cupach, 2007). Despite being widely denounced by heterosexual individuals who were socialized in monogamous cultures such as the United States (even by those who have themselves committed infidelity, although this condemnation is not as fervent), it is a commonly reported negative event in romantic relationships (Laumann et al., 1994). Estimates of the occurrence of sexual infidelity vary markedly across studies, in part because disparate definitions of sexual infidelity are used. Because sexual infidelity includes but is not limited to prohibited sexual intercourse with someone outside of the primary relationship, prevalence estimates will necessarily vary according to whether more or less inclusive conceptualizations are employed.

Some sources indicate that as many as 40% of married men and 25% of married women have had extramarital sexual relationships (Tsapelas et al., 2011), although other sources put the number at less than 25% of spouses (while agreeing that prevalence estimates are higher for husbands than wives; Blow & Hartnett, 2005). These estimates can reach as high as 70% for partners in dating relationships as opposed to marriage, although some estimates are considerably lower, topping out at around 33% (e.g., Allen &

Baucom, 2006; Tafoya & Spitzberg, 2007). Taken together, these percentages paint a picture that suggests that the incidence of infidelity in both married and dating relationships is relatively high (particularly for the latter group)—and these numbers are likely to be underreported, given the nature of the behavior and the strong perceptions of immorality surrounding it (Prins et al., 1993).

Given that sexual infidelity is usually seen as a severely negative and highly consequential violation of acceptable and appropriate behavior in monogamous, heterosexual relationships, it follows that the occurrence of this transgression will elicit a response from the transgressed-against partner, and this response will have implications for the continuance or termination of the relationship (Shackelford et al., 2002). Two responses to relationship transgressions are possible: relationship-destructive responses such as revenge (see Yoshimura & Boon, 2018, for an overview) or dissolution (see "Relationship Dissolution Following Infidelity"), and relationship-protective responses such as forgiveness. Although some may wonder whether a severe transgression such as infidelity can or should be forgiven (a point we return to later), research has shown that sometimes individuals can subvert their natural tendency to respond to hurtful events in kind and instead choose to respond munificently by forgiving the offender (Rusbult et al., 1991).

Granting Forgiveness for a Partner's Infidelity

Forgiveness is a crucial consideration in the aftermath of a partner's sexual infidelity, as the willingness and ability to forgive a partner may enable the repair and continuance of the relationship (if continuance is desired). Even if posttransgression relationship continuance is not the goal, forgiveness has many individual benefits for the forgiveness granter as well as for the forgiveness seeker. Despite the primarily positive nature of forgiveness-granting, some drawbacks have been identified as well.

Conceptualizations of Forgiveness

The concerted study of forgiveness began in the mid-1980s, and numerous competing conceptualizations of forgiveness are found in literatures from psychological, therapeutic, and communication perspectives. These definitions vary in terms of their specificity and inclusiveness, and in terms of which aspects of the forgiveness process are highlighted. For example, McCullough and colleagues (2000) defined forgiveness with an eye toward the redirection of motivations, as an "intraindividual prosocial change toward a perceived transgressor that is situated within a specific interpersonal context" (p. 9). Fincham and colleagues (2005) also take a motivational view in identifying two elements of forgiveness: decreasing negative motivations and increasing positive motivations. Previously, and more specifically, Enright and colleagues (1998) defined interpersonal forgiveness as the "willingness to abandon one's right to resentment, negative judgment, and indifferent behaviors toward one who unjustly injured us, while fostering the undeserved qualities of compassion, generosity and even love toward him or her" (pp. 46–47). Relying on earlier work by Exline and colleagues (2003), Worthington and Sandage (2016) parsed two types of forgiveness: decisional and emotional. Decisional forgiveness is a change in behavioral intention to treat the offender "as a person of value, to forswear revenge, and to act in ways that forbear expression of anger about the transgression" (Worthington & Sandage, 2016, p. 22). Emotional forgiveness includes a transformation of negative affect to "some improved state," which could range from "less negative unforgiving emotions" to positive emotions (Worthington & Sandage, 2016, p. 23).

Therapeutic forgiveness approaches examine how forgiveness can heal enduring or otherwise traumatic pain in close relationships (e.g., marriage, family), and how relationships might be renegotiated or newly envisioned after a close other's destructive behavior. Hargrave (1994) distinguishes between exonerating and forgiving; the latter entails giving the transgressor the opportunity to compensate for their hurtful behavior and also requires an overt act of forgiving. Hargrove and Sells (1997) define forgiveness as allowing the offender to reestablish relational trust by behaving in a trustworthy manner, and encouraging open and honest discussion of the relational transgression so the transgressor and the transgressed-against partner can rebuild a better relationship. Enright and the Human Development Study Group (1991) identified active psychological processes that could be relevant to forgiveness interventions, including confronting anger, experiencing a change of heart and feeling empathy toward the offender, accepting/absorbing the pain caused by the offender, and committing to forgiveness. Similarly, other therapeutic approaches focus on specific cognitions, affect, and behavior on the part of the offended party to explain how interpersonal forgiveness is ultimately achieved (Enright & Fitzgibbons, 2000; Worthington, 1998).

Communication perspectives share some commonalities with therapeutic approaches. As with those approaches, in addition to personal consequences, consequences for the relationship between the offender and the offended are of concern to communication scholars who study forgiveness. Similar constructs are often explored as part of the forgiveness process, including emotional reactions to the offense, empathy, compassion, forbearance, benevolence, and apologies (Kelley et al., 2019). The communicative strategies used by offenders to seek forgiveness and the strategies used by transgressed-against partners to convey forgiveness to the offender are obvious areas of attention in this literature (Kelley, 1998; Kelley & Waldron, 2005). Forgiveness styles and how they are associated with individual and relational welfare have also been investigated (Merolla, 2017).

Although the various conceptualizations differ in important ways and highlight specific aspects of the forgiveness process, an area of agreement is the central claim that forgiveness entails an intrapersonal, other-oriented transformation that occurs after consideration of the offense and its personal implications in which cognitions, motivations, affect, and behavior toward the transgressor become less negative and more positive (Enright, 2001; McCullough et al., 2000). Fundamentally, forgiveness requires an internal prosocial change in the way we choose to think about the transgression and the pain it caused, willingly foregoing negative emotions and the urge to retaliate (Exline & Baumeister, 2000; Worthington, 2001). Such change should not be temporary in nature, as a relinquishment or transformation of negative affect should be maintained (Merolla, 2008). These perspectives point to both the psychological and psychosocial bases of forgiveness.

A number of scholars position or otherwise call attention to the interpersonal, psychosocial aspects of forgiveness as well as the psychological ones (McCullough et al., 2000). Forgiveness is inherently directed at another person with whom an individual has some sort of social or personal relationship (i.e., forgiveness is in relation to another person, except in the case of self-forgiveness; see Hall & Fincham, 2005) and is often communicated in some way to the transgressor (Fincham, 2000; Kelley, 1998; North, 1998). In fact, some scholars have proposed that forgiveness is not transmitted unilaterally from the offended partner to the offender as much as it is constructed through the interplay of meaning-making discourses between the transgressor and the transgressed-against partner (Pederson, 2014). In these ways, forgiveness is also clearly an interpersonal construct.

DISTINCTION OF FORGIVENESS FROM RELATED CONCEPTS

Perhaps the area of greatest conceptual agreement among those who study the topic is found in what forgiveness is not rather than in what it is. Scholars tend to agree that forgiveness is distinct from condoning, pardoning, excusing, justifying, forgetting, and (usually, although not always) reconciling (Enright & Coyle, 1998; Freedman, 1998). Forgiveness may be granted even when the transgressor has no reasonable claim to such magnanimity. Forgiveness may be granted despite the awareness that a less prosocial response would be justified.

As not all scholars agree that forgiveness is or should be distinguished conceptually from reconciliation, further explication of the relationship between these two concepts is necessary. In the forgiveness literature, reconciliation has been characterized as the reinstatement of the trust that was damaged or broken entirely as a result of a partner's transgression (Fincham, 2000). If this definition of reconciliation is adopted, then it would seem that reconciliation entails forgiveness. However, in research unrelated to the study of forgiveness, communication scholars have used the term "reconciliation" to refer to former romantic partners who revert back to the previous romantic relationship state (Bevan et al., 2003). Recognizing that partners may go through several cycles of breakups and reconciliations, this ongoing process has also been referred to as an on-again/off-again relationship (Dailey et al., 2009). Some forgiveness scholars, however, have used the term reunion to describe the rekindling of the romantic relationship after it has terminated due to a partner's transgression (Fincham, 2000). If these definitions are adopted, then forgiveness and reconciliation—as well as forgiveness and reunion—are clearly distinct. Former partners can reconcile or reunify their romantic relationship without having forgiven the transgression that tore them apart (although it appears obvious that forgiveness would ease such a transition).

Beyond the debate about whether reconciliation and forgiveness are or should be treated as distinct concepts, accommodation has been identified as the construct that is most similar to forgiveness. Accommodation is the willingness to respond to another's hurtful behavior by inhibiting the tendency to react in harmful ways (e.g., by seeking revenge) and instead to react in constructive ways that facilitate continuance of the relationship with the offender (Fincham, 2000; Rusbult et al., 1991). Although this conceptualization of accommodation has clear overlap with some definitions of forgiveness (particularly the motivation-based approaches), accommodative processes may be enacted for reasons other than having forgiven a partner. As examples, if the offending partner's potentially destructive behavior is reframed as being not so destructive, or if it is minimized as having few relational implications, or if it is ultimately excused or justified by the offended partner, then forgiveness is not relevant (Fincham, 2000). Put succinctly, accommodation may occur along with forgiveness, but it may also occur in the absence of it.

Measurement of Forgiveness

Measures of forgiveness have flourished accordingly with empirical investigations of forgiveness in recent years. In early empirical work on forgiveness, the focus was largely on measures of forgiveness of others. Assessments of self-forgiveness and the forgiveness of members of other groups (i.e., when the offense is attributed to cultural differences, interaction dynamics, or stereotypes that are specific to the groups in question) have emerged. Further, measures of forgiveness tend to be pitched at differing levels of specificity, including forgiveness of a particular offense, relationship-level forgiveness across transgressions that are committed by the same offender, and a dispositional notion of forgivingness as a trait that is consistent across situations and over time (Hoyt & McCullough, 2005). As the focus of this chapter is forgiveness for a partner's infidelity, relevant measures at this level of specificity are the primary focus of the following overview.

FORGIVENESS OF A SPECIFIC TRANSGRESSION

Most measures of forgiveness of others are self-report in nature, as exemplified by the Enright Forgiveness Inventory, the Transgression-Related Interpersonal Motivations Inventory, and the Decision to Forgive Scale—all of which are included here as often-used assessments of forgiveness of a specific offense, such as an infidelity transgression. The Enright Forgiveness Inventory (EFI) was one of the first assessments of forgiveness and it is still in frequent use today (Enright & Rique, 2004; Subkoviak et al., 1995). This 60-item inventory was intended to assess cognitions, affect, and behavior in response to having been hurt "deeply" and "unfairly" (Subkoviak et al., 1995, p. 644), yet evidence suggests that it may be unidimensional rather than multidimensional. This scale has been recommended specifically for clinical applications, as it is sensitive to changes in forgiveness in clinical samples (Enright & Rique, 2004). The EFI has been used to explore outcomes of infidelity, specifically. For example, Sodani et al. (2019) applied it in their investigation of forgiveness and the marital quality of women who were affected by infidelity.

The most frequently used assessment of transgression-specific forgiveness is the Transgression-Related Interpersonal Motivations Inventory (TRIM), a measure that is consonant with motivation-based conceptualizations of forgiveness. The original TRIM contained 12 items and assessed two dimensions indicative of unforgiveness: avoidance and revenge motivations (McCullough et al., 1998). In this assessment, increased motivations to avoid and to take revenge against the transgressor are thought to be representative of unforgiveness. Although the original 12-item scale demonstrated sound psychometric properties, conceptually speaking, low levels of unforgiveness do not necessarily equate to forgiveness (Wade & Worthington, 2003). To remedy this potential shortcoming of the scale, McCullough and colleagues added 6 items to the original measure that were intended to assess a third dimension of goodwill toward the transgressor, termed benevolence motivations (McCullough et al., 2003, 2006; McCullough & Hoyt, 2002). Elevated benevolence motivations, often used as an independent subscale, are thought to be representative of increased forgiveness. The TRIM inventory has been used to understand responses to infidelity, and is perhaps best employed in the quest to understand severe and exceedingly hurtful events as opposed to transgressions that are less severe in nature (Paleari et al., 2009). For example, Denes et al. (2020b) examined the associations between perceptions of blame and intent and the TRIM dimensions in the context of imagined same-sex infidelity in a heterosexual relationship. Denes et al. (2020a) also explored differences in the TRIM dimensions based on the motivation for engaging in same-sex infidelity while in a heterosexual relationship.

Gordon and Baucom (2003) developed the 23-item Forgiveness Inventory (FI) to apply specifically to marital betrayals such as a partner's infidelity. This measure assesses three phases of the forgiveness process including cognitive, affective, and behavioral items that are representative of nonforgiveness and forgiveness. Research with the scale has supported the three-dimensional factor structure and has revealed good reliability and convergent validity across samples (Gordon et al., 2009). The FI has demonstrated its utility in therapeutic interventions as well as outside of them (Gordon et al., 2004).

The 10-item Marital Offence-Specific Forgiveness Scale (MOFS) was introduced to apply to serious transgressions such as infidelity and shows great promise (Paleari et al., 2009). This measure is also bidimensional, reflecting positive (benevolence) and negative (avoidance/resentment) dimensions, as does the TRIM inventory. Work with the MOFS (which has been translated into German and adapted for Turkish samples) has distinguished forgiveness in the context of marriage from related constructs such as empathy, attributions, rumination, trait forgivingness, and marital quality. The scale has also demonstrated convergent validity, test-retest reliability, measurement equivalence across wives and husbands, and does not appear to exhibit social desirability bias (Fincham, 2020).

A more recently proffered assessment of forgiveness for a specific transgression that shows early potential is the 8-item Decision to Forgive Scale (DTFS; D. Davis, Hook, Van Tongeren, DeBlaere, Rice, & Worthington, 2015). Already quite heuristic despite its nascence, the DTFS has demonstrated good psychometric qualities in the forms of discriminant validity (e.g., from the avoidance and revenge motivations in the TRIM) and internal reliability. As an assessment of decisional forgiveness, it appears to be distinct from assessments of achieved forgiveness (sometimes referred to as emotional forgiveness). Achieved forgiveness is more than just the decision to forgive, which likely precedes emotional or achieved forgiveness—it is the end state and the ultimate goal of the forgiveness process (Worthington, 2006). This distinction suggests the potential utility of the DTFS in clinical and therapeutic contexts as well as empirical ones. As noted earlier in this chapter, infidelity is considered a severe relational transgression. As such, these measures, which each focus on forgiveness for a specific transgression (including but not limited to infidelity) offer a valuable means of assessing forgiveness of infidelity.

FORGIVENESS OF A TRANSGRESSOR ACROSS VARIOUS OFFENSES IN A PARTICULAR RELATIONSHIP

Few dyadic or relationship-level assessments of forgiveness exist, particularly in comparison to the number of other measures that are pitched at very high and very low levels of specificity, respectively. The most frequently used relationship-level assessment of forgiveness is the 6-item Marital Dispositional Forgiveness Scale (MDFS; Fincham & Beach, 2002). This brief scale is bidimensional, featuring items that reflect both positive (e.g., willing to let "bygones be bygones") and negative (e.g., wanting to see the transgressor "hurt and miserable") dimensions. This bidimensionality is a benefit of this assessment over other unidimensional measures, as conceptualizations of forgiveness entail more than merely the lessening of negative cognitions, motivations, affect, and behavior—they usually include increases in positive thoughts, motivations, emotions, and actions. Although not intended specifically to assess forgiveness of a partner's repeated infidelity transgressions, the scale has potential for such use.

Dispositional or Trait Forgiveness

Beyond addressing forgiveness for relational transgressions, measures have considered forgiveness as a disposition or trait that individuals possess (i.e., some individuals are predisposed to forgive more than others, which may impact forgiveness for a partner's infidelity). Numerous trait forgivingness measures are available in the literature. One of the most commonly employed dispositional assessments of forgiveness is the 10-item Trait Forgivingness Scale (TFS; Berry & Worthington, 2001; Berry et al., 2005). This scale includes both negatively and positively worded items and has demonstrated sound psychometric properties, including convergent validity with the Transgression Narrative Test of Forgivingness (TFNT; Berry et al., 2001). The TFNT is a scenario-based assessment that presents participants with five paragraph-long scenarios related to forgiveness of offenders (i.e., friend, fairly close friend, distant cousin, former classmate, current classmate) for various offenses (e.g., forgetting to drop off a job application for you, an act of violence toward you brought on by alcohol consumption, etc.). Participants rate the extent to which they would be likely to forgive the person for the situation described in each scenario. Berry et al. (2001) indicate good psychometric value for the scale in the forms of test-retest reliability and stability of item locations, and they recommend its use in interventions as well as basic research.

According to a recent analysis by McElroy-Heltzel and colleagues (2020), the Enright Forgiveness Inventory, the Transgression-Related Interpersonal Motivations Inventory, the Decision to Forgive Scale, the Marital Dispositional Forgiveness Scale, and the Trait Forgivingness Scale are currently the "strongest available measures" of other-forgiveness (p. 79). Yet, the measures described here and the empirical study of forgiveness more broadly are not without their limitations, including concerns regarding monomethod bias, self-report assessments, social desirability bias, and the need for longitudinal assessments of forgiveness that can capture the transgressed-against person's change in cognitions, motivations, emotions, and behaviors toward the transgressor. Given the severity and stigma surrounding infidelity, as well as its potential long-term consequences for individuals and their relationships, it is important to consider such limitations when choosing an appropriate measure for assessing forgiveness following infidelity.

Antecedents and Correlates of Forgiveness for a Partner's Infidelity

Having established a basic understanding of the many conceptualizations and measurements of forgiveness, we turn now to a discussion of the various individual, dispositional factors as well as relationship, situational, social network, intervention-based, and physiological considerations that have been shown to impact the extent to which the offended forgives an offense. Common precursors or correlates of offenses and of forgiveness of a partner's infidelity more specifically are discussed. Because comparatively few studies have investigated forgiveness after spousal infidelity, the discussion provided throughout this chapter is accordingly broadened to forgiveness after transgressions (Shrout & Weigel, 2017). Where relevant, findings are organized according to a number of theoretical perspectives that are commonly used to frame studies of forgiveness for a partner's severe transgressions.

INDIVIDUAL, DISPOSITIONAL FACTORS

All of the Big Five personality traits have demonstrated associations with forgiveness, although some of these characteristics (i.e., neuroticism and agreeableness) have a markedly stronger impact on forgiveness than others. Neuroticism, which can encourage people to focus particular attention on negative, self-relevant stimuli, is moderately negatively associated with forgiveness (e.g., McCullough & Hoyt, 2002; Reed & Derryberry, 1995a). Conversely, agreeableness, which often manifests as a prosocial proclivity toward cooperation with others and has been associated with empathy for others, is moderately positively related with forgiveness and negatively associated with retaliation decisions (e.g., Hilbig et al., 2016; McCullough & Hoyt, 2002). Agreeableness has been positively linked with forgiveness for infidelity transgressions, specifically (Brose et al., 2005). The remaining three factors of personality are not as closely associated with forgiveness, although small, positive relationships have been seen for conscientiousness, extraversion, and openness to new experiences (e.g., Balliet, 2010; Worthington, 1998). Narcissistic entitlement—one particular way in which narcissists' self-focus exerts itself by the presumption that one deserves special, preferential treatment from others—has also been associated negatively with forgiveness of others (e.g., Exline et al., 2004; Strelan, 2007).

Attachment theory (Bowlby, 1969; Hazan & Shaver, 1987) has demonstrated its utility as a framework for understanding forgiveness processes in close relationships, and it is clear that attachment-related anxiety and avoidance can hinder the transformational processes that are central to forgiveness (e.g., Mikulincer et al., 2006). Research has demonstrated that anxious and avoidant attachment styles are negatively related to dispositional forgivingness, but they appear to impact forgivingness through different mechanisms. That is, anxiously attached individuals—already preoccupied with uncertainties about the relationship—tend to ruminate more about offenses such as infidelity, while individuals with an avoidant attachment style—who seek increased distance under conditions of relationship threat—exhibit decreased empathy for transgressors, devaluing them and the relationship (Burnette et al., 2009; Chung, 2014). Insecurely attached individuals have been shown to make less benign attributions for partner transgressions, which are also associated with less forgiveness (Kimmes & Durtschi, 2016). Further, securely attached individuals display more dispositional forgivingness as well as more state forgiveness for betrayals, while insecurely attached individuals wish to avoid the transgressor (an indicator of nonforgiveness) after an offense (Lawler-Row et al., 2006).

Forgiveness has long been associated with most major religions, particularly Christianity (Marty, 1998; Rye et al., 2000). More specifically, positive relationships between religion or spirituality and forgiveness have received support, particularly when trait elements of religion/spirituality are associated with trait-based assessments of forgivingness (Davis et al., 2013; McCullough & Worthington, 1999). Religious individuals view their marriage as sacred, which endorses forgiveness and self-sacrificial behaviors (Mahoney, 2010). Praying for the well-being of a romantic partner increases both offender's and offended's reports of forgiveness for wrongdoings (Fincham & May, 2017). Further, a notion of covenantal forgiveness has been posited that is explicitly relevant to recovering from marital infidelity (Sauerheber & Ponton, 2017). If spouses understand their relationship as covenantal or having sacred qualities and thereby fundamental to their spirituality, then forgiveness itself becomes covenantal, and is therefore more likely to be granted for a spouse's infidelity (Mahoney et al., 1999).

Some aspects of mindfulness have been associated with forgiveness or unforgiveness after a partner's infidelity for individuals whose partners have a history of infidelity transgressions. Specifically, higher levels of nonreactivity (i.e., psychologically detaching oneself from an experience and avoiding an immediate reaction) have been predictive of greater forgiveness for infidelity, while a decreased ability to act with awareness and being more judgmental of one's own thoughts and feelings regarding a partner's past infidelity have been predictive of greater nonforgiveness (Johns et al., 2015). In addition, the ability to maintain autonomy and differentiate oneself from one's partner in emotional situations has been associated with increased forgiveness following a partner's infidelity (Khaddouma et al., 2015). Transgressed-against partners appear more likely to forgive to the extent that they are higher in empathy and perspective-taking (e.g., Fincham et al., 2002).

RELATIONSHIP CHARACTERISTICS

Strong evidence exists for the claim that pretransgression relationship constructs influence forgiveness. These pretransgression relationship considerations are influenced by (although not limited to) those identified by interdependence theory (Kelley & Thibaut, 1978) and the investment model (Rusbult, 1980). Both theoretical perspectives are concerned with predicting commitment to close relationships. Relational satisfaction, an antecedent of commitment, is predictive of appraising the offender's apology as more sincere in nature, which in turn predicts forgiveness (Schumann, 2012). An imbalance in receiving and granting forgiveness between wives and husbands has been related to a diminishment of individual and relational well-being for wives over time (Paleari et al., 2011). Marital quality has been shown to predict forgiveness (and in turn, forgiveness predicts marital quality in a bidirectional causal relationship; Fincham & Beach, 2007). Further, strength of the bond between spouses prior to the occurrence of partner infidelity is associated with increased emotional forgiveness (i.e., the restoration of positive emotions; Chi et al., 2019).

SITUATIONAL FEATURES

Forgiveness of a partner's sexual infidelity transgression may depend on a number of factors, including offense- and offender-related considerations that are specific to the situation. For example, sexual infidelity is most likely to be forgiven when the behavior is viewed as an isolated occurrence, and when the transgressor apologizes for their offense (Gunderson & Ferrari, 2008). Other research has also shown that forgiveness is encouraged when the offender demonstrates regret and sincerely apologizes (Carmody & Gordon, 2011). Discovery method may also play a role in forgiveness, as discoveries that entail more face threat (e.g., unsolicited third-party disclosures, catching a partner "red handed") are less likely to be forgiven as compared to other discovery methods that allow the offender to make some sort of redress attempt (e.g., the offending partner provides an unsolicited disclosure of the transgression; Afifi et al., 2001). Enduring and situational characteristics of the offender may come into play as well, as some research has shown that offender conscientiousness as well as the offender's ability to appear honest and humble are associated with increased benevolence motivations (Carmody & Gordon, 2011). In addition, transgressed-against partners are less likely to forgive under conditions of elevated rumination and recollection of a larger number of previous transgressions (Fincham et al., 2002; McCullough et al., 2001).

Research from an attribution theory perspective (Heider, 1958) has shed light on the role of the transgressed-against partner's attributions for the offender's transgression in the forgiveness process. Put simply, attribution theory is concerned with how people develop causal explanations for events and behaviors (Fiske & Taylor, 1991). Attributions may be internal (when the cause of a behavior/event is attributed to some enduring, dispositional characteristic) or external (when the cause of a behavior/event is attributed to some temporary, situational factor). Attributions for the transgressor's behavior are influential and adaptive, as infidelity that is attributed to external, situational causes (e.g., intoxication) as opposed to internal, enduring personality flaws (e.g., a lack of morality) is also more likely to be forgiven (Fincham, 2000; Hall & Fincham, 2006). Benign attributions are more likely to be made by those in highly committed relationships, and these benign attributions in turn enhance forgiveness (Finkel et al., 2002). More specifically, benign attributions and empathy can be facilitated by perceiving that the offender wishes to reconcile and by the transgressed-against partner's solidarity-oriented personality characteristics (i.e., the proclivity to maintain cohesion and harmony in relationships; Chi et al., 2019). In turn, benign attributions and empathy are associated with increased decisional forgiveness (i.e., choosing to eschew bitterness and thoughts of revenge), which subsequently increases emotional forgiveness.

SOCIAL NETWORK INFLUENCES

Relationships do not exist in a vacuum, and social network members may implicitly or explicitly encourage or discourage forgiveness of a romantic partner's infidelity transgression. Social network members have been shown to encourage termination of the relationship rather than forgiveness following a partner's infidelity, and offended parties (both dating partners and spouses) who elected to forgive a partner were viewed as less competent and weaker than those who terminated the relationship (Smith et al., 2014).

INTERVENTIONS THAT PROMOTE FORGIVENESS

Various forgiveness interventions are available that purport to foster forgiveness following a partner's infidelity. Two empirically validated forgiveness interventions—the decision-based model of forgiveness of marital infidelity and the integrative model of forgiveness—provide evidence that forgiveness can be facilitated and marital satisfaction can be increased, even after severe transgressions such as a partner's infidelity. The forgiveness interventions discussed below outline various steps, stages, and specific factors that comprise the forgiveness process.

DiBlasio's (2000) decision-based model of forgiveness of marital infidelity identifies 13 steps in the forgiveness process. The steps commence with discussions of what decision-based forgiveness is and why it is advantageous. Personal accountability is encouraged, wherein partners seek forgiveness and take responsibility for their transgression. Reasons for the infidelity are identified and discussed, as are emotional reactions. Partners are encouraged to recognize that forgiveness is a choice that must be maintained. Formal and ceremonial rituals of asking for and granting forgiveness, as well as committing to forgiveness in the long-term, comprise the last steps of the model.

Gordon et al. (2004) developed an integrative model of forgiveness that addresses the trauma caused by a partner's infidelity (Baucom et al., 2011; Gordon & Baucom, 1998, 1999). The model includes three stages. In the first stage, dealing with the impact of the infidelity, partners attempt to accept what has happened and limit the negative emotional and behavioral fallout from the transgression. In the second stage, partners explore reasons for the infidelity, come to terms with the enduring impacts, and consider potential responses to intervention efforts. Understanding why the infidelity occurred can help transgressed-against partners feel less vulnerable moving forward, which sets the stage for forgiveness. In the final stage, partners build on what they have learned to develop a plan about how to proceed, whether that may entail creating a more functional relationship or coming to grips with the end of their relationship.

A more recent intervention specifically developed to facilitate forgiveness after infidelity transgressions is Fife and colleagues' (2013) interpersonal forgiveness model. This approach to enabling forgiveness incorporates and synthesizes some of the constructs that have been identified in the forgiveness literature as impacting the forgiveness process. In this model, precursors of forgiveness are identified (i.e., commit to treatment, manage the crisis, explore the primary relationship prior to the infidelity, establish appropriate relationship boundaries, and define forgiveness), along with factors that encourage forgiveness: empathy, humility, commitment and hope, and apology. Apologies must include taking responsibility for the transgression, sincerely expressing remorse, pledging future fidelity, committing to do the necessary work of relationship repair, and directly asking for forgiveness.

Finally, a prescriptive model outlining the communication tasks that are required in the process of forgiveness has been forwarded (Merolla, 2017; Waldron & Kelley, 2008; Waldron et al., 2019). These seven tasks include confronting the transgression, managing the resultant negative affect (e.g., anger, shock, embarrassment, fear), engaging in sense-making or attempts to understand why the transgression occurred, forgiveness-seeking by the offending partner, forgiveness-granting by the offended partner (or minimally, indicating a willingness to begin the forgiveness process), renegotiating the relational covenant by clarifying the rules and values that will govern the post-transgression relationship, and finally, continuing to monitor and maintain the renegotiated relationship, and if that fails, considering redefining the relationship.

PHYSIOLOGICAL CONSIDERATIONS

Although still comparatively limited, research on the physiology and psychophysiology of forgiveness for transgressions has flourished since the mid-2000s (see also Crowley & Allred, 2020, for a review). Some early work in this regard examined the stress hormone cortisol, finding that following a recent, significant transgression, individuals who appraised the transgressor as more agreeable experienced decreased plasma cortisol and increased self-reported forgiveness after simulating a speech to the transgressor (Tabak & McCullough, 2011). Related work indicates that those who ruminate more than usual about a nontraumatic but hurtful transgression produce more salivary cortisol over the course of several weeks (McCullough et al., 2007b). Rumination has also been shown to decrease resting heart rate variability, and anger rumination is associated with elevated diastolic and systolic blood pressure (Larsen et al., 2012; Witvliet et al., 2011). These findings are relevant to the study of forgiveness, as rumination is associated with the transgressed-against partner's vengeful responses rather than forgiving ones (e.g., McCullough et al., 2007a). As such, these findings suggest that increased rumination, as well as the elevated production of the primary stress hormone and reduced cardiac regulation, are linked with unforgiveness. Conversely, forgiveness imagery results in decreased diastolic and systolic blood pressure (Larsen et al, 2012).

The steroid hormone testosterone has been associated with precursors to unforgiveness, including more anger rumination (Herschl et al., 2012) and less empathy (Hermans et al., 2006). In a longitudinal experimental investigation of severe transgressions in dating relationships, for those who engaged in expressive writing about the experience (as compared to writing about an unrelated topic), testosterone levels were positively related to direct forgiveness and negatively related to conditional forgiveness (Crowley et al., 2018).

The neuropeptide oxytocin has been implicated in forgiveness processes for women. After preparing and delivering a recorded speech intended for the person who transgressed against them, women's plasma oxytocin levels were associated with lower levels of forgiveness and relational distress (Tabak et al., 2011). Outside of the context of relationship transgressions (i.e., financial betrayal in a trust game), similar results have been seen for women, wherein oxytocin is associated with more punitiveness and less forgiveness (Yao et al., 2014).

Functional magnetic resonance imaging has been used to investigate how cognitive reappraisals influence affective states, which may in turn impact forgiveness processes. In a small sample of participants who were asked to imagine hurtful events and reappraise them in a forgiving manner, a neural network associated with empathy (i.e., the inferior parietal lobe), regulating emotion via cognition (i.e., the dorsolateral prefrontal cortex), and perspective-taking (i.e., the precuneus) was implicated in the reappraisal of transgressions from negative to more positive, which is a requirement of forgiveness (Ricciardi et al., 2013). Further, brain waves (specifically, the late positive potential [LPP], a slow-wave response that occurs after exposure to stimuli) have been assessed in response to individuals who were asked to ruminate on and reappraise a recent transgression (Baker et al., 2017). Particular types of reappraisals—specifically, compassionate reappraisals that emphasize the transgressor's humanity, as opposed to benefit reappraisals that focus on personal insights gained or strengths realized in dealing with the transgression—activated a complex blend of affect indicative of empathy and forgiveness. Strong evidence exists for compassionate appraisals in increasing empathy and forgiveness (e.g., Witvliet et al., 2010), and compassionate reappraisals may be indicated by an increase in the "smile muscle" response (Witvliet et al., 2011) and may reduce cardiac stress (Witvliet et al., 2015).

Evidence from this body of research clearly demonstrates the presence of physiological forerunners to and correlates of forgiveness for transgressions such as infidelity. In addition to physiological antecedents, some research has focused on physical precursors of forgiveness. Those who do not engage in frequent physical activity (e.g., aerobic and stretching exercises) may exhibit a decreased readiness to forgive romantic partners (Struthers et al., 2017).

CROSS-CULTURAL SIMILARITIES AND DIFFERENCES

Literature on characteristics that facilitate forgiveness has been limited primarily to Western cultures, although scholars have identified some cross-cultural similarities with regard to predictors of forgiveness. Most research on the role of culture in forgiveness focuses on similarities and differences between individuals socialized in individualistic versus collectivistic cultures. Some cognitive processes such as rumination have been negatively related to forgiveness in individualistic cultures (e.g., the United States) and in collectivistic cultures (e.g., the Javanese; Kurniati et al., 2017). Empathy and benign attributions have been associated with forgiveness following a spouse's infidelity transgression in Chinese samples (Chi et al., 2019). Offender behaviors such as offering an apology have been shown to increase willingness to forgive in samples from the United States, China, and The Netherlands, but this relationship is weaker for those who were socialized in honor cultures such as Turkey (McCullough & Witvliet, 2001; Merolla et al., 2012; Shafa et al., 2017). There appear to be more similarities than differences in tendencies toward forgiveness across cultures that have been studied, although some scholars have found that people in collectivistic cultures report elevated levels of trait forgivingness (Paz et al., 2008; Suwartono et al., 2007).

Cross-cultural differences regarding forgiveness have emerged as well. For example, forgiveness has sometimes been shown to differ between those socialized in individualistic versus collectivistic cultures. In individualistic cultures, much emphasis is placed on the intrapersonal processes and benefits of forgiveness, such as an internal release of negative affect and cognitions. Conversely, forgiveness may be more important interpersonally in collectivistic cultures, for preserving social harmony and repairing or reconciling relationships (Ho & Fung, 2011; Hook et al., 2009). In terms of communicating forgiveness, Chinese individuals have been shown to be more likely than American individuals to communicate forgiveness indirectly by minimizing the offense (Merolla et al., 2012).

Communicating Forgiveness

Communication scholars have investigated the strategies by which forgiveness is expressed to a transgressor as an important part of the forgiveness process (Waldron & Kelley, 2008). Although forgiveness may be granted and not truly felt or meant (called hollow forgiveness by Baumeister et al., 1998), most strategies and styles of forgiveness that have been identified reflect agreed-upon notions of the intrapersonal processes that must accompany interpersonal forgiveness.

In early research on the communication of forgiveness, Kelley (1998) identified three ways that individuals communicate forgiveness across various types of close relationships: directly (explicitly communicating forgiveness), indirectly (minimizing the offense), and conditionally (forgiving provisionally, with stipulations). Later, Waldron and Kelley (2005, 2008) expanded Kelley's (1998) original typology of three forgiveness-granting strategies into five. These include explicit declarations of forgiveness, discussion of the transgression, nonverbal displays that imply forgiveness (e.g., positive facial expressions and affectionate behaviors), minimizing or downplaying the transgression and/or its impact, and conditional forgiveness. Conditional and indirect forms of forgiveness-granting are more likely to be used when romantic partners commit transgressions that are perceived to be more severe and blameworthy, such as infidelity (Merolla, 2008).

Although both of these typologies include conditional forgiveness, whether anything short of total forgiveness constitutes true forgiveness is debated by forgiveness scholars (Enright, 2001; Fincham, 2000). Conditional forgiveness implies that some level of negative affect and distrust of the transgressor remains, which is at odds with most conceptions of forgiveness as a transformation of negative cognitions, motivations, emotions, and behaviors. Supporting the notion that perhaps conditional forgiveness is not really forgiveness at all, some research has shown that direct forgiveness serves to strengthen the primary relationship whereas more conditional forms of forgiveness weaken the relationship (Merolla & Zhang, 2011; Waldron & Kelley, 2005). Conditional forgiveness may create a power imbalance in the relationship, wherein the transgressed-against partner is able to constrain the choices of the offender (Kloeber & Waldron, 2017). Conditional forgiveness may be face-threatening for and feel manipulative to the offender, which seems to be at odds with both anecdotal and scholarly notions of forgiveness (Merolla, 2017). Conditional forgiveness appears to reflect or potentially incite negative effects for the forgiveness granter as well, as this type of forgiveness communication has been associated with higher levels of ongoing negative affect (Merolla, 2008). Other scholars have found that when individuals conditionally forgive, what they have really done is identified conditions for how to rebuild or reconcile the relationship, which again highlights the interconnections among forgiveness, repair, and reconciliation (Kloeber, 2011).

Merolla and colleagues identified four overarching forms of forgiveness, which differ along two dimensions: direct-indirect and healing-threatening (Merolla et al., 2017). The four styles of forgiveness communication include: engaging (direct and healing), de-emphasizing (indirect but healing), conditional (direct yet threatening), and suppressing (indirect and threatening). Engaging explicitly communicates forgiveness and encourages discussion of the transgression and its consequences. De-emphasizing downplays the offense by suggesting that negative affect has lessened and that the offense does not require discussion or further attention. Conditional communicates forgiveness with stipulations and demands for debt repayment or future promises (e.g., for behavior change). Finally, suppressing entails withholding any communication of forgiveness (called silent forgiveness by Baumeister et al., 1998). Although limited research currently exists with this typology, studies have shown that in the context of friendship, offenders usually prefer their forgiveness to be communicated in an engaging manner, followed by de-emphasizing, conditional, and suppressing styles (Merolla et al., 2017).

Informed by research on forgiveness-granting across related disciplines, Merolla (2017) assembled an expanded typology of 15 forgiveness-granting communicative strategies (as opposed to more general styles) culled from extant literatures. These strategies include those discussed previously, in addition to strategies such as using time to promote forgiveness, reinitiating contact, making a kind gesture, demonstrating forgiveness nonverbally (e.g., through hugs or smiles), returning to normal communication patterns, and requesting some sort of third-party intervention to assist with facilitating forgiveness. Forgiveness-granting strategies may be selected based on the transgressed-against partner's goals (e.g., to express love, to continue the relationship, to restore personal or partner well-being, to ease personal pain, etc.) and/or the forgiver's perception of the offender's potential response.

Existing work explicitly focused on how forgiveness is granted and the effects of granting forgiveness in particular ways has provided insight into the communicative aspects of forgiveness. As others have argued, a necessary next step in research regarding the interpersonal communication of forgiveness is direct observation of attempts to communicate forgiveness and a better understanding of how such attempts influence the relationship long-term, perhaps by collecting at-home recordings of couples' interactions related to forgiveness (e.g., Alberts et al., 2005).

Seeking Forgiveness for a Transgression

Comparatively limited scholarship focuses explicitly on the transgressor who is seeking forgiveness. However, if forgiveness is critical to paving the way for relational repair, reconciliation, and continuance, then it is important to examine the offender's behavior in the wake of a severe transgression such as infidelity. In other words, it seems obvious that the way in which (if at all) an offender seeks forgiveness for transgressions will impact the forgiveness process, both intrapersonally and interpersonally. As such, scholars from psychology and from communication fields have explored forgiveness-seeking.

Scholars in the realms of psychology and communication have engaged in concurrent research on the concept of forgiveness-seeking. From the psychology realm, Enright and the Human Development Study Group (1996) identified a four-stage model of receiving forgiveness from another (i.e., uncovering, decision, work, and outcome). Although many processes are identified, those related to seeking forgiveness primarily occur at the decision phase of the model, where offenders experience a desire to be forgiven that may include forgiveness-seeking behaviors (apologies and making amends). More specifically, individual, dispositional, and developmental factors that bear on the posttransgression forgiveness process have been investigated. The transgressed-against partner's developmental level of reasoning about forgiveness—the idea that people's understanding of forgiveness develops over time, beginning with a focus on punishment and retribution and progressing to the ethical, conscience-driven desire to maintain the individual rights of and to demonstrate care and love for all people—may be important in forgiving a close other's offenses (Enright et al., 1989). Across various types of relationships (e.g., romantic, friends, family), developmental level of reasoning about forgiveness has been positively associated with forgiveness-seeking (even after controlling for age), narcissism and self-monitoring have been inversely associated with forgiveness-seeking, and religiosity demonstrated no significant relationship with forgiveness-seeking (Sandage et al., 2000). Agreeableness may facilitate forgiveness-seeking, whereas openness and paranoid tendencies may discourage it (Chiaramello et al., 2008).

Imagining a favorable response as a result of forgiveness-seeking (i.e., envisioning being forgiven by the transgressed-against partner) has been shown to improve affective and physiological states, which may embolden the offender to seek forgiveness (Witvliet et al., 2002). Studies have shown that the transgressor's rumination about the offense can weaken their ability to regulate emotional and cardiac responses, perhaps influencing their ability to seek or efficacy in seeking forgiveness (da Silva et al., 2017). Guilt appears to be a primary motivation for forgiveness-seeking, as it has been shown to mediate the relationships between forgiveness and transgression severity, rumination, responsibility, and commitment (Riek et al., 2014). In this study, perhaps surprisingly, shame did not motivate transgressors to seek forgiveness.

Communication scholars have turned their attention to identifying the strategic communication practices that offenders use when forgiveness-seeking, and the impact of these strategies on the relationship between the offender and the offended. Analyzing recalled forgiveness narratives in which participants were asked to recount a time when they had forgiven a romantic partner and to specify the forgiveness-seeking communication of the offending partner in that narrative, five distinct forgiveness-seeking strategies were identified: explicit acknowledgement of the offense (e.g., apologizing, expressing regret, taking responsibility, asking directly for forgiveness), nonverbal assurances (e.g., behaving in an especially nice and affectionate manner), compensation (e.g., doing or buying something for the transgressed-against partner, offering to "do anything" in exchange for forgiveness), explanation (e.g., explaining the reasons for or circumstances surrounding the offense and otherwise discussing the transgression), and humor (e.g., joking about the situation, trying to get the transgressed-against partner to see the humorous side of the event; Kelley, 1998; Kelley & Waldron, 2005; Waldron & Kelley, 2008). Further, the results of this study suggest that explicit acknowledgment, nonverbal assurance, and compensation were related to relational recovery after an offense (and humor was not often used, especially in cases of more severe transgressions where it is clearly inappropriate). In the case of particularly severe transgressions such as a partner's infidelity, communication in the form of explicit forgiveness-seeking (and granting) can facilitate repair of relational damage.

Certain aspects of a forgiveness-seeker's communication have been clearly and consistently linked with successful forgiveness-seeking, including accounts and apologies (Hargrave, 1994). Transgressors who acknowledge the harm caused by their behavior, and who offer an apology for the offense, can convert the affective tone of the encounter and encourage forgiveness (Metts, 1994; Morse & Metts, 2011). Taking responsibility for the offense makes it easier for the transgressed-against partner to release their negative affect and to consider prosocial courses of action, such as forgiveness (Enright et al., 1992). The relationship between apologies and forgiveness is clearly established (McCullough et al., 1997). Across transgressions, including infidelity, the transgressed-against partner's perception of the offender's remorse decreases internal attributions for the offender's behavior, and increases empathy and forgiveness (Davis & Gold, 2011). Offenders who sincerely apologize, exhibit regret, accept responsibility for their behavior, commit to forswearing the behavior in the future, and perhaps offer to make reparations for their offense are more likely to draw the offended person's empathy, which in turn can lead to forgiveness (Metts & Cupach, 2007; Scher & Darley, 1997).

Outcomes of Forgiveness

Forgiveness has been shown to have a variety of benefits or positive consequences for the granter, the seeker, and the relationship between them (see "Renewed Love between Partners Following Infidelity"). Positive outcomes have been identified for mental, physical, physiological, and relationship health and well-being. Conversely, forgiveness may also have negative relational outcomes, and there is an emerging debate among scholars as to when and whether forgiveness is a healthy response to major relational transgressions (e.g., infidelity, intimate partner violence) or significant relationship breaches (e.g., divorce), as some transgressions may be "unforgivable" (Kelley, 1998). Both benefits and drawbacks of forgiveness are discussed here.

Beneficial Outcomes for the Forgiver

Research on the positive outcomes of forgiveness for the transgressed-against partner is relevant to the stress-and-coping model of forgiveness (Lazarus & Folkman, 1984). In brief, this model posits that transgressions incite a stress response, and forgiveness is an adaptive way of coping with that stress (Strelan & Covic, 2006; Worthington & Scherer, 2004). As such, this model suggests that forgiveness should be associated with any number of positive or enhanced outcomes. Forgiveness has been associated with improved psychological health (e.g., Griffin et al., 2015), better physical health (e.g., Cheadle & Toussaint, 2015), and decreased physiological stress (e.g., Larkin et al., 2015), among other beneficial outcomes. These are discussed in more detail, below.

MENTAL HEALTH

A plethora of studies have explored the associations between granting forgiveness and psychological health consequences. Across relationship types, forgiveness-granting has been associated with decreased anxiety, depression, stress, and negative affect; in addition, it improves positive affect and overall life satisfaction (Riek & Mania, 2012; Toussaint et al., 2016). Conversely, unforgiveness has been related to increased subclinical anxiety and depressive symptoms (J. Davis et al., 2015). When a partner commits frequent offenses, regularly forgiving that partner has been shown to predict a greater sense of meaning in life over a six-month timeframe (Van Tongeren et al., 2014). Offense-specific forgiveness has been associated with decreased posttraumatic stress disorder symptoms after experiencing a major trauma (e.g., physical abuse; Orcutt et al., 2008). In a study of college-aged women who had experienced severe transgressions (e.g., infidelity, abuse), women who were assigned to forgiveness interventions experienced decreased depressive symptoms and increased existential well-being over time (Rye & Pargament, 2002). Similarly, in another sample of college-aged women, forgiveness of an offense was related to decreased depression, anxiety, and stress over an average of 9 months later (Orcutt, 2006).

Research with forgiveness interventions such as Enright's Process Model of Interpersonal Forgiveness (2001)—a four-phase model of forgiveness including uncovering, decision, work, and deepening—has shown convincingly that forgiveness is associated with psychological well-being, and that the benefits of forgiveness are maintained over time (Freedman & Enright, 2020). At the intersection of mental and physical health, forgiveness has also been shown to be associated with decreased somatic symptoms (Lawler-Row, 2010; Webb et al., 2012), whereas conditional forgiveness is associated with increased somatic symptoms (Krause & Ellison, 2003). Advantageous mental health outcomes for the forgiver are amplified when the offender makes amends for their transgression (Luchies et al., 2010; Schumann, 2012).

PHYSICAL AND PHYSIOLOGICAL HEALTH

Empirical studies investigating the link between granting forgiveness and physical health outcomes have proliferated in recent years, although collectively, this specific area of inquiry represents a small fraction of the forgiveness literature. Those studies that are available demonstrate a consistent, positive association between forgiveness and a number of physical health outcomes—an association that has been shown to be mediated by stress (Green et al., 2012; Toussaint et al., 2001, 2016). Relatedly, unforgiveness has been shown to produce physiological responses consistent with stress responses (Witvliet et al., 2001, 2002). With regard to forgiveness for a betrayal transgression more specifically, those who report greater trait forgivingness and state forgiveness (particularly the latter) have reported better health (Lawler et al., 2005). Forgiveness for a transgression has also been associated with improved sleep quality by reducing rumination (Caraballo et al., 2008).

Granting forgiveness has physiological and psychophysiological benefits as well, including improved cardiovascular functioning and reduced tension (Witvliet et al., 2008). Transgressed-against partner's conciliatory behaviors during discussions of unresolved transgressions also predict decreased blood pressure for both the offended and the offender (Hannon et al., 2012). Even individual-level interventions aimed at promoting forgiveness can benefit physiological outcomes. For example, Crowley (2014) found that an expressive writing intervention aimed at reframing a traumatic event (i.e., an experience of hate speech) assisted in finding forgiveness and benefited cortisol recovery. The physiological outcomes of forgiveness may also garner long-term benefits. For example, forgiveness interventions for couples have been associated with decreases in salivary cortisol reactivity up to one month after the intervention (Worthington et al., 2015).

Early studies of the physiology of forgiveness examined cardiovascular effects such as heart rate and blood pressure, finding that low levels of state forgiveness and trait forgivingness are associated with higher diastolic and systolic blood pressure (Lawler et al., 2003). Further, trait forgivingness has been related to decreased blood pressure, whereas state forgiveness has been related to decreased heart rate (Lawler-Row et al., 2008).

Research with other interventions provide some additional evidence of the impact of forgiveness on physiological outcomes. For example, Forgiveness and Reconciliation through Experiencing Empathy (FREE) contains steps from the REACH forgiveness model (Worthington, 2006), a five-step model that facilitates the transformation of emotions related to the experience of a transgression. REACH entails recalling the hurt; emotionally replacing negative affect with empathy, sympathy, compassion, or love; the altruistic gift of forgiveness; commitment to the forgiveness; and holding onto forgiveness in the face of doubt. Research with FREE has shown a reduction in cortisol reactivity up to one month following treatment (Worthington et al., 2015).

RELATIONSHIP FUNCTIONING

Granting forgiveness has obvious implications for the health, quality, and longevity of the primary relationship (Fennell, 1993). This is true of dispositional forgivingness as well as for transgression-specific forgiveness (e.g., Braithwaite et al., 2011). Forgiveness has been identified as a way to manage the uncertainty that occurs when relationships have been damaged by a transgression (Emmers & Canary, 1996). More specifically, forgiveness of a moderately to highly harmful betrayal in romantic relationships, including sexual infidelity, has been associated with both partners' subsequent perception that the offense has been resolved, which in turn was linked to improved relational quality (Hannon et al., 2010). Further, forgiveness for a transgression predicted wives' and husbands' self-reports of increased relationship satisfaction, closeness, trust in the partner, and effective conflict resolution over a 6-month time frame (Paleari et al., 2009). Wives' forgiveness for a transgression has been shown to predict more effective conflict communication (i.e., arguing) one year later (Fincham et al., 2007).

Forgiveness has been linked with relationship commitment, such that increased benevolence motivations and decreased avoidance and revenge motivations (which together are representative of forgiveness, as assessed by the TRIM) are associated with increased commitment to the primary relationship (Tsang et al., 2006). Similarly, in the context of imagined same-sex infidelity in a heterosexual relationship, Denes et al. (2020b) found that the more individuals blamed their partner for the infidelity, the more revenge and avoidance (and the less benevolence) they expected to show. In turn, greater avoidance and less benevolence predicted greater intentions to end the relationship. When examining the motivations for engaging in same-sex infidelity in heterosexual relationships, Denes et al. (2020a) further found that women were the most likely to show benevolence and least likely to exert revenge, engage in avoidance, or terminate the relationship when they were asked to imagine that their male partner cheated for reasons of sexual experimentation. Conversely, women were the most likely to avoid or seek revenge when they were asked to imagine that the infidelity was motivated by sociosexuality (i.e., their partner cheated because "he simply enjoys having more sex with more partners;" Denes et al., 2020a, p. 8). If partners desire post-transgression relationship repair and reconciliation, forgiveness can help enable these processes (Karremans & Van Lange, 2004). On the other hand, unforgiveness for a severe relational transgression has been associated with decreases in relationship commitment for romantic partners over time (Ysseldyk & Wohl, 2012).

Changes in forgiveness for an emotional injury following an emotion-focused therapeutic intervention have been associated with elevated trust and marital satisfaction (Greenberg et al., 2010). Similarly, increased forgiveness and improved marital satisfaction (along with diminished depressive symptoms) were observed at 3.5 months following an intervention that focused specifically on marital education and forgiveness (Baskin et al., 2011).

These studies provide clear evidence that forgiveness-granting can have a number of personal health benefits (psychological, physical, and physiological) for the transgressed-against partner, as well as for their relationship with the offender. Not surprisingly, positive effects have also been identified for the transgressor.

Beneficial Outcomes for the Offender

Considerably less research has exerted focused attention on understanding the consequences of receiving forgiveness for the offender, although these are naturally expected to be positive in nature. A few studies that have directly examined transgressor outcomes reveal similar benefits for both the forgiver and the offender. For example, offenders have been shown to experience physical/physiological health benefits such as decreased blood pressure after having been forgiven (Hannon et al., 2012). Being forgiven has relational implications for the transgressor as well. In the context of dating relationships, perceptions of having been forgiven are associated with an increase in the offender's trust in the transgressed-against partner, which in turn predicts the offender's satisfaction with the relationship, which subsequently impacts the offender's commitment to the relationship (Wieselquist, 2009).

Unfavorable Outcomes of Forgiveness

Despite the positive reputation of forgiveness and the numerous benefits that have been documented, it is not a magic bullet for relational ills. There is a dark side of forgiveness wherein costs are sometimes entailed, including exploitation risk of continued partner offenses for the forgiveness granter (Burnette et al., 2012). Evolutionary perspectives on forgiveness suggest that an adaptive forgiveness system takes into account both exploitation risk and the value of the primary relationship, or the benefits versus costs of continuing a relationship with the transgressor, when considering forgiveness (Burnette et al., 2012). The offender's posttransgression behavior in the form of amends for the offense can influence this process, as better-quality amends (as discussed previously) cue perceptions of decreased exploitation risk and increased relationship value in the future for the transgressed-against partner.

As granting forgiveness for transgressions can render the forgiver susceptible to being reoffended, increased distress is experienced after forgiving exploitative partners if forgiveness is granted for the sake of the relationship (e.g., to continue a dysfunctional codependent relationship) versus for the sake of one's self (Gabriels & Strelan, 2018; Strelan et al., 2017). Other unfavorable outcomes for the forgiver have been identified that are dependent on particular personality characteristics of the offender. For example, the tendency to forgive less agreeable spouses has been negatively associated with changes in self-respect over time (Luchies et al., 2010), a result which may have emerged because the partner continued to reoffend.

Recent research has linked forgiveness to the likelihood that a transgressor will reoffend, perhaps because forgiveness removes negative or undesired outcomes for the transgressor (e.g., the offended partner's anger; McNulty, 2010). Across several studies with various designs (i.e., survey, experimental, longitudinal, diary) and assessments of forgiveness, forgiving a partner for a transgression has been shown to encourage that partner to reoffend, if the offender is lower in agreeableness (McNulty & Russell, 2016). Results such as these have not led scholars to conclude that forgiveness is disadvantageous, but its effects are evidently nuanced (Overall & McNulty, 2017). Forgiveness—particularly for severe transgressions such as infidelity—may need to be supplemented with partner regulation behaviors (i.e., communicative strategies that explicitly express opposition to the partner's behavior, such as requiring change and blaming the partner), lest the offending partner feel free to continue their hurtful behavior unchecked (Russell et al., 2018).

Other deleterious consequences for the forgiveness granter have emerged. Forgiveness may undermine one's sense of relational justice (Kelley et al., 2019). When the partner is a frequent offender, the tendency to forgive has been associated with declines in relationship satisfaction for the forgiver (McNulty, 2008). Forgiveness that is not deserved or justified (e.g., because of the severity and/or frequency of the partner's offense) may serve to prolong an unhealthy relationship, and it can also diminish the forgiveness granter's mental health (Luchies et al., 2010). Women's forgiveness of a partner's abuse may reinforce unequal power distributions and may be equated with tolerance of abuse (Lamb, 2002). Dominant abusers who are able to elicit empathy from their female targets are more likely to be forgiven, implicating a vicious cycle wherein empathy-driven forgiveness is associated with continued patterns of abuse (Tsang & Stanford, 2007).

Forgiveness can have negative extradyadic implications as well, given that it may influence the forgiver's relationship with third parties (i.e., those who have a close relationship with the offended). Some research has shown that third parties (e.g., close friends or family members of the offended) are less willing to forgive offenders, even after the transgressed-against partner has granted forgiveness. Transgressed-against partners seem more likely to forgive offending partners because of a high level of commitment to the relationship (which is absent for third parties) and because of a tendency to make more benign attributions for the offender's behavior (a tendency which third parties do not share; Green et al., 2008). In this way, forgiveness of a partner for a major transgression can have ramifications for the forgiveness granter's extradyadic relationships with friends and family members who may disagree with the decision to forgive.

Conclusion

As discussed in this chapter, a romantic partner's infidelity is one of the most severe transgressions that partners can experience—so severe that many people who are affected by infidelity consider the offense to be unforgivable. Yet, forgiveness is possible, and if such a benevolent response is chosen, available evidence from the realms of psychology and communication points to numerous benefits for the self, the partner, and the relationship. However, forgiveness has to "occur in the right way and for the right reasons" (North, 1998, p. 20). Forgiveness-granting and forgiveness-seeking are promoted or hindered by a number of factors relevant to the consideration of a partner's infidelity, including the presence and quality of offender amends. Despite its largely constructive impact, forgiveness is not a universal panacea following the experience of a partner's infidelity, and in fact may lead to destructive consequences such as the continuance of an unhealthy relationship with potential for exploitation risk.

References

Afifi, W. A., Falato, W. L., & Weiner, J. L. (2001). Identity concerns following a severe relational transgression: The role of discovery method for the relational outcomes of infidelity. *Journal of Social and Personal Relationships, 18*(2), 291–308. https://doi.org/10.1177/0265407501182007

Alberts, J. K., Yoshimura, C. G., Rabby, M., & Loschiavo, R. (2005). Mapping the topography of couples' daily conversation. *Journal of Social and Personal Relationships, 22*(3), 299–322. https://doi.org/10.1177/0265407505050941

Allen, E. S., & Baucom, D. H. (2006). Dating, marital, and hypothetical extradyadic involvements: How do they compare? *Journal of Sex Research, 43*(4), 307–317. https://doi.org/10.1080/00224490609552330

Apostolou, M. (2019). The evolution of same-sex attraction in women. *Journal of Individual Differences, 40*, 104–110. https://doi.org/10.1027/1614-0001/a000281

Balliet, D. (2010). Communication and cooperation in social dilemmas: A meta-analytic review. *Journal of Conflict Resolution, 54*(1), 39–57. https://doi.org/10.1177/0022002709352443

Baker, J. C., Williams, J. K., Witvliet, C. V., & Hill, P. C. (2017). Positive reappraisals after an offense: Event-related potentials and emotional effects of benefit-finding and compassion. *Journal of Positive Psychology, 12*(4), 373–384. https://doi.org/10.1080/17439760.2016.1209540

Baskin, T. W., Rhody, M., Schoolmeesters, S., & Ellingson, M. (2011). Supporting special-needs adoptive couples: Assessing an intervention to enhance forgiveness, increase marital satisfaction, and prevent depression. *Counseling Psychologist, 39*(7), 933–955. https://doi.org/10.1177/0011000010397554

Baucom, D. H., Snyder, D. K., & Gordon, K. C. (2011). *Helping couples get past the affair: A clinician's guide.* Guilford Press.

Baumeister, R. F., Exline, J. J., & Sommer, K. L. (1998). The victim role, grudge theory, and two dimensions of forgiveness. In E. L. Worthington, Jr. (Ed.), *Dimensions of forgiveness: Psychological research and theological perspectives* (pp. 79–104). Templeton Foundation Press.

Berry, J. W., & Worthington, E. L., Jr. (2001). Forgivingness, relationship quality, stress while imagining relationship events, and physical and mental health. *Journal of Counseling Psychology, 48*(4), 447–455. https://doi.org/10.1037/0022-0167.48.4.447

Berry, J. W., Worthington, E. L., Jr., O'Connor, L. E., Parrott, L., & Wade, N. G. (2005). Forgivingness, vengeful rumination, and affective traits. *Journal of Personality, 73*(1), 183–226. https://doi.org/10.1111/j.1467-6494.2004.00308.x

Berry, J. W., Worthington, E. L., Jr., Parrott, L., O'Connor, L. E., & Wade, N. G. (2001). Dispositional forgivingness: Development and construct validity of the Transgression Narrative Test of Forgivingness (TNTF). *Personality and Social Psychology Bulletin, 27*(10), 1277–1290. https://doi.org/10.1177/01461672012710004

Bevan, J. L., Cameron, K. A., & Dillow, M. R. (2003). One more try: Compliance-gaining strategies associated with romantic reconciliation attempts. *Southern Communication Journal, 68*(2), 121–135. https://doi.org/10.1080/10417940309373255

Blow, A. J., & Hartnett, K. (2005). Infidelity in committed relationships I: A methodological review. *Journal of Marital and Family Therapy, 31*(2), 183–216. https://doi.org/10.1111/j.1752-0606.2005.tb01555.x

Bowlby, J. (1969). *Attachment and loss* (Vol. 1). Random House.

Braithwaite, S. R., Selby, E. A., & Fincham, F. D. (2011). Forgiveness and relationship satisfaction: Mediating mechanisms. *Journal of Family Psychology, 25*(4), 551–559. https://doi.org/10.1037/a0024526

Brose, L. A., Rye, M. S., Lutz-Zois, C., & Ross, S. R. (2005). Forgiveness and personality traits. *Personality and Individual Differences, 39*(1), 35–46. https://doi.org/10.1016/j.paid.2004.11.001

Burnette, J. L., Davis, D. E., Green, J. D., Worthington, E. L., Jr., & Bradfield, E. (2009). Insecure attachment and depressive symptoms: The mediating role of rumination, empathy, and forgiveness. *Personality and Individual Differences, 46*(3), 276–280. https://doi.org/10.1016/j.paid.2008.10.016

Burnette, J. L., McCullough, M. E., Van Tongeren, D. R., & Davis, D. E. (2012). Forgiveness results from integrating information about relationship value and exploitation risk. *Personality and Social Psychology Bulletin, 38*(3), 345–356. https://doi.org/10.1177/0146167211424582

Caraballo, R., Rye, M. S., Pan, W., Kirschman, K. J. B., Lutz-Zois, C., & Lyons, A. M. (2008). Negative affect and anger rumination as mediators between forgiveness and sleep quality. *Journal of Behavioral Medicine, 31*(6), 478–488. https://doi.org/10.1007/s10865-008-9172-5

Carmody, P., & Gordon, K. (2011). Offender variables: Unique predictors of benevolence, avoidance, and revenge? *Personality and Individual Differences, 50*(7), 1012–1017. https://doi.org/10.1016/j.paid.2010.12.037

Cheadle, A. C., & Toussaint, L. L. (2015). Forgiveness and physical health in healthy populations. In L. L. Toussaint, E. L. Worthington, Jr., & D. R. Williams (Eds.), *Forgiveness and health: Scientific evidence and theories relating forgiveness to better health* (pp. 91–106). Springer. https://doi.org/10.1007/978-94-017-9993-5_7

Chi, P., Tang, Y., Worthington, E. L., Chan, C. L., Lam, D. O., & Lin, X. (2019). Intrapersonal and interpersonal facilitators of forgiveness following spousal infidelity: A stress and coping perspective. *Journal of Clinical Psychology, 75*(10), 1896–1915. https://doi.org/10.1002/jclp.22825

Chiaramello, S., Sastre, M. T. M., & Mullet, E. (2008). Seeking forgiveness: Factor structure, and relationships with personality and forgivingness. *Personality and Individual Differences, 45*(5), 383–388. https://doi.org/10.1016/j.paid.2008.05.009

Chung, M. S. (2014). Pathways between attachment and marital satisfaction: The mediating roles of rumination, empathy, and forgiveness. *Personality and Individual Differences, 70*, 246–251. https://doi.org/10.1016/j.paid.2014.06.032

Clarke, V., Braun, V., & Wooles, K. (2015). Thou shalt not covet another man? Exploring constructions of same-sex and different-sex infidelity using story completion. *Journal of Community & Applied Social Psychology, 25*(2), 153–166. https://doi.org/10.1002/casp.2204

Compton, B. L., & Bowman, J. M. (2017). Perceived cross-orientation infidelity: Heterosexual perceptions of same-sex cheating in exclusive relationships. *Journal of Homosexuality, 64*(11), 1469–1483. https://doi.org/10.1080/00918369.2016.1244447

Confer, J. C., & Cloud, M. D. (2011). Sex differences in response to imagining a partner's heterosexual or homosexual affair. *Personality and Individual Differences, 50*, 129–134. https://doi.org/10.1016/j.paid.2010.09.007

Crowley, J. P. (2014). Expressive writing to cope with hate speech: Assessing psychobiological stress recovery and forgiveness promotion for lesbian, gay, bisexual, or queer victims of hate speech. *Human Communication Research, 40*(2), 238–261. https://doi.org/10.1111/hcre.12020

Crowley, J. P., & Allred, R. A. (2020). The physiological substrate of forgiveness. In L. Aloia, A. Denes, & J. P. Crowley (Eds.), *The Oxford handbook of the physiology of interpersonal communication* (pp. 191–209). Oxford University Press.

Crowley, J. P., Denes, A., Makos, S., & Whitt, J. (2018). Threats to courtship and the physiological response: Testosterone mediates the association between relational uncertainty and disclosure for dating partner recipients of relational transgressions. *Adaptive Human Behavior and Physiology, 4*(3), 264–282. https://doi.org/10.1007/s40750-018-0092-5

Dailey, R. M., Pfiester, A., Jin, B., Beck, G., & Clark, G. (2009). On-again/off-again dating relationships: How are they different from other dating relationships? *Personal Relationships, 16*(1), 23–47. https://doi.org/10.1111/j.1475-6811.2009.01208.x

Da Silva, S. P., Witvliet, C., & Riek, B. (2017). Self-forgiveness and forgiveness-seeking in response to rumination: Cardiac and emotional responses of transgressors. *Journal of Positive Psychology, 12*(4), 362–372. https://doi.org/10.1080/17439760.2016.1187200

Davis, D. E., Hook, J. N., Van Tongeren, D. R., DeBlaere, C., Rice, K. G., & Worthington, E. L., Jr. (2015). Making a decision to forgive. *Journal of Counseling Psychology, 62*(3), 280–288. https://doi.org/10.1037/cou0000054

Davis, D. E., Worthington, E. L., Jr., Hook, J. N., & Hill, P. C. (2013). Research on religion/spirituality and forgiveness: A meta-analytic review. *Psychology of Religion and Spirituality, 5*(4), 233–241. https://doi.org/10.1037/a0033637

Davis, J. L., Green, J. D., Reid, C. A., Moloney, J. M., & Burnette, J. (2015). Forgiveness and health in nonmarried dyadic relationships. In L. L. Toussaint, E. L. Worthington, Jr., & D. R. Williams (Eds.), *Forgiveness and health: Scientific evidence and theories relating forgiveness to better health* (pp. 239–253). Springer. https://doi.org/10.1007/978-94-017-9993-5_16

Davis, J. R., & Gold, G. J. (2011). An examination of emotional empathy, attributions of stability, and the link between perceived remorse and forgiveness. *Personality and Individual Differences, 50*(3), 392–397. https://doi.org/10.1016/j.paid.2010.10.031

Denes, A., Dillow, M. R., DelGreco, M., Lannutti, P. J., & Bevan, J. (2020b). Forgive and forget? Examining the influence of blame and intentionality on forgiveness following hypothetical same-sex infidelity in the context of heterosexual romantic relationships. *Journal of Sex Research, 57*(4), 482–497. https://doi.org/10.1080/00224499.2019.1612831

Denes, A., Dillow, M.R., Lannutti, P.J., & Bevan, J. (2020a). Acceptable experimentation? Investigating reasons for same-sex infidelity and women's anticipated responses to a male partner's hypothetical same-sex infidelity. *Personality & Individual Differences, 160*. https://doi.org/10.1016/j.paid.2020.109929

Denes, A., Lannutti, P. J., & Bevan, J. L. (2015). Same-sex infidelity in heterosexual relationships: Communicative responses, jealousy-related emotions, and relational outcomes. *Personal Relationships, 22*(3), 414–430. https://doi.org/10.1080/03637751.2015.1068432

DiBlasio, F. A. (2000). Decision-based forgiveness treatment in cases of marital infidelity. *Psychotherapy: Theory, Research, Practice, Training, 37*(2), 149–158. https://doi.org/10.1037/h0087834

Dillow, M. R., Malachowski, C. C., Brann, M., & Weber, K. D. (2011). An experimental examination of the effects of communicative infidelity motives on communication and relational outcomes in romantic relationships. *Western Journal of Communication, 75*(5), 473–499. https://doi.org/10.1080/10570314.2011.588986

Emmers, T. M., & Canary, D. J. (1996). The effect of uncertainty reducing strategies on young couples' relational repair and intimacy. *Communication Quarterly, 44*(2), 166–182. https://doi.org/10.1080/01463379609370008

Enright, R. D. (2001). *Forgiveness is a choice*. American Psychological Association.

Enright, R. D., & Coyle, C. T. (1998). Researching the process model of forgiveness within psychological interventions. In E. L. Worthington Jr. (Ed.), *Dimensions of forgiveness* (pp. 139–161). Templeton Foundation Press.

Enright, R. D., & Fitzgibbons, R. P. (2000). *Helping clients forgive: An empirical guide for resolving anger and restoring hope.* American Psychological Association. https://doi.org/10.1037/10381-000

Enright, R. D., Freedman, S., & Rique, J. (1998). The psychology of interpersonal forgiveness. In R. D. Enright & J. North (Eds.), *Exploring forgiveness* (pp. 46–62). The University of Wisconsin Press.

Enright, R. D., Gassin, E. A., & Wu, C. R. (1992). Forgiveness: A developmental view. *Journal of Moral Education, 21*(2), 99–114. https://doi.org/10.1080/0305724920210202

Enright, R. D., & the Human Development Study Group. (1991). The moral development of forgiveness. In W. Kertines & J. Gerwitz (Eds.), *Handbook of moral behavior and development* (pp. 123–152). Hillsdale, NJ: Erlbaum.

Enright R. D., & Rique J. (2004). *The Enright Forgiveness Inventory (EFI) user's manual*. Mind Garden Press.

Enright, R. D., Santos, M. J. D., & Al-Mabuk, R. (1989). The adolescent as forgiver. *Journal of Adolescence, 12*(1), 95–110. https://doi.org/10.1016/0140-1971(89)90092-4

Exline, J. L., & Baumeister, R. L. (2000). Expressing forgiveness and repentance: Benefits and barriers. In M. C. McCullough, K. I. Pargament, & C. E. Thoresen (Eds.), *Forgiveness: Theory, research, and practice* (pp. 133–155). Guilford Press.

Exline, J. J., Baumeister, R. F., Bushman, B. J., Campbell, W. K., & Finkel, E. J. (2004). Too proud to let go: Narcissistic entitlement as a barrier to forgiveness. *Journal of Personality and Social Psychology, 87*(6), 894–912. https://doi.org/10.1037/0022-3514.87.6.894

Exline, J. J., Worthington, E. L., Jr., Hill, P., & McCullough, M. E. (2003). Forgiveness and justice: A research agenda for social and personality psychology. *Personality and Social Psychology Review*, *7*(4), 337–348. https://doi.org/10.1207/s15327957pspr0704_06

Fennell, D. L. (1993). Characteristics of long-term first marriages. *Journal of Mental Health Counseling*, *15*(4), 446–460.

Fife, S. T., Weeks, G. R., & Stellberg-Filbert, J. (2013). Facilitating forgiveness in the treatment of infidelity: An interpersonal model. *Journal of Family Therapy*, *35*(4), 343–367. https://doi.org/10.1111/j.1467-6427.2011.00561.x

Fincham, F. D. (2000). The kiss of the porcupines: From attributing responsibility to forgiving. *Personal Relationships*, *7*(1), 1–23. https://doi.org/10.1111/j.1475-6811.2000.tb00001.x

Fincham, F. D. (2020). Forgiveness in marriage. In E. L. Worthington, Jr., & N. G. Wade (Eds.), *Handbook of forgiveness* (2nd ed., pp. 142–152). Routledge. https://doi.org/10.4324/9781351123341-14

Fincham, F. D., & Beach, S. R. H. (2002). Forgiveness in marriage: Implications for psychological aggression and constructive communication. *Personal Relationships*, *9*(3), 239–251. https://doi.org/10.1111/1475-6811.00016

Fincham, F., & Beach, S. R. (2007). Forgiveness and marital quality: Precursor or consequence in well-established relationships? *Journal of Positive Psychology*, *2*(4), 260–268. https://doi.org/10.1080/17439760701552360

Fincham, F. D., Beach, S. R., & Davila, J. (2007). Longitudinal relations between forgiveness and conflict resolution in marriage. *Journal of Family Psychology*, *21*(3), 542–545. https://doi.org/10.1037/0893-3200.21.3.542

Fincham, F. D., Hall, J. H., & Beach, S. R. H. (2005). "Til lack of forgiveness doth us part": Forgiveness and marriage. In E. L. Worthington Jr. (Ed.), *Handbook of forgiveness* (pp. 207–225). Routledge.

Fincham, F. D., & May, R. W. (2017). Prayer and forgiveness: Beyond relationship quality and extension to marriage. *Journal of Family Psychology*, *31*(6), 734–741. https://doi.org/10.1037/fam0000331

Fincham, F. D., Paleari, F. G., & Regalia, C. (2002). Forgiveness in marriage: The role of relationship quality, attributions, and empathy. *Personal Relationships*, *9*(1), 27–37. https://doi.org/10.1111/1475-6811.00002

Finkel, E. J., Rusbult, C. E., Kumashiro, M., & Hannon, P. A. (2002). Dealing with betrayal in close relationships: Does commitment promote forgiveness? *Journal of Personality and Social Psychology*, *82*(6), 956–974. https://doi.org/10.1037/0022-3514.82.6.956

Fiske, S. T., & Taylor, S. E. (1991). *Social cognition* (2nd ed.). McGraw-Hill.

Freedman, S. (1998). Forgiveness and reconciliation: The importance of understanding how they differ. *Counseling and Values*, *42*(3), 200–216. https://doi.org/10.1002/j.2161-007X.1998.tb00426.x

Freedman, S., & Enright, R. D. (2019). A review of the empirical research using Enright's process model of interpersonal forgiveness. In E. L. Worthington, Jr. & N. G. Wade (Eds.), *Handbook of forgiveness* (2nd ed., pp. 266–276). Routledge. https://doi.org/10.4324/9781351123341-25

Furman, W., & Buhrmester, D. (2009). Methods and measures: The network of relationships inventory: Behavioral systems version. *International Journal of Behavioral Development*, *33*(5), 470–478. https://doi.org/10.1177/0165025409342634

Gabriels, J. B., & Strelan, P. (2018). For whom we forgive matters: Relationship focus magnifies, but self-focus buffers against the negative effects of forgiving an exploitative partner. *British Journal of Social Psychology*, *57*(1), 154–173. https://doi.org/10.1111/bjso.12230

Gordon, K. C., & Baucom, D. H. (1998). Understanding betrayals in marriage: A synthesized model of forgiveness. *Family Process*, *37*(4), 425–449. https://doi.org/10.1111/j.1545-5300.1998.00425.x

Gordon, K. C., & Baucom, D. H. (1999). A multitheoretical intervention for promoting recovery from extramarital affairs. *Clinical Psychology: Science and Practice*, *6*(4), 382–399. https://doi.org/10.1093/clipsy.6.4.382

Gordon, K. C., & Baucom, D. H (2003). Forgiveness and marriage: Preliminary support for a measure based on a model of recovery from marital betrayal. *American Journal of Family Therapy*, *31*(3), 179–199. https://doi.org/10.1080/01926180301115

Gordon, K. C., Baucom, D. H., & Snyder, D. K. (2004). An integrative intervention for promoting recovery from extramarital affairs. *Journal of Marital and Family Therapy*, *30*(2), 213–231. https://doi.org/10.1111/j.1752-0606.2004.tb01235.x

Gordon, K. C., Hughes, F. M., Tomcik, N. D., Dixon, L. J., & Litzinger, S. C. (2009). Widening spheres of impact: The role of forgiveness in marital and family functioning. *Journal of Family Psychology, 23*(1), 1–13. https://doi.org/10.1037/a0014354

Green, J. D., Burnette, J. L., & Davis, J. L. (2008). Third-party forgiveness: (Not) forgiving your close other's betrayer. *Personality and Social Psychology Bulletin, 34*(3), 407–418. https://doi.org/10.1177/0146167207311534

Green, M., DeCourville, N., & Sadava, S. (2012). Positive affect, negative affect, stress, and social support as mediators of the forgiveness-health relationship. *Journal of Social Psychology, 152*(3), 288–307. https://doi.org/10.1080/00224545.2011.603767

Greenberg, L., Warwar, S., & Malcolm, W. (2010). Emotion-focused couples therapy and the facilitation of forgiveness. *Journal of Marital and Family Therapy, 36*(1), 28–42. https://doi.org/10.1111/j.1752-0606.2009.00185.x

Griffin, B. J., Worthington, E. L., Lavelock, C. R., Wade, N. G., & Hoyt, W. T. (2015). Forgiveness and mental health. In L. L. Toussaint, E. L. Worthington, Jr., & D. R. Williams (Eds.), *Forgiveness and health: Scientific evidence and theories relating forgiveness to better health* (pp. 77–90). Springer. https://doi.org/10.1007/978-94-017-9993-5_6

Gunderson, P. R., & Ferrari, J. R. (2008). Forgiveness of sexual cheating in romantic relationships: Effects of discovery method, frequency of offense, and presence of apology. *North American Journal of Psychology, 10*(1), 1–14.

Hall, J. H., & Fincham, F. D. (2005). Self-forgiveness: The stepchild of forgiveness. *Journal of Social and Clinical Psychology, 24*(5), 621–637. https://doi.org/10.1521/jscp.2005.24.5.621

Hall, J. H., & Fincham, F. D. (2006). Relationship dissolution following infidelity: The roles of attributions and forgiveness. *Journal of Social and Clinical Psychology, 25*(5), 508–522. https://doi.org/10.1521/jscp.2006.25.5.508

Hannon, P. A., Finkel, E. J., Kumashiro, M., & Rusbult, C. E. (2012). The soothing effects of forgiveness on victims' and perpetrators' blood pressure. *Personal Relationships, 19*(2), 279–289. https://doi.org/10.1111/j.1475-6811.2011.01356.x

Hannon, P. A., Rusbult, C. E., Finkel, E. J., & Kumashiro, M. (2010). In the wake of betrayal: Amends, forgiveness, and the resolution of betrayal. *Personal Relationships, 17*(2), 253–278.

Hargrave, T. D. (1994). Families and forgiveness: A theoretical and therapeutic framework. *Family Journal, 2*(4), 339–348. https://doi.org/10.1177/1066480794024007

Hargrave, T. D., & Sells, J. N. (1997). The development of a forgiveness scale. *Journal of Marital and Family Therapy, 23*(1), 41–62. https://doi.org/10.1111/j.17520606.1997.tb00230.x

Hazan, C., & Shaver, P. (1987). Romantic love conceptualized as an attachment process. *Journal of Personality and Social Psychology, 52*(3), 511–524. https://doi.org/10.1037/0022-3514.52.3.511

Heider, F. (1958). *The psychology of interpersonal relations*. New York, NY: Wiley.

Hermans, E. J., Putnam, P., & Van Honk, J. (2006). Testosterone administration reduces empathetic behavior: A facial mimicry study. *Psychoneuroendocrinology, 31*(7), 859–866. https://doi.org/10.1016/j.psyneuen.2006.04.002

Herschl, L. C., Highland, K. B., & McChargue, D. E. (2012). Prenatal exposure to testosterone interacts with lifetime physical abuse to predict anger rumination and cognitive flexibility among incarcerated methamphetamine users. *American Journal on Addictions, 21*(4), 363–369. https://doi.org/10.1111/j.1521-0391.2012.00246.x

Hilbig, B. E., Thielmann, I., Klein, S. A., & Henninger, F. (2016). The two faces of cooperation: On the unique role of HEXACO Agreeableness for forgiveness versus retaliation. *Journal of Research in Personality, 64*, 69–78. https://doi.org/10.1016/j.jrp.2016.08.004

Ho, M. Y., & Fung, H. H. (2011). A dynamic process model of forgiveness: A cross-cultural perspective. *Review of General Psychology, 15*(1), 77–84. https://doi.org/10.1037/a0022605

Hook, J. N., Worthington, E. L., Jr., & Utsey, S. O. (2009). Collectivism, forgiveness, and social harmony. *Counseling Psychologist, 37*(6), 821-847. https://doi.org/10.1177/0011000008326546

Hoyt, W. T., Fincham, F. D., McCullough, M. E., Maio, G., & Davila, J. (2005). Responses to interpersonal transgressions in families: Forgivingness, forgivability, and relationship-specific effects. *Journal of Personality and Social Psychology, 89*(3), 375–394. https://doi.org/10.1037/0022-3514.89.3.375

Hoyt, W. T., & McCullough, M. E. (2005). Issues in the multimodal measurement of forgiveness. In E. L. Worthington, Jr., (Ed.), *Handbook of forgiveness* (pp. 109–123). Routledge. https://doi.org/10.4324/9780203955673

Hughes, S. M., Harrison, M. A., & Gallup, G. G., Jr. (2004). Sex differences in mating strategies: Mate guarding, infidelity and multiple concurrent sex partners. *Sexualities, Evolution, & Gender, 6*(1), 3–13. https://doi.org/10.1080/14616660410001733588

Johns, K. N., Allen, E. S., & Gordon, K. C. (2015). The relationship between mindfulness and forgiveness of infidelity. *Mindfulness, 6*(6), 1462–1471. https://doi.org/10.1007/s12671-015-0427-2

Karremans, J. C., & Van Lange, P. A. (2004). Back to caring after being hurt: The role of forgiveness. *European Journal of Social Psychology, 34*(2), 207–227. https://doi.org/10.1002/ejsp.192

Kelley, D. L. (1998). The communication of forgiveness. *Communication Studies, 49*(3), 255–271. https://doi.org/10.1080/10510979809368535

Kelley, H. H., & Thibaut, J. W. (1978). *Interpersonal relations: A theory of interdependence*. Wiley.

Kelley, D. L., & Waldron, V. R. (2005). An investigation of forgiveness-seeking communication and relational outcomes. *Communication Quarterly, 53*(3), 339–358. https://doi.org/10.1080/01463370500101097

Kelley, D. L., Waldron, V. R., & Kloeber, D. N. (2019). *A communicative approach to conflict, forgiveness, and reconciliation: Reimagining our relationships*. Routledge. https://doi.org/10.4324/9781315166353-8

Khaddouma, A., Gordon, K. C., & Bolden, J. (2015). Zen and the art of sex: Examining associations among mindfulness, sexual satisfaction, and relationship satisfaction in dating relationships. *Sexual and Relationship Therapy, 30*(2), 268–285. https://doi.org/10.1080/14681994.2014.992408

Kloeber, D. N. (2011). *Voicing conditional forgiveness*. Arizona State University.

Kloeber, D. N., & Waldron, V. R. (2017). Expressing and suppressing conditional forgiveness in serious romantic relationships. In J. A. Samp (Ed.), *Communicating interpersonal conflict in close relationships. Contexts, challenges, and opportunities* (pp. 250–266). Routledge. https://doi.org/10.4324/9781315774237

Kimmes, J. G., & Durtschi, J. A. (2016). Forgiveness in romantic relationships: The roles of attachment, empathy, and attributions. *Journal of Marital and Family Therapy, 42*(4), 645–658. https://doi.org/10.1111/jmft.12171

Kowalski, R. M. (1997). *Aversive interpersonal behaviors*. Springer Series in Social/Clinical Psychology. Springer. https://doi.org/10.1007/978-1-4757-9354-3_10

Krause, N., & Ellison, C. G. (2003). Forgiveness by God, forgiveness of others, and psychological well–being in late life. *Journal for the Scientific Study of Religion, 42*(1), 77–93. https://doi.org/10.1111/1468-5906.00162

Kurniati, N. M. T., Worthington, E. L., Kristi Poerwandari, E., Ginanjar, A. S., & Dwiwardani, C. (2017). Forgiveness in Javanese collective culture: The relationship between rumination, harmonious value, decisional forgiveness and emotional forgiveness. *Asian Journal of Social Psychology, 20*(2), 113–127. https://doi.org/10.1111/ajsp.12173

Lamb, S. (2002). Women, abuse, and forgiveness: A special case. In. S. Lamb & J. G. Murphy (Eds.), *Before forgiving: Cautionary views of forgiveness in psychotherapy* (pp. 155–171). Oxford University Press. https://doi.org/10.1093/acprof:oso/9780195145205.003.0009

Larkin, K. T., Goulet, C., & Cavanaugh, C. (2015). Forgiveness and physiological concomitants and outcomes. In L. L. Toussaint, E. L. Worthington, Jr., & D. R. Williams (Eds.), *Forgiveness and health: Scientific evidence and theories relating forgiveness to better health* (pp. 61–76). Springer. https://doi.org/10.1007/978-94-017-9993-5_5

Larsen, B. A., Darby, R. S., Harris, C. R., Nelkin, D. K., Milam, P. E., & Christenfeld, N. J. (2012). The immediate and delayed cardiovascular benefits of forgiving. *Psychosomatic Medicine, 74*(7), 745–750. https://doi.org/10.1097/psy.0b013e31825fe96c

Laumann, E. O., Gagnon, J. H., Michael, R. T., & Michaels, S. (1994). *Sex in America*. CSG Enterprise.

Laumann, E. O., Gagnon, J. H., Michael, R. T., & Michaels, S. (2000). *The social organization of sexuality: Sexual practices in the United States*. University of Chicago Press.

Lawler, K. A., Younger, J. W., Piferi, R. L., Billington, E., Jobe, R., Edmondson, K., & Jones, W. H. (2003). A change of heart: Cardiovascular correlates of forgiveness in response to interpersonal conflict. *Journal of Behavioral Medicine, 26*(5), 373–393. https://doi.org/10.1023/a:1025771716686

Lawler, K. A., Younger, J. W., Piferi, R. L., Jobe, R. L., Edmondson, K. A., & Jones, W. H. (2005). The unique effects of forgiveness on health: An exploration of pathways. *Journal of Behavioral Medicine, 28*(2), 157–167. https://doi.org/10.1007/s10865-005-3665-2

Lawler-Row, K. A. (2010). Forgiveness as a mediator of the religiosity—Health relationship. *Psychology of Religion and Spirituality*, *2*(1), 1–16. https://doi.org/10.1037/a0017584

Lawler-Row, K. A., Karremans, J. C., Scott, C., Edlis-Matityahou, M., & Edwards, L. (2008). Forgiveness, physiological reactivity and health: The role of anger. *International Journal of Psychophysiology*, *68*(1), 51–58. https://doi.org/10.1016/j.ijpsycho.2008.01.001

Lawler-Row, K. A., Younger, J. W., Piferi, R. L., & Jones, W. H. (2006). The role of adult attachment style in forgiveness following an interpersonal offense. *Journal of Counseling & Development*, *84*(4), 493–502. https://doi.org/10.1002/j.1556-6678.2006.tb00434.x

Lazarus, R. S., & Folkman, S. (1984). *Stress, appraisal, and coping*. Springer. https://doi.org/10.1017/s0033291700031652

Luchies, L. B., Finkel, E. J., Coy, A. E., Reid, C. A., Van Tongeren, D. R., Davis, J. L., & Green, J. D. (2019). People feel worse about their forgiveness when mismatches between forgiveness and amends create adaptation risks. *Journal of Social and Personal Relationships*, *36*(2), 681–705. https://doi.org/10.1177/0265407517740983

Luchies, L. B., Finkel, E. J., McNulty, J. K., & Kumashiro, M. (2010). The doormat effect: When forgiving erodes self-respect and self-concept clarity. *Journal of Personality and Social Psychology*, *98*(5), 734–749. https://doi.org/10.1037/a0020156

Mahoney, A. (2010). Religion in families, 1999–2009: A relational spirituality framework. *Journal of Marriage and Family*, *72*(4), 805–827. https://doi.org/10.1111/j.1741-3737.2010.00732.x

Mahoney, A., Pargament, K. I., Jewell, T., Swank, A. B., Scott, E., Emery, E., & Rye, M. (2017). Marriage and the spiritual realm: The role of proximal and distal religious constructs and marital functioning. *Journal of Family Psychology*, *13*(3), 321–338.

Marty, M. E. (1998). The ethos of Christian forgiveness. In E. L. Worthington, Jr., (Ed.), *Dimensions of forgiveness: Psychological research and theological perspectives* (pp. 9–28). Templeton Foundation Press.

Merolla, A. J., Zhang, S., McCullough, J. L., & Sun, S. (2017). How do you like your forgiveness? Communication style preferences and effects. *Communication Studies*, *68*(5), 568–587. https://doi.org/10.1080/10510974.2017.1377743

Merolla, A. J., Zhang, S., & Sun, S. (2013). Forgiveness in the United States and China: Antecedents, consequences, and communication style comparisons. *Communication Research*, *40*(5), 595–622. https://doi.org/10.1177/0093650212446960

McCullough, M. E. (2008). *Beyond revenge: The evolution of the forgiveness instinct*. Jossey-Bass.

McCullough, M. E., Bellah, C. G., Kilpatrick, S. D., & Johnson, J. L. (2001). Vengefulness: Relationships with forgiveness, rumination, well-being, and the Big Five. *Personality and Social Psychology Bulletin*, *27*(5), 601–610. https://doi.org/10.1177/0146167201275008

McCullough, M. E., Bono, G., & Root, L. M. (2007a). Rumination, emotion, and forgiveness: Three longitudinal studies. *Journal of Personality and Social Psychology*, *92*(3), 490–505. https://doi.org/10.1037/0022-3514.92.3.490

McCullough, M. E., Fincham, F. D., & Tsang, J. A. (2003). Forgiveness, forbearance, and time: The temporal unfolding of transgression-related interpersonal motivations. *Journal of Personality and Social Psychology*, *84*(3), 540–557. https://doi.org/10.1037/0022-3514.84.3.540

McCullough, M. E., & Hoyt, W. T. (2002). Transgression-related motivational dispositions: Personality substrates of forgiveness and their links to the Big Five. *Personality and Social Psychology Bulletin*, *28*(11), 1556–1573. https://doi.org/10.1177/014616702237583

McCullough, M. E., Orsulak, P., Brandon, A., & Akers, L. (2007b). Rumination, fear, and cortisol: An in vivo study of interpersonal transgressions. *Health Psychology*, *26*(1), 126–132. https://doi.org/10.1037/0278-6133.26.1.126

McCullough, M. E., Pargament, K. I., & Thoresen, C. E. (2000). *Forgiveness: Theory, research, and practice*. Guilford Press.

McCullough, M. E., Rachal, K., Sandage, S. J., Worthington, E. L., Jr., Brown, S. W., & Hight, T. L. (1998). Interpersonal forgiving in close relationships: II. Theoretical elaboration and measurement. *Journal of Personality and Social Psychology*, *75*(6), 1586–1603. https://doi.org/10.1037/0022-3514.75.6.1586

McCullough, M. E., Root, L. M., & Cohen, A. D. (2006). Writing about the benefits of an interpersonal transgression facilitates forgiveness. *Journal of Consulting and Clinical Psychology*, *74*(5), 887–897. https://doi.org/10.1037/0022-006x.74.5.887

McCullough, M. E., & Witvliet, C. V. (2001). The psychology of forgiveness. In C. R. Snyder & S. J. Lopez (Eds.), *Handbook of positive psychology* (pp. 446–455). Oxford.

McCullough, M. E., & Worthington, E. L., Jr. (1999). Religion and the forgiving personality. *Journal of Personality, 67*(6), 1141–1164. https://doi.org/10.1111/1467-6494.00085

McCullough, M. E., Worthington, E. L., Jr. & Rachal, K. C. (1997). Interpersonal forgiving in close relationships. *Journal of Personality and Social Psychology, 73*(2), 321–336. https://doi.org/10.1037/0022-3514.73.2.321

McElroy-Heltzel, S. E., Davis, D. E., Ordaz, A. C., Griffin, B. J., & Hook, J. N. (2020). Measuring forgiveness and self-forgiveness. In E. L. Worthington Jr. & N. G. Wade (Eds.), *Handbook of forgiveness* (2nd ed., pp. 74–84). Routledge. https://doi.org/10.4324/9781351123341-8

McNulty, J. K. (2008). Forgiveness in marriage: Putting the benefits into context. *Journal of Family Psychology, 22*(1), 171–175. https://doi.org/10.1037/0893-3200.22.1.171

McNulty, J. K. (2010). Forgiveness increases the likelihood of subsequent partner transgressions in marriage. *Journal of Family Psychology, 24*(6), 787–790. https://doi.org/10.1037/a0021678

McNulty, J. K., & Russell, V. M. (2016). Forgive and forget, or forgive and regret? Whether forgiveness leads to less or more offending depends on offender agreeableness. *Personality and Social Psychology Bulletin, 42*(5), 616–631. https://doi.org/10.1177/0146167216637841

Merolla, A. J. (2008). Communicating forgiveness in friendships and dating relationships. *Communication Studies, 59*(2), 114–131. https://doi.org/10.1080/10510970802062428

Merolla, A. J. (2017). Forgiveness following conflict: What it is, why it happens, and how it's done. In J. A. Samp (Ed.), *Communicating interpersonal conflict in close relationships: Contexts, challenges, and opportunities* (pp. 227–249). Routledge. https://doi.org/10.4324/9781315774237

Merolla, A. J., & Zhang, S. (2011). In the wake of transgressions: Examining forgiveness communication in personal relationships. *Personal Relationships, 18*(1), 79–95. https://doi.org/10.1111/j.1475-6811.2010.01323.x

Metts, S. (1994). Relational transgressions. In W. R. Cupach & B. H. Spitzberg (Eds.), *The dark side of interpersonal communication* (pp. 217–239). Hillsdale, NJ: Erlbaum. https://doi.org/10.4324/9780203936849

Metts, S., & Cupach, W. R. (2007). Responses to relational transgressions: Hurt, anger, and sometimes forgiveness. In B. H. Spitzberg & W. R. Cupach (Eds.), *The dark side of interpersonal communication* (2nd ed., pp. 243–274). Routledge. https://doi.org/10.4324/9780203936849

Mikulincer, M., Shaver, P. R., & Slav, K. (2006). Attachment, mental representations of others, and gratitude and forgiveness in romantic relationships. In M. Mikulincer & G. S. Goodman (Eds.), *Dynamics of romantic love: Attachment, caregiving, and sex* (pp. 190–215). New York, NY: Guilford.

Morse, C. R., & Metts, S. (2011). Situational and communicative predictors of forgiveness following a relational transgression. *Western Journal of Communication, 75*(3), 239–258. https://doi.org/10.1080/10570314.2011.571652

Newell, S. E., & Stutman, R. K. (1988). The social confrontation episode. *Communication Monographs, 55*(3), 266–285. https://doi.org/10.1080/03637758809376172

North, J. (1998). The "ideal" of forgiveness: A philosopher's exploration. In R. D. Enright & J. North (Eds.), *Exploring forgiveness* (pp. 15–45). University of Wisconsin Press.

Orcutt, H. K. (2006). The prospective relationship of interpersonal forgiveness and psychological distress symptoms among college women. *Journal of Counseling Psychology, 53*(3), 350–361. https://doi.org/10.1037/0022-0167.53.3.350

Orcutt, H. K., Pickett, S. M., & Pope, E. B. (2008). The relationship of offense-specific forgiveness to posttraumatic stress disorder symptoms in college students. *Journal of Aggression, Maltreatment & Trauma, 16*(1), 72–91. https://doi.org/10.1080/10926770801920776

Overall, N. C., & McNulty, J. K. (2017). What type of communication during conflict is beneficial for intimate relationships?. *Current Opinion in Psychology, 13*, 1–5. https://doi.org/10.1016/j.copsyc.2016.03.002

Paleari, F. G., Regalia, C., & Fincham, F. D. (2009). Measuring offence-specific forgiveness inmarriage: The Marital Offence-specific Forgiveness Scale (MOFS). *Psychological Assessment, 21*(2), 194–209. https://doi.org/10.1037/a0016068

Paleari, F. G., Regalia, C., & Fincham, F. D. (2011). Inequity in forgiveness: Implications for personal and relational well-being. *Journal of Social and Clinical Psychology, 30*(3), 297–324. https://doi.org/10.1521/jscp.2011.30.3.297

Paz, R., Neto, F., & Mullet, E. (2008). Forgiveness: A China-Western Europe comparison. *Journal of Psychology*, *142*(2), 147–158. https://doi.org/10.3200/jrlp.142.2.147-158

Pederson, J. R. (2014). Competing discourses of forgiveness: A dialogic perspective. *Communication Studies*, *65*(4), 353–369. https://doi.org/10.1080/10510974.2013.833526

Perlman, D., & Carcedo, R. J. (2011). Overview of the dark side of relationships research. In W. R. Cupach & B. H. Spitzberg (Eds.), *The dark side of close relationships II* (pp. 1–37). Routledge. https://doi.org/10.4135/9781412958479.n123

Prins, K. S., Buunk, B. P., & VanYperen, N. W. (1993). Equity, normative disapproval and extramarital relationships. *Journal of Social and Personal Relationships*, *10*(1), 39–53. https://doi.org/10.1177/0265407593101003

Reed, M. A., & Derryberry, D. (1995a). Temperament and attention to positive and negative trait information. *Personality and Individual Differences*, *18*(1), 135–147. https://doi.org/10.1016/0191-8869(94)00121-8

Reed, M. A., & Derryberry, D. (1995b). Temperament and response processing: Facilitatory and inhibitory consequences of positive and negative motivational states. *Journal of Research in Personality*, *29*(1), 59–84. https://doi.org/10.1006/jrpe.1995.1004

Ricciardi, E., Rota, G., Sani, L., Gentili, C., Gaglianese, A., Guazzelli, M., & Pietrini, P. (2013). How the brain heals emotional wounds: The functional neuroanatomy of forgiveness. *Frontiers in Human Neuroscience*, *7*, 1–9. https://doi.org/10.3389/fnhum.2013.00839

Riek, B. M., Luna, L. M. R., & Schnabelrauch, C. A. (2014). Transgressors' guilt and shame: A longitudinal examination of forgiveness seeking. *Journal of Social and Personal Relationships*, *31*(6), 751–772. https://doi.org/10.1177/0265407513503595

Riek, B. M., & Mania, E. W. (2012). The antecedents and consequences of interpersonal forgiveness: A meta-analytic review. *Personal Relationships*, *19*(2), 304–325. https://doi.org/10.1111/j.1475-6811.2011.01363.x

Rusbult, C. E. (1980). Commitment and satisfaction in romantic associations: A test of the investment model. *Journal of Experimental Social Psychology*, *16*(2), 172–186. https://doi.org/10.1016/0022-1031(80)90007-4

Rusbult, C., Verette, J., Whitney, G. A., Slovik, L.F., & Lipkus, I. (1991). Accommodation processes in close relationships: Theory and preliminary empirical evidence. *Journal of Personality and Social Psychology*, *60*(1), 53–79. https://doi.org/10.1037/0022-3514.60.1.53

Russell, V. M., Baker, L. R., McNulty, J. K., & Overall, N. C. (2018). "You're forgiven, but don't do it again!" Direct partner regulation buffers the costs of forgiveness. *Journal of Family Psychology*, *32*(4), 435–444. https://doi.org/10.1037/fam0000409

Rye, M. S., & Pargament, K. I. (2002). Forgiveness and romantic relationships in college: Can it heal the wounded heart? *Journal of Clinical Psychology*, *58*(4), 419–441. https://doi.org/10.1002/jclp.1153

Rye, M. S., Pargament, K. I., Ali, M. A., Beck, G. L., Dorff, E. N., Hallisey, C., Narayanan, V., & Williams, J. G. (2000). Religious perspectives on forgiveness. In M. E. McCullough, K. I. Pargament, & C. E. Thoresen (Eds.), *Forgiveness: Theory, Research, and Practice* (17–40). Guilford.

Sagarin, B. J., Becker, D. V., Guadagno, R. E., Nicastle, L. D., & Millevoi, A. (2003). Sex differences (and similarities) in jealousy: The moderating influence of infidelity experience and sexual orientation of the infidelity. *Evolution and Human Behavior*, *24*(1), 17–23. https://doi.org/10.1016/S1090-5138(02)00106-X

Sagarin, B. J., Becker, D. V., Guadagno, R. E., Wilkinson, W. W., & Nicastle, L. D. (2012). A reproductive threat based model of evolved sex differences in jealousy. *Evolutionary Psychology*, *10*(3), 487–503. https://doi.org/10.1177/147470491201000307

Sandage, S. J., Worthington, E. L., Jr., Hight, T. L., & Berry, J. W. (2000). Seeking forgiveness: Theoretical context and an initial empirical study. *Journal of Psychology and Theology*, *28*(1), 21–35. https://doi.org/10.1177/009164710002800102

Sauerheber, J. D., & Ponton, R. F. (2017). Healing from infidelity: The role of covenantal forgiveness. *Journal of Psychology and Christianity*, *36*(1), 51–62.

Scher, S. J., & Darley, J. M. (1997). How effective are the things people say to apologize? Effects of the realization of the apology speech act. *Journal of Psycholinguistic Research*, *26*(1), 127–140. https://doi.org/10.1023/a:1025068306386

Schumann, K. (2012). Does love mean never having to say you're sorry? Associations between relationship satisfaction, perceived apology sincerity, and forgiveness. *Journal of Social and Personal Relationships*, *29*(7), 997–1010. https://doi.org/10.1177/0265407512448277

Shackelford, T. K., & Buss, D. M. (1997). Cues to infidelity. *Personality and Social Psychology Bulletin*, *23*(10), 1034–1045. https://doi.org/10.1177/01461672972310004

Shackelford, T. K., Buss, D. M., & Bennett, K. (2002). Forgiveness or breakup: Sex differences in responses to a partner's infidelity. *Cognition & Emotion*, *16*(2), 299–307. https://doi.org/10.1080/02699930143000202

Shafa, S., Harinck, F., & Ellemers, N. (2017). Sorry seems to be the hardest word: Cultural differences in apologizing effectively. *Journal of Applied Social Psychology*, *47*(10), 553–567. https://doi.org/10.1111/jasp.12460

Shrout, M. R., & Weigel, D. J. (2017). Infidelity's aftermath: Appraisals, mental health, and health-compromising behaviors following a partner's infidelity. *Journal of Social and Personal Relationships*, *35*(8), 1067–1091. https://doi.org/10.1177/0265407517704091

Smith, H., Goode, C., Balzarini, R., Ryan, D., & Georges, M. (2014). The cost of forgiveness: Observers prefer victims who leave unfaithful romantic partners. *European Journal of Social Psychology*, *44*(7), 758–773. https://doi.org/10.1002/ejsp.2054

Sodani, M., Gholammohammadi, H., Khojastehmehr, R., & Abbaspour, Z. (2019). An investigation into the effectiveness of Robert Enright Forgiveness Inventory on the marital quality of women affected by infidelity. *Biomedical Research*, *30*(4), 563–570. https://doi.org/10.35841/biomedicalresearch.30-18-172

Strelan, P. (2007). Who forgives others, themselves, and situations? The roles of narcissism, guilt, self-esteem, and agreeableness. *Personality and Individual Differences*, *42*(2), 259–269. https://doi.org/10.1016/j.paid.2006.06.017

Strelan, P., & Covic, T. (2006). A review of forgiveness process models and a coping framework to guide future research. *Journal of Social and Clinical Psychology*, *25*(10), 1059–1085. https://doi.org/10.1521/jscp.2006.25.10.1059

Strelan, P., Crabb, S., Chan, D., & Jones, L. (2017). Lay perspectives on the costs and risks of forgiving. *Personal Relationships*, *24*(2), 392–407. https://doi.org/10.1111/pere.12189

Struthers, C. W., van Monsjou, E., Ayoub, M., & Guilfoyle, J. R. (2017). Fit to forgive: Effect of mode of exercise on capacity to override grudges and forgiveness. *Frontiers in Psychology*, *8*, 1–10. https://doi.org/10.3389/fpsyg.2017.00538

Subkoviak, M. J., Enright, R. D., Wu, C. R., Gassin, E. A., Freedman, S., Olson, L. M., & Sarinopoulos, I. (1995). Measuring interpersonal forgiveness in late adolescence and middle adulthood. *Journal of Adolescence*, *18*(6), 641–655. https://doi.org/10.1006/jado.1995.1045

Suwartono, C., Prawasti, C. Y., & Mullet, E. (2007). Effect of culture on forgivingness: A Southern Asia–Western Europe comparison. *Personality and Individual Differences*, *42*(3), 513–523. https://doi.org/10.1016/j.paid.2006.07.027

Tabak, B. A., & McCullough, M. E. (2011). Perceived transgressor agreeableness decreases cortisol response and increases forgiveness following recent interpersonal transgressions. *Biological Psychology*, *87*(3), 386–392. https://doi.org/10.1016/j.biopsycho.2011.05.001

Tabak, B. A., McCullough, M. E., Szeto, A., Mendez, A. J., & McCabe, P. M. (2011). Oxytocin indexes relational distress following interpersonal harms in women. *Psychoneuroendocrinology*, *36*(1), 115–122. https://doi.org/10.1016/j.psyneuen.2010.07.004

Tafoya, M. A., & Spitzberg, B. H. (2007). The dark side of infidelity: Its nature, prevalence, and communicative functions. In B. H. Spitzberg & W. R. Cupach (Eds.), *The dark side of interpersonal communication* (2nd ed., pp. 201–242). Erlbaum. https://doi.org/10.4324/9780203936849

Toussaint, L., Shields, G. S., Dorn, G., & Slavich, G. M. (2016). Effects of lifetime stress exposure on mental and physical health in young adulthood: How stress degrades and forgiveness protects health. *Journal of Health Psychology*, *21*(6), 1004–1014. https://doi.org/10.1177/1359105314544132

Toussaint, L. L., Williams, D. R., Musick, M. A., & Everson, S. A. (2001). Forgiveness and health: Age differences in a US probability sample. *Journal of Adult Development*, *8*(4), 249–257. https://doi.org/10.1023/a:1011394629736

Tsang, J. A., McCullough, M. E., & Fincham, F. D. (2006). The longitudinal association between forgiveness and relationship closeness and commitment. *Journal of Social and Clinical Psychology*, *25*(4), 448–472. https://doi.org/10.1521/jscp.2006.25.4.448

Tsang, J. A., & Stanford, M. S. (2007). Forgiveness for intimate partner violence: The influence of victim and offender variables. *Personality and Individual Differences*, *42*(4), 653–664. https://doi.org/10.1016/j.paid.2006.08.017

Tsapelas, I., Fisher, H. E., & Aron, A. (2011). Infidelity: When, where, why. In W. R. Cupach & B. R. Spitzberg (Eds.), *The dark side of close relationships II* (pp. 175–196). Routledge.

Van Tongeren, D. R., Green, J. D., Hook, J. N., Davis, D. E., Davis, J. L., & Ramos, M. (2015). Forgiveness increases meaning in life. *Social Psychological and Personality Science*, *6*(1), 47–55. https://doi.org/10.1177/1948550614541298

Wade, N. G., & Worthington, E. L., Jr. (2003). Overcoming interpersonal offenses: Is forgiveness the only way to deal with unforgiveness? *Journal of Counseling and Development*, *81*(3), 343–353. https://doi.org/10.1002/j.1556-6678.2003.tb00261.x

Waldron, V. R., & Kelley, D. L. (2005). Forgiving communication as a response to relational transgressions. *Journal of Social and Personal Relationships*, *22*(6), 723–742. https://doi.org/10.1177/0265407505056445

Waldron, V. R., & Kelley, D. L. (2008). *Communicating forgiveness*. Sage. https://doi.org/10.4135/9781483329536

Webb, J. R., Toussaint, L., & Conway-Williams, E. (2012). Forgiveness and health: Psycho-spiritual integration and the promotion of better healthcare. *Journal of Health Care Chaplaincy*, *18*(1–2), 57–73. https://doi.org/10.1080/08854726.2012.667317

Wiederman, W. W., & LaMar, L. (1998). "Not with him you don't!": Gender and emotional reactions to sexual infidelity during courtship. *Journal of Sex Research*, *35*(3), 288–297. https://doi.org/10.1080/00224499809551945

Wieselquist, J. (2009). Interpersonal forgiveness, trust, and the investment model of commitment. *Journal of Social and Personal Relationships*, *26*(4), 531–548. https://doi.org/10.1177/0265407509347931

Witvliet, C., DeYoung, N. J., Hofelich, A. J., & DeYoung, P. A. (2011). Compassionate reappraisal and emotion suppression as alternatives to offense-focused rumination: Implications for forgiveness and psychophysiological well-being. *Journal of Positive Psychology*, *6*(4), 286–299. https://doi.org/10.1080/17439760.2011.577091

Witvliet, C. V., Hofelich Mohr, A. J., Hinman, N. G., & Knoll, R. W. (2015). Transforming or restraining rumination: The impact of compassionate reappraisal versus emotion suppression on empathy, forgiveness, and affective psychophysiology. *Journal of Positive Psychology*, *10*(3), 248–261. https://doi.org/10.1080/17439760.2014.941381

Witvliet, C., Knoll, R. W., Hinman, N. G., & DeYoung, P. A. (2010). Compassion-focused reappraisal, benefit-focused reappraisal, and rumination after an interpersonal offense: Emotion-regulation implications for subjective emotion, linguistic responses, and physiology. *Journal of Positive Psychology*, *5*(3), 226–242. https://doi.org/10.1080/17439761003790997

Witvliet, C., Ludwig, T., & Bauer, D. J. (2002). Please forgive me: Transgressors' emotions and physiology during imagery of seeking forgiveness and victim responses. *Journal of Psychology and Christianity*, *21*, 219–233.

Witvliet, C., Ludwig, T. E., & Laan, K. L. V. (2001). Granting forgiveness or harboring grudges: Implications for emotion, physiology, and health. *Psychological Science*, *12*(2), 117–123. https://doi.org/10.1111/1467-9280.00320

Witvliet, C. V., Worthington, E. L., Root, L. M., Sato, A. F., Ludwig, T. E., & Exline, J. J. (2008). Retributive justice, restorative justice, and forgiveness: An experimental psychophysiology analysis. *Journal of Experimental Social Psychology*, *44*(1), 10–25. https://doi.org/10.1016/j.jesp.2007.01.009

Worthington, E. L., Jr. (1998). An empathy-humility-commitment model of forgiveness applied within family dyads. *Journal of Family Therapy*, *20*(1), 59–76. https://doi.org/10.1111/1467-6427.00068

Worthington, E. L., Jr. (2001). *Five steps to forgiveness: The art and science of forgiving*. Crown House Publishing.

Worthington, E. L., Jr. (2006). *Forgiveness and reconciliation: Theory and application*. Brunner-Routledge.

Worthington, E. L., Jr., Berry, J. W., Hook, J. N., Davis, D. E., Scherer, M., Griffin, B. J., . . . Sharp, C. B. (2015). Forgiveness-reconciliation and communication-conflict-resolution interventions versus retested controls in early married couples. *Journal of Counseling Psychology*, *62*(1), 14. https://doi.org/10.1037/cou0000045

Worthington, E. L., Jr., & Sandage, S. J. (2016). *Forgiveness and spirituality in psychotherapy: A relational approach*. American Psychological Association. https://doi.org/10.1037/14712-013

Worthington, E. L., & Scherer, M. (2004). Forgiveness is an emotion-focused coping strategy that can reduce health risks and promote health resilience: Theory, review, and hypotheses. *Psychology & Health*, *19*(3), 385–405. https://doi.org/10.1080/0887044042000196674

Ysseldyk, R., & Wohl, M. J. (2012). I forgive therefore I'm committed: A longitudinal examination of commitment after a romantic relationship transgression. *Canadian Journal of Behavioural Science/Revue Canadienne des sciences du comportement, 44*(4), 257–263. https://doi.org/10.1037/a0025463

Yao, S., Zhao, W., Cheng, R., Geng, Y., Luo, L., & Kendrick, K. M. (2014). Oxytocin makes females, but not males, less forgiving following betrayal of trust. *International Journal of Neuropsychopharmacology, 17*(11), 1785–1792. https://doi.org/10.1017/S146114571400090X

Yoshimura, S. M., & Boon, S. D. (2018). *Communicating revenge in interpersonal relationships*. Lexington Books.

CHAPTER 20

Formation of a Primary Relationship with an Infidelity Partner

Charlene F. Belu *and* Lucia F. O'Sullivan

Abstract

Infidelity can have devastating effects on romantic relationships, but it can also provide the foundation for new relationships. This chapter reviews research examining relationships formed from infidelity, drawing on the mate poaching literature. Mate poaching is a form of infidelity that occurs when a person successfully attracts someone who already is in an exclusive relationship into a new relationship. The chapter begins by providing a conceptual model to help understand some of the dynamics contributing to the initiation of new relationships from experiences of infidelity. It then discusses how common it is for primary relationships to develop from this form of infidelity and then it outlines the traits associated with individuals who form relationships from infidelity. It next reviews the research examining the quality of relationships formed from infidelity and discuss some of the processes that may explain these findings. It concludes by identifying limitations of the current literature and potential avenues for future research in this research domain.

Key Words: infidelity, mate poaching, relationship quality, attractive alternative, relationship

Introduction

Infidelity occurs with the formation of a new, clandestine intimate partnership contrary to an explicit (or implicit) agreement to be exclusive with one's primary partner (Glass, 2002). These secondary relationships might be transitory in nature, lasting for one night, weeks, or months, or might coexist alongside the primary relationship for years (Davies et al., 2019; Schmitt & Buss, 2001; Schmitt & ISDP, 2004). The popular literature and media are replete with examples of one-time encounters, concurrent liaisons of serially unfaithful individuals, and long-term mistresses or paramours that last a lifetime. When, however, does that secondary partnership supersede the primary relationship, ultimately replacing it as a "new" primary relationship? We review here what is known about the personal characteristics, relationship characteristics, and contexts associated with the formation of a primary relationship with an infidelity partner. We also examine the quality of new primary relationships that evolve from infidelity.

High-quality romantic relationships provide many psychological and physiological benefits to the individual (Loving & Slatcher, 2013; Pietromanaco & Collins, 2017), including longer life expectancy (Dupre et al., 2009; Robles et al., 2014) and reduced stress (Braithwaite et al., 2010; Kamp Dush & Amato, 2005). Infidelity can disrupt relationship processes dramatically. Few events in life cause more personal distress than learning an intimate partner has been unfaithful. Romantic and sexual exclusivity is typically endorsed as an imperative in intimate relationships and, indeed, violating that exclusivity in the form of infidelity is one of the leading causes of relationship strain, discord, divorce, and dissolution (Amato & Previti, 2003; Cano & O'Leary, 2000).

Relationships That Evolve From Infidelity

Many argue that expecting romantic and sexual exclusivity over the entire course of a relationship is unreasonable, and that humans are not especially good at resisting the appeal of an attractive alternative (Finkel et al., 2014; Lee & O'Sullivan, 2019; Miller 1997, 2008). However, exclusivity in one's intimate relationships is an expected standard around the world for established intimate relationships (Treas & Giesen, 2000; Watkins & Boon, 2015). A large body of work, however, reveals that many people do not maintain exclusivity in their relationships despite strong intentions to do so and despite awareness of the strong standard for monogamy and of the social prohibition against connecting intimately with others outside the pair bond. Depending on which behaviors are assessed and how individuals are asked, estimates indicate that 1%–38% of married or cohabiting people report having engaged in some type of infidelity in their current relationship (Hall & Fincham, 2009; Luo et al., 2010; Mark et al., 2011; Thompson & O'Sullivan, 2016). The rates are even higher among those in less committed relationships, such as dating relationships, and when assessing the wider range of sexual behaviors beyond intercourse alone (Luo et al., 2010; Thompson & O'Sullivan, 2016).

Individuals known to have engaged in infidelity are frequently viewed with disdain by peers and experience stigma and shame for violating a partner's trust by engaging in infidelity (Hall & Fincham, 2009; Sharpe et al., 2013). It is in regard to this disreputable context that we explore the quality and characteristics of relationships that evolve from infidelity. It is unclear how often intimate relationships begin before an existing relationship has ended. However, we have gained insights into this topic from research on mate poaching, which is attracting someone into a sexual or romantic encounter or relationship who is already in an exclusive intimate relationship (Belu & O'Sullivan, 2018; Davies et al., 2007; Foster et al., 2014; Schmitt & Buss, 2001), as well as a nascent body of work on "back-burner relationships" (Banas et al., 2021; Borzea & Dillow, 2017; Dibble & Drouin, 2014; Dibble et al., 2015, 2018).

Conceptual Background

Competition for mates has always been a part of our evolutionary history. One question that emerges is: When does a primary relationship get trumped by a secondary one following infidelity? Proponents of evolutionary psychological theory argue that we are drawn to those who represent opportunities to increase reproductive success (Buss & Schmitt, 2019). Because of the high investment that offspring demand of women as child bearers and primary caretakers, women are drawn to cues in men that represent a capacity to invest in offspring that may result from a pairing; mating with extradyadic partners provides a means to accrue additional resources (Buss & Schmitt, 2019; Buss et al., 2017; Trivers, 1972). Partner change occurs when an alternate partner offers a greater level of resources and even though this relationship may have been formed in infidelity, research indicates that partners likely are quick to establish that the relationship be exclusive once formed (Buss et al., 2017; Watkins & Boone, 2015).

Men's ancestral reproductive success was maximized by mating with as many partners as possible, a strategy that is compromised by women's need for resources to help ensure survival of offspring (Buss & Schmitt, 1993). Men are drawn to cues of fertility, a metric that offspring will be healthy and any investments in the raising of offspring will likely pay off in terms of genetic representation in the next generation. New partners provide opportunities to reproduce (sexual variety), although again, exclusivity is required to ensure paternal certainty (Buss & Schmitt, 2019). The mate switching hypothesis suggests that people have adaptations to detect when their romantic partner is not providing as many benefits as could be obtained elsewhere (Buss et al., 2017). This adaptation requires monitoring of potential alternatives even after someone has formed a romantic relationship, and potentially engaging in infidelity to assess and secure attractive alternatives (Buss et al., 2017). Research has revealed that both men and women cultivate backup partners and sometimes maintain communication with these individuals to keep or establish the possibility of a romantic or sexual relationship in the future (Borzea & Dillow, 2017; Dibble & Drouin, 2014; Dibble et al., 2015).

While evolutionary psychological theory provides a useful framework for understanding the appeal of alternative others in the context of mating strategies more broadly, exchange-based theories and models of interpersonal romantic relationships (e.g., Interdependence Theory; Kelley & Thibault, 1978; Investment Model of developing relationships; Rusbult, 1980) provide a proximal framework for understanding which relationships will endure. Proponents hold that relationships survive when rewards accrued in a relationship generally outweigh costs, our expectations for relationships are at least met if not exceeded, and our investment in the relationship is high in terms of time, resources, and material goods. However, a fourth factor in this theory that helps predict relationship longevity (or its demise) is an individual's perception of the quality of his or her alternatives. Quality alternatives might comprise the appeal of being single again, unfettered by a committed relationship, spending more time with friends and loved ones, or the appeal of an attractive, viable, alternative partner (Rusbult, 1980). Proponents argue that individuals continually assess their current relationship and compare it to alternative possible relationships. This framework helps us to understand better the relationships formed from infidelity.

The Appeal of Attractive Others

In past generations, women were often isolated for the most part in the home, and spent time socializing with other women during the day, but with few others. In Western cultures now, a great proportion of both men's and women's time is spent at work outside of the home, a context in which we typically mix with others away from our partners, generating potential opportunities to connect intimately with others (Blow & Hartnett, 2005; Finkel et al., 2014). The rapid and widespread uptake of digital technologies makes it easy to connect privately with prospective, new, or former partners. Moreover, the fragmentation of extended family networks, increased mobilization required by many professions, and heightened demands placed on our primary relationships to meet a range of personal, practical, and intimate needs weaken our resolve to maintain exclusivity when faced with an attractive alternative partner (Finkel et al., 2014).

Many people are drawn toward attractive others, and this attentional bias is sometimes difficult to suppress, even for those already in an exclusive relationship (Maner et al., 2003; Sui & Lui, 2009). Attention to attractive alternatives (i.e., noticing or being distracted by attractive individuals other than one's partner) can pose a threat to one's relationship if a viable relationship alternative is perceived to be superior, available, and attainable, thereby increasing the saliency of this individual (Buss & Greiling, 1999; Cole et al., 2016; Miller, 2008; Rusbult, 1983; Thibaut & Kelley, 1959). A more salient attractive alternative is more likely to alter the perceived quality of the most desirable alternative to one's relationship, which is associated with decreased commitment and relationship longevity (Thibaut & Kelley, 1959). Chronic attention to alternatives is associated with lower relationship quality, infidelity, and relationship breakup (McNulty et al., 2018; Miller, 1997, 2008). However, it is unclear when a particular attraction to an alternative leads to infidelity, as attraction to an alternative is a necessary but not sufficient criterion for infidelity (Belu & O'Sullivan, 2019).

Attraction to an alternative partner leads to infidelity when a number of conditions have been met (see Figure 20.1). First, connecting sexually or romantically with an extradyadic other constitutes infidelity only in the context of a primary relationship that has an implicit or explicit agreement to be exclusive. Second, an individual must notice or attend to an attractive alternative and recognize the appeal of that alternative by developing an attraction to them, colloquially described as a "crush." The next condition is that this attraction is communicated to the potential partner either verbally or nonverbally. There has to be bilateral communication of attraction in order for the individuals to be aware of reciprocated interest. This usually takes the form of flirting, which is an expression of attraction, typically indirect in form (Hall et al., 2010; Hall & Xing, 2015). Being attracted to another and having a flirtatious relationship does not in itself typically

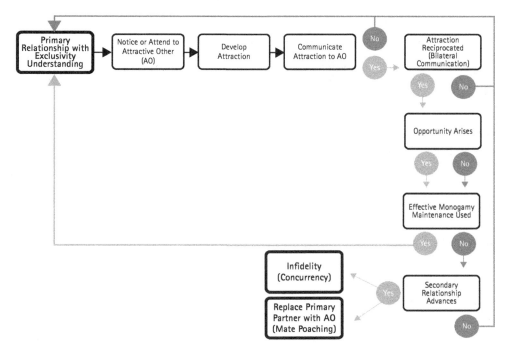

Figure 20.1 Model Depicting Progression of Attraction to Alternate Partner to Infidelity.

comprise infidelity. These scenarios can be harmless in many respects, affirming interactions that bolster one's esteem and provide a diversion on occasion (Mullinax et al., 2016; O'Sullivan et al., 2022).

A growing body of research has examined how individuals committed to their primary relationships react in scenarios where they must interact with an attractive alternative partner. Most of this work shows that those higher in commitment are more reluctant to interact with attractive others, and when they do they tend to engage in a range of monogamy maintenance strategies to ensure that exclusivity is maintained in their relationship (Lee & O'Sullivan, 2018, 2019). Some of these maintenance strategies are not conscious. For example, people discount the attractive alternative, derogate the attractiveness of the alternative, and suppress thoughts of the alternative by thinking of their love for their partner (Gagné et al., 2008; Gonzaga et al., 2008; Johnson & Rusbult, 1989; Karremans et al., 2011; Lydon et al., 1999, 2003; Simpson et al., 1990). More recently, researchers have begun to explore more intentional behaviors that individuals in relationships engage in to maintain monogamy, such as reducing their interaction with an attractive other or enhancing the quality of their romantic relationship (Lee & O'Sullivan, 2018, 2019). Whether individuals engage in such monogamy maintenance efforts is a precondition of infidelity, such that those who do not are more prone to infidelity. However, another factor is opportunity. Even if an individual and an attractive other both wish to initiate an extradyadic relationship together, there must be opportunity to do so and awareness by one or both partners of that opportunity. In addition, those who perceive their attractive alternative to be higher in mate value than their current relationship partner are more likely to consider moving from one relationship to the other (Arnocky, 2020). With each of these preconditions in place, the secondary relationship might advance toward infidelity, and, ultimately, mate switching where a new primary relationship is established between the extradyadic partners. In some instances, this mate switching will also constitute mate poaching.

Mate poaching is a form of infidelity that occurs when an individual successfully initiates a romantic or sexual relationship with someone who they know to be in an exclusive relationship (Belu & O'Sullivan, 2018; Davies et al., 2007, 2019; Foster et al., 2014). The relationships formed from mate poaching can be short-term sexual relationships that are brief and primarily sexual in nature (Moran & Wade, 2017; Schmitt & Buss, 2001; Schmitt & ISDP, 2004). However, such relationships can also be longer-term sexual and/or romantic relationships (i.e., affairs) where someone is involved in more than one relationship concurrently or these relationships can form the basis for a new exclusive relationship (Davies et al., 2019; Schmitt & Buss, 2001; Schmitt & ISDP, 2004).

Those involved in successful mate poached relationships are either poachers, poached, or copoachers (Schmitt & Buss, 2001; Schmitt & ISDP, 2004). Poachers are the individuals who attract another away from an exclusive relationship and poached individuals are those who are attracted away from an exclusive relationship. Copoachers are those who both attract someone away from an exclusive relationship and are attracted away from their own exclusive relationship (Schmitt & Buss, 2001; Schmitt & ISDP, 2004).

Although mate poaching is a form of infidelity, not all those who are involved in mate poaching will have violated an agreement between partners to be exclusive (Belu & O'Sullivan, 2020). For example, poachers who are single would not be considered to have engaged in infidelity if they successfully poach another's partner away. However, those who are poached from a relationship, or who are co-poached, would be considered to have engaged in infidelity. In short, when successful mate poaching occurs, infidelity has occurred for one or both participants in the mate poaching process.

Prevalence of Mate Poaching

Despite the preference for monogamy in romantic relationships, mate poaching is common and appears to be a cultural universal (Schmitt & ISDP, 2004; Thompson & O'Sullivan, 2016; Treas & Giesen, 2000). In a study of nearly 17,000 people in relationships in 53 countries, approximately 44% of women and 57% of men have attempted to poach someone for a long-term relationship at least once in their lifetime (Schmitt & ISDP, 2004). Of those who have attempted to poach at least once in their lifetime, 81% of men and women report having successfully poached someone for a long-term relationship (Schmitt & ISDP, 2004). Furthermore, 63% of men and 54% of women report that someone has attempted to poach them for a long-term relationship, and 52% of men and 48% of women report having been successfully poached into a long-term relationship (Schmitt & ISDP, 2004). In North America specifically, 52% of women and 63% of men have attempted to poach someone into a long-term relationship, and of those who have attempted to poach, 77% of men and 80% of women report that they have successfully poached someone into a long-term relationship (Schmitt & ISDP, 2004).

The majority of people in many cultures, then, report having poached a partner from another relationship, and this finding is reinforced by reports of being a target of a poaching attempt (Schmitt & ISDP, 2004). With regard to being poached, 72% of men and 75% of women report that someone has attempted to poach them into a long-term relationship, and 52% of men and 48% of women report being successfully poached into a long-term relationship (Schmitt & ISDP, 2004). However, although someone may have formed a new long-term relationship, it is unclear how many of these long-term relationships were long-term affairs or resulted in the formation of new, exclusive relationships.

Cross-culturally, 12% of men and 8% of women reported poaching their partner into their current romantic relationship, and 10% of men and 14% of women reported that they had been poached into their current relationship (Schmitt & ISDP, 2004). In North American samples, the percentage of current relationships reported to be formed as a result of poaching were 10% and 8% for men and women, respectively (Schmitt & ISDP, 2004). Eleven percent of men and 14% of women reported that their current relationship was formed after they were poached from a previous relationship (Schmitt & ISDP, 2004). Overall, three percent of people reported that they were copoached into their current relationship (Schmitt & ISDP, 2004). This suggests that anywhere from 8% to 14% of current romantic relationships are formed from mate poaching. More recent North American data suggest that 59%–64% of individuals have successfully poached someone into a new, exclusive relationship and 34% of individuals have been successfully poached into a new, exclusive relationship (Davies et al., 2019).

Researchers also have explored the frequency with which someone attempt to poach or has been the target of attempted poaching. Across cultures, men rarely report attempting to poach someone for a long-term relationship, but they do so more often than do women. This pattern is also found when specifically examining poaching frequency among North American men and women (Schmitt & ISDP, 2004). With regard to the frequency of being poached, men and women reported that seldom does someone attempt to poach them from their relationship. However, this occurs slightly more frequently among North American men and women than among men and women residing on other continents (Schmitt & ISDP, 2004). Overall, it seems that most people have at least one experience poaching or being poached across their lifetime, but neither event is a frequent occurrence.

Recent work has explored whether some individuals are more likely to form relationships from mate poaching than others (Belu & O'Sullivan, 2020). Belu and O'Sullivan (2020) asked 774 US adults aged 25 to 40 in romantic relationships whether they had any experience with mate poaching, either as a poacher, a poached individual, or a copoached individual. Almost half (44%) of their sample had no experience with poached relationships, a small minority had just one experience with mate poaching (19%) and just over a third (37%) had two or more experiences with mate poaching. Belu and O'Sullivan (2020) used targeted recruitment to obtain a higher number of those in poached relationships, so these proportions are an overrepresentation of how common mate poached relationships are. However, it is clear that most who have been involved in mate poaching have been involved more than once. In short, mate poaching, a form of infidelity, is a relatively common occurrence cross-culturally. Many people have experience forming at least one relationship from infidelity, and a substantial minority of people have started more than one relationship in infidelity. Who are these individuals who are willing to knowingly draw someone out of an exclusive relationship, or be drawn out of an exclusive relationship?

Predicting Who Engages in Infidelity

One trait that consistently stands out as a strong predictor of who engages in infidelity or lures someone else's partner away is sociosexuality (Rodrigues et al., 2017a; Rodrigues et al., 2017b; Seal et al., 1994; Simpson & Gangestad, 1991). Sociosexuality refers to one's comfort with and willingness to engage in sexual relations with someone without commitment (Penke & Asendorpf, 2008). Sociosexual orientation consists of three key components: behavior (i.e., a history of sex without commitment), attitudes (i.e., beliefs about sex without commitment and the need for emotional intimacy prior to sex) and desire (i.e., one's subjective sexual arousal, fantasy, and sexual motivations toward people to whom one is not committed) (Penke & Asendorpf, 2008).

Individuals who are in relationships formed from mate poaching report significantly less restricted sociosexual orientations than do those who form relationships serially (Belu & O'Sullivan, 2020). Those with less restricted sociosexual orientation have more favorable views toward sex without commitment (e.g., sex without love), have engaged in more sex without commitment, and have more sexual desire toward individuals with whom they are not in a committed relationship (Penke & Asendorpf, 2008). Individuals in poached relationships are significantly less restricted in each of these facets of sociosexual orientation when compared to their non-poached peers (Belu & O'Sullivan, 2020).

Those who are successfully poached out of an exclusive relationship are lower in agreeableness (e.g., kindness, generosity) as well as conscientiousness (e.g., organization, reliability) and higher in neuroticism (e.g., negative emotionality; Costa & McRae, 2008; Foster et al., 2014; Schmitt & Buss, 2001; Schmitt & ISDP, 2004). Successful poachers tend to endorse higher levels of openness to experience (e.g., creativity, imagination) and extraversion (e.g., sociability, positive emotionality; Kardum et al., 2015; Schmitt & ISDP, 2004).

The Dark Triad traits consist of Machiavellianism, subclinical narcissism, and subclinical psychopathy (Paulhus & Williams, 2002). Subclinical narcissism and subclinical psychopathy are positively associated with whether one has successfully poached someone from an exclusive relationship into a new long-term relationship (Jonason et al., 2010). These traits are also associated with whether someone has been poached from an exclusive relationship into a new long-term relationship (Foster et al., 2014; Jonason et al., 2010). These aversive interpersonal traits tend to be even better predictors of mate poaching than the Big Five traits (Kardum et al., 2015).

Schmitt and Buss (2001) found that successful poachers perceived themselves to be more sexually attractive and less faithful to their romantic partners. Those who were successfully poached from a partner perceived themselves to be less monogamous, more erotophilic, and less invested in their romantic relationship (Schmitt & Buss, 2001). In another study of predictors of poaching and being poached, physical attractiveness was the only factor among women that predicted success in poaching an individual (Sunderani et al., 2013). In line with traits that cue dominance, successful mate poaching by males was best predicted by their height, greater self-esteem, criminal tendencies, and greater display of cold affect (Sunderani et al., 2013). Targets of mate poaching attempts were higher on average in physical attractiveness (Sunderani et al., 2013).

Together, these profiles indicate that the traits that characterize those who engage in infidelity or who are likely to be lured away from an exclusive relationship are not traits conducive to long-term committed relationships. They tend to reflect greater sexual interest in others, a preference for short-term relationships, a tendency toward negative social interactions as well as a lack of empathy and caring for others, traits that are especially problematic when paired with higher levels of physical attractiveness (Botwin et al., 1997; Jonason & Buss, 2012; Jonason et al., 2009; Mitchell et al., 2019; Vater & Schröder-Abé, 2015). These traits tend to be associated with lower levels of passion, lesser sexual and relationship satisfaction, and lower relationship quality overall (Ali & Chamorro-Premuzic, 2010; Bourbonnaise & Durand, 2018; Botwin et al., 1997; Campbell & Foster, 2002; Foster et al., 2006; Kardum et al., 2021; Vater & Schröder-Abé, 2015; Webster et al., 2015).

Relationship Quality and Related Outcomes

An important issue examined in the literature concerns the quality of relationships that are formed from infidelity (Belu & O'Sullivan, 2020 Foster et al., 2014). The research to date demonstrates that successful poaching is common and that more than half of people have formed a relationship from poaching at least once in their lifetime (Belu & O'Sullivan, 2020; Schmitt & ISDP, 2004). The research also demonstrates that poachers, poached, and copoached people possess characteristics that are perceived to be more negative and are often associated with problems in relationship functioning (Botwin et al., 1997; Foster et al., 2014; Vater & Schröder-Abé, 2015). If the type of people that engage in these relationships have more problematic personality characteristics or have characteristics that lend to more dysfunctional relationships, what kind of relationship quality can be expected when a relationship is formed from infidelity? There is a dearth of research on the topic but what exists gives us insight into the quality of relationships formed from mate poaching, a type of infidelity.

Across three studies, Foster and colleagues (2014) explored the functioning of relationships formed from being poached out of an exclusive relationship. In the first study, 84 young adults around 19 years of age in romantic relationships participated in a longitudinal study that collected data over 12 weeks at four different time points (each three weeks apart). These romantic relationships were 15 months long, on average. Participants indicated whether they were in a relationship that had formed as a result of being poached from a previous exclusive relationship. They also rated the quality of their relationship on an array of indices (i.e., commitment, satisfaction, investment, perceived quality of alternatives, attention to alternatives, infidelity). At baseline, participants who reported that they were poached by their current partner reported lower commitment to, satisfaction with, and investment in their current romantic relationship compared to their nonpoached peers. They also perceived themselves to have greater quality of alternatives to their current romantic relationship and reported higher attention to alternatives. However, at baseline, those who were poached were not any more likely to report a greater degree of infidelity while in their current relationship. Over the length of the study, poached individuals reported lower commitment and satisfaction with their relationship. In addition, they maintained similar levels of attention to alternatives and engaged in a similar degree of infidelity, whereas their nonpoached counterparts decreased in these areas.

The second study by Foster and colleagues (2014) sought to replicate these findings as well as explore associations with personality characteristics. Another sample of 138 participants around 20 years of age in romantic relationships assessed their relationship quality via the same indicators used in the study described above. In addition, they were assessed with regard to the following: Big Five personality traits, narcissism, attachment, and sociosexual orientation. Participants completed measures at baseline and five additional time points over 10 weeks. With regard to relationship functioning, individuals who were poached reported lower commitment, lower satisfaction, and higher perceived quality of alternatives at baseline than their nonpoached peers. They also endorsed higher attention to alternatives and reported engaging in a greater degree of infidelity at baseline. However, in contrast to the findings of the first study, those who were poached did not report greater levels of relationship dysfunction at follow up. Thus, those who were poached into their current relationship reported lower levels of relationship quality in some domains that did not further deteriorate with time.

After establishing that poached individuals report lower levels of relationship quality at baseline, Foster and colleagues (2014) sought to examine the link between personality characteristics and relationship functioning. Those who were poached reported greater levels of subclinical narcissism. In addition, narcissism partially accounted for an individual's endorsement of a greater degree of infidelity. A more unrestricted sociosexual orientation approached significance as a predictor of relationship quality, but these analyses were underpowered.

To replicate these previous findings and to assess the link between sociosexual orientation and relationship quality, a third study was conducted (Foster et al., 2014). Two hundred nineteen participants (68% female) in romantic relationships, 20 years of age, on average, were recruited. Those who reported being poached into their current relationship were less satisfied, committed, and invested in their current relationship compared to those who were not in a relationship formed from poaching. They also attended more to alternatives and perceived a higher quality of alternatives to their current relationship. Those who were poached were also more likely to report having engaged in infidelity with an attractive other. This lower level of relationship functioning was in part accounted for by sociosexual orientation. In essence, those who were poached and had positive attitudes toward, desire for, and had engaged in sexual behavior without commitment were more likely to report poorer relationship functioning in their current relationship.

This work was expanded on by Belu and O'Sullivan (2018) using 675 participants aged 25–40 years, who explored the perspectives of poachers, poached, and copoached. Heterosexual adults (55% women; average age of 31) in romantic relationships indicated whether their current romantic relationship was a result of poaching. The quality of their current relationship was also assessed. Consistent with Foster and colleagues (2014), individuals who were in relationships formed from poaching reported lower levels of commitment, relationship satisfaction, and trust, and higher levels of jealousy compared to their nonpoached peers. However, when asked, these individuals perceived themselves to be in a higher-quality relationship than their previous one (Belu & O'Sullivan, 2015). Those who formed their relationship from poaching also were more likely to report having engaged in infidelity in their current relationship. When comparing the reports of poachers (who have not engaged in infidelity) to poached individuals, those who were poached reported lower levels of commitment to their current relationship than poachers did. Copoachers reported engaging in infidelity at rates similar to their poached or poaching peers (Belu & O'Sullivan, 2018).

Other research has explored whether one's history of mate poaching is linked with poorer quality relationships (Belu & O'Sullivan, 2020). Are there differences between those who have formed a relationship from mate poaching just once, perhaps an opportunistic experience, and those who use mate poaching as a relationship formation strategy more consistently (Belu & O'Sullivan, 2020)? If those who are involved in poaching possess more undesirable personality characteristics that are linked to relationship dysfunction (Botwin et al., 1997; Foster et al., 2014; Vater & Schröder-Abé, 2015), would those with a more extensive history of mate poaching be more likely to possess these traits? If so, is this associated with relationship dysfunction?

When comparing individuals in romantic relationships who had never formed a relationship from poaching, who had formed just one relationship from poaching, or who had formed two or more relationships from poaching (i.e., serial poachers), those who used poaching as a relationship formation strategy reported lower commitment, relationship satisfaction, sexual satisfaction, and trust in their current romantic relationship. These individuals also reported higher levels of jealousy than those who had formed a relationship from poaching just once and those who had never formed a relationship from mate poaching. Those who had poached just once only differed from those who had no poaching history with regard to jealousy; they reported higher levels of jealousy.

Of particular interest here, those who engaged in serial poaching were also more likely to report engaging in sexual infidelity: 55% of those who had a history of mate poaching two or more times had engaged in sexual infidelity (i.e., sexual touching, oral sex, intercourse) while in their current relationship, compared to their peers with no history (22%) or just one experience of poaching (23%). Serial poachers were also more likely to have engaged in emotional infidelity (i.e., emotional closeness, affection toward someone other than one's partner) (56%) than their one-time (27%) or no experience (17%) counterparts.

Those who rely on mate poaching as a strategy to form relationships report lower commitment, relationship satisfaction, sexual satisfaction, and trust in the current relationship (Belu & O'Sullivan, 2020). Individuals who formed more relationships from mate poaching also reported a greater degree of jealousy in their current relationship. As mate poaching history increased, so did the odds of reporting sexual and emotional infidelity.

Finally, Belu and O'Sullivan (2020) investigated the link between sociosexual orientation and relationship quality of those with mate poached relationships. Sociosexual desire (i.e., one's arousal for someone one is not committed to) is the facet of sociosexual orientation that partially explained the association between mate poaching history and relationship quality. Those with a history of poaching reported more unrestricted sociosexual desire, which is associated with lower relationship quality. However, mate poaching history is linked to lower relationship quality even after accounting for one's sociosexual desire, suggesting that there remains more to be examined when considering the link between mate poaching history and relationship quality.

Sociosexual desire may reflect a proclivity to pay more attention to attractive alternatives (Miller, 1997). When someone pays more attention to someone attractive who is not their partner, their romantic relationship is at risk (Lydon, 2010; Lydon & Karremans, 2015). When someone pays more attention to someone else, they are provided greater opportunity to collect additional information about this individual. If it is then judged that this attractive alternative possesses more positive qualities than one's romantic partner, someone may be left feeling like there are better options available to them (i.e., higher perceived quality of alternatives). The greater one's perceived quality of alternatives, the less committed they are to their romantic relationship (Drigotas & Rusbult, 1992).

In summary, relationships that are started from infidelity are poorer in quality than those that are not formed from infidelity. These relationships tend to be lower in commitment, relationship satisfaction, investment, and trust. These relationships also tend to involve a greater degree of jealousy than relationships not formed from poaching. Mate poached individuals also report greater attention to alternatives, and higher perceived quality of alternatives to their current relationship. Those with a greater history of poaching report lower relationship quality in their current romantic relationships, and sociosexual desire appears to be important.

Critique of the Literature and Future Directions

While in a romantic relationship, individuals are often surrounded by attractive alternatives that are hard to ignore. Although monogamy is valued across cultures, infidelity is common, and some romantic relationships are formed from infidelity. Yet very little is known about who is more likely to enter these relationships, under what circumstances, and the quality of the resulting relationship. What is known is drawn from the literature on mate poaching, a form of infidelity. We know that many people have some experience with mate poaching, ranging from mate poaching attempts and multiple mate poaching successes. Those who poach others or are successfully poached from an exclusive relationship tend to possess characteristics that are linked with poor relationship functioning. Relationships formed from poaching also tend to be of lower quality than those relationships formed serially.

Many people have experience with both attempting to poach someone from an existing exclusive relationship and with someone else attempting to poach them from a relationship. About half of people report successfully poaching or being poached into a relationship at some point in their lives. A small minority of current relationships are the direct result of successful poaching. Poachers and poached individuals tend to have traits that are perceived to be more negative in nature and tend to be linked with relationship dysfunction or dissolution. Not surprisingly, relationships formed from poaching tend to be of lower relationship quality. Sociosexuality is a particularly relevant characteristic associated with lower relationship quality. However, sociosexuality is just one mechanism and there are likely a multitude of factors that contribute to relationship quality. For example, those who have more experience poaching someone from a relationship may fear that their partner will leave them as well, which may lead to increased mate guarding or behavioral changes that disrupt healthy relationship functioning.

It is important to note that the mate poaching literature is limited in a number of ways. When examining the characteristics of poachers, poached, and co-poached individuals, it is useful to differentiate the types of relationships that these individuals are pursuing. There are likely differences between someone who consistently poaches for short-term sexual relationships and someone who poaches with the intention of forming a new, exclusive relationship, possibly because they feel irretrievably in love. Research could explore the relationships formed from infidelity by those who have not engaged in this behavior before. In addition, there are relationships formed from infidelity that did not occur in the context of mate poaching. Mate poaching requires that the poacher know that the target of their efforts is in a relationship, and that this relationship is exclusive. Not all infidelity occurs under these circumstances, and a broader examination of relationships formed from infidelity is warranted.

Future research should also better examine the quality of the relationship one was in when infidelity occurred and the quality of the new relationship. Although those in relationships formed from mate poaching perceive themselves to be in higher-quality relationships than before, these reports are likely to be biased by retrospective recall. Longitudinal tracking of individuals in relationships would allow for a more accurate assessment of the quality of the relationship that someone is being poached or copoached from. Some could argue that those who form relationships from infidelity, despite the distress and disruption it may cause, are engaging in adaptive mate switching, moving from a lower-quality relationship to a higher-quality one (Buss et al., 2017). Research to date suggests that relationships formed from mate poaching are lower in quality than their non-poached counterparts. Accordingly, it would also be valuable to examine the predictors of high-quality relationships formed from infidelity. For example, if someone with lower levels of sociosexuality forms a relationship from infidelity, possibly because they are leaving a bad relationship, will they report higher levels of relationship quality than their more unrestricted counterparts?

Another important avenue to research is the process by which attraction to another results in infidelity, and formation of a new relationship. Although we have proposed a model of this process, this remains to be tested. It would also be worth investigating which strategies may be used when intending to form a short-term liaison versus a long-term relationship, and the effectiveness of these strategies.

References

Ali, F., & Chamorro-Premuzic, T. (2010). The dark side of love and life satisfaction: Associations with intimate relationships, psychopathy and Machiavellianism. *Personality and Individual Differences*, 48, 228–233. https://doi.org/10.1016/j.paid.2009.10.016

Amato, P. R., & Previti, D. (2003). People's reasons for divorcing: Gender, social class, the life course, and adjustment. *Journal of Family Issues*, 24, 602–626. https://doi.org/10.1177/0192513X03024005002

Arnocky, S. (2020). Mate-value moderates the relationship between intrasexual competitiveness and successful mate poaching. *Evolutionary Psychological Science*, 6, 346–353. https://doi.org/10.1007/s40806-020-00242-0

Banas, J. A., Dibble, J. L., Bessarabova, E., & Drouin, M. (2021). Simmering on the back burner or playing with fire? Examining the consequences of back-burner digital communication among ex-partners. *Cyberpsychology, Behavior, and Social Networking*, 24, 473–479. https://doi.org/10.1089/cyber.2020.0717

Belu, C. F., & O'Sullivan, L. F. (2015). *Mate poaching and the quality of relationships that emerge from it.* Paper presented at the annual meeting of the Canadian Sex Research Forum, Kelowna, BC.

Belu, C. F., & O'Sullivan, L. F. (2018). Why find my own when I can take yours? The quality of relationships that arise from successful mate poaching. *Journal of Relationship Research*, 9, E6. https://doi.org/10.1017/jrr.2018.5

Belu, C. F., & O'Sullivan, L. F. (2019). Roving eyes: Predictors of crushes in ongoing romantic relationships and implications for relationship quality. *Journal of Relationships Research, 10*, E2. https://doi.org/10.1017/jrr.2018.21

Belu, C. F., & O'Sullivan, L. F. (2020). Once a poacher always a poacher? Mate poaching history and its association with relationship quality. *Journal of Sex Research, 57*, 508–521. https://doi.org/10.1080/00224499.2019.1610150

Blow, A. J., & Hartnett, K. (2005). Infidelity in committed relationships II: A substantive review. *Journal of Marital and Family Therapy, 31*, 217–233. https://doi.org/10.1111/j.1752-0606.2005.tb01556.x.

Borzea, D., & Dillow, M. R. (2017). Dispositional characteristics of individuals involved in back burner relationships. *Communication Research Reports, 34*, 316–325. https://doi.org/10.1080/08824096.2017.1350572

Botwin, M. D., Buss, D. M., & Shackelford, T. K. (1997). Personality and mate preferences: Five factors in mate selection and marital satisfaction. *Journal of Personality, 65*, 107–136. http://dx.doi.org/10.1111/j.1467-6494.1997.tb00531.x.

Bourbonnais, K., & Durand, G. (2018). The incremental validity of the triarchic model of psychopathy in replicating "the dark side of love and life satisfaction: Associations with intimate relationships, psychopathy and Machiavellianism. *Quantitative Methods for Psychology, 14*, r12–r17. https://doi.org/10.20982/tqmp.14.3.r001

Braithwaite, S. R., Delevi, R., & Fincham, F. D. (2010). Romantic relationships and the physical and mental health of college students. *Personal Relationships, 17*, 1–12. https://doi.org/10.1111/j.1475-6811.2010.01248.x

Buss, D. M., Goetz, C., Duntley, J. D., Asao, K., & Conroy-Beam, D. (2017). The mate switching hypothesis. *Personality and Individual Differences, 104*, 143–149. https://doi.org/10.1016/j.paid.2016.07.022

Buss, D. M., & Greiling, H. (1999). Adaptive individual differences. *Journal of Personality, 67*, 209–243. https://doi.org/10.1111/1467-6494.00053

Buss, D. M., & Schmitt, D. P. (1993). Sexual strategies theory: An evolutionary perspective on human mating. *Psychological Review, 100*, 204–232. https://doi.org/10.1037/0033-295X.100.2.204

Buss, D. M., & Schmitt, D. P. (2019). Mate preferences and their behavioral manifestations. *Annual Review of Psychology, 4*, 77–110. https://doi.org/10.1146/annurev-psych-010418-103408

Campbell, W. K., & Foster, C. A. (2002). Narcissism and commitment in romantic relationships: An investment model analysis. *Personality and Social Psychology Bulletin, 28*, 484–495. https://doi.org/10.1177/0146167202287006

Cano, A., & O'Leary, K. D. (2000). Infidelity and separations precipitate major depressive episodes and symptoms of nonspecific depression and anxiety. *Journal of Consulting and Clinical Psychology, 68*, 774–781. https://doi.org/10.1037/0022-006X.68.5.774

Cole, S., Trope, Y., & Balcetis, E. (2016). In the eye of the betrothed: Perceptual downgrading of attractive alternative romantic partners. *Personality and Social Psychology Bulletin, 42*, 879–892. https://doi.org/10.1177/0146167216646546

Costa, P. T., & McCrae, R. R. (2008). The revised neo personality inventory (neo-pi-r). In G. J. Boyle, G. Matthews, & D. H. Saklofske (Eds.), *The SAGE handbook of personality theory and assessment: Personality measurement and testing* (Volume 2, pp. 179–198). Sage.

Davies, A. P., Shackelford, T. K., & Hass, R. G. (2007). When a "poach'" is not a poach: Re-defining human mate poaching and re-estimating its frequency. *Archives of Sexual Behavior, 36*, 702–716. https://doi.org/10.1007/s10508-006-9158-8

Davies, A. P., Tratner, A. E., & Shackelford, T. K. (2019). Not clearly defined, not reliably measured, and not replicable: Revisiting the definition and measurement of human mate poaching. *Personality and Individual Differences, 145*, 103–105. https://doi.org/10.1016/j.paid.2019.03.036

Dibble, J. L., & Drouin, M. (2014). Using modern technology to keep in touch with back burners: An investment model analysis. *Computers in Human Behavior, 34*, 96–100. https://doi.org/10.1016/j.chb.2014.01.042

Dibble, J. L., Drouin, M., Aune, K. S., & Boller, R. R. (2015). Simmering on the back burner: Communication with and disclosure of relationship alternatives. *Communication Quarterly, 63*, 329–344. https://doi.org/10.1080/01463373.2015.1039719

Dibble, J. L., Punyanunt-Carter, N. M., & Drouin, M. (2018). Maintaining relationship alternatives electronically: Positive relationship maintenance in back burner relationships. *Communication Research Reports, 35*, 200–209. https://doi.org/10.1080/08824096.2018.1425985

Drigotas, S. M., & Rusbult, C. E. (1992). Should I stay or should I go? A dependence model of breakups. *Journal of Personality and Social Psychology, 62*, 62–87. https://doi.org/10.1037/0022-3514.62.1.62

Dupre, M. E., Beck, A. N., & Meadows, S. O. (2009). Marital trajectories and mortality among US adults. *American Journal of Epidemiology, 170*, 546–555. https://doi.org/10.1093/aje/kwp194

Finkel, E. J., Hui, C. M., Carswell, K. L., & Larson, G. M. (2014). The suffocation of marriage: Climbing Mount Maslow without enough oxygen. *Psychological Inquiry, 25*, 1–41. https://doi-org.proxy.hil.unb.ca/10.1080/1047840X.2014.863723.

Foster, J. D., Jonason, P. K., Shrira, I., Campbell, W. K., Shiverdecker, L. K., & Varner, S. C. (2014). What do you get when you make somebody else's partner your own? An analysis of relationships formed via mate poaching. *Journal of Research in Personality, 52*, 78–90. https://doi.org/10.1016/j.jrp.2014.07.00

Foster, J. D., Shrira, I., & Campbell, W. K. (2006). Theoretical models of narcissism, sexuality, and relationship commitment. *Journal of Social and Personal Relationships, 23*, 367–386. https://doi.org/10.1177/0265407506064204

Gagné, F., Khan, A., Lydon, J., & To, M. (2008). When flattery gets you nowhere: *Canadian Journal of Behavioral Science/Canadian Journal of Behavioral Science, 40*, 59–68. https://doi.org/10.1037/0008-400X.40.2.59

Glass, S. P. (2002). Couple therapy after the trauma of infidelity. In A. S. Gurman & N. S. Jacobson (Eds.), *Clinical handbook of couple therapy* (3rd ed., pp. 488–507). Guilford Press.

Gonzaga, G. C., Haselton, M. G., Smurda, J., Davies, M. S., & Poore, J. C. (2008). Love, desire, and the suppression of thoughts of romantic alternatives. *Evolution and Human Behavior, 29*, 119–126. https://doi.org/10.1016/j.evolhumbehav.2007.11.003

Hall, J. A., Carter, S., Cody, M. J., & Albright, J. M. (2010). Individual differences in the communication of romantic interest: Development of the flirting styles inventory. *Communication Quarterly, 58*, 365–393. https://doi.org/10.1080/01463373.2010.524874

Hall, J. H., & Fincham, F. D. (2009). Psychological distress: Precursor or consequence of dating infidelity? *Personality and Social Psychology Bulletin, 35*, 143–159. https://doi.org/10.1177/0146167208327189

Hall, J. A., & Xing, C. (2015). The verbal and nonverbal correlates of the five flirting styles. *Journal of Nonverbal Behavior, 39*, 41–68. https://doi.org/10.1007/s10919-014-0199-8

Johnson, D. J., & Rusbult, C. E. (1989). Resisting temptation: Devaluation of alternative partners as a means of maintaining commitment in close relationships. *Journal of Personality and Social Psychology, 57*, 967–980. https://doi.org/10.1037/0022-3514.57.6.967

Jonason, P. K., & Buss, D. M. (2012). Avoiding entangling commitments: Tactics for implementing a short-term mating strategy. *Personality and Individual Differences, 52*, 606–610. https://doi.org/10.1016/j.paid.2011.12.015

Jonason, P. K., Li, N. P., & Buss, D. M. (2010). The costs and benefits of the Dark Triad: Implications for mate poaching and mate retention tactics. *Personality and Individual Differences, 48*, 373–378. https://doi.org/10.1016/j.paid.2009.11.003

Jonason, P. K., Li, N. P., Webster, G. D., & Schmitt, D. P. (2009). The Dark Triad: Facilitating a short-term mating strategy in men. *European Journal of Personality, 23*, 5–18. https://doi.org/10.1002/per.698

Kamp Dush, C. M., & Amato, P. R. (2005). Consequences of relationship status and quality for subjective well-being. *Journal of Social and Personal Relationships, 22*, 607–627. https://doi.org/10.1177/0265407505056438

Kardum, I., Hudek-Knezevic, J., & Mehic, N. (2021). Personality and mate poaching. In Shackleford, T. K., Weekes-Shackelford V.A. (Eds.) *Encyclopedia of Evolutionary Psychological Science.* Springer. https://doi.org/10.1007/978-3-319-19650-3_1750

Kardum, I., Hudek-Knezevic, J., Schmitt, D. P., & Grundler, P. (2015). Personality and mate poaching experiences. *Personality and Individual Differences, 75*, 7–12. https://doi.org/10.1016/j.paid.2014.10.048

Karremans, J. C., Dotsch, R., & Corneille, O. (2011). Romantic relationship status biases memory of faces of attractive opposite-sex others: Evidence from a reverse-correlation paradigm. *Cognition, 121*, 422–426. https://doi.org/10.1016/j.cognition.2011.07.008

Kelley, H. H., & Thibaut, J. W. (1978). *Interpersonal relations: A theory of interdependence.* Wiley.

Lee, B. H., & O'Sullivan, L. F. (2018). Ain't misbehavin? Monogamy maintenance strategies in heterosexual romantic relationships. *Personal Relationships, 25*, 205–232. https://doi.org/10.1111/pere.12235

Lee, B. H., & O'Sullivan, L. F. (2019). Walk the line: How successful are efforts to maintain monogamy in intimate relationships? *Archives of Sexual Behavior, 48*, 1735–1748. https://doi.org/10.1007/s10508-018-1376-3

Loving, T. J., & Slatcher, R. B. (2013). Romantic relationships and health. In J. A. Simpson & L. Campbell (Eds.), *The Oxford handbook of close relationships* (pp. 617–637). Oxford University Press.

Luo, S., Cartun, M. A., & Snider, A. G. (2010). Assessing extradyadic behavior: A review, a new measure, and two new models. *Personality and Individual Differences, 49*, 155–163. https://doi.org/10.1016/j.paid.2010.03.033

Lydon, J. E. (2010). How to forego forbidden fruit: The regulation of attractive alternatives as a commitment mechanism. *Social and Personality Psychology Compass, 4*, 635–644. https://doi.org/10.1111/j.1751-9004.2010.00283.x

Lydon, J. E., Fitzsimons, G. M., & Naidoo, L. (2003). Devaluation versus enhancement of attractive alternatives: A critical test using the calibration paradigm. *Personality and Social Psychology Bulletin, 29*, 349–359. https://doi.org/10.1177/0146167202250202

Lydon, J., & Karremans, J. C. (2015). Relationship regulation in the face of eye candy: A motivated cognition framework for understanding responses to attractive alternatives. *Current Opinion in Psychology, 1*, 76–80. https://doi.org/10.1016/j.copsyc.2015.01.011

Lydon, J. E., Meana, M., Sepinwall, D., Richards, N., & Mayman, S. (1999). The commitment calibration hypothesis: When do people devalue attractive alternatives? *Personality and Social Psychology Bulletin, 25*, 152–161. https://doi.org/10.1177/0146167299025002002

Maner, J. K., Kenrick, D. T., Becker, D. V., Delton, A. W., Hofer, B., Wilbur, C. J., & Neuberg, S. L. (2003). Sexually selective cognition: Beauty captures the mind of the beholder. *Journal of Personality and Social Psychology, 85*, 1107–1120. https://doi.org/10.1037/0022-3514.85.6.1107

Mark, K. P., Janssen, E., & Milhausen, R. R. (2011). Infidelity in heterosexual couples: Demographic, interpersonal, and personality-related predictors of extradyadic sex. *Archives of Sexual Behavior, 40*, 971–982. https://doi.org/10.1007/s10508-011-9771-z

McNulty, J. K., Meltzer, A. L., Makhanova, A., & Maner, J. K. (2018). Attentional and evaluative biases help people maintain relationships by avoiding infidelity. *Journal of Personality and Social Psychology, 115*, 75–96. https://doi.org/10.1037/pspi0000127

Miller, R. S. (1997). Inattentive and contented: Relationship commitment and attention to alternatives. *Journal of Personality and Social Psychology, 73*, 758–766. https://doi.org/10.1037/0022-3514.73.4.758

Miller, R. S. (2008). Attending to temptation: The operation (and perils) of attention to alternatives in close relationships. In J. P. Forgas & J. Fitness (Eds.), *Social relationships: Cognitive, affective, and motivational processes* (pp. 321–337). Psychology Press.

Mitchell, V. E., Mogilski, J. K., Zeigler-Hill, V., & Welling, L. L. (2019). Mate poaching strategies are differentially associated with pathological personality traits and risk-taking in men and women. *Personality and Individual Differences, 142*, 110–115. https://doi.org/10.1016/j.paid.2019.01.045

Moran, J., & Wade, T. J. (2017). Sex and the perceived effectiveness of short-term mate poaching acts in college students. *Human Ethology Bulletin, 32*, 109–128. https://doi.org/10.22330/heb/323/109-128.

Mullinax, M., Barnhart, K. J., Mark, K., & Herbenick, D. (2016). Women's experiences with feelings and attractions for someone outside their primary relationship. *Journal of Sex & Marital Therapy, 42*, 1–17. https://doi.org/10.1080/0092623X.2015.1061076

O'Sullivan, L. F., Belu, C. F., & Garcia, J. R. (2022). Loving you from afar: Attraction to others ("crushes") among adults in exclusive relationships, communication, perceived outcomes, and expectations of future intimate involvement. *Journal of Social and Personal Relationships, 39*, 413–434. https://doi.org/10.1177/02654075211038612

Paulhus, D. L., & Williams, K. M. (2002). The dark triad of personality: Narcissism, Machiavellianism, and psychopathy. *Journal of Research in Personality, 36*, 556–563. https://doi.org/10.1016/S0092-6566(02)00505-6

Penke, L., & Asendorpf, J. B. (2008). Beyond global sociosexual orientations: A more differentiated look at sociosexuality and its effects on courtship and romantic relationships. *Journal of Personality and Social Psychology, 95*, 1113–1135. https://doi.org/10.1037/0022-3514.95.5.1113

Pietromonaco, P. R., & Collins, N. L. (2017). Interpersonal mechanisms linking close relationships to health. *The American psychologist, 72*, 531–542. https://doi.org/10.1037/amp0000129

Robles, T. F., Slatcher, R. B., Trombello, J. M., & McGinn, M. M. (2014). Marital quality and health: A meta-analytic review. *Psychological Bulletin, 140*, 140–187. https://doi.org/10.1037/a0031859

Rodrigues, D., Lopes, D., & Pereira, M. (2017b). Sociosexuality, commitment, sexual infidelity, and perceptions of infidelity: Data from the second love web site. *Journal of Sex Research, 54*, 241–253. https://doi.org/10.1080/00224499.2016.1145182

Rodrigues, D., Lopes, D., & Smith, C. V. (2017a). Caught in a "bad romance"? Reconsidering the negative association between sociosexuality and relationship functioning. *Journal of Sex Research, 54*, 1118–1127. https://doi.org/10.1080/00224499.2016.1252308

Rusbult, C. E. (1980). Commitment and satisfaction in romantic associations: A test of the investment model. *Journal of Experimental Social Psychology, 60*, 53–78. https://doi.org/10.1016/0022-1031(80)90007-4

Rusbult, C. E. (1983). A longitudinal test of the investment model: The development (and deterioration) of satisfaction and commitment in heterosexual involvements. *Journal of Personality and Social Psychology, 45*, 101–117. https://doi.org/10.1037/0022-3514.45.1.101

Sharpe, D. I., Walters, A. S., & Goren, M. J. (2013). Effect of cheating experience on attitudes toward infidelity. *Sexuality & Culture, 17*, 643–658. https://doi.org/10.1007/s12119-013-9169-2

Schmitt, D. P., & Buss, D. M. (2001). Human mate poaching: Tactics and temptations for infiltrating existing mateships. *Journal of Personality and Social Psychology, 80*, 894–917. https://doi.org/10.1037/0022-3514.80.6.894

Schmitt, D. P., & International Sexuality Description Project. (2004). Patterns and universals of mate poaching across 53 nations: The effects of sex, culture, and personality on romantically attracting another person's partner. *Journal of Personality and Social Psychology, 86*, 560–584. https://doi.org/10.1037/0022-3514.86.4.560

Seal, D. W., Agostinelli, G., & Hannett, C. A. (1994). Extradyadic romantic involvement: Moderating effects of sociosexuality and gender. *Sex Roles, 31*, 1–22. https://doi.org/10.1007/BF01560274

Simpson, J. A., & Gangestad, S. W. (1991). Individual differences in sociosexuality: Evidence for convergent and discriminant validity. *Journal of Personality and Social Psychology, 60*, 870–883. https://doi.org/10.1037//0022-3514.60.6.870

Simpson, J. A., Gangestad, S. W., & Lerma, M. (1990). Perception of physical attractiveness: Mechanisms involved in the maintenance of romantic relationships. *Journal of Personality and Social Psychology, 59*, 1192–1201. https://doi.org/10.1037/0022-3514.59.6.1192

Sui, J., & Liu, C. H. (2009). Can beauty be ignored? Effects of facial attractiveness on covert attention. *Psychonomic Bulletin & Review, 16*, 276–281. https://doi.org/10.3758/PBR.16.2.276

Sunderani, S., Arnocky, S., & Vaillancourt, T. (2013). Individual differences in mate poaching: An examination of hormonal, dispositional, and behavioral mate-value traits. *Archives of Sexual Behavior, 42*, 533–542. https://doi.org/10.1007/s10508-012-9974-y

Thibaut, J. W., & Kelley, H. H. (1959). *The social psychology of groups*. Wiley.

Thompson, A. E., & O'Sullivan, L. F. (2016). Drawing the line: The development of a comprehensive assessment of infidelity judgments. *Journal of Sex Research, 53*, 910–926. https://doi.org/10.1080/00224499.2015.1062840

Treas, J., & Giesen, D. (2000). Sexual infidelity among married and cohabiting Americans. *Journal of Marriage and Family, 62*, 48–62. https://doi.org/10.1111/j.1741-3737.2000.00048.x

Trivers, R. L. (1972). Parental investment and sexual selection. In B. Campbell (Ed.), *Sexual selection and the descent of man* (pp. 136–177). Aldine.

Vater, A., & Schröder-Abé, M. (2015). Explaining the link between personality and relationship satisfaction: Emotion regulation and interpersonal behaviour in conflict discussions. *European Journal of Personality, 29*, 201–215. https://doi.org/10.1002/per.1993

Watkins, S. J., & Boon, S. D. (2015). Expectations regarding partner fidelity in dating relationships. *Journal of Social and Personal Relationships, 33*, 237–256. https://doi.org/10.1177/0265407515574463

Webster, G. D., Laurenceau, J. P., Smith, C. V., Mahaffey, A. L., Bryan, A. D., & Brunell, A. B. (2015). An investment model of sociosexuality, relationship satisfaction, and commitment: Evidence from dating, engaged, and newlywed couples. *Journal of Research in Personality, 55*, 112–126. https://doi.org/10.1016/j.jrp.2015.02.004

CHAPTER 21

Renewed Love Between Partners Following Infidelity

T. Joel Wade, Rebecca L. Burch, *and* Maryanne L. Fisher

Abstract

Infidelity has gained significant research attention within evolutionary and social psychology, but the bulk of this work pertains to issues surrounding defining infidelity, documenting its prevalence, or how people immediately react to infidelity in their relationships. Significantly less research has focused on what transpires in the relationship in the longer-term after the infidelity, and after the faithful partner fully realizes what has occurred. The research that does exist tends to pertain to sex differences in reactions, with men being far less optimistic about the future of their existing relationships. Others have examined the effect of the type of infidelity on relationship termination. This chapter focuses on how couples decide, and the methods they use, to continue relationships and rekindle love after infidelity has occurred.

Key Words: infidelity, adultery, breakup, renewal, romantic relationship

Introduction

Your cheatin' heart will pine some day and crave the love you threw away. The time will come when you'll be blue, your cheatin' heart will tell on you.

—*Hank Williams*

Infidelity in an exclusive relationship represents a significant betrayal to one's partner. Such relationships involve a social contract, whereby one is expected to remain exclusive to the partner, whether it be sexually, emotionally, or both. Infidelity can also involve resources in which a partner uses the couple's pooled resources for selfish gains. Despite the fact that most people in the United States (referred to as "American" in this chapter) consider it morally unacceptable (Newport & Himelfarb, 2013), prevalence rates for sexual infidelity during a marriage remain over 20% (Fincham & May, 2017). Although infidelity is the leading cause of divorce (Betzig, 1989), 60%–75% of couples who have experienced an infidelity remain together (Solomon & Teagno, 2006). The country music legend Hank Williams, in the song "Your Cheatin' Heart," presents feelings a spurned lover hopes their partner may have after becoming involved in an infidelity. He describes feeling a sense of loss, regret, and feeling blue on the part of the cheater, which also implies a hope for revenge or reunion on the part of the cheatee. If someone feels this level of remorse following infidelity, or still wishes for reunion with an unfaithful lover, is it possible to renew love with a partner? Is this type of remorse necessary before attempting to rekindle one's relationship? What steps must be undertaken to re-establish oneself as an invested, committed partner, or forgive an unfaithful one?

Overview of Research on Infidelity
Defining Infidelity

Infidelity has been well studied in the scholarly literature on sexuality and includes research conducted by those using an evolutionary perspective. Moreover, it has been examined not only in humans but in other species as well, which highlights the relevance of using evolutionary-based perspectives. Monogamous species have exhibited "infidelity" (Barash & Lipton, 2002) and then continued on with their long-term relationships, presumably with their partners none the wiser (Ford, 1983; Hill et al., 1994; Richardson, 1987). In performing this research, rather than use the term "infidelity," researchers use "extrapair copulation" to describe these behaviors, as most species presumably have no concept of "infidelity" or the intricacies of social contracts.

Infidelity, incidentally, stems from the Latin *infidelitas*, or "lack of faith." Humans, as serial monogamists, are very capable of understanding the concept of "faith" and the expectation of monogamy. Indeed, the vast majority of human cultures practice a commitment-codifying ritual, a pair bonding ceremony, with similar themes and symbolic practices in those ceremonies (Burch, 2019). In fact, Treas and Giesen (2000), using the National Health and Social Life Survey data (Laumann et al., 1994) found that nearly 99% of married persons expected their spouse to have sex only in marriage, and 99% assumed their partner expected sexual exclusivity of them.

This commitment is widely seen as requisite in humans because of altricial young; human parents need assistance at least until the child is capable of independent eating and movement. Not surprisingly, Fisher (2016) argues that most human pair bonds last exactly this long, approximately four years. Within just these four years, we have reproductive goals of both sexes that pressure relationships to be monogamous. Women, with the increased burden of childcare, need monogamous relationships to prevent abandonment and loss of resources that they and their children need to survive. Men need monogamy to prevent sexual infidelity and cuckoldry. Alexander and Noonan (1979) theorized that the human mating system shifted to monogamy as men had to stay close to women to ensure paternity (when women evolved concealed ovulation), and this "daddy at home" could provide benefits, like increased investment and assurance of paternity. Let us be clear on this point, however; men and women need monogamy on the part of *their partner* to meet these reproductive goals. Fidelity, on the part of your partner, is highly adaptive.

Moreover, humans often do not just have one child, or one relationship that spans four years. Humans show a great deal of variation and flexibility in behavior, as well as having multiple children, so this "four year itch," as Fisher coins it, may continue to itch for much longer as more children require investment. The average number of children raised by women in traditional cultures is closer to six than just one (Wood, 1994). Given the importance of commitment to the survival of spouses and children through investment, food provisioning, protection, and social influence, it is not surprising that humans can have severe reactions to both infidelity and the dissolution of a relationship in response to infidelity. There is a great deal to lose.

Infidelity, although well studied, is challenging to define. Indeed, simply defining it is said to have been "a topic of discussion in the scholarly literature for at least 20 years" (Hertlein & Weeks, 2007, p. 96; and note that this statement is from more than a decade ago). Arriving at an agreed upon definition is important, as it affects documented prevalence rates, types of behaviors that are included, treatments for couples by counsellors or therapists, and so on. Moller and Vossler (2015) point out that, depending on the definition, rates vary between 1.2% and 85.5%, with more conservative rates (for random samples that are representative of the general American public) around 25%. Even a behavior which may seem straightforward to regard as infidelity—for example sexual intercourse with someone other than one's partner—can be difficult to define as such, given some couples do not see it as a breach of their relationship contract (e.g., those who engage in swinging, polyamorous couples, or some gay couples; see Moller & Vossler, 2015). For our purposes, we define infidelity as an act involving an extradyadic intimate partner that breaches a social contract of expected romantic and/or sexual exclusivity. We acknowledge that sexual behavior is the primary component of most infidelity, but other forms, such as technological or online behaviors, romantic or affectionate behaviors, or solitary behaviors may be involved (see Thompson & O'Sullivan, 2016).

Types of Infidelity

While it may seem unnecessary to spend so much time defining and categorizing infidelity, the outcomes have a considerable effect on whether a relationship can withstand its impact (as we shall see later). There are numerous types of infidelity, including sexual, emotional, and resource infidelity (see Buss & Duntley, 2011; Wade et al., in press). Sexual infidelity may be considered as sexual intercourse or extradyadic sexual activities other than intercourse (Moller & Vossler, 2015). Emotional infidelity typically refers to betraying one's emotional commitment, such as feeling love toward an alternative mate. It occurs when an individual who is in a committed relationship becomes emotionally involved with (e.g., feels romantic love toward) an extradyadic person (Brase et al., 2004). Resource infidelity involves one partner using the couple's pooled resources for their own goals at the expense of their partner's goals (Buss & Duntley, 2011). This chapter focuses on emotional infidelity and sexual infidelity, as they are the most commonly documented.

Buss and colleagues (1999) define sexual infidelity as one's partner having sexual intercourse with someone but they are certain that they will not form a deep emotional attachment to that person. In contrast, emotional infidelity involves one's partner forming a deep emotional attachment to that person, yet they are sure that they will not have sexual relations with that person. More recently, Guitar and associates (2017) reported that the most common theme for definitions of sexual infidelity was some mention of sexual activity with an individual other than one's partner, while emotional infidelity involved the most common theme of attending important events with someone else, closely followed by deceiving one's partner about feelings toward them, and being attached/dedicated emotionally to someone other than one's partner.

This division in the types of infidelity is echoed by research on the motives people report for engaging in infidelity. Barta and Kiene (2005) document that motives such as dissatisfaction (e.g., feeling a lack of love toward one's partner), neglect (e.g., feeling one's partner was not spending enough time with them, or mistreatment), anger (e.g., wanting to "get back" at the partner for a transgression), and sexual desire (e.g., wanting to pursue sexual activities, greater sexual frequency, or sexual variety) lead to infidelity. These motives map onto emotional or sexual needs not being met in the relationship, and hence may lead to emotional or sexual infidelity. Selterman et al. (2017) extended these findings and report that there are additional motives, including one's lack of love and feeling low commitment to their primary partner, a desire to enhance one's esteem or popularity, and wanting to have a variety of sexual partners. They also identify situational factors, such as the influence of alcohol, on the decision to engage in an infidelity.

One of the most robust findings within the evolutionary psychological literature pertains to sex differences in distress following a partner's sexual versus emotional infidelity (Buss et al., 1992; Buss et al., 1999). Due to the risks involved in investing in children who are biologically unrelated (i.e., paternal uncertainty), men are argued to be more sensitive to women's sexual infidelity. Throughout evolutionary history, men have sought to establish paternal confidence to avoid investing time, resources, and energy in children who are not biologically related to them (e.g., Daly et al., 1982). Thus, men's sexual jealousy evolved as a cuckoldry avoidance mechanism, because they are not assured of paternity and are at risk of providing for the progeny of another man (Daly et al., 1982).

Hence, it is argued that men are more likely to express jealousy when their partners commit sexual infidelity but less so over emotional infidelity. In contrast, emotional infidelity may signal a lack of dedication toward one's mate, including that one is potentially withdrawing from the relationship. Women have historically relied on men's resources (e.g., Hrdy, 1981), which are presumably allocated toward mates with whom they feel emotionally loyal. Women have full maternal confidence, and thus they should be more threatened by emotional infidelity than by sexual infidelity, because their mating strategy involves finding and retaining a mate willing to provide investment over the long-term in children. Consequently, emotional infidelity should be most concerning for women, as it signals an increase in the probability that a man's time, attention, and, ultimately, resources will be redirected to a rival woman and her children (Daly et al., 1982).

Incidence of Infidelity

To begin, it is notable that the overwhelming majority of Americans consider infidelity morally wrong. A 2013 Gallup poll of 1,535 American adults revealed that at the top of a list of 20 morally wrong behaviors was having an affair, which 94% of respondents deemed morally wrong. For context, the next behaviors were human cloning (87%), polygamy (86%), and suicide (84%; Newport & Himelfarb, 2013). Less than 5% of all societies are as strict about forbidding extramarital intercourse as American society (Carroll, 2018). In light of the number of people who consider it morally wrong, how many individuals actually engage in infidelity?

Issues surrounding how to define infidelity means that it is challenging to provide accurate estimates of its prevalence. Older national surveys of Americans revealed approximately 20% to 25% of respondents state they had at least one sexual affair during their lifetime (Atkins et al., 2001; Laumann et al., 1994). Wiederman and Hurd (1999) reported that 68% of women and 75% of men admitted to participating in some form of sexual cheating. There are also patterns in prevalence rates of sexuality infidelity; Adamopoulou (2013) reported several fascinating patterns in sexual infidelity in romantic relationships (both married and nonmarried). Infidelity fluctuates with the seasons and peaks in the summer and is not related to socioeconomic status or sex/gender. Among Americans, those who commit infidelity are equally split among men and women. Those who cheat are more likely to be less religious, less educated, and poorer than noncheaters. In line with other research, they are more dissatisfied with their current partner, and they have been in their current relationship for longer than noncheaters. Cheaters also report having numerous relationships that lasted less than 6 months, and perhaps most importantly, are much more likely to have cheated in past relationships.

Marriages, though, show lower rates of infidelity than cohabiting and dating relationships (the incidence is also lower if the person has children; Adamopoulou, 2013). In their review of the literature, Fincham and May (2017) report that approximately 2% to 4% of spouses report that they have had sexual interactions with an extradyadic person in the past year. They further document that lifetime estimates of infidelity are higher, occurring in approximately 20%–25% of marriages.

It is key to note that all infidelity is not equivalent. Although 90% of affairs occur because emotional needs are not met (Carroll, 2018), women and men apparently do not perceive their affairs in an equivalent manner. Women report that their affairs are more emotional than sexual, while men report that their affairs are more sexual than emotional (Glass & Wright, 1985). Seventy-seven percent of women who committed infidelity reported that they did so because they fell in love with a person outside of their relationship. This result is compared to only 43% of men who reported it was "for love."

Interestingly, however, 75% of men and only 55% of women reported the infidelity was for sexual gratification (Glass & Wright, 1992). This distinction corresponds to which type of infidelity most distresses each sex: both men and women report engaging more often in the type of infidelity they find most distressing in their partners.

Responses to Partner Infidelity

As mentioned previously, most research on infidelity, particularly research guided by an evolutionary perspective, focuses on suspicions of partner infidelity or attempts to prevent it from occurring. There are entire books written on infidelity (Barash & Lipton, 2002; Rosenberg, 2018), jealousy (Buss, 2000), mate guarding (Platek & Shackelford, 2006), and violence that is often the result of all three (Buss, 2006; Daly & Wilson, 1988). These usually deal with worst case scenarios and criminal acts, and do not provide much specific guidance for "victims" or "perpetrators." Burch and Gallup have conducted several studies on fears of infidelity and flaws in the current treatment of the associated violence (Burch & Gallup, 2020, 2004, 2000). They found that for men in court-mandated domestic violence treatment programs, suspicion of infidelity was the leading cause of violence, beginning with mate guarding behaviors, then escalating to sexual and physical violence (Burch & Gallup, 2020). They also found that, contrary to common beliefs, the violence not only continued but worsened when the partner was pregnant (Burch & Gallup, 2004), and spilled over into violence against children in the home (Burch & Gallup, 2000). The researchers suggested that violence treatment programs focus on jealousy as the main factor in not only violence in the relationship, but in the home as a whole. Male jealousy, whether founded in reality or not, has dire implications for female partners and children.

On the other hand, there are dozens of self-help and therapeutic psychology books on the market for "dealing with" or "recovering from" a partner's infidelity. While these therapeutic books can be helpful, not all are based in research. What does the research literature tell us? Sharpsteen and Kirkpatrick (1997) surveyed a wide range of potential responses to partner infidelity, the most prominent being vengefulness, sadness, and fear. Shackelford et al. (2000) asked participants to generate labels for emotions felt in reaction to partner infidelity, and found feelings of undesirability or insecurity (which accounted for the largest percentage of variance), followed by hostile and vengeful emotions, depression and hurt, and feeling helpless and abandoned. The Hank Williams quote at the beginning of this chapter aptly illustrates this well. Physical symptoms/feelings, such as feeling nauseated, sickened, shocked, and tired were also offered, as well as the expected "humiliated" or "violent." Interestingly, not all of the emotions were negative; participants also offered happy/glad, and content/relieved (see Shackelford et al., 2000, for complete list).

While men are more likely to engage in affairs for sexual gratification, they are much more distressed by their female partners engaging in sexual affairs, and while women are more likely to cheat "for love," they are more distressed by emotional infidelity. Shackelford et al. (2000) found that, among college students, the sexes nominated dissimilar emotions in response to different infidelities. Women's ratings of helpless/abandoned and shocked were higher than men's ratings for both types of infidelity, but the sex difference was greater for emotional infidelity than for sexual infidelity. Men's ratings of homicidal/suicidal were higher than women's ratings for both types of infidelity, but this difference was greater for emotional infidelity than for sexual infidelity. A later study asked participants to choose which type of infidelity was more difficult to deal with; men more than women found it more difficult to forgive a mate's sexual infidelity and were more prone to end the relationship following their partner's sexual infidelity (Shackelford et al., 2002).

When all of this work is combined, it reveals interesting patterns. Men are more likely to cheat for sexual gratification. Women are more likely to forgive this type of transgression, particularly if it is a solitary event (Shackelford et al., 2002). Consequently, sexual infidelity by the male partner, particularly with little emotional connection, is less likely to doom a marriage to divorce. However, men are far less optimistic if women engage in sexual infidelity, and women are more likely to do so if they are in love, which combines both emotional and sexual infidelity. While some have found that sexual infidelity is the strongest predictor of divorce (Tulane et al., 2011), others have found that emotional affairs are comparable in their damage to marriages (Parker & Wampler, 2003) and in sum, the combination of both emotional and sexual infidelity is the most damaging to marriages (Carroll, 2018).

There are evolutionary factors to consider. A man with an unfaithful partner not only faces embarrassment because his partner sexually cheated on him, but also there is an increased probability of taking care of another man's child due to cuckoldry. Women, given their greater investment in children, are argued to be particularly concerned with abandonment by their partners, and may be more forgiving to continue the relationship and the investment in their family. This importance of family needs repeated emphasis; children are an enormous investment. This particular pattern is found throughout the human species, with women agreeing to share husbands (polygyny) if it ensures their survival and that of their children (J. Brown, 1981).

Continuation of Romantic Relationship

As mentioned previously, there are several factors playing a role in forgiveness for infidelity, many having to do with the infidelity itself. However, some factors in forgiveness, and much of the decision to continue the relationship, have to do with the relationship itself. Weiss (1975) reported that most separated couples give some fleeting thoughts to reconciling and the number of couples reconciling was equal to the number of couples who divorced. Similarly, Wineberg (1994, 1995) found that 10% of married women reported having separated and reconciled their marriages, and 30% of women who reconciled their marriages reported still being together one year later. More recently, Solomon and Teagno (2006) report that 60%–75% of couples who have experienced an infidelity stay together. However, while those individuals stay together, they may not rekindle their love for their partner. Instead, they may remain united for pragmatic reasons, such as the presence of children, financial exigencies, or due to a fear of being single (Solomon & Teagno, 2006).

Cyclical Relationships

One might assume that since being in a relationship leads to the release of oxytocin which bonds couples together (Carter, 1992), it might be hard for an individual to just end a relationship if a partner commits infidelity. Thus, one might see a pattern in some relationships of breaking up and then getting back together. Indeed, while research has not examined infidelity and cyclical relationships, prior research indicates that cyclic romantic relationships are common (see Cupach & Metts, 2002; Davis et al., 2000; Waters, 2015).

Also, a predominant reason for renewing a relationship among partners is that there is lingering love and feelings for the partner (Dailey et al., 2011). However, data reveal that some partners in cyclic relationships report less love and understanding than partners in noncyclic relationships (Dailey et al., 2009). Given these findings, it might be harder for some couples than for others to rekindle their relationship after an infidelity occurs. For example, individuals in cyclical relationships may feel even less love and understanding following an infidelity, especially if they previously felt low levels of positive emotions toward their partner compared to those not in cyclical relationships.

Renewal of Love

Thus far, we have discussed how one may seek a "continuation of the relationship," but this may be a far cry from a "renewal of love." Partners may choose to stay together to co-parent, or for financial or social reasons; none of these decisions may include love for each other. How do partners renew their romantic relationships after infidelity?

Forgiveness

One way to start the process of relationship renewal is by forgiving the partner who committed the infidelity. Hall and Fincham (2006) report that relationships are less likely to dissolve if the transgressions are forgiven. Forgiveness is also important because rumination over wrongs and clinging to conflicts has negative psychological and physiological effects for victims (Witvliet et al., 2001). Also, forgiving a transgressor has been linked to improved immune system functioning and immediate and long-term improved cardiovascular health for victims (see Larsen et al., 2012; McCullough et al., 1997; Worthington, 1998). Additionally, Allan and McKillop (2010) report that the results from a controlled laboratory study show that individuals who forgive have better self-reported health and better health habits. So, forgiving a partner after infidelity can have benefits for individuals in relationships, and for the relationships themselves.

But what factors determine whether infidelity is forgiven?

Relationship quality plays a role. Finkel and colleagues (2002) suggested that victims in high-quality relationships are more likely to empathize and identify extenuating circumstances for their partners' transgressions, making the transgression less personal, less hurtful, and easier to forgive. However, lower-quality relationships are more likely to involve deception; people less committed to their partners are more likely to use deception as an attempt to withdraw from the relationship (Cole, 2001). Thus, a strong trusting relationship would initially have less infidelity and deception, so having an affair would appear rare and out of character. However, "forgiving infidelity is not an easy task, especially when victims do not view these transgressions as unplanned, isolated incidents" (Gunderson & Ferrari, 2008, p. 3). Not surprisingly, one-time transgressions were more likely to be forgiven and repeated transgressions led to less forgiveness (Gunderson & Ferrari, 2008). Unfortunately, Adamopoulou (2013) found that people who were unfaithful with their current partner had a history of being unfaithful in the past. Whether the partner is aware of this or not is an important factor; the concern of repeated transgressions into the future would be a sizeable stumbling block for those who wish to continue their relationship.

How the infidelity was discovered also plays a role. Afifi, Falato, and Weiner (2001) determined four different discovery methods for sexual infidelity: (1) unsolicited partner discovery, where the perpetrator admits to the infidelity without the victim knowing anything previously; (2) solicited partner discovery, where the perpetrator admits to the transgression after he or she has been suspected and questioned by the victim; (3) "red-handed" discovery, where the victim catches the perpetrator in the act; and (4) unsolicited third-party discovery, where the victim is told about the transgression by someone else. There was a clear linear pattern, with unsolicited partner discovery the most likely to be forgiven and unsolicited third-party discovery the least likely to be forgiven. While one may think that "red handed" would be the least likely to be forgiven, "third-party" discovery also adds the insult of social embarrassment and loss of privacy. It would also be expected that unsolicited partner confessions would more often be seen as an "out of character mistake," and the confession, as a first step to apology, would create steps to rebuild trust in the relationship. These findings about confession also bring up the importance of apologies in soliciting forgiveness. Gunderson and Ferrari (2008) found that having the perpetrator apologize led to increased partner forgiveness, speed to forgiveness, hope for the continuation of the relationship, and decreased termination of the relationship.

But, in order to renew the relationship, individuals have to move beyond the infidelity in a positive manner. How should that process occur? Worthington (1998) reports that having empathy for the transgressor allows the aggrieved party to begin the forgiving process. When individuals develop empathy for the transgressor they reduce their negative arousal and begin to have positive emotions toward them (Witvliet et al., 2001). Basically, as Thoresen et al. (1998) point out, forgiving allows the victim to shed their negative feelings toward the offender and adopt a compassionate attitude toward them, while not absolving the transgressor of their offense (Enright & Coyle, 1998, Witvliet et al., 2001).

As we have already seen, the sexes react to sexual and emotional infidelity differently. Shackelford et al. (2002) report that women are more likely to forgive a partner for committing a sexual infidelity while men are more likely to forgive a partner who committed an emotional infidelity. This distinction occurs due to sex-specific, obligatory, parental investment (Trivers, 1972). As earlier reviewed, the minimum of men's obligate investment is at the genetic level; they provide sperm. So, a partner's commission of sexual infidelity could lead to a man contributing his resources toward the care of another man's child. Women, in contrast, assume a far larger minimum investment via gestation, lactation, and postnatal childcare. Women can gain significant advantages if they have a mate who provides parental investment in the form of resource contributions. Women are most likely to lose that contribution if the partner forms an emotional bond with another woman and, hence, the argument is that women find emotional infidelity more distressing than men (Buss, 1995; Weiderman & Kendall, 1999). These sex differences are robust across cultures also (Buunk et al., 1996) and are reflected in each sex's attitude toward the two types of infidelity, as well as their emotional reactions and preferences (Tagler & Jeffers, 2013). It must be noted that this model, while robust, remains open to criticism. Researchers have documented that men vary considerably in their willingness and ability to parentally invest in children (Sokol-Chang et al., 2017).

Attributions play a role as well. Hall and Fincham (2006) and Shrout and Weigel (2019) report that individuals who make fewer internal attributions that blame the transgressor report more forgiveness and are less likely to end a relationship following a partner's sexual infidelity. Shrout and Weigel (2019) found this result based on hypothetical infidelity scenarios, but the scenarios used were rated as being very realistic by participants. However, the hypothetical scenarios in Shrout and Weigel's (2019) research only focused on sexual infidelity and the responses of individuals. But, other research focusing on both members of the couple's responses (Friesen et al., 2005) examined infidelity as well as any other type of transgressions, making it hard to know exactly how a commission of infidelity alone affects both partners' decisions about forgiveness.

More recently, Grøntvedt et al. (2020), in a cross-sectional study, examined forgiveness for sexual and emotional infidelity among both partners. They investigated how the perceived threat to the relationship (severity of the transgression), relationship quality, blame, and likelihood of forgiveness affected breakup likelihood. They collected data from 92 heterosexual romantic couples and hypothesized that forgiveness would be the main predictor of breakup and that partner blame would be mediated by forgiveness. Their participants read two separate vignettes describing a partner who had been sexually unfaithful in one scenario and emotionally unfaithful in the other scenario. Their scenarios made it clear that the partner had been discovered cheating, admitted the infidelity, and had shown remorse and apologized. Participants then responded by rating how threatening the transgression would be to the relationship of those involved, level of blame, internal forgiveness (keeping distance versus wanting revenge), and likelihood of a breakup. Using path analysis, for sexual infidelity, they found that the likelihood of breakup was directly related to a lack of internal forgiveness and the perceived level of threat. For emotional infidelity they found that perceived threat was the main predictor of breakup for men and women. Also, the effect of blame only affected emotional infidelity, and was accounted for by the "keeping distance" aspect of forgiveness for victims of both sexes. But, forgiveness had a greater effect for women's relationship dissolution decisions than for men's relationship dissolution decisions. So, the effect of forgiveness is similar for both sexes. The issue then becomes how long it takes to forgive a partner for committing sexual versus emotional infidelity, and whether there are sex differences therein.

Wade et al. (2017) presented a sample of 120 men and women with two separate vignettes describing a partner's commission of sexual and emotional infidelity. The researchers asked them to indicate how long they would take to forgive their partner for committing the infidelity using a number and indicating whether the number referred to days, weeks, months, or years. They found that men and women did not differ in the length of time they listed. However, the amount of time to forgive a sexual infidelity and the amount of time to forgive an emotional infidelity significantly differed. The average number of days to forgive a hypothetical sexual infidelity was 110.22 days while the average number of days to forgive a hypothetical emotional infidelity was 54.04 days. Additionally, the background demographics of the sample did not matter. There were no significant effects for: having been cheated on sexually or emotionally previously, having sexual relationship experience, being currently in a relationship or not, or using hormonal birth control (for women). They explained this finding in terms of prior research which found that individuals feel that a partner's sexual infidelity is more hurtful than a partner's emotional infidelity (Weinstein & Wade, 2011). This result is intriguing because it indicates that the amount of time individuals take to forgive an infidelity is independent of whether the infidelity is the more upsetting type of infidelity reported in prior research.

Love

Fisher (1992) reports that love is a potent emotion which can positively influence many areas of life. For instance, Aron et al. (1995) report that falling in love leads to higher self-efficacy and self-esteem. In addition, individuals report that mutual love is a vital precondition for their selection of a mate (Buss, 1988a; Hill, 1945; Hudson & Henze, 1969; McGinnis, 1958).

Love is also multifarious, and exists in a variety of forms. One type is passionate love, which causes an individual to erotically venerate another individual; this feeling is incessant (Fisher, 1992, 2004; Jankowiak & Paladino, 2008). Passionate love facilitates our identification of potential long-term mates (Fisher et al., 2002) and, unsurprisingly, is universal (D. Brown, 1992; Jankowiak & Paladino, 2008). The second type of love is known as romantic love, or as Jankowiak and Paladino (2008) call it, comfort love. This type of love involves feelings of friendship, understanding, and concern for the welfare of another person (Harvey & Wenzel, 2001; Hatfield & Rapson, 1996; Jankowiak & Paladino, 2008). The aforementioned type of love is also universal (Fisher, 2004; Jankowiak & Paladino, 2008). In fact, 151 of 166 different cultures examined all show evidence of some form of love (Jankowiak & Paladino, 2008). Bartels and Zeki (2004) report that passionate and romantic love share a common neural mechanism, and Fisher (2004) also makes a hefty case for the universality of love with distinctive brain chemistry and neuroanatomical activation. Thus, researchers conclude that we are neurologically oriented to fall in love (Jankowiak & Paladino, 2008).

Love is also an old emotion, in terms of our evolutionary heritage (Fisher, 1992). According to Fuentes (2002), love is said to have arisen about 1.8 million years ago, evolving out of our need to bond with one another to increase our ability to survive, and to direct aspects of reproduction (Buss, 1988a; Fisher, 1998). Indeed, the research of Harlow and Zimmerman (1959) and Bowlby (1982) indicates that being attached to another individual increases one's ability to survive and thrive. Additionally, Jankowiak and Fisher (1992) report that humans evolved the propensity to experience romantic love to acquire and maintain a commitment from a mate.

Fisher (2004) reports that love evolved for men to become strongly attached to women so that they stayed in close proximity while women were raising their children. Women are typically the primarily caregivers for young children (Sear & Mace, 2008), but help from men was advantageous for child survival. For example, fathers in some hunter-gatherers societies compensate for a mother's decreased foraging while nursing (Marlowe, 2000; but see also Sokol-Chang et al., 2017). Men join women in providing sustenance accumulation, shelter location, security, and the conveying of life skills to children (Fisher, 2004). Also, becoming romantically attached enhanced one's ability to have a genetic legacy via having children who themselves survived and had children. Thus, Fisher (1992) points out that surviving the pull of attachment long enough to raise a child through infancy nurtured one's own DNA. Modern hunter-gatherer groups face infant mortality rates of around 23% and child mortality rates of 46% and, hence, any advantages that increased the likelihood of a child surviving to adulthood would be important (Volk & Atkinson, 2008).

Predictably then, Fisher et al. (2002), Hatfield and Rapson (1996), and Tennov (1979) report that men and women express romantic love with the same intensity. Jankowiak and Paladino (2008) also report that men and women are united in the meaning and purpose of love. Moreover, neurobiological research shows that the levels of estradiol, progesterone, DHEAS, and androstenedione do not differ between men and women in love (Marazziti & Canale, 2004).

However, from an evolutionary perspective men and women would not be expected to engage in the same love acts because they have different parental investment concerns when it comes to mate selection. Men's obligatory parental investment is minimal (mostly genetic, as we reviewed earlier) and, consequently, their reproductive fitness concerns center around future offspring production. Men were, and are, faced with the adaptive problem of finding the best possible mates to bear their offspring, but also with the problem of raising children successfully (Buss, 1989). In contrast, due to their much higher minimum parental investment, women's reproductive fitness concerns center around securing a mate who will exhibit strong parental investment, and who has high genetic quality (Buss, 1989). Women were, and are, concerned with finding men who are the most willing and best able to genetically and financially invest in their offspring (Buss, 1989), as well as dedicate time, protect, and transfer life skills to children.

Given these preferences, women and men display different assets to obtain the mates they desire. Women display assets that indicate fertility and successful mothering potential while men display assets that indicate status and genetic quality (Buss, 1988b; Buss & Dedden, 1990). Therefore, it was not surprising that Buss (1988a) found seven love act goals that men and women express differently: resource display, exclusivity, commitment, sexual intimacy, reproduction, resource sharing, and parental investment. While the other love act goals are self-explanatory, with regard to resource display, men try to prove their status and financial capabilities, alerting their potential partners to their capacity to provide for future children (Buss, 1988a). Conversely, women expend effort to dress up and look attractive for their potential partners. By doing so, women are displaying their beauty, youthfulness, and health, factors and determinants of a reproductively valuable female (Buss, 1988a). Therefore, the resource a woman displays is her ability to produce children.

Which love acts do men and women engage in? Wade et al. (2009) conducted three studies to address this question, examining the love acts used, their prototypicality, and their perceived effectiveness. Study 1 relied on act nomination and found 43 love acts, many of which exemplified the categories identified in Buss's (1988a) love act research. Examples of the top love acts reported were had sex, he gave or purchased flowers for her, he gave her a gift, he took her out to dinner, she verbally expressed her love by saying I love you, she was comfortable displaying her affection for him in public, and held hands. Also, men nominated more love acts that involve resource display while women more often nominated love acts that relate to displaying their reproductive value, consistent with Buss's (1988a) findings, and consistent with parental investment theory. Study 2 found that love acts related to exclusivity were rated as the most prototypical love acts. However, surprisingly, love acts related to displaying reproductive value, and love acts related to resource display, were not rated as the most prototypical love acts. Study 3 found that love acts exemplifying exclusivity were rated as the most effective way to show a partner that one loves him or her. Specifically, the acts rated as most effective were they got married, he proposed, he shared his emotional feelings with her, they are not afraid to be completely honest with one another, he never cheated, they supported and advised one another, they moved in together, and she said I love you. This last study highlights the challenges one faces when attempting to rekindle love after an infidelity, given that the most effective love acts are those that reinforce exclusivity to a partner.

Rekindling Love

When conflicts occur, sometimes expelling a mate can be adaptive (Wade et al., 2018). Mate expulsion provides individuals the opportunity to extract themselves from relationships that may compromise their own or their offspring's well-being, or their reproductive opportunities, and can provide occasions for personal development and transformation (Slotter et al., 2010; Tashiro & Frazier, 2003). But, there can be severe costs concomitant with mate expulsion, such as increased psychological anguish (Field et al., 2010; Morris et al., 2015; Sbarra, 2006), diminished life satisfaction (Rhoades et al., 2011), lowered offspring welfare (Amato & Keith, 1991), and economic adversity (Avellar & Smock, 2005). Also, Wade et al. (2018) posit that additional problems of a partner trying to enact retributive justice and stalking behavior (Lukacs & Quan-Haase, 2015; Perilloux & Buss, 2008), recurrent relationship rekindling (i.e., on-again/off-again relationships; Dailey et al., 2009), friendship loss (Schneider & Kenny, 2000), family disapprobation (MacDonald et al., 2012), and substance abuse (Larson & Sweeten, 2012) may also occur as a consequence of mate expulsion. Last, Fisher (2006) contends that mate expulsion is physiologically painful because the rejection from a partner involves subcortical reward/gain loss areas of the brain that are central for survival (Fisher et al., 2010). So, to moderate these costs individuals may use positive mate retention strategies such as more affection, acquiescing to a partner's demands, self-debasement, sexual inducements, and appearance enhancement (see Buss, 1988c; Buss & Shackelford, 1997; Kaighobadi et al., 2010) to forestall mate expulsion in an attempt to rekindle love. Reconciliation actions can also be used to prevent mate expulsion decisions (Wade et al., 2018). Since there are adaptive benefits associated with forgiveness and reconciliation it is likely that reconciliation behaviors have been shaped, to some extent, by natural selection to facilitate individual actions when dealing with the repeated adaptive problems that routinely occur after relationship conflict. A similar argument has been previously used to explain why people feel guilt after an infidelity (Fisher et al., 2008).

Prior research has not directly examined how individuals go about rekindling love after an infidelity has occurred. But, Wade and Brown (2012), Wade and Mogilski (2013), and Wade and Mogilski (2018) report that men are more likely to expel a mate due to a lack of sexual access whereas women are more likely to expel a mate due to a lack of emotional access. Sexual access and emotional access are related to motivations to commit sexual and emotional infidelity, respectively. For example, a partner who feels they are not receiving the amount or type of sex desired may seek to address that deficit with another partner. Similarly, a partner who feels they are not getting their desired emotional sustenance may seek to address that deficit by engaging emotionally with another partner. Thus, at the very least, individuals attempting to rekindle love must consider what may have been missing in their relationship, in terms of the gap between what was desired versus present.

Wade et al.'s (2018) research on reconciliation after romantic conflict provides evidence of how one might go about rekindling love after an infidelity occurs. They conducted two studies to examine reconciliation actions after a romantic conflict has occurred. Study 1 used an act nomination procedure to identify the actions individuals report using to reconcile after a romantic conflict. Two hundred twenty responses were nominated, and grouped into the following categories: give gifts, do nice gestures, give in or give up, take some space, spend time together, wait for partner to apologize, give sex/sexual favors, argue with partner, make partner laugh, drink alcohol, forgive your partner, take the blame/admit being wrong, compromise, forget it/pretend it did not occur, ignore/avoid partner, vent to a friend, cry, apologize, cook a meal, kiss/hug/affection, and communicate. They found that the most common responses reported by women (from most to least frequent) were apologizing, communication, gifts, affection, and sexual favors. The most common responses reported by men (from most to least frequent) were gifts, apologizing, nice gestures, sex/sexual favors, spending time together, and communication. Additionally, men reported giving gifts and nice gestures more often than women did, while women reported giving more communication and giving more affection compared to men. Study 2 examined which of the aforementioned categories of actions are perceived as most effective for reconciliation after a romantic conflict. Wade et al. (2018) found that men rated the acts give sex/sexual favors and do nice gestures, as more effective actions for a partner to perform to get them to reconcile than women. Women rated the acts spend time together and apologize as more effective for a partner to perform to get them to reconcile than men. Also, in general, communicate, apologize, forgive partner, spend time together, compromise, and give a kiss/hug/affection were rated as most effective. So, an avenue to rekindling love after infidelity is for men to spend time together with their partner, and apologize to their partner, and for women to give sexual favors to their partner and do nice gestures for their partner. Also, men and women can both rekindle love after an infidelity by engaging in actions such as: communicate, apologize, forgive partner, spend time together, compromise, and give a kiss/hug/affection. These actions work because they indicate romantic investment in one's partner (see Wade et al., 2009; Wade & Vanartsdalen, 2013). Reaffirming to one's partner that one continues to love them after a romantic conflict may facilitate mate retention (Buss & Shackelford, 1997). In addition, sustaining one's romantic affiliation gives reproductive and health remunerations attendant with the creation of a long-term pair bond (Braithwaite et al., 2010; Quinlan, 2008).

Conclusion

If there is one message to glean from this chapter, it is that responses to infidelity and romantic decisions thereafter are the result of several proximate and ultimate factors. The type and frequency of infidelity, the circumstances surrounding it, how the partner learned of it, and the quality of the relationship before it, all play a role in how partners decide where the relationship will go next. And yes, in some cases money or children play a large role in that decision. What we can see, species-wide, is that there are measurable, replicable patterns in which types of infidelity are more likely to end in relationship dissolution. Fortunately, we also see measurable, replicable patterns in what helps relationships continue after infidelity occurs.

This research, while fascinating in its own right, also creates several important implications for marital and couple's therapy. Those helping couples need to first consider how the involved individuals define infidelity, and the form of infidelity that occurred. One benefit of applying evolutionary psychology in therapeutic settings is that it offers potentially effective techniques. There is an untapped opportunity for researchers to explore how clients respond to treatment that includes evolutionary explanations. For example, understanding why infidelity involving sexual behavior versus emotional commitment leads to different reactions in men and women may be useful. While research on reconciliation after conflict is directly relevant, so too is informing clients about our evolutionary heritage, and why certain types of infidelity, coupled with the way the infidelity was revealed, for example, may more readily lead to rekindling love.

It is also important to point out, as Burch and Gallup (2000, 2020) did, that infidelity, and even the suspicion of it, can be damaging to parent/child relationships as well. While that is not the focus of this chapter, it is important to include these relationships in therapeutic discourse and in research. The romantic relationship in a family does not exist in a vacuum; fear of cuckoldry can be just as detrimental for children in a family as to female partners. Future research should examine this topic with a similar focus as Wade and colleagues (Wade et al., 2009; Wade & Vanartsdalen, 2013, Wade et al., 2018). How do you repair relationships between family members (other than romantic partners) after infidelity?

In addition to how infidelity affects other members of the family, more work needs to be done on the successful continuation of relationships. As previously mentioned, a great deal of research, particularly evolutionary psychological research, focuses on the negative outcomes of infidelity. We do not dispute that focusing on negative outcomes is necessary when attempting to understand an issue, but there is a need to examine functioning relationships as well, or how relationships progress after an infidelity, which includes studying positive outcomes (Fisher et al., 2009). Many couples try and succeed in maintaining relationships after infidelity, which is seldom explored from an evolutionary perspective. What they have discovered, and what this chapter has pointed out, is that the strategies for rekindling love follow evolutionary patterns. There are behaviors that are universally more successful for salvaging a relationship, such as disclosing infidelity, admitting fault, and asking for forgiveness, and there are sex/gender specific strategies based on reproductive goals that are more successful rekindling romance. Evolutionary theorists have already done a great deal of work on the evolutionary underpinnings of mental illness and health (see the work of Nesse, 2015, for example). Reconciliation, including rekindling love, after infidelity provides a context for combining clinical and evolutionary psychology for the purpose of couple's and marital therapy. The foundation has already been laid, with global studies on marriage and marital quality measures (Cronin-Weisfeld et al., 2017) and many studies on marriage and divorce (for example, Buckle et al., 1996). Now this research has to be synthesized and applied.

Additionally, Wade et al. (in press) and Conley et al. (2017) point out that some relationships are not monogamous. Yet, there is no research that examines rekindling love in consensually nonmonogamous relationships after infidelity has occurred. Mogilski et al. (2017) highlight that these relationships involve a primary and a secondary partner, and the distress experienced is greater when the primary partner commits infidelity than when the secondary partner commits infidelity (Mogilski et al., 2019). Accordingly, it is possible that different actions may be needed to rekindle love when the infidelity involves a primary versus a secondary partner.

Lastly, there is no evolutionary theory-based research that has investigated how gay and lesbian couples rekindle love after an infidelity occurs. Since lesbian and gay couples differ from heterosexual couples in terms of whether they desire the same actions and characteristics from their relationships (Howard & Perilloux, 2017), it is possible that distinct actions would be needed to rekindle lesbian and gay relationships. Finally, as there seems to be a bourgeoning body of research examining gay and lesbian relationships, the future should yield an opportune time for combining clinical and evolutionary psychology for the purpose of applying couple's and marital therapy to these relationships. While there is much research needed, this chapter shows that rekindling love after infidelity can be understood using an evolutionary psychological perspective.

This chapter details what circumstances are more likely to lead to relationship dissolution; women committing sexual infidelity, particularly if they fall in love, carries with it the worst prognosis for the relationship continuing. We also outline the factors that will lead to greater forgiveness: if an individual has committed infidelity, it may be best to tell their partner, apologize, and ask for forgiveness, according to the reviewed literature. Last, we review methods of renewing and regenerating love in the relationship after the infidelity has occurred. In total, this chapter provides an evolutionary psychological analysis and therapeutic suggestions for dealing with infidelity in romantic relationships.

References

Adamopoulou, E. (2013). New facts on infidelity. *Economic Letters*, *121*(3), 458–462.

Afifi, W. A., Falato, W. L., & Weiner, J. L. (2001). Identity concerns following a severe relational transgression: The role of discovery method for the relational outcomes of infidelity. *Journal of Social and Personal Relationships*, *18*, 291–308.

Allan, A., & McKillop, D. (2010). The health implications of apologizing after an adverse event. *International Journal for Quality in Health Care*, *22*(2), 126–131.

Alexander, R. D., & Noonan, K. M. (1979). Concealment of ovulation, parental care, and human social evolution. Evolutionary biology and human social behavior: An anthropological perspective, 436–453.

Amato, P. R., & Keith, B. (1991). Parental divorce and the well-being of children—a meta-analysis. *Psychological Bulletin*, *110*, 26–46.

Aron, A., Paris, M., & Aron, E. (1995). Falling in love: Studies of self-concept change. *Journal of Personality and Social Psychology*, *69*(6), 1102–1112.

Atkins, D. C., Baucom, D. H., & Jacobson, N. S. (2001). Understanding infidelity: Correlates in a national random sample. *Journal of Family Psychology, 15*(4), 735–749. https://doi.org/10.1037/0893-3200.15.4.735

Avellar, S., & Smock, P. J. (2005). The economic consequences of the dissolution of cohabiting unions. *Journal of Marriage and Family, 67*(2), 315–327.

Barash, D. P., & Lipton, J. E. (2002). *The myth of monogamy: Fidelity and infidelity in animals and people.* Macmillan.

Barta, W. D., & Kiene, S. M. (2005). Motivations for infidelity in heterosexual dating couples: The roles of gender, personality differences, and sociosexual orientation. *Journal of Social and Personal Relationships, 22*(3), 339–360. https://doi.org/10.1177/0265407505052440

Bartels, A., & Zeki, S. (2004). The neural correlates of maternal and passionate love. *Neuroimage, 21,* 1155–1166.

Betzig, L. (1989). Causes of conjugal dissolution across cultural study. *Current Anthropology, 30,* 654–676.

Bowlby, J. (1982). *Attachment.* Basic Books.

Braithwaite, S. R., Delevi, R., & Fincham, F. D. (2010). Romantic relationships and the physical and mental health of college students. *Personal Relationships, 17*(1), 1–12.

Brase, G. L., Caprar, D., & Voracek, M. (2004). Sex differences in responses to relationship threats in England and Romania. *Journal of Social and Personal Relationships, 21,* 777–792.

Brown, D. (1992). *Human universals.* Basic Books.

Brown, J. E. (1981). Polygyny and family planning in sub-Saharan Africa. *Studies in family planning,* 12(8–9) 322–326.

Buckle, L., Gallup, G. G., Jr., & Rodd, Z. A. (1996). Marriage as a reproductive contract: Patterns of marriage, divorce, and remarriage. *Ethology and Sociobiology, 17*(6), 363–377.

Burch, R. L. (2019). The wedding as a reproductive ritual. *Review of General Psychology, 23*(3), 382–398.

Burch, R. L., & Gallup, G. G., Jr. (2020). Abusive men are driven by paternal uncertainty. *Evolutionary Behavioral Sciences, 14*(2), 197–209. https://doi.org/10.1037/ebs0000163

Burch, R. L., & Gallup, G. G. (2004). Pregnancy as a stimulus for domestic violence. *Journal of Family Violence, 19*(4), 243–247.

Burch, R. L., & Gallup, G. G., Jr. (2000). Perceptions of paternal resemblance predict family violence. *Evolution and Human Behavior, 21*(6), 429–435.

Buss, D. M. (1988a). *Love acts: The evolutionary biology of love.* In Robert J. Sternberg and Michael L. Barnes (Eds.). *The psychology of love* (pp. 100–118). Yale University Press.

Buss, D. M. (1988b). The evolution of human intrasexual competition: Tactics of mate attraction. *Journal of Personality and Social Psychology, 54*(4), 616–628.

Buss, D. M. (1988c). From vigilance to violence: Tactics of mate retention in American undergraduates. *Ethology and Sociobiology, 9*(5), 291–317.

Buss, D. M. (1989). Sex differences in human mate preferences: Evolutionary hypotheses tested in 37 cultures. *Behavioral and Brain Sciences, 12,* 1–49.

Buss, D. M. (1995). Psychological sex differences. Origins through sexual selection. *American Psychologist, 50*(3), 164–168.

Buss, D. M. (2000). *The dangerous passion: Why jealousy is as necessary as love and sex.* Free Press.

Buss, D. M. (2006). *The murderer next door: Why the mind is designed to kill.* Penguin.

Buss, D. M., & Dedden, L. A. (1990). Derogation of competitors. *Journal of Social and Personal Relationships, 7,* 395–422.

Buss, D. M., & Duntley, J. D. (2011). The evolution of intimate partner violence. *Aggression and Violent Behavior, 16*(5), 411–419.

Buss, D. M., Larsen, R. J., Westen, D., & Semmelroth, J. (1992). Sex differences in jealousy: Evolution, physiology, and psychology. *Psychological Science, 3,* 251–255.

Buss, D. M., & Shackelford, T. K. (1997). From vigilance to violence: Mate retention tactics in married couples. *Journal of Personality and Social Psychology, 72*(2), 346–361.

Buss, D. M., Shackelford, T. K., Kirkpatrick, L. A., Choe, J. C., Lim, H. K., Hasegawa, M., Hasegawa, T., & Bennett, K. (1999). Jealousy and beliefs about infidelity: Tests of competing hypotheses in the United States, Korea, and Japan. *Personal Relationships, 6,* 125–150.

Buunk, B. P., Angleitner, A., Oubaid, V., & Buss, D. M. (1996). Sex differences in jealousy in evolutionary and cultural perspective: Tests from the Netherlands, Germany, and the United States. *Psychological Science, 7*(6), 359–363.

Carroll, J. L. (2018). *Sexuality now: Embracing diversity.* Cengage Learning.

Carter, C.S. (1992). Oxytocin and sexual behavior. *Neuroscience and Biobehavioral Reviews, 16*, 131–144.

Cole, T. (2001). Lying to the one you love: The use of deception in romantic relationships. *Journal of Social and Personal Relationships, 18*, 107–129.

Conley, T. D., Matsick, J. L., Moors, A. C., & Ziegler, A. (2017). Investigation of consensually nonmonogamous relationships: Theories, methods, and new directions. *Perspectives on Psychological Science, 12*(2), 205–232.

Cronin-Weisfeld, C., Weisfeld, G., & Dillon, L. (2017). *The psychology of marriage: An evolutionary and cross-cultural view.* Lexington Books.

Cupach, W. R., & Metts, S. (2002). *The persistence of reconciliation attempts following the dissolution of romantic relationships.* Paper presented at the 11th International Conference on Personal Relationships. Halifax, Nova Scotia.

Dailey, R. M., Pfiester, R. A., Jin, B., Beck, G., & Clark, G. (2009). On-again/off-again dating relationships: How are they different from other dating relationships? *Personal Relationships, 16*, 23–47.

Dailey, R. M., Jin, B., Pfiester, A., & Beck, G. (2011). On-again/off-again dating relationships: What keeps partners coming back? *Journal of Social Psychology, 151*(4), 417–440.

Daly, M., & Wilson, M. (1988. *Homicide: Foundations of human behavior.* Taylor & Francis.

Daly, M., Wilson, M., & Weghorst, S. J. (1982). Male sexual jealousy. *Ethology and Sociobiology, 3*, 11–27.

Davis, K. E., Ace, A., & Andra, M. (2000). Stalking perpetrators and psychological maltreatment of partners: Anger-jealousy, attachment insecurity, need for control, and break-up context. *Violence and Victims, 15*, 407–425.

Enright, R. D., & Coyle, C. T. (1998). Researching the process model of forgiveness within psychological interventions. In E. L. Worthington Jr. (Ed.), *Dimensions of forgiveness* (pp. 139–161). Templeton Foundation Press.

Field, T., Diego, M., Pelaez, M., Deeds, O., & Delgado, J. (2010). Breakup distress and loss of intimacy in university students. *Psychology, 1*, 173–177.

Fincham, F. D., & May, R. W. (2017). Infidelity in romantic relationships. *Current Opinion in Psychology, 13*, 70–74. https://doi.org/10.1016/j.copsyc.2016.03.008

Finkel, E. J., Rusbult, C. E., Kumashiro, M., & Hannon, P. A. (2002). Dealing with betrayal in close relationships: Does commitment promote forgiveness? *Journal of Personality and Social Psychology, 82*(6), 956–974.

Fisher, H. E. (1992). *Anatomy of love: The natural history of monogamy, adultery, and divorce.* Norton and Company.

Fisher, H. E. (1998). Lust, attraction, and attachment in mammalian reproduction. *Human Nature, 9*(1), 23–52.

Fisher, H. E. (2004). *Why we love: The nature and chemistry of romantic love.* Henry Holt.

Fisher, H. (2006). Broken hearts: the nature and risks of romantic rejection. In A. C. Crouter & A. Booth (Eds.), *Romance and sex in adolescence and emerging adulthood: Risks and opportunities* (pp. 3–28). Erlbaum.

Fisher, H. E. (2016). *Anatomy of love: A natural history of mating, marriage, and why we stray (completely revised and updated with a new introduction).* Norton.

Fisher, H., Aron, A., Mashek, D., Li, H., & Brown, L. (2002). Defining the brain systems of lust, romantic attraction, and attachment. *Archives of Sexual Behavior, 31*, 413–419.

Fisher, H. E., Brown, L. L., Aron, A., Strong, G., & Mashek, D. (2010). Reward, addiction, and emotion regulation systems associated with rejection in love. *Journal of Neurophysiology, 104*(1), 51–60.

Fisher, M., Cox, A., & Shaw, S. (2009). Working towards a model of normative behavior for long-term committed relationships. *Journal of Social, Evolutionary, and Cultural Psychology, 3*, 372–385.

Fisher, M., Rekkas, P., Voracek, M., & Cox, A. (2008). Sex differences in feelings of guilt arising from infidelity. *Evolutionary Psychology, 6*, 436–446.

Ford, N. L. (1983). Variation in mate fidelity in monogamous birds. In *Current ornithology* (pp. 329–356). Springer.

Friesen, M. D., Fletcher, G. J. O., & Overall, N. C. (2005). A dyadic assessment of forgiveness in intimate relationships. *Personal Relationships, 12*, 61–77.

Fuentes, A. (2002). Patterns and trends in primate pair bond. *International Journal of Primatology, 23*(5), 953–978.

Glass, S. P., & Wright, T. L. (1985). Sex differences in types of extramarital involvement and marital dissatisfaction. *Sex Roles, 12*, 1101–1119.

Glass, S. P., & Wright, T. L. (1992). Justifications for extramarital relationships: the association between attitudes, behaviors, and gender. *Journal of Sex Research*, *29*(3), 361–387.

Grøntvedt, T. V., Kennair, L. E. O., & Bendixen, M. (2020). Breakup likelihood following hypothetical sexual or emotional infidelity: Perceived threat, blame, and forgiveness. *Journal of Relationships Research*, *11*, e7, 1–9.

Guitar, A. E., Geher, G., Kruger, D. J., Garcia, J. R., Fisher, M. L., & Fitzgerald, C. J. (2017). Defining and distinguishing sexual and emotional infidelity. *Current Psychology*, *36*(3), 434–446.

Gunderson, P. R., & Ferrari, J. R. (2008). Forgiveness of sexual cheating in romantic relationships: Effects of discovery method, frequency of offense, and presence of apology. *North American Journal of Psychology*, *10*(1), 1–14.

Hall, J. H., & Fincham, F. D. (2006). Relationship dissolution following infidelity: The roles of attributions and forgiveness. *Journal of Social and Clinical Psychology*, *25*(5), 508–522.

Harlow, H., & Zimmerman, R. R. (1959). Affectionate responses in the infant monkey. *Science*, *130*, 421–32.

Harvey, J., & Wenzel, A. (2001). *Close romantic relationships: Maintenance and enhancement*. Erlbaum.

Hatfield, E., & Rapson, R. L. (1996). *Love and sex: Cross cultural perspectives*. Allyn & Bacon.

Hertlein, K.M., & Weeks, G.A. (2007). Two roads diverging in a wood: The current state of infidelity research and treatment. *Journal of Couple and Relationship Therapy*, *6*, 95–107.

Hill, R. (1945). Campus values in mate selection. *Journal of Home Economics*, *37*, 554–558.

Hill, G. E., Montgomerie, R., Roeder, C., & Boag, P. (1994). Sexual selection and cuckoldry in a monogamous songbird: Implications for sexual selection theory. *Behavioral Ecology and Sociobiology*, *35*(3), 193–199.

Howard, R. M., & Perilloux, C. (2017). Is mating psychology most closely tied to biological sex or preferred partner's sex? *Personality and Individual Differences*, *115*, 83–89.

Hrdy, S.B. (1981). *The woman that never evolved*. Harvard University Press.

Hudson, J. W., & Henze, L. P. (1969). Campus values in mate selection: A replication. *Journal of Marriage and the Family*, *31*, 772–775.

Jankowiak, W. R., & Fisher, E. F. (1992). Romantic love: A cross-cultural perspective. *Ethnology*, *2*, 149–156.

Jankowiak, W., & Paladino, T. (2008). Desiring sex, longing for love: A tripartite conundrum. In W. Jankowiak (Ed.). *Intimacies: Love and sex across cultures*. (pp. 1–36). Columbia University Press.

Kaighobadi, F., Shackelford, T. K., & Buss, D. M. (2010). Spousal mate retention in the newlywed year and three years later. *Personality and Individual Differences*, *48*(4), 414–418.

Larsen, B. A., Darby, R. S., Harris, C. R., Nelkin, D. K., Milam, P. E., & Christenfeld, N. J. (2012). The immediate and delayed cardiovascular benefits of forgiving. *Psychosomatic Medicine*, *74*(7), 745–750.

Larson, M., & Sweeten, G. (2012). Breaking up is hard to do: Romantic dissolution, offending, and substance use during the transition to adulthood. *Criminology*, *50*, 605–636.

Laumann, E. O., Gagnon, J. H., Michael, R. T., & Michaels, S. (1994). *The social organization of sexuality: sexual practices in the United States*. University of Chicago Press.

Lukacs, V., & Quan-Haase, A. (2015). Romantic breakups on Facebook: New scales for studying post-breakup behaviors, digital distress, and surveillance. *Information, Communication & Society*, *18*, 492–508.

MacDonald, G., Marshall, T. C., Gere, J., Shimotomai, A., & Lies, J. (2012). Valuing romantic relationships: The role of family approval across cultures. *Cross-Cultural Research*, *46*, 366–393.

Marazziti, D., & Canale, D. (2004). Hormonal changes when falling in love. *Psychoneuroendocrinology*, *29*, 931–936.

Marlowe, F. (2000). Paternal investment and the human mating system. *Behavioural Processes*, *51*(1–3), 45–61.

McCullough, M. E., Worthington E. L., Jr., & Rachal, K. C. (1997). Interpersonal forgiving in close relationships. *Journal of Personality and Social Psychology*, *73*(2), 321.

McGinnis, R. (1958). Campus values in mate selection. *Social Forces*, *36*, 368–373.

Mogilski, J. K., Memering, S. L., Welling, L. L., & Shackelford, T. K. (2017). Monogamy versus consensual non-monogamy: Alternative approaches to pursuing a strategically pluralistic mating strategy. *Archives of Sexual Behavior*, *46*(2), 407–417.

Mogilski, J. K., Reeve, S. D., Nicolas, S. C., Donaldson, S. H., Mitchell, V. E., & Welling, L. L. (2019). Jealousy, consent, and comparison within monogamous and consensually non-monogamous romantic relationships. *Archives of Sexual Behavior*, *48*(6), 1811–1828.

Moller, N. P., & Vossler, A. (2015). Defining infidelity in research and couple counseling: A qualitative study. *Journal of Sex and Martial Therapy*, *41*(5), 487–497.

Morris, C. E., Reiber, C., & Roman, E. (2015). Quantitative sex differences in response to the dissolution of a romantic relationship. *Evolutionary Behavioral Sciences, 9*, 270–282.

Newport, F., & Himelfarb, I. (2013). In U.S., record-high say gay, lesbian relations morally ok. Retrieved August 11, 2020. https://news.gallup.com/poll/162689/record-high-say-gay-lesbian-relations-morally.aspx

Parker, T. S., & Wampler, K. S. (2003). How bad is it? Perceptions of the relationship impact of different types of internet sexual activities. *Contemporary Family Therapy: An International Journal, 25*, 415.

Perilloux, C., & Buss, D. M. (2008). Breaking up romantic relationships: Costs experienced and coping strategies deployed. *Evolutionary Psychology, 6*, 147470490800600119.

Platek, S. M., & Shackelford, T. K. (Eds.). (2006). *Female infidelity and paternal uncertainty: Evolutionary perspectives on male anti-cuckoldry tactics*. Cambridge University Press.

Quinlan, R. J. (2008). Human pair-bonds: Evolutionary functions, ecological variation, and adaptive development. *Evolutionary Anthropology: Issues, News, and Reviews, 17*(5), 227–238.

Rhoades, G. K., Kamp Dush, C. M., Atkins, D. C., Stanley, S. M., & Markman, H. J. (2011). Breaking up is hard to do: The impact of unmarried relationship dissolution on mental health and life satisfaction. *Journal of Family Psychology, 25*, 366–374.

Richardson, P. R. K. (1987). Aardwolf mating system: Overt cuckoldry in an apparently monogamous mammal. *South African Journal of Science, 83*(7), 405.

Rosenberg, K. P. (2018). *Infidelity: Why men and women cheat*. Hachette Books.

Sbarra, D. A. (2006). Predicting the onset of emotional recovery following nonmarital relationship dissolution: Survival analyses of sadness and anger. *Personality and Social Psychology Bulletin, 32*, 298–312.

Schneider, C. S., & Kenny, D. A. (2000). Cross-sex friends who were once romantic partners: Are they platonic friends now? *Journal of Social and Personal Relationships, 17*(3), 451–466.

Sear, R., & Mace, R. (2008). Who keeps children alive? A review of the effects of kin on child survival. *Evolution and Human Behavior, 29*(1), 1–18.

Selterman, D., Garcia, J. R., & Tsapelas, I. (2017). Motivations for extradyadic infidelity revisited. *Journal of Sex Research, 56*(3), 273–286.

Shackelford, T. K., Buss, D. M., & Bennett, K. (2002). Forgiveness or breakup: Sex differences in responses to a partner's infidelity. *Cognition & Emotion, 16*(2), 299–307.

Shackelford, T. K., LeBlanc, G. J., & Drass, E. (2000). Emotional reactions to infidelity. *Cognition & Emotion, 14*(5), 643–659.

Sharpsteen, D. J., & Kirkpatrick, L. A. (1997). Romantic jealousy and adult romantic attachment. *Journal of Personality and Social Psychology, 72*(3), 627.

Shrout, M. R., & Weigel, D. J. (2019). "Should I stay or should I go?": Understanding the noninvolved partner's decision-making process following infidelity. *Journal of Social and Personal Relationships, 36*, 400–420.

Slotter, E. B., Gardner, W. L., & Finkel, E. J. (2010). Who am I without you? The influence of romantic breakup on the self-concept. *Personality and Social Psychology Bulletin, 36*, 147–160.

Sokol-Chang, R., Burch, R., & Fisher, M L. (2017). Cooperative and competitive mothering: From bonding to rivalry in the service of childrearing. In M. L. Fisher (Ed.), *The Oxford handbook of women and competition*. Oxford University Press, 505–528.

Solomon, S. D., & Teagno, L. J. (2006). *Intimacy after infidelity: How to rebuild and affair-proof your marriage*. New Harbinger.

Tagler, M. J., & Jeffers, H. M. (2013). Sex differences in attitudes toward partner infidelity. *Evolutionary Psychology, 11*(4), 821–832.

Tashiro, T. Y., & Frazier, P. (2003). "I'll never be in a relationship like that again": Personal growth following romantic relationship breakups. *Personal Relationships, 10*, 113–128.

Tennov, D. (1979). *Love and limerence: The experience of being in love*. Stein & Day.

Thoresen, C. E., Luskin, F., & Harris, A. H. S. (1998). Science and forgiveness interventions: Reflections and recommendations. In E. L. Worthington Jr. (Ed.), *Dimensions of forgiveness* (pp. 163–190). Templeton Foundation Press.

Thompson, A. E., & O'Sullivan, L. F. (2016). Drawing the line: The development of a comprehensive assessment of infidelity judgments. *Journal of Sex Research, 53*, 910–926. https://doi.org/10.1080/00224499.2015.1062840

Treas, J., & Giesen, D. (2000). Sexual infidelity among married and cohabiting Americans. *Journal of Marriage and Family, 62*(1), 48–60.

Trivers, R. L. 1972. Parental investment and sexual selection. In B. Campbell, (Ed.) *Sexual selection and the descent of man* (pp. 136–179). Aldine.

Tulane, S., Skogrand, L., & DeFrain, J. (2011). Couples in great marriages who considered divorcing. *Marriage and Family Review, 47*, 289–310. doi:10.1080/01494929.2011.594215.

Volk, T., & Atkinson, J. (2008). Is child death the crucible of human evolution? *Journal of Social, Evolutionary, and Cultural Psychology, 2*, 247–260.

Wade, T. J., Auer, G., & Roth, T. M. (2009). What is love: Further investigation of love acts. *Journal of Social, Evolutionary, and Cultural Psychology, 3*(4), 290–304.

Wade, T. J., & Brown, K. (2012). Mate expulsion and sexual conflict. In T. Shackelford & A. Goetz (Eds.), *The Oxford handbook of sexual conflict in humans* (pp. 315–327). Oxford University Press.

Wade, T. J., Grayson, S., Salerno, K., & Moran, J. (2017). *How long does it take to forgive a partner for committing sexual or emotional infidelity?* Paper presented at the 11th Northeastern Evolutionary Psychology Society Conference, Binghamton, NY.

Wade, T. J., & Mogilski, J. (2013). *Mate expulsion decisions across sex: A conjoint analysis.* Paper presented at the 7th Northeastern Evolutionary Psychology Society Conference. Lebanon Valley College, Annville, PA.

Wade, T. J., Mogilski, J., & Schoenberg, R. (2018). Sex differences in reconciliation behavior after romantic conflict. *Evolutionary Psychological Science, 4*(1), 1–7.

Wade, T. J., Moran, J. B., & Fisher, M. L. (in press). Relationship dissatisfaction and partner access deficits. In T. Shackelford & J. Mogilski (Eds.), *The Oxford handbook of evolutionary psychology and romantic relationships.* Oxford University Press.

Wade, T. J., & Vanartsdalen, J. (2013). The Big-5 and the perceived effectiveness of love acts. *Human Ethology Bulletin, 28*(2), 3–12.

Waters, A. (2015). *A comparative analysis of cyclical vs. non-cyclical romantic relationships* [Unpublished Doctoral dissertation].

Weinstein, J. L., & Wade, T. J. (2011). Jealousy induction methods, sex, and the Big-5 personality dimensions. *Psychology, 2*(05), 517–521.

Weiss, R. S. (1975). *Marital separation.* Basic Books.

Wiederman, M. W., & Hurd, C. (1999). Extradyadic involvement during dating. *Journal of Social and Personal Relationships, 16*(2), 265–274. https://doi.org/10.1177/0265407599162008

Wiederman, M. W., & Kendall, E. (1999). Evolution, sex, and jealousy: Investigation with a sample from Sweden. *Evolution and Human Behavior, 20*(2), 121–128.

Wineberg, H. (1994). Marital reconciliation in the United States: Which couples are successful? *Journal of Marriage and the Family, 56*(1), 80–88.

Wineberg, H. (1995). An examination of ever-divorced women who attempted a marital reconciliation before becoming divorced. *Journal of Divorce & Remarriage, 22*(3–4), 129–146.

Witvliet, C. V. O., Ludwig, T. E., & Laan, K. L. V. (2001). Granting forgiveness or harboring grudges: Implications for emotion, physiology, and health. *Psychological Science, 12*(2), 117–123.

Wood, J. W. (1994). *Dynamics of human reproduction: Biology, biometry, and demography.* Routledge. https://doi.org/10.4324/9780203792780

Worthington, E. L., Jr. (1998). Empirical research in forgiveness: Looking backward, looking forward. In E. L. Worthington Jr. (Ed.), *Dimensions of forgiveness* (pp. 321–339). Templeton Foundation Press.

CHAPTER 22

Relationship Quality Between Partners Following Infidelity in the Absence of Renewed Love

Mohammad Hassan Asayesh *and* Elaheh Golpasha

Abstract

Infidelity means having any secret emotional, sexual, virtual relationship, or a combination of them outside the marital relationship. Infidelity has a significant prevalence as one of the major reasons of divorce, which causes psychological traumas in victims. Various studies in different cultures have revealed that extramarital affairs in each culture can have different meanings and, consequently, different effects, but what is obvious is that extramarital affairs in any form (emotional, sexual, online, or a combination) as a stressful event have detrimental effects on the family unit and various dimensions of victim's and his/her spouse's mental health. Research has shown that infidelity has many psychological effects on its victims. Affective experiences and reactions, cognitive experiences and reactions, psychosomatic and physical experiences and reactions, communication experiences and reactions, as well as spiritual experiences and reactions are among the psychological reactions and complex problems encountered by the victims. If the victims of infidelity are not treated, harmful consequences can last for a long time. Moreover, experts have acknowledged that couples involved in infidelity can be helped out. In this report, in addition to presenting the effects and psychological consequences of infidelity, effective factors for the treatment of these clients are discussed.

Key Words: infidelity, extramarital relationship, affairs, psychological reactions, love

Introduction

It is natural for people to enter a romantic relationship or marriage to give or receive love and affection (Buss, 2018). In such relationships, a sense of trust is a dimension of marital satisfaction. Expecting mutual trust is the foundation of couples' commitment to each other. An important and often unmentioned element of this trust is that couples experience emotional closeness and sexual relations exclusively with each other (Lusterman, 1998). A committed couple relationship is, in fact, a moral and contractual agreement whereby both parties implicitly commit themselves to love and support each other, and to provide each other peace and care. In this type of relationship, there is an expectation of sexual and emotional monogamy (Allen et al., 2005; Boekhout et al., 2003). In a public survey on 3432 people in the United States by Tsapelas et al. (2010), the results showed that 77% of the participants "believed in" or desired monogamy.

Evidently, to preserve the foundations of the family in monogamous marriages, which are the norm in different societies cross-culturally (Tsapelas et al., 2010), the principles of commitment and faithfulness are essential. Marital commitment typically implies that members of the couple have a long-term view of their marriage and make sacrifices to retain their relationship, take measures to maintain and strengthen their unity and solidarity, and remain in the relationship even during difficult times (Harmon, 2005). When members of a couple are committed to their relationship, this will lead to compassion, forgiveness, and sacrifices, motivation toward cooperation with each other, and paying more attention to each other's interests. This affects the economy of the household, and maintains the marital relationship (Zhang & Tsang, 2013).

Although monogamy is the main strategy for the human marriage and reproduction, unfaithfulness or infidelity are also common today (Buunk & Dijkstra, 2006), and is an important problem for many couples. For years, researchers and experts have discussed and analyzed marital infidelity, suggesting that it will continue to be a challenge for marriage and marital relationships (Taghi Pour et al., 2019). Many studies confirm that infidelity is a main cause of marital conflict, the disintegration of families and, in many cases, divorce (Snyder et al., 2007; Platt et al., 2008; Shackelford, 2008; Frederick & Fales, 2016).

Marital infidelity is defined as establishing physical or emotional intimacy with a person outside the relationship (Balderrama-Durbin et al., 2017). Knight (2010) considers a larger extent for defining infidelity, and regards it as having sexual, emotional, or online relationships or a combination of all. In the *Encyclopedia of Evolutionary Psychological Science* (Shackelford & Weekes-Shackelford, 2019), infidelity is defined as follows: "Infidelity may include a wide range of behaviors, depending on one's perspective. Behaviors such as flirtations, emotional involvement, and sexual intercourse may or may not be counted as infidelity. It is said that the precise identification of infidelity with full precision may be difficult" (Urganci & Sevi, 2019). We contend that infidelity refers to a conscious and secret emotional and/or sexual relationship outside of the committed couples' relationship that can be in the form of a face-to-face or online relationship, with numerous consequences for the couples' health and relationship. The effects of this phenomenon have made it a devastating problem for couples and families.

The current literature shows that unfaithfulness and infidelity as causes of divorce are on the rise (Shackelford, 2008); 20% of women and 40% of men have confessed to having at least one romantic relationship with a person other than their spouse during their lifetime (Gordon et al., 2004), while in more recent studies the probability of its occurrence in one's lifetime has been reported as 60% (Abrahamson et al., 2012). It is observed that the statistics on unfaithfulness greatly vary, which could suggest the effect of cultural, personality, and sexual factors. Although statistics on unfaithfulness differ, it is clear that these numbers have increased in recent years, and this is a red flag for the constitution of family and social health, requiring accurate solutions, proper psychological, and social interventions.

Marital infidelity is an effect with different causes which have been explained in multiple psychological and sociological theories and studies. Some of these studies indicate that sexual dissatisfaction (Rozov et al., 2015), marital conflicts, empty nest syndrome, diminished intimacy, sex addiction (Browth, 2001; as cited in Long and Young, 2007), expression of criticism about the relationship, low sex drive (Birnbaum et al., 2019), the spouse's personal characteristics (Conroy, 2014), the need for attention and power, proving one's attraction, and femininity or masculinity (Fisher, 2007) all can play a role in unfaithfulness. Although people have specific needs, expectations, motivations, and goals based on their personalities (Ferron et al., 2017) that can determine the motive for marital infidelity, by examining different cultures, one study concluded that extramarital relations can have different causes and meanings and, therefore, different effects and prevalence in different cultures (Asayesh, 2017). For instance, in Islamic countries including Iran (where the authors reside), a legal permit is issued for polygamy in certain cases, which is a culturally dependent issue and can confuse people; therefore, the outcomes of polygynous relationships is different in Iranian families because some accept while others oppose it. The first author remembers one of his clients in Iran whose husband had cheated on her. She said:

> When I realized that this was an unlawful relationship and not a temporary marriage, it was so hard on me, and the world turned upside down. After all, our religion permits temporary marriage to prevent men from sin, and they can have many wives. If it were a single woman who'd married him temporarily, I'd say she was a helpless woman in a halal relationship, so be it, and I'd forgive. But now, I feel horrible; he's committed a grave sin and destroyed my life and that of our children.

We see that the effects of unfaithfulness differ across cultures, and many sociological factors are relevant. Although it is possible to discuss these comments as a defense mechanism for psychological rationalization, the truth is that social beliefs affect the definition of marital infidelity and the experience of its outcomes. It is clear that infidelity can cause numerous problems and negative consequences for the mental health of the victims (Kachadourian et al., 2015), for marital relations (Snyder et al., 2007; Asayesh et al., 2019), and can cause adjustment problems or divorce (Whisman, 2016). Sometimes, the disclosure of unfaithfulness is a stimulant and trigger for couples to seek couples' therapy. Therefore, it is important for therapists to be aware of the psychological reactions of the spouse who is the victim of unfaithfulness, the possible reactions of both parties, the probable outcomes of those reactions, and the previous and subsequent quality of their marital relationship. Therefore, in this chapter, we aim to examine the effects of unfaithfulness on the victims and their marital relationship. To this end, a precise and comprehensive study of the effects and outcomes of unfaithfulness in marital relationship and life is required so that different aspects of this phenomenon on victims can be properly identified. Below, we discuss the outcomes of unfaithfulness and couples' psychological and relational responses after unfaithfulness to provide a better understanding of this topic and a guide for the development of effective therapeutic interventions.

Outcomes of Unfaithfulness in Marital Life

The stability and strength of the family are affected by different intrapersonal, interpersonal, and environmental factors. An important factor that disrupts the health of the family is the breach in the monopoly on emotional and sexual relations within the marital bond (Allendorf & Ghimire, 2013). Infidelity is a painful and complex experience for the victim (Shackelford et al.2008). Many studies indicate that any extramarital relation (emotional, sexual, online) can create major intra- and interpersonal distresses for both spouses (Spring, 2012; Fung et al., 2009). The damages caused by unfaithfulness and infidelity to the spouse include negative effects on individuals and the marriage; however, due to its negative consequences, infidelity also disturbs child rearing, family's health, and perhaps even the security of society (Asayesh, 2017). These consequences affect the current and future life of the couple and their children personally and socially. The results of a study by Taghi Pour et al. (2019) indicated that children, the victimized spouse, and the family experience unpleasant consequences due to infidelity. Asayesh (2017) showed that after the disclosure of unfaithfulness, the victims react in six main domains of life: emotional, cognitive, relational, behavioral, spiritual, and psychosomatic. Different problems are caused to intra- and interpersonal as well as family dimensions, and families will face problems such as marital crisis, reduced functioning in parental roles, and occupational problems, which can cause complex and extensive conflicts in the family. As the disclosure of marital unfaithfulness is a damaging event for the spouses, especially the victim, it also is often associated with distress and a loss of function of the victim in different domains; thus, infidelity can have many consequences for the marital and family relations. Therefore, based on the importance of these outcomes for family, and especially marital, relations, these effects will be explored in emotional and relational dimensions.

Emotional Effects of Infidelity on the Victim's Relationship

For any person, realizing that his/her spouse has had extramarital relations can be a bitter experience (Kessel et al., 2007). Emotional distress is often the first reaction to the spouse's unfaithfulness (Brown, 2001; Olson et al., 2002, as cited in Gordon et al., 2004; Asayesh, 2017). The natural reaction of the victim is often associated with the experience of intense and shocking emotions. When a spouse violates the sense of trust and protection, and betrays or abandons their partner, the psychological activities and nervous system of the partner are altered. With the secretion of adrenaline and other stress hormones that depend on the sympathetic nervous system, intense excitation, alertness, anxiety, restlessness, frequent wake-ups during the night, insomnia, sensitivity to noise, extreme rumination, a sense of confusion after waking up, and forgetfulness may arise. Moreover, with the release of endogenous opioids that secrete into the nerves, pain perception is weakened and the person is protected against intense emotional stress; therefore, the spectrum of emotional and physical feelings is limited, and the person may lose interest in previously pleasant relationships. The mind wanders, and concentration is disrupted. These feelings cause a sense of bewilderment, emotional paralysis, and loneliness (Spring, 2012). Kessel et al. (2007) noted that the disclosure of an extramarital relationship can cause trauma and shock and lead to the emergence of emotions such as rage, sorrow, and shame. The victim also feels pain, a sense of betrayal, and shame (Brown, 2001). Some studies show that the sense of being betrayed, abandoned, shamed, and angry are felt by the victim along with many other emotions. Other studies also indicate that unfaithfulness destroys the previous security, stability, and previous will and control in the marital relationship. In such cases, vacillating feelings of rage, overwhelming powerlessness, victimization, and abandonment are frequently reported (Brown, 2001; Spring, 2012; Cano & O'Leary, 2000; Atkins et al., 2001; Gordon et al., 2004; Snyder et al., 2007; Asayesh, 2017).

A study by Olson (2002) also showed that, after the discovery of the spouse's unfaithfulness, people show intense emotions such as denial, rage, anger, and depression. It has also been mentioned that prevalent initial reactions to the disclosure of unfaithfulness include shock, denial, and anger (Humphrey, 1987; as cited in Fife et al., 2007; Brand et al., 2007). Therefore, due to the traumatic nature of the disclosure of unfaithfulness, the victims are first shocked and experience intense excitation and range and other complex emotional responses. One of the clients of the first author said the following about the experience of the spouse's infidelity:

> I was shocked. It's too painful for me. The news of the death of a loved one isn't that bad. . . . I feel I'm asleep now. I don't think I'm awake. I cry every night.

Spring (2012) also notes that when unfaithfulness is disclosed, the victim is probably in shock, often loses his/her trust in justice in the world, and his/her sense of control over life, self-esteem, and self-concept. The victim feels abandoned, ashamed, depressed, and helpless. He/she may withdraw from life, lose contact with him/herself, and suffer from delusions; of course, these responses and experiences are predictable and common responses to difficult and shocking experiences.

We believe that these emotional reactions can profoundly affect marital relations. If emotional reactions are not taken seriously by the couple and not treated by therapists, the marital relationship will not be treated and mental health problems and divorce are predictable. The results of a study by Asayesh, Farahbakhsh, Salimi Bajestani, et al. (2017b) showed that people report various emotional reactions to the spouse's unfaithfulness. These reactions are classified into the two themes of "maladaptive emotional reactions" and "adaptive emotional reactions." "Maladaptive emotional reactions" consist of subthemes such as feelings of separation from life (including feelings of sadness, frustration, and desire for death), separation from oneself (including inadequacy and sense of abandonment), anger, hatred, cruelty, vulnerability, emotional confusion, fear and anxiety, numbness, and coldness. "Adaptive emotional reactions" consists of subthemes such as feelings of self-worth (including one's own and spouse), compassion (including toward the spouse and toward the rival), and attachment to the spouse (interest in spouse, sense of mutual ownership between the couple, and forgiveness). These reactions led to extreme compensation and the desire to rebuild the marital life. In what follows, these reactions and other emotional and cognitive qualities in the couple's relationship will be more closely examined.

There is consensus about negative reactions that people, upon hearing about the act of unfaithfulness, may show multiple negative reactions including a fear of inadequacy, self-doubt, depression, shock, and confusion (Ciarocco et al., 2012). The emotional reactions of some women to their spouses' unfaithfulness include a sense of separation from life (feeling of unhappiness, frustration, a desire to die) and separation from oneself (a sense of inadequacy and sense of abandonment). In this emotional reaction, victims of unfaithfulness find life sad and disappointing, feel empty, and have little motivation to continue living. They also have a sense of failure, inadequacy, inefficiency, fault and guilt, frailty, worthlessness, as well as abandonment, loneliness, being deceived and boycotted by the spouse. These feelings are associated with a sense of depression, loss, and mourning (Asayesh, Farahbakhsh, Salimi Bajestani, et al., 2017b), i.e., the person perceives that he/she has lost the sense of trust, honesty, worth, adequacy, competency, attraction, and reliability towards the spouse. In fact, this depression is an outcome of doubting oneself and one's spouse. One of the first author's clients, a 32-year-old woman, explained her experience of her husband's infidelity:

> I felt swindled; as if my life's been wasted. . . . I feel worthless. Life has no meaning for me anymore. I'm fed up with life. I don't care if I'm hungry or thirsty anymore. I'm depressed and hopeless.

Spring (2012) noted that the victim may experience nine forms of loss, all revolving around the main one, i.e., "loss of self." These losses include: (1) a sense of alienation; (2) losing the sense of being unique and special; (3) loss of self-esteem; (4) loss of self-confidence; (5) loss of one's control over one's thoughts, actions, and body;, (6) loss of trust; (7) loss of religious faith; (8) loss of social relationships; and (9) loss of one's will power and determination in life. These consequences can lead to further feelings of vulnerability, loss of identity, self-respect, and sense of purpose; as a result, the active internal patterns are highly affected and change (Case, 2005; Johnson, 2005; Macintosh et al., 2007, p. 129). Ciarocco et al. (2012) show that the victims' multiple negative reactions may include a sense of inadequacy, self-doubt, depression, shock, and confusion. Lusterman

(1998) notes that victims of unfaithfulness feel failure and jealousy the moment they realize their spouses' unfaithfulness.

Some victims also discuss changes in their humanitarian sense in their marital life. They report a heightened desire for revenge and to hurt their spouse; they feel an ongoing grudge and hatred; and they do not have their previous sense of compassion for others. In fact, they suffer from cruelty and repress their positive and humanitarian emotions. A 42-year-old female client with one child showed intense anger and aggression upon the disclosure of her husband's infidelity:

> That night, when I realized it and he confessed, I was really mad. I lost my control and beat him up. Beat him all over his face and body. I broke the dishes, and my son and I left the next day. I hated him; I still feel anger and hatred. . . . Sometimes, when I'm angry, I drag out the fight. I don't show him my anger on purpose; I can't help it. I can't hide my anger. I've become nervous and more aggressive.

These reactions show a lack of emotion regulation in the victim of infidelity. According to Brown (2001), becoming aware of the spouse's betrayal is associated with intense emotions such as anger, hatred, and insecurity. Miller and Maner (2008) found that after a spouse's infidelity, men often express their emotions through anger, while women show signs of depression and search deeply for the causes of infidelity. Lusterman (1998) noted that some victims of infidelity attack their spouses. It seems that, in the case of such emotional distress in the victim (whether male or female), serious treatment and emergency intervention may be required. Some victims of unfaithfulness express their wish for divorce due to extreme anger and hatred for their spouse. The reason for divorce could be emotional stress, intense anger due to the sense of oppression and injustice, conflict, irritation, and a sense of hatred and disgust toward the spouse; therefore, they find it difficult to tolerate their spouse and living with him/her, and thus prefer to end the marriage. In these cases, efforts at emotion regulation and release, providing social and therapeutic supports, and gaining time to provide full treatment are essential. Asayesh (2017) noted that this experience of anger is not always limited to the husband, and may also be extended to the third party (mistress) in the relationship or even the husband's family because they have failed to support their daughter-in-law; they may even be angry with their own family. The first author recalls that, in the counseling and psychological services clinic of the University of Tehran, he met a 37-year-old woman whose husband had been unfaithful to her. She expressed the experience of a deep and intense anger. Some of her statements are noteworthy:

> My bad psychological state began after being shocked, with fear and anger towards my husband. Back then, I was very irritable and angry; I was even angry with my step-mother who took his side. But I thought my own family was even more guilty; I said if they did such and such, he'd be attracted to us and wouldn't pursue another woman. I told my mom, "He

had no mother; if you'd given him a kiss, he might like you." My father hadn't believed in him and had belittled him. I thought everyone was guilty. I kept fighting with them and was angry with them. And I was mad at that woman, too. I still sometimes fight with her online. I'd hurt her if I could.

This client talks about anger and looks for an opportunity for revenge. It seems that the psychological injury is very deep. In some cases, unfaithfulness inflicts destructive injuries in the mind of the victim which, occasionally, causes serious crises in their marital and family life. Emotional distress is the emotional response of some victims to their spouses' unfaithfulness. This emotional reaction, which is among the most intense reactions of some victims, includes a sense of being lost, emotional shock, restlessness, suicidal ideations, madness, grudge, loss of control over oneself, and efforts for serious revenge (Asayesh, Farahbakhsh, Salimi Bajestani, et al., 2017b). This topic has been neglected to some extent in other studies.

The results of a study by Omarzu et al. (2012) show that secret extramarital relationships often cause intense emotional stress for both parties on discovery. According to Gordon et al. (2004), emotional distress in reaction to infidelity is among the first reactions of some victims toward their spouses. The report by Ciarocco et al. (2012) demonstrates that a sense of shock and confusion is among the multiple negative reactions of victims of unfaithfulness. These reactions show the severity of the damage caused by unfaithfulness. Confirming this finding, Spring (2012) mentions that the mind and body of the victim are in a state of shock; victims detach themselves from life, lose touch with their sense of self. In another study, it has been noted that this damage as a trauma sometimes causes signs and symptoms similar to those of posttraumatic stress disorder (PTSD) in the victim (Omarzu, et al., 2012; Lusterman, 1998). It has been specified that the signs of anxiety mediate the relationship between the spouse's infidelity and physical aggression, harming the spouse, mental aggression, and sexual aggression against the spouse (Arnocky et al., 2015). The first author had a client in the counseling and psychological services clinic of the University of Tehran. He was a 40-year-old man with two children who had a relatively good relationship with his wife. When he realized that his wife had sexual relations with her colleague at work, he lost his control and showed strange reactions for some months. He said:

I didn't feel well. I was crazy at that moment. I felt I'd gone mad. I didn't know what to do. I beat her up, until all her body and face were bruised. I'd never been like that. This behavior was not expected of me. . . . I thought of revenge; taking revenge on that man. Every day, I think of hitting him, or burning him, or hiring someone to kill him. . . . In the past months, I've been thinking and thinking. I've lost control over my mind. I even thought about divorce and suicide.

People who discover their spouse's extramarital relationship or unfaithfulness and the breach of faith, often experience a deep psychological and emotional stress. Sometimes, some victims attack their spouses or commit suicide or murder (Lusterman, 1998, p. 21). Beating and cursing, murdering the spouse, or committing suicide are also probable (Gordon, 2005). According to Marjorie et al. (2020), infidelity and romantic jealousy are commonly cited causes of intimate partner violence. Brown (2001) holds that realizing one's spouse's infidelity is associated with intense emotions such as anger and hatred, and some people show a risk of suicide and homicide attempts. These signs should be taken as a red flag indicating the need for intervention in crisis. People with disrupted thought content or process cannot think properly and often take dangerous actions or make inaccurate and emotional decisions. They need control, accompaniment, and sometimes pharmacotherapy; therefore, a psychiatric referral is essential along with psychotherapy. Supporting the unfaithful spouse is occasionally necessary until the risk to his/her life is resolved; in these cases, the breach of confidentiality is important to help the client and his/her spouse.

Another emotional reaction resulting from infidelity that disrupts the couple's relationship is the sense of fear and anxiety in the victims. According to Spring (2012), the nervous system and cognitive activity of victims of unfaithfulness undergo physiological changes. Since the sympathetic nervous system is alarmed, the secretion of hormones related to this system, including adrenaline, is initiated. This causes the body to show a variety of reactions, such as excitation, insomnia, and extreme rumination. According to Atkins et al. (2001), unfaithfulness has many psychological and emotional effects such as fear. Asayesh, Farahbakhsh, Salimi Bajestani, et al. (2017b) note that the sense of fear and anxiety in victims of marital infidelity includes different dimensions such as fear of the future, fear of sin and punishment, fear of children's future, fear of disgrace, panic, physical tension, stress, a sense of insecurity and danger, sensitivity and alertness, restlessness and irritability. Based on emotionally focused therapy (EFT), Macintosh et al. (2007) noted that following unfaithfulness and attachment injury, the victim may suffer from fear of reattachment, and cannot trust his/her spouse anymore; this can be a source of intense fear in the victim (Fife et al., 2007). The first author remembers a client visiting him at the counseling and psychological services clinic of the University of Tehran who was very anxious and had experienced panic attacks which persisted after the spouse's unfaithfulness. The client said:

> I've felt horrible since I realized the matter. My anxiety was much worse back then. Panic attacks began, and happened 4–5 times a day. I felt suffocated; I felt I was dying and I shivered. I lost my job because of panic attacks. I'd lost balance. I was afraid that there'd be earthquakes. I didn't leave the house. I couldn't even take a shower. I was afraid of being alone. My brother accompanied me. When the panic got worse, I visited a psychiatrist and started taking medication.

It seems that this intense anxiety toward the spouse's unfaithfulness is a psychological reaction to a serious and unbearable trauma, which has caused a critical situation for the client and his/her relationship. Whisman and Wagers (2005) concluded that major depression episodes and PTSD are the most prevalent clinical diagnoses in victims of unfaithfulness, especially women. Cano and O'Leary (2002, as cited in Brand et al., 2007) showed that women who experience the stress of their spouse's unfaithfulness run the risk of major depressive disorder six times higher than those who do not experience such stress. Moreover, Asayesh (2017) notes that unfaithfulness is a confusing and painful experience for everyone involved and can lead to disorders such as depression.

As for major depression episodes and PTSD, the measure that should be taken is the evaluation of the level of marital disorder, as well as suicidal and homicidal thoughts. Still, there are few studies that have examined the treatment of depression and PTSD in the case of unfaithfulness (Kessel et al., 2007). This critical phase necessitates psychotherapy interventions along with pharmacotherapy in the first phase of treatment for such clients.

Following the activation of anxiety and fear, some victims feel intense vulnerability in their marital life. In this situation, victims feel they are under great pressure; they feel helplessness, injury, and loss, all of which include feelings of weakness and vulnerability (Asayesh, Farahbakhsh, Salimi Bajestani, et al., 2017b). According to Lusterman (1998), the victim of unfaithfulness feels hurt, deceived, and mistrusting. Case (2005) stated that the experience of the spouse's unfaithfulness would intensify their vulnerability, which may make room for psychological disorders. Another client of the first author in said clinic said:

> I saw death with my own eyes. The world was upside down. I never expected he/she would betray me like that. He/she did not pay attention to me anymore. I feel helpless and bear all the pressure. I don't trust him/her and I'm afraid of him/her.

As demonstrated in this case, the victim suffers a great deal of vulnerability. Kessel et al. (2007) note that for the victim, understanding that his/her spouse has had an extramarital relationship can be a very damaging experience; therefore, the victims feel great vulnerability in their married life, and need the support of others, including their family or a therapist. An important injury is the injury to the couples' attachment. To explain this vulnerability, Johnson et al. (2001) conceptualize attachment injuries in the EFT treatment literature. This injury is like a wound that disrupts the ideas about the attachment necessary in a relationship. When the unfaithful spouse does not show any reassuring or calming reaction, or when the victim can no longer trust the spouse, the injury becomes worse. Thus, this sense of vulnerability and helplessness can activate the insecure attachment patterns in the victim, and this agitation and helplessness will persist as long as their attachment pattern is not reconstructed. Thus, attention should be paid to these reactions and treating them in couples' and individual therapy.

Thought and Cognition Dissociation in the Couples After Marital Infidelity

Intense emotional disturbance after the disclosure of marital unfaithfulness is often associated with cognitive distress. Unfaithfulness disrupts the victim's basic beliefs about marriage, and threatens his/her individual and marital identity (Winek & Craven, 2003). According to interpretations based on different theories, including cognitive-behavioral theory, thoughts play a major role in the creation of psychological disorders (Sharf, 2012). Research indicates that victims of unfaithfulness show different cognitive reactions to the spouse's unfaithfulness. In the study by Asayesh et al. (2018), the negative cognitive reactions of the participants included suspicion, rumination and obsessive thoughts, a change in religious beliefs, thinking about decision-making, thinking about punishing the spouse, a change in the meaning of life, self-criticism, and disrupted thinking. Some reports also noted the activation of cognitive distortions (Ghahari, 2016). Victims deal with the mentality of lack of control over an unpredictable future, and proclaim this thinking and belief in different ways and with surprise and anger.

A considerable and important cognitive disorder experienced by the victim is intense rumination about the event of unfaithfulness, which can be so severe and uncontrollable that it may disrupt daily functioning and concentration. In this cognitive state, the victims continually review the event or factors that lead to the recall of the event, and think about the consequences of unfaithfulness in their life (Brown, 2001; Glass & Wright, 2007). In the same vein, Harley and Chalmers (2013) state that the problem faced by most women whose spouses have been unfaithful is not forgiving their spouses, but forgetting the unfaithfulness. They fall prey to rumination, recall the scenes of unfaithfulness or their spouses' unjust behavior, and experience insufferable pain and discomfort because of some attitudinal and cognitive changes. This state can be an effort to overcome the severe unexperienced emotions (repressed emotions) related to the painful memory of infidelity which have caused a high degree of anxiety, fear, or anger, a mechanism also observed in people with PTSD. According to Lusterman (1998), when people realize their spouses' unfaithfulness, this unfaithfulness becomes a mental preoccupation. In the study by Asayesh (2018), the findings specified more precise dimensions of rumination and obsessive thoughts in victims. These dimensions included mental preoccupation with the event of unfaithfulness (rumination about the past), and mental preoccupation and obsessive thoughts about the effects of unfaithfulness and the future. These two dimensions comprised rumination about the event of unfaithfulness, mental preoccupation about the unfaithfulness, efforts to prove unfaithfulness, mental preoccupation with the effects of unfaithfulness on children, mental preoccupation with family honor, mental preoccupation with the spouse's behavioral changes, and mental preoccupation with the future.

Many victims of unfaithfulness suffer from cognitive distortions and disrupted thinking; as a result, they cannot reflect on their life, make correct decisions, or take the right action in their daily life, and this causes problems for the marital relationship, too. Lusterman

(1998) notes that the victim of unfaithfulness has different disappointing thoughts, and, as a result, feels emotions such as anger. The victim is angry with his/her spouse, and this emotional reaction is manifested with the following thoughts: "His/her behavior was unjust," "He/she didn't care about me," "He/she thought I was stupid," "I wasn't enough for him/her," "He/she must be laughing at me now." In some cases, the victims are angry with themselves for their deep trust in their spouse and neglecting the suspicious signs. Anger toward oneself is often accompanied by the following thoughts: "I was stupid; I was wrong to trust him/her this much," "If I'd controlled him/her, this wouldn't have happened," and "I should've been more severe on him/her." These thoughts cause further anger in the victims. In this regard, labeling, personalization, magnification, black and white thinking, fortune telling, and mind reading are among the common cognitive distortions and defenses in victims of unfaithfulness (Ghahari, 2016). These thoughts and beliefs activate the anger of the victims and show their high anxiety and mental distress. The first author recalls a 39-year-old woman whose spouse had been unfaithful and divorced her because he loved another woman. She recounted a very difficult experience: Some of her statements are noteworthy:

> When my husband said he loved her and wanted to marry her, the world turned upside down. I lost my mind. I lost my mental balance. Sometimes I crushed my pills (Xanax) in his food or tea so that he'd sleep and wouldn't go to that woman. I threatened him that I'd strike up a relationship with his friends. I really wanted him to die. I decided to take revenge many times, but I could never actually do it. I was irritable, anxious, and restless. I had severe anxiety and was sad all the time. I couldn't even tell anyone. I just wanted to deny it. My mental issues worsened gradually, and became phobic fears, depression, and suicide. I was so depressed that I attempted suicide twice that year. Once, I took all the pills at home, but my brother came and saved my life. Another time, when I was riding in my husband's car, I threw myself out and was injured. After this, I lost my self-confidence a great deal. I couldn't even drive. I lost my job. Now, I don't take risks anymore. I became so unbelievably fearful. I was even afraid of the lift; I still am, but less. Unfortunately, I get migraines and my memory never became what it used to be; maybe it was the side-effect of those pills and the suicide attempt. I haven't cried for years; I've promised myself that I wouldn't cry.

Evidently, in this case, there is serious emotional distress and thought disorder. She has lost natural functioning in her life, and even the fitness to work and drive. She does not have the capability to reflect and concentrate on or make correct decisions or take correct actions in her life. In the study by Asayesh (2018), a disorder in thought includes thought disturbance, disbelief, and cognitive distortions; these people suffer from thought disturbance, shocks, thought disorder, and mania. Cano and O'Leary (2000) note that, after unfaithfulness, disturbing thoughts and feelings and lack of concentration occur in the victim. According to Johnson et al. (2001), the emotional shock and distress resulting from unfaithfulness can lead to dissociated thinking about oneself, one's spouse, and the environment, and the ensuing helplessness becomes fixated as a new criterion and standard in one's internal working model (Macintosh et al., 2007). It seems that treatment for these people who visit the therapist alone should prioritize the treatment of the past trauma and the resulting emotional disturbance, and aim at emotion regulation, attachment model improvement, and cognitive reconstruction after reducing the load of internal negative emotions.

In addition to a thought disorder, many victims become suspicious and mistrustful of their spouses. In this cognitive reaction, the victim has a totally negative view with mistrust and hopelessness toward his/her spouse (Asayesh, 2017). Some victims state that the basic assumptions about themselves, their spouse, and the relationship (e.g., that partners can be trusted, the relationship is a safe place) are violated, and this has crushed their basic beliefs for the formation of emotional security (Snyder et al., 2007). The first author had a 35-year-old female client. Her husband had cheated on her after 5 years of marriage and having a child. She declared,

> This affected my trust in my husband. I kept checking on him. I thought, "Where is he now?" When he left for work, I wasn't at ease. I called him to see where he was. . . . Once, I decided to take revenge, and acted on it. I dated someone, but then I realized I'm not capable of doing this. We don't want just having fun and going out from a relationship.

Because of this shattered trust, the victim cannot continue the marital relationship as it was in the past. The victim does not have a proper understanding of why the infidelity has occurred, and cannot trust that the spouse would never hurt her/him again (Snyder et al., 2007). According to Johnson et al. (2001), following unfaithfulness, the victim's understanding of him/herself and the spouse is disrupted, and his/her security is injured; the victim should process new information about him/herself and the spouse. The loss of the sense of trust between couples shatters secure attachments and the relationship is disrupted. Attachment injuries are defined as follows in the EFT: "a violation of trust resulting from a betrayal or from an abandonment at a moment of intense need or vulnerability." In fact, this injury is like a wound disturbing the principles governing attachment in a relationship (Johnson et al., 2001). The outcome of this injury is a change in one's beliefs regarding the spouse and their relationship. The victim can no longer trust his/her spouse or feel secure in their relationship (Brown, 2001; Glass & Wright, 2007).

In addition to mistrust in the spouse, reactions based on suspicious and generalized pessimism about others are also identified. In this cognitive state, the victim is suspicious not only of his/her spouse, but the world and the people in it. Some victims also harbor this negative attitude toward the spouse's family, and the female or male sex (Asayesh et al., 2018). On this, Balman (1992, as cited in Lusterman, 1998) noted that people who have suffered a severe trauma feel fundamental confusion about the nature of the world cognitively and existentially. Based on Balman's reports, these people had three basic assumptions in their mind before experiencing the trauma: (1) the world is a source of goodness,

(2) the world is purposeful and meaningful, and (3) the self is valuable. Following the trauma of unfaithfulness, these assumptions are shattered. Moreover, the majority of the victims of unfaithfulness find the meaning of their life disrupted. Some lose meaning in their life, while some others find the meaning of their life changed, and feel hopeless about life and their future. The first author had a 40-year-old female client whose husband had been unfaithful to her when she was traveling. The couple did not have any children, and had been married for three years. They had many relational problems, and the husband felt depressed. She had visited with her husband for counseling. This is part of the interview on the first session:

> My image of life and its meaning has changed. The world is bleak and I'm hopeless. . . . This event has also affected my spirituality and relationship with God. My relationship with God has increased and I think about death.

Lusterman (1998) and Ghahari (2016) noted that some victims of unfaithfulness sometimes lose meaning in their life and feel empty. Confirming this, Spring (2012) notes that the victim's trust in justice in the world is sometimes lost; he/she has lost control over life, self-esteem, and self-concept; and feels helpless and empty. The meaning of life based on existentialist theories is an important bedrock for stability in one's life, without which life may feel worthless, and the person suffers many mental disorders (Frankl, 1977, as cited in Corey, 2013). Therefore, in individual and couples' therapy about infidelity and its outcomes, special attention should be paid to depression, a sense of emptiness, and the meaning of life. These victims' suicidal ideation should be checked and, if necessary, they should be referred to a psychiatrist for pharmacotherapy. Therapists should pay attention to the unfaithful spouse's depression and suicide ideation as well, and sometimes individual therapy intervention should be developed for him/her in addition to couple's therapy.

The Relational Effects of Unfaithfulness and Attachment Injury

One of the dimensions of injury resulting from unfaithfulness is the relational domain, and familial and marital relationship. People have needs, and if these needs are not met, this will have negative consequences for their well-being. These needs include the need for relationships and emotional closeness with an intimate person, which is usually met in marriage (Victor & Yang, 2012). Different studies show that unfaithfulness can have irreversible damages to the marital relationship and their need for emotional closeness (Peluso, 2007; Abrahamson et al., 2012; Hall, & Fincham, 2008). Unfaithfulness leads to a wide range of negative relational reactions such as aggression, causes mistrust trust, disrespect, and the loss of a compassionate marital relationship (Asayesh, 2017). The interpersonal effects of unfaithfulness are harmful not only to the marital life, but also to the mental health of other family members such as children (Cano & O'Leary, 2000; Johnson et al., 2001). The results of a study by Asayesh et al. (2019) showed that women show different relational reactions to the spouse's unfaithfulness. Based on their findings, victims suffer from relational dissociation and maladaptive relationships; this means that some victims report different experiences of their disturbed relationships in different domains of relationship, manifested in various dimensions such as their relationship with their spouse, parent–child relationship, relationship with their families, and relationship with God.

A relational outcome of facing the crisis of unfaithfulness is the couple's dissociated marital relations (Fife et al., 2007; Hertlein, 2011). Following unfaithfulness, the victim's understanding of him/herself and the spouse is disrupted, and his/her security is injured; the victim realizes that he/she should process new information about him/herself and the spouse (Johnson et al., 2001). Based on some studies, including Shackelford et al. (2008), Schneider et al. (2007), Knight (2010), and Asayesh (2017), in the majority of victims, the marital relationship is disturbed. This disturbance is manifested in emotional as well as sexual relations. In the study by Asayesh et al. (2019), the majority of the victims noted that they had less desire emotionally and sexually and felt more coldness and separation from their spouse, and some even felt disgusted by this. Another client of the first author in said clinic said:

> Our emotional and sexual relations are dead. Even if he approaches me for sex, I see it as what an animal would do and have no feelings about it. I don't like it. I say, well, let's be an animal for him for 20 minutes.

In this case, diminished sexual desire or even disgust toward sex with the spouse can be detected. Unfaithfulness can affect the emotional characteristics of the couple's relationship such as emotional intimacy, sexual desire and intimacy, trust, and interpersonal conflicts (Fife et al., 2007; Hertlein, 2011). Some victims of unfaithfulness do not enjoy other aspects of life either, and hunger and thirst do not matter to them. In many cases, the couples stop doing the activities they used to find pleasurable. They stop pleasurable joint activities such as going to the movies, dining out, going to parties, sexual intercourse, etc., and do not even desire to do these activities alone, and these show a disrupted marital intimacy. Based on EFT, Macintosh et al. (2007) noted that after unfaithfulness and attachment injury, the victim feels sadness, emotional detachment, and avoidance of the spouse. Moreover, marital relations, such as physical contact, verbal love, and sexual intercourse are all affected by unfaithfulness, are diminished, or lost.

Research shows that an outcome of unfaithfulness is the sense of loneliness in the victim (Rokach & Philibert-Lignières, 2015). When unfaithfulness happens in the marital life, this need is not met, and both parties suffer from the absence of intimacy and loneliness. In such cases, the victim finds the sense of intimacy and closeness disrupted, and this puts him/her in a difficult situation to maintain well-being or even life (Allen et al., 2005). The more the distance in the relationship and interpersonal intimacy, the more the sense of loneliness. One can say that fundamental fears of intimacy are prevalent in couples who have faced unfaithfulness (Weeks & Treat, 2001). It is believed that a major part of problems in marital relations is somehow associated with these fears. Following unfaithfulness and attachment injury, the victim probably feels intense anger, grief, and attachment fear of the spouse, and can no longer trust him/her (Macintosh et al., 2007; Fife et al., 2007). Attachment injury demonstrates an injured relationship (Johnson et al., 2001). In fact, after unfaithfulness and the loss of trust among the couples, the secure attachments and the mutual marital relationship are disrupted, and this may cause emotional dissociation between them. In fact, marital unfaithfulness can be a trauma for the relationship and, by disrupting attachment and emotional dissociation, can often motivate and encourage couples to seek separation, divorce, or receive counseling services (Fife et al., 2007; Hertlein, 2011). In this state, beliefs, imaginations, and experiences should be treated and alleviated at the personal and interpersonal level. To continue the relationship, painful and debilitating feelings and experiences should be treated (Johnson, 2005). Therefore, emotional interventions, especially for attachment, trust, and forgiveness, can be effective.

In addition to negative relationship-related reactions in the couple's relationship, some victims showed a sense of love and further attachment for the spouse, which has been neglected in studies. They sought to continue their marital relations (Asayesh et al., 2019). Some victims confessed that their love for their spouse has not been diminished, and that they still felt love, ownership, and yearning for their spouse. On this, another client of the first author in said clinic said,

> I didn't like to fight, and I didn't fight. Mostly, I talked to him to attract him to myself. . . . I fixed myself up and bought beautiful clothes to be attractive.

Mansoori et al. (2010) reported that some people show a sense of yearning for relationship and closeness after separation or divorce or the thought of separation and divorce. This finding was confirmed by Shackelford et al. (2000). In fact, these feelings are some kind of coping feelings for reconstructing one's life. These feelings were mostly seen in victims with a dependent personality or no sense of support from their families. These people are mostly women who, in reacting to their spouse's infidelity, try to improve their emotional and sexual relationship or make up for their own mistakes in order to save their marriage. Women who were willing to repair their life were ready to cope and try for keeping their husband for different reasons, such as fear of loneliness and divorce, fear of rejection from the family, lack of financial independence, competition with the rival (mistress), or to protect the honor of the family and children.

Another outcome of unfaithfulness is a disruption in the parent-child relationship, mentioned in some reports (Stefano & Oala, 2008; Ghahari, 2016; Spring, 2012). One of the basic needs of children is the sense of security and care, which they expect from their parents. However, children whose parents experience conflicts related to unfaithfulness experience distress, disappointment, disturbance, and hopelessness (Lusterman, 2005). The effects of a child under the effect of illegitimate relationships can be parallel to that of the victim parent (Duncombe et al., 2004). The results of a study by Taghi Pour et al. (2019) indicated that children, the victim spouse, and the family experience unpleasant consequences due to infidelity. In the study by Asayesh et al. (2019), some victims of unfaithfulness had problems in their relationship with their children, and the quality of their parent-child relationship was changed. Mothers noted that their relationship with their children manifested itself in the form of irascibility or impatience. In some cases, the father-child relationship was also disturbed. In cases where children realized their fathers' unfaithfulness, the relationship was manifested in the form of fathers' misbehaving with the children (Such as, punishment & violent behavior), negligence, lack of attention, and coldness, and the children's fear of their father, anger, hatred, and a cold emotional relationship with their father. One of the clients of the first author in said clinic, a 42-year-old woman with two children, knew that her husband was cheating on her. Her efforts to cut the relationship were not successful. She said the following about the parent–child relationship:

> My husband's unfaithfulness and my poor state have highly affected my behavior with my children. Sometimes I am aggressive and picky; sometimes I'm impatient and don't pay them enough attention. . . . My husband has become cold towards the children. He checks his phone all the time, walks in the alleys, or sits in his car. And the children don't approach him at all.

Stefano and Oala (2008) noted that the loss of function of the parental role is one of the outcomes of the spouse's unfaithfulness. Naturally, psychological pressures and emotional and cognitive dissociations resulting from unfaithfulness in the mother lead to loss of mental control, aggression, lack of concentration on daily life, including child rearing. Moreover, the disclosure of this relationship to children and observing the conflicts between parents lead to disorders in children. Since unfaithfulness affects both the parent–child relationship and children's health, in treating its effects, special attention should be paid to the role of children and the injury to the parent–child relationship (Sori, 2007). One of the findings of Asayesh et al. (2019) was an improved parent–child relationship and forming a coalition. Some victims form coalitions with their children to feel better, protect their sense of righteousness, or direct the meaning of their life toward their children. An elderly client whose husband had been unfaithful to her said, "My daughter is very protective and supportive of me. She keeps telling me, 'Don't worry, mom; if we have to, we'll throw Dad out of the house.'" By gaining their children's trust, these people try to pressure their spouse to cut ties with his/her lover. Following these coalitions with the victim, in some cases, the relationship between the unfaithful parent and children is disrupted, but sometimes these coalitions succeed in cutting off the ties between the unfaithful parent and the lover. Some victim parents leave the house with their children without filing for divorce and live in a new house. Trying to make themselves feel better, some of them try to expand their social relationships to end their isolation. Some others find companions and talk to them to find peace. Yet some others try to improve their spiritual relationship with God and strengthen it by praying and reading holy texts.

Another effect of unfaithfulness in the marital relationship is the dissociation of the family relationship and the relationship with the families of origin, and especially their parents. Some spouses disclose the matter to their families due to their need for support or to punish the unfaithful spouse. This disclosure, if it is emotional and without certain considerations, can have very destructive effects on marital relations and family relations (mostly in Eastern societies and collectivist cultures like Iran), which make it very difficult to return to the married life (Asayesh et al, 2019). The relationship of some victims with their families is disrupted after this disclosure, and their marital relationship is also disturbed. The unfaithful spouse's relationship with the victim's family is also affected beyond repair, and in some cases, the couple decides to cut ties with their parents and families. Note that the disclosure of unfaithfulness to one's parents is not always wrong. According to Ghahari (2016), in some cases the disclosure of unfaithfulness to parents may be necessary; if there is the risk of death or suicide for a spouse, or when the unfaithful partner wants to get a divorce and does not intend to try and solve the problem, social support should be sought from the family.

Conclusion

Based on what has been discussed in this chapter about the quality of a couple's relationship after infidelity, infidelity can cause major intra- and interpersonal distress for the unfaithful spouse and the victim (Spring, 2012; Fung et al., 2009). These effects are wide-ranging and will have different effects and injuries on the emotions, cognitions, relationships, attachments, and other aspects of the life of both spouses. The damages caused by unfaithfulness and infidelity to the spouse seem to be only individual or marital; however, due to its negative consequences, it disturbs child rearing, family's health, and even the security of society, in addition to marriage (Asayesh, 2017). These consequences affect the life of the couples and their children personally and socially (Taghi Pour et al., 2019).

It was also specified that all spouses who realize their spouses' unfaithfulness do not show the same degree of psychological reactions. Women's and men's perception of their spouses' extramarital relationship differs, and this difference affects their emotional reactions. These differences are due to biological, psychological, personality-related, and cultural factors (Spring, 2012); moreover, some components are influential on the intensity and quality of psychological reactions of spouses to the phenomenon of unfaithfulness. According to Fife et al. (2007), preexisting marital circumstances, how the infidelity was discovered, and the personality characteristics of the individuals involved affect the intensity and quality of the spouses' reactions and problems. For instance, sometimes, some people may be happy about unfaithfulness because of severe conflicts in their married life, and find this as an excuse for getting a divorce. In addition, the type of extramarital relationship (Peluso, 2007), the unfaithful spouse's reaction (MacDonald, 2010), having a history of unfaithfulness (Snyder et al., 2007) and sex affect people's reaction to unfaithfulness.

Some victims may suffer from some other psychological disorders such as depression, anxiety, and even PTSD, in addition to the disorder in their marital relations; thus, the therapist should be aware of the consequences of unfaithfulness for the family and individuals and adopt a correct treatment course in this process. Having a relatively complete understanding of the probable future events helps the therapist or counselor to direct the couples correctly during the heated period after the initial disclosure and during the process of treatment and recovery (Fife et al., 2007). Based on the effects of unfaithfulness on the family and the victim, if the victims do not receive proper treatment, the harmful consequences of this event may persist for a long time (Baucom et al., 2009). Research shows that couples who deal with unfaithfulness can be helped (Gordon et al., 2005; Long & Young, 2007; Asayesh, 2017). In most cases, therapists can help the couple when they draw up a plan of the common emotional reactions, what the couple may experience after the disclosure of unfaithfulness, and the process of forgiveness and recovery for the couples to enhance their understanding of the process (Olson et al., 2002). If the couples know what awaits them, and are ensured that the treatment can help them recover, their chance of participation in different stages of treatment increases (Peluso, 2007).

According to Brown (2001), since unfaithfulness and extramarital relations lead to the expression of different negative intra- and interpersonal reactions, the process of counseling for these individuals is unpredictable and does not follow a regular therapeutic pattern. Some findings indicate the importance of taking unfaithfulness into account as a relational phenomenon, denoting the importance of the relational approach in treating couples who experience infidelity (Scheeren et al., 2018). Different studies have been conducted and various theoretical models have been used in treating couples dealing with unfaithfulness. Davis and Gold (2011) examined empathy, attributions of stability, and the relationship between remorse and forgiveness. They concluded that the spouse's remorse reduces the attributions of stability and behavior stability, and increases empathy and forgiveness. Gordon et al. (2004) developed a three-stage model of forgiveness, comprising (1) exposure, (2) searching for the reason, (3) recovery to help spouses. Enright and Fitzgibbons (2004) observe that counseling reduced forgiveness, anger, anxiety, and depression in clients, and had a positive effect on their mental health. Furthermore, there are diverse ways to treat and work with marital issues, the important ones include behavioral, cognitive, psychoanalytic, and systematic (Champion & Power, 2000). Research also shows that there are different treatment models for unfaithfulness. These include EFT, forgiveness therapy, cognitive-behavioral therapy (CBT), traumatic model, and insight-oriented models. It is mentioned that the goal and planning of treatment should focus on changing traditional sex roles, accounting for infidelity and romantic jealousy, improving the communication and trust between couples (Pichon et al., 2020).

As we have mastery and emphasis over the PTC (paradox + timetable = cure) treatment method (Besharat, 2018), we believe that treatment should be offered systemically and behaviorally, but the therapists should not neglect the identification, analysis, and treatment of the fundamental factors leading to vulnerability and the unconscious content of the couple; discovering the psychological pathology of the couples, including the presence of mental disorders such as anxiety disorders, unconscious communication patterns formed based on the basic primary experiences of their relationship with their parents, and personality disorders such as narcissistic personality disorder or borderline personality disorder in either of the spouses. Having a suitable treatment plan for providing intervention for emotional and relational dimensions of the couples dealing with unfaithfulness improves emotional disorders, mitigates anxiety, and repairs their attachment pattern. Implementing therapeutic relational and behavioral techniques and exercises in the treatment sessions and assigning therapeutic homework seems to be necessary. Furthermore, the identification of the reasons for unfaithfulness and solving problems that have motivated infidelity, teaching the skills necessary to prevent unfaithfulness, and emotion-centered, relational, and systemic interventions are essential. It is recommended that more studies focus on the interventional strategies focusing on the spouses' personality characteristics, psychological disorders, and relationship simultaneously; in addition to individual and systemic treatment, the outcomes of unfaithfulness can be thus managed and resolved, thereby reducing its effects on other family members.

References

Abrahamson, I., Hussain, R., Kahn, A., & Schofield, M. J. (2012). What helps couples rebuild the relationship after infidelity? *Journal of Family Issues*, *33* (11), 1494–1519.

Allen, E. S., Atkins, D. C., Baucom, D. H., Snyder, D. K., Gordon, K. C., & Glass, S. P. (2005). Intrapersonal, interpersonal, and contextual factors in engaging in and responding to extramarital involvement. *Clinical Psychology: Science and Practice*, *12*(2), 101–130.

Allendorf, K., & Ghimire, D. J. (2013). Determinants of marital quality in an arranged marriage society. *Social Science Research*, *42*(1), 59–70.

Arnocky, S., Sunderani, S., Gomes, W., & Vaillancourt, T. (2015). Anticipated partner infidelity and men's intimate partner violence: The mediating role of anxiety. Evolutionary Behavioral Sciences., 9, 186–196

Asayesh, M. H., Farahbakhsh, K. Delavar, A., & Salimi Bajestani, H. (2018). Cognitive experiences and reactions of women to infidelity: A phenomenological study. *Journal of Qualitative Research in Health Sciences*, *7*(2), 188–203.

Asayesh, M. H., Farahbakhsh, K. Salimi Bajestani, H., & Delavar, A. (2017). Explanation of experiences and emotional reactions in women victims of infidelity: A qualitative study. *Journal of Qualitative Research in Health Sciences*, *6*(4), 355–372.

Asayesh, M. H., Farahbakhsh, K., Salimi Bajestani, H., & Delavar, A., (2019). Studying the communication reactions of female victims of infidelity: A phenomenological study. *Journal of Counseling Research*, *18*(69), 31–58.

Atkins, D. C., Baucom, D. H., & Jacobson, N. S. (2001). Understanding infidelity: Correlates in a national random sample. *Journal of Family Psychology*, *15*(4), 735–749.

Balderrama-Durbin, C., Stanton, K., Snyder, D. K., Cigrang, J. A., Talcott, G. W., Smith Slep, A. M., Heyman, R. E., & Cassidy, D. G. (2017). The risk for marital infidelity across a year-long deployment. *Journal of Family Psychology*, *31*(5),629.

Baucom, D. H., Gordon, K. C., Snyder, D. K., Atkins, D. C., & Christensen, A. (2006). Treating affair couples: Clinical considerations and initial findings. *Journal of Cognitive Psychotherapy*, *20*(4), 374–392.

Baucom, D. H., Snyder, D. K., & Gordon, K. C. (2009). *Helping couples get past the affair: A clinician's guide*. Guilford Press.

Berk, L. E. (2013). *Development through the lifespan* (6th ed). Pearson.

Besharat, M. A. (2018). *Paradox + timetable = Cure, The complete model of couple therapy by PTC method*. Rosh. (Persian).

Birnbaum, G. E., Mizrahi, M., Kovler, L., Shutzman, B., Aloni-Soroker, A., & Reis, H. T. (2019). Our fragile relationships: Relationship threat and its effect on the allure of alternative mates. *Archives of Sexual Behavior, 48*(3), 703–713.

Boekhout, B. A., Hendrick, S. S., & Hendrick, C. (2003). Exploring infidelity: Developing the relationship issues scale. *Journal of Loss and Trauma, 8*, 283–306.

Brand, R. J., Markey, C. M., Mills, A., & Hodges, S. D. (2007). Sex differences in self-reported infidelity and its correlates. *Journal of Sex Roles, 57*, 101–109.

Brown, E. M. (2001). *Patterns of infidelity and their treatment*. Psychology Press.

Buss, D. M. (2018). Sexual and emotional infidelity: Evolved gender differences in jealousy prove robust and replicable. *Perspectives on Psychological Science, 13*(2), 155–160.

Buunk, A. P., & Dijkstra, P. (2006). Temptation and threat: Extradyadic relations and jealousy. In A. L. Vangelisti & D. Perlman (Eds.), *The Cambridge handbook of personal relationships* (pp. 533–555). Cambridge University Press.

Cano, A., & O'Leary, K. D. (2000). Infidelity and separations precipitate major depressive episodes and symptoms of nonspecific depression and anxiety. *Journal of Consulting and Clinical Psychology, 68* (5), 774–781.

Case, B. (2005). Healing the wounds of infidelity through the healing power of apology and forgiveness. *Journal of Couple & Relationship Therapy, 4*(2/3), 41–55.

Champion, L., & Power, M. (2000). *Adult psychological problems* (2nd ed.). Psychological Press.

Ciarocco, N. J., Echevarria, J., & Lewandowski, G. W. (2012). Hunger for love: The influence of self-regulation on infidelity. *Journal of Social Psychology, 512*(1), 61–74.

Conroy, A. A. (2014). Marital infidelity and intimate partner violence in rural Malawi: A dyadic investigation. *Archives of Sexual Behavior, 43*(7), 1303–1314.

Corey, G. (2012). *Theory and practice of counseling and psychotherapy* (9th ed.). Cengage Learning.

Davis, J., & Gold, G. (2011). An examination of emotional empathy, attributions of stability, and the link between perceived remorse and forgiveness. *Journal of Personality and Individual Differences, 50*, 392–397.

Duncombe, J., Harrison, K., Allan, G., & Marsden, D. (2004). *The state of affairs: Explorations in infidelity and commitment*. Erlbaum.

Enright, R. D., & Fitzgibbons, R. P. (2000). *Helping clients forgive: An empirical guide for resolving anger and restoring hope*. American Psychological Association.

Ferron, A., Lussier, Y., Sabourin, S., & Brassard, A. (2017). The role of Internet pornography use and cyber infidelity in the associations between personality, attachment, and couple and sexual satisfaction. *Social Networking, 6*, 1–8.

Fife, S. T., Weeks, G. R., & Gambescia, N. (2007). The intersystems approach to treating infidelity. In P. R. Peluso (Ed.), *Infidelity: A practitioner's guide to working with couples in crisis* (pp. 71–98). Routledge.

Fisher, T. D. (2007). Sex of experimenter and social norm effects on reports of sexual behavior in young men and women. *Archives of Sexual Behavior, 36*, 89–100.

Frederick, D. A., & Fales, M. R. (2016). Upset over sexual versus emotional infidelity among gay, lesbian, bisexual, and heterosexual adults. *Archives of Sexual Behavior, 45*, 175–91.

Fung, S. C., Wong, C. W., & Tam, S. M. (2009). Familial and extramarital relations among truck drivers crossing the Hong Kong-China border. *Journal of Sex and Marital Therapy, 35*, 239–44.

Ghahari, S. (2016). *Infidelity in marriage (strategies for intervention)*. Danzheh (Persian).

Glass, S. P., & Wright, T. L. (2007). Reconstructing marriages after the trauma of infidelity. In W. K. Halford & H. J. Markman (Eds.), *Clinical handbook of marriage and couples interventions* (pp. 471–507). Wiley.

Gordon, K. C., & Baucom, D. H. (2004). Understanding betrayals in marriage: A synthesized model of forgiveness. *Family Processes, 37*(4), 425–449.

Gordon, K. C., Baucom, D. H., & Snyder, D. K. (2000). The use of forgiveness in marital therapy. In M. E. McCullough, K. I. Pargament, & C. E. Thoresen (Eds.), *Forgiveness: Theory, research, and practice*. (pp. 203–227). Guilford Press.

Gordon, K. C., Baucom, D. H., & Snyder, D. K. (2004). An integrative intervention for promoting recovery from extramarital affair. *Journal of Marital and Family Therapy, 30*(2), 213–231.

Gordon, K. C., Baucom, D. H., & Snyder, D. K. (2005b). Treating couples recovering from infidelity: An integrative approach. *Journal of Clinical Psychology, 61*(11), 1393–1405.

Gordon, K. C., Baucom, D. H., Snyder, D. K., & Dixon, L. J. (2008). Couple therapy and the treatment of affairs. In S. A. Gurman (Ed.). *Clinical handbook of couple therapy* (pp. 429–458). Guilford Press.

Hall, J. H., & Fincham, F. D. (2008). Psychological distress: Precursor or consequence of dating infidelity? *Personality and Social Psychology Bulletin*, *35*(2), 143–159.

Harmon, Kh. D. (2005), *Black man and marriage: The impact of spirituality, religiosity, and marital commitment on satisfaction* [Unpublished doctoral dissertation, University of Alabama].

Hertlein, K. M. (2011). Therapeutic dilemmas in treating internet infidelity. *American Journal of Family Therapy*, *39*(2), 162–173.

Johnson, S. M. (2005). Broken bonds: An emotionally focused approach to infidelity. *Journal of Couple & Relationship Therapy*, *4*(2/3), 17–29.

Johnson, S. M., Makinen, J. A., & Millikin, J. W. (2001). Attachment injuries in couple relationships: A new perspective on impasses in couples therapy. *Journal of Marital and Family Therapy*, *27*(2), 145–155.

Kachadourian, L. K., Smith, B. N., Taft, C. T., & Vogt, D. (2015). The impact of infidelity on combat-exposed service members. *Journal of Traumatic Stress*, *28*, 418–425.

Kessel, D. E., Moon, J. H., & Atkins, D. C. (2007). Research on couple therapy for infidelity: What do we know about helping couples when there has been an affair? In P. R. Peluso (Ed.), *Infidelity: A practitioner's guide to working with couples in crisis* (pp. 55–70). Routledge.

Long, L. L., & Young, M. E (2007). *Counseling and therapy for couples*. Thomson Brooks/Cole.

Lusterman, D. D. (1998). *Infidelity: A survival guide*. New Harbinger.

MacDonald, L. J. (2010). *How to help your spouse heal from your affair: A compact manual for the unfaithful*. Healing Counsel Press.

Macintosh, H. B., Hall, J., & Johnson, S. M. (2007). Forgive and forget: A comparison of emotionally focused and cognitive-behavioral models of forgiveness and intervention in the context of couple infidelity. In P. R. Peluso (Ed.), *Infidelity: A practitioner's guide to working with couples in crisis* (pp. 100–127). Routledge.

Marjorie, P., Treves-Kagan, S., Stern, E., Kyegombe, N, Stöckl, H., & Buller, A. M. (2020). A mixed-methods systematic review: Infidelity, romantic jealousy and intimate partner violence against women. *International Journal of Environmental Research and Public Health*, *17*, 5682.

Miller, S. L., & Maner, J. K. (2008). Coping with romantic betrayal: Sex differences in responses to partner infidelity. *Evolutionary Psychology*, *6*(3), 413–426.

Olson, M., Russell, C., Higgins-Kessler, M., & Miller, R. (2002). Emotional processes following disclosure of an extramarital affair. *Journal of Marital and Family Therapy*, *28*, 423–434.

Omarzu, J., Miller, A. N., Schultz, C., & Ashlee, T. (2012). Motivations and emotional consequences related to engaging in extramarital relationships. *International Journal of Sex Health*, *24*(2), 154–162.

Peluso, P. R. (Ed.). (2007). *Infidelity: A practitioner's guide to working with couples in crisis*. Routledge.

Pichon, M., Treves-Kagan, S., Stern, E., Kyegombe, N., Stöckl, H., & Maria Buller, A. (2020). A mixed-methods systematic review: Infidelity, romantic jealousy and intimate partner violence against women. *International Journal of Environmental Research and Public Health*, *17*, 56–82.

Platt, R. A. L., Nalbone, D. P., Casanova, G., & Wetchler, J. (2008). Parental conflict and infidelity as predictors of adult children's attachment style and infidelity. *American Journal of Family Therapy*, *36*, 149–161.

Rokach, A., & Philibert-Lignières, G. (2015). Intimacy, loneliness and infidelity. *Open Psychology Journal*, *8*(1), 71–77.

Rozov, A., Demeshkina, N., Westhof, E., Yusupov, M., & Yusupova, G. (2015). Structural insights into the translational infidelity mechanism. *Nature Communications*, *6*, 7251.

Scheeren, P., Apellániz, I. A. M., Wagner, A. (2018). Marital infidelity: The experience of men and women. *Trends in Psychology/Temas em Psicologia—Março*, *26*(1), 371–385.

Shackelford, T. K. (2001). Cohabitation and marriage. *Aggressive Behavior*, *27*, 261–284.

Shackelford, T. K., Besser, A., & Goetz, A. T. (2008). Personality, marital satisfaction, and probability of marital infidelity. *Individual Differences Research*, *6*(1), 13–25.

Shackelford, T. K., LeBlanc, G. J, & Drass, E. (2000). Emotional reactions to infidelity. *Cognition and Emotion*, *14*(5), 643–659.

Shackelford, T. K., & Weekes-Shackelford, V. A. (Eds.). (2019). *Encyclopedia of evolutionary psychological science*. Springer Nature.

Shackelford, T. K., & Buss, D. M. (2000). Marital satisfaction and spousal cost-infliction. *Personality and Individual Differences*, *28*, 917–928.

Shackelford, T. K., Buss, D. M., & Bennett, K. (2002). Forgiveness or breakup: Sex differences in responses to a partner's infidelity. *Cognition and Emotion*, *16*(2), 299–307.

Sharf, R. S. (2012). *Theories of psychotherapy and counseling: Concepts and cases*. Brooks/Cole.

Snyder, D. K., Baucom, D. H., & Gordon, K. C. (2008). An Integrative Approach to Treating Infidelity. *The Family Journal*, *16*, 300–307.

Sori, C. F. (2007). An affair to remember: Infidelity and its impact on children. In P. R. Peluso (Ed), *Infidelity: A practitioner's guide to working with couples in crisis* (pp. 247–276). Routledge.

Spring, J. A. (2012). *After the affair: Healing the pain and rebuilding trust when a partner has been unfaithful* (2nd ed. paperback). William Morrow.

Stefano, J. D., & Oala, M. (2008). Extramarital affairs: Basic considerations and essential tasks in clinical work. *Journal of Counseling and Therapy for Couples and Families*, *16*(1), 13–19.

Taghi Pour, M., Ismail, A., Wan Jaafar, W. M., & Yusop, Y. M. (2019). Infidelity in marital relationships. *Psychology & Psychological Research International Journal*, *4*(2), 000200.

Tsapelas, I., Fisher, H. E., & Aron, A. (2010). Infidelity: When, where, why. In W. R. Cupach & B. H. Spitzberg (Eds.), *The dark side of close relationships II* (pp. 175–196). Routledge.

Urganci, B., & Sevi, B. (2019). Infidelity risk. In T. K. Shackelford & V. A. Weekes-Shackelford (Eds.), *Encyclopedia of evolutionary psychological science*. Springer Nature (pp. 93–98).

Victor, C. R., & Yang, K. (2012). The prevalence of loneliness among adults: A case study of the United Kingdom. *Journal of Psychology*, *146*(1–2), 85–104.

Weeks, G. R., & Treat, S. (2001). *Couples in treatment: Techniques and approaches for effective practice* (2nd ed.). Brunner/Routledge.

Whisman, M. A. (2016). Discovery of a partner affair and major depressive episode in a probability sample of married or cohabiting adults. *Family Process*, *55*(4), 713–723.

Winek, J., & Craven, P. (2003). Healing rituals for couples recovering from adultery. *Contemporary Family Therapy*, *25*(3), 249–266.

Zhang, H., & Tsang, S. K. M. (2013). Relative income and marital happiness among urban Chinese women: The moderating role of personal commitment. *Journal of Happiness Studies*, *14*(5), 1575–1584.

CHAPTER 23

Violence and Homicide Following Partner Infidelity

Steven Arnocky, Adam Davis, Ashley Locke, Larissa McKelvie, *and* Tracy Vaillancourt

Abstract

Infidelity is one of the greatest adaptive challenges of our reproductive lives. A partner's infidelity can lead to their defection from the relationship and offspring, loss of important resources, and for men, cuckoldry. It is unsurprising, then, that humans have evolved adaptations meant to prevent, curtail, and punish a partner's infidelity. Among the most devastating of these are the perpetration of intimate partner violence, homicide, uxoricide, and filicide. This chapter reviews theory and supporting evidence that aggression has evolved, in part, as an adaptive set of behavior meant to prevent and respond to infidelity. It begins by describing the particular reproductive challenges posed by infidelity for men and women. Next, it reviews the available evidence that violence and killing is an abhorrent, yet predictable response to real or suspected infidelity, with attention paid to sex differences in these acts. The putative adaptive functions of different types of aggression toward an intimate partner, a sexual rival, and toward offspring are discussed. It then highlights the important role of perceptual biases surrounding infidelity and negative affect, including jealousy and anxiety, in mediating aggressive responses to infidelity. Finally, adaptive explanations of individual differences, cultural contexts, and environmental factors in predicting violent responses to infidelity are discussed and future directions are offered in order to highlight the pressing need for continued research on the adaptive functions of violence occurring in the shadow of infidelity.

Key Words: infidelity, intimate partner, violence, IPV, homicide, sexual proprietariness, jealousy, filicide, infanticide

Infidelity: An Important Adaptive Challenge

Humans are among the roughly 5% of mammals that exhibit social monogamy and biparental care (Kleiman, 1977). Human females are also somewhat unique among mammals in that they remain sexually receptive throughout their reproductive cycles (i.e., extended sexuality; Grebe et al., 2013) and they do not conspicuously signal their fertility status (Haselton & Gildersleeve, 2011). Although biparental care provides many benefits to offspring survival and development (see Arnocky & Carré, 2016, for review; Buss & Shackelford, 1997a; Shackelford, Goetz, et al., 2005), these extended mating relationships also confer greater risk and relevance of infidelity to an individual's reproductive success.

Sexual infidelity is both common (i.e., in up to 25% of marriages; Wiederman, 1997), and universal, spanning diverse cultural, historical, and contextual boundaries (Fincham & May, 2017). As such, infidelity represents a fundamental reproductive challenge; one for which humans appear to have evolved a suite of perceptual, emotional, and behavioral abilities, tactics, and strategies to overcome (Buss, 2013; Buss & Duntley, 2014; Goetz et al., 2005; Platek & Shackelford, 2006; Starratt et al., 2007). There are many potentially violent consequences to real or suspected infidelity, ranging from psychological, physical, or sexual violence perpetrated against the partner, physical violence perpetrated against a same-sex rival, and sometimes, the abuse and killing of children. What these apparently diverse acts and targets of aggression all have in common is, broadly, their robust links to (typically) male sexual proprietariness, which embodies men's attempts to control and monopolize the reproductive decisions of women to stymie infidelity, reduce paternity uncertainty, and prevent women's attempts to defect from the romantic relationship (Daly & Wilson, 1988; Taylor, 2012; Wilson & Daly, 1996).

Several scholars in evolutionary psychology have argued that the physiological, cognitive, and affective factors underpinning behavioral responses to infidelity, such as intimate partner violence (IPV), constitute adaptations (e.g., Barbaro, 2017; Buss & Duntley, 2011, 2014; Goetz Shackelford, Romero, et al., 2008). Adaptations may be defined as reliably occurring heritable traits that were selected because they enhanced the ability of an organism to survive and reproduce in its evolutionary past (Buss et al., 1998; Confer et al., 2010; Tooby & Cosmides, 1990). Candidates for psychological adaptations among humans include traits that: (1) contribute to reproductive success; (2) have simpler precursors in nonhuman animals, particularly close phylogenetic relatives; (3) have a direct function (i.e., they serve to overcome adaptive problems); (4) are deployed in a context-specific, cost-efficient, and goal-directed manner; (5) are flexibly responsive to evolutionarily relevant social and environmental inputs; and (6) are represented across cultures with a meaningful level of consistency. Importantly, the operation of adaptations does not require conscious awareness of their existence nor need they be good, innocuous, or ethical at an individual or societal level (Confer et al., 2010; Crippen, 2018). Many kinds of repugnant and societally damaging behavior (e.g., IPV) may constitute adaptions that require ultimate (i.e., distal) explanations that relate to their functional significance (Archer & Vaughan, 2001; Daly, 2014; Vandermassen, 2011; Welling & Nicolas, 2015). This in no way implies that the behavior under consideration is morally acceptable or immutable (i.e., the product of genetic determinism), but rather that it is not solely the product of socialization, culture, and societal structures. Nonetheless, when studying human psychology it is necessary and fruitful to consider how culture and other proximate (i.e., immediate) mechanisms contribute to produce the behavior in question, which highlights the potential complementarity of sociocultural and evolutionary theorizing (Brown et al., 2018; Daly, 2014; Goetz Shackelford, & Camilleri, 2008; Ward & Siegert, 2002).

Heritable traits that enhance fitness may co-opt existing adaptations to perform functions other than the purpose for which they had been selected (i.e., an exaptation; Havlíček et al., 2015). One example is the large trunk of elephants, which may have originally evolved to accommodate enlarged tusks (i.e., hypertrophy), but have since been exapted for several different functions (e.g., sound production, digging, and a snorkel for swimming; Brosius, 2019). Furthermore, an exapted trait can be useful for an organism's survival or reproduction in its current environment, but constitutes a byproduct of an adaptation with no proper direct function (i.e., a spandrel). Therefore, it is prudent to consider whether the perceptual, cognitive, and affective mechanisms coordinating aggression and violence in response to infidelity constitute adaptations, exaptations, or spandrels (Buss & Duntley, 2011; Goetz Shackelford, & Camilleri, 2008; Thornhill & Palmer, 2000; West, 2007; Wilson & Daly, 1996).

In this chapter, our goal is to highlight the adaptive problems posed by social monogamy, biparental care, and extended sexuality, specifically emotional infidelity (i.e., forming a deep emotional bond with someone outside the mateship) and sexual infidelity (i.e., extrapair copulations; Kruger et al., 2015). The psychological mechanisms embodying information-processing procedures that reliably manifest in response to infidelity are described and their adaptive utility is considered. Special attention is given to the sex-specific nature of aggression and violence in response to actual or suspected infidelity, as well as counterstrategies to avoid these costly actions, which arguably correspond to the unique adaptive challenges likely faced by ancestral women and men over their evolutionary histories (Buss & Duntley, 2011, 2014).

Partner/Child Abandonment

Extramarital affairs play an important role in the destabilization of mating dyads. Yet, Hall and Fincham (2006) caution that identifying how influential infidelity is to relationship dissolution is difficult because (1) mitigating factors associated with infidelity, such as incompatibility or drug use, can also influence divorce directly, and (2) those who separate following infidelity tend to include other factors within their reasoning for the breakup. Nevertheless, there is a clear positive link between infidelity and breakup of the dyad, as described more thoroughly in chapter 18 of this book. Kelly and Conley (1987) reported longitudinal data from a study in which 300 married couples were followed from the 1930s until 1980. Results showed that of those who got divorced, 32% directly cited infidelity, while additional couples cited related reasons like "wife's devotion to another man." In the British National Survey of Sexual Attitudes and Lifestyles (NATSAL; Erens et al., 2001), which included data from over 12,000 participants, 37% of those who had experienced the failure of their first live-in partnership reported infidelity as a contributing factor to the dissolution of that relationship. In modeling differential demographic and proximate factors contributing to divorce, Amato and Rogers (1997) found that infidelity was the strongest predictor of relationship dissolution.

Relationship dissolution can have drastic implications for the family and parenting structure. News articles on the topic often present vivid case examples such as:

> Alison says her oldest son, who is now five, still asks about his house and his friends and his toys, and why Daddy is choosing his new girlfriend and their son over him. She says he'd ask, "Why is Daddy living with that baby and not me? I am his first baby. I am his number one boy. How come he doesn't want to always be with me?" (Barmak, 2018).

The British Economic and Social Research Council reported that only 49% of fathers who do not live with their children say they still have regular contact with them, and that 13% never see their children (Poole et al., 2013).

Loss of Resources/Coparenting

To the extent that infidelity is a major catalyst of relationship dissolution, it is important to understand the effects of familial breakup, more generally, upon offspring. One potential outcome is the loss of paternal resource provisioning to children. In the United Kingdom, it is estimated that only 29% of those fathers who never see their children provide financial support (Poole et al., 2013). In some instances, this may be linked to the reinvestment of those resources into the offspring of another woman. Again, in the United Kingdom, three in 10 fathers who have nonresident dependent age children are also living with other dependent children (Poole et al., 2013). Loss of male resources and parental investment would have been a particularly relevant challenge for ancestral women, given their reliance upon male resource provisioning for offspring survival. It is well understood that biparental care facilitates offspring survival and reproductive fitness (see Arnocky & Vaillancourt, 2017). Data from hunter-gatherer and preindustrial Western populations converge to demonstrate that father-present children are more likely to survive than father-absent children (Hill & Hurtado, 1996; Geary, 2000). In contemporary Western society, evidence also shows that father-present children score higher on social and academic skills alongside higher income in adulthood relative to father-absent children (Geary, 2000).

Cuckoldry

The unsuspecting investment in genetically unrelated offspring, which comes at the expense of investment in one's own genetic offspring, is a reproductive challenge that is faced specifically by men. Contemporary rates of nonpaternity appear to be low in the general population, ranging between 1% and 2%, which some researchers have ascribed to the ability of modern birth control practices to regulate conception. Recent estimates for several historical populations also suggest a similarly low nonpaternity rate. However, nonpaternity rates do increase in specific populations where infidelity is ostensibly suspected more regularly, such as among those seeking paternity testing because of contested fatherhood, where rates appear to be between 10% and 30% (see Larmuseau et al., 2016, for review). Other research highlights the threat of extrapair paternity in traditional societies. For example, Scelza et al. (2020) found that among Himba pastoralists, the rate of extrapair paternity was nearly 50%, with more than two-thirds of mating relationships having at least one child resulting from extrapair copulations. Moreover, both sexes demonstrated accuracy at detecting such offspring. Therefore, cuckoldry has likely been a recurrent adaptive problem that men have evolved psychological mechanisms to reduce the risk of (Buss & Duntley, 2011).

Evidence of Violence in Response to Real or Suspected Infidelity
Intimate Partner Violence

One of the most common correlates of real or perceived infidelity is IPV, which is defined as "behavior within an intimate relationship that causes physical, sexual, or psychological harm, including acts of physical aggression, sexual coercion, psychological abuse, and controlling behavior. This definition covers violence by both current and former spouses and partners" (World Health Organization [WHO], 2017a). Examples of physical violence include throwing items at a partner, threatening, slapping, kicking, choking, burning, using a weapon against, or hitting the partner (WHO, LSHTM, & SAMRC, 2013). Examples of emotional or psychological abuse involve "insults, belittling, constant humiliation, intimidation (e.g. destroying things), threats of harm, [or] threats to take away children" (WHO & The Pan American Health Organization, 2012, p. 1). This form of violence occurs in all countries and, as such, is a widespread problem (WHO, 2002; WHO & LSHTM, 2010). Of women who have been in a relationship, an estimated 30% have experienced physical or sexual violence, or both, by an intimate partner (Devries et al., 2013; WHO, LSHTM, & SAMRC, 2013), with IPV being more likely to occur in lower income countries (WHO & LSHTM, 2010). For instance, lifetime rates of physical and sexual IPV in Tanzania have been found to be as high as 61% (Kapiga et al., 2017). In a cross-sectional study conducted by the WHO based on data from 12 countries, between 20% and 75% of women, and 45% of men, have experienced emotional abuse from an intimate partner (García-Moreno et al., 2005). The majority of the victims are girls and women, with men being the primary perpetrators (WHO & LSHTM, 2010). Importantly, IPV can also be perpetrated via digital means (i.e., cyber IPV), such as digital dating abuse, where electronic technologies (e.g., cellphones, computers, and gaming consoles) are used to control, harass, and/or aggress against mates (Bhogal et al., 2019). Among American college-aged students, some estimates of digital dating abuse victimization are as high as 74%, indicating that cyber IPV may be a particularly powerful form of partner-directed aggression (Reed et al., 2016). There appear to be no significant sex differences in the frequency of experiencing digital dating abuse; however, men may be more likely to perpetrate sexual cyber IPV and women more likely to interpret sexual digital dating abuse (e.g., "sexting") more negatively (see Reed et al., 2016).

Shields and Hanneke (1983) identified that women who committed infidelity during their prior relationship were more likely to experience sexual and physical abuse at the hands of their partner. Other researchers have also noted that suspicions and perceptions of extradyadic relations—having emotional or sexual relations with others outside of an exclusive mateship—are related to the perpetration of IPV (Neal & Lemay, 2019; Nemeth et al., 2012). For example, in their study of heterosexual couples, Nemeth et al. (2012) found that IPV was consistently triggered by infidelity. Specifically, these researchers examined the content of telephone calls between 17 heterosexual couples, in which the man was incarcerated for domestic violence. The female victims had suffered serious injuries during the attacks, such as strangulation, head trauma, bite wounds, and even lost pregnancies. Results of this qualitative examination demonstrated that across couples, violence was precipitated by suspicion or knowledge of infidelity (see Davis et al., 2019). In sub-Saharan Africa it has also been found that real or perceived extramarital relationships are common causes for IPV (Conroy, 2014; Karamagi et al., 2006). In North America, men who suspected a partner was likely to cheat reported more controlling behavior, which in turn predicted violence against intimate partners (Cousins & Gangestad, 2007). In addition, Arnocky, Sunderani, et al. (2015) supported positive correlations between anticipated partner infidelity and IPV (physical assault, partner injury, sexual coercion, and psychological aggression) in a sample of college-aged men.

From an evolutionary perspective, several scholars have posited that IPV may have evolved to prevent the diversion of key mating resources that impact reproductive success (Buss & Duntley, 2011, 2014; Shackelford, 2003; Shackelford, Goetz, et al., 2005). Generally speaking, IPV may be considered a form of cost-inflicting mate retention behavior, including emotional manipulation, controlling behavior, and physical abuse, that functions to stymie women's and men's infidelity and to reduce the likelihood of defection from the mateship (Albert & Arnocky, 2016; Davis et al., 2018; Miner, Shackelford, et al., 2009; Miner, Starratt, et al., 2009). For ancestral women, a mate's infidelity, especially emotional infidelity, could have signaled the loss of physical protection for her and her offspring, as well as the loss of provisioning and paternal investment (Buss & Duntley, 2014). In contrast, for men, infidelity, particularly sexual infidelity, could have signaled the loss of paternity, unwittingly investing parental and material resources in genetically unrelated offspring, reputation damage, and forgone opportunities to mate with other women. The sex-differentiated aspects of these adaptive challenges has led evolutionary researchers to posit that IPV may adaptively function as an anticuckoldry tactic for men to reduce the likelihood that a female partner may consort with mate poachers (i.e., individuals attempting to pry committed mates away from their relationships; Arnocky et al., 2013) or defect from the mateship as a consequence of fearing violent abuse toward her and her offspring (Barbaro, 2017; Barbaro & Shackelford, 2016; Buss & Duntley, 2011, 2014; Goetz Shackelford, Romero, et al., 2008; Kaighobadi, Shackelford, & Goetz, 2009; Platek & Shackelford, 2006).

Several lines of evidence support the potential adaptive utility of IPV in response to suspected or actual infidelity. Male sexual coercion—the use of intimidation and force toward females to heighten the probability of mating with the male aggressor and to lower the likelihood of mating with rivals—has been observed among various species of primate (Smuts, 1992; Stumpf & Boesch, 2010). Across varied cultural contexts, men's sexual jealousy (i.e., negative affect in response to a real or perceived threat of a mate's sexual infidelity; Davis et al., 2016) has been shown to be to be a potent harbinger for spousal battery (Buss, 2000; Counts, 1992; Daly & Wilson, 1988; Smuts, 1992). Specifically, domestic assault appears to function primarily to prevent infidelity, whereas in-pair sexual assault seems to be a response after infidelity has been committed (Camilleri & Quinsey, 2009; Daly & Wilson, 1992; Goetz & Shackelford, 2006). Men's sexual coercion, ranging from emotional manipulation (e.g., withholding benefits to gain sexual access to one's partner) to physical force (i.e., rape), has been linked to suspected and past female infidelity using both self- and partner-reports (Goetz & Shackelford, 2009). Moreover, perceived sexual ownership and feelings of jealousy (i.e., male sexual proprietariness) have been argued to be key factors underpinning men's heightened levels of threat and their IPV toward their pregnant partners (Taylor, 2012). Within abusive relationships, pregnant women appear to face a higher risk of physical and emotional abuse, sexual violence, stalking, threats of death and violence, as well as coercive power and control tactics by their intimate partners (Burch & Gallup; 2004; Buss & Duntley, 2011). Evidence also suggests that women carrying the child of another man are more likely to be abused by their current partner (Martin et al., 2004; Taillieu & Brownridge, 2010). Taken together, this body of evidence highlights that infidelity and IPV frequently intersect; real or suspected female infidelity likely precipitates and maintains, but does not justify, violence against women. However, it is important to acknowledge that such cross-sectional studies, while informative, are limited in their ability to examine causal mechanisms of IPV. Specifically, it is difficult to determine the extent to which infidelity directly leads to abuse, relative to the possibility of individuals who are abused perhaps being subsequently more likely to be unfaithful (Arnocky, Sunderani, et al., 2015). Further complicating the matter, some researchers have classified infidelity as a subset of IPV and a means of harming one's partner (Utley, 2017). Moreover, men who are suspected by their partner of infidelity are also more likely to perpetrate acts of IPV (WHO & LSHTM, 2010).

Nonetheless, there are reasons to question whether the physiological and psychological mechanisms underpinning IPV in response to infidelity constitute adaptations. Cost-inflicting mate retention is a risky reproductive strategy to perform because it may result in violent retaliation, even death, by one's intimate partner and increase the likelihood of termination of the relationship (discussed in Davis et al., 2018, Duntley & Shackelford, 2012, and Miner, Starratt, et al., 2009). For instance, Shackelford and Buss (2000) found that the frequency of particular cost-inflicting acts (e.g., monopolization of a mate's time, threatening to commit infidelity, and emotional manipulation) corresponded to significantly lower levels of general marital satisfaction among young American adult newlyweds. Similar results have been found for Croatian heterosexual adults in long-term romantic relationships (Salkicevic et al., 2014). Lower relationship satisfaction has been found to be an important predictor of relationship dissolution, particularly in women (Røsand et al., 2014), which brings into question the effectiveness of IPV as a means of retaining one's partner. Concern over and actual instances of IPV are also common reasons for women to terminate their pregnancies in modern society (Biggs et al., 2013; Chibber et al., 2014; Taylor, 2012; WHO, LSHTM, & SAMRC, 2013). Evidence of self-induced abortions through various different methods (e.g., ingesting toxic plants/herbs) appear across different cultural circumstances and extend back to ancient civilizations (Sensoy et al., 2015). Pregnant women who are abused by their partners also frequently experience blows to the abdomen, which can increase the risk of miscarriage (Jasinski, 2004; Morland et al., 2008; Valladares et al., 2005). Although IPV toward pregnant partners may be a response to concerns of nonpaternity to eliminate rival offspring (Buss & Duntley, 2011), it is challenging to empirically weigh the reproductive costs and benefits of killing pregnant partners or strategically injuring them to encourage miscarriage over suspicions of infidelity and lost paternity.

Female-Perpetrated IPV, Jealousy, and Infidelity

There is good evolutionary rationale to suspect that men will be the primary perpetrators of overt, risky, and damaging forms of IPV, as a consequence of male sexual proprietariness, male sexual coercion, paternity uncertainty, as well as their greater androgen levels (testosterone) and general propensity for more aggressive behavior (Carré et al., 2011; Daly & Wilson, 1988; Smuts, 1992). However, evidence suggests that, particularly in cultures that are higher in gender parity (e.g., the United States, Canada, and the United Kingdom), women and men perpetrate common forms of emotional and physical violence to a similar extent (Archer, 2006, 2018; Graham-Kevan & Archer, 2003; Straus, 2009). The majority of emotional and physical IPV appears to be bilateral, whereby both partners are engaged in mutual violence toward one another (Babcock et al., 2019; Madsen et al., 2012). Although self-defense and retaliation are commonly cited motives for women's IPV, as well as men's (Babcock et al., 2019), anger and getting a partner's attention are prevalent motivating factors for women's physical violence against their male partners (see Bair-Merritt et al., 2010, for review). Nonetheless, to date few researchers have examined, in a detailed manner, the specific reasons why women engage in unilateral (i.e., female-only) and bilateral aggression against their partners. Since jealousy has been proposed to serve a similar function in women and men (i.e., to initiate mate retention behavior to drive off rivals, prevent infidelity, and hinder defection from the mateship), suspected or actual partner infidelity may motivate women's IPV. For instance, romantically jealous women have been found to engage in more relational aggression (i.e., behavior aimed at damaging relationships and social standing) toward their mates (Arnocky et al., 2012). Relational aggression, in turn, has been linked to lower reported marital quality in longitudinal research (Coyne et al., 2017). Both partnered women and men higher in cognitive jealousy (i.e., worry and suspicions about partner infidelity) and behavioral jealousy (i.e., surveillance behavior to stymie infidelity) are more likely to be perpetrators of IPV (Rodriguez et al., 2015). Similarly, anxious jealousy (i.e., rumination about suspected partner infidelity) and preventive jealousy (i.e., action taken to prevent a partner from consorting with others where infidelity may occur) positively predicts women's and men's cost-inflicting mate retention (Davis et al., 2018). Therefore, it is evident that the perpetration of IPV is not a male-specific phenomenon, and that jealousy is an important factor underpinning women's violence directed toward their partners.

Sexual Coercion and Rape

Rape of an intimate partner is a particularly salient and abhorrent form of sexual IPV that many scholars from varying perspectives have studied. Rape is defined as a form of nonconsensual sexual behavior (e.g., forced vaginal/anal intercourse, digital penetration, oral sex, or penetration with an object) associated with sexual aggression, violence, and violations to bodily autonomy (Clutton-Brock & Parker, 1995; Thornhill & Palmer, 2000; Vandermassen, 2011; Ward & Siegert, 2002). Cross-culturally, some academics have found estimates of rape among married women to range from 10 to 14% (reviewed in Martin et al., 2007). Other researchers have found slightly higher estimates, ranging from 10% to 26% (reviewed in Kaighobadi, Shackelford, & Goetz, 2009). In the United States, women's lifetime prevalence of rape by an intimate partner has been found to be about 9% (Breiding, 2014). In the context of intimate romantic relationships, several evolutionary scholars have posited that rape may function as a sex-specific anticuckoldry tactic that is triggered by men's sexual jealousy in response to a partner's suspected or actual sexual infidelity (i.e., the cuckoldry risk hypothesis; Goetz & Shackelford, 2009; Goetz, Shackelford, et al., 2008; Lalumière et al., 2005; Platek & Shackelford, 2006; Thornhill & Thornhill, 1992; Wilson & Daly, 1992). Ancestral men, but not women, had to deal with uncertainty regarding the genetic relationship that they shared with their offspring (i.e., paternity uncertainty). Therefore, rape in response to a mate's sexual infidelity could have promoted competition with a rival's sperm in a female partner's reproductive tract to prevent cuckoldry (Goetz & Shackelford, 2009). Evidence indicates that sperm can live up to five days inside of a women's reproductive tract (Holt & Fazeli, 2016), suggesting that a relatively large window of opportunity exists for men to deploy sperm competition tactics. Although researchers have consistently argued and empirically demonstrated that men's sexual jealousy and suspicions of infidelity are key predictors of in-pair rape, cross-cultural estimates regarding the motivating factors of forced in-pair copulation are uncertain and in need of investigation (Wegner et al., 2015).

For decades scholars have debated whether rape as an anti-cuckoldry tactic is adaptive or not. It is important to stress that this question is qualitatively different from considerations of whether nonpartner rape is adaptive for less desirable men to secure reproductive opportunities with female partners (i.e., the mate deprivation hypothesis), or whether rape is an exaptation of men's relatively higher sex drives and preference for sexual variety (Camilleri & Quinsey, 2009; Goetz Shackelford, & Camilleri,, 2008; Quinsey & Lalumière, 1995; Shields & Shields, 1983; Symons, 1979; Thornhill & Palmer, 2000; Vandermassen, 2011). Many converging lines of evidence support the potential adaptive utility of rape. Forced in-pair copulation occurs in several nonhuman animals following female extrapair mating (Barash, 1977; Cheng et al., 1983; McKinney et al., 1984). Humans are also a pair-bonding and socially monogamous species, meaning that ancestral men would have had to deal with the threat of sexual infidelity and paternity uncertainty throughout their evolutionary histories (Buss & Duntley, 2011; Goetz Shackelford, Romero, et al., 2008). Despite significant variability, in-pair rape is a historically and cross-culturally universal phenomenon (reviewed in Grubin, 1992; Shackelford, Goetz, et al., 2005; Wilson & Daly, 1992, 1993). Furthermore, partner rape has a proposed direct function of encouraging sperm competition to avoid cuckoldry (Goetz & Shackelford, 2009; Shackelford & Goetz, 2007). It is also possible that ancestral men who engaged in sperm competition tactics such as rape would have had greater reproductive success relative to men who did not engage in these tactics. Perhaps surprisingly, the probability of conception as a consequence of partner rape for women is similar, sometimes higher, to that of women having consensual sex with their partners (Basile et al., 2018; Gottschall & Gottschall, 2003; McFarlane, 2007). Moreover, many researchers have supported a positive link between in-pair sexually coercive behavior (including rape) with men's suspicions of their partner's infidelity, as well as women's reports of past infidelities and future infidelity intentions (Camilleri & Quinsey, 2009; Camilleri & Miele, 2017; Goetz & Shackelford, 2009; He & Tsang, 2017; Shackelford & Goetz, 2007; Wilson & Daly, 1996). Women also appear to have evolved a suite of counteradaptations that reduce the likelihood of rape, including the formation of alliances for protection and to seek revenge against rapists, selecting physically formidable male partners who can intimidate or effectively retaliate against rapists (i.e., the bodyguard hypothesis) and the systematic avoidance of individuals and contexts wherein rape may be more likely to occur mediated through the heightened expression of anxiety and fear (see Duntley & Shackelford, 2012 for discussion).

Nonetheless, there are reasons to question the adaptive utility of partner rape as an anticuckoldry tactic for the purpose of sperm competition. In-pair rape can be an extremely risky strategy, particularly in more developed cultural contexts, resulting in severe social sanctions and legal consequences, as well as aggressive retaliation or death on behalf of kin, allies, and community members (Adams-Clark & Chrisler, 2018; Grubin, 1992; Starratt et al., 2007; Ward & Siegert, 2002). Although limited, evidence suggests that some men fail to ejaculate when they rape women (Grubin, 1992). In a similar vein, many women do not orgasm or fake orgasm when raped by their partners (Thomas et al., 2016;

Ward & Siegert, 2002), which may reduce the likelihood of conception (Wheatley & Puts, 2015). It is also possible that men's forced in-pair copulation could be an exaptation of their cost-inflicting mate retention that functions primarily to dominate, control, and intimidate their partners (i.e., sexual proprietariness; Daly & Wilson, 1988), rather than for the explicit purpose of sperm competition. It is also evident that same-sex partner rape occurs among women and men in the contexts of homosexual and bisexual relationships, and that women, at times, rape their male and female partners (Sable et al., 2006; Walker et al., 2005). Moreover, there is little evidence that in-pair rape produces concrete benefits in terms of men's reproductive success in the form of siring more genetically related offspring in comparison to men who do not use this strategy. See chapter 24 for a more detailed discussion of infidelity and sexual coercion.

Intimate Partner Homicide

Sometimes, violence against a partner extends beyond physical and emotional scars, resulting in either uxoricide (killing of a female intimate partner) or mariticide (killing of a male intimate partner; United Nations Office on Drugs and Crime [UNODC], 2019a). Globally, an estimated 24% to 48% of homicides are perpetrated by an intimate partner, and of those cases, the majority (82%) of victims are women (UNODC, 2019a, 2019b). For women, this translates to an intimate partner homicide (IPH) rate of 0.8 per 100,000 women (UNODC, 2019a). It should be noted that while other studies find somewhat lower rates for males being the victim of IPH (such as the 6% found in the meta-analysis by Stöckl et al., 2013), the general trend remains consistent: Women make up the vast majority of victims of IPH. Further, an unfortunate epiphenomenal feature of IPH exists: When the total female homicide rate decreases in a country, the proportion of IPHs increases. This is evidenced by IPH remaining consistent over time, despite a decrease in homicide generally (UNODC, 2019a). It is important to note that IPH also occurs among homosexual, bisexual, lesbian, and other couples. Relative to heterosexual couples, gay and lesbian couples face additional social and cultural stressors (e.g., public stigma, familial isolation, and the absence of social services) that may increase the risk of domestic violence and IPH (Meyer, 2003). Examining over 50,000 IPHs in the United States, Mize and Shackelford (2008) found that IPH occurred more often among gay couples relative to heterosexual couples, and that those in lesbian relationships had the lowest rates of IPH. Relative to heterosexual couples, individuals in gay and lesbian relationships more often committed IPH via stabbing, beating, and strangulation. Nonetheless, empirical work on rates of IPH across differing sexual orientations is limited and in need of further investigation.

In previous work, the killing of an intimate partner has been frequently linked to infidelity. Chimbos (1978) interviewed 34 Canadians who had killed their spouses (29 men and 5 women). Eighty-five percent of those individuals indicated that sexual matters (e.g., female denials to sexual intimacy or female infidelity) constituted the central source of disputes within their marriages, with wives' infidelity resulting in more disputes than husbands' infidelity. When related to infidelity, IPH is considered to be an extreme form of male sexual proprietariness (Daly & Wilson, 1988). This form of homicide can also be classified as an expressive homicide, in which the crime is typically unplanned and results from an overemotional state (Buss, 2000; Taylor, 2016). As a result, when men kill their partners, the perpetrator sometimes receives sympathy from others as it is perceived differently from other crimes (i.e., the crime was committed as a result of passion; Evzonas, 2018).

Several researchers have examined men's homicide of their opposite-sex intimate partners (i.e., uxoricide) from an evolutionary perspective (Buss, 2000; Daly et al., 1982; Kaighobadi, Shackelford, & Goetz, 2009; Mize et al., 2011; Peters et al., 2002; Wilson & Daly, 1993, 1996). Some scholars have posited that uxoricide may best be explained as a byproduct of men's evolved sexual strategies to seek out exclusive sexual access to their female mates in order to reduce paternity uncertainty and avoid cuckoldry (Daly & Wilson, 1988; Wilson & Daly, 1993, 1996). This has been the labeled the "slip-up" theory of IPH (Shackelford et al., 2000). Uxoricide may also be a byproduct of younger men's heightened homicidal attitudes and behavior relative to older same-sex conspecifics (i.e., routine activities theory; discussed in Mize et al., 2011, and Shackelford et al., 2000). Alternatively, other researchers have advanced the hypothesis that uxoricide may be produced by an adaptation selected to increase reproductive success (i.e., evolved homicide module theory; Duntley & Buss, 2005).

Evidence supporting uxoricide as adaptive includes: (1) male primates killing female mates in response to sexual infidelity (Smuts, 1992; Smuts & Smuts, 1993); (2) men's experience of sexual jealousy and suspicions of infidelity as reliable antecedents of uxoricide (Archer, 2013; Daly & Wilson, 1988); (3) a heightened risk of uxoricide for younger, more reproductively valuable women, particularly through more intimate means (e.g., stabbing and strangulation; Daly & Wilson, 1988; Dobash et al., 2004; Mize et al., 2011; Shackelford et al., 2000; Wilson et al., 1995); and (4) evidence of counterstrategies deployed by women to avoid uxoricide, such as killing male partners in self-defense or killing men who have previously perpetrated in-pair violence toward them (discussed in Duntley & Shackelford, 2012).

Nonetheless, uxoricide may best qualify as an evolutionary byproduct rather than the designed behavioral output of an adaptation. There are good reasons to believe that uxoricide might detract from, rather than contribute to, men's fitness in both ancestral and modern environments. Killing one's intimate partner would likely have been, and currently is in many modern cultural contexts, a high-risk strategy associated with recrimination and social exclusion by community members (Daly & Wilson, 1988; Wilson et al., 1995). Furthermore, uxoricide may signal to other potential mates that an individual male is psychologically unstable and, therefore, not a suitable relationship partner. This would likely harm men's reproductive success, particularly considering the importance heterosexual women ascribe to emotional stability as a key mate preference criterion in long-term relationships (Shackelford, Schmitt, et al., 2005). Indeed, the perpetrators of uxoricide are significantly more likely to have been diagnosed with personality disorders (reviewed in Dutton & Kerry, 1999). Although rare, the occurrence of suicide following uxoricide (i.e., uxoricide-suicide; Liem et al., 2009) would obviously preclude men from establishing new mateships, as well as producing and investing in offspring.

Intrasexual Homicide

Infidelity-related killings are not limited to the romantic partner, but can also extend to killing of the mate poacher. Homicide involves the killing of another with the intent to cause serious bodily harm or death (WHO, 2017b). Across the globe, 464,000 individuals are victims of homicide annually, according to data from 2017 (UNODC, 2019c), meaning that the global homicide rate is 6.1 for every 100,000 individuals (UNODC, 2019c). The most frequently victimized demographic are males between the ages of 15 and 29 years, though age trends for victimization are comparable between the sexes (UNODC, 2019d). Attesting to this, the WHO (2017a) reported that the global male population is victimized at a rate of 10.3 homicides per every 100,000, whereas the global female population is victimized at a rate of 2.4 homicides per every 100,000. Furthermore, approximately 90% of all recorded homicides are perpetrated by males (UNODC, 2019c).

Researchers have consistently demonstrated that as the severity and risky nature of aggressive interpersonal behavior increases, males are significantly more likely to be the perpetrators, particularly in regard to same-sex homicide of unrelated conspecifics (Archer, 2009; Daly & Wilson, 1990; Goetz, Shackelford, Romero, et al., 2008). Indeed, several homicide cases have shown how men catching their female partners in the act of infidelity results in the male lover being killed in a crime of passion (Buss, 2000). For example, researchers have studied specific typologies of male–male violence, such as the killing of a female mate's new male partner. Approximately 10% of male–male homicides in Japan during the years 1950 and 1960 were motivated by sexual jealousy (10.6% and 9.9%, respectively; Hiraiwa-Hasegawa, 2005). Unsurprisingly, sexual jealousy has been argued and shown to be a key motivating factor in men's killing of same-sex rivals that threaten the integrity of their mateships and who increase the risk of paternity uncertainty (Arnocky & Carré, 2016; Buss, 2013; Daly & Wilson, 1988; Davis et al., 2016; Duntley & Buss, 2005).

In some instances, when a person murders another as a result of sexual infidelity (e.g., finding a spouse committing acts of sexual infidelity in the moment), there are laws that sympathize with the perpetrator. For example, Philip Barton Key was murdered by Daniel Sickles in 1859, as a result of Key's affair with Sickles's wife (Keetley, 2008). In this case, Sickles was acquitted because his action was judged to be the result of an "uncontrollable instinct." In Canada, an individual can have a murder charge reduced from murder to manslaughter if they killed another in the heat of passion because of provocation, providing partial defense (Dayan, 2018). The defense of provocation is also used in other countries, like in the Commonwealth Caribbean (Wheatle, 2016). However, there are criticisms of this legal "provocation" defense, and some scholars and advocates wish to abolish the law. Some countries have followed this scholarly advice (Grant & Parles, 2017; Wheatle, 2016) and, as a consequence, this defense has been removed in some jurisdictions, such as in Australia (which has implemented the offence of defensive homicide; Fitz-Gibbon & Pickering, 2012), and in the United Kingdom. The United Kingdom has replaced the aforementioned defense with an alternative: loss of control. This defense is an attempt to target the gendered operation of the provocation defense. Whereas the provocation defense allowed sexual infidelity to partially excuse the act of homicide, the "loss of control"' defense does not allow for such a justification in IPH cases. Of note, the current state of this legal defense may change as there is case law attempting to make sexual infidelity a mitigating factor once more (Horder & Fitz-Gibbon, 2015; Kesserling, 2016; Slater, 2012; Wake, 2012). Meanwhile, other countries continue to uphold this legal defense (see, for example, Dressler, 2002; Gruber, 2015). The motivating factor of infidelity in male–male homicide is also evidenced by studies of hypothetical scenarios involving individuals who have not committed a crime. Miller and Maner (2008) asked undergraduate students to write about their anticipated reactions to an imagined infidelity. In response to partner infidelity, men reported they would experience stronger feelings of anger and a greater propensity for violence than women. Compared to women, men also reported being significantly more likely to perpetrate violence against the interloper than against their romantic partner.

Several lines of evidence converge to illustrate how same-sex violence, such as homicide, in response to infidelity may be adaptive. There is evidence that in many primate species, males violently attack and sometimes kill same-sex conspecifics if they encroach on their mating territory or attempt to copulate with mated females in both polyandrous and monogamous mating systems (discussed in French et al., 2018). In humans, same-sex violence and homicide to compete for mates and in response to suspected or actual infidelity has also been observed in many different cultures and across time (Blake & Denson, 2017; Daly & Wilson, 1988). These acts have plausible direct functions as an anticuckoldry tactic to reduce the likelihood of siring genetically unrelated offspring and as a mate retention tactic to remove intrasexual competitors from the mating arena (Buss, 2002, 2013; Kaighobadi et al., 2012). Homicidal ideation and violent retaliation (including same-sex homicide) are also reliably predicted by men's sexual jealousy, anticipated partner infidelity, and women's past infidelity (Buss, 2000, 2006, 2013; Duntley & Buss, 2005). There also appear to be antihomicide defenses that function as counterstrategies to reduce the likelihood of being killed by conspecifics, such as avoiding situations where stranger homicide may be more likely to occur (e.g., lower socioeconomic areas and dark alleys; see Duntley & Shackelford, 2012).

Nonetheless, similar to uxoricide, killing conspecifics is a very risky strategy that may inhibit, rather than promote, men's reproductive success. As a highly social species that evolved in small nomadic hunter-gatherer communities (Richerson & Boyd, 1998), it is likely that men killing same-sex group members over suspected infidelity would have been met with strong disapproval, and would signal to available mates that an individual is dangerous and potentially psychologically unstable (Daly & Wilson, 1998; Wilson et al., 1995). The same could be said in most developed modern circumstances where homicide is met with legal consequences and public disapproval. However, in patriarchal cultural contexts wherein men are able to subjugate and acquire dominion over women, it is possible for men to kill in a more religiously and socially "acceptable" manner (e.g., honor killings; Buss & Shackelford, 1997b; Wilson & Daly, 1996). Perhaps in these settings men could experience heightened reproductive success, but this again casts some doubt on the idea that men's same-sex homicide is universally adaptive.

Filicide

Filicide is the act of a parent killing their child. Researchers have further operationalized the constructs of neonaticide (i.e., the killing of a newborn on the first day of life) and infanticide (i.e., the killing of a genetically related or unrelated infant during their first year of life by conspecifics). Filicide is also a well-documented phenomenon occurring across diverse cultural contexts and throughout time (Adinkrah, 2003; Almeida & Viera, 2017; Friedman et al., 2012; Hrdy, 1999; UNODC 2019e). In Canada, the vast majority of child homicide victims are killed by a family member. Usually this family member is a parent, and this pattern of results has been quite consistent (e.g., in Canada since Statistics Canada began reporting these values in the mid-1970s; Statistics Canada, 2009). Of the children killed annually in the United States, parents are responsible for an estimated 61% of murders of children under the age of 5 years (Friedman et al., 2005), and similar rates have been cited for the United Kingdom (see Martin, 2006). On average, 450 children are murdered by their parents each year in the United States and about 30 in Canada (Statistics Canada, 2009). Sometimes, there is a combination of murder and suicide in filicide cases. When considering filicide broadly, men appear to be the perpetrators more often than women. In Canada, data collected from 1997–2006 shows that the perpetrating parent is typically the father rather than the mother (Statistics Canada, 2009). However, there appear to be important differences in terms of the victim's age. Empirical work indicates that mothers commit neonaticide far more often than fathers (Fox & Fridel, 2017; Goetting, 1988) and that this pattern seems to reverse in cases of filicide involving older children (Kunz & Bahr, 1996). These fathers committing filicide also tend to have lower socioeconomic standing (Campion et al., 1988; Marleau et al., 1999) and use more violent means of perpetrating the act (e.g., stabbing; Marleau et al., 1999).

Researchers have outlined at least five underlying motives for filicide, one of which includes spousal revenge perpetrated primarily to cause harm to one's partner. Ostensibly this could relate to infidelity, yet we are unaware of empirical data on whether suspicion or confirmation of infidelity, or of discovery of cuckoldry, serves as a reliable impetus for violence against the offspring. Nevertheless, sexual jealousy and sexual infidelity have been invoked by many authors as key motivating factors in contributing to paternal filicide (Adinkrah, 2003; Archer, 2013; Daly & Wilson, 1984, 1988; Friedman et al., 2012; West, 2007). In support of this idea, there have been highly publicized cases which provide anecdotal evidence that some men cite infidelity as a reason for killing their children. News reports of different cases containing statements like "A Tennessee man is accused of beating a 4-month-old baby to death after discovering that he wasn't the infant boy's father" (Georgantopoulos, 2019), "A man is due to be sentenced today for killing a baby boy when doubts emerged over whether or not he was the father" (Hartley-Parkinson, 2019), and "A hospital radiographer was jailed for life for murdering his three-year-old daughter . . . after discovering sexually explicit emails sent by his wife . . . to a part-time judge whom she had met on the internet" (Martin, 2006) are easy to find among international news headlines. Such cases are not limited only to responses to infidelity. One news report noted, "A Colorado father was sentenced to three consecutive lifetimes in prison after . . . [planning] . . . the August murders of his pregnant wife and two young daughters—apparently in the hope of starting a new life with his girlfriend" (Selk, 2018).

From an evolutionary perspective, discontinuing investment in offspring when confronted with information that one is not the biological father makes sense. Killing that offspring might simultaneously punish one's female partner, reducing her reproductive success and the success of an intrasexual rival—behavior that is seen in some other mammalian species, such as lions and various primates, as well as many species of insects, amphibians, fish, and birds (e.g., Hrdy, 1979; Smuts & Smuts, 1993). Yet in humans, there are inherent risks to using such behavior, including ambiguity of potentially eliminating one's own offspring and the retaliation by others in the social group. For men, a key proposed direct function of filicide is the avoidance of investing limited resources in genetically unrelated offspring when faced with high levels of paternal uncertainty (Daly & Wilson, 1988, 2008; West et al., 2009).

Moreover, step-parents who do not share a genetic relationship with their offspring are significantly more likely to kill children within the family structure than are genetic parents and they tend to use methods of killing that are less immediate that thus produce more pain (e.g., beating and bludgeoning; Daly & Wilson, 1994; Weekes-Shackelford & Shackelford, 2004). Partner revenge has also been shown to be an important motivating factor for paternal filicide, particularly in response to infidelity, relationship dissolution, and loss of custody (Palermo, 2003; Resnick, 2016; West, 2007; West et al., 2009). It is possible that this behavior could function to deter a female partner's sexual infidelity, perhaps even as an extreme means of punishing a mate's infidelity threat (a key cost-inflicting form of mate retention; Barbaro et al., 2015; Starratt et al., 2007).

Conversely, some scholars have posited that male infanticide could be an exaptation of men's aggressive intrasexual rivalry (Bartlett et al., 1993). Some data support this idea. For instance, aggressive men are more likely to engage in spousal homicide and filicide (reviewed in Palombit, 2015). Nonetheless, currently it seems to be an inadequate hypothesis given how highly goal-directed, context-specific, and patterned infanticide is among humans and nonhuman animals (West, 2007). Furthermore, the "byproduct" argument for infanticide in response to infidelity does not adequately address observations of maternal filicide in response to infidelity (Friedman et al., 2012).

However tempting it may be to make adaptive conclusions about filicide based on these case examples, the reality is that "spousal revenge," as the motive underlying filicide which seems to best fit with real or suspected infidelity, appears to be rare compared to other reasons, such as altruistic killing and acute psychosis (Resnick, 1969). Moreover, some studies show that mothers rather than fathers are more likely to kill younger children, especially between the ages of 1 and 4 years. There is no genetic reason why infidelity would bear on women's willingness to invest in a child, since they are not susceptible to cuckoldry. One could speculate that perhaps the threat of loss of male resources or desire to attract a new mate (which could be inhibited by a child) might bear on this behavior in women. Indeed, anthropologists have noted that in some cultures filicide is directly linked to the availability of resources, and the likelihood of that offspring being able to attract important resources. One of the most striking examples of this link can be found in the anthropological literature on Inuit populations. In the early 20th century, it was noted that Inuit women would kill their children by way of freezing, drowning, or suffocation, under the "stress of unbearable economic conditions" (Garber, 1947). In these circumstances, female infants were far more likely to be killed than male infants, ostensibly because "boy babies will grow up to become producers and providers" (Garber, 1947). Poverty and a lack of resources, coupled with child characteristics that confer greater burden or threat to survival have been cited in contemporary societies as explanations of infanticide as well (e.g., Friedman et al., 2012; Hilari et al., 2009). Some studies have linked the likelihood of being a lone parent to infanticide; especially when social, economic, and cultural influences hinder a woman's ability to raise a child alone (e.g., Friedman et al., 2012; Rattigan, 2012). To the extent that a male's infidelity could result in his abandonment of his partner and offspring, the loss of those resources could function as a tipping point for the viability of the offspring toward the mother's reproductive fitness. Nevertheless, there is little empirical evidence directly linking filicide to infidelity. In Croatia, Marcikić et al. (2006) found evidence of fear of infidelity being discovered by a husband, along with socioeconomic hardships, as motivating factors for infanticide. Similarly, Friedman and Resnick (2007) note that women's spousal revenge filicide "most often occurs after learning of spousal infidelities or in the course of child custody disputes" (p. 139). Future researchers should seek to more thoroughly investigate putative links between infidelity and filicide.

Social-Cognitive and Emotional Adaptations Linked to Infidelity and Violence

Sensitivity to Cues of Partner Infidelity

Given the adaptive challenges associated with a partner's infidelity (e.g., cuckoldry), researchers have argued that humans have evolved a constellation of perceptual, cognitive, and affective mechanisms that operate to gauge looming threats that infidelity may transpire and to detect that infidelity has occurred (Andrews et al., 2008; Buss, 2002; Shackelford & Buss, 1997). For instance, researchers have identified that perception of a romantic partner's actions may serve as a cue to emotional and sexual infidelity in a long-term partner, such as reluctance to spend time with, acting guilty/anxious toward, and sexual disinterest/boredom with one's mate (Shackelford & Buss, 1997). Another strong predictor of future partner infidelity is whether that individual has committed infidelity in the past (Baker & Bellis, 1995). Other researchers have focused on more subtle cues, such as perceptions of vocal pitch. Women perceive men with more masculine (low-pitched) voices as more likely to be unfaithful than men with more feminized voices, whereas men perceive women with more feminine voices as being more likely to be unfaithful in comparison to women with more masculinized voices (O'Connor et al., 2011). Interestingly, women who more often rate men with lower voice pitch as likely to commit infidelity are more likely to prefer these men as short-term sexual partners, as opposed to long-term romantic partners (O'Connor et al., 2014). Furthermore, some researchers have shown that individuals accurately rate the vocal pitch of those who have previously committed infidelity as more likely to have been unfaithful (Hughes & Harrison, 2017; Schild et al., 2020). Importantly, there are sex differences in the monitoring tendencies and the accuracy of infidelity inferences that correspond to the divergent adaptive problems that have differentially impinged on women's and men's reproductive success over their evolutionary histories, as we discuss next.

Evolutionary scholars have argued that the costs of failing to detect a partner's infidelity would have been more detrimental to the reproductive success of ancestral men relative to ancestral women because of men's paternity uncertainty (Andrews et al., 2008; Kruger et al., 2015). Men would, therefore, benefit more by falsely assuming infidelity (a false-positive), because the opposite act of failing to detect a true infidelity (a false-negative) could lead to cuckoldry. This phenomenon, grounded within error management theory, has been termed the "infidelity overperception bias" (see Goetz & Causey, 2009). Indeed, heterosexual men have been shown to be more suspicious of a partner's potential future sexual infidelity (Goetz & Causey, 2009), even when their partners say that they have been faithful (Andrews et al., 2008). Men also appear to be more accurate in their inferences of infidelity than women (Brand et al., 2007; Andrews et al., 2008). Further, there is some evidence that women may have difficulty in detecting male sexual infidelity. In one study of adults living in economically disadvantaged communities in India, 22% of men had reported extramarital sex, yet only 6% of wives reported knowledge of these sexual liaisons (Schensul et al., 2006). Nonetheless, because of the heightened likelihood of IPH faced by women over suspected and actual sexual infidelity (Wilson & Daly, 1988), selection has likely favored more effective ways of hiding and disguising cues to infidelity among women as adaptive counterstrategies (Duntley & Shackelford, 2012).

Through the rivalry sensitivity hypothesis, it has also been suggested that women and men may have evolved different detection strategies and sensitivities to cues and sources of infidelity (Ein-Dor et al., 2015). Specifically, women focus their attention on threats to infidelity from potential rivals (other women), compared to men who focus on monitoring their own partner's intents to commit infidelity (Ein-Dor et al., 2015). Women were more likely than men to state that an ambiguous gaze from an attractive same-sex stranger was threatening (i.e., a "zone defense"; Ein-Dor et al., 2015). This demonstrates that the focus of women's sensitivity to threats is on potential rivals, arguable because women lack the capacity to physically dominate (and thus prevent infidelity by) their partner. Conversely, men were more likely to appraise gazes of their own partners toward strangers as threatening, demonstrating sensitivity to within-couple threats (i.e., a "person-to-person defense"; Ein-Dor et al., 2015). An alternative explanation of these findings might be that because men are generally less discriminating in their mate choice (especially for short-term affairs), that female interest in one's partner represents a greater threat than the reverse, given that women likely receive much more attention from potential suitors than men. Consequently, a more efficient strategy for males would be to monitor the partner rather than all male rivals. According to evolutionary psychologists, information that signals a reproductive threat should then promote an affective response, which in turn would elicit an appropriate behavioral outcome (see Arnocky et al., 2012, for review). Indeed, knowledge or suspicion of infidelity has been robustly linked to a constellation of emotions including jealousy and anxiety, which in turn appear to motivate violence in some circumstances.

Emotional, Sexual, and Morbid Jealousy

Evolutionary scholars argue that romantic jealousy functions to promote actions aimed at retaining one's mate, such as being vigilant to the presence of intrasexual rivals (Albert & Arnocky, 2016; Arnocky et al., 2012; Buss, 2002; Davis et al., 2018). In support of its adaptive utility, researchers have observed sex differences in the types of infidelity that are most strongly tied to jealousy, which map on to the specific adaptive challenges likely faced by ancestral women and men. As described earlier in this chapter in the section on IPV, men face the adaptive challenges of paternal uncertainty and cuckoldry in relation to women's sexual infidelity. Males tend to be more upset and likely to express sexual jealousy if their partner commits sexual infidelity, referring to sexual activity with someone other than one's long-term partner (Buss, 2013; Davis et al., 2016; Kruger et al., 2015; Shackelford & Buss, 1997). In contrast, women face the adaptive challenge of securing and retaining male physical protection, provisioning, and paternal investment for their offspring. Men's emotional infidelity (i.e., establishing a strong emotional attachment with someone outside the mateship), therefore, is particularly distressful for women and elicits their emotional jealousy.

Across varied samples and methods, meta-analytic work supports the hypothesis that heterosexual men experience more psychological distress than women over a partner's sexual infidelity, whereas the opposite pattern has been documented in regard to a partner's emotional infidelity (see Edlund & Sagarin, 2017). These sex differences in jealousy have proven replicable across cultures that significantly differ socially, economically, and politically, including China, Japan, Chile, Spain, Romania, Ireland, Sweden, and The Netherlands (Buss, 2018). There is also evidence that these sex differences occur in response to the actual experience of infidelity (Edlund & Sagarin, 2017). Similar findings have also been reported for heterosexual women and men expressing morbid jealousy, denoting an excessive and delusional experience of jealousy over suspected infidelity (Easton et al., 2007). This sex difference does, however, appear to be more pronounced among heterosexual couples and attenuated among homosexual partners (Harris, 2003). Results are more mixed when considering women's and men's physiological reactions to infidelity. Some have supported the predicted sex difference in distress over sexual and emotional infidelity (e.g., Buss et al., 1992), whereas other scholars have found that men generally show greater physiological activity to sexual compared to emotional imagery even in the absence of infidelity cues (Harris, 2000).

There also appears to be a corresponding sex difference in forgiveness of infidelity. Men report being more likely to break up with their partner if she has committed a sexual infidelity compared to emotional infidelity, whereas the reverse was true of women (Shackelford et al., 2002). In a situation where participants were told to imagine that both sexual and emotional aspects of an infidelity were involved, the majority of men indicated that the sexual aspect would be the most difficult to forgive (Shackelford et al., 2002). Perhaps the tendency for males to overperceive and fail to forgive sexual infidelity has implications for the perpetration of violence as a means of curtailing such threats (see chapter 10 for a more thorough discussion of sex differences in jealousy).

Understanding sex differences in sexual jealousy is important because of the abundance of evidence linking male sexual proprietariness and jealousy to partner-directed violence in the face of real, suspected, or anticipated infidelity (Buss & Duntley, 2011; Daly et al., 1982). Wilson and Daly (1996) have noted that men's antipathy for female infidelity and attempts to leave the relationship resoundingly underlies violence toward, and killing of, women. Victims and perpetrators ascribe men's violent and autonomy-limiting behavior toward women as most frequently motivated by jealousy (see Wilson & Daly, 1996 for review). Easton and Shackelford (2009) found that morbidly jealous men, more than women, used physical violence, attempted to kill, and actually killed their romantic partners. In another study looking at the emotional reactions to infidelity, men, compared to women, provided higher ratings for emotions surrounding feeling homicidal and suicidal (Shackelford et al., 2000). Sex differences in infidelity-related emotions have also been explored at the neural level. One study found that compared to neutral situations, during situations which evoked jealousy, men showed greater activation than women in the brain regions involved in sexual/aggressive behaviors such as the amygdala and hypothalamus (Takahashi et al., 2006). This provides support for the idea that men and women may have different neuropsychological modules to process sexual and emotional infidelity.

Anxiety and Anxious Attachment

Parallel to work on jealousy, researchers have also recognized anxiety (i.e., worry and apprehension of things to come) as a core component of sexual proprietariness, such that the "threat of losing one's mate to a rival evokes jealousy that includes not only anxiety but also seeking of reassurance and aggression to try to avert loss" (Marks & Nesse, 1994, p. 252). Indeed, anxiety has been linked to the perpetration of aggression in humans and other species (see Arnocky, Sunderani, Gomes, et al., 2015, for review). Baumeister and Tice (1990) argued that anxiety evolved in part to facilitate the maintenance of important relationships by promoting corrective action in the face of social exclusion (see Buss, 1990). Rodriguez et al. (2015) found that anxious individuals reported more jealousy when they were less trusting of their partner and that low trust predicted perpetration of nonphysical partner violence (e.g., making fun of the partner and screaming at the partner) more among anxious individuals. Like jealousy, one's mate value also appears to interact with the experience of anxious emotions. For instance, Phillips (2010) found that women and men lower in mate value reported greater insecurity and anxiety in response to a partner's infidelity.

In spite of the vast body of research implicating jealousy concerning violence related to real or suspected infidelity, there is relatively limited empirical work wherein these relations are statistically modeled. If negative affect serves the adaptive function of motivating behavioral responses to information about reproductive threats, then we can expect variables such as jealousy and anxiety to mediate the links between infidelity (reproductive threat) and aggression (behavioral response). Arnocky, Sunderani, Gomes, et al. (2015) explored whether anxiety mediated links between anticipated partner infidelity and the perpetration of IPV in a sample of undergraduate men. They found that symptoms of anxiety mediated relations between anticipated partner infidelity and physical aggression, partner injury, psychological aggression, and sexual aggression toward a partner. These studies provide initial evidence that negative affect likely mediate links between cues to a reproductive threat, such as infidelity, and aggressive reactions to such threats.

Evolutionary scholars have also implicated the role of anxiety in people's romantic attachment orientations, which putatively function to coordinate cognitive, affective, and behavioral responses to relationship threats such as infidelity and relationship dissolution (see Barbaro et al., 2016). Specifically, attachment anxiety embodies feelings of insecurity in a romantic relationship, encouraging hypervigilance to relationship threats and an excessive dependence on one's partner for assurance. Individuals with anxious attachments are prone to consider a wider range of behavior as signaling infidelity (Kruger et al., 2013), express more jealousy (Kim et al., 2018), and deploy cost-inflicting mate retention at a higher frequency (Barbaro et al., 2016). Men and women with an anxious attachment are also more likely to psychologically aggress against, physically assault, and sexually coerce their romantic partners (Barbaro & Shackelford, 2019). Using path analysis to model the direction of effects and to infer causal relations, Barbaro et al. (2019) found that anxious attachment positively predicted heightened perceptions of future infidelity, which explained women's and men's use of cost-inflicting mate retention. Collectively, these studies provide important evidence that negative trait and attachment affectivity mediate the links between cues to a reproductive threat, such as infidelity, and aggressive reactions to such threats.

Individual Differences in Violence
Mate Value

On the mating market, women and men who are lower in mate value are competitively disadvantaged, which places them at a greater risk of partner infidelity or mate defection (Miner, Starratt, et al., 2009). Mate value embodies a constellation of factors such as kindness, honesty, physical attractiveness, and loyalty, several of which vary in importance according to biological sex. Women tend to value indicators of resource holding potential (e.g., status, ambition, and wealth) and physical formidability in a partner more than men, whereas men tend to desire cues to health, reproductive value (e.g., youth, physical appearance), and parenting ability in a partner more than women (Fisher et al., 2008; Shackelford, Schmitt, et al., 2005). Evolutionary scholars have posited that individuals of lower mate value should be more likely to resort to more high-risk and damaging (i.e., cost-inflicting) forms of mate retention. In support of this idea, Graham-Kevan and Archer (2009) found that both women and men with lower mate value were more controlling and more physically aggressive toward their partners. Similarly, Davis et al. (2019) found that poorer reported physical health (a putative marker of lower mate value), corresponded to engaging in more cost-inflicting mate retention among women and men. Sela et al. (2017) found that individuals who perceived themselves to be more replaceable relative to their mates and less likely to be able to replace their partners (i.e., a mate value discrepancy), were more likely to perform both cost-inflicting and benefit-provisioning acts (e.g., gift giving, complimenting one's partner, and going out to expensive restaurants).

Although relevant to both sexes, men, like the males of most other mammals, have greater reproductive variability than women (i.e., Bateman's principle). Therefore, men of lower mate value are predicted to have a vested interest in retaining their partners at whatever the cost. Women are also more frequently the targets of men's mate poaching efforts (Sunderani et al., 2013), suggesting, again, that lower mate value men may have to guard their partners more vigorously and resort to cost-inflicting tactics more often than their higher mate value same-sex counterparts. Miner, Shackelford, et al. (2009) showed that lower mate value men used more partner-directed verbal aggression in comparison to higher mate value men. Furthermore, Miner, Starratt, et al. (2009) found that men higher on mate value used healthier, positive, and less risky mate retention (i.e., benefit-provisioning acts) and fewer cost-inflicting forms of mate retention toward their female partners. Taller men who are generally regarded as more attractive by women (i.e., higher mate value) have also been shown to exhibit lower jealousy than their shorter counterparts (Brewer & Riley 2009; Buunk et al. 2008). Moreover, Buunk and Massar (2019) found in a sample of men from Nicaragua that lower mate value predicted increased perpetration of IPV. Danel et al. (2017) found that women who reported their own mate value as being significantly higher than their male partner's (i.e., a mate value discrepancy) also reported more controlling behavior by their partners. Nonetheless, aggression and IPV in relation to low mate value is not limited to men. In a sample of over 500 women who were currently in heterosexual relationships, Arnocky et al. (2012) found that women who perceived themselves as less physically attractive than other women (i.e., lower in mate value) engaged in more relational aggression toward their partners. Importantly, women's mate value also varies predictably over development and cyclically across the phases of the menstrual cycle, which evolutionary scholars predict to influence the likelihood of infidelity and men's mate retention efforts (Gangestad et al., 2002; Pillsworth & Haselton, 2006).

Differences in Fertility Status and Reproductive Value

As stated in the section on IPH, younger women are higher in reproductive value than their older same-sex counterparts and face a higher risk of uxoricide (Daly & Wilson, 1988; Mize et al., 2011). Younger women are also more likely to experience vigorous mate retention efforts by their male partners, including greater surveillance and controlling behavior (Buss & Shackelford, 1997; Graham-Kevan & Archer, 2009; Shackelford et al., 2000). Women's fertility status has also been found to predict men's mate retention behavior. For instance, in a Caribbean village, men who were partnered with pregnant women (who were thus not at present risk of impregnation by another male) spent less time with, and were less aggressive toward, their partners in comparison to men whose partners were fecund (i.e., capable of producing offspring; Flinn, 1988). Furthermore, women's fertility shifts significantly across the phases of their menstrual cycles, peaking during the periovulatory phase, and evidence suggests that men can detect subtle changes in women's fertility status across the cycle (Haselton & Gildersleeve, 2011). Consequently, men self-report and women report that their partners engage in more mate retention behavior around ovulation (Gangestad et al., 2002; Pillsworth & Haselton, 2006). Individual differences are but one source of variance underpinning responses to infidelity. Social and ecological parameters have also been shown to influence how people respond to real or suspected infidelity.

Social-Ecological Contexts Influencing Responses to Infidelity

Across varied disciplines and subdisciplinary branches of study, many researchers have inappropriately argued that either individual differences or social-cultural processes account for perceptions of infidelity and IPV, particularly when examining the sex- and gender-differentiated aspects of these relations. However, human psychology manifests through a confluence of proximate (i.e., immediate) and ultimate (i.e., distal) mechanisms, underscoring the necessity of studying physiology, attitudes, values, emotions, personality, demographic characteristics, development, socialization practices, societal structures, features of the physical environment, ecology, and phylogeny in trying to understand how (a proximate question) and why (an ultimate question) infidelity and IPV occur (Brown et al., 2018; Daly, 2014; Goetz, Shackelford, & Camilleri, 2008; Ward & Siegert, 2002). One cultural-level variable that has received a significant amount of attention from researchers, relates to societies wherein men control a disproportionate amount of power over women (i.e., patriarchal cultures).

Patriarchy and Cultures of Honor

Sociocultural researchers have highlighted the importance of the internalization of masculine ideologies that are more prevalent in patriarchal cultures when attempting to comprehend male-perpetrated IPV in response to infidelity (Brown et al., 2018; Brown & Osterman, 2012; Osterman & Brown, 2011). In these cultures, individual men tend to seek power and dominion over women and are more likely to treat them as sexual objects. One example is cultures of honor—contexts within which individuals feel obligated and emboldened to protect their reputations. In such cultures, men internalize norms through socialization processes where women are viewed as conquests, which becomes linked to men's sexual proprietariness (Buss & Shackelford, 1997b; Daly & Wilson, 1988; Wilson & Daly, 1996). Therefore, from sociocultural and evolutionary perspectives, we should expect men in honor cultures to feel more justified in expressing deleterious forms of jealousy (e.g., possessive jealousy) and engaging in a greater frequency of IPV as a reputation management strategy when threats to their honor are triggered. Several researchers have shown how men living in cultures of honor are more tolerant of male jealousy and male perpetrated IPV in comparison to men who have not been socialized by these cultures (Vandello et al., 2009). Brown et al. (2018) also showed that in American states with a stronger culture of honor, there were higher rates of rape, physical dating violence, and economic deprivation. On the point of economic deprivation, evolutionary scholars have emphasized how situations of resource scarcity are predicted to engender more risky, damaging, and violent intrasexual competition and intergroup aggression among conspecifics for access to those limited resource (Allen et al., 2016; Cox, 2008; Daly & Wilson, 1988).

Income Inequality, Resource Scarcity, and Environmental Unpredictability

Conflict arises among individuals when there is variability in the ability to access, defend, and secure limited resources that contribute to survival or reproductive success, whether it is food, shelter, or mates (Daly & Wilson, 1990). Evolutionary investigators have convincingly shown that one of the best predictors of aggression and violence (e.g., homicide and IPV) is income inequality, wherein those with fewer resource, such as those in poverty, compete more fiercely when they feel like there is nothing to lose because the benefits of violence outweigh the potential costs (Balci & Ayranci, 2005; Daly & Wilson, 1988; Daly et al., 2001; Flynn & Graham, 2010). Both women and men in situations typified by income inequality increase their intrasexual rivalry in sex-specific ways that correspond to the adaptive challenges faced by ancestral women and men. For women, poverty may engender more self-promotion to attract mates (e.g., emphasizing cues to promiscuity), competitor derogation to lower the mate value of rivals, as well as competition for access to men who are capable of providing resources and parental investment (Blake & Brooks, 2019; Campbell, 1999). In these situations, women may be more likely to commit infidelity to acquire better quality sexual and romantic partners (Cox, 2008). In slight contrast, men in these situations may increase their violent tendencies to retain romantic partners, fight off rivals, and remove competitors from the mating arena (i.e., homicide), and due to an inability to attract and maintain mateships through self-promoting cues to resource holding, status, and parental investment (Daly, 2017; Daly & Wilson, 1988).

Evolutionary scholars have pointed to environmental unpredictability (i.e., the degree of fluctuation and stochasticity in early developmental environments) as another important contextual variable that influences perceptions of infidelity and more violent forms of mate retention behavior. For example, Barbaro and Shackelford (2019) showed that retrospective accounts of unpredictability in childhood were linked to IPV (e.g., physical assault), which was explained (i.e., mediated) by anxious attachment. However, this effect was significantly stronger for men in comparison to women, perhaps because men may benefit from riskier reproductive strategies than women as a consequence of women's greater obligatory parental investment.

Another salient cue to resource scarcity is the relative number of sexually available mates within a population in a particular geographic location (i.e., the operational sex ratio; Arnocky et al., 2016).

Sex Ratios and Perceived Mate Availability

Infidelity rates and intentions have been linked to population operational sex ratios largely within the context of female-biased regions (i.e., more reproductive-aged women relative to men) exhibiting a more unrestricted sociosexual orientation relative to male-biased (i.e., more reproductive aged men relative to women) regions (Schmitt, 2005).

This effect has also been observed experimentally. Arnocky et al. (2016) found that men primed with perceived mate abundance exhibited less restricted sociosexual attitudes and more intended infidelity relative to men primed with perceived mate scarcity. In another study, individuals who were primed with the same mate-availability scenarios also exhibited increased intrasexual competitiveness, jealousy, and indirect and physical (men only) aggression toward a hypothetical mate poacher when primed with mate scarcity versus abundance (Arnocky et al., 2014). This suggests that whereas perception of mate abundance may promote infidelity, perceptions of mate scarcity may promote effort aimed at preventing partner defection.

Conclusions and Future Research Directions

Human mating relies largely on the provision of reproductively relevant resources by relationship partners. Infidelity represents an important threat to this process, introducing risk of cuckoldry, diversion of physical and emotional resources, and potential dissolution of the mateship and abandonment of offspring. Accordingly, evolutionary psychologists have argued that humans have evolved a suite of perceptual, cognitive, affective, and behavioral traits which serve, in part, to counteract the threat of infidelity. Some of the most devastating of these include various forms of IPV (e.g., rape and uxoricide, homicide, and filicide). These actions, though repugnant, may have facilitated ancestral reproductive fitness via their functions related to deterring infidelity or defection, isolating the partner, punishing infidelity to reduce its future occurrence, eliminating the competition, competing with other men's sperm, or eliminating the partner or resultant children who do not pose strong likelihood of passing on one's genes. Sex differences in these violent actions may reflect the differential risks associated with resource loss versus cuckoldry and acquisition of new partners which vary between men and women, along with the risk associated with violence perpetration, which is inherently more detrimental to women than it is to men. Varying degrees of evidence have linked men's sexual proprietariness to these vicious and unconscionable acts, suggesting that jealousy and related emotions such as anxiety play an important role in promoting these actions in response to a real or perceived infidelity. Moreover, individual differences, such as mate value, as well as social-ecological factors, including cultures of honor, income inequality, and mate scarcity, may play a role in moderating these links.

Despite the power of an evolutionary perspective in delineating why individuals engage in violence in response to suspected or actual infidelity, the sex-differentiated aspects of the behavior, and the moderating factors engendering same-sex and partner-directed abuse and the killing of offspring, there are still many areas in need of further investigation. For instance, there is ongoing debate regarding whether the physiological and psychological mechanisms underpinning violent behavior over infidelity actually constitute adaptations or exaptations (e.g., rape). Concrete evidence is needed regarding actual outcomes linked to reproductive success concerning sexually coercive behavior, including rape. Similarly, there is little evidence supporting the notion that various forms of cost-inflicting mate retention (e.g., IPV) work to retain desired partners and whether the reproductive benefits of the behavior outweigh the potential costs. Contextual factors such as perceptions of mate availability or resource availability would also benefit greatly from examining potential links to mate retention and violence. For instance, one could administer a mate availability or resource availability priming manipulation and examine subsequent attitudes toward mate retention effort and partner violence. Several researchers have linked vocal pitch to perceptions of infidelity (e.g., O'Connell et al., 2014; O'Connell et al., 2011); however, few scholars have examined the associations between vocal pitch in relation to actual infidelity outcomes (see Hughes & Harrison, 2017; Schild et al., 2020). There exists an even larger gap in the literature regarding the relations between vocal pitch and mate retention behavior, which would contribute to extant literature on perceptual threat detection and behavioral responses to potential infidelity. Similarly, many researchers have shown how particular characteristics in intrasexual rivals elicit women's and men's jealousy and suspicions of infidelity (e.g., Buss et al., 2000; Dijkstra & Buunk, 2002); however, few scholars have modeled how these characteristics then promote mate retention behavior in response to looming infidelity threats (Nascimento & Little, 2019). Researchers have also begun to examine different forms of cyber IPV from an evolutionary perspective; although, limited work has been conducted from this viewpoint in identifying the cognitive (e.g., perceptions of infidelity) and affective factors (e.g., jealousy) that precipitate digital dating abuse (Bhogal et al., 2019). Taken together, the growing evidence in support of perceptual, emotional, and behavioral adaptations can together inform a better understanding of violence in response to real or suspected infidelity.

References

Adams-Clark, A. A., & Chrisler, J. C. (2018). What constitutes rape? The effect of marital status and type of sexual act on perceptions of rape scenarios. *Violence Against Women, 24*(16), 1867–1886. https://doi.org/10.1177/1077801218755975

Adinkrah, M. (2003). Men who kill their own children: Paternal filicide incidents in contemporary Fiji. *Child Abuse & Neglect, 27*(5), 557–568. https://doi.org/10.1016/S0145-2134(03)00041-3

Albert, G., & Arnocky, S. (2016). Use of mate retention strategies. In T. K. Shackelford & V. A. Weekes-Shackelford (Eds.), *The encyclopedia of evolutionary psychological science*. Springer. https://doi.org/10.1007/978-3-319-16999-6_151-1

Allen, M. W., Bettinger, R. L., Codding, B. F., Jones, T. L., & Schwitalla, A. W. (2016). Resource scarcity drives lethal aggression among prehistoric hunter-gatherers in central California. *Proceedings of the National Academy of Sciences, 113*(43), 12120–12125. https://doi.org/10.1073/pnas.1607996113

Almeida, F., & Vieira, D. N. (2017). Profiling in violent crimes: The perpetrator and the victim in cases of filicide. In W. Petherick & G. Sinnamon (Eds.), *The psychology of criminal and antisocial behavior* (pp. 167–209). Academic Press.

Amato, P. R., & Rogers, S. J. (1997). A longitudinal study of marital problems and subsequent divorce. *Journal of Marriage and the Family, 59*(3), 612–624. https://doi.org/10.2307/353949

Andrews, P. W., Gangestad, S. W., Miller, G. F., Haselton, M. G., Thornhill, R., & Neale, M. C. (2008). Sex differences in detecting sexual infidelity. *Human Nature, 19*(4), 347. https://doi.org/10.1007/s12110-008-9051-3

Archer, J. (2001). Evolving theories of behavior. *The Psychologist, 14*(8), 414–419. http://facelab.org/debruine/Teaching/EvPsych/files/Archer_2001.pdf

Archer, J. (2006). Cross-cultural differences in physical aggression between partners: A social-role analysis. *Personality and Social Psychology Review, 10*(2), 133–153. https://doi.org/10.1207/s15327957pspr1002_3

Archer, J. (2009). Does sexual selection explain human sex differences in aggression? *Behavioral and Brain Sciences, 32*, 249–311. https://doi.org/10.1017/S0140525X09990951

Archer, J. (2013). Can evolutionary principles explain patterns of family violence? *Psychological Bulletin, 139*(2), 403–440. https://doi.org/10.1037/a0029114

Archer, J. (2018). Violence to partners: Gender symmetry revisited. In J. L. Ireland, C. A. Ireland, & P. Burch (Eds.), *International handbook on aggression* (pp. 155–169). Routledge.

Archer, J., & Vaughan, A. E. (2001). Evolutionary theories of rape. *Psychology, Evolution & Gender, 3*(1), 95–101. https://doi.org/10.1080/14616660110049609

Arnocky, S., & Carré, J. M. (2016). Intrasexual rivalry among men. In T. K. Shackelford & V. A. Weekes-Shackelford (Eds.), *The encyclopedia of evolutionary psychological science*. Springer. https://doi.org/10.1007/978-3-319-16999-6_874-1

Arnocky, S., Ribout, A., Mirza, R. S., & Knack, J. M. (2014). Perceived mate intrasexual competition, jealousy and mate-guarding behavior. *Journal of Evolutionary Psychology, 12*(1), 45–64. https://doi.org/10.1556/JEP.12.2014.1.3

Arnocky, S., Sunderani, S., Gomes, W., & Vaillancourt, T. (2015). Anticipated partner infidelity and men's intimate partner violence: The mediating role of anxiety. *Evolutionary Behavioral Sciences, 9*(3), 186–196. https://doi.org/10.1177/1474704915593666

Arnocky, S., Sunderani, S., Miller, J., & Vaillancourt, T. (2012). Jealousy mediates the relationship between attractiveness comparison and females' indirect aggression. *Personal Relationships, 19*(2), 290–303. https://doi.org/10.1111/j.1475-6811.2011.01362.x

Arnocky, S., Sunderani, S., & Vaillancourt, T. (2013). Mate-poaching and mating success in humans. *Journal of Evolutionary Psychology, 11*(2), 65–83. https://doi.org/10.1556/JEP.11.2013.2.2

Arnocky, S., & Vaillancourt, T. (2012). A multi-informant longitudinal study on the relationship between aggression, peer victimization, and dating status in adolescence. *Evolutionary Psychology, 10*(2), 253–270. https://doi.org/10.1177/147470491201000207

Arnocky, S., & Vaillancourt, T. (2017). Sexual competition among women: A review of the theory and supporting evidence. In M. Fisher (Ed.), *The Oxford handbook of women and competition* (pp. 25–39). Oxford University Press.

Arnocky, S., Woodruff, N., & Schmitt, D. P. (2016). Men's sociosexuality is sensitive to changes in mate availability. *Personal Relationships, 23*(1), 172–181. https://doi.org/10.1111/pere.12118

Babcock, J. C., Snead, A. L., Bennett, V. E., & Armenti, N. A. (2019). Distinguishing subtypes of mutual violence in the context of self-defense: Classifying types of partner violent couples using a modified Conflict Tactics Scale. *Journal of Family Violence, 34*(7), 687–696. https://doi.org/10.1007/s10896-018-0012-2

Bair-Merritt, M. H., Shea Crowne, S., Thompson, D. A., Sibinga, E., Trent, M., & Campbell, J. (2010). Why do women use intimate partner violence? A systematic review of women's motivations. *Trauma, Violence, & Abuse, 11*(4), 178–189. https://doi.org/10.1177/1524838010379003

Balci, Y. G., & Ayranci, U. (2005). Physical violence against women: Evaluation of women assaulted by spouses. *Journal of Clinical Forensic Medicine, 12*(5), 258–263. https://doi.org/10.1016/j.jcfm.2005.03.006

Barash, D. P. (1977). Sociobiology of rape in mallards (*Anas platyrhynchos*): Responses of the mated male. *Science, 197*(4305), 788–789. https://science.sciencemag.org/content/197/4305/788

Barbaro, N. (2017). Violence to control women's sexuality. In T. K. Shackelford & V. A. Weekes-Shackelford (Eds.), *Encyclopedia of evolutionary psychological science*. Springer. https://doi.org/10.1007/978-3-319-16999-6_898-1pp. 8407–8412.

Barbaro, N., Pham, M. N., & Shackelford, T. K. (2015). Solving the problem of partner infidelity: Individual mate retention, coalitional mate retention, and in-pair copulation frequency. *Personality and Individual Differences, 82*, 67–71. https://doi.org/10.1016/j.paid.2015.02.033

Barbaro, N., Pham, M. N., Shackelford, T. K., & Zeigler-Hill, V. (2016). Insecure romantic attachment dimensions and frequency of mate retention behaviors. *Personal Relationships, 23*(3), 605–618. https://doi.org/10.1111/pere.12146

Barbaro, N., Sela, Y., Atari, M., Shackelford, T. K., & Zeigler-Hill, V. (2019). Romantic attachment and mate retention behavior: The mediating role of perceived risk of partner infidelity. *Journal of Social and Personal Relationships, 36*(3), 940–956. https://doi.org/10.1177/0265407517749330

Barbaro, N., & Shackelford, T. K. (2016). Female-directed violence as a form of sexual coercion in humans (*Homo sapiens*). *Journal of Comparative Psychology, 130*, 321–327. https://doi.org/10.1037/com0000038

Barbaro, N., & Shackelford, T. K. (2019). Environmental unpredictability in childhood is associated with anxious romantic attachment and intimate partner violence perpetration. *Journal of Interpersonal Violence, 34*(2), 240–269. https://doi.org/10.1177/0886260516640548

Barkow, J. H., Cosmides, L., & Tooby, J. (Eds.). (1992). *The adapted mind: Evolutionary psychology and the generation of culture*. Oxford University Press.

Barmak, S. (2018, December 7). *What happens after the affair—when you have kids*. Today's Parent. https://www.macleans.ca/society/life/what-happens-after-the-affair-when-you-have-kids/

Bartlett, T. Q., Sussman, R. W., & Cheverud, J. M. (1993). Infant killing in primates: A review of observed cases with specific reference to the sexual selection hypothesis. *American Anthropologist, 95*(4), 958–990. https://doi.org/10.1525/aa.1993.95.4.02a00090

Basile, K. C., Smith, S. G., Liu, Y., Kresnow, M. J., Fasula, A. M., Gilbert, L., & Chen, J. (2018). Rape-related pregnancy and association with reproductive coercion in the US. *American Journal of Preventive Medicine, 55*(6), 770–776. https://doi.org/10.1016/j.amepre.2018.07.028

Baumeister, R. F., & Tice, D. M. (1990). Point-counterpoints: Anxiety and social exclusion. *Journal of Social and Clinical Psychology, 9*(2), 165–195. https://doi.org/10.1521/jscp.1990.9.2.165

Bhogal, M. S., Rhead, C., & Tudor, C. (2019). Understanding digital dating abuse from an evolutionary perspective: Further evidence for the role of mate value discrepancy. *Personality and Individual Differences, 151*, 109552 https://doi.org/10.1016/j.paid.2019.109552

Biggs, M. A., Gould, H., & Foster, D. G. (2013). Understanding why women seek abortions in the US. *BMC Women's Health, 13*, 1–13.. https://doi.org/10.1186/1472-6874-13-29

Blake, K. R., & Brooks, R. C. (2019). Status anxiety mediates the positive relationship between income inequality and sexualization. *Proceedings of the National Academy of Sciences, 116*(50), 25029–25033. https://doi.org/10.1073/pnas.1909806116

Blake, K. R., & Denson, T. F. (2017). Contexts for men's aggression against men. In T. K. Shackelford & V. A. Weekes-Shackelford (Eds.), *Encyclopedia of evolutionary psychological science*. Springer. (pp. 1–10). https://doi.org/10.1007/978-3-319-16999-6

Breiding, M. J. (2014). *Prevalence and characteristics of sexual violence, stalking, and intimate partner violence victimization—National Intimate Partner and Sexual Violence Survey, United States, 2011*. Centers for Disease Control and Prevention. https://www.cdc.gov/mmwr/preview/mmwrhtml/ss6308a1.htm

Brewer, G., & Riley, C. (2009). Height, relationship satisfaction, jealousy, and mate retention. *Evolutionary Psychology, 7*(3), 477–489. https://doi.org/10.1177/147470490900700310

Brown, R. P., Baughman, K., & Carvallo, M. (2018). Culture, masculine honor, and violence toward women. *Personality and Social Psychology Bulletin, 44*(4), 538–549. https://doi.org/10.1177/0146167217744195

Brown, R. P., & Osterman, L. L. (2012). Culture of honor, violence, and homicide. In T. Shackelford & V. W. Shackelford (Eds.), *Oxford handbook of evolutionary perspectives on violence, homicide, and war* (pp. 218–232). Oxford University Press.

Burch, R. L., & Gallup, G. G., Jr. (2004). Pregnancy as a stimulus for domestic violence. *Journal of Family Violence, 19*, 243–247. https://doi.org/10.1023/B:JOFV.0000032634.40840.48

Buss, D. M. (1990). The evolution of anxiety and social exclusion. *Journal of Social and Clinical Psychology, 9*(2), 196–201. https://doi.org/10.1521/jscp.1990.9.2.196

Buss, D. M. (2000). *The dangerous passion: Why jealousy is as necessary as love and sex*. Free Press.

Buss, D. M. (2002). Human mate guarding. *Neuroendocrinology Letters, 23*, 23–29. https://www.ncbi.nlm.nih.gov/pubmed/12496732

Buss, D. M. (2006). *The murderer next door: Why the mind is designed to kill*. Penguin.

Buss, D. M. (2013). Sexual jealousy. *Psihologijske Teme, 22*(2), 155–182. https://hrcak.srce.hr/108507

Buss, D. M. (2018). Sexual and emotional infidelity: Evolved gender differences in jealousy prove robust and replicable. *Perspectives on Psychological Science, 13*(2), 155–160. https://doi.org/10.1177/1745691617698225

Buss, D. M., & Duntley, J. D. (2011). The evolution of intimate partner violence. *Aggression & Violent Behavior, 16*, 411–419. https://doi.org/10.1016/j.avb.2011.04.015

Buss, D. M., & Duntley, J. D. (2014). Intimate partner violence in evolutionary perspective. In T. K. Shackelford & R. D. Hansen (Eds.), *The evolution of violence* (pp. 1–22). Springer.

Buss, D. M., Haselton, M. G., Shackelford, T. K., Bleske, A. L., & Wakefield, J. C. (1998). Adaptations, exaptations, and spandrels. *American Psychologist, 53*(5), 533–548. https://doi.org/10.1037//0003-066x.53.5.533

Buss, D. M., Larsen, R. J., Westen, D., & Semmelroth, J. (1992). Sex differences in jealousy: Evolution, physiology, and psychology. *Psychological Science, 3*(4), 251–255. https://doi.org/10.1111/j.1467-9280.1992.tb00038.x

Buss, D. M., & Shackelford, T. K. (1997a). From vigilance to violence: Mate retention tactics in married couples. *Journal of Personality and Social Psychology, 72*(2), 346–361. https://doi.org/10.1037/0022-3514.72.2.346

Buss, D. M., & Shackelford, T. K. (1997b). Human aggression in evolutionary psychological perspective. *Clinical Psychology Review, 17*(6), 605–619. https://doi.org/10.1016/S0272-7358(97)00037-8

Buss, D. M., Shackelford, T. K., Kirkpatrick, L. A., Choe, J. C., Lim, H. K., Hasegawa, M., Hasegawa, T., & Bennett, K. (1999). Jealousy and the nature of beliefs about infidelity: Tests of competing hypotheses about sex differences in the United States, Korea, and Japan. *Personal Relationships, 6*, 125–150. https://doi.org/10.1111/j.1475-6811.1999.tb00215.x

Buss, D. M., Shackelford, T. K., & McKibbin, W. F. (2008). The mate retention inventory-shortform (MRI-SF). *Personality and Individual Differences, 44*, 322–334. https://doi.org/10.1016/j.paid.2007.08.013

Buunk, A. P., & Massar, K. (2021). Intimate partner violence in Nicaragua: The role of possessive jealousy, intrasexual competitiveness, life history, mate value, and stress. *Journal of Interpersonal Violence, 36* (15 – 16), NP8101 – NP818123. https://doi.org/10.1177/0886260519842854

Buunk, A. P., Park, J. H., Zurriaga, R., Klavina, L., & Massar, K. (2008). Height predicts jealousy differently for men and women. *Evolution and Human Behavior, 29*(2), 133– 139. https://doi.org/10.1016/j.evolhumbehav.2007.11.006

Camilleri, J. A., & Miele, M. M. (2017). Perpetrators of intimate partner sexual violence: Characteristics, motivations, and implications for assessment and intervention. In L. McOrmond-Plummer, J. Y. Levy-Peck, & P. Easteal (Eds), *Perpetrators of intimate partner sexual violence: Prevention, recognition, and intervention* (pp. 55–66). Routledge.

Camilleri, J. A., & Quinsey, V. L. (2009). Testing the cuckoldry risk hypothesis of partner sexual coercion in community and forensic samples. *Evolutionary Psychology, 7*(2), 164–178. https://doi.org/10.1177/147470490900700203

Campbell, A. (1999). Staying alive: Evolution, culture, and women's intrasexual aggression. *Behavioral and Brain Sciences, 22*(2), 203–214. https://doi.org/10.1017/S0140525X99001818

Campion, J. F., Cravens, J. M., & Covan, F. (1988). A study of filicidal men. *American Journal of Psychiatry, 145*, 1141–1144. https://doi.org/10.1176/ajp.145.9.1141

Carré, J. M., McCormick, C. M., & Hariri, A. R. (2011). The social neuroendocrinology of human aggression. *Psychoneuroendocrinology, 36*(7), 935–944. https://doi.org/10.1016/j.psyneuen.2011.02.001

Cheng, K. M., Burns, J. T., & McKinney, F. (1983). Forced copulation in captive mallards III. Sperm competition. *The Auk, 100*(2), 302–310. https://doi.org/10.1093/auk/100.2.302

Chibber, K. S., Biggs, M. A., Roberts, S. C., & Foster, D. G. (2014). The role of intimate partners in women's reasons for seeking abortion. *Women's Health Issues, 24*(1), e131– e138. https://doi.org/10.1016/j.whi.2013.10.007

Chimbos, P. D. (1978). *Marital violence: A study of interspouse homicide*. R & E Research Associates.

Clutton-Brock, T. H., & Parker, G. A. (1995). Sexual coercion in animal societies. *Animal Behavior, 49* (5), 1345–1365. https://doi.org/10.1006/anbe.1995.0166

Confer, J. C., Easton, J. A., Fleischman, D. S., Goetz, C. D., Lewis, D. M., Perilloux, C., & Buss, D. M. (2010). Evolutionary psychology: Controversies, questions, prospects, and limitations. *American Psychologist, 65*(2), 110–126. https://doi.org/10.1037/a0018413

Conroy, A. (2014). Marital infidelity and intimate partner violence in rural Malawi: A dyadic investigation. *Archives of Sexual Behavior, 43*(7), 1303–1314. https://doi.org/ 10.1007/s10508-014-0306-2

Counts, D. A. (1992). "All men do it": Wife beating in Kaliai, Papua New Guinea. In D. A. Counts, J. K. Brown, & J. C. Campbell (Eds.), *Sanctions and sanctuary: Cultural perspectives on the beating of wives* (pp. 63–76). Westview Press.

Cousins, A. J., & Gangestad, S. W. (2007). Perceived threats of female infidelity, male proprietariness, and violence in college dating couples. *Violence and Victims, 22*(6), 651– 668. https://doi.org/10.1891/088667007782793156

Cox, D. (2008, January 9). *The evolutionary biology and economics of sexual behavior and infidelity*. Paper prepared for the *American Economic Association ASSA Meetings*, San Francisco.

Coyne, S. M., Nelson, D. A., Carroll, J. S., Smith, N. J., Yang, C., Holmgren, H. G., & Johnson, C. (2017). Relational aggression and marital quality: A five-year longitudinal study. *Journal of Family Psychology, 31*(3), 282–293. http://dx.doi.org/10.1037/fam0000274

Crippen, T. (2018). Evolutionary behavioral science: Core principles, common misconceptions, and a troubling tendency. In R. L. Hopcroft (Ed.), *The Oxford handbook of evolution, biology, and society* (pp. 423–450). Oxford University Press.

Daly, M. (2014). Evolutionary perspectives on sex, gender, and crime. In R. Gartner & B. McCarthy (Eds.), *The Oxford handbook of gender, sex, and crime* (pp. 245–259). Oxford University Press.

Daly, M. (2017). *Killing the competition: Economic inequality and homicide*. Routledge.

Daly, M., & Wilson, M. (1988). *Homicide*. Aldine de Gruyter.

Daly, M., & Wilson, M. (1990). Killing the competition. *Human Nature, 1*(1), 81–107. https://doi.org/10.1007/BF02692147

Daly, M., & Wilson, M. (1992). The man who mistook his wife for a chattel. In J. H. Barkow, L. Cosmides, & J. Tooby (Eds.), *The adapted mind: Evolutionary psychology and the generation of culture* (pp. 289–322). Oxford University Press.

Daly, M., & Wilson, M. I. (1994). Some differential attributes of lethal assaults on small children by stepfathers versus genetic fathers. *Ethology and Sociobiology, 15*, 207–217. https://doi.org/10.1016/0162-3095(94)90014-0

Daly, M., & Wilson, M. (2008). Is the "Cinderella effect" controversial? In C. Crawford & D. Krebs (Eds.), *Foundations of evolutionary psychology* (pp. 383–400). Taylor & Francis/Erlbaum.

Daly, M., Wilson, M., & Vasdev, S. (2001). Income inequality and homicide rates in Canada and the United States. *Canadian Journal of Criminology, 43*, 219–236. https://psycnet.apa.org/record/2003- 99209-003

Daly, M., Wilson, M., & Weghorst, S. J. (1982). Male sexual jealousy. *Ethology and Sociobiology, 3*, 11–27. https://doi.org/10.1016/0162-3095(82)90027-9

Danel, D. P., Siennicka, A., Glińska, K., Fedurek, P., Nowak Szczepańska, N., Jankowska, E. A., & Lewandowski, Z. (2017). Female perception of a partner's mate value discrepancy and controlling behavior in romantic relationships. *Acta Ethologica, 20*(1), 1–8. https://doi.org/10.1007/s10211-016-0240-5

Davis, A. C., Belanger, J., Mattsson, A., & Arnocky, S. (2019). Hostility mediates the relations between self-perceived physical health status and cost-inflicting mate retention. *Evolutionary Behavioral Sciences, 16* (1), 1 – 13. . https://doi.org/10.1037/ebs0000188

Davis, A. C., Desrochers, J., DiFilippo, A., Vaillancourt, T., & Arnocky, S. (2018). Type of jealousy differentially predicts cost-inflicting and benefit-provisioning mate retention. *Personal Relationships, 25*(4), 596–610. https://doi.org/10.1111/pere.12262

Davis, A. C., Vaillancourt, T., & Arnocky, S., & (2016). Men's sexual jealousy. In T. K. Shackelford & V. A. Weekes-Shackelford (Eds.), *The encyclopedia of evolutionary psychological science*. Springer(pp. 1 – 8). . https://doi.org/10.1007/978-3-319-16999-6_871-1

Davis, A., Vaillancourt, T., Arnocky, S., & Doyel, R. (2019). Women's gossip as an intrasexual competition strategy: An evolutionary approach to gender and discrimination. In F. Giardini & R. Wittek (Eds.), *The Oxford handbook of gossip and reputation* (pp. 303–321). Oxford University Press. https://doi.org/10.1093/oxfordhb/9780190494087.013.16

Dayan, H. (2018). *Femicide and the law: American criminal doctrines*. Routledge.

Devries, K. M., Mak, J. Y., Garcia-Moreno, C., Petzold, M., Child, J. C., Falder, G., . . . Pallitto, C. (2013). The global prevalence of intimate partner violence against women. *Science, 340*(6140), 1527–1528. https://science.sciencemag.org/content/340/6140/1527

Dijkstra, P., & Buunk, B. P. (2002). Sex differences in the jealousy-evoking effect of rival characteristics. *European Journal of Social Psychology, 32*(6), 829–852. https://doi.org/10.1002/ejsp.125

Dobash, R. E., Dobash, R. P., Cavanagh, K., & Lewis, R. (2004). Not an ordinary killer just an ordinary guy: When men murder an intimate woman partner. *Violence Against Women, 10*, 577–605. https://doi.org/10.1177/1077801204265015

Dressler, J. (2002). Why keep the provocation defence: Some reflections on a difficult subject. *Minnesota Law Review, 86*, 959–1002. https://heinonline.org/HOL/LandingPage?handle=hein.journals/mnlr86&div=27&id=&page=

Duntley, J. D., & Buss, D. M. (2005). The plausibility of adaptations for homicide. In P. Carruthers, S. Laurence, & S. Stich (Eds.), *The innate mind: Structure and contents* (pp. 291–304). Oxford University Press.

Duntley, J. D., & Shackelford, T. K. (2012). Adaptations to avoid victimization. *Aggression and Violent Behavior*, *17*(1), 59–71. https://doi.org/10.1016/j.avb.2011.09.008

Dutton, D. G., & Kerry, G. (1999). Modus operandi and personality disorder in incarcerated spousal killers. *International Journal of Law and Psychiatry*, *22*, 287–299. https://doi.org/10.1016/s0160-2527(99)00010-2

Ein-Dor, T., Perry-Paldi, A., Hirschberger, G., Birnbaum, G. E., & Deutsch, D. (2015). Coping with mate poaching: Gender differences in detection of infidelity-related threats. *Evolution and Human Behavior*, *36*(1), 17–24. https://doi.org/10.1016/j.evolhumbehav.2014.08.002

Erens, B., McManus, S., Field, J., Korovessis, C., Johnson, A., Fenton, K., et al. (2001). *National survey of sexual attitudes and lifestyles II: Technical report*. National Centre for Social Research. http://www.natsal.ac.uk/media/2081/technical_report.pdf

Evzonas, N. (2018). Jealousy as a driving force for murder. *Psychoanalytic Review*, *105*(3), 257–277. https://doi.org/10.1521/prev.2018.105.3.257

Fincham, F. D., & May, R. W. (2017). Infidelity in romantic relationships. *Current Opinion in Psychology*, *13*, 70–74. https://doi.org/10.1016/j.copsyc.2016.03.008

Fisher, M., Cox, A., Bennett, S., & Gavric, D. (2008). Components of self-perceived mate value. *Journal of Social, Evolutionary, and Cultural Psychology*, *2*(4), 156–168. http://dx.doi.org/10.1037/h0099347

Fitz-Gibbon, K., & Pickering, S. (2012). Homicide law reform in Victoria, Australia: From provocation to defensive homicide and beyond. *British Journal of Criminology*, *52*(1), 159–180. https://doi.org/10.1093/bjc/azr060

Flynn, A., & Graham, K. (2010). "Why did it happen?": A review and conceptual framework for research on perpetrators' and victims' explanations for intimate partner violence. *Aggression and Violent Behavior*, *15*(3), 239–251. https://doi.org/10.1016/j.avb.2010.01.002

Fox, J. A., & Fridel, E. E. (2017). Gender differences in patterns and trends in US homicide, 1976–2015. *Violence and Gender*, *4*(2), 37–43. https://doi.org/10.1089/vio.2017.0016

French, J. A., Cavanaugh, J., Mustoe, A. C., Carp, S. B., & Womack, S. L. (2018). Social monogamy in non-human primates: Phylogeny, phenotype, and physiology. *Journal of Sex Research*, *55*(4-5), 410–434. https://doi.org/10.1080/00224499.2017.1339774

Friedman, S. H., Cavney, J., & Resnick, P. J. (2012). Mothers who kill: Evolutionary underpinnings and infanticide law. *Behavioral Sciences & the Law*, *30*(5), 585–597. https://doi.org/10.1002/bsl.2034

Friedman, S. H., Horwitz, S. M., & Resnick, P. J. (2005). Child murder by mothers: A critical analysis of the current state of knowledge and a research agenda. *American Journal of Psychiatry*, *162*(9), 1578–1587. https://doi.org/10.1176/appi.ajp.162.9.1578

Friedman, S. H., & Resnick, P. J. (2007). Child murder by mothers: Patterns and prevention. *World Psychiatry*, *6*(3), 137–141. https://www.ncbi.nlm.nih.gov/pmc/articles/PMC2174580/

Gangestad, S. W., Thornhill, R., & Garver, C. E. (2002). Changes in women's sexual interests and their partners' mate retention tactics across the menstrual cycle: Evidence for shifting conflicts of interest. *Proceedings of the Royal Society of London: B Biological Sciences*, *269*, 975–982. https://doi.org/10.1098/rspb.2001.1952

Garber, C. M. (1947). Eskimo infanticide. *Scientific Monthly*, *64*(2), 98–102. https://www.jstor.org/stable/19306

García-Moreno, C., Jansen, H. A. F. M., Ellsberg, M., Heise, L., & Watts, C. (2005). *WHO multi-country study on women's health and domestic violence against women*. World Health Organization. https://www.who.int/reproductivehealth/publications/violence/24159358X/en/

Geary, D. (2000). Evolution and proximate expression of human paternal investment. *Psychological Bulletin*, *126*, 55–77. https://doi.org/10.1037/0033-2909.126.1.55

Genest, A., & Mathieu, C. (2014). Intimate partner violence: The role of attachment on men's anger. *Partner Abuse*, *5*, 375–387. http://dx.doi.org/10.1891/1946-6560.5.4.375

Georgantopoulos, M. A. (2019, April 25). A man allegedly killed a 4-month-old baby when he found out he wasn't the father. *BuzzFeed News*. https://www.buzzfeednews.com/article/maryanngeorgantopoulos/tennessee-memphis-man-kills-baby-not-father

Giordano, P. C., Copp, J. E., Longmore, M. A., & Manning, W. D. (2016). Anger, control, and intimate partner violence in young adulthood. *Journal of Family Violence*, *31*(1), 1–13. https://doi.org/10.1007/s10896-015-9753-3

Goetting, A. (1988). When parents kill their young children: Detroit 1982–1986. *Journal of Family Violence, 3*, 339–346. https://doi.org/10.1007/BF00989982

Goetz, A. T., & Causey, K. (2009). Sex differences in perceptions of infidelity: Men often assume the worst. *Evolutionary Psychology, 7*(2), 253–263. https://doi.org/10.1177/147470490900700208

Goetz, A. T., & Shackelford, T. K. (2006). Sexual coercion and forced in-pair copulation as sperm competition tactics in humans. *Human Nature, 17*, 265–282. https://doi.org/10.1007/s12110-006-1009-8

Goetz, A. T., & Shackelford, T. K. (2009). Sexual coercion in intimate relationships: A comparative analysis of the effects of women's infidelity and men's dominance and control. *Archives of Sexual Behavior, 38*(2), 226–234. https://doi.org/10.1007/s10508- 008-9353-x

Goetz, A. T., Shackelford, T. K., & Camilleri, J. A. (2008). Proximate and ultimate explanations are required for a comprehensive understanding of partner rape. *Aggression and Violent Behavior, 13*, 119–123. https://doi.org/10.1016/j.avb.2008.02.002

Goetz, A. T., Shackelford, T. K., Romero, G. A., Kaighobadi, F., & Miner, E. J. (2008). Punishment, proprietariness, and paternity: Men's violence against women from an evolutionary perspective. *Aggression and Violent Behavior, 13*(6), 481–489. https://doi.org/10.1016/j.avb.2008.07.004

Goetz, A. T., Shackelford, T. K., Weekes-Shackelford, V. A., Euler, H. A., Hoier, S., Schmitt, D.P., & LaMunyon, C. W. (2005). Mate retention, semen displacement, and human sperm competition: A preliminary investigation of tactics to prevent and correct female infidelity. *Personality and Individual Differences, 38*(4), 749–763. https://doi.org/10.1016/j.paid.2004.05.028

Gottschall, J. A., & Gottschall, T. A. (2003). Are per-incident rape-pregnancy rates higher than per-incident consensual pregnancy rates? *Human Nature, 14*(1), 1–20. https://doi.org/10.1007/s12110-003-1014-0

Graham-Kevan, N., & Archer, J. (2003). Intimate terrorism and common couple violence: A test of Johnson's predictions in four British samples. *Journal of Interpersonal Violence, 18*(11), 1247–1270. https://doi.org/10.1177/0886260503256656

Graham-Kevan, N., & Archer, J. (2009). Control tactics and partner violence in heterosexual relationships. *Evolution and Human Behavior, 30*(6), 445–452. https://doi.org/10.1016/j.evolhumbehav.2009.06.007

Grant, I., & Parles, D. (2017). Equality and the defence of provocation: Irreconcilable differences. *Dalhousie Law Journal, 40*(2), 455–495. https://commons.allard.ubc.ca/cgi/viewcontent.cgi?article=1505&context=fac_pubs

Grebe, N. M., Gangestad, S. W., Garver-Apgar, C. E., & Thornhill, R. (2013). Women's luteal-phase sexual proceptivity and the functions of extended sexuality. *Psychological Science, 24*(10), 2106–2110. https://doi.org/10.1177/0956797613485965

Gruber, A. (2015). A provocative defense. *California Law Review, 103*, 273–333. https://heinonline.org/HOL/LandingPage?handle=hein.journals/calr103&div=11&id=&page=

Grubin, D. (1992). Sexual offending: A cross-cultural comparison. *Annual Review of Sex Research, 3*(1), 201–217. https://doi.org/10.1080/10532528.1992.10559879

Hall, J. H., & Fincham, F. D. (2006). Relationship dissolution following infidelity: The roles of attributions and forgiveness. *Journal of Social and Clinical Psychology, 25*(5), 508–522. https://doi.org/10.1521/jscp.2006.25.5.508

Hartley-Parkinson, R. (2019, June 5). Man killed baby boy after being told he was "possibly" not the child's father. *Metro News.* https://metro.co.uk/2019/06/05/man-killed-baby-boy-told-possibly-not-childs-father-9812454/

Haselton, M. G., & Gildersleeve, K. (2011). Can men detect ovulation? *Current Directions in Psychological Science, 20*(2), 87–92. https://doi.org/10.1177/0963721411402668

Havlíček, J., Cobey, K. D., Barrett, L., Klapilová, K., & Roberts, S. C. (2015). The spandrels of Santa Barbara? A new perspective on the peri-ovulation paradigm. *Behavioral Ecology, 26*(5), 1249–1260. https://doi.org/10.1093/beheco/arv064

He, S., & Tsang, S. (2017). Perceived female infidelity and male sexual coercion concerning first sex in Chinese college students' dating relationships: The mediating role of male partners' attachment insecurity. *Personality and Individual Differences, 111*, 146–152. https://doi.org/10.1016/j.paid.2017.02.016

Hilari, C. D., Condori, I., & Dearden, K. A. (2009). When is deliberate killing of young children justified? Indigenous interpretations of infanticide in Bolivia. *Social Science & Medicine, 68*(2), 352–361. https://doi.org/10.1016/j.socscimed.2008.10.009

Hill, K., & Hurtado, M. (1996). *Ache life history: The ecology and demography of a foraging people.* Aldine de Gruyter.

Hiraiwa-Hasegawa, M. (2005). Homicide by men in Japan, and its relationship to age, resources and resources. *Evolution and Human Behavior*, *26*, 332–343. https://doi.org/10.1016/j.evolhumbehav.2004.12.003

Horder, J., & Fitz-Gibbon, K. (2015). When sexual infidelity triggers murder: Examining the impact of homicide law reform on judicial attitudes in sentencing. *Cambridge Law Journal*, *74*(2), 307–328. https://doi.org/10.1017/S0008197315000318

Holt, W. V., & Fazeli, A. (2016). Sperm storage in the female reproductive tract. *Annual Review of Animal Biosciences*, *4*, 291–310. https://doi.org/10.1146/annurev-animal-021815-111350

Hrdy, S. B. (1979). Infanticide among animals: A review, classification, and examination of the implications for the reproductive strategies of females. *Ethology and Sociobiology*, *1*(1), 13–40. https://doi.org/10.1016/0162-3095(79)90004-9

Hrdy, S. B. (1999). *Mother nature: A history of mothers, infants and natural selection*, Pantheon/Random House.

Hughes, S. M., & Harrison, M. A. (2017). Your cheatin' voice will tell on you: Detection of past infidelity from voice. *Evolutionary Psychology*, *15*(2), 1–12. https://doi.org/10.1177/1474704917711513

Jasinski, J. L. (2004). Pregnancy and domestic violence: A review of the literature. *Trauma, Violence, & Abuse*, *5*(1), 47–64. https://doi.org/10.1177/1524838003259322

Kaighobadi, F., Shackelford, T. K., & Goetz, A. T. (2009). From mate retention to murder: Evolutionary psychological perspectives on men's partner-directed violence. *Review of General Psychology*, *13*(4), 327–334. https://doi.org/10.1037/a0017254

Kaighobadi, F., Shackelford, T. K., & Goetz, A. T. (2012). Sexual conflict in mateships: From mate retention to murder. In T. K. Shackelford & A. T. Goetz (Eds.), *Oxford handbook of sexual conflict in humans* (pp. 269–279). Oxford University Press.

Kaighobadi, F., Starratt, V. G., Shackelford, T. K., & Popp, D. (2008). Male mate retention mediates the relationship between female sexual infidelity and female directed violence. *Personality and Individual Differences*, *44*, 1422–1431. https://doi.org/10.1016/j.paid.2007.12.010

Kapiga, S., Harvey, S., Muhammad, A. K., Stöckl, H., Mshana, G., Hashim, R., Hansen, C., Lees, S., & Watts, C. (2017). Prevalence of intimate partner violence and abuse and associated factors among women enrolled into a cluster randomised trial in northwestern Tanzania. *BMC Public Health*, *17*(1), 1–11. https://doi.org/10.1186/s12889-017-4119-9

Karamagi, C. A., Tumwine, J. K., Tylleskar, T., & Heggenhougen, K. (2006). Intimate partner violence against women in eastern Uganda: Implications for HIV prevention. *BMC Public Health*, *6*(1), 1–12. https://doi.org/10.1186/1471-2458-6-284

Keetley, D. (2008). From anger to jealousy: Explaining domestic homicide in antebellum America. *Journal of Social History*, *42*(2), 269–297. https://www.jstor.org/stable/27696441

Kelly, E. L., & Conley, J. J. (1987). Personality and compatibility: A prospective analysis of marital stability and marital satisfaction. *Journal of Personality and Social Psychology*, *52* (1), 27–40. https://doi.org/10.1037/0022-3514.52.1.27

Kesserling, K. (2016). No greater provocation? Adultery and the mitigation of murder in English law. *American Society for Legal History*, *34*(1), 199–225. https://doi.org/10.1017/S0738248015000681

Kim, K. J., Feeney, B. C., & Jakubiak, B. K. (2018). Touch reduces romantic jealousy in the anxiously attached. *Journal of Social and Personal Relationships*, *35*(7), 1019–1041. https://doi.org/10.1177/0265407517702012

Kleiman, D. G. (1977). Monogamy in mammals. *Quarterly Review of Biology*, *52*(1), 39–69. https://doi.org/10.1086/409721

Kruger, D. J., Fisher, M. L., Edelstein, R. S., Chopik, W. J., Fitzgerald, C. J., & Strout, S. L. (2013). Was that cheating? Perceptions vary by sex, attachment anxiety, and behavior. *Evolutionary Psychology*, *11*(1), 159–171. https://doi.org/10.1177/147470491301100115

Kruger, D. J., Fisher, M. L., Fitzgerald, C. J., Garcia, J. R., Geher, G., & Guitar, A. E. (2015). Sexual and emotional aspects are distinct components of infidelity and unique predictors of anticipated distress. *Evolutionary Psychological Science*, *1*(1), 44–51. https://doi.org/10.1007/s40806-015-0010-z

Kunz, J., & Bahr, S. J. (1996). A profile of parental homicide against children. *Journal of Family Violence*, *11*(4), 347–362. https://doi.org/10.1007/BF02333422

Lalumière, M. L., Harris, G. T., Quinsey, V. L., & Rice, M. E. (Eds.). (2005). *The causes of rape: Understanding individual differences in male propensity for sexual aggression*. American Psychological Association. https://doi.org/10.1037/10961-000

Larmuseau, M. H. D., Matthijs, K., & Wenseleers, T. (2016). Cuckolded fathers rare in human populations. *Trends in Ecology & Evolution*, *31*(5), 327–329. https://doi.org/10.1016/j.tree.2016.03.004

Liem, M., Postulart, M., & Nieuwbeerta, P. (2009). Homicide-suicide in the Netherlands: An epidemiology. *Homicide Studies*, *13*(2), 99–123. https://doi.org/10.1177/1088767908330833

Madsen, C., Stith, S., Thomsen, C., & McCollum, E. (2012). Therapy-seeking violent couples: Bilateral and unilateral violence. *Partner Abuse*, *3*(1), 43–58. https://doi.org/10.1891/1946-6560.3.1.43

Marcikić, M., Dumenčić, B., Matuzalem, E., Marjanović, K., Požgain, I., & Ugljarević, M. (2006). Infanticide in eastern Croatia. *Collegium Antropologicum*, *30*(2), 437–442. https://www.ncbi.nlm.nih.gov/pubmed/16848164

Marks, I. F. M., & Nesse, R. M. (1994). Fear and fitness: An evolutionary analysis of anxiety disorders. *Ethology & Sociobiology*, *15*(5–6), 247–261. http://dx.doi.org/10.1016/0162-3095(94)90002-7

Marleau, J. D., Poulin, B., Webanck, T., Roy, R. R., & Laporte, L. (1999). Paternal filicide: A study of 10 men. *Canadian Journal of Psychiatry*, *44*, 57–63. https://doi.org/10.1177/070674379904400107

Martin, E. K., Taft, C. T., & Resick, P. A. (2007). A review of marital rape. *Aggression and Violent Behavior*, *12*(3), 329–347. https://doi.org/10.1016/j.avb.2006.10.003

Martin, L. (2006, November 5). Fathers who kill their children. *Guardian*. https://www.theguardian.com/uk/2006/nov/05/ukcrime.lornamartin

Martin, S. L., Harris-Brit, A., Li, Y., Moracco, K. E., Kupper, L. L., & Campbell, J. C. (2004). Changes in intimate partner violence during pregnancy. *Journal of Family Violence*, *19*, 201–210. https://doi.org/10.1023/B:JOFV.0000032630.50593.93

McFarlane, J. (2007). Pregnancy following partner rape: What we know and what we need to know. *Trauma, Violence, & Abuse*, *8*(2), 127–134. https://doi.org/10.1177/1524838007301222

McKinney, F., Cheng, K. M., & Bruggers, D. J. (1984). Sperm competition in apparently monogamous birds. In R. L. Smith (Ed.), *Sperm competition and evolution of animal mating systems* (pp. 523–545). Academic Press.

Meyer, I. H. (2003). Prejudice, social stress, and mental health in lesbian, gay, and bisexual populations: Conceptual issues and research evidence. *Psychological Bulletin*, *129*(5), 674–697. https://dx.doi.org/10.1037%2F0033-2909.129.5.674

Miller, S. L., & Maner, J. K. (2008). Coping with romantic betrayal: Sex differences in responses to partner infidelity. *Evolutionary Psychology*, *6*(3), 413–426. https://doi.org/10.1177/147470490800600305

Miner, E. J., Shackelford, T. K., & Starratt, V. G. (2009). Mate value of romantic partners predicts men's partner-directed verbal insults. *Personality and Individual Differences*, *46*, 135–139. https://doi.org/10.1016/j.paid.2008.09.015

Miner, E. J., Starratt, V. G., & Shackelford, T. K. (2009). It's not all about her: Men's mate value and mate retention. *Personality and Individual Differences*, *47*, 214–218. https://doi.org/10.1016/j.paid.2009.03.002

Mize, K. D., Shackelford, T. K., & Weekes-Shackelford, V. A. (2011). Younger women incur excess risk of uxoricide by stabbing and other hands-on killing methods. *Personality and Individual Differences*, *50*(7), 1120–1125. https://doi.org/10.1016/j.paid.2011.01.038

Morland, L. A., Leskin, G. A., Rebecca Block, C., Campbell, J. C., & Friedman, M. J. (2008). Intimate partner violence and miscarriage: Examination of the role of physical and psychological abuse and posttraumatic stress disorder. *Journal of Interpersonal Violence*, *23*(5), 652–669. https://doi.org/10.1177/0886260507313533

Nascimento, B. S., & Little, A. (2020). Mate retention behaviors and jealousy in hypothetical mate-poaching situations: Measuring the effects of sex, context, and rivals' attributes. *Evolutionary Psychological Science*, *6*(1), 20–29. https://doi.org/10.1007/s40806-019-00207-y

Neal, A. M., & Lemay, E. P. (2019). The wandering eye perceives more threats: Projection of attraction to alternative partners predicts anger and negative behavior in romantic relationships. *Journal of Social and Personal Relationships*, *36*(2), 450–468. https://doi.org/10.1177/0265407517734398

Nemeth, J. M., Bonomi, A. E., Lee, M. A., & Ludwin, J. M. (2012). Sexual infidelity as trigger for intimate partner violence. *Journal of Women's Health*, *21*(9), 942–949. https://doi.org/10.1089/jwh.2011.3328

O'Connor, J. J., Pisanski, K., Tigue, C. C., Fraccaro, P. J., & Feinberg, D. R. (2014). Perceptions of infidelity risk predict women's preferences for low male voice pitch in short-term overlong-term relationship contexts. *Personality and Individual Differences*, *56*, 73–77. https://doi.org/10.1016/j.paid.2013.08.029

O'Connor, J. J., Re, D. E., & Feinberg, D. R. (2011). Voice pitch influences perceptions of sexual infidelity. *Evolutionary Psychology*, *9*(1), 64–78. https://doi.org/10.1177/147470491100900109

Osterman, L. L., & Brown, R. P. (2011). Culture of honor and violence against the self. *Personality and Social Psychology Bulletin*, *37*, 1611–1623. https://doi.org/10.1177/0146167211418529

Palermo, M. T. (2003). Preventing filicide in families with autistic children. *International Journal of Offender Therapy and Comparative Criminology*, *47*(1), 47–57. https://doi.org/10.1177/0306624X02239274

Palombit, R. A. (2015). Infanticide. In P. Whelehan, & A. Bolin (Eds.), *The international encyclopedia of human sexuality* (pp. 583–625). Wiley.

Peters, J., Shackelford, T. K., & Buss, D. M. (2002). Understanding domestic violence against women: Using evolutionary psychology to extend the feminist functional analysis. *Violence and Victims*, *17*(2), 255–264. https://doi.org/10.1891/vivi.17.2.255.33644

Phillips, A. (2010). Indignation or insecurity: The influence of mate value on distress in response to infidelity. *Evolutionary Psychology*, *8*(4), 736–750. https://doi.org/10.1177/147470491000800413

Pillsworth, E. G., & Haselton, M. G. (2006). Male sexual attractiveness predicts differential ovulatory shifts in female extra-pair attraction and male mate retention. *Evolution and Human Behavior*, *27*(4), 247–258. https://doi.org/10.1016/j.evolhumbehav.2005.10.002

Platek, S. M., & Shackelford, T. K. (Eds.). (2006). *Female infidelity and paternal uncertainty: Evolutionary perspectives on male anti-cuckoldry tactics*. Cambridge University Press.

Poole, E., Speight, S., O'Brien, M., Connolly, S., & Aldrich, M. (2013, November 15). *What do we know about non-resident fathers?* Understanding Society. https://www.understandingsociety.ac.uk/research/publications/522028

Quinsey, V. L., & Lalumière, M. L. (1995). Evolutionary perspectives on sexual offending. *Sexual Abuse: A Journal of Research and Treatment*, *7*(4), 301–315. https://doi.org/10.1007/BF02256834

Rattigan, C. (2012). *"What else could I do?": Single mothers and infanticide, 1900–1950*. Irish Academic Press.

Reed, L. A., Tolman, R. M., & Ward, L. M. (2016). Snooping and sexting: Digital media as a context for dating aggression and abuse among college students. *Violence Against Women*, *22*(13), 1556–1576. https://doi.org/10.1177/1077801216630143

Resnick, P. J. (1969). Child murder by parents: A psychiatric review of filicide. *American Journal of Psychiatry*, *126* (3), 325–334. https://doi.org/10.1176/ajp.126.3.325

Resnick, P. J. (2016). Filicide in the United States. *Indian Journal of Psychiatry*, *58*(Suppl 2), S203–S209. https://www.ncbi.nlm.nih.gov/pmc/articles/PMC5282617/

Richerson, P. J., & Boyd, R. (1998). The evolution of human ultra-sociality. In I. Eibl-Eibisfeldt & F. Salter (Eds.), *Ideology, warfare, and indoctrinability* (pp. 71–95). Berghan Books.

Rodriguez, L. M., DiBello, A. M., Øverup, C. S., & Neighbors, C. (2015). The price of distrust: Trust, anxious attachment, jealousy, and partner abuse. *Partner Abuse*, *6*, 298–319. https://doi.org/10.1891/1946-6560.6.3.298

Røsand, G. M. B., Slinning, K., Røysamb, E., & Tambs, K. (2014). Relationship dissatisfaction and other risk factors for future relationship dissolution: A population-based study of 18,523 couples. *Social Psychiatry and Psychiatric Epidemiology*, *49*(1), 109–119. https://doi.org/10.1007/s00127-013-0681-3

Sable, M. R., Danis, F., Mauzy, D. L., & Gallagher, S. K. (2006). Barriers to reporting sexual assault for women and men: Perspectives of college students. *Journal of American College Health*, *55*(3), 157–162. https://doi.org/10.3200/JACH.55.3.157-162

Salkicevic, S., Stanic, A. L., & Grabovac, M. T. (2014). Good mates retain us right: Investigating the relationship between mate retention strategies, mate value, and relationship satisfaction. *Evolutionary Psychology*, *12*(5), 1038–1052. https://doi.org/10.1177/147470491401200512

Scelza, B. A., Prall, S. P., Swinford, N., Gopalan, S., Atkinson, E. G., McElreath, R., . . . Henn, B. M. (2020). High rate of extrapair paternity in a human population demonstrates diversity in human reproductive strategies. *Science Advances*, *6*(8), eaay6195. doi:10.1126/sciadv.aay6195

Schild, C., Stern, J., & Zettler, I. (2020). Linking men's voice pitch to actual and perceived trustworthiness across domains. *Behavioral Ecology*, *31*(1), 164–175. https://doi.org/10.1093/beheco/arz173

Schmitt, D. P. (2005). Sociosexuality from Argentina to Zimbabwe: A 48-nation study of sex, culture, and strategies of human mating. *Behavioral and Brain Sciences*, *28*(2), 247–275. https://doi.org/10.1017/S0140525X05000051

Sela, Y., Mogilski, J. K., Shackelford, T. K., Zeigler-Hill, V., & Fink, B. (2017). Mate value discrepancy and mate retention behaviors of self and partner. *Journal of Personality*, *85*(5), 730–740. https://doi.org/10.1111/jopy.12281

Selk, A. (2018, November 18). He killed his wife and daughters "for a fresh start," a prosecutor said. He'll spend the rest of his life in prison. *Washington Post*. https://www.washingtonpost.com/crime-law/2018/11/19/kids-are-my-life-dad-said-his-missing-family-hes-being-sentenced-their-murders/

Sensoy, N., Dogan, N., Sen, K., Aslan, H., & Baser, A. T. (2015). Unwanted pregnancy and traditional self-induced abortion methods known among women aged 15 to 49. *Journal of the Pakistan Medical Association*, 65(5), 452–456. https://www.ncbi.nlm.nih.gov/pubmed/26028375

Shackelford, T. K. (2003). Preventing, correcting, and anticipating female infidelity: Three adaptive problems of sperm competition. *Evolution and Cognition*, 9(1), 90–96. https://www.researchgate.net/publication/284080152_Preventing_correcting_and_anticip ating_female_infidelity_Three_adaptive_problems_of_sperm_competition

Shackelford, T. K., & Buss, D. M. (1997). Cues to infidelity. *Personality and Social Psychology Bulletin*, 12(10), 1034–1045. https://doi.org/10.1177/01461672972310004

Shackelford, T. K., & Buss, D. M. (2000). Marital satisfaction and spousal cost-infliction. *Personality and Individual Differences*, 28(5), 917–928. https://doi.org/10.1016/S0191-8869(99)00150-6

Shackelford, T. K., Buss, D. M., & Peters, J. (2000). Wife killing: Risk to women as a function of age. *Violence and Victims*, 15(3), 273–282. https://www.ncbi.nlm.nih.gov/pubmed/11200102

Shackelford, T. K., & Goetz, A. T. (2007). Adaptation to sperm competition in humans. *Current Directions in Psychological Science*, 16(1), 47–50. https://doi.org/10.1111/j.1467-8721.2007.00473.x

Shackelford, T. K., Goetz, A. T., Buss, D. M., Euler, H. A., & Hoier, S. (2005). When we hurt the ones we love: Predicting violence against women from men's mate retention. *Personal Relationships*, 12(4), 447–463. https://doi.org/10.1111/j.1475- 6811.2005.00125.x

Shackelford, T. K., Schmitt, D. P., & Buss, D. M. (2005). Universal dimensions of human mate preferences. *Personality and Individual Differences*, 39(2), 447–458. https://doi.org/10.1016/j.paid.2005.01.023

Shields, N. M., & Hanneke, C. R. (1983). Battered wives' reactions to marital rape. In D. Finkelhor, R. J. Gelles, G. T. Hotaling, & M. A. Straus (Eds.), *The dark side of families: Current family violence research* (pp. 131–148). Sage.

Shields, W. M., & Shields, L. M. (1983). Forcible rape: An evolutionary perspective. *Ethology and Sociobiology*, 4, 115–136. https://doi.org/10.1016/0162-3095(83)90026-2

Slater, J. (2012). Sexual infidelity and loss of self-control: Context or camouflage? *Denning Law Journal*, 24, 153–168. https://heinonline.org/HOL/LandingPage?handle= hein.journals/denlj24&div=9&id=&page=

Smuts, B. (1992). Male aggression against women: An evolutionary perspective. *Human Nature*, 3(1), 1–44. https://doi.org/10.1007/BF02692265

Smuts, B. B., & Smuts, R. W. (1993). Male aggression and sexual coercion of females in nonhuman primates and other mammals: Evidence and theoretical implications. In P. J. B. Slater, J. S. Rosenblatt, C. T. Snowdon, & M. Milinski (Eds.), *Advances in the study of behavior* (pp. 1–63). Academic Press.

Starratt, V. G., Shackelford, T. K., Goetz, A. T., & McKibbin, W. F. (2007). Male mate retention behaviors vary with risk of partner infidelity and sperm competition. *Acta Psychologica Sinica*, 39(3), 523–527. https://psycnet.apa.org/record/2007-06914-015

Statistics Canada. (2009, October). *Family violence in Canada: A statistical profile 2008*. https://www150.statcan.gc.ca/n1/pub/85-224-x/85-224-x2008000-eng.pdf

Stöckl, H., Devries, K., Rotstein, A., Abrahams, N., Campbell, J., Watts, C., & Moreno, C. (2013). The global prevalence of intimate partner homicide: A systematic review. *Lancet*, 382(9895), 1–7. http://dx.doi.org/10.1016/S0140-6736(13)61030-2

Straus, M. A. (2009). Why the overwhelming evidence on partner physical violence by women has not been perceived and is often denied. *Journal of Aggression, Maltreatment & Trauma*, 18(6), 552–571. https://doi.org/10.1080/10926770903103081

Stumpf, R. M., & Boesch, C. (2010). Male aggression and sexual coercion in wild West African chimpanzees, *Pan troglodytes verus*. *Animal Behaviour*, 79(2), 333–342. https://doi.org/10.1016/j.anbehav.2009.11.008

Symons, D. (1979). *The evolution of human sexuality*. Oxford University Press.

Taillieu, T. L., & Brownridge, D. A. (2010). Violence against pregnant women: Prevalence, patterns, risk factors, theories, and directions for future research. *Aggression and Violent Behavior*, 15, 14–35. https://doi.org/10.1016/j.avb.2009.07.013

Taylor, R. (2012). The importance of "sexual proprietariness" in theoretical framing and interpretation of pregnancy-associated intimate partner violence and femicide: Through the eyes of a junior scholar. *Homicide Studies*, 16(4), 346–358. https://doi.org/10.1177/1088767912460238

Taylor, R. (2016). Homicide. In W. G. Jennings (Ed.), *The encyclopedia of crime and punishment* (pp. 1–8). Wiley.

Thomas, E. J., Stelzl, M., & Lafrance, M. N. (2017). Faking to finish: Women's accounts of feigning sexual pleasure to end unwanted sex. *Sexualities, 20*(3), 281–301. https://doi.org/10.1177/1363460716649338

Thornhill, R., & Palmer, C. T. (2000). Why men rape. *New York Academy of Sciences, 40*(1), 30–36. https://www.csus.edu/indiv/m/merlinos/thornhill.html

Thornhill, R., & Thornhill, N. W. (1992). The evolutionary psychology of men's coercive sexuality. *Behavioral and Brain Sciences, 15*(2), 363–375. https://doi.org/10.1017/S0140525X00069120

Tooby, J., & Cosmides, L. (1990). The past explains the present: Emotional adaptations and the structure of ancestral environments. *Ethology and Sociobiology, 11*(4–5), 375–424. https://doi.org/10.1016/0162-3095(90)90017-Z

United Nations Office on Drugs and Crime (UNODC). (2019a). *Global study on homicide: Gender-related killing of women and girls*. United Nations. https://www.unodc.org/documents/data-and-analysis/gsh/Booklet_5.pdf

United Nations Office on Drugs and Crime (UNODC). (2019b). *Global study on homicide: Understanding homicide—typologies, demographic factors, mechanisms and contributors*. United Nations. https://www.unodc.org/documents/data-and-analysis/gsh/Booklet_3.pdf

United Nations Office on Drugs and Crime (UNODC). (2019c). *Global study on homicide: Executive summary*. United Nations. https://www.unodc.org/documents/data-and-analysis/gsh/Booklet1.pdf

United Nations Office on Drugs and Crime (UNODC). (2019d). *Global study on homicide: Homicide trends, patterns, and criminal justice response*. United Nations. https://www.unodc.org/documents/data-and-analysis/gsh/Booklet2.pdf

United Nations Office on Drugs and Crime (UNODC). (2019e). *Global study on homicide: Killing of children and young adults*. United Nations. https://www.unodc.org/documents/data-and-analysis/gsh/Booklet_6new.pdf

Utley, E. A. (2017). Infidelity's coexistence with intimate partner violence: An interpretive description of women who survived a partner's sexual affair. *Western Journal of Communication, 81*(4), 426–445. https://doi.org/10.1080/10570314.2017.1279744

Valladares, E., Peña, R., Persson, L. A., & Högberg, U. (2005). Violence against pregnant women: Prevalence and characteristics. A population-based study in Nicaragua. *BJOG: An International Journal of Obstetrics & Gynaecology, 112*, 1243–1248. https://doi.org/10.1111/j.1471-0528.2005.00621.x

Vandello, J. A., Cohen, D., Grandon, R., & Franiuk, R. (2009). Stand by your man: Indirect prescriptions for honorable violence and feminine loyalty in Canada, Chile, and the United States. *Journal of Cross-Cultural Psychology, 40*, 81–104. https://doi.org/10.1177/0022022108326194

Vandermassen, G. (2011). Evolution and rape: A feminist Darwinian perspective. *Sex Roles, 64*(9–10), 732–747. https://doi.org/10.1007/s11199-010-9895-y

Walker, J., Archer, J., & Davies, M. (2005). Effects of rape on men: A descriptive analysis. *Archives of Sexual Behavior, 34*(1), 69–80. https://doi.org/10.1007/s10508-005-1001-0

Wake, N. (2012). Loss of control beyond sexual infidelity. *Journal of Criminal Law, 76*(3), 193–197. https://doi.org/10.1350/jcla.2012.76.3.766

Ward, T., & Siegert, R. (2002). Rape and evolutionary psychology: A critique of Thornhill and Palmer's theory. *Aggression and Violent Behavior, 7*(2), 145–168. https://doi.org/10.1016/S1359-1789(00)00042-2

Weekes-Shackelford, V. A., & Shackelford, T. K. (2004). Methods of filicide: Stepparents and genetic parents kill differently. *Violence and Victims, 19*(1), 75–81. https://doi.org/10.1891/vivi.19.1.75.33232

Wegner, R., Abbey, A., Pierce, J., Pegram, S. E., & Woerner, J. (2015). Sexual assault perpetrators' justifications for their actions: Relationships to rape supportive attitudes, incident characteristics, and future perpetration. *Violence Against Women, 21*(8), 1018–1037. https://doi.org/10.1177/1077801215589380

Welling, L. L., & Nicolas, S. C. (2015). The Darwinian mystique? Synthesizing evolutionary psychology and feminism. In V. Ziegler-Hill, L. Welling, & T. K. Shackelford (Eds.), *Evolutionary perspectives on social psychology* (pp. 203–214). Springer.

West, S. G. (2007). An overview of filicide. *Psychiatry (Edgmont), 4*(2), 48–57. https://www.ncbi.nlm.nih.gov/pmc/articles/PMC2922347/

West, S. G., Friedman, S. H., & Resnick, P. J. (2009). Fathers who kill their children: An analysis of the literature. *Journal of Forensic Sciences, 54*(2), 463–468. https://doi.org/10.1111/j.1556-4029.2008.00964.x

Wheatle, S. (2016). The constitutionality of the "homosexual advance defence" in the commonwealth Caribbean. *Equal Rights Review*, *16*, 38–60. https://ssrn.com/abstract=2815808

Wheatley, J. R., & Puts, D. A. (2015). Evolutionary science of female orgasm. In T. K. Shackelford & R. Hansen (Eds.), *The evolution of sexuality* (pp. 123–148). Springer.

Wiederman M. W. (1997). Extramarital sex: Prevalence and correlates in a national survey. *Journal of Sex Research*, *34*, 167–174. https://doi.org/10.1080/00224499709551881

Wilson, M., & Daly, M. (1992). The man who mistook his wife for a chattel. In J. H. Barkow, L. Cosmides, & J. Tooby (Eds.), *The adapted mind* (pp. 289–322). Oxford University Press.

Wilson, M., & Daly, M. (1993). An evolutionary psychological perspective on male sexual proprietariness and violence against wives. *Violence and Victims*, *8*(3), 271–294. https://www.ncbi.nlm.nih.gov/pubmed/8186185

Wilson, M., & Daly, M. (1996). Male sexual proprietariness and violence against wives. *Current Directions in Psychological Science*, *5*(1), 2–7. https://www.jstor.org/stable/20182377

Wilson, M., Daly, M., & Daniele, A. (1995). Familicide: The killing of spouse and children. *Aggressive Behavior*, *21*(4), 275–291. https://doi.org/10.1002/1098-2337(1995)21:4<275::AID-AB2480210404>3.0.CO;2-S

World Health Organization (WHO). (2002). *World report on violence and health*. World Health Organization. https://www.who.int/violence_injury_prevention/violence/world_report/en/introduction.pdf

World Health Organization (WHO). (2017a). *Intimate partner violence*. World Health Organization. http://apps.who.int/violence-info/intimate-partner-violence/

World Health Organization (WHO). (2017b). *Homicide: WHO global health estimates* (2015 update). World Health Organization. http://apps.who.int/violence-info/homicide/

World Health Organization & London School of Hygiene and Tropical Medicine (WHO & LSHTM). (2010). *Preventing intimate partner and sexual violence against women: Taking action and generating evidence*. World Health Organization. https://www.who.int/violence_injury_prevention/publications/violence/9789241564007_eng.pdf

World Health Organization, London School of Hygiene and Tropical Medicine, & South American Medical Research Council (WHO, LSHTM, & SAMRC). (2013). *Global and regional estimates of violence against women: Prevalence and health effects of intimate partner violence and non-partner sexual violence*. World Health Organization. https://www.who.int/reproductivehealth/publications/violence/9789241564625/en/

World Health Organization (WHO) & The Pan American Health Organization (2012). *Understanding and addressing violence against women*. https://apps.who.int/iris/bitstream/handle/10665/77432/WHO_RHR_12.36_eng.pdf;jsessionid=D85F19141A724EDFB62BDB65F4D7F753?sequence=1.

Wright, M. F. (2017). Intimate partner aggression and adult attachment insecurity: The mediation of jealousy and anger. *Evolutionary Behavioral Sciences*, *11*(2), 187–198. http://dx.doi.org/10.1037/ebs0000097

CHAPTER 24

Male Sexual Coercion in Response to Mate Infidelity

Lidia Dengelegi Abrams *and* Mike Abrams

Abstract

Abstract: The power to restrain women's sexuality has taken many forms.. Historically, men have been entitled and even encouraged to reprimand their wives physically, and forced sex was not excluded as a means of rebuke and control. Marital rape, which many have been considered an oxymoron as one could not rape something owned, has been used to punish a woman judged to be unfaithful. The long list of restraints and coercive acts served the ultimate purpose of limiting women's sexual access, or desirability, to competing males. To better understand these processes, this chapter explores the often brutal but evolutionarily old control strategies that have been deployed when males have feared or suspected infidelity. Intimate partner violence is often paired with sexual coercion when female infidelity is suspected. Sexual coercion is one of several methods of mate guarding, preventing or avenging cuckoldry. The variables that affect the decision to apply coercive methods and other tactics of mate guarding are discussed. Research is presented indicating sexual selection pressures (i.e., evolution) is the ultimate cause of forced in-pair copulation, notwithstanding the proximate causes of religion, culture, traditions, thoughts, feelings, and beliefs of the men and women involved in the dynamic of sexual coercion in response to real or perceived female infidelity. Case studies of couples experiencing the dynamics of female infidelity and male sexual coercion are presented, along with an evolutionarily informed cognitive therapy that may provide a useful treatment mechanism.

Key Words: sexual coercion, infidelity, forced in-pair copulation, informed, cognitive therapy, evolutionary perspective

One legacy of our distant past is sexual coercion in which the male (usually) physically forces a female (usually) to engage in sexual activity. This has been the modal use of the term "sexual coercion." The most extreme form of sexual coercion is rape, but there are many other types of sexual coercion. In this chapter we explore a wide range of actions and inactions that lead to physical or emotional distress and ultimately sexual coercion, in the context of intimate heterosexual relationships. This dynamic has been termed "forced in-pair copulation" or FIPC (Goetz & Shackelford, 2006). Evolutionary psychologists have documented that men have evolved psychological adaptations to counter the dangers of cuckoldry, instigated by their female partner's sexual relationship with a rival. Men have been shown to engage in various behaviors to decrease the chance of extramarital sexual activity on the part of their spouse (i.e., mate guarding) and also to decrease the likelihood that the female extramarital activity, if it occurs, results in insemination (sperm competition–related activities; Goetz & Shackelford, 2006).

When female infidelity is suspected, it has been shown that the male partner will engage in increasing mate guarding and increased frequency and amount of insemination, in an attempt to prevent insemination by a competitor (Buss, 1988; Shackelford et al., 2006). When female infidelity becomes known, the relationship may end, or otherwise its dynamics tend to drastically change for the worse. The cuckolded mate may become increasingly anxious about his own mate value, the potential loss of respect, love, and resources provided by the cuckolding spouse, and about potentially suffering the shame and decrease in status and mate value if the cuckoldry becomes known to others (Buss, 2006). The issue of paternity becomes central to the man's efforts, as he becomes focused on avoiding the prospect of raising another man's child, having his wife focus her energies on raising another man's child. If the man chooses to stay in the relationship, retaining not just the relationship but also reproductive exclusivity with the spouse becomes a primary driving force. The cuckolded spouse will choose one or more of a variety of strategies to re-establish himself as her only sexual partner. Mate retention strategies vary based on the man's personality, level of psychological adjustment and self-esteem, perceived mate value, and attitudes and beliefs about gender roles (Salwen & O'Leary, 2013; Starrat et al., 2008; Arnocky et al., 2015). While some men will try to regain their partner's attentions with affection and sharing of resources, others attempt to increase their dominance and control over their cheating spouse (Goetz & Shackelford, 2009). They will also manipulate, pressure, coerce, and guilt their partner into being available sexually to them and to the exclusion of others (Camilleri & Quinsey, 2009). A subset of the latter group has also been shown to resort to physical coercion or rape, as a form of aggression, intimidation, and punishment, as well as to assert their reproductive primacy, as explained by sperm competition theory (DeLecca & Pham, 2021). Societal mores and beliefs about gender roles and potential punishment for in-couple rape contribute to the extent to which jealousy and anxiety about being cuckolded results in sexual coercion or assault of the unfaithful partner (Snead & Babcock, 2019). As laws and societal mores indicate that there would be negative consequences to FIPC, also called intimate partner sexual abuse, has decreased to an extent, it continues to be concerning reality in all modern societies (Fanslow et. al, 2021; Zukauskiem et al., 2019; Abrahams et al., 2004).

Intimate Partner Violence (IPV) and Sexual Coercion

Love, marriage, and committed bonds do not preclude violence, which can plague a relationship for disturbingly long durations. In the majority of heterosexual relationships that include violence, it is the man who aggresses against the woman (Breiding et al., 2014). And since men are considerably stronger than women, their assaults inflict more damage. This strength differential explains the higher rate of intimate partner injury in women than in men. One in 7 women versus 1 in 25 men have been injured by their partner (https://ncadv.org/STATISTICS). IPV is more likely to occur in established relationships and especially in relationships experiencing many and varied conflicts; this is also true for rape (Finkelhor & Yllo, 1987). In couples in which one partner has become disaffected for reasons including decreased sexual interest from their partner or increased interest in an extrapair partner, men more than women

engage in IPV, including rape or FIPC, an extreme form of mate guarding or mate retention. Research indicates that male mate guarding, even in its most violent manifestations, is an adaptation to prevent infidelity and cuckolding. Such findings include that there is an increased rate of FIPC when a man feels less desirable than his partner, and when she is in, or close to, estrus (e.g., Buss & Shackelford, 1997; Goetz et al., 2005).

Sexual violence and coercion are estimated to be experienced by 10%–26% of women within marriage (Goetz et al., 2018; Finkelhor & Yllo, 1987 Hadi, 2000; Navarro-Mantas, 2021; Painter & Farrington, 1998. Some authors relate the male propensity to sexually abuse their partners with a male need for control and domination (Basile, 2002; Bergen, 1996), yet this does not appear to be the general rule, as sexual violence does not correlate with dominance in the relationship (Gage & Hutchinson, 2006). Goetz and associates (2008) postulate that a need for dominance and control may be the proximate causes of IPV, but this need is ultimately in the service of an evolutionary goal: to limit a partner's sexual autonomy and reduce paternity uncertainty. Indeed, Goetz and Shackelford (2009) show that proximate factors for mate controlling behavior are necessary for FIPC, but so are ultimate causes, driven by suspected female infidelity. This is supported by a study (Shackelford et al., 2005) finding that male violence toward their partners is connected with direct guarding behavior, intrasexual negative inducements (e.g., threatening a perceived competitor), public displays of possession of their partners, as well as monopolization of a partner's time and emotional manipulation. On the other side of the spectrum are males who use positive inducements, such as displaying fondness or care toward their partners, and who are not violent to their partners.

The definition of sexual coercion as physically forced intercourse is quite narrow. It excludes many acts of sex other than intercourse, as well as a wide range of actions that intimidate, slander, embarrass, or distress someone, perhaps using their sexuality, or sexual history, in order to control them. Sexually coercive acts can be in response to behaviors found provocative in the partner, or they may be meant to punish, deter, and control. In our clinical practice we have seen (a) forced sex after a man was sexually humiliated by his partner's negative statements about his mate worth, (b) insults about her physical appearance when the husband suspected that his wife enjoyed attention from others too much, and (c) forced fellatio and anal sex as punishment for suspected unfaithfulness. Acts of physical abuse—punching, slapping, shoving, choking, etc., sometimes accompany the sexual coercion. Following these behaviors, the relationship sometimes but not always ends. There is often shame in the abused partner, and the abuse may not be revealed to anyone other than a psychologist.

Sexual coercion can include verbal intimidation, the manipulation of shared assets (e.g., Shackelford & Goetz, 2004), sexual withholding, nonconsensual sexually sadistic acts, and verbal emotional abuse. An aversive action meant to induce or restrict sexual behavior can be considered sexual coercion (Poppen & Segal, 1988, Johnson & Sigler, 2000; Marshall & Holtzworth-Munroe, 2002). These tactics are in contrast to the more socially acceptable forms of persuasion that include enhancing one's appearance, providing social or financial resources, inducing sexual arousal, arranging conducive circumstances, or even encouraging intoxication (Felson, 1993).

Sexual coercion is often linked to infidelity for several reasons, and perceived relationship imbalances sometimes underlie the infidelity. It is common for people to justify their own infidelity based on their belief that they contribute more to the relationship than their spouse. This can be based on their feeling more attractive, earning more, having superior academic credentials, or excelling in any attribute they believe is crucial for success. Partners in relationships are continually assessing their own and their mate's "market value," and their self-appraised mate value will often guide the treatment of their partner and decision of whether to be unfaithful.

Since humans, along with most mammals, are not naturally exclusively monogamous (Barash & Lipton (2001), it follows that sustained monogamy requires effort. Based on the increasing frequency of breakups over time, it seems that the effort to sustain monogamy increases with time as well. The half-life of monogamous bonds diminishes as a result of several common challenges to fidelity. Among these is the tendency of partners to continuously assess their own mate value relative to their current partner and potential new partners. This challenge to relationship fidelity is exacerbated by the inevitable change of a person's status, appearance, health, and emotional stability over the life span. When time treats one partner more harshly than the other, there will emerge an increased disparity in relative mate value. Of course, this does not inevitably lead to the relationship's demise. Conjugate or companionate love can foster a bond that is resistant to the allure of another potential partner. Or, less ideally, ancillary factors like parental obligations or economic barriers can attenuate the attraction of a more desirable new mate. Unhappily, many relationships do not develop a strong enough familial bond, and neither do they have structural obstacles to revoking a commitment. The combination of relationship fragility and the common practice of evaluating potential new partners may motivate a partner's focus on someone who seems to offer more. A man's or woman's finding someone they believe to be both available and more suitable can lead to a breakdown in the continuing effort to sustain monogamy. For example, a woman who has a close friendship with a male coworker of a higher status or more physically attractive than her husband may progress to a sexual affair if her husband loses his job or otherwise becomes less desirable in her eyes. In situations such as these, the affair may be a first step in establishing a new relationship. Infidelity may be a step in the process of finding a new partner.

An affair facilitating an exit from a relationship leads to grief, anger, and feelings of betrayal, but in most cases the rancor does not extend beyond hostile words and attorney letters. In some dysfunctional relationships, however, violence between partners precludes a safe exit. Instead, the relationship is sustained through violence and coercion.

There are individual differences in how couples negotiate real or perceived infidelity. Issues of self-control, psychological adjustment, beliefs about women's roles, family background and traditions, self-esteem and self-acceptance, attachment anxiety and other factors affect how much damage is done to each other, to the relationship, and to any children in the family. Salwen and O'Leary (2013) found that an overall maladaptive behavioral style consisting of psychological aggression, dominance, and jealousy is related to the use of sexual coercion. Camilleri and Quinsey (2009) hypothesize that there are three routes to sexually coercive behavior: young male syndrome (young males are more likely to commit sexual crimes, and it might have been adaptive in ancestral settings as males who behaved in such a way gained the advantage at a time when there was the harshest competition for females), competitive disadvantage (operationalized as neurodevelopmental insults, and lower intelligence) and psychopathy. The first two characteristics, if related to partner sexual violence, may demonstrate that sexual violence in the relationship is related to mate guarding and sexual competition, as these two groups remain vulnerable to other males attempting to "steal" their partners. The researchers found a relationship between psychopathy and partner-directed sexual aggression. Still, two-thirds of those who committed partner rape were not psychopaths and were likely affected by the strong evolutionary forces discussed here.

Is Rape a Natural Form of Sexuality?

Close to half a century ago, feminists such as Susan Brownmiller (1975) opined that men control women through acts of sexual coercion, of which the most pernicious form is rape. Brownmiller further argued that rape is not sex, but solely a violent act with the tacit goal of female subjugation. This constructivist argument that rape is not a variant of sexuality (in humans and other species) is an example of the moralistic fallacy. This fallacy ensues when one asserts a natural behavior is intrinsically good or appropriate; and conversely, iniquitous acts cannot be natural. The same logic was used to condemn homosexuality—reproduction is natural and homosexuality, which does not lead to reproduction, therefore must be wrong. By extension, an abhorrent act like rape cannot be a natural sexual behavior because it is immoral. However, the evidence, even if not socially palatable, supports the contrary. In their studies, Thornhill and Thornhill (1992) found that male sexual arousal and performance level were the same in coercive situations as in consensual mating situations; men can be equally aroused to perform by sexual acts either involving or not involving coercion. Rape is certainly an act of sex, even if criminal and cruel, even if used as an act of coercion (Abrams, 2016).

Sexual asymmetry in reproduction leads to males being less discriminating in sexual partners, more motivated to seek multiple partners, and more motivated to include copulation in communication with the opposite sex. On the other hand, females have evolved to be more discriminative, which is why coercive sexuality in males has been adaptive—forcing oneself on a desirable but uninterested partner has led to more offspring (Smuts, 1992). And on the other hand, undesirable consequences of rape for males (threat of female's family retaliation, etc.) did not lead to the selection against rape, suggesting that its overall benefit was higher than the cost. Thornhill and Thornhill (1992) found that younger males and males of lower socioeconomic status were more likely to be coercive, which suggests that the males who face the greatest competition in access to females or are in a disadvantageous position undertake more drastic measures to increase the probability of securing sexual access to women.

Rape and other forms of sexual coercion may represent exaggerated dominant and submissive behaviors that evolved to facilitate reproduction. The fact that females of all species are less cautious and aggressive when sexually aroused exemplifies the link between submissiveness and sexuality. In fact, in most female mammals, it is common to exhibit less anxiety and aggression during estrus (Byrnes & Bridges, 2006; Hyde & Sawyer, 1977; Rodriguez-Sierra et al., 1984). Otherwise aggressive female animals will assume submissive postures to permit penetration when sexually aroused (Pfaff et al., 1978). For example, females like the lion and the hyena (East et al., 1993) are fearsome predators, yet will become passive when aroused and adopt a submissive posture for intromission. This behavior is explained by a submission circuit in the mammalian brain (e.g., Pfaff et al., 1994). This circuit is at least partially mediated by estrogen and other hormones responsible for ovulation. Many of these hormones have been shown to suppress cautionary behaviors on the part of a female to allow a potentially dangerous male to get close enough to mate (Ciaccio et al., 1979; Swanson & Payne, 1970). This natural calming that encourages sexual submission is essential for reproduction since all females from the hyena to the human take considerable risks when allowing copulation. Evolution had to provide mechanisms that attenuate the natural caution against predation in order to facilitate reproduction. Freud (1933) wrote about the sexual dimension of dominance and submission. However, he incorrectly argued that the sexual submissiveness of women led to the development of sexual masochism, which he considered an essential aspect of the female psyche. This is a pervasive psychoanalytic theme that has never been evidenced. Today, most evolutionary psychologists would argue that Freud conflated the suspension of defensiveness that precedes female sexual receptivity with masochism (Abrams, 2016). Freud, along with the more evidence-oriented von Krafft-Ebing, theorized that sadism in men was an exaggeration of the aggressive male sex drive and not necessarily pathological. The link between submission and sexual receptivity exists in both men and women, but it is more common in women (Abrams, 2016). However, even if women possess an innate inclination to be submissive during sex, it is erroneous to conclude that this is linked to submissiveness in any domain other than sex and that it is a pathway to masochism. Permitting oneself to be vulnerable during sexual encounters is distinct from the desire to be harmed or degraded. In fact, sexual masochism as a paraphilic sexual preference appears to be more common in men than women. If women were innately masochistic, then the evidence that men commonly find masochistic fantasies more arousing than women do would be a paradox. This is the finding of a study that focused on masochistic sexual fantasies of college students (Abrams et al., 2019; Donnelly & Fraser, 1998). Interestingly, men's submission fantasies are often centered on arousal by BDSM (bondage-discipline sadomasochism), whereas female submission fantasies are more likely to be about being dominated by a sexually committed male (Abrams, 2016). This is concordant with women's universal preference for taller or physically larger males (Buss, 2004). Mating with a larger man was adaptive during epochs in which women and their progeny required physical protection for survival. Thus, it is likely that a fantasy of a sexually dominating male is an expression of the desire for a strong and socially dominant mate. In modern societies it is common for socially dominant women to have fantasies of sexual submission to dominant men (Hawley & Hensley, 2009), which suggests that modern females still have modules for sexual submission. And the aggressiveness, still linked to male sexuality, is expressed through intrusive mate guarding, rageful jealously, physical violence with competing males, etc., further suggesting dominance and submission underlying sexuality. There is certainly overlap in male and female responses; some men acquire a more submissive sexual response and some women a more aggressive one. These orientations also vary by degree, in most extreme forms being labeled sadism and masochism. Sadism takes the desire for dominance and exaggerates it to the point in which inflicting pain or humiliation produces or enhances sexual pleasure. In contrast, when the urge for subjugation increases to an extreme, sexual masochism ensues. Humiliation, subjugation, or pain become necessary or sufficient for sexual satisfaction. Since sadism and masochistic fantasies are nearly ubiquitous (Brown et al., 2020; Joyal & Carpentier, 2017), they are likely related to reproductive adaptations associated with the domination and submission involved in sexual reproduction.

Evolutionary Perspectives

Evolution through natural selection has become the cogent consolidating principle for psychology. Evolutionary psychology has become an increasingly applied field, looking beyond the descriptions of psychological phenomena to find the ultimate reasons for their existence. Since all paradigm shifts bring resistance and contentions, it is inevitable that this would be the case for evolutionary psychology. Especially so in the case of sexual violence, in which the premise that modules for violent behavior are adaptations is misconstrued as an excuse for the behavior. Yet it is inaccurate to presume that when evolutionary psychologists argue that something is natural, it is ipso facto good. The schism between many behaviors that occur in nature and those that are morally acceptable or even tolerable caused consternation in Charles Darwin. He observed that natural selection had no direction or morality and at times seemed quite cruel. Darwin, who originally trained to be an Anglican priest, had his faith in both God and a just world challenged by his observations. In a letter to his colleague Asa Gray, he wrote:

> Owing to this struggle for life, any variation, however slight, and from whatever cause proceeding, if it be in any degree profitable to an individual of any species, in its infinitely complex relations to other organic beings and to external nature, will tend to the preservation of that individual, and will generally be inherited by its offspring. The offspring, also, will thus have a better chance of surviving, for, of the many individuals of any species which are periodically born, but a small number can survive (Darwin, 1996, p. 52).
>
> There seems to me too much misery in the world. I cannot persuade myself that a beneficent & omnipotent God would have designedly created the Ichneumonidæ with the express intention of their feeding within the living bodies of caterpillars, or that a cat should play with mice. Not believing this, I see no necessity in the belief that the eye was expressly designed. On the other hand, I cannot anyhow be contented to view this wonderful universe & especially the nature of man, & to conclude that everything is the result of brute force. I am inclined to look at everything as resulting from designed laws, with the details, whether good or bad, left to the working out of what we may call chance. (Levine, 2011, p. 12).

Darwin was evidently troubled by the amorality and cruelty of nature; however, as contrary as his observations may have been to a just world, he did not deny their reality, nor did his contemporaries accuse him of advocating or defending these behaviors. Darwin viewed them as adaptations that arose to give their bearers an advantage for survival. *And this is the case for sexual violence*, which overlies several behavioral penchants that increased fitness during our ancestral past. Since moral virtue was not an attribute that added to fitness during the epochs in which the preponderance of hominin and human behavior evolved, violence had many upsides and fewer downsides. It is apparent that our psyches contain the residue of violent and often cruel ancestors. It is hard to imagine that this would not be the case given the continued prevalence of violent jealousy, mate guarding, and sexual competition even with modern legal and cultural prohibitions against such behaviors. In epochs during which there was no codification of social behavior or prescribed punishments for sexual or other violence these were likely to be more common. That a majority of human societies now condemn rape and sexual coercion is unlikely to change evolved mechanisms for sexual jealousy and sperm competition, which have been effective for spreading men's genes for many thousands of years (Kaighobadi et al., 2009). Given the fact that these mechanisms were effective, males in current societies are the descendants of the males who used them to their advantage.

The essential debate is whether sexual coercion is an expression of a discrete evolved mechanism versus byproduct of other evolved male tendencies such as aggressiveness, hypersexuality, and general coerciveness (e.g., Thornhill & Thornhill, 1992). The position that rape is an evolved behavior has been met with vitriolic controversy. Despite the question remaining open, the evidence suggests that there is no specific mechanism for rape (Buss, 2021). Instead, it is a byproduct of the traits mentioned above. However, the evidence also indicates that sexual coercion probably overlies an evolved mechanism for several reasons, foremost of which is that social learning alone cannot explain it (Thornhill & Thornhill, 1992). In addition, all polygynous male animals are prone to sexual aggression and intrasexual violence (Lindenfors & Tullberg, (2011). There is no reason to believe that human males are an exception.

Sexual coercion, like most behaviors associated with sexuality, can be traced to a person's genome, as measured by heritability. For example, a Finnish study (Westerlund et al., 2010) revealed that genetic differences explained 54% of sociosexual behavior, 23% of sociosexual attitudes, and 20%–25% of sexual coercion. Additionally, in studies of familial aggregation (Långström, et al., 2015), genetic differences explained 40% of sexual coercion and shared environments explained only 2% of sexual coercion among first order relatives. Such data directly contradicts the standard social science model, which holds that sexual coercion is learned. It is particularly interesting that genetic differences only explained 19% of rape while they explained 46% of child molestation. This suggests that rape is a special form of sexual coercion, compared to paraphilic sexual violence.

FIPC and Sperm Competition

Much of the literature has focused on proximate, nonevoluntary analyses of sexual coercion: culture, social roles, attitudes, beliefs, etc. There is no question that all these play a role in the frequency, intensity, and specific expression of FIPC. The focus of this chapter, however, is the common occurrence of in-pair sexual coercion throughout the centuries and across cultures, leading to the need to address if and how it could have arisen due to natural selection.

Rape as an adaptive behavior is typically discussed in relation to men attempting to copulate with a large number of different partners, as their costs for fathering these offspring may be minimal (since they can choose not to take on parenting tasks), and the benefits in terms of spreading one's own genetic material can be large. Partner rape seems illogical in this sense, as it could potentially endanger the reproductive health of one's partner, and the male already has sexual access to his partner. In particular, sexual coercion increases the risk for unintended pregnancy and includes strategies such as condom manipulation and pressure by the male partner for the woman to become pregnant (Walker & Rowlands, 2019). In addition to unwanted pregnancies, this type of sexual abuse can leave young women with sexually transmitted infections and long-term psychological damage (De Visser et al., 2007; Agardh et al., 2012). Violence toward a pregnant partner can result in other negative consequences, including miscarriage, delayed or absent prenatal care, stillbirth, premature labor, injury to the fetus, and low birth weight of the infant (Berhanie et al., 2019). Despite all these disadvantages, FIPC is not rare. And behaviors that exist with some regularity are likely to have evolved because of their adaptiveness.

Sexual coercion in intimate relationships has been explained through an evolutionary lens as a response to paternity uncertainty and sexual jealousy Goetz & Shackelford, 2006; Goetz et al., 2008; Lalumière et al., 2005; Thornhill & Thornhill, 1992; Wilson & Daly, 1992), as a way of engaging in sperm competition. Sperm competition is a type of post-copulatory competition, engaged in by males who may have not been able to repel other males from their partner, that is, their mate guarding behaviors were not successful, but they still try to increase their chance of fathering a child with that partner (Shackelford & Goetz, 2006; Shackelford et al., 2006). This phenomenon has been documented in many animal species, especially in birds, which are socially monogamous but sometimes copulate with other partners, the same behaviors commonly seen in humans. Some of the features that have evolved to help win, or alternatively, to avoid sperm competition include testis size (related to the amount of sperm that can be deposited into a female reproductive tract), mate guarding behaviors (either proximate, such as staying close to and monitoring the female, or remote, such as a copulatory plug in some insects), sperm displacement (often seen in insects and some birds), frequent in-pair copulation, ejaculate adjustment, and forced in-pair copulation (often seen in birds, immediately after a female partner's extrapair copulations (Gallup & Burch, 2006; Shackelford & Goetz, 2006).

In avian species, forced copulation seems to follow extrapair copulation, apparently supporting this hypothesis (Birkhead et al., 1989; Cheng et al., 1983). In humans, many studies suggest the existence of this relationship; sexual coercion in relationships is likely to follow male accusations of his female partner's infidelity (Finkelhor & Yllo, 1987 Russell, 1982; McKibbin et al., 2011). For example, one older study (Shields & Hanneke, 1983) reports that almost half of the women who were beaten and raped by their husbands previously engaged in extrapair sexual activity, unlike women who were beaten but not raped (23% engaged in extrapair copulation), and nonvictimized women (10%). The main question is not whether sperm competition is one of the determinants of intimate partner sexual coercion, but instead the relative importance that it plays in such behaviors.

One measure of the risk of the female partner's infidelity has been operationalized as the proportion of time that the couple has spent apart since the last in-pair intercourse. The higher this proportion is, the more the risk that the female was unfaithful and hence inseminated by another male increases. If this proportion is correlated with sexual coercion, it would suggest that this behavior is a tactic to address the problem of sperm competition. Alternatively, if the time that has passed from the last intercourse, regardless of time spent apart, correlates with sexual coercion, this would suggest that coercion stems simply from sexual frustration, and perhaps does not have anything to do with female infidelity. Shackelford and colleagues (2002, 2006, 2007) have shown that males who have spent a greater proportion of time away from their partners since the last copulation perceived their partner as more sexually attractive to themselves and to other potential partners; they had more interest in copulating with their partner, were more persistent in their efforts to copulate with their partner, and estimate a higher level of interest in their partner for engaging in sexual activity with them, although they expressed higher distress at the partner's imagined rejection following time apart. These relationships were independent of total time since the last copulation and of relationship satisfaction, although those variables were also connected with relationship satisfaction. Not surprisingly, when the likelihood of female infidelity was judged high, men's assessment of their partner's interest in them sexually was lowered rather than increased. The practically certain existence of sperm competition in humans does not function as a conscious strategy, such that males calculate the probability of females being unfaithful and then judging what reaction could minimize the paternity uncertainty. Instead, the evolved psychological mechanisms surrounding increased sexual interest in one's partner likely motivate the behaviors that would present the adaptive reactions to sperm competition (Conroy & Gray, 2014).

The perception of female infidelity seems to be related to shorter copulation, which may be a means for the male to enter the sperm competition more quickly (Barbaro et al., 2015). Camilleri and Quinsey (2009) emphasize that sexual coercion as the reaction to perceived infidelity is likely to happen only when the infidelity cues have happened recently, i.e., when there is still a viable chance for the male to enter the sperm competition. Again, it is unlikely that males consciously calculate the probability of female infidelity and adjust their responses accordingly (Shackelford et al., 2002). The connection between these variables signals the existence of an underlying evolved mechanism that helps men increase their paternity likelihood.

McKibbin and associates (2011) found that several types of sexual coercion (resource manipulation and violence, commitment manipulation, and defection threat) were significantly positively correlated with the amount of time spent apart since the last in-pair intercourse, thus supporting the sperm competition hypothesis. The correlations of coercive behaviors and total time since last intercourse were insignificant for the sample overall. This correlation was moderated by perceived likelihood of infidelity—the correlation persisted in males who perceived their partners to be likely to commit infidelity, but not in males who believed their partners would remain faithful. These results speak in favor of sperm competition theory, but they also demonstrate that males base their calculations of risk of being cuckolded not only on objective measures such as time spent apart, but also on some measure of trust or prediction they form in regard to their partners.

Also in support of the notion that FIPC constitutes a form of sperm competition, Goetz and Shackelford (2006) and others find that it most often occurs in cases of suspected female infidelity or by a low status male competing with one with higher mate value. Real or perceived mate value discrepancies affect the likelihood of partner violence and FIPC. Starratt et al. (2008), for example, found a correlation between partner directed insults and accusations of sexual infidelity and sexual coercion. This study suggests that there is a mechanism, commonly found in men but also sometimes in women, that responds in several, more or less acceptable ways, to perceived infidelity. In this model, insults may be a way to lower the partner's self-perceived mate value and hence increase their dedication to the current relationship and divert them from cheating.

FIPC can be a reaction to the female's sexual rejection of her partner, which could signal possible infidelity. Finkelhor and Yllo (1987) have found that rape in a committed partnership happens more often toward the end of the relationship and less often in the earlier phases.

Males are more likely to express mate retention behaviors, including FIPC, when their partner is perceived to have greater reproductive value, when she is more likely to commit infidelity, and when she is near ovulation (Buss & Shackelford, 1997; Gangestad et al., 2002; Goetz et al., 2005). These authors further find that FIPC is correlated with other mate retention behaviors—threats, blackmail, limiting access to funds, transportation, and socialization—in an effort to prevent competing males from inseminating one's partner, as a way to increase reproductive success.

Camilleri and Quinsey (2009) found that sexual coercion does not accompany all doubts regarding female infidelity. When these doubts were not supported by several infidelity cues, many men were likely to engage in sexual coaxing behaviors such as massage, kissing, and other ways to initiate consensual intercourse. On the other hand, sexual coercion commonly followed doubts confirmed by multiple cues of infidelity. There are many differences in how different men within different relationships within different societies attempt to defend against cuckoldry and loss of a mate. Starratt et al. (2008) find a correlation between partner-directed insults and accusations of sexual infidelity and sexual coercion. Resource manipulation, commitment manipulation, and defection threats are correlated with accusations of infidelity and partner insults. Insults such as derogating her physical attractiveness, her value as a partner, her mental capacity, or her value as a person correlate with sexual coercion and can be seen as a type of mate guarding. Lowering the partner's perceived self-value and self-esteem is meant to diminish her likelihood of attempting to stray.

A study by Jones and associates (2007) shows that individuals who express high mating effort, characterized by short-term relationships and inconsistent partner-guarding, are more likely to be upset over sexual infidelity than emotional infidelity. Conversely, individuals with low mating effort, who conduct more mate guarding behaviors, but in a way that preserves the future of a relationship, are more likely to be upset by emotional infidelity than sexual infidelity. Moreover, the high-mating-effort individuals are more likely to react punitively to all types of infidelity.

Clinical Approach to Treatment of FIPC

The authors have worked with many couples dealing with infidelity and FIPC, at varying levels of intensity and violence. Below we present and comment on actual cases, with names and identifiers changed, and our approach taken to help the couple understand and cope with the dynamics involved and to make the best decisions moving forward. Our form of treatment has its' roots in Albert Ellis's rational-emotive behavioral therapy (Ellis, 1962) and Beck's and others' cognitive-behavioral therapy (Abrams, 2020). We found that offering clients psychoeducation about evolutionarily based tendencies and behaviors makes self-acceptance and other-acceptance possible. This leads to decreased emotional distress and better ability to make rational decisions about oneself and one's relationships. We call this therapy informed cognitive therapy, or ICT (Abrams, 2020.

Maggie and Jeff

Jeff came to therapy, in his words, because his wife "made him." She told him he needed to change, or she couldn't be with him. To get the whole picture, we eventually got his wife Maggie into therapy as well. Their story: They met in college. He was a business major, ambitious about his future. She was studying sociology, interested in human rights, helping the world. Jeff was—and is—handsome, and Maggie fell for him hard. He grew to like her, too, although she was not quite his type, a bit plain and on the heavy side. Yet she was so wonderful to him, he realized he could not let her go. After college they married. She was in love with him, and he loved her, in his way. Jeff did well in his securities job, working hard and charming male and female customers alike. Maggie worked for nonprofits, happy to lend a hand to anyone in need. They fell into a routine involving little time together—he working overtime and she going to various political meetings at night. Except, he wasn't always working overtime. Jeff had developed his own routine involving short and longer-term relationships with women he would meet. Maggie had gained more weight; he was less and less attracted to her. His excuse: stress from his long hours. They rarely had sex, and when they did it was brief, more as a fulfillment of his obligations. But then, a few years into the marriage, he happened to look at her phone and could not believe that his frumpy wife was the object of someone's attention, even adoration. She was talking extensively to a male coworker, and it wasn't clear whether anything untoward had happened. He confronted her, she denied it, but he couldn't be sure. In addition to feeling angry and betrayed, he felt a strange excitement stirring. For the first time in years he felt attracted to Maggie, in a new way. Rather than arguing with her, he acted on his newfound attraction. They made love and Maggie was amazed at how good it was. She felt that maybe he wasn't so angry, maybe everything was okay. Jeff did in fact have intermittent angry outbursts (Despite the fact that he was regularly sleeping with other women, Maggie's doing so was not okay with him.). In between the angry periods, he was having sex with her more. He couldn't understand it himself—the great anger he felt at his wife's flirtations with another man, when he was not even attracted to her anymore, and his own days were full of extramarital dalliances.

While at first Maggie welcomed Jeff's sexual attentions, she started feeling awkward about it. She felt there was something impersonal about their encounters that she didn't understand. She was confused, after years of having thought that Jeff had not much of a sex drive. Also, she felt that this all had to do with her coworker's attentions to her. Jeff would now get angry if she said "no" to sex, or would taunt her that she would probably want to do it with her coworker, not him. She would feel guilty, give in, but not enjoy the sexual experience. She started not liking Jeff. She wished things were back to the way they were, not much sex between them but love, friendship, and understanding. She questioned why they were even together, he seemed so obsessed with having sex with her and talking about her coworker.

This had been going on for about 10 months, and the relationship had gone from almost no sex to obligatory sex twice a week or Jeff would not be content. It became a chore for Maggie, and it cast a negative light on their relationship. Jeff told her that he was trying to give her what she needed at home so she wouldn't have to go elsewhere, but it seemed that it was more that Jeff was driven to have sex with her and it was not about making her happy, nor about being attracted to her. Jeff on his end said that in a strange way he did become attracted to Maggie, not that he suddenly liked her body type, but he wanted to possess her sexually nonetheless. The fact that another man found her attractive intrigued him, even as it angered him. He noted in an individual session that this newly found urge to have sex with his wife was beginning to interfere with his outside liaisons, causing complaints from his paramours. He did love Maggie, and he wanted to have her, not lose her to another man. And yes, there was an angry aspect, he should have her or nobody else. Maggie never found out about Jeff's affairs. Her complaints about him arose only from the change he underwent when he thought she was cheating on him. Which she had only come close to.

Comment: Jeff's behavior was explained to Maggie from an evolutionary perspective—that he felt compelled to mate-guard. And perhaps she could enjoy his interest in her, regardless of how it came to be. Jeff came to have a better understanding of his strange reaction to Maggie's suspected infidelity. He also became more confident when getting more evidence that Maggie in fact did not cheat on him. This lessened his sexual obsession with her, which Maggie didn't mind. Maggie admitted that she had felt neglected and unappreciated, hence the flirtation. Both worked on accepting the other's less than perfect behaviors, and the couple learned to communicate better and understand what each wanted from the other. Maggie came to feel more appreciated. In the end they settled back into a life of limited sex but with once again growing conjugal love. Jeff continued with his affairs, as he bluntly stated that no one could take his freedom away, but less frequently, as he found his home life to be more satisfying.

Nick and Loraine

Nick came in for therapy for help in deciding what to do about his marriage. He has been faithful, hard-working, a good father. Yet he found out that his wife had cheated on him. It had gone on for some months. She claims she's lost her head, this man seduced her. Nick even knows the person. He is horrified and mortified with the embarrassment of his wife choosing to cuckold him with this man he knows. He is angry at her betrayal, doesn't know if he can or if he should forgive her. Also, he feels so inadequate. He remembers times when she's made fun of his thin frame, slightly deprecating things she's said humorously now don't seem so funny. He feels a strong need to fight back, somehow, to punish her, to prove that he's worthy, to keep her from leaving him. Or should he leave? There are three children in the marriage, one with mild autism. With the money they both make, they do okay, but add a second household and the children would be deprived.

He doesn't know if he can trust her. Will she do it again? He can't help but still love her, maybe even more now, with a bitter poignancy. She has discontinued her affair, gave all kinds of excuses but repented, promised she'd never contact the man again, never do anything like this again. Nick is comparing himself to the other man—who is smarter, who is richer, better looking? He comes out ahead in many ways, but the doubt keeps gnawing at him that he is not good enough. Would he feel better with a woman who wouldn't do something like this to him? Should he brave it and move on?

Asked about their sex life, it has changed. Before he discovered the infidelity, Nick and his wife had a nice sexual relationship, never the most important part of their lives together. They had so much else in common, both being teachers and artists. Ever since he found out about the infidelity, Nick sees his wife as more of a sexual being. He looks at her and wants to have sex with her, whether or not she's in the mood. They argue, then they have sex. It's not a joyous experience, more like something he feels must happen. It feels reassuring, having had sex with her. Also, he has developed a fetish; every time he has sex with his wife, as foreplay, he insists that they go through a fantasy of her being with another man. She complains bitterly about this, says it terrifies her, as it's the very thing that makes Nick furious with her. Yet now it's also the very thing that turns him on! Him getting to have sex with the woman wanted, possessed by another man and winning her in the end. He gets that she doesn't like this roleplay, but he feels that she owes him; it's the least she could do to oblige him. The frequency of their sexual intimacy has somewhat increased, in between episodes of bitter fighting and recriminations. He watches her like a hawk, follows her to activities he would normally skip. He feels relatively safe when she's with the kids, but at other times he must know where she is at all times. He goes with her, sometimes follows her, and always spies on her electronically. He is checking her emails and phone regularly, he put a tracker on her car, spends a good amount of time monitoring her actions. He's obsessed with her cheating. His sleep is poor; he has been gaining weight from stress. He lost his voice once from yelling too much. He yells, she cries, locks herself in the room; he once broke the door down and insisted she prove her dedication to him by having sex with him. No, he didn't rape her, but kind of gave her no choice. Sometimes it seems like they now hate each other, engaged in a battle that may never end. Is this any kind of life, he wonders?

Comment: Nick was devastated by Loraine's deceit. Yet, he didn't want to give her up. He found himself engaging in a level of sexual coercion, coming to fetishize her infidelity. He now routinely did a huge amount of mate guarding. The relationship was nothing like it used to be, when they trusted each other. Yet the love was there, and they wanted to hold on to the marriage, for the children and for financial reasons. Actually, despite Nick's concerns, his mate value appeared quite comparable to hers; there was no discrepancy for him to worry about that would lead to more infidelity. This issue was discussed, as well as the fact that his insecurities led to more anger and distress for the family. Nick was obsessed with the idea that women don't cheat, it's men that cheat, so if Loraine did, she is a particularly bad person. This was challenged and discussed at length, leading to Nick having a bit more acceptance and understanding.

Discussing and normalizing each partner's actions and reactions led to less distress. Nick agreed to go into individual therapy to work on his deep-seated insecurities that his wife's infidelity had brought out full-force. Loraine also went to therapy to understand her motivations better and to help her make better decisions in the future, all the while with the understanding that what she did was not good for the family, but neither was it evil, awful, or unheard of; that she is not a terrible person deserving of infinite punishment.

Feelings run high and judgments are harsh when infidelity occurs. In a way it is ironic, as it does happen so often. But each individual's reactions appear to have been shaped by evolutionary forces. In men, the feelings of betrayal and hurt are underlined by the evolutionary urge to mate guard and prevent cuckoldry and sperm competition. An understanding of this seeps in slowly as the feelings are intense. On the other hand, couples who decide that it is to their benefit to stay together despite the difficulties can benefit from support and understanding and normalization of human sexual behavior and of the imperfectness of relationships.

Alan and Sandy

Alan, a tall, good-looking man, is married to Sandy, an attractive woman herself, who openly goes to parties where there is swinging and sex with multiple partners, and BDSM. She tells Alan that this is what makes her happy, and if he cares about her he should not object. Alan doesn't much like it, but agrees that Sandy should do what makes her happy. He tries his best to be a good husband and father to their child in the meanwhile. He doesn't much care for the swinging scene for himself. Ironically, Sandy pays lip service to both of them being free to explore, but when Alan takes a small step in that direction with a pretty woman, Sandy does not take it well at all. Sandy is a strong-willed woman, she imposes her wishes with impunity. She doesn't much like having sex with Alan; he's submissive and boring. But, he lets her do what she wants.

This couple came for couple therapy for the expected reasons, stress and distress over Sandy's assertively upholding her rights to party, so to speak, and Alan not quite having equality in the relationship. In addition to the out-in-the-open infidelities, he also had to put up with her criticisms of him—his skin was too dry, he should lose a few pounds, go to the gym. Not that this would make her want to be monogamous with him, but it would help her be more attracted to him. Sandy openly states that she is not very attracted to her husband, although she certainly loves him. Sex is just not the best part of the relationship. Alan wishes it was a better part of the relationship.

Comment: Alan and Sandy are both intelligent, they are both professionals. They love each other. They differ from the norm in that she has a stronger desire than most women for multiple sex partners and for being dominated and hurt during sex. Alan differs from most men in that he is particularly accepting of his wife, not that he is thrilled with her choices. What he wants is a better sexual relationship with his wife. He is not the dominant type and has no interest in introducing bondage and sadism into his sex life. Still, there was room for improvement in their sex life. In therapy we worked on ways to improve it, using both behavioral suggestions and disputations of rigid or irrational beliefs about how conjugal sex "should" be. A little progress was made. Sandy further learned to be less critical of Alan's appearance. It was explored in therapy, but Sandy has no intention of giving up her promiscuous lifestyle. Alan will never like it, but apparently he can live with it. So, with a little improvement from their therapy sessions, they stay together and raise their son.

Informed Cognitive Therapy (ICT) as a Cognitive-Behavioral Therapy (CBT) for Treatment of FIPC

Cognitive-behavioral therapy (CBT) is the term used for a range of conceptually related therapies that strive to be evidence based, focusing on helping clients address cognitive distortions, misperceptions, misinterpretations of each other's intentions and behaviors, or irrational beliefs (Dobson & Dobson, 2009). Informed cognitive therapy (ICT) builds on CBT by using an evolutionarily informed perspective. In the case of sexual aggressive and nonaggressive behaviors, it recognizes that there are strong underlying evolutionary forces at play, beyond individual frailties. Clients who come to understand these evolutionary influences on their psyche and their behavior can move forward better. They can choose to fight their innately programmed urges, but know that this is a difficult task and must be done for good reasons. The naturalistic fallacy—that certain behaviors feel so good and ego-congruent that they must be right— is challenged. Yes, extrapair sexual activity is natural in humans and animals, as is intimate partner violence and sexual coercion. But these may still not be moral or right, or even right for the individual engaging in them. Persons who choose to have monogamous relationships often gain a great deal from this alliance. However, most will have to fight hard to overcome the natural urges for extrapair activity, as well as urges to control and punish a partner for their infidelities.

Learning to tolerate frustration and delay gratification can lead to a fuller, more gratifying life than giving in to sexual and aggressive urges. ICT simultaneously lifts some of the burden of the responsibility for the evolutionarily propelled urges, while also challenging clients to use this understanding to take control over their actions and their lives.

References

Abrahams, N., Jewkes, R., Hoffman, M., & Laubsher, R. (2004). Sexual violence against intimate partners in Cape Town: prevalence and risk factors reported by men. *Bulletin of the World Health Organization, 82,* 330–337.

Abrams, M. (2016). *Sexuality and its disorders: Development, cases, and treatment.* SAGE Publications.

Abrams, M. (2020). *The new CBT: Clinical evolutionary psychology.* Cognella Academic Publishing.

Abrams, M., Milisavljević, M., & Šoškić, A. (2019). Childhood abuse: Differential gender effects on mental health and sexuality. *Sexologies, 28,* e89–e96.Agardh A., Tumwine G., Asamoah B.O., & Cantor-Graae E. (2012). The invisible suffering: Sexual coercion, interpersonal violence, and mental health—A cross-sectional study among university students in South-Western Uganda. *PLoS One, 7,* e51424.

Arnocky, S., Sunderani, S., Gomes, W., & Vaillancourt, T. (2015). Anticipated partner infidelity and men's intimate partner violence: The mediating role of anxiety. *Evolutionary Behavioral Sciences, 9,* 186–196.

Barbaro, N., Pham, M. N., & Shackelford, T. K. (2015). Solving the problem of partner infidelity: Individual mate retention, coalitional mate retention, and in-pair copulation frequency. *Personality and Individual Differences, 82,* 67–71.

Barash, D. P., & Lipton, J. E. (2001). *The myth of monogamy: Fidelity and infidelity in animals and people.* W. H. Freeman/Times Books/Henry Holt.

Basile, K. C. (2002). Prevalence of wife rape and other intimate partner sexual coercion in a nationally representative sample of women. *Violence and Victims, 17,* 511–524.

Bergen, R. K. (1996). *Wife rape* (Vol. 2). Sage.

Berhanie, E., Gebregziabher, D., Berihu, H., Gerezgiher, A., & Kidane, G. (2019). Intimate partner violence during pregnancy and adverse birth outcomes: A case-control study. *Reproductive Health, 16,* 22.

Birkhead, T. R., Hunter, F. M., & Pellatt, J. E. (1989). Sperm competition in the zebra finch, Taeniopygia guttata. *Animal Behaviour, 38,* 935–950.

Breiding, M. J., Chen, J., & Black, M. C. (2014). Intimate partner violence in the United States--2010. *CDC.*

Brown, A., Barker, E. D., & Rahman, Q. (2020). A systematic scoping review of the prevalence, etiological, psychological, and interpersonal factors associated with BDSM. *Journal of Sex Research, 57,* 781 – 811.

Brownmiller, S. (1975). *Against our will: Men, women and rape.* Simon & Schuster (Pelican Books ed., 1986).

Buss, D. M. (1988). From vigilance to violence: Tactics of mate retention in American undergraduates. *Ethology and Sociobiology, 9,* 291–317.

Buss, D. M. (2004. *The evolution of desire: Strategies in human mating.* Basic Books.

Buss, D. M. (2006). *The murderer next door: Why the mind is designed to kill.* Penguin Random House.

Buss, D. M. (2021). *When men behave badly: The hidden roots of sexual deception, harassment, and assault.* Little, Brown, Spark.

Buss, D. M., & Shackelford, T. K. (1997). From vigilance to violence: mate retention tactics in married couples. *Journal of Personality and Social Psychology, 72,* 346–361.Byrnes, E. M., & Bridges, R. S. (2006). Reproductive experience alters anxiety-like behavior in the female rat. *Hormones and Behavior, 50,* 70–76.

Camilleri, J. A., & Quinsey, V. L. (2009). Testing the cuckoldry risk hypothesis of partner sexual coercion in community and forensic samples. *Evolutionary Psychology, 7,* 14 - 178.

Cheng, K. M., Burns, J. T., & McKinney, F. (1983). Forced copulation in captive mallards III. Sperm competition. *The Auk, 100,* 302–310.

Ciaccio, L. A., Lisk, R. D., & Reuter, L. A. (1979). Prelordotic behavior in the hamster: A hormonally modulated transition from aggression to sexual receptivity. *Journal of Comparative and Physiological Psychology, 93,* 771.

Conroy, L. P., & Gray, D. A. (2014). Forced copulation as a conditional alternative strategy in camel crickets. *Behavioral Ecology and Sociobiology, 68,* 1431–1439.

Darwin, C. (1996). *The origin of species.* (G. Beer, Ed.). Oxford University Press. (Original work published 1859.)

DeLecce, T., & Pham, M. N. (2021). Sperm competition theory. In T. K. Shackleford (Ed.), *The SAGE handbook of evolutionary psychology: Foundations of evolutionary psychology* (pp. 222–240). Sage Reference.

de Visser, R. O., Rissel, C. E., Richters, J., & Smith, A. M. (2007). The impact of sexual coercion on psychological, physical, and sexual well-being in a representative sample of Australian women. *Archives of Sexual Behavior*, *36*, 676–686.

Dobson, D., & Dobson, K. S. (2009). *Evidence-based practice of cognitive-behavioral therapy*. Guilford Press.

Donnelly, D., & Fraser, J. (1998). Gender differences in sado-masochistic arousal among college students. *Sex Roles*, *39*, 391–407.

East, M. L., Hofer, H., & Wickler, W. (1993). The erect "penis" is a flag of submission in a female-dominated society: Greetings in Serengeti spotted hyenas. *Behavioral Ecology and Sociobiology*, *33*, 355–370.

Ellis, A. (1962). *Reason and emotion in psychotherapy*. Citadel Press.

Fanslow, J., Hashemi, L., Gulliver, P., & McIntosh, T. (2021). A century of sexual abuse victimisation: A birth cohort analysis. *Social Science & Medicine*, *270*, Article 113574.

Felson, R. B. (1993). Motives for sexual coercion. In R. B. Felson & J. T. Tedeschi (Eds.), *Aggression and violence: Social interactionist perspectives* (pp. 233–253). American Psychological Association.

Finkelhor, D., & Yllo, K. (1987). *License to rape: Sexual abuse of wives*. Free Press.

Freud, S. (1933). New introductory lectures on psychoanalysis. *Standard Edition*, 223–182. London: Hogarth Press.

Gage, A. J., & Hutchinson, P. L. (2006). Power, control, and intimate partner sexual violence in Haiti. *Archives of Sexual Behavior*, *35*, 11–24.

Gallup Jr, G. G., & Burch, R. L. (2006). The semen displacement hypothesis: Semen hydraulics and the intra-pair copulation proclivity model of female infidelity. In S. M. Platek & T. K. Shackelford (Eds.), *Female infidelity and paternal uncertainty: Evolutionary perspectives on male anti-cuckoldry tactics*, 129–140. Cambridge University Press.

Gangestad, S. W., Thornhill, R., & Garver, C. E. (2002). Changes in women's sexual interests and their partner's mate–retention tactics across the menstrual cycle: evidence for shifting conflicts of interest. *Proceedings of the Royal Society of London. Series B: Biological Sciences*, *269*, 975–982.

Goetz, A. T., & Shackelford, T. K. (2006). Sexual coercion and forced in-pair copulation as sperm competition tactics in humans. *Human Nature*, *17*, 265–282.

Goetz, A. T., & Shackelford, T. K. (2009). Sexual coercion in intimate relationships: A comparative analysis of the effects of women's infidelity and men's dominance and control. *Archives of Sexual Behavior*, *38*, 226–234.

Goetz, A. T., Shackelford, T. K., & Camilleri, J. A. (2008). Proximate and ultimate explanations are required for a comprehensive understanding of partner rape. *Aggression and Violent Behavior*, *13*, 119–123.

Goetz, A. T., Shackelford, T. K., Weekes-Shackelford, V. A., Euler, H. A., Hoier, S., Schmitt, D. P., & LaMunyon, C. W. (2005). Mate retention, semen displacement, and human sperm competition: A preliminary investigation of tactics to prevent and correct female infidelity. *Personality and Individual Differences*, *38*, 749–763.

Hadi, A. (2000). Prevalence and correlates of the risk of marital sexual violence in Bangladesh. *Journal of Interpersonal Violence*, *15*, 787–805.

Hawley, P. H., & Hensley, W. A., IV. (2009). Social dominance and forceful submission fantasies: Feminine pathology or power? *Journal of Sex Research*, *46*, 568–585.

Hyde, J. S., & Sawyer, T. F. (1977). Estrous cycle fluctuations in aggressiveness of house mice. *Hormones and Behavior*, *9*, 290–295.

Johnson, I. M., & Sigler, R. T. (2000). Forced sexual intercourse among intimates. *Journal of Family Violence*, *15*, 95–108.

Jones, D. N., Figueredo, A. J., Dickey, E. D., & Jacobs, W. J. (2007). Relations among individual differences in reproductive strategies, sexual attractiveness, affective and punitive intentions, and imagined sexual or emotional infidelity. *Evolutionary Psychology*, *5*, 387–410.

Joyal, C.C., & Carpentier, J. (2017). The prevalence of paraphilic interests and behaviors in the general population: A provincial survey. *Journal of Sex Research*, *54*, 161–171.

Kaighobadi, F., Shackelford, T. K., Popp, D., Moyer, R. M., Bates, V. M., & Liddle, J. R. (2009). Perceived risk of female infidelity moderates the relationship between men's personality and partner-directed violence. *Journal of Research in Personality*, *43*, 1033–1039.

Lalumière, M. L., Harris, G. T., Quinsey, V. L., & Rice, M. E. (2005). Contextual and Situational Factors. In M. L. Lalumière, G. T. Harris, V. L. Quinsey, & M. E. Rice, *The causes of rape: Understanding individual differences in male propensity for sexual aggression* (pp. 143–157). American Psychological Association.

Långström, N., Babchishin, K. M., Fazel, S., Lichtenstein, P., & Frisell, T. (2015). Sexual offending runs in families: A 37-year nationwide study. *International Journal of Epidemiology, 44*, 713–720.

Levine, G. (2011). *Darwin the writer*. Oxford University Press.

Lindenfors, P., & Tullberg, B. S. (2011). Evolutionary aspects of aggression the importance of sexual selection. *Advances in Genetics, 75*, 7–22.

Marshall, A. D., & Holtzworth-Munroe, A. (2002). Varying forms of husband sexual aggression: Predictors and subgroup differences. *Journal of Family Psychology, 16*, 286.

McKibbin, W. F., Starratt, V. G., Shackelford, T. K., & Goetz, A. T. (2011). Perceived risk of female infidelity moderates the relationship between objective risk of female infidelity and sexual coercion in humans (*Homo sapiens*). *Journal of Comparative Psychology, 125*, 370.

Navarro-Mantas, L., Velásquez, M. J., Lemus, S. D., & Megías, J. L. (2021). Prevalence and sociodemographic predictors of intimate partner violence against women in El Salvador. *Journal of Interpersonal Violence, 36*, NP3547–NP3573.

Painter, K., & Farrington, D. P. (1998). Marital violence in Great Britain and its relationship to marital and non-marital rape. *International Review of Victimology, 5*, 257–276.

Poppen, P. J., & Segal, N. J. (1988). The influence of sex and sex role orientation on sexual coercion. *Sex Roles: A Journal of Research, 19*, 689–701.

Pfaff, D. W., Diakow, C., Montgomery, M., & Jenkins, F. A. (1978). X-ray cinematographic analysis of lordosis in female rats. *Journal of Comparative and Physiological Psychology, 92*, 937.

Pfaff, D. W., Schwartz-Giblin, S., McCarthy, M. M., and Kow, L.-M. (1994). Cellular and molecular mechanisms of female reproductive behaviors. In E. Knobil and J. D. Neill (Eds.), *The Physiology of Reproduction, 2nd ed.*, pp. 107–220. Raven Press.

Rodriguez-Sierra, J. F., Howard, J. L., Pollard, G. T., & Hendricks, S. E. (1984). Effect of ovarian hormones on conflict behavior. *Psychoneuroendocrinology, 9*, 293–300.

Russell, D. E. H. (1982). *Rape in marriage*. Macmillian.

Salwen, J. K., & O'Leary, K. D. (2013). Adjustment problems and maladaptive relational style: A mediational model of sexual coercion in intimate relationships. *Journal of Interpersonal Violence, 28*, 1969–1988.

Shackelford, T. K., & Goetz, A. T. (2004). Men's sexual coercion in intimate relationships: Development and initial validation of the Sexual Coercion in Intimate Relationships Scale. *Violence and Victims, 19*, 541–556.

Shackelford, T. K., Goetz, A. T., Guta, F. E., & Schmitt, D. P. (2006). Mate guarding and frequent in-pair copulation in humans: Concurrent or compensatory anti-cuckoldry tactics? *Human Nature, 17*, 239–252.

Shackelford, T. K., Goetz, A. T., McKibbin, W. F., & Starratt, V. G. (2007). Absence makes the adaptations grow fonder: Proportion of time apart from partner, male sexual psychology, and sperm competition in humans (*Homo sapiens*). *Journal of Comparative Psychology, 121*, 214–220.

Shackelford, T. K., LeBlanc, G. J., Weekes-Shackelford, V. A., Bleske-Rechek, A. L., Euler, H. A., & Hoier, S. (2002) Psychological adaptation to human sperm competition. *Evolution and Human Behavior, 23*, 123–138.

Shields, N. M., & Hanneke, C. R. (1983). Attribution processes in violent relationships: Perceptions of violent husbands and their wives. *Journal of Applied Social Psychology, 13*, 515–527.

Snead, A. L., & Babcock, J. C. (2019). Differential predictors of intimate partner sexual coercion versus physical assault perpetration. *Journal of Sexual Aggression, 25*, 146–160. https://doi.org/10.1080/13552600.2019.1581282

Smuts, B. (1992). Male aggression against women. *Human Nature, 3*, 1–44.

Starratt, V. G., Goetz, A. T., Shackelford, T. K., McKibbin, W. F., & Stewart-Williams, S. (2008). Men's partner-directed insults and sexual coercion in intimate relationships. *Journal of Family Violence, 23*, 315–323.

Swanson, H. H., & Payne, A. P. (1970). Agonistic behaviour between pairs of hamsters of the same and opposite sex in a neutral observation area. *Behaviour, 36*, 259–269.

Thornhill, R., & Nancy, W. (1992). The evolutionary psychology of men's coercive sexuality. *Behavioral and Brain Sciences, 15*, 363–421.

Walker, S., & Rowlands, S (2019). Reproductive control by others: Means, perpetrators and effects. *British Medical Journal: MJ Sexual & Reproductive Health, 45*, 61–67.

Westerlund, M., Santtila, P., Johansson, A., Varjonen, M., Witting, K., Jern, P., . . . Sandnabba, N. K. (2010). Does unrestricted sociosexual behaviour have a shared genetic basis with sexual coercion? *Psychology, Crime & Law, 16,* 5–23.

Wilson, M., & Daly, M. (1992). The man who mistook his wife for a chattel. In J. H. Barkow, L. Cosmides, & J. Tooby (Eds.), *The adapted mind: Evolutionary psychology and the generation of culture,* 289–322. Oxford University Press.

Žukauskienė, R., Kaniušonytė, G., Bakaitytė, A., & Truskauskaitė-Kunevičienė, I. (2021). Prevalence and patterns of intimate partner violence in a nationally representative sample in Lithuania. *Journal of Family Violence, 36,* 117–130.

CHAPTER 25

Consequences of Infidelity in Nonhuman Animals

Yu-Hsun Hsu

Abstract

Infidelity occurs in many socially monogamous animals. While infidelity may affect both sexes via sexually transmitted diseases, in general infidelity is beneficial to mated males but more often costly to mated females. Unfaithful females are therefore expected to receive either direct benefits (i.e., benefits increasing female survival, offspring survival, or number of offspring), indirect benefits (i.e., genetic benefits increasing the number of grandoffspring), or both, in order to balance the costs of infidelity. However, recent meta-analyses have provided only limited support for these adaptive explanations of female infidelity. Emerging hypotheses therefore posit that infidelity might be nonadaptive to females and is presumably maintained in females as a byproduct of other traits favored by selection. This chapter discusses our current understanding of the potential consequences of infidelity in socially monogamous nonhuman animals, including costs and benefits for both sexes, and suggests directions for future studies.

Key Words: extrapair mating, extrapair paternity, polyandry, multiple mating, good genes

Infidelity in Nonhuman Animals

Various mating systems have evolved in wild animals. It was once thought that most if not all socially monogamous animals were faithful to their partners; for example, a study in the late 1960s reported that more than 90% of surveyed passerine families were monogamous (Lack, 1968). However, the application of molecular techniques to wild animals (Burke & Bruford, 1987; Goossens et al., 1998) and field observations of animal behaviors (Birkhead et al., 1987; Palombit, 1994; Reichard, 1995) have revealed that infidelity in socially monogamous wild animals is more common than previously expected. Among passerines, where social monogamy is the most common mating system, infidelity occurs in more than 76% of studied species (reviewed in Brouwer & Griffith, 2019). In mammals, where social monogamy is less common, perhaps due to sex-skewed parental care, infidelity has been reported in several species across taxa (Barelli et al., 2013; Fietz et al., 2000; Goossens et al., 1998; Reichard, 1995). By contrast, infidelity is relatively rare in fishes (Rueger et al., 2019) and invertebrates such as beetles (Dillard, 2017).

An interesting feature of infidelity in wild animals is the large variation of extrapair paternity rates both within and between species. Several comparative studies have attempted to attribute this large variation of extrapair paternity rates to ecological or other environmental factors, but the explainable ratios are limited (Brouwer & Griffith, 2019; Griffith et al., 2002; Isvaran & Clutton-Brock, 2007; Lifjeld et al., 2019). The difficulty of explaining the variation of extrapair paternity rates indicates that the evolutionary basis of fidelity in socially monogamous animals is not yet fully understood.

To improve our understanding of infidelity, it is essential to explicitly investigate the consequences of this behavior. The aim of this chapter is therefore to review the current understanding of the consequences of infidelity. In the following sections, the benefits and costs of infidelity will be discussed separately for females and males.

Costs of Infidelity

Females: Reduced Paternal Investment from Social Mates

Perhaps the most important cost of female infidelity is reduced paternal investment from social mates. Parental investment is a costly adult behavior that increases offspring survival (Trivers, 1972). According to a meta-analysis, avian males in artificially enlarged nests, which may result in higher paternal investment than usual, had reduced survival (Santos & Nakagawa, 2012). Therefore, males are expected to justify their paternal investment to optimize their fitness.

In socially monogamous species, males are expected to reduce their paternal investment when paternity uncertainty or the availability of other breeding opportunities increases (the parental care adjustment hypothesis; Grafen, 1980; Maynard-Smith, 1977). This hypothesis has been supported since early empirical studies where infidelity in wild animals was confirmed by DNA fingerprinting (Burke et al., 1989; Dixon et al., 1994). A comparative study of birds (Arnqvist & Kirkpatrick, 2005) and a recent comparative analysis across birds, fish, mammals, and insects (Griffin et al., 2013) provided further support for this hypothesis by showing that males significantly reduce paternal investment in response to female infidelity.

Despite the evidence supporting the parental care adjustment hypothesis, the detailed mechanisms by which males decide to reduce paternal investment have not been investigated until recently. For example, a comparative study showed that males only reduce paternal investment when both the costs of paternal investment are relatively high and there is a high risk of paternity loss (Griffin et al., 2013). That is, in a species where there is little cost of future reproductive success, males may continue to provide unreduced paternal investment to their offspring. Another recent study analyzing a long-term dataset of house sparrows (*Passer domesticus*) reported a within-male adjustment of paternal investment in response to female infidelity, which was relatively consistent within each female (Schroeder et al., 2016). In the same study, a similar adjustment was not observed in response to alien young resulting from cross-fostering, indicating that males may not adjust their efforts based on offspring recognition. Thus, future studies should continue to investigate the mechanisms underlying the link between infidelity and reduced paternal investment in order to better understand the costs of female infidelity.

Males: Paternity Loss

For a socially monogamous male, seeking opportunities for extrapair mating may be traded off with securing paternity in his own nest (Hill et al., 2011). An early comparative avian study reported that under a high risk of cuckoldry, males tend to guard their mates more intensively by copulating multiple times in order to secure their paternity through sperm competition (Møller & Birkhead, 1991). In other species, males use alternative strategies to guard their mates and secure paternity. For example, male Seychelles warblers (*Acrocephalus sechellensis*) follow their mates closely during her most fertile periods. After artificially terminating mate guarding in some pairs by adding model eggs, researchers found that males with reduced mate guarding were more likely to be cuckolded, despite spending time protecting the model eggs instead of seeking extrapair copulation (Komdeur et al., 1999, 2007).

However, this positive relationship between mate guarding and cuckoldry avoidance is subject to limitations. Theoretical modeling has suggested that males only favor guarding over extrapair mating when guarding is efficient and can maximize their overall reproductive success; that is, there may not be a linear correlation between extrapair activities and the likelihood of being cuckolded (Harts & Kokko, 2013; Kokko & Morrell, 2005). The proposed trade-off between seeking infidelity and cuckoldry avoidance was further challenged by a study of a wild house sparrow (*Passer domesticus*) population in which increased male annual extrapair paternity could not explain male annual paternity loss (Supporting Information in Hsu et al., 2017). In red-backed fairy-wrens (*Malurus melanocephalus*), attractive males tended to seek extrapair copulation, whereas unattractive males invested in guarding their own mates; however, overall reproductive success was similar between attractive and unattractive males (Dowling & Webster, 2017). These results indicate that males maximize their fitness by deploying mating tactics according to their own quality or attractiveness and that seeking extrapair copulation may not be as costly as previously thought. A recent meta-analysis supported these findings by showing a weak positive correlation between paternity protection behaviors (including mate guarding and frequent copulation) and paternity gain and a negative correlation between male protection behaviors and male quality (Harts et al., 2016).

In summary, although recent studies suggest that the cost of male infidelity through paternity loss may be lower than previously predicted, the understanding of such cost remains insufficient.

Both Sexes: Sexually Transmitted Diseases (STDs)

Another cost of infidelity is exposure to sexually transmitted diseases (STDs). Unlike the reduction of paternal investment and the trade-off between paternity loss and mate guarding, STDs affect both sexes. As early as 1986, the spread of STDs was suggested to be more prevalent in larger breeding groups than in smaller breeding groups of geese (Stipkovits et al., 1986). A study in passerines further supported a higher transmission probability of STDs in promiscuous and polyandrous species than in monogamous species, indicating that multiple mating can facilitate disease transmission (Poiani & Wilks, 2000).

STDs were first suggested to affect the evolution of mating behaviors and mating systems, including extrapair mating in socially monogamous species, almost 30 years ago (reviewed in Sheldon, 1993). However, despite this early recognition of the influence of STDs, few studies have directly examined this influence (Hillgarth, 1996; Lombardo & Thorpe, 2000; Westneat & Rambo, 2000). There are only a handful of empirical studies (Wagner, 1991), presumably because of the difficulty of collecting data and tracking the transmitted pathways in wild animals. Nevertheless, a theoretical model suggested that STDs may act as a frequency-dependent stabilizing evolutionary force on female infidelity (Kokko, Ranta, et al., 2002). Several follow-up theoretical studies examined how STDs may shape the evolution of mate choice (Ashby, 2020) or influence different mating systems (Ashby & Gupta, 2013). In general, the increased risk of STDs makes infidelity costly to the participating individuals, but there is insufficient information to quantify the influence of STDs on infidelity in nonhuman animals.

Female Benefits of Infidelity

Given that infidelity is costly to females through reduced paternal investment and increased risk of STDs, it has been assumed that females should be able to obtain benefits from infidelity in order for this behavior to evolve or be maintained. This assumption is especially relevant for birds, where infidelity has been reported in more than 76% of studied species (reviewed in Brouwer & Griffith, 2019). What are these benefits?

The benefits of infidelity for females can be categorized as direct and indirect. Direct benefits increase female fitness either by increasing their own survival or increasing the number of offspring (Darwin, 1859). Although the concept of direct benefits is straightforward and commonly accepted, evidence of direct benefits of female infidelity is relatively limited. As an indirect benefit, an unfaithful female may produce offspring with enhanced fitness and thus an increased number of grandoffspring (Fisher, 1930). Such indirect benefits are difficult to demonstrate but have been the focus of studies of female infidelity in wild animals in recent decades.

Direct Benefits

FEMALE SURVIVAL

A direct benefit of mating outside the pair-bond is increased female survival. For example, females may obtain resources from extrapair males. Male great gray shrikes (*Lanius excubitor*) offer prey as nuptial gifts to both within-pair and extrapair females, but the prey gifted to extrapair females is significantly larger than that gifted to social mates (Tryjanowski & Hromada, 2005). In this population, females can obtain direct benefits from infidelity both in the form of extra energy from nuptial gifts and an increased number of offspring.

Mating with aggressive extrapair males also may increase female survival. Male barn swallows (*Hirundo rustica*) have been observed to harass neighboring females through frequent chasing with the intention of forced mating (Møller, 1985). Forced mating by males with extrapair females is also common among waterfowl such as mallards (*Anas platyrhynchos*), white-cheeked pintails (*Anas bahamensis*), and lesser scaups (*Aythya affinis*), with vigorous chasing aerially, terrestrially, and even underwater (reviewed in McKinney & Evarts, 1998). For females of these species, resisting extrapair copulation can be too costly, and therefore females may accept aggressive courting from extrapair males in order to increase their survival.

FEMALE REPRODUCTIVE SUCCESS

Perhaps the most commonly accepted direct benefit of female extrapair mating is fertilization insurance. Four years after the first published report of extrapair offspring in house sparrows (*Passer domesticus*; Burke & Bruford, 1987), cuckoldry in this species was reported to be more frequent in broods with infertile eggs (Wetton & Parkin, 1991). According to the fertilization hypothesis, females engage in extrapair mating or multiple mating as insurance against infertility or genetic incompatibility with their social partners. In a comparative study using hatching rates to indicate fertilization success, the proportion of extrapair offspring sired by a male was positively correlated with hatching rate in 113 bird species (Reding, 2015). Interestingly, a recent experiment in zebra finches (*Taeniopygia guttata*) showed that repeated hatching failure did not increase female responsiveness towards extrapair males (Ihle et al., 2013). Moreover, if a female experiencing reproductive failure assessed her potential future mates by engaging in extrapair mating, a clear causal relationship between reproductive failure and divorce would be expected. However, convincing evidence, either through observation or manipulation, supporting such causality is lacking for monogamous species (reviewed in Ihle et al., 2013).

Alternatively, females may enjoy increased reproductive success due to extra paternal investment from extrapair mating. American crows (*Corvus brachyrhynchos*) are socially monogamous birds that breed cooperatively. In a population where extrapair mating occurred both between and within groups, males provided significantly higher paternal investment to broods with within-group extrapair offspring than to other broods (Townsend et al., 2010). This increased paternal investment was substantial enough to compensate for the costs of inbreeding due to within-group extrapair mating. Nevertheless, in most species, males provide no nuptial gifts to extrapair females nor paternal investment to extrapair offspring (but see Santema & Kempenaers, 2021 for a rare case), and thus evidence supporting the direct benefits hypothesis for females is scarce.

Last but not least, female infidelity may improve female reproductive success in species with infanticide. While females are always confident of their maternity, males are always uncertain of their paternity. Therefore, in species where males may kill the young of other males, mating with multiple males may reduce the likelihood of infanticide because these males may either protect the offspring or be less likely to kill offspring due to paternity confusion (Wolff & MacDonald, 2004). Supportive evidence of the infanticide avoidance hypothesis mostly comes from mammals, especially primates, either in the rare cases of social monogamy with extrapair mating or in socially polyandrous species (Borries et al., 2011; Klemme & Ylönen, 2010; Opie et al., 2013, but see Lukas & Clutton-Brock, 2014, for nonsupportive evidence). Studies testing this hypothesis in passerines, where social monogamy is common, are scarce (Robertson & Stutchbury, 1988), presumably because infanticide is rare in this taxon. The infanticide avoidance hypothesis is therefore unable to explain the common occurrence of infidelity in passerines.

Indirect Benefits

GOOD GENES HYPOTHESIS

The good genes hypothesis was originally proposed to explain female preferences in general. According to this hypothesis, females prefer males with heritable traits indicating high quality (Fisher, 1930; Hamilton & Zuk, 1982). By mating with these males, females can produce high-quality offspring. These high-quality offspring are expected to have high lifetime reproductive success, thus increasing the number of grandoffspring of the focal female. Adapting good genes hypothesis to female infidelity implies that females will mate with extrapair males with greater heritable quality than their within-pair male (Houtman, 1992). In socially monogamous species, even the best male can only form a social pair-bond with one female at a time. Therefore, most females in the population cannot form social bonds with their most preferred male(s). Instead, these females may engage in extrapair mating with higher quality males in order to produce offspring of higher fitness.

Body Size

According to the good genes hypothesis, extrapair males are expected to exhibit higher quality than within-pair males. The male trait most frequently used to test the good genes hypothesis is male body size. A male with larger body size is likely to win more intrasexual competitions and thus obtain better territory, richer food resources, and better protection against predators. Several body size indicators, such as height and weight, have moderate to high heritability. For example, in Savannah sparrows (*Passerculus sandwichensis*), the highest and lowest estimated heritability of recorded body size indicators were 0.651 ± 0.155 (tarsus length) and 0.160 ± 0.182 (bill width) (Cava et al., 2019), respectively. Therefore, offspring sired by extrapair males with larger body size are likely to be larger and to inherit high quality on competition and antipredator ability. However, the results of body size comparisons between extrapair and within-pair males are inconsistent. For example, in blue tits (*Cyanistes caeruleus*), the tarsus was longer in extrapair males than in the within-pair males they cuckolded, but similarly significant effects were not observed for wing length in the same population (Kempenaers et al., 1997) or in other populations of the same species (Charmantier et al., 2004). The results for other species are also inconsistent, with most studies reporting insignificant differences between extrapair males and the within-pair males they cuckolded (Forstmeier, 2002; Grant & Grant, 2011; Hsu et al., 2015). In rare cases, extrapair males are smaller than the within-pair males they cuckolded. For example, extrapair males had shorter wings than within-pair males in orange-tufted sunbirds (*Nectarinia osea osea*), although these males did not differ in body mass and bill length (Zilberman et al., 1999).

To reveal general trends, a recent meta-analysis examined whether extrapair males are larger than the within-pair males they cuckolded in passerines, the nonhuman taxa with the greatest number of studies of female infidelity. After considering phylogenetic relationships between species, body size indicators did not differ between extrapair males and the within-pair males they cuckolded (Hsu et al., 2015). These results remained the same after separating studies by trait category, such as wing length, body mass, tarsus length, and bill length and width.

Male Age

Male age is another trait often used to test the good genes hypothesis. By successfully living longer, a male demonstrates his ability to forage, evade predators, and survive bad weather. Females are therefore expected to prefer mating with older extrapair males, assuming these male viability characteristics are heritable (Kokko, Brooks, et al., 2002; Kokko & Lindstrom, 1996). Supporting evidence for this preference has been reported for several species, such as migratory purple martins (*Progne subis*; Tarof et al., 2012) and blue tits (*Cyanistes caeruleus*; Delhey et al., 2007). However, some studies have reported that extrapair males were younger than the within-pair males they cuckolded (Leisler et al., 2000; Tarvin et al., 2005) or that there were no significant differences in age (Gil et al., 2007; Hill et al., 2011).

Compared with studies of morphology, fewer studies have tested age differences between extrapair males and the within-pair males they cuckolded, possibly due to the logistical difficulties of collecting male age data. In order to collect age and paternity data from a wild population, the majority of individuals of a population must be monitored for several years. A meta-analysis based on published data suggested a trend in which extrapair males were older than the within-pair males they cuckolded (Hsu et al., 2015). Although the sample size was small, publication bias was negligible in this meta-analysis (Hsu et al., 2015).

SEXY SON HYPOTHESIS

Apart from male life-history traits such as body size and age, females may prefer to mate with males with exaggerated secondary sexual traits in order to produce attractive offspring that will have higher lifetime reproductive success. First proposed by Fisher (1930), the sexy son hypothesis was supported by a quantitative genetic model constructed by Lande (1981). This model demonstrated that female preference for a particular male trait can coevolve with male display of that trait through genetic correlation. When adapted to explain female infidelity, this hypothesis postulates that females tend to mate with attractive extrapair males in order to produce attractive offspring and, in turn, a higher number of grandoffspring. According to this hypothesis, extrapair males are expected to be more attractive than the within-pair males they cuckolded. For the common rosefinch (*Carpodacus erythrinus*), extrapair males displayed better overall sexual ornamentation (a measure comprising hue, brightness, and saturation) than the within-pair males they cuckolded (Albrecht et al., 2009). Similarly, extrapair males in kingbirds (*Tyrannus tyrannus*) performed better in several measurements of singing than the within-pair males they cuckolded (Dolan et al., 2007).

Interestingly, a meta-analysis of passerine studies showed that the attractiveness of extrapair males was not significantly different from that of the within-pair males they cuckolded (Hsu et al., 2015), even though there were more studies testing the sexy son hypothesis than the good genes hypothesis. However, in species where males attract females by song characteristics, extrapair males performed significantly better than the within-pair males they cuckolded, whereas no difference was observed in species in which males attract females by ornaments.

GENETIC COMPATIBILITY HYPOTHESIS

The genetic compatibility hypothesis posits that female preference relies on the level of genetic compatibility of a chosen male and the focal female (Brown, 1997). That is, to maximize the heterozygosity and thus the fitness of her offspring, a female is expected to mate with the male that is most compatible or most genetically dissimilar with her (Kempenaers, 2007; Mays & Hill, 2004). In contrast to the good genes and sexy son hypotheses, which imply that female preference is based on absolute criteria according to which one or a few superior males are favored by all females, the genetic compatibility hypothesis considers female preference to be based on a criterion related to the genetic composition of each female. Therefore, the most suitable male partner is different for each female within the same population.

When adapting the genetic compatibility hypothesis to explain female infidelity, a female is expected to mate with extrapair males that are genetically more compatible with the focal female than her within-pair mate. Mating with genetically dissimilar extrapair males can reduce inbreeding, especially in small populations where inbreeding depression may occur (but see Duthie & Reid, 2016; Reid et al., 2015).

Supportive evidence for the genetic compatibility hypothesis has been reported for several species, including house finches (*Haemorthous mexicanus*; Oh & Badyaev, 2006), tree swallows (*Tachycineta bicolor*; Whittingham & Dunn, 2010), and great reed warblers (*Acrocephalus arundinaceus*; Bensch et al., 1994). However, many studies do not support this prediction and report differences that are either insignificant (Grant & Grant, 2011; Suter et al., 2007) or in the opposite direction (Ferretti et al., 2011; Freeman-Gallant et al., 2006). A meta-analysis in passerines reported that the genetic similarity between a female and her extrapair mate was no different from that between the same female and her within-pair mate (Hsu et al., 2015). This result persisted even after dividing the analysis into studies based on genetic markers such as MHC and those based on neutral markers such as microsatellite and DNA fingerprinting.

PATERNITY EFFECTS ON OFFSPRING FITNESS

It could be argued that the genetic benefits of infidelity to females are obscured by a lack of sufficiently precise measurements. For example, the failure to find support for the good genes hypothesis or sexy son hypothesis may indicate that the examined life-history or sexually selected traits are not chosen by females. Similarly, with respect to the genetic compatibility hypothesis, females using relative criteria for male genetics might target extrapair males with the most optimal genetic compatibility instead of males that are the most dissimilar (Mays et al., 2008).

One general prediction for all three of these hypotheses is that offspring resulting from infidelity (hereafter referred to as "extrapair offspring") are expected to have higher fitness than within-pair offspring. After all, increased offspring fitness and an increased number of grandoffspring are considered the core indirect benefits to females. Evidence for this prediction is inconsistent. A four-year study of blue tits (*Cyanistes caeruleus*) reported that extrapair offspring had higher genetic heterozygosity than their maternal half-siblings, that is, the within-pair offspring of their social fathers (Foerster et al., 2003). Moreover, the same study also reported that offspring successfully fledged and recruited tended to have higher heterozygosity than those failed to recruit, indicating that producing highly heterozygous extrapair offspring is beneficial to females. In an 8-year study of dark-eyed juncos (*Junco hyemalis*), extrapair offspring had higher reproductive success than within-pair offspring (Gerlach et al., 2012), suggesting a more straightforward indirect benefit to unfaithful females. However, several studies have found nonsupportive evidence. For example, a meta-analysis of data from 10 studies found no significant difference in survival between extrapair and within-pair offspring (Akçay & Roughgarden, 2007). Studies of several species have also reported that extrapair offspring had either similar or lower fitness than within-pair offspring (Hsu et al., 2014; Sardell, Arcese, & Reid, 2012; Schmoll et al., 2009).

There are several potential reasons for these inconclusive results. First, paternity may affect offspring fitness at different life-history stages. For example, in house sparrows (*Passer domesticus*), extrapair and within-pair offspring performed similarly in hatching success and nestling survival, but extrapair offspring performed worse in the probability of recruitment and lifetime reproductive success (Hsu et al., 2014). Similarly, in coal tits (*Periparus ater*), the fitness of recruited extrapair and within-pair offspring was similar as measured by lifespan and age at first reproduction, but male extrapair offspring had a higher lifetime reproductive success than male within-pair offspring (Schmoll et al., 2009).

Second, the results may vary depending on to whom the extrapair offspring was compared with. Because females in most species mate more than once in a lifetime, these females may engage in extrapair mating in some broods but mate solely with their social partners in other broods. Therefore, it is important to define the extrapair and within-pair offspring under comparison. For example, in house sparrows (*Passer domesticus*), extrapair offspring and within-pair offspring from unfaithful mothers had similar fitness, but these extrapair offspring performed worse on recruitment and reproductive success than within-pair offspring produced by faithful females (Hsu et al., 2014). In song sparrows (*Melospiza melodia*), hatchlings sired by male extrapair offspring had greater recruiting opportunities than hatchlings sired by male within-pair offspring (Sardell, Arcese, & Reid, 2012). The same study found no effect of paternity status on hatchlings produced by female extrapair offspring (Sardell, Arcese, & Reid, 2012), indicating a sex-specific effect of paternity status. Interestingly, when limiting the comparison to extrapair offspring and their maternal half-siblings (i.e., within-brood comparison) in mixed broods of the same population, neither an advantage of paternity status nor a sex-specific effect was detected. On the contrary, extrapair offspring were reported to produce similar or lower lifetime reproductive success than their maternal half-siblings (Sardell et al., 2012). These conflicting results highlight the importance of defining the units being compared because different comparisons can yield different results for offspring fitness.

Context-Dependent Hypothesis

Given the accumulating evidence challenging the indirect benefits explanations of female infidelity, some researchers have argued for the inclusion of possible interactions between paternity effects and environmental effects. The key assumption of this context-dependent hypothesis is an interaction between genotype and environment; that is, the same genotypes may show phenotypically plastic responses to different environments (Qvarnstrom, 2001; Schmoll, 2011). According to this hypothesis, the difference in offspring fitness may be large enough to be detectable in some, usually stressful environmental conditions. Therefore, females are expected to obtain indirect benefits from infidelity under these specific environmental conditions but not from the other conditions(Schmoll, 2011; Schmoll et al., 2005).

To support the context-dependent hypothesis, evidence showing variations in fitness differences between offspring depending on environmental context is needed (O'Brien & Dawson, 2007). In coal tits (*Periparus ater*), the recruitment probability decreased with increasing hatching date, but this effect was less pronounced in extrapair offspring than in their maternal half-siblings (i.e., within-pair offspring from the same broods). Therefore, extrapair offspring had a higher probability of recruitment than their maternal half-siblings only if they hatched later in the season and not if they hatched early in the season (Schmoll et al., 2005). Similarly, in common yellowthroats (*Geothlypis trichas*), extrapair nestlings had stronger immune responses than within-pair nestlings only in colder and thus more stressful years (Garvin et al., 2006). However, nonsupportive evidence has also been reported. In red bishops (*Euplectes orix*), extrapair nestlings had weaker immune responses than within-pair nestlings under stressful environmental conditions (i.e., hotter temperature; Edler & Friedl, 2008).

The current results from studies testing the context-dependent hypothesis in natural conditions can potentially be a coincidence with normal annual variation, because the comparisons were between offspring produced in different years (Edler & Friedl, 2008; Garvin et al., 2006; O'Brien & Dawson, 2007), with the exception of the coal tit study (Schmoll et al., 2005). To control the environmental factor, Arct et al. (2013) conducted a manipulation experiment in which they increased environmental stress by artificially enlarging the brood size of blue tits (*Cyanistes caeruleus*). They found that compared to within-pair offspring, extrapair offspring had significantly stronger immune responses in nests with enlarged broods. By contrast, extrapair offspring had weaker immune responses in control nests, but this difference was not significant. However, another manipulation experiment reported opposite results: in pied flycatchers (*Ficedula hypoleuca*) in Spain, extrapair offspring was smaller and lighter than within-pair offspring in enlarged broods (Moreno et al., 2013).

In general, observational and experimental studies of the context-dependent hypothesis are scarce. Observational studies require continually collecting data for multiple years, which is costly, without prior information about a "stressful condition" that a research team can target. Experimental studies are restricted by the need for manageable sample sizes. However, these deficiencies might be partly overcome by the recent emergence of comparative analyses such as meta-analyses and phylogenetic comparative analyses.

For species distributed across temporal zones, latitude could be used as an indicator of environmental difficulty, as higher latitudes are associated with more severe winters and thus greater survival stress. According to the context-dependent hypothesis, females would be expected to benefit more from infidelity at higher latitudes, and thus an increase in extrapair paternity rates with latitude would be predicted. However, a recently published phylogenetic mixed model for socially monogamous avian species showed the opposite: within noncolonial species, populations distributed at higher latitudes had lower extrapair paternity rates (Brouwer & Griffith, 2019). In a subsequent analysis of four species that were sampled in more than 10 different populations, this trend remained supported for noncolonial blue tits (*Cyanistes caeruleus*), pied flycatchers (*Ficedula hypoleuca*), and great tits (*Parus major*), presumably due to the trade-off between seeking extrapair mating and parental care (Brouwer & Griffith, 2019). Nevertheless, latitude can also be an indicator of other variables, such as breeding synchrony, which was the focus of the original authors (Brouwer & Griffith, 2019). Further studies are required to tease these variables apart.

Summary of Benefits of Infidelity to Females

Several hypotheses have been proposed to explain female infidelity. These hypotheses consider both direct benefits, i.e., an increased female survival and female reproductive success, and indirect benefits, i.e., an increased number of grandoffspring of the focal females. However, empirical evidence from case studies, comparative studies, and meta-analyses supporting these explanations is limited. Rather than indicating the absence of benefits of infidelity for females, the accumulated results suggest infidelity may be beneficial to females either generally in all conditions, or specifically in certain conditions. However, regardless of form, these benefits are too trivial to solely explain the prevalence of female infidelity in some wild animal taxa.

Nonadaptive Infidelity in Females

The persistent failure of adaptive explanations of female infidelity calls for alternative explanations for why females mate outside of their pair bonds. One possible explanation is that infidelity is nonadaptive in females; that is, female infidelity could simply be a byproduct of other traits favored by selection in the population. In this case, females may continually engage in extrapair mating as long as the influence of infidelity, whether positive, negative, or neutral, is weak enough that it can be neglected.

Several hypotheses of nonadaptive explanations of female infidelity have gained attention in the past decade. Most of these hypotheses are based on the core assumption that male infidelity is favored by selection. Males can increase their annual and lifetime reproductive success through infidelity (Albrecht et al., 2007), and the costs of infidelity to males are generally small because most males in socially monogamous species do not provide paternal investment to their extrapair offspring (see the earlier sections "Males: Paternity Loss" and "Both Sexes: Sexually Transmitted Diseases (STDs)" for detailed discussions of the costs of infidelity to males). Since infidelity requires the participation of two individuals, female infidelity is expected to result as a byproduct of male infidelity.

Male Manipulation Hypothesis

The male manipulation hypothesis considers that larger or older males are more experienced in increasing their reproductive success through infidelity by higher investment on reproduction; courting, convincing, or forcing extrapair females to mate with them (reviewed in Westneat & Stewart, 2003; Lifjeld et al., 2022). Based on this hypothesis, compared to the within-pair males they cuckold, extrapair males are expected to be (1) larger, in order to convince or even force females to mate with them; or (2) older, so that these males are better at attracting females to mate with them, assuming male age is positively correlated with mating experience. These predictions are similar to those of the good genes hypothesis. However, as we discussed in the section "Indirect Benefits," current evidence only supports that extrapair males tend to be older and not that extrapair males are usually larger than within-pair males (Cleasby & Nakagawa, 2012; Hsu et al., 2015). Because both adaptive and nonadaptive explanations of female infidelity predict that extrapair males are larger than the within-pair males they cuckolded, I will discuss male age effects on extrapair paternity and offspring fitness separately later in this chapter

Genetic Constraints in Females

Genetic constraints are another possible explanation of the prevalence of female infidelity even in the absence of benefits to females. It is possible that the alleles responsible for female infidelity have extra pleiotropic effects favored by selection in the population, either in males (i.e., intersexual correlation hypothesis) or in females (i.e., intrasexual correlation hypothesis). Both hypotheses require infidelity to be heritable. In a captive zebra finch (*Taeniopygia guttata*) population, both female extrapair response (heritability, h^2, was estimated to be 0.578 ± 0.117) and extrapair paternity (h^2 = 0.147 ± 0.071) were heritable, although the heritability of male extrapair paternity was weak (h^2 = 0.060 ± 0.059; Supplemental information in Forstmeier et al., 2011). However, the most recent study of the same population estimated weak heritability of all three traits: female extrapair response, h^2 = 0.043 ± 0.019; female extrapair paternity, h^2 = 0.057 ± 0.026; and male extrapair paternity, h^2 = 0.025 ± 0.021 (Supporting information in Wang et al., 2020). Similarly, the h^2 values of both female and male extrapair paternity in song sparrows (*Melospiza melodia*) were low to moderate, although with relatively larger variance (Reid et al., 2011a, 2011b, 2014; Reid & Wolak, 2018). The weak h^2 of extrapair mating was also reported in a recent study in pied flycatchers (*Ficedula hypoleuca*), where the estimated h^2 of the extrapair offspring number was low across female-specific, male-specific, and the joint estimation (Grinkov et al., 2020).

INTERSEXUAL CORRELATION HYPOTHESIS

The intersexual correlation hypothesis posits that nonadaptive female infidelity evolves and is maintained by a set of genes whose pleotropic effects also enhance male promiscuity via increased male reproductive success (reviewed in Forstmeier et al., 2014). That is, because engaging in extrapair mating is beneficial to males, if extrapair mating behaviors are under the same set of genetic controls in both sexes, then the daughters of these males are likely to engage in extrapair mating even if infidelity does not increase these daughters' fitness per se. This hypothesis is supported by a recent theoretical study with a two-locus model. In this model, nonadaptive female infidelity can evolve by hitchhiking with male promiscuity, but only when female infidelity is cost-free (Lyu et al., 2018).

This hypothesis requires a positive between-sex genetic correlation (r_{MF}) between female and male extrapair mating behaviors. Supportive evidence has been reported in zebra finches (*Taeniopygia guttata*), where the r_{MF} of female and male extrapair mating was estimated to be moderate (r_{MF} = 0.6; Forstmeier et al., 2011) compared with other behavioral traits (r_{MF} = 0.77; reviewed in Poissant et al., 2010). However, this finding was challenged recently in a study re-examining the r_{MF} of female and male extrapair mating after manipulating male courtship rates in the same captive zebra finch population. The latest study reported an r_{MF} close to zero between male courtship rates and female extrapair paternity and a negative r_{MF} between male extrapair siring success and female extrapair paternity (Wang et al., 2020). These results challenge the major assumption of the intersexual correlation hypothesis of female infidelity and call for further studies in other species before any general conclusions can be drawn.

INTRASEXUAL CORRELATION HYPOTHESIS

Female infidelity can also evolve and be maintained by the correlation between female responsiveness and other female traits under selection, such as female fecundity, which can increase female reproductive success (Forstmeier et al., 2011; Wang et al., 2020), or personality traits that may alter female mating behaviors (Patrick et al., 2012). Alternatively, if female acceptance of courting from their within-pair males and female acceptance of costly infidelity are controlled by the same set of alleles, positive selection of the former may increase the latter (Arnqvist & Kirkpatrick, 2005). Only limited empirical studies have analyzed the additive genetic correlation between female infidelity and other female traits. In captive zebra finches (*Taeniopygia guttata*), the additive genetic correlation between female fecundity and female extrapair response was moderate (0.41 ± 0.21; Wang et al., 2020). In song sparrows (*Melospiza melodia*), however, the genetic correlation between female annual reproductive success and female extrapair reproduction was not significantly different from zero (Reid, 2012). Further empirical and theoretical studies are therefore required to evaluate this hypothesis.

Effects of Male Age on Female Infidelity

Male Age is Associated with Extrapair Paternity

Although age-dependent reproductive success has been reported in several species (Froy et al., 2013; Hayward et al., 2013; Schroeder et al., 2012), the age-dependent trajectory of extrapair paternity success has rarely been addressed (Hsu et al., 2017; Lebigre et al., 2013). This is intriguing because male age effects on extrapair paternity are among the most robust findings in studies of infidelity in nonhuman animals. Extrapair males are generally older than within-pair males (reviewed in Hsu et al., 2015), and older males tend to sire more extrapair offspring within the same populations (reviewed in Cleasby & Nakagawa, 2012).

However, it is not clear whether the association between male age and extrapair paternity is due to a between-male age effect, in which higher-quality males live longer and sire more extrapair offspring throughout their lifetimes (i.e., selective disappearance), or a within-male age effect, in which extrapair paternity by the same male increases with age. A recent study applied a within-individual analysis in order to distinguish within-male and between-male effects of age in a wild house sparrow (*Passer domesticus*) population (Hsu et al., 2017). In this study, within the same male, extrapair paternity success was reported to increase with age early in life but decline with age later in life, even after considering the terminal effect. Interestingly, there was no significant between-individual age effect on male extrapair paternity success (Hsu et al., 2017). The questions that remain are why do males attain more extrapair paternity success as they age, and what are the consequences in terms of offspring fitness?

Male Age Effects on Female Infidelity
BENEFITS OF OLDER MALES

Older males can attain higher extrapair paternity success through various pathways. First, older males may be preferred by females. One commonly accepted assumption is that older males are often high-quality males with proven viability (Trivers, 1972). This assumption is supported by theoretical studies showing that female preference for older males can evolve in various conditions where both female preference and male quality are heritable (Kokko, 1998; Kokko & Lindstrom, 1996; Manning, 1985, but see Hansen & Price, 1995). Second, older males are often experienced breeders and can engage in more extrapair matings by attracting females with better timing and frequency or by higher investment on reproduction (Poesel et al., 2006; Lifjeld et al., 2022). Last but not least, older males may gain higher extrapair paternity through sperm competition. In several species, the size of testes often increases with male age, which may lead to higher sperm production per ejaculation and thus higher fertilization success (Laskemoen et al., 2008).

COSTS OF OLDER MALES

The major costs of mating with older males are the costs associated with senescence, which takes various forms. For example, physiological senescence of muscles and body mass may weaken a male's foraging ability and territory-holding potential, leading to reduced survival (Hamalainen et al., 2014; Hindle et al., 2009). Similarly, germline senescence in older males may occur through the accumulation of mutations with male age. Such germline senescence may result in offspring with lower genetic quality and thus lower offspring fitness (Kong et al., 2012; Pizzari et al., 2008). The expected results of male senescence are in line with the predictions of the Lansing effect, a transgenerational effect where offspring sired by older males tend to have shorter lifespans and reduced lifetime fitness than offspring sired by younger males (Lansing, 1954).

In the case of extrapair paternity, because males usually do not provide direct benefits such as food resources and paternal investment to extrapair females or extrapair offspring, physiological senescence of muscles and body mass has relatively low impact. By contrast, germline senescence is expected to be a major disadvantage to females mating with aging males outside of pair bonds.

Male Extrapair Mating Behavior and Extrapair Paternity

The male manipulation hypothesis, as explained in the section "Male Manipulation Hypothesis", posits that older and more experienced males can obtain more extrapair paternity because these males are better at convincing females to engage in extrapair mating. This hypothesis is based on the assumption that male age influences male mating behaviors, which will further translate into male extrapair reproductive success. This assumption is difficult to test because copulation, especially extrapair copulation, is challenging to observe in most species. Nevertheless, some studies have successfully tested this correlation. In blue tits (*Cyanistes caeruleus*), older males started singing their dawn song earlier in the morning than second-year males. Males singing earlier in the morning had more mating partners and thus more mating opportunities (Poesel et al., 2006). In a study of captive house sparrows (*Passer domesticus*) there was no correlation between male age and male extrapair mating behavior (Girndt et al., 2018). This is intriguing because male age was associated with male extrapair paternity gain both in this studied captive population and in a wild house sparrow population that had been monitored for more than a decade (Hsu et al., 2017). This difference between the age-related proportions of extrapair mating behaviors and extrapair paternity gain could be a result of sperm competition. In captive house sparrows, sperm morphological traits and sperm load (indicated by the measure of cloacal protuberance volume) did not differ with male age, but older males delivered almost three times more sperm to females (Girndt et al., 2019).

Effects of Male Age on Offspring Fitness

The age-dependent trajectory of paternity success starts lower, increases more steeply and declines later for extrapair paternity than for within-pair paternity, but the proportion of extrapair paternity among all paternity increases with male age within the same individual (Hsu et al., 2017). That is, extrapair offspring are particularly prone to paternal age effects. Interestingly, in a wild population of house sparrows (*Passer domesticus*) where the extrapair males were known to be older than the within-pair males they cuckolded, the fitness of extrapair offspring was reported to be lower than that of within-pair offspring (Hsu et al., 2014, 2015). On the contrary, in blue tits (*Cyanistes caeruleus*), although extrapair males were in general older than the within-pair males they cuckolded, extrapair offspring were more likely to survive than within-pair offspring in the same population (Kempenaers et al., 1997).

In short, although studies of several species have shown that extrapair males are older than within-pair males (reviewed in Hsu et al., 2015) and that older parents tend to produce offspring with decreased fitness (Bouwhuis et al., 2010; Schroeder et al., 2015), investigations of the connections between the age effects of extrapair males and offspring fitness remain scarce. That is, there is insufficient evidence to draw any general conclusions on whether mating with older extrapair males is beneficial or not to the unfaithful females.

Conclusion

In summary, infidelity is beneficial to males with little cost but is costly to females with little confirmed benefits (Figure 25.1). Current evidence indicates that female infidelity is more likely to be maintained by a positive correlation, either behaviorally or genetically, with male infidelity, which is favored by selection, than by positive selection on this behavior in females per se. This conclusion represents a big breakthrough in our understanding of animal infidelity in the last decade, as accumulated evidence has challenged the long-accepted adaptive explanations of female infidelity and shifted our attention toward the nonadaptive explanations.

Although most studies of animal infidelity have focused on testing the indirect benefits hypothesis, some studies have considered more than one selection force in animal infidelity. For example, a comparative study reported significant direct costs and nonsignificant indirect benefits of female infidelity, suggesting that female infidelity could be an outcome

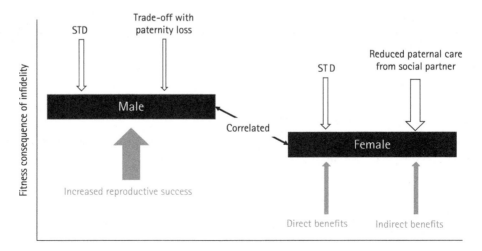

Figure 25.1 Illustration of the costs (white arrows) and benefits (grey arrows) of male and female infidelity that influence their fitness consequences. This width of each arrow indicates the magnitude of the impact based on current evidence.

of sexual conflicts (Arnqvist & Kirkpatrick, 2005). Integrative points of view have also been developed for some study systems (i.e., specific populations of wild animals), such as house sparrows (*Passer domesticus*) on Lundy Island, United Kingdom (Hsu et al., 2014, 2015, 2017; Schroeder et al., 2016); song sparrows (*Melospiza melodia*) on Mandarte Island, Canada (Reid et al., 2011a, 2015; Reid & Sardell, 2012; Reid & Wolak, 2018; Sardell, Arcese, & Reid, 2012; Sardell, Arcese, Keller, et al., 2012); and a captive population of zebra finches (*Taeniopygia guttata*) in Seewiesen, Germany (Forstmeier et al., 2011; Ihle et al., 2013; Wang et al., 2020).

Nevertheless, much work remains unfinished. First, our current understanding on the costs of infidelity for both sexes are insufficient to provide representative estimations. Therefore, there is a need for more studies of the impact of STDs or paternity loss due to the trade-off with seeking extrapair mating. Second, integrative studies considering multiple selection forces in animal infidelity, both empirical and theoretical, can provide an overview of the overall fitness consequences of this behavior. Such an overview may help improve our understanding of the high variation of extrapair paternity rates both between and within species (reviewed in Brouwer & Griffith, 2019).

References

Akçay, E., & Roughgarden, J. (2007). Extra-pair paternity in birds: Review of the genetic benefits. *Evolutionary Ecology Research*, 9(5), 855–868.

Albrecht, T., Schnitzer, J., Kreisinger, J., Exnerova, A., Bryja, J., & Munclinger, P. (2007). Extrapair paternity and the opportunity for sexual selection in long-distant migratory passerines. *Behavioral Ecology*, 18(2), 477–486. https://doi.org/10.1093/beheco/arm001

Albrecht, T., Vinkler, M., Schnitzer, J., Polakova, R., Munclinger, P., & Bryja, J. (2009). Extra-pair fertilizations contribute to selection on secondary male ornamentation in a socially monogamous passerine. *Journal of Evolutionary Biology*, 22(10), 2020–2030. https://doi.org/10.1111/j.1420-9101.2009.01815.x

Arct, A., Drobniak, S. M., Podmokla, E., Gustafson, L., & Cichon, M. (2013). Benefits of extra-pair mating may depend on environmental conditions—An experimental study in the blue tit (*Cyanistes caeruleus*). *Behavioral Ecology and Sociobiology*, 67(11), 1809–1815. https://doi.org/10.1007/s00265-013-1588-4

Arnqvist, G., & Kirkpatrick, M. (2005). The evolution of infidelity in socially monogamous passerines: The strength of direct and indirect selection on extrapair copulation behavior in females. *American Naturalist*, 165(S5), S26–37. https://doi.org/10.1086/429350

Ashby, B. (2020). Antagonistic coevolution between hosts and sexually transmitted infections. *Evolution*, 71(1), 43–56. https://doi.org/doi.org/10.1111/evo.13883

Ashby, B., & Gupta, S. (2013). Sexually transmitted infections in polygamous mating systems. *Philosophical Transactions of the Royal Society B: Biological Sciences*, 368(1613), 20120048. https://doi.org/10.1098/rstb.2012.0048

Barelli, C., Matsudaira, K., Wolf, T., Roos, C., Heistermann, M., Hodges, K., Ishida, T., Malaivijitnond, S., & Reichard, U. H. (2013). Extra-pair paternity confirmed in wild white-handed gibbons. *American Journal of Primatology*, 75(12), 1185–1195. https://doi.org/10.1002/ajp.22180

Bensch, S., Hasselquist, D., & Vonschantz, T. (1994). Genetic similarity between parents predicts hatching failure—Nonincestuous inbreeding in the great reed warbler. *Evolution*, 48(2), 317–326. https://doi.org/10.1111/j.1558-5646.1994.tb01314.x

Birkhead, T. R., Atkin, L., & Møller, A. P. (1987). Copulation behaviour of birds. *Behaviour*, 101(13), 101–138. https://doi.org/10.1163/156853987X00396

Borries, C., Savini, T., & Koenig, A. (2011). Social monogamy and the threat of infanticide in larger mammals. *Behavioral Ecology and Sociobiology*, 65, 685–693. https://doi.org/10.1007/s00265-010-1070-5

Bouwhuis, S., Charmantier, A., Verhulst, S., & Sheldon, B. C. (2010). Trans-generational effects on ageing in a wild bird population. *Journal of Evolutionary Biology*, *23*, 636–642. https://doi.org/10.1111/j.1420-9101.2009.01929.x

Brouwer, L., & Griffith, S. C. (2019). Extra-pair paternity in birds. *Molecular Ecology*, *28*(22), 4864–4882. https://doi.org/10.1111/mec.15259

Brown, J. L. (1997). A theory of mate choice based on heterozygosity. *Behavioral Ecology*, *8*(1), 60–65. https://doi.org/10.1093/beheco/8.1.60

Burke, T., & Bruford, M. W. (1987). DNA fingerprinting in birds. *Nature*, *327*(6118), 149–152. https://doi.org/10.1038/327149a0

Burke, T., Davies, N. B., Bruford, M. W., & Hatchwell, B. J. (1989). Parental care and mating behaviour of polyandrous dunnocks *Prunella modularis* related to paternity by DNA fingerprinting. *Nature*, *338*, 249–251. https://doi.org/10.1038/338249a0

Cava, J. A., Perlut, N. G., & Travis, S. E. (2019). Heritability and evolvability of morphological traits of Savannah sparrows (*Passerculus sandwichensis*) breeding in agricultural grasslands. *PLoS One*, *14*(1), e0210472. https://doi.org/10.1371/journal.pone.0210472

Charmantier, A., Blondel, J., Perret, P., & Lambrechts, M. M. (2004). Do extra-pair paternities provide genetic benefits for female blue tits *Parus caeruleus*? *Journal of Avian Biology*, *35*(6), 524–532. https://doi.org/10.1111/j.0908-8857.2004.03296.x

Cleasby, I. R., & Nakagawa, S. (2012). The influence of male age on within-pair and extra-pair paternity in passerines. *Ibis*, *154*(2), 318–324. https://doi.org/10.1111/j.1474-919X.2011.01209.x

Darwin, C. (1859). *On the origin of species by means of natural selection, or preservation of favoured races in the struggle for life*. London:John Murray.

Delhey, K., Peters, A., Johnsen, A., & Kempenaers, B. (2007). Fertilization success and UV ornamentation in blue tits *Cyanistes caeruleus*: Correlational and experimental evidence. *Behavioral Ecology*, *18*(2), 399–409. https://doi.org/10.1093/beheco/arl096

Dillard, J. R. (2017). High rates of extra-pair paternity in a socially monogamous beetle with biparental care. *Ecological Entomology*, *42*(1), 1–10. https://doi.org/10.1111/een.12346

Dixon, A., Ross, D., Omalley, S. L. C., & Burke, T. (1994). Paternal investment inversely related to degree of extra-pair paternity in the reed bunting. *Nature*, *371*(6499), 698–700. https://doi.org/10.1038/371698a0

Dolan, A. C., Murphy, M. T., Redmond, L. J., Sexton, K., & Duffield, D. (2007). Extrapair paternity and the opportunity for sexual selection in a socially monogamous passerine. *Behavioral Ecology*, *18*(6), 985–993. https://doi.org/10.1093/beheco/arm068

Dowling, J., & Webster, M. S. (2017). Working with what you've got: Unattractive males show greater mate guarding effort in a duetting songbird. *Biology Letters*, *13*(1), 20160682. https://doi.org/10.1098/rsbl.2016.0682

Duthie, A. B., & Reid, J. M. (2016). Evolution of inbreeding avoidance and inbreeding preference through mate choice among interacting relatives. *American Naturalist*, *188*(6), 651–667. https://doi.org/10.1086/688919

Edler, R., & Friedl, T. W. P. (2008). Within-pair young are more immunocompetent than extrapair young in mixed-paternity broods of the red bishop. *Animal Behaviour*, *75*, 391–401. https://doi.org/10.1016/j.anbehav.2007.05.004

Ferretti, V., Massoni, V., Bulit, F., Winkler, D. W., & Lovette, I. J. (2011). Heterozygosity and fitness benefits of extrapair mate choice in white-rumped swallows (*Tachycineta leucorrhoa*). *Behavioral Ecology*, *22*(6), 1178–1186. https://doi.org/10.1093/beheco/arr103

Fietz, J., Zischler, H., Schwiegk, C., Tomiuk, J., Dausmann, K. H., & Ganzhorn, J. U. (2000). High rates of extra-pair young in the pair-living fat-tailed dwarf lemur, *Cheirogaleus medius*. *Behavioral Ecology and Sociobiology*, *49*, 8–17. https://doi.org/10.1007/s002650000269

Fisher, R. A. (1930). *The genetical theory of natural selection*. Clarendon Press. https://doi.org/10.5962/bhl.title.27468

Foerster, K., Delhey, K., Johnsen, A., Lifjeld, J. T., & Kempenaers, B. (2003). Females increase offspring heterozygosity and fitness through extra-pair matings. *Nature*, *425*(6959), 714–717. https://doi.org/10.1038/nature01969

Forstmeier, W. (2002). Factors contributing to male mating success in the polygynous dusky warbler (*Phylloscopus fuscatus*). *Behaviour*, *139*, 1361–1381. http://www.jstor.org/stable/4535992

Forstmeier, W., Martin, K., Bolund, E., Schielzeth, H., & Kempenaers, B. (2011). Female extrapair mating behavior can evolve via indirect selection on males. *Proceedings of the National Academy of Sciences, 108*(26), 10608–10613. https://doi.org/10.1073/pnas.1103195108

Forstmeier, W., Nakagawa, S., Griffith, S. C., & Kempenaers, B. (2014). Female extra-pair mating: Adaptation or genetic constraint? *Trends in Ecology and Evolution, 29*(8), 456–464. https://doi.org/10.1016/j.tree.2014.05.005

Freeman-Gallant, C. R., Wheelwright, N. T., Meiklejohn, K. E., & Sollecito, S. V. (2006). Genetic similarity, extrapair paternity, and offspring quality in Savannah sparrows (*Passerculus sandwichensis*). *Behavioral Ecology, 17*(6), 952–958. https://doi.org/10.1093/beheco/arl031

Froy, H., Phillips, R. A., Wood, A. G., Nussey, D. H., & Lewis, S. (2013). Age-related variation in reproductive traits in the wandering albatross: Evidence for terminal improvement following senescence. *Ecology Letters, 16*(5), 642–649. https://doi.org/10.1111/ele.12092

Garvin, J. C., Abroe, B., Pedersen, M. C., Dunn, P. O., & Whittingham, L. A. (2006). Immune response of nestling warblers varies with extra-pair paternity and temperature. *Molecular Ecology, 15*(12), 3833–3840. https://doi.org/10.1111/j.1365-294X.2006.03042.x

Gerlach, N. M., McGlothlin, J. W., Parker, P. G., & Ketterson, E. D. (2012). Promiscuous mating produces offspring with higher lifetime fitness. *Proceedings of the Royal Society B: Biological Sciences, 279*, 860–866. https://doi.org/10.1098/rspb.2011.1547

Gil, D., Slater, P. J. B., & Graves, J. A. (2007). Extra-pair paternity and song characteristics in the willow warbler *Phylloscopus trochilus*. *Journal of Avian Biology, 38*(3), 291–297. https://doi.org/10.1111/J.2007.0908-8857.03868.x

Girndt, A., Chng, C. W. T., Burke, T., & Schroeder, J. (2018). Male age is associated with extra-pair paternity, but not with extra-pair mating behaviour. *Scientific Reports, 8*, 8378. https://doi.org/10.1038/s41598-018-26649-1

Girndt, A., Cockburn, G., Sánchez-Tójar, A., Hertel, M., Burke, T., & Schroeder, J. (2019). Male age and its association with reproductive traits in captive and wild house sparrows. *Journal of Evolutionary Biology, 32*(12), 1432–1443. https://doi.org/10.1111/jeb.13542

Goossens, B., Graziani, L., Waits, L. P., Farand, E., Magnolon, S., Coulon, J., Bel, M. C., Taberlet, P., & Allainé, D. (1998). Extra-pair paternity in the monogamous Alpine marmot revealed by nuclear DNA microsatellite analysis. *Behavioral Ecology and Sociobiology, 43*(4–5), 281–288. https://doi.org/10.1007/s002650050492

Grafen, A. (1980). Opportunity cost, benefit and degree of relatedness. *Animal Behaviour, 28*(3), 967–968. https://doi.org/10.1016/S0003-3472(80)80160-6

Grant, P. R., & Grant, B. R. (2011). Causes of lifetime fitness of Darwin's finches in a fluctuating environment. *Proceedings of the National Academy of Sciences, 108*(2), 674–679. https://doi.org/10.1073/pnas.1018080108

Griffin, A. S., Alonzo, S. H., & Cornwallis, C. K. (2013). Why do cuckolded males provide paternal care? *PLoS Biology, 11*(3), e1001520. https://doi.org/10.1371/journal.pbio.1001520

Griffith, S. C., Owens, I. P. F., & Thuman, K. A. (2002). Extra pair paternity in birds: A review of interspecific variation and adaptive function. *Molecular Ecology, 11*(11), 2195–2212. https://doi.org/10.1046/j.1365-294X.2002.01613.x

Grinkov, V. G., Bauer, A., Sternberg, H., & Wink, M. (2020). Heritability of the extra-pair mating behavior of the pied flycatcher in Western Siberia. *PeerJ, 8*, e9571. http://doi.org/10.7717/peerj.9571

Hamalainen, A., Dammhahn, M., Aujard, F., Eberle, M., Hardy, I., Kappeler, P. M., Perret, M., Schliehe-Diecks, S., & Kraus, C. (2014). Senescence or selective disappearance? Age trajectories of body mass in wild and captive populations of a small-bodied primate. *Proceedings of the Royal Society B: Biological Sciences, 281*, 20140830. https://doi.org/10.1098/rspb.2014.0830

Hamilton, W. D., & Zuk, M. (1982). Heritable true fitness and bright birds—A role for parasites. *Science, 218*(4570), 384–387. https://doi.org/10.1126/science.7123238

Hansen, T. F., & Price, D. K. (1995). Good genes and old age: Do old mates provide superior genes? *Journal of Evolutionary Biology, 8*(6), 759–778. https://doi.org/10.1046/j.1420-9101.1995.8060759.x

Harts, A. M. F., Booksmythe, I., & Jennions, M. D. (2016). Mate guarding and frequent copulation in birds: A meta-analysis of their relationship to paternity and male phenotype. *Evolution, 70*(12), 2789–2808. https://doi.org/10.1111/evo.13081

Harts, A. M. F., & Kokko, H. (2013). Understanding promiscuity: When is seeking additional mates better than guarding an already found one? *Evolution, 67*(10), 2838–2848. https://doi.org/10.1111/evo.12163

Hayward, A. D., Wilson, A. J., Pilkington, J. G., Clutton-Brock, T. H., Pemberton, J. M., & Kruuk, L. E. B. (2013). Reproductive senescence in female Soay sheep: Variation across traits and contributions of individual ageing and selective disappearance. *Functional Ecology, 27*(1), 184–195. https://doi.org/10.1111/1365-2435.12029

Hill, C. E., Akcay, C., Campbell, S. E., & Beecher, M. D. (2011). Extrapair paternity, song, and genetic quality in song sparrows. *Behavioral Ecology, 22*(1), 73–81. https://doi.org/10.1093/beheco/arq171

Hillgarth, N. (1996). Ectoparasite transfer during mating in ring-necked pheasants *Phasianus colchicus*. *Journal of Avian Biology, 27*(3), 260–262. https://doi.org/10.2307/3677232

Hindle, A. G., Horning, M., Mellish, J.-A. E., & Lawler, J. M. (2009). Diving into old age: Muscular senescence in a large-bodied, long-lived mammal, the Weddell seal (*Leptonychotes weddellii*). *Journal of Experimental Biology, 212*(6), 790–796. https://doi.org/10.1242/jeb.025387.

Houtman, A. M. (1992). Female zebra finches choose extra-pair copulations with genetically attractive males. *Proceedings of the Royal Society B: Biological Sciences, 249*(1324), 3–6. https://doi.org/10.1098/rspb.1992.0075

Hsu, Y.-H., Schroeder, J., Winney, I., Burke, T., & Nakagawa, S. (2014). Costly infidelity: Low lifetime fitness of extra-pair offspring in a passerine bird. *Evolution, 68*(10), 2873–2884. https://doi.org/10.1111/evo.12475

Hsu, Y.-H., Schroeder, J., Winney, I., Burke, T., & Nakagawa, S. (2015). Are extra-pair males different from cuckolded males? A case study and a meta-analytic examination. *Molecular Ecology, 24*(7), 1558–1571. https://doi.org/10.1111/mec.13124

Hsu, Y.-H., Simons, M. J. P., Schroeder, J., Grindt, A., Winney, I. S., Burke, T., Nakagawa, S., Girndt, A., Winney, I. S., Burke, T., & Nakagawa, S. (2017). Age-dependent trajectories differ between within-pair and extra-pair paternity success. *Journal of Evolutionary Biology, 30*(5), 951–959. https://doi.org/10.1111/jeb.13058

Ihle, M., Kempenaers, B., & Forstmeier, W. (2013). Does hatching failure breed infidelity? *Behavioral Ecology, 24*(1), 119–127. https://doi.org/10.1093/beheco/ars142

Isvaran, K., & Clutton-Brock, T. (2007). Ecological correlates of extra-group paternity in mammals. *Proceedings of the Royal Society B: Biological Sciences, 274*(1607), 219–224. https://doi.org/10.1098/rspb.2006.3723

Kempenaers, B. (2007). Mate choice and genetic quality: A review of the heterozygosity theory. *Advances in the Study of Behavior, 37*, 189–278. https://doi.org/10.1016/S0065-3454(07)37005-8

Kempenaers, B., Verheyren, G. R., & Dhondt, A. A. (1997). Extrapair paternity in the blue tit (*Parus caeruleus*): Female choice, male characteristics, and offspring quality. *Behavioral Ecology, 8*(5), 481–492. https://doi.org/10.1093/beheco/8.5.481

Klemme, I., & Ylönen, H. (2010). Polyandry enhances offspring survival in an infanticidal species. *Biology Letters, 6*, 24–26. https://doi.org/10.1098/rsbl.2009.0500

Kokko, H. (1998). Good genes, old age and life-history trade-offs. *Evolutionary Ecology, 12*(6), 739–750. https://doi.org/10.1023/A:1006541701002

Kokko, H., Brooks, R., McNamara, J. M., & Houston, A. I. (2002). The sexual selection continuum. *Proceedings of the Royal Society B: Biological Sciences, 269*(1498), 1331–1340. https://doi.org/10.1098/rspb.2002.2020

Kokko, H., & Lindstrom, J. (1996). Evolution of female preference for old mates. *Proceedings of the Royal Society B: Biological Sciences, 263*(1376), 1533–1538. https://doi.org/10.1098/rspb.1996.0224

Kokko, H., & Morrell, L. J. (2005). Mate guarding, male attractiveness, and paternity under social monogamy. *Behavioral Ecology, 16*(4), 724–731. https://doi.org/10.1093/beheco/ari050

Kokko, H., Ranta, E., Ruxton, G., & Lundberg, P. (2002). Sexually transmitted disease and the evolution of mating systems. *Evolution, 56*(6), 1091–1100. https://doi.org/10.1111/j.0014-3820.2002.tb01423.x

Komdeur, J., Burke, T., & Richardson, D. S. (2007). Explicit experimental evidence for the effectiveness of proximity as mate-guarding behaviour in reducing extra-pair fertilization in the Seychelles warbler. *Molecular Ecology, 16*(17), 3679–3688. https://doi.org/10.1111/j.1365-294X.2007.03420.x

Komdeur, J., Kraaijeveld-Smit, F., Kraaijeveld, K., & Edelaar, P. (1999). Explicit experimental evidence for the role of mate guarding in minimizing loss of paternity in the Seychelles warbler. *Proceedings of the Royal Society B: Biological Sciences, 266*(1433), 2075–2081. https://doi.org/10.1098/rspb.1999.0890

Kong, A., Frigge, M. L., Masson, G., Besenbacher, S., Sulem, P., Magnusson, G., Gudjonsson, S. A., Sigurdsson, A., Jonasdottir, A., Jonasdottir, A., Wong, W. S. W., Sigurdsson, G., Walters, G. B., Steinberg, S., Helgason, H., Thorleifsson, G., Gudbjartsson, D. F., Helgason, A., Magnusson, O. T., . . . Stefansson, K. (2012). Rate of de novo mutations and the importance of father's age to disease risk. *Nature*, *488*(7412), 471–475. https://doi.org/10.1038/nature11396

Lack, D. L. (1968). *Ecological adaptations for breeding in birds* (1st ed.). Methuen.

Lande, R. (1981). Models of speciation by sexual selection on polygenic traits. *Proceedings of the National Academy of Sciences*, *78*(6), 3721–3725. https://doi.org/10.1073/pnas.78.6.3721

Lansing, A. I. (1954). A nongenic factor in the longevity of rotifers. *Annals of the New York Academy of Sciences*, *57*(5), 455–464. https://doi.org/10.1111/j.1749-6632.1954.tb36418.x

Laskemoen, T., Fossoy, F., Rudolfsen, G., & Lifjeld, J. T. (2008). Age-related variation in primary sexual characters in a passerine with male age-related fertilization success, the bluethroat *Luscinia svecica*. *Journal of Avian Biology*, *39*(3), 322–328. https://doi.org/10.1111/j.0908-8857.2008.04178.x

Lebigre, C., Arcese, P., & Reid, J. M. (2013). Decomposing variation in male reproductive success: Age-specific variances and covariances through extra-pair and within-pair reproduction. *Journal of Animal Ecology*, *82*(4), 872–883. https://doi.org/10.1111/1365-2656.12063

Leisler, B., Beier, J., Staudter, H., & Wink, M. (2000). Variation in extra-pair paternity in the polygynous great reed warbler (*Acrocephalus arundinaceus*). *Journal Fur Ornithologie*, *141*(1), 77–84. https://doi.org/10.1007/BF01651774

Lifjeld, J. T., Gohli, J., Albrecht, T., Garcia-Del-Rey, E., Johannessen, L. E., Kleven, O., Marki, P. Z., Omotoriogun, T. C., Rowe, M., & Johnsen, A. (2019). Evolution of female promiscuity in Passerides songbirds. *BMC Evolutionary Biology*, *19*, 169. https://doi.org/10.1186/s12862-019-1493-1

Lifjeld, J.T., Kleven, O., Fossøy, F., Jacobsen, F., Laskemoen, T., Rudolfsen, G., & Robertson, R. J. (2022). When older males sire more offspring—Increased attractiveness or higher fertility? *Behavioral Ecology and Sociobiology* 76, 61. https://doi.org/10.1007/s00265-022-03170-0

Lombardo, M. P., & Thorpe, P. A. (2000). Microbes in tree swallow semen. *Journal of Wildlife Diseases*, *36*, 460–468. https://doi.org/10.7589/0090-3558-36.3.460

Lukas, D., & Clutton-Brock, T. (2014). Evolution of social monogamy in primates is not consistently associated with male infanticide. *Proceedings of the National Academy of Sciences*, *111*(17), E1674. https://doi.org/10.1073/pnas.1401012111

Lyu, N., Servedio, M. R., & Sun, Y. H. (2018). Nonadaptive female pursuit of extrapair copulations can evolve through hitchhiking. *Ecology and Evolution*, *8*(7), 3685–3692. https://doi.org/10.1002/ece3.3915

Manning, J. T. (1985). Choosy females and correlates of male age. *Journal of Theoretical Biology*, *116*(3), 349–354. https://doi.org/10.1016/S0022-5193(85)80273-3

Maynard-Smith, J. (1977). Parental investment: A prospective analysis. *Animal Behaviour*, *25*, 1–9. https://doi.org/10.1016/0003-3472(77)90062-8

Mays, H. L., Albrecht, T., Liu, M., & Hill, G. E. (2008). Female choice for genetic complementarity in birds: A review. *Genetica*, *134*(1), 147–158. https://doi.org/10.1007/s10709-007-9219-5

Mays, H. L., & Hill, G. E. (2004). Choosing mates: Good genes versus genes that are a good fit. *Trends in Ecology & Evolution*, *19*(10), 554–559. https://doi.org/10.1016/j.tree.2004.07.018

McKinney, F., & Evarts, S. (1998). Sexual coercion in waterfowl and other birds. *Ornithological Monographs*. *49*, 163–195 https://doi.org/10.2307/40166723

Møller, A. P. (1985). Mixed reproductive strategy and mate guarding in a semi-colonial passerine, the swallow *Hirundo rustica*. *Behavioral Ecology and Sociobiology*, *17*, 401–408. https://doi.org/10.1007/BF00293220

Møller, A. P., & Birkhead, T. R. (1991). Frequent copulations and mate guarding as alternative paternity guards in birds: A comparative study. *Behaviour*, *118*(3/4), 170–186. https://doi.org/10.1163/156853991X00274

Moreno, J., Martínez, J. G., González-Braojos, S., Ruiz-De-Castañeda, R., Cantarero, A., & Sánchez-Tójar, A. (2013). Extra-pair matings, context-dependence and offspring quality: A brood manipulation experiment in pied flycatchers. *Behaviour*, *150*(3–4), 359–380. https://doi.org/10.1163/1568539X-00003056

O'Brien, E. L., & Dawson, R. D. (2007). Context-dependent genetic benefits of extra-pair mate choice in a socially monogamous passerine. *Behavioral Ecology and Sociobiology*, *61*(5), 775–782. https://doi.org/10.1007/s00265-006-0308-8

Oh, K. P., & Badyaev, A. V. (2006). Adaptive genetic complementarity in mate choice coexists with selection for elaborate sexual traits. *Proceedings of the Royal Society B: Biological Sciences, 273*(1596), 1913–1919. https://doi.org/10.1098/rspb.2006.3528

Opie, C., Atkinson, Q. D., Dunbar, R. I. M., & Shultz, S. (2013). Male infanticide leads to social monogamy in primates. *Proceedings of the National Academy of Sciences, 110*(33), 13328–13332. https://doi.org/10.1073/pnas.1307903110

Palombit, R. A. (1994). Extra-pair copulations in a monogamous ape. *Animal Behaviour, 47*(3), 721–723. https://doi.org/10.1006/anbe.1994.1097

Patrick, S. C., Chapman, J. R., Dugdale, H. L., Quinn, J. L., & Sheldon, B. C. (2012). Promiscuity, paternity and personality in the great tit. *Proceedings of the Royal Society B: Biological Sciences, 279*(1734), 1724–1730. https://doi.org/10.1098/rspb.2011.1820

Pizzari, T., Dean, R., Pacey, A., Moore, H., & Bonsall, M. B. (2008). The evolutionary ecology of pre- and post-meiotic sperm senescence. *Trends in Ecology & Evolution, 23*(3), 131–140. https://doi.org/10.1016/j.tree.2007.12.003

Poesel, A., Kunc, H. P., Foerster, K., Johnsen, A., & Kempenaers, B. (2006). Early birds are sexy: Male age, dawn song and extrapair paternity in blue tits, *Cyanistes* (formerly *Parus*) *caeruleus*. *Animal Behaviour, 72*, 531–538. https://doi.org/10.1016/j.anbehav.2005.10.022

Poiani, A., & Wilks, C. (2000). Sexually transmitted diseases: A possible cost of promiscuity in birds? *The Auk, 117*(4), 1061–1065.https://doi.org/ 10.1093/auk/117.4.1061

Poissant, J., Wilson, A. J., & Coltman, D. W. (2010). Sex-specific genetic variance and the evolution of sexual dimorphism: A systematic review of cross-sex genetic correlations. *Evolution, 64*(1), 97–107. https://doi.org/10.1111/j.1558-5646.2009.00793.x

Qvarnstrom, A. (2001). Context-dependent genetic benefits from mate choice. *Trends in Ecology & Evolution, 16*(1), 5–7. https://doi.org/10.1016/S0169-5347(00)02030-9

Reding, L. (2015). Increased hatching success as a direct benefit of polyandry in birds. *Evolution, 69*(1), 264–270. https://doi.org/10.1111/evo.12553

Reichard, U. (1995). Extra-pair copulations in a monogamous Gibbon (*Hylobates lar*). *Ethology, 100*(2), 99–112. https://doi.org/10.1111/j.1439-0310.1995.tb00319.x

Reid, J. M. (2012). Predicting evolutionary responses to selection on polyandry in the wild: Additive genetic covariances with female extra-pair reproduction. *Proceedings of the Royal Society B: Biological Sciences, 279*(1747), 4652–4660. https://doi.org/10.1098/rspb.2012.1835

Reid, J. M., Arcese, P., Keller, L. F., Germain, R. R., Duthie, A. B., Losdat, S., Wolak, M. E., & Nietlisbach, P. (2015). Quantifying inbreeding avoidance through extra-pair reproduction. *Evolution, 69*(1), 59–74. https://doi.org/10.1111/evo.12557

Reid, J. M., Arcese, P., Sardell, R. J., & Keller, L. F. (2011a). Additive genetic variance, heritability, and inbreeding depression in male extra-pair reproductive success. *American Naturalist, 177*(2), 177–187. https://doi.org/10.1086/657977

Reid, J. M., Arcese, P., Sardell, R. J., & Keller, L. F. (2011b). Heritability of female extra-pair paternity rate in song sparrows (*Melospiza melodia*). *Proceedings of the Royal Society B: Biological Sciences, 278*(1708), 1114–1120. https://doi.org/10.1098/rspb.2010.1704

Reid, J. M., & Sardell, R. J. (2012). Indirect selection on female extra-pair reproduction? Comparing the additive genetic value of maternal half-sib extra-pair and within-pair offspring. *Proceedings of the Royal Society B: Biological Sciences, 279*(1734), 1700–1708. https://doi.org/10.1098/rspb.2011.2230

Reid, J. M., & Wolak, M. E. (2018). Is there indirect selection on female extra-pair reproduction through cross-sex genetic correlations with male reproductive fitness? *Evolution Letters, 2*(2), 159–168. https://doi.org/10.1002/evl3.56

Robertson, R. J., & Stutchbury, B. J. (1988). Experimental evidence for sexually selected infanticide in tree swallows. *Animal Behaviour, 36*, 749–753. https://doi.org/10.1016/S0003-3472(88)80158-1

Rueger, T., Harrison, H. B., Gardiner, N. M., Berumen, M. L., & Jones, G. P. (2019). Extra-pair mating in a socially monogamous and paternal mouth-brooding cardinalfish. *Molecular Ecology, 28*(10), 2625–2635. https://doi.org/10.1111/mec.15103

Santema, P., & Kempenaers, B. (2021). Offspring provisioning by extra-pair males in blue tits. *Journal of Avian Biology, 52*(5). doi:10.1111/jav.02755

Santos, E. S. A., & Nakagawa, S. (2012). The costs of parental care: A meta-analysis of the trade-off between parental effort and survival in birds. *Journal of Evolutionary Biology*, *25*, 1911–1917. https://doi.org/10.1111/j.1420-9101.2012.02569.x

Sardell, R. J., Arcese, P., Keller, L. F., & Reid, J. M. (2012). Are there indirect fitness benefits of female extra-pair reproduction? Lifetime reproductive success of within-pair and extra-pair offspring. *American Naturalist*, *179*(6), 779–793. https://doi.org/10.1086/665665

Sardell, R. J., Arcese, P., & Reid, J. M. (2012). Offspring fitness varies with parental extra-pair status in song sparrows, *Melospiza melodia*. *Proceedings of the Royal Society B: Biological Sciences*, *279*(1744), 4078–4086. https://doi.org/10.1098/rspb.2012.1139

Schmoll, T. (2011). A review and perspective on context-dependent genetic effects of extra-pair mating in birds. *Journal of Ornithology*, *152*, 265–277. https://doi.org/10.1007/s10336-011-0683-4

Schmoll, T., Dietrich, V., Winkel, W., Epplen, J. T., Schurr, F., & Lubjuhn, T. (2005). Paternal genetic effects on offspring fitness are context dependent within the extrapair mating system of a socially monogamous passerine. *Evolution*, *59*(3), 645–657. https://doi.org/10.1554/04-090

Schmoll, T., Schurr, F. M., Winkel, W., Epplen, J. T., & Lubjuhn, T. (2009). Lifespan, lifetime reproductive performance and paternity loss of within-pair and extra-pair offspring in the coal tit *Periparus ater*. *Proceedings of the Royal Society B: Biological Sciences*, *276*(1655), 337–345. https://doi.org/10.1098/rspb.2008.1116

Schroeder, J., Burke, T., Mannarelli, M. E., Dawson, D. A., & Nakagawa, S. (2012). Maternal effects and heritability of annual productivity. *Journal of Evolutionary Biology*, *25*(1), 149–156. https://doi.org/10.1111/j.1420-9101.2011.02412.x

Schroeder, J., Hsu, Y.-H. H., Winney, I., Simons, M. J. P., Nakagawa, S., & Burke, T. (2016). Predictably philandering females prompt poor paternal provisioning. *American Naturalist*, *188*(2), 219–230. https://doi.org/10.1086/687243

Schroeder, J., Nakagawa, S., Rees, M., Mannarelli, M.-E., & Burke, T. (2015). Reduced fitness in progeny from old parents in a natural population. *Proceedings of the National Academy of Sciences*, *112*(13), 4021–4025. https://doi.org/10.1073/pnas.1422715112

Sheldon, B. C. (1993). Sexually transmitted disease in birds: Occurrence and evolutionary significance. *Philosophical Transactions of the Royal Society B: -Biological Sciences*, *339*(1290), 491–497. https://doi.org/10.1098/rstb.1993.0044

Stipkovits, L., Varga, Z., Czifra, G., & Dobos-Kovacs, M. (1986). Occurrence of mycoplasmas in geese affected with inflammation of the cloaca and phallus. *Avian Pathology*, *15*(2), 289–299. https://doi.org/10.1080/03079458608436289

Suter, S. M., Keiser, M., Feignoux, R., & Meyer, D. R. (2007). Reed bunting females increase fitness through extra-pair mating with genetically dissimilar males. *Proceedings of the Royal Society B: Biological Sciences*, *274*(1627), 2865–2871. https://doi.org/10.1098/rspb.2007.0799

Tarof, S. A., Kramer, P. M., Tautin, J., & Stutchbury, B. J. M. (2012). Effects of known age on male paternity in a migratory songbird. *Behavioral Ecology*, *23*(2), 313–321. https://doi.org/10.1093/beheco/arr188

Tarvin, K. A., Webster, M. S., Tuttle, E. M., & Pruett-Jones, S. (2005). Genetic similarity of social mates predicts the level of extrapair paternity in splendid fairy-wrens. *Animal Behaviour*, *70*, 945–955. https://doi.org/10.1016/j.anbehav.2005.01.012

Townsend, A. K., Clark, A. B., & McGowan, K. J. (2010). Direct benefits and genetic costs of extrapair paternity for female American crows (*Corvus brachyrhynchos*). *American Naturalist*, *175*(1), E1–E9. https://doi.org/10.1086/648553

Trivers, R. L. (1972). Parental investment and sexual selection. In B. Campbell (Ed.), *Sexual selection and the descent of man* (pp. 136–179). Aldine.

Tryjanowski, P., & Hromada, M. (2005). Do males of the great grey shrike, *Lanius excubitor*, trade food for extrapair copulations? *Animal Behaviour*, *69*(3), 529–533. https://doi.org/10.1016/j.anbehav.2004.06.009

Wagner, R. H. (1991). The use of extrapair copulations for mate appraisal by razorbills, *Alca torda*. *Behavioral Ecology*, *2*(3), 198–203. https://doi.org/10.1093/beheco/2.3.198

Wang, D., Forstmeier, W., Martin, K., Wilson, A., & Kempenaers, B. (2020). The role of genetic constraints and social environment in explaining female extra-pair mating. *Evolution*, *74*(3), 544-558. https://doi.org/10.1111/evo.13905

Westneat, D. F., & Rambo, T. B. (2000). Copulation exposes female red-winged blackbirds to bacteria in male semen. *Journal of Avian Biology*, *31*(1), 1–7. https://doi.org/10.1034/j.1600-048X.2000.310101.x

Westneat, D. F., & Stewart, I. R. K. (2003). Extra-pair paternity in birds: Causes, correlates, and conflict. *Annual Review of Ecology, Evolution, and Systematics, 34,* 365–396. https://doi.org/10.1146/annurev.ecolsys.34.011802.132439

Wetton, J. H., & Parkin, D. T. (1991). An association between fertility and cuckoldry in the house sparrow, *Passer domesticus. Proceedings of the Royal Society B: Biological Sciences, 245*(1314), 227–233. https://doi.org/10.1098/rspb.1991.0114

Whittingham, L. A., & Dunn, P. O. (2010). Fitness benefits of polyandry for experienced females. *Molecular Ecology, 19*(11), 2328–2335. https://doi.org/10.1111/j.1365-294X.2010.04640.x

Wolff, J. O., & MacDonald, D. W. (2004). Promiscuous females protect their offspring. *Trends in Ecology and Evolution, 19*(3), 127–134. https://doi.org/10.1016/j.tree.2003.12.009

Zilberman, R., Moav, B., & Yom-Tov, Y. (1999). Extra-pair paternity in the socially monogamous orange-tufted sunbird (*Nectarinia osea osea*). *Israel Journal of Zoology, 45*(3), 407–421. https://doi.org/10.1080/00212210.1999.10689008

CHAPTER 26

Future Directions for Theory and Research on the Predictors, Nature, and Consequences of Infidelity

Tara DeLecce

Abstract

This handbook has presented the current state of the research on the predictors, nature, and consequences of infidelity from a variety of perspectives, including social, clinical, and evolutionary. Although significant advances have been made to understand infidelity, there remain many unanswered questions, leaving plentiful avenues for future directions. This concluding chapter will address in more detail several remaining issues mentioned in previous chapters. Most importantly, "infidelity" lacks a definition that is standardized across studies, and a clearer understanding could be achieved given adequate methods to define infidelity, even if this means converting the construct of infidelity from unidimensional to multidimensional. Once this is accomplished, other issues surrounding infidelity can be explored. Specifically, in addition to a lack of research addressing non-heterosexual dyadic relationships, there is a lack of research on the nature of infidelity in relationships that are polyamorous or entail some degree of socially acceptable nonmonogamy. Relatedly, little research has investigated the consequences of infidelity in cultures that place less value on maintaining monogamy. Furthermore, there is an overreliance on cross-sectional research featuring relatively young participants, which does not address the impact of infidelity across the lifespan, including in the postreproductive years. The remainder of the chapter provides suggestions for ways to incorporate these missing issues into the infidelity literature.

Key Words: infidelity definition, polyamorous infidelity, postreproductive infidelity, nonmonogamy norms, polygynous infidelity, polyandrous infidelity

Standardizing the Definition of Infidelity

The arguably most important limitation in infidelity research is the lack of a standard definition for infidelity. It is not uncommon to see infidelity measures consisting of an ambiguous assessment of, "Have you ever engaged in an affair?" with the most specific definition often being that of sexual intercourse with a person other than one's regular partner. Studies on infidelity are less likely to measure emotional infidelity, and neither is this type of infidelity clearly defined in most studies. The use of broad questions of "sexual and/or emotional" or more usually "sexual infidelity" limits the conclusions that can be reached about infidelity. This is an issue that has been recognized for decades, with researchers offering suggestions for improvement in the past. However, little effort has been made to standardize the definition of infidelity.

For example, in 1983, Thompson proposed a system of descriptors to define infidelity. This system consisted of three parts. The first part addresses whether the extrapair relationship is sanctioned by the primary relationship, the second part addresses the relationship outside of which the behavior occurs such as whether it is only extramarital sex or extramarital cohabiting. The third part addresses whether sexual intercourse occurs, the frequency of it if it does occur, friendship, and other dyadic behaviors (Thompson, 1983). In 2005, a methodological review of the literature to that point revealed that it was still common to see infidelity defined and measured through single-item questions about extradyadic sex, despite recommendations to avoid this practice from the 1980s (Blow & Hartnett, 2005). The authors of this methodological review offered their own suggestions to improve the definition of infidelity for research purposes. They offered a more inclusive definition of infidelity, as follows: "Infidelity is a sexual and/or emotional act engaged in by one person within a committed relationship, where such an act occurs outside of the primary relationship and constitutes a breach of trust and/or violation of agreed-upon norms (overt and covert) by one or both individuals in that relationship in relation to romantic/emotional or sexual exclusivity" (Blow & Hartnett, 2005, pp. 191–192).

As for measuring the different components of this definition, the authors suggest to first ask participants whether a breach of trust occurred either in terms of emotional or sexual exclusivity ("yes" or "no"). Then, the severity of the breach of trust is further examined along a continuum in two separate questions (which had been incorporated successfully in previous research): one asking about extradyadic emotional involvement, and the other asking about extradyadic sexual involvement. The emotional involvement continuum would range from no emotional involvement to extremely deep emotional involvement. The sexual involvement continuum would range from no sexual involvement to kissing, petting, sexual intimacy without intercourse, and then sexual intimacy with intercourse (Blow & Hartnett, 2005; Glass & Wright, 1985, 1992).

Very few studies have incorporated this advice (but see Kruger et al, 2013; Mattingly et al, 2010); however, Luo and colleagues (2010) attempted to capture all the various types of extradyadic behaviors. Going beyond measuring them on a continuum, this study used factor analysis for better statistical precision for assessing specific extradyadic behaviors. They created a new measure called the Extradyadic Behavior Inventory (EDI), which contains 23 items asking about face-to-face extradyadic behaviors as well as 13 items asking about online extradyadic behaviors. The face-to-face behaviors were inspired from a review of behaviors assessed in previous studies, such as receiving and giving genital (or nongenital) stimulation, oral sex (both giving and receiving), kissing, vaginal intercourse, masturbating in another's presence, talking dirty, flirting, meeting with a romantic interest in secret, and experiencing a deep emotional attachment. The online behaviors included flirting, keeping a communication partner secret, masturbating online or over the phone, phone sex, cybersex, sharing intimate pictures, visiting dating websites, sharing intimate details of one's life, and discussing one's complaints about the primary partner. The exploratory factor analysis of these items yielded three factors: a face-to-face extradyadic behaviors factor, an online emotional extradyadic behaviors factor, and an online sexual extradyadic behaviors factor (Luo, et al, 2010).

The use of exploratory factor analysis to define infidelity was extended in 2011 with the development and validation of the Perceptions of Dating Infidelity Scale (PDIS), using both exploratory and confirmatory factor analysis (Wilson et al.,, 2011). This scale assesses three factors: ambiguous behaviors, explicit behaviors, and deceptive behaviors. Ambiguous behaviors refer to behaviors with someone other than one's partner that could be a sign of infidelity, such as going out to eat or getting drinks with someone else, going dancing with someone else, or talking on the phone and/or through the internet with someone else. Explicit behaviors most often are considered clear signs of infidelity, and mainly consist of sexual behaviors. Deceptive behaviors involve some type of deception from one's regular partner such as lying or withholding information about their whereabouts or activities.

More recently, both exploratory and confirmatory factor analysis were used to develop and validate the Definitions of Infidelity Questionnaire (DIQ; Thompson & O'Sullivan, 2016). The DIQ consists of four factors: sexual/explicit behaviors, technology/online behaviors, emotional/affectionate behaviors, and solitary behaviors. The DIQ includes 32 items, with examples of sexual behaviors including vaginal, oral, and anal sex, sending explicit messages, and browsing dating websites among the technology behaviors, liking on social media, and providing emotional support among examples of emotional behaviors, and masturbating alone and/or watching pornography among examples of solitary behaviors. The development of the DIQ included multivariate validity analyses, a separate study to establish temporal consistency, and large sample sizes.

However, even the developers of the DIQ concede there are limitations to defining infidelity. They note that infidelity cannot be considered adequately defined until such research includes samples from more diverse populations, including different age groups and cultures (especially non-WEIRD cultures; Thompson & O'Sullivan, 2016). Toward this aim, Romero-Palencia and colleagues (2007) developed a scale in Spanish using a Mexican sample via exploratory factor analysis, known as the Multidimensional Inventory of Infidelity (IMIN). The IMIN assesses four factors: Infidelity tendency, reasons for infidelity, beliefs in infidelity, and consequences of infidelity. The IMIN was further validated through confirmatory factor analysis with a Colombian sample (Munévar et al.,, 2021). Overall, although these are advances in developing a comprehensive and multidimensional definition of infidelity that are beginning to include ideations of infidelity from diverse populations, it is still unlikely that a standard measure can be relied on until each of these multidimensional instruments (the PDIS, DIQ, and IMIN) are directly compared to one another to investigate which model provides the best fit to data. It would also be useful to translate these instruments into several different languages for invariance testing in different cultures, not just for North America and South America.

Polyamorous Infidelity

Another theme from the chapters in this handbook is the suggestion for researchers to commit to decoupling nonconsensual from consensual nonmonogamy when conducting infidelity research. Most studies appear to have conflated these relationship types, which may have produced unreliable statistics on aspects of infidelity, such as its prevalence. Consensual nonmonogamy is another reason a multidimensional definition of infidelity is needed, one that covers not only extradyadic sex, but the context of the extradyadic sex, in terms of whether there is deception and/or secrecy, and whether sexual and/or emotional monogamy is expected in the primary relationship.

Functionally and behaviorally, infidelity and consensual nonmonogamy are distinct, especially in terms of greater and more detailed communication within consensually nonmonogamous couples, and a different set of moral norms within communities of nonmonogamous people compared to traditional monogamous couples. Although some research has investigated how couples overcome infidelity in monogamous couples, there is less research investigating how couples overcome infidelity (or, more accurately, rule violations) in consensually nonmonogamous couples, and little research that compares and contrasts how couples with these differing monogamy agreements deal with infidelity.

Perhaps part of the reason there is less research on infidelity in polyamorous or consensually nonmonogamist couples is that it is more difficult to define than in monogamous relationships. In fact, many polyamorists reject the idea of placing restrictions on what people can and cannot do in these types of relationships; instead, they contend there should be more focus on what people should or can do rather than what they should not or cannot do (Wosick-Correa, 2010). Within polyamorous relationships, there is an emphasis on agentic fidelity, or remaining loyal to the process of establishing agreements and rules, respecting oneself and one's partners through following the rules, and being self-aware (Wosick-Correa, 2010). Despite this attitude of not wanting to enforce restrictions on behavior, most people in consensually nonmonogamous relationships report an agreement or set of rules or boundaries for partners. It is not uncommon for partners to report a feeling of "specialness" with at least one of the partners, perhaps one they feel closer to than the others, and this specialness is maintained by doing some activities uniquely with that partner, such as only spending the night with that partner (Wosick-Correa, 2010). Violations of these rules are typically not perceived as cheating in the traditional sense, but there are times when this is viewed as "cheating." For instance, one heterosexual woman in a polyamorous relationship gave this response in an interview when asked if she ever "cheated" in the relationship:

What a good question, because by definition it's almost a contradiction in terms. I can't say that I have cheated. Generally, I think that there are some people who "do poly" a whole lot better than others. . . . I guess to me if you have rules and then break those rules, you've cheated. But I don't like that term because, again, it's a contradiction since cheating implies [stops in mid-sentence with a blank stare]—well it's like "pseudo-cheating." You are 'cause you're breaking rules but you aren't because the rules are different than normal rules about monogamy. (cited in Wosick-Correa, 2010, p. 13).

In this same study, 18% of participants responded "yes" when asked if they ever cheated in a consensually nonmonogamous relationship, and 12% reported that their primary partner cheated on them. When people in polyamorous relationships do feel that cheating has occurred, their response is often different than a typical response in traditional, monogamous relationships. Those in monogamous relationships are prone to respond to partner infidelity by dissolution of the relationship, whereas 87% of the time, those in polyamorous relationships respond to rule violations or "cheating" by renegotiating the rules (Wosick-Correa, 2010).

Another distinctive feature of nonmonogamous relationships is that instances of nonmonogamy (those that fit the negotiated rules) can be responded to with compersion, which is when a person takes joy in a partner's pleasure in sexual and relational encounters with others (Balzarini et al., 2021). In a study of a large sample of participants in polyamorous relationships (over 3,500), compared to a sample of participants in monogamous relationships, are more likely to report compersion in response to a hypothetical scenario featuring their partner involved in extradyadic relations (Balzarini, et al., 2021). Other research indicates that compersion only occurs when the extrapair activity is within the boundaries established for the relationship. Extradyadic behavior that violates these boundaries produces distress, just as any extradyadic behavior does for monogamous couples. Furthermore, those in consensually nonmonogamous relationships report feeling more distress at the thought of their primary partner entering another relationship without their consent compared to a secondary partner doing the same (Mogilski et al, 2019). Relatedly, those in consensually nonmonogamous relationships engage in more mate retention with primary partners compared to secondary partners, and downplay how pleasurable their sexual experiences are with others when discussing those experiences with their primary partner (Mogilski et al., 2017). Taken together, perhaps compersion is not the only reaction to consensual extradyadic activity; perhaps it is associated with a mix of positive and negative emotions. The extent to which extradyadic behavior in a polyamorous relationship may produce positive or negative reactions may depend on the structure of the relationship. According to one study comparing different types of polyamorous relationships, latent class analysis revealed three distinct types: consensual nonmonogamy in which both partners have low interest in monogamy and high levels of mutual consent and communication regarding extradyadic activity, partially open relationships in which there is less openness, consent, and communication between partners about extradyadic activity, and one-sided relationships, in which one partner desires monogamy while the other does not and, therefore, engages in extradyadic activity. On examination of the functioning of each of these three types of polyamorous relationships, consensual nonmonogamous relationships were higher functioning compared to partially open and one-sided relationships (Hangen et al., 2020).

Additional studies that compare and contrast different arrangements on the monogamy continuum will help illuminate how people set rules for extradyadic activity, communicate effectively, and solve problems as a result of rule violations or infidelity in their relationships. Such research may have important clinical implications in terms of helping therapists assist clients to navigate consensually nonmonogamous relationships or to renegotiate relationship boundaries after rule violations. This could also mean that different interventions may be necessary for coping with primary partner infidelity compared to secondary partner infidelity. Similarly, future research could use other measures besides self-report to assess reactions to infidelity and/or rule violations in polyamorous relationships. It is possible that reports of compersion are a result of social desirability concerns associated with self-report than a genuinely positive reaction to infidelity. The finding that people spend more time mate guarding primary partners and portray to their primary partners that their extradyadic sexual experiences is less pleasurable it actually was makes this plausible. Attempts to use both physiological measures (e.g., skin conductance, cortisol levels) along with self-reports to assess reactions to infidelity, as in previous research with monogamous couples (see Buss et al., 1992), would provide a more comprehensive understanding of how partners in polyamorous relationships react to infidelity and/or rule violations. Reactions could be further moderated by other reproductive hormones, including both testosterone and estrogen at different times throughout the ovulatory cycle.

Impact of Infidelity in Societies Without Monogamy Norms

Current research on polyamorous relationship dynamics is typically approached from a perspective that assumes monogamy at the societal level. In other words, research thus far on polyamorous relationships has focused on samples from predominantly Western societies in which monogamy is legally imposed and polyamorous individuals are not representative of the majority. However, this ignores a sizable portion of the global human population—cultures in which having more than one spouse is legal and socially acceptable. In these cultures, many features of infidelity (e.g., sexual intercourse with another, emotional attachment to another) would not be considered as such, especially for men who are polygynously mated and women who are polyandrously mated, as such behaviors with more than one individual are socially acceptable and lack the secrecy associated with the taboo nature of infidelity. How, then, would infidelity be perceived in such contexts?

Polygyny is the most common nonmonogamous mating system. The most commonly researched version of polygyny is that imposed by Islamic law, which states the following conditions: Men cannot have more than four wives at a time, only men who can financially support more than one wife are allowed to exceed one wife, and when men do have multiple wives, they must all be given equal attention and receive the same treatment (Chamie, 1986). Even in cultures that allow polygyny, typically only a minority of men meet the criteria for practicing polygyny, but this differs by region as well. For instance, in sub-Saharan African nations, polygyny ranges from approximately 20%–40%, but in Middle Eastern countries rates of polygyny are lower, between 2% and 12%. Despite the allowance of four wives, demographic research on polygynous Muslim cultures reveals that, in more than 90% of cases, men have two wives, with the probability of having three wives ranging between 3% and 7% and the likelihood of four wives around 1% (Chamie, 1986). Given that the typical polygynous Muslim population would involve families consisting of one husband and two wives, this is the arrangement that should be the focus of infidelity research in polygynous marriages.

Among existing research on polygynous marriages, there is evidence that women are more upset by their husbands taking on additional wives than by legally unrecognized infidelity, especially if the infidelity is short-term (Liversage, 2019). Research on the addition of wives has revealed that adding a wife is associated with conflict between cowives, and reduced attention and/or investment in children before the new wife entered the family (Al-Krenawi & Graham, 1999; Elbedour, et al, 2002). In fact, there has even been coined the psychiatric diagnosis "first wife syndrome" in Arabic polygynous societies, in which women who were the first wife in a polygynous marriage experience difficulty coping with the introduction of other wives and is marked by symptoms such as psychosomatic pain, anxiety, and fatigue (Al-Sherbiny, 2005). In a study using a Tanzanian sample that specifically addresses infidelity rather than the addition of wives, there is a preference among wives for husbands to engage in infidelity. They indicate that although they preferred a monogamous and loving marriage, they know this is not possible and it is preferred for husbands to have casual, secret, and (most importantly) short-term flings rather than add a new wife. In Tanzania, the addition of a new wife is a greater threat to marriage and is more likely to lead to divorce from the first wife (Keefe, 2019). This qualitative study suggests that infidelity may have less of an emotional impact than in societies that only allow monogamy.

There is a need for research directly addressing the nature and impact of infidelity in polygynous marriages, especially quantitative research. One speculation from an evolutionary perspective could be that a husband's infidelity is truly less upsetting than the addition of a new wife in polygynous cultures because the new wife is officially recognized as another individual with which previous wives must share their husbands' resources, along with any offspring produced from the newly acquired wife. In the case of legally unrecognized or even secret infidelity, alternatively, the likelihood of a polygynous husband investing substantial resources into these secret affair partners is much lower, which ultimately means that this is less of a threat to women's investment from their husbands.

There is even less literature on polyandrous marriages, let alone infidelity in such marriages in terms of the shared wife engaging in intercourse or an emotional affair with another man other than her culturally recognized husbands. Research on women's infidelity in which there is less of a negative impact usually focuses on contexts in which couples are legally (and/or socially) monogamously married, but the infidelity of wives is tolerated, usually because husbands are engaging in infidelity themselves. For instance, in the small-scale Himba society of Namibia, husbands and wives both report distress over their spouse's infidelity; however, men are expected to invest equally in children they know are not biologically theirs, and there is a lack of a violent response to being cuckolded by their wives as is often seen in other societies (Prall & Scelza, 2020; Scelza, 2014). It is likely that the reason for a dearth of research on infidelity in polyandrous marriages is because polyandry is practiced only in very few small societies ranging from a few hundred to 80,000 individuals, and it is not legally recognized like polygyny (Gautam & Kshatriya, 2011). Nevertheless, a complete understanding of the nature of infidelity along with its consequences requires investigations of infidelity across all human mating systems.

Yet another speculation from an evolutionary perspective regarding infidelity in the context of polyandry is that perhaps cohusbands may prefer for wives to have only publicly recognized husbands and may find secret infidelity more upsetting. From a male perspective, paternity uncertainty is a recurrent adaptive problem, and, even in the case of polyandrous mating arrangements, usually cohusbands are brothers and share a portion of genes. In this case, paternity confusion is not so detrimental to the passage of one's genes to the next generation. When there are even more affair partners, and especially secret ones, paternity confusion and cuckoldry become an even bigger threat to male reproductive success, especially if affair partners are not genetically related to the cohusbands. At least when all cohusbands are publicly recognized and known, cohusbands can use this information to appropriately deploy prudent sperm allocation to increase the chances of achieving paternity.

Consequences of Infidelity Across the Lifespan

One of the weaknesses of infidelity research is that it lacks information on the impact of infidelity across the lifespan. Researchers have relied on retrospective, cross-sectional studies, usually featuring younger participants in the prime of their reproductive years. This leaves open the question of how infidelity is perceived in later life, especially in the postreproductive years. It could be argued that infidelity, especially sexual infidelity, would be viewed less harshly for a few reasons, at least from an evolutionary perspective. For men specifically, a postreproductive aged partner's infidelity would not lead to investment in nongenetically related children as a result, and thus would not be a threat to reproductive success. For women specifically, their children have likely reached adulthood, so their partner's infidelity would not lead to a redirection of the partner's resources away from her own children in a way that would decrease the children's chances of survival; once again, infidelity under these circumstances would not be a threat to reproductive success.

On the other hand, infidelity in the postreproductive years could be associated with threats to kin investment rather than direct threats to reproduction. This may make emotional infidelity more of a threat than sexual infidelity. In the typical scenario, an older man who has been married for many years has an affair and leaves his wife, along with revoking his life savings from their children's inheritance, especially if he is able to start a new family with a younger partner, thus potentially investing more in the younger children than in in grandchildren. This is a legitimate concern, as research on patterns of estate divisions in Canada reveal that people bequeath the largest percentage of their estate to their biological offspring, which is consistent with predictions about with kin-based altruism. The second-largest percentage typically goes to a spouse (Smith et al., 1987). Another study examining over 145,000 estates in Sweden corroborated these findings (Elinder et al., 2021). In the case of an elderly woman's infidelity, this may lead to discord between not only her spouse but also adult offspring (or other family members) due to reputational concerns, which may compromise a family's status. Some research suggests that scrutiny outside the family is a concern for adult offspring when they learn of a parent's infidelity (Thorson, 2009). Alternatively, it could be that, in the later years, people place higher priority in other areas of their lives, such as their health, due to the increased incidence of chronic disease and disability (Træen et al., 2017). Under these conditions, perhaps infidelity would not have the dramatic impact that it would on younger couples.

The scant amount of cross-sectional research on infidelity among older couples does little to address how infidelity affects relationships at this life stage, although the General Social Survey (conducted by the University of Chicago) suggests that affairs by spouses over the age of 60 years have increased between 1991 and 2006 (Smith et al., 2011). This is not just an American trend, as this has also been documented in Canada, Britain, Italy, France, and Japan (Brown et al., 2018). Empirical and clinical research routinely omits older couples (Ivey et al., 2000; Story et al., 2007). To further compound the problem, older couples are less likely to seek counseling for infidelity than are younger couples, so less is known about the prevalence and nature of infidelity in the older demographic (Gardner & Poole, 2009). Of the research that does exist, one interesting set of case studies following eight dementia patients in their 70s and 80s (three female, five male) indicates that sexual infidelity is still a concern, and one of the more common features of dementia is delusional jealousy over a spouse's real or imagined sexual infidelity, with this paranoia stronger for men than women, and stronger in those with a history of spousal infidelity (Sibisi, 1999). Research reviewing clinical cases of couples ranging in age from 55 to 75 years seeking infidelity counseling found that men are more likely to engage in sexual infidelity compared to women, which mirrors trends in younger couples (Weeks et al., 2003; Williamson & Brimhall, 2017). Additionally, common themes found in infidelity circumstances at this later life stage include men feeling weaker and less "manly" due to health problems and/or retirement and the resulting feeling of loss of identity, and women feeling unattractive due to physiological changes associated with menopause and age. When partners feel this way, they are more likely to withdraw from one another, which increases the risk of infidelity (Williamson & Brimhall, 2017).

Longitudinal research will help to understand how infidelities develop, and how the nature and consequences of infidelity may change over time. Longitudinal research may also help researchers identify participants prior to extradyadic experiences and gain not only a more complete picture of the length and nature of the extradyadic involvement, but also produce a less biased sample. Currently, there are few longitudinal studies examining infidelity. One study followed 72 heterosexual couples from their engagement and then yearly during their marriage for 8 years (Allen, et al, 2008). Couples who had experienced infidelity were compared to those who did not over the 8-year time span, and it was revealed that in marriages in which the man committed infidelity, there were lower levels of male sexual and relational satisfaction along with more problematic communication patterns before marriage. For marriages in which the woman committed infidelity, there were higher levels of male sexual satisfaction before marriage, but greater negative communication (especially compared to couples who did not experience infidelity) was still present. One of the longest running longitudinal studies included a sample of over 1,400 married couples across a 17-year period and concluded that infidelity is both a cause and a consequence of poor marital quality (Previti & Amato, 2004). The results of this study revealed that, for the most part, couples do not engage in infidelity until they either start thinking about divorce or discussing the possibility of divorce with their spouses. This suggests that people commit infidelity to assess alternative partners in anticipation of an impending divorce. Furthermore, the results indicated that sexual infidelity does further negatively impact a marriage, regardless of prior levels of unhappiness, through an additional decline in marital satisfaction and further increase in divorce proneness. Similarly, a 12-year longitudinal study using the same participants that included various marital problems in addition to infidelity discovered that extramarital sex was a powerful predictor of divorce compared to other problems such as substance abuse (Amato & Rogers, 1997). Besides these notable exceptions, most longitudinal research on infidelity ranges from 1 month to 5 years (see Altgelt et al., 2018; Hall & Fincham, 2009; Ritchie et al., 2020), which may not provide a sufficient observation period to understand the long-term consequences of infidelity. Additionally, all these studies involved samples less than 55 years of age 55; even the study spanning 17 years had a mean participant age of 35 years at the start of data collection. Therefore, there are few examinations of infidelity among couples in their postreproductive years. Future research, both cross-sectional and longitudinal, should incorporate couples in their 60s and older to illuminate the experience of infidelity and its surrounding issues at this point in the lifespan.

Conclusions

To conclude, there is still much to be investigated to reach a comprehensive understanding of infidelity. The first step is to develop a standardized and multidimensional definition of infidelity along with a standardized instrument to measure infidelity and its several dimensions across studies. Also, research on how infidelity impacts mating arrangements other than monogamy is limited, with little research on infidelity in polyandrous marriages. It could be that, in nonmonogamous contexts, infidelity does not warrant a negative response (or a less severe negative response). In addition, longitudinal research on how infidelity affects relationships at different points across the lifespan, especially beyond the reproductive years, is lacking. It is important to know whether the consequences of infidelity at the age of 20 years are as severe as those at the age of 70 years, for example, and to identify important differences between experiences at these time points in the lifespan. These gaps in the literature need to be filled to better identify the predictors, nature, and consequences of infidelity.

References

Al-Krenawi, A., & Graham, J. R., 1999. The story of Bedouin-Arab women in a polygamous marriage. *Women's Studies International Forum, 22*, 497–509.

Al-Sherbiny, L. A. M. (2005). The case of first wife in polygamy. *Electronic Arab Psychological Review Quarterly Edition, 8*, 18–26.

Allen, E. S., Rhoades, G. K., Stanley, S. M., Markman, H. J., Williams, T., Melton, J., & Clements, M. L. (2008). Premarital precursors of marital infidelity. *Family Process, 47*, 243–259.

Altgelt, E. E., Reyes, M. A., French, J. E., Meltzer, A. L., & McNulty, J. K. (2018). Who is sexually faithful? Own and partner personality traits as predictors of infidelity. *Journal of Social and Personal Relationships, 35*, 600–614.

Amato, P. R., & Rogers, S. J. (1997). A longitudinal study of marital problems and subsequent divorce. *Journal of Marriage and the Family, 59*, 612–624.

Balzarini, R. N., McDonald, J. N., Kohut, T., Lehmiller, J. J., Holmes, B. M., & Harman, J. J. (2021). Compersion: When jealousy-inducing situations don't (just) induce jealousy. *Archives of Sexual Behavior, 50*, 1311–1324.

Blow, A. J., & Hartnett, K. (2005). Infidelity in committed relationships I: A methodological review. *Journal of Marital and Family Therapy, 31*, 183–216.

Brown, S. L., Lin, I. F., Hammersmith, A. M., & Wright, M. R. (2018). Later life marital dissolution and repartnership status: A national portrait. *Journals of Gerontology: Series B, 73*, 1032–1042.

Buss, D. M., Larsen, R. J., Westen, D., & Semmelroth, J. (1992). Sex differences in jealousy: Evolution, physiology, and psychology. *Psychological Science, 3*, 251–256.

Chamie, J. (1986). Polygyny among Arabs. *Population Studies, 40*, 55–66.

Elbedour, S., Onwuegbuzie, A. J., Caridine, C., & Abu-Saad, H., 2002. The effect of polygamous marital structure on behavioral, emotional, and academic adjustment in children: A comprehensive review of the literature. *Clinical Child and Family Psychology Review, 5*, 255–271.

Elinder, M., Engström, P., & Erixson, O. (2021). The last will: Estate divisions as a testament of to whom altruism is directed. *Plos One, 16*, e0254492.

Gardner, P. J., & Poole, J. M. (2009). One story at a time: Narrative therapy, older adults, and addictions. *Journal of Applied Gerontology, 28*, 600–620.

Gautam, R. K., & Kshatriya, G. K. (2011). Polyandry: A case study of Kinnauras. *Indian Journal of Physical Anthropology and Human Genetics, 30*, 145–161.

Glass, S. P., & Wright, T. L. (1985). Sex differences in type of extramarital involvement and marital dissatisfaction. *Sex Roles, 12*, 1101–1120.

Glass, S. P., & Wright, T. L. (1992). Justifications for extramarital relationships: The association between attitudes, behaviors, and gender. *Journal of Sex Research, 29*, 361–387.

Hall, J. H., & Fincham, F. D. (2009). Psychological distress: Precursor or consequence of dating infidelity? *Personality and Social Psychology Bulletin, 35*, 143–159.

Hangen, F., Crasta, D., & Rogge, R. D. (2020). Delineating the boundaries between nonmonogamy and infidelity: Bringing consent back into definitions of consensual nonmonogamy with latent profile analysis. *Journal of Sex Research, 57*, 438–457.

Ivey, D. C., Wieling, E., & Harris, S. M. (2000). Save the young—The elderly have lived their lives: Ageism in marriage and family therapy. *Family Process, 39*, 163–175.

Keefe, S. (2019). " Looking outside the marriage": Polygyny, infidelity, and divorce in coastal Tanzania. *Gendered Perspectives on International Development: Working Papers, 314*, 1–20.

Kruger, D. J., Fisher, M. L. Edelstein, R. S., Chopik, W. J., Fitzgerald, C. J. & Strout, S. L. (2013). Was that cheating? Perceptions vary by sex, attachment anxiety, and behavior. *Evolutionary Psychology, 11*, 147470491301100115.

Liversage, A. (2019). Polygamy, wellbeing, and ill-being amongst ethnic Muslim minorities. In M. Tiilikainen, M. Al-Sharmani, & S. Mustasaari (Eds.), *Wellbeing of Transnational Muslim Families* (pp. 78–93). Routledge.

Luo, S., Cartun, M. A., & Snider, A. G. (2010). Assessing dyadic behavior: A review, a new measure, and two new models. *Personality and Individual Differences, 49*, 155–163.

Mattingly, B. A., Wilson, K., Clark, E. M., Bequette, A. W., & Weidler, D. J. (2010). Foggy faithfulness: Relationship quality, religiosity, and the perceptions of dating infidelity scale in an adult sample. *Journal of Family Issues, 31*, 1465–1480.

Mogilski, J. K., Memering, S. L., Welling, L. L., & Shackelford, T. K. (2017). Monogamy versus consensual non-monogamy: Alternative approaches to pursuing a strategically pluralistic mating strategy. *Archives of Sexual Behavior, 46*, 407–417.

Mogilski, J. K., Reeve, S. D., Nicolas, S. C., Donaldson, S. H., Mitchell, V. E., & Welling, L. L. (2019). Jealousy, consent, and compersion within monogamous and consensually non-monogamous romantic relationships. *Archives of Sexual Behavior, 48*, 1811–1828.

Munévar, F. R., Patino, L. E. P, Ortegon, L. M., Rodriguez, M. C., Zapata, C. D., & Nino, Y. R. (2021). Validation of the Multidimensional Inventory of Infidelity (IMIN) in Colombian population/Validacion del Inventario Multidimensional de Infidelidad (IMIN) en poblacion colombiana. *International Journal of Psychological Research, 14*, 33–48.

Palencia, A. R., Aragón, S. R., & Loving, R. D. (2007). Development of the multidimensional inventory of infidelity (IMIN). *Ibero-American Journal of Diagnosis and Evaluation-e Avaliação Psicológica, 1*, 121–147.

Prall, S. P., & Scelza, B. A. (2020). Why men invest in non-biological offspring: Paternal care and paternity confidence among Himba pastoralists. *Proceedings of the Royal Society B, 287*, 20192890.

Previti, D., & Amato, P. R. (2004). Is infidelity a cause or a consequence of poor marital quality? *Journal of Social and Personal Relationships, 21*, 217–230.

Ritchie, L. L., Stanley, S. M., Rhoades, G. K., & Markman, H. J. (2020). Romantic alternative monitoring increases ahead of infidelity and break-up. *Journal of Social and Personal Relationships, 38*, 711 – 724.

Scelza, B. A. (2014). Jealousy in a small-scale, natural fertility population: The roles of paternity, investment and love in jealous response. *Evolution and Human Behavior, 35*, 103–108.

Sibisi, C. D. (1999). The phenomenology of delusional jealousy in late life. *International Journal of Geriatric Psychiatry, 14*, 398–399.

Smith, M. S., Kish, B. J., & Crawford, C. B. (1987). Inheritance of wealth as human kin investment. *Ethology and Sociobiology, 8*, 171–182.

Smith, T. W., Marsden, P. V., & Hout, M. (2011). *General social survey, 1972–2010 cumulative file* [data file and codebook]. National Opinion Research.

Story, T. N., Berg, C. A., Smith, T. W., Beveridge, R., Henry, N. J., & Pearce, G. (2007). Age, marital satisfaction, and optimism as predictors of positive sentiment override in middle-aged and older married couples. *Psychology and Aging, 22*, 719–727.

Thompson, A. E., & O'Sullivan, L. F. (2016). Drawing the line: The development of a comprehensive assessment of infidelity judgments. *Journal of Sex Research, 53*, 910–926.

Thompson, A. P. (1983). Extramarital sex: A review of the research literature. *Journal of Sex Research, 19*, 1–22.

Thorson, A. R. (2009). Adult children's experiences with their parent's infidelity: Communicative protection and access rules in the absence of divorce. *Communication Studies, 60*, 32–48.

Træn, B., Hald, G. M., Graham, C. A., Enzlin, P., Janssen, E., Kvalem, I. L., . . . Štulhofer, A. (2017). Sexuality in older adults (65+)—An overview of the literature, part 1: Sexual function and its difficulties. *International Journal of Sexual Health, 29*, 1–10.

Weeks, G. R., Gambescia, N., & Jenkins, R. E. (2003). *Treating infidelity: Therapeutic dilemmas and effective strategies.* Norton.

Williamson, M. E., & Brimhall, A. S. (2017). A journey of remembering: A narrative framework for older couples experiencing infidelity. *Journal of Couple & Relationship Therapy, 16*, 232–252.

Wilson, K., Mattingly, B. A., Clark, E. M., Weidler, D. J., & Bequette, A. W. (2011). The gray area: Exploring attitudes toward infidelity and the development of the Perceptions of Dating Infidelity Scale. *Journal of Social Psychology, 151*, 63–86.

Wosick-Correa, K. (2010). Agreements, rules and agentic fidelity in polyamorous relationships. *Psychology & Sexuality, 1*, 44–61.

INDEX

For the benefit of digital users, indexed terms that span two pages (e.g., 52–53) may, on occasion, appear on only one of those pages.

Tables and figures are indicated by *t* and *f* following the page number.

A

Abell, L., 12*t*
Abraham, J., 264
Abrams, M., 267–68
ACEs model, 329–30
Adamopoulou, E., 267, 268, 475, 479
Adams, H. M., 12*t*
Afifi, W. A., 479
Africa
    attitudes towards infidelity, 354, 359–60
    cross-cultural research, 143, 146, 359–60
    operational sex ratio, 96–97
    polygyny in, 607
    race/ethnicity, 41–43, 47–48
African Americans
    attitude toward infidelity, 34–36, 354
    ecological model adaptation, 50–51
    infidelity predictors, 31–32, 46
    infidelity prevalence, 52–53, 400
    man sharing, 34–35
    operational sex ratio, 34–35, 94
    power relationships, 30
age differences
    cross-cultural research, 144
    good genes hypothesis, 582–83
    lifespan studies, 608–10
    nonhuman animals studies, 589–92
    novelty-seeking, 217
    offspring fitness, 590–92
    testosterone levels, 64, 75–76
aggression. *See* violence/homicide
Agostinelli, G., 216
agreeableness, 5*t*, 6–8, 11, 145–46, 157, 220, 241–42, 276–77, 379–82, 425–26, 434, 440, 460
Alavi, M., 12*t*
alcohol use history, 146
Alexander, R. D., 472
Allan, A., 478
Allan, G., 319–20
Allen, E. S., 16–17, 16*t*, 218–19, 318, 320, 401
Altgelt, E. E., 4–6, 5*t*, 7, 8, 9–10, 12*t*, 22
Amato, P. R., 335–36, 400–1, 403, 409, 518
amygdala, 243
Apostolou, M., 44
Archer, J., 537
arginine vasopressin receptor 1A gene (AVPR1A), 74
Arnocky, S., 521, 536, 540–41
Aron, A., 481
Arsena, A. R., 225
Arslan, R. C., 296, 304
Asayesh, M. H., 496, 497–98, 501, 502, 503, 504–5, 506–7, 508–9
Asendorpf, J. B., 20, 20*t*, 69–70
asexuality, 174–75
Ashdown, B. K., 116
AshleyMadison.com, 93–94, 156–57, 160, 263, 366
Asia, 43–44, 48
    attitudes towards infidelity, 354–56, 360
    cross-cultural research, 143–44, 147–48
    emotional *vs.* sexual aspects, 354–56
    online infidelity perceptions, 163, 364
    race/ethnicity, 43–44, 48
Asian Americans, 30, 31–32, 36–38, 47–48, 49, 53
Atkins, D. C., 12*t*, 114, 142–43, 320, 401
attachment insecurity
    anxiety, 16–18, 16*t*, 218–19, 383–85, 426, 536–37
    avoidance, 16*t*, 17, 18–19, 218–19, 383–85, 404, 426, 536–37
    consensual nonmonogamy and, 384–85
    deception/secrecy, 273, 276–77
    divorce, 403–4, 409
    emotional infidelity and, 158
    forgiveness and, 426
    gender differences, 383, 384
    infidelity and, 15–19, 16*t*, 32–33
    long-term infidelities, 322–23
    mate poaching, 462
    in nonheterosexual relationships, 382–86
    novelty-seeking, 218–20
    of partner, 16*t*
    violence/homicide, 536–37
attribution theory, 428
avians. *See* bird studies

B

back-up mate theory, 218
Baker, R. R., 296
Banfield, S., 319–20
Baptist, J., 332
Barbaro, N., 536–37
Barta, W. D., 5*t*, 20*t*, 145–46, 322, 474
Bartels, A., 481–82

Bateman's principle, 537–38
Bauch, C. T., 130
Baucom, D. H., 16–17, 16t, 218–19, 334, 423
Baumeister, R. F., 536
Beach, F. A., 237
Bellis, M. A., 296
Belu, C. F., 459–60, 463–64
benefit-provisioning strategies, 298–99
Beougher, S. C., 376, 377
Bergen, K. M., 161
Berry, J. W., 424–25
Betzig, L., 325
Big Five personality traits
　agreeableness, 5t, 6–8, 11, 145–46, 157, 220, 241–42, 276–77, 379–82, 425–26, 434, 440, 460
　conscientiousness, 4–6, 5t, 10–11, 44, 145, 149, 157, 220, 241–42, 379–82, 425–26, 460
　consensual nonmonogamy and, 381–82
　cross-cultural research, 144–46, 149
　extraversion, 5t, 8, 10–11, 73–74, 145, 149, 220, 276–77, 379–82, 425–26, 460
　forgiveness, 425–26, 434, 440
　gender differences, 4–7, 8–10
　infidelity and, 4–11
　integrative data analysis, 9
　longitudinal studies, 7–8
　long-term infidelities, 323
　mate poaching, 460, 462
　mate switching, 241–42
　neuroticism, 5t, 8–9, 10–11, 144–45, 149, 157, 159, 180, 220, 276–77, 380, 425–26, 460
　novelty-seeking, 220
　openness to experience, 5t, 9–11, 145, 149, 220, 380, 425–26, 460
　of partner, 4–8, 9, 10–11
　predicting infidelity, 180
　research associations, 22–23
　sexual orientation differences, 379–82
binegativity/biphobia, 179–80
bioecological model, 50–51
bird studies
　brain size, 125–26
　context-dependent hypothesis, 585–87
　extrapair fertilizations (EPFs), 124, 126
　female reproductive success, 580–81
　female survival benefits, 580
　forced copulation, 564
　genetic benefits of polygamy, 239–40
　genetic compatibility hypothesis, 583–84
　genetic constraints in females, 588–89
　good genes hypothesis, 581–83
　intersexual correlation hypothesis, 588–89
　intrasexual correlation hypothesis, 589
　intraspecific brood parasitism (IBP), 124, 126
　long-term infidelities, 126
　male age effects, 589–92
　male manipulation hypothesis, 591
　mate guarding, 125, 578
　monogamy, 122, 124–27
　offspring fitness, 584–85, 590–92
　operational sex ratio, 89
　paternal investment, 577–78
　paternity loss, 589–90
　polygamy, 237, 239–40
　sexual/genetic monogamy, 126–27
　sexy son hypothesis, 583
　social monogamy, 124–26
　STDs, 579
Blow, A. J., 52, 350, 366–67
Blumstein, P., 375, 378
Bogaert, A. F., 16–17, 16t
Booth, A., 67
Borelli, J. L., 404
Boston Marriage, 174–75
Bourassa, K. J., 404, 405–6
Bourdage, J. S., 5t
Bowlby, J., 482
Bowman, J. M., 186
Brewer, G., 12t, 221
Broude, G. J., 360–61
Brown, E. M., 499, 501, 511
Brown, K., 484
Brown, R. P., 539
Brownmiller, S., 559–60
Burch, R. L., 476, 486
Buss, D. M., 5t, 10, 12t, 13, 14, 102, 154, 155–56, 158, 215, 218, 236–37, 238–39, 267–68, 269, 298–99, 317, 354–56, 461, 474, 483, 522–23
Buunk, A. P., 146–47, 148–49, 354–56, 537–38
Buunk, B., 357–58
Byers, E. S., 350–51

C

Camilleri, J. A., 559, 565, 566
Campbell, K., 16t, 47, 52
Campbell, W. K., 12t
Cano, A., 502, 504–5
Carbello, L., 125–26
Carey, M. P., 35–36, 52–53
Case, B., 502
Catholicism, 29
Chan, S., 43
Cherkas, L. F., 134
Chesler, P., 96
children impacts
　child/partner abandonment, 518–19
　deception/secrecy, 276
　long-term infidelities, 337–39
　monogamy vs. multiple sexual partners, 215
　parent-child relationship, 508–9
Chimbos, P. D., 526–27
Choi, K. H., 35
Chou, J., 160–61
Christensen, H. T., 351–52
Ciarocco, N. J., 500
Cloud, M. D., 185
Clutton-Brock, T. H., 123, 127
Cobey, K., 300
cognitive-behavioral therapy (CBT), 571–72
cognitive dissonance theory, 110–11
Cohen, D., 45
compersion, 388, 605–6
competition. See intrasexual competition
competitive disadvantage, 559
Compton, B. L., 186
computer-mediated communication (CMC), 330–31
concubinage, 96
Confer, J. C., 185
confession solicitation tactics, 268–69

congruency hypothesis, 302
Conley, J. J., 518
Conley, T. D., 487
conscientiousness, 4–6, 5t, 10–11, 44, 145, 149, 157, 220, 241–42, 379–82, 425–26, 460
consensual nonmonogamy
　attachment insecurity and, 384–85
　Big Five personality traits and, 381–82
　characterization, 390, 391, 604–6
　nonconsensual vs., 388–89
context-dependent hypothesis, 585–87
Cook, C. T., 34–35
Coolidge effect, 213–14, 225–26
Cooper, A., 263, 329
cortisol, 73–74, 430
Costa, P. T. Jr., 146
cost-inflicting strategies, 298–99
Cravens, J. D., 328
Crenshaw, K., 48–49
cross-cultural research
　affective touch, 357
　age differences, 144
　alcohol use history, 146
　attitudes towards infidelity, 148–49, 351–54, 359–60
　behavioral ecological approach, 356–60
　Big Five personality traits, 144–46, 149
　cultural dimensions model, 366
　demographic factors, 142–44
　detection of infidelity, 359
　divorce, 353
　emotional/affectionate behaviors, 141–42
　emotional vs. sexual aspects, 354–57
　extradyadic behavior types, 141–42
　female infidelity constraints, 94–97
　forgiveness, 353, 431–32
　frequency of extramarital partnerships, 356
　gender differences, 143–44, 149, 351–52, 353, 354–57
　gender expectations, 183, 184–85
　ideological factors, 148–49
　income/education/occupational status, 142–43
　infidelity impacts, 606–8
　intersectionality of identities, 183–84
　intimate partner violence (IPV), 520–21
　IPH, 526–27
　jealousy, 184, 535
　limitations of, 365–67
　long-term infidelities, 43
　love, 481–82
　Machiavellianism and infidelity, 221
　mate poaching, 211–12, 459
　nature/definition of infidelity, 349–51
　nonheterosexual relationships, 182–85
　novelty-seeking, 216–17, 219
　online infidelity, 162–64
　operational sex ratio, 92–93, 94–97
　paternal investment, 356–57, 358, 359–60
　patterns historically, 95–96, 140–41
　polyamory/polygyny, 362
　polygyny, 358–59
　pornography, 362–66
　predicting infidelity, 184–85
　quality of alternatives, 142–43
　race/ethnicity, 32, 41–45, 46–47, 52
　relational factors, 146–47
　religiosity, 148, 149
　satisfaction, 46–48
　sexual behaviors, 141–42
　sexual coercion, 524
　sexual/romantic interactions history, 147–48
　social support, 183
　socioeconomic status (SES), 142–43
　solitary behaviors, 142
　technology-facilitated infidelity, 141
　testosterone studies, 76
　wife sharing/lending, 360–61
Crowley, J. P., 437
cuckoldry, 272–73, 277–78, 300, 472, 477, 486, 519–20, 532–34, 569–70, 578
cultural differences. See cross-cultural research
cyber-cheating, 263. See also online infidelity
cybersex, 155, 326–27, 328, 332, 349–50, 362–63, 364–65

D

Dabbs, M. Jr., 67
Dalla, R. L., 40
Dark Triad, 11–15, 12t, 157, 159, 179, 180, 220–22, 241–42, 266–67, 276–77, 461
Darwin, C., 86, 561–62
dating websites, 114, 141, 160–61, 263, 350–51, 603
Davis, A. C., 537
Davis, J., 511
deception/secrecy
　attachment insecurity, 273
　children, 276
　choice to conceal or reveal, 278–80
　concepts, definitions, 262
　cuckoldry, 272–73, 277–78, 300, 472, 477, 486, 519–20, 532–34, 569–70, 578
　Dark Triad, 266–67, 276–77
　detection, factors influencing, 272–74
　detection mechanisms, 267–70
　discovery aftermath, 281–84, 569–70
　divorce, 283
　facial cues, 270
　forgiveness and, 282
　gaslighting, 262–63
　gender differences, 272–73, 278, 279–80, 283
　implicit behavioral cues, 269–70
　infidelity defined by, 260–62
　by infidelity partner, 276–77
　information-seeking strategies, 268–69
　long-term infidelities, 243, 245
　loss in partner trust, 265
　mate poaching, 275–76
　nature of, 262–63
　online infidelity, 263–65, 364–65
　oral sex as detection strategy, 269
　prevalence, 262
　previous experience, 272
　prior infidelity risk, 267

deception/secrecy (cont.)
   projection-detection relationship, 273–74
   renewed love and, 479
   sociosexuality and, 265–66
   suspicion/jealousy, 274
   targets of, 274–76
   traits related to, 265–67
   voice cues, 271
   withdrawal patterns, 270
Decision to Forgive Scale, 422–23, 424, 425
deficit model of infidelity, 104, 212, 383
Definitions of Infidelity Questionnaire (DIQ), 603
de Miguel, A., 299
Denes, A., 185–86, 187, 417–18, 423, 438
DeWall, C. N., 16t, 18, 19
diathesis-stress model study, 107–8
DiBlasio, F. A., 429
discounting hypothesis, 183
divorce
   attachment insecurity, 403–4, 409
   cross-cultural research, 353
   deception/secrecy, 283
   decisional factors, 401–2
   demographics, 400
   depression/major depressive disorder, 407–8
   divorce-stress-adjustment model, 403, 409
   emotion regulation/suppression, 403–6, 409
   entrapment, 407
   gender differences, 408, 410, 484
   humiliation, 407–8, 410
   impacts of, 519
   infidelity detection and, 402, 406–9
   long-term infidelities, 335–36
   mate switching, 245–46
   motivations, 401, 499, 518
   narrative coherence, 404–6
   negative outcomes following, 403, 407–8, 484
   in nonheterosexual relationships, 410
   novelty-seeking and, 211–12, 215
   online infidelity, 328
   operational sex ratio and, 93–94
   posttraumatic growth, 408–9
   predictors of, 480–81
   prevalence, 400
   race/ethnicity, 36–37
   reconciliation tactics, 402
   recovery, 402–4, 408
   relationship factors, 108
   satisfaction and, 36–37, 522–23
   self-concept disturbances, 404–6
   symptom vs. cause, 400–1
   technology effects, 410–11
   testosterone relationship to, 68
   therapeutic approach to, 411
Djamba, Y. K., 143
Docan, C. A., 363–64
Docan-Morgan, T., 363–64
Donohoe, F., 40–41, 47, 53–54
dopaminergic reward pathway, 222–23
Dowd, M. M., 267–68, 270, 279, 281–82
DRD4, 222–24
Drigotas, S., 16t
dual mating strategy hypothesis, 72, 245, 293, 294–95, 296–97, 303–4
Duncombe, J., 337–38
Durante, K. M., 72–73, 225
Düsing, C., 86

E

Eastwick, P. W., 224–25
EDI. See infidelity generally
Ellis, A., 567
Ellison, P. T., 76
Emery, R. E., 408
Emlen, S., 87
emotional invalidation, 107–8
Enright, R. D., 419–20, 434, 436, 511
Enright Forgiveness Inventory (EFI), 422–23, 425
equity theory, 104–5
erotic chatting, 263–65, 362–64
espionage, 268
estradiol, 62, 72–73, 77, 290–91, 296–97, 299–300
ethnicity. See race/ethnicity
European Americans, 30–31, 37–38
exchange orientation, infidelity and, 146
exhibitionism, 159
Exline, J. L., 419–20
expressiveness, 380
extended sexuality theory, 293–94, 296–97
Extradyadic Behavior Inventory (EDI), 602–3
extradyadic involvements (EDI). See infidelity generally
extraversion, 5t, 8, 10–11, 73–74, 145, 149, 220, 276–77, 379–82, 425–26, 460
Eyre, S. L., 35

F

Falato, W. L., 479
Farahbakhsh, K., 497–98, 501
fast life strategy, 218
fertilization hypothesis, 580
Fife, S. T., 429, 510
Figueredo, A. J., 218
filicide, 530–32
Fincham, F. D., 22, 44, 148–49, 334–35, 419–20, 475, 478, 480, 518
Finkelhor, D., 566
first wife syndrome, 607
Fish, J. N., 16t
Fisher, A. E., 218
Fisher, H., 237, 242
Fisher, H. E., 472, 481, 482, 484
Fisher, M. L., 67
Fisher, R. A., 86, 583
Fitzgibbons, R. P., 511
five factor model of personality. See Big Five personality traits
Fleming, A. S., 292–93
Foo, Y. Z., 291–92
forced in-pair copulation (FIPC), 555–57, 563–72
Ford, C. S., 237
forgiveness
   accommodation vs., 422
   antecedents/correlates, 425–32
   attachment insecurity and, 426
   attributions role, 480
   Big Five personality traits, 425–26, 434, 440
   communicative infidelity, 417
   communicative strategies, 420, 432–33, 435, 440

conceptualizations of, 419–22
conditional, 432–33
cross-cultural research, 353, 431–32
deception/secrecy and, 282
decision-based model, 428–29
dispositional, 438
dispositional/trait, 424–25
emotional, 419–20
evolutionary psychology, 252
exoneration *vs.*, 420
expectations of, 256
exploitation risk/reoffense, 439–40
facilitation of, 411
forms of, 433
gender differences, 417–18, 438, 480–81, 535
granting, 419–33
individual differences in, 281, 425–27
integrative model, 428–29
interpersonal forgiveness model, 429
interventions, 428–30, 437
long-term infidelities, 336–37
measurement of, 422–24
mental health benefits, 436
mindfulness and, 427
motivations, 419–20
outcomes, 333, 336–37, 402, 435–40, 479, 480–81
physical/physiological benefits, 437, 439
physiology/psychophysiology, 430–31
prescriptive model, 429–30
prevalence of infidelity, 418–19
reappraisals, fMRI studies, 430–31
reconciliation/reunion *vs.*, 421–22
as reconciliation tactic, 402
relational justice/power effects, 440
relationship commitment and, 438
relationship-destructive responses, 419
relationship factors, 427
relationship function benefits, 438–39
relationship-protective responses, 419
relationship quality and, 479

relationship transgressions and, 415–19
religiosity and, 426
renewed love and, 478–81
same-sex infidelity, 417–18
seeking, 433–35
sexual *vs.* emotional infidelity, 416–17
situational factors, 427–28
social network influences, 428
of specific transgression, 422–24, 436, 438
stress-and-coping model, 436
therapeutic, 420
third party relationships, 440
of transgressor/various offenses, 424
Forgiveness and Reconciliation through Experiencing Empathy (FREE), 437
Forgiveness Inventory (FI), 423
Foster, J. D., 462–63
Freud, S., 560–61
Friedman, S. H., 532
Fuentes, A., 482

G

Gallup, G. G. Jr., 476, 486
Garcia, J. R., 222–23
Gass, G. Z., 284
Gavrilets, S., 130–31
gender differences
 African Americans, 34
 Africans, 42–43
 Asian Americans, 38
 attachment anxiety, 16–17
 attachment insecurity, 383
 Big Five personality traits, 4–7, 8–10
 cross-cultural research, 143–44, 149, 351–52, 353, 354–57
 deception/secrecy, 283
 divorce, 408, 410, 484
 forgiveness, 417–18, 438, 480–81, 535
 group perceptions, 29, 47–48
 infidelity detection strategies, 272–73
 infidelity disclosure, 279–80
 infidelity prevalence, 400
 infidelity rates, 211–12
 intrasexual competition, 62–63, 64–65
 jealousy, 185–86, 535–36
 Latin Americans, 38–39

 long-term infidelities, 278, 318–19, 320–21, 322, 341
 love act goals, 483
 mate poaching, 272, 458–59
 mate retention, 566
 mate switching, 241–42, 243–46
 mating strategies, 90–91
 Middle East, 44
 motivations, 156, 476–77
 narcissism, 13, 221
 Native Americans, 40–41
 nonheterosexual relationships, 180, 379
 novelty-seeking, 213–16, 217–18, 225–26
 online infidelity, 156, 326–27
 operational sex ratio, 94
 perceptions of cheating, 187
 perceptions of infidelity, 154
 primary relationship/infidelity relationship, 212–13
 race/ethnicity, 32–33, 38
 relationship length, 113–14
 relationship satisfaction, 105–6
 response to deception/infidelity, 278
 same-sex infidelity, 417–18
 in same-sex infidelity response, 185–86, 417–18
 self-control/self-regulation, 224–25
 sexual dimorphism, 71–72
 sexual satisfaction, 109
 sexual *vs.* emotional infidelity, 158, 474–75, 480–81
 sociosexuality, 69–70
 violence/homicide, 541
gendered racism, 49
gender ratio imbalance, 33, 34–35, 46, 50–51. *See also* operational sex ratio
General Social Survey (GSS), 31–32, 217, 319–20, 352–53, 609–10
genetic compatibility hypothesis, 583–84
Ghahari, S., 506, 510
Gibbs, J. L., 330–31
Gibson, K. A., 5*t*, 144, 145–46
Giesen, D., 472
girlfriend experience, 160
Glass, S. P., 318–19, 321, 322
Goetz, A. T., 557, 565–66

Gold, G., 511
Gomes, W., 536
Gonzalez-Lopez, G., 38–39
good genes hypothesis, 245, 581–83
Gordon, K. C., 334, 423, 429, 500, 511
GPS software, 163–64
Graham, S. M., 146
Graham-Kevan, N., 537
Grammer, K., 64–65
Gray, P. B., 76
Grøntvedt, T., 302–3, 480–81
Guitar, A. E., 261, 316–17, 474

H

Hackathorn, J., 116
Hall, J. H., 334–35, 478, 480, 518
Hanneke, C. R., 521
Hargrave, T. D., 420
Harlow, H., 482
Harris, C. R., 341
Harrison, K., 339–40
Harrison, M. A., 271
Hartnett, K., 52, 350, 366–67
Haseli, A., 50, 51–52, 144
Haselton, M. G., 278
Hatfield, E., 482
Helsper, E. J., 332
Hendrick, C., 353
Hendrick, S., 353
Henline, B. H., 327, 363–64
Hertlein, K. M., 329–30
Hickle, K. E., 39
HIV/STIs, 35, 38, 41–42, 43, 47–48, 94, 579
Hoff, C. C., 376, 377
Hofstede, G., 366
Holmes, W. M., 407–8
homicide. *See* violence/homicide
honor culture, 45, 96, 539
hormones. *See also* ovulatory cycle
   estradiol, 62, 72–73, 77, 290–91, 296–97, 299–300
   extradyadic behavior regulation by, 67–76
   facial masculinity preferences, 72
   mating *vs.* parenting, 62–63, 66–67, 71, 76–77
   monogamy, 65–66
   ovulation and, 63–64, 65, 73
   polyamory, 66, 140–41
   polygamy, 75–76
   progesterone, 62, 72–73, 77, 290–91
   research limitations, 74–76
   sexual dimorphism, 71–72, 291–92
   shoulder-to-hip ratios, 73
   testosterone (*see* testosterone)
   waist-to-hip ratios, 73
Horwitz, A. V., 407–8
Hrdy, S. B., 358–59
Hsieh, C., 160–61
Hughes, S. M., 213–14, 271
Human Relations Area Files (HRAF), 357–58
Hunyady, O., 12t
Hupka, R. B., 357–58
Hurd, C., 262, 475
hyperpersonal model, 330–31

I

immunocompetence handicap hypothesis, 291–92
impulsivity, infidelity and, 4
infanticide, 530, 532, 581
infidelity generally
   adverse reactions to, 243
   classification categories, 261–62
   concepts, definitions, 21, 140–41, 315–17, 349–51, 363–64, 472–73, 494
   context role in, 22–23
   definition standardization, 601–4
   distorted cognitions associated with, 255–57
   factors predicting, 3–4
   family members effects, 486
   group perceptions of, 29
   impacts, 211–12
   lifespan studies of, 608–10
   partner responses to, 476–77
   perceptions of, 454
   predictors of, 21–22, 180, 184–85, 324–25, 533
   prevalence, 61–62, 154–55, 166, 211–12, 239–43, 262, 375–78, 418–19, 454, 475–76, 494
   reproductive behaviors in, 62
   research methodology, 15, 21–22
   types of, 473–75
infidelity overperception bias, 533–34
informed cognitive therapy (ICT), 571–72
instrumentality, 380
integrative data analyses
   attachment anxiety, 16–17
   Big Five personality traits, 9
   narcissism, 11–13
interdependence model, 45–47, 427
interdependence theory, 103
Internet addiction disorder, 165
interrogation, 268–69
intersectionality model, 45, 48–50
intersexual correlation hypothesis, 588–89
intimate partner homicide (IPH), 526–28
intimate partner violence (IPV), 517, 520–24, 536, 537–40, 541, 556–59
intrasexual competition
   gender differences, 62–63, 64–65
   hormonal influences, 62–63, 64–65
   male age, 582–83
   male body size, 581–82
   mate poaching, 455
   mate switching as survival attribute, 240–42
   operational sex ratio, 90–91
   sexual coercion, 524–25
   sperm competition, 563–66
intrasexual correlation hypothesis, 589
investment model of commitment, 46, 103–4, 109–10, 212, 427
Ishola, C. A., 42

J

Jahan, Y., 44
Jain, G., 365–66
Jankowiak, W., 359, 481–82
jealousy
   as adaptive, 154, 238
   compersion *vs.*, 388
   cross-cultural research, 184, 535
   Dark Triad and, 179
   emotional, 534–36
   emotional *vs.* sexual infidelity, 354–56, 566
   evoked sexual, cross-cultural variations, 357–58
   evolution of, 474–75

filicide and, 530–31
gender differences, 185–86, 535–36
hormonal contraceptives and, 300–3
hormonal effects on, 298–300
morbid, 534–36
nonheterosexual relationships, 164
as normative, 183, 274
online infidelity, 155–56, 159
paternal investment and, 356–57, 358
sexual, 534–36
steroid hormones effects, 303–4
as violence/homicide motivation, 522, 523–24, 534–36
Johnson, D. J., 112
Johnson, S. M., 502, 504–5
Jonason, P. K., 219
Jones, D. N., 12t, 221, 222, 566
Joseph, P. N., 213–14
Judaism, 29

K
Kalantar, S., 44
Kelley, D. L., 432
Kelly, E. L., 518
Kessel, D. E., 496–97, 502
Key, Philip Barton, 528–29
keyboard loggers, 163–64
Kiene, S. M., 5t, 20t, 145–46, 322, 474
Kimuna, S. R., 143
kin investment, 609
Kinsey, A., 74–75
Kirkpatrick, L. A., 476
Kitson, G. C., 407–8
Klapilová, K., 302–3
Knodel, J., 43
Kongnyuy, E. J., 146
Kruger, D. J., 278, 280, 350–51
Kwena, Z., 42–43

L
Labrecque, L. T., 319–20, 324–25, 352–53
Lambert, C. T., 129
Lambert, N. M., 270
Lande, R., 583
Lang, G., 43
LaSala, M. C., 376, 377
Latin Americans, 29, 37–40, 47–48, 53–54, 148, 162–63

Lawson, A., 212–13
L-DOPA, 222–23
Lee, L. A., 403–4
lek paradox, 239–40
Levine, E. C., 182
LGBTQ+. *See also* nonheterosexual relationships; same-sex infidelity
attachment insecurity in, 382–86
concepts, definitions, 173
felt experiences, 386–88, 391
infidelity prevalence, 375–78
IPH prevalence, 526
motivations, 390–91
personality role in, 379–82
renewed love, 487
Li, N. P., 72–73
Li, Y. M., 163
life history theory, 62–63
Lippa, R. A., 216–17
Little, A., 213–14
Little, A. C., 301–2
Liu, C., 109, 213
Liu-Farrer, G., 43–44
longitudinal studies, 608–10
long-term infidelities
attachment insecurity, 322–23
back burner relationships, 331–32
bird studies, 126
boundary setting, 332–33, 338–39
children impacts, 337–39
commitment and, 103–4
concepts, definitions, 315–17, 340
contextual factors as predictive, 324–25
cross-cultural studies, 43
cultural influence effects, 325
deception/secrecy, 243, 245
divorce, 335–36
emotional infidelity, 198, 316–17, 318–20, 322–23
family/friends impacts, 337–40
forgiveness, 336–37
gender differences, 278, 318–19, 320–21, 322, 341
hormonal contraceptives and, 301–2
individual factors as predictor, 320–23

literature limitations, 340–42
mammals, 127–28, 133
measurement of, 340–41
motivations, 320–25, 329–33
nonheterosexual relationships, 174–75, 341
noninvolved partner impacts, 328, 333–35
novelty-seeking, 213–15, 223, 225–26
online infidelity, 155–56, 161, 325–33
operational sex ratio, 89–91, 93, 97, 325
opportunity effects, 324–25
outcomes of, 333–37
ovulatory cycle in, 291–94, 298, 301–2
partner similarity as predictive, 51–52
personality traits, 323
positive outcomes, 336–37
predictors of, 320–25
prevalence of, 317–20
reconciliation, 336–37
relational factors as predictive, 323–24
relationship dissolution, 325
reproductive benefits, 90–91, 153–54, 225–26
research designs, 341
sampling, 341
sexual infidelity, 317–19
sociosexuality, 323
sugar daddy model, 160–61
testosterone level effects, 64, 68–72, 75
work status effects, 324–25
Lopez, V., 53–54
Lukas, D., 123, 127
Lung, E., 5t, 9–10
Luo, S., 350–51, 602–3
Lusterman, D. D., 499, 502, 503–4, 506
lying. *See* deception/secrecy

M
Macauda, M. M., 354
Machiavellianism
infidelity and, 12t, 14–15, 157, 179, 180, 220–22, 266–67
mate poaching, 461
Macintosh, H. B., 501, 507
Madathil, J., 44
Mahambrey, M., 5t, 10

male manipulation hypothesis, 588, 591
mammals
  hormonal regulation in, 127–28, 560–61
  long-term infidelities, 127–28, 133
  male infanticide/provisioning, 127
  mate guarding in, 127, 128
  mate switching as survival attribute, 240–42
  monogamy in, 127–29
  operational sex ratio, 88, 89
  pair bonding/parental care, 127–28
  paternal investment, 577
  peak fertility signs in, 294
  sexual/genetic monogamy, 129
  social monogamy in, 127–29
  submission/sexual receptivity behaviors in, 560–61
Maner, J. K., 499, 528–29
manipulation, 159
man-sharing, 34–35
Marcikić, M., 532
marianismo/machismo, 38–39
Marin, R. A., 335–36
Marital Dispositional Forgiveness Scale (MDFS), 424, 425
Marital Offence-Specific Forgiveness Scale (MOFS), 423
marital separation. *See* divorce
mariticide, 526
Marjorie, P., 501
Mark, K. P., 51–52, 109
Marlowe, F. W., 358–59
Marsden, D., 337–38
Martins, A., 146–47, 216–17
masochistic sexual fantasies study, 560–61
Massar, K., 537–38
Mass-Observation Archive (M-OA), 319–20
mate deprivation hypothesis, 524–25
mate expulsion. *See* divorce
mate guarding, 123, 125, 127, 128, 132–33, 238, 272, 294–95, 298–99, 300, 476, 556, 564, 567–70, 578
mate poaching
  attractive others, 456–58, 457f

Big Five personality traits, 460, 462
case study, 250–51
characterization, 454
cross-cultural research, 211–12, 459
Dark Triad traits and, 221, 461
deception/secrecy, 275–76
evolutionary psychology, 455–56
factors affecting, 147, 212–13, 245–46
gender differences, 272, 458–59
hormonal modulation in, 70–71, 72–73, 74–75
individual factors, 459–60
intrasexual competition, 455
IPV and, 521–23
literature critique, 465–66
mate value perceptions, 537–38
motivations, 457–58
paternal investment, 455
prediction of, 460–61
prevalence of, 61–62, 458–60, 465
profiles, 461
race/ethnicity in, 35, 46, 52–53
relationship quality and, 438, 461–65, 466
relationship success, 455–56
resistance strategies, 457–58
as self-expansion, 111–12, 212–13
serial poaching, 463–64
sociosexuality and, 460, 462, 464
value of in forgiveness, 439
mate retention, 298–99, 521–23, 556, 566, 567–70
mate switching
  as adaptive, 455
  antecedents, 241, 244–45, 252–53
  case studies, 246–51
  CBT, 254–57
  counseling, 248–49, 253–54
  couples assessment, 251–53
  divorce, 245–46
  evolutionary psychology, 237–40, 246, 252
  as exit strategy, 243–49, 253, 279–80, 283
  explanations/rationalizations, 241

fMRI studies, 242
gender differences, 241–42, 243–46
good genes hypothesis, 245
infidelity detection, 237–38
infidelity prevalence/incidence, 239–43
man seeking younger woman, 246–49
marketability self-assessment, 236–37
motivations, 457–58
romantic infidelity, 238–43
sexual infidelity, 237–38
as survival attribute, 240–42
twin studies, 241–42
woman seeking mate fitness, 249–51
Mattingly, B. A, 20t
May, R. W., 22, 475
Maykovich, M. K., 351–52
Mbago, M. C., 147–48
McAlister, A., 143
McBride, M. C., 161
McCabe, M. P., 319–20
McCrae, R. R., 146
McCullough, M. E., 419–20, 423
McDaniel, B. T., 264
McElreath, R., 130
McElroy-Heltzel, S. E., 425
McKibbin, W. F., 565
McKillop, D., 478
McNulty, J. K., 12t, 13, 16t, 19–20, 20t, 22–23, 221
menstrual cycle. *See* ovulatory cycle
Merolla, A. J., 433
Middle East, 44–45
Middle Eastern Americans, 30
migrant labor system, 42
Mileham, B. L. A., 327–28, 330, 363–64
Miller, A. N., 318
Miller, S. L., 499, 528–29
Miner, E. J., 537–38
misattributed paternity, 277–78
Mitsunaga, T. M., 147–48
Mogilski, J. K., 484, 487
Moller, N. P., 364–65, 473
Mongeau, P. A., 282–83
monogamy
  biparental care, 122–23
  bird studies, 122, 124–27
  children *vs.* multiple sexual partners, 215

concepts, definitions, 122
distribution across species, 121–22
genetic benefits of, 133–34, 153–54, 472
heritability of female infidelity, 134
hormone effects on, 65–66
in humans, 132–33, 134
infanticide, 123
lifetime prevalence, 131–32
maintenance strategies, 457–58, 558–59
male provisioning, 129–30
in mammals, 122, 127–29
mate guarding, 123, 125, 127, 128, 132–33
nonpaternity measurement, 133
paternal care, 129–30
polygyny (*see* polygamy)
primates, 123, 128
race/ethnicity, 181
re-pairing, 122
serial, 129–30
sexual/genetic, 122, 123–24, 126–27, 129, 132–33, 175
short-term mating, 131
social, 122, 124–26, 130–32, 175
theoretical perspectives on, 122–24
Moors, A. C., 379, 381
Morrisey, L., 322
motivations. *See also* novelty-seeking
anonymity, 329–31
choice to conceal or reveal infidelity, 278–80
divorce, 401, 499, 518
forgiveness, 419–20
gender differences, 156, 476–77
infidelity generally, 474, 475–77, 495
in-pair relationship maintenance, 282–83
long-term infidelities, 320–25, 329–33
mate poaching, 457–58
mate switching, 457–58
nonheterosexual relationships, 390–91
online infidelity, 329–33, 364
partner/spousal revenge, 531–32

predictive factors, online infidelity, 156
reconnecting with past partners, 331
same-sex infidelity, 418
sexual coercion, 522, 524–25
Multidimensional Inventory of Infidelity (IMIN), 603–4
Murdock, G. P., 359

N

narcissism
forgiveness-seeking and, 434
infidelity and, 11–14, 12*t*, 159, 179, 180, 220–22, 241–42, 266–67
mate poaching, 461, 462–63
sociosexuality and, 13–14
National Health and Social Life Survey, 109, 213
National Survey of Sexual Health and Behavior, 382
Native Americans, 30, 31–32, 40–41, 47, 53–54
Negy, C., 362
neonaticide, 530
Neudorf, D. L., 125
neuroticism, 5*t*, 8–9, 10–11, 144–45, 149, 157, 159, 180, 220, 276–77, 380, 425–26, 460
Nichols, W. C., 284
nonheterosexual relationships. *See also* LGBTQ+
asexuality, 174–75
attachment style in, 382–86
casual *vs.* committed, 176–77
characterization, 172–75
communication factors, 185–87, 377
consensual nonmonogamy, 187–88, 390, 391
couples longitudinal studies, 389–90
cultural differences in, 182–85
divorce in, 410
felt experiences, 386–88, 391
gender differences, 180, 379
individual differences impacts, 179–80
infidelity in, 175–76
jealousy, 164
long-term infidelities, 174–75, 341
marriage equality impacts, 177
motivations, 390–91

nonconsensual *vs.* consensual nonmonogamy, 388–89
nonmonogamy, 373–75
online infidelity, 164–65, 166
open relationships, 173–74, 187–88, 261, 376
open *vs.* closed, 177
ovulatory cycle, 295, 304–5
pansexuality, 173
personality impacts, 179–80
personality role in, 379–82
polyamory, 173–74, 187–88, 377
polyfidelity, 173–74, 187–88
polygyny (*see* polygyny)
predictions, 177–79, 180, 181–82, 184–85, 187–88
prevalence of infidelity in, 375–78
queerplatonic, 174–75
race/ethnicity, 181–82
same-sex infidelity, 185–86
sexual orientation differences in, 378–79
sexual *vs.* emotional infidelity, 175–76
sexual *vs.* social monogamy, 175
swinging lifestyle, 177, 187–88, 362
third-party perceptions, 185–87
nonhuman animals studies. *See also* bird studies; mammals
context-dependent hypothesis, 585–87
female reproductive success, 580–81
female survival benefits, 580
genetic compatibility hypothesis, 583–84
genetic constraints in females, 588–89
good genes hypothesis, 581–83
infidelity benefits, 579–87
infidelity generally, 576–77, 592*f*
intersexual correlation hypothesis, 588–89
intrasexual correlation hypothesis, 589
male age effects, 589–92
male manipulation hypothesis, 588, 591
mate poaching, 521–22

INDEX | 623

nonhuman animals studies (*cont.*)
  nonadaptive infidelity, 587–89
  offspring fitness, 584–85, 590–92
  operational sex ratio, 88, 89
  paternal investment, 577–79, 580–81
  paternity loss, 578, 589–90
  sexually transmitted diseases, 579
  sexy son hypothesis, 583
Noonan, K. M., 472
Norton, A. M., 332
novelty-seeking
  acceptability/likelihood relationship, 216–17
  age impacts on, 217
  attachment theory, 218–20
  back-up mate theory, 218
  Big Five personality traits, 220
  cross-cultural research, 216–17, 219
  Dark Triad traits, 220–22
  divorce and, 211–12, 215
  dual-mating strategy, 217–18
  fast life strategy, 218
  fertility status and, 225
  gender differences, 225–26
  genetic basis of, 217–18, 222–24, 226
  infidelity and, 211–12
  long-term infidelities, 213–15, 223, 225–26
  marital satisfaction, 212–13, 225–26
  mating strategies, 215
  parental investment theory, 214–15
  self-control/self-regulation in, 224–25, 226–27
  sexual strategies theory, 185, 215
  sexy son hypothesis, 217–18
  sociosexual orientation and, 216–17

O

Oala, M., 509
O'Connor, J. J. M., 271
Octaviana, B. N., 264
Ogwokhademhe, M., 42
Olderbak, S. G., 218
O'Leary, K. D., 502, 504–5, 559
Olson, M., 497
Omarzu, J., 147, 318, 321–22, 500

online infidelity
  anonymity, 329–31
  back burner relationships, 331–32
  boundary setting, 332–33
  concepts, definitions, 165–66, 327, 332–33, 363–66
  cultural differences, 162–64
  cybersex, 155, 326–27, 328, 332, 349–50, 362–63, 364–65
  dating websites, 114, 141, 160–61, 263, 350–51, 603
  deception/secrecy, 263–65, 364–65
  divorce, 328
  emotional, 154, 158–62, 264, 363–64
  erotic chatting, 263–65, 362–64
  evolutionary psychology, 154–55
  experiences of, 327–28
  fidelity/fidelity management, 163–64
  gender differences, 156, 326–27
  Internet addiction, 165
  jealousy, 155–56, 159
  long-term infidelities, 155–56, 161, 325–33
  monogamy genetic benefits, 153–54
  motivations, 329–33, 364
  noninvolved partner impacts, 328, 333–35
  nontraditional relationships, 166
  pair-bonded couples, 158
  perceptions of, 158–59
  personality trait correlates, 159
  phone sex, 363
  pornography, 155, 264–65, 326, 349–50, 362–66
  predictors of, 159, 167
  prevalence, 154–55, 166
  race/ethnicity, 162–63
  reconnecting with past partners, 331
  same-sex couples, 164–65, 166
  satisfaction and, 328, 364
  sexting, 141, 155–58
  sexual, 154, 155–58, 363–64
  social media, 157, 161, 165, 264, 331–32, 410–11
  studies, 156–58

  therapeutic approach to, 159–60
  virtual relationships, 363–64
openness to experience, 5t, 9–11, 145, 149, 220, 380, 425–26, 460
open relationships, 173–74, 187–88, 261, 376
operational sex ratio
  African Americans, 94
  bird studies, 89
  concubinage, 96
  cross-species behavioral patterns, 87–90
  cultural patterns historically, 92–93, 95–96
  definitions of, 87
  divorce and, 93–94
  female infidelity constraints, 94–97
  fish studies, 88, 89
  gender differences, 94
  infidelity and, 93–94
  insect studies, 88
  intrasexual competition, 90–91
  long-term infidelities, 89–91, 93, 97, 325
  mating strategies, 90–91
  nonhuman primates studies, 88, 89
  patterns associated with, 90–91
  polyandry, 91–92
  polygyny, 91–92, 96
  power relationships, 94–97
  principles of, 86–87
  race/ethnicity influences, 33, 34–35, 46, 50–51
  reproductive value, 90
  social norms enforcement, 94–95
  violence/homicide, 540–41
  workplace environments, 94
Ophir, A. G., 127–28
opioids, 496–97
oral contraceptives (OCs), 73, 300–3
Oring, L., 87
Orzeck, T., 5t, 9–10
Ostovich, J. M., 216
O'Sullivan, L. F., 459–60, 463–64
ovulatory cycle. *See also* hormones

congruency hypothesis, 302
dual mating hypothesis, 293, 294–95, 296–97, 303–4
estrogen, 290, 296–97, 299–300, 303–4
extended sexuality theory, 293–94, 296–97
female mate preference theories, 291–95
fertility cue detection, 299
hormonal contraceptives and, 300–3
infidelity and, 73
in long-term infidelities, 291–94, 298, 301–2
male counter-strategies, 298–300
mate attraction effects, 63–65, 71–72, 73, 290–91
mating strategies, 292–94
nonheterosexual relationships, 295, 304–5
overview, 289–91
parental investment theory, 292
progesterone, 290, 296–97, 303–4
research designs, 304–5
sexual desire/behavior changes, 295–97, 300–3
steroid hormones, 303–4, 560–61
strategic pluralism theory, 292–93
oxytocin, 74, 127–28, 223, 226, 430, 478
oxytocin receptor gene (OXTR), 74
Oyediran, K., 42

P

Paladino, T., 481–82
Panayiotou, R., 44
pansexuality, 173
Pardiwalla, A., 160
parental care adjustment hypothesis, 577–78
parental investment theory, 214–15, 292, 472–73, 474–75, 480, 482–83. *See also* paternal investment theory
Parker, M. L., 16t, 52
Parker, T. S., 326–27
Parkinson's disease, 222–23
Parsons, J. T., 181

partner/child abandonment, 518–19
partner qualities. *See also* relationship factors
attachment anxiety, 17–18
attachment avoidance, 18
Big Five personality traits, 4–8, 9, 10–11
deception/secrecy, 276–77
emotional invalidation, 107–8
felt experiences, 386–88, 391
gaslighting, 262–63
Machiavellianism, 14–15
narcissism, 13
power, 30–31
as predictive, 21–22
psychopathy, 14
race/ethnicity, 33
responses to infidelity, 476–77
sociosexuality, 20, 20t
sociosexuality/testosterone relationships, 70–71
Partner Selection Game study, 224–25
paternal investment theory. *See also* parental investment theory
cross-cultural research, 356–57, 358, 359–60
jealousy and, 356–57, 358
mate poaching, 455
paternity fraud, 277–78
patriarchy/honor culture, 45, 96, 539
Pazhoohi, F., 358–59
Penke, L., 20, 20t, 69–70
Penn, C. D., 37
Perceptions of Dating Infidelity Scale (PDIS), 261–62, 603
personality. *See* Big Five personality traits; Dark Triad
Pham, M. N., 269
Phillips, A., 536
phone sex, 363
Pickens, J. C., 332
pillow talk, 107
Pillsworth, E. G., 72–73
polyamory
characterization, 173–74
hormones, 66, 140–41
as infidelity, 362, 604–6
research limitations, 187–88
sexual agreements, 377

polyandry
infidelity impacts, 608
operational sex ratio, 91–92
prevalence, 360
polyfidelity, 173–74, 187–88
polygamy, 75–76, 237
polygyny
child mortality rate in predicting, 358–59
as infidelity, 362
infidelity impacts, 606–7
operational sex ratio, 91–92, 96
prevalence of, 121–22, 129–30, 237
polymorphisms, genetic, 222–23
pornography, 155, 264–65, 326, 349–50, 362–66
Prall, S. P., 359–60
Prestage, G., 377
Previti, D., 400–1
primary relationship/infidelity partner. *See* mate poaching
primate studies. *See* nonhuman animals studies
Process Model of Interpersonal Forgiveness, 436
progesterone, 62, 72–73, 77
psychological distress, infidelity and, 146
psychopathy
infidelity and, 12t, 14, 146, 157, 179, 220–22, 266–67
in mate poaching, 461
in sexual coercion, 559
PTSD, 334, 500, 502, 511
Puerto Rican Americans, 35–36, 354
Puts, D. A., 70, 75

Q

queerplatonic, 174–75
Quinlan, M. B., 359
Quinlan, R. J., 359
Quinsey, V. L., 559, 565, 566

R

race/ethnicity
acculturation effects, 37–38, 53–54
Africa (*see* Africa)
African Americans, 30, 31–32, 34–36, 46, 50–51, 52–53, 354
Asia (*see* Asia)
Asian Americans, 30, 31–32, 36–38, 47–48, 49, 53

race/ethnicity (cont.)
  bioecological model, 50–51
  clinical practice, 51–52
  common EDI predictors, 31–33
  concepts, definitions, 29–31
  contextual factors, 28–29, 32, 52
  cross-cultural research, 32, 41–45, 46–47, 52
  divorce, 36–37
  double standards, 35–36
  emotions/well-being relationships, 52–53
  environmental factors, 33, 36, 51, 53
  ethnic minorities, 35, 39–40, 51
  European Americans, 30–31, 37–38
  focus group studies, 35
  gender differences, 32–33, 38
  gender ratio imbalance, 33, 34–35, 46, 50–51
  HIV/STIs, 35, 38, 41–42, 43, 47–48, 94
  honor culture, 45
  identity and, 30–31, 181
  infidelity and, 31
  infidelity prevalence, 400
  interdependence model, 45–47
  intersectionality model, 45, 48–50
  Latin Americans, 29, 37–40, 47–48, 53–54, 148, 162–63
  in mate poaching, 35, 46, 52–53
  Middle East, 44–45
  Middle Eastern Americans, 30
  monogamy, 181
  Native Americans, 30, 31–32, 40–41, 47, 53–54
  nonheterosexual/alternative relationships, 52
  nonheterosexual relationships, 181–82
  online infidelity, 162–63
  partner qualities, 33
  partners' compatibility, 51–52
  patriarchy, 29, 47–48
  peer pressure, 39–40
  power relationships, 30–31, 33, 38–39, 43, 47–48
  predicting infidelity, 181–82
  Puerto Rican Americans, 35–36, 354
  religiosity, 29, 32–33, 35, 44
  social exchange theory, 45–47
  social status, 39–40, 41
  socioeconomic status (SES), 30, 53
  sugar daddy model, 42, 43, 46–47
  symbolic interaction theory, 47–48
  violence, 39, 43
  WASP norms, 32, 37–38, 47, 52
Randall, H. E., 350–51
rape, 559–63. *See also* sexual coercion
Rapson, R. L., 482
rational-emotive behavioral therapy, 567
REACH forgiveness model, 437
Reich, N., 44
Reissman, C. K., 406–7
relationship dissolution. *See* divorce
relationship factors. *See also* partner qualities
  assortative mating, 114–15
  commitment, 146–47
  commitment, hormonal influences, 296–97
  communication and satisfaction, 106–9, 185–87
  cross-cultural research, 146–47
  cyber-infidelity, 114
  derogation of alternatives, 112–13
  divorce, 108, 401–2
  employment, 114
  forgiveness, 427
  gender and satisfaction, 105–6
  identity, 111
  income level, 115
  infidelity prediction, 101–3
  investment model of commitment, 46, 103–4, 109–10
  investments, 110–12
  motivation research, 115–16
  opportunities for infidelity, 114–15
  power relationships, 107–8, 146–47
  as predictive of long-term infidelities, 323–24
  prevention of infidelity, 116
  quality of alternatives, 112–13, 558–59
  relationship type/length, 113–14
  religiosity, 35
  research designs, 115
  sacrifice and commitment, 110
  satisfaction (*see* satisfaction)
  self-expansion model (SEM), 111–12
  sexual satisfaction, 16–17, 33, 104–6, 109–10
religiosity
  cross-cultural research, 148, 149
  forgiveness and, 426
  infidelity and, 4–6
  infidelity prevalence, 400
  race/ethnicity, 29, 32–33, 35, 44
  relationship factors, 35
renewed love
  cyclical relationships, 478
  deception/secrecy and, 479
  detection of infidelity, 479
  forgiveness and, 478–81
  infidelity research overview, 472–77
  love as factor, 481–83
  reconciliation actions, 484–85
  rekindling, 484–85
  relationship continuation, 477–78
  relationship quality and, 479
  therapeutic approach, 486
Resnick, P. J., 532
Righetti, F., 299
rivalry sensitivity hypothesis, 534
Roberts, S. C., 302
Rodrigues, D., 20t
Rodriguez, L. M., 536
Rogers, S., 335–36, 401
Rogers, S. J., 518
romantic friendships, 174–75
Romero-Palencia, A. R., 603–4
Roscoe, B., 261–62
Rubin, J. D., 181
rumination, 430, 431, 434, 496–97, 503
Rusbult, C. E., 46, 112, 212
Russell, V. M., 5t, 8, 9–10, 16t, 17, 18–19, 322–23, 383–84

S

Sabini, J., 216
Sadava, S., 16–17, 16t
Salimi Bajestani, H., 497–98, 501
Salwen, J. K., 559
same-sex infidelity. *See also* LGBTQ+
  concepts, definitions, 417
  gender differences in response to, 185–86, 417–18
  in heterosexual relationships, 417–18, 423, 438
  intrasexual homicide, 528–30
  motivations, 418
  online infidelity, 164–65, 166
  studies of, 375, 417–18
Samson, C., 212–13
Sandage, S. J., 419–20
Sandhu, D. S., 44
satisfaction. *See also* relationship factors
  attachment insecurity and, 383, 385
  automatic attitudes toward partners, 23–24
  characterization, 104–10, 146–47
  commitment and, 68, 103
  communication and, 106–9
  cross-cultural studies, 46–48
  divorce and, 36–37, 522–23
  forgiveness and, 427, 440
  gender and, 105–6
  hormonal contraceptives and, 301–2
  infidelity prevalence, 400–1
  mate poaching and, 462–63
  online infidelity and, 328, 364
  partner incompatibility in, 33, 51–52
  personality effects, 149
  as predictive, 42–43, 47–48
  as protective, 44, 46, 105
  relationship, 105
  sexual, 109–10
  testosterone effects on, 64, 70, 76–77
Sbarra, D. A., 403–4, 408
Scelza, B. A., 356–57, 359–60, 519–20
Scheele, D., 223
Schmitt, D. P., 5t, 9–10, 144–45, 215, 216–17, 219, 275, 317, 461

Schneider, J. P., 265, 328
Schultz, C., 318
Schulz, B. E., 282–83
Schwartz, P., 375, 378
Scott, J., 352–53
Seal, D., 20t, 217
Seal, D. W., 216
Second Love, 263
secrecy. *See* deception/secrecy
Seeking Arrangement, 160
Sela, Y., 537
self-esteem, infidelity and, 146
self-expansion model (SEM), 111–12, 212–13
Sells, J. N., 420
Selterman, D., 474
Sen, S., 365–66
sensation seeking, 381
sexting, 141, 155–58
sexual coercion. *See also* violence/homicide
  clinical approach to, 567–71
  cognitive-behavioral therapy (CBT), 571–72
  concepts, definitions, 555–56, 557–58
  cross-cultural studies, 524
  evolutionary perspectives, 561–63, 569–70
  extended sexuality theory and, 293–94
  forced in-pair copulation (FIPC), 555–57, 563–72
  heritability measures, 563
  honor culture and, 96
  infidelity cues and, 564–66
  in-pair rape, 524–26
  IPV and, 520–22, 556–59
  mate retention/guarding, 556, 559, 567–70
  motivations, 522, 524–25
  paternity in, 556
  power relationships, 558, 559–61, 570–71
  quality of alternatives, 112–13, 142–43, 558–59
  rape as natural sexuality, 559–66
  routes to, 559
  time spent apart, 564–65
sexual dimorphism, 71–72, 291–92
sexually transmitted diseases (STDs), 35, 38, 41–42, 43, 47–48, 94, 579

sexual sensation seeking, 381
sexual strategies theory, 185, 215, 292–93
sexy son hypothesis, 217–18, 583
Shackelford, T. K., 4–6, 5t, 7, 9–10, 12t, 13, 14, 102, 269, 275, 476, 480, 507, 508, 522–23, 535–36, 537–38, 557, 564–66
Sharpsteen, D. J., 476
Sheets, V., 183
Shen, H. H., 43
Shields, N. M., 521
Shrout, M. R., 480
Sichona, F. J., 147–48
Sickles, Daniel, 528–29
Slepian, M. L., 279
Smart, J., 43
Smith, C. V., 5t
Smith, D. J., 42
Smith, I., 142–43
Smith, T. E., 282
SO. *See* sociosexuality
social exchange theory, 45–47
social media, 157, 161, 165, 264, 331–32, 410–11
sociosexuality
  deception/secrecy and, 265–66, 276–77
  gender differences, 69–70
  infidelity and, 19–21, 20t, 32–33, 146
  long-term infidelities, 323
  mate poaching and, 460, 462, 464
  narcissism and, 13–14
  novelty-seeking and, 216–17
  predictive value of, 69
  testosterone and, 69–71
Solomon, S. D., 477–78
Southern Belle archetype, 95
sperm competition, 563–66
Splenda daddies, 160
Spring, J. A., 497, 498–99, 500, 501, 506
spyware, 163–64
Standard Cross-Cultural Sample, 358–59, 360
Starratt, V. G., 537–38, 565–66
Stefano, J. D., 509
Stephenson, R., 41–42
Stevenson, A., 329–30
strategic pluralism theory, 292–93
sugar babies, 160–61
Sugar Baby University, 160

sugar daddy model, 42, 43, 46–47, 160–61
sugaring, 160–61
sugar mamma, 160–61
Sunderani, S., 521, 536
surveillance behaviors, 163–64
Sweeney, M. M., 407–8
swinging lifestyle, 177, 187–88, 362

T

Taghi Pour, M., 496, 508–9
Teagno, L. J., 477–78
technology-facilitated infidelity, 141. *See also* online infidelity
Tennov, D., 482
testosterone
 age-related declines in, 64, 75–76
 cross-cultural studies of, 76
 demographic variables and infidelity, 75–76
 divorce relationship to, 68
 effects on forgiveness, 430
 environmental cues responses, 75
 extradyadic behavior regulation by, 67–72
 feedback regulation of, 70
 functions in females, 64–66, 290–92
 functions in males, 63–64, 291–92
 immunocompetence effects, 64
 infidelity and, 62, 67, 68, 71–72
 long-term infidelities and, 64, 68–72, 75
 mate acquisition behavior, 63–64
 mating *vs.* parenting, 66–67
 motherhood and, 65–66
 ovulation and, 63–64, 65
 relationship commitment and, 68, 69, 75
 relationship orientation and, 68
 satisfaction effects, 64, 70, 76–77
 sexual dimorphism, 71–72, 291–92
 sociosexual orientation and, 69–71
 vocal frequencies effects, 71–72

Thapa, R., 43
thin slice theory, 271
third-person emotional bond development, 141–42
Thompson, A. P., 319, 354–56, 602
Thoresen, C. E., 479
Thornhill, R., 269
Thornhill, R./N. W., 559–60
Thorson, A. R., 338
Tice, D. M., 536
Tidwell, N. D., 224–25
Timmerman, A., 318
Tinder study, 157
Toplu-Demirtaş, E., 44, 148–49
Trait Forgivingness Scale (TFS), 424–25
Transgression Narrative Test of Forgivingness (TFNT), 424–25
Transgression-Related Interpersonal Motivations Inventory (TRIM), 423, 425
Treas, J., 472
Triple A model, 329–30
Trivers, R., 214, 292

U

unfaithfulness. *See also* infidelity generally
 adaptive emotional reactions, 497–98
 anger, 503–4
 attachment injuries, 502, 506–10
 coalition formation, 509
 commitment/faithfulness, 493–94
 concepts, definitions, 494
 depression, 498, 511
 emotional effects of, 496–502, 510–11
 emotion regulation and, 497–99
 family/family of origin relationship, 510
 fear/anxiety, 501–2, 503–4, 507–8, 511
 forgiveness and, 479
 humanitarian sense changes, 499
 infidelity effects, 495–96
 infidelity motivations, 495
 infidelity prevalence, 494
 intervention signs, 501
 loneliness, 507–8
 loss forms, 498–99
 major depression, 502
 maladaptive emotional reactions, 497–98, 506–7
 mate poaching and, 438, 461–65, 466
 meaning of life disruption, 505–6
 outcomes of, 496
 parent-child relationship, 508–9
 PTC treatment method, 511–12
 quality of alternatives, 112–13, 142–43
 relational effects of, 506–10
 renewed love and, 479
 rumination, 496–97, 503
 separation from oneself/life, 498
 sexual desire/disgust toward sex, 507
 suspicion/mistrust, 505–6
 therapeutic approach, 511
 thought/cognition dissociation, 503–6, 507
 vulnerability, 502
Utley, E., 52–53
uxoricide, 526, 527–28, 538

V

Vandello, J. A., 45
vasopressin, 74, 127–28, 223
Vera Cruz, G., 353
violence/homicide. *See also* sexual coercion
 anxiety/anxious attachment, 536–37
 cuckoldry, 272–73, 277–78, 300, 472, 477, 486, 519–20, 532–34, 569–70
 environmental unpredictability, 540
 fertility status/reproductive value, 538
 filicide, 530–32
 gender differences, 541
 honor culture/patriarchy, 45, 96, 539
 income inequality, 540
 infanticide, 530, 532, 581
 infidelity as adaptive, 516–20
 infidelity cues sensitivity, 533–34
 intimate partner homicide (IPH), 526–28

intimate partner violence (IPV), 517, 520–24, 536, 537–40, 541
intrasexual homicide, 528–30
jealousy as motivation for, 522, 523–24, 534–36
loss of control defense, 528–29
mate retention, 541–42
mate value perceptions, 537–38
partner/child abandonment, 518–19
perceived mate availability, 540–41
provocation defense, 528–29
resource scarcity, 540
resources/coparenting loss, 519
as response, 476, 501
sex ratios, 540–41
sexual coercion/rape, 524–26
sexual proprietariness, 516–17, 522, 526–27, 539
social-ecological contexts, 539–41
uxoricide, 526, 527–28, 538
vocal pitch, 533, 541–42
Vossler, A., 364–65, 473

W

Wade, T. J., 481, 484–87
Waldron, V. R., 432
Wampler, K. S., 326–27
Watson, N. V., 75
Weigel, D. J., 276, 339, 480
Weinberg, M. S., 353
Weiner, J. L., 479
Weiser, D. A., 12t, 20t, 36–37, 221, 222, 276, 315–16, 339
Weiss, R. S., 477–78
Welling, L. L., 71
West, R. J. D., 125–26
Whisman, M., 319–20, 324–25, 407–8
Whisman, M. A., 5t, 352–53, 502
White, D. R., 359
white privilege, 30
Whiting, J. B., 332
Whitty, M. T., 155, 326, 332, 362
Widman, L., 12t, 13, 22–23, 221
Widmer, E. D., 31–32
Wiederman, M. W., 262, 475
Williams, L. R., 39–40, 53–54
Williams, S. S., 279

Wilson, K., 261–62, 266, 280, 350–51
Wineberg, H., 477–78
Wiysonge, C. S., 146
Wolfe, M. D., 183
work spouse relationships, 161–62
Worthington, E. L. Jr., 419–20, 479
Wright, D. W., 47
Wright, T. L., 318–19, 321, 322
Wu, E. D., 36

Y

Yang, Y., 43
Yllo, K., 566
Young, K. S., 264
young male syndrome, 559
Yuan, S., 36–37

Z

Zayas, V., 21–22
Zeki, S., 481–82
Zhang, N., 147
Zhang, Y., 144
Zietsch, B. P., 223
Zilioli, S., 75
Zimmerman, R. R., 482